CLR via C#, Third Edition

Jeffrey Richter

PUBLISHED BY
Microsoft Press
A Division of Microsoft Corporation
One Microsoft Way
Redmond, Washington 98052-6399

Library of Congress Control Number: 2009943026

Printed and bound in the United States of America.

1 2 3 4 5 6 7 8 9   WCT   5 4 3 2 1 0

A CIP catalogue record for this book is available from the British Library.

Microsoft Press books are available through booksellers and distributors worldwide. For further information about international editions, contact your local Microsoft Corporation office or contact Microsoft Press International directly at fax (425) 936-7329. Visit our Web site at www.microsoft.com/mspress. Send comments to msinput@microsoft.com.

Acquisitions Editor: Ben Ryan
Developmental Editor: Devon Musgrave
Project Editor: Valerie Woolley
Editorial Production: Custom Editorial Productions, Inc.
Technical Reviewer: Christophe Nasarre; Technical Review services provided by Content Master, a member of CM Group, Ltd.
Cover: Tom Draper Design

Body Part No. X16-61995

Table of Contents

What do you think of this book? We want to hear from you!

Microsoft is interested in hearing your feedback so we can continually improve our books and learning resources for you. To participate in a brief online survey, please visit:

www.microsoft.com/learning/booksurvey/

What do you think of this book? We want to hear from you!

Microsoft is interested in hearing your feedback so we can continually improve our books and learning resources for you. To participate in a brief online survey, please visit:

www.microsoft.com/learning/booksurvey/

Foreword

At first, when Jeff asked me to write the foreword for his book, I was so flattered! He must really respect me, I thought. Ladies, this is a common thought process error—trust me, he doesn't respect you. It turns out that I was about #14 on his list of potential foreword writers and he had to settle for me. Apparently, none of the other candidates (Bill Gates, Steve Ballmer, Catherine Zeta-Jones, . . .) were that into him. At least he bought me dinner.

But no one can tell you more about this book than I can. I mean, Catherine could give you a mobile makeover, but I know all kinds of stuff about reflection and exceptions and C# language updates because he has been talking on and on about it for years. This is standard dinner conversation in our house! Other people talk about the weather or stuff they heard at the water cooler, but we talk about .NET. Even Aidan, our six-year-old, asks questions about Jeff's book. Mostly about when he will be done writing it so they can play something "cool." Grant (age 2) doesn't talk yet, but his first word will probably be "Sequential."

In fact, if you want to know how this all started, it goes something like this. About 10 years ago, Jeff went to a "Secret Summit" at Microsoft. They pulled in a bunch of industry experts (Really, how do you get this title? Believe me, this isn't Jeff's college degree), and unveiled the new COM. Late that night in bed (in our house, this is what we discuss in bed), he talked about how COM is dead. And he was enchanted. Lovestruck, actually. In a matter of days he was hanging around the halls of Building 42 on Microsoft's Redmond campus, hoping to learn more about this wonderful .NET. The affair hasn't ended, and this book is what he has to show for it.

For years, Jeff has told me about threading. He really likes this topic. One time, in New Orleans, we went on a two-hour walk, alone, holding hands, and he spoke the whole time about how he had enough content for a threading book: The art of threading. How misunderstood threading in Windows is. It breaks his heart, all those threads out there. Where do they all go? Why were they created if no one had a plan for them? These are the questions of the universe to Jeff, the deeper meanings in life. Finally, in this book, he has written it down. It is all here. Believe me folks, if you want to know about threading, no one has thought about it more or worked with it more than Jeff has. And all those wasted hours of his life (he can't get them back) are here at your disposal. Please read it. Then send him an e-mail about how that information changed your life. Otherwise, he is just another tragic literary figure whose life ended without meaning or fulfillment. He will drink himself to death on diet soda.

This edition of the book even includes a new chapter about the runtime serializer. Turns out, this is not a new breakfast food for kids. When I figured out it was more computer talk and not something to put on my grocery list, I tuned it out. So I don't know what it says, but it is in here and you should read it (with a glass of milk).

My hope is that now he is finished talking about garbage collection in theory and can get on with actually collecting our garbage and putting it on the curb. Seriously people, how hard is that?

Folks, here is the clincher—this is Jeffrey Richter's magnum opus. This is it. There will be no more books. Of course, we say this every time he finishes one, but this time we really mean it. So, 13 books (give or take) later, this is the best and the last. Get it fast, because there are only a limited number and once they are gone—poof. No more. Just like QVC or something. Back to real life for us, where we can discuss the important things, like what the kids broke today and whose turn is it to change the diapers.

Kristin Trace (Jeffrey's wife)

November 24, 2009

A typical family breakfast at the Richter household

Introduction

It was October 1999 when some people at Microsoft first demonstrated the Microsoft .NET Framework, the common language runtime (CLR), and the C# programming language to me. The moment I saw all of this, I was impressed and I knew that it was going to change the way I wrote software in a very significant way. I was asked to do some consulting for the team and immediately agreed. At first, I thought that the .NET Framework was an abstraction layer over the Win32 API and COM. As I invested more and more of my time into it, however, I realized that it was much bigger. In a way, it is its own operating system. It has its own memory manager, its own security system, its own file loader, its own error handling mechanism, its own application isolation boundaries (AppDomains), its own threading models, and more. This book explains all these topics so that you can effectively design and implement software applications and components for this platform.

I have spent a good part of my life focusing on threading, concurrent execution, parallelism, synchronization, and so on. Today, with multicore computers becoming so prevalent, these subjects are becoming increasingly important. A few years ago, I decided to create a book dedicated to threading topics. However, one thing led to another and I never produced the book. When it came time to revise this book, I decided to incorporate all the threading information in here. So this book covers the .NET Framework's CLR and the C# programming language, and it also has my threading book embedded inside it (see Part V, "Threading").

It is October 2009 as I write this text, making it 10 years now that I've worked with the .NET Framework and C#. Over the 10 years, I have built all kinds of applications and, as a consultant to Microsoft, have contributed quite a bit to the .NET Framework itself. As a partner in my own company, Wintellect (*http://Wintellect.com*), I have worked with numerous customers to help them design software, debug software, performance-tune software, and solve issues they have with the .NET Framework. All these experiences have really helped me learn the spots that people have trouble with when trying to be productive with the .NET Framework. I have tried to sprinkle knowledge from these experiences through all the topics presented in this book.

Who This Book Is For

The purpose of this book is to explain how to develop applications and reusable classes for the .NET Framework. Specifically, this means that I intend to explain how the CLR works and the facilities that it offers. I'll also discuss various parts of the Framework Class Library (FCL). No book could fully explain the FCL—it contains literally thousands of types now, and this number continues to grow at an alarming rate. Therefore, here I'm concentrating on the core types that every developer needs to be aware of. And while this book isn't specifically about Windows Forms, Windows Presentation Foundation (WPF), Silverlight, XML Web services,

Web Forms, and so on, the technologies presented in the book are applicable to *all* these application types.

The book addresses Microsoft Visual Studio 2010, .NET Framework version 4.0, and version 4.0 of the C# programming language. Since Microsoft tries to maintain a large degree of backward compatibility when releasing a new version of these technologies, many of the things I discuss in this book apply to earlier versions as well. All the code samples use the C# programming language as a way to demonstrate the behavior of the various facilities. But, since the CLR is usable by many programming languages, the book's content is still quite applicable for the non-C# programmer.

> **Note** You can download the code shown in the book from Wintellect's Web site (*http://Wintellect.com*). In some parts of the book, I describe classes in my own Power Threading Library. This library is available free of charge and can also be downloaded from Wintellect's Web site.

Today, Microsoft offers several versions of the CLR. There is the desktop/server version, which runs on 32-bit x86 versions of Microsoft Windows as well as 64-bit x64 and IA64 versions of Windows. There is the Silverlight version, which is produced from the same source code base as the desktop/server version of the .NET Framework's CLR. Therefore, everything in this book applies to building Silverlight applications, with the exception of some differences in how Silverlight loads assemblies. There is also a "lite" version of the .NET Framework called the .NET Compact Framework, which is available for Windows Mobile phones and other devices running the Windows CE operating system. Much of the information presented in this book is applicable to developing applications for the .NET Compact Framework, but this platform is not the primary focus of this book.

On December 13, 2001, ECMA International (*http://www.ecma-international.org/*) accepted the C# programming language, portions of the CLR, and portions of the FCL as standards. The standards documents that resulted from this have allowed other organizations to build ECMA-compliant versions of these technologies for other CPU architectures, as well as other operating systems. In fact, Novell produces Moonlight (*http://www.mono-project.com/Moonlight*), an open-source implementation of Silverlight (*http://Silverlight.net*) that is primarily for Linux and other UNIX/X11-based operating systems. Moonlight is based on the ECMA specifications. Much of the content in this book is about these standards; therefore, many will find this book useful for working with any runtime/library implementation that adheres to the ECMA standard.

Note My editors and I have worked hard to bring you the most accurate, up-to-date, in-depth, easy-to-read, painless-to-understand, bug-free information. Even with this fantastic team assembled, however, things inevitably slip through the cracks. If you find any mistakes in this book (especially bugs) or have some constructive feedback, I would greatly appreciate it if you would contact me at *JeffreyR@Wintellect.com*.

Dedication

To Kristin Words cannot express how I feel about our life together. I cherish our family and all our adventures. I'm filled each day with love for you.

To Aidan (age 6) and Grant (age 2) You both have been an inspiration to me and have taught me to play and have fun. Watching the two of you grow up has been so rewarding and enjoyable for me. I am lucky to be able to partake in your lives. I love and appreciate you more than you could ever know.

Acknowledgments

I couldn't have written this book without the help and technical assistance of many people. In particular, I'd like to thank my family. The amount of time and effort that goes into writing a book is hard to measure. All I know is that I could not have produced this book without the support of my wife, Kristin, and my two sons, Aidan and Grant. There were many times when we wanted to spend time together but were unable to due to book obligations. Now that the book project is completed, I really look forward to adventures we will all share together.

For this book revision, I truly had some fantastic people helping me. Christophe Nasarre, who I've worked with on several book projects, has done just a phenomenal job of verifying my work and making sure that I'd said everything the best way it could possibly be said. He has truly had a significant impact on the quality of this book. As always, the Microsoft Press editorial team is a pleasure to work with. I'd like to extend a special thank you to Ben Ryan, Valerie Woolley, and Devon Musgrave. Also, thanks to Jean Findley and Sue McClung for their editing and production support.

Support for This Book

Every effort has been made to ensure the accuracy of this book. As corrections or changes are collected, they will be added to a Microsoft Knowledge Base article accessible via the Microsoft Help and Support site. Microsoft Press provides support for books, including instructions for finding Knowledge Base articles, at the following Web site:

http://www.microsoft.com/learning/support/books/

If you have questions regarding the book that are not answered by visiting the site above or viewing a Knowledge Base article, send them to Microsoft Press via e-mail to mspinput@microsoft.com.

Please note that Microsoft software product support is not offered through these addresses.

We Want to Hear from You

We welcome your feedback about this book. Please share your comments and ideas via the following short survey:

http://www.microsoft.com/learning/booksurvey

Your participation will help Microsoft Press create books that better meet your needs and standards.

> **Note** We hope that you will give us detailed feedback via our survey. If you have questions about our publishing program, upcoming titles, or Microsoft Press in general, we encourage you to interact with us via Twitter at *http://twitter.com/MicrosoftPress*. For support issues, use only the e-mail address shown above.

Chapter 1
The CLR's Execution Model

The Microsoft .NET Framework introduces many new concepts, technologies, and terms. My goal in this chapter is to give you an overview of how the .NET Framework is designed, introduce you to some of the new technologies the framework includes, and define many of the terms you'll be seeing when you start using it. I'll also take you through the process of building your source code into an application or a set of redistributable components (files) that contain types (classes, structures, etc.) and then explain how your application will execute.

Compiling Source Code into Managed Modules

OK, so you've decided to use the .NET Framework as your development platform. Great! Your first step is to determine what type of application or component you intend to build. Let's just assume that you've completed this minor detail; everything is designed, the specifications are written, and you're ready to start development.

Now you must decide which programming language to use. This task is usually difficult because different languages offer different capabilities. For example, in unmanaged C/C++, you have pretty low-level control of the system. You can manage memory exactly the way you want to, create threads easily if you need to, and so on. Microsoft Visual Basic 6, on the other hand, allows you to build UI applications very rapidly and makes it easy for you to control COM objects and databases.

The common language runtime (CLR) is just what its name says it is: a runtime that is usable by different and varied programming languages. The core features of the CLR (such as memory management, assembly loading, security, exception handling, and thread synchronization) are available to any and all programming languages that target it—period. For example, the runtime uses exceptions to report errors, so all languages that target the runtime also get errors reported via exceptions. Another example is that the runtime also allows you to create a thread, so any language that targets the runtime can create a thread.

In fact, at runtime, the CLR has no idea which programming language the developer used for the source code. This means that you should choose whatever programming language allows you to express your intentions most easily. You can develop your code in any programming language you desire as long as the compiler you use to compile your code targets the CLR.

So, if what I say is true, what is the advantage of using one programming language over another? Well, I think of compilers as syntax checkers and "correct code" analyzers. They examine your source code, ensure that whatever you've written makes some sense, and then output code that describes your intention. Different programming languages allow you to develop using different syntax. Don't underestimate the value of this choice. For mathematical or financial applications, expressing your intentions by using APL syntax can save many days of development time when compared to expressing the same intention by using Perl syntax, for example.

Microsoft has created several language compilers that target the runtime: C++/CLI, C# (pronounced "C sharp"), Visual Basic, F# (pronounced "F sharp"), Iron Python, Iron Ruby, and an Intermediate Language (IL) Assembler. In addition to Microsoft, several other companies, colleges, and universities have created compilers that produce code to target the CLR. I'm aware of compilers for Ada, APL, Caml, COBOL, Eiffel, Forth, Fortran, Haskell, Lexico, LISP, LOGO, Lua, Mercury, ML, Mondrian, Oberon, Pascal, Perl, Php, Prolog, RPG, Scheme, Smalltalk, and Tcl/Tk.

Figure 1-1 shows the process of compiling source code files. As the figure shows, you can create source code files written in any programming language that supports the CLR. Then you use the corresponding compiler to check the syntax and analyze the source code. Regardless of which compiler you use, the result is a *managed module*. A managed module is a standard 32-bit Microsoft Windows portable executable (PE32) file or a standard 64-bit Windows portable executable (PE32+) file that requires the CLR to execute. By the way, managed assemblies always take advantage of Data Execution Prevention (DEP) and Address Space Layout Randomization (ASLR) in Windows; these two features improve the security of your whole system.

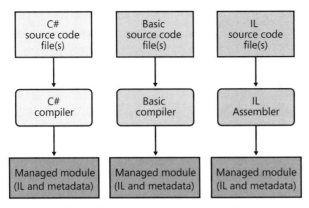

FIGURE 1-1 Compiling source code into managed modules

Table 1-1 describes the parts of a managed module.

TABLE 1-1 Parts of a Managed Module

Part	Description
PE32 or PE32+ header	The standard Windows PE file header, which is similar to the Common Object File Format (COFF) header. If the header uses the PE32 format, the file can run on a 32-bit or 64-bit version of Windows. If the header uses the PE32+ format, the file requires a 64-bit version of Windows to run. This header also indicates the type of file: GUI, CUI, or DLL, and contains a timestamp indicating when the file was built. For modules that contain only IL code, the bulk of the information in the PE32(+) header is ignored. For modules that contain native CPU code, this header contains information about the native CPU code.
CLR header	Contains the information (interpreted by the CLR and utilities) that makes this a managed module. The header includes the version of the CLR required, some flags, the **MethodDef** metadata token of the managed module's entry point method (**Main** method), and the location/size of the module's metadata, resources, strong name, some flags, and other less interesting stuff.
Metadata	Every managed module contains metadata tables. There are two main types of tables: tables that describe the types and members defined in your source code and tables that describe the types and members referenced by your source code.
IL code	Code the compiler produced as it compiled the source code. At runtime, the CLR compiles the IL into native CPU instructions.

Native code compilers produce code targeted to a specific CPU architecture, such as x86, x64, or IA64. All CLR-compliant compilers produce IL code instead. (I'll go into more detail about IL code later in this chapter.) IL code is sometimes referred to as *managed code* because the CLR manages its execution.

In addition to emitting IL, every compiler targeting the CLR is required to emit full *metadata* into every managed module. In brief, metadata is a set of data tables that describe what is defined in the module, such as types and their members. In addition, metadata also has tables indicating what the managed module references, such as imported types and their members. Metadata is a superset of older technologies such as COM's Type Libraries and Interface Definition Language (IDL) files. The important thing to note is that CLR metadata is far more complete. And, unlike Type Libraries and IDL, metadata is always associated with the file that contains the IL code. In fact, the metadata is always embedded in the same EXE/DLL as the code, making it impossible to separate the two. Because the compiler produces the metadata and the code at the same time and binds them into the resulting managed module, the metadata and the IL code it describes are never out of sync with one another.

Metadata has many uses. Here are some of them:

- Metadata removes the need for native C/C++ header and library files when compiling because all the information about the referenced types/members is contained in the file that has the IL that implements the type/members. Compilers can read metadata directly from managed modules.

- Microsoft Visual Studio uses metadata to help you write code. Its IntelliSense feature parses metadata to tell you what methods, properties, events, and fields a type offers, and in the case of a method, what parameters the method expects.

- The CLR's code verification process uses metadata to ensure that your code performs only "type-safe" operations. (I'll discuss verification shortly.)

- Metadata allows an object's fields to be serialized into a memory block, sent to another machine, and then deserialized, re-creating the object's state on the remote machine.

- Metadata allows the garbage collector to track the lifetime of objects. For any object, the garbage collector can determine the type of the object and, from the metadata, know which fields within that object refer to other objects.

In Chapter 2, "Building, Packaging, Deploying, and Administering Applications and Types," I'll describe metadata in much more detail.

Microsoft's C#, Visual Basic, F#, and the IL Assembler always produce modules that contain managed code (IL) and managed data (garbage-collected data types). End users must have the CLR (presently shipping as part of the .NET Framework) installed on their machine in order to execute any modules that contain managed code and/or managed data in the same way that they must have the Microsoft Foundation Class (MFC) library or Visual Basic DLLs installed to run MFC or Visual Basic 6 applications.

By default, Microsoft's C++ compiler builds EXE/DLL modules that contain unmanaged (native) code and manipulate unmanaged data (native memory) at runtime. These modules don't require the CLR to execute. However, by specifying the **/CLR** command-line switch, the C++ compiler produces modules that contain managed code, and of course, the CLR must then be installed to execute this code. Of all of the Microsoft compilers mentioned, C++ is unique in that it is the only compiler that allows the developer to write both managed and unmanaged code and have it emitted into a single module. It is also the only Microsoft compiler that allows developers to define both managed and unmanaged data types in their source code. The flexibility provided by Microsoft's C++ compiler is unparalleled by other compilers because it allows developers to use their existing native C/C++ code from managed code and to start integrating the use of managed types as they see fit.

Combining Managed Modules into Assemblies

The CLR doesn't actually work with modules, it works with assemblies. An *assembly* is an abstract concept that can be difficult to grasp initially. First, an assembly is a logical grouping of one or more modules or resource files. Second, an assembly is the smallest unit of reuse, security, and versioning. Depending on the choices you make with your compilers or tools, you can produce a single-file or a multifile assembly. In the CLR world, an assembly is what we would call a *component*.

In Chapter 2, I'll go over assemblies in great detail, so I don't want to spend a lot of time on them here. All I want to do now is make you aware that there is this extra conceptual notion that offers a way to treat a group of files as a single entity.

Figure 1-2 should help explain what assemblies are about. In this figure, some managed modules and resource (or data) files are being processed by a tool. This tool produces a single PE32(+) file that represents the logical grouping of files. What happens is that this PE32(+) file contains a block of data called the *manifest*. The manifest is simply another set of metadata tables. These tables describe the files that make up the assembly, the publicly exported types implemented by the files in the assembly, and the resource or data files that are associated with the assembly.

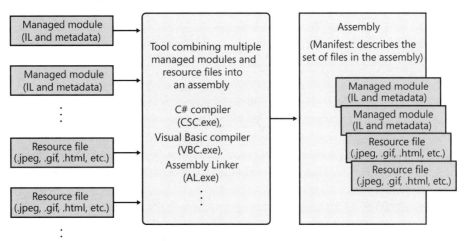

FIGURE 1-2 Combining managed modules into assemblies

By default, compilers actually do the work of turning the emitted managed module into an assembly; that is, the C# compiler emits a managed module that contains a manifest. The manifest indicates that the assembly consists of just the one file. So, for projects that have just one managed module and no resource (or data) files, the assembly will be the managed module, and you don't have any additional steps to perform during your build process. If you want to group a set of files into an assembly, you'll have to be aware of more tools (such as the assembly linker, AL.exe) and their command-line options. I'll explain these tools and options in Chapter 2.

An assembly allows you to decouple the logical and physical notions of a reusable, securable, versionable component. How you partition your code and resources into different files is completely up to you. For example, you could put rarely used types or resources in separate files that are part of an assembly. The separate files could be downloaded on demand from the Web as they are needed at runtime. If the files are never needed, they're never down-loaded, saving disk space and reducing installation time. Assemblies allow you to break up the deployment of the files while still treating all of the files as a single collection.

An assembly's modules also include information about referenced assemblies (including their version numbers). This information makes an assembly *self-describing*. In other words, the CLR can determine the assembly's immediate dependencies in order for code in the assembly to execute. No additional information is required in the registry or in Active Directory Domain Services (AD DS). Because no additional information is needed, deploying assemblies is much easier than deploying unmanaged components.

Loading the Common Language Runtime

Each assembly you build can be either an executable application or a DLL containing a set of types for use by an executable application. Of course, the CLR is responsible for man-aging the execution of code contained within these assemblies. This means that the .NET Framework must be installed on the host machine. Microsoft has created a redistribution package that you can freely ship to install the .NET Framework on your customers' machines. Some versions of Windows ship with the .NET Framework already installed.

You can tell if the .NET Framework has been installed by looking for the MSCorEE.dll file in the %SystemRoot%\System32 directory. The existence of this file tells you that the .NET Framework is installed. However, several versions of the .NET Framework can be installed on a single machine simultaneously. If you want to determine exactly which versions of the .NET Framework are installed, examine the subkeys under the following registry key:

HKEY_LOCAL_MACHINE\SOFTWARE\Microsoft\NET Framework Setup\NDP

The .NET Framework SDK includes a command-line utility called CLRVer.exe that shows all of the CLR versions installed on a machine. This utility can also show which version of the CLR is being used by processes currently running on the machine by using the **–all** switch or passing the ID of the process you are interested in.

Before we start looking at how the CLR loads, we need to spend a moment discussing 32-bit and 64-bit versions of Windows. If your assembly files contain only type-safe managed code, you are writing code that should work on both 32-bit and 64-bit versions of Windows. No source code changes are required for your code to run on either version of Windows. In fact, the resulting EXE/DLL file produced by the compiler will run on 32-bit Windows as well as the x64 and IA64 versions of 64-bit Windows! In other words, the one file will run on any machine that has a version of the .NET Framework installed on it.

On extremely rare occasions, developers want to write code that works only on a specific version of Windows. Developers might do this when using unsafe code or when interoperating with unmanaged code that is targeted to a specific CPU architecture. To aid these developers, the C# compiler offers a **/platform** command-line switch. This switch allows you to specify whether the resulting assembly can run on x86 machines running 32-bit Windows versions only, x64 machines running 64-bit Windows only, or Intel Itanium machines running 64-bit Windows only. If you don't specify a platform, the default is **anycpu**, which indicates that the resulting assembly can run on any version of Windows. Users of Visual Studio can set a project's target platform by displaying the project's property pages, clicking the Build tab, and then selecting an option in the Platform Target list (see Figure 1-3).

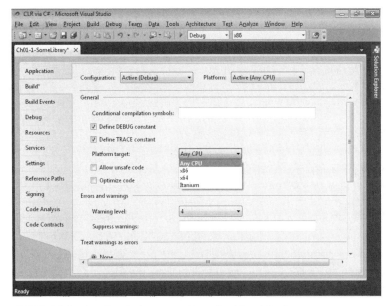

FIGURE 1-3 Setting the platform target by using Visual Studio

Depending on the platform switch, the C# compiler will emit an assembly that contains either a PE32 or PE32+ header, and the compiler will also emit the desired CPU architecture (or agnostic) into the header as well. Microsoft ships two SDK command-line utilities, DumpBin.exe and CorFlags.exe, that you can use to examine the header information emitted in a managed module by the compiler.

When running an executable file, Windows examines this EXE file's header to determine whether the application requires a 32-bit or 64-bit address space. A file with a PE32 header can run with a 32-bit or 64-bit address space, and a file with a PE32+ header requires a 64-bit address space. Windows also checks the CPU architecture information embedded inside the header to ensure that it matches the CPU type in the computer. Lastly, 64-bit versions of Windows offer a technology that allows 32-bit Windows applications to run. This technology is called *WoW64* (for Windows on Windows64). This technology even allows 32-bit applications with x86 native code in them to run on an Itanium machine, because the WoW64 technology can emulate the x86 instruction set; albeit with a significant performance cost.

Table 1-2 shows two things. First, it shows what kind of managed module you get when you specify various **/platform** command-line switches to the C# compiler. Second, it shows how that application will run on various versions of Windows.

TABLE 1-2 **Effects of /platform on Resulting Module and at Runtime**

/platform Switch	Resulting Managed Module	x86 Windows	x64 Windows	IA64 Windows
anycpu (the default)	PE32/agnostic	Runs as a 32-bit application	Runs as a 64-bit application	Runs as a 64-bit application
x86	PE32/x86	Runs as a 32-bit application	Runs as a WoW64 application	Runs as a WoW64 application
x64	PE32+/x64	Doesn't run	Runs as a 64-bit application	Doesn't run
Itanium	PE32+/Itanium	Doesn't run	Doesn't run	Runs as a 64-bit application

After Windows has examined the EXE file's header to determine whether to create a 32-bit process, a 64-bit process, or a WoW64 process, Windows loads the x86, x64, or IA64 version of MSCorEE.dll into the process's address space. On an x86 version of Windows, the x86 version of MSCorEE.dll can be found in the C:\Windows\System32 directory. On an x64 or IA64 version of Windows, the x86 version of MSCorEE.dll can be found in the C:\Windows\SysWow64 directory, whereas the 64-bit version (x64 or IA64) can be found in the C:\Windows\System32 directory (for backward compatibility reasons). Then, the process's primary thread calls a method defined inside MSCorEE.dll. This method initializes the CLR, loads the EXE assembly, and then calls its entry point method (**Main**). At this point, the managed application is up and running.[1]

---

[1] Your code can query **Environment**'s **Is64BitOperatingSystem** property to determine if it is running on a 64-bit version of Windows. Your code can also query **Environment**'s **Is64BitProcess** property to determine if it is running in a 64-bit address space.

> **Note** Assemblies built by using version 1.0 or 1.1 of Microsoft's C# compiler contain a PE32 header and are CPU-architecture agnostic. However, at load time, the CLR considers these assemblies to be x86 only. For executable files, this improves the likelihood of the application actually working on a 64-bit system because the executable file will load in WoW64, giving the process an environment very similar to what it would have on a 32-bit x86 version of Windows.

If an unmanaged application calls **LoadLibrary** to load a managed assembly, Windows knows to load and initialize the CLR (if not already loaded) in order to process the code contained within the assembly. Of course, in this scenario, the process is already up and running, and this may limit the usability of the assembly. For example, a managed assembly compiled with the **/platform:x86** switch will not be able to load into a 64-bit process at all, whereas an executable file compiled with this same switch would have loaded in WoW64 on a computer running a 64-bit version of Windows.

Executing Your Assembly's Code

As mentioned earlier, managed assemblies contain both metadata and IL. IL is a CPU-independent machine language created by Microsoft after consultation with several external commercial and academic language/compiler writers. IL is a much higher-level language than most CPU machine languages. IL can access and manipulate object types and has instructions to create and initialize objects, call virtual methods on objects, and manipulate array elements directly. It even has instructions to throw and catch exceptions for error handling. You can think of IL as an object-oriented machine language.

Usually, developers will program in a high-level language, such as C#, C++/CLI, or Visual Basic. The compilers for these high-level languages produce IL. However, as any other machine language, IL can be written in assembly language, and Microsoft does provide an IL Assembler, ILAsm.exe. Microsoft also provides an IL Disassembler, ILDasm.exe.

Keep in mind that any high-level language will most likely expose only a subset of the facilities offered by the CLR. However, the IL assembly language allows a developer to access all of the CLR's facilities. So, should your programming language of choice hide a facility the CLR offers that you really want to take advantage of, you can choose to write that portion of your code in IL assembly or perhaps another programming language that exposes the CLR feature you seek.

The only way for you to know what facilities the CLR offers is to read documentation specific to the CLR itself. In this book, I try to concentrate on CLR features and how they are exposed or not exposed by the C# language. I suspect that most other books and articles will present the CLR via a language perspective, and that most developers will come to believe that the CLR offers only what the developer's chosen language exposes. As long as your language allows you to accomplish what you're trying to get done, this blurred perspective isn't a bad thing.

Important I think this ability to switch programming languages easily with rich integration between languages is an awesome feature of the CLR. Unfortunately, I also believe that developers will often overlook this feature. Programming languages such as C# and Visual Basic are excellent languages for performing I/O operations. APL is a great language for performing advanced engineering or financial calculations. Through the CLR, you can write the I/O portions of your application in C# and then write the engineering calculations part in APL. The CLR offers a level of integration between these languages that is unprecedented and really makes mixed-language programming worthy of consideration for many development projects.

To execute a method, its IL must first be converted to native CPU instructions. This is the job of the CLR's JIT (just-in-time) compiler.

Figure 1-4 shows what happens the first time a method is called.

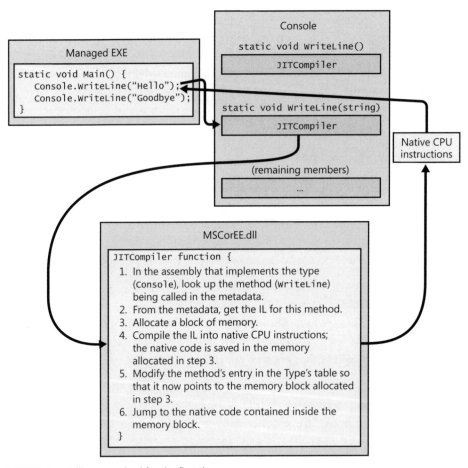

FIGURE 1-4 Calling a method for the first time

Just before the **Main** method executes, the CLR detects all of the types that are referenced by **Main**'s code. This causes the CLR to allocate an internal data structure that is used to manage access to the referenced types. In Figure 1-4, the **Main** method refers to a single type, **Console**, causing the CLR to allocate a single internal structure. This internal data structure contains an entry for each method defined by the **Console** type. Each entry holds the address where the method's implementation can be found. When initializing this structure, the CLR sets each entry to an internal, undocumented function contained inside the CLR itself. I call this function **JITCompiler**.

When **Main** makes its first call to **WriteLine**, the **JITCompiler** function is called. The **JITCompiler** function is responsible for compiling a method's IL code into native CPU instructions. Because the IL is being compiled "just in time," this component of the CLR is frequently referred to as a *JITter* or a *JIT compiler*.

> **Note** If the application is running on an x86 version of Windows or in WoW64, the JIT compiler produces x86 instructions. If your application is running as a 64-bit application on an x64 or Itanium version of Windows, the JIT compiler produces x64 or IA64 instructions, respectively.

When called, the **JITCompiler** function knows what method is being called and what type defines this method. The **JITCompiler** function then searches the defining assembly's metadata for the called method's IL. **JITCompiler** next verifies and compiles the IL code into native CPU instructions. The native CPU instructions are saved in a dynamically allocated block of memory. Then, **JITCompiler** goes back to the entry for the called method in the type's internal data structure created by the CLR and replaces the reference that called it in the first place with the address of the block of memory containing the native CPU instructions it just compiled. Finally, the **JITCompiler** function jumps to the code in the memory block. This code is the implementation of the **WriteLine** method (the version that takes a **String** parameter). When this code returns, it returns to the code in **Main**, which continues execution as normal.

Main now calls **WriteLine** a second time. This time, the code for **WriteLine** has already been verified and compiled. So the call goes directly to the block of memory, skipping the **JITCompiler** function entirely. After the **WriteLine** method executes, it returns to **Main**. Figure 1-5 shows what the process looks like when **WriteLine** is called the second time.

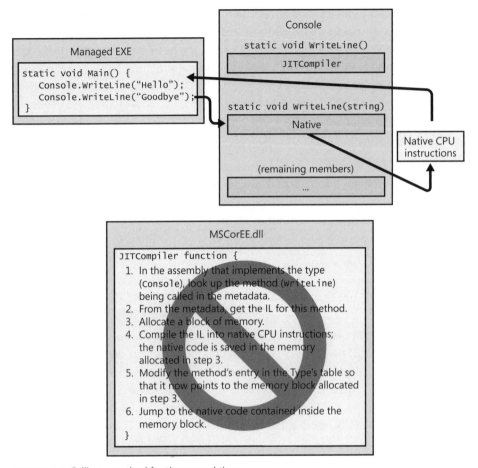

FIGURE 1-5 Calling a method for the second time

A performance hit is incurred only the first time a method is called. All subsequent calls to the method execute at the full speed of the native code because verification and compilation to native code don't need to be performed again.

The JIT compiler stores the native CPU instructions in dynamic memory. This means that the compiled code is discarded when the application terminates. So if you run the application again in the future or if you run two instances of the application simultaneously (in two different operating system processes), the JIT compiler will have to compile the IL to native instructions again.

For most applications, the performance hit incurred by JIT compiling isn't significant. Most applications tend to call the same methods over and over again. These methods will take the performance hit only once while the application executes. It's also likely that more time is spent inside the method than calling the method.

You should also be aware that the CLR's JIT compiler optimizes the native code just as the back end of an unmanaged C++ compiler does. Again, it may take more time to produce the optimized code, but the code will execute with much better performance than if it hadn't been optimized.

There are two C# compiler switches that impact code optimization: **/optimize** and **/debug**. The following table shows the impact these switches have on the quality of the IL code generated by the C# compiler and the quality of the native code generated by the JIT compiler:

Compiler Switch Settings	C# IL Code Quality	JIT Native Code Quality
/optimize- /debug- (this is the default)	Unoptimized	Optimized
/optimize- /debug(+/full/pdbonly)	Unoptimized	Unoptimized
/optimize+ /debug(-/+/full/pdbonly)	Optimized	Optimized

With **/optimize-**, the unoptimized IL code produced by the C# compiler contains many no-operation (NOP) instructions and also branches that jump to the next line of code. These instructions are emitted to enable the edit-and-continue feature of Visual Studio while debugging and the extra instructions also make code easier to debug by allowing breakpoints to be set on control flow instructions such as **for**, **while**, **do**, **if**, **else**, **try**, **catch**, and **finally** statement blocks. When producing optimized IL code, the C# compiler will remove these extraneous NOP and branch instructions, making the code harder to single-step through in a debugger as control flow will be optimized. Also, some function evaluations may not work when performed inside the debugger. However, the IL code is smaller, making the resulting EXE/DLL file smaller, and the IL tends to be easier to read for those of you (like me) who enjoy examining the IL to understand what the compiler is producing.

Furthermore, the compiler produces a Program Database (PDB) file only if you specify the **/debug(+/full/pdbonly)** switch. The PDB file helps the debugger find local variables and map the IL instructions to source code. The **/debug:full** switch tells the JIT compiler that you intend to debug the assembly, and the JIT compiler will track what native code came from each IL instruction. This allows you to use the just-in-time debugger feature of Visual Studio to connect a debugger to an already-running process and debug the code easily. Without the **/debug:full** switch, the JIT compiler does not, by default, track the IL to native code information which makes the JIT compiler run a little faster and also uses a little less memory. If you start a process with the Visual Studio debugger, it forces the JIT compiler to track the IL to native code information (regardless of the **/debug** switch) unless you turn off the Suppress JIT Optimization On Module Load (Managed Only) option in Visual Studio.

When you create a new C# project in Visual Studio, the Debug configuration of the project has **/optimize-** and **/debug:full** switches, and the Release configuration has **/optimize+** and **/debug:pdbonly** switches specified.

For those developers coming from an unmanaged C or C++ background, you're probably thinking about the performance ramifications of all this. After all, unmanaged code is compiled for a specific CPU platform, and, when invoked, the code can simply execute. In this managed environment, compiling the code is accomplished in two phases. First, the compiler passes over the source code, doing as much work as possible in producing IL. But to execute the code, the IL itself must be compiled into native CPU instructions at runtime, requiring more memory to be allocated and requiring additional CPU time to do the work.

Believe me, since I approached the CLR from a C/C++ background myself, I was quite skeptical and concerned about this additional overhead. The truth is that this second compilation stage that occurs at runtime does hurt performance, and it does allocate dynamic memory. However, Microsoft has done a lot of performance work to keep this additional overhead to a minimum.

If you too are skeptical, you should certainly build some applications and test the performance for yourself. In addition, you should run some nontrivial managed applications Microsoft or others have produced, and measure their performance. I think you'll be surprised at how good the performance actually is.

You'll probably find this hard to believe, but many people (including me) think that managed applications could actually outperform unmanaged applications. There are many reasons to believe this. For example, when the JIT compiler compiles the IL code into native code at runtime, the compiler knows more about the execution environment than an unmanaged compiler would know. Here are some ways that managed code can outperform unmanaged code:

- A JIT compiler can determine if the application is running on an Intel Pentium 4 CPU and produce native code that takes advantage of any special instructions offered by the Pentium 4. Usually, unmanaged applications are compiled for the lowest-common-denominator CPU and avoid using special instructions that would give the application a performance boost.

- A JIT compiler can determine when a certain test is always false on the machine that it is running on. For example, consider a method that contains the following code:

```
if (numberOfCPUs > 1) {
  . . .
}
```

  This code could cause the JIT compiler to not generate any CPU instructions if the host machine has only one CPU. In this case, the native code would be fine-tuned for the host machine; the resulting code is smaller and executes faster.

- The CLR could profile the code's execution and recompile the IL into native code while the application runs. The recompiled code could be reorganized to reduce incorrect branch predictions depending on the observed execution patterns. Current versions of the CLR do not do this, but future versions might.

These are only a few of the reasons why you should expect future managed code to execute better than today's unmanaged code. As I said, the performance is currently quite good for most applications, and it promises to improve as time goes on.

If your experiments show that the CLR's JIT compiler doesn't offer your application the kind of performance it requires, you may want to take advantage of the NGen.exe tool that ships with the .NET Framework SDK. This tool compiles all of an assembly's IL code into native code and saves the resulting native code to a file on disk. At runtime, when an assembly is loaded, the CLR automatically checks to see whether a precompiled version of the assembly also exists, and if it does, the CLR loads the precompiled code so that no compilation is required at runtime. Note that NGen.exe must be conservative about the assumptions it makes regarding the actual execution environment, and for this reason, the code produced by NGen.exe will not be as highly optimized as the JIT compiler–produced code. I'll discuss NGen.exe in more detail later in this chapter.

IL and Verification

IL is stack-based, which means that all of its instructions push operands onto an execution stack and pop results off the stack. Because IL offers no instructions to manipulate registers, it is easy for people to create new languages and compilers that produce code targeting the CLR.

IL instructions are also typeless. For example, IL offers an **add** instruction that adds the last two operands pushed on the stack. There are no separate 32-bit and 64-bit versions of the **add** instruction. When the **add** instruction executes, it determines the types of the operands on the stack and performs the appropriate operation.

In my opinion, the biggest benefit of IL isn't that it abstracts away the underlying CPU. The biggest benefit IL provides is application robustness and security. While compiling IL into native CPU instructions, the CLR performs a process called *verification*. Verification examines the high-level IL code and ensures that everything the code does is safe. For example, verification checks that every method is called with the correct number of parameters, that each parameter passed to every method is of the correct type, that every method's return value is used properly, that every method has a return statement, and so on. The managed module's metadata includes all of the method and type information used by the verification process.

In Windows, each process has its own virtual address space. Separate address spaces are necessary because you can't trust an application's code. It is entirely possible (and unfortunately, all too common) that an application will read from or write to an invalid memory address. By placing each Windows process in a separate address space, you gain robustness and stability; one process can't adversely affect another process.

By verifying the managed code, however, you know that the code doesn't improperly access memory and can't adversely affect another application's code. This means that you can run multiple managed applications in a single Windows virtual address space.

Because Windows processes require a lot of operating system resources, having many of them can hurt performance and limit available resources. Reducing the number of processes by running multiple applications in a single OS process can improve performance, require fewer resources, and be just as robust as if each application had its own process. This is another benefit of managed code as compared to unmanaged code.

The CLR does, in fact, offer the ability to execute multiple managed applications in a single OS process. Each managed application executes in an AppDomain. By default, every managed EXE file will run in its own separate address space that has just the one AppDomain. However, a process hosting the CLR (such as Internet Information Services [IIS] or Microsoft SQL Server) can decide to run AppDomains in a single OS process. I'll devote part of Chapter 22, "CLR Hosting and AppDomains," to a discussion of AppDomains.

Unsafe Code

By default, Microsoft's C# compiler produces safe code. *Safe code* is code that is verifiably safe. However, Microsoft's C# compiler allows developers to write unsafe code. Unsafe code is allowed to work directly with memory addresses and can manipulate bytes at these addresses. This is a very powerful feature and is typically useful when interoperating with unmanaged code or when you want to improve the performance of a time-critical algorithm.

However, using unsafe code introduces a significant risk: unsafe code can corrupt data structures and exploit or even open up security vulnerabilities. For this reason, the C# compiler requires that all methods that contain unsafe code be marked with the **unsafe** keyword. In addition, the C# compiler requires you to compile the source code by using the **/unsafe** compiler switch.

When the JIT compiler attempts to compile an unsafe method, it checks to see if the assembly containing the method has been granted the **System.Security.Permissions.Security Permission** with the **System.Security.Permissions.SecurityPermissionFlag**'s **SkipVerification** flag set. If this flag is set, the JIT compiler will compile the unsafe code and allow it to execute. The CLR is trusting this code and is hoping the direct address and byte manipulations do not cause any harm. If the flag is not set, the JIT compiler throws either a **System.InvalidProgramException** or a **System.Security.VerificationException**, preventing the method from executing. In fact, the whole application will probably terminate at this point, but at least no harm can be done.

> **Note** By default, assemblies that load from the local machine or via network shares are granted full trust, meaning that they can do anything, which includes executing unsafe code. However, by default, assemblies executed via the Internet are not granted the permission to execute unsafe code. If they contain unsafe code, one of the aforementioned exceptions is thrown. An administrator/end user can change these defaults; however, the administrator is taking full responsibility for the code's behavior.

Microsoft supplies a utility called PEVerify.exe, which examines all of an assembly's methods and notifies you of any methods that contain unsafe code. You may want to consider running PEVerify.exe on assemblies that you are referencing; this will let you know if there may be problems running your application via the intranet or Internet.

You should be aware that verification requires access to the metadata contained in any dependent assemblies. So when you use PEVerify to check an assembly, it must be able to locate and load all referenced assemblies. Because PEVerify uses the CLR to locate the dependent assemblies, the assemblies are located using the same binding and probing rules that would normally be used when executing the assembly. I'll discuss these binding and probing rules in Chapter 2 and Chapter 3, "Shared Assemblies and Strongly Named Assemblies."

IL and Protecting Your Intellectual Property

Some people are concerned that IL doesn't offer enough intellectual property protection for their algorithms. In other words, they think that you could build a managed module and that someone else could use a tool, such as an IL Disassembler, to easily reverse engineer exactly what your application's code does.

Yes, it's true that IL code is higher-level than most other assembly languages, and, in general, reverse engineering IL code is relatively simple. However, when implementing server-side code (such as a Web service, Web form, or stored procedure), your assembly resides on your server. Because no one outside of your company can access the assembly, no one outside of your company can use any tool to see the IL—your intellectual property is completely safe.

If you're concerned about any of the assemblies you do distribute, you can obtain an obfuscator utility from a third-party vendor. These utilities scramble the names of all of the private symbols in your assembly's metadata. It will be difficult for someone to un-scramble the names and understand the purpose of each method. Note that these obfuscators can provide only a little protection because the IL must be available at some point for the CLR to JIT compile it.

If you don't feel that an obfuscator offers the kind of intellectual property protection you desire, you can consider implementing your more sensitive algorithms in some un-managed module that will contain native CPU instructions instead of IL and metadata. Then you can use the CLR's interoperability features (assuming that you have ample permissions) to communicate between the managed and unmanaged portions of your application. Of course, this assumes that you're not worried about people reverse engineering the native CPU instructions in your unmanaged code.

The Native Code Generator Tool: NGen.exe

The NGen.exe tool that ships with the .NET Framework can be used to compile IL code to native code when an application is installed on a user's machine. Since the code is compiled at install time, the CLR's JIT compiler does not have to compile the IL code at runtime, and this *can* improve the application's performance. The NGen.exe tool is interesting in two scenarios:

- **Improving an application's startup time**   Running NGen.exe can improve startup time because the code will already be compiled into native code so that compilation doesn't have to occur at runtime.

- **Reducing an application's working set**   If you believe that an assembly will be loaded into multiple processes simultaneously, running NGen.exe on that assembly can reduce the applications' working set. The reason is because the NGen.exe tool compiles the IL to native code and saves the output in a separate file. This file can be memory-mapped into multiple-process address spaces simultaneously, allowing the code to be shared; not every process needs its own copy of the code.

When a setup program invokes NGen.exe on an application or a single assembly, all of the assemblies for that application or the one specified assembly have their IL code compiled into native code. A new assembly file containing only this native code instead of IL code is created by NGen.exe. This new file is placed in a folder under the directory with a name like C:\Windows\Assembly\NativeImages_v4.0.#####_64. The directory name includes the version of the CLR and information denoting whether the native code is compiled for x86 (32-bit version of Windows), x64, or Itanium (the latter two for 64-bit versions of Windows).

Now, whenever the CLR loads an assembly file, the CLR looks to see if a corresponding NGen'd native file exists. If a native file cannot be found, the CLR JIT compiles the IL code as usual. However, if a corresponding native file does exist, the CLR will use the compiled code contained in the native file, and the file's methods will not have to be compiled at runtime.

On the surface, this sounds great! It sounds as if you get all of the benefits of managed code (garbage collection, verification, type safety, and so on) without all of the performance problems of managed code (JIT compilation). However, the reality of the situation is not as rosy as it would first seem. There are several potential problems with respect to NGen'd files:

- **No intellectual property protection**   Many people believe that it might be possible to ship NGen'd files without shipping the files containing the original IL code, thereby keeping their intellectual property a secret. Unfortunately, this is not possible. At runtime, the CLR requires access to the assembly's metadata (for functions such as reflection and serialization); this requires that the assemblies that contain IL and metadata be shipped. In addition, if the CLR can't use the NGen'd file for some reason (described below), the CLR gracefully goes back to JIT compiling the assembly's IL code, which must be available.

- **NGen'd files can get out of sync**   When the CLR loads an NGen'd file, it compares a number of characteristics about the previously compiled code and the current execution environment. If any of the characteristics don't match, the NGen'd file cannot be used, and the normal JIT compiler process is used instead. Here is a partial list of characteristics that must match:

  - ❏ CLR version: this changes with patches or service packs
  - ❏ CPU type: this changes if you upgrade your processor hardware
  - ❏ Windows OS version: this changes with a new service pack update
  - ❏ Assembly's identity module version ID (MVID): this changes when recompiling
  - ❏ Referenced assembly's version IDs: this changes when you recompile a referenced assembly
  - ❏ Security: this changes when you revoke permissions (such as declarative inheritance, declarative link-time, **SkipVerification**, or **UnmanagedCode** permissions), that were once granted

  Note that it is possible to run NGen.exe in update mode. This tells the tool to run NGen.exe on all of the assemblies that had previously been NGen'd. Whenever an end user installs a new service pack of the .NET Framework, the service pack's installation program will run NGen.exe in update mode automatically so that NGen'd files are kept in sync with the version of the CLR installed.

- **Inferior execution-time performance**   When compiling code, NGen can't make as many assumptions about the execution environment as the JIT compiler can. This causes NGen.exe to produce inferior code. For example, NGen won't optimize the use of certain CPU instructions; it adds indirections for static field access because the actual address of the static fields isn't known until runtime. NGen inserts code to call class constructors everywhere because it doesn't know the order in which the code will execute and if a class constructor has already been called. (See Chapter 8, "Methods," for more about class constructors.) Some NGen'd applications actually perform about 5 percent slower when compared to their JIT-compiled counterpart. So, if you're considering using NGen.exe to improve the performance of your application, you should compare NGen'd and non-NGen'd versions to be sure that the NGen'd version doesn't actually run slower! For some applications, the reduction in working set size improves performance, so using NGen can be a net win.

Due to all of the issues just listed, you should be very cautious when considering the use of NGen.exe. For server-side applications, NGen.exe makes little or no sense because only the first client request experiences a performance hit; future client requests run at high speed. In addition, for most server applications, only one instance of the code is required, so there is no working set benefit. Also, note that NGen'd images cannot be shared across AppDomains, so there is no benefit to NGen'ing an assembly that will be used in a cross-AppDomain scenario (such as ASP.NET).

For client applications, NGen.exe might make sense to improve startup time or to reduce working set if an assembly is used by multiple applications simultaneously. Even in a case in which an assembly is not used by multiple applications, NGen'ing an assembly could improve working set. Moreover, if NGen.exe is used for all of a client application's assemblies, the CLR will not need to load the JIT compiler at all, reducing working set even further. Of course, if just one assembly isn't NGen'd or if an assembly's NGen'd file can't be used, the JIT compiler will load, and the application's working set increases.

The Framework Class Library

The .NET Framework includes the *Framework Class Library (FCL)*. The FCL is a set of DLL assemblies that contain several thousand type definitions in which each type exposes some functionality. Microsoft is producing additional libraries such as the Windows SideShow Managed API SDK[2] and the DirectX SDK. These additional libraries provide even more types, exposing even more functionality for your use. In fact, Microsoft is producing many libraries at a phenomenal rate, making it easier than ever for developers to use various Microsoft technologies.

Here are just some of the kinds of applications developers can create by using these assemblies:

- **Web services**   Methods that can process messages sent over the Internet very easily using Microsoft's ASP.NET XML Web Service technology or Microsoft's Windows Communication Foundation (WCF) technology.

- **Web Forms HTML-based applications (Web sites)**   Typically, ASP.NET Web Forms applications will make database queries and Web service calls, combine and filter the returned information, and then present that information in a browser by using a rich HTML-based user interface.

- **Rich Windows GUI applications**   Instead of using a Web Forms page to create your application's UI, you can use the more powerful, higher-performance functionality offered by the Windows desktop via Microsoft's Windows Forms technology or Windows Presentation Foundation (WPF) technology. GUI applications can take advantage of controls, menus, and mouse and keyboard events, and they can exchange information directly with the underlying operating system. Windows Forms applications can also make database queries and consume Web services.

- **Rich Internet Applications (RIAs)**   Using Microsoft's Silverlight technology, you can build rich GUI applications that are deployed via the Internet. These applications can run inside or outside of a Web browser. They also run on non-Windows operating systems, and on mobile devices.

---

[2] Incidentally, I personally was contracted by Microsoft to develop this SDK.

- **Windows console applications**   For applications with very simple UI demands, a console application provides a quick and easy way to build an application. Compilers, utilities, and tools are typically implemented as console applications.

- **Windows services**   Yes, it is possible to build service applications that are controllable via the Windows Service Control Manager (SCM) by using the .NET Framework.

- **Database stored procedures**   Microsoft's SQL Server, IBM's DB2, and Oracle's database servers allow developers to write their stored procedures using the .NET Framework.

- **Component library**   The .NET Framework allows you to build stand-alone assemblies (components) containing types that can be easily incorporated into any of the previously mentioned application types.

Because the FCL contains literally thousands of types, a set of related types is presented to the developer within a single namespace. For example, the **System** namespace (which you should become most familiar with) contains the **Object** base type, from which all other types ultimately derive. In addition, the **System** namespace contains types for integers, characters, strings, exception handling, and console I/O as well as a bunch of utility types that convert safely between data types, format data types, generate random numbers, and perform various math functions. All applications will use types from the **System** namespace.

To access any of the framework's features, you need to know which namespace contains the types that expose the facilities you're after. A lot of types allow you to customize their behavior; you do so by simply deriving your own type from the desired FCL type. The object-oriented nature of the platform is how the .NET Framework presents a consistent programming paradigm to software developers. Also, developers can easily create their own namespaces containing their own types. These namespaces and types merge seamlessly into the programming paradigm. Compared to Win32 programming paradigms, this new approach greatly simplifies software development.

Most of the namespaces in the FCL present types that can be used for any kind of application. Table 1-3 lists some of the more general namespaces and briefly describes what the types in that namespace are used for. This is a very small sampling of the namespaces available. Please see the documentation that accompanies the various Microsoft SDKs to gain familiarity with the ever-growing set of namespaces that Microsoft is producing.

TABLE 1-3 Some General FCL Namespaces

Namespace	Description of Contents
System	All of the basic types used by every application
System.Data	Types for communicating with a database and processing data
System.IO	Types for doing stream I/O and walking directories and files

Namespace	Description of Contents
System.Net	Types that allow for low-level network communications and working with some common Internet protocols.
System.Runtime.InteropServices	Types that allow managed code to access unmanaged OS platform facilities such as COM components and functions in Win32 or custom DLLs
System.Security	Types used for protecting data and resources
System.Text	Types to work with text in different encodings, such as ASCII and Unicode
System.Threading	Types used for asynchronous operations and synchronizing access to resources
System.Xml	Types used for processing Extensible Markup Language (XML) schemas and data

This book is about the CLR and about the general types that interact closely with the CLR. So the content of this book is applicable to all programmers writing applications or components that target the CLR. Many other good books exist that cover specific application types such as Web Services, Web Forms, Windows Forms, etc. These other books will give you an excellent start at helping you build your application. I tend to think of these application-specific books as helping you learn from the top down because they concentrate on the application type and not on the development platform. In this book, I'll offer information that will help you learn from the bottom up. After reading this book and an application-specific book, you should be able to easily and proficiently build any kind of application you desire.

The Common Type System

By now, it should be obvious to you that the CLR is all about types. Types expose functionality to your applications and other types. Types are the mechanism by which code written in one programming language can talk to code written in a different programming language. Because types are at the root of the CLR, Microsoft created a formal specification—the Common Type System (CTS)—that describes how types are defined and how they behave.

Note In fact, Microsoft has been submitting the CTS as well as other parts of the .NET Framework, including file formats, metadata, IL, and access to the underlying platform (P/Invoke) to ECMA for the purpose of standardization. The standard is called the Common Language Infrastructure (CLI) and is the ECMA-335 specification. In addition, Microsoft has also submitted portions of the FCL, the C# programming language (ECMA-334), and the C++/CLI programming language. For information about these industry standards, please go to the ECMA Web site that pertains to Technical Committee 39: *www.ecma-international.org/*. You can also refer to Microsoft's own Web site: *http://msdn.microsoft.com/en-us/netframework/aa569283.aspx*. In addition, Microsoft has applied their Community Promise to the ECMA-334 and ECMA-335 specifications. For more information about this, see *http://www.microsoft.com/interop/cp/default.mspx*.

The CTS specification states that a type can contain zero or more members. In Part II, "Designing Types," I'll cover all of these members in great detail. For now, I want just to give you a brief introduction to them:

- **Field**   A data variable that is part of the object's state. Fields are identified by their name and type.

- **Method**   A function that performs an operation on the object, often changing the object's state. Methods have a name, a signature, and modifiers. The signature specifies the number of parameters (and their sequence), the types of the parameters, whether a value is returned by the method, and if so, the type of the value returned by the method.

- **Property**   To the caller, this member looks like a field. But to the type implementer, it looks like a method (or two). Properties allow an implementer to validate input parameters and object state before accessing the value and/or calculating a value only when necessary. They also allow a user of the type to have simplified syntax. Finally, properties allow you to create read-only or write-only "fields."

- **Event**   An event allows a notification mechanism between an object and other interested objects. For example, a button could offer an event that notifies other objects when the button is clicked.

The CTS also specifies the rules for type visibility and access to the members of a type. For example, marking a type as *public* (called **public**) exports the type, making it visible and accessible to any assembly. On the other hand, marking a type as *assembly* (called **internal** in C#) makes the type visible and accessible to code within the same assembly only. Thus, the CTS establishes the rules by which assemblies form a boundary of visibility for a type, and the CLR enforces the visibility rules.

A type that is visible to a caller can further restrict the ability of the caller to access the type's members. The following list shows the valid options for controlling access to a member:

- **Private**   The member is accessible only by other members in the same class type.

- **Family**   The member is accessible by derived types, regardless of whether they are within the same assembly. Note that many languages (such as C++ and C#) refer to family as **protected**.

- **Family and assembly**   The member is accessible by derived types, but only if the derived type is defined in the same assembly. Many languages (such as C# and Visual Basic) don't offer this access control. Of course, IL Assembly language makes it available.

- **Assembly**   The member is accessible by any code in the same assembly. Many languages refer to *assembly* as **internal**.

- **Family or assembly**   The member is accessible by derived types in any assembly. The member is also accessible by any types in the same assembly. C# refers to *family or assembly* as **protected internal**.

- **Public**   The member is accessible by any code in any assembly.

In addition, the CTS defines the rules governing type inheritance, virtual methods, object life-time, and so on. These rules have been designed to accommodate the semantics expressible in modern-day programming languages. In fact, you won't even need to learn the CTS rules per se because the language you choose will expose its own language syntax and type rules in the same way that you're familiar with today. And it will map the language-specific syntax into IL, the "language" of the CLR, when it emits the assembly during compilation.

When I first started working with the CLR, I soon realized that it is best to think of the language and the behavior of your code as two separate and distinct things. Using C++, you can define your own types with their own members. Of course, you could have used C# or Visual Basic to define the same type with the same members. Sure, the syntax you use for defining the type is different depending on the language you choose, but the behavior of the type will be identical regardless of the language because the CLR's CTS defines the behavior of the type.

To help clarify this idea, let me give you an example. The CTS allows a type to derive from only one base class. So, while the C++ language supports types that can inherit from multiple base types, the CTS can't accept and operate on any such type. To help the developer, Microsoft's C++/CLI compiler reports an error if it detects that you're attempting to create managed code that includes a type deriving from multiple base types.

Here's another CTS rule. All types must (ultimately) inherit from a predefined type: **System.Object**. As you can see, **Object** is the name of a type defined in the **System** namespace. This **Object** is the root of all other types and therefore guarantees that every type instance has a minimum set of behaviors. Specifically, the **System.Object** type allows you to do the following:

- Compare two instances for equality.
- Obtain a hash code for the instance.
- Query the true type of an instance.
- Perform a shallow (bitwise) copy of the instance.
- Obtain a string representation of the instance object's current state.

The Common Language Specification

COM allows objects created in different languages to communicate with one another. On the other hand, the CLR now integrates all languages and allows objects created in one language to be treated as equal citizens by code written in a completely different language. This integration is possible because of the CLR's standard set of types, metadata (self-describing type information), and common execution environment.

While this language integration is a fantastic goal, the truth of the matter is that programming languages are very different from one another. For example, some languages don't treat symbols with case-sensitivity, and some don't offer unsigned integers, operator overloading, or methods to support a variable number of arguments.

If you intend to create types that are easily accessible from other programming languages, you need to use only features of your programming language that are guaranteed to be available in all other languages. To help you with this, Microsoft has defined a Common Language Specification (CLS) that details for compiler vendors the minimum set of features their compilers must support if these compilers are to generate types compatible with other components written by other CLS-compliant languages on top of the CLR.

The CLR/CTS supports a lot more features than the subset defined by the CLS, so if you don't care about interlanguage operability, you can develop very rich types limited only by the language's feature set. Specifically, the CLS defines rules that externally visible types and methods must adhere to if they are to be accessible from any CLS-compliant programming language. Note that the CLS rules don't apply to code that is accessible only within the defining assembly. Figure 1-6 summarizes the ideas expressed in this paragraph.

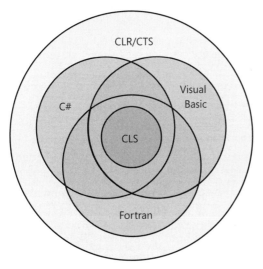

FIGURE 1-6 Languages offer a subset of the CLR/CTS
and a superset of the CLS (but not necessarily the same superset)

As Figure 1-6 shows, the CLR/CTS offers a set of features. Some languages expose a large subset of the CLR/CTS. A programmer willing to write in IL assembly language, for example, is able to use all of the features the CLR/CTS offers. Most other languages, such as C#, Visual Basic, and Fortran, expose a subset of the CLR/CTS features to the programmer. The CLS defines the minimum set of features that all languages must support.

If you're designing a type in one language, and you expect that type to be used by another language, you shouldn't take advantage of any features that are outside of the CLS in its public and protected members. Doing so would mean that your type's members might not be accessible by programmers writing code in other programming languages.

In the following code, a CLS-compliant type is being defined in C#. However, the type has a few non–CLS-compliant constructs causing the C# compiler to complain about the code.

```
using System;

// Tell compiler to check for CLS compliance
[assembly: CLSCompliant(true)]

namespace SomeLibrary {
    // Warnings appear because the class is public
    public sealed class SomeLibraryType {

        // Warning: Return type of 'SomeLibrary.SomeLibraryType.Abc()'
        // is not CLS-compliant
        public UInt32 Abc() { return 0; }

        // Warning: Identifier 'SomeLibrary.SomeLibraryType.abc()'
        // differing only in case is not CLS-compliant
        public void abc() { }

        // No warning: this method is private
        private UInt32 ABC() { return 0; }
    }
}
```

In this code, the **[assembly:CLSCompliant(true)]** attribute is applied to the assembly. This attribute tells the compiler to ensure that any publicly exposed type doesn't have any construct that would prevent the type from being accessed from any other programming language. When this code is compiled, the C# compiler emits two warnings. The first warning is reported because the method **Abc** returns an unsigned integer; some other programming languages can't manipulate unsigned integer values. The second warning is because this type exposes two public methods that differ only by case and return type: **Abc** and **abc**. Visual Basic and some other languages can't call both of these methods.

Interestingly, if you were to delete **public** from in front of **'sealed class SomeLibraryType'** and recompile, both warnings would go away. The reason is that the **SomeLibraryType** type would default to **internal** and would therefore no longer be exposed outside of the assembly. For a complete list of CLS rules, refer to the "Cross-

Language Interoperability" section in the .NET Framework SDK documentation (*http://msdn.microsoft.com/en-us/library/730f1wy3.aspx*).

Let me distill the CLS rules to something very simple. In the CLR, every member of a type is either a field (data) or a method (behavior). This means that every programming language must be able to access fields and call methods. Certain fields and certain methods are used in special and common ways. To ease programming, languages typically offer additional abstractions to make coding these common programming patterns easier. For example, languages expose concepts such as enums, arrays, properties, indexers, delegates, events, constructors, finalizers, operator overloads, conversion operators, and so on. When a compiler comes across any of these things in your source code, it must translate these constructs into fields and methods so that the CLR and any other programming language can access the construct.

Consider the following type definition, which contains a constructor, a finalizer, some overloaded operators, a property, an indexer, and an event. Note that the code shown is there just to make the code compile; it doesn't show the correct way to implement a type.

```
using System;

internal sealed class Test {
   // Constructor
   public Test() {}

   // Finalizer
   ~Test() {}

   // Operator overload
   public static Boolean operator == (Test t1, Test t2) {
      return true;
   }
   public static Boolean operator != (Test t1, Test t2) {
      return false;
   }

   // An operator overload
   public static Test operator + (Test t1, Test t2) { return null; }

   // A property
   public String AProperty {
      get { return null; }
      set { }
   }

   // An indexer
   public String this[Int32 x] {
      get { return null; }
      set { }
   }

   // An event
   public event EventHandler AnEvent;
}
```

When the compiler compiles this code, the result is a type that has a number of fields and methods defined in it. You can easily see this by using the IL Disassembler tool (ILDasm.exe) provided with the .NET Framework SDK to examine the resulting managed module, which is shown in Figure 1-7.

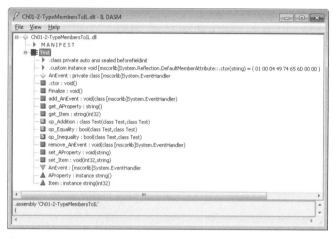

FIGURE 1-7 ILDasm showing Test type's fields and methods (obtained from metadata)

Table 1-4 shows how the programming language constructs got mapped to the equivalent CLR fields and methods.

TABLE 1-4 Test Type's Fields and Methods (Obtained from Metadata)

Type Member	Member Type	Equivalent Programming Language Construct
AnEvent	Field	Event; the name of the field is **AnEvent** and its type is **System.EventHandler**.
.ctor	Method	Constructor.
Finalize	Method	Finalizer.
add_AnEvent	Method	**Event add accessor** method.
get_AProperty	Method	**Property get accessor** method.
get_Item	Method	**Indexer get accessor** method.
op_Addition	Method	+ operator.
op_Equality	Method	== operator.
op_Inequality	Method	!= operator.
remove_AnEvent	Method	**Event remove accessor** method.
set_AProperty	Method	**Property set accessor** method.
set_Item	Method	**Indexer set accessor** method.

The additional nodes under the **Test** type that aren't mentioned in Table 1-4—**.class**, **.custom**, **AnEvent**, **AProperty**, and **Item**—identify additional metadata about the type. These nodes don't map to fields or methods; they just offer some additional information about the type that the CLR, programming languages, or tools can get access to. For example, a tool can see that the **Test** type offers an event, called **AnEvent**, which is exposed via the two methods (**add_AnEvent** and **remove_AnEvent**).

Interoperability with Unmanaged Code

The .NET Framework offers a ton of advantages over other development platforms. However, very few companies can afford to redesign and re-implement all of their existing code. Microsoft realizes this and has constructed the CLR so that it offers mechanisms that allow an application to consist of both managed and unmanaged parts. Specifically, the CLR supports three interoperability scenarios:

- **Managed code can call an unmanaged function in a DLL**   Managed code can easily call functions contained in DLLs by using a mechanism called P/Invoke (for Platform Invoke). After all, many of the types defined in the FCL internally call functions exported from Kernel32.dll, User32.dll, and so on. Many programming languages will expose a mechanism that makes it easy for managed code to call out to unmanaged functions contained in DLLs. For example, a C# application can call the **CreateSemaphore** function exported from Kernel32.dll.

- **Managed code can use an existing COM component (server)**   Many companies have already implemented a number of unmanaged COM components. Using the type library from these components, a managed assembly can be created that describes the COM component. Managed code can access the type in the managed assembly just as any other managed type. See the TlbImp.exe tool that ships with the .NET Framework SDK for more information. At times, you might not have a type library or you might want to have more control over what TlbImp.exe produces. In these cases, you can manually build a type in source code that the CLR can use to achieve the proper interoperability. For example, you could use DirectX COM components from a C# application.

- **Unmanaged code can use a managed type (server)**   A lot of existing unmanaged code requires that you supply a COM component for the code to work correctly. It's much easier to implement these components by using managed code so that you can avoid all of the code having to do with reference counting and interfaces. For example, you could create an ActiveX control or a shell extension in C#. See the TlbExp.exe and RegAsm.exe tools that ship with the .NET Framework SDK for more information.

 Note Microsoft now makes available the source code for the Type Library Importer tool and a P/Invoke Interop Assistant tool to help developers needing to interact with native code. These tools and their source code can be downloaded from *http://CLRInterop.CodePlex.com/*.

Chapter 2
Building, Packaging, Deploying, and Administering Applications and Types

Before we get into the chapters that explain how to develop programs for the Microsoft .NET Framework, let's discuss the steps required to build, package, and deploy your applications and their types. In this chapter, I'll focus on the basics of how to build assemblies that are for your application's sole use. In Chapter 3, "Shared Assemblies and Strongly Named Assemblies," I'll cover the more advanced concepts you'll need to understand, including how to build and use assemblies containing types that will be shared by multiple applications. In both chapters, I'll also talk about the ways an administrator can affect the execution of an application and its types.

Today, applications consist of several types, which are typically created by you and Microsoft. In addition, there are many component vendors creating and selling types that other companies can use to reduce a software project's development time. If these types are developed using any language that targets the common language runtime (CLR), they can all work together seamlessly; a type written in one language can use another type as its base class without concern for the language the base type was developed in.

In this chapter, I'll also explain how these types are built and packaged into files for deployment. In the process, I'll take you on a brief historical tour of some of the problems that the .NET Framework is solving.

.NET Framework Deployment Goals

Over the years, Microsoft Windows has gotten a reputation for being unstable and complicated. This reputation, whether deserved or not, is the result of many different factors. First, all applications use dynamic-link libraries (DLLs) from Microsoft or other vendors. Because an application executes code from various vendors, the developer of any one piece of code can't be 100 percent sure how someone else is going to use it. Although this kind of interaction can potentially cause all kinds of trouble, in practice, these problems don't typically arise because applications are tested and debugged before they are deployed.

Users, however, frequently run into problems when one company decides to update its code and ships new files to them. These new files are supposed to be backward-compatible with the previous files, but who knows for sure? In fact, when one vendor updates its code, it usually finds it impossible to retest and debug all of the already-shipped applications to ensure that the changes will have no undesirable effect.

I'm sure that everyone reading this book has experienced some variation of this problem: when installing a new application, you discover that it has somehow corrupted an already-installed application. This predicament is known as "DLL hell." This type of instability puts fear into the hearts and minds of the typical computer user. The end result is that users have to carefully consider whether to install new software on their machines. Personally, I've decided not to try out certain applications out of fear that it might adversely affect some application I really rely on.

The second reason that contributed to the aforementioned reputation of Windows is installation complexities. Today, when most applications are installed, they affect all parts of the system. For example, installing an application causes files to be copied to various directories, updates registry settings, and installs shortcuts on your desktop and Start menu. The problem with this is that the application isn't isolated as a single entity. You can't easily back up the application since you must copy the application's files and also the relevant parts of the registry. In addition, you can't easily move the application from one machine to another; you must run the installation program again so that all files and registry settings are set properly. Finally, you can't easily uninstall or remove the application without having this nasty feeling that some part of the application is still lurking on your machine.

The third reason has to do with security. When applications are installed, they come with all kinds of files, many of them written by different companies. In addition, Web applications frequently have code (like ActiveX controls) that is downloaded in such a way that users don't even realize that code is being installed on their machine. Today, this code can perform any operation, including deleting files or sending e-mail. Users are right to be terrified of installing new applications because of the potential damage they can cause. To make users comfortable, security must be built into the system so that the users can explicitly allow or disallow code developed by various companies to access their system's resources.

The .NET Framework addresses the DLL hell issue in a big way, as you'll see while reading this chapter and Chapter 3. It also goes a long way toward fixing the problem of having an application's state scattered all over a user's hard disk. For example, unlike COM, types no longer require settings in the registry. Unfortunately, applications still require shortcut links. As for security, the .NET Framework includes a security model called *code access security*. Whereas Windows security is based on a user's identity, code access security is based on permissions that host applications that loading components can control. A host application like Microsoft Silverlight can grant just a few permissions to downloaded code, while a locally installed (self-hosting) application could run with full trust (all permissions). As you'll see, the .NET Framework enables users to control what gets installed and what runs, and in general, to control their machines, more than Windows ever did.

Building Types into a Module

In this section, I'll show you how to turn your source file, containing various types, into a file that can be deployed. Let's start by examining the following simple application:

```
public sealed class Program {
    public static void Main() {
        System.Console.WriteLine("Hi");
    }
}
```

This application defines a type, called **Program**. This type has a single public, static method called **Main**. Inside **Main** is a reference to another type called **System.Console**. **System.Console** is a type implemented by Microsoft, and the Intermediate Language (IL) code that implements this type's methods is in the MSCorLib.dll file. So our application defines a type and also uses another company's type.

To build this sample application, put the preceding code into a source code file, say, Program.cs, and then execute the following command line:

```
csc.exe /out:Program.exe /t:exe /r:MSCorLib.dll Program.cs
```

This command line tells the C# compiler to emit an executable file called Program.exe (**/out:Program.exe**). The type of file produced is a Win32 console application (**/t[arget]:exe**).

When the C# compiler processes the source file, it sees that the code references the **System.Console** type's **WriteLine** method. At this point, the compiler wants to ensure that this type exists somewhere, that it has a **WriteLine** method, and that the argument being passed to this method matches the parameter the method expects. Since this type is not defined in the C# source code, to make the C# compiler happy, you must give it a set of assemblies that it can use to resolve references to external types. In the command line above,

I've included the **/r[eference]:MSCorLib.dll** switch, which tells the compiler to look for external types in the assembly identified by the MSCorLib.dll file.

MSCorLib.dll is a special file in that it contains all the core types: **Byte**, **Char**, **String**, **Int32**, and many more. In fact, these types are so frequently used that the C# compiler automatically references the MSCorLib.dll assembly. In other words, the following command line (with the **/r** switch omitted) gives the same results as the line shown earlier:

```
csc.exe /out:Program.exe /t:exe Program.cs
```

Furthermore, because the **/out:Program.exe** and the **/t:exe** command-line switches also match what the C# compiler would choose as defaults, the following command line gives the same results too:

```
csc.exe Program.cs
```

If, for some reason, you really don't want the C# compiler to reference the MSCorLib.dll assembly, you can use the **/nostdlib** switch. Microsoft uses this switch when building the MSCorLib.dll assembly itself. For example, the following command line will generate an error when CSC.exe attempts to compile the Program.cs file because the **System.Console** type is defined in MSCorLib.dll:

```
csc.exe /out:Program.exe /t:exe /nostdlib Program.cs
```

Now, let's take a closer look at the Program.exe file produced by the C# compiler. What exactly is this file? Well, for starters, it is a standard portable executable (PE) file. This means that a machine running 32-bit or 64-bit versions of Windows should be able to load this file and do something with it. Windows supports two types of applications, those with a console user interface (CUI) and those with a graphical user interface (GUI). Because I specified the **/t:exe** switch, the C# compiler produced a CUI application. You'd use the **/t:winexe** switch to cause the C# compiler to produce a GUI application.

Response Files

Before leaving the discussion about compiler switches, I'd like to spend a moment talking about *response files*. A response file is a text file that contains a set of compiler command-line switches. When you execute CSC.exe, the compiler opens response files and uses any switches that are specified in them as though the switches were passed to CSC.exe on the command line. You instruct the compiler to use a response file by specifying its name on the command line prepended by an @ sign. For example, you could have a response file called MyProject.rsp that contains the following text:

```
/out:MyProject.exe
/target:winexe
```

To cause CSC.exe to use these settings, you'd invoke it as follows:

```
csc.exe @MyProject.rsp CodeFile1.cs CodeFile2.cs
```

This tells the C# compiler what to name the output file and what kind of target to create. As you can see, response files are very convenient because you don't have to manually express the desired command-line arguments each time you want to compile your project.

The C# compiler supports multiple response files. In addition to the files you explicitly specify on the command line, the compiler automatically looks for files called CSC.rsp. When you run CSC.exe, it looks in the current directory for a local CSC.rsp file—you should place any project-specific settings in this file. The compiler also looks in the directory containing the CSC.exe file for a global CSC.rsp file. Settings that you want applied to all of your projects should go in this file. The compiler aggregates and uses the settings in all of these response files. If you have conflicting settings in the local and global response files, the settings in the local file override the settings in the global file. Likewise, any settings explicitly passed on the command line override the settings taken from a local response file.

When you install the .NET Framework, it installs a default global CSC.rsp file in the %SystemRoot%\Microsoft.NET\Framework\v*X.X.X*directory (where *X.X.X* is the version of the .NET Framework you have installed). The 4.0 version of this file contains the following switches:

```
# This file contains command-line options that the C#
# command line compiler (CSC) will process as part
# of every compilation, unless the "/noconfig" option
# is specified.

# Reference the common Framework libraries
/r:Accessibility.dll
/r:Microsoft.CSharp.dll
/r:System.Configuration.dll
/r:System.Configuration.Install.dll
/r:System.Core.dll
/r:System.Data.dll
/r:System.Data.DataSetExtensions.dll
/r:System.Data.Linq.dll
/r:System.Deployment.dll
/r:System.Device.dll
/r:System.DirectoryServices.dll
/r:System.dll
/r:System.Drawing.dll
/r:System.EnterpriseServices.dll
/r:System.Management.dll
/r:System.Messaging.dll
/r:System.Numerics.dll
/r:System.Runtime.Remoting.dll
/r:System.Runtime.Serialization.dll
/r:System.Runtime.Serialization.Formatters.Soap.dll
/r:System.Security.dll
```

```
/r:System.ServiceModel.dll
/r:System.ServiceProcess.dll
/r:System.Transactions.dll
/r:System.Web.Services.dll
/r:System.Windows.Forms.Dll
/r:System.Xml.dll
/r:System.Xml.Linq.dll
```

Because the global CSC.rsp file references all of the assemblies listed, you do not need to explicitly reference these assemblies by using the C# compiler's **/reference** switch. This response file is a big convenience for developers because it allows them to use types and namespaces defined in various Microsoft-published assemblies without having to specify a **/reference** compiler switch for each when compiling.

Referencing all of these assemblies could slow the compiler down a bit. But if your source code doesn't refer to a type or member defined by any of these assemblies, there is no impact to the resulting assembly file, nor to run-time execution performance.

> **Note**   When you use the **/reference** compiler switch to reference an assembly, you can specify a complete path to a particular file. However, if you do not specify a path, the compiler will search for the file in the following places (in the order listed):
>
> - Working directory.
> - The directory that contains the CSC.exe file itself. MSCorLib.dll is always obtained from this directory. The path looks something like this: %SystemRoot%\Microsoft.NET\Framework \v4.0.#####.
> - Any directories specified using the **/lib** compiler switch.
> - Any directories specified using the **LIB** environment variable.

Of course, you're welcome to add your own switches to the global CSC.rsp file if you want to make your life even easier, but this makes it more difficult to replicate the build environment on different machines: you have to remember to update the CSC.rsp the same way on each build machine. Also, you can tell the compiler to ignore both local and global CSC.rsp files by specifying the **/noconfig** command-line switch.

A Brief Look at Metadata

Now we know what kind of PE file we've created. But what exactly is in the Program.exe file? A managed PE file has four main parts: the PE32(+) header, the CLR header, the metadata, and the IL. The PE32(+) header is the standard information that Windows expects. The CLR header is a small block of information that is specific to modules that require the CLR (managed modules). The header includes the major and minor version number of the CLR that the module was built for: some flags, a **MethodDef** token (described later) indicating the module's entry point method if this module is a CUI or GUI executable, and an optional strong-name digital signature (discussed in Chapter 3). Finally, the header contains the size and offsets of certain metadata tables contained within the module. You can see the exact format of the CLR header by examining the **IMAGE_COR20_HEADER** defined in the CorHdr.h header file.

The metadata is a block of binary data that consists of several tables. There are three categories of tables: definition tables, reference tables, and manifest tables. Table 2-1 describes some of the more common definition tables that exist in a module's metadata block.

TABLE 2-1 Common Definition Metadata Tables

Metadata Definition Table Name	Description
ModuleDef	Always contains one entry that identifies the module. The entry includes the module's file name and extension (without path) and a module version ID (in the form of a GUID created by the compiler). This allows the file to be renamed while keeping a record of its original name. However, renaming a file is strongly discouraged and can prevent the CLR from locating an assembly at runtime, so don't do this.
TypeDef	Contains one entry for each type defined in the module. Each entry includes the type's name, base type, and flags (**public**, **private**, etc.) and contains indexes to the methods it owns in the MethodDef table, the fields it owns in the FieldDef table, the properties it owns in the PropertyDef table, and the events it owns in the EventDef table.
MethodDef	Contains one entry for each method defined in the module. Each entry includes the method's name, flags (**private**, **public**, **virtual**, **abstract**, **static**, **final**, etc.), signature, and offset within the module where its IL code can be found. Each entry can also refer to a ParamDef table entry in which more information about the method's parameters can be found.
FieldDef	Contains one entry for every field defined in the module. Each entry includes flags (**private**, **public**, etc.), type, and name.
ParamDef	Contains one entry for each parameter defined in the module. Each entry includes flags (**in**, **out**, **retval**, etc.), type, and name.
PropertyDef	Contains one entry for each property defined in the module. Each entry includes flags, type, and name.
EventDef	Contains one entry for each event defined in the module. Each entry includes flags and name.

As the compiler compiles your source code, everything your code defines causes an entry to be created in one of the tables described in Table 2-1. Metadata table entries are also created as the compiler detects the types, fields, methods, properties, and events that the source code references. The metadata created includes a set of reference tables that keep a record of the referenced items. Table 2-2 shows some of the more common reference metadata tables.

TABLE 2-2 Common Reference Metadata Tables

Metadata Reference Table Name	Description
AssemblyRef	Contains one entry for each assembly referenced by the module. Each entry includes the information necessary to bind to the assembly: the assembly's name (without path and extension), version number, culture, and public key token (normally a small hash value generated from the publisher's public key, identifying the referenced assembly's publisher). Each entry also contains some flags and a hash value. This hash value was intended to be a checksum of the referenced assembly's bits. The CLR completely ignores this hash value and will probably continue to do so in the future.
ModuleRef	Contains one entry for each PE module that implements types referenced by this module. Each entry includes the module's file name and extension (without path). This table is used to bind to types that are implemented in different modules of the calling assembly's module.
TypeRef	Contains one entry for each type referenced by the module. Each entry includes the type's name and a reference to where the type can be found. If the type is implemented within another type, the reference will indicate a TypeRef entry. If the type is implemented in the same module, the reference will indicate a ModuleDef entry. If the type is implemented in another module within the calling assembly, the reference will indicate a ModuleRef entry. If the type is implemented in a different assembly, the reference will indicate an AssemblyRef entry.
MemberRef	Contains one entry for each member (fields and methods, as well as property and event methods) referenced by the module. Each entry includes the member's name and signature and points to the TypeRef entry for the type that defines the member.

There are many more tables than what I listed in Tables 2-1 and 2-2, but I just wanted to give you a sense of the kind of information that the compiler emits to produce the metadata information. Earlier I mentioned that there is also a set of manifest metadata tables; I'll discuss these a little later in the chapter.

Various tools allow you to examine the metadata within a managed PE file. My personal favorite is ILDasm.exe, the IL Disassembler. To see the metadata tables, execute the following command line:

```
ILDasm Program.exe
```

This causes ILDasm.exe to run, loading the Program.exe assembly. To see the metadata in a nice, human-readable form, select the View/MetaInfo/Show! menu item (or press CTRL+M). This causes the following information to appear:

```
============================================================
ScopeName : Program.exe
MVID      : {CA73FFE8-0D42-4610-A8D3-9276195C35AA}
============================================================
Global functions
------------------------------------------------------

Global fields
------------------------------------------------------

Global MemberRefs
------------------------------------------------------

TypeDef #1 (02000002)
------------------------------------------------------
    TypDefName: Program   (02000002)
    Flags     : [Public] [AutoLayout] [Class] [Sealed] [AnsiClass]
                [BeforeFieldInit]   (00100101)
    Extends   : 01000001 [TypeRef] System.Object
    Method #1 (06000001) [ENTRYPOINT]
    ------------------------------------------------------
        MethodName: Main (06000001)
        Flags     : [Public] [Static] [HideBySig] [ReuseSlot]   (00000096)
        RVA       : 0x00002050
        ImplFlags : [IL] [Managed]   (00000000)
        CallCnvntn: [DEFAULT]
        ReturnType: Void
        No arguments.

    Method #2 (06000002)
    ------------------------------------------------------
        MethodName: .ctor (06000002)
        Flags     : [Public] [HideBySig] [ReuseSlot] [SpecialName]
                    [RTSpecialName] [.ctor]   (00001886)
        RVA       : 0x0000205c
        ImplFlags : [IL] [Managed]   (00000000)
        CallCnvntn: [DEFAULT]
        hasThis
        ReturnType: Void
        No arguments.


TypeRef #1 (01000001)
------------------------------------------------------
Token:            0x01000001
ResolutionScope:  0x23000001
TypeRefName:      System.Object
    MemberRef #1 (0a000004)
    ------------------------------------------------------
        Member: (0a000004) .ctor:
        CallCnvntn: [DEFAULT]
        hasThis
        ReturnType: Void
        No arguments.

TypeRef #2 (01000002)
```

```
------------------------------------------------------
Token:            0x01000002
ResolutionScope:  0x23000001
TypeRefName:      System.Runtime.CompilerServices.CompilationRelaxationsAttribute
   MemberRef #1 (0a000001)
   ------------------------------------------------------
      Member: (0a000001) .ctor:
      CallCnvntn: [DEFAULT]
      hasThis
      ReturnType: Void
      1 Arguments
         Argument #1:  I4

TypeRef #3 (01000003)
------------------------------------------------------
Token:            0x01000003
ResolutionScope:  0x23000001
TypeRefName:      System.Runtime.CompilerServices.RuntimeCompatibilityAttribute
   MemberRef #1 (0a000002)
   ------------------------------------------------------
      Member: (0a000002) .ctor:
      CallCnvntn: [DEFAULT]
      hasThis
      ReturnType: Void
      No arguments.
TypeRef #4 (01000004)
------------------------------------------------------
Token:            0x01000004
ResolutionScope:  0x23000001
TypeRefName:      System.Console
   MemberRef #1 (0a000003)
   ------------------------------------------------------
      Member: (0a000003) WriteLine:
      CallCnvntn: [DEFAULT]
      ReturnType: Void
      1 Arguments
         Argument #1:  String

Assembly
------------------------------------------------------
   Token: 0x20000001
   Name : Program
   Public Key   :
   Hash Algorithm : 0x00008004
   Version: 0.0.0.0
   Major Version: 0x00000000
   Minor Version: 0x00000000
   Build Number: 0x00000000
   Revision Number: 0x00000000
   Locale: <null>
   Flags : [none] (00000000)
   CustomAttribute #1 (0c000001)
   ------------------------------------------------------
      CustomAttribute Type: 0a000001
      CustomAttributeName:
```

```
      System.Runtime.CompilerServices.CompilationRelaxationsAttribute ::
          instance void .ctor(int32)
      Length: 8
      Value : 01 00 08 00 00 00 00 00                         >              <
      ctor args: (8)

   CustomAttribute #2 (0c000002)
   -----------------------------------------------------------
      CustomAttribute Type: 0a000002
      CustomAttributeName: System.Runtime.CompilerServices.RuntimeCompatibilityAttribute ::
          instance void .ctor()
      Length: 30
      Value : 01 00 01 00 54 02 16 57  72 61 70 4e 6f 6e 45 78 >    T  WrapNonEx<
            : 63 65 70 74 69 6f 6e 54  68 72 6f 77 73 01        >ceptionThrows  <
      ctor args: ()

AssemblyRef #1 (23000001)
-----------------------------------------------------------
   Token: 0x23000001
   Public Key or Token: b7 7a 5c 56 19 34 e0 89
   Name: mscorlib
   Version: 4.0.0.0
   Major Version: 0x00000004
   Minor Version: 0x00000000
   Build Number: 0x00000000
   Revision Number: 0x00000000
   Locale: <null>
   HashValue Blob:
   Flags: [none] (00000000)


User Strings
-------------------------------------------------------
70000001 : ( 2) L"Hi"


Coff symbol name overhead:  0
============================================================
============================================================
============================================================
```

Fortunately, ILDasm processes the metadata tables and combines information where appropriate so that you don't have to parse the raw table information. For example, in the dump above, you see that when ILDasm shows a TypeDef entry, the corresponding member definition information is shown with it before the first TypeRef entry is displayed.

You don't need to fully understand everything you see here. The important thing to remember is that Program.exe contains a TypeDef whose name is **Program.** This type identifies a public sealed class that is derived from **System.Object** (a type referenced from another assembly). The **Program** type also defines two methods: **Main** and **.ctor** (a constructor).

Main is a public, static method whose code is IL (as opposed to native CPU code, such as x86). **Main** has a **void** return type and takes no arguments. The constructor method (always shown with a name of **.ctor**) is public, and its code is also IL. The constructor has a **void** return type, has no arguments, and has a **this** pointer, which refers to the object's memory that is to be constructed when the method is called.

I strongly encourage you to experiment with using ILDasm. It can show you a wealth of information, and the more you understand what you're seeing, the better you'll understand the CLR and its capabilities. As you'll see, I'll use ILDasm quite a bit more in this book.

Just for fun, let's look at some statistics about the Program.exe assembly. When you select ILDasm's View/Statistics menu item, the following information is displayed:

```
File size            : 3584
 PE header size      : 512 (496 used)    (14.29%)
 PE additional info  : 1415              (39.48%)
 Num.of PE sections  : 3
 CLR header size     : 72                ( 2.01%)
 CLR meta-data size  : 612               (17.08%)
 CLR additional info : 0                 ( 0.00%)
 CLR method headers  : 2                 ( 0.06%)
 Managed code        : 18                ( 0.50%)
 Data                : 2048              (57.14%)
 Unaccounted         : -1095             (-30.55%)

 Num.of PE sections  : 3
   .text    - 1024
   .rsrc    - 1536
   .reloc   - 512

 CLR meta-data size  : 612
   Module          -    1 (10 bytes)
   TypeDef         -    2 (28 bytes)    0 interfaces, 0 explicit layout
   TypeRef         -    4 (24 bytes)
   MethodDef       -    2 (28 bytes)    0 abstract, 0 native, 2 bodies
   MemberRef       -    4 (24 bytes)
   ParamDef        -    2 (12 bytes)
   CustomAttribute-    2 (12 bytes)
   Assembly        -    1 (22 bytes)
   AssemblyRef     -    1 (20 bytes)
   Strings         -  184 bytes
   Blobs           -   68 bytes
   UserStrings     -    8 bytes
   Guids           -   16 bytes
   Uncategorized   -  168 bytes

 CLR method headers : 2
   Num.of method bodies  - 2
   Num.of fat headers    - 0
   Num.of tiny headers   - 2

 Managed code : 18
   Ave method size - 9
```

Here you can see the size (in bytes) of the file and the size (in bytes and percentages) of the various parts that make up the file. For this very small Program.cs application, the PE header and the metadata occupy the bulk of the file's size. In fact, the IL code occupies just 18 bytes. Of course, as an application grows, it will reuse most of its types and references to other types and assemblies, causing the metadata and header information to shrink considerably as compared to the overall size of the file.

> **Note** By the way, ILDasm.exe does have a bug in it that affects the file size information shown. In particular, you cannot trust the **Unaccounted** information.

Combining Modules to Form an Assembly

The Program.exe file discussed in the previous section is more than just a PE file with metadata; it is also an *assembly*. An assembly is a collection of one or more files containing type definitions and resource files. One of the assembly's files is chosen to hold a *manifest*. The manifest is another set of metadata tables that basically contain the names of the files that are part of the assembly. They also describe the assembly's version, culture, publisher, publicly exported types, and all of the files that comprise the assembly.

The CLR operates on assemblies; that is, the CLR always loads the file that contains the manifest metadata tables first and then uses the manifest to get the names of the other files that are in the assembly. Here are some characteristics of assemblies that you should remember:

- An assembly defines the reusable types.
- An assembly is marked with a version number.
- An assembly can have security information associated with it.

An assembly's individual files don't have these attributes—except for the file that contains the manifest metadata tables.

To package, version, secure, and use types, you must place them in modules that are part of an assembly. In most cases, an assembly consists of a single file, as the preceding Program.exe example does. However, an assembly can also consist of multiple files: some PE files with metadata and some resource files such as .gif or .jpg files. It might help you to think of an assembly as a logical EXE or a DLL.

I'm sure that many of you reading this are wondering why Microsoft has introduced this new assembly concept. The reason is that an assembly allows you to decouple the logical and physical notions of reusable types. For example, an assembly can consist of several types. You could put the frequently used types in one file and the less frequently used types in another file. If your assembly is deployed by downloading it via the Internet, the file with the infrequently used types might not ever have to be downloaded to the client if the client never accesses the types. For example, an independent software vendor (ISV) specializing in UI controls might choose to implement Active Accessibility types in a separate module (to satisfy Microsoft's Logo requirements). Only users who require the additional accessibility features would require this module to be downloaded.

You configure an application to download assembly files by specifying a **codeBase** element (discussed in Chapter 3) in the application's configuration file. The **codeBase** element identifies a URL pointing to where all of an assembly's files can be found. When attempting to load an assembly's file, the CLR obtains the **codeBase** element's URL and checks the machine's download cache to see if the file is present. If it is, the file is loaded. If the file isn't in the cache, the CLR downloads the file into the cache from the location the URL points to. If the file can't be found, the CLR throws a `FileNotFoundException` exception at runtime.

I've identified three reasons to use multifile assemblies:

- You can partition your types among separate files, allowing for files to be incrementally downloaded as described in the Internet download scenario. Partitioning the types into separate files also allows for partial or piecemeal packaging and deployment for applications you purchase and install.

- You can add resource or data files to your assembly. For example, you could have a type that calculates some insurance information. This type might require access to some actuarial tables to make its computations. Instead of embedding the actuarial tables in your source code, you could use a tool (such as the Assembly Linker, AL.exe, discussed later) so that the data file is considered to be part of the assembly. By the way, this data file can be in any format—a text file, a Microsoft Office Excel spreadsheet, a Microsoft Office Word table, or whatever you like—as long as your application knows how to parse the file's contents.

- You can create assemblies consisting of types implemented in different programming languages. For example, you can implement some types in C#, some types in Microsoft Visual Basic, and other types in other languages. When you compile the types written with C# source code, the compiler produces a module. When you compile other types written with Visual Basic source code, the compiler produces a separate module. You can then use a tool to combine all of these modules into a single assembly. To developers using the assembly, the assembly appears to contain just a bunch of types; developers won't even know that different programming languages were used. By the way, if you prefer, you can run ILDasm.exe on each of the modules to obtain an IL source code file. Then you can run ILAsm.exe and pass it all of the IL source code files. ILAsm.exe will produce a single file containing all of the types. This technique requires your source code compiler to produce IL-only code.

> **Important** To summarize, an assembly is a unit of reuse, versioning, and security. It allows you to partition your types and resources into separate files so that you, and consumers of your assembly, get to determine which files to package together and deploy. Once the CLR loads the file containing the manifest, it can determine which of the assembly's other files contain the types and resources the application is referencing. Anyone consuming the assembly is required to know only the name of the file containing the manifest; the file partitioning is then abstracted away from the consumer and can change in the future without breaking the application's behavior.
>
> If you have multiple types that can share a single version number and security settings, it is recommended that you place all of the types in a single file rather than spread the types out over separate files, let alone separate assemblies. The reason is performance. Loading a file/assembly takes the CLR and Windows time to find the assembly, load it, and initialize it. The fewer files/assemblies loaded the better, because loading fewer assemblies helps reduce working set and also reduces fragmentation of a process's address space. Finally, nGen.exe can perform better optimizations when processing larger files.

To build an assembly, you must select one of your PE files to be the keeper of the manifest. Or you can create a separate PE file that contains nothing but the manifest. Table 2-3 shows the manifest metadata tables that turn a managed module into an assembly.

TABLE 2-3 Manifest Metadata Tables

Manifest Metadata Table Name	Description
AssemblyDef	Contains a single entry if this module identifies an assembly. The entry includes the assembly's name (without path and extension), version (major, minor, build, and revision), culture, flags, hash algorithm, and the publisher's public key (which can be **null**).
FileDef	Contains one entry for each PE and resource file that is part of the assembly (except the file containing the manifest since it appears as the single entry in the AssemblyDef table). The entry includes the file's name and extension (without path), hash value, and flags. If this assembly consists only of its own file, the FileDef table has no entries.
ManifestResourceDef	Contains one entry for each resource that is part of the assembly. The entry includes the resource's name, flags (**public** if visible outside the assembly and **private** otherwise), and an index into the FileDef table indicating the file that contains the resource file or stream. If the resource isn't a stand-alone file (such as .jpg or a .gif), the resource is a stream contained within a PE file. For an embedded resource, the entry also includes an offset indicating the start of the resource stream within the PE file.
ExportedTypesDef	Contains one entry for each public type exported from all of the assembly's PE modules. The entry includes the type's name, an index into the FileDef table (indicating which of this assembly's files implements the type), and an index into the TypeDef table. *Note*: To save file space, types exported from the file containing the manifest are not repeated in this table because the type information is available using the metadata's TypeDef table.

The existence of a manifest provides a level of indirection between consumers of the assembly and the partitioning details of the assembly and makes assemblies self-describing. Also, note that the file containing the manifest has metadata information that indicates which files are part of the assembly, but the individual files themselves do not have metadata information that specifies that they are part of the assembly.

> **Note** The assembly file that contains the manifest also has an AssemblyRef table in it. This table contains an entry for all of the assemblies referenced by all of the assembly's files. This allows tools to open an assembly's manifest and see its set of referenced assemblies without having to open the assembly's other files. Again, the entries in the AssemblyRef table exist to make an assembly self-describing.

The C# compiler produces an assembly when you specify any of the following command-line switches: **/t[arget]:exe**, **/t[arget]:winexe**, or **/t[arget]:library**. All of these switches cause the compiler to generate a single PE file that contains the manifest metadata tables. The resulting file is either a CUI executable, a GUI executable, or a DLL, respectively.

In addition to these switches, the C# compiler supports the **/t[arget]:module** switch. This switch tells the compiler to produce a PE file that doesn't contain the manifest metadata tables. The PE file produced is always a DLL PE file, and this file must be added to an assembly before the CLR can access any types within it. When you use the **/t:module** switch, the C# compiler, by default, names the output file with an extension of .netmodule.

> **Important** Unfortunately, the Microsoft Visual Studio integrated development environment (IDE) doesn't natively support the ability for you to create multifile assemblies. If you want to create multifile assemblies, you must resort to using command-line tools.

There are many ways to add a module to an assembly. If you're using the C# compiler to build a PE file with a manifest, you can use the **/addmodule** switch. To understand how to build a multifile assembly, let's assume that we have two source code files:

- RUT.cs, which contains rarely used types

- FUT.cs, which contains frequently used types

Let's compile the rarely used types into their own module so that users of the assembly won't need to deploy this module if they never access the rarely used types:

```
csc /t:module RUT.cs
```

This line causes the C# compiler to create a RUT.netmodule file. This file is a standard DLL PE file, but, by itself, the CLR can't load it.

Next let's compile the frequently used types into their own module. We'll make this module the keeper of the assembly's manifest because the types are used so often. In fact, because this module will now represent the entire assembly, I'll change the name of the output file to JeffTypes.dll instead of calling it FUT.dll:

```
csc /out:JeffTypes.dll /t:library /addmodule:RUT.netmodule FUT.cs
```

This line tells the C# compiler to compile the FUT.cs file to produce the JeffTypes.dll file. Because **/t:library** is specified, a DLL PE file containing the manifest metadata tables is emitted into the JeffTypes.dll file. The **/addmodule:RUT.netmodule** switch tells the compiler that RUT.netmodule is a file that should be considered part of the assembly. Specifically, the **/addmodule** switch tells the compiler to add the file to the FileDef manifest metadata table and to add RUT.netmodule's publicly exported types to the ExportedTypesDef manifest metadata table.

Once the compiler has finished all of its processing, the two files shown in Figure 2-1 are created. The module on the right contains the manifest.

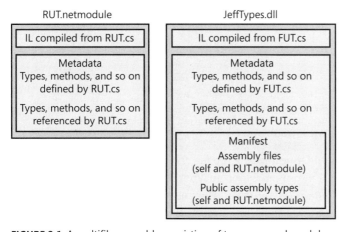

FIGURE 2-1 A multifile assembly consisting of two managed modules, one with a manifest

The RUT.netmodule file contains the IL code generated by compiling RUT.cs. This file also contains metadata tables that describe the types, methods, fields, properties, events, and so on that are defined by RUT.cs. The metadata tables also describe the types, methods, and so on that are referenced by RUT.cs. The JeffTypes.dll is a separate file. Like RUT.netmodule, this file includes the IL code generated by compiling FUT.cs and also includes similar definition and reference metadata tables. However, JeffTypes.dll contains the additional manifest metadata tables, making JeffTypes.dll an assembly. The additional manifest metadata tables describe all of the files that make up the assembly (the JeffTypes.dll file itself and the RUT.netmodule file). The manifest metadata tables also include all of the public types exported from JeffTypes.dll and RUT.netmodule.

> **Note** In reality, the manifest metadata tables don't actually include the types that are exported from the PE file that contains the manifest. The purpose of this optimization is to reduce the number of bytes required by the manifest information in the PE file. So statements like "The manifest metadata tables also include all the public types exported from JeffTypes.dll and RUT.netmodule" aren't 100 percent accurate. However, this statement does accurately reflect what the manifest is logically exposing.

Once the JeffTypes.dll assembly is built, you can use ILDasm.exe to examine the metadata's manifest tables to verify that the assembly file does in fact have references to the RUT.netmodule file's types. Here is what the FileDef and ExportedTypesDef metadata tables look like:

```
File #1 (26000001)
-------------------------------------------------------
    Token: 0x26000001
    Name : RUT.netmodule
    HashValue Blob : e6 e6 df 62 2c a1 2c 59  97 65 0f 21 44 10 15 96  f2 7e db c2
    Flags : [ContainsMetaData]   (00000000)


ExportedType #1 (27000001)
-------------------------------------------------------
    Token: 0x27000001
    Name: ARarelyUsedType
    Implementation token: 0x26000001
    TypeDef token: 0x02000002
    Flags     : [Public] [AutoLayout] [Class] [Sealed] [AnsiClass]
                [BeforeFieldInit](00100101)
```

From this, you can see that RUT.netmodule is a file considered to be part of the assembly with the token 0x26000001. From the ExportedTypesDef table, you can see that there is a publicly exported type, **ARarelyUsedType.** The implementation token for this type is 0x26000001, which indicates that the type's IL code is contained in the RUT.netmodule file.

> **Note** For the curious, metadata tokens are 4-byte values. The high byte indicates the type of token (0x01=TypeRef, 0x02=TypeDef, 0x23=AssemblyRef, 0x26=FileRef, 0x27=ExportedType). For the complete list, see the **CorTokenType** enumerated type in the CorHdr.h file included with the .NET Framework SDK. The three lower bytes of the token simply identify the row in the corresponding metadata table. For example, the implementation token 0x26000001 refers to the first row of the FileRef table. For most tables, rows are numbered starting with 1, not 0. For the TypeDef table, rows actually start with 2.

Any client code that consumes the JeffTypes.dll assembly's types must be built using the **/r[eference]:JeffTypes.dll** compiler switch. This switch tells the compiler to load the JeffTypes.dll assembly and all of the files listed in its FileDef table when searching for an external type. The compiler requires all of the assembly's files to be installed and accessible. If you were to delete the RUT.netmodule file, the C# compiler would produce the following error: "`fatal error CS0009: Metadata file 'C:\JeffTypes.dll' could not be opened– 'Error importing module 'RUT.netmodule' of assembly 'C:\JeffTypes.dll'–The system cannot find the file specified'`". This means that to build a new assembly, all of the files from a referenced assembly *must* be present.

As the client code executes, it calls methods. When a method is called for the first time, the CLR detects the types that the method references as a parameter, a return value, or as a local variable. The CLR then attempts to load the referenced assembly's file that contains the manifest. If the type being accessed is in this file, the CLR performs its internal bookkeeping, allowing the type to be used. If the manifest indicates that the referenced type is in a different file, the CLR attempts to load the necessary file, performs its internal bookkeeping, and allows the type to be accessed. The CLR loads assembly files only when a method referencing a type in an unloaded assembly is called. This means that to run an application, all of the files from a referenced assembly *do not* need to be present.

Adding Assemblies to a Project by Using the Visual Studio IDE

If you're using the Visual Studio IDE to build your project, you'll have to add any assemblies that you want to reference to your project. To do so, open Solution Explorer, right-click the project you want to add a reference to, and then select the Add Reference menu item. This causes the Add Reference dialog box, shown in Figure 2-2, to appear.

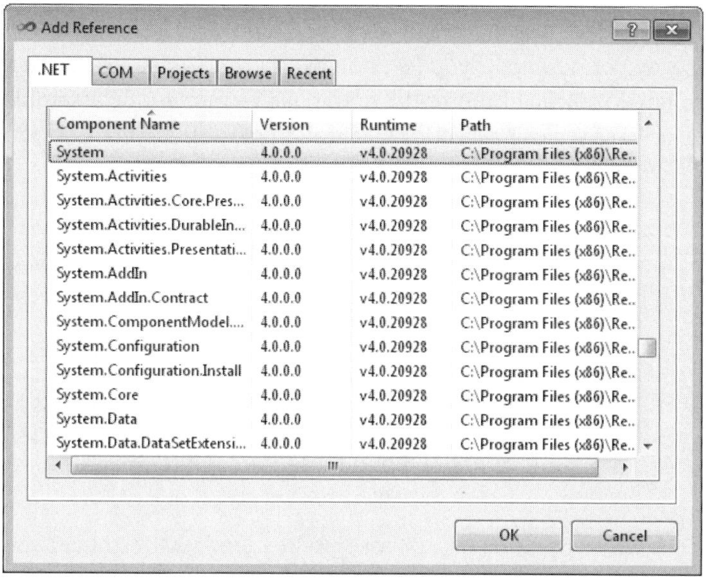

FIGURE 2-2 The Add Reference dialog box in Visual Studio

To have your project reference an assembly, select the desired assembly from the list. If the assembly you want isn't in the list, click the Browse tab to navigate to the desired assembly (file containing a manifest) to add the assembly reference. The COM tab on the Add Reference dialog box allows an unmanaged COM server to be accessed from within managed source code via a managed proxy class automatically generated by Visual Studio. The Projects tab allows the current project to reference an assembly that is created by another project in the same solution. The Recent tab allows you to select an assembly that you recently added to another project.

To make your own assemblies appear in the .NET tab's list, add the following subkey to the registry:

HKEY_LOCAL_MACHINE\SOFTWARE\Microsoft\.NETFramework\AssemblyFolders\MyLibName

MyLibName is a unique name that you create—Visual Studio doesn't display this name. After creating the subkey, change its default string value so that it refers to a directory path (such as C:\Program Files\MyLibPath) containing your assembly's files. Using HKEY_LOCAL_MACHINE adds the assemblies for all users on a machine; use HKEY_CURRENT_USER instead to add the assemblies for a specific user.

Using the Assembly Linker

Instead of using the C# compiler, you might want to create assemblies by using the Assembly Linker utility, AL.exe. The Assembly Linker is useful if you want to create an assembly consisting of modules built from different compilers (if your compiler doesn't support the equivalent of C#'s **/addmodule** switch) or perhaps if you just don't know your assembly packaging requirements at build time. You can also use AL.exe to build resource-only assemblies, called *satellite* assemblies, which are typically used for localization purposes. I'll talk about satellite assemblies later in the chapter.

The AL.exe utility can produce an EXE or a DLL PE file that contains only a manifest describing the types in other modules. To understand how AL.exe works, let's change the way the JeffTypes.dll assembly is built:

```
csc /t:module RUT.cs
csc /t:module FUT.cs
al  /out:JeffTypes.dll /t:library FUT.netmodule RUT.netmodule
```

Figure 2-3 shows the files that result from executing these statements.

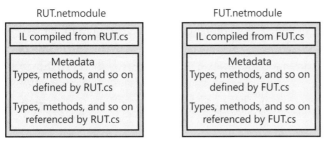

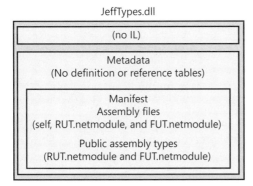

FIGURE 2-3 A multifile assembly consisting of three managed modules, one with a manifest

In this example, two separate modules, RUT.netmodule and FUT.netmodule, are created. Neither module is an assembly because they don't contain manifest metadata tables. Then a third file is produced: JeffTypes.dll, which is a small DLL PE file (because of the **/t[arget]:library** switch) that contains no IL code but has manifest metadata tables indicating that RUT.netmodule and FUT.netmodule are part of the assembly. The resulting assembly consists of three files: JeffTypes.dll, RUT.netmodule, and FUT.netmodule. The Assembly Linker has no way to combine multiple files into a single file.

The AL.exe utility can also produce CUI and GUI PE files by using the **/t[arget]:exe** or **/t[arget]:winexe** command-line switches. But this is very unusual since it would mean that you'd have an EXE PE file with just enough IL code in it to call a method in another module. You can specify which method in a module should be used as an entry point by adding the **/main** command-line switch when invoking AL.exe. The following is an example of how to call the Assembly Linker, AL.exe, by using the **/main** command-line switch:

```
csc /t:module /r:JeffTypes.dll Program.cs
al /out:Program.exe /t:exe /main:Program.Main Program.netmodule
```

Here the first line builds the Program.cs file into a Program.netmodule file. The second line produces a small Program.exe PE file that contains the manifest metadata tables. In addition, there is a small global function named **__EntryPoint** that is emitted by AL.exe because of the **/main:Program.Main** command-line switch. This function, **__EntryPoint**, contains the following IL code:

```
.method privatescope static void __EntryPoint$PST06000001() cil managed
{
  .entrypoint
  // Code size       8 (0x8)
  .maxstack  8
  IL_0000:  tail.
  IL_0002:  call         void [.module 'Program.netmodule']Program::Main()
  IL_0007:  ret
} // end of method 'Global Functions'::__EntryPoint
```

As you can see, this code simply calls the **Main** method contained in the **Program** type defined in the Program.netmodule file. The **/main** switch in AL.exe isn't that useful because it's unlikely that you'd ever create an assembly for an application that didn't have its entry point in the PE file that contains the manifest metadata tables. I mention the switch here only to make you aware of its existence.

With the code that accompanies this book, I have created a Ch02-3-BuildMultiFileLibrary.bat file that encapsulates all the steps required to build a multifile assembly. The Ch02-4-AppUsingMultiFileLibrary project in Visual Studio invokes this batch file as a prebuild command-line step. You can examine this project to see how to integrate building and referencing a multifile assembly from within Visual Studio.

Adding Resource Files to an Assembly

When using AL.exe to create an assembly, you can add a file as a resource to the assembly by using the **/embed[resource]** switch. This switch takes a file (any file) and embeds the file's contents into the resulting PE file. The manifest's ManifestResourceDef table is updated to reflect the existence of the resources.

AL.exe also supports a **/link[resource]** switch, which also takes a file containing resources. However, the **/link[resource]** switch updates the manifest's ManifestResourceDef and FileDef tables, indicating that the resource exists and identifying which of the assembly's files contains it. The resource file is not embedded into the assembly PE file; it remains separate and must be packaged and deployed with the other assembly files.

Like AL.exe, CSC.exe also allows you to combine resources into an assembly produced by the C# compiler. The C# compiler's **/resource** switch embeds the specified resource file into the resulting assembly PE file, updating the ManifestResourceDef table. The compiler's **/linkresource** switch adds an entry to the ManifestResourceDef and the FileDef manifest tables to refer to a stand-alone resource file.

One last note about resources: it's possible to embed standard Win32 resources into an assembly. You can do this easily by specifying the pathname of a .res file with the **/win32res** switch when using either AL.exe or CSC.exe. In addition, you can quickly and easily embed a standard Win32 icon resource into an assembly file by specifying the pathname of the .ico file with the **/win32icon** switch when using either AL.exe or CSC.exe. Within Visual Studio, you can add resource files to your assembly by displaying your project's properties and then clicking the Application tab. The typical reason an icon is embedded is so that Windows Explorer can show an icon for a managed executable file.

> **Note** Managed assembly files also contain Win32 manifest resource information in them. By default, the C# compiler automatically produces this manifest information but you can tell it not to by using the **/nowin32manifest** switch. The default manifest produced by the C# compiler looks like this:
>
> ```xml
> <?xml version="1.0" encoding="UTF-8" standalone="yes"?>
> <assembly xmlns="urn:schemas-microsoft-com:asm.v1" manifestVersion="1.0">
>     <assemblyIdentity version="1.0.0.0" name="MyApplication.app" />
>         <trustInfo xmlns="urn:schemas-microsoft-com:asm.v2">
>             <security>
>                 <requestedPrivileges xmlns="urn:schemas-microsoft-com:asm.v3">
>                     <requestedExecutionLevel level="asInvoker" uiAccess="false"/>
>                 </requestedPrivileges>
>             </security>
>         </trustInfo>
> </assembly>
> ```

Assembly Version Resource Information

When AL.exe or CSC.exe produces a PE file assembly, it also embeds into the PE file a standard Win32 version resource. Users can examine this resource by viewing the file's properties. Application code can also acquire and examine this information at runtime by calling **System.Diagnostics.FileVersionInfo**'s static **GetVersionInfo** method. Figure 2-4 shows the Details tab of the JeffTypes.dll Properties dialog box.

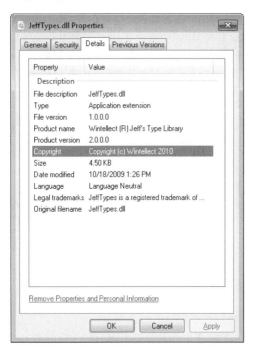

FIGURE 2-4 The Details tab of the JeffTypes.dll Properties dialog box

When building an assembly, you should set the version resource fields by using custom attributes that you apply at the assembly level in your source code. Here's what the code that produced the version information in Figure 2-4 looks like:

```
using System.Reflection;

// FileDescription version information:
[assembly: AssemblyTitle("JeffTypes.dll")]

// Comments version information:
[assembly: AssemblyDescription("This assembly contains Jeff's types")]

// CompanyName version information:
[assembly: AssemblyCompany("Wintellect")]

// ProductName version information:
[assembly: AssemblyProduct("Wintellect (R) Jeff's Type Library")]

// LegalCopyright version information:
[assembly: AssemblyCopyright("Copyright (c) Wintellect 2010")]

// LegalTrademarks version information:
[assembly:AssemblyTrademark("JeffTypes is a registered trademark of Wintellect")]

// AssemblyVersion version information:
[assembly: AssemblyVersion("3.0.0.0")]
```

```
// FILEVERSION/FileVersion version information:
[assembly: AssemblyFileVersion("1.0.0.0")]

// PRODUCTVERSION/ProductVersion version information:
[assembly: AssemblyInformationalVersion("2.0.0.0")]

// Set the Language field (discussed later in the "Culture" section)
[assembly:AssemblyCulture("")]
```

> **Important** Unfortunately, the Windows Explorer Properties dialog box is missing entries for some of the attributes. In particular, it would be great if the value of the **AssemblyVersion** attribute were shown because the CLR uses this value when loading assemblies, as we'll discuss in Chapter 3.

Table 2-4 shows the version resource fields and the custom attributes that correspond to them. If you're using AL.exe to build your assembly, you can use command-line switches to set this information instead of using the custom attributes. The second column in Table 2-4 shows the AL.exe command-line switch that corresponds to each version resource field. Note that the C# compiler doesn't offer these command-line switches and that, in general, using custom attributes is the preferred way to set this information.

TABLE 2-4 **Version Resource Fields and Their Corresponding AL.exe Switches and Custom Attributes**

Version Resource	AL.exe Switch	Custom Attribute/Comment
FILEVERSION	**/fileversion**	`System.Reflection.AssemblyFileVersionAttribute`.
PRODUCTVERSION	**/productversion**	`System.Reflection.AssemblyInformationalVersionAttribute`.
FILEFLAGSMASK	(none)	Always set to **VS_FFI_FILEFLAGSMASK** (defined in WinVer.h as **0x0000003F**).
FILEFLAGS	(none)	Always **0**.
FILEOS	(none)	Currently always **VOS__WINDOWS32**.
FILETYPE	**/target**	Set to **VFT_APP** if **/target:exe** or **/target:winexe** is specified; set to **VFT_DLL** if **/target:library** is specified.
FILESUBTYPE	(none)	Always set to **VFT2_UNKNOWN**. (This field has no meaning for **VFT_APP** and **VFT_DLL**.)
AssemblyVersion	**/version**	`System.Reflection.AssemblyVersionAttribute`.
Comments	**/description**	`System.Reflection.AssemblyDescriptionAttribute`.
CompanyName	**/company**	`System.Reflection.AssemblyCompanyAttribute`.
FileDescription	**/title**	`System.Reflection.AssemblyTitleAttribute`.

Version Resource	AL.exe Switch	Custom Attribute/Comment
FileVersion	**/version**	**System.Reflection. AssemblyFileVersionAttribute**.
InternalName	**/out**	Set to the name of the output file specified (without the extension).
LegalCopyright	**/copyright**	**System.Reflection.AssemblyCopyrightAttribute**.
LegalTrademarks	**/trademark**	**System.Reflection.AssemblyTrademarkAttribute**.
OriginalFilename	**/out**	Set to the name of the output file (without a path).
PrivateBuild	(none)	Always blank.
ProductName	**/product**	**System.Reflection.AssemblyProductAttribute**.
ProductVersion	**/productversion**	**System.Reflection. AssemblyInformationalVersionAttribute**.
SpecialBuild	(none)	Always blank.

Important When you create a new C# project in Visual Studio, an AssemblyInfo.cs file is created automatically for you. This file contains all of the assembly version attributes described in this section, plus a few additional attributes that I'll cover in Chapter 3. You can simply open the AssemblyInfo.cs file and modify your assembly-specific information. Visual Studio also provides a dialog box that you can use to edit the assembly version information in this file. To see this dialog box, in Solution Explorer, double-click your project's Properties entry, and on the Application tab, click Assembly Information; you'll see a dialog box like the one shown in Figure 2-5.

FIGURE 2-5 Visual Studio's Assembly Information dialog box

Version Numbers

In the previous section, you saw that several version numbers can be applied to an assembly. All of these version numbers have the same format: each consists of four period-separated parts, as shown in Table 2-5.

TABLE 2-5 Format of Version Numbers

	Major Number	Minor Number	Build Number	Revision Number
Example:	2	5	719	2

Table 2-5 shows an example of a version number: 2.5.719.2. The first two numbers make up the public perception of the version. The public will think of this example as version 2.5 of the assembly. The third number, 719, indicates the build of the assembly. If your company builds its assembly every day, you should increment the build number each day as well. The last number, 2, indicates the revision of the build. If for some reason your company has to build an assembly twice in one day, maybe to resolve a hot bug that is halting other work, the revision number should be incremented.

Microsoft uses this version-numbering scheme, and it's highly recommended that you use this scheme as well. Future versions of the CLR will offer better support for loading new versions of an assembly and for rolling back to a previous version of an assembly if a new version actually breaks an existing application. To accomplish this versioning support, the CLR will expect that a version of an assembly that fixes one or more bugs will have the same major/minor version, and the build/revision numbers will indicate a servicing version containing the update(s). When loading an assembly, the CLR will automatically find the latest installed servicing version that matches the major/minor version of the assembly being requested.

You'll notice that an assembly has three version numbers associated with it. This is very unfortunate and leads to a lot of confusion. Let me explain each version number's purpose and how it is expected to be used:

- **AssemblyFileVersion**   This version number is stored in the Win32 version resource. This number is for information purposes only; the CLR doesn't examine this version number in any way. Typically, you set the major and minor parts to represent the version you want the public to see. Then you increment the build and revision parts each time a build is performed. Ideally, Microsoft's tool (such as CSC.exe or AL.exe) would automatically update the build and revision numbers for you (based on the date and time when the build was performed), but unfortunately, they don't. This version number can be seen when using Windows Explorer and is typically used to identify a specific version of an assembly when troubleshooting a customer's system.

- **AssemblyInformationalVersion**   This version number is also stored in the Win32 version resource, and again, this number is for information purposes only; the CLR doesn't examine or care about it in any way. This version number exists to indicate the version of the product that includes this assembly. For example, version 2.0 of a product might contain several assemblies; one of these assemblies is marked as version 1.0 since it's a new assembly that didn't ship in version 1.0 of the same product. Typically, you set the major and minor parts of this version number to represent the public version of your product. Then you increment the build and revision parts each time you package a complete product with all its assemblies.

- **AssemblyVersion**   This version number is stored in the AssemblyDef manifest metadata table. The CLR uses this version number when binding to strongly named assemblies (discussed in Chapter 3). This number is extremely important and is used to uniquely identify an assembly. When starting to develop an assembly, you should set the major, minor, build, and revision numbers and shouldn't change them until you're ready to begin work on the next deployable version of your assembly. When you build an assembly, this version number of the referenced assembly is embedded in the AssemblyRef table's entry. This means that an assembly is tightly bound to a specific version of a referenced assembly.

Culture

Like version numbers, assemblies also have a culture as part of their identity. For example, I could have an assembly that is strictly for German, another assembly for Swiss German, another assembly for U.S. English, and so on. Cultures are identified via a string that contains a primary and a secondary tag (as described in RFC 1766). Table 2-6 shows some examples.

TABLE 2-6 **Examples of Assembly Culture Tags**

Primary Tag	Secondary Tag	Culture
de	(none)	German
de	AT	Austrian German
de	CH	Swiss German
en	(none)	English
en	GB	British English
en	US	U.S. English

In general, if you create an assembly that contains code, you don't assign a culture to it. This is because code doesn't usually have any culture-specific assumptions built into it. An assembly that isn't assigned a culture is referred to as being *culture neutral*.

If you're designing an application that has some culture-specific resources to it, Microsoft highly recommends that you create one assembly that contains your code and your application's default (or fallback) resources. When building this assembly, don't specify a culture. This is the assembly that other assemblies will reference when they create and manipulate types it publicly exposes.

Now you can create one or more separate assemblies that contain only culture-specific resources—no code at all. Assemblies that are marked with a culture are called *satellite assemblies*. For these satellite assemblies, assign a culture that accurately reflects the culture of the resources placed in the assembly. You should create one satellite assembly for each culture you intend to support.

You'll usually use the AL.exe tool to build a satellite assembly. You won't use a compiler because the satellite assembly should have no code contained within it. When using AL.exe, you specify the desired culture by using the **/c[ulture]:text** switch, where **text** is a string such as "en-US," representing U.S. English. When you deploy a satellite assembly, you should place it in a subdirectory whose name matches the culture text. For example, if the application's base directory is C:\MyApp, the U.S. English satellite assembly should be placed in the C:\MyApp\en-US subdirectory. At runtime, you access a satellite assembly's resources by using the **System.Resources.ResourceManager** class.

> **Note** It is possible to create a satellite assembly that contains code, though this practice is discouraged. If you prefer, you can specify the culture by using the **System.Reflection.AssemblyCultureAttribute** custom attribute instead of using AL.exe's **/culture** switch, for example, as shown here:
>
> ```
> // Set assembly's culture to Swiss German
> [assembly:AssemblyCulture("de-CH")]
> ```

Normally, you shouldn't build an assembly that references a satellite assembly. In other words, an assembly's AssemblyRef entries should all refer to culture-neutral assemblies. If you want to access types or members contained in a satellite assembly, you should use reflection techniques as discussed in Chapter 23, "Assembly Loading and Reflection."

Simple Application Deployment (Privately Deployed Assemblies)

Throughout this chapter, I've explained how you build modules and how you combine those modules into an assembly. At this point, I'm ready to explain how to package and deploy all of the assemblies so that users can run the application.

Assemblies don't dictate or require any special means of packaging. The easiest way to package a set of assemblies is simply to copy all of the files directly. For example, you could put all of the assembly files on a CD-ROM and ship it to the user with a batch file setup program that just copies the files from the CD to a directory on the user's hard drive. Because the assemblies include all of the dependent assembly references and types, the user can just run the application and the runtime will look for referenced assemblies in the application's directory. No modifications to the registry are necessary for the application to run. To uninstall the application, just delete all the files—that's it!

Of course, you can package and install the assembly files by using other mechanisms, such as .cab files (typically used for Internet download scenarios to compress files and reduce download times). You can also package the assembly files into an MSI file for use by the Windows Installer service (MSIExec.exe). Using MSI files allows assemblies to be installed on demand the first time the CLR attempts to load the assembly. This feature isn't new to MSI; it can perform the same demand-load functionality for unmanaged EXE and DLL files as well.

> **Note** Using a batch file or some other simple "installation software" will get an application onto the user's machine; however, you'll need more sophisticated installation software to create shortcut links on the user's desktop and Start menu. Also, you can easily back up and restore the application or move it from one machine to another, but the various shortcut links will require special handling.

Of course, Visual Studio has a built-in mechanism that you can use to publish an application by displaying a project's Properties pages and clicking the Publish tab. You can use the options available on the Publish tab to cause Visual Studio to produce an MSI file and copy the resulting MSI file to a Web site, FTP server, or file path. The MSI file can also install any prerequisite components such as the .NET Framework or Microsoft SQL Server 2008 Express Edition. Finally, the application can automatically check for updates and install them on the user's machine by taking advantage of ClickOnce technology.

Assemblies deployed to the same directory as the application are called *privately deployed assemblies* because the assembly files aren't shared with any other application (unless the other application is also deployed to the same directory). Privately deployed assemblies are a big win for developers, end users, and administrators because they can simply be copied to an application's base directory, and the CLR will load them and execute the code in them. In addition, an application can be uninstalled by simply deleting the assemblies in its directory. This allows simple backup and restore as well.

This simple install/move/uninstall scenario is possible because each assembly has metadata indicating which referenced assembly should be loaded; no registry settings are required. In addition, the referencing assembly scopes every type. This means that an application always binds to the same type it was built and tested with; the CLR can't load a different assembly that just happens to provide a type with the same name. This is different from COM, in which types are recorded in the registry, making them available to any application running on the machine.

In Chapter 3, I'll discuss how to deploy shared assemblies that are accessible by multiple applications.

Simple Administrative Control (Configuration)

The user or the administrator can best determine some aspects of an application's execution. For example, an administrator might decide to move an assembly's files on the user's hard disk or to override information contained in the assembly's manifest. Other scenarios also exist related to versioning; I'll talk about some of these in Chapter 3.

To allow administrative control over an application, a configuration file can be placed in the application's directory. An application's publisher can create and package this file. The setup program would then install this configuration file in the application's base directory. In addition, the machine's administrator or an end user could create or modify this file. The CLR interprets the content of this file to alter its policies for locating and loading assembly files.

These configuration files contain Extensible Markup Language (XML) and can be associated with an application or with the machine. Using a separate file (vs. registry settings) allows the file to be easily backed up and also allows the administrator to copy the application to another machine—just copy the necessary files and the administrative policy is copied too.

In Chapter 3, we'll explore this configuration file in more detail. But I want to give you a taste of it now. Let's say that the publisher of an application wants its application deployed with the JeffTypes assembly files in a different directory than the application's assembly file. The desired directory structure looks like this:

```
AppDir directory (contains the application's assembly files)
    Program.exe
    Program.exe.config (discussed below)

    AuxFiles subdirectory (contains JeffTypes' assembly files)
        JeffTypes.dll
        FUT.netmodule
        RUT.netmodule
```

Since the JeffTypes files are no longer in the application's base directory, the CLR won't be able to locate and load these files; running the application will cause a **System.IO.FileNotFoundException** exception to be thrown. To fix this, the publisher creates an XML configuration file and deploys it to the application's base directory. The name of this file must be the name of the application's main assembly file with a .config extension: Program.exe.config, for this example. The configuration file should look like this:

```
<configuration>
    <runtime>
        <assemblyBinding xmlns="urn:schemas-microsoft-com:asm.v1">
            <probing privatePath="AuxFiles" />
        </assemblyBinding>
    </runtime>
</configuration>
```

Whenever the CLR attempts to locate an assembly file, it always looks in the application's directory first, and if it can't find the file there, it looks in the AuxFiles subdirectory. You can specify multiple semicolon-delimited paths for the probing element's **privatePath** attribute. Each path is considered relative to the application's base directory. You can't specify an absolute or a relative path identifying a directory that is outside of the application's base directory. The idea is that an application can control its directory and its subdirectories but has no control over other directories.

Probing for Assembly Files

When the CLR needs to locate an assembly, it scans several subdirectories. Here is the order in which directories are probed for a culture-neutral assembly (where **firstPrivatePath** and **secondPrivatePath** are specified via the config file's **privatePath** attribute):

```
AppDir\AsmName.dll
AppDir\AsmName\AsmName.dll
AppDir\firstPrivatePath\AsmName.dll
AppDir\firstPrivatePath\AsmName\AsmName.dll
AppDir\secondPrivatePath\AsmName.dll
AppDir\secondPrivatePath\AsmName\AsmName.dll
...
```

In this example, no configuration file would be needed if the JeffTypes assembly files were deployed to a subdirectory called JeffTypes, since the CLR would automatically scan for a subdirectory whose name matches the name of the assembly being searched for.

If the assembly can't be found in any of the preceding subdirectories, the CLR starts all over, using an .exe extension instead of a .dll extension. If the assembly still can't be found, a **FileNotFoundException** is thrown.

For satellite assemblies, similar rules are followed except that the assembly is expected to be in a subdirectory, whose name matches the culture, of the application's base directory. For example, if AsmName.dll has a culture of "en-US" applied to it, the following directories are probed:

```
C:\AppDir\en-US\AsmName.dll
C:\AppDir\en-US\AsmName\AsmName.dll
C:\AppDir\firstPrivatePath\en-US\AsmName.dll
C:\AppDir\firstPrivatePath\en-US\AsmName\AsmName.dll
C:\AppDir\secondPrivatePath\en-US\AsmName.dll
C:\AppDir\secondPrivatePath\en-US\AsmName\AsmName.dll

C:\AppDir\en-US\AsmName.exe
C:\AppDir\en-US\AsmName\AsmName.exe
C:\AppDir\firstPrivatePath\en-US\AsmName.exe
C:\AppDir\firstPrivatePath\en-US\AsmName\AsmName.exe
C:\AppDir\secondPrivatePath\en-US\AsmName.exe
C:\AppDir\secondPrivatePath\en-US\AsmName\AsmName.exe
```

```
C:\AppDir\en\AsmName.dll
C:\AppDir\en\AsmName\AsmName.dll
C:\AppDir\firstPrivatePath\en\AsmName.dll
C:\AppDir\firstPrivatePath\en\AsmName\AsmName.dll
C:\AppDir\secondPrivatePath\en\AsmName.dll
C:\AppDir\secondPrivatePath\en\AsmName\AsmName.dll

C:\AppDir\en\AsmName.exe
C:\AppDir\en\AsmName\AsmName.exe
C:\AppDir\firstPrivatePath\en\AsmName.exe
C:\AppDir\firstPrivatePath\en\AsmName\AsmName.exe
C:\AppDir\secondPrivatePath\en\AsmName.exe
C:\AppDir\secondPrivatePath\en\AsmName\AsmName.exe
```

As you can see, the CLR probes for files with either an .exe or .dll file extension. Since probing can be very time-consuming (especially when the CLR is looking for files over a network), in the XML configuration file, you can specify one or more **culture** elements to limit the probing that the CLR performs when looking for satellite assemblies.

The name and location of this XML configuration file is different depending on the application type:

- For executable applications (EXEs), the configuration file must be in the application's base directory, and it must be the name of the EXE file with ".config" appended to it.

- For Microsoft ASP.NET Web Form applications, the file must be in the Web application's virtual root directory and is always named Web.config. In addition, subdirectories can also contain their own Web.config file, and the configuration settings are inherited. For example, a Web application located at *http://Wintellect.com/Training* would use the settings in the Web.config files contained in the virtual root directory and in its Training subdirectory.

As mentioned at the beginning of this section, configuration settings apply to a particular application and to the machine. When you install the .NET Framework, it creates a Machine.config file. There is one Machine.config file per version of the CLR you have installed on the machine.

The Machine.config file is located in the following directory:

%SystemRoot%\Microsoft.NET\Framework\version\CONFIG

Of course, %SystemRoot% identifies your Windows directory (usually C:\WINDOWS), and *version* is a version number identifying a specific version of the .NET Framework (something like v4.0.#####).

Settings in the Machine.config file represent default settings that affect all applications running on the machine. An administrator can create a machine-wide policy by modifying the single Machine.config file. However, administrators and users should avoid modifying this file because it contains many settings related to various things, making it much more difficult to navigate. Plus, you want the application's settings to be backed up and restored, and keeping an application's settings in the application-specific configuration file enables this.

Chapter 3
Shared Assemblies and Strongly Named Assemblies

In Chapter 2, "Building, Packaging, Deploying, and Administering Applications and Types," I talked about the steps required to build, package, and deploy an assembly. I focused on what's called private deployment, in which assemblies are placed in the application's base directory (or a subdirectory thereof) for the application's sole use. Deploying assemblies privately gives a company a large degree of control over the naming, versioning, and behavior of the assembly.

In this chapter, I'll concentrate on creating assemblies that can be accessed by multiple applications. The assemblies that ship with the Microsoft .NET Framework are an excellent example of globally deployed assemblies, because all managed applications use types defined by Microsoft in the .NET Framework Class Library (FCL).

As I mentioned in Chapter 2, Microsoft Windows has a reputation for being unstable. The main reason for this reputation is the fact that applications are built and tested using code implemented by someone else. After all, when you write an application for Windows, your application is calling into code written by Microsoft developers. Also, a large number of companies make controls that application developers can incorporate into their own applications. In fact, the .NET Framework encourages this, and many control vendors have appeared over time.

As time marches on, Microsoft developers and control developers modify their code: they fix bugs, patch security flaws, add features, and so on. Eventually, the new code makes its way onto the user's machine. The user's applications that were previously installed and working fine are no longer using the same code that the applications were built and tested with. As a result, the applications' behavior is no longer predictable, which contributes to the instability of Windows.

File versioning is a very difficult problem to solve. In fact, I assert that if you take a file that is used by other code files and change just one bit in the file—change a 0 to a 1 or a 1 to a 0—there's absolutely no way to guarantee that code that used the file before it was changed will now work just as well if it uses the new version of the file. One of the reasons why this statement is true is that a lot of applications exploit bugs, either knowingly or unknowingly. If a later version of a file fixes a bug, the application no longer runs as expected.

So here's the problem: How do you fix bugs and add features to a file and also guarantee that you don't break some application? I've given this question a lot of thought and have come to one conclusion: It's just not possible. But, obviously, this answer isn't good enough. Files will ship with bugs, and companies will always want to provide new features. There must be a way to distribute new files with the hope that the applications will work just fine. And if the application doesn't work fine, there has to be an *easy* way to restore the application to its last-known good state.

In this chapter, I'll explain the infrastructure that the .NET Framework has in place to deal with versioning problems. Let me warn you: What I'm about to describe is complicated. I'm going to talk about a lot of algorithms, rules, and policies that are built into the common language runtime (CLR). I'm also going to mention a lot of tools and utilities that the application developer must use. This stuff is complicated because, as I've mentioned, the versioning problem is difficult to address and to solve.

Two Kinds of Assemblies, Two Kinds of Deployment

The CLR supports two kinds of assemblies: *weakly named assemblies* and *strongly named assemblies*.

Important By the way, you won't find the term *weakly named assembly* in any of the .NET Framework documentation. Why? Because I made it up. In fact, the documentation has no term to identify a weakly named assembly. I decided to coin the term so that I can talk about assemblies without any ambiguity as to what kind of assembly I'm referring to.

Weakly named assemblies and strongly named assemblies are structurally identical—that is, they use the same portable executable (PE) file format, PE32(+) header, CLR header, metadata, manifest tables, and Intermediate Language (IL) that we examined in Chapter 1, "The CLR's Execution Model," and Chapter 2. And you use the same tools, such as the C# compiler and AL.exe, to build both kinds of assemblies. The real difference between weakly named and strongly named assemblies is that a strongly named assembly is signed with a publisher's public/private key pair that uniquely identifies the assembly's publisher. This key pair allows the assembly to be uniquely identified, secured, and versioned, and it allows the assembly to be deployed anywhere on the user's machine or even on the Internet. This ability to uniquely identify an assembly allows the CLR to enforce certain known-to-be-safe policies when an application tries to bind to a strongly named assembly. This chapter is dedicated to explaining what strongly named assemblies are and what policies the CLR applies to them.

An assembly can be deployed in two ways: privately or globally. A privately deployed assembly is an assembly that is deployed in the application's base directory or one of its subdirectories. A weakly named assembly can be deployed only privately. I talked about privately deployed assemblies in Chapter 2. A globally deployed assembly is an assembly that is deployed into some well-known location that the CLR looks in when it's searching for the assembly. A strongly named assembly can be deployed privately or globally. I'll explain how to create and deploy strongly named assemblies in this chapter. Table 3-1 summarizes the kinds of assemblies and the ways that they can be deployed.

TABLE 3-1 How Weakly and Strongly Named Assemblies Can Be Deployed

Kind of Assembly	Can Be Privately Deployed	Can Be Globally Deployed
Weakly named	Yes	No
Strongly named	Yes	Yes

> **Note** It is highly recommended that you strongly name all of your assemblies. In fact, it is likely that future versions of the CLR will require all assemblies to be strongly named, and the ability to create weakly named assemblies will be deprecated. Weakly named assemblies are a problem because it is possible to have several different assemblies all with the same weak name. On the other hand, giving an assembly a strong name uniquely identifies that assembly. If the CLR can uniquely identify an assembly, it can apply more policies to it related to versioning or backward compatibility. It is Microsoft's plan to endow future versions of the CLR with these policies to make versioning simpler. In fact, just eliminating the ability to make weakly named assemblies makes understanding the CLR's versioning policies simpler.

Giving an Assembly a Strong Name

If multiple applications are going to access an assembly, the assembly must be placed in a well-known directory, and the CLR must know to look in this directory automatically when a reference to the assembly is detected. However, we have a problem: Two (or more) companies could produce assemblies that have the same file name. Then, if both of these assemblies get copied into the same well-known directory, the last one installed wins, and all of the applications that were using the old assembly no longer function as desired. (This is exactly why DLL hell exists today in Windows, in which shared DLLs are all just copied into the System32 directory.)

Obviously, differentiating assemblies simply by using a file name isn't good enough. The CLR needs to support some mechanism that allows assemblies to be uniquely identified. This is what the term *strongly named assembly* refers to. A strongly named assembly consists of four attributes that uniquely identify the assembly: a file name (without an extension), a version number, a culture identity, and a public key. Since public keys are very large numbers, we frequently use a small hash value derived from a public key. This hash value is called a *public key token*. The following assembly identity strings (sometimes called an *assembly display name*) identify four completely different assembly files:

```
"MyTypes, Version=1.0.8123.0, Culture=neutral, PublicKeyToken=b77a5c561934e089"

"MyTypes, Version=1.0.8123.0, Culture="en-US", PublicKeyToken=b77a5c561934e089"

"MyTypes, Version=2.0.1234.0, Culture=neutral, PublicKeyToken=b77a5c561934e089"

"MyTypes, Version=1.0.8123.0, Culture=neutral, PublicKeyToken=b03f5f7f11d50a3a"
```

The first string identifies an assembly file called MyTypes.exe or MyTypes.dll (you can't actually determine the file extension from an assembly identity string). The company producing the assembly is creating version 1.0.8123.0 of this assembly, and nothing in the assembly is sensitive to any one culture because **Culture** is set to **neutral**. Of course, any company could produce a MyTypes.dll (or MyTypes.exe) assembly file that is marked with a version number of 1.0.8123.0 and a neutral culture.

There must be a way to distinguish this company's assembly from another company's assembly that happens to have the same attributes. For several reasons, Microsoft chose to use standard public/private key cryptographic technologies instead of any other unique identification technique such as GUIDs, URLs, or URNs. Specifically, cryptographic techniques provide a way to check the integrity of the assembly's bits as they are installed on a machine, and they also allow permissions to be granted on a per-publisher basis. I'll discuss these techniques later in this chapter. So a company that wants to uniquely mark its assemblies must create a public/private key pair. Then the public key can be associated with the assembly. No two companies should have the same public/private key pair, and this distinction is what allows two companies to create assemblies that have the same name, version, and culture without causing any conflict.

> **Note** The **System.Reflection.AssemblyName** class is a helper class that makes it easy for you to build an assembly name and to obtain the various parts of an assembly's name. The class offers several public instance properties, such as **CultureInfo**, **FullName**, **KeyPair**, **Name**, and **Version**. The class also offers a few public instance methods, such as **GetPublicKey**, **GetPublicKeyToken**, **SetPublicKey**, and **SetPublicKeyToken**.

In Chapter 2, I showed you how to name an assembly file and how to apply an assembly version number and a culture. A weakly named assembly can have assembly version and culture attributes embedded in the manifest metadata; however, the CLR always ignores the version number and uses only the culture information when it's probing subdirectories looking for the satellite assembly. Because weakly named assemblies are always privately deployed, the CLR simply uses the name of the assembly (tacking on a .dll or an .exe extension) when searching for the assembly's file in the application's base directory or in any of the application's subdirectories specified in the Extensible Markup Language (XML) configuration file's probing element's **privatePath** XML attribute.

A strongly named assembly has a file name, an assembly version, and a culture. In addition, a strongly named assembly is signed with the publisher's private key.

The first step in creating a strongly named assembly is to obtain a key by using the Strong Name utility, SN.exe, that ships with the .NET Framework SDK and Microsoft Visual Studio. This utility offers a whole slew of features depending on the command-line switch you specify. Note that all SN.exe's command-line switches are case-sensitive. To generate a public/private key pair, you run SN.exe as follows:

```
SN -k MyCompany.snk
```

This line tells SN.exe to create a file called MyCompany.snk. This file will contain the public and private key numbers persisted in a binary format.

Public key numbers are very big. If you want to, after creating the file that contains the public and private key, you can use the SN.exe utility again to see the actual public key. To do this, you must execute the SN.exe utility twice. First, you invoke SN.exe with the **–p** switch to create a file that contains only the public key (MyCompany.PublicKey):

```
SN -p MyCompany.snk MyCompany.PublicKey
```

Then, you invoke SN.exe, passing it the **–tp** switch and the file that contains just the public key:

```
SN -tp MyCompany.PublicKey
```

When I execute this line, I get the following output:

```
Microsoft (R) .NET Framework Strong Name Utility  Version 4.0.20928.1
Copyright (c) Microsoft Corporation.  All rights reserved.

Public key is
002400000480000094000000060200000024000052534131000400000010001003f9d621b702111
850be453b92bd6a58c020eb7b804f75d67ab302047fc786ffa3797b669215afb4d814a6f294010
b233bac0b8c8098ba809855da256d964c0d07f16463d918d651a4846a62317328cac893626a550
69f21a125bc03193261176dd629eace6c90d36858de3fcb781bfc8b817936a567cad608ae672b6
1fb80eb0

Public key token is 3db32f38c8b42c9a
```

The SN.exe utility doesn't offer any way for you to display the private key.

The size of public keys makes them difficult to work with. To make things easier for the developer (and for end users too), *public key tokens* were created. A public key token is a 64-bit hash of the public key. SN.exe's **-tp** switch shows the public key token that corresponds to the complete public key at the end of its output.

Now that you know how to create a public/private key pair, creating a strongly named assembly is simple. When you compile your assembly, you use the **/keyfile:<file>** compiler switch:

```
csc /keyfile:MyCompany.snk Program.cs
```

When the C# compiler sees this switch, the compiler opens the specified file (MyCompany.snk), signs the assembly with the private key, and embeds the public key in the manifest. Note that you sign only the assembly file that contains the manifest; the assembly's other files can't be signed explicitly.

If you are using Visual Studio, you can create a new public/private key file by displaying the properties for your project, clicking the Signing tab, selecting the Sign The Assembly check box, and then choosing the <New...> option from the Choose A Strong Name Key File combo box.

Here's what it means to sign a file: When you build a strongly named assembly, the assembly's FileDef manifest metadata table includes the list of all the files that make up the assembly. As each file's name is added to the manifest, the file's contents are hashed, and this hash value is stored along with the file's name in the FileDef table. You can override the default hash algorithm used with AL.exe's **/algid** switch or apply the assembly-level **System.Reflection.AssemblyAlgorithmIdAttribute** custom attribute in one of the assembly's source code files. By default, a SHA-1 algorithm is used, and this should be sufficient for almost all applications.

After the PE file containing the manifest is built, the PE file's entire contents (except for any Authenticode Signature, the assembly's strong name data, and the PE header checksum) are hashed, as shown in Figure 3-1. The hash algorithm used here is always SHA-1 and can't be overridden. This hash value is signed with the publisher's private key, and the resulting RSA digital signature is stored in a reserved section (not included in the hash) within the PE file. The CLR header of the PE file is updated to reflect where the digital signature is embedded within the file.

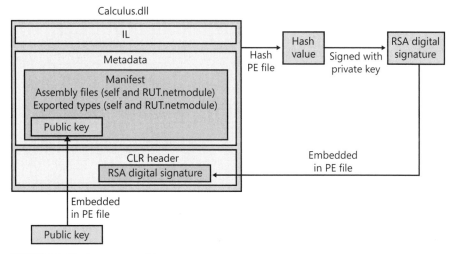

FIGURE 3-1 Signing an assembly

The publisher's public key is also embedded into the AssemblyDef manifest metadata table in this PE file. The combination of the file name, the assembly version, the culture, and the public key gives this assembly a strong name, which is guaranteed to be unique. There is no way that two companies could each produce an assembly named *OurLibrary* with the same public/private keys unless the companies share this key pair with each other.

At this point, the assembly and all of its files are ready to be packaged and distributed.

As described in Chapter 2, when you compile your source code, the compiler detects the types and members that your code references. You must specify the referenced assemblies to the compiler. For the C# compiler, you use the **/reference** compiler switch. Part of the compiler's job is to emit an AssemblyRef metadata table inside the resulting managed module. Each entry in the AssemblyRef metadata table indicates the referenced assembly's name (without path and extension), version number, culture, and public key information.

> **Important** Because public keys are such large numbers, and a single assembly might reference many assemblies, a large percentage of the resulting file's total size would be occupied with public key information. To conserve storage space, Microsoft hashes the public key and takes the last 8 bytes of the hashed value. These reduced public key values—known as public key tokens—are what are actually stored in an AssemblyRef table. In general, developers and end users will see public key token values much more frequently than full public key values.
>
> Note, however, that the CLR never uses public key tokens when making security or trust decisions because it is possible that several public keys could hash to a single public key token.

The AssemblyRef metadata information (obtained by using ILDasm.exe) for the JeffTypes.dll file that I discussed in Chapter 2 is shown here:

```
AssemblyRef #1 (23000001)
-------------------------------------------------------
Token: 0x23000001
Public Key or Token: b7 7a 5c 56 19 34 e0 89
Name: mscorlib
Version: 4.0.0.0
Major Version: 0x00000004
Minor Version: 0x00000000
Build Number: 0x00000000
Revision Number: 0x00000000
Locale: <null>
HashValue Blob:
Flags: [none] (00000000)
```

From this, you can see that JeffTypes.dll references a type that is contained in an assembly matching the following attributes:

```
"MSCorLib, Version=4.0.0.0, Culture=neutral, PublicKeyToken=b77a5c561934e089"
```

Unfortunately, ILDasm.exe uses the term *Locale* when it really should be using *Culture*.

If you look at JeffTypes.dll's AssemblyDef metadata table, you see the following:

```
Assembly
-------------------------------------------------------
Token: 0x20000001
Name : JeffTypes
Public Key    :
Hash Algorithm : 0x00008004
Version: 3.0.0.0
Major Version: 0x00000003
Minor Version: 0x00000000
Build Number: 0x00000000
Revision Number: 0x00000000
Locale: <null>
Flags : [none] (00000000)
```

This is equivalent to the following:

```
"JeffTypes, Version=3.0.0.0, Culture=neutral, PublicKeyToken=null"
```

In this line, no public key token is specified because in Chapter 2, the JeffTypes.dll assembly wasn't signed with a public/private key pair, making it a weakly named assembly. If I had used SN.exe to create a key file compiled with the **/keyfile** compiler switch, the resulting assembly would have been signed. If I had then used ILDasm.exe to explore the new assembly's metadata, the AssemblyDef entry would have bytes appearing after the Public Key field, and the assembly would be strongly named. By the way, the AssemblyDef entry always stores the full public key, not the public key token. The full public key is necessary to ensure that the file hasn't been tampered with. I'll explain the tamper resistance of strongly named assemblies later in this chapter.

The Global Assembly Cache

Now that you know how to create a strongly named assembly, it's time to learn how to deploy this assembly and how the CLR uses the information to locate and load the assembly.

If an assembly is to be accessed by multiple applications, the assembly must be placed into a well-known directory, and the CLR must know to look in this directory automatically when a reference to the assembly is detected. This well-known location is called the global assembly cache (GAC), which can usually be found in the following directory (assuming that Windows is installed in the C:\Windows directory):

```
C:\Windows\Assembly
```

The GAC directory is structured: It contains many subdirectories, and an algorithm is used to generate the names of these subdirectories. You should never manually copy assembly files into the GAC; instead, you should use tools to accomplish this task. These tools know the GAC's internal structure and how to generate the proper subdirectory names.

While developing and testing, the most common tool for installing a strongly named assembly into the GAC is GACUtil.exe. Running this tool without any command-line arguments yields the following usage:

```
Microsoft (R) .NET Global Assembly Cache Utility.  Version 4.0.20928.1
Copyright (c) Microsoft Corporation.  All rights reserved.

Usage: Gacutil <command> [ <options> ]
Commands:
  /i <assembly_path> [ /r <...> ] [ /f ]
    Installs an assembly to the global assembly cache.

  /il <assembly_path_list_file> [ /r <...> ] [ /f ]
    Installs one or more assemblies to the global assembly cache.

  /u <assembly_display_name> [ /r <...> ]
    Uninstalls an assembly from the global assembly cache.

  /ul <assembly_display_name_list_file> [ /r <...> ]
    Uninstalls one or more assemblies from the global assembly cache.

  /l [ <assembly_name> ]
    List the global assembly cache filtered by <assembly_name>

  /lr [ <assembly_name> ]
    List the global assembly cache with all traced references.

  /cdl
    Deletes the contents of the download cache

  /ldl
    Lists the contents of the download cache
```

```
/?
   Displays a detailed help screen

Options:
 /r <reference_scheme> <reference_id> <description>
   Specifies a traced reference to install (/i, /il) or uninstall (/u, /ul).

 /f
   Forces reinstall of an assembly.

 /nologo
   Suppresses display of the logo banner

 /silent
   Suppresses display of all output
```

As you can see, you can invoke GACUtil.exe, specifying the **/i** switch to install an assembly into the GAC, and you can use GACUtil.exe's **/u** switch to uninstall an assembly from the GAC. Note that you can't ever place a weakly named assembly into the GAC. If you pass the file name of a weakly named assembly to GACUtil.exe, it displays the following error message: **"Failure adding assembly to the cache: Attempt to install an assembly without a strong name."**

> **Note** By default, the GAC can be manipulated only by a user belonging to the Windows Administrators group. GACUtil.exe will fail to install or uninstall an assembly if the user invoking the execution of the utility isn't a member of this group.

Using GACUtil.exe's **/i** switch is very convenient for developer testing. However, if you use GACUtil.exe to deploy an assembly in a production environment, it's recommended that you use GACUtil.exe's **/r** switch in addition to specifying the **/i** or **/u** switch to install or uninstall the assembly. The **/r** switch integrates the assembly with the Windows install and uninstall engine. Basically, it tells the system which application requires the assembly and then ties the application and the assembly together.

> **Note** If a strongly named assembly is packaged in a cabinet (.cab) file or is compressed in some way, the assembly's file must first be decompressed to temporary file(s) before you use GACUtil.exe to install the assembly's files into the GAC. Once the assembly's files have been installed, the temporary file(s) can be deleted.

The GACUtil.exe tool doesn't ship with the end-user .NET Framework redistributable package. If your application includes some assemblies that you want deployed into the GAC, you should use the Windows Installer (MSI), because MSI is the only tool that is guaranteed to be on end-user machines and capable of installing assemblies into the GAC.

Important Globally deploying assembly files into the GAC is a form of registering the assembly, although the actual Windows registry isn't affected in any way. Installing assemblies into the GAC breaks the goal of simple application installation, backup, restore, moving, and uninstall. So it is recommended that you avoid global deployment and use private deployment whenever possible.

What is the purpose of "registering" an assembly in the GAC? Well, say two companies each produce an OurLibrary assembly consisting of one file: OurLibrary.dll. Obviously, both of these files can't go in the same directory because the last one installed would overwrite the first one, surely breaking some application. When you install an assembly into the GAC, dedicated subdirectories are created under the C:\Windows\Assembly directory, and the assembly files are copied into one of these subdirectories.

Normally, no one examines the GAC's subdirectories, so the structure of the GAC shouldn't really matter to you. As long as the tools and the CLR know the structure, all is good.

Building an Assembly That References a Strongly Named Assembly

Whenever you build an assembly, the assembly will have references to other strongly named assemblies. This is true because **System.Object** is defined in MSCorLib.dll, which is strongly named. However, it's likely that an assembly will reference types in other strongly named assemblies published either by Microsoft, a third party, or your own organization. In Chapter 2, I showed you how to use CSC.exe's **/reference** compiler switch to specify the assembly file names you want to reference. If the file name is a full path, CSC.exe loads the specified file and uses its metadata information to build the assembly. As mentioned in Chapter 2, if you specify a file name without a path, CSC.exe attempts to find the assembly by looking in the following directories (in order of their presentation here):

1. Working directory.

2. The directory that contains the CSC.exe file itself. This directory also contains the CLR DLLs.

3. Any directories specified using the **/lib** compiler switch.

4. Any directories specified using the LIB environment variable.

So if you're building an assembly that references Microsoft's System.Drawing.dll, you can specify the **/reference:System.Drawing.dll** switch when invoking CSC.exe. The compiler will examine the directories shown earlier and will find the System.Drawing.dll file in the directory that contains the CSC.exe file itself, which is the same directory that contains the DLLs for the version of the CLR the compiler is tied to. Even though this is the directory where the assembly is found at compile time, this isn't the directory where the assembly will be loaded from at runtime.

You see, when you install the .NET Framework, two copies of Microsoft's assembly files are actually installed. One set is installed into the compiler/CLR directory, and another set is installed into a GAC subdirectory. The files in the compiler/CLR directory exist so that you can easily build your assembly, whereas the copies in the GAC exist so that they can be loaded at runtime.

The reason that CSC.exe doesn't look in the GAC for referenced assemblies is that you'd have to know the path to the assembly file and the structure of the GAC is undocumented. Alternatively, CSC.exe could allow you to specify a still long but slightly nicer-looking string, such as "System.Drawing, Version=v4.0.0.0, Culture=neutral, PublicKeyToken=b03f5f7f11d50a3a." Both of these solutions were deemed worse than having the assembly files installed twice on the user's hard drive.

> **Note** When building an assembly, you may want to refer to another assembly that has an x86 as well as an x64 version of itself available. Fortunately, the GAC subdirectories can actually hold an x86 and an x64 version of the same assembly. However, since the assemblies have the same file name, you cannot have different versions of these assemblies in the compiler/CLR directory. However, it shouldn't matter. When you install the .NET Framework on a machine, the x86, x64, or IA64 version of the assemblies are installed in the compiler/CLR directory. When you build an assembly, you can reference whatever version of the files were installed because all of the versions contain identical metadata and differ only by their code. At runtime, the proper version of the assembly will be loaded from the GAC. I'll discuss how the CLR determines where to load the assembly from at runtime later in this chapter.

Strongly Named Assemblies Are Tamper-Resistant

Signing an assembly with a private key ensures that the holder of the corresponding public key produced the assembly. When the assembly is installed into the GAC, the system hashes the contents of the file containing the manifest and compares the hash value with the RSA digital signature value embedded within the PE file (after unsigning it with the public key). If the values are identical, the file's contents haven't been tampered with, and you know that you have the public key that corresponds to the publisher's private key. In addition, the system hashes the contents of the assembly's other files and compares the hash values with the hash values stored in the manifest file's FileDef table. If any of the hash values don't match, at least one of the assembly's files has been tampered with, and the assembly will fail to install into the GAC.

> **Important** This mechanism ensures only that a file's content hasn't been tampered with. The mechanism doesn't allow you to tell who the publisher is unless you're absolutely positive that the publisher produced the public key you have and you're sure that the publisher's private key was never compromised. Another way to know the identity of the publisher is if the publisher associated its identity with the assembly by using Microsoft's Authenticode technology.

When an application needs to bind to an assembly, the CLR uses the referenced assembly's properties (name, version, culture, and public key) to locate the assembly in the GAC. If the referenced assembly can be found, its containing subdirectory is returned, and the file holding the manifest is loaded. Finding the assembly this way assures the caller that the assembly loaded at runtime came from the same publisher that built the assembly the code was compiled against. This assurance is possible because the public key token in the referencing assembly's AssemblyRef table corresponds to the public key in the referenced assembly's AssemblyDef table. If the referenced assembly isn't in the GAC, the CLR looks in the application's base directory and then in any of the private paths identified in the application's configuration file; then, if the application was installed using MSI, the CLR asks MSI to locate the assembly. If the assembly can't be found in any of these locations, the bind fails, and a `System.IO.FileNotFoundException` is thrown.

When strongly named assembly files are loaded from a location other than the GAC (via the application's base directory or via a **codeBase** element in a configuration file), the CLR compares hash values when the assembly is loaded. In other words, a hash of the file is performed every time an application executes and loads the assembly. This performance hit is a tradeoff for being certain that the assembly file's content hasn't been tampered with. When the CLR detects mismatched hash values at runtime, it throws a `System.IO.FileLoadException`.

> **Note** When a strongly named assembly is installed in the GAC, the system ensures that the file containing the manifest hasn't been tampered with. This check occurs only once, at installation time. In addition, to improve performance, the CLR does not check if a strongly named assembly has been tampered with if the assembly is fully trusted and is being loaded into a fully trusted AppDomain. On the other hand, when a strongly named assembly is loaded from a directory other than the GAC, the CLR verifies the assembly's manifest file to ensure that the file's contents have not been tampered with, causing an additional performance hit every time this file is loaded.

Delayed Signing

Earlier in this chapter, I discussed how the SN.exe tool can produce public/private key pairs. This tool generates the keys by making calls into the Crypto API provided by Windows. These keys can be stored in files or other storage devices. For example, large organizations (such as Microsoft) will maintain the returned private key in a hardware device that stays locked in a vault; only a few people in the company have access to the private key. This precaution prevents the private key from being compromised and ensures the key's integrity. The public key is, well, public and freely distributed.

When you're ready to package your strongly named assembly, you'll have to use the secure private key to sign it. However, while developing and testing your assembly, gaining access to the secure private key can be a hassle. For this reason, the .NET Framework supports *delayed signing*, sometimes referred to as *partial signing*. Delayed signing allows you to build an assembly by using only your company's public key; the private key isn't necessary. Using the public key allows assemblies that reference your assembly to embed the correct public key value in their AssemblyRef metadata entries. It also allows the assembly to be placed in the GAC appropriately. If you don't sign the file with your company's private key, you lose all of the tampering protection afforded to you because the assembly's files won't be hashed, and a digital signature won't be embedded in the file. This loss of protection shouldn't be a problem, however, because you use delayed signing only while developing your own assembly, not when you're ready to package and deploy the assembly.

Basically, you get your company's public key value in a file and pass the file name to whatever utility you use to build the assembly. (As I have shown earlier in this chapter, you can use SN.exe's **–p** switch to extract a public key from a file that contains a public/private key pair.) You must also tell the tool that you want the assembly to be delay signed, meaning that you're not supplying a private key. For the C# compiler, you do this by specifying the **/delaysign** compiler switch. In Visual Studio, you display the properties for your project, click the Signing tab, and then select the Delay Sign Only check box. If you're using AL.exe, you can specify the **/delay[sign]** command-line switch.

When the compiler or AL.exe detects that you're delay signing an assembly, it will emit the assembly's AssemblyDef manifest entry, which will contain the assembly's public key. Again, the presence of the public key allows the assembly to be placed in the GAC. It also allows you to build other assemblies that reference this assembly; the referencing assemblies will have the correct public key in their AssemblyRef metadata table entries. When creating the resulting assembly, space is left in the resulting PE file for the RSA digital signature. (The utility can determine how much space is necessary from the size of the public key.) Note that the file's contents won't be hashed at this time either.

At this point, the resulting assembly doesn't have a valid signature. Attempting to install the assembly into the GAC will fail because a hash of the file's contents hasn't been done—the file appears to have been tampered with. On every machine on which the assembly needs to be installed into the GAC, you must prevent the system from verifying the integrity of the assembly's files. To do this, you use the SN.exe utility, specifying the **–Vr** command-line switch. Executing SN.exe with this switch also tells the CLR to skip checking hash values for any of the assembly's files when loaded at runtime. Internally, SN's **–Vr** switch adds the assembly's identity under the following registry subkey: HKEY_LOCAL_MACHINE\SOFTWARE \Microsoft\StrongName\Verification.

Important When using any utility that manipulates the registry, make sure that you run the 64-bit version of the utility on a 64-bit machine. By default, the 32-bit x86 utilities are installed in C:\Program Files (x86)\Microsoft SDKs\Windows\v7.0A\bin\NETFX 4.0 Tools, and the 64-bit x64 utilities are installed in C:\Program Files (x86)\Microsoft SDKs\Windows\v7.0A\bin \NETFX 4.0 Tools\x64.

When you're finished developing and testing the assembly, you need to officially sign it so that you can package and deploy it. To sign the assembly, use the SN.exe utility again, this time with the **–R** switch and the name of the file that contains the actual private key. The **–R** switch causes SN.exe to hash the file's contents, sign it with the private key, and embed the RSA digital signature in the file where the space for it had previously been reserved. After this step, you can deploy the fully signed assembly. On the developing and testing machines, don't forget to turn verification of this assembly back on by using SN.exe's **–Vu** or **–Vx** command-line switch. The following list summarizes the steps discussed in this section to develop your assembly by using the delayed signing technique:

1. While developing an assembly, obtain a file that contains only your company's public key, and compile your assembly by using the **/keyfile** and **/delaysign** compiler switches:

   ```
   csc /keyfile:MyCompany.PublicKey /delaysign MyAssembly.cs
   ```

2. After building the assembly, execute the following line so that the CLR will trust the assembly's bytes without performing the hash and comparison. This allows you to in-stall the assembly in the GAC (if you desire). Now, you can build other assemblies that reference the assembly, and you can test the assembly. Note that you have to execute the following command line only once per machine; it's not necessary to perform this step each time you build your assembly.

   ```
   SN.exe –Vr MyAssembly.dll
   ```

3. When ready to package and deploy the assembly, obtain your company's private key, and then execute the line below. You can install this new version in the GAC if you desire, but don't attempt to install it in the GAC until executing step 4.

   ```
   SN.exe –R MyAssembly.dll MyCompany.PrivateKey
   ```

4. To test in real conditions, turn verification back on by executing the following com-mand line:

   ```
   SN –Vu MyAssembly.dll
   ```

At the beginning of this section, I mentioned how organizations keep their key pairs in a hardware device such as a smart card. To keep these keys secure, you must make sure that the key values are never persisted in a disk file. Cryptographic service providers (CSPs) offer containers that abstract the location of these keys. Microsoft, for example, uses a CSP that has a container that, when accessed, obtains the private key from a hardware device.

If your public/private key pair is in a CSP container, you'll have to specify different switches to the CSC.exe, AL.exe, and SN.exe programs: When compiling (CSC.exe), specify the **/keycontainer** switch instead of the **/keyfile** switch; when linking (AL.exe), specify its **/keyname** switch instead of its **/keyfile** switch; and when using the Strong Name program (SN.exe) to add a private key to a delay-signed assembly, specify the **–Rc** switch instead of the **–R** switch. SN.exe offers additional switches that allow you to perform operations with a CSP.

Important Delayed signing is also useful whenever you want to perform some other operation to an assembly before you package it. For example, you may want to run an obfuscator over your assembly. You can't obfuscate an assembly after it's been fully signed because the hash value will be incorrect. So, if you want to obfuscate an assembly file or perform any other type of post-build operation, you should use delayed signing, perform the post-build operation, and then run SN.exe with the –**R** or –**Rc** switch to complete the signing process of the assembly with all of its hashing.

Privately Deploying Strongly Named Assemblies

Installing assemblies into the GAC offers several benefits. The GAC enables many applications to share assemblies, reducing physical memory usage on the whole. In addition, it's easy to deploy a new version of the assembly into the GAC and have all applications use the new version via a publisher policy (described later in this chapter). The GAC also provides side-by-side management for an assembly's different versions. However, the GAC is usually secured so that only an administrator can install an assembly into it. Also, installing into the GAC breaks the simple copy deployment story.

Although strongly named assemblies can be installed into the GAC, they certainly don't have to be. In fact, it's recommended that you deploy assemblies into the GAC only if the assembly is intended to be shared by many applications. If an assembly isn't intended to be shared, it should be deployed privately. Deploying privately preserves the simple copy install deployment story and better isolates the application and its assemblies. Also, the GAC isn't intended to be the new C:\Windows\System32 dumping ground for common files. The reason is because new versions of assemblies don't overwrite each other; they are installed side by side, eating up disk space.

In addition to deploying a strongly named assembly in the GAC or privately, a strongly named assembly can be deployed to some arbitrary directory that a small set of applications know about. For example, you might be producing three applications, all of which want to share a strongly named assembly. Upon installation, you can create three directories: one for each application and an additional directory for the assembly you want shared. When you install each application into its directory, also install an XML configuration file, and have the shared assembly's **codeBase** element indicate the path of the shared assembly. Now at runtime, the CLR will know to look in the strongly named assembly's directory for the shared assembly. For the record, this technique is rarely used and is somewhat discouraged because no single application controls when the assembly's files should be uninstalled.

> **Note** The configuration file's **codeBase** element actually identifies a URL. This URL can refer to any directory on the user's machine or to a Web address. In the case of a Web address, the CLR will automatically download the file and store it in the user's download cache (a subdirectory under C:\Users*UserName*\Local Settings\Application Data\Assembly, where *UserName* is the name of the Windows user account currently signed on). When referenced in the future, the CLR will compare the timestamp of the downloaded file with the timestamp of the file at the specified URL. If the timestamp of the file at the URL is newer, the CLR will download the new version of the file and load it. If the previously downloaded file is newer, the CLR will load this file and will not download the file again (improving performance). An example of a configuration file containing a **codeBase** element is shown later in this chapter.

How the Runtime Resolves Type References

At the beginning of Chapter 2, we saw the following source code:

```
public sealed class Program {
    public static void Main() {
        System.Console.WriteLine("Hi");
    }
}
```

This code is compiled and built into an assembly, say Program.exe. When you run this application, the CLR loads and initializes. Then the CLR reads the assembly's CLR header, looking for the MethodDefToken that identifies the application's entry point method (**Main**). From the MethodDef metadata table, the offset within the file for the method's IL code is located and JIT-compiled into native code, which includes having the code verified for type safety. The native code then starts executing. Following is the IL code for the **Main** method. To obtain this output, I ran ILDasm.exe, chose the View menu's Show Bytes menu item, and then double-clicked the **Main** method in the tree view.

```
.method public hidebysig static void  Main() cil managed
// SIG: 00 00 01
{
  .entrypoint
  // Method begins at RVA 0x2050
  // Code size       11 (0xb)
  .maxstack  8
  IL_0000:  /* 72   | (70)000001       */
            ldstr      "Hi"
  IL_0005:  /* 28   | (0A)000003       */
            call       void [mscorlib]System.Console::WriteLine(string)
  IL_000a:  /* 2A   |                  */
            ret
} // end of method Program::Main
```

When JIT-compiling this code, the CLR detects all references to types and members and loads their defining assemblies (if not already loaded). As you can see, the IL code above has a reference to **System.Console.WriteLine**. Specifically, the IL **call** instruction references metadata token 0A000003. This token identifies entry 3 in the MemberRef metadata table (table 0A). The CLR looks up this MemberRef entry and sees that one of its fields refers to an entry in a TypeRef table (the **System.Console** type). From the TypeRef entry, the CLR is directed to an AssemblyRef entry: "mscorlib, Version=4.0.0.0, Culture=neutral, PublicKeyToken=b77a5c561934e089". At this point, the CLR knows which assembly it needs. Now the CLR must locate the assembly in order to load it.

When resolving a referenced type, the CLR can find the type in one of three places:

- **Same file**   Access to a type that is in the same file is determined at compile time (sometimes referred to as *early bound*). The type is loaded out of the file directly, and execution continues.

- **Different file, same assembly**   The runtime ensures that the file being referenced is, in fact, in the assembly's FileRef table of the current assembly's manifest. The runtime then looks in the directory where the assembly's manifest file was loaded. The file is loaded, its hash value is checked to ensure the file's integrity, the type's member is found, and execution continues.

- **Different file, different assembly**   When a referenced type is in a different assembly's file, the runtime loads the file that contains the referenced assembly's manifest. If this file doesn't contain the type, the appropriate file is loaded. The type's member is found, and execution continues.

> **Note** The ModuleDef, ModuleRef, and FileDef metadata tables refer to files using the file's name and its extension. However, the AssemblyRef metadata table refers to assemblies by file name without an extension. When binding to an assembly, the system automatically appends .dll and .exe file extensions while attempting to locate the file by probing the directories as mentioned in the "Simple Administrative Control (Configuration)" section in Chapter 2.

If any errors occur while resolving a type reference—file can't be found, file can't be loaded, hash mismatch, and so on—an appropriate exception is thrown.

> **Note** If you want, your code can register callback methods with **System.AppDomain**'s **AssemblyResolve**, **ReflectionOnlyAssemblyResolve**, and **TypeResolve** events. In your callback methods, you can execute code that resolves the binding problem and allows the application to continue running without throwing an exception.

In the previous example, the CLR determines that **System.Console** is implemented in a different assembly than the caller. The CLR must search for the assembly and load the PE file that contains the assembly's manifest. The manifest is then scanned to determine the PE file that implements the type. If the manifest file contains the referenced type, all is well. If the type is in another of the assembly's files, the CLR loads the other file and scans its metadata to locate the type. The CLR then creates its internal data structures to represent the type, and the JIT compiler completes the compilation for the **Main** method. Finally, the **Main** method can start executing.

Figure 3-2 illustrates how type binding occurs.

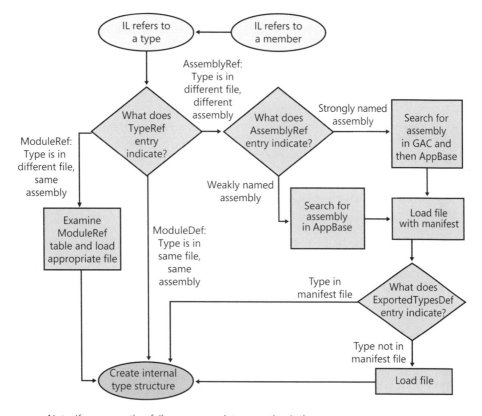

Note: If any operation fails, an appropriate exception is thrown.

FIGURE 3-2 Flowchart showing how, given IL code that refers to a method or type, the CLR uses metadata to locate the proper assembly file that defines a type

Important Strictly speaking, the example just described isn't 100 percent correct. For references to methods and types defined in an assembly that does not ship with the .NET Framework, the discussion is correct. However, the .NET Framework assemblies (including MSCorLib.dll) are closely tied to the version of the CLR that's running. Any assembly that references .NET Framework assemblies always binds to the version that matches the CLR's version. This is called *unification*, and Microsoft does this because they test all of the .NET Framework assemblies with a particular version of the CLR; therefore, unifying the code stack helps ensure that applications will work correctly.

So in the previous example, the reference to **System.Console**'s **WriteLine** method binds to whatever version of MSCorLib.dll matches the version of the CLR, regardless of what version of MSCorLib.dll is referenced in the assembly's AssemblyRef metadata table.

There is one more twist to this story: To the CLR, all assemblies are identified by name, version, culture, and public key. However, the GAC identifies assemblies using name, version, culture, public key, and CPU architecture. When searching the GAC for an assembly, the CLR figures out what type of process the application is currently running in: 32-bit x86 (possibly using the WoW64 technology), 64-bit x64, or 64-bit IA64. Then, when searching the GAC for an assembly, the CLR first searches for a CPU architecture–specific version of the assembly. If it does not find a matching assembly, it then searches for a CPU-agnostic version of the assembly.

In this section, you saw how the CLR locates an assembly when using a default policy. However, an administrator or the publisher of an assembly can override the default policy. In the next two sections, I'll describe how to alter the CLR's default binding policy.

> **Note** The CLR supports the ability to move a type (class, structure, enum, interface, or del-
> egate) from one assembly to another. For example, in .NET 3.5, the **System.TimeZoneInfo**
> class is defined in the System.Core.dll assembly. But in .NET 4.0, Microsoft moved this class
> to the MSCorLib.dll assembly. Normally, moving a type from one assembly to another would
> break applications. However, the CLR offers a **System.Runtime.CompilerServices.**
> **TypeForwardedToAttribute** attribute, which can be applied to the original assembly (such as
> System.Core.dll). The parameter that you pass to this attribute's constructor is of type
> **System.Type** and it indicates the new type (that is now defined in MSCorLib.dll)
> that applications should now use. The CLR's binder uses this information. Since the
> **TypeForwardedToAttribute**'s constructor takes a **Type**, the assembly containing this
> attribute will be dependent on the new assembly defining the type.
>
> If you take advantage of this feature, then you should also apply the **System.Runtime.**
> **CompilerServices.TypeForwardedFromAttribute** attribute to the type in the new assem-
> bly and pass to this attribute's constructor a string with the full name of the assembly that used
> to define the type. This attribute typically is used for tools, utilities, and serialization. Since the
> **TypeForwardedFromAttribute**'s constructor takes a **String**, the assembly containing this
> attribute is not dependent on the assembly that used to define the type.

Advanced Administrative Control (Configuration)

In the section "Simple Administrative Control (Configuration)" in Chapter 2, I gave a brief introduction to how an administrator can affect the way the CLR searches and binds to as-semblies. In that section, I demonstrated how a referenced assembly's files can be moved to a subdirectory of the application's base directory and how the CLR uses the application's XML configuration file to locate the moved files.

Having discussed only the probing element's **privatePath** attribute in Chapter 2, I'm going to discuss the other XML configuration file elements in this section. Following is an XML configuration file:

```xml
<?xml version="1.0"?>
<configuration>
    <runtime>
        <assemblyBinding xmlns="urn:schemas-microsoft-com:asm.v1">
            <probing privatePath="AuxFiles;bin\subdir" />

            <dependentAssembly>

                <assemblyIdentity name="JeffTypes"
                  publicKeyToken="32ab4ba45e0a69a1" culture="neutral"/>

                <bindingRedirect
                  oldVersion="1.0.0.0" newVersion="2.0.0.0" />

                <codeBase version="2.0.0.0"
                  href="http://www.Wintellect.com/JeffTypes.dll" />

            </dependentAssembly>

            <dependentAssembly>

                <assemblyIdentity name="TypeLib"
                  publicKeyToken="1f2e74e897abbcfe" culture="neutral"/>

                <bindingRedirect
                  oldVersion="3.0.0.0-3.5.0.0" newVersion="4.0.0.0" />

                <publisherPolicy apply="no" />

            </dependentAssembly>

        </assemblyBinding>
    </runtime>
</configuration>
```

This XML file gives a wealth of information to the CLR. Here's what it says:

- **probing element**   Look in the application base directory's AuxFiles and bin\subdir subdirectories when trying to find a weakly named assembly. For strongly named assemblies, the CLR looks in the GAC or in the URL specified by the **codeBase** element. The CLR looks in the application's private paths for a strongly named assembly only if no **codeBase** element is specified.

- **First dependentAssembly, assemblyIdentity, and bindingRedirect elements** When attempting to locate version 1.0.0.0 of the culture-neutral JeffTypes assembly published by the organization that controls the 32ab4ba45e0a69a1 public key token, locate version 2.0.0.0 of the same assembly instead.

- **codeBase element**   When attempting to locate version 2.0.0.0 of the culture-neutral JeffTypes assembly published by the organization that controls the 32ab4ba45e0a69a1 public key token, try to find it at the following URL: *www.Wintellect.com/JeffTypes.dll*. Although I didn't mention it in Chapter 2, a **codeBase** element can also be used with weakly named assemblies. In this case, the assembly's version number is ignored and should be omitted from the XML's **codeBase** element. Also, the **codeBase** URL must refer to a directory under the application's base directory.

- Second **dependentAssembly**, **assemblyIdentity**, and **bindingRedirect** elements When attempting to locate version 3.0.0.0 through version 3.5.0.0 inclusive of the culture-neutral TypeLib assembly published by the organization that controls the 1f2e74e897abbcfe public key token, locate version 4.0.0.0 of the same assembly instead.

- **publisherPolicy element**   If the organization that produces the TypeLib assembly has deployed a publisher policy file (described in the next section), the CLR should ignore this file.

When compiling a method, the CLR determines the types and members being referenced. Using this information, the runtime determines, by looking in the referencing assembly's AssemblyRef table, the assembly that was originally referenced when the calling assembly was built. The CLR then looks up the assembly/version in the application's configuration file and applies any version number redirections; the CLR is now looking for this assembly/version.

If the **publisherPolicy** element's **apply** attribute is set to **yes**—or if the element is omitted —the CLR examines the GAC for the new assembly/version and applies any version number redirections that the publisher of the assembly feels is necessary; the CLR is now looking for this assembly/version. I'll talk more about publisher policy in the next section. Finally, the CLR looks up the new assembly/version in the machine's Machine.config file and applies any version number redirections there.

At this point, the CLR knows the version of the assembly that it should load, and it attempts to load the assembly from the GAC. If the assembly isn't in the GAC, and if there is no **codeBase** element, the CLR probes for the assembly as I described in Chapter 2. If the configuration file that performs the last redirection also contains a **codeBase** element, the CLR attempts to load the assembly from the **codeBase** element's specified URL.

Using these configuration files, an administrator can really control what assembly the CLR decides to load. If an application is experiencing a bug, the administrator can contact the publisher of the errant assembly. The publisher can send the administrator a new assembly that the administrator can install. By default, the CLR won't load this new assembly because the already-built assemblies don't reference the new version. However, the administrator can modify the application's XML configuration file to instruct the CLR to load the new assembly.

If the administrator wants all applications on the machine to pick up the new assembly, the administrator can modify the machine's Machine.config file instead, and the CLR will load the new assembly whenever an application refers to the old assembly.

If the new assembly doesn't fix the original bug, the administrator can delete the binding redirection lines from the configuration file, and the application will behave as it did before. It's important to note that the system allows the use of an assembly that doesn't exactly match the assembly version recorded in the metadata. This extra flexibility is very handy.

Publisher Policy Control

In the scenario described in the previous section, the publisher of an assembly simply sent a new version of the assembly to the administrator, who installed the assembly and manually edited the application's or machine's XML configuration files. In general, when a publisher fixes a bug in an assembly, the publisher would like an easy way to package and distribute the new assembly to all of the users. But the publisher also needs a way to tell each user's CLR to use the new assembly version instead of the old assembly version. Sure, each user could modify his or her application's or machine's XML configuration file, but this is terribly inconvenient and error prone. What the publisher needs is a way to create policy information that is installed on the user's computer when the new assembly is installed. In this section, I'll show how an assembly's publisher can create this policy information.

Let's say that you're a publisher of an assembly and that you've just created a new version of your assembly that fixes some bugs. When you package your new assembly to send out to all of your users, you should also create an XML configuration file. This configuration file looks just like the configuration files we've been talking about. Here's an example file (called JeffTypes.config) for the JeffTypes.dll assembly:

```
<configuration>
   <runtime>
      <assemblyBinding xmlns="urn:schemas-microsoft-com:asm.v1">
         <dependentAssembly>

            <assemblyIdentity name="JeffTypes"
              publicKeyToken="32ab4ba45e0a69a1" culture="neutral"/>

            <bindingRedirect
              oldVersion="1.0.0.0" newVersion="2.0.0.0" />

            <codeBase version="2.0.0.0"
              href="http://www.Wintellect.com/JeffTypes.dll"/>

         </dependentAssembly>
      </assemblyBinding>
   </runtime>
</configuration>
```

Of course, publishers can set policies only for the assemblies that they themselves create. In addition, the elements shown here are the only elements that can be specified in a publisher policy configuration file; you can't specify the **probing** or **publisherPolicy** elements, for example.

This configuration file tells the CLR to load version 2.0.0.0 of the JeffTypes assembly whenever version 1.0.0.0 of the assembly is referenced. Now you, the publisher, can create an assembly that contains this publisher policy configuration file. You create the publisher policy assembly by running AL.exe as follows:

```
AL.exe /out:Policy.1.0.JeffTypes.dll
       /version:1.0.0.0
       /keyfile:MyCompany.snk
       /linkresource:JeffTypes.config
```

Let me explain the meaning of AL.exe's command-line switches:

- **/out**   This switch tells AL.exe to create a new PE file, called Policy.1.0.JeffTypes.dll, which contains nothing but a manifest. The name of this assembly is very important. The first part of the name, *Policy,* tells the CLR that this assembly contains publisher policy information. The second and third parts of the name, *1.0,* tell the CLR that this publisher policy assembly is for any version of the JeffTypes assembly that has a major and minor version of 1.0. Publisher policies apply to the major and minor version numbers of an assembly only; you can't create a publisher policy that is specific to individual builds or revisions of an assembly. The fourth part of the name, *JeffTypes,* indicates the name of the assembly that this publisher policy corresponds to. The fifth and last part of the name, *dll,* is simply the extension given to the resulting assembly file.

- **/version**   This switch identifies the version of the publisher policy assembly; this version number has nothing to do with the JeffTypes assembly itself. You see, publisher policy assemblies can also be versioned. Today, the publisher might create a publisher policy redirecting version 1.0.0.0 of JeffTypes to version 2.0.0.0. In the future, the publisher might want to direct version 1.0.0.0 of JeffTypes to version 2.5.0.0. The CLR uses this version number so that it knows to pick up the latest version of the publisher policy assembly.

- **/keyfile**   This switch causes AL.exe to sign the publisher policy assembly by using the publisher's public/private key pair. This key pair must also match the key pair used for all versions of the JeffTypes assembly. After all, this is how the CLR knows that the same publisher created both the JeffTypes assembly and this publisher policy file.

- **/linkresource**   This switch tells AL.exe that the XML configuration file is to be considered a separate file of the assembly. The resulting assembly consists of two files, both of which must be packaged and deployed to the users along with the new version of the JeffTypes assembly. By the way, you can't use AL.exe's **/embedresource** switch to embed the XML configuration file into the assembly file, making a single file assembly, because the CLR requires the XML file to be contained in its own separate file.

Once this publisher policy assembly is built, it can be packaged together with the new JeffTypes.dll assembly file and deployed to users. The publisher policy assembly must be installed into the GAC. Although the JeffTypes assembly can also be installed into the GAC, it doesn't have to be. It could be deployed into an application's base directory or some other directory identified by a **codeBase** URL.

> **Important** A publisher should create a publisher policy assembly only when deploying an update or a service pack version of an assembly. When doing a fresh install of an application, no publisher policy assemblies should be installed.

I want to make one last point about publisher policy. Say that a publisher distributes a publisher policy assembly, and for some reason, the new assembly introduces more bugs than it fixes. If this happens, the administrator would like to tell the CLR to ignore the publisher policy assembly. To have the runtime do this, the administrator can edit the application's configuration file and add the following **publisherPolicy** element:

```
<publisherPolicy apply="no"/>
```

This element can be placed as a child element of the **<assemblyBinding>** element in the application's configuration file so that it applies to all assemblies, or as a child element of the **<dependantAssembly>** element in the application's configuration file to have it apply to a specific assembly. When the CLR processes the application's configuration file, it will see that the GAC shouldn't be examined for the publisher policy assembly. So the CLR will continue to operate using the older version of the assembly. Note, however, that the CLR will still examine and apply any policy specified in the Machine.config file.

> **Important** A publisher policy assembly is a way for a publisher to make a statement about the compatibility of different versions of an assembly. If a new version of an assembly isn't intended to be compatible with an earlier version, the publisher shouldn't create a publisher policy assembly. In general, use a publisher policy assembly when you build a new version of your assembly that fixes a bug. You should test the new version of the assembly for backward compatibility. On the other hand, if you're adding new features to your assembly, you should consider the assembly to have no relationship to a previous version, and you shouldn't ship a publisher policy assembly. In addition, there's no need to do any backward compatibility testing with such an assembly.

Chapter 4
Type Fundamentals

In this chapter, I will introduce information that is fundamental to working with types and the common language runtime (CLR). In particular, I'll discuss the minimum set of behaviors that you can expect every type to have. I'll also describe type safety, namespaces, assemblies, and the various ways you can cast objects from one type to another. Finally, I'll conclude this chapter with an explanation of how types, objects, thread stacks, and the managed heap all relate to one another at runtime.

All Types Are Derived from `System.Object`

The runtime requires every type to ultimately be derived from the **System.Object** type. This means that the following two type definitions are identical:

```
// Implicitly derived from Object
class Employee {
...
}
```

```
// Explicitly derived from Object
class Employee : System.Object {
...
}
```

Because all types are ultimately derived from **System.Object**, you are guaranteed that every object of every type has a minimum set of methods. Specifically, the **System.Object** class offers the public instance methods listed in Table 4-1.

TABLE 4-1 **Public Methods of** `System.Object`

Public Method	Description
`Equals`	Returns **true** if two objects have the same value. For more information about this method, see the "Object Equality and Identity" section in Chapter 5, "Primitive, Reference, and Value Types."
`GetHashCode`	Returns a hash code for this object's value. A type should override this method if its objects are to be used as a key in a hash table collection. The method should provide a good distribution for its objects. It is unfortunate that this method is defined in **Object** because most types are never used as keys in a hash table; this method should have been defined in an interface. For more information about this method, see the "Object Hash Codes" section in Chapter 5.
`ToString`	By default, returns the full name of the type (**this.GetType().FullName**). However, it is common to override this method so that it returns a **String** object containing a representation of the object's state. For example, the core types, such as **Boolean** and **Int32**, override this method to return a string representation of their values. It is also common to override this method for debugging purposes; you can call it and get a string showing the values of the object's fields. In fact, Microsoft Visual Studio's debugger calls this function automatically to show you a string representation of an object. Note that **ToString** is expected to be aware of the **CultureInfo** associated with the calling thread. Chapter 14, "Chars, Strings, and Working with Text," discusses **ToString** in greater detail.
`GetType`	Returns an instance of a **Type**-derived object that identifies the type of the object used to call **GetType**. The returned **Type** object can be used with the reflection classes to obtain metadata information about the object's type. Reflection is discussed in Chapter 23, "Assembly Loading and Reflection." The **GetType** method is nonvirtual, which prevents a class from overriding this method and lying about its type, violating type safety.

In addition, types that derive from **System.Object** have access to the protected methods listed in Table 4-2.

TABLE 4-2 **Protected Methods of** `System.Object`

Protected Method	Description
`MemberwiseClone`	This nonvirtual method creates a new instance of the type and sets the new object's instance fields to be identical to the **this** object's instance fields. A reference to the new instance is returned.
`Finalize`	This virtual method is called when the garbage collector determines that the object is garbage before the memory for the object is reclaimed. Types that require cleanup when collected should override this method. I'll talk about this important method in much more detail in Chapter 21, "Automatic Memory Management (Garbage Collection)."

The CLR requires all objects to be created using the **new** operator. The following line shows how to create an **Employee** object:

```
Employee e = new Employee("ConstructorParam1");
```

Here's what the **new** operator does:

1. It calculates the number of bytes required by all instance fields defined in the type and all of its base types up to and including **System.Object** (which defines no instance fields of its own). Every object on the heap requires some additional members—called the type object pointer and the sync block index—used by the CLR to manage the object. The bytes for these additional members are added to the size of the object.

2. It allocates memory for the object by allocating the number of bytes required for the specified type from the managed heap; all of these bytes are then set to zero (0).

3. It initializes the object's type object pointer and sync block index members.

4. The type's instance constructor is called, passing it any arguments (the string "**ConstructorParam1**" in the preceding example) specified in the call to **new**. Most compilers automatically emit code in a constructor to call a base class's constructor. Each constructor is responsible for initializing the instance fields defined by the type whose constructor is being called. Eventually, **System.Object**'s constructor is called, and this constructor method does nothing but return. You can verify this by using ILDasm.exe to load MSCorLib.dll and examine **System.Object**'s constructor method.

After **new** has performed all of these operations, it returns a reference (or pointer) to the newly created object. In the preceding code example, this reference is saved in the variable **e**, which is of type **Employee**.

By the way, the **new** operator has no complementary **delete** operator; that is, there is no way to explicitly free the memory allocated for an object. The CLR uses a garbage-collected environment (described in Chapter 21) that automatically detects when objects are no longer being used or accessed and frees the object's memory automatically.

Casting Between Types

One of the most important features of the CLR is type safety. At runtime, the CLR always knows what type an object is. You can always discover an object's exact type by calling the **GetType** method. Because this method is nonvirtual, it is impossible for a type to spoof another type. For example, the **Employee** type can't override the **GetType** method and have it return a type of **SuperHero**.

Developers frequently find it necessary to cast an object to various types. The CLR allows you to cast an object to its type or to any of its base types. Your choice of programming language dictates how to expose casting operations to the developer. For example, C# doesn't require any special syntax to cast an object to any of its base types, because casts to base types are considered safe implicit conversions. However, C# does require the developer to explicitly cast an object to any of its derived types since such a cast could fail at runtime. The following code demonstrates casting to base and derived types:

```
// This type is implicitly derived from System.Object.
internal class Employee {
   ...
}


public sealed class Program {
   public static void Main() {
      // No cast needed since new returns an Employee object
      // and Object is a base type of Employee.
      Object o = new Employee();

      // Cast required since Employee is derived from Object.
      // Other languages (such as Visual Basic) might not require
      // this cast to compile.
      Employee e = (Employee) o;
   }
}
```

This example shows what is necessary for your compiler to compile your code. Now I'll explain what happens at runtime. At runtime, the CLR checks casting operations to ensure that casts are always to the object's actual type or any of its base types. For example, the following code will compile, but at runtime, an **InvalidCastException** will be thrown:

```
internal class Employee {
   ...
}
internal class Manager : Employee {
   ...
}


public sealed class Program {
   public static void Main() {
      // Construct a Manager object and pass it to PromoteEmployee.
      // A Manager IS-A Object: PromoteEmployee runs OK.
      Manager m = new Manager();
      PromoteEmployee(m);

      // Construct a DateTime object and pass it to PromoteEmployee.
      // A DateTime is NOT derived from Employee. PromoteEmployee
      // throws a System.InvalidCastException exception.
      DateTime newYears = new DateTime(2010, 1, 1);
      PromoteEmployee(newYears);
   }

   public static void PromoteEmployee(Object o) {
      // At this point, the compiler doesn't know exactly what
      // type of object o refers to. So the compiler allows the
      // code to compile. However, at runtime, the CLR does know
      // what type o refers to (each time the cast is performed) and
      // it checks whether the object's type is Employee or any type
      // that is derived from Employee.
```

```
        Employee e = (Employee) o;
        ...
    }
}
```

In the **Main** method, a **Manager** object is constructed and passed to **PromoteEmployee**. This code compiles and executes because **Manager** is ultimately derived from **Object**, which is what **PromoteEmployee** expects. Once inside **PromoteEmployee**, the CLR confirms that **o** refers to an object that is either an **Employee** or a type that is derived from **Employee**. Because **Manager** is derived from **Employee**, the CLR performs the cast and allows **PromoteEmployee** to continue executing.

After **PromoteEmployee** returns, **Main** constructs a **DateTime** object and passes it to **PromoteEmployee**. Again, **DateTime** is derived from **Object**, and the compiler compiles the code that calls **PromoteEmployee** with no problem. However, inside **PromoteEmployee**, the CLR checks the cast and detects that **o** refers to a **DateTime** object and is therefore not an **Employee** or any type derived from **Employee**. At this point, the CLR can't allow the cast and throws a **System.InvalidCastException**.

If the CLR allowed the cast, there would be no type safety, and the results would be unpredictable, including the possibility of application crashes and security breaches caused by the ability of types to easily spoof other types. Type spoofing is the cause of many security breaches and compromises an application's stability and robustness. Type safety is therefore an extremely important part of the CLR.

By the way, the proper way to declare the **PromoteEmployee** method would be to specify an **Employee** type instead of an **Object** type as its parameter so that the compiler produces a compile-time error, saving the developer from waiting until a runtime exception occurs to discover a problem. I used **Object** so that I could demonstrate how the C# compiler and the CLR deal with casting and type-safety.

Casting with the C# **is** and **as** Operators

Another way to cast in the C# language is to use the **is** operator. The **is** operator checks whether an object is compatible with a given type, and the result of the evaluation is a **Boolean: true** or **false**. The **is** operator will never throw an exception. The following code demonstrates:

```
Object o = new Object();
Boolean b1 = (o is Object);    // b1 is true.
Boolean b2 = (o is Employee); // b2 is false.
```

If the object reference is **null**, the **is** operator always returns **false** because there is no object available to check its type.

The **is** operator is typically used as follows:

```
if (o is Employee) {
   Employee e = (Employee) o;
   // Use e within the remainder of the 'if' statement.
}
```

In this code, the CLR is actually checking the object's type twice: The **is** operator first checks to see if **o** is compatible with the **Employee** type. If it is, inside the **if** statement, the CLR again verifies that **o** refers to an **Employee** when performing the cast. The CLR's type checking improves security, but it certainly comes at a performance cost, because the CLR must determine the actual type of the object referred to by the variable (**o**), and then the CLR must walk the inheritance hierarchy, checking each base type against the specified type (**Employee**). Because this programming paradigm is quite common, C# offers a way to simplify this code and improve its performance by providing an **as** operator:

```
Employee e = o as Employee;
if (e != null) {
   // Use e within the 'if' statement.
}
```

In this code, the CLR checks if **o** is compatible with the **Employee** type, and if it is, **as** returns a non-**null** reference to the same object. If **o** is not compatible with the **Employee** type, the **as** operator returns **null**. Notice that the **as** operator causes the CLR to verify an object's type just once. The **if** statement simply checks whether **e** is **null**; this check can be performed faster than verifying an object's type.

The **as** operator works just as casting does except that the **as** operator will never throw an exception. Instead, if the object can't be cast, the result is **null**. You'll want to check to see whether the resulting reference is **null**, or attempting to use the resulting reference will cause a **System.NullReferenceException** to be thrown. The following code demonstrates:

```
Object o = new Object();    // Creates a new Object object
Employee e = o as Employee; // Casts o to an Employee
// The cast above fails: no exception is thrown, but e is set to null.

e.ToString();  // Accessing e throws a NullReferenceException.
```

To make sure you understand everything just presented, take the following quiz. Assume that these two class definitions exist:

```
internal class B {     // Base class
}

internal class D : B { // Derived class
}
```

Now examine the lines of C# code in Table 4-3. For each line, decide whether the line would compile and execute successfully (marked OK below), cause a compile-time error (CTE), or cause a run-time error (RTE).

TABLE 4-3 Type-Safety Quiz

Statement	OK	CTE	RTE
`Object o1 = new Object();`	✓		
`Object o2 = new B();`	✓		
`Object o3 = new D();`	✓		
`Object o4 = o3;`	✓		
`B b1 = new B();`	✓		
`B b2 = new D();`	✓		
`D d1 = new D();`	✓		
`B b3 = new Object();`		✓	
`D d2 = new Object();`		✓	
`B b4 = d1;`	✓		
`D d3 = b2;`		✓	
`D d4 = (D) d1;`	✓		
`D d5 = (D) b2;`	✓		
`D d6 = (D) b1;`			✓
`B b5 = (B) o1;`			✓
`B b6 = (D) b2;`	✓		

> **Note** C# allows a type to define conversion operator methods as discussed in the "Conversion Operator Methods" section of Chapter 9, "Parameters." These methods are invoked only when using a cast expression; they are never invoked when using C#'s **as** or **is** operator.

Namespaces and Assemblies

Namespaces allow for the logical grouping of related types, and developers typically use them to make it easier to locate a particular type. For example, the **System.Text** namespace defines a bunch of types for performing string manipulations, and the **System.IO** namespace defines a bunch of types for performing I/O operations. Here's some code that constructs a **System.IO.FileStream** object and a **System.Text.StringBuilder** object:

```
public sealed class Program {
   public static void Main() {
      System.IO.FileStream fs = new System.IO.FileStream(...);
      System.Text.StringBuilder sb = new System.Text.StringBuilder();
   }
}
```

As you can see, the code is pretty verbose; it would be nice if there were some shorthand way to refer to the **FileStream** and **StringBuilder** types to reduce typing. Fortunately, many compilers do offer mechanisms to reduce programmer typing. The C# compiler provides this mechanism via the **using** directive. The following code is identical to the previous example:

```
using System.IO;    // Try prepending "System.IO."
using System.Text;  // Try prepending "System.Text."

public sealed class Program {
    public static void Main() {
        FileStream fs = new FileStream(...);
        StringBuilder sb = new StringBuilder();
    }
}
```

To the compiler, a namespace is simply an easy way of making a type's name longer and more likely to be unique by preceding the name with some symbols separated by dots. So the compiler interprets the reference to **FileStream** in this example to mean **System.IO.FileStream**. Similarly, the compiler interprets the reference to **StringBuilder** to mean **System.Text.StringBuilder**.

Using the C# **using** directive is entirely optional; you're always welcome to type out the fully qualified name of a type if you prefer. The C# **using** directive instructs the compiler to try prepending different prefixes to a type name until a match is found.

> **Important** The CLR doesn't know anything about namespaces. When you access a type, the CLR needs to know the full name of the type (which can be a really long name containing periods) and which assembly contains the definition of the type so that the runtime can load the proper assembly, find the type, and manipulate it.

In the previous code example, the compiler needs to ensure that every type referenced exists and that my code is using that type in the correct way: calling methods that exist, passing the right number of arguments to these methods, ensuring that the arguments are the right type, using the method's return value correctly, and so on. If the compiler can't find a type with the specified name in the source files or in any referenced assemblies, it prepends **System.IO.** to the type name and checks if the generated name matches an existing type. If the compiler still can't find a match, it prepends **System.Text.** to the type's name. The two **using** directives shown earlier allow me to simply type **FileStream** and **StringBuilder** in my code—the compiler automatically expands the references to **System.IO.FileStream** and **System.Text.StringBuilder**. I'm sure you can easily imagine how much typing this saves, as well as how much cleaner your code is to read.

When checking for a type's definition, the compiler must be told which assemblies to examine by using the **/reference** compiler switch as discussed in Chapter 2, "Building, Packaging, Deploying, and Administering Applications and Types," and Chapter 3, "Shared Assemblies and Strongly Named Assemblies." The compiler will scan all of the referenced assemblies looking for the type's definition. Once the compiler finds the proper assembly, the assembly information and the type information is emitted into the resulting managed module's metadata. To get the assembly information, you must pass the assembly that defines any referenced types to the compiler. The C# compiler, by default, automatically looks in the MSCorLib.dll assembly even if you don't explicitly tell it to. The MSCorLib.dll assembly contains the definitions of all of the core Framework Class Library (FCL) types, such as **Object**, **Int32**, **String**, and so on.

As you might imagine, there are some potential problems with the way that compilers treat namespaces: it's possible to have two (or more) types with the same name in different namespaces. Microsoft strongly recommends that you define unique names for types. However, in some cases, it's simply not possible. The runtime encourages the reuse of components. Your application might take advantage of a component that Microsoft created and another component that Wintellect created. These two companies might both offer a type called **Widget**—Microsoft's **Widget** does one thing, and Wintellect's **Widget** does something entirely different. In this scenario, you had no control over the naming of the types, so you can differentiate between the two widgets by using their fully qualified names when referencing them. To reference Microsoft's **Widget**, you would use **Microsoft.Widget**, and to reference Wintellect's **Widget**, you would use **Wintellect.Widget**. In the following code, the reference to **Widget** is ambiguous, so the C# compiler generates the following message: **"error CS0104: 'Widget' is an ambiguous reference"**:

```
using Microsoft;  // Try prepending "Microsoft."
using Wintellect; // Try prepending "Wintellect."

public sealed class Program {
   public static void Main() {
      Widget w = new Widget();// An ambiguous reference
   }
}
```

To remove the ambiguity, you must explicitly tell the compiler which **Widget** you want to create:

```
using Microsoft;  // Try prepending "Microsoft."
using Wintellect; // Try prepending "Wintellect."

public sealed class Program {
   public static void Main() {
      Wintellect.Widget w = new Wintellect.Widget(); // Not ambiguous
   }
}
```

There's another form of the C# **using** directive that allows you to create an alias for a single type or namespace. This is handy if you have just a few types that you use from a namespace and don't want to pollute the global namespace with all of a namespace's types. The following code demonstrates another way to solve the ambiguity problem shown in the preceding code:

```
using Microsoft;  // Try prepending "Microsoft."
using Wintellect; // Try prepending "Wintellect."

// Define WintellectWidget symbol as an alias to Wintellect.Widget
using WintellectWidget = Wintellect.Widget;

public sealed class Program {
   public static void Main() {
      WintellectWidget w = new WintellectWidget(); // No error now
   }
}
```

These methods of disambiguating a type are useful, but in some scenarios, you need to go further. Imagine that the Australian Boomerang Company (ABC) and the Alaskan Boat Corporation (ABC) are each creating a type, called **BuyProduct**, which they intend to ship in their respective assemblies. It's likely that both companies would create a namespace called **ABC** that contains a type called **BuyProduct**. Anyone who tries to develop an application that needs to buy both boomerangs and boats would be in for some trouble unless the programming language provides a way to programmatically distinguish between the assemblies, not just between the namespaces. Fortunately, the C# compiler offers a feature called *extern aliases* that *gives* you a way to work around this rarely occurring problem. Extern aliases also give you a way to access a single type from two (or more) different versions of the same assembly. For more information about extern aliases, see the C# Language Specification.

In your library, when you're designing types that you expect third parties to use, you should define these types in a namespace so that compilers can easily disambiguate them. In fact, to reduce the likelihood of conflict, you should use your full company name (not an acronym or abbreviation) to be your top-level namespace name. Referring to the Microsoft .NET Framework SDK documentation, you can see that Microsoft uses a namespace of "Microsoft" for Microsoft-specific types. (See the **Microsoft.CSharp**, **Microsoft.VisualBasic**, and **Microsoft.Win32** namespaces as examples.)

Creating a namespace is simply a matter of writing a namespace declaration into your code as follows (in C#):

```
namespace CompanyName {
   public sealed class A {               // TypeDef: CompanyName.A
   }

   namespace X {
      public sealed class B { ... }       // TypeDef: CompanyName.X.B
   }
}
```

The comment on the right of the class definitions above indicates the real name of the type the compiler will emit into the type definition metadata table; this is the real name of the type from the CLR's perspective.

Some compilers don't support namespaces at all, and other compilers are free to define what "namespace" means to a particular language. In C#, the **namespace** directive simply tells the compiler to prefix each type name that appears in source code with the namespace name so that programmers can do less typing.

How Namespaces and Assemblies Relate

Be aware that a namespace and an assembly (the file that implements a type) aren't necessarily related. In particular, the various types belonging to a single namespace might be implemented in multiple assemblies. For example, the **System.IO.FileStream** type is implemented in the MSCorLib.dll assembly, and the **System.IO.FileSystemWatcher** type is implemented in the System.dll assembly. In fact, the .NET Framework doesn't even ship a System.IO.dll assembly.

A single assembly can contain types in different namespaces. For example, the **System.Int32** and **System.Text.StringBuilder** types are both in the MSCorLib.dll assembly.

When you look up a type in the .NET Framework SDK documentation, the documentation will clearly indicate the namespace that the type belongs to and also the assembly that the type is implemented in. In Figure 4-1, you can clearly see (right above the Syntax section) that the **ResXFileRef** type is part of the **System.Resources** namespace and that the type is implemented in the System.Windows.Forms.dll assembly. To compile code that references the **ResXFileRef** type, you'd add a **using System.Resources;** directive to your source code, and you'd use the **/r:System.Windows.Forms.dll** compiler switch.

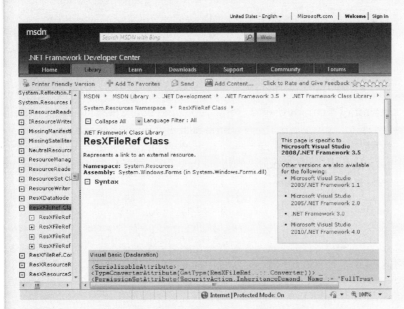

FIGURE 4-1 SDK documentation showing namespace and assembly information for a type

How Things Relate at Runtime

In this section, I'm going to explain the relationship at runtime between types, objects, a thread's stack, and the managed heap. Furthermore, I will also explain the difference between calling static methods, instance methods, and virtual methods. Let's start off with some fundamentals of computers. What I'm about to describe is not specific to the CLR at all, but I'm going to describe it so that we have a working foundation, and then I'll modify the discussion to incorporate CLR-specific information.

Figure 4-2 shows a single Microsoft Windows process that has the CLR loaded into it. In this process there may be many threads. When a thread is created, it is allocated a 1-MB stack. This stack space is used for passing arguments to a method and for local variables defined within a method. In Figure 4-2, the memory for one thread's stack is shown (on the right). Stacks build from high-memory addresses to low-memory addresses. In the figure, this thread has been executing some code, and its stack has some data on it already (shown as the shaded area at the top of the stack). Now, imagine that the thread has executed some code that calls the **M1** method.

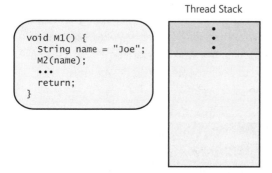

FIGURE 4-2 A thread's stack with the **M1** method about to be called

All but the simplest of methods contain some *prologue code*, which initializes a method before it can start doing its work. These methods also contain *epilogue code*, which cleans up a method after it has performed its work so that it can return to its caller. When the **M1** method starts to execute, its prologue code allocates memory for the local **name** variable from the thread's stack (see Figure 4-3).

Thread Stack

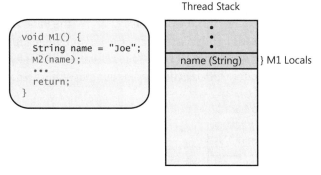

FIGURE 4-3 Allocating **M1**'s local variable on the thread's stack

Then, **M1** calls the **M2** method, passing in the **name** local variable as an argument. This causes the address in the **name** local variable to be pushed on the stack (see Figure 4-4). Inside the **M2** method, the stack location will be identified using the parameter variable named **s**. (Note that some architectures pass arguments via registers to improve performance, but this distinction is not important for this discussion.) Also, when a method is called, the address indicating where the called method should return to in the calling method is pushed on the stack (also shown in Figure 4-4).

Thread Stack

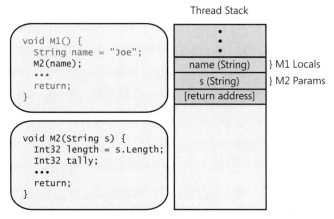

FIGURE 4-4 M1 pushes arguments and the return address on the thread's stack when calling **M2**.

When the **M2** method starts to execute, its prologue code allocates memory for the local **length** and **tally** variables from the thread's stack (see Figure 4-5). Then the code inside method **M2** executes. Eventually, **M2** gets to its return statement, which causes the CPU's instruction pointer to be set to the return address in the stack, and **M2**'s stack frame is unwound so that it looks the way it did in Figure 4-3. At this point, **M1** is continuing to execute its code that immediately follows the call to **M2**, and its stack frame accurately reflects the state needed by **M1**.

Eventually, **M1** will return back to its caller by setting the CPU's instruction pointer to be set to the return address (not shown on the figures, but it would be just above the **name** argument on the stack), and **M1**'s stack frame is unwound so that it looks the way it did in Figure 4-2. At this point, the method that called **M1** continues to execute its code that immediately follows the call to **M1**, and its stack frame accurately reflects the state needed by that method.

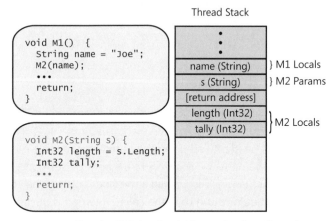

FIGURE 4-5 Allocating **M2**'s local variables on the thread's stack

Now, let's start gearing the discussion toward the CLR. Let's say that we have these two class definitions:

```
internal class Employee {
    public          Int32     GetYearsEmployed()  { ... }
    public virtual  String    GetProgressReport() { ... }
    public static   Employee  Lookup(String name) { ... }
}

internal sealed class Manager : Employee {
    public override String    GetProgressReport() { ... }
}
```

Our Windows process has started, the CLR is loaded into it, the managed heap is initialized, and a thread has been created (along with its 1 MB of stack space). This thread has already executed some code, and this code has decided to call the **M3** method. All of this is shown in Figure 4-6. The **M3** method contains code that demonstrates how the CLR works; this is not code that you would normally write, because it doesn't actually do anything useful.

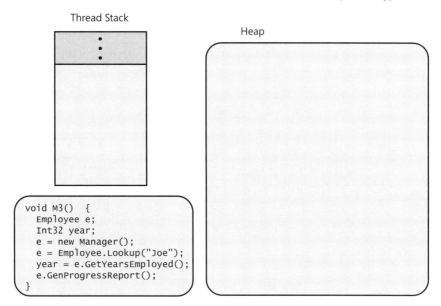

FIGURE 4-6 The CLR loaded in a process, its heap initialized, and a thread's stack with the **M3** method about to be called

As the just-in-time (JIT) compiler converts **M3**'s Intermediate Language (IL) code into native CPU instructions, it notices all of the types that are referred to inside **M3**: **Employee**, **Int32**, **Manager**, and **String** (because of **"Joe"**). At this time, the CLR ensures that the assemblies that define these types are loaded. Then, using the assembly's metadata, the CLR extracts information about these types and creates some data structures to represent the types themselves. The data structures for the **Employee** and **Manager** type objects are shown in Figure 4-7. Since this thread already executed some code prior to calling **M3**, let's assume that the **Int32** and **String** type objects have already been created (which is likely because these are commonly used types), and so I won't show them in the figure.

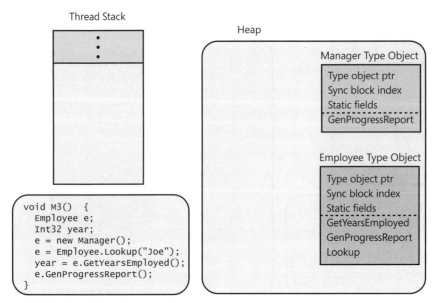

FIGURE 4-7 The **Employee** and **Manager** type objects are created just as **M3** is being called.

Let's take a moment to discuss these type objects. As discussed earlier in this chapter, all objects on the heap contain two overhead members: the type object pointer and the sync block index. As you can see, the **Employee** and **Manager** type objects have both of these members. When you define a type, you can define static data fields within it. The bytes that back these static data fields are allocated within the type objects themselves. Finally, inside each type object is a method table with one entry per method defined within the type. This is the method table that was discussed in Chapter 1, "The CLR's Execution Model." Since the **Employee** type defines three methods (**GetYearsEmployed**, **GetProgressReport**, and **Lookup**), there are three entries in **Employee**'s method table. Since the **Manager** type defines one method (an override of **GetProgressReport**), there is just one entry in **Manager**'s method table.

Now, after the CLR has ensured that all of the type objects required by the method are created and the code for **M3** has been compiled, the CLR allows the thread to execute **M3**'s native code. When **M3**'s prologue code executes, memory for the local variables must be allocated from the thread's stack, as shown in Figure 4-8. By the way, the CLR automatically initializes all local variables to **null** or **0** (zero) as part of the method's prologue code. However, the C# compiler issues a **"Use of unassigned local variable"** error message if you write code that attempts to read from a local variable that you have not explicitly initialized in your source code.

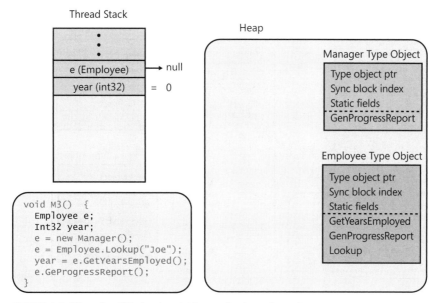

FIGURE 4-8 Allocating **M3**'s local variables on the thread's stack

Then, **M3** executes its code to construct a **Manager** object. This causes an instance of the **Manager** type, a **Manager** object, to be created in the managed heap, as shown in Figure 4-9. As you can see, the **Manager** object—as do all objects—has a type object pointer and sync block index. This object also contains the bytes necessary to hold all of the instance data fields defined by the **Manager** type, as well as any instance fields defined by any base classes of the **Manager** type (in this case, **Employee** and **Object**). Whenever a new object is created on the heap, the CLR automatically initializes the internal type object pointer member to refer to the object's corresponding type object (in this case, the **Manager** type object). Furthermore, the CLR initializes the sync block index and sets all of the object's instance fields to **null** or **0** (zero) prior to calling the type's constructor, a method that will likely modify some of the instance data fields. The **new** operator returns the memory address of the **Manager** object, which is saved in the variable **e** (on the thread's stack).

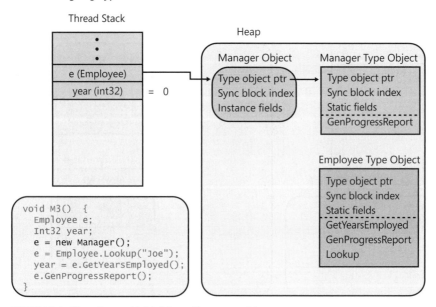

FIGURE 4-9 Allocating and initializing a **Manager** object

The next line of code in **M3** calls **Employee**'s static **Lookup** method. When calling a static method, the JIT compiler locates the type object that corresponds to the type that defines the static method. Then, the JIT compiler locates the entry in the type object's method table that refers to the method being called, JITs the method (if necessary), and calls the JITted code. For our discussion, let's say that **Employee**'s **Lookup** method queries a database to find Joe. Let's also say that the database indicates that Joe is a manager at the company, and therefore, internally, the **Lookup** method constructs a new **Manager** object on the heap, initializes it for Joe, and returns the address of this object. The address is saved in the local variable **e**. The result of this operation is shown in Figure 4-10.

Note that **e** no longer refers to the first **Manager** object that was created. In fact, since no variable refers to this object, it is a prime candidate for being garbage collected in the future, which will reclaim (free) the memory used by this object.

The next line of code in **M3** calls **Employee**'s nonvirtual instance **GetYearsEmployed** method. When calling a nonvirtual instance method, the JIT compiler locates the type object that corresponds to the type of the variable being used to make the call. In this case, the variable **e** is defined as an **Employee**. (If the **Employee** type didn't define the method being called, the JIT compiler walks down the class hierarchy toward **Object** looking for this method. It can do this because each type object has a field in it that refers to its base type; this information is not shown in the figures.) Then, the JIT compiler locates the entry in the type object's method table that refers to the method being called, JITs the method (if necessary), and then calls the JITted code. For our discussion, let's say that **Employee**'s **GetYearsEmployed** method returns **5** because Joe has been employed at the company for five years. The integer is saved in the local variable **year**. The result of this operation is shown in Figure 4-11.

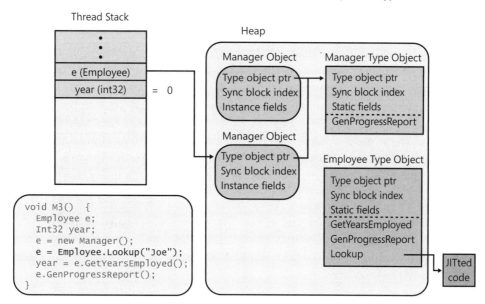

FIGURE 4-10 **Employee**'s static **Lookup** method allocates and initializes a **Manager** object for Joe

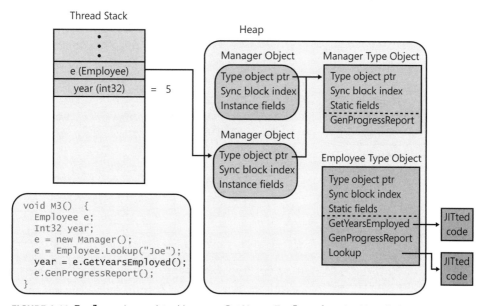

FIGURE 4-11 **Employee**'s nonvirtual instance **GetYearsEmployed** method is called, returning **5**

The next line of code in **M3** calls **Employee**'s virtual instance **GetProgressReport** method. When calling a virtual instance method, the JIT compiler produces some additional code in the method, which will be executed each time the method is invoked. This code will first look in the variable being used to make the call and then follow the address to the calling object. In this case, the variable **e** points to the **Manager** object representing "Joe." Then, the code will examine the object's internal type object pointer member; this member refers to the actual type of the object. The code then locates the entry in the type object's method table that refers to the method being called, JITs the method (if necessary), and calls the JITted code. For our discussion, **Manager**'s **GetProgressReport** implementation is called because **e** refers to a **Manager** object. The result of this operation is shown in Figure 4-12.

Note that if **Employee**'s **Lookup** method had discovered that Joe was just an **Employee** and not a **Manager**, **Lookup** would have internally constructed an **Employee** object whose type object pointer member would have referred to the **Employee** type object, causing **Employee**'s implementation of **GetProgressReport** to execute instead of **Manager**'s implementation.

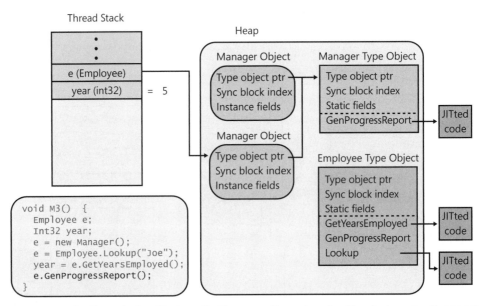

FIGURE 4-12 **Employee**'s virtual instance **GetProgressReport** method is called, causing **Manager**'s override of this method to execute

At this point, we have discussed the relationship between source code, IL, and JITted code. We have also discussed the thread's stack, arguments, local variables, and how these arguments and variables refer to objects on the managed heap. You also see how objects contain a pointer to their type object (containing the static fields and method table). We have also discussed how the JIT compiler determines how to call static methods, nonvirtual instance methods, and virtual instance methods. All of this should give you great insight into how the

CLR works, and this insight should help you when architecting and implementing your types, components, and applications. Before ending this chapter, I'd like to give you just a little more insight as to what is going on inside the CLR.

You'll notice that the **Employee** and **Manager** type objects both contain type object pointer members. This is because type objects are actually objects themselves. When the CLR creates type objects, the CLR must initialize these members. "To what?" you might ask. Well, when the CLR starts running in a process, it immediately creates a special type object for the **System.Type** type (defined in MSCorLib.dll). The **Employee** and **Manager** type objects are "instances" of this type, and therefore, their type object pointer members are initialized to refer to the **System.Type** type object, as shown in Figure 4-13.

Of course, the **System.Type** type object is an object itself and therefore also has a type object pointer member in it, and it is logical to ask what this member refers to. It refers to itself because the **System.Type** type object is itself an "instance" of a type object. And now you should understand the CLR's complete type system and how it works. By the way, **System.Object**'s **GetType** method simply returns the address stored in the specified object's type object pointer member. In other words, the **GetType** method returns a pointer to an object's type object, and this is how you can determine the true type of any object in the system (including type objects).

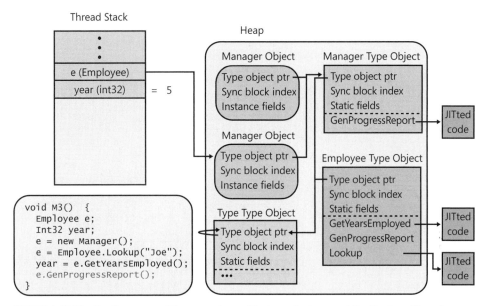

FIGURE 4-13 The **Employee** and **Manager** type objects are instances of the **System.Type** type.

Chapter 5
Primitive, Reference, and Value Types

In this chapter, I'll discuss the different kinds of types you'll run into as a Microsoft .NET Framework developer. It is crucial for all developers to be familiar with the different behaviors that these types exhibit. When I was first learning the .NET Framework, I didn't fully understand the difference between primitive, reference, and value types. This lack of clarity led me to unwittingly introduce subtle bugs and performance issues into my code. By explaining the differences between the types here, I'm hoping to save you some of the headaches that I experienced while getting up to speed.

Programming Language Primitive Types

Certain data types are so commonly used that many compilers allow code to manipulate them using simplified syntax. For example, you could allocate an integer by using the following syntax:

```
System.Int32 a = new System.Int32();
```

But I'm sure you'd agree that declaring and initializing an integer by using this syntax is rather cumbersome. Fortunately, many compilers (including C#) allow you to use syntax similar to the following instead:

```
int a = 0;
```

This syntax certainly makes the code more readable and generates identical Intermediate Language (IL) to that which is generated when **System.Int32** is used. Any data types the compiler directly supports are called *primitive types*. Primitive types map directly to types existing in the Framework Class Library (FCL). For example, in C#, an **int** maps directly to the

`System.Int32` type. Because of this, the following four lines of code all compile correctly and produce the exact same IL:

```
int        a = 0;                        // Most convenient syntax
System.Int32 a = 0;                      // Convenient syntax
int        a = new int();                // Inconvenient syntax
System.Int32 a = new System.Int32();     // Most inconvenient syntax
```

Table 5-1 shows the FCL types that have corresponding primitives in C#. For the types that are compliant with the Common Language Specification (CLS), other languages will offer similar primitive types. However, languages aren't required to offer any support for the non–CLS-compliant types.

TABLE 5-1   C# Primitives with Corresponding FCL Types

Primitive Type	FCL Type	CLS-Compliant	Description
sbyte	System.SByte	No	Signed 8-bit value
byte	System.Byte	Yes	Unsigned 8-bit value
short	System.Int16	Yes	Signed 16-bit value
ushort	System.Uint16	No	Unsigned 16-bit value
int	System.Int32	Yes	Signed 32-bit value
uint	System.Uint32	No	Unsigned 32-bit value
long	System.Int64	Yes	Signed 64-bit value
ulong	System.UInt64	No	Unsigned 64-bit value
char	System.Char	Yes	16-bit Unicode character (**char** never represents an 8-bit value as it would in unmanaged C++.)
float	System.Single	Yes	IEEE 32-bit floating point value
double	System.Double	Yes	IEEE 64-bit floating point value
bool	System.Boolean	Yes	A **true/false** value
decimal	System.Decimal	Yes	A 128-bit high-precision floating-point value commonly used for financial calculations in which rounding errors can't be tolerated. Of the 128 bits, 1 bit represents the sign of the value, 96 bits represent the value itself, and 8 bits represent the power of 10 to divide the 96-bit value by (can be anywhere from 0 to 28). The remaining bits are unused.
string	System.String	Yes	An array of characters
object	System.Object	Yes	Base type of all types

Primitive Type	FCL Type	CLS-Compliant	Description
dynamic	System.Object	Yes	To the common language runtime (CLR), **dynamic** is identical to **object**. However, the C# compiler allows **dynamic** variables to participate in dynamic dispatch using a simplified syntax. For more information, see "The **dynamic** Primitive Type" section at the end of this chapter.

Another way to think of this is that the C# compiler automatically assumes that you have the following **using** directives (as discussed in Chapter 4, "Type Fundamentals") in all of your source code files:

```
using sbyte  = System.SByte;
using byte   = System.Byte;
using short  = System.Int16;
using ushort = System.UInt16;
using int    = System.Int32;
using uint   = System.UInt32;
...
```

The C# language specification states, "As a matter of style, use of the keyword is favored over use of the complete system type name." I disagree with the language specification; I prefer to use the FCL type names and completely avoid the primitive type names. In fact, I wish that compilers didn't even offer the primitive type names and forced developers to use the FCL type names instead. Here are my reasons:

- I've seen a number of developers confused, not knowing whether to use **string** or **String** in their code. Because in C# **string** (a keyword) maps exactly to **System.String** (an FCL type), there is no difference and either can be used. Similarly, I've heard some developers say that **int** represents a 32-bit integer when the application is running on a 32-bit OS and that it represents a 64-bit integer when the application is running on a 64-bit OS. This statement is absolutely false: in C#, an **int** always maps to **System.Int32**, and therefore it represents a 32-bit integer regardless of the OS the code is running on. If programmers would use **Int32** in their code, then this potential confusion is also eliminated.

- In C#, **long** maps to **System.Int64**, but in a different programming language, **long** could map to an **Int16** or **Int32**. In fact, C++/CLI does treat **long** as an **Int32**. Someone reading source code in one language could easily misinterpret the code's intention if he or she were used to programming in a different programming language. In fact, most languages won't even treat **long** as a keyword and won't compile code that uses it.

- The FCL has many methods that have type names as part of their method names. For example, the **BinaryReader** type offers methods such as **ReadBoolean**, **ReadInt32**, **ReadSingle**, and so on, and the **System.Convert** type offers methods such as **ToBoolean**, **ToInt32**, **ToSingle**, and so on. Although it's legal to write the following code, the line with **float** feels very unnatural to me, and it's not obvious that the line is correct:

```
BinaryReader br = new BinaryReader(...);
float  val = br.ReadSingle();   // OK, but feels unnatural
Single val = br.ReadSingle();   // OK and feels good
```

- Many programmers that use C# exclusively tend to forget that other programming languages can be used against the CLR, and because of this, C#-isms creep into the class library code. For example, Microsoft's FCL is almost exclusively written in C# and developers on the FCL team have now introduced methods into the library such as **Array**'s **GetLongLength**, which returns an **Int64** value that is a **long** in C# but not in other languages (like C++/CLI). Another example is **System.Linq.Enumerable**'s **LongCount** method.

For all of these reasons, I'll use the FCL type names throughout this book.

In many programming languages, you would expect the following code to compile and execute correctly:

```
Int32  i = 5;    // A 32-bit value
Int64  l = i;    // Implicit cast to a 64-bit value
```

However, based on the casting discussion presented in Chapter 4, you wouldn't expect this code to compile. After all, **System.Int32** and **System.Int64** are different types, and neither one is derived from the other. Well, you'll be happy to know that the C# compiler does compile this code correctly, and it runs as expected. Why? The reason is that the C# compiler has intimate knowledge of primitive types and applies its own special rules when compiling the code. In other words, the compiler recognizes common programming patterns and produces the necessary IL to make the written code work as expected. Specifically, the C# compiler supports patterns related to casting, literals, and operators, as shown in the following examples.

First, the compiler is able to perform implicit or explicit casts between primitive types such as these:

```
Int32  i = 5;           // Implicit cast from Int32  to Int32
Int64  l = i;           // Implicit cast from Int32  to Int64
Single s = i;           // Implicit cast from Int32  to Single
Byte   b = (Byte) i;    // Explicit cast from Int32  to Byte
Int16  v = (Int16) s;   // Explicit cast from Single to Int16
```

C# allows implicit casts if the conversion is "safe," that is, no loss of data is possible, such as converting an **Int32** to an **Int64**. But C# requires explicit casts if the conversion is potentially unsafe. For numeric types, "unsafe" means that you could lose precision or magnitude as a result of the conversion. For example, converting from **Int32** to **Byte** requires an explicit cast because precision might be lost from large **Int32** numbers; converting from **Single** to **Int16** requires a cast because **Single** can represent numbers of a larger magnitude than **Int16** can.

Be aware that different compilers can generate different code to handle these cast operations. For example, when casting a **Single** with a value of 6.8 to an **Int32**, some compilers could generate code to put a 6 in the **Int32**, and others could perform the cast by rounding the result up to 7. By the way, C# always truncates the result. For the exact rules that C# follows for casting primitive types, see the "Conversions" section in the C# language specification.

In addition to casting, primitive types can be written as *literals*. A literal is considered to be an instance of the type itself, and therefore, you can call instance methods by using the instance as shown here:

```
Console.WriteLine(123.ToString() + 456.ToString());  // "123456"
```

Also, if you have an expression consisting of literals, the compiler is able to evaluate the expression at compile time, improving the application's performance.

```
Boolean found = false;     // Generated code sets found to 0
Int32 x = 100 + 20 + 3;    // Generated code sets x to 123
String s = "a " + "bc";    // Generated code sets s to "a bc"
```

Finally, the compiler automatically knows how and in what order to interpret operators (such as +, -, *, /, %, &, ^, |, ==, !=, >, <, >=, <=, <<, >>, ~, !, ++, --, and so on) when used in code:

```
Int32 x = 100;                            // Assignment operator
Int32 y = x + 23;                         // Addition and assignment operators
Boolean lessThanFifty = (y < 50);  // Less-than and assignment operators
```

Checked and Unchecked Primitive Type Operations

Programmers are well aware that many arithmetic operations on primitives could result in an overflow:

```
Byte b = 100;
b = (Byte) (b + 200);        // b now contains 44 (or 2C in Hex).
```

> **Important** When performing the arithmetic operation above, the first step requires that all operand values be expanded to 32-bit values (or 64-bit values if any operand requires more than 32 bits). So **b** and **200** (values requiring less than 32 bits) are first converted to 32-bit values and then added together. The result is a 32-bit value (300 in decimal, or 12C in hexadecimal) that must be cast to a **Byte** before the result can be stored back in the variable **b**. C# doesn't perform this cast for you implicitly, which is why the **Byte** cast on the second line of the preceding code is required.

In most programming scenarios, this silent overflow is undesirable and if not detected causes the application to behave in strange and unusual ways. In some rare programming scenarios (such as calculating a hash value or a checksum), however, this overflow is not only acceptable but is also desired.

Different languages handle overflows in different ways. C and C++ don't consider overflows to be an error and allow the value to wrap; the application continues running. Microsoft Visual Basic, on the other hand, always considers overflows to be errors and throws an exception when it detects one.

The CLR offers IL instructions that allow the compiler to choose the desired behavior. The CLR has an instruction called **add** that adds two values together. The **add** instruction performs no overflow checking. The CLR also has an instruction called **add.ovf** that also adds two values together. However, **add.ovf** throws a **System.OverflowException** if an overflow occurs. In addition to these two IL instructions for the add operation, the CLR also has similar IL instructions for subtraction (**sub/sub.ovf**), multiplication (**mul/mul.ovf**), and data conversions (**conv/conv.ovf**).

C# allows the programmer to decide how overflows should be handled. By default, overflow checking is turned off. This means that the compiler generates IL code by using the versions of the add, subtract, multiply, and conversion instructions that don't include overflow checking. As a result, the code runs faster—but developers must be assured that overflows won't occur or that their code is designed to anticipate these overflows.

One way to get the C# compiler to control overflows is to use the **/checked+** compiler switch. This switch tells the compiler to generate code that has the overflow-checking versions of the add, subtract, multiply, and conversion IL instructions. The code executes a little slower because the CLR is checking these operations to determine whether an overflow occurred. If an overflow occurs, the CLR throws an **OverflowException**.

In addition to having overflow checking turned on or off globally, programmers can control overflow checking in specific regions of their code. C# allows this flexibility by offering **checked** and **unchecked** operators. Here's an example that uses the **unchecked** operator:

```
UInt32 invalid = unchecked((UInt32) (-1));  // OK
```

And here is an example that uses the **checked** operator:

```
Byte b = 100;
b = checked((Byte) (b + 200));     // OverflowException is thrown
```

In this example, **b** and **200** are first converted to 32-bit values and are then added together; the result is 300. Then 300 is converted to a **Byte** due to the explicit cast; this generates the **OverflowException**. If the **Byte** were cast outside the **checked** operator, the exception wouldn't occur:

```
b = (Byte) checked(b + 200);      // b contains 44; no OverflowException
```

In addition to the **checked** and **unchecked** operators, C# also offers **checked** and **unchecked** statements. The statements cause all expressions within a block to be checked or unchecked:

```
checked {                         // Start of checked block
   Byte b = 100;
   b = (Byte) (b + 200);          // This expression is checked for overflow.
}                                 // End of checked block
```

In fact, if you use a **checked** statement block, you can now use the += operator with the **Byte**, which simplifies the code a bit:

```
checked {          // Start of checked block
   Byte b = 100;
   b += 200;       // This expression is checked for overflow.
}                  // End of checked block
```

> **Important** Because the only effect that the **checked** operator and statement have is to determine which versions of the add, subtract, multiply, and data conversion IL instructions are produced, calling a method within a **checked** operator or statement has no impact on that method, as the following code demonstrates:
>
> ```
> checked {
>    // Assume SomeMethod tries to load 400 into a Byte.
>    SomeMethod(400);
>    // SomeMethod might or might not throw an OverflowException.
>    // It would if SomeMethod were compiled with checked instructions.
> }
> ```

In my experience, I've seen a lot of calculations produce surprising results. Typically, this is due to invalid user input, but it can also be due to values returned from parts of the system that a programmer just doesn't expect. And so, I now recommend that programmers do the following:

- Use signed data types (such as **Int32** and **Int64**) instead of unsigned numeric types (such as **UInt32** and **UInt64**) wherever possible. This allows the compiler to detect more overflow/underflow errors. In addition, various parts of the class library (such as **Array**'s and **String**'s **Length** properties) are hard-coded to return signed values, and less casting is required as you move these values around in your code. Fewer casts make source code cleaner and easier to maintain. In addition, unsigned numeric types are not CLS-compliant.

- As you write your code, explicitly use **checked** around blocks where an unwanted overflow might occur due to invalid input data, such as processing a request with data supplied from an end user or a client machine. You might want to catch **OverflowException** as well, so that your application can gracefully recover from these failures.

- As you write your code, explicitly use **unchecked** around blocks where an overflow is OK, such as calculating a checksum.

- For any code that doesn't use **checked** or **unchecked**, the assumption is that you *do* want an exception to occur on overflow, for example, calculating something (such as prime numbers) where the inputs are known, and overflows are bugs.

Now, as you develop your application, turn on the compiler's **/checked+** switch for debug builds. Your application will run more slowly because the system will be checking for overflows on any code that you didn't explicitly mark as **checked** or **unchecked**. If an exception occurs, you'll easily detect it and be able to fix the bug in your code. For the release build of your application, use the compiler's **/checked-**switch so that the code runs faster and overflow exceptions won't be generated. To change the Checked setting in Microsoft Visual Studio, display the properties for your project, select the Build tab, click Advanced, and then select the Check For Arithmetic Overflow/underflow" option, as shown in Figure 5-1.

If your application can tolerate the slight performance hit of always doing checked operations, then I recommend that you compile with the **/checked** command-line option even for a release build because this can prevent your application from continuing to run with corrupted data and possible security holes. For example, you might perform a multiplication to calculate an index into an array; it is much better to get an **OverflowException** as opposed to accessing an incorrect array element due to the math wrapping around.

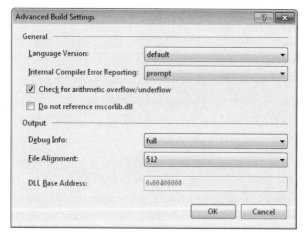

FIGURE 5-1 Changing the compiler's default setting for performing checked arithmetic using Visual Studio's Advanced Build Settings dialog box

Important The **System.Decimal** type is a very special type. Although many programming languages (C# and Visual Basic included) consider **Decimal** a primitive type, the CLR does not. This means that the CLR doesn't have IL instructions that know how to manipulate a **Decimal** value. If you look up the **Decimal** type in the .NET Framework SDK documentation, you'll see that it has public static methods called **Add**, **Subtract**, **Multiply**, **Divide**, and so on. In addition, the **Decimal** type provides operator overload methods for +, -, *, /, and so on.

When you compile code that uses **Decimal** values, the compiler generates code to call **Decimal**'s members to perform the actual operation. This means that manipulating **Decimal** values is slower than manipulating CLR primitive values. Also, because there are no IL instructions for manipulating **Decimal** values, the **checked** and **unchecked** operators, statements, and compiler switches have no effect. Operations on **Decimal** values always throw an **OverflowException** if the operation can't be performed safely.

Similarly, the **System.Numerics.BigInteger** type is also special in that it internally uses an array of **UInt32**s to represent an arbitrarily large integer whose value has no upper or lower bound. Therefore, operations on a **BigInteger** never result in an **OverflowException**. However, a **BigInteger** operation may throw an **OutOfMemoryException** if the value gets too large and there is insufficient available memory to resize the array.

Reference Types and Value Types

The CLR supports two kinds of types: *reference types* and *value types*. While most types in the FCL are reference types, the types that programmers use most often are value types. Reference types are always allocated from the managed heap, and the C# **new** operator returns the memory address of the object—the memory address refers to the object's bits. You need to bear in mind some performance considerations when you're working with reference types. First, consider these facts:

- The memory must be allocated from the managed heap.
- Each object allocated on the heap has some additional overhead members associated with it that must be initialized.
- The other bytes in the object (for the fields) are always set to zero.
- Allocating an object from the managed heap could force a garbage collection to occur.

If every type were a reference type, an application's performance would suffer greatly. Imagine how poor performance would be if every time you used an **Int32** value, a memory allocation occurred! To improve performance for simple, frequently used types, the CLR offers lightweight types called *value types*. Value type instances are usually allocated on a thread's stack (although they can also be embedded as a field in a reference type object). The variable representing the instance doesn't contain a pointer to an instance; the variable contains the fields of the instance itself. Because the variable contains the instance's fields, a pointer doesn't have to be dereferenced to manipulate the instance's fields. Value type instances don't come under the control of the garbage collector, so their use reduces pressure in the managed heap and reduces the number of collections an application requires over its lifetime.

The .NET Framework SDK documentation clearly indicates which types are reference types and which are value types. When looking up a type in the documentation, any type called a *class* is a reference type. For example, the **System.Exception** class, the **System.IO.FileStream** class, and the **System.Random** class are all reference types. On the other hand, the documentation refers to each value type as a *structure* or an *enumeration*. For example, the **System.Int32** structure, the **System.Boolean** structure, the **System.Decimal** structure, the **System.TimeSpan** structure, the **System.DayOfWeek** enumeration, the **System.IO.FileAttributes** enumeration, and the **System.Drawing.FontStyle** enumeration are all value types.

If you look more closely at the documentation, you'll notice that all of the structures are immediately derived from the **System.ValueType** abstract type. **System.ValueType** is itself immediately derived from the **System.Object** type. By definition, all value types must be derived from **System.ValueType**. All enumerations are derived from the **System.Enum** abstract type, which is itself derived from **System.ValueType**. The CLR and all programming languages give enumerations special treatment. For more information about enumerated types, refer to Chapter 15, "Enumerated Types and Bit Flags."

Even though you can't choose a base type when defining your own value type, a value type can implement one or more interfaces if you choose. In addition, all value types are sealed, which prevents a value type from being used as a base type for any other reference type or value type. So, for example, it's not possible to define any new types using **Boolean**, **Char**, **Int32**, **Uint64**, **Single**, **Double**, **Decimal**, and so on as base types.

> **Important** For many developers (such as unmanaged C/C++ developers), reference types and value types will seem strange at first. In unmanaged C/C++, you declare a type, and then the code that uses the type gets to decide if an instance of the type should be allocated on the thread's stack or in the application's heap. In managed code, the developer defining the type indicates where instances of the type are allocated; the developer using the type has no control over this.

The following code and Figure 5-2 demonstrate how reference types and value types differ:

```
// Reference type (because of 'class')
class  SomeRef { public Int32 x; }

// Value type (because of 'struct')
struct SomeVal { public Int32 x; }

static void ValueTypeDemo() {
   SomeRef r1 = new SomeRef();    // Allocated in heap
   SomeVal v1 = new SomeVal();    // Allocated on stack
```

```
r1.x = 5;                      // Pointer dereference
v1.x = 5;                      // Changed on stack
Console.WriteLine(r1.x);       // Displays "5"
Console.WriteLine(v1.x);       // Also displays "5"
// The left side of Figure 5-2 reflects the situation
// after the lines above have executed.

SomeRef r2 = r1;               // Copies reference (pointer) only
SomeVal v2 = v1;               // Allocate on stack & copies members
r1.x = 8;                      // Changes r1.x and r2.x
v1.x = 9;                      // Changes v1.x, not v2.x
Console.WriteLine(r1.x);       // Displays "8"
Console.WriteLine(r2.x);       // Displays "8"
Console.WriteLine(v1.x);       // Displays "9"
Console.WriteLine(v2.x);       // Displays "5"
// The right side of Figure 5-2 reflects the situation
// after ALL of the lines above have executed.
}
```

In this code, the **SomeVal** type is declared using **struct** instead of the more common **class**. In C#, types declared using **struct** are value types, and types declared using **class** are reference types. As you can see, the behavior of reference types and value types differs quite a bit. As you use types in your code, you must be aware of whether the type is a reference type or a value type because it can greatly affect how you express your intentions in the code.

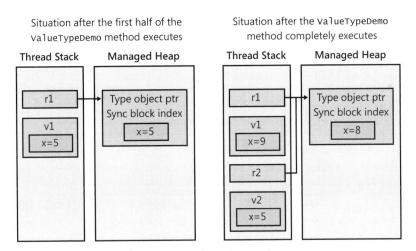

FIGURE 5-2 Visualizing the memory as the code executes

In the preceding code, you saw this line:

```
SomeVal v1 = new SomeVal();    // Allocated on stack
```

The way this line is written makes it look as if a **SomeVal** instance will be allocated on the managed heap. However, the C# compiler knows that **SomeVal** is a value type and produces code that allocates the **SomeVal** instance on the thread's stack. C# also ensures that all of the fields in the value type instance are zeroed.

The preceding line could have been written like this instead:

```
SomeVal v1;    // Allocated on stack
```

This line also produces IL that allocates the instance on the thread's stack and zeroes the fields. The only difference is that C# "thinks" that the instance is initialized if you use the **new** operator. The following code will make this point clear:

```
// These two lines compile because C# thinks that
// v1's fields have been initialized to 0.
SomeVal v1 = new SomeVal();
Int32 a = v1.x;

// These two lines don't compile because C# doesn't think that
// v1's fields have been initialized to 0.
SomeVal v1;
Int32 a = v1.x;   // error CS0170: Use of possibly unassigned field 'x'
```

When designing your own types, consider carefully whether to define your types as value types instead of reference types. In some situations, value types can give better performance. In particular, you should declare a type as a value type if *all* the following statements are true:

- The type acts as a primitive type. Specifically, this means that it is a fairly simple type that has no members that modify any of its instance fields. When a type offers no members that alter its fields, we say that the type is *immutable*. In fact, it is recommended that many value types mark all their fields as **readonly** (discussed in Chapter 7, "Constants and Fields").
- The type doesn't need to inherit from any other type.
- The type won't have any other types derived from it.

The size of instances of your type is also a condition to take into account because by default, arguments are passed by value, which causes the fields in value type instances to be copied, hurting performance. Again, a method that returns a value type causes the fields in the instance to be copied into the memory allocated by the caller when the method returns, hurting performance. So, in addition to the previous conditions, you should declare a type as a value type if one of the following statements is true:

- Instances of the type are small (approximately 16 bytes or less).
- Instances of the type are large (greater than 16 bytes) and are not passed as method parameters or returned from methods.

The main advantage of value types is that they're not allocated as objects in the managed heap. Of course, value types have several limitations of their own when compared to reference types. Here are some of the ways in which value types and reference types differ:

- Value type objects have two representations: an *unboxed* form and a *boxed* form (discussed in the next section). Reference types are always in a boxed form.

- Value types are derived from **System.ValueType**. This type offers the same methods as defined by **System.Object**. However, **System.ValueType** overrides the **Equals** method so that it returns **true** if the values of the two objects' fields match. In addition, **System.ValueType** overrides the **GetHashCode** method to produce a hash code value by using an algorithm that takes into account the values in the object's instance fields. Due to performance issues with this default implementation, when defining your own value types, you should override and provide explicit implementations for the **Equals** and **GetHashCode** methods. I'll cover the **Equals** and **GetHashCode** methods at the end of this chapter.

- Because you can't define a new value type or a new reference type by using a value type as a base class, you shouldn't introduce any new virtual methods into a value type. No methods can be abstract, and all methods are implicitly sealed (can't be overridden).

- Reference type variables contain the memory address of objects in the heap. By default, when a reference type variable is created, it is initialized to **null**, indicating that the reference type variable doesn't currently point to a valid object. Attempting to use a **null** reference type variable causes a **NullReferenceException** to be thrown. By contrast, value type variables always contain a value of the underlying type, and all members of the value type are initialized to 0. Since a value type variable isn't a pointer, it's not possible to generate a **NullReferenceException** when accessing a value type. The CLR does offer a special feature that adds the notion of nullability to a value type. This feature, called *nullable types*, is discussed in Chapter 19, "Nullable Value Types."

- When you assign a value type variable to another value type variable, a field-by-field copy is made. When you assign a reference type variable to another reference type variable, only the memory address is copied.

- Because of the previous point, two or more reference type variables can refer to a single object in the heap, allowing operations on one variable to affect the object referenced by the other variable. On the other hand, value type variables are distinct objects, and it's not possible for operations on one value type variable to affect another.

- Because unboxed value types aren't allocated on the heap, the storage allocated for them is freed as soon as the method that defines an instance of the type is no longer active. This means that a value type instance doesn't receive a notification (via a **Finalize** method) when its memory is reclaimed.

Note In fact, it would be quite odd to define a value type with a **Finalize** method since the method would be called only on boxed instances. For this reason, many compilers (including C#, C++/CLI, and Visual Basic) don't allow you to define **Finalize** methods on value types. Although the CLR allows a value type to define a **Finalize** method, the CLR won't call this method when a boxed instance of the value type is garbage collected.

How the CLR Controls the Layout of a Type's Fields

To improve performance, the CLR is capable of arranging the fields of a type any way it chooses. For example, the CLR might reorder fields in memory so that object references are grouped together and data fields are properly aligned and packed. However, when you define a type, you can tell the CLR whether it must keep the type's fields in the same order as the developer specified them or whether it can reorder them as it sees fit.

You tell the CLR what to do by applying the **System.Runtime.InteropServices. StructLayoutAttribute** attribute on the class or structure you're defining. To this attribute's constructor, you can pass **LayoutKind.Auto** to have the CLR arrange the fields, **LayoutKind.Sequential** to have the CLR preserve your field layout, or **LayoutKind.Explicit** to explicitly arrange the fields in memory by using offsets. If you don't explicitly specify the **StructLayoutAttribute** on a type that you're defining, your compiler selects whatever layout it determines is best.

You should be aware that Microsoft's C# compiler selects **LayoutKind.Auto** for reference types (classes) and **LayoutKind.Sequential** for value types (structures). It is obvious that the C# compiler team believes that structures are commonly used when interoperating with unmanaged code, and for this to work, the fields must stay in the order defined by the programmer. However, if you're creating a value type that has nothing to do with interoperability with unmanaged code, you probably want to override the C# compiler's default. Here's an example:

```
using System;
using System.Runtime.InteropServices;

// Let the CLR arrange the fields to improve
// performance for this value type.
[StructLayout(LayoutKind.Auto)]
internal struct SomeValType {
   private readonly Byte m_b;
   private readonly Int16 m_x;
   ...
}
```

The **StructLayoutAttribute** also allows you to explicitly indicate the offset of each field by passing **LayoutKind.Explicit** to its constructor. Then you apply an instance of the **System.Runtime.InteropServices.FieldOffsetAttribute** attribute to each field passing to this attribute's constructor an **Int32** indicating the offset (in bytes) of the field's first byte from the beginning of the instance. Explicit layout is typically used to simulate what would be a *union* in unmanaged C/C++ because you can have multiple fields starting at the same offset in memory. Here is an example:

```
using System;
using System.Runtime.InteropServices;

// The developer explicitly arranges the fields of this value type.
[StructLayout(LayoutKind.Explicit)]
internal struct SomeValType {
    [FieldOffset(0)]
    private readonly Byte m_b; // The m_b and m_x fields overlap each

    [FieldOffset(0)]
    private readonly Int16 m_x; // other in instances of this type
}
```

It should be noted that it is illegal to define a type in which a reference type and a value type overlap. It is possible to define a type in which multiple reference types overlap at the same starting offset; however, this is unverifiable. It is legal to define a type in which multiple value types overlap; however, all of the overlapping bytes must be accessible via public fields for the type to be verifiable.

Boxing and Unboxing Value Types

Value types are lighter weight than reference types because they are not allocated as objects in the managed heap, not garbage collected, and not referred to by pointers. However, in many cases, you must get a reference to an instance of a value type. For example, let's say that you wanted to create an **ArrayList** object (a type defined in the **System.Collections** namespace) to hold a set of **Point** structures. The code might look like this:

```
// Declare a value type.
struct Point {
    public Int32 x, y;
}

public sealed class Program {
    public static void Main() {
        ArrayList a = new ArrayList();
        Point p;                 // Allocate a Point (not in the heap).
        for (Int32 i = 0; i < 10; i++) {
            p.x = p.y = i;   // Initialize the members in the value type.
            a.Add(p);            // Box the value type and add the
                                 // reference to the Arraylist.
        }
        ...
    }
}
```

With each iteration of the loop, a **Point**'s value type fields are initialized. Then the **Point** is stored in the **ArrayList.** But let's think about this for a moment. What is actually being stored in the **ArrayList**? Is it the **Point** structure, the address of the **Point** structure, or something else entirely? To get the answer, you must look up **ArrayList**'s **Add** method and see what type its parameter is defined as. In this case, the **Add** method is prototyped as follows:

```
public virtual Int32 Add(Object value);
```

From this, you can plainly see that **Add** takes an **Object** as a parameter, indicating that **Add** requires a reference (or pointer) to an object on the managed heap as a parameter. But in the preceding code, I'm passing **p**, a **Point**, which is a value type. For this code to work, the **Point** value type must be converted into a true heap-managed object, and a reference to this object must be obtained.

It's possible to convert a value type to a reference type by using a mechanism called *boxing*. Internally, here's what happens when an instance of a value type is boxed:

1. Memory is allocated from the managed heap. The amount of memory allocated is the size required by the value type's fields plus the two additional overhead members (the type object pointer and the sync block index) required by all objects on the managed heap.

2. The value type's fields are copied to the newly allocated heap memory.

3. The address of the object is returned. This address is now a reference to an object; the value type is now a reference type.

The C# compiler automatically produces the IL code necessary to box a value type instance, but you still need to understand what's going on internally so that you're aware of code size and performance issues.

In the preceding code, the C# compiler detected that I was passing a value type to a method that requires a reference type, and it automatically emitted code to box the object. So at runtime, the fields currently residing in the **Point** value type instance **p** are copied into the newly allocated **Point** object. The address of the boxed **Point** object (now a reference type) is returned and is then passed to the **Add** method. The **Point** object will remain in the heap until it is garbage collected. The **Point** value type variable (**p**) can be reused because the **ArrayList** never knows anything about it. Note that the lifetime of the boxed value type extends beyond the lifetime of the unboxed value type.

Note It should be noted that the FCL now includes a new set of generic collection classes that make the non-generic collection classes obsolete. For example, you should use the **System.Collections.Generic.List<T>** class instead of the **System.Collections.ArrayList** class. The generic collection classes offer many improvements over the non-generic equivalents. For example, the API has been cleaned up and improved, and the performance of the collection classes has been greatly improved as well. But one of the biggest improvements is that the generic collection classes allow you to work with collections of value types without requiring that items in the collection be boxed/unboxed. This in itself greatly improves performance because far fewer objects will be created on the managed heap thereby reducing the number of garbage collections required by your application. Furthermore, you will get compile-time type safety, and your source code will be cleaner due to fewer casts. This will all be explained in further detail in Chapter 12, "Generics."

Now that you know how boxing works, let's talk about unboxing. Let's say that you want to grab the first element out of the **ArrayList** by using the following code:

```
Point p = (Point) a[0];
```

Here you're taking the reference (or pointer) contained in element 0 of the **ArrayList** and trying to put it into a **Point** value type instance, **p**. For this to work, all of the fields contained in the boxed **Point** object must be copied into the value type variable, **p**, which is on the thread's stack. The CLR accomplishes this copying in two steps. First, the address of the **Point** fields in the boxed **Point** object is obtained. This process is called *unboxing*. Then, the values of these fields are copied from the heap to the stack-based value type instance.

Unboxing is *not* the exact opposite of boxing. The unboxing operation is much less costly than boxing. Unboxing is really just the operation of obtaining a pointer to the raw value type (data fields) contained within an object. In effect, the pointer refers to the unboxed portion in the boxed instance. So, unlike boxing, unboxing doesn't involve the copying of any bytes in memory. Having made this important clarification, it is important to note that an unboxing operation is typically followed by copying the fields.

Obviously, boxing and unboxing/copy operations hurt your application's performance in terms of both speed and memory, so you should be aware of when the compiler generates code to perform these operations automatically and try to write code that minimizes this code generation.

Internally, here's exactly what happens when a boxed value type instance is unboxed:

1. If the variable containing the reference to the boxed value type instance is **null**, a **NullReferenceException** is thrown.

2. If the reference doesn't refer to an object that is a boxed instance of the desired value type, an **InvalidCastException** is thrown.[1]

The second item above means that the following code will *not* work as you might expect:

```
public static void Main() {
    Int32  x = 5;
    Object o = x;         // Box x; o refers to the boxed object
    Int16  y = (Int16) o; // Throws an InvalidCastException
}
```

Logically, it makes sense to take the boxed **Int32** that **o** refers to and cast it to an **Int16**. However, when unboxing an object, the cast must be to the exact unboxed value type—**Int32** in this case. Here's the correct way to write this code:

```
public static void Main() {
    Int32  x = 5;
    Object o = x;                 // Box x; o refers to the boxed object
    Int16  y = (Int16)(Int32) o; // Unbox to the correct type and cast
}
```

I mentioned earlier that an unboxing operation is frequently followed immediately by a field copy. Let's take a look at some C# code demonstrating that unbox and copy operations work together:

```
public static void Main() {
    Point p;
    p.x = p.y = 1;
    Object o = p;    // Boxes p; o refers to the boxed instance

    p = (Point) o;   // Unboxes o AND copies fields from boxed
                     // instance to stack variable
}
```

On the last line, the C# compiler emits an IL instruction to unbox **o** (get the address of the fields in the boxed instance) and another IL instruction to copy the fields from the heap to the stack-based variable **p**.

Now look at this code:

```
public static void Main() {
    Point p;
    p.x = p.y = 1;
```

---
[1] The CLR also allows you to unbox a value type into a nullable version of the same value type. This is discussed in Chapter 19.

```
    Object o = p;    // Boxes p; o refers to the boxed instance

    // Change Point's x field to 2
    p = (Point) o;   // Unboxes o AND copies fields from boxed
                     // instance to stack variable
    p.x = 2;         // Changes the state of the stack variable
    o = p;           // Boxes p; o refers to a new boxed instance
}
```

The code at the bottom of this fragment is intended only to change **Point**'s **x** field from **1** to **2**. To do this, an unbox operation must be performed, followed by a field copy, followed by changing the field (on the stack), followed by a boxing operation (which creates a whole new boxed instance in the managed heap). Hopefully, you see the impact that boxing and unboxing/copying operations have on your application's performance.

Some languages, such as C++/CLI, allow you to unbox a boxed value type without copying the fields. Unboxing returns the address of the unboxed portion of a boxed object (ignoring the object's type object pointer and sync block index overhead). You can now use this pointer to manipulate the unboxed instance's fields (which happen to be in a boxed object on the heap). For example, the previous code would be much more efficient if written in C++/CLI, because you could change the value of **Point**'s **x** field within the already boxed **Point** instance. This would avoid both allocating a new object on the heap and copying all of the fields twice!

> **Important** If you're the least bit concerned about your application's performance, you must be aware of when the compiler produces the code that performs these operations. Unfortunately, many compilers implicitly emit code to box objects, and so it is not obvious when you write code that boxing is occurring. If I am concerned about the performance of a particular algorithm, I always use a tool such as ILDasm.exe to view the IL code for my methods and see where the **box** IL instructions are.

Let's look at a few more examples that demonstrate boxing and unboxing:

```
public static void Main() {
    Int32   v = 5;          // Create an unboxed value type variable.
    Object o = v;           // o refers to a boxed Int32 containing 5.
    v = 123;                // Changes the unboxed value to 123

    Console.WriteLine(v + ", " + (Int32) o); // Displays "123, 5"
}
```

In this code, can you guess how many boxing operations occur? You might be surprised to discover that the answer is three! Let's analyze the code carefully to really understand what's going on. To help you understand, I've included the IL code generated for the **Main** method shown in the preceding code. I've commented the code so that you can easily see the individual operations.

```
.method public hidebysig static void  Main() cil managed
{
  .entrypoint
  // Code size       45 (0x2d)
  .maxstack  3
  .locals init (int32 V_0,
          object V_1)
  // Load 5 into v.
  IL_0000:  ldc.i4.5
  IL_0001:  stloc.0

  // Box v and store the reference pointer in o.
  IL_0002:  ldloc.0
  IL_0003:  box         [mscorlib]System.Int32
  IL_0008:  stloc.1

  // Load 123 into v.
  IL_0009:  ldc.i4.s   123
  IL_000b:  stloc.0

  // Box v and leave the pointer on the stack for Concat.
  IL_000c:  ldloc.0
  IL_000d:  box         [mscorlib]System.Int32

  // Load the string on the stack for Concat.
  IL_0012:  ldstr       ", "

  // Unbox o: Get the pointer to the In32's field on the stack.
  IL_0017:  ldloc.1
  IL_0018:  unbox.any [mscorlib]System.Int32

  // Box the Int32 and leave the pointer on the stack for Concat.
  IL_001d:  box         [mscorlib]System.Int32

  // Call Concat.
  IL_0022:  call        string [mscorlib]System.String::Concat(object,
                                                               object,
                                                               object)

  // The string returned from Concat is passed to WriteLine.
  IL_0027:  call        void [mscorlib]System.Console::WriteLine(string)

  // Return from Main terminating this application.
  IL_002c:  ret
} // end of method App::Main
```

First, an **Int32** unboxed value type instance (**v**) is created on the stack and initialized to **5**. Then a variable (**o**) typed as **Object** is created, and is initialized to point to **v**. But because reference type variables must always point to objects in the heap, C# generated the proper IL code to box and store the address of the boxed copy of **v** in **o**. Now the value **123** is placed into the unboxed value type instance **v**; this has no effect on the boxed **Int32** value, which keeps its value of **5**.

Next is the call to the **WriteLine** method. **WriteLine** wants a **String** object passed to it, but there is no string object. Instead, these three items are available: an unboxed **Int32** value type instance (**v**), a **String** (which is a reference type), and a reference to a boxed **Int32** value type instance (**o**) that is being cast to an unboxed **Int32**. These must somehow be combined to create a **String**.

To create a **String**, the C# compiler generates code that calls the **String** object's static **Concat** method. There are several overloaded versions of the **Concat** method, all of which perform identically—the only difference is in the number of parameters. Because a string is being created from the concatenation of three items, the compiler chooses the following version of the **Concat** method:

```
public static String Concat(Object arg0, Object arg1, Object arg2);
```

For the first parameter, **arg0**, **v** is passed. But **v** is an unboxed value parameter and **arg0** is an **Object**, so **v** must be boxed and the address to the boxed **v** is passed for **arg0**. For the **arg1** parameter, the **","** string is passed as a reference to a **String** object. Finally, for the **arg2** parameter, **o** (a reference to an **Object**) is cast to an **Int32**. This requires an unboxing operation (but no copy operation), which retrieves the address of the unboxed **Int32** contained inside the boxed **Int32**. This unboxed **Int32** instance must be boxed again and the new boxed instance's memory address passed for **Concat**'s **arg2** parameter.

The **Concat** method calls each of the specified objects' **ToString** method and concatenates each object's string representation. The **String** object returned from **Concat** is then passed to **WriteLine** to show the final result.

I should point out that the generated IL code is more efficient if the call to **WriteLine** is written as follows:

```
Console.WriteLine(v + ", " + o);// Displays "123, 5"
```

This line is identical to the earlier version except that I've removed the **(Int32)** cast that preceded the variable **o**. This code is more efficient because **o** is already a reference type to an **Object** and its address can simply be passed to the **Concat** method. So, removing the cast saved two operations: an unbox and a box. You can easily see this savings by rebuilding the application and examining the generated IL code:

```
.method public hidebysig static void  Main() cil managed
{
  .entrypoint
  // Code size       35 (0x23)
  .maxstack  3
  .locals init (int32 V_0,
          object V_1)

  // Load 5 into v.
  IL_0000:  ldc.i4.5
```

```
    IL_0001:  stloc.0

    // Box v and store the reference pointer in o.
    IL_0002:  ldloc.0
    IL_0003:  box          [mscorlib]System.Int32
    IL_0008:  stloc.1

    // Load 123 into v.
    IL_0009:  ldc.i4.s    123
    IL_000b:  stloc.0

    // Box v and leave the pointer on the stack for Concat.
    IL_000c:  ldloc.0
    IL_000d:  box          [mscorlib]System.Int32

    // Load the string on the stack for Concat.
    IL_0012:  ldstr        ", "

    // Load the address of the boxed Int32 on the stack for Concat.
    IL_0017:  ldloc.1

    // Call Concat.
    IL_0018:  call         string [mscorlib]System.String::Concat(object,
                                                                  object,
                                                                  object)

    // The string returned from Concat is passed to WriteLine.
    IL_001d:  call         void [mscorlib]System.Console::WriteLine(string)

    // Return from Main terminating this application.
    IL_0022:  ret
} // end of method App::Main
```

A quick comparison of the IL for these two versions of the **Main** method shows that the version without the **(Int32)** cast is 10 bytes smaller than the version with the cast. The extra unbox/box steps in the first version are obviously generating more code. An even bigger concern, however, is that the extra boxing step allocates an additional object from the managed heap that must be garbage collected in the future. Certainly, both versions give identical results, and the difference in speed isn't noticeable, but extra, unnecessary boxing operations occurring in a loop cause the performance and memory usage of your application to be seriously degraded.

You can improve the previous code even more by calling **WriteLine** like this:

```
Console.WriteLine(v.ToString() + ", " + o);    // Displays "123, 5"
```

Now **ToString** is called on the unboxed value type instance **v**, and a **String** is returned. String objects are already reference types and can simply be passed to the **Concat** method without requiring any boxing.

Let's look at yet another example that demonstrates boxing and unboxing:

```
public static void Main() {
    Int32 v = 5;                 // Create an unboxed value type variable.
    Object o = v;                // o refers to the boxed version of v.

    v = 123;                     // Changes the unboxed value type to 123
    Console.WriteLine(v);        // Displays "123"

    v = (Int32) o;               // Unboxes and copies o into v
    Console.WriteLine(v);        // Displays "5"
}
```

How many boxing operations do you count in this code? The answer is one. The reason that
there is only one boxing operation is that the **System.Console** class defines a **WriteLine**
method that accepts an **Int32** as a parameter:

```
public static void WriteLine(Int32 value);
```

In the two calls to **WriteLine** above, the variable **v**, an **Int32** unboxed value type instance, is
passed by value. Now it may be that **WriteLine** will box this **Int32** internally, but you have
no control over that. The important thing is that you've done the best you could and have
eliminated the boxing from your own code.

If you take a close look at the FCL, you'll notice many overloaded methods that differ based
on their value type parameters. For example, the **System.Console** type offers several overloaded versions of the **WriteLine** method:

```
public static void WriteLine(Boolean);
public static void WriteLine(Char);
public static void WriteLine(Char[]);
public static void WriteLine(Int32);
public static void WriteLine(UInt32);
public static void WriteLine(Int64);
public static void WriteLine(UInt64);
public static void WriteLine(Single);
public static void WriteLine(Double);
public static void WriteLine(Decimal);
public static void WriteLine(Object);
public static void WriteLine(String);
```

You'll also find a similar set of overloaded methods for **System.Console**'s **Write** method,
System.IO.BinaryWriter's **Write** method, **System.IO.TextWriter**'s **Write** and **WriteLine**
methods, **System.Runtime.Serialization.SerializationInfo**'s **AddValue** method,
System.Text.StringBuilder's **Append** and **Insert** methods, and so on. Most of these
methods offer overloaded versions for the sole purpose of reducing the number of boxing
operations for the common value types.

If you define your own value type, these FCL classes will not have overloads of these methods
that accept your value type. Furthermore, there are a bunch of value types already defined
in the FCL for which overloads of these methods do not exist. If you call a method that does
not have an overload for the specific value type that you are passing to it, you will always end

up calling the overload that takes an **Object**. Passing a value type instance as an **Object** will cause boxing to occur, which will adversely affect performance. If you are defining your own class, you can define the methods in the class to be generic (possibly constraining the type parameters to be value types). Generics give you a way to define a method that can take any kind of value type without having to box it. Generics are discussed in Chapter 12.

One last point about boxing: if you know that the code that you're writing is going to cause the compiler to box a single value type repeatedly, your code will be smaller and faster if you manually box the value type. Here's an example:

```
using System;

public sealed class Program {
    public static void Main() {
        Int32 v = 5;    // Create an unboxed value type variable.

#if INEFFICIENT
        // When compiling the following line, v is boxed
        // three times, wasting time and memory.
        Console.WriteLine("{0}, {1}, {2}", v, v, v);
#else
        // The lines below have the same result, execute
        // much faster, and use less memory.
        Object o = v;   // Manually box v (just once).

        // No boxing occurs to compile the following line.
        Console.WriteLine("{0}, {1}, {2}", o, o, o);
#endif
    }
}
```

If this code is compiled with the **INEFFICIENT** symbol defined, the compiler will generate code to box **v** three times, causing three objects to be allocated from the heap! This is extremely wasteful since each object will have exactly the same contents: **5**. If the code is compiled without the **INEFFICIENT** symbol defined, **v** is boxed just once, so only one object is allocated from the heap. Then, in the call to **Console.WriteLine**, the reference to the single boxed object is passed three times. This second version executes *much* faster and allocates less memory from the heap.

In these examples, it's fairly easy to recognize when an instance of a value type requires boxing. Basically, if you want a reference to an instance of a value type, the instance must be boxed. Usually this happens because you have a value type instance and you want to pass it to a method that requires a reference type. However, this situation isn't the only one in which you'll need to box an instance of a value type.

Recall that unboxed value types are lighter-weight types than reference types for two reasons:

■   They are not allocated on the managed heap.

■   They don't have the additional overhead members that every object on the heap has: a type object pointer and a sync block index.

Because unboxed value types don't have a sync block index, you can't have multiple threads synchronize their access to the instance by using the methods of the **System.Threading.Monitor** type (or by using C#'s **lock** statement).

Even though unboxed value types don't have a type object pointer, you can still call virtual methods (such as **Equals**, **GetHashCode**, or **ToString**) inherited or overridden by the type. If your value type overrides one of these virtual methods, then the CLR can invoke the method nonvirtually because value types are implicitly sealed and cannot have any types derived from them. In addition, the value type instance being used to invoke the virtual method is not boxed. However, if your override of the virtual method calls into the base type's implementation of the method, then the value type instance does get boxed when calling the base type's implementation so that a reference to a heap object get passed to the **this** pointer into the base method.

However, calling a nonvirtual inherited method (such as **GetType** or **MemberwiseClone)** always requires the value type to be boxed because these methods are defined by **System.Object**, so the methods expect the **this** argument to be a pointer that refers to an object on the heap.

In addition, casting an unboxed instance of a value type to one of the type's interfaces requires the instance to be boxed, because interface variables must always contain a reference to an object on the heap. (I'll talk about interfaces in Chapter 13, "Interfaces.") The following code demonstrates:

```
using System;

internal struct Point : IComparable {
   private readonly Int32 m_x, m_y;

   // Constructor to easily initialize the fields
   public Point(Int32 x, Int32 y) {
      m_x = x;
      m_y = y;
   }

   // Override ToString method inherited from System.ValueType
   public override String ToString() {
      // Return the point as a string
      return String.Format("({0}, {1})", m_x, m_y);
   }

   // Implementation of type-safe CompareTo method
   public Int32 CompareTo(Point other) {
      // Use the Pythagorean Theorem to calculate
      // which point is farther from the origin (0, 0)
      return Math.Sign(Math.Sqrt(m_x * m_x + m_y * m_y)
```

```
                    - Math.Sqrt(other.m_x * other.m_x + other.m_y * other.m_y));
    }


    // Implementation of IComparable's CompareTo method
    public Int32 CompareTo(Object o) {
        if (GetType() != o.GetType()) {
            throw new ArgumentException("o is not a Point");
        }
        // Call type-safe CompareTo method
        return CompareTo((Point) o);
    }
}


public static class Program {
    public static void Main() {
        // Create two Point instances on the stack.
        Point p1 = new Point(10, 10);
        Point p2 = new Point(20, 20);

        // p1 does NOT get boxed to call ToString (a virtual method).
        Console.WriteLine(p1.ToString());// "(10, 10)"

        // p DOES get boxed to call GetType (a non-virtual method).
        Console.WriteLine(p1.GetType());// "Point"

        // p1 does NOT get boxed to call CompareTo.
        // p2 does NOT get boxed because CompareTo(Point) is called.
        Console.WriteLine(p1.CompareTo(p2));// "-1"

        // p1 DOES get boxed, and the reference is placed in c.
        IComparable c = p1;
        Console.WriteLine(c.GetType());// "Point"

        // p1 does NOT get boxed to call CompareTo.
        // Since CompareTo is not being passed a Point variable,
        // CompareTo(Object) is called which requires a reference to
        // a boxed Point.
        // c does NOT get boxed because it already refers to a boxed Point.
        Console.WriteLine(p1.CompareTo(c));// "0"

        // c does NOT get boxed because it already refers to a boxed Point.
        // p2 does get boxed because CompareTo(Object) is called.
        Console.WriteLine(c.CompareTo(p2));// "-1"

        // c is unboxed, and fields are copied into p2.
        p2 = (Point) c;

        // Proves that the fields got copied into p2.
        Console.WriteLine(p2.ToString());// "(10, 10)"
    }
}
```

This code demonstrates several scenarios related to boxing and unboxing:

- **Calling ToString**   In the call to **ToString**, **p1** doesn't have to be boxed. At first, you'd think that **p1** would have to be boxed because **ToString** is a virtual method that is inherited from the base type, **System.ValueType**. Normally, to call a virtual method, the CLR needs to determine the object's type in order to locate the type's method table. Since **p1** is an unboxed value type, there's no type object pointer. However, the just-in-time (JIT) compiler sees that **Point** overrides the **ToString** method, and it emits code that calls **ToString** directly (nonvirtually) without having to do any boxing. The compiler knows that polymorphism can't come into play here since **Point** is a value type, and no type can derive from it to provide another implementation of this virtual method. Note that if **Point**'s **ToString** method internally calls **base.ToString()**, then the value type instance would be boxed when calling **System.ValueType**'s **ToString** method.

- **Calling GetType**   In the call to the nonvirtual **GetType** method, **p1** does have to be boxed. The reason is that the **Point** type inherits **GetType** from **System.Object**. So to call **GetType**, the CLR must use a pointer to a type object, which can be obtained only by boxing **p1**.

- **Calling CompareTo (first time)**   In the first call to **CompareTo**, **p1** doesn't have to be boxed because **Point** implements the **CompareTo** method, and the compiler can just call it directly. Note that a **Point** variable (**p2**) is being passed to **CompareTo**, and therefore the compiler calls the overload of **CompareTo** that accepts a **Point** parameter. This means that **p2** will be passed by value to **CompareTo** and no boxing is necessary.

- **Casting to IComparable**   When casting **p1** to a variable (**c**) that is of an interface type, **p1** must be boxed because interfaces are reference types by definition. So **p1** is boxed, and the pointer to this boxed object is stored in the variable **c**. The following call to **GetType** proves that **c** does refer to a boxed **Point** on the heap.

- **CallingCompareTo (second time)**   In the second call to **CompareTo**, **p1** doesn't have to be boxed because **Point** implements the **CompareTo** method, and the compiler can just call it directly. Note that an **IComparable** variable (**c**) is being passed to **CompareTo**, and therefore, the compiler calls the overload of **CompareTo** that accepts an **Object** parameter. This means that the argument passed must be a pointer that refers to an object on the heap. Fortunately, **c** does refer to a boxed **Point**, and therefore, that memory address in **c** can be passed to **CompareTo**, and no additional boxing is necessary.

- **Calling CompareTo (third time)**   In the third call to **CompareTo**, **c** already refers to a boxed **Point** object on the heap. Since **c** is of the **IComparable** interface type, you can call only the interface's **CompareTo** method that requires an **Object** parameter. This means that the argument passed must be a pointer that refers to an object on the heap. So **p2** is boxed, and the pointer to this boxed object is passed to **CompareTo**.

■ **Casting to Point**   When casting **c** to a **Point**, the object on the heap referred to by **c** is unboxed, and its fields are copied from the heap to **p2**, an instance of the **Point** type residing on the stack.

I realize that all of this information about reference types, value types, and boxing might be overwhelming at first. However, a solid understanding of these concepts is critical to any .NET Framework developer's long-term success. Trust me: having a solid grasp of these concepts will allow you to build efficient applications faster and easier.

Changing Fields in a Boxed Value Type by Using Interfaces (and Why You Shouldn't Do This)

Let's have some fun and see how well you understand value types, boxing, and unboxing. Examine the following code, and see whether you can figure out what it displays on the console:

```
using System;

// Point is a value type.
internal struct Point {
   private Int32 m_x, m_y;

   public Point(Int32 x, Int32 y) {
      m_x = x;
      m_y = y;
   }

   public void Change(Int32 x, Int32 y) {
      m_x = x; m_y = y;
   }

   public override String ToString() {
      return String.Format("({0}, {1})", m_x, m_y);
   }
}

public sealed class Program {
   public static void Main() {
      Point p = new Point(1, 1);

      Console.WriteLine(p);

      p.Change(2, 2);
      Console.WriteLine(p);

      Object o = p;
      Console.WriteLine(o);

      ((Point) o).Change(3, 3);
      Console.WriteLine(o);
   }
}
```

Very simply, **Main** creates an instance (**p**) of a **Point** value type on the stack and sets its **m_x** and **m_y** fields to **1**. Then, **p** is boxed before the first call to **WriteLine**, which calls **ToString** on the boxed **Point**, and **(1, 1)** is displayed as expected. Then, **p** is used to call the **Change** method, which changes the values of **p**'s **m_x** and **m_y** fields on the stack to **2**. The second call to **WriteLine** requires **p** to be boxed again and displays **(2, 2)**, as expected.

Now, **p** is boxed a third time, and **o** refers to the boxed **Point** object. The third call to **WriteLine** again shows **(2, 2)**, which is also expected. Finally, I want to call the **Change** method to update the fields in the boxed **Point** object. However, **Object** (the type of the variable **o**) doesn't know anything about the **Change** method, so I must first cast **o** to a **Point**. Casting **o** to a **Point** unboxes **o** and copies the fields in the boxed **Point** to a temporary **Point** on the thread's stack! The **m_x** and **m_y** fields of this temporary point are changed to **3** and **3**, but the boxed **Point** isn't affected by this call to **Change**. When **WriteLine** is called the fourth time, **(2, 2)** is displayed again. Many developers do *not* expect this.

Some languages, such as C++/CLI, let you change the fields in a boxed value type, but C# does not. However, you can fool C# into allowing this by using an interface. The following code is a modified version of the previous code:

```
using System;

// Interface defining a Change method
internal interface IChangeBoxedPoint {
   void Change(Int32 x, Int32 y);
}


// Point is a value type.
internal struct Point : IChangeBoxedPoint {
   private Int32 m_x, m_y;

   public Point(Int32 x, Int32 y) {
      m_x = x;
      m_y = y;
   }

   public void Change(Int32 x, Int32 y) {
      m_x = x; m_y = y;
   }

   public override String ToString() {
      return String.Format("({0}, {1})", m_x, m_y);
   }
}

public sealed class Program {
   public static void Main() {
      Point p = new Point(1, 1);

      Console.WriteLine(p);
```

```
        p.Change(2, 2);
        Console.WriteLine(p);

        Object o = p;
        Console.WriteLine(o);

        ((Point) o).Change(3, 3);
        Console.WriteLine(o);

        // Boxes p, changes the boxed object and discards it
        ((IChangeBoxedPoint) p).Change(4, 4);
        Console.WriteLine(p);

        // Changes the boxed object and shows it
        ((IChangeBoxedPoint) o).Change(5, 5);
        Console.WriteLine(o);
    }
}
```

This code is almost identical to the previous version. The main difference is that the **Change** method is defined by the **IChangeBoxedPoint** interface, and the **Point** type now implements this interface. Inside **Main**, the first four calls to **WriteLine** are the same and produce the same results I had before (as expected). However, I've added two more examples at the end of **Main**.

In the first example, the unboxed **Point**, **p**, is cast to an **IChangeBoxedPoint**. This cast causes the value in **p** to be boxed. **Change** is called on the boxed value, which does change its **m_x** and **m_y** fields to **4** and **4**, but after **Change** returns, the boxed object is immediately ready to be garbage collected. So the fifth call to **WriteLine** displays **(2, 2)**. Many developers won't expect this result.

In the last example, the boxed **Point** referred to by **o** is cast to an **IChangeBoxedPoint**. No boxing is necessary here because **o** is already a boxed **Point**. Then **Change** is called, which *does* change the boxed **Point**'s **m_x** and **m_y** fields. The interface method **Change** has allowed me to change the fields in a boxed **Point** object! Now, when **WriteLine** is called, it displays **(5, 5)** as expected. The purpose of this whole example is to demonstrate how an interface method is able to modify the fields of a boxed value type. In C#, this isn't possible without using an interface method.

> **Important** Earlier in this chapter, I mentioned that value types should be immutable: that is, they should not define any members that modify any of the type's instance fields. In fact, I recommended that value types have their fields marked as **readonly** so that the compiler will issue errors should you accidentally write a method that attempts to modify a field. The previous example should make it very clear to you why value types should be immutable. The unexpected behaviors shown in the previous example all occur when attempting to call a method that modifies the value type's instance fields. If after constructing a value type, you do not call any methods that modify its state, you will not get confused when all of the boxing and unboxing/field copying occurs. If the value type is immutable, you will end up just copying the same state around, and you will not be surprised by any of the behaviors you see.

A number of developers reviewed the chapters of this book. After reading through some of my code samples (such as the preceding one), these reviewers would tell me that they've sworn off value types. I must say that these little value type nuances have cost me days of debugging time, which is why I spend time pointing them out in this book. I hope you'll remember some of these nuances and that you'll be prepared for them if and when they strike you and your code. Certainly, you shouldn't be scared of value types. They are useful, and they have their place. After all, a program needs a little **Int32** love now and then. Just keep in mind that value types and reference types have very different behaviors depending on how they're used. In fact, you should take the preceding code and declare the **Point** as a **class** instead of a **struct** to appreciate the different behavior that results. Finally, you'll be very happy to know that the core value types that ship in the FCL—**Byte**, **Int32**, **UInt32**, **Int64**, **UInt64**, **Single**, **Double**, **Decimal**, **BigInteger**, **Complex**, all **enums**, and so on—are all immutable, so you should experience no surprising behavior when using any of these types.

Object Equality and Identity

Frequently, developers write code to compare objects with one another. This is particularly true when placing objects in a collection and you're writing code to sort, search, or compare items in a collection. In this section, I'll discuss object equality and identity, and I'll also discuss how to define a type that properly implements object equality.

The **System.Object** type offers a virtual method named **Equals**, whose purpose is to return **true** if two objects contain the same value. The implementation of **Object**'s **Equals** method looks like this:

```
public class Object {
   public virtual Boolean Equals(Object obj) {

      // If both references point to the same object,
      // they must have the same value.
      if (this == obj) return true;

      // Assume that the objects do not have the same value.
      return false;
   }
}
```

At first, this seems like a reasonable default implementation of **Equals:** it returns **true** if the **this** and **obj** arguments refer to the same exact object. This seems reasonable because **Equals** knows that an object must have the same value as itself. However, if the arguments refer to different objects, **Equals** can't be certain if the objects contain the same values, and therefore, **false** is returned. In other words, the default implementation of **Object**'s **Equals** method really implements identity, not value equality.

Unfortunately, as it turns out, **Object**'s **Equals** method is not a reasonable default, and it should have never been implemented this way. You immediately see the problem when you start thinking about class inheritance hierarchies and how to properly override **Equals**. Here is how to properly implement an **Equals** method internally:

1. If the **obj** argument is **null**, return **false** because the current object identified by **this** is obviously not **null** when the nonstatic **Equals** method is called.

2. If the **this** and **obj** arguments refer to the same object, return **true**. This step can improve performance when comparing objects with many fields.

3. If the **this** and **obj** arguments refer to objects of different types, return **false**. Obviously, checking if a **String** object is equal to a **FileStream** object should result in a **false** result.

4. For each instance field defined by the type, compare the value in the **this** object with the value in the **obj** object. If any fields are not equal, return **false**.

5. Call the base class's **Equals** method so it can compare any fields defined by it. If the base class's **Equals** method returns **false**, return **false;** otherwise, return **true**.

So Microsoft should have implemented **Object**'s **Equals** like this:

```
public class Object {
   public virtual Boolean Equals(Object obj) {
      // The given object to compare to can't be null
      if (obj == null) return false;

      // If objects are different types, they can't be equal.
      if (this.GetType() != obj.GetType()) return false;

      // If objects are same type, return true if all of their fields match
      // Since System.Object defines no fields, the fields match
      return true;
   }
}
```

But, since Microsoft didn't implement **Equals** this way, the rules for how to implement **Equals** are significantly more complicated than you would think. When a type overrides **Equals**, the override should call its base class's implementation of **Equals** unless it would be calling **Object**'s implementation. This also means that since a type can override **Object**'s **Equals** method, this **Equals** method can no longer be called to test for identity. To fix this, **Object** offers a static **ReferenceEquals** method, which is implemented like this:

```
public class Object {
   public static Boolean ReferenceEquals(Object objA, Object objB) {
      return (objA == objB);
   }
}
```

You should always call **ReferenceEquals** if you want to check for identity (if two references point to the same object). You shouldn't use the C# == operator (unless you cast both operands to **Object** first) because one of the operands' types could overload the == operator, giving it semantics other than identity.

As you can see, the .NET Framework has a very confusing story when it comes to object equality and identity. By the way, **System.ValueType** (the base class of all value types) does override **Object**'s **Equals** method and is correctly implemented to perform a value equality check (not an identity check). Internally, **ValueType**'s **Equals** is implemented this way:

1. If the **obj** argument is **null**, return **false**.

2. If the **this** and **obj** arguments refer to objects of different types, return **false**.

3. For each instance field defined by the type, compare the value in the **this** object with the value in the **obj** object by calling the field's **Equals** method. If any fields are not equal, return **false**.

4. Return **true**. **Object**'s **Equals** method is not called by **ValueType**'s **Equals** method.

Internally, **ValueType**'s **Equals** method uses reflection (covered in Chapter 23, "Assembly Loading and Reflection") to accomplish step #3 above. Since the CLR's reflection mechanism is slow, when defining your own value type, you should override **Equals** and provide your own implementation to improve the performance of value equality comparisons that use instances of your type. Of course, in your own implementation, do not call **base.Equals**.

When defining your own type, if you decide to override **Equals**, you must ensure that it adheres to the four properties of equality:

- **Equals** must be reflexive; that is, **x.Equals(x)** must return **true**.
- **Equals** must be symmetric; that is, **x.Equals(y)** must return the same value as **y.Equals(x)**.
- **Equals** must be transitive; that is, if **x.Equals(y)** returns **true** and **y.Equals(z)** returns **true**, then **x.Equals(z)** must also return **true**.
- **Equals** must be consistent. Provided that there are no changes in the two values being compared, **Equals** should consistently return **true** or **false**.

If your implementation of **Equals** fails to adhere to all of these rules, your application will behave in strange and unpredictable ways.

When overriding the **Equals** method, there are a few more things that you'll probably want to do:

- **Have the type implement the System.IEquatable<T> interface's Equals method** This generic interface allows you to define a type-safe **Equals** method. Usually, you'll implement the **Equals** method that takes an **Object** parameter to internally call the type-safe **Equals** method.

- **Overload the == and !=operator methods**   Usually, you'll implement these operator methods to internally call the type-safe **Equals** method.

Furthermore, if you think that instances of your type will be compared for the purposes of sorting, you'll want your type to also implement **System.IComparable**'s **CompareTo** method and **System.IComparable<T>**'s type-safe **CompareTo** method. If you implement these methods, you'll also want to overload the various comparison operator methods (<, <=, >, >=) and implement these methods internally to call the type-safe **CompareTo** method.

Object Hash Codes

The designers of the FCL decided that it would be incredibly useful if any instance of any object could be placed into a hash table collection. To this end, **System.Object** provides a virtual **GetHashCode** method so that an **Int32** hash code can be obtained for any and all objects.

If you define a type and override the **Equals** method, you should also override the **GetHashCode** method. In fact, Microsoft's C# compiler emits a warning if you define a type that overrides **Equals** without also overriding **GetHashCode**. For example, compiling the following type yields this warning: "**warning CS0659: 'Program' overrides Object.Equals(object o) but does not override Object.GetHashCode()**".

```
public sealed class Program {
    public override Boolean Equals(Object obj) { ... }
}
```

The reason why a type that defines **Equals** must also define **GetHashCode** is that the implementation of the **System.Collections.Hashtable** type, the **System.Collections. Generic.Dictionary** type, and some other collections require that any two objects that are equal must have the same hash code value. So if you override **Equals**, you should override **GetHashCode** to ensure that the algorithm you use for calculating equality corresponds to the algorithm you use for calculating the object's hash code.

Basically, when you add a key/value pair to a collection, a hash code for the key object is obtained first. This hash code indicates which "bucket" the key/value pair should be stored in. When the collection needs to look up a key, it gets the hash code for the specified key object. This code identifies the "bucket" that is now searched sequentially, looking for a stored key object that is equal to the specified key object. Using this algorithm of storing and looking up keys means that if you change a key object that is in a collection, the collection will no longer be able to find the object. If you intend to change a key object in a hash table, you should remove the original object/value pair, modify the key object, and then add the new key object/value pair back into the hash table.

Defining a **GetHashCode** method can be easy and straightforward. But depending on your data types and the distribution of data, it can be tricky to come up with a hashing algorithm that returns a well-distributed range of values. Here's a simple example that will probably work just fine for **Point** objects:

```
internal sealed class Point {
    private readonly Int32 m_x, m_y;
    public override Int32 GetHashCode() {
        return m_x ^ m_y;  // m_x XOR'd with m_y
    }
    ...
}
```

When selecting an algorithm for calculating hash codes for instances of your type, try to follow these guidelines:

- Use an algorithm that gives a good random distribution for the best performance of the hash table.

- Your algorithm can also call the base type's **GetHashCode** method, including its return value. However, you don't generally want to call **Object**'s or **ValueType**'s **GetHashCode** method, because the implementation in either method doesn't lend itself to high-performance hashing algorithms.

- Your algorithm should use at least one instance field.

- Ideally, the fields you use in your algorithm should be immutable; that is, the fields should be initialized when the object is constructed, and they should never again change during the object's lifetime.

- Your algorithm should execute as quickly as possible.

- Objects with the same value should return the same code. For example, two **String** objects with the same text should return the same hash code value.

System.Object's implementation of the **GetHashCode** method doesn't know anything about its derived type and any fields that are in the type. For this reason, **Object**'s **GetHashCode** method returns a number that is guaranteed to uniquely identify the object within the AppDomain; this number is guaranteed not to change for the lifetime of the object. After the object is garbage collected, however, its unique number can be reused as the hash code for a new object.

Note If a type overrides **Object**'s **GetHashCode** method, you can no longer call it to get a unique ID for the object. If you want to get a unique ID (within an AppDomain) for an object, the FCL provides a method that you can call. In the **System.Runtime.CompilerServices** namespace, see the **RuntimeHelpers** class's public, static **GetHashCode** method that takes a reference to an **Object** as an argument. **RuntimeHelpers**' **GetHashCode** method returns a unique ID for an object even if the object's type overrides **Object**'s **GetHashCode** method. This method got its name because of its heritage, but it would have been better if Microsoft had named it something like **GetUniqueObjectID**.

`System.ValueType`'s implementation of **GetHashCode** uses reflection (which is slow) and XORs some of the type's instance fields together. This is a naïve implementation that might be good for some value types, but I still recommend that you implement **GetHashCode** yourself because you'll know exactly what it does, and your implementation will be faster than **ValueType**'s implementation.

> **Important** If you're implementing your own hash table collection for some reason, or you're implementing any piece of code in which you'll be calling **GetHashCode**, you should *never, ever persist hash code values*. The reason is that hash code values are subject to change. For example, a future version of a type might use a different algorithm for calculating the object's hash code.

There is a company that was not heeding this important warning. On their Web site, users could create new accounts by selecting a user name and a password. The Web site then took the password **String**, called **GetHashCode**, and persisted the hash code value in a database. When users logged back on to the Web site, they entered their password. The Web site would call **GetHashCode** again and compare the hash code value with the stored value in the database. If the hash codes matched, the user would be granted access. Unfortunately, when the company upgraded to a new version of the CLR, **String**'s **GetHashCode** method had changed, and it now returned a different hash code value. The end result was that no user was able to log on to the Web site anymore!

The dynamic Primitive Type

C# is a type-safe programming language. This means that all expressions resolve into an instance of a type and the compiler will generate only code that is attempting to perform an operation that is valid for this type. The benefit of a type-safe programming language over a non–type-safe programming language is that many programmer errors are detected at compile time, helping to ensure that the code is correct before you attempt to execute it. In addition, compile-time languages can typically produce smaller and faster code since they make more assumptions at compile time and bake those assumptions into the resulting IL and metadata.

However, there are also many occasions when a program has to act on information that it doesn't know about until it is running. While you can use type-safe programming languages (like C#) to interact with this information, the syntax tends to be clumsy, especially since you tend to work a lot with strings, and performance is hampered as well. If you are writing a pure C# application, then the only occasion you have for working with runtime-determined information is when you are using reflection (discussed in Chapter 23). However, many developers also use C# to communicate with components that are not implemented in C#. Some of these components could be .NET-dynamic languages such as Python or Ruby, or COM objects that support the **IDispatch** interface (possibly implemented in native C or C++), or

HTML Document Object Model (DOM) objects (implemented using various languages and technologies). Communicating with HTML DOM objects is particularly useful when building a Microsoft Silverlight application.

To make it easier for developers using reflection or communicating with other components, the C# compiler offers you a way to mark an expression's type as **dynamic**. You can also put the result of an expression into a variable and you can mark a variable's type as **dynamic.** This **dynamic** expression/variable can then be used to invoke a member such as a field, a property/indexer, a method, delegate, and unary/binary/conversion operators. When your code invokes a member using a dynamic expression/variable, the compiler generates special IL code that describes the desired operation. This special code is referred to as the *payload*. At runtime, the payload code determines the exact operation to execute based on the actual type of the object now referenced by the **dynamic** expression/variable.

Here is some code to demonstrate what I'm talking about:

```
Private static class DynamicDemo {
    public static void Main() {
        for (Int32 demo = 0; demo < 2; demo++) {
            dynamic arg = (demo == 0) ? (dynamic) 5 : (dynamic) "A";
            dynamic result = Plus(arg);
            M(result);
        }
    }

    private static dynamic Plus(dynamic arg) { return arg + arg; }

    private static void M(Int32 n) { Console.WriteLine("M(Int32): " + n); }
    private static void M(String s) { Console.WriteLine("M(String): " + s); }
}
```

When I execute **Main**, I get the following output:

```
M(Int32): 10
M(String): AA
```

To understand what's happening, let's start by looking at the **Plus** method. This method has declared its parameter's type as **dynamic**, and inside the method, the argument is used as the two operands to the binary + operator. Since **arg** is **dynamic**, the C# compiler emits payload code that will examine the actual type of **arg** at runtime and determine what the + operator should actually do.

The first time **Plus** is called, **5** (an **Int32**), is passed, so **Plus** will return the value **10** (also an **Int32**) back to its caller. This puts this result in the **result** variable (declared as a **dynamic** type). Then, the **M** method is called, passing it **result**. For the call to **M**, the compiler will emit payload code that will, at runtime, examine the actual type of the value being passed to **M** and determine which overload of the **M** method to call. When **result** contains an **Int32**, the overload of **M** that takes an **Int32** parameter is called.

The second time **Plus** is called, "A" (a **String**) is passed, so **Plus** will return "AA" (the result of concatenating "A" with itself) back to its caller, which puts this result in the **result** variable. Then, the **M** method is called again, passing it **result**. This time, the payload code determines that the actual type being passed to **M** is a **String** and calls the overload of **M** that takes a **String** parameter.

When the type of a field, method parameter, method return type, or local variable, is specified as **dynamic**, the compiler converts this type to the **System.Object** type and applies an instance of **System.Runtime.CompilerServices.DynamicAttribute** to the field, parameter, or return type in metadata. If a local variable is specified as **dynamic**, then the variable's type will also be of type **Object**, but the **DynamicAttribute** is not applied to the local variable since its usage is self-contained within the method. Since **dynamic** is really the same as **Object**, you cannot write methods whose signature differs only by **dynamic** and **Object**.

It is also possible to use **dynamic** when specifying generic type arguments to a generic class (reference type), a structure (value type), an interface, a delegate, or a method. When you do this, the compiler converts **dynamic** to **Object** and applies **DynamicAttribute** to the various pieces of metadata where it makes sense. Note that the generic code that you are using has already been compiled and will consider the type to be **Object**; no dynamic dispatch will be performed because the compiler did not produce any payload code in the generic code.

Any expression can implicitly be cast to **dynamic** since all expressions result in a type that is derived from **Object**.[2] Normally, the compiler does not allow you to write code that implicitly casts an expression from **Object** to another type; you must use explicit cast syntax. However, the compiler does allow you to cast an expression from **dynamic** to another type using implicit cast syntax:

```
Object o1 = 123;       // OK: Implicit cast from Int32 to Object (boxing)
Int32 n1 = o;          // Error: No implicit cast from Object to Int32
Int32 n2 = (Int32) o;  // OK: Explicit cast from Object to Int32 (unboxing)

dynamic d1 = 123;      // OK: Implicit cast from Int32 to dynamic (boxing)
Int32 n3 = d;          // OK: Implicit cast from dynamic to Int32 (unboxing)
```

While the compiler allows you to omit the explicit cast when casting from **dynamic** to some other type, the CLR will validate the cast at runtime to ensure that type safety is maintained. If the object's type is not compatible with the cast, the CLR will throw an **InvalidCastException** exception.

Note that the result of evaluating a **dynamic** expression is a dynamic expression. Examine this code:

```
dynamic d = 123;
var result = M(d);  // Note: 'var result' is the same as 'dynamic result'
```

---

[2] And, as always, value types will be boxed.

Here, the compiler allows the code to compile because it doesn't know at compile time which **M** method it will call. Therefore, it also does not know what type of result **M** will return. And so, the compiler assumes that the **result** variable is of type **dynamic** itself. You can verify this by placing your mouse over **var** in the Visual Studio editor; the IntelliSense window will indicate **'dynamic: Represents an object whose operations will be resolved at runtime.'** If the **M** method invoked at runtime has a return type of **void**, no exception is thrown; instead, **result** will be assigned a value of **null**.

> **Important** Do not confuse **dynamic** and **var**. Declaring a local variable using **var** is just a syntactical shortcut that has the compiler infer the specific data type from an expression. The **var** keyword can be used only for declaring local variables inside a method while the **dynamic** keyword can be used for local variables, fields, and arguments. You cannot cast an expression to **var** but you can cast an expression to **dynamic**. You must explicitly initialize a variable declared using **var** while you do not have to initialize a variable declared with **dynamic**. For more information about C#'s **var**, see the "Implicitly Typed Local Variables" section in Chapter 9, "Parameters."

However, when converting from **dynamic** to another static type, the result's type is, of course, the static type. Similarly, when constructing a type by passing one or more **dynamic** arguments to its constructor, the result is the type of object you are constructing:

```
dynamic d = 123;
var x = (Int32) d;         // Conversion: 'var x' is the same as 'Int32 x'
var dt = new DateTime(d);  // Construction: 'var dt' is the same as 'DateTime dt'
```

If a **dynamic** expression is specified as the collection in a **foreach** statement or as a resource in a **using** statement, the compiler will generate code that attempts to cast the expression to the non-generic **System.IEnumerable** interface or to the **System.IDisposable** interface, respectively. If the cast succeeds, the expression is used and the code runs just fine. If the cast fails, a **Microsoft.CSharp.RuntimeBinder.RuntimeBinderException** exception is thrown.

> **Important** A **dynamic** expression is really the same type as **System.Object**. The compiler assumes that whatever operation you attempt on the expression is legal, so the compiler will not generate any warnings or errors. However, exceptions will be thrown at runtime if you attempt to execute an invalid operation. In addition, Visual Studio cannot offer any IntelliSense support to help you write code against a **dynamic** expression. You cannot define an extension method (discussed in Chapter 8, "Methods") that extends **dynamic**, although you can define one that extends **Object**. And, you cannot pass a lambda expression or anonymous method (both discussed in Chapter 17, "Delegates") as an argument to a **dynamic** method call since the compiler cannot infer the types being used.

Here is an example of some C# code that uses COM **IDispatch** to create a Microsoft Office Excel workbook and places a string in cell A1:

```
using Microsoft.Office.Interop.Excel;
...
public static void Main() {
   Application excel = new Application();
   excel.Visible = true;
   excel.Workbooks.Add(Type.Missing);
   ((Range)excel.Cells[1, 1]).Value = "Text in cell A1"; // Put this string in cell A1
}
```

Without the **dynamic** type, the value returned from **excel.Cells[1, 1]** is of type **Object**, which must be cast to the **Range** type before its **Value** property can be accessed. However, when producing a runtime callable wrapper assembly for a COM object, any use of **VARIANT** in the COM method is really converted to **dynamic**; this is called *dynamification*. Therefore, since **excel.Cells[1, 1]** is of type **dynamic**, you do not have to explicitly cast it to the **Range** type before its **Value** property can be accessed. Dynamification can greatly simplify code that interoperates with COM objects. Here is the simpler code:

```
using Microsoft.Office.Interop.Excel;
...
public static void Main() {
   Application excel = new Application();
   excel.Visible = true;
   excel.Workbooks.Add(Type.Missing);
   excel.Cells[1, 1].Value = "Text in cell A1"; // Put this string in cell A1
}
```

The code below shows how to use reflection to call a method ("Contains") on a **String** target ("Jeffrey Richter") passing it a **String** argument ("ff") and storing the **Int32** result in a local variable (**result**):

```
Object target = "Jeffrey Richter";
Object arg = "ff";

// Find a method on the target that matches the desired argument types
Type[] argTypes = newType[] { arg.GetType() };
MethodInfo method = target.GetType().GetMethod("Contains", argTypes);

// Invoke the method on the target passing the desired arguments
Object[] arguments = newObject[] { arg };
Boolean result = Convert.ToBoolean(method.Invoke(target, arguments));
```

Using C#'s **dynamic** type, this code can be rewritten with greatly improved syntax:

```
dynamic target = "Jeffrey Richter";
dynamic arg = "ff";
Boolean result = target.Contains(arg);
```

Earlier, I mentioned that the C# compiler emits payload code that, at runtime, figures out what operation to perform based on the actual type of an object. This payload code uses a class known as a *runtime binder*. Different programming languages define their own runtime binders that encapsulate the rules of that language. The code for the C# runtime binder is in the Microsoft.CSharp.dll assembly, and you must reference this assembly when you build projects that use the **dynamic** keyword. This assembly is referenced in the compiler's default response file, CSC.rsp. It is the code in this assembly that knows to produce code (at runtime) that performs addition when the + operator is applied to two **Int32** objects and concatenation when applied to two **String** objects.

At runtime, the Microsoft.CSharp.dll assembly will have to load into the AppDomain, which hurts your application's performance and increases memory consumption. Microsoft.CSharp.dll also loads System.dll and System.Core.dll. If you are using **dynamic** to help you interoperate with COM components, then System.Dynamic.dll will also load. And when the payload code executes, it generates dynamic code at runtime; this code will be in an in-memory assembly called "Anonymously Hosted DynamicMethods Assembly." The purpose of this code is to improve the performance of dynamic dispatch in scenarios where a particular call site is making many invocations using dynamic arguments that have the same runtime type.

Due to all the overhead associated with C#'s built-in dynamic evaluation feature, you should consciously decide that you are getting sufficient syntax simplification from the **dynamic** feature to make it worth the extra performance hit of loading all these assemblies and the extra memory that they consume. If you have only a couple places in your program where you need **dynamic** behavior, it might be more efficient to just do it the old-fashioned way, by calling reflection methods (for managed objects) or with manual casting (for COM objects).

At runtime, the C# runtime binder resolves a dynamic operation according to the runtime type of the object. The binder first checks to see if the type implements the **IDynamicMetaObjectProvider** interface. If the object does implement this interface, then the interface's **GetMetaObject** method is called, which returns a **DynamicMetaObject**-derived type. This type can process all of the member, method, and operator bindings for the object. Both the **IDynamicMetaObjectProvider** interface and the **DynamicMetaObject** base class are defined in the **System.Dynamic** namespace, and both are in the System.Core.dll assembly.

Dynamic languages, such as Python and Ruby, endow their types with **DynamicMetaObject**-derived types so that they can be accessed in a way appropriate for them when manipulated from other programming languages (like C#). Similarly, when accessing a COM component, the C# runtime binder will use a **DynamicMetaObject**-derived type that knows how to communicate with a COM component. The COM **DynamicMetaObject**-derived type is defined in the System.Dynamic.dll assembly.

If the type of the object being used in the dynamic expression does not implement the **IDynamicMetaObjectProvider** interface, then the C# compiler treats the object like an instance of an ordinary C#-defined type and performs operations on the object using reflection.

Chapter 6
Type and Member Basics

In Chapters 4 and 5, I focused on types and what operations are guaranteed to exist on all instances of any type. I also explained how all types fall into one of two categories: reference types and value types. In this and the subsequent chapters in this part, I'll show how to design types by using the different kinds of members that can be defined within a type. In Chapters 7 through 11, I'll discuss the various members in detail.

The Different Kinds of Type Members

A type can define zero or more of the following kinds of members:

- **Constants**   A constant is a symbol that identifies a never-changing data value. These symbols are typically used to make code more readable and maintainable. Constants are always associated with a type, not an instance of a type. Logically, constants are always static members. Discussed in Chapter 7, "Constants and Fields."

- **Fields**   A field represents a read-only or read/write data value. A field can be static, in which case the field is considered part of the type's state. A field can also be instance (nonstatic), in which case it's considered part of an object's state. I strongly encourage you to make fields private so that the state of the type or object can't be corrupted by code outside of the defining type. Discussed in Chapter 7.

- **Instance constructors**   An instance constructor is a special method used to initialize a new object's instance fields to a good initial state. Discussed in Chapter 8, "Methods."

- **Type constructors**   A type constructor is a special method used to initialize a type's static fields to a good initial state. Discussed in Chapter 8.

- **Methods** A method is a function that performs operations that change or query the state of a type (static method) or an object (instance method). Methods typically read and write to the fields of the type or object. Discussed in Chapter 8.

- **Operator overloads** An operator overload is a method that defines how an object should be manipulated when certain operators are applied to the object. Because not all programming languages support operator overloading, operator overload methods are not part of the Common Language Specification (CLS). Discussed in Chapter 8.

- **Conversion operators** A conversion operator is a method that defines how to implicitly or explicitly cast or convert an object from one type to another type. As with operator overload methods, not all programming languages support conversion operators, so they're not part of the CLS. Discussed in Chapter 8.

- **Properties** A property is a mechanism that allows a simple, field-like syntax for setting or querying part of the logical state of a type (static property) or object (instance property) while ensuring that the state doesn't become corrupt. Properties can be parameterless (very common) or parameterful (fairly uncommon but used frequently with collection classes). Discussed in Chapter 10, "Properties."

- **Events** A static event is a mechanism that allows a type to send a notification to one or more static or instance methods. An instance (nonstatic) event is a mechanism that allows an object to send a notification to one or more static or instance methods. Events are usually raised in response to a state change occurring in the type or object offering the event. An event consists of two methods that allow static or instance methods to register and unregister interest in the event. In addition to the two methods, events typically use a delegate field to maintain the set of registered methods. Discussed in Chapter 11, "Events."

- **Types** A type can define other types nested within it. This approach is typically used to break a large, complex type down into smaller building blocks to simplify the implementation.

Again, the purpose of this chapter isn't to describe these various members in detail but to set the stage and explain what these various members all have in common.

Regardless of the programming language you're using, the corresponding compiler must process your source code and produce metadata and Intermediate Language (IL) code for each kind of member in the preceding list. The format of the metadata is identical regardless of the source programming language you use, and this feature is what makes the CLR a *common language* runtime. The metadata is the common information that all languages produce and consume, enabling code in one programming language to seamlessly access code written in a completely different programming language.

This common metadata format is also used by the CLR, which determines how constants, fields, constructors, methods, properties, and events all behave at runtime. Simply stated, metadata is the key to the whole Microsoft .NET Framework development platform; it enables the seamless integration of languages, types, and objects.

The following C# code shows a type definition that contains an example of all the possible members. The code shown here will compile (with warnings), but it isn't representative of a type that you'd normally create; most of the methods do nothing of any real value. Right now, I just want to show you how the compiler translates this type and its members into metadata. Once again, I'll discuss the individual members in the next few chapters.

```
using System;

public sealed class SomeType {                          //  1

   // Nested class
   private class SomeNestedType { }                     //  2

   // Constant, read-only, and static read/write field
   private const    Int32  c_SomeConstant = 1;          //  3
   private readonly String m_SomeReadOnlyField = "2";   //  4
   private static   Int32  s_SomeReadWriteField = 3;    //  5

   // Type constructor
   static SomeType() { }                                //  6

   // Instance constructors
   public SomeType(Int32 x) { }                         //  7
   public SomeType() { }                                //  8

   // Instance and static methods
   private String InstanceMethod() { return null; }     //  9
   public static void Main() {}                         // 10

   // Instance property
   public Int32 SomeProp {                              // 11
      get { return 0; }                                 // 12
      set { }                                           // 13
   }

   // Instance parameterful property (indexer)
   public Int32 this[String s] {                        // 14
      get { return 0; }                                 // 15
      set { }                                           // 16
   }

   // Instance event
   public event EventHandler SomeEvent;                 // 17
}
```

If you were to compile the type just defined and examine the metadata in ILDasm.exe, you'd see the output shown in Figure 6-1.

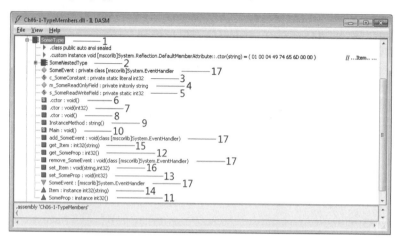

FIGURE 6-1 ILDasm.exe output showing metadata from preceding code

Notice that all the members defined in the source code cause the compiler to emit some metadata. In fact, some of the members cause the compiler to generate additional members as well as additional metadata. For example, the event member (17) causes the compiler to emit a field, two methods, and some additional metadata. I don't expect you to fully understand what you're seeing here now. But as you read the next few chapters, I encourage you to look back to this example to see how the member is defined and what effect that has on the metadata produced by the compiler.

Type Visibility

When defining a type at file scope (versus defining a type nested within another type), you can specify the type's visibility as being either **public** or **internal**. A **public** type is visible to all code within the defining assembly as well as all code written in other assemblies. An **internal** type is visible to all code within the defining assembly, and the type is not visible to code written in other assemblies. If you do not explicitly specify either of these when you define a type, the C# compiler sets the type's visibility to **internal** (the more restrictive of the two). Here are some examples:

```
using System;

// The type below has public visibility and can be accessed by code
// in this assembly as well as code written in other assemblies.
public class ThisIsAPublicType { ... }

// The type below has internal visibility and can be accessed by code
// in this assembly only.
internal class ThisIsAnInternalType { ... }

// The type below is internal because public/internal
// was not explicitly stated
class ThisIsAlsoAnInternalType { ... }
```

Friend Assemblies

Imagine the following scenario: A company has one team, TeamA, that is defining a bunch of utility types in one assembly, and they expect these types to be used by members in another team, TeamB. For various reasons such as time schedules or geographical location, or perhaps different cost centers or reporting structures, these two teams cannot build all of their types into a single assembly; instead, each team produces its own assembly file.

In order for TeamB's assembly to use TeamA's types, TeamA must define all of their utility types as **public.** However, this means that their types are publicly visible to any and all assemblies; developers in another company could write code that uses the public utility types, and this is not desirable. Maybe the utility types make certain assumptions that TeamB ensures when they write code that uses TeamA's types. What we'd like to have is a way for TeamA to define their types as **internal** while still allowing TeamB to access the types. The CLR and C# support this via *friend assemblies*. This friend assembly feature is also useful when you want to have one assembly containing code that performs unit tests against the internal types within another assembly.

When an assembly is built, it can indicate other assemblies it considers "friends" by using the **InternalsVisibleTo** attribute defined in the **System.Runtime.CompilerServices** namespace. The attribute has a string parameter that identifies the friend assembly's name and public key (the string you pass to the attribute must not include a version, culture, or processor architecture). Note that friend assemblies can access *all* of an assembly's **internal** types as well as these type's **internal** members. Here is an example of how an assembly can specify two other strongly named assemblies named "Wintellect" and "Microsoft" as its friend assemblies:

```
using System;
using System.Runtime.CompilerServices; // For InternalsVisibleTo attribute

// This assembly's internal types can be accessed by any code written
// in the following two assemblies (regardless of version or culture):
[assembly:InternalsVisibleTo("Wintellect, PublicKey=12345678...90abcdef")]
[assembly:InternalsVisibleTo("Microsoft, PublicKey=b77a5c56...1934e089")]

internal sealed class SomeInternalType { ... }
internal sealed class AnotherInternalType { ... }
```

Accessing the above assembly's **internal** types from a friend assembly is trivial. For example, here's how a friend assembly called "Wintellect" with a public key of "12345678...90abcdef" can access the internal type **SomeInternalType** in the assembly above:

```
using System;

internal sealed class Foo {
    private static Object SomeMethod() {
        // This "Wintellect" assembly accesses the other assembly's
```

```
        // internal type as if it were a public type
        SomeInternalType sit = new SomeInternalType();
        return sit;
    }
}
```

Since the **internal** members of the types in an assembly become accessible to friend assemblies, you should think carefully about what accessibility you specify for your type's
members and which assemblies you declare as your friends. Note that the C# compiler requires you to use the **/out:<file>** compiler switch when compiling the friend assembly (the
assembly that does not contain the **InternalsVisibleTo** attribute). The switch is required
because the compiler needs to know the name of the assembly being compiled in order to
determine if the resulting assembly should be considered a friend assembly. You would think
that the C# compiler could determine this on its own since it normally determines the output
file name on its own; however, the compiler doesn't decide on an output file name until it
is finished compiling the code. So requiring the **/out:<file>** compiler switch improves the
performance of compiling significantly.

Also, if you are compiling a module (as opposed to an assembly) using C#'s **/t:module**
switch, and this module is going to become part of a friend assembly, you need to compile
the module by using the C# compiler's **/moduleassemblyname:<string>** switch as well. This
tells the compiler what assembly the module will be a part of so the compiler can allow code
in the module to access the other assembly's internal types.

> **Important** The friend assembly feature should be used only by assemblies that ship on the
> same schedule and probably even ship together. The reason is because the interdependency
> between friend assemblies is so high that shipping the friend assemblies on different schedules
> will most likely cause compatibility problems. If you expect the assemblies to ship on different
> schedules, you should try to design **public** classes that can be consumed by any assembly and
> limit accessibility via a LinkDemand requesting the **StrongNameIdentityPermission.**

Member Accessibility

When defining a type's member (which includes nested types), you can specify the member's
accessibility. A member's accessibility indicates which members can be legally accessed from
referent code. The CLR defines the set of possible accessibility modifiers, but each programming language chooses the syntax and term it wants developers to use when applying the
accessibility to a member. For example, the CLR uses the term *Assembly* to indicate that a
member is accessible to any code within the same assembly, whereas the C# term for this is
internal.

Table 6-1 shows the six accessibility modifiers that can be applied to a member. The rows of
the table are in order from most restrictive (*Private*) to least restrictive (*Public*).

TABLE 6-1 **Member Accessibility**

CLR Term	C# Term	Description
Private	**private**	The member is accessible only by methods in the defining type or any nested type.
Family	**protected**	The member is accessible only by methods in the defining type, any nested type, or one of its derived types without regard to assembly.
Family and Assembly	(not supported)	The member is accessible only by methods in the defining type, any nested type, or by any derived types defined in the same assembly.
Assembly	**internal**	The member is accessible only by methods in the defining assembly.
Family or Assembly	**protected internal**	The member is accessible by any nested type, any derived type (regardless of assembly), or any methods in the defining assembly.
Public	**public**	The member is accessible to all methods in any assembly.

Of course, for any member to be accessible, it must be defined in a type that is visible. For example, if AssemblyA defines an **internal** type with a **public** method, code in AssemblyB cannot call the **public** method because the **internal** type is not visible to AssemblyB.

When compiling code, the language compiler is responsible for checking that the code is referencing types and members correctly. If the code references some type or member incorrectly, the compiler has the responsibility of emitting the appropriate error message. In addition, the just-in-time (JIT) compiler also ensures that references to fields and methods are legal when compiling IL code into native CPU instructions at runtime. For example, if the JIT compiler detects code that is improperly attempting to access a private field or method, the JIT compiler throws a **FieldAccessException** or a **MethodAccessException**, respectively.

Verifying the IL code ensures that a referenced member's accessibility is properly honored at runtime, even if a language compiler ignored checking the accessibility. Another, more likely, possibility is that the language compiler compiled code that accessed a **public** member in another type (in another assembly); but at runtime, a different version of the assembly is loaded, and in this new version, the **public** member has changed and is now **protected** or **private.**

In C#, if you do not explicitly declare a member's accessibility, the compiler usually (but not always) defaults to selecting **private** (the most restrictive of them all). The CLR requires that all members of an interface type be public. The C# compiler knows this and forbids the programmer from explicitly specifying accessibility on interface members; the compiler just makes all the members **public** for you.

> **More Info**   See the "Declared Accessibility" section in the C# Language Specification for the complete set of C# rules about what accessibilities can be applied to types and members and what default accessibilities C# selects based on the context in which the declaration takes place.

Furthermore, you'll notice the CLR offers an accessibility called *Family and Assembly.* However, C# doesn't expose this in the language. The C# team felt that this accessibility was for the most part useless and decided not to incorporate it into the C# language.

When a derived type is overriding a member defined in its base type, the C# compiler requires that the original member and the overriding member have the same accessibility. That is, if the member in the base class is **protected**, the overriding member in the derived class must also be **protected.** However, this is a C# restriction, not a CLR restriction. When deriving from a base class, the CLR allows a member's accessibility to become less restrictive but not more restrictive. For example, a class can override a **protected** method defined in its base class and make the overridden method **public** (more accessible). However, a class cannot override a **protected** method defined in its base class and make the overridden method **private** (less accessible). The reason a class cannot make a base class method more restricted is because a user of the derived class could always cast to the base type and gain access to the base class's method. If the CLR allowed the derived type's method to be less accessible, it would be making a claim that was not enforceable.

Static Classes

There are certain classes that are never intended to be instantiated, such as **Console, Math, Environment,** and **ThreadPool.** These classes have only **static** members and, in fact, the classes exist simply as a way to group a set of related members together. For example, the **Math** class defines a bunch of methods that do math-related operations. C# allows you to define non-instantiable classes by using the C# **static** keyword. This keyword can be applied only to classes, not structures (value types) because the CLR always allows value types to be instantiated and there is no way to stop or prevent this.

The compiler enforces many restrictions on a **static** class:

- The class must be derived directly from **System.Object** because deriving from any other base class makes no sense since inheritance applies only to objects, and you cannot create an instance of a **static** class.

- The class must not implement any interfaces since interface methods are callable only when using an instance of a class.

- The class must define only **static** members (fields, methods, properties, and events). Any instance members cause the compiler to generate an error.

- The class cannot be used as a field, method parameter, or local variable because all of these would indicate a variable that refers to an instance, and this is not allowed. If the compiler detects any of these uses, the compiler issues an error.

Here is an example of a **static** class that defines some **static** members; this code compiles (with a warning) but the class doesn't do anything interesting:

```
using System;

public static class AStaticClass {
   public static void AStaticMethod() { }

   public static String AStaticProperty {
      get { return s_AStaticField; }
      set { s_AStaticField = value; }
   }

   private static String s_AStaticField;

   public static event EventHandler AStaticEvent;
}
```

If you compile the code above into a library (DLL) assembly and look at the result by using ILDasm.exe, you'll see what is shown in Figure 6-2. As you can see in Figure 6-2, defining a class by using the **static** keyword causes the C# compiler to make the class both **abstract** and **sealed**. Furthermore, the compiler will not emit an instance constructor method into the type. Notice that there is no instance constructor (**.ctor**) method shown in Figure 6-2.

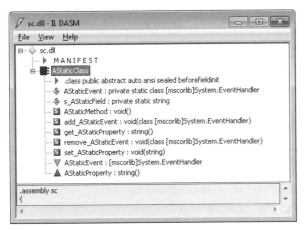

FIGURE 6-2 ILDasm.exe showing the class as abstract sealed in metadata

Partial Classes, Structures, and Interfaces

In this section, I discuss partial classes, structures, and interfaces. It should be noted that this feature is offered entirely by the C# compiler (some other compilers also offer this feature); the CLR knows nothing about partial classes, structures, and interfaces.

The **partial** keyword tells the C# compiler that the source code for a single class, structure, or interface definition may span one or more source code files. There are three main reasons why you might want to split the source code for a type across multiple files:

- **Source control**   Suppose a type's definition consists of a lot of source code, and a programmer checks it out of source control to make changes. No other programmer will be able to modify the type at the same time without doing a merge later. Using the **partial** keyword allows you to split the code for the type across multiple source code files, each of which can be checked out individually so that multiple programmers can edit the type at the same time.

- **Splitting a class or structure into distinct logical units within a single file**   I some-times create a single type that provides multiple features so that the type can provide a complete solution. To simplify my implementation, I will sometimes declare the same partial type repeatedly within a single source code file. Then, in each part of the partial type, I implement one feature with all its fields, methods, properties, events, and so on. This allows me to easily see all the members that provide a single feature grouped to-gether, which simplifies my coding. Also, I can easily comment out a part of the partial type to remove a whole feature from the class and replace it with another implementa-tion (via a new part of the partial type).

- **Code spitters**   In Microsoft Visual Studio, when you create a new Windows Forms or Web Forms project, some source code files are created automatically as part of the project. These source code files contain templates that give you a head start at building these kinds of projects. When you use the Visual Studio designers and drag and drop controls onto the Windows form or Web form, Visual Studio writes source code for you automatically and spits this code into the source code files. This really improves your productivity. Historically, the generated code was emitted into the same source code file that you were working on. The problem with this is that you might edit the gener-ated code accidentally and cause the designers to stop functioning correctly. Starting with Visual Studio 2005, when you create a new Windows form, Web form, user control, and so on, Visual Studio creates two source code files: one for your code and the other for the code generated by the designer. Since the designer code is in a separate file, you'll be far less likely to accidentally edit it.

The **partial** keyword is applied to the types in all files. When the files are compiled together, the compiler combines the code to produce one type that is in the resulting .exe or .dll assembly file (or .netmodule module file). As I stated in the beginning of this section, the partial types feature is completely implemented by the C# compiler; the CLR knows nothing about partial types at all. This is why all of the source code files for the type must use the same programming language, and they must all be compiled together as a single compilation unit.

Components, Polymorphism, and Versioning

Object-oriented programming (OOP) has been around for many, many years. When it was first used in the late 1970s/early 1980s, applications were much smaller in size and all the code to make the application run was written by one company. Sure, there were operating systems back then and applications did make use of what they could out of those operating systems, but the operating systems offered very few features compared with the operating systems of today.

Today, software is much more complex and users demand that applications offer rich features such as GUIs, menu items, mouse input, tablet input, printer output, networking, and so on. For this reason, our operating systems and development platforms have grown substantially over recent years. Furthermore, it is no longer feasible or even cost effective for application developers to write all of the code necessary for their application to work the way users expect. Today, applications consist of code produced by many different companies. This code is stitched together using an object-oriented paradigm.

Component Software Programming (CSP) is OOP brought to this level. Here are some attributes of a component:

- A component (an assembly in .NET) has the feeling of being "published."
- A component has an identity (a name, version, culture, and public key).
- A component forever maintains its identity (the code in an assembly is never statically linked into another assembly; .NET always uses dynamic linking).
- A component clearly indicates the components it depends upon (reference metadata tables).
- A component should document its classes and members. C# offers this by allowing in-source Extensible Markup Language (XML) documentation along with the compiler's **/doc** command-line switch.
- A component must specify the security permissions it requires. The CLR's code access security (CAS) facilities enable this.
- A component publishes an interface (object model) that won't change for any servicings. A *servicing* is a new version of a component whose intention is to be backward compatible with the original version of the component. Typically, a servicing version includes bug fixes, security patches, and possibly some small feature enhancements. But a servicing cannot require any new dependencies or any additional security permissions.

As indicated by the last bullet, a big part of CSP has to do with versioning. Components will change over time and components will ship on different time schedules. Versioning introduces a whole new level of complexity for CSP that didn't exist with OOP, with which all code was written, tested, and shipped as a single unit by a single company. In this section, I'm going to focus on component versioning.

In .NET, a version number consists of four parts: a *major* part, a *minor* part, a *build* part, and a *revision* part. For example, an assembly whose version number is 1.2.3.4 has a major part of 1, a minor part of 2, a build part of 3, and a revision part of 4. The major/minor parts are typically used to represent a consistent and stable feature set for an assembly and the build/revision parts are typically used to represent a servicing of this assembly's feature set.

Let's say that a company ships an assembly with version 2.7.0.0. If the company later wants to fix a bug in this component, they would produce a new assembly in which only the build/revision parts of the version are changed, something like version 2.7.1.34. This indicates that the assembly is a servicing whose intention is to be backward compatible with the original component (version 2.7.0.0).

On the other hand, if the company wants to make a new version of the assembly that has significant changes to it and is therefore not intended to be backward compatible with the original assembly, the company is really creating a new component and the new assembly should be given a version number in which the major/minor parts are different from the existing component (version 3.0.0.0, for example).

> **Note** I have just described how you should think of version numbers. Unfortunately, the CLR doesn't treat version numbers this way. Today, the CLR treats a version number as an opaque value, and if an assembly depends on version 1.2.3.4 of another assembly, the CLR tries to load version 1.2.3.4 only (unless a binding redirection is in place).

Now that we've looked at how we use version numbers to update a component's identity to reflect a new version, let's take a look at some of the features offered by the CLR and programming languages (such as C#) that allow developers to write code that is resilient to changes that may be occurring in components that they are using.

Versioning issues come into play when a type defined in a component (assembly) is used as the base class for a type in another component (assembly). Obviously, if the base class versions (changes) underneath the derived class, the behavior of the derived class changes as well, probably in a way that causes the class to behave improperly. This is particularly true in polymorphism scenarios in which a derived type overrides virtual methods defined by a base type.

C# offers five keywords that you can apply to types and/or type members that impact component versioning. These keywords map directly to features supported in the CLR to support component versioning. Table 6-2 contains the C# keywords related to component versioning and indicates how each keyword affects a type or type member definition.

TABLE 6-2 C# Keywords and How They Affect Component Versioning

C# Keyword	Type	Method/Property/Event	Constant/Field
abstract	Indicates that no in-stances of the type can be constructed	Indicates that the derived type must override and implement this member before instances of the derived type can be constructed	(not allowed)
virtual	(not allowed)	Indicates that this member can be overridden by a derived type	(not allowed)
override	(not allowed)	Indicates that the derived type is overriding the base type's member	(not allowed)
sealed	Indicates that the type cannot be used as a base type	Indicates that the member cannot be overridden by a derived type. This keyword can be applied only to a method that is overriding a virtual method.	(not allowed)
new	When applied to a nested type, method, property, event, constant, or field, indicates that the member has no relationship to a similar member that may exist in the base class		

I will demonstrate the value and use of all these keywords in the upcoming section titled "Dealing with Virtual Methods When Versioning Types." But before we get to a versioning scenario, let's focus on how the CLR actually calls virtual methods.

How the CLR Calls Virtual Methods, Properties, and Events

In this section, I will be focusing on methods, but this discussion is relevant to virtual properties and virtual events as well. Properties and events are actually implemented as methods; this will be shown in their corresponding chapters.

Methods represent code that performs some operation on the type (static methods) or an instance of the type (nonstatic methods). All methods have a name, a signature, and a return value (that may be **void**). The CLR allows a type to define multiple methods with the same name as long as each method has a different set of parameters or a different return value. So it's possible to define two methods with the same name and same parameters as long as the methods have a different return type. However, except for IL assembly language, I'm not aware of any language that takes advantage of this "feature"; most languages (including C#) require that methods differ by parameters and ignore a method's return type when deter-mining uniqueness. (C# actually relaxes this restriction when defining conversion operator methods; see Chapter 8 for details.)

The **Employee** class shown below defines three different kinds of methods:

```
internal class Employee {
   // A nonvirtual instance method
   public         Int32    GetYearsEmployed() { ... }

   // A virtual method (virtual implies instance)
   public virtual String   GetProgressReport() { ... }

   // A static method
   public static  Employee Lookup(String name) { ... }
}
```

When the compiler compiles this code, the compiler emits three entries in the resulting assembly's method definition table. Each entry has flags set indicating if the method is instance, virtual, or static.

When code is written to call any of these methods, the compiler emitting the calling code examines the method definition's flags to determine how to emit the proper IL code so that the call is made correctly. The CLR offers two IL instructions for calling a method:

- The **call** IL instruction can be used to call static, instance, and virtual methods. When the **call** instruction is used to call a static method, you must specify the type that defines the method that the CLR should call. When the **call** instruction is used to call an instance or virtual method, you must specify a variable that refers to an object. The **call** instruction assumes that this variable is not **null.** In other words, the type of the variable itself indicates which type defines the method that the CLR should call. If the variable's type doesn't define the method, base types are checked for a matching method. The **call** instruction is frequently used to call a virtual method nonvirtually.

- The **callvirt** IL instruction can be used to call instance and virtual methods, not static methods. When the **callvirt** instruction is used to call an instance or virtual method, you must specify a variable that refers to an object. When the **callvirt** IL instruction is used to call a nonvirtual instance method, the type of the variable indicates which type defines the method that the CLR should call. When the **callvirt** IL instruction is used to call a virtual instance method, the CLR discovers the actual type of the object being used to make the call and then calls the method polymorphically. In order to determine the type, the variable being used to make the call must not be **null.** In other words, when compiling this call, the JIT compiler generates code that verifies that the variable's value is not **null.** If it is **null,** the **callvirt** instruction causes the CLR to throw a **NullReferenceException.** This additional check means that the **callvirt** IL instruction executes slightly more slowly than the **call** instruction. Note that this **null** check is performed even when the **callvirt** instruction is used to call a nonvirtual instance method.

So now, let's put this together to see how C# uses these different IL instructions:

```
using System;

public sealed class Program {
   public static void Main() {
      Console.WriteLine(); // Call a static method

      Object o = new Object();
      o.GetHashCode(); // Call a virtual instance method
      o.GetType();     // Call a nonvirtual instance method
   }
}
```

If you were to compile the code above and look at the resulting IL, you'd see the following:

```
.method public hidebysig static void Main() cil managed {
 .entrypoint
 // Code size 26 (0x1a)
 .maxstack 1
 .locals init (object V_0)
 IL_0000: call void System.Console::WriteLine()
 IL_0005: newobj instance void System.Object::.ctor()
 IL_000a: stloc.0
 IL_000b: ldloc.0
 IL_000c: callvirt instance int32 System.Object::GetHashCode()
 IL_0011: pop
 IL_0012: ldloc.0
 IL_0013: callvirt instance class System.Type System.Object::GetType()
 IL_0018: pop
 IL_0019: ret
} // end of method Program::Main
```

Notice that the C# compiler uses the **call** IL instruction to call **Console**'s **WriteLine** method. This is expected because **WriteLine** is a static method. Next, notice that the **callvirt** IL instruction is used to call **GetHashCode**. This is also expected, since **GetHashCode** is a virtual method. Finally, notice that the C# compiler also uses the **callvirt** IL instruction to call the **GetType** method. This is surprising since **GetType** is not a virtual method. However, this works because while JIT-compiling this code, the CLR will know that **GetType** is not a virtual method, and so the JIT-compiled code will simply call **GetType** nonvirtually.

Of course, the question is, why didn't the C# compiler simply emit the **call** instruction instead? The answer is because the C# team decided that the JIT compiler should generate code to verify that the object being used to make the call is not **null**. This means that calls to nonvirtual instance methods are a little slower than they could be. It also means that the C# code shown below will cause a **NullReferenceException** to be thrown. In some other programming languages, the intention of the code shown below would run just fine:

```
using System;

public sealed class Program {
    public Int32 GetFive() { return 5; }
    public static void Main() {
        Program p = null;
        Int32 x = p.GetFive(); // In C#, NullReferenceException is thrown
    }
}
```

Theoretically, the code above is fine. Sure, the variable **p** is **null**, but when calling a nonvirtual method (**GetFive**), the CLR needs to know just the data type of **p**, which is **Program**. If **GetFive** did get called, the value of the **this** argument would be **null**. Since the argument is not used inside the **GetFive** method, no **NullReferenceException** would be thrown. However, because the C# compiler emits a **callvirt** instruction instead of a **call** instruction, the code above will end up throwing the **NullReferenceException.**

> **Important** If you define a method as nonvirtual, you should never change the method to virtual in the future. The reason is because some compilers will call the nonvirtual method by using the **call** instruction instead of the **callvirt** instruction. If the method changes from nonvirtual to virtual and the referencing code is not recompiled, the virtual method will be called nonvirtually, causing the application to produce unpredictable behavior. If the referencing code is written in C#, this is not a problem, since C# calls all instance methods by using **callvirt.** But this could be a problem if the referencing code was written using a different programming language.

Sometimes, the compiler will use a **call** instruction to call a virtual method instead of using a **callvirt** instruction. At first, this may seem surprising, but the code below demonstrates why it is sometimes required:

```
internal class SomeClass {
    // ToString is a virtual method defined in the base class: Object.
    public override String ToString() {

        // Compiler uses the 'call' IL instruction to call
        // Object's ToString method nonvirtually.

        // If the compiler were to use 'callvirt' instead of 'call', this
        // method would call itself recursively until the stack overflowed.
        return base.ToString();
    }
}
```

When calling **base.ToString** (a virtual method), the C# compiler emits a **call** instruction to ensure that the **ToString** method in the base type is called nonvirtually. This is required because if **ToString** were called virtually, the call would execute recursively until the thread's stack overflowed, which obviously is not desired.

Compilers tend to use the **call** instruction when calling methods defined by a value type since value types are sealed. This implies that there can be no polymorphism even for their virtual methods, which causes the performance of the call to be faster. In addition, the nature of a value type instance guarantees it can never be **null,** so a **NullReferenceException** will never be thrown. Finally, if you were to call a value type's virtual method virtually, the CLR would need to have a reference to the value type's type object in order to refer to the method table within it. This requires boxing the value type. Boxing puts more pressure on the heap, forcing more frequent garbage collections and hurting performance.

Regardless of whether **call** or **callvirt** is used to call an instance or virtual method, these methods always receive a hidden **this** argument as the method's first parameter. The **this** argument refers to the object being operated on.

When designing a type, you should try to minimize the number of virtual methods you define. First, calling a virtual method is slower than calling a nonvirtual method. Second, virtual methods cannot be inlined by the JIT compiler, which further hurts performance. Third, virtual methods make versioning of components more brittle, as described in the next section. Fourth, when defining a base type, it is common to offer a set of convenience over-loaded methods. If you want these methods to be polymorphic, the best thing to do is to make the most complex method virtual and leave all of the convenience overloaded methods nonvirtual. By the way, following this guideline will also improve the ability to version a component without adversely affecting the derived types. Here is an example:

```
public class Set {
    private Int32 m_length = 0;

    // This convenience overload is not virtual
    public Int32 Find(Object value) {
        return Find(value, 0, m_length);
    }

    // This convenience overload is not virtual
    public Int32 Find(Object value, Int32 startIndex) {
        return Find(value, startIndex, m_length - startIndex);
    }

    // The most feature-rich method is virtual and can be overridden
    public virtual Int32 Find(Object value, Int32 startIndex, Int32 endIndex) {
        // Actual implementation that can be overridden goes here...
    }

    // Other methods go here
}
```

Using Type Visibility and Member Accessibility Intelligently

With the .NET Framework, applications are composed of types defined in multiple assemblies produced by various companies. This means that the developer has little control over the components he or she is using and the types defined within those components. The developer typically doesn't have access to the source code (and probably doesn't even know what programming language was used to create the component), and components tend to version with different schedules. Furthermore, due to polymorphism and protected members, a base class developer must trust the code written by the derived class developer. And, of course, the developer of a derived class must trust the code that he is inheriting from a base class. These are just some of the issues that you need to really think about when designing components and types.

In this section, I'd like to say just a few words about how to design a type with these issues in mind. Specifically, I'm going to focus on the proper way to set type visibility and member accessibility so that you'll be most successful.

First, when defining a new type, compilers should make the class sealed by default so that the class cannot be used as a base class. Instead, many compilers, including C#, default to unsealed classes and allow the programmer to explicitly mark a class as sealed by using the **sealed** keyword. Obviously, it is too late now, but I think that today's compilers have chosen the wrong default and it would be nice if this could change with future compilers. There are three reasons why a sealed class is better than an unsealed class:

- **Versioning**   When a class is originally sealed, it can change to unsealed in the future without breaking compatibility. However, once a class is unsealed, you can never change it to sealed in the future as this would break all derived classes. In addition, if the unsealed class defines any unsealed virtual methods, ordering of the virtual method calls must be maintained with new versions or there is the potential of breaking derived types in the future.

- **Performance**   As discussed in the previous section, calling a virtual method doesn't perform as well as calling a nonvirtual method because the CLR must look up the type of the object at runtime in order to determine which type defines the method to call. However, if the JIT compiler sees a call to a virtual method using a sealed type, the JIT compiler can produce more efficient code by calling the method nonvirtually. It can do this because it knows there can't possibly be a derived class if the class is sealed. For example, in the code below, the JIT compiler can call the virtual **ToString** method nonvirtually:

```
using System;
public sealed class Point {
    private Int32 m_x, m_y;

    public Point(Int32 x, Int32 y) { m_x = x; m_y = y; }
```

```
    public override String ToString() {
       return String.Format("({0}, {1})", m_x, m_y);
    }

    public static void Main() {
       Point p = new Point(3, 4);

       // The C# compiler emits the callvirt instruction here but the
       // JIT compiler will optimize this call and produce code that
       // calls ToString nonvirtually because p's type is Point,
       // which is a sealed class
       Console.WriteLine(p.ToString());
    }
}
```

- **Security and predictability**   A class must protect its own state and not allow itself to ever become corrupted. When a class is unsealed, a derived class can access and manipulate the base class's state if any data fields or methods that internally manipulate fields are accessible and not private. In addition, a virtual method can be overridden by a derived class, and the derived class can decide whether to call the base class's implementation. By making a method, property, or event virtual, the base class is giving up some control over its behavior and its state. Unless carefully thought out, this can cause the object to behave unpredictably, and it opens up potential security holes.

The problem with a sealed class is that it can be a big inconvenience to users of the type. Occasionally, developers want to create a class derived from an existing type in order to attach some additional fields or state information for their application's own use. In fact, they may even want to define some helper or convenience methods on the derived type to manipulate these additional fields. Since sealed classes restrict this ability, I made a proposal to the CLR team that they introduce a new class modifier called **closed.**

A closed class can be used as a base class, but its behavior is closed and not subject to interference by a derived class. Basically, a closed base class would prohibit a derived class from accessing any of the base class's non-public members. This would allow the base class to change with the knowledge that it will not impact a derived class. Ideally, compilers would change the default access modifier for types to **closed** because this would be the safest choice without being too restrictive. It is too early to know if this idea will make its way into the CLR and programming languages. However, I am very hopeful it will someday.

By the way, you could almost accomplish today what **closed** is designed to do; it's just that it is very inconvenient. Basically, when you implement your class, make sure you seal all the virtual methods you inherit (including the methods defined by **System.Object**). Also, don't define any methods that may become a versioning burden in the future such as protected or virtual methods. Here is an example:

```
public class SimulatedClosedClass : Object {
   public sealed override Boolean Equals(Object obj) {
      return base.Equals(obj);
   }
   public sealed override Int32 GetHashCode() {
      return base.GetHashCode();
   }
   public sealed override String ToString() {
      return base.ToString();
   }
   // Unfortunately, C# won't let you seal the Finalize method

   // Define additional public or private members here...
   // Do not define any protected or virtual members
}
```

Unfortunately, the compilers and the CLR do not support closed types today. Here are the guidelines I follow when I define my own classes:

- When defining a class, I always explicitly make it **sealed** unless I truly intend for the class to be a base class that allows specialization by derived classes. As stated earlier, this is the opposite of what C# and many other compilers default to today. I also default to making the class **internal** unless I want the class to be publicly exposed outside of my assembly. Fortunately, if you do not explicitly indicate a type's visibility, the C# compiler defaults to internal. If I really feel that it is important to define a class that others can derive but I do not want to allow specialization, I will simulate creating a closed class by using the above technique of sealing the virtual methods that my class inherits.

- Inside the class, I always define my data fields as **private** and I never waver on this. Fortunately, C# does default to making fields **private.** I'd actually prefer it if C# mandated that all fields be private and that you could not make fields **protected, internal, public,** and so on. Exposing state is the easiest way to get into problems, have your object behave unpredictably, and open potential security holes. This is true even if you just declare some fields as **internal.** Even within a single assembly, it is too hard to track all code that references a field, especially if several developers are writing code that gets compiled into the same assembly.

- Inside the class, I always define my methods, properties, and events as **private** and nonvirtual. Fortunately, C# defaults to this as well. Certainly, I'll make a method, property, or event **public** to expose some functionality from the type. I try to avoid making any of these members **protected** or **internal,** as this would be exposing my type to some potential vulnerability. However, I would sooner make a member **protected** or **internal** than I would make a member **virtual** because a virtual member gives up a lot of control and really relies on the proper behavior of the derived class.

- There is an old OOP adage that goes like this: when things get too complicated, make more types. When an implementation of some algorithm starts to get complicated, I define helper types that encapsulate discrete pieces of functionality. If I'm defining these helper types for use by a single über-type, I'll define the helper types nested within the über-type. This allows for scoping and also allows the code in the nested, helper type to reference the private members defined in the über-type. However, there is a design guideline rule, enforced by the Code Analysis tool (FxCopCmd.exe) in Visual Studio, which indicates that publicly exposed nested types should be defined at file or assembly scope and not be defined within another type. This rule exists because some developers find the syntax for referencing nested types cumbersome. I appreciate this rule, and I never define public nested types.

Dealing with Virtual Methods When Versioning Types

As was stated earlier, in a Component Software Programming environment, versioning is a very important issue. I talked about some of these versioning issues in Chapter 3, "Shared Assemblies and Strongly Named Assemblies," when I explained strongly named assemblies and discussed how an administrator can ensure that an application binds to the assemblies that it was built and tested with. However, other versioning issues cause source code compatibility problems. For example, you must be very careful when adding or modifying members of a type if that type is used as a base type. Let's look at some examples.

CompanyA has designed the following type, **Phone:**

```
namespace CompanyA {
   public class Phone {
      public void Dial() {
         Console.WriteLine("Phone.Dial");
         // Do work to dial the phone here.
      }
   }
}
```

Now imagine that CompanyB defines another type, **BetterPhone,** which uses CompanyA's **Phone** type as its base:

```
namespace CompanyB {
   public class BetterPhone : CompanyA.Phone {
      public void Dial() {
         Console.WriteLine("BetterPhone.Dial");
         EstablishConnection();
         base.Dial();
      }

      protected virtual void EstablishConnection() {
         Console.WriteLine("BetterPhone.EstablishConnection");
         // Do work to establish the connection.
      }
   }
}
```

When CompanyB attempts to compile its code, the C# compiler issues the following message: "**warning CS0108: 'CompanyB.BetterPhone.Dial()' hides inherited member 'CompanyA.Phone.Dial()'. Use the new keyword if hiding was intended.**" This warning is notifying the developer that **BetterPhone** is defining a **Dial** method, which will hide the **Dial** method defined in **Phone.** This new method could change the semantic meaning of **Dial** (as defined by CompanyA when it originally created the **Dial** method).

It's a very nice feature of the compiler to warn you of this potential semantic mismatch. The compiler also tells you how to remove the warning by adding the **new** keyword before the definition of **Dial** in the **BetterPhone** class. Here's the fixed **BetterPhone** class:

```
namespace CompanyB {
    public class BetterPhone : CompanyA.Phone {

        // This Dial method has nothing to do with Phone's Dial method.
        public new void Dial() {
            Console.WriteLine("BetterPhone.Dial");
            EstablishConnection();
            base.Dial();
        }

        protected virtual void EstablishConnection() {
            Console.WriteLine("BetterPhone.EstablishConnection");
            // Do work to establish the connection.
        }
    }
}
```

At this point, CompanyB can use **BetterPhone.Dial** in its application. Here's some sample code that CompanyB might write:

```
public sealed class Program {
    public static void Main() {
        CompanyB.BetterPhone phone = new CompanyB.BetterPhone();
        phone.Dial();
    }
}
```

When this code runs, the following output is displayed:

```
BetterPhone.Dial
BetterPhone.EstablishConnection
Phone.Dial
```

This output shows that CompanyB is getting the behavior it desires. The call to **Dial** is calling the new **Dial** method defined by **BetterPhone,** which calls the virtual **EstablishConnection** method and then calls the **Phone** base type's **Dial** method.

Now let's imagine that several companies have decided to use CompanyA's **Phone** type. Let's further imagine that these other companies have decided that the ability to establish a connection in the **Dial** method is a really useful feature. This feedback is given to CompanyA, which now revises its **Phone** class:

```
namespace CompanyA {
    public class Phone {
        public void Dial() {
            Console.WriteLine("Phone.Dial");
            EstablishConnection();
            // Do work to dial the phone here.
        }

        protected virtual void EstablishConnection() {
            Console.WriteLine("Phone.EstablishConnection");
            // Do work to establish the connection.
        }
    }
}
```

Now when CompanyB compiles its **BetterPhone** type (derived from this new version of CompanyA's **Phone**), the compiler issues this message: **"warning CS0114: 'CompanyB.BetterPhone.EstablishConnection()' hides inherited member 'CompanyA.Phone.EstablishConnection()'. To make the current member override that implementation, add the override keyword. Otherwise, add the new keyword."**

The compiler is alerting you to the fact that both **Phone** and **BetterPhone** offer an **EstablishConnection** method and that the semantics of both might not be identical; simply recompiling **BetterPhone** can no longer give the same behavior as it did when using the first version of the **Phone** type.

If CompanyB decides that the **EstablishConnection** methods are not semantically identical in both types, CompanyB can tell the compiler that the **Dial** and **EstablishConnection** method defined in **BetterPhone** is the correct method to use and that it has no relationship with the **EstablishConnection** method defined in the **Phone** base type. CompanyB informs the compiler of this by adding the **new** keyword to the **EstablishConnection** method:

```
namespace CompanyB {
    public class BetterPhone : CompanyA.Phone {

        // Keep 'new' to mark this method as having no
        // relationship to the base type's Dial method.
        public new void Dial() {
            Console.WriteLine("BetterPhone.Dial");
            EstablishConnection();
            base.Dial();
        }

        // Add 'new' to mark this method as having no
        // relationship to the base type's EstablishConnection method.
        protected new virtual void EstablishConnection() {
            Console.WriteLine("BetterPhone.EstablishConnection");
            // Do work to establish the connection.
        }
    }
}
```

In this code, the **new** keyword tells the compiler to emit metadata, making it clear to the CLR that **BetterPhone**'s **EstablishConnection** method is intended to be treated as a new function that is introduced by the **BetterPhone** type. The CLR will know that there is no relationship between **Phone**'s and **BetterPhone**'s methods.

When the same application code (in the **Main** method) executes, the output is as follows:

```
BetterPhone.Dial
BetterPhone.EstablishConnection
Phone.Dial
Phone.EstablishConnection
```

This output shows that **Main**'s call to **Dial** calls the new **Dial** method defined by **BetterPhone.Dial**, which in turn calls the virtual **EstablishConnection** method that is also defined by **BetterPhone**. When **BetterPhone**'s **EstablishConnection** method returns, **Phone**'s **Dial** method is called. **Phone**'s **Dial** method calls **EstablishConnection,** but because **BetterPhone**'s **EstablishConnection** is marked with **new, BetterPhone**'s **EstablishConnection** method isn't considered an override of **Phone**'s virtual **EstablishConnection** method. As a result, **Phone**'s **Dial** method calls **Phone**'s **EstablishConnection** method—this is the expected behavior.

> **Note** If the compiler treated methods as overrides by default (as a native C++ compiler does), the developer of **BetterPhone** couldn't use the method names **Dial** and **EstablishConnection.** This would most likely cause a ripple effect of changes throughout the entire source code base, breaking source and binary compatibility. This type of pervasive change is undesirable, especially in any moderate-to-large project. However, if changing the method name causes only moderate updates in the source code, you should change the name of the methods so the two different meanings of **Dial** and **EstablishConnection** don't confuse other developers.

Alternatively, CompanyB could have gotten the new version of CompanyA's **Phone** type and decided that **Phone**'s semantics of **Dial** and **EstablishConnection** are exactly what it's been looking for. In this case, CompanyB would modify its **BetterPhone** type by removing its **Dial** method entirely. In addition, because CompanyB now wants to tell the compiler that **BetterPhone**'s **EstablishConnection** method is related to **Phone**'s **EstablishConnection** method, the **new** keyword must be removed. Simply removing the **new** keyword isn't enough, though, because now the compiler can't tell exactly what the intention is of **BetterPhone**'s **EstablishConnection** method. To express his intent exactly, the CompanyB developer must also change **BetterPhone**'s **EstablishConnection** method from **virtual** to **override.** The following code shows the new version of **BetterPhone**:

```
namespace CompanyB {
   public class BetterPhone : CompanyA.Phone {

   // Delete the Dial method (inherit Dial from base).

   // Remove 'new' and change 'virtual' to 'override' to
   // mark this method as having a relationship to the base
   // type's EstablishConnection method.
   protected override void EstablishConnection() {
      Console.WriteLine("BetterPhone.EstablishConnection");
      // Do work to establish the connection.
   }
 }
}
```

Now when the same application code (in the **Main** method) executes, the output is as follows:

```
Phone.Dial
BetterPhone.EstablishConnection
```

This output shows that **Main**'s call to **Dial** calls the **Dial** method defined by **Phone** and inherited by **BetterPhone.** Then when **Phone**'s **Dial** method calls the virtual **EstablishConnection** method, **BetterPhone**'s **EstablishConnection** method is called because it overrides the virtual **EstablishConnection** method defined by **Phone**.

Chapter 7
Constants and Fields

In this chapter, I'll show you how to add data members to a type. Specifically, we'll look at constants and fields.

Constants

A *constant* is a symbol that has a never-changing value. When defining a constant symbol, its value must be determinable at compile time. The compiler then saves the constant's value in the assembly's metadata. This means that you can define a constant only for types that your compiler considers primitive types. In C#, the following types are primitives and can be used to define constants: **Boolean**, **Char**, **Byte**, **SByte**, **Int16**, **UInt16**, **Int32**, **UInt32**, **Int64**, **UInt64**, **Single**, **Double**, **Decimal**, and **String**. However, C# also allows you to define a constant variable of a non-primitive type if you set the value to **null**:

```
using System;

public sealed class SomeType {
   // SomeType is not a primitive type but C# does allow
   // a constant variable of this type to be set to 'null'.
   public const SomeType Empty = null;
}
```

Because a constant value never changes, constants are always considered to be part of the defining type. In other words, constants are always considered to be static members, not instance members. Defining a constant causes the creation of metadata.

When code refers to a constant symbol, compilers look up the symbol in the metadata of the assembly that defines the constant, extract the constant's value, and embed the value in the emitted Intermediate Language (IL) code. Because a constant's value is embedded directly in code, constants don't require any memory to be allocated for them at runtime. In addition, you can't get the address of a constant and you can't pass a constant by reference. These constraints also mean that constants don't have a good cross-assembly versioning story, so you should use them only when you know that the value of a symbol will never change.

(Defining **MaxInt16** as **32767** is a good example.) Let me demonstrate exactly what I mean. First, take the following code and compile it into a DLL assembly:

```
using System;

public sealed class SomeLibraryType {
   // NOTE: C# doesn't allow you to specify static for constants
   // because constants are always implicitly static.
   public const Int32 MaxEntriesInList = 50;
}
```

Then use the following code to build an application assembly:

```
using System;

public sealed class Program {
   public static void Main() {
      Console.WriteLine("Max entries supported in list: "
         + SomeLibraryType.MaxEntriesInList);
   }
}
```

You'll notice that this application code references the **MaxEntriesInList** constant defined in the **SomeLibraryType** class. When the compiler builds the application code, it sees that **MaxEntriesInList** is a constant literal with a value of **50** and embeds the **Int32** value of **50** right inside the application's IL code, as you can see in the IL code shown below. In fact, after building the application assembly, the DLL assembly isn't even loaded at runtime and can be deleted from the disk.

```
.method public hidebysig static void  Main() cil managed
{
  .entrypoint
  // Code size       25 (0x19)
  .maxstack  8
  IL_0000:  nop
  IL_0001:  ldstr      "Max entries supported in list: "
  IL_0006:  ldc.i4.s   50
  IL_0008:  box        [mscorlib]System.Int32
  IL_000d:  call       string [mscorlib]System.String::Concat(object, object)
  IL_0012:  call       void [mscorlib]System.Console::WriteLine(string)
  IL_0017:  nop
  IL_0018:  ret
} // end of method Program::Main
```

This example should make the versioning problem obvious to you. If the developer changes the **MaxEntriesInList** constant to **1000** and only rebuilds the DLL assembly, the application assembly is not affected. For the application to pick up the new value, it will have to be re-compiled as well. You can't use constants if you need to have a value in one assembly picked up by another assembly at runtime (instead of compile time). Instead, you can use **readonly** fields, which I'll discuss next.

Fields

A *field* is a data member that holds an instance of a value type or a reference to a reference type. Table 7-1 shows the modifiers that can be applied to a field.

TABLE 7-1 Field Modifiers

CLR Term	C# Term	Description
Static	`static`	The field is part of the type's state, as opposed to being part of an object's state.
Instance	(default)	The field is associated with an instance of the type, not the type itself.
InitOnly	`readonly`	The field can be written to only by code contained in a constructor method.
Volatile	`volatile`	Code that accessed the field is not subject to some thread-unsafe optimizations that may be performed by the compiler, the CLR, or by hardware. Only the following types can be marked `volatile`: all reference types, `Single`, `Boolean`, `Byte`, `SByte`, `Int16`, `UInt16`, `Int32`, `UInt32`, `Char`, and all enumerated types with an underlying type of `Byte`, `SByte`, `Int16`, `UInt16`, `Int32`, or `UInt32`. Volatile fields are discussed in Chapter 28, "Primitive Thread Synchronization Constructs."

As Table 7-1 shows, the common language runtime (CLR) supports both type (static) and instance (nonstatic) fields. For type fields, the dynamic memory required to hold the field's data is allocated inside the type object, which is created when the type is loaded into an AppDomain (see Chapter 22, "CLR Hosting and AppDomains"), which typically happens the first time any method that references the type is just-in-time (JIT)–compiled. For instance fields, the dynamic memory to hold the field is allocated when an instance of the type is constructed.

Because fields are stored in dynamic memory, their value can be obtained at runtime only. Fields also solve the versioning problem that exists with constants. In addition, a field can be of any data type, so you don't have to restrict yourself to your compiler's built-in primitive types (as you do for constants).

The CLR supports **readonly** fields and **read/write** fields. Most fields are **read/write** fields, meaning the field's value might change multiple times as the code executes. However, **readonly** fields can be written to only within a constructor method (which is called only once, when an object is first created). Compilers and verification ensure that **readonly** fields are not written to by any method other than a constructor. Note that reflection can be used to modify a **readonly** field.

Let's take the example from the "Constants" section and fix the versioning problem by using a static **readonly** field. Here's the new version of the DLL assembly's code:

```
using System;

public sealed class SomeLibraryType {
    // The static is required to associate the field with the type.
    public static readonly Int32 MaxEntriesInList = 50;
}
```

This is the only change you have to make; the application code doesn't have to change at all, although you must rebuild it to see the new behavior. Now when the application's **Main** method runs, the CLR will load the DLL assembly (so this assembly is now required at run time) and grab the value of the **MaxEntriesInList** field out of the dynamic memory allocated for it. Of course, the value will be **50**.

Let's say that the developer of the DLL assembly changes the **50** to **1000** and rebuilds the assembly. When the application code is re-executed, it will automatically pick up the new value: **1000**. In this case, the application code doesn't have to be rebuilt—it just works (although its performance is adversely affected). A caveat: this scenario assumes that the new version of the DLL assembly is not strongly named and the versioning policy of the application is such that the CLR loads this new version.

The following example shows how to define a **readonly** static field that is associated with the type itself, as well as **read/write** static fields and **readonly** and **read/write** instance fields, as shown here:

```
public sealed class SomeType {
    // This is a static read-only field; its value is calculated and
    // stored in memory when this class is initialized at run time.
    public static readonly Random s_random = new Random();

    // This is a static read/write field.
    private static Int32 s_numberOfWrites = 0;

    // This is an instance read-only field.
    public readonly String Pathname = "Untitled";

    // This is an instance read/write field.
    private System.IO.FileStream m_fs;

    public SomeType(String pathname) {
        // This line changes a read-only field.
        // This is OK because the code is in a constructor.
        this.Pathname = pathname;
    }

    public String DoSomething() {
        // This line reads and writes to the static read/write field.
        s_numberOfWrites = s_numberOfWrites + 1;

        // This line reads the read-only instance field.
        return Pathname;
    }
}
```

In this code, many of the fields are initialized inline. C# allows you to use this convenient inline initialization syntax to initialize a class's constants and **read/write** and **readonly** fields. As you'll see in Chapter 8, "Methods," C# treats initializing a field inline as shorthand syntax for initializing the field in a constructor. Also, in C#, there are some performance issues to consider when initializing fields by using inline syntax versus assignment syntax in a constructor. These performance issues are discussed in Chapter 8 as well.

> **Important** When a field is of a reference type and the field is marked as **readonly**, it is the reference that is immutable, not the object that the field refers to. The following code demonstrates:
>
> ```
> public sealed class AType {
>     // InvalidChars must always refer to the same array object
>     public static readonly Char[] InvalidChars = new Char[] { 'A', 'B', 'C' };
> }
>
> public sealed class AnotherType {
>     public static void M() {
>         // The lines below are legal, compile, and successfully
>         // change the characters in the InvalidChars array
>         AType.InvalidChars[0] = 'X';
>         AType.InvalidChars[1] = 'Y';
>         AType.InvalidChars[2] = 'Z';
>
>         // The line below is illegal and will not compile because
>         // what InvalidChars refers to cannot be changed
>         AType.InvalidChars = new Char[] { 'X', 'Y', 'Z' };
>     }
> }
> ```

Chapter 8
Methods

This chapter focuses on the various kinds of methods that you'll run into, including instance constructors and type constructors, as well as how to define methods to overload operators and type conversions (for implicit and explicit casting). We'll also talk about extension methods, which allow you to logically add your own instance methods to already existing types, and partial methods, which allow you to spread a type's implementation into multiple parts.

Instance Constructors and Classes (Reference Types)

Constructors are special methods that allow an instance of a type to be initialized to a good state. Constructor methods are always called .ctor (for *constructor*) in a method definition metadata table. When creating an instance of a reference type, memory is allocated for the instance's data fields, the object's overhead fields (type object pointer and sync block index) are initialized, and then the type's instance constructor is called to set the initial state of the object.

When constructing a reference type object, the memory allocated for the object is always zeroed out before the type's instance constructor is called. Any fields that the constructor doesn't explicitly overwrite are guaranteed to have a value of **0** or **null**.

Unlike other methods, instance constructors are never inherited. That is, a class has only the instance constructors that the class itself defines. Since instance constructors are never inherited, you cannot apply the following modifiers to an instance constructor: **virtual**, **new**, **override**, **sealed**, or **abstract**. If you define a class that does not explicitly define any constructors, the C# compiler defines a default (parameterless) constructor for you whose implementation simply calls the base class's parameterless constructor.

For example, if you define the following class:

```
public class SomeType {
}
```

it is as though you wrote the code like this:

```
public class SomeType {
    public SomeType() : base() { }
}
```

If the class is **abstract**, the compiler-produced default constructor has **protected** accessibility; otherwise, the constructor is given **public** accessibility. If the base class doesn't offer a parameterless constructor, the derived class must explicitly call a base class constructor or the compiler will issue an error. If the class is **static** (**sealed** and **abstract**), the compiler will not emit a default constructor at all into the class definition.

A type can define several instance constructors. Each constructor must have a different signature, and each can have different accessibility. For verifiable code, a class's instance constructor must call its base class's constructor before accessing any of the inherited fields of the base class. The C# compiler will generate a call to the default base class's constructor automatically if the derived class's constructor does not explicitly invoke one of the base class's constructors. Ultimately, **System.Object**'s public, parameterless constructor gets called. This constructor does nothing—it simply returns. This is because **System.Object** defines no instance data fields, and therefore its constructor has nothing to do.

In a few situations, an instance of a type can be created without an instance constructor being called. In particular, calling **Object**'s **MemberwiseClone** method allocates memory, initializes the object's overhead fields, and then copies the source object's bytes to the new object. Also, a constructor is usually not called when deserializing an object with the runtime serializer. The deserialization code allocates memory for the object without calling a constructor using the **System.Runtime.Serialization.FormatterServices** type's **GetUninitializedObject** or **GetSafeUninitializedObject** methods (as discussed in Chapter 24, "Runtime Serialization").

> **Important** You should not call any virtual methods within a constructor that can affect the object being constructed. The reason is if the virtual method is overridden in the type being instantiated, the derived type's implementation of the overridden method will execute, but all of the fields in the hierarchy have not been fully initialized. Calling a virtual method would therefore result in unpredictable behavior.

C# offers a simple syntax that allows the initialization of fields defined within a reference type when an instance of the type is constructed:

```
internal sealed class SomeType {
    private Int32 m_x = 5;
}
```

When a **SomeType** object is constructed, its **m_x** field will be initialized to **5**. How does this happen? Well, if you examine the Intermediate Language (IL) for **SomeType**'s constructor method (also called **.ctor**), you'll see the code shown here:

```
.method public hidebysig specialname rtspecialname
        instance void  .ctor() cil managed
{
  // Code size        14 (0xe)
  .maxstack   8
  IL_0000:  ldarg.0
  IL_0001:  ldc.i4.5
  IL_0002:  stfld        int32 SomeType::m_x
  IL_0007:  ldarg.0
  IL_0008:  call         instance void [mscorlib]System.Object::.ctor()
  IL_000d:  ret
} // end of method SomeType::.ctor
```

In this code, you see that **SomeType**'s constructor contains code to store a **5** into **m_x** and then calls the base class's constructor. In other words, the C# compiler allows the convenient syntax that lets you initialize the instance fields inline and translates this to code in the constructor method to perform the initialization. This means that you should be aware of code explosion, as illustrated by the following class definition:

```
internal sealed class SomeType {
    private Int32  m_x = 5;
    private String m_s = "Hi there";
    private Double m_d = 3.14159;
    private Byte   m_b;

    // Here are some constructors.
    public SomeType()         { ... }
    public SomeType(Int32 x)  { ... }
    public SomeType(String s) { ...; m_d = 10; }
}
```

When the compiler generates code for the three constructor methods, the beginning of each method includes the code to initialize **m_x**, **m_s**, and **m_d**. After this initialization code, the compiler inserts a call to the base class's constructor, and then the compiler appends to the method the code that appears in the constructor methods. For example, the code generated for the constructor that takes a **String** parameter includes the code to initialize **m_x**, **m_s**, and **m_d**, call the base class's (**Object**'s) constructor, and then overwrite **m_d** with the value **10**. Note that **m_b** is guaranteed to be initialized to **0** even though no code exists to explicitly initialize it.

> **Note** The compiler initializes any fields using the convenient syntax before calling a base class's constructor to maintain the impression that these fields always have a value as the source code appearance dictates. The potential problem occurs when a base class's constructor invokes a virtual method that calls back into a method defined by the derived class. If this happens, the fields initialized using the convenient syntax have been initialized before the virtual method is called.

Because there are three constructors in the preceding class, the compiler generates the code to initialize **m_x**, **m_s**, and **m_d** three times—once per constructor. If you have several initialized instance fields and a lot of overloaded constructor methods, you should consider defining the fields without the initialization, creating a single constructor that performs the common initialization, and having each constructor explicitly call the common initialization constructor. This approach will reduce the size of the generated code. Here is an example using C#'s ability to explicitly have a constructor call another constructor by using the **this** keyword:

```csharp
internal sealed class SomeType {
    // Do not explicitly initialize the fields here
    private Int32  m_x;
    private String m_s;
    private Double m_d;
    private Byte   m_b;

    // This constructor sets all fields to their default.
    // All of the other constructors explicitly invoke this constructor.
    public SomeType() {
        m_x = 5;
        m_s = "Hi there";
        m_d = 3.14159;
        m_b = 0xff;
    }

    // This constructor sets all fields to their default, then changes m_x.
    public SomeType(Int32 x) : this() {
        m_x = x;
    }

    // This constructor sets all fields to their default, then changes m_s.
    public SomeType(String s) : this() {
        m_s = s;
    }

    // This constructor sets all fields to their default, then changes m_x & m_s.
    public SomeType(Int32 x, String s) : this() {
        m_x = x;
        m_s = s;
    }
}
```

Instance Constructors and Structures (Value Types)

Value type (**struct**) constructors work quite differently from reference type (**class**) constructors. The common language runtime (CLR) always allows the creation of value type instances, and there is no way to prevent a value type from being instantiated. For this reason, value types don't actually even need to have a constructor defined within them, and the C# compiler doesn't emit default parameterless constructors for value types. Examine the following code:

```
internal struct Point {
   public Int32 m_x, m_y;
}
internal sealed class Rectangle {
   public Point m_topLeft, m_bottomRight;
}
```

To construct a **Rectangle**, the **new** operator must be used, and a constructor must be specified. In this case, the default constructor automatically generated by the C# compiler is called. When memory is allocated for the **Rectangle**, the memory includes the two instances of the **Point** value type. For performance reasons, the CLR doesn't attempt to call a constructor for each value type field contained within the reference type. But as I mentioned earlier, the fields of the value types are initialized to **0/null**.

The CLR does allow you to define constructors on value types. The only way that these constructors will execute is if you write code to explicitly call one of them, as in **Rectangle**'s constructor, shown here:

```
internal struct Point {
   public Int32 m_x, m_y;

   public Point(Int32 x, Int32 y) {
      m_x = x;
      m_y = y;
   }
}

internal sealed class Rectangle {
   public Point m_topLeft, m_bottomRight;

   public Rectangle() {
      // In C#, new on a value type calls the constructor to
      // initialize the value type's fields.
      m_topLeft    = new Point(1, 2);
      m_bottomRight = new Point(100, 200);
   }
}
```

A value type's instance constructor is executed only when explicitly called. So if **Rectangle**'s constructor didn't initialize its **m_topLeft** and **m_bottomRight** fields by using the **new** operator to call **Point**'s constructor, the **m_x** and **m_y** fields in both **Point** fields would be **0**.

In the **Point** value type defined earlier, no default parameterless constructor is defined. However, let's rewrite that code as follows:

```
internal struct Point {
   public Int32 m_x, m_y;

   public Point() {
      m_x = m_y = 5;
   }
}

internal sealed class Rectangle {
   public Point m_topLeft, m_bottomRight;

   public Rectangle() {
   }
}
```

Now when a new **Rectangle** is constructed, what do you think the **m_x** and **m_y** fields in the two **Point** fields, **m_topLeft** and **m_bottomRight**, would be initialized to: **0** or **5**? (Hint: This is a trick question.)

Many developers (especially those with a C++ background) would expect the C# compiler to emit code in **Rectangle**'s constructor that automatically calls **Point**'s default parameterless constructor for the **Rectangle**'s two fields. However, to improve the runtime performance of the application, the C# compiler doesn't automatically emit this code. In fact, many compilers will never emit code to call a value type's default constructor automatically, even if the value type offers a parameterless constructor. To have a value type's parameterless constructor execute, the developer must add explicit code to call a value type's constructor.

Based on the information in the preceding paragraph, you should expect the **m_x** and **m_y** fields in **Rectangle**'s two **Point** fields to be initialized to **0** in the code shown earlier because there are no explicit calls to **Point**'s constructor anywhere in the code.

However, I did say that my original question was a trick question. The trick part is that C# doesn't allow a value type to define a parameterless constructor. So the previous code won't actually compile. The C# compiler produces the following message when attempting to compile that code: **"error CS0568: Structs cannot contain explicit parameterless constructors."**

C# purposely disallows value types from defining parameterless constructors to remove any confusion a developer might have about when that constructor gets called. If the constructor can't be defined, the compiler can never generate code to call it automatically. Without a parameterless constructor, a value type's fields are always initialized to **0/null**.

> **Note** Strictly speaking, value type fields are guaranteed to be **0/null** when the value type is a field nested within a reference type. However, stack-based value type fields are not guaranteed to be **0/null**. For verifiability, any stack-based value type field must be written to prior to being read. If code could read a value type's field prior to writing to the field, a security breach is possible. C# and other compilers that produce verifiable code ensure that all stack-based value types have their fields zeroed out or at least written to before being read so that a verification exception won't be thrown at run time. For the most part, this means that you can assume that your value types have their fields initialized to **0**, and you can completely ignore everything in this note.

Keep in mind that although C# doesn't allow value types with parameterless constructors, the CLR does. So if the unobvious behavior described earlier doesn't bother you, you can use another programming language (such as IL assembly language) to define your value type with a parameterless constructor.

Because C# doesn't allow value types with parameterless constructors, compiling the following type produces the following message: **"error CS0573: 'SomeValType.m_x': cannot have instance field initializers in structs."**

```
internal struct SomeValType {
    // You cannot do inline instance field initialization in a value type
    private Int32 m_x = 5;
}
```

In addition, because verifiable code requires that every field of a value type be written to prior to any field being read, any constructors that you do have for a value type must initialize all of the type's fields. The following type defines a constructor for the value type but fails to initialize all of the fields:

```
internal struct SomeValType {
    private Int32 m_x, m_y;

    // C# allows value types to have constructors that take parameters.
    public SomeValType(Int32 x) {
        m_x = x;
        // Notice that m_y is not initialized here.
    }
}
```

When compiling this type, the C# compiler produces the following message: **"error CS0171: Field 'SomeValType.m_y' must be fully assigned before control leaves the constructor."** To fix the problem, assign a value (usually **0**) to **y** in the constructor.

As an alternative way to initialize all the fields of a value type, you can actually do this:

```
// C# allows value types to have constructors that take parameters.
public SomeValType(Int32 x) {
   // Looks strange but compiles fine and initializes all fields to 0/null
   this = new SomeValType();

   m_x = x; // Overwrite m_x's 0 with x
   // Notice that m_y was initialized to 0.
}
```

In a value type's constructor, **this** represents an instance of the value type itself and you can actually assign to it the result of **new**ing up an instance of the value type, which really just zeroes out all the fields. In a reference type's constructor, **this** is considered read-only and so you cannot assign to it at all.

Type Constructors

In addition to instance constructors, the CLR also supports type constructors (also known as *static constructors, class constructors,* or *type initializers*). A type constructor can be applied to interfaces (although C# doesn't allow this), reference types, and value types. Just as instance constructors are used to set the initial state of an instance of a type, type constructors are used to set the initial state of a type. By default, types don't have a type constructor defined within them. If a type has a type constructor, it can have no more than one. In addition, type constructors never have parameters. In C#, here's how to define a reference type and a value type that have type constructors:

```
internal sealed class SomeRefType {
   static SomeRefType() {
      // This executes the first time a SomeRefType is accessed.
   }
}

internal struct SomeValType {
   // C# does allow value types to define parameterless type constructors.
   static SomeValType() {
      // This executes the first time a SomeValType is accessed.
   }
}
```

You'll notice that you define type constructors just as you would parameterless instance constructors, except that you must mark them as **static**. Also, type constructors should always be private; C# makes them **private** for you automatically. In fact, if you explicitly mark a type constructor as **private** (or anything else) in your source code, the C# compiler issues the following error: **"error CS0515: 'SomeValType.SomeValType()': access modifiers are not allowed on static constructors."** Type constructors should be private to prevent any developer-written code from calling them; the CLR is always capable of calling a type constructor.

> **Important** While you can define a type constructor within a value type, you should never actu-ally do this because there are times when the CLR will not call a value type's static type construc-tor. Here is an example:
>
> ```
> internal struct SomeValType {
>    static SomeValType() {
>       Console.WriteLine("This never gets displayed");
>    }
>    public Int32 m_x;
> }
>
> public sealed class Program {
>    public static void Main() {
>       SomeValType[] a = new SomeValType[10];
>       a[0].m_x = 123;
>       Console.WriteLine(a[0].m_x);    // Displays 123
>    }
> }
> ```

The calling of a type constructor is a tricky thing. When the just-in-time (JIT) compiler is compiling a method, it sees what types are referenced in the code. If any of the types define a type constructor, the JIT compiler checks if the type's type constructor has already been executed for this AppDomain. If the constructor has never executed, the JIT compiler emits a call to the type constructor into the native code that the JIT compiler is emitting. If the type constructor for the type has already executed, the JIT compiler does not emit the call since it knows that the type is already initialized. (For an example of this, see the "Type Constructor Performance" section later in this chapter.)

Now, after the method has been JIT-compiled, the thread starts to execute it and will eventu-ally get to the code that calls the type constructor. In fact, it is possible that multiple threads will be executing the same method concurrently. The CLR wants to ensure that a type's con-structor executes only once per AppDomain. To guarantee this, when a type constructor is called, the calling thread acquires a mutually exclusive thread synchronization lock. So if multiple threads attempt to simultaneously call a type's static constructor, only one thread will acquire the lock and the other threads will block. The first thread will execute the code in the static constructor. After the first thread leaves the constructor, the waiting threads will wake up and will see that the constructor's code has already been executed. These threads will not execute the code again; they will simply return from the constructor method. In addition, if any of these methods ever get called again, the CLR knows that the type constructor has already executed and will ensure that the constructor is not called again.

> **Note** Since the CLR guarantees that a type constructor executes only once per AppDomain and is thread-safe, a type constructor is a great place to initialize any singleton objects required by the type.

Within a single thread, there is a potential problem that can occur if two type constructors contain code that reference each other. For example, ClassA has a type constructor containing code that references ClassB, and ClassB has a type constructor containing code that references ClassA. In this situation, the CLR still guarantees that each type constructor's code executes only once; however, it cannot guarantee that ClassA's type constructor code has run to completion before executing ClassB's type constructor. You should certainly try to avoid writing code that sets up this scenario. In fact, since the CLR is responsible for calling type constructors, you should always avoid writing any code that requires type constructors to be called in a specific order.

Finally, if a type constructor throws an unhandled exception, the CLR considers the type to be unusable. Attempting to access any fields or methods of the type will cause a **System.TypeInitializationException** to be thrown.

The code in a type constructor has access only to a type's static fields, and its usual purpose is to initialize those fields. As it does with instance fields, C# offers a simple syntax that allows you to initialize a type's static fields:

```
internal sealed class SomeType {
   private static Int32 s_x = 5;
}
```

> **Note** While C# doesn't allow a value type to use inline field initialization syntax for instance fields, it does allow you to use it for static fields. In other words, if you change the **SomeType** type above from a **class** to a **struct**, the code will compile and work as expected.

When this code is built, the compiler automatically generates a type constructor for **SomeType**. It's as if the source code had originally been written as follows:

```
internal sealed class SomeType {
   private static Int32 s_x;
   static SomeType() { s_x = 5; }
}
```

Using ILDasm.exe, it's easy to verify what the compiler actually produced by examining the IL for the type constructor. Type constructor methods are always called **.cctor** (for *class constructor*) in a method definition metadata table.

In the code below, you see that the **.cctor** method is **private** and **static**. In addition, notice that the code in the method does in fact load a **5** into the static field **s_x**.

```
.method private hidebysig specialname rtspecialname static
        void  .cctor() cil managed
{
  // Code size       7 (0x7)
  .maxstack  8
  IL_0000:  ldc.i4.5
  IL_0001:  stsfld      int32 SomeType::s_x
  IL_0006:  ret
} // end of method SomeType::.cctor
```

Type constructors shouldn't call a base type's type constructor. Such a call isn't necessary because none of a type's static fields is shared or inherited from its base type.

> **Note** Some languages, such as Java, expect that accessing a type causes its type constructor and all of its base type's type constructors to be called. In addition, interfaces implemented by the types must also have their type constructors called. The CLR doesn't offer this behavior. However, the CLR does offer compilers and developers the ability to provide this behavior via the **RunClassConstructor** method offered by the **System.Runtime.CompilerServices.RuntimeHelpers** type. Any language that requires this behavior would have its compiler emit code into a type's type constructor that calls this method for all base types. When using the **RunClassConstructor** method to call a type constructor, the CLR knows if the type constructor has executed previously and, if it has, the CLR won't call it again.

Finally, assume that you have this code:

```
internal sealed class SomeType {
    private static Int32 s_x = 5;

    static SomeType() {
        s_x = 10;
    }
}
```

In this case, the C# compiler generates a single type constructor method. This constructor first initializes **s_x** to **5** and then initializes **s_x** to **10**. In other words, when the C# compiler generates IL code for the type constructor, it first emits the code required to initialize the static fields followed by the explicit code contained in your type constructor method.

> **Important** Developers occasionally ask me if there's a way to get some code to execute when a type is unloaded. You should first know that types are unloaded only when the AppDomain unloads. When the AppDomain unloads, the object that identifies the type becomes unreachable, and the garbage collector reclaims the type object's memory. This behavior leads many developers to believe that they could add a static **Finalize** method to the type, which will automatically get called when the type is unloaded. Unfortunately, the CLR doesn't support static **Finalize** methods. All is not lost, however. If you want some code to execute when an AppDomain unloads, you can register a callback method with the **System.AppDomain** type's **DomainUnload** event.

Type Constructor Performance

In the previous section, I mentioned that calling a type constructor is a tricky thing. And I explained some of the trickiness about it: the JIT compiler has to decide whether to emit the code to call it, and the CLR ensures that calls to it are thread-safe. As it turns out, this is the just the beginning of the tricky stuff. There is more about this that is performance-related.

As discussed already, when compiling a method, the JIT compiler determines whether it must emit a call to execute a type constructor into the method. If the JIT compiler decides to emit the call, it must decide where it should emit the call. There are two possibilities here:

- The JIT compiler can emit the call immediately before code that would create the first instance of the type or immediately before code that accesses a noninherited field or member of the class. This is called *precise* semantics because the CLR will call the type constructor at precisely the right time.

- The JIT compiler can emit the call sometime before code first accesses a static field or a static or instance method, or invokes an instance constructor. This is called *before-field-init* semantics because the CLR guarantees only that the static constructor will run some time before the member is accessed; it could run much earlier.

The before-field-init semantics is preferred since it gives the CLR a lot of freedom as to when it can call the type constructor, and the CLR takes advantage of this whenever possible to produce code that executes faster. For example, the CLR might pick different times to call the type constructor based on whether the type is loaded in an AppDomain or loaded domain-neutral or whether the code is being JIT-compiled or NGen'd.

By default, language compilers choose which of these semantics makes the most sense for the type you're defining and informs the CLR of this choice by setting the **beforefieldinit** flag in the row of the type definition metadata table. In this section, I'll focus on what the C# compiler does and how this impacts performance. Let's start by examining the following code:

```
using System;
using System.Diagnostics;

///////////////////////////////////////////////////////////////////////

// Since this class doesn't explicitly define a type constructor,
// C# marks the type definition with BeforeFieldInit in the metadata.
internal sealed class BeforeFieldInit {
   public static Int32 s_x = 123;
}

// Since this class does explicitly define a type constructor,
// C# doesn't mark the type definition with BeforeFieldInit in the metadata.
internal sealed class Precise {
   public static Int32 s_x;
```

```
      static Precise() { s_x = 123; }
}

//////////////////////////////////////////////////////////////////////////

public sealed class Program {
   public static void Main() {
      const Int32 iterations = 1000 * 1000 * 1000;
      PerfTest1(iterations);
      PerfTest2(iterations);
   }


   // When this method is JIT compiled, the type constructors for
   // the BeforeFieldInit and Precise classes HAVE NOT executed yet
   // and therefore, calls to these constructors are embedded in
   // this method's code, making it run slower
   private static void PerfTest1(Int32 iterations) {
      Stopwatch sw = Stopwatch.StartNew();
      for (Int32 x = 0; x < iterations; x++) {
         // The JIT compiler hoists the code to call BeforeFieldInit's
         // type constructor so that it executes before the loop starts
         BeforeFieldInit.s_x = 1;
      }
      Console.WriteLine("PerfTest1: {0} BeforeFieldInit", sw.Elapsed);

      sw = Stopwatch.StartNew();
      for (Int32 x = 0; x < iterations; x++) {
         // The JIT compiler emits the code to call Precise's
         // type constructor here so that it checks whether it
         // has to call the constructor with each loop iteration
         Precise.s_x = 1;
      }
      Console.WriteLine("PerfTest1: {0} Precise", sw.Elapsed);
   }

   // When this method is JIT compiled, the type constructors for
   // the BeforeFieldInit and Precise classes HAVE executed
   // and therefore, calls to these constructors are NOT embedded
   // in this method's code, making it run faster
   private static void PerfTest2(Int32 iterations) {
      Stopwatch sw = Stopwatch.StartNew();
      for (Int32 x = 0; x < iterations; x++) {
         BeforeFieldInit.s_x = 1;
      }
      Console.WriteLine("PerfTest2: {0} BeforeFieldInit", sw.Elapsed);

      sw = Stopwatch.StartNew();
      for (Int32 x = 0; x < iterations; x++) {
         Precise.s_x = 1;
      }
      Console.WriteLine("PerfTest2: {0} Precise", sw.Elapsed);
   }
}

///////////////////////////// End of File /////////////////////////////////
```

When I build and run the code above, I get the following output:

```
PerfTest1: 00:00:01.9619358 BeforeFieldInit
PerfTest1: 00:00:06.2374912 Precise
PerfTest2: 00:00:03.1576608 BeforeFieldInit
PerfTest2: 00:00:03.1557822 Precise
```

When the C# compiler sees a class with static fields that use inline initialization (the **BeforeFieldInit** class), the compiler emits the class's type definition table entry with the **BeforeFieldInit** metadata flag. When the C# compiler sees a class with an explicit type constructor (the **Precise** class), the compiler emits the class's type definition table entry without the **BeforeFieldInit** metadata flag. The rationale behind this is as follows: initialization of static fields needs to be done before the fields are accessed, whereas an explicit type constructor can contain arbitrary code that can have observable side effects; this code may need to run at a precise time.

As you can see from the output, this decision comes with a huge performance impact. When **PerfTest1** runs, the top loop executes in about 1.96 seconds versus the bottom loop, which took about 6.24 seconds to run—the bottom loop took about 3 times longer to execute. When **PerfTest2** runs, the times are much closer in value because the JIT compiler knew that the types' constructors were already called, and therefore the native code doesn't contain any calls to the type constructor methods.

It would be nice if C# gave programmers the ability to set the **BeforeFieldInit** flag explicitly in their source code instead of the compiler making this decision based on whether a type constructor is created implicitly or explicitly. This way, developers would have more direct control over the performance and semantics of their code.

Operator Overload Methods

Some programming languages allow a type to define how operators should manipulate instances of the type. For example, a lot of types (such as **System.String**, **System.Decimal**, and **System.DateTime**) overload the equality (==) and inequality (!=) operators. The CLR doesn't know anything about operator overloading because it doesn't even know what an operator is. Your programming language defines what each operator symbol means and what code should be generated when these special symbols appear.

For example, in C#, applying the + symbol to primitive numbers causes the compiler to generate code that adds the two numbers together. When the + symbol is applied to **String** objects, the C# compiler generates code that concatenates the two strings together. For inequality, C# uses the != symbol, while Microsoft Visual Basic uses the <> symbol. Finally, the ^ symbol means exclusive OR (XOR) in C#, but it means exponent in Visual Basic.

Although the CLR doesn't know anything about operators, it does specify how languages should expose operator overloads so that they can be readily consumed by code written in a different programming language. Each programming language gets to decide for itself whether it will support operator overloads, and if it does, the syntax for expressing and using them. As far as the CLR is concerned, operator overloads are simply methods.

Your choice of programming language determines whether or not you get the support of operator overloading and what the syntax looks like. When you compile your source code, the compiler produces a method that identifies the behavior of the operator. The CLR specification mandates that operator overload methods be **public** and **static** methods. In addition, C# (and many other languages) requires that at least one of the operator method's parameters must be the same as the type that the operator method is defined within. The reason for this restriction is that it enables the C# compiler to search for a possible operator method to bind to in a reasonable amount of time.

Here is an example of an operator overload method defined in a C# class definition:

```
public sealed class Complex {
   public static Complex operator+(Complex c1, Complex c2) { ... }
}
```

The compiler emits a metadata method definition entry for a method called **op_Addition**; the method definition entry also has the **specialname** flag set, indicating that this is a "special" method. When language compilers (including the C# compiler) see a + operator specified in source code, they look to see if one of the operand's types defines a **specialname** method called **op_Addition** whose parameters are compatible with the operand's types. If this method exists, the compiler emits code to call this method. If no such method exists, a compilation error occurs.

Tables 8-1 and 8-2 show the set of unary and binary operators that C# supports being over-loaded, their symbols, and the corresponding Common Language Specification (CLS) method name that the compiler emits. I'll explain the tables' third columns in the next section.

TABLE 8-1 C# Unary Operators and Their CLS-Compliant Method Names

C# Operator Symbol	Special Method Name	Suggested CLS-Compliant Method Name
+	op_UnaryPlus	Plus
-	op_UnaryNegation	Negate
!	op_LogicalNot	Not
~	op_OnesComplement	OnesComplement
++	op_Increment	Increment
--	op_Decrement	Decrement
(none)	op_True	IsTrue {get;}
(none)	op_False	IsFalse {get;}

TABLE 8-2 C# Binary Operators and Their CLS-Compliant Method Names

C# Operator Symbol	Special Method Name	Suggested CLS-Compliant Method Name
+	op_Addition	Add
−	op_Subtraction	Subtract
*	op_Multiply	Multiply
/	op_Division	Divide
%	op_Modulus	Mod
&	op_BitwiseAnd	BitwiseAnd
|	op_BitwiseOr	BitwiseOr
^	op_ExclusiveOr	Xor
<<	op_LeftShift	LeftShift
>>	op_RightShift	RightShift
==	op_Equality	Equals
!=	op_Inequality	Compare
<	op_LessThan	Compare
>	op_GreaterThan	Compare
<=	op_LessThanOrEqual	Compare
>=	op_GreaterThanOrEqual	Compare

The CLR specification defines many additional operators that can be overloaded, but C# does not support these additional operators. Therefore, they are not in mainstream use, so I will not list them here. If you are interested in the complete list, please see the ECMA specifications (www.ecma-international.org/publications/standards/Ecma-335.htm) for the Common Language Infrastructure (CLI), Partition I, Concepts and Architecture, Sections 10.3.1 (unary operators) and 10.3.2 (binary operators).

Note If you examine the core numeric types (**Int32**, **Int64**, **UInt32**, and so on) in the Framework Class Library (FCL), you'll see that they don't define any operator overload methods. The reason they don't is that compilers look specifically for operations on these primitive types and emit IL instructions that directly manipulate instances of these types. If the types were to offer methods and if compilers were to emit code to call these methods, a run-time performance cost would be associated with the method call. Plus, the method would ultimately have to execute some IL instructions to perform the expected operation anyway. This is the reason why the core FCL types don't define any operator overload methods. Here's what this means to you: If the programming language you're using doesn't support one of the core FCL types, you won't be able to perform any operations on instances of that type.

Operators and Programming Language Interoperability

Operator overloading can be a very useful tool, allowing developers to express their thoughts with succinct code. However, not all programming languages support operator overloading. When using a language that doesn't support operator overloading, the language will not know how to interpret the + operator (unless the type is a primitive in that language), and the compiler will emit an error. When using languages that do not support operator overloading, the language should allow you to call the desired **op_*** method directly (such as **op_Addition**).

If you are using a language that doesn't support + operator overloading to be defined in a type, obviously, this type could still offer an **op_Addition** method. From C#, you might expect that you could call this **op_Addition** method by using the + operator, but you cannot. When the C# compiler detects the + operator, it looks for an **op_Addition** method that has the **specialname** metadata flag associated with it so that the compiler knows for sure that the **op_Addition** method is intended to be an operator overload method. Because the **op_Addition** method is produced by a language that doesn't support operator overloads, the method won't have the **specialname** flag associated with it, and the C# compiler will produce a compilation error. Of course, code in any language can explicitly call a method that just happens to be named **op_Addition**, but the compilers won't translate a usage of the + symbol to call this method.

Jeff's Opinion About Microsoft's Operator Method Name Rules

I'm sure that all of these rules about when you can and can't call an operator overload method seem very confusing and overly complicated. If compilers that supported operator overloading just didn't emit the **specialname** metadata flag, the rules would be a lot simpler, and programmers would have an easier time working with types that offer operator overload methods. Languages that support operator overloading would support the operator symbol syntax, and all languages would support calling the various **op_** methods explicitly. I can't come up with any reason why Microsoft made this so difficult, and I hope that they'll loosen these rules in future versions of their compilers.

For a type that defines operator overload methods, Microsoft recommends that the type also define friendlier public static methods that call the operator overload methods internally. For example, a public-friendly named method called **Add** should be defined by a type that overloads the **op_Addition** method. The third column in Tables 8-1 and 8-2 lists the recommended friendly name for each operator. So the **Complex** type shown earlier should be defined this way:

```
public sealed class Complex {
    public static Complex operator+(Complex c1, Complex c2) { ... }
    public static Complex Add(Complex c1, Complex c2) { return(c1 + c2); }
}
```

Certainly, code written in any programming language can call any of the friendly operator methods, such as **Add**. Microsoft's guideline that types offer these friendly method names complicates the story even more. I feel that this additional complication is unnecessary, and that calling these friendly named methods would cause an additional performance hit unless the JIT compiler is able to inline the code in the friendly named method. Inlining the code would cause the JIT compiler to optimize the code, removing the additional method call and boosting runtime performance.

Note For an example of a type that overloads operators and uses the friendly method names as per Microsoft's design guidelines, see the **System.Decimal** class in the FCL.

Conversion Operator Methods

Occasionally, you need to convert an object from one type to an object of a different type. For example, I'm sure you've had to convert a **Byte** to an **Int32** at some point in your life. When the source type and the target type are a compiler's primitive types, the compiler knows how to emit the necessary code to convert the object.

If the source type or target type is not a primitive, the compiler emits code that has the CLR perform the conversion (cast). In this case, the CLR just checks if the source object's type is the same type as the target type (or derived from the target type). However, it is sometimes natural to want to convert an object of one type to a completely different type. For example, the **System.Xml.Linq.XElement** class allows you to convert an Extensible Markup Language (XML) element to a **Boolean**, **(U)Int32**, **(U)Int64**, **Single**, **Double**, **Decimal**, **String**, **DateTime**, **DateTimeOffset**, **TimeSpan**, **Guid**, or the nullable equivalent of any of these types (except **String**). You could also imagine that the FCL included a **Rational** data type and that it might be convenient to convert an **Int32** object or a **Single** object to a **Rational** object. Moreover, it also might be nice to convert a **Rational** object to an **Int32** or a **Single** object.

To make these conversions, the **Rational** type should define public constructors that take a single parameter: an instance of the type that you're converting from. You should also define public instance **ToXxx** methods that take no parameters (just like the very popular **ToString** method). Each method will convert an instance of the defining type to the **Xxx** type. Here's how to correctly define conversion constructors and methods for a **Rational** type:

```
public sealed class Rational {
    // Constructs a Rational from an Int32
    public Rational(Int32 num) { ... }

    // Constructs a Rational from a Single
    public Rational(Single num) { ... }
```

```
    // Convert a Rational to an Int32
    public Int32 ToInt32() { ... }

    // Convert a Rational to a Single
    public Single ToSingle() { ... }
}
```

By invoking these constructors and methods, a developer using any programming language can convert an **Int32** or a **Single** object to a **Rational** object and convert a **Rational** object to an **Int32** or a **Single** object. The ability to do these conversions can be quite handy, and when designing a type, you should seriously consider what conversion constructors and methods make sense for your type.

In the previous section, I discussed how some programming languages offer operator overloading. Well, some programming languages (such as C#) also offer conversion operator overloading. *Conversion operators* are methods that convert an object from one type to another type. You define a conversion operator method by using special syntax. The CLR specification mandates that conversion overload methods be **public** and **static** methods. In addition, C# (and many other languages) requires that either the parameter or the return type must be the same as the type that the conversion method is defined within. The reason for this restriction is that it enables the C# compiler to search for a possible operator method to bind to in a reasonable amount of time. The following code adds four conversion operator methods to the **Rational** type:

```
public sealed class Rational {
    // Constructs a Rational from an Int32
    public Rational(Int32 num) { ... }

    // Constructs a Rational from a Single
    public Rational(Single num) { ... }

    // Convert a Rational to an Int32
    public Int32 ToInt32() { ... }

    // Convert a Rational to a Single
    public Single ToSingle() { ... }

    // Implicitly constructs and returns a Rational from an Int32
    public static implicit operator Rational(Int32 num) {
        return new Rational(num);
    }

    // Implicitly constructs and returns a Rational from a Single
    public static implicit operator Rational(Single num) {
        return new Rational(num);
    }

    // Explicitly returns an Int32 from a Rational
    public static explicit operator Int32(Rational r) {
        return r.ToInt32();
    }
}
```

```
    // Explicitly returns a Single from a Rational
    public static explicit operator Single(Rational r) {
        return r.ToSingle();
    }
}
```

For conversion operator methods, you must indicate whether a compiler can emit code to call a conversion operator method implicitly or whether the source code must explicitly indicate when the compiler is to emit code to call a conversion operator method. In C#, you use the **implicit** keyword to indicate to the compiler that an explicit cast doesn't have to appear in the source code in order to emit code that calls the method. The **explicit** keyword allows the compiler to call the method only when an explicit cast exists in the source code.

After the **implicit** or **explicit** keyword, you tell the compiler that the method is a conversion operator by specifying the **operator** keyword. After the **operator** keyword, you specify the type that an object is being cast to; in the parentheses, you specify the type that an object is being cast from.

Defining the conversion operators in the preceding **Rational** type allows you to write code like this (in C#):

```
public sealed class Program {
    public static void Main() {
        Rational r1 = 5;          // Implicit cast from Int32  to Rational
        Rational r2 = 2.5F;       // Implicit cast from Single to Rational

        Int32  x = (Int32)  r1;   // Explicit cast from Rational to Int32
        Single s = (Single) r2;   // Explicit cast from Rational to Single
    }
}
```

Under the covers, the C# compiler detects the casts (type conversions) in the code and internally generates IL code that calls the conversion operator methods defined by the **Rational** type. But what are the names of these methods? Well, compiling the **Rational** type and examining its metadata shows that the compiler produces one method for each conversion operator defined. For the **Rational** type, the metadata for the four conversion operator methods looks like this:

```
public static Rational op_Implicit(Int32 num)
public static Rational op_Implicit(Single num)
public static Int32    op_Explicit(Rational r)
public static Single   op_Explicit(Rational r)
```

As you can see, methods that convert an object from one type to another are always named **op_Implicit** or **op_Explicit**. You should define an implicit conversion operator only when precision or magnitude isn't lost during a conversion, such as when converting an **Int32** to a **Rational**. However, you should define an explicit conversion operator if precision or magnitude is lost during the conversion, as when converting a **Rational** object to an **Int32**. If an explicit conversion fails, you should indicate this by having your explicit conversion operator method throw an **OverflowException** or an **InvalidOperationException**.

> **Note** The two **op_Explicit** methods take the same parameter, a **Rational**. However, the methods differ by their return value, an **Int32** and a **Single**. This is an example of two methods that differ only by their return type. The CLR fully supports the ability for a type to define multiple methods that differ only by return type. However, very few languages expose this ability. As you're probably aware, C++, C#, Visual Basic, and Java are all examples of languages that don't support the definition of multiple methods that differ only by their return type. A few languages (such as IL assembly language) allow the developer to explicitly select which of these methods to call. Of course, IL assembly language programmers shouldn't take advantage of this ability because the methods they define can't be callable from other programming languages. Even though C# doesn't expose this ability to the C# programmer, the compiler does take advantage of this ability internally when a type defines conversion operator methods.

C# has full support for conversion operators. When it detects code where you're using an object of one type and an object of a different type is expected, the compiler searches for an implicit conversion operator method capable of performing the conversion and generates code to call that method. If an implicit conversion operator method exists, the compiler emits a call to it in the resulting IL code. If the compiler sees source code that is explicitly casting an object from one type to another type, the compiler searches for an implicit or explicit conversion operator method. If one exists, the compiler emits the call to the method. If the compiler can't find an appropriate conversion operator method, it issues an error and doesn't compile the code.

> **Note** C# generates code to invoke explicit conversion operators when using a cast expression; they are never invoked when using C#'s **as** or **is** operators.

To really understand operator overload methods and conversion operator methods, I strongly encourage you to examine the **System.Decimal** type as a role model. **Decimal** defines several constructors that allow you to convert objects from various types to a **Decimal**. It also offers several **ToXxx** methods that let you convert a **Decimal** object to another type. Finally, the type defines several conversion operators and operator overload methods as well.

Extension Methods

The best way to understand C#'s *extension methods* feature is by way of an example. In the "**StringBuilder** Members" section in Chapter 14, "Chars, Strings, and Working with Text," I mention how the **StringBuilder** class offers fewer methods than the **String** class for manipulating a string and how strange this is, considering that the **StringBuilder** class is the preferred way of manipulating a string because it is mutable. So, let's say that you would like to define some of these missing methods yourself to operate on a **StringBuilder**. For example, you might want to define your own **IndexOf** method as follows:

```
public static class StringBuilderExtensions {
   public static Int32 IndexOf(StringBuilder sb, Char value) {
      for (Int32 index = 0; index < sb.Length; index++)
         if (sb[index] == value) return index;
      return -1;
   }
}
```

Now that you have defined this method, you can use it as the following code demonstrates:

```
StringBuilder sb = new StringBuilder("Hello. My name is Jeff.");    // The initial string

// Change period to exclamation and get # characters in 1st sentence (5).
Int32 index = StringBuilderExtensions.IndexOf(sb.Replace('.', '!'), '!');
```

This code works just fine, but is it not ideal from a programmer's perspective. The first problem is that a programmer who wants to get the index of a character within a **StringBuilder** must know that the **StringBuilderExtensions** class even exists. The second problem is that the code does not reflect the order of operations that are being performed on the **StringBuilder** object, making the code difficult to write, read, and maintain. The programmer wants to call **Replace** first and then call **IndexOf**; but when you read the last line of code from left to right, **IndexOf** appears first on the line and **Replace** appears second. Of course, you could alleviate this problem and make the code's behavior more understandable by rewriting it like this:

```
// First, change period to exclamation mark
sb.Replace('.', '!');

// Now, get # characters in 1st sentence (5)
Int32 index = StringBuilderExtensions.IndexOf(sb, '!');
```

However, a third problem exists with both versions of this code that affects understanding the code's behavior. The use of **StringBuilderExtensions** is overpowering and detracts a programmer's mind from the operation that is being performed: **IndexOf**. If the **StringBuilder** class had defined its own **IndexOf** method, then we could rewrite the code above as follows:

```
// Change period to exclamation and get # characters in 1st sentence (5).
Int32 index = sb.Replace('.', '!').IndexOf('!');
```

Wow, look how great this is in terms of code maintainability! In the **StringBuilder** object, we're going to replace a period with an exclamation mark and then find the index of the exclamation mark.

Now, I can explain what C#'s extension methods feature does. It allows you to define a static method that you can invoke using instance method syntax. Or, in other words, we can now define our own **IndexOf** method and the three problems mentioned above go away. To turn the **IndexOf** method into an extension method, we simply add the **this** keyword before the first argument:

```
public static class StringBuilderExtensions {
   public static Int32 IndexOf(this StringBuilder sb, Char value) {
      for (Int32 index = 0; index < sb.Length; index++)
         if (sb[index] == value) return index;
      return -1;
   }
}
```

Now, when the compiler sees code like this:

```
Int32 index = sb.IndexOf('X');
```

the compiler first checks if the **StringBuilder** class or any of its base classes offers an instance method called **IndexOf** that takes a single **Char** parameter. If an existing instance method exists, then the compiler produces IL code to call it. If no matching instance method exists, then the compiler will look at any static classes that define static methods called **IndexOf** that take as their first parameter a type matching the type of the expression being used to invoke the method. This type must also be marked with the **this** keyword. In this example, the expression is **sb**, which is of the **StringBuilder** type. In this case, the compiler is looking specifically for an **IndexOf** method that takes two parameters: a **StringBuilder** (marked with the **this** keyword) and a **Char**. The compiler will find our **IndexOf** method and produce IL code that calls our static method.

OK—so this now explains how the compiler improves the last two problems related to code understandability that I mentioned earlier. However, I haven't yet addressed the first problem: how does a programmer know that an **IndexOf** method even exists that can operate on a **StringBuilder** object? The answer to this question is found in Microsoft Visual Studio's Intellisense feature. In the editor, when you type a period, Visual Studio's IntelliSense window opens to show you the list of instance methods that are available. Well, that IntelliSense window also shows you any extension methods that exist for the type of expression you have to the left of the period. Figure 8-1 shows Visual Studio's IntelliSense window; the icon for an extension method has a down arrow next to it, and the tooltip next to the method indicates that the method is really an extension method. This is truly awesome because it is now easy to define your own methods to operate on various types of objects and have other programmers discover your methods naturally when using objects of these types.

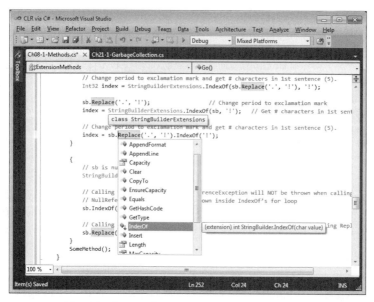

FIGURE 8-1 Visual Studio's IntelliSense window, showing extension methods

Rules and Guidelines

There are some additional rules and guidelines that you should know about extension methods:

- C# supports extension methods only; it does not offer extension properties, extension events, extension operators, and so on.

- Extension methods (methods with **this** before their first argument) must be declared in non-generic, static classes. However, there is no restriction on the name of the class; you can call it whatever you want. Of course, an extension method must have at least one parameter, and only the first parameter can be marked with the **this** keyword.

- The C# compiler looks only for extension methods defined in static classes that are themselves defined at the file scope. In other words, if you define the static class nested within another class, the C# compiler will emit the following message: **"error CS1109: Extension method must be defined in a top-level static class; StringBuilderExtensions is a nested class."**

- Since the static classes can have any name you want, it takes the C# compiler time to find extension methods as it must look at all the file-scope static classes and scan their static methods for a match. To improve performance and also to avoid considering an extension method that you may not want, the C# compiler requires that you "import" extension methods. For example, if someone has defined a **StringBuilderExtensions** class in a **Wintellect** namespace, then a programmer who wants to have access to this class's extension methods must put a **using Wintellect;** directive at the top of his or her source code file.

- It is possible that multiple static classes could define the same extension method. If the compiler detects that two or more extension methods exist, then the compiler issues the following message: **"error CS0121: The call is ambiguous between the following methods or properties: 'StringBuilderExtensions. IndexOf(string, char)' and 'AnotherStringBuilderExtensions. IndexOf(string, char)'."** To fix this error, you must modify your source code. Specifically, you cannot use the instance method syntax to call this static method anymore; instead you must now use the static method syntax where you explicitly indicate the name of the static class to explicitly tell the compiler which method you want to invoke.

- You should use this feature sparingly, as not all programmers are familiar with it. For example, when you extend a type with an extension method, you are actually extending derived types with this method as well. Therefore, you should not define an extension method whose first parameter is **System.Object**, as this method will be callable for all expression types and this will really pollute Visual Studio's IntelliSense window.

- There is a potential versioning problem that exists with extension methods. If, in the future, Microsoft adds an **IndexOf** instance method to their **StringBuilder** class with the same prototype as my code is attempting to call, then when I recompile my code, the compiler will bind to Microsoft's **IndexOf** instance method instead of my static **IndexOf** method. Because of this, my program will experience different behavior. This versioning problem is another reason why this feature should be used sparingly.

Extending Various Types with Extension Methods

In this chapter, I demonstrated how to define an extension method for a class, **StringBuilder**. I'd like to point out that since an extension method is really the invocation of a static method, the CLR does not emit code ensuring that the value of the expression used to invoke the method is not **null**:

```
// sb is null
StringBuilder sb = null;

// Calling extension method: NullReferenceException will NOT be thrown when calling IndexOf
// NullReferenceException will be thrown inside IndexOf's for loop
sb.IndexOf('X');

// Calling instance method: NullReferenceException WILL be thrown when calling Replace
sb.Replace('.', '!');
```

I'd also like to point out that you can define extension methods for interface types as the following code shows:

```
public static void ShowItems<T>(this IEnumerable<T> collection) {
    foreach (var item in collection)
        Console.WriteLine(item);
}
```

The extension method above can now be invoked using any expression that results in a type that implements the **IEnumerable<T>** interface:

```
public static void Main() {
   // Shows each Char on a separate line in the console
   "Grant".ShowItems();

   // Shows each String on a separate line in the console
   new[] { "Jeff", "Kristin" }.ShowItems();

   // Shows each Int32 value on a separate line in the console
   new List<Int32>() { 1, 2, 3 }.ShowItems();
}
```

Important Extension methods are the cornerstone of Microsoft's Language Integrated Query (LINQ) technology. For a great example of a class that offers many extension methods, see the static **System.Linq.Enumerable** class and all its static extension methods in the Microsoft .NET Framework SDK documentation. Every extension method in this class extends either the **IEnumerable** or **IEnumerable<T>** interface.

You can define extension methods for delegate types, too. For an example of this, turn to page 278 in Chapter 11, "Events." You can also add extension methods to enumerated types. I show an example of this in the "Adding Methods to Enumerated Types" section in Chapter 15, "Enumerated Types and Bit Flags."

And last but not least, I want to point out that the C# compiler allows you to create a delegate (see Chapter 17, "Delegates," for more information) that refers to an extension method over an object:

```
public static void Main () {
   // Create an Action delegate that refers to the static ShowItems extension method
   // and has the first argument initialized to reference the "Jeff" string.
   Action a = "Jeff".ShowItems;
   .
   .
   .
   // Invoke the delegate which calls ShowItems passing it a reference to the "Jeff" string.
   a();
}
```

In the code above, the C# compiler generates IL code to construct an **Action** delegate. When creating a delegate, the constructor is passed the method that should be called and is also passed a reference to an object that should be passed to the method's hidden **this** parameter. Normally, when you create a delegate that refers to a static method, the object reference is **null** since static methods don't have a **this** parameter. However, in this example, the C# compiler generated some special code that creates a delegate that refers to a static method (**ShowItems**) and the target object of the static method is the reference to the "Jeff" string. Later, when the delegate is invoked, the CLR will call the static method and will pass to it the reference to the "Jeff" string. This is a little hacky, but it works great and it feels natural so long as you don't think about what is happening internally.

The Extension Attribute

It would be best if this concept of extension methods was not C#-specific. Specifically, we want programmers to define a set of extension methods in some programming language and for people in other programming languages to take advantage of them. For this to work, the compiler of choice must support searching static types and methods for potentially matching extension methods. And compilers need to do this quickly so that compilation time is kept to a minimum.

In C#, when you mark a static method's first parameter with the **this** keyword, the compiler internally applies a custom attribute to the method and this attribute is persisted in the resulting file's metadata. The attribute is defined in the System.Core.dll assembly, and it looks like this:

```
// Defined in the System.Runtime.CompilerServices namespace
[AttributeUsage(AttributeTargets.Method | AttributeTargets.Class | AttributeTargets.
Assembly)]
public sealed class ExtensionAttribute : Attribute {
}
```

In addition, this attribute is applied to the metadata for any static class that contains at least one extension method. And this attribute is also applied to the metadata for any assembly that contains at least one static class that contains an extension method. So now, when compiling code that invokes an instance method that doesn't exist, the compiler can quickly scan all the referenced assemblies to know which ones contain extension methods. Then it can scan only these assemblies for static classes that contain extension methods, and it can scan just the extension methods for potential matches to compile the code as quickly as possible.

Note The **ExtensionAttribute** class is defined in the System.Core.dll assembly. This means that the resulting assembly produced by the compiler will have a reference to System.Core.dll embedded in it even if I do not use any types from System.Core.dll and do not even reference System.Core.dll when compiling my code. However, this is not too bad a problem because the **ExtensionAttribute** is used only at compile time; at runtime, System.Core.dll will not have to be loaded unless the application consumes something else in this assembly.

Partial Methods

Imagine that you use a tool that produces a C# source code file containing a type definition. The tool knows that there are potential places within the code it produces where you might want to customize the type's behavior. Normally, customization would be done by having the tool-produced code invoke virtual methods. The tool-produced code would also have to contain definitions for these virtual methods, and the way these methods would be implemented is to do nothing and simply return. Now, if you want to customize the behavior of the class, you'd define your own class, derive it from the base class, and then override any virtual methods implementing it so that it has the behavior you desire. Here is an example:

```
// Tool-produced code in some source code file:
internal class Base {
   private String m_name;

   // Called before changing the m_name field
   protected virtual void OnNameChanging(String value) {
   }

   public String Name {
      get { return m_name; }
      set {
         OnNameChanging(value.ToUpper());  // Inform class of potential change
         m_name = value;                   // Change the field
      }
   }
}
```

```
// Developer-produced code in some other source code file:
internal class Derived : Base {
   protected override void OnNameChanging(string value) {
      if (String.IsNullOrEmpty(value))
         throw new ArgumentNullException("value");
   }
}
```

Unfortunately, there are two problems with the code above:

- The type must be a class that is not sealed. You cannot use this technique for sealed classes or for value types (because value types are implicitly sealed). In addition, you cannot use this technique for static methods since they cannot be overridden.

- There are efficiency problems here. A type is being defined just to override a method; this wastes a small amount of system resources. And, even if you do not want to override the behavior of **OnNameChanging**, the base class code still invokes a virtual method which simply does nothing but return. Also, **ToUpper** is called whether **OnNameChanging** accesses the argument passed to it or not.

C#'s partial methods feature allows you the option of overriding the behavior or a type while fixing the aforementioned problems. The code below uses partial methods to accomplish the same semantic as the previous code:

```
// Tool-produced code in some source code file:
internal sealed partial class Base {
   private String m_name;

   // This defining-partial-method-declaration is called before changing the m_name field
   partial void OnNameChanging(String value);

   public String Name {
      get { return m_name; }
      set {
         OnNameChanging(value.ToUpper());   // Inform class of potential change
         m_name = value;                    // Change the field
      }
   }
}

// Developer-produced code in some other source code file:
internal sealed partial class Base {

   // This implementing-partial-method-declaration is called before m_name is changed
   partial void OnNameChanging(String value) {
      if (String.IsNullOrEmpty(value))
         throw new ArgumentNullException("value");
   }
}
```

There are several things to notice about this new version of the code:

- The class is now sealed (although it doesn't have to be). In fact, the class could be a static class or even a value type.

- The tool-produced code and the developer-produced code are really two partial definitions that ultimately make up one type definition. For more information about partial types, see the "Partial Classes, Structures, and Interfaces" section in Chapter 6, "Type and Member Basics."

- The tool-produced code defined a partial method declaration. This method is marked with the **partial** token and it has no body.

- The developer-produced code implemented the partial method declaration. This method is also marked with the **partial** token and it has a body.

Now, when you compile this code, you see the same effect as the original code I showed you. Again, the big benefit here is that you can rerun the tool and produce new code in a new source code file, but your code remains in a separate file and is unaffected. And, this technique works for sealed classes, static classes, and value types.

> **Note** In Visual Studio's editor, if you type in **partial** and press the spacebar, the IntelliSense window shows you all the enclosing type's defined partial method declarations that do not yet have matching implementing partial method declarations. You can then easily select a partial method from the IntelliSense window and Visual Studio will produce the method prototype for you automatically. This is a very nice feature that enhances productivity.

But, there is another big improvement we get with partial methods. Let's say that you do not need to modify the behavior of the tool-produced type. In this case, you do not supply your source code file at all. If you just compile the tool-produced code by itself, the compiler produces IL code and metadata as if the tool-produced code looked like this:

```
// Logical equivalent of tool-produced code if there is no
// implementing partial method declaration:
internal sealed class Base {
   private String m_name;

   public String Name {
      get { return m_name; }
      set {
         m_name = value;                    // Change the field
      }
   }
}
```

That is, if there is no implementing partial method declaration, the compiler will not emit any metadata representing the partial method. In addition, the compiler will not emit any IL instructions to call the partial method. And the compiler will not emit code that evaluates any arguments that would have been passed to the partial method. In this example, the compiler will not emit code to call the **ToUpper** method. The result is that there is less metadata/IL, and the runtime performance is awesome!

> **Note** Partial methods work similarly to the **System.Diagnostics.ConditionalAttribute** attribute. However, partial methods work within a single type only while the **ConditionalAttribute** can be used to optionally invoke methods defined in another type.

Rules and Guidelines

There are some additional rules and guidelines that you should know about partial methods:

- They can only be declared within a partial class or struct.

- Partial methods must always have a return type of **void**, and they cannot have any parameters marked with the **out** modifier. These restrictions are in place because at runtime, the method may not exist and so you can't initialize a variable to what the method might return because the method might not exist. Similarly, you can't have an

out parameter because the method would have to initialize it and the method might not exist. A partial method may have **ref** parameters, may be generic, may be instance or static, and may be marked as **unsafe**.

- Of course, the defining partial method declaration and the implementing partial method declaration must have identical signatures. If both have custom attributes applied to them, then the compiler combines both methods' attributes together. Any attributes applied to a parameter are also combined.

- If there is no implementing partial method declaration, then you cannot have any code that attempts to create a delegate that refers to the partial method. Again, the reason is that the method doesn't exist at runtime. The compiler produces this message: **"error CS0762: Cannot create delegate from method 'Base.OnNameChanging(string)' because it is a partial method without an implementing declaration"**.

- Partial methods are always considered to be private methods. However, the C# compiler forbids you from putting the **private** keyword before the partial method declaration.

Chapter 9
Parameters

This chapter focuses on the various ways of passing parameters to a method, including how to optionally specify parameters, specify parameters by name, and pass parameters by reference, as well as how to define methods that accept a variable number of arguments.

Optional and Named Parameters

When designing a method's parameters, you can assign default values to some of or all the parameters. Then, code that calls these methods can optionally not specify some of the arguments, thereby accepting the default values. In addition, when you call a method, you can specify arguments by using the name of their parameters. Here is some code that demonstrates using both optional and named parameters:

```
public static class Program {
   private static Int32 s_n = 0;

   private static void M(Int32 x = 9, String s = "A",
      DateTimedt = default(DateTime), Guidguid = new Guid()) {

      Console.WriteLine("x={0}, s={1}, dt={2}, guid={3}", x, s, dt, guid);
   }

   public static void Main() {
      // 1. Same as: M(9, "A", default(DateTime), new Guid());
      M();

      // 2. Same as: M(8, "X", default(DateTime), new Guid());
      M(8, "X");

      // 3. Same as: M(5, "A", DateTime.Now, Guid.NewGuid());
      M(5, guid: Guid.NewGuid(), dt: DateTime.Now);
```

```
    // 4. Same as: M(0, "1", default(DateTime), new Guid());
    M(s_n++, s_n++.ToString());

    // 5. Same as: String t1 = "2"; Int32 t2 = 3;
    //              M(t2, t1, default(DateTime), new Guid());
    M(s: (s_n++).ToString(), x: s_n++);
  }
}
```

When I run this program, I get the following output:

```
x=9, s=A, dt=1/1/0001 12:00:00 AM, guid=00000000-0000-0000-0000-000000000000
x=8, s=X, dt=1/1/0001 12:00:00 AM, guid=00000000-0000-0000-0000-000000000000
x=5, s=A, dt=7/2/2009 10:14:25 PM, guid=d24a59da-6009-4aae-9295-839155811309
x=0, s=1, dt=1/1/0001 12:00:00 AM, guid=00000000-0000-0000-0000-000000000000
x=3, s=2, dt=1/1/0001 12:00:00 AM, guid=00000000-0000-0000-0000-000000000000
```

As you can see, whenever arguments are left out at the call site, the C# compiler embeds the parameter's default value. The third and fifth calls to M use C#'s named parameter feature. In the two calls, I'm explicitly passing a value for **x** and I'm indicating that I want to pass an argument for the parameters named **guid** and **dt**.

When you pass arguments to a method, the compiler evaluates the arguments from left to right. In the fourth call to M, the value in **s_n** (0) is passed for **x**, then **s_n** is incremented, and **s_n** (1) is passed as a string for **s** and then **s_n** is incremented again to 2. When you pass arguments by using named parameters, the compiler still evaluates the arguments from left to right. In the fifth call to M, the value in **s_n** (2) is converted to a string and saved in a temporary variable (**t1**) that the compiler creates. Next, **s_n** is incremented to 3 and this value is saved in another temporary variable (**t2**) created by the compiler, and then **s_n** is incremented again to 4. Ultimately, M is invoked, passing it **t2**, **t1**, a default **DateTime**, and a new **Guid**.

Rules and Guidelines

There are some additional rules and guidelines that you should know about when defining a method that specifies default values for some of its parameters:

- You can specify default values for the parameters of methods, constructor methods, and parameterful properties (C# indexers). You can also specify default values for parameters that are part of a delegate definition. Then, when invoking a variable of this delegate type, you can omit the arguments and accept the default values.

- Parameters with default values must come after any parameters that do not have default values. That is, once you define a parameter as having a default value, then all parameters to the right of it must also have default values. For example, in the definition of my **M** method, I would get a compiler error if I removed the default value (**"A"**) for **s**. There is one exception to this rule: a **params** array parameter (discussed later in this chapter) must come after all parameters (including those that have default values), and the array cannot have a default value itself.

- Default values must be constant values known at compile time. This means that you can set default values for parameters of types that C# considers to be primitive types, as shown in Table 5-1 in Chapter 5, "Primitive, Reference, and Value Types." This also includes enumerated types, and any reference type can be set to **null**. For a parameter of an arbitrary value type, you can set the default value to be an instance of the value type, with all its fields containing zeroes. You can use the **default** keyword or the **new** keyword to express this; both syntaxes produce identical Intermediate Language (IL) code. Examples of both syntaxes are used by my **M** method for setting the default value for the **dt** parameter and **guid** parameter, respectively.

- Be careful not to rename parameter variables because any callers who are passing arguments by parameter name will have to modify their code. For example, in the declaration of my **M** method, if I rename the **dt** variable to **dateTime**, then my third call to **M** in the earlier code will cause the compiler to produce the following message: "**error CS1739: The best overload for 'M' does not have a parameter named 'dt'.**"

- Be aware that changing a parameter's default value is potentially dangerous if the method is called from outside the module. A call site embeds the default value into its call. If you later change the parameter's default value and do not recompile the code containing the call site, then it will call your method passing the old default value. You might want to consider using a default value of **0/null** as a sentinel to indicate default behavior; this allows you to change your default without having to recompile all the code with call sites. Here is an example:

```
// Don't do this:
private static String MakePath(String filename = "Untitled") {
    return String.Format(@"C:\{0}.txt", filename);
}

// Do this instead:
private static String MakePath(String filename = null) {
    // I am using the null-coalescing operator (??) here; see Chapter 19
    return String.Format(@"C:\{0}.txt", filename ?? "Untitled");
}
```

- You cannot set default values for parameters marked with either the **ref** or **out** keywords because there is no way to pass a meaningful default value for these parameters.

There are some additional rules and guidelines that you should know about when calling a method using optional or named parameters:

- Arguments can be passed in any order; however, named arguments must always appear at the end of the argument list.

- You can pass arguments by name to parameters that do not have default values, but all required arguments must be passed (by position or by name) for the compiler to compile the code.

- C# doesn't allow you to omit arguments between commas, as in `M(1, ,DateTime.Now)`, because this could lead to unreadable comma-counting code. Pass arguments by way of their parameter name if you want to omit some arguments for parameters with default values.

- To pass an argument by parameter name that requires **ref/out**, use syntax like this:

```
// Method declaration:
private static void M(ref Int32 x) { ... }

// Method invocation:
Int32 a = 5;
M(x: ref a);
```

> **Note** C#'s optional and named parameter features are really convenient when writing C# code that interoperates with the COM object model in Microsoft Office. And, when calling a COM component, C# also allows you to omit **ref/out** when passing an argument by reference to simplify the coding even more. When not calling a COM component, C# requires that the **out/ref** keyword be applied to the argument.

The DefaultParameterValue and Optional Attributes

It would be best if this concept of default and optional arguments was not C#-specific. Specifically, we want programmers to define a method indicating which parameters are optional and what their default value should be in some programming language and then give programmers working in other programming languages the ability to call them. For this to work, the compiler of choice must allow the caller to omit some arguments and have a way of determining what those arguments' default values should be.

In C#, when you give a parameter a default value, the compiler internally applies the `System.Runtime.InteropServices.OptionalAttribute` custom attribute to the parameter, and this attribute is persisted in the resulting file's metadata. In addition, the compiler applies `System.Runtime.InteropServices.DefaultParameterValueAttribute` to the parameter and persists this attribute in the resulting file's metadata. Then, `DefaultParameterValueAttribute`'s constructor is passed the constant value that you specified in your source code.

Now, when a compiler sees that you have code calling a method that is missing some arguments, the compiler can ensure that you've omitted optional arguments, grab their default values out of metadata, and embed the values in the call for you automatically.

Implicitly Typed Local Variables

C# supports the ability to infer the type of a method's local variable from the type of expression that is used to initialize it. Here is some sample code demonstrating the use of this feature:

```
private static void ImplicitlyTypedLocalVariables() {
    var name = "Jeff";
    ShowVariableType(name);      // Displays: System.String

    // var n = null;             // Error
    var x = (Exception)null;     // OK, but not much value
    ShowVariableType(x);         // Displays: System.Exception

    var numbers = new Int32[] { 1, 2, 3, 4 };
    ShowVariableType(numbers); // Displays: System.Int32[]

    // Less typing for complex types
    var collection = new Dictionary<String, Single>() { { ".NET", 4.0f } };

    // Displays: System.Collections.Generic.Dictionary`2[System.String,System.Single]
    ShowVariableType(collection);

    foreach (var item in collection) {
        // Displays: System.Collections.Generic.KeyValuePair`2[System.String,System.Single]
        ShowVariableType(item);
    }
}

private static void ShowVariableType<T>(T t) {
    Console.WriteLine(typeof(T));
}
```

The first line of code inside the **ImplicitlyTypedLocalVariables** method is introducing a new local variable using the C# **var** token. To determine the type of the **name** variable, the compiler looks at the type of the expression on the right side of the assignment operator (=). Since **"Jeff"** is a string, the compiler infers that **name**'s type must be **String**. To prove that the compiler is inferring the type correctly, I wrote the **ShowVariableType** method. This generic method infers the type of its argument, and then it shows the type that it inferred on the console. I added what **ShowVariableType** displayed as comments inside the **ImplicitlyTypedLocalVariables** method for easy reading.

The second assignment (commented out) inside the **ImplicitlyTypedLocalVariables** method would produce a compiler error ("**error CS0815: Cannot assign <null> to an implicitly-typed local variable**") because **null** is implicitly castable to any reference type or nullable value type; therefore, the compiler cannot infer a distinct type for it. However, on the third assignment, I show that it is possible to initialize an implicitly typed local variable with **null** if you explicitly specify a type (**Exception**, in my example). While this is possible, it is not that useful because you could also write **Exception x = null;** to get the same result.

In the fourth assignment, you see some real value of using C#'s implicitly typed local variable feature. Without this feature, you'd have to specify **Dictionary<String, Single>** on both sides of the assignment operator. Not only is this a lot of typing, but if you ever decide to change the collection type or any of the generic parameter types, then you would have to modify your code on both sides of the assignment operator, too.

In the **foreach** loop, I also use **var** to have the compiler automatically infer the type of the elements inside the collection. This demonstrates that it is possible and quite useful to use **var** with **foreach**, **using**, and **for** statements. It can also be useful when experimenting with code. For example, you initialize an implicitly typed local variable from the return type of a method, and as you develop your method, you might decide to change its return type. If you do this, the compiler will automatically figure out that the return type has changed and automatically change the type of the variable! This is great, but of course, other code in the method that uses that variable may no longer compile if the code accesses members using the variable assuming that it was the old type.

In Microsoft Visual Studio, you can hold the mouse cursor over **var** in your source code and the editor will display a tooltip showing you the type that the compiler infers from the expression. C#'s implicitly typed local variable feature must be used when working with anonymous types within a method; see Chapter 10, "Properties," for more details.

You cannot declare a method's parameter type using **var**. The reason for this should be obvious to you since the compiler would have to infer the parameter's type from the argument being passed at a callsite and there could be no call sites or many call sites. In addition, you cannot declare a type's field using **var**. There are many reasons why C# has this restriction. One reason is that fields can be accessed by several methods and the C# team feels that this contract (the type of the variable) should be stated explicitly. Another reason is that allowing this would permit an anonymous type (discussed in Chapter 10) to leak outside of a single method.

Important Do not confuse **dynamic** and **var**. Declaring a local variable using **var** is just a syntactical shortcut that has the compiler infer the specific data type from an expression. The **var** keyword can be used only for declaring local variables inside a method while the **dynamic** keyword can be used for local variables, fields, and arguments. You cannot cast an expression to **var**, but you can cast an expression to **dynamic**. You must explicitly initialize a variable declared using **var** while you do not have to initialize a variable declared with **dynamic**. For more information about C#'s **dynamic** type, see the "The dynamic Primitive Type" section in Chapter 5.

Passing Parameters by Reference to a Method

By default, the common language runtime (CLR) assumes that all method parameters are passed by value. When reference type objects are passed, the reference (or pointer) to the object is passed (by value) to the method. This means that the method can modify the object and the caller will see the change. For value type instances, a copy of the instance is passed to the method. This means that the method gets its own private copy of the value type and the instance in the caller isn't affected.

> **Important** In a method, you must know whether each parameter passed is a reference type or a value type because the code you write to manipulate the parameter could be markedly different.

The CLR allows you to pass parameters by reference instead of by value. In C#, you do this by using the **out** and **ref** keywords. Both keywords tell the C# compiler to emit metadata indicating that this designated parameter is passed by reference, and the compiler uses this to generate code to pass the address of the parameter rather than the parameter itself.

From the CLR's perspective, **out** and **ref** are identical—that is, the same IL is produced regardless of which keyword you use, and the metadata is also identical except for 1 bit, which is used to record whether you specified **out** or **ref** when declaring the method. However, the C# compiler treats the two keywords differently, and the difference has to do with which method is responsible for initializing the object being referred to. If a method's parameter is marked with **out**, the caller isn't expected to have initialized the object prior to calling the method. The called method can't read from the value, and the called method must write to the value before returning. If a method's parameter is marked with **ref**, the caller must initialize the parameter's value prior to calling the method. The called method can read from the value and/or write to the value.

Reference and value types behave very differently with **out** and **ref**. Let's look at using **out** and **ref** with value types first:

```
public sealed class Program {
   public static void Main() {
      Int32 x;                 // x is uninitialized
      GetVal(out x);           // x doesn't have to be initialized.
      Console.WriteLine(x);    // Displays "10"
   }

   private static void GetVal(out Int32 v) {
      v = 10;   // This method must initialize v.
   }
}
```

In this code, **x** is declared in **Main**'s stack frame. The address of **x** is then passed to **GetVal**. **GetVal**'s **v** is a pointer to the **Int32** value in **Main**'s stack frame. Inside **GetVal**, the **Int32** that **v** points to is changed to **10**. When **GetVal** returns, **Main**'s **x** has a value of **10**, and 10 is displayed on the console. Using **out** with large value types is efficient because it prevents instances of the value type's fields from being copied when making method calls.

Now let's look at an example that uses **ref** instead of **out**:

```
public sealed class Program {
   public static void Main() {
      Int32 x = 5;          // x is initialized
      AddVal(ref x);        // x must be initialized.
      Console.WriteLine(x); // Displays "15"
   }

   private static void AddVal(ref Int32 v) {
      v += 10;   // This method can use the initialized value in v.
   }
}
```

In this code, **x** is also declared in **Main**'s stack frame and is initialized to **5**. The address of **x** is then passed to **AddVal**. **AddVal**'s **v** is a pointer to the **Int32** value in **Main**'s stack frame. Inside **AddVal**, the **Int32** that **v** points to is required to have a value already. So, **AddVal** can use the initial value in any expression it desires. **AddVal** can also change the value, and the new value will be "returned" to the caller. In this example, **AddVal** adds **10** to the initial value. When **AddVal** returns, **Main**'s **x** will contain **15**, which is what gets displayed in the console.

To summarize, from an IL or a CLR perspective, **out** and **ref** do exactly the same thing: they both cause a pointer to the instance to be passed. The difference is that the compiler helps ensure that your code is correct. The following code that attempts to pass an uninitialized value to a method expecting a **ref** parameter produces the following message: "**error CS0165: Use of unassigned local variable 'x'.**"

```
public sealed class Program {
   public static void Main() {
      Int32 x;              // x is not initialized.

      // The following line fails to compile, producing
      // error CS0165: Use of unassigned local variable 'x'.
      AddVal(ref x);

      Console.WriteLine(x);
   }

   private static void AddVal(ref Int32 v) {
      v += 10;   // This method can use the initialized value in v.
   }
}
```

Important I'm frequently asked why C# requires that a call to a method must specify **out** or **ref**. After all, the compiler knows whether the method being called requires **out** or **ref** and should be able to compile the code correctly. It turns out that the compiler can indeed do the right thing automatically. However, the designers of the C# language felt that the caller should explicitly state its intention. This way at the call site, it's obvious that the method being called is expected to change the value of the variable being passed.

In addition, the CLR allows you to overload methods based on their use of **out** and **ref** parameters. For example, in C#, the following code is legal and compiles just fine:

```
public sealed class Point {
   static void Add(Point p) { ... }
   static void Add(ref Point p) { ... }
}
```

It's not legal to overload methods that differ only by **out** and **ref** because the metadata representation of the method's signature for the methods would be identical. So I couldn't also define the following method in the preceding **Point** type:

```
static void Add(out Point p) { ... }
```

If you attempt to include the last **Add** method in the **Point** type, the C# compiler issues this message: "`error CS0663: 'Add' cannot define overloaded methods that differ only on ref and out.`"

Using **out** and **ref** with value types gives you the same behavior that you already get when passing reference types by value. With value types, **out** and **ref** allow a method to manipulate a single value type instance. The caller must allocate the memory for the instance, and the callee manipulates that memory. With reference types, the caller allocates memory for a pointer to a reference object, and the callee manipulates this pointer. Because of this behavior, using **out** and **ref** with reference types is useful only when the method is going to "return" a reference to an object that it knows about. The following code demonstrates:

```
using System;
using System.IO;

public sealed class Program {
   public static void Main() {
      FileStream fs;   // fs is uninitialized

      // Open the first file to be processed.
      StartProcessingFiles(out fs);

      // Continue while there are more files to process.
      for (; fs != null; ContinueProcessingFiles(ref fs)) {

         // Process a file.
         fs.Read(...);
      }
   }
}
```

```
    private static void StartProcessingFiles(out FileStream fs) {
        fs = new FileStream(...);    // fs must be initialized in this method
    }

    private static void ContinueProcessingFiles(ref FileStream fs) {
        fs.Close();   // Close the last file worked on.

        // Open the next file, or if no more files, "return" null.
        if (noMoreFilesToProcess) fs = null;
        else fs = new FileStream (...);
    }
}
```

As you can see, the big difference with this code is that the methods that have **out** or **ref** reference type parameters are constructing an object, and the pointer to the new object is returned to the caller. You'll also notice that the **ContinueProcessingFiles** method can manipulate the object being passed into it before returning a new object. This is possible because the parameter is marked with the **ref** keyword. You can simplify the preceding code a bit, as shown here:

```
using System;
using System.IO;

public sealed class Program {
    public static void Main() {
        FileStream fs = null;    // Initialized to null (required)

        // Open the first file to be processed.
        ProcessFiles(ref fs);

        // Continue while there are more files to process.
        for (; fs != null; ProcessFiles(ref fs)) {

            // Process a file.
            fs.Read(...);
        }
    }

    private static void ProcessFiles(ref FileStream fs) {
        // Close the previous file if one was open.
        if (fs != null) fs.Close();   // Close the last file worked on.

        // Open the next file, or if no more files, "return" null.
        if (noMoreFilesToProcess) fs = null;
        else fs = new FileStream (...);
    }
}
```

Here's another example that demonstrates how to use the **ref** keyword to implement a method that swaps two reference types:

```
public static void Swap(ref Object a, ref Object b) {
   Object t = b;
   b = a;
   a = t;
}
```

To swap references to two **String** objects, you'd probably think that you could write code like this:

```
public static void SomeMethod() {
   String s1 = "Jeffrey";
   String s2 = "Richter";

   Swap(ref s1, ref s2);
   Console.WriteLine(s1);   // Displays "Richter"
   Console.WriteLine(s2);   // Displays "Jeffrey"
}
```

However, this code won't compile. The problem is that variables passed by reference to a method must be of the same type as declared in the method signature. In other words, **Swap** expects two **Object** references, not two **String** references. To swap the two **String** references, you must do this:

```
public static void SomeMethod() {
   String s1 = "Jeffrey";
   String s2 = "Richter";

   // Variables that are passed by reference
   // must match what the method expects.
   Object o1 = s1, o2 = s2;
   Swap(ref o1, ref o2);

   // Now cast the objects back to strings.
   s1 = (String) o1;
   s2 = (String) o2;

   Console.WriteLine(s1);   // Displays "Richter"
   Console.WriteLine(s2);   // Displays "Jeffrey"
}
```

This version of **SomeMethod** does compile and execute as expected. The reason why the parameters passed must match the parameters expected by the method is to ensure that type safety is preserved. The following code, which thankfully won't compile, shows how type safety could be compromised.

```
internal sealed class SomeType {
   public Int32 m_val;
}

public sealed class Program {
   public static void Main() {
      SomeType st;
```

```
    // The following line generates error CS1503: Argument '1':
    // cannot convert from 'ref SomeType' to 'ref object'.
    GetAnObject(out st);

    Console.WriteLine(st.m_val);
}

private static void GetAnObject(out Object o) {
    o = new String('X', 100);
}
}
```

In this code, **Main** clearly expects **GetAnObject** to return a **SomeType** object. However, because **GetAnObject**'s signature indicates a reference to an **Object**, **GetAnObject** is free to initialize **o** to an object of any type. In this example, when **GetAnObject** returned to **Main**, **st** would refer to a **String**, which is clearly not a **SomeType** object, and the call to **Console.WriteLine** would certainly fail. Fortunately, the C# compiler won't compile the preceding code because **st** is a reference to **SomeType**, but **GetAnObject** requires a reference to an **Object**.

You can use generics to fix these methods so that they work as you'd expect. Here is how to fix the **Swap** method shown earlier:

```
public static void Swap<T>(ref T a, ref T b) {
    T t = b;
    b = a;
    a = t;
}
```

And now, with **Swap** rewritten as above, the following code (identical to that shown before) will compile and run perfectly:

```
public static void SomeMethod() {
    String s1 = "Jeffrey";
    String s2 = "Richter";

    Swap(ref s1, ref s2);
    Console.WriteLine(s1);   // Displays "Richter"
    Console.WriteLine(s2);   // Displays "Jeffrey"
}
```

For some other examples that use generics to solve this problem, see **System.Threading**'s **Interlocked** class with its **CompareExchange** and **Exchange** methods.

Passing a Variable Number of Arguments to a Method

It's sometimes convenient for the developer to define a method that can accept a variable number of arguments. For example, the **System.String** type offers methods allowing an arbitrary number of strings to be concatenated together and methods allowing the caller to specify a set of strings that are to be formatted together.

To declare a method that accepts a variable number of arguments, you declare the method as follows:

```
static Int32 Add(params Int32[] values) {
   // NOTE: it is possible to pass the 'values'
   // array to other methods if you want to.

   Int32 sum = 0;
   if (values != null) {
      for (Int32 x = 0; x < values.Length; x++)
         sum += values[x];
   }
   return sum;
}
```

Everything in this method should look very familiar to you except for the **params** keyword that is applied to the last parameter of the method signature. Ignoring the **params** keyword for the moment, it's obvious that this method accepts an array of **Int32** values and iterates over the array, adding up all of the values. The resulting **sum** is returned to the caller.

Obviously, code can call this method as follows:

```
public static void Main() {
   // Displays "15"
   Console.WriteLine(Add(new Int32[] { 1, 2, 3, 4, 5 } ));
}
```

It's clear that the array can easily be initialized with an arbitrary number of elements and then passed off to **Add** for processing. Although the preceding code would compile and work correctly, it is a little ugly. As developers, we would certainly prefer to have written the call to **Add** as follows:

```
public static void Main() {
   // Displays "15"
   Console.WriteLine(Add(1, 2, 3, 4, 5));
}
```

You'll be happy to know that we can do this because of the **params** keyword. The **params** keyword tells the compiler to apply an instance of the **System.ParamArrayAttribute** custom attribute to the parameter.

When the C# compiler detects a call to a method, the compiler checks all of the methods with the specified name, where no parameter has the **ParamArray** attribute applied. If a method exists that can accept the call, the compiler generates the code necessary to call the method. However, if the compiler can't find a match, it looks for methods that have a **ParamArray** attribute to see whether the call can be satisfied. If the compiler finds a match, it emits code that constructs an array and populates its elements before emitting the code that calls the selected method.

In the previous example, no **Add** method is defined that takes five **Int32**-compatible arguments; however, the compiler sees that the source code has a call to **Add** that is being passed a list of **Int32** values and that there is an **Add** method whose array-of-**Int32** parameter is marked with the **ParamArray** attribute. So the compiler considers this a match and generates code that coerces the parameters into an **Int32** array and then calls the **Add** method. The end result is that you can write the code, easily passing a bunch of parameters to **Add**, but the compiler generates code as though you'd written the first version that explicitly constructs and initializes the array.

Only the last parameter to a method can be marked with the **params** keyword (**ParamArrayAttribute**). This parameter must also identify a single-dimension array of any type. It's legal to pass **null** or a reference to an array of **0** entries as the last parameter to the method. The following call to **Add** compiles fine, runs fine, and produces a resulting sum of **0** (as expected):

```
public static void Main() {
    // Both of these lines display "0"
    Console.WriteLine(Add());      // passes new Int32[0] to Add
    Console.WriteLine(Add(null)); // passes null to Add: more efficient (no array allocated)
}
```

So far, all of the examples have shown how to write a method that takes an arbitrary number of **Int32** parameters. How would you write a method that takes an arbitrary number of parameters where the parameters could be any type? The answer is very simple: just modify the method's prototype so that it takes an **Object[]** instead of an **Int32[]**. Here's a method that displays the **Type** of every object passed to it:

```
public sealed class Program {
    public static void Main() {
        DisplayTypes(new Object(), new Random(), "Jeff", 5);
    }

    private static void DisplayTypes(params Object[] objects) {
        if (objects != null) {
            foreach (Object o in objects)
                Console.WriteLine(o.GetType());
        }
    }
}
```

Running this code yields the following output:

```
System.Object
System.Random
System.String
System.Int32
```

Important Be aware that calling a method that takes a variable number of arguments incurs an additional performance hit unless you explicitly pass **null**. After all, an array object must be allocated on the heap, the array's elements must be initialized, and the array's memory must ultimately be garbage collected. To help reduce the performance hit associated with this, you may want to consider defining a few overloaded methods that do not use the **params** keyword. For some examples, look at the **System.String** class's **Concat** method, which has the following overloads:

```
public sealed class String : Object, ... {
    public static string Concat(object arg0);
    public static string Concat(object arg0, object arg1);
    public static string Concat(object arg0, object arg1, object arg2);
    public static string Concat(params object[] args);

    public static string Concat(string str0, string str1);
    public static string Concat(string str0, string str1, string str2);
    public static string Concat(string str0, string str1, string str2, string str3);
    public static string Concat(params string[] values);
}
```

As you can see, the **Concat** method defines several overloads that do not use the **params** key-word. These versions of the **Concat** method are the most frequently called overloads, and these overloads exist in order to improve performance for the most common scenarios. The overloads that use the **params** keyword are there for the less common scenarios; these scenarios will suffer a performance hit, but fortunately, they are rare.

Parameter and Return Type Guidelines

When declaring a method's parameter types, you should specify the weakest type possible, preferring interfaces over base classes. For example, if you are writing a method that manipulates a collection of items, it would be best to declare the method's parameter by using an interface such as **IEnumerable<T>** rather than using a strong data type such as **List<T>** or even a stronger interface type such as **ICollection<T>** or **IList<T>**:

```
// Desired: This method uses a weak parameter type
public void ManipulateItems<T>(IEnumerable<T> collection) { ... }

// Undesired: This method uses a strong parameter type
public void ManipulateItems<T>(List<T> collection) { ... }
```

The reason, of course, is that someone can call the first method passing in an array object, a **List<T>** object, a **String** object, and so on—any object whose type implements **IEnumerable<T>**. The second method allows only **List<T>** objects to be passed in; it will not accept an array or a **String** object. Obviously, the first method is better because it is much more flexible and can be used in a much wider range of scenarios.

Naturally, if you are writing a method that requires a list (not just any enumerable object), then you should declare the parameter type as an **IList<T>**. You should still avoid declaring the parameter type as **List<T>**. Using **IList<T>** allows the caller to pass arrays and any other objects whose type implements **IList<T>**.

Note that my examples talked about collections, which are designed using an interface architecture. If we were talking about classes designed using a base class architecture, the concept still applies. So, for example, if I were implementing a method that processed bytes from a stream, we'd have this:

```
// Desired: This method uses a weak parameter type
public void ProcessBytes(Stream someStream) { ... }

// Undesired: This method uses a strong parameter type
public void ProcessBytes(FileStream fileStream) { ... }
```

The first method can process bytes from any kind of stream: a **FileStream**, a **NetworkStream**, a **MemoryStream**, and so on. The second method can operate only on a **FileStream**, making it far more limited.

On the flip side, it is usually best to declare a method's return type by using the strongest type possible (trying not to commit yourself to a specific type). For example, it is better to declare a method that returns a **FileStream** object as opposed to returning a **Stream** object:

```
// Desired: This method uses a strong return type
public FileStream OpenFile() { ... }

// Undesired: This method uses a weak return type
public Stream OpenFile() { ... }
```

Here, the first method is preferred because it allows the method's caller the option of treating the returned object as either a **FileStream** object or as a **Stream** object. Meanwhile, the second method requires that the caller treat the returned object as a **Stream** object. Basically, it is best to let the caller have as much flexibility as possible when calling a method, allowing the method to be used in the widest range of scenarios.

Sometimes you want to retain the ability to change the internal implementation of a method without affecting the callers. In the example just shown, the **OpenFile** method is unlikely to ever change its internal implementation to return anything other than a **FileStream** object (or an object whose type is derived from **FileStream**). However, if you have a method that returns a **List<String>** object, you might very well want to change the internal implementation of this method in the future so that it would instead return a **String[]**. In the cases in which you want to leave yourself some flexibility to change what your method returns, choose a weaker return type. For example:

```
// Flexible: This method uses a weaker return type
public IList<String> GetStringCollection() { ... }

// Inflexible: This method uses a stronger return type
public List<String> GetStringCollection() { ... }
```

In this example, even though the **GetStringCollection** method uses a **List<String>** object internally and returns it, it is better to prototype the method as returning an **IList<String>** instead. In the future, the **GetStringCollection** method could change its internal collection to use a **String[]**, and callers of the method won't be required to change any of their source code. In fact, they won't even have to recompile their code. Notice in this example that I'm using the strongest of the weakest types. For instance, I'm not using an **IEnumerable<String>** or even **ICollection<String>**.

Const-ness

In some languages, such as unmanaged C++, it is possible to declare methods or parameters as a constant that forbids the code in an instance method from changing any of the object's fields or prevents the code from modifying any of the objects passed into the method. The CLR does not provide for this, and many programmers have been lamenting this missing feature. Since the CLR doesn't offer this feature, no language (including C#) can offer this feature.

First, you should note that in unmanaged C++, marking an instance method or parameter as **const** ensured only that the programmer could not write normal code that would modify the object or parameter. Inside the method, it was always possible to write code that could mutate the object/parameter by either casting away the **const**-ness or by getting the address of the object/argument and then writing to the address. In a sense, unmanaged C++ lied to programmers, making them believe that their constant objects/arguments couldn't be written to even though they could.

When designing a type's implementation, the developer can just avoid writing code that manipulates the object/arguments. For example, strings are immutable because the **String** class doesn't offer any methods that can change a string object.

Also, it would be very difficult for Microsoft to endow the CLR with the ability to verify that a constant object/argument isn't being mutated. The CLR would have to verify at each write that the write was not occurring to a constant object, and this would hurt performance significantly. Of course, a detected violation would result in the CLR throwing an exception. Furthermore, constant support adds a lot of complexity for developers. For example, if a type is immutable, all derived types would have to respect this. In addition, an immutable type would probably have to consist of fields that are also of immutable types.

These are just some of the reasons why the CLR does not support constant objects/arguments.

Chapter 10
Properties

In this chapter, I'll talk about properties. Properties allow source code to call a method by using a simplified syntax. The common language runtime (CLR) offers two kinds of properties: parameterless properties, which are simply called *properties*, and parameterful properties, which are called different names by different programming languages. For example, C# calls parameterful properties *indexers*, and Microsoft Visual Basic calls them *default properties*. I'll also talk about initializing properties using object and collection initializers as well as ways to package a bunch of properties together using C#'s anonymous types and the **System.Tuple** type.

Parameterless Properties

Many types define state information that can be retrieved or altered. Frequently, this state information is implemented as field members of the type. For example, here's a type definition that contains two fields:

```
public sealed class Employee {
   public String Name; // The employee's name
   public Int32  Age;  // The employee's age
}
```

If you were to create an instance of this type, you could easily get or set any of this state information with code similar to the following:

```
Employee e = new Employee();
e.Name = "Jeffrey Richter";  // Set the employee's Name.
e.Age  = 45;                 // Set the employee's Age.

Console.WriteLine(e.Name);   // Displays "Jeffrey Richter"
```

Querying and setting an object's state information in the way I just demonstrated is very common. However, I would argue that the preceding code should never be implemented as shown. One of the hallmarks of object-oriented design and programming is *data encapsulation*. Data encapsulation means that your type's fields should never be publicly exposed because it's too easy to write code that improperly uses the fields, corrupting the object's state. For example, a developer could easily corrupt an **Employee** object with code like this:

```
e.Age = -5; // How could someone be -5 years old?
```

There are additional reasons for encapsulating access to a type's data field. For example, you might want access to a field to execute some side effect, cache some value, or lazily create some internal object. You might also want access to the field to be thread-safe. Or perhaps the field is a logical field whose value isn't represented by bytes in memory but whose value is instead calculated using some algorithm.

For any of these reasons, when designing a type, I strongly suggest that all of your fields be **private**. Then, to allow a user of your type to get or set state information, you expose methods for that specific purpose. Methods that wrap access to a field are typically called accessor methods. These accessor methods can optionally perform sanity checking and ensure that the object's state is never corrupted. For example, I'd rewrite the previous class as follows:

```
public sealed class Employee {
    private String m_Name;    // Field is now private
    private Int32  m_Age;     // Field is now private

    public String GetName() {
        return(m_Name);
    }

    public void SetName(String value) {
        m_Name = value;
    }

    public Int32 GetAge() {
        return(m_Age);
    }

    public void SetAge(Int32 value) {
        if (value < 0)
            throw new ArgumentOutOfRangeException("value",  value.ToString(),
                "The value must be greater than or equal to 0");
        m_Age = value;
    }
}
```

Although this is a simple example, you should still be able to see the enormous benefit you get from encapsulating the data fields. You should also be able to see how easy it is to make read-only or write-only properties: just don't implement one of the accessor methods. Alternatively, you could allow only derived types to modify the value by marking the **SetXxx** method as **protected**.

Encapsulating the data as shown earlier has two disadvantages. First, you have to write more code because you now have to implement additional methods. Second, users of the type must now call methods rather than simply refer to a single field name.

```
e.SetName("Jeffrey Richter");        // updates the employee's name
String EmployeeName = e.GetName();   // retrieves the employee's name
e.SetAge(41);                        // Updates the employee's age
e.SetAge(-5);                        // Throws ArgumentOutOfRangeException
Int32 EmployeeAge = e.GetAge();      // retrieves the employee's age
```

Personally, I think these disadvantages are quite minor. Nevertheless, programming languages and the CLR offer a mechanism called *properties* that alleviates the first disadvantage a little and removes the second disadvantage entirely.

The class shown here uses properties and is functionally identical to the class shown earlier:

```
public sealed class Employee {
    private String m_Name;
    private Int32  m_Age;

    public String Name {
        get { return(m_Name); }
        set { m_Name = value; } // The 'value' keyword always identifies the new value.
    }

    public Int32 Age {
        get { return(m_Age); }
        set {
            if (value < 0)     // The 'value' keyword always identifies the new value.
                throw new ArgumentOutOfRangeException("value",  value.ToString(),
                    "The value must be greater than or equal to 0");
            m_Age = value;
        }
    }
}
```

As you can see, properties complicate the definition of the type slightly, but the fact that they allow you to write your code as follows more than compensates for the extra work:

```
e.Name = "Jeffrey Richter";    // "sets" the employee name
String EmployeeName = e.Name;  // "gets" the employee's name
e.Age = 41;                    // "sets" the employee's age
e.Age = -5;                    // Throws ArgumentOutOfRangeException
Int32 EmployeeAge = e.Age;     // "gets" the employee's age
```

You can think of properties as *smart fields*: fields with additional logic behind them. The CLR supports static, instance, abstract, and virtual properties. In addition, properties can be marked with any accessibility modifier (discussed in Chapter 6, "Type and Member Basics") and defined within an interface (discussed in Chapter 13, "Interfaces").

Each property has a name and a type (which can't be **void**). It isn't possible to overload properties (that is, have two properties with the same name if their types are different).

When you define a property, you typically specify both a **get** and a **set** method. However, you can leave out the **set** method to define a read-only property or leave out the **get** method to define a write-only property.

It's also quite common for the property's **get/set** methods to manipulate a private field defined within the type. This field is commonly referred to as the *backing field*. The **get** and **set** methods don't have to access a backing field, however. For example, the **System.Threading.Thread** type offers a **Priority** property that communicates directly with the operating system; the **Thread** object doesn't maintain a field for a thread's priority. Another example of properties without backing fields are those read-only properties calculated at runtime—for example, the length of a zero-terminated array or the area of a rectangle when you have its height and width.

When you define a property, depending on its definition, the compiler will emit either two or three of the following items into the resulting managed assembly:

- A method representing the property's **get** accessor method. This is emitted only if you define a **get** accessor method for the property.

- A method representing the property's **set** accessor method. This is emitted only if you define a **set** accessor method for the property.

- A property definition in the managed assembly's metadata. This is always emitted.

Refer back to the **Employee** type shown earlier. As the compiler compiles this type, it comes across the **Name** and **Age** properties. Because both properties have **get** and **set** accessor methods, the compiler emits four method definitions into the **Employee** type. It's as though the original source were written as follows:

```
public sealed class Employee {
    private String m_Name;
    private Int32  m_Age;

    public String get_Name(){
        return m_Name;
    }
    public void   set_Name(String value) {
        m_Name = value; // The argument 'value' always identifies the new value.
    }

    public Int32 get_Age() {
        return m_Age;
    }

    public void  set_Age(Int32 value) {
        if (value < 0)      // The 'value' always identifies the new value.
            throw new ArgumentOutOfRangeException("value", value.ToString(),
                "The value must be greater than or equal to 0");
        m_Age = value;
    }
}
```

The compiler automatically generates names for these methods by prepending **get_** or **set_** to the property name specified by the developer.

C# has built-in support for properties. When the C# compiler sees code that's trying to get or set a property, the compiler actually emits a call to one of these methods. If you're using a programming language that doesn't directly support properties, you can still access properties by calling the desired accessor method. The effect is exactly the same; it's just that the source code doesn't look as pretty.

In addition to emitting the accessor methods, compilers also emit a property definition entry into the managed assembly's metadata for each property defined in the source code. This entry contains some flags and the type of the property, and it refers to the **get** and **set** accessor methods. This information exists simply to draw an association between the abstract concept of a "property" and its accessor methods. Compilers and other tools can use this metadata, which can be obtained by using the **System.Reflection.PropertyInfo** class. The CLR doesn't use this metadata information and requires only the accessor methods at runtime.

Automatically Implemented Properties

If you are creating a property to simply encapsulate a backing field, then C# offers a simplified syntax known as *automatically implemented properties* (AIPs), as shown here for the **Name** property:

```
public sealed class Employee {
   // This property is an automatically implemented property
   public String Name { get; set; }

   private Int32  m_Age;


   public Int32 Age {
      get { return(m_Age); }
      set {
         if (value < 0)      // The 'value' keyword always identifies the new value.
            throw new ArgumentOutOfRangeException("value", value.ToString(),
               "The value must be greater than or equal to 0");
         m_Age = value;
      }
   }
}
```

When you declare a property and do not provide an implementation for the **get/set** methods, then the C# compiler will automatically declare for you a private field. In this example, the field will be of type **String**, the type of the property. And, the compiler will automatically implement the **get_Name** and **set_Name** methods for you to return the value in the field and to set the field's value, respectively.

You might wonder what the value of doing this is, as opposed to just declaring a **public String** field called **Name**. Well, there is a big difference. Using the AIP syntax means that you have created a property. Any code that accesses this property is actually calling **get** and **set** methods. If you decide later to implement the **get** and/or **set** method yourself instead of accepting the compiler's default implementation, then any code that accesses the property will not have to be recompiled. However, if you declared **Name** as a field and then you later change it to a property, then all code that accessed the field will have to be recompiled so that it now accesses the property methods.

- Personally, I do not like the compiler's AIP feature, so I usually avoid it for the following reason: The syntax for a field declaration can include initialization so that you are declaring and initializing the field in one line of code. However, there is no convenient syntax to set an AIP to an initial value. Therefore, you must explicitly initialize each AIP in each constructor method.

- The runtime serialization engines persist the name of the field in a serialized stream. The name of the backing field for an AIP is determined by the compiler, and it could actually change the name of this backing field every time you recompile your code, negating the ability to deserialize instances of any types that contain an AIP. Do not use the AIP feature with any type you intend to serialize or deserialize.

- When debugging, you cannot put a breakpoint on an AIP **get** or **set** method, so you cannot easily detect when an application is getting or setting this property. You can set breakpoints on manually implemented properties, which can be quite handy when tracking down bugs.

You should also know that when you use AIPs, the property must be readable and writable; that is, the compiler must produce both **get** and **set** methods. This makes sense because a write-only field is not useful without the ability to read its value; likewise, a read-only field would always have its default value. In addition, since you do not know the name of the compiler-generated backing field, your code must always access the property by using the property name. And, if you decide you want to explicitly implement one of the accessor methods, then you must explicitly implement both accessor methods and you are not using the AIP feature anymore. For a single property, the AIP feature is an all-or-nothing deal.

Defining Properties Intelligently

Personally, I don't like properties and I wish that they were not supported in the Microsoft .NET Framework and its programming languages. The reason is that properties look like fields, but they are methods. This has been known to cause a phenomenal amount of confusion. When a programmer sees code that appears to be accessing a field, there are many assumptions that the programmer makes that may not be true for a property. For example,

- A property may be read-only or write-only; field access is always readable and writable. If you define a property, it is best to offer both **get** and **set** accessor methods.

■ A property method may throw an exception; field access never throws an exception.

■ A property cannot be passed as an **out** or **ref** parameter to a method; a field can. For example, the following code will not compile:

```
using System;

public sealed class SomeType {
   private static String Name {
      get { return null; }
      set {}
   }

   static void MethodWithOutParam(out String n) { n = null; }

   public static void Main() {
      // For the line of code below, the C# compiler emits the following:
      // error CS0206: A property or indexer may not
      // be passed as an out or ref parameter
      MethodWithOutParam(out Name);
   }
}
```

■ A property method can take a long time to execute; field access always completes immediately. A common reason to use properties is to perform thread synchronization, which can stop the thread forever, and therefore, a property should not be used if thread synchronization is required. In that situation, a method is preferred. Also, if your class can be accessed remotely (for example, your class is derived from **System.MarshalByRefObject**), calling the property method will be very slow, and therefore, a method is preferred to a property. In my opinion, classes derived from **MarshalByRefObject** should never use properties.

■ If called multiple times in a row, a property method may return a different value each time; a field returns the same value each time. The **System.DateTime** class has a read-only **Now** property that returns the current date and time. Each time you query this property, it will return a different value. This is a mistake, and Microsoft wishes that they could fix the class by making **Now** a method instead of a property. **Environment**'s **TickCount** property is another example of this mistake.

■ A property method may cause observable side effects; field access never does. In other words, a user of a type should be able to set various properties defined by a type in any order he or she chooses without noticing any different behavior in the type.

■ A property method may require additional memory or return a reference to something that is not actually part of the object's state, so modifying the returned object has no effect on the original object; querying a field always returns a reference to an object that is guaranteed to be part of the original object's state. Working with a property that returns a copy can be very confusing to developers, and this characteristic is frequently not documented.

It has come to my attention that people use properties far more often than they should. If you examine this list of differences between properties and fields, you'll see that there are very few circumstances in which defining a property is actually useful and will not cause confusion for developers. The only thing that properties buy you is some simplified syntax; there is no performance benefit compared to calling a non-property method, and understandability of the code is reduced. If I had been involved in the design of the .NET Framework and compilers, I would have not offered properties at all; instead, I would have programmers actually implement **GetXxx** and **SetXxx** methods as desired. Then, if compilers wanted to offer some special, simplified syntax for calling these methods, so be it. But I'd want the compiler to use syntax that is different from field access syntax so that programmers really understand what they are doing—a method call.

Properties and the Visual Studio Debugger

Microsoft Visual Studio allows you to enter an object's property in the debugger's watch window. When you do this, every time you hit a breakpoint, the debugger calls into the property's **get** accessor method and displays the returned value. This can be quite helpful in tracking down bugs, but it can also cause bugs to occur and hurt your debugging performance. For example, let's say that you have created a **FileStream** for a file on a network share and then you add **FileStream**'s **Length** property to the debugger's watch window. Now, every time you hit a breakpoint, the debugger will call **Length**'s **get** accessor method, which internally makes a network request to the server to get the current length of the file!

Similarly, if your property's **get** accessor method has a side effect, then this side effect will execute every time you hit a breakpoint. For example, let's say that your property's **get** accessor method increments a counter every time it is called; this counter will now be incremented every time you hit a breakpoint, too. Because of these potential problems, Visual Studio allows you to turn off property evaluation for properties shown in watch windows. To turn property evaluation off in Visual Studio, select Tools, Options, Debugging, and General and in the list box in Figure 10-1, and clear the Enable Property Evaluation And Other Implicit Function Calls option. Note that even with this item cleared, you can add the property to the watch window and manually force Visual Studio to evaluate it by clicking the force evaluation circle in the watch window's Value column.

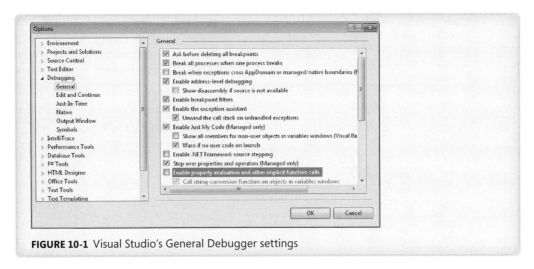

FIGURE 10-1 Visual Studio's General Debugger settings

Object and Collection Initializers

It is very common to construct an object and then set some of the object's public properties (or fields). To simplify this common programming pattern, the C# language supports a special object initialization syntax. Here is an example:

```
Employee e = new Employee() { Name = "Jeff", Age = 45 };
```

With this one statement, I am constructing an **Employee** object, calling its parameterless constructor, and then setting its public **Name** property to **"Jeff"** and its public **Age** property to **45**. In fact, the code above is identical to this, which you could verify by examining the Intermediate Language (IL) for both of these code fragments:

```
Employee e = new Employee();
e.Name = "Jeff";
e.Age = 45;
```

The real benefit of the object initializer syntax is that it allows you to code in an expression context (as opposed to a statement context), permitting composability of functions, which in turn increases code readability. For example, I can now write this:

```
String s = new Employee() { Name = "Jeff", Age = 45 }.ToString().ToUpper();
```

So now, in one statement, I have constructed an **Employee** object, called its constructor, initialized two public properties, and then, using the resulting expression, called **ToString** on it followed by calling **ToUpper**. For more about composability of functions, see the "Extension Methods" section in Chapter 8, "Methods."

As a small side note, C# also lets you omit the parentheses before the open brace if you want to call a parameterless constructor. The line below produces the same IL as the line above:

```
String s = new Employee { Name = "Jeff", Age = 45 }.ToString().ToUpper();
```

If a property's type implements the **IEnumerable** or **IEnumerable<T>** interface, then the property is considered to be a collection, and initializing a collection is an additive operation as opposed to a replacement operation. For example, suppose I have the following class definition:

```
public sealed class Classroom {
   private List<String> m_students = new List<String>();
   public List<String> Students { get { return m_students; } }

   public Classroom() {}
}
```

I can now have code that constructs a **Classroom** object and initializes the **Students** collection as follows:

```
public static void M() {
   Classroom classroom = new Classroom {
      Students = { "Jeff", "Kristin", "Aidan", "Grant" }
   };

   // Show the 4 students in the classroom
   foreach (var student in classroom.Students)
      Console.WriteLine(student);
}
```

When compiling this code, the compiler sees that the **Students** property is of type **List<String>** and that this type implements the **IEnumerable<String>** interface. Now, the compiler assumes that the **List<String>** type offers a method called **Add** (because most collection classes actually offer an **Add** method that adds items to the collection). The compiler then generates code to call the collection's **Add** method. So, the code shown above is converted by the compiler into this:

```
public static void M() {
   Classroom classroom = new Classroom();
   classroom.Students.Add("Jeff");
   classroom.Students.Add("Kristin");
   classroom.Students.Add("Aidan");
   classroom.Students.Add("Grant");

   // Show the 4 students in the classroom
   foreach (var student in classroom.Students)
      Console.WriteLine(student);
}
```

If the property's type implements **IEnumerable** or **IEnumerable<T>** but the type doesn't offer an **Add** method, then the compiler does not let you use the collection initialize syntax to add items to the collection; instead, the compiler issues something like the following message: "**error CS0117: 'System.Collections.Generic.IEnumerable<string>' does not contain a definition for 'Add'.**"

Some collection's **Add** methods take multiple arguments. For example, **Dictionary**'s **Add** method:

```
public void Add(TKey key, TValue value);
```

You can pass multiple arguments to an **Add** method by using nested braces in a collection initializer, as follows:

```
var table = new Dictionary<String, Int32> {
   { "Jeffrey", 1 }, { "Kristin", 2 }, { "Aidan", 3 }, { "Grant", 4 }
};
```

The line above is identical to:

```
var table = new Dictionary<String, Int32>();
table.Add("Jeffrey", 1);
table.Add("Kristin", 2);
table.Add("Aidan", 3);
table.Add("Grant", 4);
```

Anonymous Types

C#'s anonymous type feature allows you to automatically declare an immutable tuple type using a very simple and succinct syntax. A *tuple type*[1] is a type that contains a collection of properties that are usually related to each other in some way. In the top line of the code below, I am defining a class with two properties (**Name** of type **String**, and **Year** of type **Int32**), constructing an instance of this type, and setting its **Name** property to **"Jeff"** and its **Year** property to **1964**.

```
// Define a type, construct an instance of it, & initialize its properties
var o1 = new { Name = "Jeff", Year = 1964 };

// Display the properties on the console:
Console.WriteLine("Name={0}, Year={1}", o1.Name, o1.Year);// Displays: Name=Jeff, Year=1964
```

This top line of code creates an anonymous type because I did not specify a type name after the **new** keyword, so the compiler will create a type name for me automatically and not tell me what it is (which is why it is called an anonymous type). The line of code uses the object initializer syntax discussed in the previous section to declare the properties and also to initialize these properties. Also, since I (the developer) do not know the name of the type at compile time, I do not know what type to declare the variable **o1** as. However, this is not a problem, as I can use C#'s implicitly typed local variable feature (**var**), as discussed in

---

[1] The term originated as an abstraction of the sequence: single, double, triple, quadruple, quintuple, *n*-tuple.

Chapter 9, "Parameters," to have the compiler infer the type from the expression on the right of the assignment operator (=).

Now, let's focus on what the compiler is actually doing. When you write a line of code like this:

```
var o = new { property1 = expression1, ..., propertyN = expressionN };
```

the compiler infers the type of each expression, creates private fields of these inferred types, creates public read-only properties for each of the fields, and creates a constructor that accepts all these expressions. The constructor's code initializes the private read-only fields from the expression results passed in to it. In addition, the compiler overrides **Object**'s **Equals**, **GetHashCode**, and **ToString** methods and generates code inside all these methods. In effect, the class that the compiler generates looks like this:

```
[CompilerGenerated]
internal sealed class <>f__AnonymousType0<...>: Object {
   private readonly t1 f1;
   public  t1 p1 { get { return f1; } }

   ...

   private readonly tn fn;
   public  tn pn { get { return fn; } }

   public <>f__AnonymousType0<...>(t1 a1, ..., tn an) {
      f1 = a1; ...; fn = an; // Set all fields
   }

   public override Boolean Equals(Object value) {
      // Return false if any fields don't match; else true
   }

   public override Int32 GetHashCode() {
      // Returns a hash code generated from each fields' hash code
   }

   public override String ToString() {
      // Return comma-separated set of property name = value pairs
   }
}
```

The compiler generates **Equals** and **GetHashCode** methods so that instances of the anonymous type can be placed in a hash table collection. The properties are readonly as opposed to read/write to help prevent the object's hashcode from changing. Changing the hashcode for an object used as a key in a hashtable can prevent the object from being found. The compiler generates the **ToString** method to help with debugging. In the Visual Studio debugger, you can place the mouse cursor over a variable that refers to an instance of an anonymous type, and Visual Studio will invoke the **ToString** method and show the resulting string in a datatip window. By the way, Visual Studio's IntelliSense will suggest the property names as you write code in the editor—a very nice feature.

The compiler supports two additional syntaxes for declaring a property inside an anonymous type where it can infer the property names and types from variables:

```
String Name = "Grant";
DateTime dt = DateTime.Now;

// Anonymous type with two properties
//  1. String Name property set to Grant
//  2. Int32 Year property set to the year inside the dt
var o2 = new { Name, dt.Year };
```

In this example, the compiler determines that the first property should be called **Name**. Since **Name** is the name of a local variable, the compiler sets the type of the property to be the same type as the local variable: **String**. For the second property, the compiler uses the name of the field/property: **Year**. **Year** is an **Int32** property of the **DateTime** class and therefore the **Year** property in the anonymous type will also be an **Int32**. Now, when the compiler constructs an instance of this anonymous type, it will set the instance's **Name** property to the same value that is in the **Name** local variable so the **Name** property will refer to the same **"Grant"** string. The compiler will set the instance's **Year** property to the same value that is returned from **dt**'s **Year** property.

The compiler is very intelligent about defining anonymous types. If the compiler sees that you are defining multiple anonymous types in your source code that have the identical structure, the compiler will create just one definition for the anonymous type and create multiple instances of that type. By "same structure," I mean that the anonymous types have the same type and name for each property and that these properties are specified in the same order. In the code examples above, the type of variable **o1** and the type of variable **o2** will be the same type because the two lines of code are defining an anonymous type with a **Name/String** property and a **Year/Int32** property, and **Name** comes before **Year**.

Since the two variables are of the same type, we get to do some cool things, such as checking if the two objects contain equal values and assigning a reference to one object into the other's variable, as follows:

```
// One type allows equality and assignment operations.
Console.WriteLine("Objects are equal: " + o1.Equals(o2));
o1 = o2;   // Assignment
```

Also, because of this type identity, we can create an implicitly typed array (discussed in the "Initializing Array Elements" section in Chapter 16, "Arrays") of anonymous types:

```
// This works because all of the objects are of the same anonymous type
var people = new[] {
    o1,  // From earlier in this section
    new { Name = "Kristin", Year = 1970 },
    new { Name = "Aidan", Year = 2003 },
    new { Name = "Grant", Year = 2008 }
};
```

```
// This shows how to walk through the array of anonymous types (var is required)
foreach (var person in people)
    Console.WriteLine("Person={0}, Year={1}", person.Name, person.Year);
```

Anonymous types are most commonly used with the Language Integrated Query (LINQ) technology, where you perform a query that results in a collection of objects that are all of the same anonymous type. Then, you process the objects in the resulting collection. All this takes place in the same method. Here is an example that returns all the files in my document directory that have been modified within the past seven days:

```
String myDocuments = Environment.GetFolderPath(Environment.SpecialFolder.MyDocuments);
var query =
        from pathname in Directory.GetFiles(myDocuments)
        let LastWriteTime = File.GetLastWriteTime(pathname)
        where LastWriteTime > (DateTime.Now - TimeSpan.FromDays(7))
        orderby LastWriteTime
        select new { Path = pathname, LastWriteTime };// Set of anonymous type objects

foreach (var file in query)
    Console.WriteLine("LastWriteTime={0}, Path={1}", file.LastWriteTime, file.Path);
```

Instances of anonymous types are not supposed to leak outside of a method. A method cannot be prototyped as accepting a parameter of an anonymous type because there is no way to specify the anonymous type. Similarly, a method cannot indicate that it returns a reference to an anonymous type. While it is possible to treat an instance of an anonymous type as an **Object** (since all anonymous types are derived from **Object**), there is no way to cast a variable of type **Object** back into an anonymous type because you don't know the name of the anonymous type at compile time. If you want to pass a tuple around, then you should consider using the **System.Tuple** type discussed in the next section.

The **System.Tuple** Type

In the **System** namespace, Microsoft has defined several generic **Tuple** types (all derived from **Object**) that differ by arity (the number of generic parameters). Here is what the simplest and most complex ones essentially look like:

```
// This is the simplest:
[Serializable]
public class Tuple<T1> {
    private T1 m_Item1;
    public Tuple(T1 item1) { m_Item1 = item1; }
    public T1 Item1 { get { return m_Item1; } }
}


// This is the most complex:
[Serializable]
public class Tuple<T1, T2, T3, T4, T5, T6, T7, TRest> {
    private T1 m_Item1; private T2 m_Item2; private T3 m_Item3; private T4 m_Item4;
    private T5 m_Item5; private T6 m_Item6; private T7 m_Item7; private TRestm_Rest;
```

```
    public Tuple(T1 item1, T2 item2, T3 item3, T4 item4, T5 item5, T6 item6, T7 item7,
        TRest t) {
        m_Item1 = item1; m_Item2 = item2; m_Item3 = item3; m_Item4 = item4;
        m_Item5 = item5; m_Item6 = item6; m_Item7 = item7; m_Rest = rest;
    }

    public T1 Item1 { get { return m_Item1; } }
    public T2 Item2 { get { return m_Item2; } }
    public T3 Item3 { get { return m_Item3; } }
    public T4 Item4 { get { return m_Item4; } }
    public T5 Item5 { get { return m_Item5; } }
    public T6 Item6 { get { return m_Item6; } }
    public T7 Item7 { get { return m_Item7; } }
    public TRest Rest { get { return m_Rest; } }
}
```

Like anonymous types, once a **Tuple** is created, it is immutable (all properties are read-only). I don't show it here, but the **Tuple** classes also offer **CompareTo**, **Equals**, **GetHashCode**, and **ToString** methods, as well as a **Size** property. In addition, all the **Tuple** types implement the **IStructuralEquatable**, **IStructuralComparable**, and **IComparable** interfaces so that you can compare two **Tuple** objects with each other to see how their fields compare with each other. Refer to the SDK documentation to learn more about these methods and interfaces.

Here is an example of a method that uses a **Tuple** type to return two pieces of information back to a caller:

```
// Returns minimum in Item1 & maximum in Item2
private static Tuple<Int32, Int32>MinMax(Int32 a, Int32 b) {
    return new Tuple<Int32, Int32>(Math.Min(a, b), Math.Max(a, b));
}

// This shows how to call the method and how to use the returned Tuple
private static void TupleTypes() {
    varminmax = MinMax(6, 2);
    Console.WriteLine("Min={0}, Max={1}", minmax.Item1, minmax.Item2); // Min=2, Max=6
}
```

Of course, it is very important that the producer and consumer of the **Tuple** have a clear understanding of what is being returned in the **Item#** properties. With anonymous types, the properties are given actual names based on the source code that defines the anonymous type. With **Tuple** types, the properties are assigned their **Item#** names by Microsoft and you cannot change this at all. Unfortunately, these names have no real meaning or significance, so it is up to the producer and consumer to assign meanings to them. This also reduces code readability and maintainability so you should add comments to your code explaining what the producer/consumer understanding is.

The compiler can only infer generic types when calling a generic method, not when you are calling a constructor. For this reason, the **System** namespace also includes a non-generic, static **Tuple** class containing a bunch of static **Create** methods which can infer generic types from arguments. This class acts as a factory for creating **Tuple** objects, and it exists simply to simplify your code. Here is a rewrite of the **MinMax** method shown earlier using the static **Tuple** class:

```
// Returns minimum in Item1 & maximum in Item2
private static Tuple<Int32, Int32>MinMax(Int32 a, Int32 b) {
   return Tuple.Create(Math.Min(a, b), Math.Max(a, b));    // Simpler syntax
}
```

If you want to create a **Tuple** with more than eight elements in it, then you would pass another **Tuple** for the **Rest** parameter as follows:

```
var t = Tuple.Create(0, 1, 2, 3, 4, 5, 6, Tuple.Create(7, 8));
Console.WriteLine("{0}, {1}, {2}, {3}, {4}, {5}, {6}, {7}, {8}",
   t.Item1, t.Item2, t.Item3, t.Item4, t.Item5, t.Item6, t.Item7,
   t.Rest.Item1.Item1, t.Rest.Item1.Item2);
```

> **Note** In addition to anonymous types and the **Tuple** types, you might want to take a look at the **System.Dynamic.ExpandoObject** class (defined in the System.Core.dll assembly). When you use this class with C#'s **dynamic** type (discussed in Chapter 5, "Primitive, Reference, and Value Types"), you have another way of grouping a set of properties (key/value pairs) together. The result is not compile-time type-safe, but the syntax looks nice (although you get no IntelliSense support), and you can pass **ExpandoObject** objects between C# and dynamic languages like Python. Here's some sample code that uses an **ExpandoObject**:
>
> ```
> dynamic e = new System.Dynamic.ExpandoObject();
> e.x = 6;        // Add an Int32 'x' property whose value is 6
> e.y = "Jeff"; // Add a String 'y' property whose value is "Jeff"
> e.z = null;   // Add an Object 'z' property whose value is null
>
> // See all the properties and their values:
> foreach (var v in (IDictionary<String, Object>)e)
>    Console.WriteLine("Key={0}, V={1}", v.Key, v.Value);
>
>
> // Remove the 'x' property and its value
> var d = (IDictionary<String, Object>)e;
> d.Remove("x");
> ```

Parameterful Properties

In the previous section, the **get** accessor methods for the properties accepted no parameters. For this reason, I called these properties *parameterless properties*. These properties are easy to understand because they have the feel of accessing a field. In addition to these field-like properties, programming languages also support what I call *parameterful properties*, whose **get** accessor methods accept one or more parameters and whose **set** accessor methods accept two or more parameters. Different programming languages expose parameterful properties in different ways. Also, languages use different terms to refer to parameterful properties: C# calls them *indexers* and Visual Basic calls them *default properties*. In this section, I'll focus on how C# exposes its indexers by using parameterful properties.

In C#, parameterful properties (indexers) are exposed using an array-like syntax. In other words, you can think of an indexer as a way for the C# developer to overload the **[]** operator. Here's an example of a **BitArray** class that allows array-like syntax to index into the set of bits maintained by an instance of the class:

```csharp
using System;

public sealed class BitArray {
    // Private array of bytes that hold the bits
    private Byte[] m_byteArray;
    private Int32  m_numBits;

    // Constructor that allocates the byte array and sets all bits to 0
    public BitArray(Int32 numBits) {
        // Validate arguments first.
        if (numBits <= 0)
            throw new ArgumentOutOfRangeException("numBits must be > 0");

        // Save the number of bits.
        m_numBits = numBits;

        // Allocate the bytes for the bit array.
        m_byteArray = new Byte[(numBits + 7) / 8];
    }

    // This is the indexer (parameterful property).
    public Boolean this[Int32 bitPos] {

        // This is the indexer's get accessor method.
        get {
            // Validate arguments first
            if ((bitPos < 0) || (bitPos >= m_numBits))
                throw new ArgumentOutOfRangeException("bitPos");

            // Return the state of the indexed bit.
            return (m_byteArray[bitPos / 8] & (1 << (bitPos % 8))) != 0;
        }

        // This is the indexer's set accessor method.
        set {
            if ((bitPos < 0) || (bitPos >= m_numBits))
                throw new ArgumentOutOfRangeException("bitPos", bitPos.ToString());
            if (value) {
                // Turn the indexed bit on.
                m_byteArray[bitPos / 8] = (Byte)
                    (m_byteArray[bitPos / 8] | (1 << (bitPos % 8)));
            } else {
                // Turn the indexed bit off.
                m_byteArray[bitPos / 8] = (Byte)
                    (m_byteArray[bitPos / 8] & ~(1 << (bitPos % 8)));
            }
        }
    }
}
```

Using the **BitArray** class's indexer is incredibly simple:

```
// Allocate a BitArray that can hold 14 bits.
BitArray ba = new BitArray(14);

// Turn all the even-numbered bits on by calling the set accessor.
for (Int32 x = 0; x < 14; x++) {
   ba[x] = (x % 2 == 0);
}

// Show the state of all the bits by calling the get accessor.
for (Int32 x = 0; x < 14; x++) {
   Console.WriteLine("Bit " + x + " is " + (ba[x] ? "On" : "Off"));
}
```

In the **BitArray** example, the indexer takes one **Int32** parameter, **bitPos**. All indexers must have at least one parameter, but they can have more. These parameters (as well as the return type) can be of any data type (except **void**). An example of an indexer that has more than one parameter can be found in the **System.Drawing.Imaging.ColorMatrix** class, which ships in the System.Drawing.dll assembly.

It's quite common to create an indexer to look up values in an associative array. In fact, the **System.Collections.Generic.Dictionary** type offers an indexer that takes a key and returns the value associated with the key. Unlike parameterless properties, a type can offer multiple, overloaded indexers as long as their signatures differ.

Like a parameterless property's **set** accessor method, an indexer's **set** accessor method also contains a hidden parameter, called **value** in C#. This parameter indicates the new value desired for the "indexed element."

The CLR doesn't differentiate parameterless properties and parameterful properties; to the CLR, each is simply a pair of methods and a piece of metadata defined within a type. As mentioned earlier, different programming languages require different syntax to create and use parameterful properties. The fact that C# requires **this[...]** as the syntax for expressing an indexer was purely a choice made by the C# team. What this choice means is that C# allows indexers to be defined only on instances of objects. C# doesn't offer syntax allowing a developer to define a static indexer property, although the CLR does support static parameterful properties.

Because the CLR treats parameterful properties just as it does parameterless properties, the compiler will emit either two or three of the following items into the resulting managed assembly:

- A method representing the parameterful property's **get** accessor method. This is emitted only if you define a **get** accessor method for the property.

- A method representing the parameterful property's **set** accessor method. This is emitted only if you define a **set** accessor method for the property.

- A property definition in the managed assembly's metadata, which is always emitted. There's no special parameterful property metadata definition table because, to the CLR, parameterful properties are just properties.

For the **BitArray** class shown earlier, the compiler compiles the indexer as though the original source code were written as follows:

```
public sealed class BitArray {

    // This is the indexer's get accessor method.
    public Boolean get_Item(Int32 bitPos) { /* ... */ }

    // This is the indexer's set accessor method.
    public void    set_Item(Int32 bitPos, Boolean value)  { /* ... */ }
}
```

The compiler automatically generates names for these methods by prepending **get_** and **set_** to the *indexer name*. Because the C# syntax for an indexer doesn't allow the developer to specify an *indexer name*, the C# compiler team had to choose a default name to use for the accessor methods; they chose **Item**. Therefore, the method names emitted by the compiler are **get_Item** and **set_Item**.

When examining the .NET Framework Reference documentation, you can tell if a type offers an indexer by looking for a property named **Item**. For example, the **System.Collections.Generic.List** type offers a public instance property named **Item**; this property is **List**'s indexer.

When you program in C#, you never see the name of **Item**, so you don't normally care that the compiler has chosen this name for you. However, if you're designing an indexer for a type that code written in other programming languages will be accessing, you might want to change the default name, **Item**, given to your indexer's **get** and **set** accessor methods. C# allows you to rename these methods by applying the **System.Runtime.CompilerServices.IndexerNameAttribute** custom attribute to the indexer. The following code demonstrates how to do this:

```
using System;
using System.Runtime.CompilerServices;

public sealed class BitArray {

    [IndexerName("Bit")]
    public Boolean this[Int32 bitPos] {
        // At least one accessor method is defined here
    }
}
```

Now the compiler will emit methods called **get_Bit** and **set_Bit** instead of **get_Item** and **set_Item**. When compiling, the C# compiler sees the **IndexerName** attribute, and this tells the compiler how to name the methods and the property metadata; the attribute itself is not emitted into the assembly's metadata.[2]

Here's some Visual Basic code that demonstrates how to access this C# indexer:

```
' Construct an instance of the BitArray type.
Dim ba as New BitArray(10)

' Visual Basic uses () instead of [] to specify array elements.
Console.WriteLine(ba(2))        ' Displays True or False

' Visual Basic also allows you to access the indexer by its name.
Console.WriteLine(ba.Bit(2))    ' Displays same as previous line
```

In C#, a single type can define multiple indexers as long as the indexers all take different parameter sets. In other programming languages, the **IndexerName** attribute allows you to define multiple indexers with the same signature because each can have a different name. The reason C# won't allow you to do this is because its syntax doesn't refer to the indexer by name; the compiler wouldn't know which indexer you were referring to. Attempting to compile the following C# source code causes the compiler to generate the following message: "**error C0111: Type 'SomeType' already defines a member called 'this' with the same parameter types.**"

```
using System;
using System.Runtime.CompilerServices;

public sealed class SomeType {

   // Define a get_Item accessor method.
   public Int32 this[Boolean b] {
      get { return 0; }
   }

   // Define a get_Jeff accessor method.
   [IndexerName("Jeff")]
   public String this[Boolean b] {
      get { return null; }
   }
}
```

You can clearly see that C# thinks of indexers as a way to overload the [] operator, and this operator can't be used to disambiguate parameterful properties with different method names and identical parameter sets.

By the way, the **System.String** type is an example of a type that changed the name of its indexer. The name of **String**'s indexer is **Chars** instead of **Item**. This read-only property allows you to get an individual character within a string. For programming languages that don't use [] operator syntax to access this property, **Chars** was decided to be a more meaningful name.

---

[2] For this reason, the **IndexerNameAttribute** class is not part of the ECMA standardization of the CLI and the C# language.

Selecting the Primary Parameterful Property

C#'s limitations with respect to indexers brings up the following two questions:

- What if a type is defined in a programming language that does allow the developer to define several parameterful properties?
- How can this type be consumed from C#?

The answer to both questions is that a type must select one of the parameterful property names to be the default property by applying an instance of **System.Reflection.DefaultMemberAttribute** to the class itself. For the record, **DefaultMemberAttribute** can be applied to a class, a structure, or an interface. In C#, when you compile a type that defines a parameterful property, the compiler automatically applies an instance of **DefaultMember** attribute to the defining type and takes it into account when you use the **IndexerName** attribute. This attribute's constructor specifies the name that is to be used for the type's default parameterful property.

So, in C#, if you define a type that has a parameterful property and you don't specify the **IndexerName** attribute, the defining type will have a **DefaultMember** attribute indicating **Item**. If you apply the **IndexerName** attribute to a parameterful property, the defining type will have a **DefaultMember** attribute indicating the string name specified in the **IndexerName** attribute. Remember, C# won't compile the code if it contains parameterful properties with different names.

For a language that supports several parameterful properties, one of the property method names must be selected and identified by the type's **DefaultMember** attribute. This is the only parameterful property that C# will be able to access.

When the C# compiler sees code that is trying to get or set an indexer, the compiler actually emits a call to one of these methods. Some programming languages might not support parameterful properties. To access a parameterful property from one of these languages, you must call the desired accessor method explicitly. To the CLR, there's no difference between parameterless properties and parameterful properties, so you use the same **System.Reflection.PropertyInfo** class to find the association between a parameterful property and its accessor methods.

The Performance of Calling Property Accessor Methods

For simple **get** and **set** accessor methods, the just-in-time (JIT) compiler *inlines* the code so that there's no runtime performance hit as a result of using properties rather than fields. Inlining is when the code for a method (or accessor method, in this case) is compiled directly in the method that is making the call. This removes the overhead associated with making a call at runtime at the expense of making the compiled method's code bigger. Because property accessor methods typically contain very little code, inlining them can make the native code smaller and can make it execute faster.

Note that the JIT compiler does not inline property methods when debugging code because inlined code is harder to debug. This means that the performance of accessing a property can be fast in a release build and slow in a debug build. Field access is fast in both debug and release builds.

Property Accessor Accessibility

Occasionally, when designing a type, it is desired to have one accessibility for a **get** accessor method and a different accessibility for a **set** accessor method. The most common scenario is to have a public **get** accessor and a protected **set** accessor:

```
public class SomeType {
    private String m_name;
    public String Name {
        get { return m_name; }
        protected set {m_name = value; }
    }
}
```

As you can see from the code above, the **Name** property is itself declared as a **public** property, and this means that the **get** accessor method will be public and therefore callable by all code. However, notice that the **set** accessor is declared as **protected** and will be callable only from code defined within **SomeType** or from code in a class that is derived from **SomeType**.

When defining a property with accessor methods that have different accessibilities, C# syntax requires that the property itself must be declared with the least-restrictive accessibility and that more restrictive accessibility be applied to just one of the accessor methods. In the example above, the property is **public**, and the **set** accessor is **protected** (more restrictive than **public**).

Generic Property Accessor Methods

Since properties are really just methods, and because C# and the CLR allow methods to be generic, sometimes people want to define properties that introduce their own generic type parameters (as opposed to using the enclosing type's generic type parameter). However, C# does not allow this. The main reason why properties cannot introduce their own generic type parameters is because they don't make sense conceptually. A property is supposed to represent a characteristic of an object that can be queried or set. Introducing a generic type parameter would mean that the behavior of the querying/setting could be changed, but conceptually, a property is not supposed to have behavior. If you want your object to expose some behavior—generic or not—define a method, not a property.

Chapter 11
Events

In this chapter, I'll talk about the last kind of member a type can define: events. A type that defines an event member allows the type (or instances of the type) to notify other objects that something special has happened. For example, the **Button** class offers an event called **Click**. When a **Button** object is clicked, one or more objects in an application may want to receive notification about this event in order to perform some action. Events are type members that allow this interaction. Specifically, defining an event member means that a type is offering the following capabilities:

- A method can register its interest in the event.

- A method can unregister its interest in the event.

- Registered methods will be notified when the event occurs.

Types can offer this functionality when defining an event because they maintain a list of the registered methods. When the event occurs, the type notifies all of the registered methods in the collection.

The common language runtime's (CLR's) event model is based on *delegates*. A delegate is a type-safe way to invoke a callback method. Callback methods are the means by which objects receive the notifications they subscribed to. In this chapter, I'll be using delegates, but I won't fully explain all their details until Chapter 17, "Delegates."

To help you fully understand the way events work within the CLR, I'll start with a scenario in which events are useful. Suppose you want to design an e-mail application. When an e-mail message arrives, the user might like the message to be forwarded to a fax machine or a pager. In architecting this application, let's say that you'll first design a type, called **MailManager**, that receives the incoming e-mail messages. **MailManager** will expose an event called **NewMail**. Other types (such as **Fax** and **Pager**) may register interest in this event. When **MailManager** receives a new e-mail message, it will raise the event, causing the message to be distributed to each of the registered objects. Each object can process the message in any way it desires.

When the application initializes, let's instantiate just one **MailManager** instance—the application can then instantiate any number of **Fax** and **Pager** types. Figure 11-1 shows how the application initializes and what happens when a new e-mail message arrives.

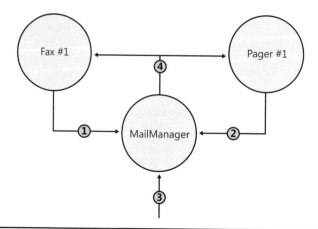

1. A method in the Fax object registers interest with the MailManager's event.
2. A method in the Pager object registers interest with the MailManager's event.
3. A new mail message arrives at MailManager.
4. The MailManager object fires the notification off to all the registered methods, which process the mail message as desired

FIGURE 11-1 Architecting an application to use events

Here's how the application illustrated in Figure 11-1 works: The application initializes by constructing an instance of **MailManager**. **MailManager** offers a **NewMail** event. When the **Fax** and **Pager** objects are constructed, they register an instance method with **MailManager**'s **NewMail** event so that **MailManager** knows to notify the **Fax** and **Pager** objects when new e-mail messages arrive. Now, when **MailManager** receives a new e-mail message (sometime in the future), it will raise the **NewMail** event, giving all of the registered methods an opportunity to process the new message in any way they want.

Designing a Type That Exposes an Event

There are many steps a developer must take in order to define a type that exposes one or more event members. In this section, I'll walk through each of the necessary steps. The **MailManager** sample application (which can be downloaded from *http://wintellect.com*) shows all of the source code for the **MailManager** type, the **Fax** type, and the **Pager** type. You'll notice that the **Pager** type is practically identical to the **Fax** type.

Step #1: Define a type that will hold any additional information that should be sent to receivers of the event notification

When an event is raised, the object raising the event may want to pass some additional information to the objects receiving the event notification. This additional information needs to be encapsulated into its own class, which typically contains a bunch of private fields along with some read-only public properties to expose these fields. By convention, classes that hold event information to be passed to the event handler should be derived from **System.EventArgs**, and the name of the class should be suffixed with **EventArgs**. In this example, the **NewMailEventArgs** class has fields identifying who sent the message (**m_from**), who is receiving the message (**m_to**), and the subject of the message (**m_subject**).

```
// Step #1: Define a type that will hold any additional information that
// should be sent to receivers of the event notification
internal class NewMailEventArgs : EventArgs {

   private readonly String m_from, m_to, m_subject;

   public NewMailEventArgs(String from, String to, String subject) {
      m_from = from; m_to = to; m_subject = subject;
   }

   public String From    { get { return m_from;    } }
   public String To      { get { return m_to;      } }
   public String Subject { get { return m_subject; } }
}
```

> **Note** The **EventArgs** class is defined in the Microsoft .NET Framework Class Library (FCL) and is implemented like this:
>
> ```
> [ComVisible(true), Serializable]
> public class EventArgs {
>    public static readonly EventArgs Empty = new EventArgs();
>    public EventArgs() {  }
> }
> ```
>
> As you can see, this type is nothing to write home about. It simply serves as a base type from which other types can derive. Many events don't have any additional information to pass on. For example, when a **Button** notifies its registered receivers that it has been clicked, just invoking the callback method is enough information. When you're defining an event that doesn't have any additional data to pass on, just use **EventArgs.Empty** rather than constructing a new **EventArgs** object.

Step #2: Define the event member

An event member is defined using the C# keyword **event**. Each event member is given accessibility (which is almost always **public** so that other code can access the event member), a type of delegate indicating the prototype of the method(s) that will be called, and a name (which can be any valid identifier). Here is what the event member in our **MailManager** class looks like:

```
internal class MailManager {

   // Step #2: Define the event member
   public event EventHandler<NewMailEventArgs> NewMail;
   ...
}
```

NewMail is the name of this event. The type of the event member is **EventHandler<NewMailEventArgs>**, which means that all receivers of the event notification must supply a callback method whose prototype matches that of the **EventHandler<NewMailEventArgs>** delegate type. Since the generic **System.EventHandler** delegate is defined as follows:

```
public delegate void EventHandler<TEventArgs>(Object sender, TEventArgs e)
   where TEventArgs: EventArgs;
```

the method prototypes must look like this:

```
void MethodName(Object sender, NewMailEventArgs e);
```

> **Note** A lot of people wonder why the event pattern requires the **sender** parameter to always be of type **Object**. After all, since the **MailManager** will be the only type raising an event with a **NewMailEventArgs** object, it makes more sense for the callback method to be prototyped like this:
>
> ```
> void MethodName(MailManager sender, NewMailEventArgs e);
> ```
>
> The pattern requires the **sender** parameter to be of type **Object** mostly because of inheritance. What if **MailManager** were used as a base class for **SmtpMailManager**? In this case, the callback method should have the **sender** parameter prototyped as **SmtpMailManager** instead of **MailManager**, but this can't happen because **SmtpMailManager** just inherited the **NewMail** event. So the code that was expecting **SmtpMailManager** to raise the event must still have to cast the **sender** argument to **SmtpMailManager**. In other words, the cast is still required, so the **sender** parameter might as well be typed as **Object**.
>
> The next reason for typing the **sender** parameter as **Object** is just flexibility. It allows the delegate to be used by multiple types that offer an event that passes a **NewMailEventArgs** object. For example, a **PopMailManager** class could use the delegate even if this class were not derived from **MailManager**.

The event pattern also requires that the delegate definition and the callback method name the **EventArgs**-derived parameter **e**. The only reason for this is to add additional consistency to the pattern, making it easier for developers to learn and implement the pattern. Tools that spit out source code (such as Microsoft Visual Studio) also know to call the parameter **e**.

Finally, the event pattern requires all event handlers to have a return type of **void**. This is necessary because raising an event might call several callback methods, and there is no way to get the return values from all of them. Having a return type of **void** doesn't allow the callbacks to return a value. Unfortunately, there are some event handlers in the FCL, such as **ResolveEventHandler**, that did not follow Microsoft's own prescribed pattern because it returns an object of type **Assembly**.

Step #3: Define a method responsible for raising the event to notify registered objects that the event has occurred

By convention, the class should define a protected, virtual method that is called by code internally within the class and its derived classes when the event is to be raised. This method takes one parameter, a **NewMailEventArgs** object, which includes the information passed to the objects receiving the notification. The default implementation of this method simply checks if any objects have registered interest in the event and, if so, the event will be raised, thereby notifying the registered methods that the event has occurred. Here is what the method in our **MailManager** class looks like:

```
internal class MailManager {
    ...
    // Step #3: Define a method responsible for raising the event
    // to notify registered objects that the event has occurred
    // If this class is sealed, make this method private and nonvirtual
    protected virtual void OnNewMail(NewMailEventArgs e) {

        // Copy a reference to the delegate field now into a temporary field for thread safety
        EventHandler<EventArgs> temp =
            Interlocked.CompareExchange(ref NewMail, null, null);

        // If any methods registered interest with our event, notify them
        if (temp != null) temp(this, e);
    }
    ...
}
```

Raising an Event in a Thread-Safe Way

When the .NET Framework first shipped, the recommended way for developers to raise an event was by using code similar to this:

```
// Version 1
protected virtual void OnNewMail(NewMailEventArgs e) {
    if (NewMail != null) NewMail(this, e);
}
```

The problem with the **OnNewMail** method is that the thread could see that **NewMail** is not **null**, and then, just before invoking **NewMail**, another thread could remove a delegate from the chain making **NewMail null**, resulting in a **NullReferenceException** being thrown. To fix this race condition, many developers write the **OnNewMail** method as follows:

```
// Version 2
protected void OnNewMail(NewMailEventArgs e) {
    EventHandler<NewMailEventArgs> temp = NewMail;
    if (temp != null) temp(this, e);
}
```

The thinking here is that a reference to **NewMail** is copied into a temporary variable, **temp**, which refers to the chain of delegates at the moment the assignment is performed. Now, this method compares **temp** and **null** and invokes **temp**, so it doesn't matter if another thread changes **NewMail** after the assignment to **temp**. Remember that delegates are immutable and this is why this technique works in theory. However, what a lot of developers don't realize is that this code could be optimized by the compiler to remove the local **temp** variable entirely. If this happens, this version of the code is identical to the first version, so a **NullReferenceException** is still possible.

To really fix this code, you should rewrite **OnNewMail** like this:

```
// Version 3
protected void OnNewMail(NewMailEventArgs e) {
    EventHandler<NewMailEventArgs> temp = Thread.VolatileRead(ref NewMail);
    if (temp != null) temp(this, e);
}
```

The call to **VolatileRead** forces **NewMail** to be read at the point of the call and the reference really has to be copied to the **temp** variable now. Then, **temp** will be invoked only if it is not **null**. Unfortunately, it is impossible to write the code as shown because there isn't a generic overload of the **VolatileRead** method. However, there is a generic overload of **Interlocked.CompareExchange**, which you can use:

```
// Version 4
protected void OnNewMail(NewMailEventArgs e) {
    EventHandler<NewMailEventArgs> temp =
        Interlocked.CompareExchange(ref NewMail, null, null);
    if (temp != null) temp(this, e);
}
```

Here, **CompareExchange** changes the **NewMail** reference to **null** if it is **null** and does not alter **NewMail** if it is not **null**. In other words, **CompareExchange** doesn't change the value in **NewMail** at all, but it does return the value inside **NewMail** in an atomic, thread-safe way. See Chapter 28, "Primitive Thread Synchronization Constructs," for more information about the **Thread.VolatileRead** and **Interlocked.CompareExchange** methods.

While the fourth version of this code is the best, technically correct version, you can actually use the second version because the just-in-time (JIT) compiler is aware of this pattern and it knows not to optimize away the local **temp** variable. Specifically, all of Microsoft's JIT compilers respect the invariant of not introducing new reads to heap memory and therefore, caching a reference in a local variable ensures that the heap reference is accessed only once. This is not documented and, in theory, it could change, which is why you should use the fourth version. But in reality, Microsoft's JIT compiler would never embrace a change that would break this pattern because too many applications would break.[1] In addition, events are mostly used in single-threaded scenarios (Windows Forms, Windows Presentation Foundation, and Microsoft Silverlight) and so thread safety is not an issue anyway.

It is very important to note that due to this thread race condition, it is also possible that a method will be invoked after it has been removed from the event's delegate chain.

As a convenience, you could define an extension method (as discussed in Chapter 8, "Methods") that encapsulates this thread-safety logic. Define the extension method like this:

```
public static class EventArgExtensions {
    public static void Raise<TEventArgs>(this TEventArgs e,
        Object sender, ref EventHandler<TEventArgs> eventDelegate)
        where TEventArgs : EventArgs {

        // Copy a reference to the delegate field now into a temporary field for thread safety
        EventHandler<TEventArgs> temp =
            Interlocked.CompareExchange(ref eventDelegate, null, null);

        // If any methods registered interest with our event, notify them
        if (temp != null) temp(sender, e);
    }
}
```

And now, we can rewrite the **OnNewMail** method as follows:

```
protected virtual void OnNewMail(NewMailEventArgs e) {
    e.Raise(this, ref m_NewMail);
}
```

---

[1] This was actually told to me by a member of Microsoft's JIT compiler team.

A class that uses **MailManager** as a base type is free to override the **OnNewMail** method. This capability gives the derived class control over the raising of the event. The derived class can handle the new e-mail message in any way it sees fit. Usually, a derived type calls the base type's **OnNewMail** method so that the registered method(s) receive the notification. However, the derived class might decide to disallow the event from being forwarded.

Step #4: Define a method that translates the input into the desired event

Your class must have some method that takes some input and translates it into the raising of the event. In my **MailManager** example, the **SimulateNewMail** method is called to indicate that a new e-mail message has arrived into **MailManager**:

```
internal class MailManager {

    // Step #4: Define a method that translates the
    // input into the desired event
    public void SimulateNewMail(String from, String to, String subject) {

        // Construct an object to hold the information we wish
        // to pass to the receivers of our notification
        NewMailEventArgs e = new NewMailEventArgs(from, to, subject);

        // Call our virtual method notifying our object that the event
        // occurred. If no type overrides this method, our object will
        // notify all the objects that registered interest in the event
        OnNewMail(e);
    }
}
```

SimulateNewMail accepts information about the message and constructs a **NewMailEventArgs** object, passing the message information to its constructor. **MailManager**'s own virtual **OnNewMail** method is then called to formally notify the **MailManager** object of the new e-mail message. Usually, this causes the event to be raised, notifying all of the registered methods. (As mentioned before, a class using **MailManager** as a base class can override this behavior.)

How the Compiler Implements an Event

Now that you know how to define a class that offers an event member, let's take a closer look at what an event really is and how it works. In the **MailManager** class, we have a line of code that defines the event member itself:

```
public event EventHandler<NewMailEventArgs> NewMail;
```

When the C# compiler compiles the line above, it translates this single line of source code into the following three constructs:

```
// 1. A PRIVATE delegate field that is initialized to null
private EventHandler<NewMailEventArgs> NewMail = null;

// 2. A PUBLIC add_Xxx method (where Xxx is the Event name)
// Allows methods to register interest in the event.
public void add_NewMail(EventHandler<NewMailEventArgs> value) {
    // The loop and the call to CompareExchange is all just a fancy way
    // of adding a delegate to the event in a thread-safe way
    EventHandler<NewMailEventArgs>prevHandler;
    EventHandler<NewMailEventArgs> newMail = this.NewMail;
    do {
        prevHandler = newMail;
        EventHandler<NewMailEventArgs>newHandler =
            (EventHandler<NewMailEventArgs>) Delegate.Combine(prevHandler, value);
        newMail = Interlocked.CompareExchange<EventHandler<NewMailEventArgs>>(
            ref this.NewMail, newHandler, prevHandler);
    } while (newMail != prevHandler);
}

// 3. A PUBLIC remove_Xxx method (where Xxx is the Event name)
// Allows methods to unregister interest in the event.
public void remove_NewMail(EventHandler<NewMailEventArgs> value) {
    // The loop and the call to CompareExchange is all just a fancy way
    // of removing a delegate from the event in a thread-safe way
    EventHandler<NewMailEventArgs> prevHandler;
    EventHandler<NewMailEventArgs> newMail = this.NewMail;
    do {
        prevHandler = newMail;
        EventHandler<NewMailEventArgs> newHandler =
            (EventHandler<NewMailEventArgs>) Delegate.Remove(prevHandler, value);
        newMail = Interlocked.CompareExchange<EventHandler<NewMailEventArgs>>(
            ref this.NewMail, newHandler, prevHandler);
    } while (newMail != prevHandler);
}
```

The first construct is simply a field of the appropriate delegate type. This field is a reference to the head of a list of delegates that will be notified when this event occurs. This field is initialized to **null**, meaning that no listeners have registered interest in the event. When a method registers interest in the event, this field refers to an instance of the **EventHandler<NewMailEventArgs>** delegate, which may refer to additional **EventHandler<NewMailEventArgs>** delegates. When a listener registers interest in an event, the listener is simply adding an instance of the delegate type to the list. Obviously, unregistering means removing the delegate from the list.

You'll notice that the delegate field, **NewMail** in this example, is always **private** even though the original line of source code defines the event as **public**. The reason for making the delegate field **private** is to prevent code outside the defining class from manipulating it improperly. If the field were **public**, any code could alter the value in the field and potentially wipe out all of the delegates that have registered interest in the event.

The second construct the C# compiler generates is a method that allows other objects to register their interest in the event. The C# compiler automatically names this function by prepending **add_** to the event's name (**NewMail**). The C# compiler automatically generates the code that is inside this method. The code always calls **System.Delegate**'s static **Combine** method, which adds the instance of a delegate to the list of delegates and returns the new head of the list, which gets saved back in the field.

The third construct the C# compiler generates is a method that allows an object to unregister its interest in the event. Again, the C# compiler automatically names this function by prepending **remove_** to the event's name (**NewMail**). The code inside this method always calls **Delegate**'s static **Remove** method, which removes the instance of a delegate from the list of delegates and returns the new head of the list, which gets saved back in the field.

> **Warning** If you attempt to remove a method that was never added, then **Delegate**'s **Remove** method internally does nothing. That is, you get no exception or warning of any type; the event's collection of methods remains unchanged.

> **Note** The **add** and **remove** methods use a well-known pattern to update a value in a thread-safe way. This pattern is discussed in the "The Interlocked Anything Pattern" section of Chapter 28."

In this example, the **add** and **remove** methods are **public**. The reason they are **public** is that the original line of source code declared the event to be **public**. If the event had been declared **protected**, the **add** and **remove** methods generated by the compiler would also have been declared **protected**. So, when you define an event in a type, the accessibility of the event determines what code can register and unregister interest in the event, but only the type itself can ever access the delegate field directly. Event members can also be declared as **static** or **virtual**, in which case the **add** and **remove** methods generated by the compiler would be either **static** or **virtual**, respectively.

In addition to emitting the aforementioned three constructs, compilers also emit an event definition entry into the managed assembly's metadata. This entry contains some flags and the underlying delegate type, and refers to the **add** and **remove** accessor methods. This information exists simply to draw an association between the abstract concept of an "event" and its accessor methods. Compilers and other tools can use this metadata, and this information can also be obtained by using the **System.Reflection.EventInfo** class. However, the CLR itself doesn't use this metadata information and requires only the accessor methods at runtime.

Designing a Type That Listens for an Event

The hard work is definitely behind you at this point. In this section, I'll show you how to define a type that uses an event provided by another type. Let's start off by examining the code for the **Fax** type:

```
internal sealed class Fax {
    // Pass the MailManager object to the constructor
    public Fax(MailManager mm) {

        // Construct an instance of the EventHandler<NewMailEventArgs>
        // delegate that refers to our FaxMsg callback method.
        // Register our callback with MailManager's NewMail event
        mm.NewMail += FaxMsg;
    }

    // This is the method the MailManager will call
    // when a new e-mail message arrives
    private void FaxMsg(Object sender, NewMailEventArgs e) {

        // 'sender' identifies the MailManager object in case
        // we want to communicate back to it.

        // 'e' identifies the additional event information
        // the MailManager wants to give us.

        // Normally, the code here would fax the e-mail message.
        // This test implementation displays the info in the console
        Console.WriteLine("Faxing mail message:");
        Console.WriteLine("    From={0}, To={1}, Subject={2}",
            e.From, e.To, e.Subject);
    }

    // This method could be executed to have the Fax object unregister
    // itself with the NewMail event so that it no longer receives
    // notifications
    public void Unregister(MailManager mm) {

        // Unregister with MailManager's NewMail event
        mm.NewMail -= FaxMsg;
    }
}
```

When the e-mail application initializes, it would first construct a **MailManager** object and save the reference to this object in a variable. Then the application would construct a **Fax** object, passing the reference to the **MailManager** object as a parameter. In the **Fax** constructor, the **Fax** object registers its interest in **MailManager**'s **NewMail** event using C#'s **+=** operator:

```
mm.NewMail += FaxMsg;
```

Because the C# compiler has built-in support for events, the compiler translates the use of the += operator into the following line of code to add the object's interest in the event:

```
mm.add_NewMail(new EventHandler<NewMailEventArgs>(this.FaxMsg));
```

As you can see, the C# compiler is generating code that will construct an **EventHandler<NewMailEventArgs>** delegate object that wraps the **Fax** class's **FaxMsg** method. Then, the C# compiler calls the **MailManager**'s **add_NewMail** method, passing it the new delegate. Of course, you can verify all of this by compiling the code and looking at the IL with a tool such as ILDasm.exe.

Even if you're using a programming language that doesn't directly support events, you can still register a delegate with the event by calling the **add** accessor method explicitly. The effect is identical; the source code will just not look as pretty. It's the **add** method that registers the delegate with the event by adding it to the event's list of delegates.

When the **MailManager** object raises the event, the **Fax** object's **FaxMsg** method gets called. The method is passed a reference to the **MailManager** object as the first parameter, **sender**. Most of the time, this parameter is ignored, but it can be used if the **Fax** object wants to access members of the **MailManager** object in response to the event notification. The second parameter is a reference to a **NewMailEventArgs** object. This object contains any additional information the designer of **MailManager** and **NewMailEventArgs** thought would be useful to the event receivers.

From the **NewMailEventArgs** object, the **FaxMsg** method has easy access to the message's sender, the message's recipient, and the message's subject. In a real **Fax** object, this information would be faxed somewhere. In this example, the information is simply displayed in the console window.

When an object is no longer interested in receiving event notifications, it should unregister its interest. For example, the **Fax** object would unregister its interest in the **NewMail** event if the user no longer wanted his or her e-mail forwarded to a fax. As long as an object has registered one of its methods with an event, the object can't be garbage collected. If your type implements **IDisposable**'s **Dispose** method, the implementation should cause it to unregister interest in all events. (See Chapter 21, "Automatic Memory Management (Garbage Collection)," for more information about **IDisposable**.)

Code that demonstrates how to unregister for an event is shown in **Fax**'s **Unregister** method. This method is practically identical to the code shown in the **Fax** constructor. The only difference is that this code uses -= instead of +=. When the C# compiler sees code using the -= operator to unregister a delegate with an event, the compiler emits a call to the event's **remove** method:

```
mm.remove_NewMail(new EventHandler<NewMailEventArgs>(FaxMsg));
```

As with the += operator, even if you're using a programming language that doesn't directly support events, you can still unregister a delegate with the event by calling the **remove** accessor method explicitly. The **remove** method unregisters the delegate from the event by scanning the list for a delegate that wraps the same method as the one passed in. If a match is found, the existing delegate is removed from the event's list of delegates. If a match isn't found, no error occurs, and the list is unaltered.

By the way, C# requires your code to use the += and -= operators to add and remove delegates from the list. If you try to call the **add** or **remove** method explicitly, the C# compiler produces the CS0571 "`cannot explicitly call operator or accessor`" error message.

Explicitly Implementing an Event

The `System.Windows.Forms.Control` type defines about 70 events. If the `Control` type implemented the events by allowing the compiler to implicitly generate the **add** and **remove** accessor methods and delegate fields, every `Control` object would have 70 delegate fields in it just for the events! Since most programmers care about just a few events, an enormous amount of memory would be wasted for each object created from a `Control`-derived type. By the way, the ASP.NET `System.Web.UI.Control` and the Windows Presentation Foundation (WPF) `System.Windows.UIElement` type also offer many events that most programmers do not use.

In this section, I discuss how the C# compiler allows a class developer to explicitly implement an event, allowing the developer to control how the **add** and **remove** methods manipulate the callback delegates. I'm going to demonstrate how explicitly implementing an event can be used to efficiently implement a class that offers many events. However, there are certainly other scenarios where you might want to explicitly implement a type's event.

To efficiently store event delegates, each object that exposes events will maintain a collection (usually a dictionary) with some sort of event identifier as the key and a delegate list as the value. When a new object is constructed, this collection is empty. When interest in an event is registered, the event's identifier is looked up in the collection. If the event identifier is there, the new delegate is combined with the list of delegates for this event. If the event identifier isn't in the collection, the event identifier is added with the delegate.

When the object needs to raise an event, the event identifier is looked up in the collection. If the collection doesn't have an entry for the event identifier, nothing has registered interest in the event and no delegates need to be called back. If the event identifier is in the collection, the delegate list associated with the event identifier is invoked. Implementing this design pattern is the responsibility of the developer who is designing the type that defines the events; the developer using the type has no idea how the events are implemented internally.

Here is an example of how you could accomplish this pattern. First, I implemented an **EventSet** class that represents a collection of events and each event's delegate list as follows:

```
using System;
using System.Collections.Generic;

// This class exists to provide a bit more type safety and
// code maintainability when using EventSet
public sealed class EventKey : Object { }

public sealed class EventSet {
    // The private dictionary used to maintain EventKey -> Delegate mappings
    private readonly Dictionary<EventKey, Delegate> m_events =
        newDictionary<EventKey, Delegate>();

    // Adds an EventKey -> Delegate mapping if it doesn't exist or
    // combines a delegate to an existing EventKey
    public void Add(EventKey eventKey, Delegate handler) {
        Monitor.Enter(m_events);
        Delegate d;
        m_events.TryGetValue(eventKey, out d);
        m_events[eventKey] = Delegate.Combine(d, handler);
        Monitor.Exit(m_events);
    }

    // Removes a delegate from an EventKey (if it exists) and
    // removes the EventKey -> Delegate mapping the last delegate is removed
    public void Remove(EventKey eventKey, Delegate handler) {
        Monitor.Enter(m_events);
        // Call TryGetValue to ensure that an exception is not thrown if
        // attempting to remove a delegate from an EventKey not in the set
        Delegate d;
        if (m_events.TryGetValue(eventKey, out d)) {
            d = Delegate.Remove(d, handler);

            // If a delegate remains, set the new head else remove the EventKey
            if (d != null) m_events[eventKey] = d;
            else m_events.Remove(eventKey);
        }
        Monitor.Exit(m_events);
    }

    // Raises the event for the indicated EventKey
    public void Raise(EventKey eventKey, Object sender, EventArgs e) {
        // Don't throw an exception if the EventKey is not in the set
        Delegate d;
        Monitor.Enter(m_events);
        m_events.TryGetValue(eventKey, out d);
        Monitor.Exit(m_events);

        if (d != null) {
            // Because the dictionary can contain several different delegate types,
            // it is impossible to construct a type-safe call to the delegate at
            // compile time. So, I call the System.Delegate type's DynamicInvoke
            // method, passing it the callback method's parameters as an array of
```

```
    // objects. Internally, DynamicInvoke will check the type safety of the
    // parameters with the callback method being called and call the method.
    // If there is a type mismatch, then DynamicInvoke will throw an exception.
    d.DynamicInvoke(newObject[] { sender, e });
    }
}
```

> **Note** The FCL defines a type, **System.ComponentModel.EventHandlerList**, which does
> essentially the same thing as my **EventSet** class. The **System.Windows.Forms.Control** and
> **System.Web.UI.Control** types use the **EventHandlerList** type internally to maintain their
> sparse set of events. You're certainly welcome to use the FCL's **EventHandlerList** type if
> you'd like. The difference between the **EventHandlerList** type and my **EventSet** type is that
> **EventHandlerList** uses a linked list instead of a hash table. This means that accessing elements
> managed by the **EventHandlerList** is slower than using my **EventSet**. In addition, the
> **EventHandlerList** doesn't offer any thread-safe way to access the events; you would have to
> implement your own thread-safe wrapper around the **EventHandlerList** collection if you need
> to do this.

Now, I show a class that uses my **EventSet** class. This class has a field that refers to an
EventSet object, and each of this class's events is explicitly implemented so that each event's
add method stores the specified callback delegate in the **EventSet** object and each event's
remove method eliminates the specified callback delegate (if found):

```
using System;

// Define the EventArgs-derived type for this event.
public class FooEventArgs : EventArgs { }

public class TypeWithLotsOfEvents {

    // Define a private instance field that references a collection.
    // The collection manages a set of Event/Delegate pairs.
    // NOTE: The EventSet type is not part of the FCL, it is my own type.
    private readonly EventSet m_eventSet = newEventSet();

    // The protected property allows derived types access to the collection.
    protected EventSet EventSet { get { return m_eventSet; } }

    #region Code to support the Foo event (repeat this pattern for additional events)
    // Define the members necessary for the Foo event.
    // 2a. Construct a static, read-only object to identify this event.
    // Each object has its own hash code for looking up this
    // event's delegate linked list in the object's collection.
    protected static readonly EventKey s_fooEventKey = newEventKey();

    // 2d. Define the event's accessor methods that add/remove the
    // delegate from the collection.
    public event EventHandler<FooEventArgs> Foo {
        add     { m_eventSet.Add(s_fooEventKey, value); }
        remove { m_eventSet.Remove(s_fooEventKey, value); }
    }

}
```

```
// 2e. Define the protected, virtual On method for this event.
protected virtual void OnFoo(FooEventArgs e) {
   m_eventSet.Raise(s_fooEventKey, this, e);
}

// 2f. Define the method that translates input to this event.
public void SimulateFoo() {OnFoo(newFooEventArgs());}
#endregion
}
```

Code that uses the **TypeWithLotsOfEvents** type can't tell whether the events have been implemented implicitly by the compiler or explicitly by the developer. They just register the events using normal syntax. Here is some code demonstrating this:

```
public sealed class Program {
   public static void Main() {
      TypeWithLotsOfEvents twle = newTypeWithLotsOfEvents();

      // Add a callback here
      twle.Foo += HandleFooEvent;

      // Prove that it worked
      twle.SimulateFoo();
   }

   private static void HandleFooEvent(object sender, FooEventArgs e) {
      Console.WriteLine("Handling Foo Event here...");
   }
}
```

Chapter 12
Generics

Developers who are familiar with object-oriented programming know the benefits it offers. One of the big benefits that make developers extremely productive is code reuse, which is the ability to derive a class that inherits all of the capabilities of a base class. The derived class can simply override virtual methods or add some new methods to customize the behavior of the base class to meet the developer's needs. *Generics* is another mechanism offered by the common language runtime (CLR) and programming languages that provides one more form of code reuse: algorithm reuse.

Basically, one developer defines an algorithm such as sorting, searching, swapping, comparing, or converting. However, the developer defining the algorithm doesn't specify what data type(s) the algorithm operates on; the algorithm can be generically applied to objects of different types. Another developer can then use this existing algorithm as long as he or she indicates the specific data type(s) the algorithm should operate on, for example, a sorting algorithm that operates on `Int32`s, `String`s, etc., or a comparing algorithm that operates on `DateTime`s, `Version`s, etc.

Most algorithms are encapsulated in a type, and the CLR allows the creation of generic reference types as well as generic value types, but it does not allow the creation of generic enumerated types. In addition, the CLR allows the creation of generic interfaces and generic delegates. Occasionally, a single method can encapsulate a useful algorithm, and therefore, the CLR allows the creation of generic methods that are defined in a reference type, value type, or interface.

Let's look at a quick example. The Framework Class Library (FCL) defines a generic list algorithm that knows how to manage a set of objects; the data type of these objects is not specified by the generic algorithm. Someone wanting to use the generic list algorithm can specify the exact data type to use with it later.

The FCL class that encapsulates the generic list algorithm is called **List<T>** (pronounced *List of Tee*), and this class is defined in the **System.Collections.Generic** namespace. Here is what this class definition looks like (the code is severely abbreviated):

```
[Serializable]
public class List<T> : IList<T>, ICollection<T>, IEnumerable<T>,
    IList, ICollection, IEnumerable {

    public List();
    public void Add(T item);
    public Int32 BinarySearch(T item);
    public void Clear();
    public Boolean Contains(T item);
    public Int32 IndexOf(T item);
    public Boolean Remove(T item);
    public void Sort();
    public void Sort(IComparer<T> comparer);
    public void Sort(Comparison<T> comparison);
    public T[] ToArray();

    public Int32 Count { get; }
    public T this[Int32 index] { get; set; }
}
```

The programmer who defined the generic **List** class indicates that it works with an unspecified data type by placing the **<T>** immediately after the class name. When defining a generic type or method, any variables it specifies for types (such as **T**) are called *type parameters*. **T** is a variable name that can be used in source code anywhere a data type can be used. For example, in the **List** class definition, you see **T** being used for method parameters (the **Add** method accepts a parameter of type **T**) and return values (the **ToArray** method returns a single-dimension array of type **T**). Another example is the indexer method (called **this** in C#). The indexer has a **get** accessor method that returns a value of type **T** and a **set** accessor method that accepts a parameter of type **T**. Since the **T** variable can be used anywhere that a data type can be specified, it is also possible to use **T** when defining local variables inside a method or when defining fields inside a type.

> **Note** Microsoft's design guidelines state that generic parameter variables should either be called **T** or at least start with an uppercase **T** (as in **TKey** and **TValue**). The uppercase **T** stands for *type*, just as an uppercase **I** stands for *interface* (as in **IComparable**).

Now that the generic **List<T>** type has been defined, other developers can use this generic algorithm by specifying the exact data type they would like the algorithm to operate on. When using a generic type or method, the specified data types are referred to as *type arguments*. For example, a developer might want to work with the **List** algorithm by specifying a **DateTime** type argument. Here is some code that shows this:

```
private static void SomeMethod() {
    // Construct a List that operates on DateTime objects
    List<DateTime> dtList = new List<DateTime>();

    // Add a DateTime object to the list
    dtList.Add(DateTime.Now);        // No boxing

    // Add another DateTime object to the list
    dtList.Add(DateTime.MinValue); // No boxing

    // Attempt to add a String object to the list
    dtList.Add("1/1/2004");          // Compile-time error

    // Extract a DateTime object out of the list
    DateTime dt = dtList[0];         // No cast required
}
```

Generics provide the following big benefits to developers as exhibited by the code just shown:

- **Source code protection**   The developer using a generic algorithm doesn't need to have access to the algorithm's source code. With C++ templates or Java's generics, however, the algorithm's source code must be available to the developer who is using the algorithm.

- **Type safety**   When a generic algorithm is used with a specific type, the compiler and the CLR understand this and ensure that only objects compatible with the specified data type are used with the algorithm. Attempting to use an object of an incompatible type will result in either a compiler error or a runtime exception being thrown. In the example, attempting to pass a **String** object to the **Add** method results in the compiler issuing an error.

- **Cleaner code**   Since the compiler enforces type safety, fewer casts are required in your source code, meaning that your code is easier to write and maintain. In the last line of **SomeMethod**, a developer doesn't need to use a (**DateTime**) cast to put the result of the indexer (querying element at index 0) into the **dt** variable.

- **Better performance**   Before generics, the way to define a generalized algorithm was to define all of its members to work with the **Object** data type. If you wanted to use the algorithm with value type instances, the CLR had to box the value type instance prior to calling the members of the algorithm. As discussed in Chapter 5, "Primitive, Reference, and Value Types," boxing causes memory allocations on the managed heap, which causes more frequent garbage collections, which, in turn, hurt an application's

performance. Since a generic algorithm can now be created to work with a specific value type, the instances of the value type can be passed by value, and the CLR no longer
has to do any boxing. In addition, since casts are not necessary (see the previous bullet),
the CLR doesn't have to check the type safety of the attempted cast, and this results in
faster code too.

To drive home the performance benefits of generics, I wrote a program that tests the performance of the generic **List** algorithm against the FCL's non-generic **ArrayList** algorithm. In
fact, I tested the performance of these two algorithms by using both value type objects and
reference type objects. Here is the program itself:

```
using System;
using System.Collections;
using System.Collections.Generic;
using System.Diagnostics;

public static class Program {
   public static void Main() {
      ValueTypePerfTest();
      ReferenceTypePerfTest();
   }

   private static void ValueTypePerfTest() {
      const Int32 count = 10000000;

      using (new OperationTimer("List<Int32>")) {
         List<Int32> l = new List<Int32>(count);
         for (Int32 n = 0; n < count; n++) {
            l.Add(n);
            Int32 x = l[n];
         }
         l = null;   // Make sure this gets GC'd
      }

      using (new OperationTimer("ArrayList of Int32")) {
         ArrayList a = new ArrayList();
         for (Int32 n = 0; n < count; n++) {
            a.Add(n);
            Int32 x = (Int32) a[n];
         }
         a = null;   // Make sure this gets GC'd
      }
   }

   private static void ReferenceTypePerfTest() {
      const Int32 count = 10000000;

      using (new OperationTimer("List<String>")) {
         List<String> l = new List<String>();
         for (Int32 n = 0; n < count; n++) {
            l.Add("X");
            String x = l[n];
         }
```

```
            l = null;   // Make sure this gets GC'd
        }

        using (new OperationTimer("ArrayList of String")) {
            ArrayList a = new ArrayList();
            for (Int32 n = 0; n < count; n++) {
                a.Add("X");
                String x = (String) a[n];
            }
            a = null;   // Make sure this gets GC'd
        }
    }
}

// This class is useful for doing operation performance timing
internal sealed class OperationTimer : IDisposable {
    private Int64  m_startTime;
    private String m_text;
    private Int32  m_collectionCount;

    public OperationTimer(String text) {
        PrepareForOperation();

        m_text = text;
        m_collectionCount = GC.CollectionCount(0);

        // This should be the last statement in this
        // method to keep timing as accurate as possible
        m_startTime = Stopwatch.GetTimestamp();
    }

    public void Dispose() {
        Console.WriteLine("{0,6:###.00} seconds (GCs={1,3}) {2}",
            (Stopwatch.GetTimestamp() - m_startTime) /
                (Double) Stopwatch.Frequency,
            GC.CollectionCount(0) - m_collectionCount, m_text);
    }

    private static void PrepareForOperation() {
        GC.Collect();
        GC.WaitForPendingFinalizers();
        GC.Collect();
    }
}
```

When I compile and run a release build (with optimizations turned on) of this program on my computer, I get the following output:

```
 .10 seconds (GCs=  0) List<Int32>
3.02 seconds (GCs= 45) ArrayList of Int32
 .47 seconds (GCs=  6) List<String>
 .51 seconds (GCs=  6) ArrayList of String
```

The output here shows that using the generic **List** algorithm with the **Int32** type is much faster than using the non-generic **ArrayList** algorithm with **Int32**. In fact, the difference is phenomenal: .1 second versus 3 seconds. That's 30 times faster! In addition, using a value type (**Int32**) with **ArrayList** causes a lot of boxing operations to occur, which results in 45 garbage collections. Meanwhile, the **List** algorithm required 0 garbage collections.

The result of the test using reference types is not as momentous. Here we see that the times and number of garbage collections are about the same. So it doesn't appear that the generic **List** algorithm is of any benefit here. However, keep in mind that when using a generic algorithm, you also get cleaner code and compile-time type safety. So while the performance improvement is not huge, the other benefits you get when using a generic algorithm are usually an improvement.

> **Note** You do need to realize that the CLR generates native code for each method the first time the method is called for a particular data type. This will increase an application's working set size, which will hurt performance. I will talk about this more in the "Generics Infrastructure" section of this chapter.

Generics in the Framework Class Library

Certainly, the most obvious use of generics is with collection classes, and the FCL defines several generic collection classes available for your use. Most of these classes can be found in the **System.Collections.Generic** namespace and the **System.Collections.ObjectModel** namespace. There are also thread-safe generic collection classes available in the **System.Collections.Concurrent** namespace. Microsoft recommends that programmers use the generic collection classes and now discourages use of the non-generic collection classes for several reasons. First, the non-generic collection classes are not generic, and so you don't get the type safety, cleaner code, and better performance that you get when you use generic collection classes. Second, the generic classes have a better object model than the non-generic classes. For example, fewer methods are virtual, resulting in better performance, and new members have been added to the generic collections to provide new functionality.

The collection classes implement many interfaces, and the objects that you place into the collections can implement interfaces that the collection classes use for operations such as sorting and searching. The FCL ships with many generic interface definitions so that the benefits of generics can be realized when working with interfaces as well. The commonly used interfaces are contained in the **System.Collections.Generic** namespace.

The new generic interfaces are not a replacement for the old non-generic interfaces; in many scenarios, you will have to use both. The reason is backward compatibility. For example, if the **List<T>** class implemented only the **IList<T>** interface, no code could consider a **List<DateTime>** object an **IList**.

I should also point out that the **System.Array** class, the base class of all array types, offers many static generic methods, such as **AsReadOnly**, **BinarySearch**, **ConvertAll**, **Exists**, **Find**, **FindAll**, **FindIndex**, **FindLast**, **FindLastIndex**, **ForEach**, **IndexOf**, **LastIndexOf**, **Resize**, **Sort**, and **TrueForAll**. Here are examples showing what some of these methods look like:

```
public abstract class Array : ICloneable, IList, ICollection, IEnumerable,
    IStructuralComparable, IStructuralEquatable {

    public static void  Sort<T>(T[] array);
    public static void  Sort<T>(T[] array, IComparer<T> comparer);

    public static Int32 BinarySearch<T>(T[] array, T value);
    public static Int32 BinarySearch<T>(T[] array, T value,
        IComparer<T> comparer);
    ...
}
```

Here is code that demonstrates how to use some of these methods:

```
public static void Main() {
    // Create & initialize a byte array
    Byte[] byteArray = new Byte[] { 5, 1, 4, 2, 3 };

    // Call Byte[] sort algorithm
    Array.Sort<Byte>(byteArray);

    // Call Byte[] binary search algorithm
    Int32 i = Array.BinarySearch<Byte>(byteArray, 1);
    Console.WriteLine(i);   // Displays "0"
}
```

Wintellect's Power Collections Library

At Microsoft's request, Wintellect has produced the Power Collections library to bring some of the C++ Standard Template Library's collection classes to the CLR programmer. This library is a set of collection classes that anyone can download and use free of charge. See *http://Wintellect.com* for details. These collection classes are generic themselves and make extensive use of generics. Table 12-1 shows a list of some of the collection classes you'll find in the Power Collections library.

TABLE 12-1 Generic Collection Classes from Wintellect's Power Collections Library

Collection Class	Description
BigList<T>	Collection of ordered **T** objects. Very efficient when working with more than 100 items.
Bag<T>	Collection of unordered **T** objects. The collection is hashed, and duplicates are allowed.
OrderedBag<T>	Collection of ordered **T** objects. Duplicates are allowed.
Set<T>	Collection of unordered **T** items. Duplicates are not allowed.
OrderedSet<T>	Collection of ordered **T** items. Duplicates are not allowed.
Deque<T>	Double-ended queue. Similar to a list but more efficient for adding/removing items at the beginning than a list.
OrderedDictionary<TKey,TValue>	Dictionary in which keys are ordered, and each can have one value.
MultiDictionary<TKey,TValue>	Dictionary in which a key can have multiple values. Keys are hashed, duplicates are allowed, and items are unordered.
OrderedMultiDictionary<TKey,TValue>	Dictionary in which keys are ordered, and each can have multiple values (also maintained in sorted order). Duplicate keys are allowed.

Generics Infrastructure

Generics were added to version 2.0 of the CLR, and it was a major task that required many people working for quite some time. Specifically, to make generics work, Microsoft had to do the following:

- Create new Intermediate Language (IL) instructions that are aware of type arguments.

- Modify the format of existing metadata tables so that type names and methods with generic parameters could be expressed.

- Modify the various programming languages (C#, Microsoft Visual Basic .NET, etc.) to support the new syntax, allowing developers to define and reference generic types and methods.

- Modify the compilers to emit the new IL instructions and the modified metadata format.

- Modify the just-in-time (JIT) compiler to process the new type-argument–aware IL instructions that produce the correct native code.

- Create new reflection members so that developers can query types and members to determine if they have generic parameters. Also, new reflection emit members had to be defined so that developers could create generic type and method definitions at runtime.

- Modify the debugger to show and manipulate generic types, members, fields, and local variables.

- Modify the Microsoft Visual Studio IntelliSense feature to show specific member prototypes when using a generic type or a method with a specific data type.

Now let's spend some time discussing how the CLR handles generics internally. This information could impact how you architect and design a generic algorithm. It could also impact your decision to use an existing generic algorithm or not.

Open and Closed Types

In various chapters throughout this book, I have discussed how the CLR creates an internal data structure for each and every type in use by an application. These data structures are called *type objects*. Well, a type with generic type parameters is still considered a type, and the CLR will create an internal type object for each of these. This applies to reference types (classes), value types (structs), interface types, and delegate types. However, a type with generic type parameters is called an *open type*, and the CLR does not allow any instance of an open type to be constructed (similar to how the CLR prevents an instance of an interface type from being constructed).

When code references a generic type, it can specify a set of generic type arguments. If actual data types are passed in for all of the type arguments, the type is called a *closed type*, and the CLR does allow instances of a closed type to be constructed. However, it is possible for code referencing a generic type to leave some generic type arguments unspecified. This creates a new open type object in the CLR, and instances of this type cannot be created. The following code should make this clear:

```
using System;
using System.Collections.Generic;

// A partially specified open type
internal sealed class DictionaryStringKey<TValue> :
    Dictionary<String, TValue> {
}

public static class Program {
    public static void Main() {
        Object o = null;

        // Dictionary<,> is an open type having 2 type parameters
        Type t = typeof(Dictionary<,>);
```

```
            // Try to create an instance of this type (fails)
            o = CreateInstance(t);
            Console.WriteLine();

            // DictionaryStringKey<> is an open type having 1 type parameter
            t = typeof(DictionaryStringKey<>);

            // Try to create an instance of this type (fails)
            o = CreateInstance(t);
            Console.WriteLine();

            // DictionaryStringKey<Guid> is a closed type
            t = typeof(DictionaryStringKey<Guid>);

            // Try to create an instance of this type (succeeds)
            o = CreateInstance(t);

            // Prove it actually worked
            Console.WriteLine("Object type=" + o.GetType());
        }

    private static Object CreateInstance(Type t) {
        Object o = null;
        try {
            o = Activator.CreateInstance(t);
            Console.Write("Created instance of {0}", t.ToString());
        }
        catch (ArgumentException e) {
            Console.WriteLine(e.Message);
        }
        return o;
    }
}
```

When I compile the code above and run it, I get the following output:

```
Cannot create an instance of System.Collections.Generic.
Dictionary`2[TKey,TValue] because Type.ContainsGenericParameters is true.

Cannot create an instance of DictionaryStringKey`1[TValue] because
Type.ContainsGenericParameters is true.

Created instance of DictionaryStringKey`1[System.Guid]
Object type=DictionaryStringKey`1[System.Guid]
```

As you can see, **Activator**'s **CreateInstance** method throws an **ArgumentException** when you ask it to construct an instance of an open type. In fact, the exception's string message indicates that the type still contains some generic parameters.

In the output, you'll notice that the type names end with a backtick (`) followed by a number. The number indicates the type's *arity*, which indicates the number of type parameters required by the type. For example, the **Dictionary** class has an arity of 2 since it requires that types be specified for **TKey** and **TValue**. The **DictionaryStringKey** class has an arity of 1 since it requires just one type to be specified for **TValue**.

I should also point out that the CLR allocates a type's static fields inside the type object (as discussed in Chapter 4, "Type Fundamentals"). So each closed type has its own static fields. In other words, if **List<T>** defined any static fields, these fields are not shared between a **List<DateTime>** and a **List<String>**; each closed type object has its own static fields. Also, if a generic type defines a static constructor (discussed in Chapter 8, "Methods"), this constructor will execute once per closed type. Sometimes people define a static constructor on a generic type to ensure that the type arguments will meet certain criteria. For example, if you wanted to define a generic type that can be used only with enumerated types, you could do the following:

```
internal sealed class GenericTypeThatRequiresAnEnum<T> {
   static GenericTypeThatRequiresAnEnum() {
      if (!typeof(T).IsEnum) {
         throw new ArgumentException("T must be an enumerated type");
      }
   }
}
```

The CLR has a feature, called *constraints*, that offers a better way for you to define a generic type indicating what type arguments are valid for it. I'll discuss constraints later in this chapter. Unfortunately, constraints do not support the ability to limit a type argument to enumerated types only, which is why the previous example requires a static constructor to ensure that the type is an enumerated type.

Generic Types and Inheritance

A generic type is a type, and as such, it can be derived from any other type. When you use a generic type and specify type arguments, you are defining a new type object in the CLR, and the new type object is derived from whatever type the generic type was derived from. In other words, since **List<T>** is derived from **Object**, **List<String>** and **List<Guid>** are also derived from **Object**. Similarly, since **DictionaryStringKey<TValue>** is derived from **Dictionary<String, TValue>**, **DictionaryStringKey<Guid>** is also derived from **Dictionary<String, Guid>**. Understanding that specifying type arguments doesn't have anything to do with inheritance hierarchies will help you to recognize what kind of casting you can and can't do.

For example, if a linked-list node class is defined like this:

```
internal sealed class Node<T> {
   public T m_data;
   public Node<T> m_next;

   public Node(T data) : this(data, null) {
   }

   public Node(T data, Node<T> next) {
      m_data = data; m_next = next;
```

```
      }

   public override String ToString() {
      return m_data.ToString() +
         ((m_next != null) ? m_next.ToString() : String.Empty);
   }
}
```

then I can write some code to build up a linked list that would look something like this:

```
private static void SameDataLinkedList() {
   Node<Char> head = new Node<Char>('C');
   head = new Node<Char>('B', head);
   head = new Node<Char>('A', head);
   Console.WriteLine(head.ToString());
}
```

In the **Node** class just shown, the **m_next** field must refer to another node that has the same kind of data type in its **m_data** field. This means that the linked list must contain nodes in which all data items are of the same type (or derived type). For example, I can't use the **Node** class to create a linked list in which one element contains a **Char**, another element contains a **DateTime**, and another element contains a **String**. Well, I could if I use **Node<Object>** everywhere, but then I would lose compile-time type safety, and value types would get boxed.

So a better way to go would be to define a non-generic **Node** base class and then define a generic **TypedNode** class (using the **Node** class as a base class). Now, I can have a linked list in which each node can be of a specific data type (not **Object**), get compile-time type safety and avoid the boxing of value types. Here are the new class definitions:

```
internal class Node {
   protected Node m_next;

   public Node(Node next) {
      m_next = next;
   }
}

internal sealed class TypedNode<T> : Node {
   public T m_data;

   public TypedNode(T data) : this(data, null) {
   }

   public TypedNode(T data, Node next) : base(next) {
      m_data = data;
   }

   public override String ToString() {
      return m_data.ToString() +
         ((m_next != null) ? m_next.ToString() : String.Empty);
   }
}
```

I can now write code to create a linked list in which each node is a different data type. The code could look something like this:

```
private static void DifferentDataLinkedList() {
   Node head = new TypedNode<Char>('.');
   head = new TypedNode<DateTime>(DateTime.Now, head);
   head = new TypedNode<String>("Today is ", head);
   Console.WriteLine(head.ToString());
}
```

Generic Type Identity

Sometimes generic syntax confuses developers. After all, there can be a lot of less-than (<) and greater-than (>) signs sprinkled throughout your source code, and this hurts readability. To improve syntax, some developers define a new non-generic class type that is derived from a generic type and that specifies all of the type arguments. For example, to simplify code like this:

```
List<DateTime> dtl= new List<DateTime>();
```

Some developers might first define a class like this:

```
internal sealed class DateTimeList : List<DateTime> {
   // No need to put any code in here!
}
```

Now, the code that creates a list can be rewritten more simply (without less-than and greater-than signs) like this:

```
DateTimeList dtl = new DateTimeList();
```

While this seems like a convenience, especially if you use the new type for parameters, local variables, and fields, you should never define a new class explicitly for the purpose of making your source code easier to read. The reason is because you lose type identity and equivalence, as you can see in the following code:

```
Boolean sameType = (typeof(List<DateTime>) == typeof(DateTimeList));
```

When the code above runs, **sameType** will be initialized to **false** because you are comparing two different type objects. This also means that a method prototyped as accepting a **DateTimeList** will not be able to have a **List<DateTime>** passed to it. However, a method prototyped as accepting a **List<DateTime>** can have a **DateTimeList** passed to it since **DateTimeList** is derived from **List<DateTime>**. Programmers may become easily confused by all of this.

Fortunately, C# does offer a way to use simplified syntax to refer to a generic closed type while not affecting type equivalence at all; you can use the good old **using** directive at the top of your source code file. Here is an example:

```
using DateTimeList = System.Collections.Generic.List<System.DateTime>;
```

Here, the **using** directive is really just defining a symbol called **DateTimeList**. As the code compiles, the compiler substitutes all occurrences of **DateTimeList** with **System.Collections.Generic.List<System.DateTime>**. This just allows developers to use a simplified syntax without affecting the actual meaning of the code, and therefore, type identity and equivalence are maintained. So now, when the following line executes, **sameType** will be initialized to **true**.

```
Boolean sameType = (typeof(List<DateTime>) == typeof(DateTimeList));
```

As another convenience, you can use C#'s implicitly typed local variable feature, where the compiler infers the type of a method's local variable from the type of the expression you are assigning to it:

```
using System;
using System.Collections.Generic;
...
internal sealed class SomeType {
   private static void SomeMethod () {

      // Compiler infers that DateTimeList is of type
      // System.Collections.Generic.List<System.DateTime>
      var dtl = List<DateTime>();
      ...
   }

}
```

Code Explosion

When a method that uses generic type parameters is JIT-compiled, the CLR takes the method's IL, substitutes the specified type arguments, and then creates native code that is specific to that method operating on the specified data types. This is exactly what you want and is one of the main features of generics. However, there is a downside to this: the CLR keeps generating native code for every method/type combination. This is referred to as *code explosion*. This can end up increasing the application's working set substantially, thereby hurting performance.

Fortunately, the CLR has some optimizations built into it to reduce code explosion. First, if a method is called for a particular type argument, and later, the method is called again using the same type argument, the CLR will compile the code for this method/type combination just once. So if one assembly uses **List<DateTime>**, and a completely different assembly (loaded in the same AppDomain) also uses **List<DateTime>**, the CLR will compile the methods for **List<DateTime>** just once. This reduces code explosion substantially.

The CLR has another optimization: the CLR considers all reference type arguments to be identical, and so again, the code can be shared. For example, the code compiled by the CLR for **List<String>**'s methods can be used for **List<Stream>**'s methods, since **String** and **Stream** are both reference types. In fact, for any reference type, the same code will be used. The CLR can perform this optimization because all reference type arguments or variables are really just pointers (all 32 bits on a 32-bit Windows system and 64 bits on a 64-bit Windows system) to objects on the heap, and object pointers are all manipulated in the same way.

But if any type argument is a value type, the CLR must produce native code specifically for that value type. The reason is because value types can vary in size. And even if two value types are the same size (such as **Int32** and **UInt32**, which are both 32 bits), the CLR still can't share the code because different native CPU instructions can be used to manipulate these values.

Generic Interfaces

Obviously, the ability to define generic reference and value types was the main feature of generics. However, it was critical for the CLR to also allow generic interfaces. Without generic interfaces, any time you tried to manipulate a value type by using a non-generic interface (such as **IComparable**), boxing and a loss of compile-time type safety would happen again. This would severely limit the usefulness of generic types. And so the CLR does support generic interfaces. A reference or value type can implement a generic interface by specifying type arguments, or a type can implement a generic interface by leaving the type arguments unspecified. Let's look at some examples.

Here is the definition of a generic interface that ships as part of the FCL (in the **System.Collections.Generic** namespace):

```
public interface IEnumerator<T> : IDisposable, IEnumerator {
    T Current { get; }
}
```

Here is an example of a type that implements this generic interface and that specifies type arguments. Notice that a **Triangle** object can enumerate a set of **Point** objects. Also note that the **Current** property is of the **Point** data type:

```
internal sealed class Triangle : IEnumerator<Point> {
    private Point[] m_vertices;

    // IEnumerator<Point>'s Current property is of type Point
    public Point Current { get { ... } }

    ...
}
```

Now let's look at an example of a type that implements the same generic interface but with the type arguments left unspecified:

```
internal sealed class ArrayEnumerator<T> : IEnumerator<T> {
   private T[] m_array;

   // IEnumerator<T>'s Current property is of type T
   public T Current { get { ... } }

   ...
}
```

Notice that an **ArrayEnumerator** object can enumerate a set of **T** objects (where **T** is unspecified allowing code using the generic **ArrayEnumerator** type to specify a type for **T** later). Also note that the **Current** property is now of the unspecified data type **T**. Much more information about generic interfaces is presented in Chapter 13, "Interfaces."

Generic Delegates

The CLR supports generic delegates to ensure that any type of object can be passed to a callback method in a type-safe way. Furthermore, generic delegates allow a value type instance to be passed to a callback method without any boxing. As discussed in Chapter 17, "Delegates," a delegate is really just a class definition with four methods: a constructor, an **Invoke** method, a **BeginInvoke** method, and an **EndInvoke** method. When you define a delegate type that specifies type parameters, the compiler defines the delegate class's methods, and the type parameters are applied to any methods having parameters/return values of the specified type parameter.

For example, if you define a generic delegate like this:

```
public delegate TReturn CallMe<TReturn, TKey, TValue>(TKey key, TValue value);
```

The compiler turns that into a class that logically looks like this:

```
public sealed class CallMe<TReturn, TKey, TValue> : MulticastDelegate {
   public CallMe(Object object, IntPtr method);
   public virtual TReturn Invoke(TKey key, TValue value);
   public virtual IAsyncResult BeginInvoke(TKey key, TValue value,
      AsyncCallback callback, Object object);
   public virtual TReturn EndInvoke(IAsyncResult result);
}
```

> **Note** It is recommended that you use the generic **Action** and **Func** delegates that come predefined in the Framework Class Library (FCL) wherever possible. I describe these delegate types in the "Enough with the Delegate Definitions Already (Generic Delegates)" section of Chapter 17, "Delegates."

Delegate and Interface Contravariant and Covariant Generic Type Arguments

Each of a delegate's generic type parameters can be marked as covariant or contravariant. This feature allows you to cast a variable of a generic delegate type to the *same delegate type* where the generic parameter types differ. A generic type parameter can be any one of the following:

- **Invariant**   Meaning that that generic type parameter cannot be changed. I have shown only invariant generic type parameters so far in this chapter.

- **Contravariant**   Meaning that the generic type parameter can change from a class to a class derived from it. In C#, you indicate contravariant generic type parameters with the **in** keyword. Contravariant generic type parameters can appear only in input positions such as a method's argument.

- **Covariant**   Meaning that the generic type argument can change from a class to one of its base classes. In C#, you indicate covariant generic type parameters with the **out** keyword. Covariant generic type parameters can appear only in output positions such as a method's return type.

For example, let's say that the following delegate type definition exists (which, by the way, it does):

```
public delegate TResult Func<in T, out TResult>(T arg);
```

Here, the generic type parameter **T** is marked with the **in** keyword, making it contravariant; and the generic type parameter **TResult** is marked with the **out** keyword, making it covariant.

So now, if I have a variable declared as follows:

```
Func<Object, ArgumentException> fn1 = null;
```

I can cast it to another **Func** type, where the generic type parameters are different:

```
Func<String, Exception>fn2 = fn1;// No explicit cast is required here
Exception e = fn2("");
```

What this is saying is that **fn1** refers to a function that accepts an **Object** and returns an **ArgumentException**. The **fn2** variable wants to refer to a method that takes a **String** and returns an **Exception**. Since you can pass a **String** to a method that wants an **Object** (because **String** is derived from **Object**), and since you can take the result of a method that returns an **ArgumentException** and treat it as an **Exception** (because **Exception** is a base class of **ArgumentException**), the code above compiles and is known at compile time to preserve type safety.

Note Variance applies only if the compiler can verify that a reference conversion exists between types. In other words, variance is not possible for value types because boxing would be required. In my opinion, this restriction is what makes these variance features not that useful. For example, if I have the following method:

```
voidProcessCollection(IEnumerable<Object> collection) { ... }
```

I can't call it passing in a reference to a **List<DateTime>** object since a reference conversion doesn't exist between the **DateTime** value type and **Object** even though **DateTime** is derived from **Object**. You solve this problem by declaring **ProcessCollection** as follows:

```
void ProcessCollection<T>(IEnumerable<T> collection) { ... }
```

Plus, the big benefit of **ProcessCollection(IEnumerable<Object> collection)** is that there is only one version of the JITted code. However, with **ProcessCollection<T>(IEnumerable<T> collection)**, there is also only one version of the JITted code shared by all Ts that are reference types. You do get other versions of JITted code for Ts that are value types, but now you can at least call the method passing it a collection of value types.

Also, variance is not allowed on a generic type parameter if an argument of that type is passed to a method using the **out** or **ref** keyword. For example, the line of code below causes the compiler to generate the following error message: "**Invalid variance: The type parameter 'T' must be invariantly valid on 'SomeDelegate<T>.Invoke(ref T)'. 'T' is contravariant.**"

```
delegate void SomeDelegate<in T>(ref T t);
```

When using delegates that take generic arguments and return values, it is recommended to always specify the **in** and **out** keywords for contravariance and covariance whenever possible, as doing this has no ill effects and enables your delegate to be used in more scenarios.

Like delegates, an interface with generic type parameters can have its type parameters be contravariant or covariant. Here is an example of an interface with a contravariant generic type parameter:

```
public interface IEnumerator<out T> : IEnumerator {
    Boolean MoveNext();
    T Current { get; }
}
```

Since **T** is contravariant, it is possible to have the following code compile and run successfully:

```
// This method accepts an IEnumerable of any reference type
Int32 Count(IEnumerable<Object> collection) { ... }

...
// The call below passes an IEnumerable<String> to Count
Int32 c = Count(new[] { "Grant" });
```

Important Sometimes developers ask why they must explicitly put **in** or **out** on generic type parameters. They think the compiler should be able to examine the delegate or interface declaration and automatically detect what generic type parameters can be contravariant and covariant. While it is true that the compiler could detect this automatically, the C# team believes that you are declaring a contract and that you should be explicit about what you want to allow. For example, it would be bad if the compiler determined that a generic type parameter could be contravariant and then, in the future, you added a member to an interface that had the type parameter used in an output position. The next time you compile, the compiler would determine that the type parameter should be invariant, but all code sites that reference the other members might now produce errors if they had used the fact that the type parameter had been contravariant.

For this reason, the compiler team forces you to be explicit when declaring a generic type parameter. Then, if you attempt to use this type parameter in a context that doesn't match how you declared it, the compiler issues an error letting you know that you are attempting to break the contract. If you then decide to break the contract by adding **in** or **out** on generic type parameters, you should expect to have to modify some of the code sites that were using the old contract.

Generic Methods

When you define a generic class, struct, or interface, any methods defined in these types can refer to a type parameter specified by the type. A type parameter can be used as a method's parameter, a method's return value, or as a local variable defined inside the method. However, the CLR also supports the ability for a method to specify its very own type parameters. And these type parameters can also be used for parameters, return values, or local variables. Here is a somewhat contrived example of a type that defines a type parameter and a method that has its very own type parameter:

```
internal sealed class GenericType<T> {
   private T m_value;

   public GenericType(T value) { m_value = value; }

   public TOutput Converter<TOutput>() {
      TOutput result = (TOutput) Convert.ChangeType(m_value, typeof(TOutput));
      return result;
   }
}
```

In this example, you can see that the **GenericType** class defines its own type parameter (**T**), and the **Converter** method defines its own type parameter (**TOutput**). This allows a **GenericType** to be constructed to work with any type. The **Converter** method can convert the object referred to by the **m_value** field to various types depending on what type argument is passed to it when called. The ability to have type parameters and method parameters allows for phenomenal flexibility.

A reasonably good example of a generic method is the **Swap** method:

```
private static void Swap<T>(ref T o1, ref T o2) {
    T temp = o1;
    o1 = o2;
    o2 = temp;
}
```

Code can now call **Swap** like this:

```
private static void CallingSwap() {
    Int32 n1 = 1, n2 = 2;
    Console.WriteLine("n1={0}, n2={1}", n1, n2);
    Swap<Int32>(ref n1, ref n2);
    Console.WriteLine("n1={0}, n2={1}", n1, n2);

    String s1 = "Aidan", s2 = "Grant";
    Console.WriteLine("s1={0}, s2={1}", s1, s2);
    Swap<String>(ref s1, ref s2);
    Console.WriteLine("s1={0}, s2={1}", s1, s2);
}
```

Using generic types with methods that take **out** and **ref** parameters can be particularly interesting because the variable you pass as an **out/ref** argument must be the same type as the method's parameter to avoid a potential type safety exploit. This issue related to **out/ref** parameters is discussed toward the end of the "Passing Parameters by Reference to a Method" section in Chapter 9, "Parameters." In fact, the **Interlocked** class's **Exchange** and **CompareExchange** methods offer generic overloads for precisely this reason[1]:

```
public static class Interlocked {
    public static T Exchange<T>(ref T location1, T value) where T: class;
    public static T CompareExchange<T>(
        ref T location1, T value, T comparand) where T: class;
}
```

Generic Methods and Type Inference

For many developers, the C# generic syntax can be confusing with all of its less-than and greater-than signs. To help improve code creation, readability, and maintainability, the C# compiler offers *type inference* when calling a generic method. Type inference means that the compiler attempts to determine (or infer) the type to use automatically when calling a generic method. Here is some code that demonstrates type inference:

```
private static void CallingSwapUsingInference() {
    Int32 n1 = 1, n2 = 2;
    Swap(ref n1, ref n2);// Calls Swap<Int32>

    String s1 = "Aidan";
    Object s2 = "Grant";
    Swap(ref s1, ref s2);// Error, type can't be inferred
}
```

---

[1] The **where** clause will be explained in the "Verifiability and Constraints" section later in this chapter.

In this code, notice that the calls to **Swap** do not specify type arguments in less-than/greater-than signs. In the first call to **Swap**, the C# compiler was able to infer that **n1** and **n2** are **Int32**s, and therefore, it should call **Swap** by using an **Int32** type argument.

When performing type inference, C# uses the variable's data type, not the actual type of the object referred to by the variable. So in the second call to **Swap**, C# sees that **s1** is a **String** and **s2** is an **Object** (even though it happens to refer to a **String**). Since **s1** and **s2** are variables of different data types, the compiler can't accurately infer the type to use for **Swap**'s type argument, and it issues the following message: "**error CS0411: The type arguments for method 'Program.Swap<T>(ref T, ref T)' cannot be inferred from the usage. Try specifying the type arguments explicitly.**"

A type can define multiple methods with one of its methods taking a specific data type and another taking a generic type parameter, as in the following example:

```
private static void Display(String s) {
   Console.WriteLine(s);
}

private static void Display<T>(T o) {
   Display(o.ToString());  // Calls Display(String)
}
```

Here are some ways to call the **Display** method:

```
Display("Jeff");            // Calls Display(String)
Display(123);               // Calls Display<T>(T)
Display<String>("Aidan");   // Calls Display<T>(T)
```

In the first call, the compiler could actually call either the **Display** method that takes a **String** or the generic **Display** method (replacing **T** with **String**). However, the C# compiler always prefers a more explicit match over a generic match, and therefore, it generates a call to the non-generic **Display** method that takes a **String**. For the second call, the compiler can't call the non-generic **Display** method that takes a **String**, so it must call the generic **Display** method. By the way, it is fortunate that the compiler always prefers the more explicit match; if the compiler had preferred the generic method, because the generic **Display** method calls **Display** again (but with a **String** returned by **ToString**), there would have been infinite recursion.

The third call to **Display** specifies a generic type argument, **String**. This tells the compiler not to try to infer type arguments but instead to use the type arguments that I explicitly specified. In this case, the compiler also assumes that I must really want to call the generic **Display** method, so the generic **Display** will be called. Internally, the generic **Display** method will call **ToString** on the passed-in string, which results in a string that is then passed to the non-generic **Display** method.

Generics and Other Members

In C#, properties, indexers, events, operator methods, constructors, and finalizers cannot themselves have type parameters. However, they can be defined within a generic type, and the code in these members can use the type's type parameters.

C# doesn't allow these members to specify their own generic type parameters because Microsoft's C# team believes that developers would rarely have a need to use these members as generic. Furthermore, the cost of adding generic support to these members would be quite high in terms of designing adequate syntax into the language. For example, when you use a **+** operator in code, the compiler could call an operator overload method. There is no way to indicate any type arguments in your code along with the **+** operator.

Verifiability and Constraints

When compiling generic code, the C# compiler analyzes it and ensures that the code will work for any type that exists today or that may be defined in the future. Let's look at the following method:

```
private static Boolean MethodTakingAnyType<T>(T o) {
   T temp = o;
   Console.WriteLine(o.ToString());
   Boolean b = temp.Equals(o);
   return b;
}
```

This method declares a temporary variable (**temp**) of type **T**, and then the method performs a couple of variable assignments and a few method calls. This method works for any type. If **T** is a reference type, it works. If **T** is a value or enumeration type, it works. If **T** is an interface or delegate type, it works. This method works for all types that exist today or that will be defined tomorrow because every type supports assignment and calls to methods defined by **Object** (such as **ToString** and **Equals**).

Now look at the following method:

```
private static T Min<T>(T o1, T o2) {
   if (o1.CompareTo(o2) < 0) return o1;
   return o2;
}
```

The **Min** method attempts to use the **o1** variable to call the **CompareTo** method. But there are lots of types that do not offer a **CompareTo** method, and therefore, the C# compiler can't compile this code and guarantee that this method would work for all types. If you attempt to compile the above code, the compiler issues the following message: "**error CS0117: 'T' does not contain a definition for 'CompareTo'.**"

So it would seem that when using generics, you can declare variables of a generic type, perform some variable assignments, call methods defined by **Object**, and that's about it! This makes generics practically useless. Fortunately, compilers and the CLR support a mechanism called *constraints* that you can take advantage of to make generics useful again.

A constraint is a way to limit the number of types that can be specified for a generic argument. Limiting the number of types allows you to do more with those types. Here is a new version of the **Min** method that specifies a constraint (in bold):

```
public static T Min<T>(T o1, T o2) where T : IComparable<T> {
   if (o1.CompareTo(o2) < 0) return o1;
   return o2;
}
```

The C# **where** token tells the compiler that any type specified for **T** must implement the generic **IComparable** interface of the same type (**T**). Because of this constraint, the compiler now allows the method to call the **CompareTo** method since this method is defined by the **IComparable<T>** interface.

Now, when code references a generic type or method, the compiler is responsible for ensuring that a type argument that meets the constraints is specified. For example, the following code causes the compiler to issue the following message: "**error CS0311: The type 'object' cannot be used as type parameter 'T' in the generic type or method 'SomeType.Min<T>(T, T)'. There is no implicit reference conversion from 'object' to 'System.IComparable<object>'.**"

```
private static void CallMin() {
   Object o1 = "Jeff", o2 = "Richter";
   Object oMin = Min<Object>(o1, o2);  // Error CS0311
}
```

The compiler issues the error because **System.Object** doesn't implement the **IComparable<Object>** interface. In fact, **System.Object** doesn't implement any interfaces at all.

Now that you have a sense of what constraints are and how they work, we'll start to look a little deeper into them. Constraints can be applied to a generic type's type parameters as well as to a generic method's type parameters (as shown in the **Min** method). The CLR doesn't allow overloading based on type parameter names or constraints; you can overload types or methods based only on arity. The following examples show what I mean:

```
// It is OK to define the following types:
internal sealed class AType {}
internal sealed class AType<T> {}
internal sealed class AType<T1, T2> {}

// Error: conflicts with AType<T> that has no constraints
internal sealed class AType<T> where T : IComparable<T> {}
```

```
// Error: conflicts with AType<T1, T2>
internal sealed class AType<T3, T4> {}

internal sealed class AnotherType {
    // It is OK to define the following methods:
    private static void M() {}
    private static void M<T>() {}
    private static void M<T1, T2>() {}

    // Error: conflicts with M<T> that has no constraints
    private static void M<T>() where T : IComparable<T> {}

    // Error: conflicts with M<T1, T2>
    private static void M<T3, T4>() {}
}
```

When overriding a virtual generic method, the overriding method must specify the same number of type parameters, and these type parameters will inherit the constraints specified on them by the base class's method. In fact, the overriding method is not allowed to specify any constraints on its type parameters at all. However, it can change the names of the type parameters. Similarly, when implementing an interface method, the method must specify the same number of type parameters as the interface method, and these type parameters will inherit the constraints specified on them by the interface's method. Here is an example that demonstrates this rule by using virtual methods:

```
internal class Base {
    public virtual void M<T1, T2>()
        where T1 : struct
        where T2 : class {
    }
}

internal sealed class Derived : Base {
    public override void M<T3, T4>()
        where T3 : EventArgs  // Error
        where T4 : class       // Error
        { }
}
```

Attempting to compile the code above causes the compiler to issue the following message: "**error CS0460: Constraints for override and explicit interface implementation methods are inherited from the base method so cannot be specified directly.**" If we remove the two **where** lines from the **Derived** class's M<**T3, T4**> method, the code will compile just fine. Notice that you can change the names of the type parameters (as in the example: from **T1** to **T3** and **T2** to **T4**); however, you cannot change (or even specify) constraints.

Now let's talk about the different kinds of constraints the compiler/CLR allows you to apply to a type parameter. A type parameter can be constrained using a *primary constraint*, a *secondary constraint*, and/or a *constructor constraint*. I'll talk about these three kinds of constraints in the next three sections.

Primary Constraints

A type parameter can specify zero primary constraints or one primary constraint. A primary constraint can be a reference type that identifies a class that is not sealed. You cannot specify one of the following special reference types: **System.Object**, **System.Array**, **System.Delegate**, **System.MulticastDelegate**, **System.ValueType**, **System.Enum**, or **System.Void**.

When specifying a reference type constraint, you are promising the compiler that a specified type argument will either be of the same type or of a type derived from the constraint type. For example, see the following generic class:

```
internal sealed class PrimaryConstraintOfStream<T> where T : Stream {
    public void M(T stream) {
        stream.Close();// OK
    }
}
```

In this class definition, the type parameter **T** has a primary constraint of **Stream** (defined in the **System.IO** namespace). This tells the compiler that code using **PrimaryConstraintOfStream** must specify a type argument of **Stream** or a type derived from **Stream** (such as **FileStream**). If a type parameter doesn't specify a primary constraint, **System.Object** is assumed. However, the C# compiler issues an error message ("**error CS0702: Constraint cannot be special class 'object'** ") if you explicitly specify **System.Object** in your source code.

There are two special primary constraints: **class** and **struct**. The **class** constraint promises the compiler that a specified type argument will be a reference type. Any class type, interface type, delegate type, or array type satisfies this constraint. For example, see the following generic class:

```
internal sealed class PrimaryConstraintOfClass<T> where T : class {
    public void M() {
        T temp = null;// Allowed because T must be a reference type
    }
}
```

In this example, setting **temp** to **null** is legal because **T** is known to be a reference type, and all reference type variables can be set to **null**. If **T** were unconstrained, the code above would not compile because **T** could be a value type, and value type variables cannot be set to **null**.

The **struct** constraint promises the compiler that a specified type argument will be a value type. Any value type, including enumerations, satisfies this constraint. However, the compiler and the CLR treat any **System.Nullable<T>** value type as a special type, and nullable types do not satisfy this constraint. The reason is because the **Nullable<T>** type constrains its type parameter to **struct**, and the CLR wants to prohibit a recursive type such as **Nullable<Nullable<T>>**. Nullable types are discussed in Chapter 19, "Nullable Value Types."

Here is an example class that constrains its type parameter by using the **struct** constraint:

```
internal sealed class PrimaryConstraintOfStruct<T> where T : struct {
    public static T Factory() {
        // Allowed because all value types implicitly
        // have a public, parameterless constructor
        return new T();
    }
}
```

In this example, **new**ing up a **T** is legal because **T** is known to be a value type, and all value types implicitly have a public, parameterless constructor. If **T** were unconstrained, constrained to a reference type, or constrained to **class**, the above code would not compile because some reference types do not have public, parameterless constructors.

Secondary Constraints

A type parameter can specify zero or more secondary constraints where a secondary constraint represents an interface type. When specifying an interface type constraint, you are promising the compiler that a specified type argument will be a type that implements the interface. And since you can specify multiple interface constraints, the type argument must specify a type that implements all of the interface constraints (and all of the primary constraints too, if specified). Chapter 13 discusses interface constraints in detail.

There is another kind of secondary constraint called a *type parameter constraint* (sometimes referred to as a *naked type constraint*). This kind of constraint is used much less often than an interface constraint. It allows a generic type or method to indicate that there must be a relationship between specified type arguments. A type parameter can have zero or more type constraints applied to it. Here is a generic method that demonstrates the use of a type parameter constraint:

```
private static List<TBase> ConvertIList<T, TBase>(IList<T> list)
    where T : TBase {
    List<TBase> baseList = new List<TBase>(list.Count);
    for (Int32 index = 0; index < list.Count; index++) {
        baseList.Add(list[index]);
    }
    return baseList;
}
```

The **ConvertIList** method specifies two type parameters in which the **T** parameter is constrained by the **TBase** type parameter. This means that whatever type argument is specified for **T**, the type argument must be compatible with whatever type argument is specified for **TBase**. Here is a method showing some legal and illegal calls to **ConvertIList**:

```
private static void CallingConvertIList() {
   // Construct and initialize a List<String> (which implements IList<String>)
   IList<String> ls = new List<String>();
   ls.Add("A String");

   // Convert the IList<String> to an IList<Object>
   IList<Object> lo = ConvertIList<String, Object>(ls);

   // Convert the IList<String> to an IList<IComparable>
   IList<IComparable> lc = ConvertIList<String, IComparable>(ls);

   // Convert the IList<String> to an IList<IComparable<String>>
   IList<IComparable<String>> lcs =
      ConvertIList<String, IComparable<String>>(ls);

   // Convert the IList<String> to an IList<String>
   IList<String> ls2 = ConvertIList<String, String>(ls);

   // Convert the IList<String> to an IList<Exception>
   IList<Exception> le = ConvertIList<String, Exception>(ls);// Error
}
```

In the first call to **ConvertIList**, the compiler ensures that **String** is compatible with **Object**. Since **String** is derived from **Object**, the first call adheres to the type parameter constraint. In the second call to **ConvertIList**, the compiler ensures that **String** is compatible with **IComparable**. Since **String** implements the **IComparable** interface, the second call adheres to the type parameter constraint. In the third call to **ConvertIList**, the compiler ensures that **String** is compatible with **IComparable<String>**. Since **String** implements the **IComparable<String>** interface, the third call adheres to the type parameter constraint. In the fourth call to **ConvertIList**, the compiler knows that **String** is compatible with itself. In the fifth call to **ConvertIList**, the compiler ensures that **String** is compatible with **Exception**. Since **String** is not compatible with **Exception**, the fifth call doesn't adhere to the type parameter constraint, and the compiler issues the following message: "**error CS0311: The type 'string' cannot be used as type parameter 'T' in the generic type or method 'Program.ConvertIList<T,TBase>(System.Collections. Generic.IList<T>)'. There is no implicit reference conversion from 'string' to 'System.Exception'.**"

Constructor Constraints

A type parameter can specify zero constructor constraints or one constructor constraint. When specifying a constructor constraint, you are promising the compiler that a specified type argument will be a non-abstract type that implements a public, parameterless constructor. Note that the C# compiler considers it an error to specify a constructor constraint with the **struct** constraint because it is redundant; all value types implicitly offer a public, parameterless constructor. Here is an example class that constrains its type parameter by using the constructor constraint:

```
internal sealed class ConstructorConstraint<T> where T : new() {
    public static T Factory() {
        // Allowed because all value types implicitly
        // have a public, parameterless constructor and because
        // the constraint requires that any specified reference
        // type also have a public, parameterless constructor
        return new T();
    }
}
```

In this example, **new**ing up a **T** is legal because **T** is known to be a type that has a public, parameterless constructor. This is certainly true of all value types, and the constructor constraint requires that it be true of any reference type specified as a type argument.

Sometimes, developers would like to declare a type parameter by using a constructor constraint whereby the constructor takes various parameters itself. As of now, the CLR (and therefore the C# compiler) supports only parameterless constructors. Microsoft feels that this will be good enough for almost all scenarios, and I agree.

Other Verifiability Issues

In the remainder of this section, I'd like to point out a few other code constructs that have unexpected behavior when used with generics due to verifiability issues and how constraints can be used to make the code verifiable again.

Casting a Generic Type Variable

Casting a generic type variable to another type is illegal unless you are casting to a type compatible with a constraint:

```
private static void CastingAGenericTypeVariable1<T>(T obj) {
    Int32  x = (Int32) obj;    // Error
    String s = (String) obj;   // Error
}
```

The compiler issues an error on both lines above because **T** could be any type, and there is no guarantee that the casts will succeed. You can modify this code to get it to compile by casting to **Object** first:

```
private static void CastingAGenericTypeVariable2<T>(T obj) {
    Int32  x = (Int32) (Object) obj;    // No error
    String s = (String) (Object) obj;   // No error
}
```

While this code will now compile, it is still possible for the CLR to throw an **InvalidCastException** at runtime .

If you are trying to cast to a reference type, you can also use the C# **as** operator. Here is code modified to use the **as** operator with **String** (since **Int32** is a value type):

```
private static void CastingAGenericTypeVariable3<T>(T obj) {
    String s = obj as String;  // No error
}
```

Setting a Generic Type Variable to a Default Value

Setting a generic type variable to **null** is illegal unless the generic type is constrained to a reference type.

```
private static void SettingAGenericTypeVariableToNull<T>() {
    T temp = null;     // CS0403 - Cannot convert null to type parameter 'T' because it could
                       // be a non-nullable value type. Consider using 'default(T)' instead
}
```

Since **T** is unconstrained, it could be a value type, and setting a variable of a value type to **null** is not possible. If **T** were constrained to a reference type, setting **temp** to **null** would compile and run just fine.

Microsoft's C# team felt that it would be useful to give developers the ability to set a variable to a default value. So the C# compiler allows you to use the **default** keyword to accomplish this:

```
private static void SettingAGenericTypeVariableToDefaultValue<T>() {
    T temp = default(T);  // OK
}
```

The use of the **default** keyword above tells the C# compiler and the CLR's JIT compiler to produce code to set **temp** to **null** if **T** is a reference type and to set **temp** to all-bits-zero if **T** is a value type.

Comparing a Generic Type Variable with null

Comparing a generic type variable to **null** by using the == or != operator is legal regardless of whether the generic type is constrained:

```
private static void ComparingAGenericTypeVariableWithNull<T>(T obj) {
    if (obj == null) { /* Never executes for a value type */ }
}
```

Since **T** is unconstrained, it could be a reference type or a value type. If **T** is a value type, **obj** can never be **null**. Normally, you'd expect the C# compiler to issue an error because of this. However, the C# compiler does not issue an error; instead, it compiles the code just fine. When this method is called using a type argument that is a value type, the JIT compiler sees that the **if** statement can never be true, and the JIT compiler will not emit the native code for the **if** test or the code in the braces. If I had used the != operator, the JIT compiler would not emit the code for the **if** test (since it is always true), and it will emit the code inside the **if**'s braces.

By the way, if **T** had been constrained to a **struct**, the C# compiler would issue an error because you shouldn't be writing code that compares a value type variable with **null** since the result is always the same.

Comparing Two Generic Type Variables with Each Other

Comparing two variables of the same generic type is illegal if the generic type parameter is not known to be a reference type:

```
private static void ComparingTwoGenericTypeVariables<T>(T o1, T o2) {
    if (o1 == o2) { }  // Error
}
```

In this example, **T** is unconstrained, and whereas it is legal to compare two reference type variables with one another, it is not legal to compare two value type variables with one another unless the value type overloads the == operator. If **T** were constrained to **class**, this code would compile, and the == operator would return **true** if the variables referred to the same object, checking for exact identity. Note that if **T** were constrained to a reference type that overloaded the **operator** == method, the compiler would emit calls to this method when it sees the == operator. Obviously, this whole discussion applies to uses of the != operator too.

When you write code to compare the primitive value types—**Byte**, **Int32**, **Single**, **Decimal**, etc.—the C# compiler knows how to emit the right code. However, for non-primitive value types, the C# compiler doesn't know how to emit the code to do comparisons. So if **ComparingTwoGenericTypeVariables** method's **T** were constrained to **struct**, the compiler would issue an error. And you're not allowed to constrain a type parameter to a specific value type because it is implicitly sealed, and therefore no types exist that are derived from the value type. Allowing this would make the generic method constrained to a specific type, and the C# compiler doesn't allow this because it is more efficient to just make a non-generic method.

Using Generic Type Variables as Operands

Finally, it should be noted that there are a lot of issues about using operators with generic type operands. In Chapter 5, I talked about C# and how it handles its primitive types: **Byte**, **Int16**, **Int32**, **Int64**, **Decimal**, and so on. In particular, I mentioned that C# knows how to interpret operators (such as +, -, *, and /) when applied to the primitive types. Well, these operators can't be applied to variables of a generic type because the compiler doesn't know the type at compile time. This means that you can't use any of these operators with variables of a generic type. So it is impossible to write a mathematical algorithm that works on an arbitrary numeric data type. Here is an example of a generic method that I'd like to write:

```
private static T Sum<T>(T num) where T : struct {
   T sum = default(T) ;
   for (T n = default(T) ; n < num ; n++)
      sum += n;
   return sum;
}
```

I've done everything possible to try to get this method to compile. I've constrained **T** to **struct**, and I'm using **default(T)** to initialize **sum** and **n** to **0**. But when I compile this code, I get the following three errors:

- **error CS0019: Operator '<' cannot be applied to operands of type 'T' and 'T'**

- **error CS0023: Operator '++' cannot be applied to operand of type 'T'**

- **error CS0019: Operator '+=' cannot be applied to operands of type 'T' and 'T'**

This is a severe limitation on the CLR's generic support, and many developers (especially in the scientific, financial, and mathematical world) are very disappointed by this limitation. Many people have tried to come up with techniques to work around this limitation by using reflection (see Chapter 23, "Assembly Loading and Reflection"), operator overloading, and so on. But all of these cause a severe performance penalty or hurt readability of the code substantially. Hopefully, this is an area that Microsoft will address in a future version of the CLR and the compilers.

Chapter 13
Interfaces

Many programmers are familiar with the concept of multiple inheritance: the ability to define a class that is derived from two or more base classes. For example, imagine a class named **TransmitData**, whose function is to transmit data, and another class named **ReceiveData**, whose function is to receive data. Now imagine that you want to create a class named **SocketPort**, whose function is to transmit and receive data. In order to accomplish this, you would want to derive **SocketPort** from both **TransmitData** and **ReceiveData**.

Some programming languages allow multiple inheritance, making it possible for the **SocketPort** class to be derived from the two base classes, **TransmitData** and **ReceiveData**. However, the common language runtime (CLR)—and therefore all managed programming languages—does not support multiple inheritance. Rather than not offer any kind of multiple inheritance at all, the CLR does offer scaled-down multiple inheritance via *interfaces*. This chapter will discuss how to define and use interfaces as well as provide some guidelines to help you determine when to use an interface rather than a base class.

Class and Interface Inheritance

In the Microsoft .NET Framework, there is a class called `System.Object` that defines four public instance methods: `ToString`, `Equals`, `GetHashCode`, and `GetType`. This class is the root or ultimate base class of all other classes—all classes will inherit `Object`'s four instance methods. This also means that code written to operate on an instance of the `Object` class can actually perform operations on an instance of any class.

Since someone at Microsoft has implemented `Object`'s methods, any class derived from `Object` is actually inheriting the following:

- **The method signatures**   This allows code to think that it is operating on an instance of the `Object` class, when in fact, it could be operating on an instance of some other class.

- **The implementation of these methods**   This allows the developer defining a class derived from `Object` not to be required to implement `Object`'s methods manually.

In the CLR, a class is always derived from one and only one class (that must ultimately be derived from `Object`). This base class provides a set of method signatures and implementations for these methods. And a cool thing about defining a new class is that it can become the base class for another class defined in the future by some other developer—all of the method signatures and their implementations will be inherited by the new derived class.

The CLR also allows developers to define an *interface*, which is really just a way to give a name to a set of method signatures. These methods do not come with any implementation at all. A class inherits an interface by specifying the interface's name, and the class must explicitly provide implementations of the interface's methods before the CLR will consider the type definition to be valid. Of course, implementing interface methods can be tedious, which is why I referred to interface inheritance as a scaled-down mechanism to achieve multiple inheritance. The C# compiler and the CLR actually allow a class to inherit several interfaces, and of course, the class must provide implementations for all of the inherited interface methods.

One of the great features of class inheritance is that it allows instances of a derived type to be substituted in all contexts that expect instances of a base type. Similarly, interface inheritance allows instances of a type that implements the interface to be substituted in all contexts that expect instances of the named interface type. We will now look at how to define interfaces to make our discussion more concrete.

Defining an Interface

As mentioned in the previous section, an interface is a named set of method signatures. Note that interfaces can also define events, parameterless properties, and parameterful properties (indexers in C#) because all of these are just syntax shorthands that map to methods anyway, as shown in previous chapters. However, an interface cannot define any constructor methods. In addition, an interface is not allowed to define any instance fields.

Although the CLR does allow an interface to define static methods, static fields, constants, and static constructors, a Common Language Infrastructure (CLI)–compliant interface must not have any of these static members because some programming languages aren't able to define or access them. In fact, C# prevents an interface from defining any of these static members.

In C#, you use the **interface** keyword to define an interface, giving it a name and its set of instance method signatures. Here are the definitions of a few interfaces defined in the Framework Class Library (FCL):

```
public interface IDisposable {
   void Dispose();
}

public interface IEnumerable {
   IEnumerator GetEnumerator();
}

public interface IEnumerable<out T> : IEnumerable {
   new IEnumerator<T> GetEnumerator();
}

public interface ICollection<T> : IEnumerable<T>, IEnumerable {
   void    Add(T item);
   void    Clear();
   Boolean Contains(T item);
   void    CopyTo(T[] array, Int32 arrayIndex);
   Boolean Remove(T item);
   Int32   Count      { get; } // Read-only property
   Boolean IsReadOnly { get; } // Read-only property
}
```

To the CLR, an interface definition is just like a type definition. That is, the CLR will define an internal data structure for the interface type object, and reflection can be used to query features of the interface type. Like types, an interface can be defined at file scope or defined nested within another type. When defining the interface type, you can specify whatever visibility/accessibility (**public**, **protected**, **internal**, etc.) you desire.

By convention, interface type names are prefixed with an uppercase **I**, making it easy to spot an interface type in source code. The CLR does support generic interfaces (as you can see from some of the previous examples) as well as generic methods in an interface. I will discuss some of the many features offered by generic interfaces later in this chapter and in Chapter 12, "Generics," in which I cover generics more broadly.

An interface definition can "inherit" other interfaces. However, I use the word *inherit* here rather loosely because interface inheritance doesn't work exactly as does class inheritance. I prefer to think of interface inheritance as including the contract of other interfaces.

For example, the **ICollection<T>** interface definition includes the contracts of the **IEnumerable<T>** and **IEnumerable** interfaces. This means that:

- Any class that inherits the **ICollection<T>** interface must implement all of the methods defined by the **ICollection<T>**, **IEnumerable<T>**, and **IEnumerable** interfaces.

- Any code that expects an object whose type implements the **ICollection<T>** interface can assume that the object's type also implements the methods of the **IEnumerable<T>** and **IEnumerable** interfaces.

Inheriting an Interface

In this section, I'll show how to define a type that implements an interface, and then I'll show how to create an instance of this type and use the object to call the interface's methods. C# actually makes this pretty simple, but what happens behind the scenes is a bit more complicated. I'll explain what is happening behind the scenes later in this chapter.

The **System.IComparable<T>** interface is defined (in MSCorLib.dll) as follows:

```
public interface IComparable<in T> {
   Int32 CompareTo(T other);
}
```

The following code shows how to define a type that implements this interface and also shows code that compares two **Point** objects:

```
using System;


// Point is derived from System.Object and implements IComparable<T> for Point.
public sealed class Point : IComparable<Point> {
   private Int32 m_x, m_y;

   public Point(Int32 x, Int32 y) {
      m_x = x;
      m_y = y;
   }

   // This method implements IComparable<T>.CompareTo() for Point
   public Int32 CompareTo(Point other) {
      return Math.Sign(Math.Sqrt(m_x * m_x + m_y * m_y)
         - Math.Sqrt(other.m_x * other.m_x + other.m_y * other.m_y));
   }

   public override String ToString() {
      return String.Format("({0}, {1})", m_x, m_y);
   }
}
```

```
public static class Program {
    public static void Main() {
        Point[] points = new Point[] {
            new Point(3, 3),
            new Point(1, 2),
        };

        // Here is a call to Point's IComparable<T> CompareTo method
        if (points[0].CompareTo(points[1]) > 0) {
            Point tempPoint = points[0];
            points[0] = points[1];
            points[1] = tempPoint;
        }
        Console.WriteLine("Points from closest to (0, 0) to farthest:");
        foreach (Point p in points)
            Console.WriteLine(p);
    }
}
```

The C# compiler requires that a method that implements an interface be marked as public. The CLR requires that interface methods be marked as virtual. If you do not explicitly mark the method as virtual in your source code, the compiler marks the method as virtual and sealed; this prevents a derived class from overriding the interface method. If you explicitly mark the method as virtual, the compiler marks the method as virtual (and leaves it unsealed); this allows a derived class to override the interface method.

If an interface method is sealed, a derived class cannot override the method. However, a derived class can re-inherit the same interface and can provide its own implementation for the interface's methods. When calling an interface's method on an object, the implementation associated with the object's type is called. Here is an example that demonstrates this:

```
using System;

public static class Program {
    public static void Main() {
        /*********************** First Example *************************/
        Base b = new Base();

        // Calls Dispose by using b's type: "Base's Dispose"
        b.Dispose();

        // Calls Dispose by using b's object's type: "Base's Dispose"
        ((IDisposable)b).Dispose();


        /*********************** Second Example ************************/
        Derived d = new Derived();

        // Calls Dispose by using d's type: "Derived's Dispose"
        d.Dispose();

        // Calls Dispose by using d's object's type: "Derived's Dispose"
```

```
            ((IDisposable)d).Dispose();


            /*********************** Third Example *************************/
            b = new Derived();

            // Calls Dispose by using b's type: "Base's Dispose"
            b.Dispose();

            // Calls Dispose by using b's object's type: "Derived's Dispose"
            ((IDisposable)b).Dispose();
        }
    }

// This class is derived from Object and it implements IDisposable
internal class Base : IDisposable {
    // This method is implicitly sealed and cannot be overridden
    public void Dispose() {
        Console.WriteLine("Base's Dispose");
    }
}

// This class is derived from Base and it re-implements IDisposable
internal class Derived : Base, IDisposable {
    // This method cannot override Base's Dispose. 'new' is used to indicate
    // that this method re-implements IDisposable's Dispose method
    new public void Dispose() {
        Console.WriteLine("Derived's Dispose");

        // NOTE: The next line shows how to call a base class's implementation (if desired)
        // base.Dispose();
    }
}
```

More About Calling Interface Methods

The FCL's **System.String** type inherits **System.Object**'s method signatures and their implementations. In addition, the **String** type also implements several interfaces: **IComparable**, **ICloneable**, **IConvertible**, **IEnumerable**, **IComparable<String>**, **IEnumerable<Char>**, and **IEquatable<String>**. This means that the **String** type isn't required to implement (or override) the methods its **Object** base type offers. However, the **String** type must implement the methods declared in all of the interfaces.

The CLR allows you to define field, parameter, or local variables that are of an interface type. Using a variable of an interface type allows you to call methods defined by that interface. In addition, the CLR will allow you to call methods defined by **Object** because all classes inherit **Object**'s methods. The following code demonstrates this:

```
// The s variable refers to a String object.
String s = "Jeffrey";
// Using s, I can call any method defined in
// String, Object, IComparable, ICloneable, IConvertible, IEnumerable, etc.

// The cloneable variable refers to the same String object
ICloneable cloneable = s;
// Using cloneable, I can call any method declared by the
// ICloneable interface (or any method defined by Object) only.

// The comparable variable refers to the same String object
IComparable comparable = s;
// Using comparable, I can call any method declared by the
// IComparable interface (or any method defined by Object) only.

// The enumerable variable refers to the same String object
// At run time, you can cast a variable from one interface to another as
// long as the object's type implements both interfaces.
IEnumerable enumerable = (IEnumerable) comparable;
// Using enumerable, I can call any method declared by the
// IEnumerable interface (or any method defined by Object) only.
```

In this code, all of the variables refer to the same "Jeffrey" **String** object that is in the managed heap, and therefore, any method that I call while using any of these variables affects the one "Jeffrey" **String** object. However, the type of the variable indicates the action that I can perform on the object. The **s** variable is of type **String**, and therefore, I can use **s** to call any members defined by the **String** type (such as the **Length** property). I can also use the variable **s** to call any methods inherited from **Object** (such as **GetType**).

The **cloneable** variable is of the **ICloneable** interface type, and therefore, using the **cloneable** variable, I can call the **Clone** method defined by this interface. In addition, I can call any method defined by **Object** (such as **GetType**) because the CLR knows that all types derive from **Object**. However, using the **cloneable** variable, I cannot call public methods defined by **String** itself or any methods defined by any other interface that **String** implements. Similarly, using the **comparable** variable, I can call **CompareTo** or any method defined by **Object**, but no other methods are callable using this variable.

Important Like a reference type, a value type can implement zero or more interfaces. However, when you cast an instance of a value type to an interface type, the value type instance must be boxed. This is because an interface variable is a reference that must point to an object on the heap so that the CLR can examine the object's type object pointer to determine the exact type of the object. Then, when calling an interface method with a boxed value type, the CLR will follow the object's type object pointer to find the type object's method table in order to call the proper method.

Implicit and Explicit Interface Method Implementations (What's Happening Behind the Scenes)

When a type is loaded into the CLR, a method table is created and initialized for the type (as discussed in Chapter 1, "The CLR's Execution Model"). This method table contains one entry for every new method introduced by the type as well as entries for any virtual methods inherited by the type. Inherited virtual methods include methods defined by the base types in the inheritance hierarchy as well as any methods defined by the interface types. So if you have a simple type defined like this:

```
internal sealed class SimpleType : IDisposable {
   public void Dispose() { Console.WriteLine("Dispose"); }
}
```

the type's method table contains entries for the following:

- All the virtual instance methods defined by **Object**, the implicitly inherited base class.

- All the interface methods defined by **IDisposable**, the inherited interface. In this example, there is only one method, **Dispose**, since the **IDisposable** interface defines just one method.

- The new method, **Dispose**, introduced by **SimpleType**.

To make things simple for the programmer, the C# compiler assumes that the **Dispose** method introduced by **SimpleType** is the implementation for **IDisposable**'s **Dispose** method. The C# compiler makes this assumption because the method is **public**, and the signatures of the interface method and the newly introduced method are identical. That is, the methods have the same parameter and return types. By the way, if the new **Dispose** method were marked as **virtual**, the C# compiler would still consider this method to be a match for the interface method.

When the C# compiler matches a new method to an interface method, it emits metadata indicating that both entries in **SimpleType**'s method table should refer to the same implementation. To help make this clearer, here is some code that demonstrates how to call the class's public **Dispose** method as well as how to call the class's implementation of **IDisposable**'s **Dispose** method:

```
public sealed class Program {
   public static void Main() {
      SimpleType st = new SimpleType();

      // This calls the public Dispose method implementation
      st.Dispose();

      // This calls IDisposable's Dispose method implementation
      IDisposable d = st;
      d.Dispose();
   }
}
```

In the first call to **Dispose**, the **Dispose** method defined by **SimpleType** is called. Then I define a variable, **d**, which is of the **IDisposable** interface type. I initialize the **d** variable to refer to the **SimpleType** object. Now when I call **d.Dispose()**, I am calling the **IDisposable** interface's **Dispose** method. Since C# requires the public **Dispose** method to also be the implementation for **IDisposable**'s **Dispose** method, the same code will execute, and, in this example, you can't see any observable difference. The output is as follows:

```
Dispose
Dispose
```

Now, let me rewrite the **SimpleType** from above so that you can see an observable difference:

```
internal sealed class SimpleType : IDisposable {
    public void Dispose() { Console.WriteLine("public Dispose"); }
    void IDisposable.Dispose() { Console.WriteLine("IDisposable Dispose"); }
}
```

Without changing the **Main** method shown earlier, if we just recompile and rerun the program, the output will be this:

```
public Dispose
IDisposable Dispose
```

In C#, when you prefix the name of a method with the name of the interface that defines the method (**IDisposable.Dispose** as in this example), you are creating an *explicit interface method implementation* (EIMI). Note that when you define an explicit interface method in C#, you are not allowed to specify any accessibility (such as **public** or **private**). However, when the compiler generates the metadata for the method, its accessibility is set to private, preventing any code using an instance of the class from simply calling the interface method. The only way to call the interface method is through a variable of the interface's type.

Also note that an EIMI method cannot be marked as **virtual** and therefore cannot be overridden. This is because the EIMI method is not really part of the type's object model; it's a way of attaching an interface (set of behaviors or methods) onto a type without making the behaviors/methods obvious. If all of this seems a bit kludgy to you, you *are* understanding it correctly—this is all a bit kludgy. Later in this chapter, I'll show some valid reasons for using EIMIs.

Generic Interfaces

C#'s and the CLR's support of generic interfaces offers many great features for developers. In this section, I'd like to discuss the benefits offered when using generic interfaces.

First, generic interfaces offer great compile-time type safety. Some interfaces (such as the non-generic **IComparable** interface) define methods that have **Object** parameters or return types. When code calls these interface methods, a reference to an instance of any type can be passed. But this is usually not desired. The following code demonstrates:

```
private void SomeMethod1() {
    Int32 x = 1, y = 2;
    IComparable c = x;

    // CompareTo expects an Object; passing y (an Int32) is OK
    c.CompareTo(y);     // y is boxed here

    // CompareTo expects an Object; passing "2" (a String) compiles
    // but an ArgumentException is thrown at runtime
    c.CompareTo("2");
}
```

Obviously, it is preferable to have the interface method strongly typed, and this is why the FCL includes a generic **IComparable<in T>** interface. Here is the new version of the code revised by using the generic interface:

```
private void SomeMethod2() {
    Int32 x = 1, y = 2;
    IComparable<Int32> c = x;

    // CompareTo expects an Int32; passing y (an Int32) is OK
    c.CompareTo(y);     // y is not boxed here

    // CompareTo expects an Int32; passing "2" (a String) results
    // in a compiler error indicating that String cannot be cast to an Int32
    c.CompareTo("2");   // Error
}
```

The second benefit of generic interfaces is that much less boxing will occur when working with value types. Notice in **SomeMethod1** that the non-generic **IComparable** interface's **CompareTo** method expects an **Object**; passing **y** (an **Int32** value type) causes the value in **y** to be boxed. However, in **SomeMethod2**, the generic **IComparable<in T>** interface's **CompareTo** method expects an **Int32**; passing **y** causes it to be passed by value, and no boxing is necessary.

> **Note** The FCL defines non-generic and generic versions of the **IComparable**, **ICollection**, **IList**, and **IDictionary** interfaces, as well as some others. If you are defining a type, and you want to implement any of these interfaces, you should typically implement the generic versions of these interfaces. The non-generic versions are in the FCL for backward compatibility to work with code written before the .NET Framework supported generics. The non-generic versions also provide users a way of manipulating the data in a more general, less type-safe fashion.
>
> Some of the generic interfaces inherit the non-generic versions, so your class will have to implement both the generic and non-generic versions of the interfaces. For example, the generic **IEnumerable<out T>** interface inherits the non-generic **IEnumerable** interface. So if your class implements **IEnumerable<out T>**, your class must also implement **IEnumerable**.

Sometimes when integrating with other code, you may have to implement a non-generic interface because a generic version of the interface simply doesn't exist. In this case, if any of the interface's methods take or return **Object**, you will lose compile-time type safety, and you will get boxing with value types. You can alleviate this situation to some extent by using a technique I describe in the "Improving Compile-Time Type Safety with Explicit Interface Method Implementations" section near the end of this chapter.

The third benefit of generic interfaces is that a class can implement the same interface multiple times as long as different type parameters are used. The following code shows an example of how useful this could be:

```
using System;

// This class implements the generic IComparable<T> interface twice
public sealed class Number: IComparable<Int32>, IComparable<String> {
    private Int32 m_val = 5;

    // This method implements IComparable<Int32>'s CompareTo
    public Int32 CompareTo(Int32 n) {
        return m_val.CompareTo(n);
    }

    // This method implements IComparable<String>'s CompareTo
    public Int32 CompareTo(String s) {
        return m_val.CompareTo(Int32.Parse(s));
    }
}

public static class Program {
    public static void Main() {
        Number n = new Number();

        // Here, I compare the value in n with an Int32 (5)
        IComparable<Int32> cInt32 = n;
        Int32 result = cInt32.CompareTo(5);

        // Here, I compare the value in n with a String ("5")
        IComparable<String> cString = n;
        result = cString.CompareTo("5");
    }
}
```

An interface's generic type parameters can also be marked as contravariant and covariant, which allows even more flexibility for using generic interfaces. For more about contravariance and covariance, see the "Delegate and Interface Contravariant and Covariant Generic Type Arguments" section in Chapter 12.

Generics and Interface Constraints

In the previous section, I discussed the benefits of using generic interfaces. In this section, I'll discuss the benefits of constraining generic type parameters to interfaces.

The first benefit is that you can constrain a single generic type parameter to multiple interfaces. When you do this, the type of parameter you are passing in must implement *all* of the interface constraints. Here is an example:

```
public static class SomeType {
    private static void Test() {
        Int32 x = 5;
        Guid g = new Guid();

        // This call to M compiles fine because
        // Int32 implements IComparable AND IConvertible
        M(x);

        // This call to M causes a compiler error because
        // Guid implements IComparable but it does not implement IConvertible
        M(g);
    }

    // M's type parameter, T, is constrained to work only with types that
    // implement both the IComparable AND IConvertible interfaces
    private static Int32 M<T>(T t) where T : IComparable, IConvertible {
        ...
    }
}
```

This is actually quite cool! When you define a method's parameters, each parameter's type indicates that the argument passed must be of the parameter's type or be derived from it. If the parameter type is an interface, this indicates that the argument can be of any class type as long as the class implements the interface. Using multiple interface constraints actually lets the method indicate that the passed argument must implement multiple interfaces.

In fact, if we constrained **T** to a class and two interfaces, we are saying that the type of argument passed must be of the specified base class (or derived from it), and it must also implement the two interfaces. This flexibility allows the method to really dictate what callers can pass, and compiler errors will be generated if callers do not meet these constraints.

The second benefit of interface constraints is reduced boxing when passing instances of value types. In the previous code fragment, the **M** method was passed **x** (an instance of an **Int32**, which is a value type). No boxing will occur when **x** is passed to **M**. If code inside **M** does call **t.CompareTo(...)**, still no boxing occurs to make the call (boxing may still happen for arguments passed to **CompareTo**).

On the other hand, if **M** had been declared like this:

```
private static Int32 M(IComparable t) {
    ...
}
```

then in order to pass **x** to **M**, **x** would have to be boxed.

For interface constraints, the C# compiler emits certain Intermediate Language (IL) instructions that result in calling the interface method on the value type directly without boxing it. Aside from using interface constraints, there is no other way to get the C# compiler to emit these IL instructions, and therefore, calling an interface method on a value type always causes boxing.

Implementing Multiple Interfaces That Have the Same Method Name and Signature

Occasionally, you might find yourself defining a type that implements multiple interfaces that define methods with the same name and signature. For example, imagine that there are two interfaces defined as follows:

```
public interface IWindow {
    Object GetMenu();
}

public interface IRestaurant {
    Object GetMenu();
}
```

Let's say that you want to define a type that implements both of these interfaces. You'd have to implement the type's members by using explicit interface method implementations as follows:

```
// This type is derived from System.Object and
// implements the IWindow and IRestaurant interfaces.
public sealed class MarioPizzeria : IWindow, IRestaurant {

    // This is the implementation for IWindow's GetMenu method.
    Object IWindow.GetMenu() { ... }

    // This is the implementation for IRestaurant's GetMenu method.
    Object IRestaurant.GetMenu() { ... }

    // This (optional method) is a GetMenu method that has nothing
    // to do with an interface.
    public Object GetMenu() { ... }
}
```

Because this type must implement multiple and separate **GetMenu** methods, you need to tell the C# compiler which **GetMenu** method contains the implementation for a particular interface.

Code that uses a **MarioPizzeria** object must cast to the specific interface to call the desired method. The following code demonstrates:

```
MarioPizzeria mp = new MarioPizzeria();

// This line calls MarioPizzeria's public GetMenu method
mp.GetMenu();

// These lines call MarioPizzeria's IWindow.GetMenu method
IWindow window = mp;
window.GetMenu();

// These lines call MarioPizzeria's IRestaurant.GetMenu method
IRestaurant restaurant = mp;
restaurant.GetMenu();
```

Improving Compile-Time Type Safety with Explicit Interface Method Implementations

Interfaces are great because they define a standard way for types to communicate with each other. Earlier, I talked about generic interfaces and how they improve compile-time type safety and reduce boxing. Unfortunately, there may be times when you need to implement a non-generic interface because a generic version doesn't exist. If any of the interface's method(s) accept parameters of type **System.Object** or return a value whose type is **System.Object**, you will lose compile-time type safety, and you will get boxing. In this section, I'll show you how you can use EIMI to improve this situation somewhat.

Look at the very common **IComparable** interface:

```
public interface IComparable {
    Int32 CompareTo(Object other);
}
```

This interface defines one method that accepts a parameter of type **System.Object**. If I define my own type that implements this interface, the type definition might look like this:

```
internal struct SomeValueType : IComparable {
    private Int32 m_x;
    public SomeValueType(Int32 x) { m_x = x; }
    public Int32 CompareTo(Object other) {
        return(m_x - ((SomeValueType) other).m_x);
    }
}
```

Using **SomeValueType**, I can now write the following code:

```
public static void Main() {
    SomeValueType v = new SomeValueType(0);
    Object o = new Object();
    Int32 n = v.CompareTo(v); // Undesired boxing
    n = v.CompareTo(o);       // InvalidCastException
}
```

There are two characteristics of this code that are not ideal:

- **Undesired boxing**   When **v** is passed as an argument to the **CompareTo** method, it must be boxed because **CompareTo** expects an **Object**.

- **The lack of type safety**   This code compiles, but an **InvalidCastException** is thrown inside the **CompareTo** method when it attempts to cast **o** to **SomeValueType**.

Both of these issues can be fixed by using EIMIs. Here's a modified version of **SomeValueType** that has an EIMI added to it:

```
internal struct SomeValueType : IComparable {
    private Int32 m_x;
    public SomeValueType(Int32 x) { m_x = x; }

    public Int32 CompareTo(SomeValueType other) {
        return(m_x - other.m_x);
    }

    // NOTE: No public/private used on the next line
    Int32 IComparable.CompareTo(Object other) {
        return CompareTo((SomeValueType) other);
    }
}
```

Notice several changes in this new version. First, it now has two **CompareTo** methods. The first **CompareTo** method no longer takes an **Object** as a parameter; it now takes a **SomeValueType** instead. Because this parameter has changed, the code that casts **other** to **SomeValueType** is no longer necessary and has been removed. Second, changing the first **CompareTo** method to make it type-safe means that **SomeValueType** no longer adheres to the contract placed on it by implementing the **IComparable** interface. So **SomeValueType** must implement a **CompareTo** method that satisfies the **IComparable** contract. This is the job of the second **IComparable.CompareTo** method, which is an EIMI.

Having made these two changes means that we now get compile-time type safety and no boxing:

```
public static void Main() {
    SomeValueType v = new SomeValueType(0);
    Object o = new Object();
    Int32  n = v.CompareTo(v); // No boxing
    n = v.CompareTo(o);        // compile-time error
}
```

If, however, we define a variable of the interface type, we will lose compile-time type safety and experience undesired boxing again:

```
public static void Main() {
   SomeValueType v = new SomeValueType(0);
   IComparable c = v;            // Boxing!

   Object o = new Object();
   Int32  n = c.CompareTo(v); // Undesired boxing
   n = c.CompareTo(o);        // InvalidCastException
}
```

In fact, as mentioned earlier in this chapter, when casting a value type instance to an interface type, the CLR must box the value type instance. Because of this fact, two boxings will occur in the previous **Main** method.

EIMIs are frequently used when implementing interfaces such as **IConvertible**, **ICollection**, **IList**, and **IDictionary**. They let you create type-safe versions of these interfaces' methods, and they enable you to reduce boxing operations for value types.

Be Careful with Explicit Interface Method Implementations

It is critically important for you to understand some ramifications that exist when using EIMIs. And because of these ramifications, you should try to avoid EIMIs as much as possible. Fortunately, generic interfaces help you avoid EIMIs quite a bit. But there may still be times when you will need to use them (such as implementing two interface methods with the same name and signature). Here are the big problems with EIMIs:

- There is no documentation explaining how a type specifically implements an EIMI method, and there is no Microsoft Visual Studio IntelliSense support.

- Value type instances are boxed when cast to an interface.

- An EIMI cannot be called by a derived type.

Let's take a closer look at these problems.

When examining the methods for a type in the .NET Framework reference documentation, explicit interface method implementations are listed, but no type-specific help exists; you can just read the general help about the interface methods. For example, the documentation for the **Int32** type shows that it implements all of **IConvertible** interface's methods. This is good because developers know that these methods exist; however, this has been very confusing to developers because you can't call an **IConvertible** method on an **Int32** directly. For example, the following method won't compile:

```
public static void Main() {
   Int32 x = 5;
   Single s = x.ToSingle(null); // Trying to call an IConvertible method
}
```

When compiling this method, the C# compiler produces the following message: "**messagepi117: 'int' does not contain a definition for 'ToSingle'.**" This error message confuses the developer because it's clearly stating that the **Int32** type doesn't define a **ToSingle** method when, in fact, it does.

To call **ToSingle** on an **Int32**, you must first cast the **Int32** to an **IConvertible**, as shown in the following method:

```
public static void Main() {
   Int32 x = 5;
   Single s = ((IConvertible) x).ToSingle(null);
}
```

Requiring this cast isn't obvious at all, and many developers won't figure this out on their own. But an even more troublesome problem exists: casting the **Int32** value type to an **IConvertible** also boxes the value type, wasting memory and hurting performance. This is the second of the big problems I mentioned at the beginning of this section.

The third and perhaps the biggest problem with EIMIs is that they cannot be called by a derived class. Here is an example:

```
internal class Base : IComparable {

   // Explicit Interface Method Implementation
   Int32 IComparable.CompareTo(Object o) {
      Console.WriteLine("Base's CompareTo");
      return 0;
   }
}

internal sealed class Derived : Base, IComparable {

   // A public method that is also the interface implementation
   public Int32 CompareTo(Object o) {
      Console.WriteLine("Derived's CompareTo");

      // This attempt to call the base class's EIMI causes a compiler error:
      // error CS0117: 'Base' does not contain a definition for 'CompareTo'
      base.CompareTo(o);
      return 0;
   }
}
```

In **Derived**'s **CompareTo** method, I try to call **base.CompareTo**, but this causes the C# compiler to issue an error. The problem is that the **Base** class doesn't offer a public or protected **CompareTo** method that can be called; it offers a **CompareTo** method that can be called only by using a variable that is of the **IComparable** type. I could modify **Derived**'s **CompareTo** method so that it looks like this:

```
// A public method that is also the interface implementation
public Int32 CompareTo(Object o) {
   Console.WriteLine("Derived's CompareTo");

   // This attempt to call the base class's EIMI causes infinite recursion
   IComparable c = this;
   c.CompareTo(o);

   return 0;
}
```

In this version, I am casting **this** to an **IComparable** variable, **c**. And then, I use **c** to call **CompareTo**. However, the **Derived**'s public **CompareTo** method serves as the implementation for **Derived**'s **IComparableCompareTo** method, and therefore, infinite recursion occurs. This could be fixed by declaring the **Derived** class without the **IComparable** interface, like this:

```
internal sealed class Derived : Base /*, IComparable */ { ... }
```

Now the previous **CompareTo** method will call the **CompareTo** method in **Base**. But sometimes you cannot simply remove the interface from the type because you want the derived type to implement an interface method. The best way to fix this is for the base class to provide a virtual method in addition to the interface method that it has chosen to implement explicitly. Then the **Derived** class can override the virtual method. Here is the correct way to define the **Base** and **Derived** classes:

```
internal class Base : IComparable {

   // Explicit Interface Method Implementation
   Int32 IComparable.CompareTo(Object o) {
      Console.WriteLine("Base's IComparable CompareTo");
      return CompareTo(o);   // This now calls the virtual method
   }

   // Virtual method for derived classes (this method could have any name)
   public virtual Int32 CompareTo(Object o) {
      Console.WriteLine("Base's virtual CompareTo");
      return 0;
   }
}

internal sealed class Derived : Base, IComparable {

   // A public method that is also the interface implementation
   public override Int32 CompareTo(Object o) {
      Console.WriteLine("Derived's CompareTo");

      // Now, we can call Base's virtual method
      return base.CompareTo(o);
   }
}
```

Note that I have defined the virtual method above as a public method, but in some cases, you will prefer to make the method protected instead. It is fine to make this method protected instead of public, but that will necessitate other minor changes. This discussion clearly shows you that EIMIs should be used with great care. When many developers first learn about EIMIs, they think that they're cool and they start using them whenever possible. Don't do this! EIMIs are useful in some circumstances, but you should avoid them whenever possible because they make using a type much more difficult.

Design: Base Class or Interface?

I often hear the question, "Should I design a base type or an interface?" The answer isn't always clear-cut. Here are some guidelines that might help you:

- **IS-A vs. CAN-DO relationship**   A type can inherit only one implementation. If the derived type can't claim an IS-A relationship with the base type, don't use a base type; use an interface. Interfaces imply a CAN-DO relationship. If the CAN-DO functionality appears to belong with various object types, use an interface. For example, a type can convert instances of itself to another type (**IConvertible**), a type can serialize an instance of itself (**ISerializable**), etc. Note that value types must be derived from **System.ValueType**, and therefore, they cannot be derived from an arbitrary base class. In this case, you must use a CAN-DO relationship and define an interface.

- **Ease of use**   It's generally easier for you as a developer to define a new type derived from a base type than to implement all of the methods of an interface. The base type can provide a lot of functionality, so the derived type probably needs only relatively small modifications to its behavior. If you supply an interface, the new type must implement all of the members.

- **Consistent implementation**   No matter how well an interface contract is documented, it's very unlikely that everyone will implement the contract 100 percent correctly. In fact, COM suffers from this very problem, which is why some COM objects work correctly only with Microsoft Office Word or with Windows Internet Explorer. By providing a base type with a good default implementation, you start off using a type that works and is well tested; you can then modify parts that need modification.

- **Versioning**   If you add a method to the base type, the derived type inherits the new method, you start off using a type that works, and the user's source code doesn't even have to be recompiled. Adding a new member to an interface forces the inheritor of the interface to change its source code and recompile.

In the FCL, the classes related to streaming data use an implementation inheritance design. The **System.IO.Stream** class is the abstract base class. It provides a bunch of methods, such as **Read** and **Write**. Other classes—**System.IO.FileStream**, **System.IO.MemoryStream**, and **System.Net.Sockets.NetworkStream**—are derived from **Stream**. Microsoft chose an

IS-A relationship between each of these three classes and the **Stream** class because it made implementing the concrete classes easier. For example, the derived classes need to implement only synchronous I/O operations; they inherit the ability to perform asynchronous I/O operations from the **Stream** base class.

Admittedly, choosing to use inheritance for the stream classes isn't entirely clear-cut; the **Stream** base class actually provides very little implementation. However, if you consider the Microsoft Windows Forms control classes, in which **Button**, **CheckBox**, **ListBox**, and all of the other controls are derived from **System.Windows.Forms.Control**, it's easy to imagine all of the code that **Control** implements, which the various control classes simply inherit to function correctly.

By contrast, Microsoft designed the FCL collections to be interface based. The **System.Collections.Generic** namespace defines several collection-related interfaces: **IEnumerable<out T>**, **ICollection<T>**, **IList<T>**, and **IDictionary<TKey, TValue>**. Then Microsoft provided a number of classes, such as **List<T>**, **Dictionary<TKey, TValue>**, **Queue<T>**, **Stack<T>**, and so on, that implement combinations of these interfaces. Here the designers chose a CAN-DO relationship between the classes and the interfaces because the implementations of these various collection classes are radically different from one another. In other words, there isn't a lot of sharable code between a **List<T>**, a **Dictionary<TKey, TValue>**, and a **Queue<T>**.

The operations these collection classes offer are, nevertheless, pretty consistent. For example, they all maintain a set of elements that can be enumerated, and they all allow adding and removing of elements. If you have a reference to an object whose type implements the **IList<T>** interface, you can write code to insert elements, remove elements, and search for an element without having to know exactly what type of collection you're working with. This is a very powerful mechanism.

Finally, it should be pointed out that you can actually do both: define an interface *and* provide a base class that implements the interface. For example, the FCL defines the **IComparer<in T>** interface, and any type can choose to implement this interface. In addition, the FCL provides an abstract base class, **Comparer<T>**, which implements this interface and provides a default implementation for the non-generic **IComparable**'s **Compare** method. Having both an interface definition and a base class offers great flexibility because developers can now choose whichever they prefer.

Chapter 14
Chars, Strings, and Working with Text

In this chapter, I'll explain the mechanics of working with individual characters and strings in the Microsoft .NET Framework. I'll start by talking about the **System.Char** structure and the various ways that you can manipulate a character. Then I'll go over the more useful **System.String** class, which allows you to work with immutable strings. (Once created, strings can't be modified in any way.) After examining strings, I'll show you how to perform various operations efficiently to build a string dynamically via the **System.Text.StringBuilder** class. With the string basics out of the way, I'll then describe how to format objects into strings and how to efficiently persist or transmit strings by using various encodings. Finally, I'll discuss the **System.Security.SecureString** class, which can be used to protect sensitive string data such as passwords and credit card information.

Characters

In the .NET Framework, characters are always represented in 16-bit Unicode code values, easing the development of global applications. A character is represented with an instance of the **System.Char** structure (a value type). The **System.Char** type is pretty simple. It offers two public read-only constant fields: **MinValue**, defined as **'\0'**, and **MaxValue**, defined as **'\uffff'**.

Given an instance of a **Char**, you can call the static **GetUnicodeCategory** method, which returns a value of the **System.Globalization.UnicodeCategory** enumerated type. This value indicates whether the character is a control character, a currency symbol, a lowercase letter, an uppercase letter, a punctuation character, a math symbol, or another character (as defined by the Unicode standard).

To ease developing, the **Char** type also offers several static methods, such as **IsDigit**, **IsLetter**, **IsWhiteSpace**, **IsUpper**, **IsLower**, **IsPunctuation**, **IsLetterOrDigit**, **IsControl**, **IsNumber**, **IsSeparator**, **IsSurrogate**, **IsLowSurrogate**, **IsHighSurrogate**, and **IsSymbol**. Most of these methods call **GetUnicodeCategory** internally and simply return **true** or **false** accordingly. Note that all of these methods take either a single character for a parameter or a **String** and the index of a character within the **String** as parameters.

In addition, you can convert a single character to its lowercase or uppercase equivalent in a culture-agnostic way by calling the static **ToLowerInvariant** or **ToUpperInvariant** method. Alternatively, the **ToLower** and **ToUpper** methods convert the character by using the culture information associated with the calling thread (which the methods obtain internally by querying the static **CurrentCulture** property of the **System.Threading.Thread** class). You can also specify a particular culture by passing an instance of the **CultureInfo** class to these methods. **ToLower** and **ToUpper** require culture information because letter casing is a culture-dependent operation. For example, Turkish considers the uppercase of U+0069 (LATIN LOWERCASE LETTER I) to be U+0130 (LATIN UPPERCASE LETTER I WITH DOT ABOVE), whereas other cultures consider the result to be U+0049 (LATIN CAPITAL LETTER I).

Besides these static methods, the **Char** type also offers a few instance methods of its own. The **Equals** method returns **true** if two **Char** instances represent the same 16-bit Unicode code point. The **CompareTo** methods (defined by the **IComparable/IComparable<Char>** interfaces) return a comparison of two **Char** instances; this comparison is not culture-sensitive. The **ConvertFromUtf32** method produces a string consisting of two UTF-16 characters from a single UTF-32 character. The **ConvertToUtf32** produces a UTF-16 character from a low/high surrogate pair or from a string. The **ToString** method returns a **String** consisting of a single character. The opposite of **ToString** is **Parse/TryParse**, which takes a single-character **String** and returns its UTF-16 code point.

The last method, **GetNumericValue**, returns the numeric equivalent of a character. I demonstrate this method in the following code:

```
using System;

public static class Program {
    public static void Main() {
        Double d;                           // '\u0033' is the "digit 3"
        d = Char.GetNumericValue('\u0033'); // '3' would work too
        Console.WriteLine(d.ToString());    // Displays "3"

        // '\u00bc' is the "vulgar fraction one quarter ('¼')"
        d = Char.GetNumericValue('\u00bc');
        Console.WriteLine(d.ToString());    // Displays "0.25"

        // 'A' is the "Latin capital letter A"
        d = Char.GetNumericValue('A');
        Console.WriteLine(d.ToString());    // Displays "-1"
    }
}
```

Finally, three techniques allow you to convert between various numeric types to **Char** instances and vice versa. The techniques are listed here in order of preference:

- **Casting**   The easiest way to convert a **Char** to a numeric value such as an **Int32** is simply by casting. Of the three techniques, this is the most efficient because the compiler emits Intermediate Language (IL) instructions to perform the conversion, and no methods have to be called. In addition, some languages (such as C#) allow you to indicate whether the conversion should be performed using checked or unchecked code (discussed in Chapter 5, "Primitive, Reference, and Value Types").

- **Use the Convert type**   The **System.Convert** type offers several static methods that are capable of converting a **Char** to a numeric type and vice versa. All of these methods perform the conversion as a checked operation, causing an **OverflowException** to be thrown if the conversion results in the loss of data.

- **Use the IConvertible interface**   The **Char** type and all of the numeric types in the .NET Framework Class Library (FCL) implement the **IConvertible** interface. This interface defines methods such as **ToUInt16** and **ToChar**. This technique is the least efficient of the three because calling an interface method on a value type requires that the instance be boxed—**Char** and all of the numeric types are value types. The methods of **IConvertible** throw a **System.InvalidCastException** if the type can't be converted (such as converting a **Char** to a **Boolean**) or if the conversion results in a loss of data. Note that many types (including the FCL's **Char** and numeric types) implement **IConvertible**'s methods as explicit interface member implementations (described in Chapter 13, "Interfaces"). This means that you must explicitly cast the instance to an **IConvertible** before you can call any of the interface's methods. All of the methods of **IConvertible** except **GetTypeCode** accept a reference to an object that implements the **IFormatProvider** interface. This parameter is useful if for some reason the conversion needs to take culture information into account. For most conversions, you can pass **null** for this parameter because it would be ignored anyway.

The following code demonstrates how to use these three techniques:

```
using System;

public static class Program {
   public static void Main() {
      Char  c;
      Int32 n;

      // Convert number <-> character using C# casting
      c = (Char) 65;
      Console.WriteLine(c);                    // Displays "A"

      n = (Int32) c;
      Console.WriteLine(n);                    // Displays "65"
```

```
        c = unchecked((Char) (65536 + 65));
        Console.WriteLine(c);                   // Displays "A"



        // Convert number <-> character using Convert
        c = Convert.ToChar(65);
        Console.WriteLine(c);                   // Displays "A"

        n = Convert.ToInt32(c);
        Console.WriteLine(n);                   // Displays "65"


        // This demonstrates Convert's range checking
        try {
            c = Convert.ToChar(70000);          // Too big for 16 bits
            Console.WriteLine(c);               // Doesn't execute
        }
        catch (OverflowException) {
            Console.WriteLine("Can't convert 70000 to a Char.");
        }


        // Convert number <-> character using IConvertible
        c = ((IConvertible) 65).ToChar(null);
        Console.WriteLine(c);                   // Displays "A"

        n = ((IConvertible) c).ToInt32(null);
        Console.WriteLine(n);                   // Displays "65"
    }
}
```

The System.String Type

One of the most used types in any application is **System.String**. A **String** represents an immutable ordered set of characters. The **String** type is derived immediately from **Object**, making it a reference type, and therefore, **String** objects (its array of characters) always live in the heap, never on a thread's stack. The **String** type also implements several interfaces (**IComparable/IComparable<String>**, **ICloneable**, **IConvertible**, **IEnumerable/IEnumerable<Char>**, and **IEquatable<String>**).

Constructing Strings

Many programming languages (including C#) consider **String** to be a primitive type—that is, the compiler lets you express literal strings directly in your source code. The compiler places these literal strings in the module's metadata, and they are then loaded and referenced at runtime.

In C#, you can't use the **new** operator to construct a **String** object from a literal string:

```
using System;

public static class Program {
    public static void Main() {
        String s = new String("Hi there.");  // <-- Error
        Console.WriteLine(s);
    }
}
```

Instead, you must use the following simplified syntax:

```
using System;

public static class Program {
    public static void Main() {
        String s = "Hi there.";
        Console.WriteLine(s);
    }
}
```

If you compile this code and examine its IL (using ILDasm.exe), you'd see the following:

```
.method public hidebysig static void  Main() cil managed
{
  .entrypoint
  // Code size       13 (0xd)
  .maxstack  1
  .locals init (string V_0)
  IL_0000:  ldstr      "Hi there."
  IL_0005:  stloc.0
  IL_0006:  ldloc.0
  IL_0007:  call       void [mscorlib]System.Console::WriteLine(string)
  IL_000c:  ret
} // end of method Program::Main
```

The **newobj** IL instruction constructs a new instance of an object. However, no **newobj** instruction appears in the IL code example. Instead, you see the special **ldstr** (load string) IL instruction, which constructs a **String** object by using a literal string obtained from metadata. This shows you that the common language runtime (CLR) does, in fact, have a special way of constructing literal **String** objects.

If you are using unsafe code, you can construct a **String** object from a **Char*** or **SByte***. To accomplish this, you would use C#'s **new** operator and call one of the constructors provided by the **String** type that takes **Char*** or **SByte*** parameters. These constructors create a **String** object, initializing the string from an array of **Char** instances or signed bytes. The other constructors don't have any pointer parameters and can be called using safe (verifiable) code written in any managed programming language.

C# offers some special syntax to help you enter literal strings into the source code. For special characters such as new lines, carriage returns, and backspaces, C# uses the escape mechanism familiar to C/C++ developers:

```
// String containing carriage-return and newline characters
String s = "Hi\r\nthere.";
```

> **Important** Although the preceding example hard-codes carriage-return and newline characters into the string, I don't recommend this practice. Instead, the **System.Environment** type defines a read-only **NewLine** property that returns a string consisting of these characters when your application is running on Microsoft Windows. However, the **NewLine** property is platform sensitive, and it returns the appropriate string required to obtain a newline by the underlying platform. So, for example, if the Common Language Infrastructure (CLI) is ported to a UNIX system, the **NewLine** property would return a string consisting of just a single character **\n**. Here's the proper way to define the previous string so that it works correctly on any platform:
>
> ```
> String s = "Hi" + Environment.NewLine + "there.";
> ```

You can concatenate several strings to form a single string by using C#'s + operator as follows:

```
// Three literal strings concatenated to form a single literal string
String s = "Hi" + " " + "there.";
```

In this code, because all of the strings are literal strings, the C# compiler concatenates them at compile time and ends up placing just one string—**"Hi there."**—in the module's metadata. Using the + operator on nonliteral strings causes the concatenation to be performed at runtime. To concatenate several strings together at runtime, avoid using the + operator because it creates multiple string objects on the garbage-collected heap. Instead, use the **System.Text.StringBuilder** type (which I'll explain later in this chapter).

Finally, C# also offers a special way to declare a string in which all characters between quotes are considered part of the string. These special declarations are called *verbatim strings* and are typically used when specifying the path of a file or directory or when working with regular expressions. Here is some code showing how to declare the same string with and without using the verbatim string character (@).

```
// Specifying the pathname of an application
String file = "C:\\Windows\\System32\\Notepad.exe";

// Specifying the pathname of an application by using a verbatim string
String file = @"C:\Windows\System32\Notepad.exe";
```

You could use either one of the preceding code lines in a program because they produce identical strings in the assembly's metadata. However, the @ symbol before the string on the second line tells the compiler that the string is a verbatim string. In effect, this tells the compiler to treat backslash characters as backslash characters instead of escape characters, making the path much more readable in your source code.

Now that you've seen how to construct a string, let's talk about some of the operations you can perform on **String** objects.

Strings Are Immutable

The most important thing to know about a **String** object is that it is immutable. That is, once created, a string can never get longer, get shorter, or have any of its characters changed. Having immutable strings offers several benefits. First, it allows you to perform operations on a string without actually changing the string:

```
if (s.ToUpperInvariant().Substring(10, 21).EndsWith("EXE")) {
   ...
}
```

Here, **ToUpperInvariant** returns a new string; it doesn't modify the characters of the string **s**. **Substring** operates on the string returned by **ToUpperInvariant** and also returns a new string, which is then examined by **EndsWith**. The two temporary strings created by **ToUpperInvariant** and **Substring** are not referenced for long by the application code, and the garbage collector will reclaim their memory at the next collection. If you perform a lot of string manipulations, you end up creating a lot of **String** objects on the heap, which causes more frequent garbage collections, thus hurting your application's performance. To perform a lot of string manipulations efficiently, use the **StringBuilder** class.

Having immutable strings also means that there are no thread synchronization issues when manipulating or accessing a string. In addition, it's possible for the CLR to share multiple identical **String** contents through a single **String** object. This can reduce the number of strings in the system—thereby conserving memory usage—and it is what string interning (discussed later in the chapter) is all about.

For performance reasons, the **String** type is tightly integrated with the CLR. Specifically, the CLR knows the exact layout of the fields defined within the **String** type, and the CLR accesses these fields directly. This performance and direct access come at a small development cost: the **String** class is sealed, which means that you cannot use it as a base class for your own type. If you were able to define your own type, using **String** as a base type, you could add your own fields, which would break the CLR's assumptions. In addition, you could break some assumptions that the CLR team has made about **String** objects being immutable.

Comparing Strings

Comparing is probably the most common operation performed on strings. There are two reasons to compare two strings with each other. We compare two strings to determine equality or to sort them (usually for presentation to a user).

In determining string equality or when comparing strings for sorting, it is highly recommended that you call one of these methods (defined by the **String** class):

```
Boolean Equals(String value, StringComparison comparisonType)
static Boolean Equals(String a, String b, StringComparison comparisonType)

static Int32 Compare(String strA, String strB, StringComparison comparisonType)
static Int32 Compare(string strA, string strB, Boolean ignoreCase, CultureInfo culture)
static Int32 Compare(String strA, String strB, CultureInfo culture, CompareOptions options)
static Int32 Compare(String strA, Int32 indexA, String strB, Int32 indexB, Int32 length,
    StringComparison comparisonType)
static Int32 Compare(String strA, Int32 indexA, String strB, Int32 indexB, Int32 length,
    CultureInfo culture, CompareOptions options)
static Int32 Compare(String strA, Int32 indexA, String strB, Int32 indexB, Int32 length,
    Boolean ignoreCase, CultureInfo culture)

Boolean StartsWith(String value, StringComparison comparisonType)
Boolean StartsWith(String value,
    Boolean ignoreCase, CultureInfo culture)

Boolean EndsWith(String value, StringComparison comparisonType)
Boolean EndsWith(String value, Boolean ignoreCase, CultureInfo culture)
```

When sorting, you should always perform case-sensitive comparisons. The reason is that if two strings differing only by case are considered to be equal, they could be ordered differently each time you sort them; this would confuse the user.

The **comparisonType** argument (in most of the methods shown above) is one of the values defined by the **StringComparison** enumerated type, which is defined as follows:

```
public enum StringComparison {
    CurrentCulture = 0,
    CurrentCultureIgnoreCase = 1,
    InvariantCulture = 2,
    InvariantCultureIgnoreCase = 3,
    Ordinal = 4,
    OrdinalIgnoreCase = 5
}
```

The **CompareOptions** argument (in two of the methods above) is one of the values defined by the **CompareOptions** enumerator type:

```
[Flags]
public enum CompareOptions {
    None = 0,
    IgnoreCase = 1,
    IgnoreNonSpace = 2,
    IgnoreSymbols  = 4,
    IgnoreKanaType = 8,
    IgnoreWidth = 0x00000010,
    Ordinal = 0x40000000,
    OrdinalIgnoreCase = 0x10000000,
    StringSort = 0x20000000
}
```

Methods that accept a **CompareOptions** argument also force you to explicitly pass in a culture. When passing in the **Ordinal** or **OrdinalIgnoreCase** flag, these **Compare** methods ignore the specified culture.

Many programs use strings for internal programmatic purposes such as path names, file names, URLs, registry keys and values, environment variables, reflection, Extensible Markup Language (XML) tags, XML attributes, and so on. Often, these strings are not shown to a user and are used only within the program. When comparing programmatic strings, you should always use **StringComparison.Ordinal** or **StringComparison.OrdinalIgnoreCase**. This is the fastest way to perform a comparison that is not to be affected in any linguistic way because culture information is not taken into account when performing the comparison.

On the other hand, when you want to compare strings in a linguistically correct manner (usually for display to an end user), you should use **StringComparison.CurrentCulture** or **StringComparison.CurrentCultureIgnoreCase**.

> **Important** For the most part, **StringComparison.InvariantCulture** and **StringComparison.InvariantCultureIgnoreCase** should not be used. Although these values cause the comparison to be linguistically correct, using them to compare programmatic strings takes longer than performing an ordinal comparison. Furthermore, the invariant culture is culture agnostic, which makes it an incorrect choice when working with strings that you want to show to an end user.

> **Important** If you want to change the case of a string's characters before performing an ordinal comparison, you should use **String**'s **ToUpperInvariant** or **ToLowerInvariant** method. When normalizing strings, it is highly recommended that you use **ToUpperInvariant** instead of **ToLowerInvariant** because Microsoft has optimized the code for performing uppercase comparisons. In fact, the FCL internally normalizes strings to uppercase prior to performing case-insensitive comparisons. We use **ToUpperInvariant** and **ToLowerInvariant** methods because the **String** class does not offer **ToUpperOrdinal** and **ToLowerOrdinal** methods. We do not use the **ToUpper** and **ToLower** methods because these are culture sensitive.

Sometimes, when you compare strings in a linguistically correct manner, you want to specify a specific culture rather than use a culture that is associated with the calling thread. In this case, you can use the overloads of the **StartsWith**, **EndsWith**, and **Compare** methods shown earlier, all of which take **Boolean** and **CultureInfo** arguments.

> **Important** The **String** type defines several overloads of the **Equals**, **StartsWith**, **EndsWith**, and **Compare** methods in addition to the versions shown earlier. Microsoft recommends that these other versions (not shown in this book) be avoided. Furthermore, **String**'s other comparison methods—**CompareTo** (required by the **IComparable** interface), **CompareOrdinal**, and the == and != operators—should also be avoided. The reason for avoiding these methods and operators is because the caller does not explicitly indicate how the string comparison should be performed, and you cannot determine from the name of the method what the default comparison will be. For example, by default, **CompareTo** performs a culture-sensitive comparison, whereas **Equals** performs an ordinal comparison. Your code will be easier to read and maintain if you always indicate explicitly how you want to perform your string comparisons.

Now, let's talk about how to perform linguistically correct comparisons. The .NET Framework uses the **System.Globalization.CultureInfo** type to represent a language/country pair (as described by the RFC 1766 standard). For example, "en-US" identifies English as written in the United States, "en-AU" identifies English as written in Australia, and "de-DE" identifies German as written in Germany. In the CLR, every thread has two properties associated with it. Each of these properties refers to a **CultureInfo** object. The two properties are:

- **CurrentUICulture** This property is used to obtain resources that are shown to an end user. It is most useful for GUI or Web Forms applications because it indicates the language that should be used when displaying UI elements such as labels and buttons. By default, when you create a thread, this thread property is set to a **CultureInfo** object, which identifies the language of the Windows version the application is running on using the Win32 **GetUserDefaultUILanguage** function. If you're running a Multilingual User Interface (MUI) version of Windows, you can set this via the "Regional and Language Options" Control Panel Settings dialog box. On a non-MUI version of Windows, the language is determined by the localized version of the OS installed (or the installed language pack) and the language is not changeable.

- **CurrentCulture** This property is used for everything that **CurrentUICulture** isn't used for, including number and date formatting, string casing, and string comparing. When formatting, both the language and country parts of the **CultureInfo** object are used. By default, when you create a thread, this thread property is set to a **CultureInfo** object, whose value is determined by calling the Win32 **GetUserDefaultLCID** method, whose value is set in the "Regional and Language" Control Panel applet.

On many computers, a thread's **CurrentUICulture** and **CurrentCulture** properties will be set to the same **CultureInfo** object, which means that they both use the same language/ country information. However, they can be set differently. For example: an application running in the United States could use Spanish for all of its menu items and other GUI elements while properly displaying all of the currency and date formatting for the United States. To do this, the thread's **CurrentUICulture** property should be set to a **CultureInfo** object initialized with a language of "es" (for Spanish), while the thread's **CurrentCulture** property should be set to a **CultureInfo** object initialized with a language/country pair of "en-US."

Internally, a **CultureInfo** object has a field that refers to a **System.Globalization. CompareInfo** object, which encapsulates the culture's character-sorting table information as defined by the Unicode standard. The following code demonstrates the difference between performing an ordinal comparison and a culturally aware string comparison:

```
using System;
using System.Globalization;

public static class Program {
   public static void Main() {
      String s1 = "Strasse";
      String s2 = "Straße";
      Boolean eq;

      // CompareOrdinal returns nonzero.
      eq = String.Compare(s1, s2, StringComparison.Ordinal) == 0;
      Console.WriteLine("Ordinal  comparison: '{0}' {2} '{1}'", s1, s2,
         eq ? "==" : "!=");

      // Compare Strings appropriately for people
      // who speak German (de) in Germany (DE)
      CultureInfo ci = new CultureInfo("de-DE");

      // Compare returns zero.
      eq = String.Compare(s1, s2, true, ci) == 0;
      Console.WriteLine("Cultural comparison: '{0}' {2} '{1}'", s1, s2,
         eq ? "==" : "!=");
   }
}
```

Building and running this code produces the following output:

```
Ordinal  comparison: 'Strasse' != 'Straße'
Cultural comparison: 'Strasse' == 'Straße'
```

> **Note** When the **Compare** method is not performing an ordinal comparison, it performs *character expansions*. A character expansion is when a character is expanded to multiple characters regardless of culture. In the above case, the German *Eszet* character 'ß' is always expanded to 'ss.' Similarly, the 'Æ' ligature character is always expanded to 'AE.' So in the code example, the second call to **Compare** will always return 0 regardless of which culture I actually pass in to it.

In some rare circumstances, you may need to have even more control when comparing strings for equality or for sorting. This could be necessary when comparing strings consisting of Japanese characters. This additional control can be accessed via the **CultureInfo** object's **CompareInfo** property. As mentioned earlier, a **CompareInfo** object encapsulates a culture's character comparison tables, and there is just one **CompareInfo** object per culture.

When you call **String**'s **Compare** method, if the caller specifies a culture, the specified culture is used, or if no culture is specified, the value in the calling thread's **CurrentCulture** property is used. Internally, the **Compare** method obtains the reference to the **CompareInfo** object for the appropriate culture and calls the **Compare** method of the **CompareInfo** object, passing along the appropriate options (such as case insensitivity). Naturally, you could call the **Compare** method of a specific **CompareInfo** object yourself if you need the additional control.

The **Compare** method of the **CompareInfo** type takes as a parameter a value from the **CompareOptions** enumerated type (as shown earlier). You can OR these bit flags together to gain significantly greater control when performing string comparisons. For a complete description of these symbols, consult the .NET Framework documentation.

The following code demonstrates how important culture is to sorting strings and shows various ways of performing string comparisons:

```
using System;
using System.Text;
using System.Windows.Forms;
using System.Globalization;
using System.Threading;

public sealed class Program {
    public static void Main() {
        String output = String.Empty;
        String[] symbol = new String[] { "<", "=", ">" };
        Int32 x;
        CultureInfo ci;

        // The code below demonstrates how strings compare
        // differently for different cultures.
        String s1 = "coté";
        String s2 = "côte";

        // Sorting strings for French in France.
        ci = new CultureInfo("fr-FR");
        x = Math.Sign(ci.CompareInfo.Compare(s1, s2));
        output += String.Format("{0} Compare: {1} {3} {2}",
            ci.Name, s1, s2, symbol[x + 1]);
        output += Environment.NewLine;

        // Sorting strings for Japanese in Japan.
        ci = new CultureInfo("ja-JP");
        x = Math.Sign(ci.CompareInfo.Compare(s1, s2));
        output += String.Format("{0} Compare: {1} {3} {2}",
            ci.Name, s1, s2, symbol[x + 1]);
        output += Environment.NewLine;
```

```
    // Sorting strings for the thread's culture
    ci = Thread.CurrentThread.CurrentCulture;
    x = Math.Sign(ci.CompareInfo.Compare(s1, s2));
    output += String.Format("{0} Compare: {1} {3} {2}",
        ci.Name, s1, s2, symbol[x + 1]);
    output += Environment.NewLine + Environment.NewLine;

    // The code below demonstrates how to use CompareInfo.Compare's
    // advanced options with 2 Japanese strings. One string represents
    // the word "shinkansen" (the name for the Japanese high-speed
    // train) in hiragana (one subtype of Japanese writing), and the
    // other represents the same word in katakana (another subtype of
    // Japanese writing).
    s1 = "しんかんせん";   // ("\u3057\u3093\u304B\u3093\u305b\u3093")
    s2 = "シンカンセン";   // ("\u30b7\u30f3\u30ab\u30f3\u30bb\u30f3")

    // Here is the result of a default comparison
    ci = new CultureInfo("ja-JP");
    x = Math.Sign(String.Compare(s1, s2, true, ci));
    output += String.Format("Simple {0} Compare: {1} {3} {2}",
        ci.Name, s1, s2, symbol[x + 1]);
    output += Environment.NewLine;

    // Here is the result of a comparison that ignores
    // kana type (a type of Japanese writing)
    CompareInfo compareInfo = CompareInfo.GetCompareInfo("ja-JP");
    x = Math.Sign(compareInfo.Compare(s1, s2, CompareOptions.IgnoreKanaType));
    output += String.Format("Advanced {0} Compare: {1} {3} {2}",
        ci.Name, s1, s2, symbol[x + 1]);

    MessageBox.Show(output, "Comparing Strings For Sorting");
  }
}
```

 Note This source code file can't be saved in ANSI or the Japanese characters will be lost. To save this file in Microsoft Visual Studio, go to the Save File As dialog box, click the down arrow that is part of the Save button and select Save With Encoding. I selected "Unicode (UTF-8 with signature) – Codepage 65001". Microsoft's C# compiler can successfully parse source code files using this code page.

Building and running this code produces the output shown in Figure 14-1.

FIGURE 14-1 String sorting results

In addition to **Compare**, the **CompareInfo** class offers the **IndexOf**, **LastIndexOf**, **IsPrefix**, and **IsSuffix** methods. Because all of these methods offer overloads that take a **CompareOptions** enumeration value as a parameter, they give you more control than the **Compare**, **IndexOf**, **LastIndexOf**, **StartsWith**, and **EndsWith** methods defined by the **String** class. Also, you should be aware that the FCL includes a **System.StringComparer** class that you can also use for performing string comparisons. This class is useful when you want to perform the same kind of comparison repeatedly for many different strings.

String Interning

As I said in the preceding section, checking strings for equality is a common operation for many applications—this task can hurt performance significantly. When performing an ordinal equality check, the CLR quickly tests to see if both strings have the same number of characters. If they don't, the strings are definitely not equal; if they do, the strings might be equal, and the CLR must then compare each individual character to determine for sure. When performing a culturally aware comparison, the CLR must always compare all of the individual characters because strings of different lengths might be considered equal.

In addition, if you have several instances of the same string duplicated in memory, you're wasting memory because strings are immutable. You'll use memory much more efficiently if there is just one instance of the string in memory and all variables needing to refer to the string can just point to the single string object.

If your application frequently compares strings for equality using case-sensitive, ordinal comparisons, or if you expect to have many string objects with the same value, you can enhance performance substantially if you take advantage of the *string interning* mechanism in the CLR. When the CLR initializes, it creates an internal hash table in which the keys are strings and the values are references to **String** objects in the managed heap. Initially, the table is empty (of course). The **String** class offers two methods that allow you to access this internal hash table:

```
public static String Intern(String str);
public static String IsInterned(String str);
```

The first method, **Intern**, takes a **String**, obtains a hash code for it, and checks the internal hash table for a match. If an identical string already exists, a reference to the already existing **String** object is returned. If an identical string doesn't exist, a copy of the string is made, the copy is added to the internal hash table, and a reference to this copy is returned. If the application no longer holds a reference to the original **String** object, the garbage collector is able to free the memory of that string. Note that the garbage collector can't free the strings that the internal hash table refers to because the hash table holds the reference to those **String** objects. **String** objects referred to by the internal hash table can't be freed until the AppDomain is unloaded or the process terminates.

As does the **Intern** method, the **IsInterned** method takes a **String** and looks it up in the internal hash table. If a matching string is in the hash table, **IsInterned** returns a reference to the interned string object. If a matching string isn't in the hash table, however, **IsInterned** returns **null**; it doesn't add the string to the hash table.

By default, when an assembly is loaded, the CLR interns all of the literal strings described in the assembly's metadata. Microsoft learned that this hurts performance significantly due to the additional hash table lookups, so it is now possible to turn this "feature" off. If an assembly is marked with a **System.Runtime.CompilerServices.CompilationRelaxationsAttribute** specifying the **System.Runtime.CompilerServices.CompilationRelaxations.NoStringInterning** flag value, the CLR *may*, according to the ECMA specification, choose not to intern all of the strings defined in that assembly's metadata. Note that, in an attempt to improve your application's performance, the C# compiler always specifies this attribute/flag whenever you compile an assembly.

Even if an assembly has this attribute/flag specified, the CLR may choose to intern the strings, but you should not count on this. In fact, you really should never write code that relies on strings being interned unless you have written code that explicitly calls the **String**'s **Intern** method yourself. The following code demonstrates string interning:

```
String s1 = "Hello";
String s2 = "Hello";
Console.WriteLine(Object.ReferenceEquals(s1, s2));   // Should be 'False'

s1 = String.Intern(s1);
s2 = String.Intern(s2);
Console.WriteLine(Object.ReferenceEquals(s1, s2));   // 'True'
```

In the first call to the **ReferenceEquals** method, **s1** refers to a **"Hello"** string object in the heap, and **s2** refers to a different **"Hello"** string object in the heap. Since the references are different, **False** should be displayed. However, if you run this on version 4.0 of the CLR, you'll see that **True** is displayed. The reason is because this version of the CLR chooses to ignore the attribute/flag emitted by the C# compiler, and the CLR interns the literal **"Hello"** string when the assembly is loaded into the AppDomain. This means that **s1** and **s2** refer to the single **"Hello"** string in the heap. However, as mentioned previously, you should never write code that relies on this behavior because a future version of the CLR might honor the attribute/flag and not intern the **"Hello"** string. In fact, version 4.0 of the CLR does honor the attribute/flag when this assembly's code has been compiled using the NGen.exe utility.

Before the second call to the **ReferenceEquals** method, the **"Hello"** string has been explicitly interned, and **s1** now refers to an interned **"Hello"**. Then by calling **Intern** again, **s2** is set to refer to the same **"Hello"** string as **s1**. Now, when **ReferenceEquals** is called the second time, we are guaranteed to get a result of **True** regardless of whether the assembly was compiled with the attribute/flag.

So now, let's look at an example to see how you can use string interning to improve performance and reduce memory usage. The **NumTimesWordAppearsEquals** method below takes two arguments: a word and an array of strings in which each array element refers to a single word. This method then determines how many times the specified word appears in the wordlist and returns this count:

```
private static Int32 NumTimesWordAppearsEquals(String word, String[] wordlist) {
   Int32 count = 0;
   for (Int32 wordnum = 0; wordnum < wordlist.Length; wordnum++) {
      if (word.Equals(wordlist[wordnum], StringComparison.Ordinal))
         count++;
   }
   return count;
}
```

As you can see, this method calls **String**'s **Equals** method, which internally compares the strings' individual characters and checks to ensure that all characters match. This comparison can be slow. In addition, the wordlist array might have multiple entries that refer to multiple **String** objects containing the same set of characters. This means that multiple identical strings might exist in the heap and are surviving ongoing garbage collections.

Now, let's look at a version of this method that was written to take advantage of string interning:

```
private static Int32 NumTimesWordAppearsIntern(String word, String[] wordlist) {
   // This method assumes that all entries in wordlist refer to interned strings.
   word = String.Intern(word);
   Int32 count = 0;
   for (Int32 wordnum = 0; wordnum < wordlist.Length; wordnum++) {
      if (Object.ReferenceEquals(word, wordlist[wordnum]))
         count++;
   }
   return count;
}
```

This method interns the word and assumes that the wordlist contains references to interned strings. First, this version might be saving memory if a word appears in the wordlist multiple times because, in this version, **wordlist** would now contain multiple references to the same single **String** object in the heap. Second, this version will be faster because determining if the specified word is in the array is simply a matter of comparing pointers.

Although the **NumTimesWordAppearsIntern** method is faster than the **NumTimesWordAppearsEquals** method, the overall performance of the application might be slower when using the **NumTimesWordAppearsIntern** method because of the time it takes to intern all of the strings when they were added to the **wordlist** array (code not shown). The **NumTimesWordAppearsIntern** method will really show its performance and memory improvement if the application needs to call the method multiple times using the same wordlist. The point of this discussion is to make it clear that string interning is useful, but it should be used with care and caution. In fact, this is why the C# compiler indicates that it doesn't want string interning to be enabled.

String Pooling

When compiling source code, your compiler must process each literal string and emit the string into the managed module's metadata. If the same literal string appears several times in your source code, emitting all of these strings into the metadata will bloat the size of the resulting file.

To remove this bloat, many compilers (include the C# compiler) write the literal string into the module's metadata only once. All code that references the string will be modified to refer to the one string in the metadata. This ability of a compiler to merge multiple occurrences of a single string into a single instance can reduce the size of a module substantially. This process is nothing new—C/C++ compilers have been doing it for years. (Microsoft's C/C++ compiler calls this *string pooling*.) Even so, string pooling is another way to improve the performance of strings and just one more piece of knowledge that you should have in your repertoire.

Examining a String's Characters and Text Elements

Although comparing strings is useful for sorting them or for detecting equality, sometimes you need just to examine the characters within a string. The **String** type offers several properties and methods to help you do this, including **Length**, **Chars** (an indexer in C#), **GetEnumerator**, **ToCharArray**, **Contains**, **IndexOf**, **LastIndexOf**, **IndexOfAny**, and **LastIndexOfAny**.

In reality, a **System.Char** represents a single 16-bit Unicode code value that doesn't necessarily equate to an abstract Unicode character. For example, some abstract Unicode characters are a combination of two code values. When combined, the U+0625 (the Arabic letter *Alef* with *Hamza* below) and U+0650 (the Arabic *Kasra*) characters form a single abstract character or *text element*.

In addition, some Unicode text elements require more than a 16-bit value to represent them. These text elements are represented using two 16-bit code values. The first code value is called the high surrogate, and the second code value is called the low surrogate. High surrogates have a value between U+D800 and U+DBFF, and low surrogates have a value between U+DC00 and U+DFFF. The use of surrogates allows Unicode to express more than a million different characters.

Surrogates are rarely used in the United States and Europe but are more commonly used in East Asia. To properly work with text elements, you should use the **System.Globalization.StringInfo** type. The easiest way to use this type is to construct an instance of it, passing its constructor a string. Then you can see how many text elements are in the string by querying the **StringInfo**'s **LengthInTextElements** property. You can then call **StringInfo**'s **SubstringByTextElements** method to extract the text element or the number of consecutive text elements that you desire.

In addition, the **StringInfo** class offers a static **GetTextElementEnumerator** method, which acquires a **System.Globalization.TextElementEnumerator** object that allows you to enumerate through all of the abstract Unicode characters contained in the string. Finally, you could call **StringInfo**'s static **ParseCombiningCharacters** method to obtain an array of **Int32** values. The length of the array indicates how many text elements are contained in the string. Each element of the array identifies an index into the string where the first code value for a new text element can be found.

The following code demonstrates the various ways of using the **StringInfo** class to manipulate a string's text elements:

```
using System;
using System.Text;
using System.Globalization;
using System.Windows.Forms;


public sealed class Program {
    public static void Main() {
        // The string below contains combining characters
        String s = "a\u0304\u0308bc\u0327";
        SubstringByTextElements(s);
        EnumTextElements(s);
        EnumTextElementIndexes(s);
    }

    private static void SubstringByTextElements(String s) {
        String output = String.Empty;

        StringInfo si = new StringInfo(s);
        for (Int32 element = 0; element < si.LengthInTextElements; element++) {
            output += String.Format(
                "Text element {0} is '{1}'{2}",
                element, si.SubstringByTextElements(element, 1),
                Environment.NewLine);
        }
        MessageBox.Show(output, "Result of SubstringByTextElements");
    }

    private static void EnumTextElements(String s) {
        String output = String.Empty;

        TextElementEnumerator charEnum =
            StringInfo.GetTextElementEnumerator(s);
        while (charEnum.MoveNext()) {
            output += String.Format(
                "Character at index {0} is '{1}'{2}",
```

```
                    charEnum.ElementIndex, charEnum.GetTextElement(),
                    Environment.NewLine);
        }
        MessageBox.Show(output, "Result of GetTextElementEnumerator");
    }

    private static void EnumTextElementIndexes(String s) {
        String output = String.Empty;

        Int32[] textElemIndex = StringInfo.ParseCombiningCharacters(s);
        for (Int32 i = 0; i < textElemIndex.Length; i++) {
            output += String.Format(
                "Character {0} starts at index {1}{2}",
                i, textElemIndex[i], Environment.NewLine);
        }
        MessageBox.Show(output, "Result of ParseCombiningCharacters");
    }
}
```

Building and running this code produces the message boxes shown in Figures 14-2, 14-3, and 14-4.

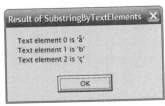

FIGURE 14-2 Result of **SubstringByTextElements**

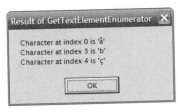

FIGURE 14-3 Result of **GetTextElementEnumerator**

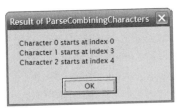

FIGURE 14-4 Result of **ParseCombiningCharacters**

Other String Operations

The **String** type also offers methods that allow you to copy a string or parts of it. Table 14-1 summarizes these methods.

TABLE 14-1 Methods for Copying Strings

Member	Method Type	Description
Clone	Instance	Returns a reference to the same object (**this**). This is OK because **String** objects are immutable. This method implements **String**'s **ICloneable** interface.
Copy	Static	Returns a new duplicate string of the specified string. This method is rarely used and exists to help applications that treat strings as tokens. Normally, strings with the same set of characters are interned to a single string. This method creates a new string object so that the references (pointers) are different even though the strings contain the same characters.
CopyTo	Instance	Copies a portion of the string's characters to an array of characters.
Substring	Instance	Returns a new string that represents a portion of the original string.
ToString	Instance	Returns a reference to the same object (**this**).

In addition to these methods, **String** offers many static and instance methods that manipulate a string, such as **Insert**, **Remove**, **PadLeft**, **Replace**, **Split**, **Join**, **ToLower**, **ToUpper**, **Trim**, **Concat**, **Format**, and so on. Again, the important thing to remember about all of these methods is that they return new string objects; because strings are immutable, once they're created, they can't be modified (using safe code).

Constructing a String Efficiently

Because the **String** type represents an immutable string, the FCL provides another type, **System.Text.StringBuilder**, which allows you to perform dynamic operations efficiently with strings and characters to create a **String**. Think of **StringBuilder** as a fancy constructor to create a **String** that can be used with the rest of the framework. In general, you should design methods that take **String** parameters, not **StringBuilder** parameters.

Logically, a **StringBuilder** object contains a field that refers to an array of **Char** structures. **StringBuilder**'s members allow you to manipulate this character array, effectively shrinking the string or changing the characters in the string. If you grow the string past the allocated array of characters, the **StringBuilder** automatically allocates a new, larger array, copies the characters, and starts using the new array. The previous array is garbage collected.

When finished using the **StringBuilder** object to construct your string, "convert" the **StringBuilder**'s character array into a **String** simply by calling the **StringBuilder**'s

ToString method. This creates a new **String** object in the heap that contains the string that was in the **StringBuilder** at the time you called **ToString**. At this point, you can continue to manipulate the string inside the **StringBuilder**, and later you can call **ToString** again to convert it into another **String** object.

Constructing a **StringBuilder** Object

Unlike with the **String** class, the CLR has no special information about the **StringBuilder** class. In addition, most languages (including C#) don't consider the **StringBuilder** class to be a primitive type. You construct a **StringBuilder** object as you would any other non-primitive type:

```
StringBuilder sb = new StringBuilder();
```

The **StringBuilder** type offers many constructors. The job of each constructor is to allocate and initialize the state maintained by each **StringBuilder** object:

- **Maximum capacity**   An **Int32** value that specifies the maximum number of characters that can be placed in the string. The default is **Int32.MaxValue** (approximately 2 billion). It's unusual to change this value. However, you might specify a smaller maximum capacity to ensure that you never create a string over a certain length. Once constructed, a **StringBuilder**'s maximum capacity value can't be changed.

- **Capacity**   An **Int32** value indicating the size of the character array being maintained by the **StringBuilder**. The default is 16. If you have some idea of how many characters you'll place in the **StringBuilder**, you should use this number to set the capacity when constructing the **StringBuilder** object.

  When appending characters to the character array, the **StringBuilder** detects if the array is trying to grow beyond the array's capacity. If it is, the **StringBuilder** automatically doubles the capacity field, allocates a new array (the size of the new capacity), and copies the characters from the original array into the new array. The original array will be garbage collected in the future. Dynamically growing the array hurts performance; avoid this by setting a good initial capacity.

- **Character array**   An array of **Char** structures that maintains the set of characters in the "string." The number of characters is always less than or equal to the capacity and maximum capacity values. You can use the **StringBuilder**'s **Length** property to obtain the number of characters used in the array. The **Length** is always less than or equal to the **StringBuilder**'s capacity value. When constructing a **StringBuilder**, you can pass a **String** to initialize the character array. If you don't specify a string, the array initially contains no characters—that is, the **Length** property returns **0**.

StringBuilder Members

Unlike a **String**, a **StringBuilder** represents a mutable string. This means that most of **StringBuilder**'s members change the contents in the array of characters and don't cause new objects to be allocated on the managed heap. A **StringBuilder** allocates a new object on only two occasions:

- You dynamically build a string whose length is longer than the capacity you've set.

- You call **StringBuilder**'s **ToString** method.

Table 14-2 summarizes **StringBuilder**'s members.

TABLE 14-2 StringBuilder Members

Member	Member Type	Description
MaxCapacity	Read-only property	Returns the largest number of characters that can be placed in the string.
Capacity	Read/write property	Gets or sets the size of the character array. Trying to set the capacity smaller than the string's length or bigger than **MaxCapacity** throws an **ArgumentOutOfRangeException**.
EnsureCapacity	Method	Guarantees that the character array is at least the size specified. If the value passed is larger than the **StringBuilder**'s current capacity, the current capacity increases. If the current capacity is already larger than the value passed to this property, no change occurs.
Length	Read/write property	Gets or sets the number of characters in the "string." This will likely be smaller than the character array's current capacity. Setting this property to **0** resets the **StringBuilder**'s contents to an empty string.
ToString	Method	The parameterless version of this method returns a **String** representing the **StringBuilder**'s character array.
Chars	Read/write indexer property	Gets or sets the character at the specified index into the character array. In C#, this is an indexer (parameterful property) that you access using array syntax (**[]**).
Clear	Method	Clears the contents of the **StringBuilder** object, the same as setting its **Length** property to **0**.
Append	Method	Appends a single object to the end of the character array, growing the array if necessary. The object is converted to a string by using the general format and the culture associated with the calling thread.
Insert	Method	Inserts a single object into the character array, growing the array if necessary. The object is converted to a string by using the general format and the culture associated with the calling thread.

Member	Member Type	Description
AppendFormat	Method	Appends the specified objects to the end of the character array, growing the array if necessary. The objects are converted to strings by using the formatting and culture information provided by the caller. **AppendFormat** is one of the most common methods used with **StringBuilder** objects.
AppendLine	Method	Appends a blank line or a string with a blank line to the end of the character array, increasing the capacity of the array if necessary.
Replace	Method	Replaces one character with another or one string with another from within the character array.
Remove	Method	Removes a range of characters from the character array.
Equals	Method	Returns **true** only if both **StringBuilder** objects have the same maximum capacity, capacity, and characters in the array.
CopyTo	Method	Copies a subset of the **StringBuilder**'s characters to a **Char** array.

One important thing to note about **StringBuilder**'s methods is that most of them return a reference to the same **StringBuilder** object. This allows a convenient syntax to chain several operations together:

```
StringBuilder sb = new StringBuilder();
String s = sb.AppendFormat("{0} {1}", "Jeffrey", "Richter").
   Replace(' ', '-').Remove(4, 3).ToString();
Console.WriteLine(s);  // "Jeff-Richter"
```

You'll notice that the **String** and **StringBuilder** classes don't have full method parity; that is, **String** has **ToLower**, **ToUpper**, **EndsWith**, **PadLeft**, **PadRight**, **Trim**, and so on. The **StringBuilder** class doesn't offer any of these methods. On the other hand, the **StringBuilder** class offers a richer **Replace** method that allows you to replace characters or strings in a portion of the string (not the whole string). It's unfortunate that there isn't complete parity between these two classes because now you must convert between **String** and **StringBuilder** to accomplish certain tasks. For example, to build up a string, convert all characters to uppercase, and then insert a string requires code like this:

```
// Construct a StringBuilder to perform string manipulations.
StringBuilder sb = new StringBuilder();

// Perform some string manipulations by using the StringBuilder.
sb.AppendFormat("{0} {1}", "Jeffrey", "Richter").Replace(" ", "-");

// Convert the StringBuilder to a String in
// order to uppercase all the characters.
String s = sb.ToString().ToUpper();
```

```
// Clear the StringBuilder (allocates a new Char array).
sb.Length = 0;

// Load the uppercase String into the StringBuilder,
// and perform more manipulations.
sb.Append(s).Insert(8, "Marc-");

// Convert the StringBuilder back to a String.
s = sb.ToString();

// Display the String to the user.
Console.WriteLine(s);  // "JEFFREY-Marc-RICHTER"
```

It's inconvenient and inefficient to have to write this code just because **StringBuilder** doesn't offer all of the operations that **String** does. In the future, I hope that Microsoft will add more string operation methods to **StringBuilder** to make it a more complete class.

Obtaining a String Representation of an Object: ToString

You frequently need to obtain a string representation of an object. Usually, this is necessary when you want to display a numeric type (such as **Byte**, **Int32**, and **Single**) or a **DateTime** object to the user. Because the .NET Framework is an object-oriented platform, every type is responsible for providing code that converts an instance's value to a string equivalent. When designing how types should accomplish this, the designers of the FCL devised a pattern that would be used consistently throughout. In this section, I'll describe this pattern.

You can obtain a string representation for any object by calling the **ToString** method. A public, virtual, parameterless **ToString** method is defined by **System.Object** and is therefore callable using an instance of any type. Semantically, **ToString** returns a string representing the object's current value, and this string should be formatted for the calling thread's current culture; that is, the string representation of a number should use the proper decimal separator, digit-grouping symbol, and other elements associated with the culture assigned to the calling thread.

System.Object's implementation of **ToString** simply returns the full name of the object's type. This value isn't particularly useful, but it is a reasonable default for the many types that can't offer a sensible string. For example, what should a string representation of a **FileStream** or a **Hashtable** object look like?

All types that want to offer a reasonable way to obtain a string representing the current value of the object should override the **ToString** method. All base types built into the FCL (**Byte**, **Int32**, **UInt64**, **Double**, and so on) override their **ToString** method and return a culturally aware string. In the Visual Studio debugger, a datatip is displayed when the mouse is placed over a particular variable. The text shown in the datatip is obtained by calling the object's **ToString** method. So, when you define a class, you should always override the **ToString** method so that you get good debugging support.

Specific Formats and Cultures

The parameterless **ToString** method has two problems. First, the caller has no control over the formatting of the string. For example, an application might want to format a number into a currency string, decimal string, percent string, or hexadecimal string. Second, the caller can't easily choose to format a string by using a specific culture. This second problem is more troublesome for server-side application code than for client-side code. On rare occasions, an application needs to format a string by using a culture other than the culture associated with the calling thread. To have more control over string formatting, you need a version of the **ToString** method that allows you to specify precise formatting and culture information.

Types that offer the caller a choice in formatting and culture implement the **System. IFormattable** interface:

```
public interface IFormattable {
    String ToString(String format, IFormatProvider formatProvider);
}
```

In the FCL, all of the base types (**Byte**, **SByte**, **Int16/UInt16**, **Int32/UInt32**, **Int64/UInt64**, **Single**, **Double**, **Decimal**, and **DateTime**) implement this interface. In addition, some other types, such as **Guid**, implement it. Finally, every enumerated type definition will automatically implement the **IFormattable** interface so that a meaningful string symbol from an instance of the enumerated type can be obtained.

IFormattable's **ToString** method takes two parameters. The first, **format**, is a string that tells the method how the object should be formatted. **ToString**'s second parameter, **formatProvider**, is an instance of a type that implements the **System.IFormatProvider** interface. This type supplies specific culture information to the **ToString** method. I'll discuss how shortly.

The type implementing the **IFormattable** interface's **ToString** method determines which format strings it's going to recognize. If you pass a format string that the type doesn't recognize, the type is supposed to throw a **System.FormatException**.

Many of the types Microsoft has defined in the FCL recognize several formats. For example, the **DateTime** type supports "d" for short date, "D" for long date, "g" for general, "M" for month/day, "s" for sortable, "T" for long time, "u" for universal time in ISO 8601 format, "U" for universal time in full date format, "Y" for year/month, and others. All enumerated types support "G" for general, "F" for flags, "D" decimal, and "X" for hexadecimal. I'll cover formatting enumerated types in more detail in Chapter 15, "Enumerated Types and Bit Flags."

Also, all of the built-in numeric types support "C" for currency, "D" for decimal, "E" for exponential (scientific) notation, "F" for fixed-point, "G" for general, "N" for number, "P" for percent, "R" for round-trip, and "X" for hexadecimal. In fact, the numeric types also support picture format strings just in case the simple format strings don't offer you exactly what you're looking for. Picture format strings contain special characters that tell the type's **ToString** method exactly how many digits to show, exactly where to place a decimal separator, exactly how many digits to place after the decimal separator, and so on. For complete information about format strings, see "Formatting Types" in the .NET Framework SDK.

For most types, calling **ToString** and passing **null** for the format string is identical to calling **ToString** and passing "G" for the format string. In other words, objects format themselves using the "General format" by default. When implementing a type, choose a format that you think will be the most commonly used format; this format is the "General format." By the way, the **ToString** method that takes no parameters assumes that the caller wants the "General format."

So now that format strings are out of the way, let's turn to culture information. By default, strings are formatted using the culture information associated with the calling thread. The parameterless **ToString** method certainly does this, and so does **IFormattable**'s **ToString** if you pass **null** for the **formatProvider** parameter.

Culture-sensitive information applies when you're formatting numbers (including currency, integers, floating point, percentages, dates, and times). The **Guid** type has a **ToString** method that returns only a string representing its value. There's no need to consider a culture when generating the **Guid**'s string because **GUID**s are used for programmatic purposes only.

When formatting a number, the **ToString** method sees what you've passed for the **formatProvider** parameter. If **null** is passed, **ToString** determines the culture associated with the calling thread by reading the **System.Threading.Thread.CurrentThread.CurrentCulture** property. This property returns an instance of the **System.Globalization.CultureInfo** type.

Using this object, **ToString** reads its **NumberFormat** or **DateTimeFormat** property, depending on whether a number or date/time is being formatted. These properties return an instance of **System.Globalization.NumberFormatInfo** or **System.Globalization. DateTimeFormatInfo**, respectively. The **NumberFormatInfo** type defines a bunch of properties, such as **CurrencyDecimalSeparator**, **CurrencySymbol**, **NegativeSign**, **NumberGroupSeparator**, and **PercentSymbol**. Likewise, the **DateTimeFormatInfo** type defines an assortment of properties, such as **Calendar**, **DateSeparator**, **DayNames**, **LongDatePattern**, **ShortTimePattern**, and **TimeSeparator**. **ToString** reads these properties when constructing and formatting a string.

When calling **IFormattable**'s **ToString** method, instead of passing **null**, you can pass a reference to an object whose type implements the **IFormatProvider** interface:

```
public interface IFormatProvider {
   Object GetFormat(Type formatType);
}
```

Here's the basic idea behind the **IFormatProvider** interface: when a type implements this interface, it is saying that an instance of the type is able to provide culture-specific formatting information and that the culture information associated with the calling thread should be ignored.

The **System.Globalization.CultureInfo** type is one of the very few types defined in the FCL that implements the **IFormatProvider** interface. If you want to format a string for, say, Vietnam, you'd construct a **CultureInfo** object and pass that object in as **ToString**'s **formatProvider** parameter. The following code obtains a string representation of a **Decimal** numeric value formatted as currency appropriate for Vietnam:

```
Decimal price = 123.54M;
String s = price.ToString("C", new CultureInfo("vi-VN"));
MessageBox.Show(s);
```

If you build and run this code, the message box shown in Figure 14-5 appears.

FIGURE 14-5 Numeric value formatted correctly to represent Vietnamese currency

Internally, **Decimal**'s **ToString** method sees that the **formatProvider** argument is not **null** and calls the object's **GetFormat** method as follows:

```
NumberFormatInfo nfi = (NumberFormatInfo)
    formatProvider.GetFormat(typeof(NumberFormatInfo));
```

This is how **ToString** requests the appropriate number-formatting information from the (**CultureInfo**) object. Number types (such as **Decimal**) request only number-formatting information. But other types (such as **DateTime**) could call **GetFormat** like this:

```
DateTimeFormatInfo dtfi = (DateTimeFormatInfo)
    formatProvider.GetFormat(typeof(DateTimeFormatInfo));
```

Actually, because **GetFormat**'s parameter can identify any type, the method is flexible enough to allow any type of format information to be requested. The types in the .NET Framework call **GetFormat**, requesting only number or date/time information; in the future, other kinds of formatting information could be requested.

By the way, if you want to obtain a string for an object that isn't formatted for any particular culture, you should call **System.Globalization.CultureInfo**'s static **InvariantCulture** property and pass the object returned as **ToString**'s **formatProvider** parameter:

```
Decimal price = 123.54M;
String s = price.ToString("C", CultureInfo.InvariantCulture);
MessageBox.Show(s);
```

If you build and run this code, the message box shown in Figure 14-6 appears. Notice the first character in the resulting string: ¤. This is the international sign for currency (U+00A4).

FIGURE 14-6 Numeric value formatted to represent a culture-neutral currency

Normally, you wouldn't display a string formatted by using the invariant culture to a user. Typically, you'd just save this string in a data file so that it could be parsed later.

In the FCL, just three types implement the **IFormatProvider** interface. The first is **CultureInfo**, which I've already explained. The other two are **NumberFormatInfo** and **DateTimeFormatInfo**. When **GetFormat** is called on a **NumberFormatInfo** object, the method checks if the type being requested is a **NumberFormatInfo**. If it is, **this** is returned; if it's not, **null** is returned. Similarly, calling **GetFormat** on a **DateTimeFormatInfo** object returns **this** if a **DateTimeFormatInfo** is requested and **null** if it's not. These two types implement this interface simply as a programming convenience. When trying to obtain a string representation of an object, the caller commonly specifies a format and uses the culture associated with the calling thread. For this reason, you often call **ToString**, passing a string for the format parameter and **null** for the **formatProvider** parameter. To make calling **ToString** easier for you, many types offer several overloads of the **ToString** method. For example, the **Decimal** type offers four different **ToString** methods:

```
// This version calls ToString(null, null).
// Meaning: General numeric format, thread's culture information
public override String ToString();

// This version is where the actual implementation of ToString goes.
// This version implements IFormattable's ToString method.
// Meaning: Caller-specified format and culture information
public String ToString(String format, IFormatProvider formatProvider);
```

```
// This version simply calls ToString(format, null).
// Meaning: Caller-specified format, thread's culture information
public String ToString(String format);

// This version simply calls ToString(null, formatProvider).
// This version implements IConvertible's ToString method.
// Meaning: General format, caller-specified culture information
public String ToString(IFormatProvider formatProvider);
```

Formatting Multiple Objects into a Single String

So far, I've explained how an individual type formats its own objects. At times, however, you want to construct strings consisting of many formatted objects. For example, the following string has a date, a person's name, and an age:

```
String s = String.Format("On {0}, {1} is {2} years old.",
    new DateTime(2010, 4, 22, 14, 35, 5), "Aidan", 7);
Console.WriteLine(s);
```

If you build and run this code where "en-US" is the thread's current culture, you'll see the following line of output:

```
On 4/22/2010 2:35:05 PM, Aidan is 7 years old.
```

String's static **Format** method takes a format string that identifies replaceable parameters using numbers in braces. The format string used in this example tells the **Format** method to replace **{0}** with the first parameter after the format string (the date/time), replace **{1}** with the second parameter after the format string ("Aidan"), and replace **{2}** with the third parameter after the format string (7).

Internally, the **Format** method calls each object's **ToString** method to obtain a string representation for the object. Then the returned strings are all appended and the complete, final string is returned. This is all fine and good, but it means that all of the objects are formatted by using their general format and the calling thread's culture information.

You can have more control when formatting an object if you specify format information within braces. For example, the following code is identical to the previous example except that I've added formatting information to replaceable parameters 0 and 2:

```
String s = String.Format("On {0:D}, {1} is {2:E} years old.",
    new DateTime(2010, 4, 22, 14, 35, 5), "Aidan", 7);
Console.WriteLine(s);
```

If you build and run this code where "en-US" is the thread's current culture, you'll see the following line of output:

```
On Thursday, April 22, 2010, Aidan is 7.000000E+000 years old.
```

When the **Format** method parses the format string, it sees that replaceable parameter 0 should have its **IFormattable** interface's **ToString** method called passing **"D"** and **null** for its two parameters. Likewise, **Format** calls replaceable parameter 2's **IFormattable** **ToString** method, passing **"E"** and **null**. If the type doesn't implement the **IFormattable** interface, **Format** calls its parameterless **ToString** method inherited from **Object** (and possibly overridden), and the default format is appended into the resulting string.

The **String** class offers several overloads of the static **Format** method. One version takes an object that implements the **IFormatProvider** interface so that you can format all of the replaceable parameters by using caller-specified culture information. Obviously, **Format** calls each object's **IFormattableToString** method, passing it whatever **IFormatProvider** object was passed to **Format**.

If you're using **StringBuilder** instead of **String** to construct a string, you can call **StringBuilder**'s **AppendFormat** method. This method works exactly as **String**'s **Format** method except that it formats a string and appends to the **StringBuilder**'s character array. As does **String**'s **Format**, **AppendFormat** takes a format string, and there's a version that takes an **IFormatProvider**.

System.Console offers **Write** and **WriteLine** methods that also take format strings and replaceable parameters. However, there are no overloads of **Console**'s **Write** and **WriteLine** methods that allow you to pass an **IFormatProvider**. If you want to format a string for a specific culture, you have to call **String**'s **Format** method, first passing the desired **IFormatProvider** object and then passing the resulting string to **Console**'s **Write** or **WriteLine** method. This shouldn't be a big deal because, as I said earlier, it's rare for client-side code to format a string by using a culture other than the one associated with the calling thread.

Providing Your Own Custom Formatter

By now it should be clear that the formatting capabilities in the .NET Framework were designed to offer you a great deal of flexibility and control. However, we're not quite finished. It's possible for you to define a method that **StringBuilder**'s **AppendFormat** method will call whenever any object is being formatted into a string. In other words, instead of calling **ToString** for each object, **AppendFormat** can call a function you define, allowing you to format any or all of the objects in any way you want. What I'm about to describe also works with **String**'s **Format** method.

Let me explain this mechanism by way of an example. Let's say that you're formatting HTML text that a user will view in an Internet browser. You want all **Int32** values to appear in bold. To accomplish this, every time an **Int32** value is formatted into a **String**, you want to surround the string with HTML bold tags: <B> and </B>. The following code demonstrates how easy it is to do this:

```
using System;
using System.Text;
using System.Threading;

public static class Program {
   public static void Main() {
      StringBuilder sb = new StringBuilder();
      sb.AppendFormat(new BoldInt32s(), "{0} {1} {2:M}", "Jeff", 123, DateTime.Now);
      Console.WriteLine(sb);
   }
}

internal sealed class BoldInt32s : IFormatProvider, ICustomFormatter {
   public Object GetFormat(Type formatType) {
      if (formatType == typeof(ICustomFormatter)) return this;
      return Thread.CurrentThread.CurrentCulture.GetFormat(formatType);
   }

   public String Format(String format, Object arg, IFormatProvider formatProvider) {
      String s;

      IFormattable formattable = arg as IFormattable;

      if (formattable == null) s = arg.ToString();
      else s = formattable.ToString(format, formatProvider);

      if (arg.GetType() == typeof(Int32))
         return "<B>" + s + "</B>";
      return s;
   }
}
```

When you compile and run this code where "en-US" is the thread's current culture, it displays the following output (your date may be different, of course):

```
Jeff <B>123</B> January 23
```

In **Main**, I'm constructing an empty **StringBuilder** and then appending a formatted string into it. When I call **AppendFormat**, the first parameter is an instance of the **BoldInt32s** class. This class implements the **IFormatProvider** interface that I discussed earlier. In addition, this class implements the **ICustomFormatter** interface:

```
public interface ICustomFormatter {
   String Format(String format, Object arg,
      IFormatProvider formatProvider);
}
```

This interface's **Format** method is called whenever **StringBuilder**'s **AppendFormat** needs to obtain a string for an object. You can do some pretty clever things inside this method that give you a great deal of control over string formatting. Let's look inside the **AppendFormat** method to see exactly how it works. The following pseudocode shows how **AppendFormat** works:

```
public StringBuilder AppendFormat(IFormatProvider formatProvider,
   String format, params Object[] args) {

   // If an IFormatProvider was passed, find out
   // whether it offers an ICustomFormatter object.
   ICustomFormatter cf = null;

   if (formatProvider != null)
      cf = (ICustomFormatter)
         formatProvider.GetFormat(typeof(ICustomFormatter));

   // Keep appending literal characters (not shown in this pseudocode)
   // and replaceable parameters to the StringBuilder's character array.
   Boolean MoreReplaceableArgumentsToAppend = true;
   while (MoreReplaceableArgumentsToAppend) {
      // argFormat refers to the replaceable format string obtained
      // from the format parameter
      String argFormat = /* ... */;

      // argObj refers to the corresponding element
      // from the args array parameter
      Object argObj = /* ... */;

      // argStr will refer to the formatted string to be appended
      // to the final, resulting string
      String argStr = null;

      // If a custom formatter is available, let it format the argument.
      if (cf != null)
         argStr = cf.Format(argFormat, argObj, formatProvider);

      // If there is no custom formatter or if it didn't format
      // the argument, try something else.
      if (argStr == null) {
         // Does the argument's type support rich formatting?
         IFormattable formattable = argObj as IFormattable;
         if (formattable != null) {
            // Yes; pass the format string and provider to
            // the type's IFormattable ToString method.
            argStr = formattable.ToString(argFormat, formatProvider);
         } else {
            // No; get the default format by using
            // the thread's culture information.
            if (argObj != null) argStr = argObj.ToString();
            else argStr = String.Empty;
         }
      }
      // Append argStr's characters to the character array field member.
      /* ... */

      // Check if any remaining parameters to format
      MoreReplaceableArgumentsToAppend = /* ... */;
   }
   return this;
}
```

When **Main** calls **AppendFormat**, **AppendFormat** calls my format provider's **GetFormat** method, passing it the **ICustomFormatter** type. The **GetFormat** method defined in my **BoldInt32s** type sees that the **ICustomFormatter** is being requested and returns a reference to itself because it implements this interface. If my **GetFormat** method is called and is passed any other type, I call the **GetFormat** method of the **CultureInfo** object associated with the calling thread.

Whenever **AppendFormat** needs to format a replaceable parameter, it calls **ICustomFormatter**'s **Format** method. In my example, **AppendFormat** calls the **Format** method defined by my **BoldInt32s** type. In my **Format** method, I check whether the object being formatted supports rich formatting via the **IFormattable** interface. If the object doesn't, I then call the simple, parameterless **ToString** method (inherited from **Object**) to format the object. If the object does support **IFormattable**, I then call the rich **ToString** method, passing it the format string and the format provider.

Now that I have the formatted string, I check whether the corresponding object is an **Int32** type, and if it is, I wrap the formatted string in **<B>** and **</B>** HTML tags and return the new string. If the object is not an **Int32**, I simply return the formatted string without any further processing.

Parsing a String to Obtain an Object: Parse

In the preceding section, I explained how to take an object and obtain a string representation of that object. In this section, I'll talk about the opposite: how to take a string and obtain an object representation of it. Obtaining an object from a string isn't a very common operation, but it does occasionally come in handy. Microsoft felt it necessary to formalize a mechanism by which strings can be parsed into objects.

Any type that can parse a string offers a public, static method called **Parse**. This method takes a **String** and returns an instance of the type; in a way, **Parse** acts as a factory. In the FCL, a **Parse** method exists on all of the numeric types as well as for **DateTime**, **TimeSpan**, and a few other types (such as the SQL data types).

Let's look at how to parse a string into a number type. Almost all of the numeric types (**Byte**, **SByte**, **Int16/UInt16**, **Int32/UInt32**, **Int64/UInt64**, **Single**, **Double**, **Decimal**, and **BigInteger**) offer at least one **Parse** method. Here I'll show you just the **Parse** method defined by the **Int32** type. (The **Parse** methods for the other numeric types work similarly to **Int32**'s **Parse** method.)

```
public static Int32 Parse(String s, NumberStyles style,
    IFormatProvider provider);
```

Just from looking at the prototype, you should be able to guess exactly how this method works. The **String** parameter, **s**, identifies a string representation of a number you want parsed into an **Int32** object. The **System.Globalization.NumberStyles** parameter, **style**, is a set of bit flags that identify characters that **Parse** should expect to find in the string. And the **IFormatProvider** parameter, **provider**, identifies an object that the **Parse** method can use to obtain culture-specific information, as discussed earlier in this chapter.

For example, the following code causes **Parse** to throw a **System.FormatException** because the string being parsed contains a leading space:

```
Int32 x = Int32.Parse(" 123", NumberStyles.None, null);
```

To allow **Parse** to skip over the leading space, change the **style** parameter as follows:

```
Int32 x = Int32.Parse(" 123", NumberStyles.AllowLeadingWhite, null);
```

See the .NET Framework SDK documentation for a complete description of the bit symbols and common combinations that the **NumberStyles** enumerated type defines.

Here's a code fragment showing how to parse a hexadecimal number:

```
Int32 x = Int32.Parse("1A", NumberStyles.HexNumber, null);
Console.WriteLine(x);  // Displays "26"
```

This **Parse** method accepts three parameters. For convenience, many types offer additional overloads of **Parse** so you don't have to pass as many arguments. For example, **Int32** offers four overloads of the **Parse** method:

```
// Passes NumberStyles.Integer for style
// and thread's culture's provider information.
public static Int32 Parse(String s);

// Passes thread's culture's provider information.
public static Int32 Parse(String s, NumberStyles style);

// Passes NumberStyles.Integer for the style parameter.
public static Int32 Parse(String s, IFormatProvider provider);

// This is the method I've been talking about in this section.
public static Int32 Parse(String s, NumberStyles style,
    IFormatProvider provider);
```

The **DateTime** type also offers a **Parse** method:

```
public static DateTime Parse(String s,
    IFormatProvider provider, DateTimeStyles styles);
```

This method works just as the **Parse** method defined on the number types except that **DateTime**'s **Parse** method takes a set of bit flags defined by the **System.Globalization.DateTimeStyles** enumerated type instead of the **NumberStyles** enumerated type. See the .NET Framework SDK documentation for a complete description of the bit symbols and common combinations the **DateTimeStyles** type defines.

For convenience, the **DateTime** type offers three overloads of the **Parse** method:

```
// Passes thread's culture's provider information
// and DateTimeStyles.None for the style
public static DateTime Parse(String s);

// Passes DateTimeStyles.None for the style
public static DateTime Parse(String s, IFormatProvider provider);

// This is the method I've been talking about in this section.
public static DateTime Parse(String s,
    IFormatProvider provider, DateTimeStyles styles);
```

Parsing dates and times is complex. Many developers have found the **Parse** method of the **DateTime** type too forgiving in that it sometimes parses strings that don't contain dates or times. For this reason, the **DateTime** type also offers a **ParseExact** method that accepts a picture format string that indicates exactly how the date/time string should be formatted and how it should be parsed. For more information about picture format strings, see the **DateTimeFormatInfo** class in the .NET Framework SDK.

> **Note** Some developers have reported the following back to Microsoft: when their application calls **Parse** frequently, and **Parse** throws exceptions repeatedly (due to invalid user input), performance of the application suffers. For these performance-sensitive uses of **Parse**, Microsoft added **TryParse** methods to all of the numeric data types, **DateTime**, **DateTimeOffset**, **TimeSpan**, and even **IPAddress**. This is what one of the two **Int32**'s two **TryParse** method overloads looks like:
>
> ```
> public static Boolean TryParse(String s, NumberStyles style,
>     IFormatProvider provider, out Int32 result);
> ```
>
> As you can see, this method returns **true** or **false** indicating whether the specified string can be parsed into an **Int32**. If the method returns **true**, the variable passed by reference to the result parameter will contain the parsed numeric value. The **TryXxx** pattern is discussed in Chapter 20, "Exceptions and State Management."

Encodings: Converting Between Characters and Bytes

In Win32, programmers all too frequently have to write code to convert Unicode characters and strings to Multi-Byte Character Set (MBCS) characters and strings. I've certainly written my share of this code, and it's very tedious to write and error-prone to use. In the CLR, all characters are represented as 16-bit Unicode code values and all strings are composed of 16-bit Unicode code values. This makes working with characters and strings easy at runtime.

At times, however, you want to save strings to a file or transmit them over a network. If the strings consist mostly of characters readable by English-speaking people, saving or transmitting a set of 16-bit values isn't very efficient because half of the bytes written would contain zeros. Instead, it would be more efficient to *encode* the 16-bit values into a compressed array of bytes and then *decode* the array of bytes back into an array of 16-bit values.

Encodings also allow a managed application to interact with strings created by non-Unicode systems. For example, if you want to produce a file readable by an application running on a Japanese version of Microsoft Windows 95, you have to save the Unicode text by using the Shift-JIS (code page 932) encoding. Likewise, you'd use Shift-JIS encoding to read a text file produced on a Japanese Windows 95 system into the CLR.

Encoding is typically done when you want to send a string to a file or network stream by using the **System.IO.BinaryWriter** or **System.IO.StreamWriter** type. Decoding is typically done when you want to read a string from a file or network stream by using the **System.IO.BinaryReader** or **System.IO.StreamReader** type. If you don't explicitly select an encoding, all of these types default to using UTF-8. (UTF stands for Unicode Transformation Format.) However, at times, you might want to explicitly encode or decode a string. Even if you don't want to explicitly do this, this section will give you more insight into the reading and writing of strings from and to streams.

Fortunately, the FCL offers some types to make character encoding and decoding easy. The two most frequently used encodings are UTF-16 and UTF-8.

- UTF-16 encodes each 16-bit character as 2 bytes. It doesn't affect the characters at all, and no compression occurs—its performance is excellent. UTF-16 encoding is also referred to as Unicode encoding. Also note that UTF-16 can be used to convert from little-endian to big-endian and vice versa.

- UTF-8 encodes some characters as 1 byte, some characters as 2 bytes, some characters as 3 bytes, and some characters as 4 bytes. Characters with a value below 0x0080 are compressed to 1 byte, which works very well for characters used in the United States. Characters between 0x0080 and 0x07FF are converted to 2 bytes, which works well for European and Middle Eastern languages. Characters of 0x0800 and above are converted to 3 bytes, which works well for East Asian languages. Finally, surrogate pairs are written out as 4 bytes. UTF-8 is an extremely popular encoding, but it's less efficient than UTF-16 if you encode many characters with values of 0x0800 or above.

Although the UTF-16 and UTF-8 encodings are by far the most common, the FCL also supports some encodings that are used less frequently:

- UTF-32 encodes all characters as 4 bytes. This encoding is useful when you want to write a simple algorithm to traverse characters and you don't want to have to deal with characters taking a variable number of bytes. For example, with UTF-32, you do not need to think about surrogates because every character is 4 bytes. Obviously, UTF-32 is not an efficient encoding in terms of memory usage and is therefore rarely used for saving or transmitting strings to a file or network. This encoding is typically used inside the program itself. Also note that UTF-32 can be used to convert from little-endian to big-endian and vice versa.

- UTF-7 encoding is typically used with older systems that work with characters that can be expressed using 7-bit values. You should avoid this encoding because it usually ends up expanding the data rather than compressing it. The Unicode Consortium has deprecated this encoding.

- ASCII encodes the 16-bit characters into ASCII characters; that is, any 16-bit character with a value of less than 0x0080 is converted to a single byte. Any character with a value greater than 0x007F can't be converted, so that character's value is lost. For strings consisting of characters in the ASCII range (0x00 to 0x7F), this encoding compresses the data in half and is very fast (because the high byte is just cut off). This encoding isn't appropriate if you have characters outside of the ASCII range because the character's values will be lost.

Finally, the FCL also allows you to encode 16-bit characters to an arbitrary code page. As with the ASCII encoding, encoding to a code page is dangerous because any character whose value can't be expressed in the specified code page is lost. You should always use UTF-16 or UTF-8 encoding unless you must work with some legacy files or applications that already use one of the other encodings.

When you need to encode or decode a set of characters, you should obtain an instance of a class derived from **System.Text.Encoding**. **Encoding** is an abstract base class that offers several static **readonly** properties, each of which returns an instance of an **Encoding**-derived class.

Here's an example that encodes and decodes characters by using UTF-8:

```
using System;
using System.Text;

public static class Program {
    public static void Main() {
        // This is the string we're going to encode.
        String s = "Hi there.";

        // Obtain an Encoding-derived object that knows how
        // to encode/decode using UTF8
        Encoding encodingUTF8 = Encoding.UTF8;

        // Encode a string into an array of bytes.
        Byte[] encodedBytes = encodingUTF8.GetBytes(s);

        // Show the encoded byte values.
        Console.WriteLine("Encoded bytes: " +
            BitConverter.ToString(encodedBytes));

        // Decode the byte array back to a string.
        String decodedString = encodingUTF8.GetString(encodedBytes);

        // Show the decoded string.
        Console.WriteLine("Decoded string: " + decodedString);
    }
}
```

This code yields the following output:

```
Encoded bytes: 48-69-20-74-68-65-72-65-2E
Decoded string: Hi there.
```

In addition to the **UTF8** static property, the **Encoding** class also offers the following static properties: **Unicode**, **BigEndianUnicode**, **UTF32**, **UTF7**, **ASCII**, and **Default**. The **Default** property returns an object that is able to encode/decode using the user's code page as specified by the Language for Non-Unicode Programs option of the Regional And Language dialog box in Control Panel. (See the **GetACP** Win32 function for more information.) However, using the **Default** property is discouraged because your application's behavior would be machine-setting dependent, so if you change the system's default code page or if your application runs on another machine, your application will behave differently.

In addition to these properties, **Encoding** also offers a static **GetEncoding** method that allows you to specify a code page (by integer or by string) and returns an object that can encode/decode using the specified code page. You can call **GetEncoding**, passing **"Shift-JIS"** or **932**, for example.

When you first request an encoding object, the **Encoding** class's property or **GetEncoding** method constructs a single object for the requested encoding and returns this object. If an already-requested encoding object is requested in the future, the encoding class simply returns the object it previously constructed; it doesn't construct a new object for each request. This efficiency reduces the number of objects in the system and reduces pressure in the garbage-collected heap.

Instead of calling one of **Encoding**'s static properties or its **GetEncoding** method, you could also construct an instance of one of the following classes: **System.Text.UnicodeEncoding**, **System.Text.UTF8Encoding**, **System.Text.UTF32Encoding**, **System.Text.UTF7Encoding**, or **System.Text.ASCIIEncoding**. However, keep in mind that constructing any of these classes creates new objects in the managed heap, which hurts performance.

Four of these classes, **UnicodeEncoding**, **UTF8Encoding**, **UTF32Encoding**, and **UTF7Encoding**, offer multiple constructors, providing you with more control over the encoding and preamble. (Preamble is sometimes referred to as a *byte order mark* or *BOM*.) The first three aforementioned classes also offer constructors that let you tell the class to throw exceptions when decoding an invalid byte sequence; you should use these constructors when you want your application to be secure and resistant to invalid incoming data.

You might want to explicitly construct instances of these encoding types when working with a **BinaryWriter** or a **StreamWriter**. The **ASCIIEncoding** class has only a single constructor and therefore doesn't offer any more control over the encoding. If you need an **ASCIIEncoding** object, always obtain it by querying **Encoding**'s **ASCII** property; this returns a reference to a single **ASCIIEncoding** object. If you construct **ASCIIEncoding** objects yourself, you are creating more objects on the heap, which hurts your application's performance.

Once you have an **Encoding**-derived object, you can convert a string or an array of characters to an array of bytes by calling the **GetBytes** method. (Several overloads of this method exist.) To convert an array of bytes to an array of characters, call the **GetChars** method or the more useful **GetString** method. (Several overloads exist for both of these methods.) The preceding code demonstrated calls to the **GetBytes** and **GetString** methods.

All **Encoding**-derived types offer a **GetByteCount** method that obtains the number of bytes necessary to encode a set of characters without actually encoding. Although **GetByteCount** isn't especially useful, you can use this method to allocate an array of bytes. There's also a **GetCharCount** method that returns the number of characters that would be decoded without actually decoding them. These methods are useful if you're trying to save memory and reuse an array.

The **GetByteCount/GetCharCount** methods aren't that fast because they must analyze the array of characters/bytes in order to return an accurate result. If you prefer speed to an exact result, you can call the **GetMaxByteCount** or **GetMaxCharCount** method instead. Both methods take an integer specifying the number of characters or number of bytes and return a worst-case value.

Each **Encoding**-derived object offers a set of public read-only properties that you can query to obtain detailed information about the encoding. See the .NET Framework SDK documentation for a description of these properties.

To illustrate most of the properties and their meanings, I wrote the following program that displays the property values for several different encodings:

```
using System;
using System.Text;

public static class Program {
    public static void Main() {
        foreach (EncodingInfo ei in Encoding.GetEncodings()) {
            Encoding e = ei.GetEncoding();
            Console.WriteLine("{1}{0}" +
                "\tCodePage={2}, WindowsCodePage={3}{0}" +
                "\tWebName={4}, HeaderName={5}, BodyName={6}{0}" +
                "\tIsBrowserDisplay={7}, IsBrowserSave={8}{0}" +
                "\tIsMailNewsDisplay={9}, IsMailNewsSave={10}{0}",

                Environment.NewLine,
                e.EncodingName, e.CodePage, e.WindowsCodePage,
                e.WebName, e.HeaderName, e.BodyName,
                e.IsBrowserDisplay, e.IsBrowserSave,
                e.IsMailNewsDisplay, e.IsMailNewsSave);
        }
    }
}
```

Running this program yields the following output (abridged to conserve paper):

```
IBM EBCDIC (US-Canada)
        CodePage=37, WindowsCodePage=1252
        WebName=IBM037, HeaderName=IBM037, BodyName=IBM037
        IsBrowserDisplay=False, IsBrowserSave=False
        IsMailNewsDisplay=False, IsMailNewsSave=False

OEM United States
        CodePage=437, WindowsCodePage=1252
        WebName=IBM437, HeaderName=IBM437, BodyName=IBM437
        IsBrowserDisplay=False, IsBrowserSave=False
        IsMailNewsDisplay=False, IsMailNewsSave=False

IBM EBCDIC (International)
        CodePage=500, WindowsCodePage=1252
        WebName=IBM500, HeaderName=IBM500, BodyName=IBM500
        IsBrowserDisplay=False, IsBrowserSave=False
        IsMailNewsDisplay=False, IsMailNewsSave=False

Arabic (ASMO 708)
        CodePage=708, WindowsCodePage=1256
        WebName=ASMO-708, HeaderName=ASMO-708, BodyName=ASMO-708
        IsBrowserDisplay=True, IsBrowserSave=True
        IsMailNewsDisplay=False, IsMailNewsSave=False

Unicode
        CodePage=1200, WindowsCodePage=1200
        WebName=utf-16, HeaderName=utf-16, BodyName=utf-16
        IsBrowserDisplay=False, IsBrowserSave=True
        IsMailNewsDisplay=False, IsMailNewsSave=False

Unicode (Big-Endian)
        CodePage=1201, WindowsCodePage=1200
        WebName=unicodeFFFE, HeaderName=unicodeFFFE, BodyName=unicodeFFFE
        IsBrowserDisplay=False, IsBrowserSave=False
        IsMailNewsDisplay=False, IsMailNewsSave=False

Western European (DOS)
        CodePage=850, WindowsCodePage=1252
        WebName=ibm850, HeaderName=ibm850, BodyName=ibm850
        IsBrowserDisplay=False, IsBrowserSave=False
        IsMailNewsDisplay=False, IsMailNewsSave=False

Unicode (UTF-8)
        CodePage=65001, WindowsCodePage=1200
        WebName=utf-8, HeaderName=utf-8, BodyName=utf-8
        IsBrowserDisplay=True, IsBrowserSave=True
        IsMailNewsDisplay=True, IsMailNewsSave=True
```

Table 14-3 covers the most commonly used methods offered by all **Encoding**-derived classes.

TABLE 14-3 Methods of the Encoding-Derived Classes

Method	Description
GetPreamble	Returns an array of bytes indicating what should be written to a stream before writing any encoded bytes. Frequently, these bytes are referred to as BOM bytes. When you start reading from a stream, the BOM bytes automatically help detect the encoding that was used when the stream was written so that the correct decoder can be used. For some **Encoding**-derived classes, this method returns an array of 0 bytes—that is, no preamble bytes. A **UTF8Encoding** object can be explicitly constructed so that this method returns a 3-byte array of 0xEF, 0xBB, 0xBF. A **UnicodeEncoding** object can be explicitly constructed so that this method returns a 2-byte array of 0xFE, 0xFF for big-endian encoding or a 2-byte array of 0xFF, 0xFE for little-endian encoding. The default is little-endian.
Convert	Converts an array of bytes specified in a source encoding to an array of bytes specified by a destination encoding. Internally, this static method calls the source encoding object's **GetChars** method and passes the result to the destination encoding object's **GetBytes** method. The resulting byte array is returned to the caller.
Equals	Returns **true** if two **Encoding**-derived objects represent the same code page and preamble setting.
GetHashCode	Returns the encoding object's code page.

Encoding and Decoding Streams of Characters and Bytes

Imagine that you're reading a UTF-16 encoded string via a **System.Net.Sockets. NetworkStream** object. The bytes will very likely stream in as chunks of data. In other words, you might first read 5 bytes from the stream, followed by 7 bytes. In UTF-16, each character consists of 2 bytes. So calling **Encoding**'s **GetString** method passing the first array of 5 bytes will return a string consisting of just two characters. If you later call **GetString**, passing in the next 7 bytes that come in from the stream, **GetString** will return a string consisting of three characters, and all of the code points will have the wrong values!

This data corruption problem occurs because none of the **Encoding**-derived classes maintains any state in between calls to their methods. If you'll be encoding or decoding characters/bytes in chunks, you must do some additional work to maintain state between calls, preventing any loss of data.

To decode chunks of bytes, you should obtain a reference to an **Encoding**-derived object (as described in the previous section) and call its **GetDecoder** method. This method returns a reference to a newly constructed object whose type is derived from the **System.Text.Decoder** class. Like the **Encoding** class, the **Decoder** class is an abstract base class. If you look in the .NET Framework SDK documentation, you won't find any classes that represent concrete implementations of the **Decoder** class. However, the FCL does define a bunch of **Decoder**-derived classes. These classes are all internal to the FCL, but the **GetDecoder** method can construct instances of these classes and return them to your application code.

All **Decoder**-derived classes offer two important methods: **GetChars** and **GetCharCount**. Obviously, these methods are used for decoding an array of bytes and work similarly to **Encoding**'s **GetChars** and **GetCharCount** methods, discussed earlier. When you call one of these methods, it decodes the byte array as much as possible. If the byte array doesn't contain enough bytes to complete a character, the leftover bytes are saved inside the decoder object. The next time you call one of these methods, the decoder object uses the leftover bytes plus the new byte array passed to it—this ensures that the chunks of data are decoded properly. **Decoder** objects are very useful when reading bytes from a stream.

An **Encoding**-derived type can be used for stateless encoding and decoding. However, a **Decoder**-derived type can be used only for decoding. If you want to encode strings in chunks, call **GetEncoder** instead of calling the **Encoding** object's **GetDecoder** method. **GetEncoder** returns a newly constructed object whose type is derived from the abstract base class **System.Text.Encoder**. Again, the .NET Framework SDK documentation doesn't contain any classes representing concrete implementations of the **Encoder** class. However, the FCL does define some **Encoder**-derived classes. As with the **Decoder**-derived classes, these classes are all internal to the FCL, but the **GetEncoder** method can construct instances of these classes and return them to your application code.

All **Encoder**-derived classes offer two important methods: **GetBytes** and **GetByteCount**. On each call, the **Encoder**-derived object maintains any leftover state information so that you can encode data in chunks.

Base-64 String Encoding and Decoding

As of this writing, the UTF-16 and UTF-8 encodings are becoming quite popular. It is also quite popular to encode a sequence of bytes to a base-64 string. The FCL does offer methods to do base-64 encoding and decoding, and you might expect that this would be accomplished via an **Encoding**-derived type. However, for some reason, base-64 encoding and decoding is done using some static methods offered by the **System.Convert** type.

To encode a base-64 string as an array of bytes, you call **Convert**'s static **FromBase64String** or **FromBase64CharArray** method. Likewise, to decode an array of bytes as a base-64 string, you call **Convert**'s static **ToBase64String** or **ToBase64CharArray** method. The following code demonstrates how to use some of these methods:

```
using System;

public static class Program {
    public static void Main() {
        // Get a set of 10 randomly generated bytes
        Byte[] bytes = new Byte[10];
```

```
new Random().NextBytes(bytes);

// Display the bytes
Console.WriteLine(BitConverter.ToString(bytes));

// Decode the bytes into a base-64 string and show the string
String s = Convert.ToBase64String(bytes);
Console.WriteLine(s);

// Encode the base-64 string back to bytes and show the bytes
bytes = Convert.FromBase64String(s);
Console.WriteLine(BitConverter.ToString(bytes));
    }
}
```

Compiling this code and running the executable file produces the following output (your output might vary from mine because of the randomly generated bytes):

```
3B-B9-27-40-59-35-86-54-5F-F1
O7knQFk1hlRf8Q==
3B-B9-27-40-59-35-86-54-5F-F1
```

Secure Strings

Often, **String** objects are used to contain sensitive data such as a user's password or credit-card information. Unfortunately, **String** objects contain an array of characters in memory, and if some unsafe or unmanaged code is allowed to execute, the unsafe/unmanaged code could snoop around the process's address space, locate the string containing the sensitive information, and use this data in an unauthorized way. Even if the **String** object is used for just a short time and then garbage collected, the CLR might not immediately reuse the **String** object's memory (especially if the **String** object was in an older generation), leaving the **String**'s characters in the process's memory, where the information could be compromised. In addition, since strings are immutable, as you manipulate them, the old copies linger in memory and you end up with different versions of the string scattered all over memory.

Some governmental departments have stringent security requirements that require very specific security guarantees. To meet these requirements, Microsoft added a more secure string class to the FCL: **System.Security.SecureString**. When you construct a **SecureString** object, it internally allocates a block of unmanaged memory that contains an array of characters. Unmanaged memory is used so that the garbage collector isn't aware of it.

These string's characters are encrypted, protecting the sensitive information from any malicious unsafe/unmanaged code. You can append, insert, remove, or set a character in the secure string by using any of these methods: **AppendChar**, **InsertAt**, **RemoveAt**, and **SetAt**. Whenever you call any of these methods, internally, the method decrypts the characters, performs the operation in place, and then re-encrypts the characters. This means that the characters are in an unencrypted state for a very short period of time. This also means that the performance of each operation is less than stellar, so you should perform as few of these operations as possible.

The **SecureString** class implements the **IDisposable** interface to provide an easy way to deterministically destroy the string's secured contents. When your application no longer needs the sensitive string information, you simply call **SecureString**'s **Dispose** method. Internally, **Dispose** zeroes out the contents of the memory buffer to make sure that the sensitive information is not accessible to malicious code, and then the buffer is freed. Internally, a **SecureString** object has a field to a **SafeBuffer**-derived object, which maintains the actual string. Since the **SafeBuffer** class is ultimately derived from **CriticalFinalizerObject**, discussed in Chapter 21, "Automatic Memory Management (Garbage Collection)," the string's characters are guaranteed to be zeroed out and have its buffer freed when it is garbage collected. Unlike a **String** object, when a **SecureString** object is collected, the encrypted string's characters will no longer be in memory.

Now that you know how to create and modify a **SecureString** object, let's talk about how to use one. Unfortunately, the most recent FCL has limited support for the **SecureString** class. In other words, there are only a few methods that accept a **SecureString** argument. In version 4 of the .NET Framework, you can pass a **SecureString** as a password when

- Working with a cryptographic service provider (CSP). See the **System.Security.Cryptography.CspParameters** class.

- Creating, importing, or exporting an X.509 certificate. See the **System.Security.Cryptography.X509Certificates.X509Certificate** and **System.Security.Cryptography.X509Certificates.X509Certificate2** classes.

- Starting a new process under a specific user account. See the **System.Diagnostics.Process** and **System.Diagnostics.ProcessStartInfo** classes.

- Constructing an event log session. See the **System.Diagnostics.Eventing.Reader.EventLogSession** class.

- Using the **System.Windows.Controls.PasswordBox** control. See this class's **SecurePassword** property.

Finally, you can create your own methods that can accept a **SecureString** object parameter. Inside your method, you must have the **SecureString** object create an unmanaged memory buffer that contains the decrypted characters before your method uses the buffer. To keep the window of opportunity for malicious code to access the sensitive data as small as possible, your code should require access to the decrypted string for as short a period of time as possible. When finished using the string, your code should zero the buffer and free it as soon as possible. Also, never put the contents of a **SecureString** into a **String**: if you do, the **String** lives unencrypted in the heap and will not have its characters zeroed out until the memory is reused after a garbage collection. The **SecureString** class does not override the

ToString method specifically to avoid exposing the sensitive data (which converting it to a **String** would do).

Here is some sample code demonstrating how to initialize and use a **SecureString** (when compiling this, you'll need to specify the **/unsafe** switch to the C# compiler):

```
using System;
using System.Security;
using System.Runtime.InteropServices;

public static class Program {
    public static void Main() {
        using (SecureString ss = new SecureString()) {
            Console.Write("Please enter password: ");
            while (true) {
                ConsoleKeyInfo cki = Console.ReadKey(true);
                if (cki.Key == ConsoleKey.Enter) break;

                // Append password characters into the SecureString
                ss.AppendChar(cki.KeyChar);
                Console.Write("*");
            }
            Console.WriteLine();

            // Password entered, display it for demonstration purposes
            DisplaySecureString(ss);
        }
        // After 'using', the SecureString is Disposed; no sensitive data in memory
    }

    // This method is unsafe because it accesses unmanaged memory
    private unsafe static void DisplaySecureString(SecureString ss) {
        Char* pc = null;
        try {
            // Decrypt the SecureString into an unmanaged memory buffer
            pc = (Char*) Marshal.SecureStringToCoTaskMemUnicode(ss);

            // Access the unmanaged memory buffer that
            // contains the decrypted SecureString
            for (Int32 index = 0; pc[index] != 0; index++)
                Console.Write(pc[index]);
        }
        finally {
            // Make sure we zero and free the unmanaged memory buffer that contains
            // the decrypted SecureString characters
            if (pc != null)
                Marshal.ZeroFreeCoTaskMemUnicode((IntPtr) pc);
        }
    }
}
```

The **System.Runtime.InteropServices.Marshal** class offers five methods that you can call to decrypt a **SecureString**'s characters into an unmanaged memory buffer. All of these methods are static, all accept a **SecureString** argument, and all return an **IntPtr**. Each of these methods has a corresponding method that you must call in order to zero the internal buffer and free it. Table 14-4 shows the **System.Runtime.InteropServices.Marshal** class's methods to decrypt a **SecureString** into a memory buffer and the corresponding method to zero and free the buffer.

TABLE 14-4 Methods of the Marshal Class for Working with Secure Strings

Method to Decrypt SecureString to Buffer	Method to Zero and Free Buffer
SecureStringToBSTR	ZeroFreeBSTR
SecureStringToCoTaskMemAnsi	ZeroFreeCoTaskMemAnsi
SecureStringToCoTaskMemUnicode	ZeroFreeCoTaskMemUnicode
SecureStringToGlobalAllocAnsi	ZeroFreeGlobalAllocAnsi
SecureStringToGlobalAllocUnicode	ZeroFreeGlobalAllocUnicode

Chapter 15
Enumerated Types and Bit Flags

In this chapter, I'll discuss enumerated types and bit flags. Since Microsoft Windows and many programming languages have used these constructs for so many years, I'm sure that many of you are already familiar with how to use enumerated types and bit flags. However, the common language runtime (CLR) and the Framework Class Library (FCL) work together to make enumerated types and bit flags real object-oriented types that offer cool new features that I suspect most developers aren't familiar with. It's amazing to me how these new features, which are the focus of this chapter, make developing application code so much easier.

Enumerated Types

An *enumerated type* is a type that defines a set of symbolic name and value pairs. For example, the **Color** type shown here defines a set of symbols, with each symbol identifying a single color:

```
internal enum Color {
   White,        // Assigned a value of 0
   Red,          // Assigned a value of 1
   Green,        // Assigned a value of 2
   Blue,         // Assigned a value of 3
   Orange        // Assigned a value of 4
}
```

Of course, programmers can always write a program using 0 to represent white, 1 to represent red, and so on. However, programmers shouldn't hard-code numbers into their code and should use an enumerated type instead, for at least two reasons:

- Enumerated types make the program much easier to write, read, and maintain. With enumerated types, the symbolic name is used throughout the code, and the programmer doesn't have to mentally map the meaning of each hard-coded value (for example, white is 0 or vice versa). Also, should a symbol's numeric value change, the code can simply be recompiled without requiring any changes to the source code. In addition, documentation tools and other utilities, such as a debugger, can show meaningful symbolic names to the programmer.

■   Enumerated types are strongly typed. For example, the compiler will report an error if I attempt to pass **Color.Orange** as a value to a method requiring a **Fruit** enumerated type as a parameter.

In the Microsoft .NET Framework, enumerated types are more than just symbols that the compiler cares about. Enumerated types are treated as first-class citizens in the type system, which allows for very powerful operations that simply can't be done with enumerated types in other environments (such as in unmanaged C++, for example).

Every enumerated type is derived directly from **System.Enum**, which is derived from **System.ValueType**, which in turn is derived from **System.Object**. So enumerated types are value types (described in Chapter 5, "Primitive, Reference, and Value Types") and can be represented in unboxed and boxed forms. However, unlike other value types, an enumerated type can't define any methods, properties, or events. However, you can use C#'s *extension methods* feature to simulate adding methods to an enumerated type. See the "Adding Methods to Enumerated Types" section at the end of this chapter for an example of this.

When an enumerated type is compiled, the C# compiler turns each symbol into a constant field of the type. For example, the compiler treats the **Color** enumeration shown earlier as if you had written code similar to the following:

```
internal struct Color : System.Enum {
    // Below are public constants defining Color's symbols and values
    public const Color White  = (Color) 0;
    public const Color Red    = (Color) 1;
    public const Color Green  = (Color) 2;
    public const Color Blue   = (Color) 3;
    public const Color Orange = (Color) 4;

    // Below is a public instance field containing a Color variable's value
    // You cannot write code that references this instance field directly
    public Int32 value__;
}
```

The C# compiler won't actually compile this code because it forbids you from defining a type derived from the special **System.Enum** type. However, this pseudo-type definition shows you what's happening internally. Basically, an enumerated type is just a structure with a bunch of constant fields defined in it and one instance field. The constant fields are emitted to the assembly's metadata and can be accessed via reflection. This means that you can get all of the symbols and their values associated with an enumerated type at runtime. It also means that you can convert a string symbol into its equivalent numeric value. These operations are made available to you by the **System.Enum** base type, which offers several static and instance methods that can be performed on an instance of an enumerated type, saving you the trouble of having to use reflection. I'll discuss some of these operations next.

Important Symbols defined by an enumerated type are constant values. So when a compiler sees code that references an enumerated type's symbol, the compiler substitutes the symbol's numeric value at compile time, and this code no longer references the enumerated type that defined the symbol. This means that the assembly that defines the enumerated type may not be required at runtime; it was required only when compiling. If you have code that references the enumerated type—rather than just having references to symbols defined by the type—the assembly containing the enumerated type's definition will be required at runtime. Some versioning issues arise because enumerated type symbols are constants instead of read-only values. I explained these issues in the "Constants" section of Chapter 7, "Constants and Fields."

For example, the **System.Enum** type has a static method called **GetUnderlyingType**, and the **System.Type** type has an instance method called **GetEnumUnderlyingType**:

```
public static Type GetUnderlyingType(Type enumType);      // Defined in System.Enum
public         Type GetEnumUnderlyingType();              // Defined in System.Type
```

These methods return the core type used to hold an enumerated type's value. Every enumerated type has an underlying type, which can be a **byte**, **sbyte**, **short**, **ushort**, **int** (the most common type and what C# chooses by default), **uint**, **long**, or **ulong**. Of course, these C# primitive types correspond to FCL types. However, to make the implementation of the compiler itself simpler, the C# compiler requires you to specify a primitive type name here; using an FCL type name (such as **Int32**) generates the following message: "**error CS1008: Type byte, sbyte, short, ushort, int, uint, long, or ulong expected.**" The following code shows how to declare an enumerated type with an underlying type of **byte** (**System.Byte**):

```
internal enum Color : byte {
   White,
   Red,
   Green,
   Blue,
   Orange
}
```

With the **Color** enumerated type defined in this way, the following code shows what **GetUnderlyingType** will return:

```
// The following line displays "System.Byte".
Console.WriteLine(Enum.GetUnderlyingType(typeof(Color)));
```

The C# compiler treats enumerated types as primitive types. As such, you can use many of the familiar operators (==, !=, <, >, <=, >=, +, -, ^, &, |, ~, ++, and --) to manipulate enumerated type instances. All of these operators actually work on the **value__** instance field inside each enumerated type instance. Furthermore, the C# compiler allows you to explicitly cast instances of an enumerated type to a different enumerated type. You can also explicitly cast an enumerated type instance to a numeric type.

Given an instance of an enumerated type, it's possible to map that value to one of several string representations by calling the **ToString** method inherited from **System.Enum**:

```
Color c = Color.Blue;
Console.WriteLine(c);                     // "Blue" (General format)
Console.WriteLine(c.ToString());          // "Blue" (General format)
Console.WriteLine(c.ToString("G"));       // "Blue" (General format)
Console.WriteLine(c.ToString("D"));       // "3"    (Decimal format)
Console.WriteLine(c.ToString("X"));       // "03"   (Hex format)
```

> **Note** When using hex formatting, **ToString** always outputs uppercase letters. In addition, the number of digits outputted depends on the enum's underlying type: 2 digits for **byte/sbyte**, 4 digits for **short/ushort**, 8 digits for **int/uint**, and 16 digits for **long/ulong**. Leading zeros are outputted if necessary.

In addition to the **ToString** method, the **System.Enum** type offers a static **Format** method that you can call to format an enumerated type's value:

```
public static String Format(Type enumType, Object value, String format);
```

Generally, I prefer to call the **ToString** method because it requires less code and it's easier to call. But using **Format** has one advantage over **ToString**: **Format** lets you pass a numeric value for the value parameter; you don't have to have an instance of the enumerated type. For example, the following code will display "Blue":

```
// The following line displays "Blue".
Console.WriteLine(Enum.Format(typeof(Color), 3, "G"));
```

> **Note** It's possible to declare an enumerated type that has multiple symbols, all with the same numeric value. When converting a numeric value to a symbol by using general formatting, **Enum**'s methods return one of the symbols. However, there's no guarantee of which symbol name is returned. Also, if no symbol is defined for the numeric value you're looking up, a string containing the numeric value is returned.

It's also possible to call **System.Enum**'s static **GetValues** method or **System.Type**'s instance **GetEnumValues** method to obtain an array that contains one element for each symbolic name in an enumerated type; each element contains the symbolic name's numeric value:

```
public static Array GetValues(Type enumType);      // Defined in System.Enum
public         Array GetEnumValues();              // Defined in System.Type
```

Using this method along with the **ToString** method, you can display all of an enumerated type's symbolic and numeric values, like so:

```
Color[] colors = (Color[]) Enum.GetValues(typeof(Color));
Console.WriteLine("Number of symbols defined: " + colors.Length);
```

```
Console.WriteLine("Value\tSymbol\n-----\t------");
foreach (Color c in colors) {
    // Display each symbol in Decimal and General format.
    Console.WriteLine("{0,5:D}\t{0:G}", c);
}
```

The previous code produces the following output:

```
Number of symbols defined: 5
Value   Symbol
-----   ------
    0   White
    1   Red
    2   Green
    3   Blue
    4   Orange
```

This discussion shows some of the cool operations that can be performed on enumerated types. I suspect that the **ToString** method with the general format will be used quite frequently to show symbolic names in a program's user interface elements (list boxes, combo boxes, and the like), as long as the strings don't need to be localized (since enumerated types offer no support for localization). In addition to the **GetValues** method, the **System.Enum** type and the **System.Type** type also offer the following methods that return an enumerated type's symbols:

```
// Returns a String representation for the numeric value
public static String GetName(Type enumType, Object value); // Defined in System.Enum
public       String GetEnumName(Object value);             // Defined in System.Type


// Returns an array of Strings: one per symbol defined in the enum
public static String[] GetNames(Type enumType);            // Defined in System.Enum
public       String[] GetEnumNames();                      // Defined in System.Type
```

I've discussed a lot of methods that you can use to look up an enumerated type's symbol. But you also need a method that can look up a symbol's equivalent value, an operation that could be used to convert a symbol that a user enters into a text box, for example. Converting a symbol to an instance of an enumerated type is easily accomplished by using one of **Enum**'s static **Parse** and **TryParse** methods:

```
public static Object Parse(Type enumType, String value);
public static Object Parse(Type enumType, String value, Boolean ignoreCase);
public static Boolean TryParse<TEnum>(String value, out TEnum result) where TEnum: struct;
public static Boolean TryParse<TEnum>(String value, Boolean ignoreCase, out TEnum result)
    where TEnum : struct;
```

Here's some code demonstrating how to use this method:

```
// Because Orange is defined as 4, 'c' is initialized to 4.
Color c = (Color) Enum.Parse(typeof(Color), "orange", true);
```

```
// Because Brown isn't defined, an ArgumentException is thrown.
c = (Color) Enum.Parse(typeof(Color), "Brown", false);

// Creates an instance of the Color enum with a value of 1
Enum.TryParse<Color>("1", false, out c);

// Creates an instance of the Color enum with a value of 23
Enum.TryParse<Color>("23", false, out c);
```

Finally, using **Enum**'s static **IsDefined** method and **Type**'s **IsEnumDefined** method,

```
public static Boolean IsDefined(Type enumType, Object value);    // Defined in System.Enum
public        Boolean IsEnumDefined(Object value);               // Defined in System.Type
```

you can determine whether a numeric value is legal for an enumerated type:

```
// Displays "True" because Color defines Red as 1
Console.WriteLine(Enum.IsDefined(typeof(Color),  1));

// Displays "True" because Color defines White as 0
Console.WriteLine(Enum.IsDefined(typeof(Color), "White"));

// Displays "False" because a case-sensitive check is performed
Console.WriteLine(Enum.IsDefined(typeof(Color), "white"));

// Displays "False" because Color doesn't have a symbol of value 10
Console.WriteLine(Enum.IsDefined(typeof(Color),  10));
```

The **IsDefined** method is frequently used for parameter validation. Here's an example:

```
public void SetColor(Color c) {
    if (!Enum.IsDefined(typeof(Color), c)) {
       throw(new ArgumentOutOfRangeException("c", c, "Invalid Color value."));
    }
    // Set color to White, Red, Green, Blue, or Orange
    ...
}
```

The parameter validation is useful because someone could call **SetColor** like this:

```
SetColor((Color) 547);
```

Because no symbol has a corresponding value of 547, the **SetColor** method will throw an **ArgumentOutOfRangeException** exception, indicating which parameter is invalid and why.

> **Important** The **IsDefined** method is very convenient, but you must use it with caution. First, **IsDefined** always does a case-sensitive search, and there is no way to get it to perform a case-insensitive search. Second, **IsDefined** is pretty slow because it uses reflection internally; if you wrote code to manually check each possible value, your application's performance would most certainly be better. Third, you should really use **IsDefined** only if the enum type itself is defined in the same assembly that is calling **IsDefined**. Here's why: Let's say the **Color** enum is defined in one assembly and the **SetColor** method is defined in another assembly. The **SetColor** method calls **IsDefined**, and if the color is **White**, **Red**, **Green**, **Blue**, or **Orange**, **SetColor** performs its work. However, if the **Color** enum changes in the future to include **Purple**, **SetColor** will now allow **Purple**, which it never expected before, and the method might execute with unpredictable results.

Finally, the **System.Enum** type offers a set of static **ToObject** methods that convert an instance of a **Byte**, **SByte**, **Int16**, **UInt16**, **Int32**, **UInt32**, **Int64**, or **UInt64** to an instance of an enumerated type.

Enumerated types are always used in conjunction with some other type. Typically, they're used for the type's method parameters or return type, properties, and fields. A common question that arises is whether to define the enumerated type nested within the type that requires it or to define the enumerated type at the same level as the type that requires it. If you examine the FCL, you'll see that an enumerated type is usually defined at the same level as the class that requires it. The reason is simply to make the developer's life a little easier by reducing the amount of typing required. So you should define your enumerated type at the same level unless you're concerned about name conflicts.

Bit Flags

Programmers frequently work with sets of bit flags. When you call the **System.IO.File** type's **GetAttributes** method, it returns an instance of a **FileAttributes** type. A **FileAttributes** type is an instance of an **Int32**-based enumerated type, in which each bit reflects a single attribute of the file. The **FileAttributes** type is defined in the FCL as follows:

```
[Flags, Serializable]
public enum FileAttributes {
    ReadOnly          = 0x0001,
    Hidden            = 0x0002,
    System            = 0x0004,
    Directory         = 0x0010,
    Archive           = 0x0020,
    Device            = 0x0040,
    Normal            = 0x0080,
    Temporary         = 0x0100,
    SparseFile        = 0x0200,
    ReparsePoint      = 0x0400,
    Compressed        = 0x0800,
    Offline           = 0x1000,
    NotContentIndexed = 0x2000,
    Encrypted         = 0x4000
}
```

To determine whether a file is hidden, you would execute code like this:

```
String file = Assembly.GetEntryAssembly().Location;
FileAttributes attributes = File.GetAttributes(file);
Console.WriteLine("Is {0} hidden? {1}", file, (attributes & FileAttributes.Hidden) != 0);
```

> **Note** The **Enum** class defines a **HasFlag** method defined as follows:
>
> ```
> public Boolean HasFlag(Enum flag);
> ```
>
> Using this method, you could rewrite the call to **Console.WriteLine** like this:
>
> ```
> Console.WriteLine("Is {0} hidden? {1}", file,
>     attributes.HasFlag(FileAttributes.Hidden));
> ```
>
> However, I recommend that you avoid the **HasFlag** method for this reason: Since it takes a parameter of type **Enum**, any value you pass to it must be boxed, requiring a memory allocation.

And here's code demonstrating how to change a file's attributes to read-only and hidden:

```
File.SetAttributes(file, FileAttributes.ReadOnly | FileAttributes.Hidden);
```

As the **FileAttributes** type shows, it's common to use enumerated types to express the set of bit flags that can be combined. However, although enumerated types and bit flags are similar, they don't have exactly the same semantics. For example, enumerated types represent single numeric values, and bit flags represent a set of bits, some of which are on, and some of which are off.

When defining an enumerated type that is to be used to identify bit flags, you should, of course, explicitly assign a numeric value to each symbol. Usually, each symbol will have an individual bit turned on. It is also common to see a symbol called **None** defined with a value of **0**, and you can also define symbols that represent commonly used combinations (see the **ReadWrite** symbol below). It's also highly recommended that you apply the **System.FlagsAttribute** custom attribute type to the enumerated type, as shown here:

```
[Flags]    // The C# compiler allows either "Flags" or "FlagsAttribute".
internal enum Actions {
    None      = 0
    Read      = 0x0001,
    Write     = 0x0002,
    ReadWrite = Actions.Read | Actions.Write,
    Delete    = 0x0004,
    Query     = 0x0008,
    Sync      = 0x0010
}
```

Because **Actions** is an enumerated type, you can use all of the methods described in the previous section when working with bit-flag enumerated types. However, it would be nice if some of those functions behaved a little differently. For example, let's say you had the following code:

```
Actions actions = Actions.Read | Actions.Delete; // 0x0005
Console.WriteLine(actions.ToString());           // "Read, Delete"
```

When **ToString** is called, it attempts to translate the numeric value into its symbolic equivalent. The numeric value is 0x0005, which has no symbolic equivalent. However, the **ToString** method detects the existence of the **[Flags]** attribute on the **Actions** type, and **ToString** now treats the numeric value not as a single value but as a set of bit flags. Because the 0x0001 and 0x0004 bits are set, **ToString** generates the following string: "Read, Delete". If you remove the **[Flags]** attribute from the **Actions** type, **ToString** would return "5."

I discussed the **ToString** method in the previous section, and I showed that it offered three ways to format the output: "G" (general), "D" (decimal), and "X" (hex). When you're formatting an instance of an enumerated type by using the general format, the type is first checked to see if the **[Flags]** attribute is applied to it. If this attribute is not applied, a symbol matching the numeric value is looked up and returned. If the **[Flags]** attribute is applied, **ToString** works like this:

1. The set of numeric values defined by the enumerated type is obtained, and the numbers are sorted in descending order.

2. Each numeric value is bitwise-ANDed with the value in the enum instance, and if the result equals the numeric value, the string associated with the numeric value is appended to the output string, and the bits are considered accounted for and are turned off. This step is repeated until all numeric values have been checked or until the enum instance has all of its bits turned off.

3. If, after all the numeric values have been checked, the enum instance is still not 0, the enum instance has some bits turned on that do not correspond to any defined symbols. In this case, **ToString** returns the original number in the enum instance as a string.

4. If the enum instance's original value wasn't 0, the string with the comma-separated set of symbols is returned.

5. If the enum instance's original value was 0 and if the enumerated type has a symbol defined with a corresponding value of 0, the symbol is returned.

6. If we reach this step, "0" is returned.

If you prefer, you could define the **Actions** type without the **[Flags]** attribute and still get the correct string by using the "F" format:

```
// [Flags]    // Commented out now
internal enum Actions {
    None      = 0
    Read      = 0x0001,
    Write     = 0x0002,
    ReadWrite = Actions.Read | Actions.Write,
    Delete    = 0x0004,
    Query     = 0x0008,
    Sync      = 0x0010
}

Actions actions = Actions.Read | Actions.Delete; // 0x0005
Console.WriteLine(actions.ToString("F"));        // "Read, Delete"
```

If the numeric value has a bit that cannot be mapped to a symbol, the returned string will contain just a decimal number indicating the original numeric value; no symbols will appear in the string.

Note that the symbols you define in your enumerated type don't have to be pure powers of 2. For example, the **Actions** type could define a symbol called **All** with a value of 0x001F. If an instance of the **Actions** type has a value of 0x001F, formatting the instance will produce a string that contains "All." The other symbol strings won't appear.

So far, I've discussed how to convert numeric values into a string of flags. It's also possible to convert a string of comma-delimited symbols into a numeric value by calling **Enum**'s static **Parse** and **TryParse** method. Here's some code demonstrating how to use this method:

```
// Because Query is defined as 8, 'a' is initialized to 8.
Actions a = (Actions) Enum.Parse(typeof(Actions), "Query", true);
Console.WriteLine(a.ToString()); // "Query"

// Because Query and Read are defined, 'a' is initialized to 9.
Enum.TryParse<Actions>("Query, Read", false, out a);
Console.WriteLine(a.ToString()); // "Read, Query"

// Creates an instance of the Actions enum with a value of 28
a = (Actions) Enum.Parse(typeof(Actions), "28", false);
Console.WriteLine(a.ToString()); // "Delete, Query, Sync"
```

When **Parse** and **TryParse** are called, the following actions are performed internally:

1. It removes all whitespace characters from the start and end of the string.

2. If the first character of the string is a digit, plus sign (+), or minus sign (-), the string is assumed to be a number, and an enum instance is returned whose numeric value is equal to the string converted to its numeric equivalent.

3. The passed string is split into a set of tokens (separated by commas), and all white space is trimmed away from each token.

4. Each token string is looked up in the enum type's defined symbols. If the symbol is not found, **Parse** throws a **System.ArgumentException** and **TryParse** returns **false**. If the symbol is found, bitwise-OR its numeric value into a running result, and then look up the next token.

5. If all tokens have been sought and found, return the running result.

You should never use the **IsDefined** method with bit flag–enumerated types. It won't work for two reasons:

- If you pass a string to **IsDefined**, it doesn't split the string into separate tokens to look up; it will attempt to look up the string as through it were one big symbol with commas in it. Since you can't define an enum with a symbol that has commas in it, the symbol will never be found.

- If you pass a numeric value to **IsDefined**, it checks if the enumerated type defines a single symbol whose numeric value matches the passed-in number. Since this is unlikely for bit flags, **IsDefined** will usually return **false**.

Adding Methods to Enumerated Types

Earlier in this chapter, I mentioned that you cannot define a method as part of an enumerated type. And, for many years, this has saddened me because there are many occasions when I would love to have been able to supply some methods to my enumerated type. Fortunately, I can now use C#'s relatively new extension method feature (discussed in Chapter 8, "Methods") to simulate adding methods to an enumerated type.

If I want to add some methods to the **FileAttributes** enumerated type, I can define a static class with extension methods as follows:

```
internal static class FileAttributesExtensionMethods {
   public static Boolean IsSet(this FileAttributes flags, FileAttributes flagToTest) {
      if (flagToTest == 0)
         throw new ArgumentOutOfRangeException("flagToTest", "Value must not be 0");
      return (flags & flagToTest) == flagToTest;
   }

   public static Boolean IsClear(this FileAttributes flags, FileAttributes flagToTest) {
      if (flagToTest == 0)
         throw new ArgumentOutOfRangeException("flagToTest", "Value must not be 0");
      return !IsSet(flags, flagToTest);
   }

   public static Boolean AnyFlagsSet(this FileAttributes flags, FileAttributes testFlags) {
      return ((flags & testFlags) != 0);
   }
```

```
   public static FileAttributes Set(this FileAttributes flags, FileAttributes setFlags) {
      return flags | setFlags;
   }

   public static FileAttributes Clear(this FileAttributes flags,
      FileAttributes clearFlags) {
      return flags & ~clearFlags;
   }

   public static void ForEach(this FileAttributes flags,
      Action<FileAttributes> processFlag) {
      if (processFlag == null) throw new ArgumentNullException("processFlag");
      for (UInt32 bit = 1; bit != 0; bit <<= 1) {
         UInt32 temp = ((UInt32)flags) & bit;
         if (temp != 0) processFlag((FileAttributes)temp);
      }
   }
}
}
```

And here is some code that demonstrates calling some of these methods. As you can see, the code looks as if I'm calling methods on the enumerated type:

```
FileAttributes fa = FileAttributes.System;
fa = fa.Set(FileAttributes.ReadOnly);
fa = fa.Clear(FileAttributes.System);
fa.ForEach(f => Console.WriteLine(f));
```

Chapter 16
Arrays

Arrays are mechanisms that allow you to treat several items as a single collection. The Microsoft .NET common language runtime (CLR) supports single-dimensional arrays, multi-dimensional arrays, and jagged arrays (that is, arrays of arrays). All array types are implicitly derived from the **System.Array** abstract class, which itself is derived from **System.Object**. This means that arrays are always reference types that are allocated on the managed heap and that your application's variable or field contains a reference to the array and not the elements of the array itself. The following code makes this clearer:

```
Int32[] myIntegers;         // Declares a reference to an array
myIntegers = new Int32[100]; // Creates an array of 100 Int32s
```

On the first line, **myIntegers** is a variable that's capable of pointing to a single-dimensional array of **Int32**s. Initially, **myIntegers** will be set to **null** because I haven't allocated an array. The second line of code allocates an array of 100 **Int32** values; all of the **Int32**s are initialized to 0. Since arrays are reference types, the memory block required to hold the 100 unboxed **Int32**s is allocated on the managed heap. Actually, in addition to the array's elements, the memory block occupied by an array object also contains a type object pointer, a sync block index, and some additional overhead members as well. The address of this array's memory block is returned and saved in the variable **myIntegers**.

You can also create arrays of reference types:

```
Control[] myControls;        // Declares a reference to an array
myControls = new Control[50]; // Creates an array of 50 Control references
```

On the first line, **myControls** is a variable capable of pointing to a single-dimensional array of **Control** references. Initially, **myControls** will be set to **null** because I haven't allocated an array. The second line allocates an array of 50 **Control** references; all of these references are initialized to **null**. Because **Control** is a reference type, creating the array creates only a bunch of references; the actual objects aren't created at this time. The address of this memory block is returned and saved in the variable **myControls**.

Figure 16-1 shows how arrays of value types and arrays of reference types look in the managed heap.

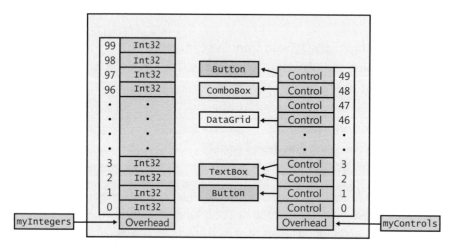

FIGURE 16-1 Arrays of value and reference types in the managed heap

In the figure, the **Controls** array shows the result after the following lines have executed:

```
myControls[1]  = new Button();
myControls[2]  = new TextBox();
myControls[3]  = myControls[2];  // Two elements refer to the same object.
myControls[46] = new DataGrid();
myControls[48] = new ComboBox();
myControls[49] = new Button();
```

Common Language Specification (CLS) compliance requires all arrays to be zero-based. This allows a method written in C# to create an array and pass the array's reference to code written in another language, such as Microsoft Visual Basic .NET. In addition, because zero-based arrays are, by far, the most common arrays, Microsoft has spent a lot of time optimizing their performance. However, the CLR does support non-zero–based arrays even though their use is discouraged. For those of you who don't care about a slight performance penalty or cross-language portability, I'll demonstrate how to create and use non-zero–based arrays later in this chapter.

Notice in Figure 16-1 that each array has some additional overhead information associated with it. This information contains the rank of the array (number of dimensions), the lower bounds for each dimension of the array (almost always 0), and the length of each dimension.

The overhead also contains the array's element type. I'll mention the methods that allow you to query this overhead information later in this chapter.

So far, I've shown examples demonstrating how to create single-dimensional arrays. When possible, you should stick with single-dimensional, zero-based arrays, sometimes referred to as *SZ arrays*, or *vectors*. Vectors give the best performance because you can use specific Intermediate Language (IL) instructions—such as **newarr**, **ldelem**, **ldelema**, **ldlen**, and **stelem**—to manipulate them. However, if you prefer to work with multi-dimensional arrays, you can. Here are some examples of multi-dimensional arrays:

```
// Create a two-dimensional array of Doubles.
Double[,] myDoubles = new Double[10, 20];

// Create a three-dimensional array of String references.
String[,,] myStrings = new String[5, 3, 10];
```

The CLR also supports jagged arrays, which are arrays of arrays. Zero-based, single-dimensional jagged arrays have the same performance as normal vectors. However, accessing the elements of a jagged array means that two or more array accesses must occur. Here are some examples of how to create an array of polygons with each polygon consisting of an array of **Point** instances:

```
// Create a single-dimensional array of Point arrays.
Point[][] myPolygons = new Point[3][];

// myPolygons[0] refers to an array of 10 Point instances.
myPolygons[0] = new Point[10];

// myPolygons[1] refers to an array of 20 Point instances.
myPolygons[1] = new Point[20];

// myPolygons[2] refers to an array of 30 Point instances.
myPolygons[2] = new Point[30];

// Display the Points in the first polygon.
for (Int32 x = 0; x < myPolygons[0].Length; x++)
    Console.WriteLine(myPolygons[0][x]);
```

Note The CLR verifies that an index into an array is valid. In other words, you can't create an array with 100 elements in it (numbered 0 through 99) and then try to access the element at index –5 or 100. Doing so will cause a **System.IndexOutOfRangeException** to be thrown. Allowing access to memory outside the range of an array would be a breach of type safety and a potential security hole, and the CLR doesn't allow verifiable code to do this. Usually, the performance degradation associated with index checking is insubstantial because the just-in-time (JIT) compiler normally checks array bounds once before a loop executes instead of at each loop iteration. However, if you're still concerned about the performance hit of the CLR's index checks, you can use unsafe code in C# to access the array. The "Array Access Performance" section later in this chapter demonstrates how to do this.

Initializing Array Elements

In the previous section, I showed how to create an array object and then I showed how to initialize the elements of the array. C# offers syntax that allows you to do these two operations in one statement. For example:

```
String[] names = new String[] { "Aidan", "Grant" };
```

The comma-separated set of tokens contained within the braces is called an *array initializer*. Each token can be an arbitrarily complex expression or, in the case of a multi-dimensional array, a nested array initializer. In the example above, I used just two simple **String** expressions.

If you are declaring a local variable in a method to refer to the initialized array, then you can use C#'s implicitly typed local variable (**var**) feature to simplify the code a little:

```
// Using C#'s implicitly typed local variable feature:
var names = new String[] { "Aidan", "Grant" };
```

Here, the compiler is inferring that the **names** local variable should be of the **String[]** type since that is the type of the expression on the right of the assignment operator (=).

You can use C#'s implicitly typed array feature to have the compiler infer the type of the array's elements. Notice the line below has no type specified between **new** and **[]**:

```
// Using C#'s implicitly typed local variable and implicitly typed array features:
var names = new[] { "Aidan", "Grant", null };
```

In the line above, the compiler examines the types of the expressions being used inside the array to initialize the array's elements, and the compiler chooses the closest base class that all the elements have in common to determine the type of the array. In this example, the compiler sees two **String**s and **null**. Since **null** is implicitly castable to any reference type (including **String**), the compiler infers that it should be creating and initializing an array of **String** references.

If you had this code,

```
// Using C#'s implicitly typed local variable & implicitly typed array features: (error)
var names = new[] { "Aidan", "Grant", 123 };
```

the compiler would issue the message "**error CS0826: No best type found for implicitly-typed array.**" This is because the base type in common between the two **String**s and the **Int32** is **Object**, which would mean that the compiler would have to create an array of **Object** references and then box the **123** and have the last array element refer to a boxed **Int32** with a value of **123**. The C# compiler team thinks that boxing array elements is too heavy-handed for the compiler to do for you implicitly, and that is why the compiler issues the error.

As an added syntactical bonus when initializing an array, you can write the following:

```
String[] names = { "Aidan", "Grant" };
```

Notice that on the right of the assignment operator (=), only the array initializer expression is given with no **new**, no type, and no **[]**s. This syntax is nice, but unfortunately, the C# compiler does not allow you to use implicitly typed local variables with this syntax:

```
// This is a local variable now (error)
var names = { "Aidan", "Grant" };
```

If you try to compile the line of code above, the compiler issues two messages: "**error CS0820: Cannot initialize an implicitly-typed local variable with an array initializer**" and "**error CS0622: Can only use array initializer expressions to assign to array types. Try using a new expression instead.**" While the compiler could make this work, the C# team thought that the compiler would be doing too much for you here. It would be inferring the type of the array, **new**'ing the array, initializing the array, and inferring the type of the local variable, too.

The last thing I'd like to show you is how to use implicitly typed arrays with anonymous types and implicitly typed local variables. Anonymous types and how type identity applies to them are discussed in Chapter 10, "Properties." Examine the code below:

```
// Using C#'s implicitly typed local, implicitly typed array, and anonymous type features:
var kids = new[] {new { Name="Aidan" }, new { Name="Grant" }};

// Sample usage (with another implicitly typed local variable):
foreach (var kid in kids)
    Console.WriteLine(kid.Name);
```

In this example, I am using an array initializer that has two expressions for the array elements. Each expression represents an anonymous type (since no type name is specified after the **new** operator). Since the two anonymous types have the identical structure (one field called **Name** of type **String**), the compiler knows that these two objects are of the exact same type. Now, I use C#'s implicitly typed array feature (no type specified between the **new** and the **[]**s so that the compiler will infer the type of the array itself, construct this array object, and initialize its references to the two instances of the one anonymous type.[1] Finally, a reference to this array object is assigned to the **kids** local variable, the type of which is inferred by the compiler due to C#'s implicitly typed local variable feature.

I show the **foreach** loop as an example of how to use this array that was just created and initialized with the two anonymous type objects. I have to use an implicitly typed local variable (**kid**) for the loop, too. When I run this code, I get the following output:

```
Aidan
Grant
```

---

[1] If you think these sentences are fun to read, you can only imagine how fun they were to write in the first place!

Casting Arrays

For arrays with reference type elements, the CLR allows you to implicitly cast the source array's element type to a target type. For the cast to succeed, both array types must have the same number of dimensions, and an implicit or explicit conversion from the source element type to the target element type must exist. The CLR doesn't allow the casting of arrays with value type elements to any other type. (However, by using the **Array.Copy** method, you can create a new array and populate its elements in order to obtain the desired effect.) The following code demonstrates how array casting works:

```
// Create a two-dimensional FileStream array.
FileStream[,] fs2dim = new FileStream[5, 10];

// Implicit cast to a two-dimensional Object array
Object[,] o2dim = fs2dim;

// Can't cast from two-dimensional array to one-dimensional array
// Compiler error CS0030: Cannot convert type 'object[*,*]' to
// 'System.IO.Stream[]'
Stream[] s1dim = (Stream[]) o2dim;

// Explicit cast to two-dimensional Stream array
Stream[,] s2dim = (Stream[,]) o2dim;

// Explicit cast to two-dimensional String array
// Compiles but throws InvalidCastException at runtime
String[,] st2dim = (String[,]) o2dim;

// Create a one-dimensional Int32 array (value types).
Int32[] i1dim = new Int32[5];

// Can't cast from array of value types to anything else
// Compiler error CS0030: Cannot convert type 'int[]' to 'object[]'
Object[] o1dim = (Object[]) i1dim;

// Create a new array, then use Array.Copy to coerce each element in the
// source array to the desired type in the destination array.
// The following code creates an array of references to boxed Int32s.
Object[] ob1dim = new Object[i1dim.Length];
Array.Copy(i1dim, ob1dim, i1dim.Length);
```

The **Array.Copy** method is not just a method that copies elements from one array to another. The **Copy** method handles overlapping regions of memory correctly, as does C's **memmove** function. C's **memcpy** function, on the other hand, doesn't handle overlapping regions correctly. The **Copy** method can also convert each array element as it is copied if conversion is required. The **Copy** method is capable of performing the following conversions:

- Boxing value type elements to reference type elements, such as copying an **Int32[]** to an **Object[]**.

- Unboxing reference type elements to value type elements, such as copying an **Object[]** to an **Int32[]**.

- Widening CLR primitive value types, such as copying elements from an **Int32[]** to a **Double[]**.

- Downcasting elements when copying between array types that can't be proven to be compatible based on the array's type, such as when casting from an **Object[]** to an **IFormattable[]**. If every object in the **Object[]** implements **IFormattable[]**, **Copy** will succeed.

Here's another example showing the usefulness of **Copy**:

```
// Define a value type that implements an interface.
internal struct MyValueType : IComparable {
    public Int32 CompareTo(Object obj) {
        ...
    }
}


public static class Program {
    public static void Main() {
        // Create an array of 100 value types.
        MyValueType[] src = new MyValueType[100];

        // Create an array of IComparable references.
        IComparable[] dest = new IComparable[src.Length];

        // Initialize an array of IComparable elements to refer to boxed
        // versions of elements in the source array.
        Array.Copy(src, dest, src.Length);
    }
}
```

As you might imagine, the Framework Class Library (FCL) takes advantage of **Array**'s **Copy** method quite frequently.

In some situations, it is useful to cast an array from one type to another. This kind of functionality is called *array covariance*. When you take advantage of array covariance, you should be aware of an associated performance penalty. Let's say you have the following code:

```
String[] sa = new String[100];
Object[] oa = sa;   // oa refers to an array of String elements
oa[5] = "Jeff";     // Perf hit: CLR checks oa's element type for String; OK
oa[3] = 5;          // Perf hit: CLR checks oa's element type for Int32; throws
                    // ArrayTypeMismatchException
```

In the code above, the **oa** variable is typed as an **Object[]**; however, it really refers to a **String[]**. The compiler will allow you to write code that attempts to put a 5 into an array element because 5 is an **Int32**, which is derived from **Object**. Of course, the CLR must ensure type safety, and when assigning to an array element, the CLR must ensure that the assignment is legal. So the CLR must check at runtime whether the array contains **Int32** elements. In this case, it doesn't, and the assignment cannot be allowed; the CLR will throw an **ArrayTypeMismatchException**.

> **Note** If you just need to make a copy of some array elements to another array, **System.Buffer**'s **BlockCopy** method executes faster than **Array**'s **Copy** method. However, **Buffer**'s **BlockCopy** supports only primitive types; it does not offer the same casting abilities as **Array**'s **Copy** method. The **Int32** parameters are expressed as byte offsets within the array, not as element indexes. **BlockCopy** is really designed for copying data that is bitwise-compatible from one array type to another blittable array type, such as copying a **Byte[]** containing Unicode characters (in the proper byte order) to a **Char[]**. This method allows programmers to partially make up for the lack of the ability to treat an array as a block of memory of any type.
>
> If you need to reliably copy a set of array elements from one array to another array, you should use **System.Array**'s **ConstrainedCopy** method. This method guarantees that the copy operation will either complete or throw an exception without destroying any data within the destination array. This allows **ConstrainedCopy** to be used in a constrained execution region (CER). In order to offer this guarantee, **ConstrainedCopy** requires that the source array's element type be the same as or derived from the destination array's element type. In addition, it will not perform any boxing, unboxing, or downcasting.

All Arrays Are Implicitly Derived from System.Array

When you declare an array variable like this,

```
FileStream[] fsArray;
```

then the CLR automatically creates a **FileStream[]** type for the AppDomain. This type will be implicitly derived from the **System.Array** type, and therefore, all of the instance methods and properties defined on the **System.Array** type will be inherited by the **FileStream[]** type, allowing these methods and properties to be called using the **fsArray** variable. This makes working with arrays extremely convenient because there are many helpful instance methods and properties defined by **System.Array**, such as **Clone**, **CopyTo**, **GetLength**, **GetLongLength**, **GetLowerBound**, **GetUpperBound**, **Length**, **Rank**, and others.

The **System.Array** type also exposes a large number of extremely useful static methods that operate on arrays. These methods all take a reference to an array as a parameter. Some of the useful static methods are **AsReadOnly**, **BinarySearch**, **Clear**, **ConstrainedCopy**, **ConvertAll**, **Copy**, **Exists**, **Find**, **FindAll**, **FindIndex**, **FindLast**, **FindLastIndex**, **ForEach**, **IndexOf**, **LastIndexOf**, **Resize**, **Reverse**, **Sort**, and **TrueForAll**. There are many overloads for each of these methods. In fact, many of the methods provide generic overloads for compile-time type safety as well as good performance. I encourage you to examine the SDK documentation to get an understanding of how useful and powerful these methods are.

All Arrays Implicitly Implement IEnumerable, ICollection, and IList

There are many methods that operate on various collection objects because the methods are declared with parameters such as **IEnumerable**, **ICollection**, and **IList**. It is possible to pass arrays to these methods because **System.Array** also implements these three interfaces. **System.Array** implements these non-generic interfaces because they treat all elements as **System.Object**. However, it would be nice to have **System.Array** implement the generic equivalent of these interfaces, providing better compile-time type safety as well as better performance.

The CLR team didn't want **System.Array** to implement **IEnumerable<T>**, **ICollection<T>**, and **IList<T>**, though, because of issues related to multi-dimensional arrays and non-zero–based arrays. Defining these interfaces on **System.Array** would have enabled these interfaces for all array types. Instead, the CLR performs a little trick: when a single-dimensional, zero–lower bound array type is created, the CLR automatically makes the array type implement **IEnumerable<T>**, **ICollection<T>**, and **IList<T>** (where **T** is the array's element type) and also implements the three interfaces for all of the array type's base types as long as they are reference types. The following hierarchy diagram helps make this clear:

```
Object
   Array (non-generic IEnumerable, ICollection, IList)
      Object[]          (IEnumerable, ICollection, IList of Object)
         String[]       (IEnumerable, ICollection, IList of String)
         Stream[]       (IEnumerable, ICollection, IList of Stream)
            FileStream[] (IEnumerable, ICollection, IList of FileStream)
      .
      .        (other arrays of reference types)
      .
```

So, for example, if you have the following line of code,

```
FileStream[] fsArray;
```

then when the CLR creates the **FileStream[]** type, it will cause this type to automatically implement the **IEnumerable<FileStream>**, **ICollection<FileStream>**, and **IList<FileStream>** interfaces. Furthermore, the **FileStream[]** type will also implement the interfaces for the base types: **IEnumerable<Stream>**, **IEnumerable<Object>**, **ICollection<Stream>**, **ICollection<Object>**, **IList<Stream>**, and **IList<Object>**. Since all of these interfaces are automatically implemented by the CLR, the **fsArray** variable could be used wherever any of these interfaces exist. For example, the **fsArray** variable could be passed to methods that have any of the following prototypes:

```
void M1(IList<FileStream> fsList) { … }
void M2(ICollection<Stream> sCollection) { … }
void M3(IEnumerable<Object> oEnumerable) { … }
```

Note that if the array contains value type elements, the array type will not implement the interfaces for the element's base types. For example, if you have the following line of code,

```
DateTime[] dtArray; // An array of value types
```

then the **DateTime[]** type will implement **IEnumerable<DateTime>**, **ICollection<DateTime>**, and **IList<DateTime>** only; it will not implement versions of these interfaces that are generic over **System.ValueType** or **System.Object**. This means that the **dtArray** variable cannot be passed as an argument to the **M3** method shown earlier. The reason for this is because arrays of value types are laid out in memory differently than arrays of reference types. Array memory layout was discussed earlier in this chapter.

Passing and Returning Arrays

When passing an array as an argument to a method, you are really passing a reference to that array. Therefore, the called method is able to modify the elements in the array. If you don't want to allow this, you must make a copy of the array and pass the copy into the method. Note that the **Array.Copy** method performs a shallow copy, and therefore, if the array's elements are reference types, the new array refers to the already existing objects.

Similarly, some methods return a reference to an array. If the method constructs and initializes the array, returning a reference to the array is fine. But if the method wants to return a reference to an internal array maintained by a field, you must decide if you want the method's caller to have direct access to this array and its elements. If you do, just return the array's reference. But most often, you won't want the method's caller to have such access, so the method should construct a new array and call **Array.Copy**, returning a reference to the new array. Again, be aware that **Array.Copy** makes a shallow copy of the original array.

If you define a method that returns a reference to an array, and if that array has no elements in it, your method can return either **null** or a reference to an array with zero elements in it. When you're implementing this kind of method, Microsoft strongly recommends that you implement the method by having it return a zero-length array because doing so simplifies the code that a developer calling the method must write. For example, this easy-to-understand code runs correctly even if there are no appointments to iterate over:

```
// This code is easier to write and understand.
Appointment[] appointments = GetAppointmentsForToday();
for (Int32 a = 0; a < appointments.Length; a++) {
    ...
}
```

The following code also runs correctly if there are no appointments to iterate over. However, this code is slightly more difficult to write and understand:

```
// This code is harder to write and understand.
Appointment[] appointments = GetAppointmentsForToday();
if (appointments != null) {
   for (Int32 a = 0, a < appointments.Length; a++) {
      // Do something with appointments[a]
   }
}
```

If you design your methods to return arrays with zero elements instead of **null**, callers of your methods will have an easier time working with them. By the way, you should do the same for fields. If your type has a field that's a reference to an array, you should consider having the field refer to an array even if the array has no elements in it.

Creating Non-Zero–Lower Bound Arrays

Earlier I mentioned that it's possible to create and work with arrays that have non-zero lower bounds. You can dynamically create your own arrays by calling **Array**'s static **CreateInstance** method. Several overloads of this method exist, allowing you to specify the type of the elements in the array, the number of dimensions in the array, the lower bounds of each dimension, and the number of elements in each dimension. **CreateInstance** allocates memory for the array, saves the parameter information in the overhead portion of the array's memory block, and returns a reference to the array. If the array has two or more dimensions, you can cast the reference returned from **CreateInstance** to an **ElementType[]** variable (where **ElementType** is some type name), making it easier for you to access the elements in the array. If the array has just one dimension, in C#, you have to use **Array**'s **GetValue** and **SetValue** methods to access the elements of the array.

Here's some code that demonstrates how to dynamically create a two-dimensional array of **System.Decimal** values. The first dimension represents calendar years from 2005 to 2009 inclusive, and the second dimension represents quarters from 1 to 4 inclusive. The code iterates over all the elements in the dynamic array. I could have hard-coded the array's bounds into the code, which would have given better performance, but I decided to use **System.Array**'s **GetLowerBound** and **GetUpperBound** methods to demonstrate their use:

```
using System;

public static class DynamicArrays {
   public static void Main() {
      // I want a two-dimensional array [2005..2009][1..4].
      Int32[] lowerBounds = { 2005, 1 };
      Int32[] lengths     = {    5, 4 };
      Decimal[,] quarterlyRevenue = (Decimal[,])
         Array.CreateInstance(typeof(Decimal), lengths, lowerBounds);

      Console.WriteLine("{0,4}  {1,9}  {2,9}  {3,9}  {4,9}",
         "Year", "Q1", "Q2", "Q3", "Q4");
      Int32 firstYear    = quarterlyRevenue.GetLowerBound(0);
```

```
        Int32 lastYear      = quarterlyRevenue.GetUpperBound(0);
        Int32 firstQuarter = quarterlyRevenue.GetLowerBound(1);
        Int32 lastQuarter  = quarterlyRevenue.GetUpperBound(1);

        for (Int32 year = firstYear; year <= lastYear; year++) {
            Console.Write(year + "  ");
            for (Int32 quarter = firstQuarter; quarter <= lastQuarter; quarter++) {
                Console.Write("{0,9:C}  ", quarterlyRevenue[year, quarter]);
            }
            Console.WriteLine();
        }
    }
}
```

If you compile and run this code, you get the following output:

Year	Q1	Q2	Q3	Q4
2005	$0.00	$0.00	$0.00	$0.00
2006	$0.00	$0.00	$0.00	$0.00
2007	$0.00	$0.00	$0.00	$0.00
2008	$0.00	$0.00	$0.00	$0.00
2009	$0.00	$0.00	$0.00	$0.00

Array Access Performance

Internally, the CLR actually supports two different kinds of arrays:

- Single-dimensional arrays with a lower bound of 0. These arrays are sometimes called SZ (for single-dimensional, zero-based) arrays or vectors.

- Single-dimensional and multi-dimensional arrays with an unknown lower bound.

You can actually see the different kinds of arrays by executing the following code (the output is shown in the code's comments):

```
using System;

public sealed class Program {
    public static void Main() {
    Array a;

    // Create a 1-dim, 0-based array, with no elements in it
    a = new String[0];
    Console.WriteLine(a.GetType());   // "System.String[]"

    // Create a 1-dim, 0-based array, with no elements in it
    a = Array.CreateInstance(typeof(String),
        new Int32[] { 0 }, new Int32[] { 0 });
    Console.WriteLine(a.GetType());   // "System.String[]"

    // Create a 1-dim, 1-based array, with no elements in it
    a = Array.CreateInstance(typeof(String),
```

```
            new Int32[] { 0 }, new Int32[] { 1 });
        Console.WriteLine(a.GetType());    // "System.String[*]"  <-- INTERESTING!

        Console.WriteLine();

        // Create a 2-dim, 0-based array, with no elements in it
        a = new String[0, 0];
        Console.WriteLine(a.GetType());    // "System.String[,]"

        // Create a 2-dim, 0-based array, with no elements in it
        a = Array.CreateInstance(typeof(String),
            new Int32[] { 0, 0 }, new Int32[] { 0, 0 });
        Console.WriteLine(a.GetType());    // "System.String[,]"

        // Create a 2-dim, 1-based array, with no elements in it
        a = Array.CreateInstance(typeof(String),
            new Int32[] { 0, 0 }, new Int32[] { 1, 1 });
        Console.WriteLine(a.GetType());    // "System.String[,]"
    }
}
```

Next to each **Console.WriteLine** is a comment that indicates the output. For the single-dimensional arrays, the zero-based arrays display a type name of **System.String[]**, whereas the 1-based array displays a type name of **System.String[*]**. The * indicates that the CLR knows that this array is not zero-based. Note that C# does not allow you to declare a variable of type **String[*]**, and therefore it is not possible to use C# syntax to access a single-dimensional, non-zero–based array. Although you can call **Array**'s **GetValue** and **SetValue** methods to access the elements of the array, this access will be slow due to the overhead of the method call.

For multi-dimensional arrays, the zero-based and 1-based arrays all display the same type name: **System.String[,]**. The CLR treats all multi-dimensional arrays as though they are *not* zero-based at runtime. This would make you think that the type name should display as **System.String[*,*]**; however, the CLR doesn't use the *s for multi-dimensional arrays because they would always be present, and the asterisks would just confuse most developers.

Accessing the elements of a single-dimensional, zero-based array is slightly faster than accessing the elements of a non-zero–based, single-dimensional array or a multi-dimensional array. There are several reasons for this. First, there are specific IL instructions—such as **newarr**, **ldelem**, **ldelema**, **ldlen**, and **stelem**—to manipulate single-dimensional, zero-based arrays, and these special IL instructions cause the JIT compiler to emit optimized code. For example, the JIT compiler will emit code that assumes that the array is zero-based, and this means that an offset doesn't have to be subtracted from the specified index when accessing an element. Second, in common situations, the JIT compiler is able to hoist the index range–checking code out of the loop, causing it to execute just once. For example, look at the following commonly written code:

```
using System;

public static class Program {
    public static void Main() {
        Int32[] a = new Int32[5];
        for(Int32 index = 0; index < a.Length; index++) {
            // Do something with a[index]
        }
    }
}
```

The first thing to notice about this code is the call to the array's **Length** property in the **for** loop's test expression. Since **Length** is a property, querying the length actually represents a method call. However, the JIT compiler knows that **Length** is a property on the **Array** class, and the JIT compiler will actually generate code that calls the property just once and stores the result in a temporary variable that will be checked with each iteration of the loop. The result is that the JITted code is fast. In fact, some developers have underestimated the abilities of the JIT compiler and have tried to write "clever code" in an attempt to help the JIT compiler. However, any clever attempts that you come up with will almost certainly impact performance negatively and make your code harder to read, reducing its maintainability. You are better off leaving the call to the array's **Length** property in the code above instead of attempting to cache it in a local variable yourself.

The second thing to notice about the code above is that the JIT compiler knows that the **for** loop is accessing array elements 0 through **Length - 1**. So the JIT compiler produces code that, at runtime, tests that all array accesses will be within the array's valid range. Specifically, the JIT compiler produces code to check if **(0 >= a.GetLowerBound(0)) && ((Length - 1) <= a.GetUpperBound(0))**. This check occurs just before the loop. If the check is good, the JIT compiler will not generate code inside the loop to verify that each array access is within the valid range. This allows array access within the loop to be very fast.

Unfortunately, as I alluded to earlier in this chapter, accessing elements of a non-zero–based single-dimensional array or of a multi-dimensional array is much slower than a single-dimensional, zero-based array. For these array types, the JIT compiler doesn't hoist index checking outside of loops, so each array access validates the specified indices. In addition, the JIT compiler adds code to subtract the array's lower bounds from the specified index, which also slows the code down, even if you're using a multi-dimensional array that happens to be zero-based.

So if performance is a concern to you, you might want to consider using an array of arrays (a jagged array) instead of a rectangular array. C# and the CLR also allow you to access an array by using unsafe (non-verifiable) code, which is, in effect, a technique that allows you to turn off the index bounds checking when accessing an array. Note that this unsafe array manipulation technique is usable with arrays whose elements are **SByte**, **Byte**, **Int16**, **UInt16**, **Int32**, **UInt32**, **Int64**, **UInt64**, **Char**, **Single**, **Double**, **Decimal**, **Boolean**, an enumerated type, or a value type structure whose fields are any of the aforementioned types.

This is a very powerful feature that should be used with extreme caution because it allows you to perform direct memory accesses. If these memory accesses are outside the bounds of the array, an exception will not be thrown; instead, you will be corrupting memory, violating type safety, and possibly opening a security hole! For this reason, the assembly containing the unsafe code must either be granted full trust or at least have the Security Permission with Skip Verification turned on.

The following C# code demonstrates three techniques (safe, jagged, and unsafe), for accessing a two-dimensional array:

```
using System;
using System.Diagnostics;

public static class Program {
    private const Int32 c_numElements = 10000;

    public static void Main() {
        const Int32 testCount = 10;
        Stopwatch sw;

        // Declare a two-dimensional array
        Int32[,] a2Dim = new Int32[c_numElements, c_numElements];

        // Declare a two-dimensional array as a jagged array (a vector of vectors)
        Int32[][] aJagged = new Int32[c_numElements][];
        for (Int32 x = 0; x < c_numElements; x++)
            aJagged[x] = new Int32[c_numElements];


        // 1: Access all elements of the array using the usual, safe technique
        sw = Stopwatch.StartNew();
        for (Int32 test = 0; test < testCount; test++)
            Safe2DimArrayAccess(a2Dim);
        Console.WriteLine("{0}: Safe2DimArrayAccess", sw.Elapsed);

        // 2: Access all elements of the array using the jagged array technique
        sw = Stopwatch.StartNew();
        for (Int32 test = 0; test < testCount; test++)
            SafeJaggedArrayAccess(aJagged);
        Console.WriteLine("{0}: SafeJaggedArrayAccess", sw.Elapsed);

        // 3: Access all elements of the array using the unsafe technique
        sw = Stopwatch.StartNew();
        for (Int32 test = 0; test < testCount; test++)
            Unsafe2DimArrayAccess(a2Dim);
        Console.WriteLine("{0}: Unsafe2DimArrayAccess", sw.Elapsed);
        Console.ReadLine();
    }

    private static Int32 Safe2DimArrayAccess(Int32[,] a) {
        Int32 sum = 0;
        for (Int32 x = 0; x < c_numElements; x++) {
            for (Int32 y = 0; y < c_numElements; y++) {
```

```
                sum += a[x, y];
            }
        }
        return sum;
    }

    private static Int32 SafeJaggedArrayAccess(Int32[][] a) {
        Int32 sum = 0;
        for (Int32 x = 0; x < c_numElements; x++) {
            for (Int32 y = 0; y < c_numElements; y++) {
                sum += a[x][y];
            }
        }
        return sum;
    }

    private static unsafe Int32 Unsafe2DimArrayAccess(Int32[,] a) {
        Int32 sum = 0;
        fixed (Int32* pi = a) {
            for (Int32 x = 0; x < c_numElements; x++) {
                Int32 baseOfDim = x * c_numElements;
                for (Int32 y = 0; y < c_numElements; y++) {
                    sum += pi[baseOfDim + y];
                }
            }
        }
        return sum;
    }
}
```

The **Unsafe2DimArrayAccess** method is marked with the **unsafe** modifier, which is required to use C#'s **fixed** statement. To compile this code, you'll have to specify the **/unsafe** switch when invoking the C# compiler or check the "Allow Unsafe Code" check box on the Build tab of the Project Properties pane in Microsoft Visual Studio.

When I run this program on my machine, I get the following output:

```
00:00:02.0017692: Safe2DimArrayAccess
00:00:01.5197844: SafeJaggedArrayAccess
00:00:01.7343436: Unsafe2DimArrayAccess
```

As you can see, the safe two-dimensional array access technique is the slowest. The safe jagged array access technique takes a little less time to complete than the safe two-dimensional array access technique. However, you should note that creating the jagged array is more time-consuming than creating the multi-dimensional array because creating the jagged array requires an object to be allocated on the heap for each dimension, causing the garbage collector to kick in periodically. So there is a trade-off: If you need to create a lot of "multi-dimensional arrays" and you intend to access the elements infrequently, it is quicker to create a multi-dimensional array. If you need to create the "multi-dimensional array" just once, and you access its elements frequently, a jagged array will give you better performance. Certainly, in most applications, the latter scenario is more common.

Finally, notice that the unsafe two-dimensional array access technique is about as fast as the safe two-dimensional array access technique, but it would be considered the fastest of them all if you also took into account that it accesses a single two-dimensional array (which is one memory allocation), as compared to creating the jagged array (which requires many memory allocations). Obviously, the unsafe technique has a time and place when it can best be used by your own code, but beware that there are three serious downsides to using this technique:

- The code that manipulates the array elements is more complicated to read and write than that which manipulates the elements using the other techniques because you are using C#'s **fixed** statement and performing memory-address calculations.

- If you make a mistake in the calculation, you are accessing memory that is not part of the array. This can result in an incorrect calculation, corruption of memory, a type-safety violation, and a potential security hole.

- Due to the potential problems, the CLR forbids unsafe code from running in reduced-security environments (like Microsoft Silverlight).

Unsafe Array Access and Fixed-Size Array

Unsafe array access is very powerful because it allows you to access:

- Elements within a managed array object that resides on the heap (as the previous section demonstrated).

- Elements within an array that resides on an unmanaged heap. The **SecureString** example in Chapter 14, "Chars, Strings, and Working with Text," demonstrated using unsafe array access on an array returned from calling the **System.Runtime. InteropServices.Marshal** class's **SecureStringToCoTaskMemUnicode** method.

- Elements within an array that resides on the thread's stack.

In cases in which performance is extremely critical, you could avoid allocating a managed array object on the heap and instead allocate the array on the thread's stack by using C#'s **stackalloc** statement (which works a lot like C's **alloca** function). The **stackalloc** statement can be used to create a single-dimensional, zero-based array of value type elements only, and the value type must not contain any reference type fields. Really, you should think of this as allocating a block of memory that you can manipulate by using unsafe pointers, and therefore, you cannot pass the address of this memory buffer to the vast majority of FCL methods. Of course, the stack-allocated memory (array) will automatically be freed when the method returns; this is where we get the performance improvement. Using this feature also requires you specify the **/unsafe** switch to the C# compiler.

The **StackallocDemo** method in the code below shows an example of how to use C#'s **stackalloc** statement:

```
using System;

public static class Program {
    public static void Main() {
        StackallocDemo();
        InlineArrayDemo();
    }

    private static void StackallocDemo() {
        unsafe {
            const Int32 width = 20;
            Char* pc = stackalloc Char[width]; // Allocates array on stack

            String s = "Jeffrey Richter";      // 15 characters

            for (Int32 index = 0; index < width; index++) {
                pc[width - index - 1] =
                    (index < s.Length) ? s[index] : '.';
            }

            // The line below displays ".....rethciR yerffeJ"
            Console.WriteLine(new String(pc, 0, width));
        }
    }

    private static void InlineArrayDemo() {
        unsafe {
            CharArray ca;                      // Allocates array on stack
            Int32 widthInBytes = sizeof(CharArray);
            Int32 width = widthInBytes / 2;

            String s = "Jeffrey Richter"; // 15 characters

            for (Int32 index = 0; index < width; index++) {
                ca.Characters[width - index - 1] =
                    (index < s.Length) ? s[index] : '.';
            }

            // The line below displays ".....rethciR yerffeJ"
            Console.WriteLine(new String(ca.Characters, 0, width));
        }
    }
}

internal unsafe struct CharArray {
    // This array is embedded inline inside the structure
    public fixed Char Characters[20];
}
```

Normally, because arrays are reference types, an array field defined in a structure is really just a pointer or reference to an array; the array itself lives outside of the structure's memory. However, it is possible to embed an array directly inside a structure as shown by the **CharArray** structure in the preceding code. To embed an array directly inside a structure, there are several requirements:

- The type must be a structure (value type); you cannot embed an array inside a class (reference type).

- The field or its defining structure must be marked with the **unsafe** keyword.

- The array field must be marked with the **fixed** keyword.

- The array must be single-dimensional and zero-based.

- The array's element type must be one of the following types: **Boolean**, **Char**, **SByte**, **Byte**, **Int32**, **UInt32**, **Int64**, **UInt64**, **Single**, or **Double**.

Inline arrays are typically used for scenarios that involve interoperating with unmanaged code where the unmanaged data structure also has an inline array. However, inline arrays can be used in other scenarios as well. The **InlineArrayDemo** method in the code shown earlier offers an example of how to use an inline array. The **InlineArrayDemo** method performs the same function as the **StackallocDemo** method; it just does it in a different way.

Chapter 17
Delegates

In this chapter, I talk about callback functions. Callback functions are an extremely useful programming mechanism that has been around for years. The Microsoft .NET Framework exposes a callback function mechanism by using *delegates*. Unlike callback mechanisms used in other platforms, such as unmanaged C++, delegates offer much more functionality. For example, delegates ensure that the callback method is type-safe, in keeping with one of the most important goals of the common language runtime (CLR). Delegates also integrate the ability to call multiple methods sequentially and support the calling of static methods as well as instance methods.

A First Look at Delegates

The C runtime's **qsort** function takes a pointer to a callback function to sort elements within an array. In Microsoft Windows, callback functions are required for window procedures, hook procedures, asynchronous procedure calls, and more. In the .NET Framework, callback methods are used for a whole slew of things. For example, you can register callback methods to get a variety of notifications such as unhandled exceptions, window state changes, menu item selections, file system changes, form control events, and completed asynchronous operations.

In unmanaged C/C++, the address of a non-member function is just a memory address. This address doesn't carry any additional information such as the number of parameters the function expects, the types of these parameters, the function's return value type, and the function's calling convention. In short, unmanaged C/C++ callback functions are not type-safe (although they are a very lightweight mechanism).

In the .NET Framework, callback functions are just as useful and pervasive as in unmanaged Windows programming. However, the .NET Framework provides a type-safe mechanism called *delegates*. I'll start off the discussion of delegates by showing you how to use them. The following code demonstrates how to declare, create, and use delegates.

```
using System;
using System.Windows.Forms;
using System.IO;


// Declare a delegate type; instances refer to a method that
// takes an Int32 parameter and returns void.
internal delegate void Feedback(Int32 value);


public sealed class Program {
   public static void Main() {
      StaticDelegateDemo();
      InstanceDelegateDemo();
      ChainDelegateDemo1(new Program());
      ChainDelegateDemo2(new Program());
   }

   private static void StaticDelegateDemo() {
      Console.WriteLine("----- Static Delegate Demo -----");
      Counter(1, 3, null);
      Counter(1, 3, new Feedback(Program.FeedbackToConsole));
      Counter(1, 3, new Feedback(FeedbackToMsgBox)); // "Program." is optional
      Console.WriteLine();
   }

   private static void InstanceDelegateDemo() {
      Console.WriteLine("----- Instance Delegate Demo -----");
      Program p = new Program();
      Counter(1, 3, new Feedback(p.FeedbackToFile));

      Console.WriteLine();
   }

   private static void ChainDelegateDemo1(Program p) {
      Console.WriteLine("----- Chain Delegate Demo 1 -----");
      Feedback fb1 = new Feedback(FeedbackToConsole);
      Feedback fb2 = new Feedback(FeedbackToMsgBox);
      Feedback fb3 = new Feedback(p.FeedbackToFile);

      Feedback fbChain = null;
      fbChain = (Feedback) Delegate.Combine(fbChain, fb1);
      fbChain = (Feedback) Delegate.Combine(fbChain, fb2);
      fbChain = (Feedback) Delegate.Combine(fbChain, fb3);
      Counter(1, 2, fbChain);

      Console.WriteLine();
      fbChain = (Feedback)
         Delegate.Remove(fbChain, new Feedback(FeedbackToMsgBox));
      Counter(1, 2, fbChain);
   }
```

```
    private static void ChainDelegateDemo2(Program p) {
        Console.WriteLine("----- Chain Delegate Demo 2 -----");
        Feedback fb1 = new Feedback(FeedbackToConsole);
        Feedback fb2 = new Feedback(FeedbackToMsgBox);
        Feedback fb3 = new Feedback(p.FeedbackToFile);

        Feedback fbChain = null;
        fbChain += fb1;
        fbChain += fb2;
        fbChain += fb3;
        Counter(1, 2, fbChain);

        Console.WriteLine();
        fbChain -= new Feedback(FeedbackToMsgBox);
        Counter(1, 2, fbChain);
    }

    private static void Counter(Int32 from, Int32 to, Feedback fb) {
        for (Int32 val = from; val <= to; val++) {
            // If any callbacks are specified, call them
            if (fb != null)
                fb(val);
        }
    }

    private static void FeedbackToConsole(Int32 value) {
        Console.WriteLine("Item=" + value);
    }

    private static void FeedbackToMsgBox(Int32 value) {
        MessageBox.Show("Item=" + value);
    }

    private void FeedbackToFile(Int32 value) {
        StreamWriter sw = new StreamWriter("Status", true);
        sw.WriteLine("Item=" + value);
        sw.Close();
    }
}
```

Now I'll describe what this code is doing. At the top, notice the declaration of the internal delegate, **Feedback**. A delegate indicates the signature of a callback method. In this example, a **Feedback** delegate identifies a method that takes one parameter (an **Int32**) and returns **void**. In a way, a delegate is very much like an unmanaged C/C++ **typedef** that represents the address of a function.

The **Program** class defines a private, static method named **Counter**. This method counts integers from the **from** argument to the **to** argument. The **Counter** method also takes an **fb**, which is a reference to a **Feedback** delegate object. **Counter** iterates through all of the integers, and for each integer, if the **fb** variable is not **null**, the callback method (specified by the **fb** variable) is called. This callback method is passed the value of the item being processed, the item number. The callback method can be designed and implemented to process each item in any manner deemed appropriate.

Using Delegates to Call Back Static Methods

Now that you understand how the **Counter** method is designed and how it works, let's see how to use delegates to call back static methods. The **StaticDelegateDemo** method that appears in the previous code sample is the focus of this section.

The **StaticDelegateDemo** method calls the **Counter** method, passing **null** in the third parameter, which corresponds to **Counter**'s **fb** parameter. Because **Counter**'s **fb** parameter receives **null**, each item is processed without calling any callback method.

Next, the **StaticDelegateDemo** method calls **Counter** a second time, passing a newly constructed **Feedback** delegate object in the third parameter of the method call. This delegate object is a wrapper around a method, allowing the method to be called back indirectly via the wrapper. In this example, the name of the static method, **Program.FeedbackToConsole**, is passed to the **Feedback** type's constructor, indicating that it is the method to be wrapped. The reference returned from the **new** operator is passed to **Counter** as its third parameter. Now when **Counter** executes, it will call the **Program** type's static **FeedbackToConsole** method for each item in the series. **FeedbackToConsole** simply writes a string to the console indicating the item being processed.

> **Note** The **FeedbackToConsole** method is defined as **private** inside the **Program** type, but the **Counter** method is able to call **Program**'s private method. In this case, you might not expect a problem because both **Counter** and **FeedbackToConsole** are defined in the same type. However, this code would work just fine even if the **Counter** method was defined in another type. In short, it is not a security or accessibility violation for one type to have code that calls another type's private member via a delegate as long as the delegate object is created by code that has ample security/accessibility.

The third call to **Counter** in the **StaticDelegateDemo** method is almost identical to the second call. The only difference is that the **Feedback** delegate object wraps the static **Program.FeedbackToMsgBox** method. **FeedbackToMsgBox** builds a string indicating the item being processed. This string is then displayed in a message box.

Everything in this example is type-safe. For instance, when constructing a **Feedback** delegate object, the compiler ensures that the signatures of **Program**'s **FeedbackToConsole** and **FeedbackToMsgBox** methods are compatible with the signature defined by the **Feedback** delegate. Specifically, both methods must take one argument (an **Int32**), and both methods must have the same return type (**void**). If **FeedbackToConsole** had been defined like this:

```
private static Boolean FeedbackToConsole(String value) {
    ...
}
```

the C# compiler wouldn't compile the code and would issue the following error: "**error CS0123: No overload for 'FeedbackToConsole' matches delegate 'Feedback'.**"

Both C# and the CLR allow for covariance and contra-variance of reference types when binding a method to a delegate. *Covariance* means that a method can return a type that is derived from the delegate's return type. *Contra-variance* means that a method can take a parameter that is a base of the delegate's parameter type. For example, given a delegate defined like this:

```
delegate Object MyCallback(FileStream s);
```

it is possible to construct an instance of this delegate type bound to a method that is prototyped like this:

```
String SomeMethod(Stream s);
```

Here, **SomeMethod**'s return type (**String**) is a type that is derived from the delegate's return type (**Object**); this covariance is allowed. **SomeMethod**'s parameter type (**Stream**) is a type that is a base class of the delegate's parameter type (**FileStream**); this contra-variance is allowed.

Note that covariance and contra-variance are supported only for reference types, not for value types or for **void**. So, for example, I cannot bind the following method to the **MyCallback** delegate:

```
Int32 SomeOtherMethod(Stream s);
```

Even though **SomeOtherMethod**'s return type (**Int32**) is derived from **MyCallback**'s return type (**Object**), this form of covariance is not allowed because **Int32** is a value type. Obviously, the reason why value types and **void** cannot be used for covariance and contra-variance is because the memory structure for these things varies, whereas the memory structure for reference types is always a pointer. Fortunately, the C# compiler will produce an error if you attempt to do something that is not supported.

Using Delegates to Call Back Instance Methods

I just explained how delegates can be used to call static methods, but they can also be used to call instance methods for a specific object. To understand how calling back an instance method works, look at the **InstanceDelegateDemo** method that appears in the code shown at the beginning of this chapter.

Notice that a **Program** object named **p** is constructed in the **InstanceDelegateDemo** method. This **Program** object doesn't have any instance fields or properties associated with it; I created it merely for demonstration purposes. When the new **Feedback** delegate object is constructed in the call to the **Counter** method, its constructor is passed **p.FeedbackToFile**. This causes the delegate to wrap a reference to the **FeedbackToFile** method, which is an instance method (not a static method). When **Counter** calls the callback method identified by its **fb** argument, the **FeedbackToFile** instance method is called, and the address of the recently constructed object **p** will be passed as the implicit **this** argument to the instance method.

The **FeedbackToFile** method works as the **FeedbackToConsole** and **FeedbackToMsgBox** methods, except that it opens a file and appends the string to the end of the file. (The Status file that the method creates can be found in the application's AppBase directory.)

Again, the purpose of this example is to demonstrate that delegates can wrap calls to instance methods as well as static methods. For instance methods, the delegate needs to know the instance of the object the method is going to operate on. Wrapping an instance method is useful because code inside the object can access the object's instance members. This means that the object can have some state that can be used while the callback method is doing its processing.

Demystifying Delegates

On the surface, delegates seem easy to use: you define them by using C#'s **delegate** keyword, you construct instances of them by using the familiar **new** operator, and you invoke the callback by using the familiar method-call syntax (except instead of a method name, you use the variable that refers to the delegate object).

However, what's really going on is quite a bit more complex than what the earlier examples illustrate. The compilers and the CLR do a lot of behind-the-scenes processing to hide the complexity. In this section, I'll focus on how the compiler and the CLR work together to implement delegates. Having this knowledge will improve your understanding of delegates and will teach you how to use them efficiently and effectively. I'll also touch on some additional features delegates make available.

Let's start by reexamining this line of code:

```
internal delegate void Feedback(Int32 value);
```

When it sees this line, the compiler actually defines a complete class that looks something like this:

```
internal class Feedback : System.MulticastDelegate {
   // Constructor
   public Feedback(Object object, IntPtr method);

   // Method with same prototype as specified by the source code
   public virtual void Invoke(Int32 value);

   // Methods allowing the callback to be called asynchronously
   public virtual IAsyncResult BeginInvoke(Int32 value,
      AsyncCallback callback, Object object);
   public virtual void EndInvoke(IAsyncResult result);
}
```

The class defined by the compiler has four methods: a constructor, **Invoke**, **BeginInvoke**, and **EndInvoke**. In this chapter, I'll concentrate on the constructor and **Invoke** methods. I'll address the **BeginInvoke** and **EndInvoke** methods in Chapter 27, "I/O-Bound Asynchronous Operations," in the "The APM and Compute-Bound Operations" section.

In fact, you can verify that the compiler did indeed generate this class automatically by examining the resulting assembly with ILDasm.exe, as shown in Figure 17-1.

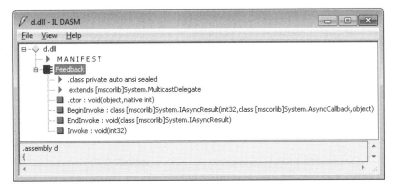

FIGURE 17-1 ILDasm.exe showing the metadata produced by the compiler for the delegate

In this example, the compiler has defined a class called **Feedback** that is derived from the **System.MulticastDelegate** type defined in the Framework Class Library (FCL). (All delegate types are derived from **MulticastDelegate**.)

> **Important** The **System.MulticastDelegate** class is derived from **System.Delegate**, which is itself derived from **System.Object**. The reason why there are two delegate classes is historical and unfortunate; there should be just one delegate class in the FCL. Sadly, you need to be aware of both of these classes because even though all delegate types you create have **MulticastDelegate** as a base class, you'll occasionally manipulate your delegate types by using methods defined by the **Delegate** class instead of the **MulticastDelegate** class. For example, the **Delegate** class has static methods called **Combine** and **Remove**. (I explain what these methods do later.) The signatures for both of these methods indicate that they take **Delegate** parameters. Because your delegate type is derived from **MulticastDelegate**, which is derived from **Delegate**, instances of your delegate type can be passed to these methods.

The class has private visibility because the delegate is declared as `internal` in the source code. If the source code had indicated `public` visibility, the **Feedback** class the compiler generated would also be public. You should be aware that delegate types can be defined within a type (nested within another type) or at global scope. Basically, because delegates are classes, a delegate can be defined anywhere a class can be defined.

Because all delegate types are derived from **MulticastDelegate**, they inherit **MulticastDelegate**'s fields, properties, and methods. Of all of these members, three non-public fields are probably most significant. Table 17-1 describes these significant fields.

TABLE 17-1 `MulticastDelegate`'s Significant Non-Public Fields

Field	Type	Description
_target	System.Object	When the delegate object wraps a static method, this field is **null**. When the delegate objects wraps an instance method, this field refers to the object that should be operated on when the callback method is called. In other words, this field indicates the value that should be passed for the instance method's implicit **this** parameter.
_methodPtr	System.IntPtr	An internal integer the CLR uses to identify the method that is to be called back.
_invocationList	System.Object	This field is usually **null**. It can refer to an array of delegates when building a delegate chain (discussed later in this chapter).

Notice that all delegates have a constructor that takes two parameters: a reference to an object and an integer that refers to the callback method. However, if you examine the source code, you'll see that I'm passing in values such as **Program.FeedbackToConsole** or **p.FeedbackToFile**. Everything you've learned about programming tells you that this code shouldn't compile!

However, the C# compiler knows that a delegate is being constructed and parses the source code to determine which object and method are being referred to. A reference to the object is passed for the constructor's **object** parameter, and a special **IntPtr** value (obtained from a **MethodDef** or **MemberRef** metadata token) that identifies the method is passed for the **method** parameter. For static methods, **null** is passed for the **object** parameter. Inside the constructor, these two arguments are saved in the **_target** and **_methodPtr** private fields, respectively. In addition, the constructor sets the **_invocationList** field to **null**. I'll postpone discussing this **_invocationList** field until the next section, "Using Delegates to Call Back Many Methods (Chaining)."

So each delegate object is really a wrapper around a method and an object to be operated on when the method is called. So if I have two lines of code that look like this:

```
Feedback fbStatic   = new Feedback(Program.FeedbackToConsole);
Feedback fbInstance = new Feedback(new Program().FeedbackToFile);
```

the **fbStatic** and **fbInstance** variables refer to two separate **Feedback** delegate objects that are initialized, as shown in Figure 17-2.

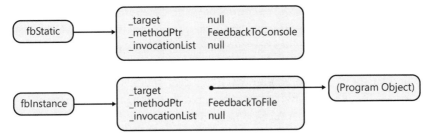

FIGURE 17-2 A variable that refers to a delegate to a static method and a variable that refers to a delegate to an instance method

The **Delegate** class defines two read-only public instance properties: **Target** and **Method**. Given a reference to a delegate object, you can query these properties. The **Target** property returns a reference to the object that will be operated on if the method is called back. Basically, the **Target** property returns the value stored in the private **_target** field. If the delegate object wraps a static method, **Target** returns **null**. The **Method** property returns a reference to a **System.Reflection.MethodInfo** object that identifies the callback method. Basically, the **Method** property has an internal mechanism that converts the value in the private **_methodPtr** field to a **MethodInfo** object and returns it.

You could use this information in several ways. For example, you could check to see if a delegate object refers to an instance method of a specific type:

```
Boolean DelegateRefersToInstanceMethodOfType(MulticastDelegate d, Type type) {
   return((d.Target != null) && d.Target.GetType() == type);
}
```

You could also write code to check if the callback method has a specific name (such as **FeedbackToMsgBox**):

```
Boolean DelegateRefersToMethodOfName(MulticastDelegate d, String methodName) {
   return(d.Method.Name == methodName);
}
```

There are many other potential uses of these properties.

Now that you know how delegate objects are constructed and what their internal structure looks like, let's talk about how the callback method is invoked. For convenience, I've repeated the code for the **Counter** method here:

```
private static void Counter(Int32 from, Int32 to, Feedback fb) {
   for (Int32 val = from; val <= to; val++) {
      // If any callbacks are specified, call them
      if (fb != null)
         fb(val);
   }
}
```

Look at the line of code just below the comment. The **if** statement first checks to see if **fb** is not **null**. If **fb** is not **null**, on the next line, you see the code that invokes the callback method. The **null** check is required because **fb** is really just a variable that *can* refer to a **Feedback** delegate object; it could also be **null**. It might seem as if I'm calling a function named **fb** and passing it one parameter (**val**). However, there is no function called **fb**. Again, because it knows that **fb** is a variable that refers to a delegate object, the compiler generates code to call the delegate object's **Invoke** method. In other words, the compiler sees this:

```
fb(val);
```

But the compiler generates code as though the source code said this:

```
fb.Invoke(val);
```

You can verify that the compiler produces code to call the delegate type's **Invoke** method by using ILDasm.exe to examine the Intermediate Language (IL) code created for the **Counter** method. Here is the IL for the **Counter** method. The instruction at IL_0009 in the figure indicates the call to **Feedback**'s **Invoke** method.

```
.method private hidebysig static void  Counter(int32 from,
                                               int32 'to',
                                               class Feedback fb) cil managed
{
  // Code size       23 (0x17)
  .maxstack  2
  .locals init (int32 V_0)
  IL_0000:  ldarg.0
  IL_0001:  stloc.0
  IL_0002:  br.s       IL_0012
  IL_0004:  ldarg.2
  IL_0005:  brfalse.s  IL_000e
  IL_0007:  ldarg.2
  IL_0008:  ldloc.0
  IL_0009:  callvirt   instance void Feedback::Invoke(int32)
  IL_000e:  ldloc.0
  IL_000f:  ldc.i4.1
  IL_0010:  add
  IL_0011:  stloc.0
  IL_0012:  ldloc.0
  IL_0013:  ldarg.1
  IL_0014:  ble.s      IL_0004
  IL_0016:  ret
} // end of method Program::Counter
```

In fact, you could modify the **Counter** method to call **Invoke** explicitly, as shown here:

```
private static void Counter(Int32 from, Int32 to, Feedback fb) {
   for (Int32 val = from; val <= to; val++) {
      // If any callbacks are specified, call them
      if (fb != null)
         fb.Invoke(val);
   }
}
```

You'll recall that the compiler defined the **Invoke** method when it defined the **Feedback** class. When **Invoke** is called, it uses the private **_target** and **_methodPtr** fields to call the desired method on the specified object. Note that the signature of the **Invoke** method matches the signature of the delegate; because the **Feedback** delegate takes one **Int32** parameter and returns **void**, the **Invoke** method (as produced by the compiler) takes one **Int32** parameter and returns **void**.

Using Delegates to Call Back Many Methods (Chaining)

By themselves, delegates are incredibly useful. But add in their support for chaining, and delegates become even more useful. *Chaining* is a set or collection of delegate objects, and it provides the ability to invoke, or call, all of the methods represented by the delegates in the set. To understand this, see the **ChainDelegateDemo1** method that appears in the code shown at the beginning of this chapter. In this method, after the **Console.WriteLine** statement, I construct three delegate objects and have variables—**fb1**, **fb2**, and **fb3**—refer to each object, as shown in Figure 17-3.

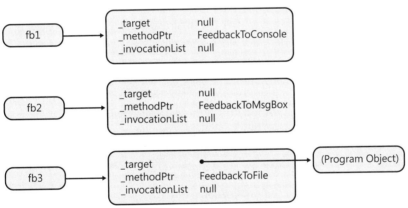

FIGURE 17-3 Initial state of the delegate objects referred to by the **fb1**, **fb2**, and **fb3** variables

The reference variable to a **Feedback** delegate object, **fbChain**, is intended to refer to a chain or set of delegate objects that wrap methods that can be called back. Initializing **fbChain** to **null** indicates that there currently are no methods to be called back. The **Delegate** class's public, static **Combine** method is used to add a delegate to the chain:

```
fbChain = (Feedback) Delegate.Combine(fbChain, fb1);
```

When this line of code executes, the **Combine** method sees that we are trying to combine **null** and **fb1**. Internally, **Combine** will simply return the value in **fb1**, and the **fbChain** variable will be set to refer to the same delegate object referred to by the **fb1** variable, as shown in Figure 17-4.

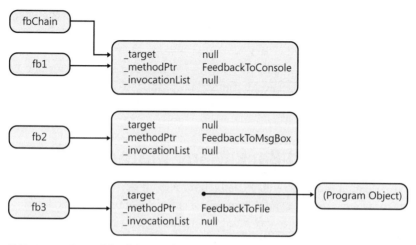

FIGURE 17-4 State of the delegate objects after inserting the first delegate in the chain

To add another delegate to the chain, the **Combine** method is called again:

```
fbChain = (Feedback) Delegate.Combine(fbChain, fb2);
```

Internally, the **Combine** method sees that **fbChain** already refers to a delegate object, so **Combine** will construct a new delegate object. This new delegate object initializes its private **_target** and **_methodPtr** fields to values that are not important for this discussion. However, what is important is that the **_invocationList** field is initialized to refer to an array of delegate objects. The first element of this array (index 0) will be initialized to refer to the delegate that wraps the **FeedbackToConsole** method (this is the delegate that **fbChain** currently refers to). The second element of the array (index 1) will be initialized to refer to the delegate that wraps the **FeedbackToMsgBox** method (this is the delegate that **fb2** refers to). Finally, **fbChain** will be set to refer to the newly created delegate object, shown in Figure 17-5.

To add the third delegate to the chain, the **Combine** method is called once again:

```
fbChain = (Feedback) Delegate.Combine(fbChain, fb3);
```

Again, **Combine** sees that **fbChain** already refers to a delegate object, and this causes a new delegate object to be constructed, as shown in Figure 17-6. As before, this new delegate object initializes the private **_target** and **_methodPtr** fields to values unimportant to this discussion, and the **_invocationList** field is initialized to refer to an array of delegate objects. The first and second elements of this array (indexes 0 and 1) will be initialized to refer to the same delegates the previous delegate object referred to in its array. The third element of the array (index 2) will be initialized to refer to the delegate that wraps the **FeedbackToFile** method (this is the delegate that **fb3** refers to). Finally, **fbChain** will be set to refer to this newly created delegate object. Note that the previously created delegate and the array referred to by its **_invocationList** field are now candidates for garbage collection.

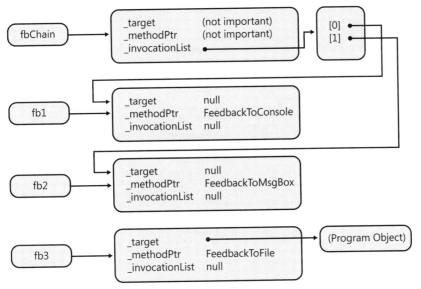

FIGURE 17-5 State of the delegate objects after inserting the second delegate in the chain

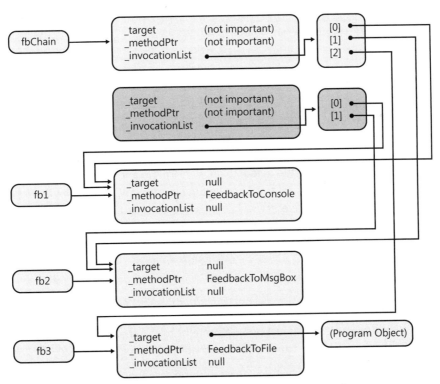

FIGURE 17-6 Final state of the delegate objects when the chain is complete

After all of the code has executed to set up the chain, the **fbChain** variable is then passed to the **Counter** method:

```
Counter(1, 2, fbChain);
```

Inside the **Counter** method is the code that implicitly calls the **Invoke** method on the **Feedback** delegate object as I detailed earlier. When **Invoke** is called on the delegate referred to by **fbChain**, the delegate sees that the private **_invocationList** field is not **null**, causing it to execute a loop that iterates through all of the elements in the array, calling the method wrapped by each delegate. In this example, **FeedbackToConsole** will get called first, followed by **FeedbackToMsgBox**, followed by **FeedbackToFile**.

Feedback's **Invoke** method is essentially implemented something like this (in pseudocode):

```
public void Invoke(Int32 value) {
   Delegate[] delegateSet = _invocationList as Delegate[];
   if (delegateSet != null) {
      // This delegate's array indicates the delegates that should be called
      foreach (Feedback d in delegateSet)
         d(value);   // Call each delegate
   } else {
      // This delegate identifies a single method to be called back
      // Call the callback method on the specified target object.
      _methodPtr.Invoke(_target, value);
      // The line above is an approximation of the actual code.
      // What really happens cannot be expressed in C#.
   }
}
```

Note that it is also possible to remove a delegate from a chain by calling **Delegate**'s public, static **Remove** method. This is demonstrated toward the end of the **ChainDelegateDemo1** method:

```
fbChain = (Feedback) Delegate.Remove(fbChain, new Feedback(FeedbackToMsgBox));
```

When **Remove** is called, it scans the delegate array (from the end toward index 0) maintained inside the delegate object referred to by the first parameter (**fbChain**, in my example). **Remove** is looking for a delegate entry whose **_target** and **_methodPtr** fields match those in the second argument (the new **Feedback** delegate, in my example). If a match is found and there is only one item left in the array, that array item is returned. If a match is found and there are multiple items left in the array, a new delegate object is constructed—the **_invocationList** array created and initialized will refer to all items in the original array except for the item being removed, of course—and a reference to this new delegate object is returned. If you are removing the only element in the chain, **Remove** returns **null**. Note that each call to **Remove** removes just one delegate from the chain; it does not remove all delegates that have matching **_target** and **_methodPtr** fields.

So far, I've shown examples in which my delegate type, **Feedback**, is defined as having a **void** return value. However, I could have defined my **Feedback** delegate as follows:

```
public delegate Int32 Feedback(Int32 value);
```

If I had, its **Invoke** method would have internally looked like this (again, in pseudocode):

```
public Int32 Invoke(Int32 value) {
   Int32 result;
   Delegate[] delegateSet = _invocationList as Delegate[];
   if (delegateSet != null) {
      // This delegate's array indicates the delegates that should be called
      foreach (Feedback d in delegateSet)
         result = d(value);   // Call each delegate
   } else {
      // This delegate identifies a single method to be called back
      // Call the callback method on the specified target object.
      result = _methodPtr.Invoke(_target, value);
      // The line above is an approximation of the actual code.
      // What really happens cannot be expressed in C#.
   }
   return result;
}
```

As each delegate in the array is called, its return value is saved in the result variable. When the loop is complete, the **result** variable will contain only the result of the last delegate called (previous return values are discarded); this value is returned to the code that called **Invoke**.

C#'s Support for Delegate Chains

To make things easier for C# developers, the C# compiler automatically provides overloads of the += and -= operators for instances of delegate types. These operators call **Delegate.Combine** and **Delegate.Remove**, respectively. Using these operators simplifies the building of delegate chains. The **ChainDelegateDemo1** and **ChainDelegateDemo2** methods in the source code shown at the beginning of this chapter produce absolutely identical IL code. The only difference between the methods is that the **ChainDelegateDemo2** method simplifies the source code by taking advantage of C#'s += and -= operators.

If you require proof that the resulting IL code is identical for the two methods, you can build the code and look at its IL for both methods by using ILDasm.exe. This will confirm that the C# compiler did in fact replace all += and -= operators with calls to the **Delegate** type's public static **Combine** and **Remove** methods, respectively.

Having More Control over Delegate Chain Invocation

At this point, you understand how to build a chain of delegate objects and how to invoke all of the objects in that chain. All items in the chain are invoked because the delegate type's **Invoke** method includes code to iterate through all of the items in the array, invoking each item. This is obviously a very simple algorithm. And although this simple algorithm is good enough for a lot of scenarios, it has many limitations. For example, the return values of the callback methods are all discarded except for the last one. Using this simple algorithm, there's no way to get the return values for all of the callback methods called. But this isn't the only limitation. What happens if one of the invoked delegates throws an exception or blocks for a very long time? Because the algorithm invoked each delegate in the chain serially, a "problem" with one of the delegate objects stops all of the subsequent delegates in the chain from being called. Clearly, this algorithm isn't robust.

For those scenarios in which this algorithm is insufficient, the **MulticastDelegate** class offers an instance method, **GetInvocationList**, that you can use to call each delegate in a chain explicitly, using any algorithm that meets your needs:

```
public abstract class MulticastDelegate : Delegate {
   // Creates a delegate array where each element refers
   // to a delegate in the chain.
   public sealed override Delegate[] GetInvocationList();
}
```

The **GetInvocationList** method operates on a **MulticastDelegate**-derived object and returns an array of **Delegate** references where each reference points to one of the chain's delegate objects. Internally, **GetInvocationList** constructs an array and initializes it with each element referring to a delegate in the chain; a reference to the array is then returned. If the **_invocationList** field is **null**, the returned array contains one element that references the only delegate in the chain: the delegate instance itself.

You can easily write an algorithm that explicitly calls each object in the array. The following code demonstrates:

```
using System;
using System.Text;

// Define a Light component.
internal sealed class Light {
   // This method returns the light's status.
   public String SwitchPosition() {
      return "The light is off";
   }
}

// Define a Fan component.
internal sealed class Fan {
   // This method returns the fan's status.
   public String Speed() {
      throw new InvalidOperationException("The fan broke due to overheating");
   }
}

// Define a Speaker component.
internal sealed class Speaker {
   // This method returns the speaker's status.
   public String Volume() {
      return "The volume is loud";
   }
}
```

```csharp
public sealed class Program {

    // Definition of delegate that allows querying a component's status.
    private delegate String GetStatus();

    public static void Main() {
        // Declare an empty delegate chain.
        GetStatus getStatus = null;

        // Construct the three components, and add their status methods
        // to the delegate chain.
        getStatus += new GetStatus(new Light().SwitchPosition);
        getStatus += new GetStatus(new Fan().Speed);
        getStatus += new GetStatus(new Speaker().Volume);

        // Show consolidated status report reflecting
        // the condition of the three components.
        Console.WriteLine(GetComponentStatusReport(getStatus));
    }

    // Method that queries several components and returns a status report
    private static String GetComponentStatusReport(GetStatus status) {

        // If the chain is empty, there is nothing to do.
        if (status == null) return null;

        // Use this to build the status report.
        StringBuilder report = new StringBuilder();

        // Get an array where each element is a delegate from the chain.
        Delegate[] arrayOfDelegates = status.GetInvocationList();

        // Iterate over each delegate in the array.
        foreach (GetStatus getStatus in arrayOfDelegates) {

            try {
                // Get a component's status string, and append it to the report.
                report.AppendFormat("{0}{1}{1}", getStatus(), Environment.NewLine);
            }
            catch (InvalidOperationException e) {
                // Generate an error entry in the report for this component.
                Object component = getStatus.Target;
                report.AppendFormat(
                    "Failed to get status from {1}{2}{0}   Error: {3}{0}{0}",
                    Environment.NewLine,
                    ((component == null) ? "" : component.GetType() + "."),
                    getStatus.Method.Name,
                    e.Message);
            }
        }

        // Return the consolidated report to the caller.
        return report.ToString();
    }
}
```

When you build and run this code, the following output appears:

```
The light is off

Failed to get status from Fan.Speed
   Error: The fan broke due to overheating

The volume is loud
```

Enough with the Delegate Definitions Already (Generic Delegates)

Many years ago, when the .NET Framework was just starting to be developed, Microsoft introduced the notion of delegates. As programmers were adding classes to the FCL, they would define new delegate types any place they introduced a callback method. Over time, many, many delegates got defined. In fact, in MSCorLib.dll alone, close to 50 delegate types are now defined. Let's just look at a few of them:

```
public delegate void TryCode(Object userData);
public delegate void WaitCallback(Object state);
public delegate void TimerCallback(Object state);
public delegate void ContextCallback(Object state);
public delegate void SendOrPostCallback(Object state);
public delegate void ParameterizedThreadStart(Object obj);
```

Do you notice anything similar about the few delegate definitions that I selected? They are really all the same: a variable of any of these delegate types must refer to a method that takes an **Object** and returns **void**. There is really no reason to have all of these delegate types defined; there really just needs to be one.

In fact, now that the .NET Framework supports generics, we really just need a few generic delegates (defined in the **System** namespace) that represent methods that take up to 16 arguments:

```
public delegate void Action();    // OK, this one is not generic
public delegate void Action<T>(T obj);
public delegate void Action<T1, T2>(T1 arg1, T2 arg2);
public delegate void Action<T1, T2, T3>(T1 arg1, T2 arg2, T3 arg3);
...
public delegate void Action<T1, ..., T16>(T1 arg1, ..., T16 arg16);
```

So the .NET Framework now ships with 17 **Action** delegates that range from having no arguments to having 16 arguments. If you ever need to call a method that has more than 16 arguments, you will be forced to define your own delegate type, but this is very unlikely.

In addition to the **Action** delegates, the .NET Framework ships with 17 **Func** delegates, which allow the callback method to return a value:

```
public delegate TResult Func<TResult>();
public delegate TResult Func<T, TResult>(T arg);
public delegate TResult Func<T1, T2, TResult>(T1 arg1, T2 arg2);
public delegate TResult Func<T1, T2, T3, TResult>(T1 arg1, T2 arg2, T3 arg3);
...
public delegate TResult Func<T1,..., T16, TResult>(T1 arg1, ..., T16 arg16);
```

It is now recommended that these delegate types be used wherever possible instead of developers defining even more delegate types in their code. This reduces the number of types in the system and also simplifies coding. However, you might have to define your own delegate if you need to pass an argument by reference using the **ref** or **out** keyword:

```
delegate void Bar(ref Int32 z);
```

You may also have to do this if you want your delegate to take a variable number of arguments via C#'s **params** keyword, if you want to specify any default values for any of your delegate's arguments, or if you need to constrain a delegate's generic type argument, as in the following code:

```
delegate void EventHandler<TEventArgs>(Object sender, TEventArgs e)
   where TEventArgs : EventArgs;
```

> **Note** The **Action** and **Func** delegate types that take 0 to 8 arguments are defined in MSCorLib.dll since methods that take this many of arguments are fairly commonplace. However, the **Action** and **Func** delegate types that take 9 to 16 arguments are defined in System.Core.dll, as methods that take this many arguments are rare. And, in fact, these delegate definitions are mostly used internally by dynamic programming languages and are not generally used by developers directly.

When using delegates that take generic arguments and return values, contra-variance and covariance come into play, and it is recommended that you always take advantage of these features because they have no ill effects and enable your delegates to be used in more scenarios. For more information about this, see the "Delegate and Interface Contravariant and Covariant Generic Type Arguments" section in Chapter 12, "Generics."

C#'s Syntactical Sugar for Delegates

Most programmers find working with delegates to be cumbersome because the syntax is so strange. For example, take this line of code:

```
button1.Click += new EventHandler(button1_Click);
```

where **button1_Click** is a method that looks something like this:

```
void button1_Click(Object sender, EventArgs e) {
   // Do something, the button was clicked...
}
```

The idea behind the first line of code is to register the address of the **button1_Click** method with a button control so that when the button is clicked, the method will be called. To most programmers, it feels quite unnatural to construct an **EventHandler** delegate object just to specify the address of the **button1_Click** method. However, constructing the **EventHandler** delegate object is required for the CLR because this object provides a wrapper that ensures that the method can be called only in a type-safe fashion. The wrapper also allows the calling of instance methods and chaining. Unfortunately, most programmers don't want to think about these details. Programmers would prefer to write the code above as follows:

```
button1.Click += button1_Click;
```

Fortunately, Microsoft's C# compiler offers programmers some syntax shortcuts when working with delegates. I'll explain all of these shortcuts in this section. One last point before we begin: what I'm about to describe really boils down to C# syntactical sugar; these new syntax shortcuts are really just giving programmers an easier way to produce the IL that must be generated so that the CLR and other programming languages can work with delegates. This also means that what I'm about to describe is specific to C#; other compilers might not offer the additional delegate syntax shortcuts.

Syntactical Shortcut #1: No Need to Construct a Delegate Object

As demonstrated already, C# allows you to specify the name of a callback method without having to construct a delegate object wrapper. Here is another example:

```
internal sealed class AClass {
   public static void CallbackWithoutNewingADelegateObject() {
      ThreadPool.QueueUserWorkItem(SomeAsyncTask, 5);
   }

   private static void SomeAsyncTask(Object o) {
      Console.WriteLine(o);
   }
}
```

Here, the **ThreadPool** class's static **QueueUserWorkItem** method expects a reference to a **WaitCallback** delegate object that contains a reference to the **SomeAsyncTask** method. Since the C# compiler is capable of inferring this on its own, it allows me to omit code that constructs the **WaitCallback** delegate object, making the code much more readable and understandable. Of course, when the code is compiled, the C# compiler does produce IL that does, in fact, new up the **WaitCallback** delegate object—we just got a syntactical shortcut.

Syntactical Shortcut #2: No Need to Define a Callback Method

In the code above, the name of the callback method, **SomeAsyncTask**, is passed to the **ThreadPool**'s **QueueUserWorkItem** method. C# allows you to write the code for the callback method inline so it doesn't have to be written inside its very own method. For example, the code above could be rewritten as follows:

```
internal sealed class AClass {
    public static void CallbackWithoutNewingADelegateObject() {
        ThreadPool.QueueUserWorkItem( obj => Console.WriteLine(obj), 5);
    }
}
```

Notice that the first "argument" to the **QueueUserWorkItem** method is code (which I italicized)! More formally, the italicized code is called a C# *lambda expression,* and it is easy to detect due to the use of C#'s lambda expression operator: =>. You may use a lambda expression in your code where the compiler would normally expect to see a delegate. And, when the compiler sees the use of this lambda expression, the compiler automatically defines a new private method in the class (**AClass**, in this example). This new method is called an *anonymous function* because the compiler creates the name of the method for you automatically, and normally, you wouldn't know its name. However, you could use a tool such as ILDasm.exe to examine the compiler-generated code. After I wrote the code above and compiled it, I was able to see, by using ILDasm.exe, that the C# compiler decided to name this method **<CallbackWithoutNewingADelegateObject>b__0** and ensured that this method took a single **Object** argument and returned **void**.

The compiler chose to start the method name with a < sign because in C#, an identifier cannot contain a < sign; this ensures that you will not accidentally define a method that coincides with the name the compiler has chosen for you. Incidentally, while C# forbids identifiers to contain a < sign, the CLR allows it, and that is why this works. Also, note that while you could access the method via reflection by passing the method name as a string, the C# language specification states that there is no guarantee of how the compiler generates the name. For example, each time you compile the code, the compiler could produce a different name for the method.

Using ILDasm.exe, you might also notice that the C# compiler applies the **System.Runtime.CompilerServices.CompilerGeneratedAttribute** attribute to this method to indicate to various tools and utilities that this method was produced by a compiler as opposed to a programmer. The code to the right of the => operator is then placed in this compiler-generated method.

> **Note** When writing a lambda expression, there is no way to apply your own custom attribute to the compiler-generated method. Furthermore, you cannot apply any method modifiers (such as **unsafe**) to the method. But this is usually not a problem because anonymous methods generated by the compiler always end up being private, and the method is either static or nonstatic depending on whether the method accesses any instance members. So there is no need to apply modifiers such as **public**, **protected**, **internal**, **virtual**, **sealed**, **override**, or **abstract** to the method.

Finally, if you write the code shown above and compile it, it's as if the C# compiler rewrote your code to look like this (comments inserted by me):

```
internal sealed class AClass {
   // This private field is created to cache the delegate object.
   // Pro: CallbackWithoutNewingADelegateObject will not create
   //      a new object each time it is called.
   // Con: The cached object never gets garbage collected
   [CompilerGenerated]
   private static WaitCallback <>9__CachedAnonymousMethodDelegate1;

   public static void CallbackWithoutNewingADelegateObject() {
      if (<>9__CachedAnonymousMethodDelegate1 == null) {
         // First time called, create the delegate object and cache it.
         <>9__CachedAnonymousMethodDelegate1 =
            new WaitCallback(<CallbackWithoutNewingADelegateObject>b__0);
      }
      ThreadPool.QueueUserWorkItem(<>9__CachedAnonymousMethodDelegate1, 5);
   }

   [CompilerGenerated]
   private static void <CallbackWithoutNewingADelegateObject>b__0(Object obj) {
      Console.WriteLine(obj);
   }
}
```

The lambda expression must match that of the **WaitCallback** delegate: it returns **void** and takes an **Object** parameter. However, I specified the name of the parameter by simply putting **obj** to the left of the => operator. On the right of the => operator, **Console.WriteLine** happens to return **void**. However, if I had placed an expression that did not return **void**, the compiler-generated code would just ignore the return value because the method that the compiler generates must have a **void** return type to satisfy the **WaitCallback** delegate.

It is also worth noting that the anonymous function is marked as **private**; this forbids any code not defined within the type from accessing the method (although reflection will reveal that the method does exist). Also, note that the anonymous method is marked as **static**; this is because the code doesn't access any instance members (which it can't since **CallbackWithoutNewingADelegateObject** is itself a static method. However, the code can reference any static fields or static methods defined within the class. Here is an example:

```
internal sealed class AClass {
   private static String sm_name;  // A static field

   public static void CallbackWithoutNewingADelegateObject() {
      ThreadPool.QueueUserWorkItem(
         // The callback code can reference static members.
         obj =>Console.WriteLine(sm_name+ ": " + obj),
         5);
   }
}
```

If the **CallbackWithoutNewingADelegateObject** method had not been static, the anonymous method's code could contain references to instance members. If it doesn't contain
references to instance members, the compiler will still produce a static anonymous method
since this is more efficient than an instance method because the additional **this** parameter is
not necessary. But, if the anonymous method's code does reference an instance member, the
compiler will produce a nonstatic anonymous method:

```
internal sealed class AClass {
   private String m_name;  // An instance field

   // An instance method
   public void CallbackWithoutNewingADelegateObject() {
      ThreadPool.QueueUserWorkItem(
         // The callback code can reference instance members.
         obj => Console.WriteLine(m_name+ ": " + obj),
         5);
   }
}
```

On the left-hand side of the => operator is where you specify the names of any arguments
that are to be passed to the lambda expression. There are some rules you must follow here.
See the examples below:

```
// If the delegate takes no arguments, use ()
Func<String> f = () => "Jeff";

// If the delegate takes 1+ arguments, you can explicitly specify the types
Func<Int32, String> f2 = (Int32 n) => n.ToString();
Func<Int32, Int32, String> f3 = (Int32 n1, Int32 n2) => (n1 + n2).ToString();

// If the delegate takes 1+ arguments, the compiler can infer the types
Func<Int32, String> f4 = (n) => n.ToString();
Func<Int32, Int32, String> f5 = (n1, n2) => (n1 + n2).ToString();

// If the delegate takes 1 argument, you can omit the ()s
Func<Int32, String> f6 = n => n.ToString();

// If the delegate has ref/out arguments, you must explicitly specify ref/out and the type
Bar b = (out Int32 n) => n = 5;
```

For the last example, assume that **Bar** is defined as follows:

```
delegate void Bar(out Int32 z);
```

On the right-hand side of the => operator is where you specify the anonymous function
body. It is very common for the body to consist of a simple or complex expression that
ultimately returns a non-**void** value. In the code just above, I was assigning lambda
expressions that returned **String**s to all the **Func** delegate variables. It is also quite
common for the body to consist of a single statement. An example of this is when I called
ThreadPool.QueueUserWorkItem, passing it a lambda expression that called
Console.WriteLine (which returns **void**).

If you want the body to consist of two or more statements, then you must enclose it in curly braces. And if the delegate expects a return value, then you must have a **return** statement inside the body. Here is an example:

```
Func<Int32, Int32, String> f7 = (n1, n2) => { Int32 sum = n1 + n2; return sum.ToString(); };
```

> **Important** In case it's not obvious, let me explicitly point out that the main benefit of lambda expressions is that they remove a level of indirection from within your source code. Normally, you'd have to write a separate method, give that method a name, and then pass the name of that method where a delegate is required. The name gives you a way to refer to a body of code, and if you need to refer to the same body of code from multiple locations in your source code, then writing a method and giving it a name is a great way to go. However, if you need to have a body of code that is referred to only once within your source code, then a lambda expression allows you to put that code directly inline without having to assign it a name, thus increasing programmer productivity.

> **Note** When C# 2.0 came out, it introduced a feature called *anonymous methods*. Like lambda expressions (introduced in C# 3.0), anonymous methods describes a syntax for creating anonymous functions. It is now recommended (in section 7.14 of the C# Language Specification) that developers use the newer lambda expression syntax rather than the older anonymous method syntax because the lambda expression syntax is more terse, making code easier to write, read, and maintain. Of course, Microsoft's C# compiler continues to support parsing both syntaxes for creating anonymous functions so that developers are not forced to modify any code that was originally written for C# 2.0. In this book, I will explain and use only the lambda expression syntax.

Syntactical Shortcut #3: No Need to Wrap Local Variables in a Class Manually to Pass Them to a Callback Method

I've already shown how the callback code can reference other members defined in the class. However, sometimes, you might like the callback code to reference local parameters or variables that exist in the defining method. Here's an interesting example:

```
internal sealed class AClass {
    public static void UsingLocalVariablesInTheCallbackCode(Int32 numToDo) {
        // Some local variables
        Int32[] squares = new Int32[numToDo];
        AutoResetEvent done = new AutoResetEvent(false);

        // Do a bunch of tasks on other threads
        for (Int32 n = 0; n < squares.Length; n++) {
            ThreadPool.QueueUserWorkItem(
                obj => {
                    Int32 num = (Int32) obj;

                    // This task would normally be more time consuming
                    squares[num] = num * num;
```

```
                    // If last task, let main thread continue running
                    if (Interlocked.Decrement(ref numToDo) == 0)
                        done.Set();
                },
                n);
        }

        // Wait for all the other threads to finish
        done.WaitOne();

        // Show the results
        for (Int32 n = 0; n < squares.Length; n++)
            Console.WriteLine("Index {0}, Square={1}", n, squares[n]);
    }
}
```

This example really shows off how easy C# makes implementing what used to be a pretty complex task. The method above defines one parameter, **numToDo**, and two local variables, **squares** and **done**. And the body of the lambda expression refers to these variables.

Now imagine that the code in the body of the lambda expression is placed in a separate method (as is required by the CLR). How would the values of the variables be passed to the separate method? The only way to do this is to define a new helper class that also defines a field for each value that you want passed to the callback code. In addition, the callback code would have to be defined as an instance method in this helper class. Then, the **UsingLocalVariablesInTheCallbackCode** method would have to construct an instance of the helper class, initialize the fields from the values in its local variables, and then construct the delegate object bound to the helper object/instance method.

> **Note** When a lambda expression causes the compiler to generate a class with parameter/local variables turned into fields, the lifetime of the objects that the variables refer to are lengthened. Usually, a parameter/local variable goes out of scope at the last usage of the variable within a method. However, turning the variable into a field causes the field to keep the object that it refers to alive for the whole lifetime of the object containing the field. This is not a big deal in most applications, but it is something that you should be aware of.

This is very tedious and error-prone work, and, of course, the C# compiler does all this for you automatically. When you write the code shown above, it's as if the C# compiler rewrites your code so that it looks something like this (comments inserted by me):

```
internal sealed class AClass {
    public static void UsingLocalVariablesInTheCallbackCode(Int32 numToDo) {

        // Some local variables
        WaitCallback callback1 = null;

        // Construct an instance of the helper class
        <>c__DisplayClass2 class1 = new <>c__DisplayClass2();
```

```
            // Initialize the helper class's fields
            class1.numToDo = numToDo;
            class1.squares = new Int32[class1.numToDo];
            class1.done = new AutoResetEvent(false);

            // Do a bunch of tasks on other threads
            for (Int32 n = 0; n < class1.squares.Length; n++) {
                if (callback1 == null) {
                    // New up delegate object bound to the helper object and
                    // its anonymous instance method
                    callback1 = new WaitCallback(
                        class1.<UsingLocalVariablesInTheCallbackCode>b__0);
                }

                ThreadPool.QueueUserWorkItem(callback1, n);
            }

            // Wait for all the other threads to finish
            class1.done.WaitOne();

            // Show the results
            for (Int32 n = 0; n < class1.squares.Length; n++)
                Console.WriteLine("Index {0}, Square={1}", n, class1.squares[n]);
        }

    // The helper class is given a strange name to avoid potential
    // conflicts and is private to forbid access from outside AClass
    [CompilerGenerated]
    private sealed class <>c__DisplayClass2 : Object {

        // One public field per local variable used in the callback code
        public Int32[] squares;
        public Int32 numToDo;
        public AutoResetEvent done;

        // public parameterless constructor
        public <>c__DisplayClass2 { }

        // Public instance method containing the callback code
        public void <UsingLocalVariablesInTheCallbackCode>b__0(Object obj) {
            Int32 num = (Int32) obj;
            squares[num] = num * num;
            if (Interlocked.Decrement(ref numToDo) == 0)
                done.Set();
        }
    }
}
```

Important Without a doubt, it doesn't take much for programmers to start abusing C#'s lambda expression feature. When I first started using lambda expressions, it definitely took me some time to get used to them. After all, the code that you write in a method is not actually inside that method, and this also can make debugging and single-stepping through the code a bit more challenging. In fact, I'm amazed at how well the Microsoft Visual Studio debugger actually handles stepping through lambda expressions in my source code.

I've set up a rule for myself: If I need my callback method to contain more than three lines of code, I will not use a lambda expression; instead, I'll write the method manually and assign it a name of my own creation. But, used judiciously, lambda expressions can greatly increase programmer productivity as well as the maintainability of your code. Below is some code in which using lambda expressions feels very natural. Without them, this code would be tedious to write, harder to read, and harder to maintain:

```
// Create an initialize a String array
String[] names = { "Jeff", "Kristin", "Aidan", "Grant" };

// Get just the names that have a lowercase 'a' in them.
Char charToFind = 'a';
names = Array.FindAll(names, name => name.IndexOf(charToFind) >= 0);

// Convert each string's characters to uppercase
names = Array.ConvertAll(names, name => name.ToUpper());

// Display the results
Array.ForEach(names, Console.WriteLine);
```

Delegates and Reflection

So far in this chapter, the use of delegates has required the developer to know up front the prototype of the method that is to be called back. For example, if **fb** is a variable that references a **Feedback** delegate (see this chapter's first program listing), to invoke the delegate, the code would look like this:

```
fb(item);   // item is defined as Int32
```

As you can see, the developer must know when coding how many parameters the callback method requires and the types of those parameters. Fortunately, the developer almost always has this information, so writing code like the preceding code isn't a problem.

In some rare circumstances, however, the developer doesn't have this information at compile time. I showed an example of this in Chapter 11, "Events," when I discussed the **EventSet** type. In this example, a dictionary maintained a set of different delegate types. At runtime, to raise an event, one of the delegates was looked up in the dictionary and invoked. At compile time, it wasn't possible to know exactly which delegate would be called and which parameters were necessary to pass to the delegate's callback method.

Fortunately, **System.Delegate** offers a few methods that allow you to create and invoke a delegate when you just don't have all the necessary information about the delegate at compile time. Here are the corresponding methods that **Delegate** defines:

```
public abstract class Delegate {
   // Construct a 'type' delegate wrapping the specified static method.
   public static Delegate CreateDelegate(Type type, MethodInfo method);
   public static Delegate CreateDelegate(Type type, MethodInfo method,
      Boolean throwOnBindFailure);
```

```
    // Construct a 'type' delegate wrapping the specified instance method.
    public static Delegate CreateDelegate(Type type,
        Object firstArgument, MethodInfo method); // firstArgument means 'this'
    public static Delegate CreateDelegate(Type type,
        Object firstArgument, MethodInfo method, Boolean throwOnBindFailure);

    // Invoke a delegate passing it parameters
    public Object DynamicInvoke(params Object[] args);
}
```

All of the **CreateDelegate** methods here construct a new object of a **Delegate**-derived type identified by the first parameter, **type**. The **MethodInfo** parameter indicates the method that should be called back; you'd use reflection APIs (discussed in Chapter 23, "Assembly Loading and Reflection") to obtain this value. If you want the delegate to wrap an instance method, you will also pass to **CreateDelegate** a **firstArgument** parameter indicating the object that should be passed as the **this** parameter (first argument) to the instance method. Finally, **CreateDelegate** normally throws an **ArgumentException** if the delegate cannot bind to the method specified by the **method** parameter. This can happen if the signature of the method identified by **method** doesn't match the signature required by the delegate identified by the **type** parameter. However, if you pass **false** for the **throwOnBindFailure** parameter, an **ArgumentException** will not be thrown; **null** will be returned instead.

> **Important** The **System.Delegate** class has many more overloads of the **CreateDelegate** method that I do not show here. You should never call any of these other methods. As a matter of fact, Microsoft regrets even defining them in the first place. The reason is because these other methods identify the method to bind to by using a **String** instead of a **MethodInfo**. This means that an ambiguous bind is possible causing your application to behave unpredictably.

System.Delegate's **DynamicInvoke** method allows you to invoke a delegate object's call-back method, passing a set of parameters that you determine at runtime. When you call **DynamicInvoke**, it internally ensures that the parameters you pass are compatible with the parameters the callback method expects. If they're compatible, the callback method is called. If they're not, an **ArgumentException** is thrown. **DynamicInvoke** returns the object the callback method returned.

The following code shows how to use the **CreateDelegate** and **DynamicInvoke** methods:

```
using System;
using System.Reflection;
using System.IO;


// Here are some different delegate definitions
internal delegate Object TwoInt32s(Int32 n1, Int32 n2);
internal delegate Object OneString(String s1);
```

```
public static class Program {
   public static void Main(String[] args) {
      if (args.Length < 2) {
         String fileName = Path.GetFileNameWithoutExtension(
            Assembly.GetEntryAssembly().Location);
      String usage =
         @"Usage:" +
         "{0}{1} delType methodName [Arg1] [Arg2]" +
         "{0}   where delType must be TwoInt32s or OneString"+
         "{0}    if delType is TwoInt32s, methodName must be Add or Subtract" +
         "{0}    if delType is OneString, methodName must be NumChars or Reverse" +
         "{0}" +
         "{0}Examples:" +
         "{0}   {1} TwoInt32s Add 123 321" +
         "{0}   {1} TwoInt32s Subtract 123 321" +
         "{0}   {1} OneString NumChars \"Hello there\"" +
         "{0}   {1} OneString Reverse  \"Hello there\"";
         Console.WriteLine(usage, Environment.NewLine, fileName);
         return;
      }

      // Convert the delType argument to a delegate type
      Type delType = Type.GetType(args[0]);
      if (delType == null) {
         Console.WriteLine("Invalid delType argument: " + args[0]);
         return;
      }

      Delegate d;
      try {
         // Convert the Arg1 argument to a method
         MethodInfo mi = typeof(Program).GetMethod(args[1],
            BindingFlags.NonPublic | BindingFlags.Static);

         // Create a delegate object that wraps the static method
         d = Delegate.CreateDelegate(delType, mi);
      }
      catch (ArgumentException) {
         Console.WriteLine("Invalid methodName argument: " + args[1]);
         return;
      }

      // Create an array that will contain just the arguments
      // to pass to the method via the delegate object
      Object[] callbackArgs = new Object[args.Length - 2];

      if (d.GetType() == typeof(TwoInt32s)) {
         try {
            // Convert the String arguments to Int32 arguments
            for (Int32 a = 2; a < args.Length; a++)
               callbackArgs[a - 2] = Int32.Parse(args[a]);
         }
         catch (FormatException) {
            Console.WriteLine("Parameters must be integers.");
            return;
         }
      }
```

```
        if (d.GetType() == typeof(OneString)) {
          // Just copy the String argument
          Array.Copy(args, 2, callbackArgs, 0, callbackArgs.Length);
        }

        try {
          // Invoke the delegate and show the result
          Object result = d.DynamicInvoke(callbackArgs);
          Console.WriteLine("Result = " + result);
        }
        catch (TargetParameterCountException) {
          Console.WriteLine("Incorrect number of parameters specified.");
        }
      }


    // This callback method takes 2 Int32 arguments
    private static Object Add(Int32 n1, Int32 n2) {
      return n1 + n2;
    }

    // This callback method takes 2 Int32 arguments
    private static Object Subtract(Int32 n1, Int32 n2) {
      return n1 - n2;
    }

    // This callback method takes 1 String argument
    private static Object NumChars(String s1) {
      return s1.Length;
    }

    // This callback method takes 1 String argument
    private static Object Reverse(String s1) {
      Char[] chars = s1.ToCharArray();
      Array.Reverse(chars);
      return new String(chars);
    }
  }
```

Chapter 18
Custom Attributes

In this chapter, I'll discuss one of the most innovative features the Microsoft .NET Framework has to offer: *custom attributes*. Custom attributes allow you to declaratively annotate your code constructs, thereby enabling special features. Custom attributes allow information to be defined and applied to almost any metadata table entry. This extensible metadata information can be queried at runtime to dynamically alter the way code executes. As you use the various .NET Framework technologies (Windows Forms, Web Forms, XML Web services, and so on), you'll see that they all take advantage of custom attributes, allowing developers to express their intentions within code very easily. A solid understanding of custom attributes is necessary for any .NET Framework developer.

Using Custom Attributes

Attributes, such as **public**, **private**, **static**, and so on, can be applied to types and members. I think we'd all agree on the usefulness of applying attributes, but wouldn't it be even more useful if we could define our own attributes? For example, what if I could define a type and somehow indicate that the type can be remoted via serialization? Or maybe I could apply an attribute to a method to indicate that certain security permissions must be granted before the method can execute.

Of course, creating and applying user-defined attributes to types and methods would be great and convenient, but it would require the compiler to be aware of these attributes so it would emit the attribute information into the resulting metadata. Because compiler vendors usually prefer not to release the source code for their compiler, Microsoft came up with another way to allow user-defined attributes. This mechanism, called *custom attributes*, is an incredibly powerful mechanism that's useful at both application design time and runtime. Anyone can define and use custom attributes, and all compilers that target the common language runtime (CLR) must be designed to recognize custom attributes and emit them into the resulting metadata.

The first thing you should realize about custom attributes is that they're just a way to associate additional information with a target. The compiler emits this additional information into the managed module's metadata. Most attributes have no meaning for the compiler; the compiler simply detects the attributes in the source code and emits the corresponding metadata.

The .NET Framework Class Library (FCL) defines literally hundreds of custom attributes that can be applied to items in your own source code. Here are some examples:

- Applying the **DllImport** attribute to a method informs the CLR that the implementation of the method is actually in unmanaged code contained in the specified DLL.

- Applying the **Serializable** attribute to a type informs the serialization formatters that an instance's fields may be serialized and deserialized.

- Applying the **AssemblyVersion** attribute to an assembly sets the version number of the assembly.

- Applying the **Flags** attribute to an enumerated type causes the enumerated type to act as a set of bit flags.

Following is some C# code with many attributes applied to it. In C#, you apply a custom attribute to a target by placing the attribute in square brackets immediately before the target. It's not important to understand what this code does. I just want you to see what attributes look like.

```
using System;
using System.Runtime.InteropServices;

[StructLayout(LayoutKind.Sequential, CharSet = CharSet.Auto)]
internal sealed class OSVERSIONINFO {
    public OSVERSIONINFO() {
        OSVersionInfoSize = (UInt32) Marshal.SizeOf(this);
    }

    public UInt32 OSVersionInfoSize = 0;
    public UInt32 MajorVersion      = 0;
    public UInt32 MinorVersion      = 0;
    public UInt32 BuildNumber       = 0;
    public UInt32 PlatformId        = 0;

    [MarshalAs(UnmanagedType.ByValTStr, SizeConst = 128)]
    public String CSDVersion        = null;
}
```

```
internal sealed class MyClass {
    [DllImport("Kernel32", CharSet = CharSet.Auto, SetLastError = true)]
    public static extern Boolean GetVersionEx([In, Out] OSVERSIONINFO ver);
}
```

In this case, the **StructLayout** attribute is applied to the **OSVERSIONINFO** class, the **MarshalAs** attribute is applied to the **CSDVersion** field, the **DllImport** attribute is applied to the **GetVersionEx** method, and the **In** and **Out** attributes are applied to **GetVersionEx**'s **ver** parameter. Every programming language defines the syntax a developer must use in order to apply a custom attribute to a target. Microsoft Visual Basic .NET, for example, requires angle brackets (<, >) instead of square brackets.

The CLR allows attributes to be applied to just about anything that can be represented in a file's metadata. Most commonly, attributes are applied to entries in the following definition tables: TypeDef (classes, structures, enumerations, interfaces, and delegates), MethodDef (including constructors), ParamDef, FieldDef, PropertyDef, EventDef, AssemblyDef, and ModuleDef. Specifically, C# allows you to apply an attribute only to source code that defines any of the following targets: assembly, module, type (class, struct, enum, interface, delegate), field, method (including constructors), method parameter, method return value, property, event, and generic type parameter.

When you're applying an attribute, C# allows you to specify a prefix specifically indicating the target the attribute applies to. The following code shows all of the possible prefixes. In many cases, if you leave out the prefix, the compiler can still determine the target an attribute applies to, as shown in the previous example. In some cases, the prefix must be specified to make your intentions clear to the compiler. The prefixes shown in italics below are mandatory.

```
using System;

[assembly: SomeAttr]        // Applied to assembly
[module:   SomeAttr]        // Applied to module

[type:     SomeAttr]        // Applied to type
internal sealed class SomeType<[typevar: SomeAttr] T> {    // Applied to generic type variable

    [field: SomeAttr]            // Applied to field
    public Int32 SomeField = 0;

    [return: SomeAttr]           // Applied to return value
    [method: SomeAttr]           // Applied to method
    public Int32 SomeMethod(
        [param: SomeAttr]        // Applied to parameter
        Int32 SomeParam) { return SomeParam; }

    [property: SomeAttr]         // Applied to property
    public String SomeProp {
        [method: SomeAttr]       // Applied to get accessor method
        get { return null; }
```

```
    }

    [event:  SomeAttr]          // Applied to event
    [field:  SomeAttr]          // Applied to compiler-generated field
    [method: SomeAttr]          // Applied to compiler-generated add & remove methods
    public event EventHandler SomeEvent;
}
```

Now that you know how to apply a custom attribute, let's find out what an attribute really is. A custom attribute is simply an instance of a type. For Common Language Specification (CLS) compliance, custom attribute classes must be derived, directly or indirectly, from the public abstract **System.Attribute** class. C# allows only CLS-compliant attributes. By examining the .NET Framework SDK documentation, you'll see that the following classes (from the earlier example) are defined: **StructLayoutAttribute**, **MarshalAsAttribute**, **DllImportAttribute**, **InAttribute**, and **OutAttribute**. All of these classes happen to be defined in the **System.Runtime.InteropServices** namespace, but attribute classes can be defined in any namespace. Upon further examination, you'll notice that all of these classes are derived from **System.Attribute**, as all CLS-compliant attribute classes must be.

> **Note** When applying an attribute to a target in source code, the C# compiler allows you to omit the **Attribute** suffix to reduce programming typing and to improve the readability of the source code. My code examples in this chapter take advantage of this C# convenience. For example, my source code contains **[DllImport(...)]** instead of **[DllImportAttribute(...)]**.

As I mentioned earlier, an attribute is an instance of a class. The class must have a public constructor so that instances of it can be created. So when you apply an attribute to a target, the syntax is similar to that for calling one of the class's instance constructors. In addition, a language might permit some special syntax to allow you to set any public fields or properties associated with the attribute class. Let's look at an example. Recall the application of the **DllImport** attribute as it was applied to the **GetVersionEx** method earlier:

```
[DllImport("Kernel32", CharSet = CharSet.Auto, SetLastError = true)]
```

The syntax of this line should look pretty strange to you because you could never use syntax like this when calling a constructor. If you examine the **DllImportAttribute** class in the documentation, you'll see that its constructor requires a single **String** parameter. In this example, **"Kernel32"** is being passed for this parameter. A constructor's parameters are called *positional parameters* and are mandatory; the parameter must be specified when the attribute is applied.

What are the other two "parameters"? This special syntax allows you to set any public fields or properties of the **DllImportAttribute** object after the object is constructed. In this example, when the **DllImportAttribute** object is constructed and **"Kernel32"** is passed to the constructor, the object's public instance fields, **CharSet** and **SetLastError**, are set to **CharSet.Auto** and **true**, respectively. The "parameters" that set fields or properties are called *named parameters* and are optional because the parameters don't have to be specified when you're applying an instance of the attribute. A little later on, I'll explain what causes an instance of the **DllImportAttribute** class to actually be constructed.

Also note that it's possible to apply multiple attributes to a single target. For example, in this chapter's first program listing, the **GetVersionEx** method's **ver** parameter has both the **In** and **Out** attributes applied to it. When applying multiple attributes to a single target, be aware that the order of attributes has no significance. Also, in C#, each attribute can be enclosed in square brackets, or multiple attributes can be comma-separated within a single set of square brackets. If the attribute class's constructor takes no parameters, the parentheses are optional. Finally, as mentioned earlier, the **Attribute** suffix is also optional. The following lines behave identically and demonstrate all of the possible ways of applying multiple attributes:

```
[Serializable][Flags]
[Serializable, Flags]
[FlagsAttribute, SerializableAttribute]
[FlagsAttribute()][Serializable()]
```

Defining Your Own Attribute Class

You know that an attribute is an instance of a class derived from **System.Attribute**, and you also know how to apply an attribute. Let's now look at how to define your own custom attribute classes. Say you're the Microsoft employee responsible for adding the bit flag support to enumerated types. To accomplish this, the first thing you have to do is define a **FlagsAttribute** class:

```
namespace System {
   public class FlagsAttribute : System.Attribute {
      public FlagsAttribute() {
      }
   }
}
```

Notice that the **FlagsAttribute** class inherits from **Attribute**; this is what makes the **FlagsAttribute** class a CLS-compliant custom attribute. In addition, the class's name has a suffix of **Attribute**; this follows the standard convention but is not mandatory. Finally, all non-abstract attributes must contain at least one public constructor. The simple **FlagsAttribute** constructor takes no parameters and does absolutely nothing.

> **Important** You should think of an attribute as a logical state container. That is, while an attribute type is a class, the class should be simple. The class should offer just one public constructor that accepts the attribute's mandatory (or positional) state information, and the class can offer public fields/properties that accept the attribute's optional (or named) state information. The class should not offer any public methods, events, or other members.
>
> In general, I always discourage the use of public fields, and I still discourage them for attributes. It is much better to use properties because this allows more flexibility if you ever decide to change how the attribute class is implemented.

So far, instances of the **FlagsAttribute** class can be applied to any target, but this attribute should really be applied to enumerated types only. It doesn't make sense to apply the attribute to a property or a method. To tell the compiler where this attribute can legally be applied, you apply an instance of the **System.AttributeUsageAttribute** class to the attribute class. Here's the new code:

```
namespace System {
   [AttributeUsage(AttributeTargets.Enum, Inherited = false)]
   public class FlagsAttribute : System.Attribute {
      public FlagsAttribute() {
      }
   }
}
```

In this new version, I've applied an instance of **AttributeUsageAttribute** to the attribute. After all, the attribute type is just a class, and a class can have attributes applied to it. The **AttributeUsage** attribute is a simple class that allows you to specify to a compiler where your custom attribute can legally be applied. All compilers have built-in support for this attribute and generate errors when a user-defined custom attribute is applied to an invalid target. In this example, the **AttributeUsage** attribute specifies that instances of the **Flags** attribute can be applied only to enumerated type targets.

Because all attributes are just types, you can easily understand the **AttributeUsageAttribute** class. Here's what the FCL source code for the class looks like:

```
[Serializable]
[AttributeUsage(AttributeTargets.Class, Inherited=true)]
public sealed class AttributeUsageAttribute : Attribute {
   internal static AttributeUsageAttribute Default =
      new AttributeUsageAttribute(AttributeTargets.All);

   internal Boolean m_allowMultiple = false;
   internal AttributeTargets m_attributeTarget = AttributeTargets.All;
   internal Boolean m_inherited = true;

   // This is the one public constructor
   public AttributeUsageAttribute(AttributeTargets validOn) {
      m_attributeTarget = validOn;
   }
```

```
internal AttributeUsageAttribute(AttributeTargets validOn,
   Boolean allowMultiple, Boolean inherited) {
   m_attributeTarget = validOn;
   m_allowMultiple = allowMultiple;
   m_inherited = inherited;
}

public Boolean AllowMultiple {
   get { return m_allowMultiple; }
   set { m_allowMultiple = value; }
}

public Boolean Inherited {
   get { return m_inherited; }
   set { m_inherited = value; }
}

public AttributeTargets ValidOn {
   get { return m_attributeTarget; }
}
}
```

As you can see, the **AttributeUsageAttribute** class has a public constructor that allows you to pass bit flags that indicate where your attribute can legally be applied. The **System.AttributeTargets** enumerated type is defined in the FCL as follows:

```
[Flags, Serializable]
public enum AttributeTargets {
   Assembly         = 0x0001,
   Module           = 0x0002,
   Class            = 0x0004,
   Struct           = 0x0008,
   Enum             = 0x0010,
   Constructor      = 0x0020,
   Method           = 0x0040,
   Property         = 0x0080,
   Field            = 0x0100,
   Event            = 0x0200,
   Interface        = 0x0400,
   Parameter        = 0x0800,
   Delegate         = 0x1000,
   ReturnValue      = 0x2000,
   GenericParameter = 0x4000,
   All              = Assembly   | Module    | Class    | Struct | Enum |
                      Constructor | Method    | Property | Field  | Event |
                      Interface   | Parameter | Delegate | ReturnValue |
                      GenericParameter
}
```

The **AttributeUsageAttribute** class offers two additional public properties that can optionally be set when the attribute is applied to an attribute class: **AllowMultiple** and **Inherited**.

For most attributes, it makes no sense to apply them to a single target more than once. For example, nothing is gained by applying the **Flags** or **Serializable** attributes more than once to a single target. In fact, if you tried to compile the code below, the compiler would report the following message: "**error CS0579: Duplicate 'Flags' attribute.**"

```
[Flags][Flags]
internal enum Color {
    Red
}
```

For a few attributes, however, it does make sense to apply the attribute multiple times to a single target. In the FCL, the **ConditionalAttribute** attribute class allows multiple instances of itself to be applied to a single target. If you don't explicitly set **AllowMultiple** to **true**, your attribute can be applied no more than once to a selected target.

AttributeUsageAttribute's other property, **Inherited**, indicates if the attribute should be applied to derived classes and overriding methods when applied on the base class. The following code demonstrates what it means for an attribute to be inherited:

```
[AttributeUsage(AttributeTargets.Class | AttributeTargets.Method, Inherited=true)]
internal class TastyAttribute : Attribute {
}

[Tasty][Serializable]
internal class BaseType {

    [Tasty] protected virtual void DoSomething() { }
}

internal class DerivedType : BaseType {
    protected override void DoSomething() { }
}
```

In this code, **DerivedType** and its **DoSomething** method are both considered **Tasty** because the **TastyAttribute** class is marked as inherited. However, **DerivedType** is not serializable because the FCL's **SerializableAttribute** class is marked as a noninherited attribute.

Be aware that the .NET Framework considers targets only of classes, methods, properties, events, fields, method return values, and parameters to be inheritable. So when you're defining an attribute type, you should set **Inherited** to **true** only if your targets include any of these targets. Note that inherited attributes do not cause additional metadata to be emitted for the derived types into the managed module. I'll say more about this a little later in the "Detecting the Use of a Custom Attribute" section.

> **Note** If you define your own attribute class and forget to apply an **AttributeUsage** attribute to your class, the compiler and the CLR will assume that your attribute can be applied to all targets, can be applied only once to a single target, and is inherited. These assumptions mimic the default field values in the **AttributeUsageAttribute** class.

Attribute Constructor and Field/Property Data Types

When defining your own custom attribute class, you can define its constructor to take parameters that must be specified by developers when they apply an instance of your attribute type. In addition, you can define nonstatic public fields and properties in your type that identify settings that a developer can optionally choose for an instance of your attribute class.

When defining an attribute class's instance constructor, fields, and properties, you must restrict yourself to a small subset of data types. Specifically, the legal set of data types is limited to the following: **Boolean**, **Char**, **Byte**, **SByte**, **Int16**, **UInt16**, **Int32**, **UInt32**, **Int64**, **UInt64**, **Single**, **Double**, **String**, **Type**, **Object**, or an enumerated type. In addition, you can use a single-dimensional, zero-based array of any of these types. However, you should avoid using arrays because a custom attribute class whose constructor takes an array is not CLS-compliant.

When applying an attribute, you must pass a compile-time constant expression that matches the type defined by the attribute class. Wherever the attribute class defines a **Type** parameter, **Type** field, or **Type** property, you must use C#'s **typeof** operator, as shown in the following code. Wherever the attribute class defines an **Object** parameter, **Object** field, or **Object** property, you can pass an **Int32**, **String**, or any other constant expression (including **null**). If the constant expression represents a value type, the value type will be boxed at runtime when an instance of the attribute is constructed.

Here's an example of an attribute and its usage:

```
using System;

internal enum Color { Red }

[AttributeUsage(AttributeTargets.All)]
internal sealed class SomeAttribute : Attribute {
   public SomeAttribute(String name, Object o, Type[] types) {
      // 'name' refers to a String
      // 'o' refers to one of the legal types (boxing if necessary)
      // 'types' refers to a 1-dimension, 0-based array of Types
   }
}

[Some("Jeff", Color.Red, new Type[] { typeof(Math), typeof(Console) })]
internal sealed class SomeType {
}
```

Logically, when a compiler detects a custom attribute applied to a target, the compiler constructs an instance of the attribute class by calling its constructor, passing it any specified parameters. Then the compiler initializes any public fields and properties using the values specified via the enhanced constructor syntax. Now that the custom attribute object is initialized, the compiler serializes the attribute object's state out to the target's metadata table entry.

Important I've found this to be the best way for developers to think of custom attributes: instances of classes that have been serialized to a byte stream that resides in metadata. Later, at runtime, an instance of the class can be constructed by deserializing the bytes contained in the metadata. In reality, what actually happens is that the compiler emits the information necessary to create an instance of the attribute class into metadata. Each constructor parameter is written out with a 1-byte type ID followed by the value. After "serializing" the constructor's parameters, the compiler emits each of the specified field and property values by writing out the field/property name followed by a 1-byte type ID and then the value. For arrays, the count of elements is saved first, followed by each individual element.

Detecting the Use of a Custom Attribute

Defining an attribute class is useless by itself. Sure, you could define attribute classes all you want and apply instances of them all you want, but this would just cause additional metadata to be written out to the assembly—the behavior of your application code wouldn't change.

In Chapter 15, "Enumerated Types and Bit Flags," you saw that applying the **Flags** attribute to an enumerated type altered the behavior of **System.Enum**'s **ToString** and **Format** methods. The reason that these methods behave differently is that they check at runtime if the enumerated type that they're operating on has the **Flags** attribute metadata associated with it. Code can look for the presence of attributes by using a technology called *reflection*. I'll give some brief demonstrations of reflection here, but I'll discuss it fully in Chapter 23, "Assembly Loading and Reflection."

If you were the Microsoft employee responsible for implementing **Enum**'s **Format** method, you would implement it like this:

```
public static String Format(Type enumType, Object value, String format) {

   // Does the enumerated type have an instance of
   // the FlagsAttribute type applied to it?
   if (enumType.IsDefined(typeof(FlagsAttribute), false)) {
      // Yes; execute code treating value as a bit flag enumerated type.
      ...
   } else {
      // No; execute code treating value as a normal enumerated type.
      ...
   }
   ...
}
```

This code calls **Type**'s **IsDefined** method, effectively asking the system to look up the metadata for the enumerated type and see whether an instance of the **FlagsAttribute** class is associated with it. If **IsDefined** returns **true**, an instance of **FlagsAttribute** is associated with the enumerated type, and the **Format** method knows to treat the value as though it contained a set of bit flags. If **IsDefined** returns **false**, **Format** treats the value as a normal enumerated type.

So if you define your own attribute classes, you must also implement some code that checks for the existence of an instance of your attribute class (on some target) and then execute some alternate code path. This is what makes custom attributes so useful!

The FCL offers many ways to check for the existence of an attribute. If you're checking for the existence of an attribute via a **System.Type** object, you can use the **IsDefined** method as shown earlier. However, sometimes you want to check for an attribute on a target other than a type, such as an assembly, a module, or a method. For this discussion, let's concentrate on the methods defined by the **System.Attribute** class. You'll recall that all CLS-compliant attributes are derived from **System.Attribute**. This class defines three static methods for retrieving the attributes associated with a target: **IsDefined**, **GetCustomAttributes**, and **GetCustomAttribute**. Each of these functions has several overloaded versions. For example, each method has a version that works on type members (classes, structs, enums, interfaces, delegates, constructors, methods, properties, fields, events, and return types), parameters, modules, and assemblies. There are also versions that allow you to tell the system to walk up the derivation hierarchy to include inherited attributes in the results. Table 18-1 briefly describes what each method does.

TABLE 18-1 System.Attribute's **Methods That Reflect over Metadata Looking for Instances of CLS-Compliant Custom Attributes**

Method	Description
IsDefined	Returns **true** if there is at least one instance of the specified **Attribute**-derived class associated with the target. This method is efficient because it doesn't construct (deserialize) any instances of the attribute class.
GetCustomAttributes	Returns an array in which each element is an instance of the specified attribute class that was applied to the target. If no attribute class is given to the method, the array contains the instances of all applied attributes, whatever class they have. Each instance is constructed (deserialized) by using the parameters, fields, and properties specified during compilation. If the target has no instances of the specified attribute class, an empty array is returned. This method is typically used with attributes that have **AllowMultiple** set to **true** or to list all applied attributes.
GetCustomAttribute	Returns an instance of the specified attribute class that was applied to the target. The instance is constructed (deserialized) by using the parameters, fields, and properties specified during compilation. If the target has no instances of the specified attribute class, **null** is returned. If the target has multiple instances of the specified attribute applied to it, a **System.Reflection.AmbiguousMatchException** exception is thrown. This method is typically used with attributes that have **AllowMultiple** set to **false**.

If you just want to see if an attribute has been applied to a target, you should call **IsDefined** because it's more efficient than the other two methods. However, you know that when an attribute is applied to a target, you can specify parameters to the attribute's constructor and optionally set fields and properties. Using **IsDefined** won't construct an attribute object, call its constructor, or set its fields and properties.

If you want to construct an attribute object, you must call either **GetCustomAttributes** or **GetCustomAttribute**. Every time one of these methods is called, it constructs new instances of the specified attribute type and sets each of the instance's fields and properties based on the values specified in the source code. These methods return references to fully constructed instances of the applied attribute classes.

When you call any of these methods, internally, they must scan the managed module's metadata, performing string comparisons to locate the specified custom attribute class. Obviously, these operations take time. If you're performance conscious, you should consider caching the result of calling these methods rather than calling them repeatedly asking for the same information.

The **System.Reflection** namespace defines several classes that allow you to examine the contents of a module's metadata: **Assembly**, **Module**, **ParameterInfo**, **MemberInfo**, **Type**, **MethodInfo**, **ConstructorInfo**, **FieldInfo**, **EventInfo**, **PropertyInfo**, and their respective ***Builder** classes. All of these classes also offer **IsDefined** and **GetCustomAttributes** methods. Only **System.Attribute** offers the very convenient **GetCustomAttribute** method.

The version of **GetCustomAttributes** defined by the reflection classes returns an array of **Object** instances (**Object[]**) instead of an array of **Attribute** instances (**Attribute[]**). This is because the reflection classes are able to return objects of non–CLS-compliant attribute classes. You shouldn't be concerned about this inconsistency because non–CLS-compliant attributes are incredibly rare. In fact, in all of the time I've been working with the .NET Framework, I've never even seen one.

> **Note** Be aware that only **Attribute**, **Type**, and **MethodInfo** classes implement reflection methods that honor the Boolean **inherit** parameter. All other reflection methods that look up attributes ignore the **inherit** parameter and do not check the inheritance hierarchy. If you need to check the presence of an inherited attribute for events, properties, fields, constructors, or parameters, you must call one of **Attribute**'s methods.

There's one more thing you should be aware of: When you pass a class to **IsDefined**, **GetCustomAttribute**, or **GetCustomAttributes**, these methods search for the application of the attribute class you specify or any attribute class derived from the specified class. If your code is looking for a specific attribute class, you should perform an additional check on the returned value to ensure that what these methods returned is the exact class you're looking for. You might also want to consider defining your attribute class to be **sealed** to reduce potential confusion and eliminate this extra check.

Here's some sample code that lists all of the methods defined within a type and displays the attributes applied to each method. The code is for demonstration purposes; normally, you wouldn't apply these particular custom attributes to these targets as I've done here.

```
using System;
using System.Diagnostics;
using System.Reflection;


[assembly: CLSCompliant(true)]


[Serializable]
[DefaultMemberAttribute("Main")]
[DebuggerDisplayAttribute("Richter", Name = "Jeff", Target = typeof(Program))]
public sealed class Program {
   [Conditional("Debug")]
   [Conditional("Release")]
   public void DoSomething() { }

   public Program() {
   }

   [CLSCompliant(true)]
   [STAThread]
   public static void Main() {
      // Show the set of attributes applied to this type
      ShowAttributes(typeof(Program));

      // Get the set of methods associated with the type
      MemberInfo[] members = typeof(Program).FindMembers(
         MemberTypes.Constructor | MemberTypes.Method,
         BindingFlags.DeclaredOnly | BindingFlags.Instance |
         BindingFlags.Public | BindingFlags.Static,
         Type.FilterName, "*");

      foreach (MemberInfo member in members) {
         // Show the set of attributes applied to this member
         ShowAttributes(member);
      }
   }

   private static void ShowAttributes(MemberInfo attributeTarget) {
      Attribute[] attributes = Attribute.GetCustomAttributes(attributeTarget);

      Console.WriteLine("Attributes applied to {0}: {1}",
         attributeTarget.Name, (attributes.Length == 0 ? "None" : String.Empty));

      foreach (Attribute attribute in attributes) {
         // Display the type of each applied attribute
         Console.WriteLine("  {0}", attribute.GetType().ToString());
```

```
            if (attribute is DefaultMemberAttribute)
                Console.WriteLine("     MemberName={0}",
                    ((DefaultMemberAttribute) attribute).MemberName);

            if (attribute is ConditionalAttribute)
                Console.WriteLine("     ConditionString={0}",
                    ((ConditionalAttribute) attribute).ConditionString);

            if (attribute is CLSCompliantAttribute)
                Console.WriteLine("     IsCompliant={0}",
                    ((CLSCompliantAttribute) attribute).IsCompliant);

            DebuggerDisplayAttribute dda = attribute as DebuggerDisplayAttribute;
            if (dda != null) {
                Console.WriteLine("     Value={0}, Name={1}, Target={2}",
                    dda.Value, dda.Name, dda.Target);
            }
        }
    }
    Console.WriteLine();
  }
}
```

Building and running this application yields the following output:

```
Attributes applied to Program:
  System.SerializableAttribute
  System.Diagnostics.DebuggerDisplayAttribute
    Value=Richter, Name=Jeff, Target=Program
  System.Reflection.DefaultMemberAttribute
    MemberName=Main

Attributes applied to DoSomething:
  System.Diagnostics.ConditionalAttribute
    ConditionString=Release
  System.Diagnostics.ConditionalAttribute
    ConditionString=Debug

Attributes applied to Main:
  System.CLSCompliantAttribute
    IsCompliant=True
  System.STAThreadAttribute

Attributes applied to .ctor: None
```

Matching Two Attribute Instances Against Each Other

Now that your code knows how to check if an instance of an attribute is applied to a target, it might want to check the fields of the attribute to see what values they have. One way to do this is to write code that explicitly checks the values of the attribute class's fields. However, **System.Attribute** overrides **Object**'s **Equals** method, and internally, this method compares the types of the two objects. If they are not identical, **Equals** returns **false**. If the types are identical, then **Equals** uses reflection to compare the values of the two attribute objects' fields (by calling **Equals** for each field). If all the fields match, then **true** is returned; otherwise, **false** is returned. You might override **Equals** in your own attribute class to remove the use of reflection, improving performance.

System.Attribute also exposes a virtual **Match** method that you can override to provide richer semantics. The default implementation of **Match** simply calls **Equals** and returns its result. The following code demonstrates how to override **Equals** and **Match** (which returns **true** if one attribute represents a subset of the other) and then shows how **Match** is used:

```
using System;


[Flags]
internal enum Accounts {
    Savings   = 0x0001,
    Checking  = 0x0002,
    Brokerage = 0x0004
}


[AttributeUsage(AttributeTargets.Class)]
internal sealed class AccountsAttribute : Attribute {
    private Accounts m_accounts;

    public AccountsAttribute(Accounts accounts) {
        m_accounts = accounts;
    }


    public override Boolean Match(Object obj) {
        // If the base class implements Match and the base class
        // is not Attribute, then uncomment the line below.
        // if (!base.Match(obj)) return false;

        // Since 'this' isn't null, if obj is null,
        // then the objects can't match
        // NOTE: This line may be deleted if you trust
        // that the base type implemented Match correctly.
        if (obj == null) return false;

        // If the objects are of different types, they can't match
        // NOTE: This line may be deleted if you trust
        // that the base type implemented Match correctly.
        if (this.GetType() != obj.GetType()) return false;

        // Cast obj to our type to access fields. NOTE: This cast
        // can't fail since we know objects are of the same type
        AccountsAttribute other = (AccountsAttribute) obj;

        // Compare the fields as you see fit
        // This example checks if 'this' accounts is a subset
        // of others' accounts
```

```
            if ((other.m_accounts & m_accounts) != m_accounts)
                return false;

            return true;    // Objects match
        }


    public override Boolean Equals(Object obj) {
        // If the base class implements Equals, and the base class
        // is not Object, then uncomment the line below.
        // if (!base.Equals(obj)) return false;

        // Since 'this' isn't null, if obj is null,
        // then the objects can't be equal
        // NOTE: This line may be deleted if you trust
        // that the base type implemented Equals correctly.
        if (obj == null) return false;

        // If the objects are of different types, they can't be equal
        // NOTE: This line may be deleted if you trust
        // that the base type implemented Equals correctly.
        if (this.GetType() != obj.GetType()) return false;

        // Cast obj to our type to access fields. NOTE: This cast
        // can't fail since we know objects are of the same type
        AccountsAttribute other = (AccountsAttribute) obj;

        // Compare the fields to see if they have the same value
        // This example checks if 'this' accounts is the same
        // as other's accounts
        if (other.m_accounts != m_accounts)
            return false;

        return true;    // Objects are equal
    }


    // Override GetHashCode since we override Equals
    public override Int32 GetHashCode() {
        return (Int32) m_accounts;
    }
}


[Accounts(Accounts.Savings)]
internal sealed class ChildAccount { }


[Accounts(Accounts.Savings | Accounts.Checking | Accounts.Brokerage)]
internal sealed class AdultAccount { }


public sealed class Program {
    public static void Main() {
        CanWriteCheck(new ChildAccount());
```

```
            CanWriteCheck(new AdultAccount());

            // This just demonstrates that the method works correctly on a
            // type that doesn't have the AccountsAttribute applied to it.
            CanWriteCheck(new Program());
    }

    private static void CanWriteCheck(Object obj) {
        // Construct an instance of the attribute type and initialize it
        // to what we are explicitly looking for.
        Attribute checking = new AccountsAttribute(Accounts.Checking);

        // Construct the attribute instance that was applied to the type
        Attribute validAccounts = Attribute.GetCustomAttribute(
            obj.GetType(), typeof(AccountsAttribute), false);

        // If the attribute was applied to the type AND the
        // attribute specifies the "Checking" account, then the
        // type can write a check
        if ((validAccounts != null) && checking.Match(validAccounts)) {
            Console.WriteLine("{0} types can write checks.", obj.GetType());
        } else {
            Console.WriteLine("{0} types can NOT write checks.", obj.GetType());
        }
    }
}
```

Building and running this application yields the following output:

```
ChildAccount types can NOT write checks.
AdultAccount types can write checks.
Program types can NOT write checks.
```

Detecting the Use of a Custom Attribute Without Creating Attribute-Derived Objects

In this section, I discuss an alternate technique for detecting custom attributes applied to a metadata entry. In some security-conscious scenarios, this alternate technique ensures that no code in an **Attribute**-derived class will execute. After all, when you call **Attribute**'s **GetCustomAttribute(s)** methods, internally, these methods call the attribute class's constructor and can also call property set accessor methods. In addition, the first access to a type causes the CLR to invoke the type's type constructor (if it exists). The constructor, set accessor, and type constructor methods could contain code that will execute whenever code is just looking for an attribute. This allows unknown code to run in the AppDomain, and this is a potential security vulnerability.

To discover attributes without allowing attribute class code to execute, you use the **System.Reflection.CustomAttributeData** class. This class defines one static method for retrieving the attributes associated with a target: **GetCustomAttributes**. This method has four overloads: one that takes an **Assembly**, one that takes a **Module**, one that takes a **ParameterInfo**, and one that takes a **MemberInfo**. This class is defined in the **System.Reflection** namespace, which is discussed in Chapter 23. Typically, you'll use the **CustomAttributeData** class to analyze attributes in metadata for an assembly that is loaded via **Assembly**'s static **ReflectionOnlyLoad** method (also discussed in Chapter 23). Briefly, **ReflectionOnlyLoad** loads an assembly in such a way that prevents the CLR from executing any code in it; this includes type constructors.

CustomAttributeData's **GetCustomAttributes** method acts as a factory. That is, when you call it, it returns a collection of **CustomAttributeData** objects in an object of type **IList<CustomAttributeData>**. The collection contains one element per custom attribute applied to the specified target. For each **CustomAttributeData** object, you can query some read-only properties to determine how the attribute object would be constructed and initialized. Specifically, the **Constructor** property indicates which constructor method *would be* called, the **ConstructorArguments** property returns the arguments that *would be* passed to this constructor as an instance of **IList<CustomAttributeTypedArgument>**, and the **NamedArguments** property returns the fields/properties that *would be* set as an instance of **IList<CustomAttributeNamedArgument>**. Notice that I say "would be" in the previous sentences because the constructor and set accessor methods will not actually be called—we get the added security by preventing any attribute class methods from executing.

Here's a modified version of a previous code sample that uses the **CustomAttributeData** class to securely obtain the attributes applied to various targets:

```
using System;
using System.Diagnostics;
using System.Reflection;
using System.Collections.Generic;


[assembly: CLSCompliant(true)]


[Serializable]
[DefaultMemberAttribute("Main")]
[DebuggerDisplayAttribute("Richter", Name="Jeff", Target=typeof(Program))]
public sealed class Program {
   [Conditional("Debug")]
   [Conditional("Release")]
   public void DoSomething() { }

   public Program() {
   }

   [CLSCompliant(true)]
   [STAThread]
   public static void Main() {
      // Show the set of attributes applied to this type
      ShowAttributes(typeof(Program));
```

```
      // Get the set of methods associated with the type
      MemberInfo[] members = typeof(Program).FindMembers(
         MemberTypes.Constructor | MemberTypes.Method,
         BindingFlags.DeclaredOnly | BindingFlags.Instance |
         BindingFlags.Public | BindingFlags.Static,
         Type.FilterName, "*");

   foreach (MemberInfo member in members) {
      // Show the set of attributes applied to this member
      ShowAttributes(member);
   }
}

private static void ShowAttributes(MemberInfo attributeTarget) {
   IList<CustomAttributeData> attributes =
      CustomAttributeData.GetCustomAttributes(attributeTarget);

   Console.WriteLine("Attributes applied to {0}: {1}",
      attributeTarget.Name, (attributes.Count == 0 ? "None" : String.Empty));

   foreach (CustomAttributeData attribute in attributes) {
      // Display the type of each applied attribute
      Type t = attribute.Constructor.DeclaringType;
      Console.WriteLine("  {0}", t.ToString());
      Console.WriteLine("    Constructor called={0}", attribute.Constructor);

      IList<CustomAttributeTypedArgument> posArgs = attribute.ConstructorArguments;
      Console.WriteLine("    Positional arguments passed to constructor:" +
         ((posArgs.Count == 0) ? " None" : String.Empty));
      foreach (CustomAttributeTypedArgument pa in posArgs) {
         Console.WriteLine("      Type={0}, Value={1}", pa.ArgumentType, pa.Value);
      }


      IList<CustomAttributeNamedArgument> namedArgs = attribute.NamedArguments;
      Console.WriteLine("    Named arguments set after construction:" +
         ((namedArgs.Count == 0) ? " None" : String.Empty));
      foreach(CustomAttributeNamedArgument na in namedArgs) {
         Console.WriteLine("      Name={0}, Type={1}, Value={2}",
            na.MemberInfo.Name, na.TypedValue.ArgumentType, na.TypedValue.Value);
      }

      Console.WriteLine();
   }
   Console.WriteLine();
}
}
```

Building and running this application yields the following output:

```
Attributes applied to Program:
  System.SerializableAttribute
    Constructor called=Void .ctor()
    Positional arguments passed to constructor: None
```

```
     Named arguments set after construction: None

   System.Diagnostics.DebuggerDisplayAttribute
     Constructor called=Void .ctor(System.String)
     Positional arguments passed to constructor:
       Type=System.String, Value=Richter
     Named arguments set after construction:
      Name=Name, Type=System.String, Value=Jeff
      Name=Target, Type=System.Type, Value=Program

   System.Reflection.DefaultMemberAttribute
     Constructor called=Void .ctor(System.String)
     Positional arguments passed to constructor:
       Type=System.String, Value=Main
     Named arguments set after construction: None


Attributes applied to DoSomething:
   System.Diagnostics.ConditionalAttribute
     Constructor called=Void .ctor(System.String)
     Positional arguments passed to constructor:
       Type=System.String, Value=Release
     Named arguments set after construction: None

   System.Diagnostics.ConditionalAttribute
     Constructor called=Void .ctor(System.String)
     Positional arguments passed to constructor:
       Type=System.String, Value=Debug
     Named arguments set after construction: None


Attributes applied to Main:
   System.CLSCompliantAttribute
     Constructor called=Void .ctor(Boolean)
     Positional arguments passed to constructor:
       Type=System.Boolean, Value=True
     Named arguments set after construction: None

   System.STAThreadAttribute
     Constructor called=Void .ctor()
     Positional arguments passed to constructor: None
     Named arguments set after construction: None


Attributes applied to .ctor: None
```

Conditional Attribute Classes

Over time, the ease of defining, applying, and reflecting over attributes has caused developers to use them more and more. Using attributes is also a very easy way to annotate your code while simultaneously implementing rich features. Lately, developers have been using attributes to assist them with design time and debugging. For example,

the Microsoft Visual Studio code analysis tool (FxCopCmd.exe) offers a
System.Diagnostics.CodeAnalysis.SuppressMessageAttribute which you can apply
to types and members in order to suppress the reporting of a specific static analysis tool rule
violation. This attribute is only looked for by the code analysis utility; the attribute is never
looked for when the program is running normally. When not using code analysis,
having **SuppressMessage** attributes sitting in the metadata just bloats the metadata, which
makes your file bigger, increases your process's working set, and hurts your application's
performance. It would be great if there were an easy way to have the compiler emit the
SuppressMessage attributes only when you intend to use the code analysis tool. Fortunately,
there is a way to do this by using conditional attribute classes.

An attribute class that has the **System.Diagnostics.ConditionalAttribute** applied to it is
called a *conditional attribute class*. Here is an example:

```
//#define TEST
#define VERIFY

using System;
using System.Diagnostics;


[Conditional("TEST")][Conditional("VERIFY")]
public sealed class CondAttribute : Attribute {
}

[Cond]
public sealed class Program {
   public static void Main() {
      Console.WriteLine("CondAttribute is {0}applied to Program type.",
         Attribute.IsDefined(typeof(Program),
            typeof(CondAttribute)) ? "" : "not ");
   }
}
```

When a compiler sees an instance of the **CondAttribute** being applied to a target, the
compiler will emit the attribute information into the metadata only if the **TEST** or **VERIFY**
symbol is defined when the code containing the target is compiled. However, the attribute
class definition metadata and implementation is still present in the assembly.

Chapter 19
Nullable Value Types

As you know, a variable of a value type can never be **null**; it always contains the value type's value itself. In fact, this is why they call these types *value* types. Unfortunately, there are some scenarios in which this is a problem. For example, when designing a database, it's possible to define a column's data type to be a 32-bit integer that would map to the **Int32** data type of the Framework Class Library (FCL). But a column in a database can indicate that the value is nullable. That is, it is OK to have no value in the row's column. Working with database data by using the Microsoft .NET Framework can be quite difficult because in the common language runtime (CLR), there is no way to represent an **Int32** value as **null**.

> **Note** Microsoft ADO.NET's table adapters do support nullable types. But unfortunately, the types in the **System.Data.SqlTypes** namespace are not replaced by nullable types, partially because there isn't a one-to-one correspondence between types. For example, the **SqlDecimal** type has a maximum of 38 digits, whereas the regular **Decimal** type can reach only 29. In addition, the **SqlString** type supports its own locale and compare options, which are not supported by the normal **String** type.

Here is another example: in Java, the **java.util.Date** class is a reference type, and therefore, a variable of this type can be set to **null**. However, in the CLR, a **System.DateTime** is a value type, and a **DateTime** variable can never be **null**. If an application written in Java wants to communicate a date/time to a Web service running the CLR, there is a problem if the Java application sends **null** because the CLR has no way to represent this and operate on it.

To improve this situation, Microsoft added the concept of nullable value types to the CLR. To understand how they work, we first need to look at the **System.Nullable<T>** class, which is defined in the FCL. Here is the logical representation of how the **System.Nullable<T>** type is defined:

```
[Serializable, StructLayout(LayoutKind.Sequential)]
public struct Nullable<T> where T : struct {

    // These 2 fields represent the state
    private Boolean hasValue = false; // Assume null
    internal T value = default(T);     // Assume all bits zero
```

457

```
    public Nullable(T value) {
        this.value = value;
        this.hasValue = true;
    }

    public Boolean HasValue { get { return hasValue; } }

    public T Value {
        get {
            if (!hasValue) {
                throw new InvalidOperationException(
                    "Nullable object must have a value.");
            }
            return value;
        }
    }

    public T GetValueOrDefault() { return value; }

    public T GetValueOrDefault(T defaultValue) {
        if (!HasValue) return defaultValue;
        return value;
    }

    public override Boolean Equals(Object other) {
        if (!HasValue) return (other == null);
        if (other == null) return false;
        return value.Equals(other);
    }

    public override int GetHashCode() {
        if (!HasValue) return 0;
        return value.GetHashCode();
    }

    public override string ToString() {
        if (!HasValue) return "";
        return value.ToString();
    }

    public static implicit operator Nullable<T>(T value) {
        return new Nullable<T>(value);
    }

    public static explicit operator T(Nullable<T> value) {
        return value.Value;
    }
}
```

As you can see, this class encapsulates the notion of a value type that can also be **null**. Since **Nullable<T>** is itself a value type, instances of it are still fairly lightweight. That is, instances can still be on the stack, and an instance is the same size as the original value type plus the size of a **Boolean** field. Notice that **Nullable**'s type parameter, **T**, is constrained to **struct**. This was done because reference type variables can already be **null**.

So now, if you want to use a nullable **Int32** in your code, you can write something like this:

```
Nullable<Int32> x = 5;
Nullable<Int32> y = null;
Console.WriteLine("x: HasValue={0}, Value={1}",  x.HasValue, x.Value);
Console.WriteLine("y: HasValue={0}, Value={1}",  y.HasValue, y.GetValueOrDefault());
```

When I compile and run this code, I get the following output:

```
x: HasValue=True, Value=5
y: HasValue=False, Value=0
```

C#'s Support for Nullable Value Types

Notice in the code that C# allows you to use fairly simple syntax to initialize the two **Nullable<Int32>** variables, **x** and **y**. In fact, the C# team wants to integrate nullable value types into the C# language, making them first-class citizens. To that end, C# offers an (arguably) cleaner syntax for working with nullable value types. C# allows the code to declare and initialize the **x** and **y** variables to be written using question-mark notation:

```
Int32? x = 5;
Int32? y = null;
```

In C#, **Int32?** is a synonym notation for **Nullable<Int32>**. But C# takes this further. C# allows you to perform conversions and casts on nullable instances. And C# also supports applying operators to nullable instances. The following code shows examples of these:

```
private static void ConversionsAndCasting() {
    // Implicit conversion from non-nullable Int32 to Nullable<Int32>
    Int32? a = 5;

    // Implicit conversion from 'null' to Nullable<Int32>
    Int32? b = null;

    // Explicit conversion from Nullable<Int32> to non-nullable Int32
    Int32 c = (Int32) a;

    // Casting between nullable primitive types
    Double? d = 5; // Int32->Double?  (d is 5.0 as a double)
    Double? e = b; // Int32?->Double? (e is null)
}
```

C# also allows you to apply operators to nullable instances. The following code shows examples of this:

```
private static void Operators() {
    Int32? a = 5;
    Int32? b = null;
```

```
   // Unary operators (+  ++   -   --   !  ~)
   a++;      // a = 6
   b = -b;  // b = null

   // Binary operators (+   -   *   /   %  &   |   ^  <<  >>)
   a = a + 3;   // a = 9
   b = b * 3;   // b = null;

   // Equality operators (==   !=)
   if (a == null) { /* no  */ } else { /* yes */ }
   if (b == null) { /* yes */ } else { /* no  */ }
   if (a != b)    { /* yes */ } else { /* no  */ }

   // Comparison operators (<>   <=   >=)
   if (a < b)     { /* no  */ } else { /* yes */ }
}
```

Here is how C# interprets the operators:

- **Unary operators (+++, −, −−, ! , ~)**   If the operand is **null**, the result is **null**.

- **Binary operators (+, −, *, /, %, &, |, ^, <<, >>)**   If either operand is **null**, the result is **null**. However, an exception is made when the **&** and **|** operators are operating on **Boolean?** operands so that the behavior of these two operators gives the same behavior as demonstrated by SQL's three-valued logic. For these two operators, if neither operand is **null**, the operator performs as expected, and if both operands are **null**, the result is **null**. The special behavior comes into play when just one of the operands is **null**. The table below lists the results produced by these two operators for all combinations of **true**, **false**, and **null**:

Operand1 → Operand2 ↓	true	false	null
true	& = **true** | = **true**	& = **false** | = **true**	& = **null** | = **true**
false	& = **false** | = **true**	& = **false** | = **false**	& = **false** | = **null**
null	& = **null** | = **true**	& = **false** | = **null**	& = **null** | = **null**

- **Equality operators (==, !=)**   If both operands are **null**, they are equal. If one operand is **null**, they are not equal. If neither operand is **null**, compare the values to determine if they are equal.

- **Relational operators (<, >, <=, >=)**   If either operand is **null**, the result is **false**. If neither operand is **null**, compare the values.

You should be aware that manipulating nullable instances does generate a lot of code. For example, see the following method:

```
private static Int32? NullableCodeSize(Int32? a, Int32? b) {
   return a + b;
}
```

When I compile this method, there is quite a bit of resulting Intermediate Language (IL) code, which also makes performing operations on nullable types slower than performing the same operation on non-nullable types. Here is the C# equivalent of the compiler-produced IL code:

```
private static Nullable<Int32> NullableCodeSize(Nullable<Int32> a, Nullable<Int32> b) {

    Nullable<Int32> nullable1 = a;
    Nullable<Int32> nullable2 = b;
    if (!(nullable1.HasValue & nullable2.HasValue)) {
        return new Nullable<Int32>();
    }
    return new Nullable<Int32>(nullable1.GetValueOrDefault() + nullable2.GetValueOrDefault());
}
```

Finally, let me point out that you can define your own value types that overload the various operators mentioned above. I discuss how to do this in the "Operator Overload Methods" section in Chapter 8, "Methods." If you then use a nullable instance of your own value type, the compiler does the right thing and invokes your overloaded operator. For example, suppose that you have a **Point** value type that defines overloads for the == and != operators as follows:

```
using System;

internal struct Point {
    private Int32 m_x, m_y;
    public Point(Int32 x, Int32 y) { m_x = x; m_y = y; }

    public static Boolean operator==(Point p1, Point p2) {
        return (p1.m_x == p2.m_x) && (p1.m_y == p2.m_y);
    }

    public static Boolean operator!=(Point p1, Point p2) {
        return !(p1 == p2);
    }
}
```

At this point, you can use nullable instances of the **Point** type and the compiler will invoke your overloaded operators:

```
internal static class Program {
    public static void Main() {
        Point? p1 = new Point(1, 1);
        Point? p2 = new Point(2, 2);

        Console.WriteLine("Are points equal? " + (p1 == p2).ToString());
        Console.WriteLine("Are points not equal? " + (p1 != p2).ToString());
    }
}
```

When I build and run the code above, I get the following output:

```
Are points equal? False
Are points not equal? True
```

C#'s Null-Coalescing Operator

C# has an operator called the *null-coalescing operator* (**??**), which takes two operands. If the operand on the left is not **null**, the operand's value is returned. If the operand on the left is **null**, the value of the right operand is returned. The null-coalescing operator offers a very convenient way to set a variable's default value.

A cool feature of the null-coalescing operator is that it can be used with reference types as well as nullable value types. Here is some code that demonstrates the use of the null-coalescing operator:

```
private static void NullCoalescingOperator() {
   Int32? b = null;

   // The line below is equivalent to:
   // x = (b.HasValue) ? b.Value : 123
   Int32 x = b ?? 123;
   Console.WriteLine(x);  // "123"

   // The line below is equivalent to:
   // String temp = GetFilename();
   // filename = (temp != null) ? temp : "Untitled";
   String filename = GetFilename() ?? "Untitled";
}
```

Some people argue that the null-coalescing operator is simply syntactic sugar for the **?:** operator, and that the C# compiler team should not have added this operator to the language. However, the null-coalescing operator offers two significant syntactic improvements. The first is that the **??** operator works better with expressions:

```
Func<String> f = () => SomeMethod() ?? "Untitled";
```

This code is much easier to read and understand than the line below, which requires variable assignments and multiple statements:

```
Func<String> f = () => { var temp = SomeMethod();
  return temp != null ? temp : "Untitled";};
```

The second improvement is that **??** works better in composition scenarios. For example, the single line

```
String s = SomeMethod1() ?? SomeMethod2() ?? "Untitled";
```

is far easier to read and understand than this chunk of code:

```
String s;
var sm1 = SomeMethod1();
if (sm1 != null) s = sm1;
else {
   var sm2 = SomeMethod2();
   if (sm2 != null) s = sm2;
   else s = "Untitled";
}
```

The CLR Has Special Support for Nullable Value Types

The CLR has built-in support for nullable value types. This special support is provided for boxing, unboxing, calling **GetType**, and calling interface methods, and it is given to nullable types to make them fit more seamlessly into the CLR. This also makes them behave more naturally and as most developers would expect. Let's take a closer look at the CLR's special support for nullable types.

Boxing Nullable Value Types

Imagine a **Nullable<Int32>** variable that is logically set to **null**. If this variable is passed to a method prototyped as expecting an **Object**, the variable must be boxed, and a reference to the boxed **Nullable<Int32>** is passed to the method. This is not ideal because the method is now being passed a non-**null** value even though the **Nullable<Int32>** variable logically contained the value of **null**. To fix this, the CLR executes some special code when boxing a nullable variable to keep up the illusion that nullable types are first-class citizens in the environment.

Specifically, when the CLR is boxing a **Nullable<T>** instance, it checks to see if it is **null**, and if so, the CLR doesn't actually box anything, and **null** is returned. If the nullable instance is not **null**, the CLR takes the value out of the nullable instance and boxes it. In other words, a **Nullable<Int32>** with a value of **5** is boxed into a boxed-**Int32** with a value of **5**. Here is some code that demonstrates this behavior:

```
// Boxing Nullable<T> is null or boxed T
Int32? n = null;
Object o = n;  // o is null
Console.WriteLine("o is null={0}", o == null);  // "True"

n = 5;
o = n;   // o refers to a boxed Int32
Console.WriteLine("o's type={0}", o.GetType()); // "System.Int32"
```

Unboxing Nullable Value Types

The CLR allows a boxed value type **T** to be unboxed into a **T** or a **Nullable<T>**. If the reference to the boxed value type is **null**, and you are unboxing it to a **Nullable<T>**, the CLR sets **Nullable<T>**'s value to **null**. Here is some code to demonstrate this behavior:

```
// Create a boxed Int32
Object o = 5;

// Unbox it into a Nullable<Int32> and into an Int32
Int32? a = (Int32?) o;  // a = 5
Int32  b = (Int32) o;  // b = 5
```

```
// Create a reference initialized to null
o = null;

// "Unbox" it into a Nullable<Int32> and into an Int32
a = (Int32?) o;       // a = null
b = (Int32)  o;       // NullReferenceException
```

Calling **GetType** via a Nullable Value Type

When calling **GetType** on a **Nullable<T>** object, the CLR actually lies and returns the type **T** instead of the type **Nullable<T>**. Here is some code that demonstrates this behavior:

```
Int32? x = 5;

// The line below displays "System.Int32"; not "System.Nullable<Int32>"
Console.WriteLine(x.GetType());
```

Calling Interface Methods via a Nullable Value Type

In the code below, I'm casting **n**, a **Nullable<Int32>**, to **IComparable<Int32>**, an interface type. However, the **Nullable<T>** type does not implement the **IComparable<Int32>** interface as **Int32** does. The C# compiler allows this code to compile anyway, and the CLR's verifier considers this code verifiable to allow you a more convenient syntax.

```
Int32? n = 5;
Int32 result = ((IComparable) n).CompareTo(5);  // Compiles & runs OK
Console.WriteLine(result);                       // 0
```

If the CLR didn't provide this special support, it would be more cumbersome for you to write code to call an interface method on a nullable value type. You'd have to cast the unboxed value type first before casting to the interface to make the call:

```
Int32 result = ((IComparable) (Int32) n).CompareTo(5);  // Cumbersome
```

This chapter is all about error handling. But it's not just about that. There are several parts to error handling. First, we'll define what an error actually is. Then, we'll talk about how to discover when your code is experiencing an error and about how to recover from this error. At this point, state becomes an issue because errors tend to come at inopportune times. It is likely that your code will be in the middle of mutating some state when it experiences the error, and your code likely will have to restore some state back to what it was prior to attempting to mutate it. Of course, we'll also talk about how your code can notify its callers that it has detected an error.

In my opinion, exception handling is the weakest area of the common language runtime (CLR) and therefore causes many problems for developers writing managed code. Over the years, Microsoft has made some significant improvements to help developers deal with errors, but I believe that there is much more that must be done before we can really have a good, reliable system. I will talk a lot about the various enhancements that have been made when dealing with unhandled exceptions, constrained execution regions, code contracts, runtime wrapped exceptions, uncatchable exceptions, and so on.

Defining "Exception"

When designing a type, you first imagine the various situations in which the type will be used. The type name is usually a noun, such as **FileStream** or **StringBuilder**. Then you define the properties, methods, events, and so on for the type. The way you define these members (property data types, method parameters, return values, and so forth) becomes the programmatic interface for your type. These members indicate actions that can be performed by the type itself or on an instance of the type. These action members are usually verbs such as **Read**, **Write**, **Flush**, **Append**, **Insert**, **Remove**, etc. When an action member cannot complete its task, the member should throw an exception.

> **Important**   An exception is when a member fails to complete the task it is supposed to perform as indicated by its name.

Look at the following class definition:

```
internal sealed class Account {
    public static void Transfer(Account from, Account to, Decimal amount) {
        from -= amount;
        to += amount;
    }
}
```

The **Transfer** method accepts two **Account** objects and a **Decimal** value that identifies an amount of money to transfer between accounts. Obviously, the goal of the **Transfer** method is to subtract money from one account and add money to another. The **Transfer** method could fail for many reasons: the **from** or **to** argument might be **null**; the **from** or **to** argument might not refer to an open account; the **from** account might have insufficient funds; the **to** account might have so much money in it that adding more would cause it to overflow; or the amount argument might be **0**, negative, or have more than two digits after the decimal place.

When the **Transfer** method is called, its code must check for all of these possibilities, and if any of them are detected, it cannot transfer the money and should notify the caller that it failed by throwing an exception. In fact, notice that the **Transfer** method's return type is **void**. This is because the **Transfer** method has no meaningful value to return; if it returns at all, it was successful. If it fails, it throws a meaningful exception.

Object-oriented programming allows developers to be very productive because you get to write code like this:

```
Boolean f = "Jeff".Substring(1, 1).ToUpper().EndsWith("E"); // true
```

Here I'm composing my intent by chaining several operations together.[1] This code was easy for me to write and is easy for others to read and maintain because the intent is obvious: Take a string, grab a portion of it, uppercase that portion, and see if it ends with an "E." This is great, but there is a big assumption being made here: no operation fails. But, of course, errors are always possible, so we need a way to handle those errors. In fact, there are many object-oriented constructs—constructors, getting/setting a property, adding/removing an event, calling an operator overload, calling a conversion operator—that have no way to return error codes, but these constructs must still be able to report an error. The mechanism provided by the Microsoft .NET Framework and all programming languages that support it is called *exception handling*.

> **Important** Many developers incorrectly believe that an exception is related to how *frequently* something happens. For example, a developer designing a file **Read** method is likely to say the following: "When reading from a file, you will eventually reach the end of its data. Since reaching the end will *always* happen, I'll design my **Read** method so that it reports the end by returning a special value; I won't have it throw an exception." The problem with this statement is that it is being made by the developer designing the **Read** method, not by the developer calling the **Read** method.
>
> When designing the **Read** method, it is impossible for the developer to know all of the possible situations in which the method gets called. Therefore, the developer can't possibly know how *often* the caller of the **Read** method will attempt to read past the end of the file. In fact, since most files contain structured data, attempting to read past the end of a file is something that *rarely* happens.

Exception-Handling Mechanics

In this section, I'll introduce the mechanics and C# constructs needed in order to use exception handling, but it's not my intention to explain them in great detail. The purpose of this chapter is to offer useful guidelines for when and how to use exception handling in your code. If you want more information about the mechanics and language constructs for using exception handling, see the .NET Framework documentation and the C# language specification. Also, the .NET Framework exception-handling mechanism is built using the Structured Exception Handling (SEH) mechanism offered by Microsoft Windows. SEH has been discussed in many resources, including my own book, *Windows via C/C++*, 5th ed. (Microsoft Press, 2007), which contains three chapters devoted to SEH.

The following C# code shows a standard usage of the exception-handling mechanism. This code gives you an idea of what exception-handling blocks look like and what their purpose is. In the subsections after the code, I'll formally describe the **try**, **catch**, and **finally** blocks and their purpose and provide some notes about their use.

---

[1] In fact, C#'s extension method feature exists in the language to allow you to chain more methods together that would not have been chainable otherwise.

```
private void SomeMethod() {

    try {
       // Put code requiring graceful recovery and/or cleanup operations here...
    }
    catch (InvalidOperationException) {
       // Put code that recovers from an InvalidOperationException here...
    }
    catch (IOException) {
       // Put code that recovers from an IOException here...
    }
    catch {
       // Put code that recovers from any kind of exception other than those above here...

       // When catching any exception, you usually re-throw the exception.
       // I explain re-throwing later in this chapter.
       throw;
    }
    finally {
       // Put code that cleans up any operations started within the try block here...
       // The code in here ALWAYS executes, regardless of whether an exception is thrown.
    }
    // Code below the finally block executes if no exception is thrown within the try block
    // or if a catch block catches the exception and doesn't throw or re-throw an exception.
}
```

This code demonstrates one possible way to use exception-handling blocks. Don't let the code scare you—most methods have simply a **try** block matched with a single **finally** block or a **try** block matched with a single **catch** block. It's unusual to have as many **catch** blocks as in this example. I put them there for illustration purposes.

The **try** Block

A *try block* contains code that requires common cleanup operations, exception-recovery operations, or both. The cleanup code should be placed in a single **finally** block. A **try** block can also contain code that might potentially throw an exception. The exception-recovery code should be placed in one or more **catch** blocks. You create one **catch** block for each kind of exception that your application can safely recover from. A **try** block must be associated with at least one **catch** or **finally** block; it makes no sense to have a **try** block that stands by itself, and C# will prevent you from doing this.

> **Important** Sometimes developers ask how much code they should put inside a single **try** block. The answer to this depends on state management. If, inside a **try** block, you execute multiple operations that could all throw the same exception type and the way that you'd recover this exception type is different depending on the operation, then you should put each operation in its own **try** block so that you can recover your state correctly.

The catch Block

A *catch block* contains code to execute in response to an exception. A **try** block can have zero or more **catch** blocks associated with it. If the code in a **try** block doesn't cause an exception to be thrown, the CLR will never execute the code contained within any of its **catch** blocks. The thread will simply skip over all of the **catch** blocks and execute the code in the **finally** block (if one exists). After the code in the **finally** block executes, execution continues with the statement following the **finally** block.

The parenthetical expression appearing after the **catch** keyword is called the *catch type*. In C#, you must specify a catch type of **System.Exception** or a type derived from **System.Exception**. For example, the previous code contains **catch** blocks for handling an **InvalidOperationException** (or any exception derived from it) and an **IOException** (or any exception derived from it). The last **catch** block (which doesn't specify a catch type) handles any exception at all except for the exception type specified by earlier **catch** blocks; this is equivalent to having a **catch** block that specifies a catch type of **System.Exception** except that you cannot access the exception information via code inside the **catch** block's braces.

> **Note** When debugging through a **catch** block by using Microsoft Visual Studio, you can see the currently thrown exception object by adding the special *$exception* variable name to a watch window.

The CLR searches from top to bottom for a matching **catch** type, and therefore you should place the more specific exception types at the top. The most-derived exception types should appear first, followed by their base types (if any), down to **System.Exception** (or an exception block that doesn't specify a catch type). In fact, the C# compiler generates an error if more specific **catch** blocks appear closer to the bottom because the **catch** block would be unreachable.

If an exception is thrown by code executing within the **try** block (or any method called from within the **try** block), the CLR starts searching for **catch** blocks whose catch type is the same type as or a base type of the thrown exception. If none of the catch types matches the exception, the CLR continues searching up the call stack looking for a catch type that matches the exception. If after reaching the top of the call stack, no **catch** block is found with a matching catch type, an unhandled exception occurs. I'll talk more about unhandled exceptions later in this chapter.

Once the CLR locates a **catch** block with a matching catch type, it executes the code in all inner **finally** blocks, starting from within the **try** block whose code threw the exception and stopping with the **catch** block that matched the exception. Note that any **finally** block associated with the **catch** block that matched the exception is not executed yet. The code in this **finally** block won't execute until after the code in the handling **catch** block has executed.

After all the code in the inner **finally** blocks has executed, the code in the handling **catch** block executes. This code typically performs some operations to deal with the exception. At the end of the **catch** block, you have three choices:

- Re-throw the same exception, notifying code higher up in the call stack of the exception.

- Throw a different exception, giving richer exception information to code higher up in the call stack.

- Let the thread fall out of the bottom of the **catch** block.

Later in this chapter, I'll offer some guidelines for when you should use each of these techniques. If you choose either of the first two techniques, you're throwing an exception, and the CLR behaves just as it did before: It walks up the call stack looking for a **catch** block whose type matches the type of the exception thrown.

If you pick the last technique, when the thread falls out of the bottom of the **catch** block, it immediately starts executing code contained in the **finally** block (if one exists). After all of the code in the **finally** block executes, the thread drops out of the **finally** block and starts executing the statements immediately following the **finally** block. If no **finally** block exists, the thread continues execution at the statement following the last **catch** block.

In C#, you can specify a variable name after a catch type. When an exception is caught, this variable refers to the **System.Exception**-derived object that was thrown. The **catch** block's code can reference this variable to access information specific to the exception (such as the stack trace leading up to the exception). Although it's possible to modify this object, you shouldn't; consider the object to be read-only. I'll explain the **Exception** type and what you can do with it later in this chapter.

> **Note** Your code can register with **AppDomain**'s **FirstChanceException** event to receive notifications as soon as an exception occurs within an AppDomain. This notification occurs before the CLR searches for any **catch** blocks. For more information about this event, see Chapter 22, "CLR Hosting and AppDomains."

The finally Block

A **finally** block contains code that's guaranteed to execute.[2] Typically, the code in a **finally** block performs the cleanup operations required by actions taken in the **try** block.

---

[2] Aborting a thread or unloading an AppDomain causes the CLR to throw a **ThreadAbortException**, which allows the **finally** block to execute. If a thread is simply killed via the Win32 **TerminateThread** function, or if the process is killed via the Win32 **TerminateProcess** function or **System.Environment**'s **FailFast** method, then the **finally** block will not execute. Of course Windows cleans up all resources that a process was using when a process terminates.

For example, if you open a file in a **try** block, you'd put the code to close the file in a **finally** block:

```
private void ReadData(String pathname) {

   FileStream fs = null;
   try {
      fs = new FileStream(pathname, FileMode.Open);
      // Process the data in the file...
   }
   catch (IOException) {
      // Put code that recovers from an IOException here...
   }
   finally {
      // Make sure that the file gets closed.
      if (fs != null) fs.Close();
   }
}
```

If the code in the **try** block executes without throwing an exception, the file is guaranteed to be closed. If the code in the **try** block does throw an exception, the code in the **finally** block still executes, and the file is guaranteed to be closed, regardless of whether the exception is caught. It's improper to put the statement to close the file after the **finally** block; the statement wouldn't execute if an exception were thrown and not caught, which would result in the file being left open (until the next garbage collection).

A **try** block doesn't require a **finally** block associated with it; sometimes the code in a **try** block just doesn't require any cleanup code. However, if you do have a **finally** block, it must appear after any and all **catch** blocks. A **try** block can have no more than one **finally** block associated with it.

When a thread reaches the end of the code contained in a **finally** block, the thread simply starts executing the statements immediately following the **finally** block. Remember that the code in the **finally** block is cleanup code. This code should execute only what is necessary to clean up operations initiated in the **try** block. The code inside **catch** and **finally** blocks should be very short and should have a high likelihood of succeeding without itself throwing an exception. Usually the code in these blocks is just one or two lines of code.

It is always possible that exception-recovery code or cleanup code could fail and throw an exception. While possible, it is unlikely and if it does happen it usually means that there is something very wrong somewhere. Most likely some state has gotten corrupted somewhere. If an exception is inadvertently thrown within a **catch** or **finally** block, the world will not come to an end—the CLR's exception mechanism will execute as though the exception were thrown after the **finally** block. However, the CLR does not keep track of the first exception that was thrown in the corresponding **try** block (if any), and you will lose any and all information (such as the stack trace) available about the first exception. Probably (and hopefully), this new exception will not be handled by your code and the exception will turn into an unhandled exception. The CLR will then terminate your process, which is good because all the corrupted state will now be destroyed. This is much better than having your application continue to run with unpredictable results and possible security holes.

Personally, I think the C# team should have chosen different language keywords for the exception-handling mechanism. What programmers want to do is try to execute some piece of code. And then, if something fails, either recover from the failure and move on or compensate to undo some state change and continue to report the failure up to a caller. Programmers also want to have guaranteed cleanup no matter what happens. The code on the left is what you have to write to make the C# compiler happy, but the code on the right is the way I prefer to think about it:

```
void Method() {
    try {
        ...
    }
    catch (XxxException) {
        ...
    }
    catch (YyyException) {
        ...
    }
    catch {
        ...; throw;
    }
    finally {
        ...
    }
}
```

```
void Method() {
    try {
        ...
    }
    handle (XxxException) {
        ...
    }
    handle (YyyException) {
        ...
    }
    compensate {
        ...
    }
    cleanup {
        ...
    }
}
```

CLS and Non-CLS Exceptions

All programming languages for the CLR must support the throwing of **Exception**-derived objects because the Common Language Specification (CLS) mandates this. However, the CLR actually allows an instance of any type to be thrown, and some programming languages will allow code to throw non–CLS-compliant exception objects such as a **String**, **Int32**, or **DateTime**. The C# compiler allows code to throw only **Exception**-derived objects, whereas code written in some other languages allow code to throw **Exception**-derived objects as well as objects that are not derived from **Exception**.

Many programmers are not aware that the CLR allows any object to be thrown to re-port an exception. Most developers believe that only **Exception**-derived objects can be thrown. Prior to version 2.0 of the CLR, when programmers wrote **catch** blocks to catch exceptions, they were catching CLS-compliant exceptions only. If a C# method called a method written in another language, and that method threw a non–CLS-compliant exception, the C# code would not catch this exception at all, leading to some security vulnerabilities.

In version 2.0 of the CLR, Microsoft introduced a new **RuntimeWrappedException** class (defined in the **System.Runtime.CompilerServices** namespace). This class is derived from **Exception**, so it is a CLS-compliant exception type. The **RuntimeWrappedException** class contains a private field of type **Object** (which can be accessed by using **RuntimeWrappedException**'s **WrappedException** read-only property). In version 2.0 of the CLR, when a non–CLS-compliant exception is thrown, the CLR automatically constructs an instance of the **RuntimeWrappedException** class and initializes its private field to refer to the object that was actually thrown. In effect, the CLR now turns all non–CLS-compliant exceptions into CLS-compliant exceptions. Any code that now catches an **Exception** type will catch non–CLS-compliant exceptions, which fixes the potential security vulnerability problem.

Although the C# compiler allows developers to throw **Exception**-derived objects only, prior to C# version 2.0, the C# compiler did allow developers to catch non–CLS-compliant exceptions by using code like this:

```
private void SomeMethod() {
   try {
      // Put code requiring graceful recovery and/or cleanup operations here...
   }
   catch (Exception e) {
      // Before C# 2.0, this block catches CLS-compliant exceptions only
      // Now, this block catches CLS- & non-CLS-compliant exceptions
      throw; // Re-throws whatever got caught
   }
   catch {
      // In all versions of C#, this block catches CLS- & non-CLS-compliant exceptions
      throw; // Re-throws whatever got caught
   }
}
```

Now, some developers were aware that the CLR supports both CLS- and non–CLS-compliant exceptions, and these developers might have written the two **catch** blocks (shown above) in order to catch both kinds of exceptions. If the above code is recompiled for CLR 2.0 or later, the second **catch** block will never execute, and the C# compiler will indicate this by issuing a warning: **"CS1058: A previous catch clause already catches all exceptions. All non-exceptions thrown will be wrapped in a System.Runtime.CompilerServices.RuntimeWrappedException."**

There are two ways for developers to migrate code from a version of the .NET Framework prior to version 2.0. First, you can merge the code from the two **catch** blocks into a single **catch** block and delete one of the **catch** blocks. This is the recommended approach. Alternatively, you can tell the CLR that the code in your assembly wants to play by the old rules. That is, tell the CLR that your **catch (Exception)** blocks should not catch an instance of the new **RuntimeWrappedException** class. And instead, the CLR should unwrap the non–CLS-compliant object and call your code only if you have a **catch** block that doesn't specify any type at all. You tell the CLR that you want the old behavior by applying an instance of the **RuntimeCompatibilityAttribute** to your assembly like this:

```
using System.Runtime.CompilerServices;
[assembly:RuntimeCompatibility(WrapNonExceptionThrows = false)]
```

Note This attribute has an assembly-wide impact. There is no way to mix wrapped and unwrapped exception styles in the same assembly. Be careful when adding new code (that expects the CLR to wrap exceptions) to an assembly containing old code (in which the CLR didn't wrap exceptions).

The System.Exception Class

The CLR allows an instance of any type to be thrown for an exception—from an **Int32** to a **String** and beyond. However, Microsoft decided against forcing all programming languages to throw and catch exceptions of any type, so they defined the **System.Exception** type and decreed that all CLS-compliant programming languages must be able to throw and catch exceptions whose type is derived from this type. Exception types that are derived from **System.Exception** are said to be CLS-compliant. C# and many other language compilers allow your code to throw only CLS-compliant exceptions.

The **System.Exception** type is a very simple type that contains the properties described in Table 20-1. Usually, you will not write any code to query or access these properties in any way. Instead, when your application terminates due to an unhandled exception, you will look at these properties in the debugger or in a report that gets generated and written out to the Windows Application event log or crash dump.

TABLE 20-1 Public Properties of the System.Exception **Type**

Property	Access	Type	Description
Message	Read-only	String	Contains helpful text indicating why the exception was thrown. The message is typically written to a log when a thrown exception is unhandled. Since end users do not see this message, the message should be as technical as possible so that developers viewing the log can use the information in the message to fix the code when producing a new version.

Property	Access	Type	Description
Data	Read-only	IDictionary	A reference to a collection of key-value pairs. Usually, the code throwing the exception adds entries to this collection prior to throwing it; code that catches the exception can query the entries and use the information in its exception-recovery processing.
Source	Read/write	String	Contains the name of the assembly that generated the exception.
StackTrace	Read-only	String	Contains the names and signatures of methods called that led up to the exception being thrown. This property is invaluable for debugging.
TargetSite	Read-only	MethodBase	Contains the method that threw the exception.
HelpLink	Read-only	String	Contains a URL (such as file://C:\MyApp\Help.htm#MyExceptionHelp) to documentation that can help a user understand the exception. Keep in mind that sound programming and security practices prevent users from ever being able to see raw unhandled exceptions, so unless you are trying to convey information to other programmers, this property is seldom used.
InnerException	Read-only	Exception	Indicates the previous exception if the current exception were raised while handling an exception. This read-only property is usually **null**. The **Exception** type also offers a public **GetBaseException** method that traverses the linked list of inner exceptions and returns the originally thrown exception.

I'd like to say a few words about **System.Exception**'s read-only **StackTrace** property. A **catch** block can read this property to obtain the stack trace indicating what methods were called that led up to the exception. This information can be extremely valuable when you're trying to detect the cause of an exception so that you can correct your code. When you access this property, you're actually calling into code in the CLR; the property doesn't simply return a string. When you construct a new object of an **Exception**-derived type, the **StackTrace** property is initialized to **null**. If you were to read the property, you wouldn't get back a stack trace; you would get back **null**.

When an exception is thrown, the CLR internally records where the **throw** instruction occurred. When a **catch** block accepts the exception, the CLR records where the exception was caught. If, inside a **catch** block, you now access the thrown exception object's **StackTrace** property, the code that implements the property calls into the CLR, which builds a string identifying all of the methods between the place where the exception was thrown and the filter that caught the exception.

> **Important** When you throw an exception, the CLR resets the starting point for the exception; that is, the CLR remembers only the location where the most recent exception object was thrown.

The following code throws the same exception object that it caught and causes the CLR to reset its starting point for the exception:

```
private void SomeMethod() {
   try { ... }
   catch (Exception e) {
      ...
      throw e;   // CLR thinks this is where exception originated.
                 // FxCop reports this as an error
   }
}
```

In contrast, if you re-throw an exception object by using the **throw** keyword by itself, the CLR doesn't reset the stack's starting point. The following code re-throws the same exception object that it caught, causing the CLR to not reset its starting point for the exception:

```
private void SomeMethod() {
   try { ... }
   catch (Exception e) {
      ...
      throw;   // This has no effect on where the CLR thinks the exception
               // originated. FxCop does NOT report this as an error
   }
}
```

In fact, the only difference between these two code fragments is what the CLR thinks is the original location where the exception was thrown. Unfortunately, when you throw or re-throw an exception, Windows does reset the stack's starting point. So if the exception becomes unhandled, the stack location that gets reported to Windows Error Reporting is the location of the last throw or re-throw, even though the CLR knows the stack location where the original exception was thrown. This is unfortunate because it makes debugging applications that have failed in the field much more difficult. Some developers have found this so intolerable that they have chosen a different way to implement their code to ensure that the stack trace truly reflects the location where an exception was originally thrown:

```
private void SomeMethod() {
   Boolean trySucceeds = false;
   try {
      ...
      trySucceeds = true;
   }
   finally {
      if (!trySucceeds) { /* catch code goes in here */ }
   }
}
```

The string returned from the **StackTrace** property doesn't include any of the methods in the call stack that are above the point where the **catch** block accepted the exception object. If you want the complete stack trace from the start of the thread up to the exception handler, you can use the **System.Diagnostics.StackTrace** type. This type defines some properties and methods that allow a developer to programmatically manipulate a stack trace and the frames that make up the stack trace.

You can construct a **StackTrace** object by using several different constructors. Some constructors build the frames from the start of the thread to the point where the **StackTrace** object is constructed. Other constructors initialize the frames of the **StackTrace** object by using an **Exception**-derived object passed as an argument.

If the CLR can find debug symbols (located in the .pdb files) for your assemblies, the string returned by **System.Exception**'s **StackTrace** property or **System.Diagnostics. StackTrace**'s **ToString** method will include source code file paths and line numbers. This information is incredibly useful for debugging.

Whenever you obtain a stack trace, you might find that some methods in the actual call stack don't appear in the stack trace string. There are two reasons for this. First, the stack is really a record of where the thread should return to, not where the thread has come from. Second, the just-in-time (JIT) compiler can inline methods to avoid the overhead of calling and returning from a separate method. Many compilers (including the C# compiler) offer a **/debug** command-line switch. When this switch is used, these compilers embed information into the resulting assembly to tell the JIT compiler not to inline any of the assembly's methods, making stack traces more complete and meaningful to the developer debugging the code.

Note The JIT compiler examines the **System.Diagnostics.DebuggableAttribute** custom attribute applied to the assembly. The C# compiler applies this attribute automatically. If this attribute has the **DisableOptimizations** flag specified, the JIT compiler won't inline the assembly's methods. Using the C# compiler's **/debug** switch sets this flag. By applying the **System.Runtime.CompilerServices.MethodImplAttribute** custom attribute to a method, you can forbid the JIT compiler from inlining the method for both debug and release builds. The following method definition shows how to forbid the method from being inlined:

```
using System;
using System.Runtime.CompilerServices;

internal sealed class SomeType {

   [MethodImpl(MethodImplOptions.NoInlining)]
   public void SomeMethod() {
      ...
   }
}
```

FCL-Defined Exception Classes

The Framework Class Library (FCL) defines many exception types (all ultimately derived from **System.Exception**). The following hierarchy shows the exception types defined in the MSCorLib.dll assembly; other assemblies define even more exception types. (The application used to obtain this hierarchy is shown in Chapter 23, "Assembly Loading and Reflection.")

```
System.Exception
    System.AggregateException
    System.ApplicationException
        System.Reflection.InvalidFilterCriteriaException
        System.Reflection.TargetException
        System.Reflection.TargetInvocationException
        System.Reflection.TargetParameterCountException
        System.Threading.WaitHandleCannotBeOpenedException
    System.InvalidTimeZoneException
    System.IO.IsolatedStorage.IsolatedStorageException
    System.Runtime.CompilerServices.RuntimeWrappedException
    System.SystemException
        System.AccessViolationException
        System.AppDomainUnloadedException
        System.ArgumentException
            System.ArgumentNullException
            System.ArgumentOutOfRangeException
            System.DuplicateWaitObjectException
            System.Globalization.CultureNotFoundException
            System.Text.DecoderFallbackException
            System.Text.EncoderFallbackException
        System.ArithmeticException
            System.DivideByZeroException
            System.NotFiniteNumberException
            System.OverflowException
        System.ArrayTypeMismatchException
        System.BadImageFormatException
        System.CannotUnloadAppDomainException
        System.Collections.Generic.KeyNotFoundException
        System.ContextMarshalException
        System.DataMisalignedException
        System.ExecutionEngineException
        System.FormatException
            System.Reflection.CustomAttributeFormatException
        System.IndexOutOfRangeException
        System.InsufficientExecutionStackException
        System.InvalidCastException
        System.InvalidOperationException
            System.ObjectDisposedException
        System.InvalidProgramException
        System.IO.IOException
            System.IO.DirectoryNotFoundException
            System.IO.DriveNotFoundException
            System.IO.EndOfStreamException
            System.IO.FileLoadException
            System.IO.FileNotFoundException
            System.IO.PathTooLongException
        System.MemberAccessException
            System.FieldAccessException
```

```
    System.MethodAccessException
    System.MissingMemberException
        System.MissingFieldException
        System.MissingMethodException
  System.MulticastNotSupportedException
  System.NotImplementedException
  System.NotSupportedException
    System.PlatformNotSupportedException
  System.NullReferenceException
  System.OperationCanceledException
      System.Threading.Tasks.TaskCanceledException
  System.OutOfMemoryException
      System.InsufficientMemoryException
  System.RankException
  System.Reflection.AmbiguousMatchException
  System.Reflection.ReflectionTypeLoadException
  System.Resources.MissingManifestResourceException
  System.Resources.MissingSatelliteAssemblyException
  System.Runtime.InteropServices.ExternalException
      System.Runtime.InteropServices.COMException
      System.Runtime.InteropServices.SEHException
  System.Runtime.InteropServices.InvalidComObjectException
  System.Runtime.InteropServices.InvalidOleVariantTypeException
  System.Runtime.InteropServices.MarshalDirectiveException
  System.Runtime.InteropServices.SafeArrayRankMismatchException
  System.Runtime.InteropServices.SafeArrayTypeMismatchException
  System.Runtime.Remoting.RemotingException
      System.Runtime.Remoting.RemotingTimeoutException
  System.Runtime.Remoting.ServerException
  System.Runtime.Serialization.SerializationException
  System.Security.Cryptography.CryptographicException
      System.Security.Cryptography.CryptographicUnexpectedOperationException
  System.Security.HostProtectionException
  System.Security.Policy.PolicyException
  System.Security.Principal.IdentityNotMappedException
  System.Security.SecurityException
  System.Security.VerificationException
  System.Security.XmlSyntaxException
  System.StackOverflowException
  System.Threading.AbandonedMutexException
  System.Threading.SemaphoreFullException
  System.Threading.SynchronizationLockException
  System.Threading.ThreadAbortException
  System.Threading.ThreadInterruptedException
  System.Threading.ThreadStartException
  System.Threading.ThreadStateException
  System.TimeoutException
  System.TypeInitializationException
  System.TypeLoadException
      System.DllNotFoundException
      System.EntryPointNotFoundException
  System.TypeUnloadedException
  System.UnauthorizedAccessException
      System.Security.AccessControl.PrivilegeNotHeldException
System.Threading.LockRecursionException
System.Threading.Tasks.TaskSchedulerException
System.TimeZoneNotFoundException
```

Microsoft's original idea was that **System.Exception** would be the base type for all exceptions and that two other types, **System.SystemException** and **System. ApplicationException**, would be the only two types immediately derived from **Exception**. Furthermore, exceptions thrown by the CLR would be derived from **SystemException**, and all application-thrown exceptions would be derived from **ApplicationException**. This way, developers could write a **catch** block that catches all CLR-thrown exceptions or all application-thrown exceptions.

However, as you can see, this rule was not followed very well; some exception types are immediately derived from **Exception** (**IsolatedStorageException**), some CLR-thrown exceptions are derived from **ApplicationException** (**TargetInvocationException**), and some application-thrown exceptions are derived from **SystemException** (**FormatException**). So it is all a big mess, and the result is that the **SystemException** and **ApplicationException** types have no special meaning at all. At this point, Microsoft would like to remove them from the exception class hierarchy, but they can't because it would break any code that already references these two types.

Throwing an Exception

When implementing your own methods, you should throw an exception when the method cannot complete its task as indicated by its name. When you want to throw an exception, there are two issues that you really need to think about and consider.

The first issue is about deciding what **Exception**-derived type are you going to throw. You really want to select a type that is meaningful here. Consider the code that is higher up the call stack and how that code might want to determine that a method failed in order to execute some graceful recovery code. You can use a type that is already defined in the FCL, but there may not be one in the FCL that matches your exact semantics. So you'll probably need to define your own type, ultimately derived from **System.Exception**.

If you want to define an exception type hierarchy, it is highly recommended that the hierarchy be shallow and wide in order to create as few base classes as possible. The reason is that base classes act as a way of treating lots of errors as one error, and this is usually dangerous. Along these lines, you should never throw a **System.Exception** object,[3] and you should use extreme caution if you throw any other base class exception type.

---

[3] In fact, the **System.Exception** class should have been marked as **abstract**, which would forbid code that tried to throw it from even compiling.

Important There are versioning ramifications here, too. If you define a new exception type derived from an existing exception type, then all code that catches the existing base type will now catch your new type as well. In some scenarios this may be desired and in some scenarios, it may not be desired. The problem is that it really depends on how code that catches the base class responds to the exception type and types derived from it. Code that never anticipated the new exception may now behave unpredictably and open security holes. The person defining the new exception type can't know about all the places where the base exception is caught and how it is handled. And so, in practice, it is impossible to make a good intelligent decision here.

The second issue is about deciding what string message are you going to pass to the exception type's constructor. When you throw an exception, you should include a string message with detailed information indicating why the method couldn't complete its task. If the exception is caught and handled, this string message is not seen. However, if the exception becomes an unhandled exception, this message is usually logged. An unhandled exception indicates a true bug in the application, and a developer must get involved to fix the bug. An end user will not have the source code or the ability to fix the code and recompile it. In fact, this string message should not be shown to an end user. So these string messages can be very technically detailed and as geeky as is necessary to help developers fix their code.

Furthermore, since all developers have to speak English (at least to some degree, since programming languages and the FCL classes and methods are in English), there is usually no need to localize exception string messages. However, you may want to localize the strings if you are building a class library that will be used by developers who speak different languages. Microsoft localizes the exception messages thrown by the FCL, since developers all over the world will be using this class library.

Defining Your Own Exception Class

Unfortunately, designing your own exception is tedious and error prone. The main reason for this is because all **Exception**-derived types should be serializable so that they can cross an AppDomain boundary or be written to a log or database. There are many issues related to serialization and they are discussed in Chapter 24, "Runtime Serialization." So, in an effort to simplify things, I made my own generic **Exception<TExceptionArgs>** class, which is defined as follows:

```
[Serializable]
public sealed class Exception<TExceptionArgs> : Exception, ISerializable
    where TExceptionArgs : ExceptionArgs {

    private const String c_args = "Args";  // For (de)serialization
    private readonly TExceptionArgs m_args;

    public  TExceptionArgs Args { get { return m_args; } }
```

```
    public Exception(String message = null, Exception innerException = null)
       : this(null, message, innerException) { }

    public Exception(TExceptionArgs args, String message = null,
       Exception innerException = null): base(message, innerException) { m_args = args; }

    // The constructor is for deserialization; since the class is sealed, the constructor is
    // private. If this class were not sealed, this constructor should be protected
    [SecurityPermission(SecurityAction.LinkDemand,
       Flags=SecurityPermissionFlag.SerializationFormatter)]
    private Exception(SerializationInfo info, StreamingContext context)
       : base(info, context) {
       m_args = (TExceptionArgs)info.GetValue(c_args, typeof(TExceptionArgs));
    }

    // The method for serialization; it's public because of the ISerializable interface
    [SecurityPermission(SecurityAction.LinkDemand,
       Flags=SecurityPermissionFlag.SerializationFormatter)]
    public override void GetObjectData(SerializationInfo info, StreamingContext context) {
       info.AddValue(c_args, m_args);
       base.GetObjectData(info, context);
    }

    public override String Message {
       get {
          String baseMsg = base.Message;
          return (m_args == null) ? baseMsg : baseMsg + " (" + m_args.Message + ")";
       }
    }

    public override Boolean Equals(Object obj) {
       Exception<TExceptionArgs> other = obj as Exception<TExceptionArgs>;
       if (obj == null) return false;
       return Object.Equals(m_args, other.m_args) && base.Equals(obj);
    }
    public override int GetHashCode() { return base.GetHashCode(); }
}
```

And the **ExceptionArgs** base class that **TExceptionArgs** is constrained to is very simple and looks like this:

```
[Serializable]
public abstract class ExceptionArgs {
   public virtual String Message { get { return String.Empty; } }
}
```

Now, with these two classes defined, I can trivially define more exception classes when I need to. To define an exception type indicating the disk is full, I simply do this:

```
[Serializable]
public sealed class DiskFullExceptionArgs : ExceptionArgs {
   private readonly String m_diskpath; // private field set at construction time

   public DiskFullExceptionArgs(String diskpath) { m_diskpath = diskpath; }
```

```
    // Public read-only property that returns the field
    public String DiskPath { get { return m_diskpath; } }

    // Override the Message property to include our field (if set)
    public override String Message {
        get {
            return (m_diskpath == null) ? base.Message : "DiskPath=" + m_diskpath;
        }
    }
}
```

And, if I have no additional data that I want to put inside the class, it gets as simple as this:

```
[Serializable]
public sealed class DiskFullExceptionArgs : ExceptionArgs { }
```

And now I can write code like this, which throws and catches one of these:

```
public static void TextException() {
    try {
        throw new Exception<DiskFullExceptionArgs>(
            new DiskFullExceptionArgs(@"C:\"), "The disk is full");
    }
    catch (Exception<DiskFullExceptionArgs> e) {
        Console.WriteLine(e.Message);
    }
}
```

> **Note** There are two issues to note about my **Exception<TExceptionArgs>** class. The first is-
> sue is that any exception type you define with it is always derived from **System.Exception**. In
> most scenarios, this is not a problem at all and, in fact, having a shallow and wide exception type
> hierarchy is preferred. The second issue is that Visual Studio's unhandled exception dialog box
> doesn't display **Exception<T>** type's generic type parameter, as you can see here:

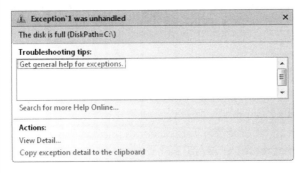

Trading Reliability for Productivity

I started writing software in 1975. I did a fair amount of BASIC programming, and as I got more interested in hardware, I switched to assembly language. Over time, I switched to the C programming language because it allowed me access to hardware with a much higher level of abstraction, making my programming easier. My background is in writing operating systems code and platform/library code, so I always work hard to make my code as small and as fast as possible since applications can only be as good as the OS and libraries they consume.

In addition to creating small and fast code, I always focused on error recovery. When allocating memory (by using C++'s **new** operator or by calling **malloc**, **HeapAlloc**, **VirtualAlloc**, etc.), I would always check the return value to ensure that the memory I requested was actually given to me. And, if the memory request failed, I always had an alternate code path ensuring that the rest of the program's state was unaffected and would let any of my callers know that I failed so that the calling code can take corrective measures too.

For some reason that I can't quite explain, this attention to detail is not done when writing code for the .NET Framework. Getting an out-of-memory situation is always possible and yet I almost never see any code containing a **catch** block to recover from an **OutOfMemoryException**. In fact, I've even had some developers tell me that the CLR doesn't let a program catch an **OutOfMemoryException**. For the record, this is absolutely not true; you can catch this exception. In fact, there are many errors that are possible when executing managed code and I hardly ever see developers write code that attempts to recover from these potential failures. In this section, I'd like to point out some of the potential failures and why it has become culturally acceptable to ignore them. I'd also like to point out some of the significant problems that can occur when ignoring these failures and suggest some ways to help mitigate these problems.

Object-oriented programming allows developers to be very productive. A big part of this is composability which makes it easy to write, read and maintain code. Take this line of code, for example:

```
Boolean f = "Jeff".Substring(1, 1).ToUpper().EndsWith("E");
```

There is a big assumption being made with the code above: no errors occur. But, of course, errors are always possible, and so we need a way to handle those errors. This is what the exception handling constructs and mechanisms are all about and why we need them as opposed to having methods that return **true/false** to indicate success/failure the way that Win32 and COM functions do.

In addition to code composability, we are productive due to all kinds of great features provided by our compilers. For example, the compiler implicitly:

- Inserts optional parameters when calling a method
- Boxes value type instances

- Constructs/initializes parameter arrays

- Binds to members of **dynamic** variables and expressions

- Binds to extension methods

- Binds/invokes overloaded operators

- Constructs delegate objects

- Infers types when calling generic methods, declaring a local variable, and using a lambda expression

- Defines/constructs closure classes for lambda expressions and iterators

- Defines/constructs/initializes anonymous types and instances of them

- Rewrites code to support Language Integrated Queries (LINQs; query expressions and expression trees)

And, the CLR itself does all kinds of great things for developers to make our lives even easier. For example, the CLR implicitly:

- Invokes virtual methods and interface methods

- Loads assemblies and JIT-compiles methods which can potentially throw `FileLoadException`, `BadImageFormatException`, `InvalidProgramException`, `FieldAccessException`, `MethodAccessException`, `MissingFieldException`, `MissingMethodException`, and `VerificationException`

- Transitions across AppDomain boundaries when accessing an object of a `MarshalByRefObject`-derived type which can potentially throw `AppDomainUnloadedException`

- Serializes and deserializes objects when crossing an AppDomain boundary

- Causes thread(s) to throw a `ThreadAbortException` when `Thread.Abort` or `AppDomain.Unload` is called

- Invokes `Finalize` methods after a garbage collection before objects have their memory reclaimed

- Creates type objects in the loader heap when using generic types

- Invokes a type's static constructor potential throwing of `TypeInitializationException`

- Throws various exceptions, including `OutOfMemoryException`, `DivideByZeroException`, `NullReferenceException`, `RuntimeWrappedException`, `TargetInvocationException`, `OverflowException`, `NotFiniteNumberException`, `ArrayTypeMismatchException`, `DataMisalignedException`, `IndexOutOfRangeException`, `InvalidCastException`, `RankException`, `SecurityException`, and more

And, of course, the .NET Framework ships with a massive class library which contains tens of thousands of types each type encapsulating common, reusable functionality. There are types for building Web form applications, Web services, rich GUI applications, working with security, manipulation of images, speech recognition, and the list goes on and on. Any of this code could throw an exception, indicating failure. And, future versions could introduce new exception types derived from existing exception types and now your **catch** blocks catch exception types that never existed before.

All of this stuff—object-oriented programming, compiler features, CLR features, and the enormous class library—is what makes the .NET Framework such a compelling software development platform.[4] My point is that all of this stuff introduces points of failure into your code which you have little control over. As long as everything is working great, all is well: we write code easily, the code is easy to read and maintain. But, when something goes wrong, it is nearly impossible to fully understand what went wrong and why. Here is an example that should really help get my point across:

```
private static Object OneStatement(Stream stream, Char charToFind) {
   return (charToFind + ": " + stream.GetType() + String.Empty + (stream.Position + 512M))
      .Where(c=>c == charToFind).ToArray();
}
```

This slightly contrived method contains just one C# statement in it, but this statement does an awful lot of work. In fact, here is the Intermediate Language (IL) the C# compiler produced for this method. (I've put some lines in boldface italics that are potential points of failure due to implicit operations that are occurring.)

```
.method private hidebysig static object OneStatement(
   class [mscorlib]System.IO.Stream stream, char charToFind) cil managed {
   .maxstack 5
   .locals init (
      [0] class Program/<>c__DisplayClass1 CS$<>8__locals2,
      [1] object[] CS$0$0000)
   L_0000: newobj instance void Program/<>c__DisplayClass1::.ctor()
   L_0005: stloc.0
   L_0006: ldloc.0
   L_0007: ldarg.1
   L_0008: stfld char Program/<>c__DisplayClass1::charToFind
   L_000d: ldc.i4.5
   L_000e: newarr object
   L_0013: stloc.1
   L_0014: ldloc.1
   L_0015: ldc.i4.0
   L_0016: ldloc.0
   L_0017: ldfld char Program/<>c__DisplayClass1::charToFind
```

---

[4] I should also add that Visual Studio's editor, IntelliSense support, code snippet support, templates, extensibility system, debugging system, and various other tools also contribute to making the platform compelling for developers. However, I leave this out of the main discussion because it has no impact on the behavior of the code at runtime.

```
L_001c: box char
L_0021: stelem.ref
L_0022: ldloc.1
L_0023: ldc.i4.1
L_0024: ldstr ": "
L_0029: stelem.ref
L_002a: ldloc.1
L_002b: ldc.i4.2
L_002c: ldarg.0
L_002d: callvirt instance class [mscorlib]System.Type [mscorlib]System.Object::GetType()
L_0032: stelem.ref
L_0033: ldloc.1
L_0034: ldc.i4.3
L_0035: ldsfld string [mscorlib]System.String::Empty
L_003a: stelem.ref
L_003b: ldloc.1
L_003c: ldc.i4.4
L_003d: ldc.i4 0x200
L_0042: newobj instance void [mscorlib]System.Decimal::.ctor(int32)
L_0047: ldarg.0
L_0048: callvirt instance int64 [mscorlib]System.IO.Stream::get_Position()
L_004d: call valuetype [mscorlib]System.Decimal
            [mscorlib]System.Decimal::op_Implicit(int64)
L_0052: call valuetype [mscorlib]System.Decimal [mscorlib]System.Decimal::op_Addition
            (valuetype [mscorlib]System.Decimal, valuetype [mscorlib]System.Decimal)
L_0057: box [mscorlib]System.Decimal
L_005c: stelem.ref
L_005d: ldloc.1
L_005e: call string [mscorlib]System.String::Concat(object[])
L_0063: ldloc.0
L_0064: ldftn instance bool Program/<>c__DisplayClass1::<M>b__0(char)
L_006a: newobj instance
            void [mscorlib]System.Func`2<char, bool>::.ctor(object, native int)
L_006f: call class [mscorlib]System.Collections.Generic.IEnumerable`1<!!0>
            [System.Core]System.Linq.Enumerable::Where<char>(
                class [mscorlib]System.Collections.Generic.IEnumerable`1<!!0>,
                class [mscorlib]System.Func`2<!!0, bool>)
L_0074: call !!0[] [System.Core]System.Linq.Enumerable::ToArray<char>
            (class [mscorlib]System.Collections.Generic.IEnumerable`1<!!0>)
L_0079: ret
}
```

As you can see, an **OutOfMemoryException** is possible when constructing the **<>c__DisplayClass1** class (a compiler-generated type), the **Object[]** array, the **Func** delegate, and boxing the **char** and **Decimal**. Memory is also allocated internally when **Concat**, **Where**, and **ToArray** are called. Constructing the **Decimal** instance could cause its type constructor to be invoked resulting in a **TypeInitializationException**.[5] And then, there are the implicit calls to **Decimal**'s **op_Implicit** operator and its **op_Addition** operator methods, which could do anything including throwing an **OverflowException**.

---

[5] By the way, **System.Char**, **System.String**, **System.Type**, and **System.IO.Stream** all define class constructors which could all potentially cause a **TypeInitializationException** to be thrown at some point in this application.

Querying **Stream**'s **Position** property is interesting. First, it is a virtual property and so my **OneStatement** method has no idea what code will actually execute which could throw any exception at all. Second, **Stream** is derived from **MarshalByRefObject** and so the stream argument could actually refer to a proxy object which itself refers to an object in another AppDomain. The other AppDomain could be unloaded and so an **AppDomainUnloadedException** could also be thrown here.

Of course, all the methods that are being called are methods that I personally have no control over since they are produced by Microsoft. And it's entirely possible that Microsoft might change how these methods are implemented in the future, so they could throw new exception types that I could not possibly know about on the day I wrote the **OneStatement** method. How can I possibly write my **OneStatement** method to be completely robust against all possible failures? By the way, the opposite is also a problem: a **catch** block could catch an exception type derived from the specified exception type and now I'm executing recovery code for a different kind of failure.

So now that you have a sense of all the possible failures, you can probably see why it has become culturally acceptable to not write truly robust and reliable code: it is simply impractical. Moreover, one could argue that it is actually impossible. The fact that errors do not occur frequently is another reason why it has become culturally acceptable. Since errors (like **OutOfMemoryException**) occur very infrequently, the community has decided to trade truly reliable code for programmer productivity.

One of the nice things about exceptions is that an unhandled one causes your application to terminate. This is nice because during testing, you will discover problems quickly and the information you get with an unhandled exception (error message and stack trace) are usually enough to allow you to fix your code. Of course, a lot of companies don't want their application to just terminate after it has been tested and deployed and so a lot of developers insert code to catch **System.Exception**, the base class of all exception types. However, the problem with catching **System.Exception** and allowing the application to continue running is that state may be corrupted.

Earlier in this chapter, I showed an **Account** class that defines a **Transfer** method whose job is to transfer money from one account to another account. What if, when this **Transfer** method is called, it successfully subtracts money from the **from** account and then throws an exception before it adds money to the **to** account? If calling code catches **System. Exception** and continues running, then the state of the application is corrupted: both the **from** and **to** accounts have less money in them then they should. Since we are talking about money here, this state corruption wouldn't just be considered a simple bug, it would definitely be considered a security bug. If the application continues running, it will attempt to perform more transfers to and from various accounts and now state corruption is running rampant within the application.

One could say that the **Transfer** method itself should catch **System.Exception** and restore money back into the **from** account. And this might actually work out OK if the **Transfer** method is simple enough. But if the **Transfer** method produces an audit record of the withdrawn money or if other threads are manipulating the same account at the same time, then attempting to undo the operation could fail as well, producing yet another thrown exception. And now, state corruption is getting worse, not better.

> **Note** One could argue that knowing *where* something went wrong is more useful than knowing *what* error occurred. For example, it might be more useful to know that transferring money out of an account failed instead of knowing that **Transfer** failed due to a **SecurityException** or **OutOfMemoryException**, etc. In fact, the Win32 error model works this way: methods return **true/false** to indicate success/failure so you know which method failed. Then, if your program cares about *why* it failed, it calls the Win32 **GetLastError** method. **System.Exception** does have a **Source** property that tells you the method that failed. But this property is a **String** that you'd have to parse, and if two methods internally call the same method, you can't tell from the **Source** property alone which method your code called that failed. Instead, you'd have to parse the **String** returned from **Exception**'s **StackTrace** property to get this information. Since this is so difficult, I've never seen anyone actually write code to do it.

There are several things you can do to *help* mitigate state corruption:

- The CLR doesn't allow a thread to be aborted when executing code inside a **catch** or **finally** block. So, we could make the **Transfer** method more robust simply by doing this:

```
public static void Transfer(Account from, Account to, Decimal amount) {
   try { /* do nothing in here */ }
   finally {
      from -= amount;
      // Now, a thread abort (due to Thread.Abort/AppDomain.Unload) can't happen here
      to += amount;
   }
}
```

   However, it is absolutely not recommended that you write all your code in **finally** blocks! You should only use this technique for modifying extremely sensitive state.

- You can use the **System.Diagnostics.Contracts.Contract** class to apply code contracts to your methods. Code contracts give you a way to validate arguments and other variables before you attempt to modify state using these arguments/variables. If the arguments/variables meet the contract, then the *chance* of corrupted state is minimized (not completely eliminated). If a contract fails, then an exception is thrown before any state has been modified. I will talk about code contracts later in this chapter.

- You can use constrained execution regions (CERs), which give you a way to take some CLR uncertainty out of the picture. For example, before entering a **try** block, you can have the CLR load any assemblies needed by code in any associated **catch** and **finally** blocks. In addition, the CLR will compile all the code in the **catch** and **finally** blocks including all the methods called from within those blocks. This will eliminate a bunch of potential exceptions (including **FileLoadException**, **BadImageFormatException**, **InvalidProgramException**, **FieldAccessException**, **MethodAccessException**, **MissingFieldException**, and **MissingMethodException**) from occurring when trying to execute error recovery code (in **catch** blocks) or cleanup code (in the **finally** block). It will also reduce the potential for **OutOfMemoryException** and some other exceptions as well. I talk about CERs later in this chapter.

■ Depending on where the state lives, you can use transactions which ensure that all state is modified or no state is modified. If the data is in a database, for example, trans-actions work well. Windows also now supports transacted registry and file operations (on an NTFS volume only) and so you might be able to use this; however the .NET Framework doesn't expose this functionality directly today. You will have to P/Invoke to native code to leverage it. See the **System.Transactions.TransactionScope** class for more details about this.

■ You can design your methods to be more explicit. For example, the **Monitor** class is typically used for taking/releasing a thread synchronization lock as follows:

```
public static class SomeType {
   private static Object s_myLockObject = new Object();

   public static void SomeMethod () {
      Monitor.Enter(s_myLockObject);  // If this throws, did the lock get taken or
                                      // not? If it did, then it won't get released!
      try {
         // Do thread-safe operation here...
      }
      finally {
         Monitor.Exit(s_myLockObject);
      }
   }
   // ...
}
```

Due to the problem shown above, the overload of **Monitor**'s **Enter** method used above is now discouraged, and it is recommended that you rewrite the above code as follows:

```
public static class SomeType {
   private static Object s_myLockObject = new Object();

   public static void SomeMethod () {
      Boolean lockTaken = false;  // Assume the lock was not taken
      try {
         // This works whether an exception is thrown or not!
         Monitor.Enter(s_myLockObject, ref lockTaken);

         // Do thread-safe operation here...
      }
```

```
        finally {
          // If the lock was taken, release it
          if (lockTaken) Monitor.Exit(s_myLockObject);
        }
      }
    }
    // ...
  }
```

While the explicitness in this code is an improvement, in the case of thread synchronization locks, the recommendation now is to not use them with exception handling at all. See Chapter 29, "Hybrid Thread Synchronization Constructs," for more details about this.

If, in your code, you have determined that state has already been corrupted beyond repair, then you should destroy any corrupted state so that it can cause no additional harm. Then, restart your application so your state initializes itself to a good condition and hopefully, the state corruption will not happen again. Since managed state cannot leak outside of an AppDomain, you can destroy any corrupted state that lives within an AppDomain by unloading the entire AppDomain by calling **AppDomain**'s **Unload** method (see Chapter 22 for details).

And, if you feel that your state is so bad that the whole process should be terminated, then you can call **Environment**'s static **FailFast** method:

```
public static void FailFast(String message);
public static void FailFast(String message, Exception exception);
```

This method terminates the process without running any active **try/finally** blocks or **Finalize** methods. This is good because executing more code while state is corrupted could easily make matters worse. However, **FailFast** will allow any **CriticalFinalizerObject**-derived objects, discussed in Chapter 21, "Automatic Memory Management (Garbage Collection), a chance to clean up. This is usually OK because they tend to just close native resources, and Windows state is probably fine even if the CLR's state or your application's state is corrupted. The **FailFast** method writes the message string and optional exception (usually the exception captured in a **catch** block) to the Windows Application event log, produces a Windows error report, creates a memory dump of your application, and then terminates the current process.

> **Important** Most of Microsoft's FCL code does not ensure that state remains good in the case of an unexpected exception. If your code catches an exception that passes through FCL code and then continues to use FCL objects, there is a chance that these objects will behave unpredictably. It's a shame that more FCL objects don't maintain their state better in the face of unexpected exceptions or call **FailFast** if their state cannot be restored.

The point of this discussion is to make you aware of the potential problems related to using the CLR's exception-handling mechanism. Most applications cannot tolerate running with a corrupted state because it leads to incorrect data and possible security holes. If you are writing an application that cannot tolerate terminating (like an operating system or database engine), then managed code is not a good technology to use. And while Microsoft Exchange Server is largely written in managed code, it uses a native database to store e-mail messages. The native database is called the Extensible Storage Engine, it ships with Windows, and can usually be found at C:\Windows\System32\EseNT.dll. Your applications can also use this engine if you'd like; search for "Extensible Storage Engine" on Microsoft's MSDN Web site.

Managed code is a good choice for applications that can tolerate an application terminating when state corruption has possibly occurred. There are many applications that fall into this category. Also, it takes significantly more resources and skills to write a robust native class library or application; for many applications, managed code is the better choice because it greatly enhances programmer productivity.

Guidelines and Best Practices

Understanding the exception mechanism is certainly important. It is equally important to understand how to use exceptions wisely. All too often, I see library developers catching all kinds of exceptions, preventing the application developer from knowing that a problem occurred. In this section, I offer some guidelines for developers to be aware of when using exceptions.

Important If you're a *class library developer* developing types that will be used by other developers, take these guidelines very seriously. You have a huge responsibility: You're trying to design the type in your class library so that it makes sense for a wide variety of applications. Remember that you don't have intimate knowledge of the code that you're calling back (via delegates, virtual methods, or interface methods). And you don't know which code is calling you. It's not feasible to anticipate every situation in which your type will be used, so don't make any policy decisions. Your code must not decide what conditions constitute an error; let the caller make that decision.

In addition, watch state very closely and try not to corrupt it. Verify arguments passed to your method by using code contracts (discussed later in this chapter). Try not to modify state at all. If you do modify state, then be ready for a failure and then try to restore state. If you follow the guidelines in this chapter, application developers will not have a difficult time using the types in your class library.

If you're an *application developer*, define whatever policy you think is appropriate. Following the design guidelines in this chapter will help you discover problems in your code before it is released, allowing you to fix them and make your application more robust. However, feel free to diverge from these guidelines after careful consideration. You get to set the policy. For example, application code can get more aggressive about catching exceptions than class library code.

Use `finally` Blocks Liberally

I think **finally** blocks are awesome! They allow you to specify a block of code that's guaranteed to execute no matter what kind of exception the thread throws. You should use **finally** blocks to clean up from any operation that successfully started before returning to your caller or allowing code following the **finally** block to execute. You also frequently use **finally** blocks to explicitly dispose of any objects to avoid resource leaking. Here's an example that has all cleanup code (closing the file) in a **finally** block:

```
using System;
using System.IO;

public sealed class SomeType {
    private void SomeMethod() {
        FileStream fs = new FileStream(@"C:\Data.bin ", FileMode.Open);
        try {
            // Display 100 divided by the first byte in the file.
            Console.WriteLine(100 / fs.ReadByte());
        }
        finally {
            // Put cleanup code in a finally block to ensure that the file gets closed regardless
            // of whether or not an exception occurs (for example, the first byte was 0).
            if (fs != null) fs.Dispose();
        }
    }
}
```

Ensuring that cleanup code always executes is so important that many programming languages offer constructs that make writing cleanup code easier. For example, the C# language automatically emits **try/finally** blocks whenever you use the **lock, using,** and **foreach** statements. The C# compiler also emits **try/finally** blocks whenever you override a class's destructor (the **Finalize** method). When using these constructs, the compiler puts the code you've written inside the **try** block and automatically puts the cleanup code inside the **finally** block. Specifically,

- When you use the **lock** statement, the lock is released inside a **finally** block.

- When you use the **using** statement, the object has its **Dispose** method called inside a **finally** block.

- When you use the **foreach** statement, the **IEnumerator** object has its **Dispose** method called inside a **finally** block.

- When you define a destructor method, the base class's **Finalize** method is called inside a **finally** block.

For example, the following C# code takes advantage of the **using** statement. This code is shorter than the code shown in the previous example, but the code that the compiler generates is identical to the code generated in the previous example.

```
using System;
using System.IO;

internal sealed class SomeType {
    private void SomeMethod() {
        using (FileStream fs = new FileStream(@"C:\Data.bin", FileMode.Open)) {
```

```
            // Display 100 divided by the first byte in the file.
            Console.WriteLine(100 / fs.ReadByte());
        }
    }
}
```

For more about the **using** statement, see Chapter 21; and for more about the **lock** statement, see Chapter 29, "Hybrid Thread Synchronization Constructs."

Don't Catch Everything

A ubiquitous mistake made by developers who have not been properly trained on the proper
use of exceptions is to use **catch** blocks too often and improperly. When you catch an
exception, you're stating that you expected this exception, you understand why it occurred,
and you know how to deal with it. In other words, you're defining a policy for the application.
This all goes back to the "Trading Reliability for Productivity" section earlier in this chapter.

All too often, I see code like this:

```
try {
    // try to execute code that the programmer knows might fail...
}
catch (Exception) {
    ...
}
```

This code indicates that it was expecting *any* and *all* exceptions and knows how to recover
from *any* and *all* situations. How can this possibly be? A type that's part of a class library
should *never, ever, under any circumstance* catch and swallow all exceptions because there is
no way for the type to know exactly how the application intends to respond to an exception.
In addition, the type will frequently call out to application code via a delegate, virtual method,
or interface method. If the application code throws an exception, another part of the application is probably expecting to catch this exception. The exception should be allowed to filter
its way up the call stack and let the application code handle the exception as it sees fit.

If the exception is unhandled, the CLR terminates the process. I'll discuss unhandled exceptions later in this chapter. Most unhandled exceptions will be discovered during testing of
your code. To fix these unhandled exceptions, you will either modify the code to look for a
specific exception, or you will rewrite the code to eliminate the conditions that cause the
exception to be thrown. The final version of the code that will be running in a production
environment should see very few unhandled exceptions and will be extremely robust.

> **Note** In some cases, a method that can't complete its task will detect that some object's state
> has been corrupted and cannot be restored. Allowing the application to continue running might
> result in unpredictable behavior or security vulnerabilities. When this situation is detected, that
> method should not throw an exception; instead, it should force the process to terminate immedi-
> ately by calling **System.Environment**'s **FailFast** method.

By the way, it *is* OK to catch **System.Exception** and execute some code inside the **catch** block's braces as long as you re-throw the exception at the bottom of that code. Catching **System.Exception** and swallowing the exception (not re-throwing it) should never be done because it hides failures that allow the application to run with unpredictable results and potential security vulnerabilities. Visual Studio's code analysis tool (FxCopCmd.exe) will flag any code that contains a **catch (Exception)** block unless there is a **throw** statement included in the block's code. The "Backing Out of a Partially Completed Operation When an Unrecoverable Exception Occurs—Maintaining State" section, coming shortly in this chapter, will discuss this pattern.

Finally, it is OK to catch an exception occurring in one thread and re-throw the exception in another thread. The Asynchronous Programming Model (discussed in Chapter 27, "I/O-Bound Asynchronous Operations") supports this. For example, if a thread pool thread executes code that throws an exception, the CLR catches and swallows the exception and allows the thread to return to the thread pool. Later, some thread should call an **EndXxx** method to determine the result of the asynchronous operation. The **EndXxx** method will throw the same exception object that was thrown by the thread pool thread that did the actual work. In this scenario, the exception is being swallowed by the first thread; however, the exception is being re-thrown by the thread that called the **EndXxx** method, so it is not being hidden from the application.

Recovering Gracefully from an Exception

Sometimes you call a method knowing in advance some of the exceptions that the method might throw. Because you expect these exceptions, you might want to have some code that allows your application to recover gracefully from the situation and continue running. Here's an example in pseudocode:

```
public String CalculateSpreadsheetCell(Int32 row, Int32 column) {
   String result;
   try {
      result = /* Code to calculate value of a spreadsheet's cell */
   }
   catch (DivideByZeroException) {
      result = "Can't show value: Divide by zero";
   }
   catch (OverflowException) {
      result = "Can't show value: Too big";
   }
   return result;
}
```

This pseudocode calculates the contents of a cell in a spreadsheet and returns a string representing the value to the caller so that the caller can display the string in the application's window. However, a cell's contents might be the result of dividing one cell by another cell. If the cell containing the denominator contains 0, the CLR will throw a **DivideByZeroException** object. In this case, the method catches this specific exception and returns a special string that will be displayed to the user. Similarly, a cell's contents might be the result of multiplying one cell by another. If the multiplied value doesn't fit in the number of bits allowed, the CLR will throw an **OverflowException** object, and again, a special string will be displayed to the user.

When you catch specific exceptions, fully understand the circumstances that cause the exception to be thrown, and know what exception types are derived from the exception type you're catching. Don't catch and handle **System.Exception** (without re-throwing) because it's not feasible for you to know all of the possible exceptions that could be thrown within your **try** block (especially if you consider the **OutOfMemoryException** or the **StackOverflowException**, to name two).

Backing Out of a Partially Completed Operation When an Unrecoverable Exception Occurs—Maintaining State

Usually, methods call several other methods to perform a single abstract operation. Some of the individual methods might complete successfully, and some might not. For example, let's say that you're serializing a set of objects to a disk file. After serializing 10 objects, an exception is thrown. (Perhaps the disk is full or the next object to be serialized isn't marked with the **Serializable** custom attribute.) At this point, the exception should filter up to the caller, but what about the state of the disk file? The file is now corrupted because it contains a partially serialized object graph. It would be great if the application could back out of the partially completed operation so that the file would be in the state it was in before any objects were serialized into it. The following code demonstrates the correct way to implement this:

```
public void SerializeObjectGraph(FileStream fs, IFormatter formatter, Object rootObj) {

   // Save the current position of the file.
   Int64 beforeSerialization = fs.Position;

   try {
      // Attempt to serialize the object graph to the file.
      formatter.Serialize(fs, rootObj);
   }
   catch {  // Catch any and all exceptions.
      // If ANYTHING goes wrong, reset the file back to a good state.
      fs.Position = beforeSerialization;

      // Truncate the file.
      fs.SetLength(fs.Position);

      // NOTE: The preceding code isn't in a finally block because
      // the stream should be reset only when serialization fails.

      // Let the caller(s) know what happened by re-throwing the SAME exception.
      throw;
   }
}
```

To properly back out of the partially completed operation, write code that catches all exceptions. Yes, catch *all* exceptions here because you don't care what kind of error occurred;

you need to put your data structures back into a consistent state. After you've caught and handled the exception, don't swallow it—let the caller know that the exception occurred. You do this by re-throwing the same exception. In fact, C# and many other languages make this easy. Just use C#'s **throw** keyword without specifying anything after **throw**, as shown in the previous code.

Notice that the **catch** block in the previous example doesn't specify any exception type because I want to catch any and all exceptions. In addition, the code in the **catch** block doesn't need to know exactly what kind of exception was thrown, just that something went wrong. Fortunately, C# lets me do this easily just by not specifying any exception type and by making the **throw** statement re-throw whatever object is caught.

Hiding an Implementation Detail to Maintain a "Contract"

In some situations, you might find it useful to catch one exception and re-throw a different exception. The only reason to do this is to maintain the meaning of a method's contract. Also, the new exception type that you throw should be a specific exception (an exception that's not used as the base type of any other exception type). Imagine a **PhoneBook** type that defines a method that looks up a phone number from a name, as shown in the following pseudocode:

```
internal sealed class PhoneBook {
    private String m_pathname;  // path name of file containing the address book

    // Other methods go here.

    public String GetPhoneNumber(String name) {
        String phone;
        FileStream fs = null;
        try {
            fs = new FileStream(m_pathname, FileMode.Open);
            // Code to read from fs until name is found goes here
            phone = /* the phone # found */
        }
        catch (FileNotFoundException e) {
            // Throw a different exception containing the name, and
            // set the originating exception as the inner exception.
            throw new NameNotFoundException(name, e);
        }
        catch (IOException e) {
            // Throw a different exception containing the name, and
            // set the originating exception as the inner exception.
            throw new NameNotFoundException(name, e);
        }
        finally {
            if (fs != null) fs.Close();
        }
        return phone;
    }
}
```

The phone book data is obtained from a file (versus a network connection or database). However, the user of the **PhoneBook** type doesn't know this because this is an implementation detail that could change in the future. So if the file isn't found or can't be read for any reason, the caller would see a `FileNotFoundException` or `IOException`, which wouldn't be anticipated. In other words, the file's existence and ability to be read is not part of the method's implied contract: There is no way the caller could have guessed this. So the **GetPhoneNumber** method catches these two exception types and throws a new `NameNotFoundException`.

When using this technique, you should catch specific exceptions that you fully understand the circumstances that cause the exception to be thrown. And, you should also know what exception types are derived from the exception type you're catching.

Throwing an exception still lets the caller know that the method cannot complete its task, and the `NameNotFoundException` type gives the caller an abstracted view as to why. Setting the inner exception to `FileNotFoundException` or `IOException` is important so that the real cause of the exception isn't lost. Besides, knowing what caused the exception could be useful to the developer of the **PhoneBook** type and possibly to a developer using the **PhoneBook** type.

Important When you use this technique, you are lying to callers about two things. First, you are lying about what actually went wrong. In my example, a file was not found but I'm reporting that a name was not found. Second, you are lying about where the failure occurred. If the `FileNotFoundException` were allowed to propagate up the call stack, its **StackTrace** property would reflect that the error occurred inside `FileStream`'s constructor. But when I swallow this exception and throw a new `NameNotFoundException`, the stack trace will indicate that the error occurred inside the **catch** block, several lines away from where the real exception was thrown. This can make debugging very difficult, so this technique should be used with great care.

Now let's say that the **PhoneBook** type was implemented a little differently. Assume that the type offers a public **PhoneBookPathname** property that allows the user to set or get the path name of the file in which to look up a phone number. Because the user is aware of the fact that the phone book data comes from a file, I would modify the **GetPhoneNumber** method so that it doesn't catch any exceptions; instead, I let whatever exception is thrown propagate out of the method. Note that I'm not changing any parameters of the **GetPhoneNumber** method, but I am changing how it's abstracted to users of the **PhoneBook** type. Users now expect a path to be part of the **PhoneBook**'s contract.

Sometimes developers catch one exception and throw a new exception in order to add additional data or context to an exception. However, if this is all you want to do, you should just catch the exception type you want, add data to the exception object's **Data** property collection, and then re-throw the same exception object:

```
private static void SomeMethod(String filename) {
   try {
      // Do whatevere here...
   }
   catch (IOException e) {
      // Add the filename to the IOException object
      e.Data.Add("Filename", filename);

      throw;   // re-throw the same exception object that now has additional data in it
   }
}
```

Here is a good use of this technique: When a type constructor throws an exception that is not caught within the type constructor method, the CLR internally catches that exception and throws a new **TypeInitializationException** instead. This is useful because the CLR emits code within your methods to implicitly call type constructors.[6] If the type constructor threw a **DivideByZeroException**, your code might try to catch it and recover from it but you didn't even know you were invoking the type constructor. So the CLR converts the **DivideByZeroException** into a **TypeInitializationException** so that you know clearly that the exception occurred due to a type constructor failing; the problem wasn't with your code.

On the other hand, here is a bad use of this technique: When you invoke a method via reflection, the CLR internally catches any exception thrown by the method and converts it to a **TargetInvocationException**. This is incredibly annoying as you must now catch the **TargetInvocationException** object and look at its **InnerException** property to discern the real reason for the failure. In fact, when using reflection, it is common to see code that looks like this:

```
private static void Reflection(Object o) {
   try {
      // Invoke a DoSomething method on this object
      var mi = o.GetType().GetMethod("DoSomething");
      mi.Invoke(o, null);   // The DoSomething method might throw an exception
   }
   catch (System.Reflection.TargetInvocationException e) {
      // The CLR converts reflection-produced exceptions to TargetInvocationException
      throw e.InnerException; // Re-throw what was originally thrown
   }
}
```

I have good news though: If you use C#'s **dynamic** primitive type (discussed in Chapter 5, "Primitive, Reference, and Value Types") to invoke a member, the compiler-generated code does not catch any and all exceptions and throw a **TargetInvocationException** object; the originally thrown exception object simply walks up the stack. For many developers, this is a good reason to prefer using C#'s **dynamic** primitive type rather than reflection.

---

6 For more information about this, see the "Type Constructors" section in Chapter 8, "Methods."

Unhandled Exceptions

When an exception is thrown, the CLR climbs up the call stack looking for **catch** blocks that match the type of the exception object being thrown. If no **catch** block matches the thrown exception type, an *unhandled exception* occurs. When the CLR detects that any thread in the process has had an unhandled exception, the CLR terminates the process. An unhandled exception identifies a situation that the application didn't anticipate and is considered to be a true bug in the application. At this point, the bug should be reported back to the company that publishes the application. Hopefully, the publisher will fix the bug and distribute a new version of the application.

Class library developers should not even think about unhandled exceptions. Only application developers need to concern themselves with unhandled exceptions, and the application should have a policy in place for dealing with unhandled exceptions. Microsoft actually recommends that application developers just accept the CLR's default policy. That is, when an application gets an unhandled exception, Windows writes an entry to the system's event log. You can see this entry by opening the Event Viewer application and then looking under Windows Logs → Application node in the tree, as shown in Figure 20-1.

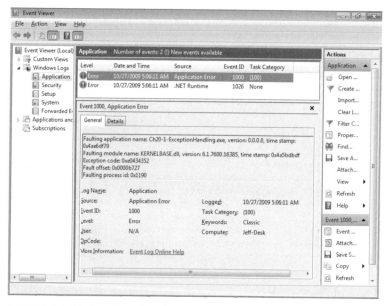

FIGURE 20-1 Windows Event log showing an application that terminated due to an unhandled exception

However, you can get more interesting details about the problem by using the Windows Action Center applet. To start the Action Center, click on the flag icon in the system tray, select Open Action Center, expand the Maintenance box, and then select the "View reliability history" link. From here, you can see the applications that have terminated due to an unhandled exception in the bottom pane, as shown in Figure 20-2.

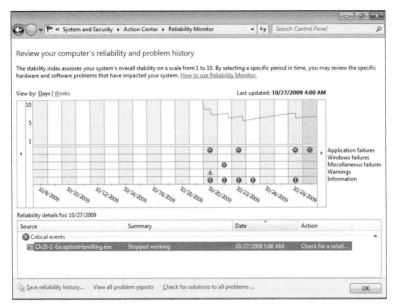

FIGURE 20-2 Reliability Monitor showing an application that terminated due to an unhandled exception

To see more details about the terminated application, double-click on a terminated application in Reliability Monitor. The details will look something like Figure 20-3 and the meaning of the problem signatures are described in Table 20-2. All unhandled exceptions produced by managed applications are placed in the CLR20r3 bucket.

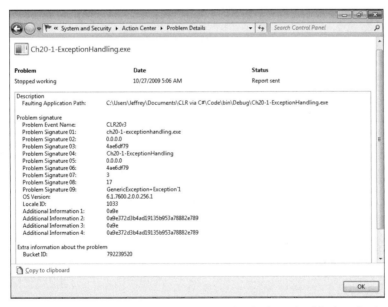

FIGURE 20-3 Reliability Monitor showing more details about the failed application

TABLE 20-2 Problem Signatures

Problem Signature	Description*
01	EXE file's name (32-character limit)
02	EXE file's assembly version number
03	EXE file's timestamp
04	EXE file's full assembly name (64-character limit)
05	Faulting assembly's version
06	Faulting assembly's timestamp
07	Faulting assembly's type and method. This value is a MethodDef metadata token (after stripping off the 0x06 high byte) identifying the method that threw the exception. From this value, you can use ILDasm.exe to determine the offending type and method.
08	Faulting method's IL instruction. This value is an offset within the faulting method of the IL instruction that threw the exception. From this value, you can use ILDasm.exe to determine the offending instruction.
09	Exception type thrown (32-character limit)

* If a string is beyond the allowed limit, then some intelligent truncations are performed, like removing "Exception" from the exception type or ".dll" from a file name. If the resulting string is still too long, then the CLR will create a value by hashing or base-64–encoding the string.

After recording information about the failing application, Windows displays the message box allowing the end user to send information about the failing application to Microsoft's servers.[7] This is called *Windows Error Reporting*, and more information about it can be found at the Windows Quality Web site (*http://WinQual.Microsoft.com*).

Companies can optionally sign up with Microsoft to view this information about their own applications and components. Signing up is free, but it does require that your assemblies be signed with a VeriSign ID (also called a Software Publisher's Digital ID for Authenticode).

Naturally, you could also develop your own system for getting unhandled exception information back to you so that you can fix bugs in your code. When your application initializes, you can inform the CLR that you have a method that you want to be called whenever any thread in your application experiences an unhandled exception.

Unfortunately, every application model Microsoft produces has its own way of tapping into unhandled exceptions. The members that you want to look up in the FCL documentation are:

- For any application, look at **System.AppDomain**'s **UnhandledException** event. Silverlight applications do not execute with enough security to register with this event.

- For a Windows Forms application, look at **System.Windows.Forms.NativeWindow**'s **OnThreadException** virtual method, **System.Windows.Forms.Application**'s **OnThreadException** virtual method, and **System.Windows.Forms.Application**'s **ThreadException** event.

---

[7] You can actually disable this message box by using P/Invoke to call Win32's **SetErrorMode** function, passing in **SEM_NOGPFAULTERRORBOX**.

- For a Windows Presentation Foundation (WPF) application, look at **System.Windows. Application**'s **DispatcherUnhandledException** event and **System.Windows. Threading.Dispatcher**'s **UnhandledException** and **UnhandledExceptionFilter** events.

- For Silverlight, look at **System.Windows.Application**'s **UnhandledException** event.

- For an ASP.NET Web Form application, look at **System.Web.UI.TemplateControl**'s **Error** event. **TemplateControl** is the base class of the **System.Web.UI.Page** and **System.Web.UI.UserControl** classes. Furthermore, you should also look at **System.Web.HttpApplication**'s **Error** event.

- For a Windows Communication Foundation application, look at **System. ServiceModel.Dispatcher.ChannelDispatcher**'s **ErrorHandlers** property.

Before I leave this section, I'd like to say a few words about unhandled exceptions that could occur in a distributed application such as a Web site or Web service. In an ideal world, a server application that experiences an unhandled exception should log it, send some kind of notification back to the client indicating that the requested operation could not complete, and then the server should terminate. Unfortunately, we don't live in an ideal world, and therefore, it may not be possible to send a failure notification back to the client. For some stateful servers (such as Microsoft SQL Server), it may not be practical to terminate the server and start a brand new instance.

For a server application, information about the unhandled exception should not be returned to the client because there is little a client could do about it, especially if the client is implemented by a different company. Furthermore, the server should divulge as little information about itself as possible to its clients to reduce that potential of the server being hacked.

Note The CLR considers some exceptions thrown by native code as *corrupted state exceptions (CSEs)* because they are usually the result of a bug in the CLR itself or in some native code for which the managed developer has no control over. By default, the CLR will not let managed code catch these exceptions and **finally** blocks will not execute. Here is the list of native Win32 exceptions that are considered CSEs:

EXCEPTION_ACCESS_VIOLATION	EXCEPTION_STACK_OVERFLOW
EXCEPTION_ILLEGAL_INSTRUCTION	EXCEPTION_IN_PAGE_ERROR
EXCEPTION_INVALID_DISPOSITION	EXCEPTION_NONCONTINUABLE_EXCEPTION
EXCEPTION_PRIV_INSTRUCTION	STATUS_UNWIND_CONSOLIDATE.

Individual managed methods can override the default and catch these exceptions by applying the **System.Runtime.ExceptionServices.HandleProcessCorruptedStateExceptionsAttribute** to the method. In addition, the method must have the **System.Security. SecurityCriticalAttribute** applied to it. You can also override the default for an entire process by setting the **legacyCorruptedStateExceptionPolicy** element in the application's Extensible Markup Language (XML) configuration file to **true**. The CLR converts most of these to a **System.Runtime.InteropServices.SEHException** object except for EXCEPTION_ ACCESS_VIOLATION, which is converted to a **System.AccessViolationException** object, and EXCEPTION_STACK_OVERFLOW, which is converted to a **System.StackOverflowException** object.

> **Note** Just before invoking a method, you could check for ample stack space by calling the **RuntimeHelper** class's **EnsureSufficientExecutionStack** method. This method checks if the calling thread has enough stack space available to execute the average method (which is not well defined). If there is insufficient stack space, the method throws an **InsufficientExecutionStackException** which you can catch. The **EnsureSufficientExecutionStack** method takes no arguments and returns **void**. This method is typically used by recursive methods.

Debugging Exceptions

The Visual Studio debugger offers special support for exceptions. With a solution open, choose Exceptions from the Debug menu, and you'll see the dialog box shown in Figure 20-4.

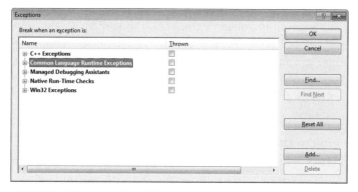

FIGURE 20-4 The Exceptions dialog box, showing the different kinds of exceptions

This dialog box shows the different kinds of exceptions that Visual Studio is aware of. For Common Language Runtime Exceptions, expanding the corresponding branch in the dialog box, as in Figure 20-5, shows the set of namespaces that the Visual Studio debugger is aware of.

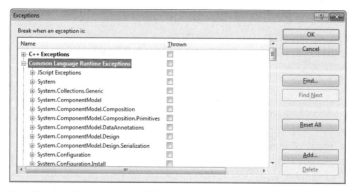

FIGURE 20-5 The Exceptions dialog box, showing CLR exceptions by namespace

If you expand a namespace, you'll see all of the **System.Exception**-derived types defined within that namespace. For example, Figure 20-6 shows what you'll see if you open the **System** namespace.

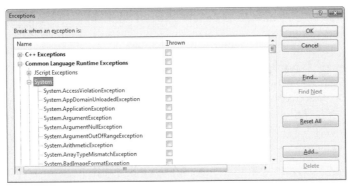

FIGURE 20-6 The Exceptions dialog box, showing CLR exceptions defined in the **System** namespace

For any exception type, if its Thrown check box is selected, the debugger will break as soon as that exception is thrown. At this point, the CLR has not tried to find any matching **catch** blocks. This is useful if you want to debug your code that catches and handles an exception. It is also useful when you suspect that a component or library may be swallowing or re-throwing exceptions, and you are uncertain where exactly to set a break point to catch it in the act.

If an exception type's Thrown check box is not selected, the debugger will also break where the exception was thrown, but only if the exception type was not handled. Developers usually leave the Thrown check box cleared because a handled exception indicates that the application anticipated the situation and dealt with it; the application continues running normally.

If you define your own exception types, you can add them to this dialog box by clicking Add. This causes the dialog box in Figure 20-7 to appear.

FIGURE 20-7 Making Visual Studio aware of your own exception type: the New Exception dialog box

In this dialog box, you first select the type of exception to be Common Language Runtime Exceptions, and then, you can enter the fully qualified name of your own exception type. Note that the type you enter doesn't have to be a type derived from **System.Exception**; non–CLS-compliant types are fully supported. If you have two or more types with the same name but in different assemblies, there is no way to distinguish the types from one another. Fortunately, this situation rarely happens.

If your assembly defines several exception types, you must add them one at a time. In the future, I'd like to see this dialog box allow me to browse for an assembly and automatically import all **Exception**-derived types into Visual Studio's debugger. Each type could then be identified by assembly as well, which would fix the problem of having two types with the same name in different assemblies.

Exception-Handling Performance Considerations

The developer community actively debates the performance of exception handling. Some people claim that exception handling performance is so bad that they refuse to even use exception handling. However, I contend that in an object-oriented platform, exception handling is not an option; it is mandatory. And besides, if you didn't use it, what would you use instead? Would you have your methods return **true/false** to indicate success/failure or perhaps some error code **enum** type? Well, if you did this, then you have the worst of both worlds: The CLR and the class library code will throw exceptions and your code will return error codes. You'd have to now deal with both of these in your code.

It's difficult to compare performance between exception handling and the more conventional means of reporting exceptions (such as **HRESULT**s, special return codes, and so forth). If you write code to check the return value of every method call and filter the return value up to your own callers, your application's performance will be seriously affected. But performance aside, the amount of additional coding you must do and the potential for mistakes is incredibly high when you write code to check the return value of every method. Exception handling is a much better alternative.

However, exception handling has a price: Unmanaged C++ compilers must generate code to track which objects have been constructed successfully. The compiler must also generate code that, when an exception is caught, calls the destructor of each successfully constructed object. It's great that the compiler takes on this burden, but it generates a lot of bookkeeping code in your application, adversely affecting code size and execution time.

On the other hand, managed compilers have it much easier because managed objects are allocated in the managed heap, which is monitored by the garbage collector. If an object is successfully constructed and an exception is thrown, the garbage collector will eventually free the object's memory. Compilers don't need to emit any bookkeeping code to track which objects are constructed successfully and don't need to ensure that a destructor has been called. Compared to unmanaged C++, this means that less code is generated by the compiler, and less code has to execute at runtime, resulting in better performance for your application.

Over the years, I've used exception handling in different programming languages, different operating systems, and different CPU architectures. In each case, exception handling is implemented differently with each implementation having its pros and cons with respect to performance. Some implementations compile exception handling constructs directly into a method, whereas other implementations store information related to exception handling in a data table associated with the method—this table is accessed only if an exception is thrown. Some compilers can't inline methods that contain exception handlers, and some compilers won't enregister variables if the method contains exception handlers.

The point is that you can't determine how much additional overhead is added to an application when using exception handling. In the managed world, it's even more difficult to tell because your assembly's code can run on any platform that supports the .NET Framework. So the code produced by the JIT compiler to manage exception handling when your assembly is running on an x86 machine will be very different from the code produced by the JIT compiler when your code is running on an x64 or IA64 processor. Also, JIT compilers associated with other CLR implementations (such as Microsoft's .NET Compact Framework or the open-source Mono project) are likely to produce different code.

Actually, I've been able to test some of my own code with a few different JIT compilers that Microsoft has internally, and the difference in performance that I've observed has been quite dramatic and surprising. The point is that you must test your code on the various platforms that you expect your users to run on, and make changes accordingly. Again, I wouldn't worry about the performance of using exception handling; because the benefits typically far outweigh any negative performance impact.

If you're interested in seeing how exception handling impacts the performance of your code, you can use the Performance Monitor tool that comes with Windows. The screen in Figure 20-8 shows the exception-related counters that are installed along with the .NET Framework.

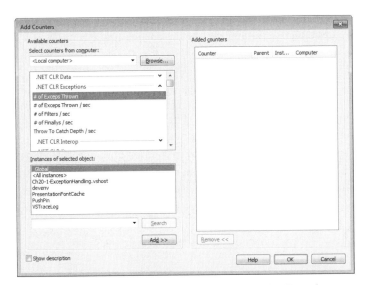

FIGURE 20-8 Performance Monitor showing the .NET CLR Exceptions counters

Occasionally, you come across a method that you call frequently that has a high failure rate. In this situation, the performance hit of having exceptions thrown can be intolerable. For example, Microsoft heard back from several customers who were calling **Int32**'s **Parse** method, frequently passing in data entered from an end user that could not be parsed. Since **Parse** was called frequently, the performance hit of throwing and catching the exceptions was taking a large toll on the application's overall performance.

To address customers' concerns and to satisfy all the guidelines described in this chapter, Microsoft added a new method to the **Int32** class. This new method is called **TryParse**, and it has two overloads that look like this:

```
public static Boolean TryParse(String s, out Int32 result);
public static Boolean TryParse(String s, NumberStyles styles,
    IFormatProvider, provider, out Int32 result);
```

You'll notice that these methods return a **Boolean** that indicates whether the **String** passed in contains characters that can be parsed into an **Int32**. These methods also return an output parameter named **result**. If the methods return **true**, **result** will contain the result of parsing the string into a 32-bit integer. If the methods return **false**, **result** will contain **0**, but you really shouldn't execute any code that looks at it anyway.

One thing I want to make absolutely clear: A **TryXxx** method's **Boolean** return value returns **false** to indicate one and only one type of failure. The method should still throw exceptions for any other type of failure. For example, **Int32**'s **TryParse** throws an **ArgumentException** if the style's argument is not valid, and it is certainly still possible to have an **OutOfMemoryException** thrown when calling **TryParse**.

I also want to make it clear that object-oriented programming allows programmers to be productive. One way that it does this is by not exposing error codes in a type's members. In other words, constructors, methods, properties, etc. are all defined with the idea that calling them won't fail. And, if defined correctly, for most uses of a member, it will not fail, and there will be no performance hit because an exception will not be thrown.

When defining types and their members, you should define the members so that it is unlikely that they will fail for the common scenarios in which you expect your types to be used. If you later hear from users that they are dissatisfied with the performance due to exceptions being thrown, then and only then should you consider adding **TryXxx** methods. In other words, you should produce the best object model first and then, if users push back, add some **TryXxx** methods to your type so that the users who experience performance trouble can benefit. Users who are not experiencing performance trouble should continue to use the non-**TryXxx** versions of the methods because this is the better object model.

Constrained Execution Regions (CERs)

Many applications don't need to be robust and recover from any and all kinds of failures. This is true of many client applications like Notepad.exe and Calc.exe. And, of course, many of us have seen Microsoft Office applications like WinWord.exe, Excel.exe, and Outlook.exe terminate due to unhandled exceptions. Also, many server-side applications, like Web servers, are stateless and are automatically restarted if they fail due to an unhandled exception. Of course some servers, like SQL Server, are all about state management and having data lost due to an unhandled exception is potentially much more disastrous.

In the CLR, we have AppDomains (discussed in Chapter 22), which contain state. When an AppDomain is unloaded, all its state is unloaded. And so, if a thread in an AppDomain experiences an unhandled exception, it is OK to unload the AppDomain (which destroys all its state) without terminating the whole process.[8]

By definition, a CER is a block of code that must be resilient to failure. Since AppDomains can be unloaded, destroying their state, CERs are typically used to manipulate any state that is shared by multiple AppDomains or processes. CERs are useful when trying to maintain state in the face of exceptions that get thrown unexpectedly. Sometimes we refer to these kinds of exceptions as *asynchronous exceptions*. For example, when calling a method, the CLR has to load an assembly, create a type object in the AppDomain's loader heap, call the type's static constructor, JIT IL into native code, and so on. Any of these operations could fail, and the CLR reports the failure by throwing an exception.

If any of these operations fail within a **catch** or `finally` block, then your error recovery or cleanup code won't execute in its entirety. Here is an example of code that exhibits the potential problem:

```
private static void Demo1() {
   try {
      Console.WriteLine("In try");
   }
   finally {
      // Type1's static constructor is implicitly called in here
      Type1.M();
   }
}

private sealed class Type1 {
   static Type1() {
      // if this throws an exception, M won't get called
      Console.WriteLine("Type1's static ctor called");
   }

   public static void M() { }
}
```

---

[8] This is definitely true if the thread lives its whole life inside a single AppDomain (like in the ASP.NET and managed SQL Server stored procedure scenarios). But you might have to terminate the whole process if a thread crosses AppDomain boundaries during its lifetime.

When I run the code above, I get the following output:

```
In try
Type1's static ctor called
```

What we want is to not even start executing the code in the **try** block above unless we know that the code in the associated **catch** and **finally** blocks is guaranteed (or as close as we can get to guaranteed) to execute. We can accomplish this by modifying the code as follows:

```
private static void Demo2() {
    // Force the code in the finally to be eagerly prepared
    RuntimeHelpers.PrepareConstrainedRegions();  // System.Runtime.CompilerServices namespace
    try {
        Console.WriteLine("In try");
    }
    finally {
        // Type2's static constructor is implicitly called in here
        Type2.M();
    }
}

public class Type2 {
    static Type2() {
        Console.WriteLine("Type2's static ctor called");
    }

    // Use this attribute defined in the System.Runtime.ConstrainedExecution namespace
    [ReliabilityContract(Consistency.WillNotCorruptState, Cer.Success)]
    public static void M() { }
}
```

Now, when I run this version of the code, I get the following output:

```
Type2's static ctor called
In try
```

The **PrepareConstrainedRegions** method is a very special method. When the JIT compiler sees this method being called immediately before a **try** block, it will eagerly compile the code in the **try**'s **catch** and **finally** blocks. The JIT compiler will load any assemblies, create any type objects, invoke any static constructors, and JIT any methods. If any of these operations result in an exception, then the exception occurs *before* the thread enters the **try** block.

When the JIT compiler eagerly prepares methods, it also walks the entire call graph eagerly preparing called methods. However, the JIT compiler only prepares methods that have the **ReliabilityContractAttribute** applied to them with either **Consistency. WillNotCorruptState** or **Consistency.MayCorruptInstance** because the CLR can't make any guarantees about methods that might corrupt AppDomain or process state. Inside a **catch** or **finally** block that you are protecting with a call to **PrepareConstrainedRegions**, you want to make sure that you only call methods with the **ReliabilityContractAttribute** set as I've just described.

The **ReliabilityContractAttribute** looks like this:

```
public sealed class ReliabilityContractAttribute : Attribute {
    public ReliabilityContractAttribute(Consistency consistencyGuarantee, Cer cer);
    public Cer Cer { get; }
    public Consistency ConsistencyGuarantee { get; }
}
```

This attribute lets a developer document the reliability contract of a particular method[9] to the method's potential callers. Both the **Cer** and **Consistency** types are enumerated types defined as follows:

```
enum Consistency {
    MayCorruptProcess, MayCorruptAppDomain, MayCorruptInstance, WillNotCorruptState
}
```

```
enum Cer { None, MayFail, Success }
```

If the method you are writing promises not to corrupt any state, use **Consistency. WillNotCorruptState**. Otherwise, document what your method does by using one of the other three possible values that match whatever state your method might corrupt. If the method that you are writing promises not to fail, use **Cer.Success**. Otherwise, use **Cer. MayFail**. Any method that does not have the **ReliabiiltyContractAttribute** applied to it is equivalent to being marked like this:

```
[ReliabilityContract(Consistency.MayCorruptProcess, Cer.None)]
```

The **Cer.None** value indicates that the method makes no CER guarantees. In other words, it wasn't written with CERs in mind; therefore, it may fail and it may or may not report that it failed. Remember that most of these settings are giving a method a way to document what it offers to potential callers so that they know what to expect. The CLR and JIT compiler do not use this information.

When you want to write a reliable method, make it small and constrain what it does. Make sure that it doesn't allocate any objects (no boxing, for example), don't call any virtual methods or interface methods, use any delegates, or use reflection because the JIT compiler can't tell what method will actually be called. However, you can manually prepare these methods by calling one of these methods defined by the **RuntimeHelpers**'s class:

```
public static void PrepareMethod(RuntimeMethodHandle method)
public static void PrepareMethod(RuntimeMethodHandle method,
    RuntimeTypeHandle[] instantiation)
public static void PrepareDelegate(Delegate d);
public static void PrepareContractedDelegate(Delegate d);
```

---

[9] You can also apply this attribute to an interface, a constructor, a structure, a class, or an assembly to affect the members inside it.

Note that the compiler and the CLR do nothing to verify that you've written your method to actually live up to the guarantees you document via the **ReliabilityContractAttribute**. If you do something wrong, then state corruption is possible.

> **Note** Even if all the methods are eagerly prepared, a method call could still result in a **StackOverflowException**. When the CLR is not being hosted, a **StackOverflowException** causes the process to terminate immediately by the CLR internally calling **Environment. FailFast**. When hosted, the **PreparedConstrainedRegions** method checks the stack to see if there is approximately 48KB of stack space remaining. If there is limited stack space, the **StackOverflowException** occurs before entering the **try** block.

You should also look at **RuntimeHelper**'s **ExecuteCodeWithGuaranteedCleanup** method which is another way to execute code with guaranteed cleanup:

```
public static void ExecuteCodeWithGuaranteedCleanup(TryCode code, CleanupCode backoutCode,
    Object userData);
```

When calling this method, you pass the body of the **try** and **finally** block as callback methods whose prototypes match these two delegates respectively:

```
public delegate void TryCode(Object userData);
public delegate void CleanupCode(Object userData, Boolean exceptionThrown);
```

And finally, another way to get guaranteed code execution is to use the **CriticalFinalizerObject** class which is explained in great detail in Chapter 21.

Code Contracts

Code contracts provide a way for you to declaratively document design decisions that you've made about your code within the code itself. The contracts take the form of

- **Preconditions**   Typically used to validate arguments.

- **Postconditions**   Used to validate state when a method terminates either due to a normal return or due to throwing an exception.

- **Object Invariants**   Used to ensure an object's fields remain in a good state through an object's entire lifetime.

Code contracts facilitate code usage, understanding, evolution, testing[10], documentation, and early error detection. You can think of preconditions, postconditions, and object invariants as parts of a method's signature. As such, you can loosen a contract with a new version of your code, but you cannot make a contract stricter with a new version without breaking backward compatibility.

---

[10] To help with automated testing, see the Pex tool created by Microsoft Research: *http://research.microsoft.com /en-us/projects/pex/*.

At the heart of the code contracts is the static **System.Diagnostics.Contracts.Contract** class:

```
public static class Contract {
   // Precondition methods: [Conditional("CONTRACTS_FULL")]
   public static void Requires(Boolean condition);
   public static void EndContractBlock();

   // Preconditions: Always
   public static void Requires<TException>(Boolean condition) where TException : Exception;

   // Postcondition methods: [Conditional("CONTRACTS_FULL")]
   public static void Ensures(Boolean condition);
   public static void EnsuresOnThrow<TException>(Boolean condition)
      where TException : Exception;

   // Special Postcondition methods: Always
   public static T Result<T>();
   public static T OldValue<T>(T value);
   public static T ValueAtReturn<T>(out T value);

   // Object Invariant methods: [Conditional("CONTRACTS_FULL")]
   public static void Invariant(Boolean condition);

   // Quantifier methods: Always
   public static Boolean Exists<T>(IEnumerable<T> collection, Predicate<T> predicate);
   public static Boolean Exists(Int32 fromInclusive, Int32 toExclusive,
      Predicate<Int32> predicate);
   public static Boolean ForAll<T>(IEnumerable<T> collection, Predicate<T> predicate);
   public static Boolean ForAll(Int32 fromInclusive, Int32 toExclusive,
      Predicate<Int32> predicate);
   // Helper methods: [Conditional("CONTRACTS_FULL")] or [Conditional("DEBUG")]
   public static void Assert(Boolean condition);
   public static void Assume(Boolean condition);

   // Infrastructure event: usually your code will not use this event
   public static event EventHandler<ContractFailedEventArgs> ContractFailed;
}
```

As indicated above, many of these static methods have the **[Conditional("CONTRACTS_ FULL")]** attribute applied to them. Some of the helper methods also have the **[Conditional("DEBUG")]** attribute applied to them. This means that the compiler will ignore any code you write that calls these methods unless the appropriate symbol is defined when compiling your code. Any methods marked with "Always" mean that the compiler always emits code to call the method. Also, the **Requires**, **Requires<TException>**, **Ensures**, **EnsuresOnThrow**, **Invariant**, **Assert**, and **Assume** methods have an additional overload (not shown) that takes a **String** message argument so you can explicitly specify a string message that should appear when the contract is violated.

By default, contracts merely serve as documentation as you would not define the **CONTRACTS_FULL** symbol when you build your project. In order to get some additional value out of using contracts, you must download additional tools and a Visual Studio property pane from *http://msdn.microsoft.com/en-us/devlabs/dd491992.aspx*. The reason why all the code contract tools are not included with Visual Studio is because this technology is relatively new and is being improved rapidly. Microsoft's DevLabs Web site can offer new versions and improvements more quickly than Visual Studio itself. After downloading and installing the additional tools, you will see your projects have a new property pane available to them, as shown in Figure 20-9.

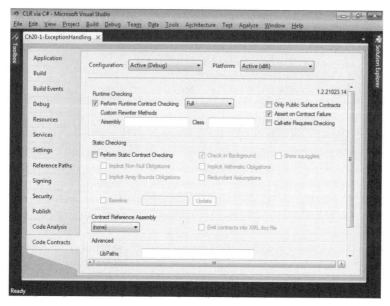

FIGURE 20-9 The Code Contracts pane for a Visual Studio project

To turn on code contract features, select the Perform Runtime Contract Checking check box and select Full from the combo box next to it. This defines the **CONTRACTS_FULL** symbol when you build your project and invokes the appropriate tools (described shortly) after building your project. Now, at runtime, when a contract is violated, **Contract**'s **ContractFailed** event is raised. Usually, developers do not register any methods with this event, but if you do, then any methods you register will receive a **ContractFailedEventArgs** object that looks like this:

```
public sealed class ContractFailedEventArgs : EventArgs {
    public ContractFailedEventArgs(ContractFailureKind failureKind,
        String message, String condition, Exception originalException);

    public ContractFailureKind FailureKind       { get; }
    public String              Message            { get; }
    public String              Condition          { get; }
    public Exception           OriginalException  { get; }

    public Boolean Handled { get; }    // true if any handler called SetHhandled
    public void SetHandled();          // Call to ignore the violation; sets Handled to true

    public Boolean Unwind { get; }     // true if any handler called SetUnwind or threw
    public void SetUnwind();           // Call to force ContractException; set Unwind to true
}
```

Multiple event handler methods can be registered with this event. Each method can process the contract violation any way it chooses. For example, a handler can log the violation, ignore the violation (by calling **SetHandled**), or terminate the process. If any method calls **SetHandled**, then the violation will be considered handled and, after all the handler methods return, the application code is allowed to continue running unless any handler calls **SetUnwind**. If a handler calls **SetUnwind**, then, after all the handler methods have completed running, a **System.Diagnostics.Contracts.ContractException** is thrown. Note that this type is internal to MSCorLib.dll and therefore you cannot write a **catch** block to catch it explicitly. Also note that if any handler method throws an unhandled exception, then the remaining handler methods are invoked and then a **ContractException** is thrown.

If there are no event handlers or if none of them call **SetHandled**, **SetUnwind**, or throw an unhandled exception, then default processing of the contract violation happens next. If the CLR is being hosted, then the host is notified that a contract failed. If the CLR is running an application on a non-interactive window station (which would be the case for a Windows service application), then **Environment.FailFast** is called to instantly terminate the process. If you compile with the Assert On Contract Failure option checked, then an assert dialog box will appear allowing you to connect a debugger to your application. If this option is not checked, then a **ContractException** is thrown.

Let's look at a sample class that is using code contracts:

```
public sealed class Item { /* ... */ }

public sealed class ShoppingCart {
    private List<Item> m_cart      = new List<Item>();
    private Decimal    m_totalCost = 0;

    public ShoppingCart() {
    }

    public void AddItem(Item item) {
        AddItemHelper(m_cart, item, ref m_totalCost);
    }

    private static void AddItemHelper(List<Item> m_cart, Item newItem,
        ref Decimal totalCost) {

        // Preconditions:
        Contract.Requires(newItem != null);
        Contract.Requires(Contract.ForAll(m_cart, s => s != newItem));

        // Postconditions:
        Contract.Ensures(Contract.Exists(m_cart, s => s == newItem));
        Contract.Ensures(totalCost >= Contract.OldValue(totalCost));
        Contract.EnsuresOnThrow<IOException>(totalCost == Contract.OldValue(totalCost));

        // Do some stuff (which could throw an IOException)...
        m_cart.Add(newItem);
        totalCost += 1.00M;
    }
}
```

```
   // Object invariant
   [ContractInvariantMethod]
   private void ObjectInvariant() {
      Contract.Invariant(m_totalCost >= 0);
   }
}
```

The **AddItemHelper** method defines a bunch of code contracts. The preconditions indicate that **newItem** must not be **null** and that the item being added to the cart is not already in the cart. The postconditions indicate that the new item must be in the cart and that the total cost must be at least as much as it was before the item was added to the cart. The postconditions also indicate that if **AddItemHelper** were to throw an **IOException** for some reason, then **totalCost** is unchanged from what it was when the method started to execute. The **ObjectInvariant** method is just a private method that, when called, makes sure that the object's **m_totalCost** field never contains a negative value.

Important All members referenced in a precondition, postcondition, or invariant test must be side-effect free. This is required because testing conditions should not change the state of the object itself. In addition, all members referenced in a precondition test must be at least as accessible as the method defining the precondition. This is required because callers of the method should be able to verify that they have met all the preconditions prior to invoking the method. On the other hand, members referenced in a postcondition or invariant test can have any accessibility as long as the code can compile. The reason why accessibility isn't important here is because postcondition and invariant tests do not affect the callers' ability to invoke the method correctly.

Important In regard to inheritance, a derived type cannot override and change the preconditions of a virtual member defined in a base type. Similarly, a type implementing an interface member cannot change the preconditions defined by that interface member. If a member does not have an explicit contract defined for it, then the member has an implicit contract that logically looks like this:

```
Contract.Requires(true);
```

And since a contract cannot be made stricter with new versions (without breaking compatibility), you should carefully consider preconditions when introducing a new virtual, abstract, or interface member. For postconditions and object invariants, contracts can be added and removed at will as the conditions expressed in the virtual/abstract/interface member and the conditions expressed in the overriding member are just logically AND-ed together.

So now you see how to declare contracts. Let's now talk about how they function at runtime. You get to declare all your precondition and postcondition contracts at the top of your methods where they are easy to find. Of course, the precondition contracts will validate their tests when the method is invoked. However, we don't want the postcondition contracts to validate their tests until the method returns. In order to get the desired behavior, the assembly produced by the C# compiler must be processed by the Code Contract Rewriter tool (CCRewrite.exe, found in C:\Program Files (x86)\Microsoft\Contracts\Bin), which produces a modified version of the assembly. After you select the Perform Runtime Contract Checking check box for your project, Visual Studio will invoke this tool for you automatically whenever you build the project. This tool analyzes the IL in all your methods and it rewrites the IL so that any postcondition contracts are executed at the end of each method. If your method has multiple return points inside it, then the CCRewrite.exe tool modifies the method's IL code so that all return points execute the postcondition code prior to the method returning.

The CCRewrite.exe tool looks in the type for any method marked with the `[ContractInvariantMethod]` attribute. The method can have any name but, by convention, people usually name the method `ObjectInvariant` and mark the method as **private** (as I've done above). The method must accept no arguments and have a **void** return type. When the CCRewrite.exe tool sees a method marked with this attribute, it inserts IL code at the end of every **public** instance method to call the `ObjectInvariant` method. This way, the object's state is checked as each method returns to ensure that no method has violated the contract. Note that the CCRewrite.exe tool does not modify a **Finalize** method or an **IDisposable**'s **Dispose** method to call the `ObjectInvariant` method because it is OK for an object's state to be altered if it is considered to be destroyed or disposed. Also note that a single type can define multiple methods with the `[ContractInvariantMethod]` attribute; this is useful when working with partial types. The CCRewrite.exe tool will modify the IL to call all of these methods (in an undefined order) at the end of each public method.

The **Assert** and **Assume** methods are unlike the other methods. First, you should not consider them to be part of the method's signature, and you do not have to put them at the beginning of a method. At runtime, these two methods perform identically: They just verify that the condition passed to them is true and throw an exception if it is not. However, there is another tool, the Code Contract Checker (CCCheck.exe) which analyzes the IL produced by the C# compiler in an attempt to statically verify that no code in the method violates a contract. This tool will attempt to prove that any condition passed to **Assert** is **true**, but it will just assume that any condition passed to **Assume** is **true** and the tool will add the expression to its body of facts known to be true. Usually, you will use **Assert** and then change an **Assert** to an **Assume** if the CCCheck.exe tool can't statically prove that the expression is true.

Let's walk through an example. Assume that I have the following type definition:

```
internal sealed class SomeType {
   private static String s_name = "Jeffrey";

   public static void ShowFirstLetter() {
      Console.WriteLine(s_name[0]);   // warning: requires unproven: index < this.Length
   }
}
```

When I build this code with the Perform Static Contract Checking function turned on, the CCCheck.exe tool produces the warning shown as a comment above. This warning is notifying me that querying the first letter of **s_name** may fail and throw an exception because it is unproven that **s_name** *always* refers to a string consisting of at least one character.

Therefore, what we'd like to do is add an assertion to the **ShowFirstLetter** method:

```
public static void ShowFirstLetter() {
   Contract.Assert(s_name.Length >= 1);    // warning: assert unproven
   Console.WriteLine(s_name[0]);
}
```

Unfortunately, when the CCCheck.exe tool analyzes this code, it is still unable to validate that **s_name** *always* refers to a string containing at least one letter, so the tool produces a similar warning. Sometimes the tool is unable to validate assertions due to limitations in the tool; future versions of the tool will be able to perform a more complete analysis.

To override shortcomings in the tool or to claim that something is true that the tool would never be able to prove, we can change **Assert** to **Assume**. If we know for a fact that no other code will modify **s_name**, then we can change **ShowFirstLetter** to this:

```
public static void ShowFirstLetter() {
   Contract.Assume(s_name.Length >= 1);    // No warning at all now!
   Console.WriteLine(s_name[0]);
}
```

With this version of the code, the CCCheck.exe tool just takes our word for it and concludes that **s_name** *always* refers to a string containing at least one letter. This version of the **ShowFirstLetter** method passes the code contract static checker without any warnings at all.

Now, let's talk about the Code Contract Reference Assembly Generator tool (CCRefGen.exe). Running the CCRewrite.exe tool to enable contract checking helps you find bugs more quickly, but all the code emitted during contract checking makes your assembly bigger and hurts its runtime performance. To improve this situation, you use the CCRefGen.exe tool to create a separate *contract reference assembly*. Visual Studio invokes this tool for you automatically if you set the Contract Reference Assembly combo box to Build. Contract assemblies are usually named *AssemName*.Contracts.dll (for example, MSCorLib.Contracts.dll), and these assemblies contain only metadata and the IL that describes the contracts—nothing else. You can identify a contract reference assembly because it will have the **System.Diagnostics. Contracts.ContractReferenceAssemblyAttribute** applied to the assembly's assembly definition metadata table. The CCRewrite.exe tool and the CCCheck.exe tool can use contract reference assemblies as input when these tools are performing their instrumentation and analysis.

The last tool, the Code Contract Document Generator tool (CCDocGen.exe), adds contract information to the XML documentation files already produced by the C# compiler when you use the compiler's **/doc:file** switch. This XML file, enhanced by the CCDocGen.exe tool, can be processed by Microsoft's Sandcastle tool to produce MSDN-style documentation that will now include contract information.

Chapter 21
Automatic Memory Management (Garbage Collection)

In this chapter, I'll discuss how managed applications construct new objects, how the managed heap controls the lifetime of these objects, and how the memory for these objects gets reclaimed. In short, I'll explain how the garbage collector in the common language runtime (CLR) works, and I'll explain various performance issues related to it. I'll also discuss how to design applications so that they use memory most efficiently.

Understanding the Basics of Working in a Garbage-Collected Platform

Every program uses resources of one sort or another, be they files, memory buffers, screen space, network connections, database resources, and so on. In fact, in an object-oriented environment, every type identifies some resource available for a program's use. To use any of these resources requires memory to be allocated to represent the type. The following steps are required to access a resource:

1. Allocate memory for the type that represents the resource by calling the Intermediate Language's (IL) **newobj** instruction, which is emitted when you use the **new** operator in C#.

2. Initialize the memory to set the initial state of the resource and to make the resource usable. The type's instance constructor is responsible for setting this initial state.

3. Use the resource by accessing the type's members (repeating as necessary).

4. Tear down the state of a resource to clean up. I'll address this topic in the section "The Dispose Pattern: Forcing an Object to Clean Up" later in this chapter.

5. Free the memory. The garbage collector is solely responsible for this step.

This seemingly simple paradigm has been one of the major sources of programming errors. How many times have programmers forgotten to free memory when it is no longer needed? How many times have programmers attempted to use memory after it had already been freed?

In the native programming world, these two application bugs are worse than most others because you usually can't predict the consequences or the timing of them. For other bugs, when you see your application misbehaving, you just fix the problem. But these two bugs cause resource leaks (memory consumption) and object corruption (destabilization), making the application perform unpredictably. In fact, there are many tools (such as Microsoft's Windows Task Manager, Process Explorer, and Performance Monitor, and Rational's Purify) that are specifically designed to help developers locate these types of bugs.

Proper resource management is very difficult and quite tedious. It distracts developers from concentrating on the real problems that they're trying to solve. It would be wonderful if some mechanism existed that simplified the mind-numbing memory-management task for developers. Fortunately, there is: garbage collection.

Garbage collection completely absolves the developer from having to track memory usage and know when to free memory. However, the garbage collector doesn't know anything about the resource represented by the type in memory, which means that a garbage collector can't know how to perform step 4 in the preceding list: tear down the state of a resource to clean up. To get a resource to clean up properly, the developer must write code that knows how to properly clean up a resource. The developer writes this code in the `Finalize`, `Dispose`, and `Close` methods, as described later in this chapter. However, as you'll see, the garbage collector can offer some assistance here too, allowing developers to skip step 4 in many circumstances.

Also, most types, including value types (including all enumeration types), collection types, `String`, `Attribute`, `Delegate`, and `Exception`, represent resources that don't require any special cleanup. For example, a `String` resource can be completely cleaned up simply by destroying the character array maintained in the object's memory.

On the other hand, a type that represents (or wraps) an unmanaged or native resource, such as a file, a database connection, a socket, a mutex, a bitmap, an icon, and so on, always requires the execution of some cleanup code when the object is about to have its memory reclaimed. In this chapter, I'll explain how to properly define types that require explicit clean-up, and I'll show you how to properly use types that offer this explicit cleanup. For now, let's examine how memory is allocated and how resources are initialized.

Allocating Resources from the Managed Heap

The CLR requires that all resources be allocated from a heap called the *managed heap*. This heap is similar to a C-runtime heap, except that you never delete objects from the managed heap—objects are automatically deleted when the application no longer needs them. This, of course, raises the question, "How does the managed heap know when the application is no longer using an object?" I'll address this question shortly.

Several garbage collection algorithms are in use today. Each algorithm is fine-tuned for a particular environment to provide the best performance. In this chapter, I'll concentrate on the garbage collection algorithm used by the Microsoft .NET Framework's CLR. Let's start off with the basic concepts.

When a process is initialized, the CLR reserves a contiguous region of address space that initially contains no backing storage. This address space region is the managed heap. The heap also maintains a pointer, which I'll call `NextObjPtr`. This pointer indicates where the next object is to be allocated within the heap. Initially, `NextObjPtr` is set to the base address of the reserved address space region.[1]

---

[1] During initialization, the CLR reserves two segments of virtual address space: one for the normal heap and one for the large object heap (discussed in the section "Large Objects" later in this chapter). The size of each segment varies. For a client application, each segment is approximately 16 MB, and for a server application, each segment is approximately 64 MB. However, there are other things that affect the segment size, such as if you are running on a 32-bit or 64-bit operating system, and also the number of CPUs in the machine (the segment size gets smaller on a machine with more CPUs). As segments fill with non-garbage objects, the CLR allocates more segments. It will continue to do this until the whole process's address space is full. So, your application's memory is limited by the process's virtual address space. You can allocate a lot more memory in a 64-bit process than you can in a 32-bit process.

The **newobj** IL instruction creates an object. Many languages (including C#, C++/CLI, and Microsoft Visual Basic) offer a **new** operator that causes the compiler to emit a **newobj** instruction into the method's IL code. The **newobj** instruction causes the CLR to perform the following steps:

1. Calculate the number of bytes required for the type's (and all of its base type's) fields.

2. Add the bytes required for an object's overhead. Each object has two overhead fields: a type object pointer and a sync block index. For a 32-bit application, each of these fields requires 32 bits, adding 8 bytes to each object. For a 64-bit application, each field is 64 bits, adding 16 bytes to each object.

3. The CLR then checks that the bytes required to allocate the object are available in the reserved region (committing storage if necessary). If there is enough free space in the managed heap, the object will fit, starting at the address pointed to by **NextObjPtr**, and these bytes are zeroed out. The type's constructor is called (passing **NextObjPtr** for the **this** parameter), and the **newobj** IL instruction (or C#'s **new** operator) returns the address of the object. Just before the address is returned, **NextObjPtr** is advanced past the object and now points to the address where the next object will be placed in the heap.

Figure 21-1 shows a managed heap consisting of three objects: A, B, and C. If a new object were to be allocated, it would be placed where **NextObjPtr** points to (immediately after object C).

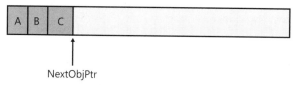

NextObjPtr

FIGURE 21-1 Newly initialized managed heap with three objects constructed in it

By contrast, let's look at how the C-runtime heap allocates memory. In a C-runtime heap, allocating memory for an object requires walking through a linked list of data structures. Once a large enough block is found, that block is split, and pointers in the linked-list nodes are modified to keep everything intact. For the managed heap, allocating an object simply means adding a value to a pointer—this is blazingly fast by comparison. In fact, allocating an object from the managed heap is nearly as fast as allocating memory from a thread's stack! In addition, most heaps (such as the C-runtime heap) allocate objects wherever they find free space. Therefore, if I create several objects consecutively, it's quite possible for these objects to be separated by megabytes of address space. In the managed heap, however, allocating several objects consecutively ensures that the objects are contiguous in memory.

In many applications, objects allocated around the same time tend to have strong relationships to each other and are frequently accessed around the same time. For example, it's very common to allocate a **FileStream** object immediately before a **BinaryWriter** object is created. Then the application would use the **BinaryWriter** object, which internally uses the `FileStream` object. In a garbage-collected environment, new objects are allocated contiguously in memory, providing performance gains resulting from locality of reference. Specifically, this means that your process's working set will be smaller than a similar application running in a non-managed environment. It's also likely that the objects that your code is using can all reside in the CPU's cache. Your application will access these objects with phenomenal speed because the CPU will be able to perform most of its manipulations without having cache misses that would force slower access to RAM.

So far, it sounds as if the managed heap is far superior to the C-runtime heap because of its simplicity of implementation and speed. But there's one little detail you should know about before getting too excited. The managed heap gains these advantages because it makes one really big assumption: that address space and storage are infinite. Obviously, this assumption is ridiculous, and the managed heap must employ a mechanism to allow it to make this assumption. This mechanism is the garbage collector. Here's how it works:

When an application calls the **new** operator to create an object, there might not be enough address space left in the region to allocate to the object. The heap detects this lack of space by adding the bytes that the object requires to the address in `NextObjPtr`. If the resulting value is beyond the end of the address space region, the heap is full, and a garbage collection must be performed.

> **Important**   What I've just said is an oversimplification. In reality, a garbage collection occurs when generation 0 is full. Some garbage collectors use generations, a mechanism whose sole purpose is to improve performance. The idea is that newly created objects are part of a young generation and objects created early in the application's lifecycle are in an old generation. Objects in generation 0 are objects that have recently been allocated and have never been examined by the garbage collector algorithm. Objects that survive a collection are promoted to another generation (such as generation 1). Separating objects into generations allows the garbage collector to collect specific generations instead of collecting all of the objects in the managed heap. I'll explain generations in more detail later in this chapter. Until then, it's easiest for you to think that a garbage collection occurs when the heap is full.

The Garbage Collection Algorithm

The garbage collector checks to see if any objects in the heap are no longer being used by the application. If such objects exist, the memory used by these objects can be reclaimed. (If no more memory is available in the heap after a garbage collection, **new** throws an `OutOfMemoryException`.) How does the garbage collector know whether the application is using an object? As you might imagine, this isn't a simple question to answer.

Every application has a set of *roots*. A single root is a storage location containing a memory pointer to a reference type object. This pointer either refers to an object in the managed heap or is set to **null**. For example, a static field (defined within a type) is considered a root. In addition, any method parameter or local variable is considered a root. Only variables that are of a reference type are considered roots; value type variables are never considered roots. Now, let's look at a concrete example starting with the following class definition:

```
internal sealed class SomeType {
   private TextWriter m_textWriter;

   public SomeType(TextWriter tw) {
      m_textWriter = tw;
   }

   public void WriteBytes(Byte[] bytes) {
      for (Int32 x = 0; x < bytes.Length; x++) {
         m_textWriter.Write(bytes[x]);
      }
   }
}
```

The first time the **WriteBytes** method is called, the just-in-time (JIT) compiler converts the method's IL code into native CPU instructions. Let's say the CLR is running on an *x86* CPU, and the JIT compiler compiles the **WriteBytes** method into the CPU instructions shown in Figure 21-2. (I added comments on the right to help you understand how the native code maps back to the original source code.)

```
         00000000 push   edi                          // Prolog
         00000001 push   esi
         00000002 push   ebx
EBX
         00000003 mov    ebx,ecx                       // ebx = this (argument)
         00000005 mov    esi,edx                       // esi = bytes array (argument)
   ESI   00000007 xor    edi,edi                       // edi = x
         00000009 cmp    dword ptr [esi+4],0           // compare bytes.Length with 0
         0000000d jle    0000002A                      // if bytes.Length <=0, go to 2a
   ECX
         0000000f mov    ecx,dword ptr [ebx+4]         // ecx = m_textWriter (field)
         00000012 cmp    edi,dword ptr [esi+4]         // compare x with bytes.Length
         00000015 jae    0000002E                      // if x >= bytes.Length, go to 2e

         00000017 movzx  edx,byte prt [esi+edi+8]      // edx = bytes[x]
EAX      0000001c mov    eax,dword ptr [ecx]           // eax = m_textWriter's type object
         0000001e call   dword ptr [eax+000000BCh]     // Call m_textWriter's Write method

         00000024 inc    edi                           // x++
         00000025 cmp    dword ptr [esi+4],edi         // compare bytes.Length with x
         00000028 jg     0000000F                      // if bytes.Length > x, go to f

         0000002a pop    ebx                           // Epilog
         0000002b pop    esi
         0000002c pop    edi
         0000002d ret                                  // return to caller

         0000002e call   76B6E337                      // Throw IndexOutOfRangeException
         00000033 int    3                             // Break in debugger
```

FIGURE 21-2 Native code produced by the JIT compiler with ranges of roots shown

As the JIT compiler produces the native code, it also creates an internal table. Logically, each entry in the table indicates a range of byte offsets in the method's native CPU instructions, and for each range, a set of memory addresses and CPU registers that contain roots.

For the **WriteBytes** method, this table reflects that the EBX register starts being a root at offset 0x00000003, the ESI register starts being a root at offset 0x00000005, and the ECX register starts being a root at offset 0x0000000f. All three of these registers stop being roots at the end of the loop (offset 0x00000028). Also note that the EAX register is a root from 0x0000001c to 0x0000001e. The EDI register is used to hold the **Int32** value represented by the variable **x** in the original source code. Since **Int32** is a value type, the JIT compiler doesn't consider the EDI register to be a root.

The **WriteBytes** method is a fairly simple method, and all of the variables that it uses can be enregistered. A more complex method could use all of the available CPU registers, and some roots would be in memory locations relative to the method's stack frame. Also note that on an *x*86 architecture, the CLR passes the first two arguments to a method via the ECX and EDX registers. For instance methods, the first argument is the **this** pointer, which is always passed in the ECX register. For the **WriteBytes** method, this is how I know that the **this** pointer is passed in the ECX register and stored in the EBX register right after the method prolog. This is also how I know that the **bytes** argument is passed in the EDX register and stored in the ESI register after the prolog.

If a garbage collection were to start while code was executing at offset 0x00000017 in the **WriteBytes** method, the garbage collector would know that the objects referred to by the EBX (**this** argument), ESI (**bytes** argument), and ECX (the **m_textWriter** field) registers were all roots and refer to objects in the heap that shouldn't be considered garbage. In addition, the garbage collector can walk up the thread's call stack and determine the roots for all of the calling methods by examining each method's internal table. The garbage collector iterates through all the type objects to obtain the set of roots stored in static fields.

When a garbage collection starts, it assumes that all objects in the heap are garbage. In other words, it is assumed that the thread's stack contains no variables that refer to objects in the heap, that no CPU registers refer to objects in the heap, and that no static fields refer to objects in the heap. The garbage collector starts what is called the *marking* phase of the collection. This is when the collector walks up the thread's stack checking all of the roots. If a root is found to refer to an object, a bit will be turned on in the object's sync block index field—this is how the object is *marked*. For example, the garbage collector might locate a local variable that points to an object in the heap. Figure 21-3 shows a heap containing several allocated objects, and the application's roots refer directly to objects A, C, D, and F. All of these objects are marked. When marking object D, the garbage collector notices that this object contains a field that refers to object H, causing object H to be marked as well. The garbage collector continues to walk through all reachable objects recursively.

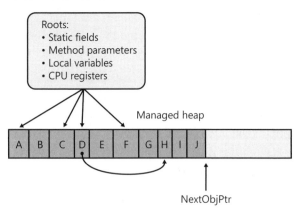

FIGURE 21-3 Managed heap before a collection

After a root and the objects referenced by its fields are marked, the garbage collector checks the next root and continues marking objects. If the garbage collector is going to mark an object that it previously marked, it can stop walking down that path. This behavior serves two purposes. First, performance is enhanced significantly because the garbage collector doesn't walk through a set of objects more than once. Second, infinite loops are prevented if you have any circular linked lists of objects.

Once all of the roots have been checked, the heap contains a set of marked and unmarked objects. The marked objects are reachable via the application's code, and the unmarked objects are unreachable. The unreachable objects are considered garbage, and the memory that they occupy can be reclaimed. The garbage collector now starts what is called the *compact phase* of the collection. This is when the collector traverses the heap linearly looking for contiguous blocks of unmarked (garbage) objects.

If small blocks are found, the garbage collector leaves the blocks alone. If large free contiguous blocks are found, however, the garbage collector shifts the nongarbage objects down in memory to compact the heap.

Naturally, moving the objects in memory invalidates all variables and CPU registers that contain pointers to the objects. So the garbage collector must revisit all of the application's roots and modify them so that each root's value points to the objects' new memory location. In addition, if any object contains a field that refers to another moved object, the garbage collector is responsible for correcting these fields as well. After the heap memory is compacted, the managed heap's **NextObjPtr** pointer is set to point to a location just after the last non-garbage object. Figure 21-4 shows the managed heap after a collection.

As you can see, a garbage collection generates a considerable performance hit, which is the major downside of using a managed heap. But keep in mind that garbage collections occur only when generation 0 is full, and until then, the managed heap is significantly faster than a C-runtime heap. Finally, the CLR's garbage collector offers some optimizations that greatly improve the performance of garbage collection. I'll discuss these optimizations later in this chapter, in the "Generations" and "Other Garbage Collection Features for Use with Native Resources" sections.

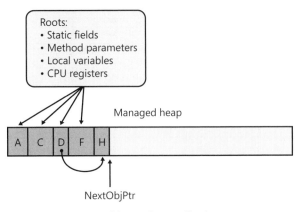

FIGURE 21-4 Managed heap after a collection

As a programmer, you should take away a couple of important points from this discussion. To start, you no longer have to implement any code to manage the lifetime of objects your application uses. And notice how the two bugs described at the beginning of this chapter no longer exist. First, it's not possible to leak objects because any object not accessible from your application's roots can be collected at some point. Second, it's not possible to access an object that is freed because the object won't be freed if it is reachable, and if it's not reachable, your application has no way to access it. Also, since a collection causes memory compaction, it is not possible for managed objects to fragment your process's virtual address space. This would sometimes be a severe problem with unmanaged heaps but is no longer an issue when using the managed heap. Using large objects (discussed later in this chapter) is an exception to this, and fragmentation of the large object heap is possible.

 Important   A type's static field roots whatever object it refers to forever or until the AppDomain that the types are loaded into is unloaded. A common way to leak memory is to have a static field refer to a collection object and then to keep adding items to the collection object. The static field keeps the collection object alive and the collection object keeps all its items alive. For this reason, it is best to avoid static fields whenever possible.

Garbage Collections and Debugging

In Figure 21-2, notice that the method's **bytes** argument (stored in the ESI register) isn't referred to after the CPU instruction at offset 0x00000028. This means that the **Byte** array object that the **bytes** argument refers to can be collected any time after the instruction at offset 0x00000028 executes (assuming that there are no other roots in the application that also refer to this array object). In other words, as soon as an object becomes unreachable, it is a candidate for collection—objects aren't guaranteed to live throughout a method's lifetime. This can have an interesting impact on your application. For example, examine the following code:

```
using System;
using System.Threading;

public static class Program {
   public static void Main() {
      // Create a Timer object that knows to call our TimerCallback
      // method once every 2000 milliseconds.
      Timer t = new Timer(TimerCallback, null, 0, 2000);

      // Wait for the user to hit <Enter>
      Console.ReadLine();
   }

   private static void TimerCallback(Object o) {
      // Display the date/time when this method got called.
      Console.WriteLine("In TimerCallback: " + DateTime.Now);

      // Force a garbage collection to occur for this demo.
      GC.Collect();
   }
}
```

Compile this code from the command prompt without using any special compiler switches.
When you run the resulting executable file, you'll see that the **TimerCallback** method is
called just once!

From examining the code above, you'd think that the **TimerCallback** method would get
called once every 2,000 milliseconds. After all, a **Timer** object is created, and the variable **t**
refers to this object. As long as the timer object exists, the timer should keep firing. But you'll
notice in the **TimerCallback** method that I force a garbage collection to occur by calling
GC.Collect().

When the collection starts, it first assumes that all objects in the heap are unreachable
(garbage); this includes the **Timer** object. Then, the collector examines the application's roots
and sees that **Main** doesn't use the **t** variable after the initial assignment to it. Therefore, the
application has no variable referring to the **Timer** object, and the garbage collection reclaims
the memory for it; this stops the timer and explains why the **TimerCallback** method is called
just once.

Let's say that you're using a debugger to step through **Main**, and a garbage collection just
happens to occur just after **t** is assigned the address of the new **Timer** object. Then, let's say
that you try to view the object that **t** refers to by using the debugger's Quick Watch window.
What do you think will happen? The debugger can't show you the object because it was just
garbage collected. This behavior would be considered very unexpected and undesirable by
most developers, so Microsoft has come up with a solution.

When the JIT compiler compiles the IL for a method into native code, it checks to see if
the assembly defining the method was compiled without optimizations and if the process
is currently being executed under a debugger. If both are true, the JIT compiler generates
the method's internal root table in such a way as to artificially extend the lifetime of all of
the variables to the end of the method. In other words, the JIT compiler will trick itself into

believing that the **t** variable in **Main** must live until the end of the method. So, if a garbage collection were to occur, the garbage collector now thinks that **t** is still a root and that the **Timer** object that **t** refers to will continue to be reachable. The **Timer** object will survive the collection, and the **TimerCallback** method will get called repeatedly until **Console. ReadLine** returns and **Main** exits. This is easy to see. Just run the same executable file under a debugger, and you'll see that the **TimerCallback** method is called repeatedly!

Now, recompile the program from a command prompt, but this time, specify the C# compiler's **/debug+** compiler-line switch. When you run the resulting executable file, you'll now see that the **TimerCallback** method is called repeatedly—even if you don't run this program under a debugger! What is happening here?

Well, when the JIT compiler compiles a method, the JIT compiler looks to see if the assembly that defines the method contains the **System.Diagnostics.DebuggableAttribute** attribute with its **DebuggingModes' DisableOptimizations** flag set. If the JIT compiler sees this flag set, it also compiles the method, artificially extending the lifetime of all variables until the end of the method. When you specify the **/debug+** compiler switch, the C# compiler emits this attribute and flag into the resulting assembly for you. Note, the C# compiler's **/optimize+** compiler switch can turn optimizations back on so this compiler switch should not be specified when performing this experiment.

The JIT compiler does this to help you with JIT debugging. You may now start your application normally (without a debugger), and if the method is called, the JIT compiler will artificially extend the lifetime of the variables to the end of the method. Later, if you decide to attach a debugger to the process, you can put a breakpoint in a previously compiled method and examine the variables.

So now you know how to build a program that works in a debug build but doesn't work correctly when you make a release build! Since no developer wants a program that works only when debugging it, there should be something we can do to the program so that it works all of the time regardless of the type of build.

You could try modifying the **Main** method to this:

```
public static void Main() {
    // Create a Timer object that knows to call our TimerCallback
    // method once every 2000 milliseconds.
    Timer t = new Timer(TimerCallback, null, 0, 2000);

    // Wait for the user to hit <Enter>
    Console.ReadLine();

    // Refer to t after ReadLine (this gets optimized away)
    t = null;
}
```

However, if you compile this (without the **/debug+** switch) and run the resulting executable file (not under the debugger), you'll see that the **TimerCallback** method is still called just once. The problem here is that the JIT compiler is an optimizing compiler, and setting a local variable or parameter variable to **null** is the same as not referencing the variable at all. In other words, the JIT compiler optimizes the **t = null;** line out of the code completely, and therefore, the program still does not work as we desire. The correct way to modify the **Main** method is as follows:

```
public static void Main() {
    // Create a Timer object that knows to call our TimerCallback
    // method once every 2000 milliseconds.
    Timer t = new Timer(TimerCallback, null, 0, 2000);

    // Wait for the user to hit <Enter>
    Console.ReadLine();

    // Refer to t after ReadLine (t will survive GCs until Dispose returns)
    t.Dispose ();
}
```

Now, if you compile this code (without the **/debug+** switch) and run the resulting executable file (not under the debugger), you'll see that the **TimerCallback** method is called multiple times, and the program is fixed. What's happening here is that the object **t** refers to is required to stay alive so that the **Dispose** instance method can be called on it (the value in **t** needs to be passed as the **this** argument to **Dispose**).

> **Note** Please don't read this whole discussion and then worry about your own objects being garbage collected prematurely. I use the **Timer** class in this discussion because it has special behavior that no other class exhibits. The "problem/feature" of **Timer** is that the existence of a **Timer** object in the heap causes something else to happen: A thread pool thread invokes a method periodically. No other type exhibits this behavior. For example, the existence of a **String** object in memory doesn't cause anything else to happen; the string just sits there. So, I use **Timer** to show how roots work and how object-lifetime works as related to the debugger, but the discussion is *not* really about how to keep objects alive. All non-**Timer** objects will live as needed by the application automatically.

Using Finalization to Release Native Resources

At this point, you should have a basic understanding of garbage collection and the managed heap, including how the garbage collector reclaims an object's memory. Fortunately for us, most types need only memory to operate. However, some types require more than just memory to be useful; some types require the use of a native resource in addition to memory.

The **System.IO.FileStream** type, for example, needs to open a file (a native resource) and store the file's handle. Then the type's **Read** and **Write** methods use this handle to manipulate the file. Similarly, the **System.Threading.Mutex** type opens a Windows mutex kernel object (a native resource) and stores its handle, using it when the **Mutex**'s methods are called.

Finalization is a mechanism offered by the CLR that allows an object to perform some grace-ful cleanup prior to the garbage collector reclaiming the object's memory. Any type that wraps a native resource, such as a file, network connection, socket, mutex, or other type, must support finalization. Basically, the type implements a method named `Finalize`. When the garbage collector determines that an object is garbage, it calls the object's `Finalize` method (if it exists). I think of it this way: Any type that implements the `Finalize` method is in effect stating that all of its objects want a last meal before they are killed.

Microsoft's C# team felt that `Finalize` methods were a special kind of method requiring special syntax in the programming language (similar to how C# requires special syntax to define a constructor). So, in C#, you must define a `Finalize` method by placing a tilde symbol (~) in front of the class name, as shown in the following code sample:

```
internal sealed class SomeType {
    // This is the Finalize method
    ~SomeType() {
        // The code here is inside the Finalize method
    }
}
```

If you were to compile this code and examine the resulting assembly with ILDasm.exe, you'd see that the C# compiler did, in fact, emit a **protected override** method named `Finalize` into the module's metadata. If you examined the `Finalize` method's IL code, you'd also see that the code inside the method's body is emitted into a **try** block, and that a call to **base. Finalize** is emitted into a **finally** block.

> **Important**   If you're familiar with C++, you'll notice that the special syntax C# requires for defining a `Finalize` method looks just like the syntax you'd use to define a C++ destructor. In fact, the C# Programming Language Specification calls this method a *destructor*. However, a `Finalize` method doesn't work like an unmanaged C++ destructor at all, and this has caused a great deal of confusion for developers migrating from one language to another.
>
> The problem is that developers mistakenly believe that using the C# destructor syntax means that the type's objects will be deterministically destructed, just as they would be in C++. However, the CLR doesn't support deterministic destruction, preventing C# from providing this mechanism.

A `Finalize` method is usually implemented to call the Win32 `CloseHandle` function, passing in the handle of the native resource. The `FileStream` type defines a file handle field, which identifies the native resource. The `FileStream` type also defines a `Finalize` method, which internally calls `CloseHandle`, passing it the file handle field; this ensures that the native file handle is closed when the managed `FileStream` object is determined to be garbage. If a type that wraps a native resource fails to define a `Finalize` method, the native resource won't be closed and will cause a resource leak that will exist until the process terminates, at which time the operating system will reclaim the native resources.

Guaranteed Finalization Using `CriticalFinalizerObject` Types

To make things simpler for developers, the `System.Runtime.ConstrainedExecution` namespace defines a `CriticalFinalizerObject` class that looks like this:

```
public abstract class CriticalFinalizerObject {
   protected CriticalFinalizerObject() { /* there is no code in here */ }

   // This is the Finalize method
   ~CriticalFinalizerObject() { /* there is no code in here */ }
}
```

I know that you're thinking that this class doesn't look too exciting, but the CLR treats this class and classes derived from it in a very special manner. In particular, the CLR endows this class with three cool features:

- The first time an object of any `CriticalFinalizerObject`-derived type is constructed, the CLR immediately JIT-compiles all of the `Finalize` methods in the inheritance hierarchy. Compiling these methods upon object construction guarantees that the native resource will be released when the object is determined to be garbage. Without this eager compiling of the `Finalize` method, it would be possible to allocate the native resource and use it, but not to get rid of it. Under low memory conditions, the CLR might not be able to find enough memory to compile the `Finalize` method, which would prevent it from executing, causing the native resource to leak. Or the resource might not be freed if the `Finalize` method contained code that referred to a type in another assembly, and the CLR failed to locate this other assembly.

- The CLR calls the `Finalize` method of `CriticalFinalizerObject`-derived types after calling the `Finalize` methods of non–`CriticalFinalizerObject`-derived types. This ensures that managed resource classes that have a `Finalize` method can access `CriticalFinalizerObject`-derived objects within their `Finalize` methods successfully. For example, the `FileStream` class's `Finalize` method can flush data from a memory buffer to an underlying disk with confidence that the disk file has not been closed yet.

- The CLR calls the `Finalize` method of `CriticalFinalizerObject`-derived types if an AppDomain is rudely aborted by a host application (such as Microsoft SQL Server or Microsoft ASP.NET). This also is part of ensuring that the native resource is released even in a case in which a host application no longer trusts the managed code running inside of it.

SafeHandle and Its Derived Types

Now, Microsoft realizes that the most-used native resources are those resources provided by Windows. And Microsoft also realizes that most Windows resources are manipulated with handles (32-bit values on a 32-bit system and 64-bit values on a 64-bit system). Again,

to make life easier and safer for developers, the **System.Runtime.InteropServices**
namespace includes a class called **SafeHandle**, which looks like this (I've added comments in
the methods to indicate what they do):

```
public abstract class SafeHandle : CriticalFinalizerObject, IDisposable {
   // This is the handle to the native resource
   protected IntPtr handle;

   protected SafeHandle(IntPtr invalidHandleValue, Boolean ownsHandle) {
      this.handle = invalidHandleValue;
      // If ownsHandle is true, then the native resource is closed when
      // this SafeHandle-derived object is collected
   }

   protected void SetHandle(IntPtr handle) {
      this.handle = handle;
   }


   // You can explicitly release the resource by calling Dispose or Close
   public void Dispose() { Dispose(true); }
   public void Close()   { Dispose(true); }

   // The default Dispose implementation (shown here) is exactly what you want.
   // Overriding this method is strongly discouraged.
   protected virtual void Dispose(Boolean disposing) {
      // The default implementation ignores the disposing argument.
      // If resource was already released, just return
      // If ownsHandle is false, return
      // Set flag indicating that this resource has been released
      // Call the virtual ReleaseHandle method
      // Call GC.SuppressFinalize(this) to prevent Finalize from being called
      // If ReleaseHandle returned true, return
      // Fire the ReleaseHandleFailed Managed Debugging Assistant (MDA)
   }

   // The default Finalize implementation (shown here) is exactly what you want.
   // Overriding this method is very strongly discouraged.
   ~SafeHandle() { Dispose(false); }

   // A derived class overrides this method to implement the code that releases the resource
   protected abstract Boolean ReleaseHandle();

   public void SetHandleAsInvalid() {
      // Set flag indicating that this resource has been released
      // Call GC.SuppressFinalize(this) to prevent Finalize from being called
   }

   public Boolean IsClosed {
      get {
         // Returns flag indicating whether resource was released
      }
   }
```

```
    public abstract Boolean IsInvalid {
        get {
            // A derived class overrides this property.
            // The implementation should return true if the handle's value doesn't
            // represent a resource (this usually means that the handle is 0 or -1)
        }
    }

    // These three methods have to do with security and reference counting;
    // I'll talk about them at the end of this section
    public void    DangerousAddRef(ref Boolean success) {...}
    public IntPtr DangerousGetHandle() {...}
    public void    DangerousRelease() {...}
}
```

The first thing to notice about the **SafeHandle** class is that it is derived from **CriticalFinalizerObject**; this ensures it gets the CLR's special treatment. The second thing to notice is that the class is abstract; it is expected that another class will be derived from **SafeHandle**, and this class will override the protected constructor, the abstract method **ReleaseHandle**, and the abstract **IsInvalid** property **get** accessor method.

In Windows, most handles are invalid if they have a value of **0** or **-1**. The **Microsoft.Win32.SafeHandles** namespace contains another helper class called **SafeHandleZeroOrMinusOneIsInvalid**, which looks like this:

```
public abstract class SafeHandleZeroOrMinusOneIsInvalid : SafeHandle {
    protected SafeHandleZeroOrMinusOneIsInvalid(Boolean ownsHandle)
        : base(IntPtr.Zero, ownsHandle) {
    }

    public override Boolean IsInvalid {
        get {
            if (base.handle == IntPtr.Zero) return true;
            if (base.handle == (IntPtr) (-1)) return true;
            return false;
        }
    }
}
```

Again, you'll notice that the **SafeHandleZeroOrMinusOneIsInvalid** class is abstract, and therefore, another class must be derived from this one to override the protected constructor and the abstract method **ReleaseHandle**. The .NET Framework provides just a few public classes derived from **SafeHandleZeroOrMinusOneIsInvalid**, including **SafeFileHandle**, **SafeRegistryHandle**, **SafeWaitHandle**, and **SafeBuffer**. Here is what the **SafeFileHandle** class looks like:

```
public sealed class SafeFileHandle : SafeHandleZeroOrMinusOneIsInvalid {
    public SafeFileHandle(IntPtr preexistingHandle, Boolean ownsHandle)
        : base(ownsHandle) {
        base.SetHandle(preexistingHandle);
    }
```

```
    protected override Boolean ReleaseHandle() {
        // Tell Windows that we want the native resource closed.
        return Win32Native.CloseHandle(base.handle);
    }
}
```

The **SafeWaitHandle** class is implemented similarly to the **SafeFileHandle** class shown above. The only reason why there are different classes with similar implementations is to achieve type safety; the compiler won't let you use a file handle as an argument to a method that expects a wait handle, and vice versa. The **SafeRegistryHandle** class's **ReleaseHandle** method calls the Win32 **RegCloseKey** function.

It would be nice if the .NET Framework included additional classes that wrap various native resources. For example, one could imagine classes such as **SafeProcessHandle**, **SafeThreadHandle**, **SafeTokenHandle**, **SafeFileMappingHandle**, **SafeViewOfFileHandle** (its **ReleaseHandle** method would call the Win32 **UnmapViewOfFile** function), **SafeLibraryHandle** (its **ReleaseHandle** method would call the Win32 **FreeLibrary** function), **SafeLocalAllocHandle** (its **ReleaseHandle** method would call the Win32 **LocalFree** function), and so on.

All of the classes just listed (and more) actually do ship with the Framework Class Library (FCL). However, these classes are not publicly exposed; they are all internal to MSCorLib.dll or System.dll. Microsoft didn't expose these classes publicly because they didn't want to do full testing of them, and they didn't want to have to take the time to document them. However, if you need any of these classes for your own work, I'd recommend that you use a tool such as ILDasm.exe or some IL decompiler tool to extract the code for these classes and integrate that code into your own project's source code. All of these classes are trivial to implement, and writing them yourself from scratch would also be quite easy.

Interoperating with Unmanaged Code by Using SafeHandle Types

As already shown, the **SafeHandle**-derived classes are extremely useful because they ensure that the native resource is freed when a garbage collection occurs. In addition to what we've already discussed, **SafeHandle** offers two more capabilities. First, the CLR gives **SafeHandle**-derived types special treatment when used in scenarios in which you are interoperating with unmanaged code. For example, let's examine the following code:

```
using System;
using System.Runtime.InteropServices;
using Microsoft.Win32.SafeHandles;

internal static class SomeType {
    [DllImport("Kernel32", CharSet=CharSet.Unicode, EntryPoint="CreateEvent")]
    // This prototype is not robust
    private static extern IntPtr CreateEventBad(
        IntPtr pSecurityAttributes, Boolean manualReset, Boolean initialState, String name);
```

```
    // This prototype is robust
    [DllImport("Kernel32", CharSet=CharSet.Unicode, EntryPoint="CreateEvent")]
    private static extern SafeWaitHandle CreateEventGood(
        IntPtr pSecurityAttributes, Boolean manualReset, Boolean initialState, String name);

    public static void SomeMethod() {
        IntPtr        handle = CreateEventBad(IntPtr.Zero, false, false, null);
        SafeWaitHandle swh   = CreateEventGood(IntPtr.Zero, false, false, null);
    }
}
```

You'll notice that the **CreateEventBad** method is prototyped as returning an **IntPtr**. Prior to version 2.0 of the .NET Framework, the **SafeHandle** class didn't exist, and you'd have to use the **IntPtr** type to represent handles. What Microsoft's CLR team discovered was that this code was not robust. You see, after **CreateEventBad** was called (which creates the native event resource), it was possible that a **ThreadAbortException** could be thrown prior to the handle being assigned to the **handle** variable. In the rare cases when this would happen, the managed code would be leaking the native resource. The only way to get the event closed would be to terminate the process.

Now, with version 2.0 and later of the .NET Framework, we can use the **SafeHandle** class to fix this potential resource leak. Notice that the **CreateEventGood** method is prototyped as returning a **SafeWaitHandle** (instead of an **IntPtr**). When **CreateEventGood** is called, the CLR calls the Win32 **CreateEvent** function. As the **CreateEvent** function returns to managed code, the CLR knows that **SafeWaitHandle** is derived from **SafeHandle**, causing the CLR to automatically construct an instance of the **SafeWaitHandle** class, passing in the handle value returned from **CreateEvent**. The **new**ing up of the **SafeWaitHandle** object and the assignment of the handle happen in unmanaged code, which cannot be interrupted by a **ThreadAbortException**. Now, it is impossible for managed code to leak this native resource. Eventually, the **SafeWaitHandle** object will be garbage collected and its **Finalize** method will be called, ensuring that the resource is released.

One last feature of **SafeHandle**-derived classes is that they prevent someone from trying to exploit a potential security hole. The problem is that one thread could be trying to use a native resource while another thread tries to free the resource. This could manifest itself as a handle-recycling exploit. The **SafeHandle** class prevents this security vulnerability by using reference counting. Internally, the **SafeHandle** class defines a private field that maintains a count. When a **SafeHandle**-derived object is set to a valid handle, the count is set to 1. Whenever a **SafeHandle**-derived object is passed as an argument to an unmanaged method, the CLR knows to automatically increment the counter. Likewise, when the unmanaged method returns to managed code, the CLR knows to decrement the counter. For example, you would prototype the Win32 **SetEvent** function as follows:

```
[DllImport("Kernel32", ExactSpelling=true)]
private static extern Boolean SetEvent(SafeWaitHandle swh);
```

Now when you call this method passing in a reference to a **SafeWaitHandle** object, the CLR will increment the counter just before the call and decrement the counter just after the call. Of course, the manipulation of the counter is performed in a thread-safe fashion. How does this improve security? Well, if another thread tries to release the native resource wrapped by the **SafeHandle** object, the CLR knows that it cannot actually release it because the resource is being used by an unmanaged function. When the unmanaged function returns, the counter is decremented to 0, and the resource will be released.

If you are writing or calling code to manipulate a handle as an **IntPtr**, you can access it out of a **SafeHandle** object, but you should manipulate the reference counting explicitly. You accomplish this via **SafeHandle**'s **DangerousAddRef** and **DangerousRelease** methods. You gain access to the raw handle via the **DangerousGetHandle** method.

I would be remiss if I didn't mention that the **System.Runtime.InteropServices** namespace also defines a **CriticalHandle** class. This class works exactly as the **SafeHandle** class in all ways except that it does not offer the reference-counting feature. The **CriticalHandle** class and the classes derived from it sacrifice security for better performance when you use it (since counters don't get manipulated). As does **SafeHandle**, the **CriticalHandle** class has two types derived from it: **CriticalHandleMinusOneIsInvalid** and **CriticalHandleZeroOrMinusOneIsInvalid**. Since Microsoft favors a more secure system over a faster system, the class library includes no types derived from either of these two classes. For your own work, I would recommend that you use **CriticalHandle**-derived types only if performance is an issue. If you can justify reducing security, you can switch to a **CriticalHandle**-derived type.

Using Finalization with Managed Resources

> **Important**   There are some people who are of the mindset that you should never use finalization with managed resources. For the most part, I agree with these people. Therefore, you may want to skip this section entirely. Using finalization with managed resources is a super-advanced way of coding and should be used only in very rare circumstances. You must have complete and intimate knowledge of the code you are calling from within a **Finalize** method. Furthermore, you must know that the behavior of code you are calling will not change with future versions. Specifically, you must know that any code you call from within a **Finalize** method does not use any other object that could have already been finalized.

While finalization is almost exclusively used to release a native resource, it can occasionally be useful with managed resources too. Here's a class that causes the computer to beep every time the garbage collector performs a collection:

```
internal sealed class GCBeep {
    ~GCBeep() { // This is the Finalize method
        Console.Beep();

        // If the AppDomain isn't unloading and if the process isn't shutting down,
        // create a new object that will get finalized at the next collection.
        if (!AppDomain.CurrentDomain.IsFinalizingForUnload() &&!Environment.HasShutdownStarted)
            new GCBeep();
    }
}
```

To use this class, you need just to construct one instance of the class. Then whenever a garbage collection occurs, the object's **Finalize** method is called, which calls **Beep** and constructs a new **GCBeep** object. This new **GCBeep** object will have its **Finalize** method called when the next garbage collection occurs. Here's a sample program that demonstrates the **GCBeep** class:

```
public static class Program {
    public static void Main() {
        // Constructing a single GCBeep object causes a beep to occur every time a GC starts.
        new GCBeep();

        // Construct a lot of 100-byte objects.
        for (Int32 x = 0; x < 10000; x++) {
            Console.WriteLine(x);
            Byte[] b = new Byte[100];
        }
    }
}
```

Note While the **GCBeep** class is useful, I provide a much more useful **GCNotification** class that allows you to instrument your application, thereby providing you a way to learn more about your application's memory usage. You'll find this class presented at the end of the "Generations" section later in this chapter.

Also be aware that a type's **Finalize** method is called even if the type's instance constructor throws an exception. So your **Finalize** method shouldn't assume that the object is in a good, consistent state. The following code demonstrates this:

```
internal sealed class TempFile {
    private String m_filename = null;
    private FileStream m_fs;

    public TempFile(String filename) {
        // The following line might throw an exception.
        m_fs = new FileStream(filename, FileMode.Create);

        // Save the name of this file.
        m_filename = filename;
    }
```

```
~TempFile() {           // This is the Finalize method
   // The right thing to do here is to test filename against null because
   // you can't be sure that filename was initialized in the constructor.
   if (m_filename != null)  File.Delete(m_filename);
}
}
```

You could write the following code instead:

```
internal sealed class TempFile {
   private String m_filename;
   private FileStream m_fs;

   public TempFile(String filename) {
      try {
         // The following line might throw an exception.
         m_fs = new FileStream(filename, FileMode.Create);

         // Save the name of this file.
         m_filename = filename;
      }
      catch {
         // If anything goes wrong, tell the GC not to call the Finalize method.
         // I'll discuss SuppressFinalize later in this chapter.
         GC.SuppressFinalize(this);

         // Let the caller know something failed.
         throw;
      }
   }

   ~TempFile() { // This is the Finalize method
      // No if statement because this  executes only if the constructor ran successfully.
      File.Delete(m_filename);
   }
}
```

When designing a type, it's best if you avoid using a **Finalize** method for several reasons all related to performance:

- Finalizable objects take longer to allocate because pointers to them must be placed on the finalization list (which I'll discuss in the "Finalization Internals" section a little later in this chapter).

- Finalizable objects get promoted to older generations, which increases memory pressure and prevents the object's memory from being collected at the time the garbage collector determines that the object is garbage. In addition, all objects referred to directly or indirectly by this object get promoted as well. (I'll discuss promotions and generations in more detail in the "Generations" section later in this chapter.)

- Finalizable objects cause your application to run slower since extra processing must occur for each object when collected.

Furthermore, be aware of the fact that you have no control over when the `Finalize` method will execute. `Finalize` methods run when a garbage collection occurs, which may happen when your application requests more memory. Also, the CLR doesn't make any guarantees as to the order in which `Finalize` methods are called, so you should avoid writing a `Finalize` method that accesses other objects whose type defines a `Finalize` method; those other objects could have been finalized already. However, it is perfectly OK to access value type instances or reference type objects that do not define a `Finalize` method. You also need to be careful when calling static methods because these methods can internally access objects that have been finalized, causing the behavior of the static method to become unpredictable.

What Causes `Finalize` Methods to Be Called?

`Finalize` methods are called at the completion of a garbage collection, which is started by one of the following five events:

- **Generation 0 is full**   When generation 0 is full, a garbage collection starts. This event is by far the most common way for `Finalize` methods to be called because it occurs naturally as the application code runs, allocating new objects.

- **Code explicitly calls `System.GC`'s static `Collect` method**   Code can explicitly request that the CLR perform a collection. Although Microsoft strongly discourages such requests, at times it might make sense for an application to force a collection.

- **Windows is reporting low memory conditions**   The CLR internally uses the Win32 `CreateMemoryResourceNotification` and `QueryMemoryResourceNotification` functions to monitor system memory overall. If Windows reports low memory, the CLR will force a garbage collection in an effort to free up dead objects to reduce the size of a process's working set.

- **The CLR is unloading an AppDomain**   When an AppDomain unloads, the CLR considers nothing in the AppDomain to be a root, and a garbage collection consisting of all generations is performed. I'll discuss AppDomains in Chapter 22, "CLR Hosting and AppDomains."

- **The CLR is shutting down**   The CLR shuts down when a process terminates normally (as opposed to an external shutdown via Task Manager, for example). During this shutdown, the CLR considers nothing in the process to be a root and calls the `Finalize` method for all objects in the managed heap. Note that the CLR does not attempt to compact or free memory here because the whole process is terminating, and Windows will reclaim all of the processes' memory.

The CLR uses a special, dedicated thread to call `Finalize` methods. For the first four events, if a `Finalize` method enters an infinite loop, this special thread is blocked, and no more `Finalize` methods can be called. This is a very bad situation because the application will never be able to reclaim the memory occupied by the finalizable objects—the application will leak memory as long as it runs.

For the fifth event, each **Finalize** method is given approximately 2 seconds to return. If a **Finalize** method doesn't return within 2 seconds, the CLR just kills the process—no more **Finalize** methods are called. Also, if it takes more than 40 seconds to call all objects' **Finalize** methods, again, the CLR just kills the process.

> **Note** These timeout values were correct at the time I wrote this text, but Microsoft might change them in the future. Code in a **Finalize** method can construct new objects. If this happens during CLR shutdown, the CLR continues collecting objects and calling their **Finalize** methods until no more objects exist or until the 40 seconds have elapsed.

Recall the **GCBeep** type presented earlier in this chapter. If a **GCBeep** object is being finalized because of the first, second, or third garbage collection reason, a new **GCBeep** object is constructed. This is OK because the application continues to run, assuming that more collections will occur in the future. However, if a **GCBeep** object is being finalized because of the fourth or fifth garbage collection reason, a new **GCBeep** object shouldn't be constructed because this object would be created while the AppDomain is unloading or the CLR is shutting down. If these new objects are created, the CLR will have a bunch of useless work to do because it will continue to call **Finalize** methods.

To prevent the construction of new **GCBeep** objects, **GCBeep**'s **Finalize** method calls **AppDomain**'s **IsFinalizingForUnload** method and also queries **System.Environment**'s **HasShutdownStarted** property. The **IsFinalizingForUnload** method returns **true** if the object's **Finalize** method is being called because the AppDomain is unloading. The **HasShutdownStarted** property returns **true** if the object's **Finalize** method is being called because the process is terminating.

Finalization Internals

On the surface, finalization seems pretty straightforward: you create an object and its **Finalize** method is called when it is collected. But once you dig in, finalization is more complicated than this.

When an application creates a new object, the **new** operator allocates the memory from the heap. If the object's type defines a **Finalize** method, a pointer to the object is placed on the *finalization list* just before the type's instance constructor is called. The finalization list is an internal data structure controlled by the garbage collector. Each entry in the list points to an object that should have its **Finalize** method called before the object's memory can be reclaimed.

Figure 21-5 shows a heap containing several objects. Some of these objects are reachable from the application's roots, and some are not. When objects C, E, F, I, and J were created, the system detected that these objects' types defined a **Finalize** method and so added pointers to these objects in the finalization list.

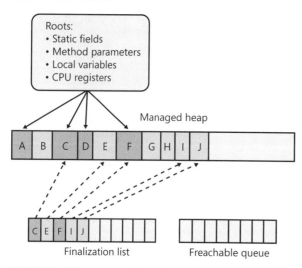

FIGURE 21-5 The managed heap showing pointers in its finalization list

> **Note** Even though **System.Object** defines a **Finalize** method, the CLR knows to ignore it; that is, when constructing an instance of a type, if the type's **Finalize** method is the one inherited from **System.Object**, the object isn't considered finalizable. One of the derived types must override **Object**'s **Finalize** method.

When a garbage collection occurs, objects B, E, G, H, I, and J are determined to be garbage. The garbage collector scans the finalization list looking for pointers to these objects. When a pointer is found, the pointer is removed from the finalization list and appended to the *freachable queue*. The freachable queue (pronounced "F-reachable") is another of the garbage collector's internal data structures. Each pointer in the freachable queue identifies an object that is ready to have its **Finalize** method called. After the collection, the managed heap looks like Figure 21-6.

In this figure, you see that the memory occupied by objects B, G, and H has been reclaimed because these objects didn't have a **Finalize** method. However, the memory occupied by objects E, I, and J couldn't be reclaimed because their **Finalize** methods haven't been called yet.

A special high-priority CLR thread is dedicated to calling **Finalize** methods. A dedicated thread is used to avoid potential thread synchronization situations that could arise if one of the application's normal-priority threads were used instead. When the freachable queue is empty (the usual case), this thread sleeps. But when entries appear, this thread wakes, removes each entry from the queue, and then calls each object's **Finalize** method. Because of the way this thread works, you shouldn't execute any code in a **Finalize** method that makes any assumptions about the thread that's executing the code. For example, avoid accessing thread-local storage in the **Finalize** method.

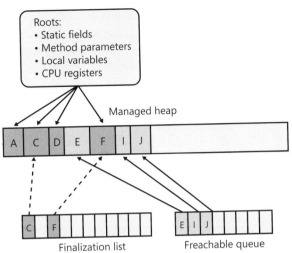

FIGURE 21-6 The managed heap showing pointers that moved from the finalization list to the freachable queue

In the future, the CLR may use multiple finalizer threads. So you should avoid writing any code that assumes that **Finalize** methods will be called serially. In other words, you will need to use thread synchronization locks if code in a **Finalize** method touches shared state. With just one finalizer thread, there could be performance and scalability issues in the scenario in which you have multiple CPUs allocating finalizable objects but only one thread executing **Finalize** methods—the one thread might not be able to keep up with the allocations.

The interaction between the finalization list and the freachable queue is fascinating. First I'll tell you how the freachable queue got its name. Well, the "f" is obvious and stands for *finalization*; every entry in the freachable queue is a reference to an object in the managed heap that should have its **Finalize** method called. But the *reachable* part of the name means that the objects are reachable. To put it another way, the freachable queue is considered a root, just as static fields are roots. So if an object is in the freachable queue, the object is reachable and is *not* garbage.

In short, when an object isn't reachable, the garbage collector considers the object to be garbage. Then when the garbage collector moves an object's reference from the finalization list to the freachable queue, the object is no longer considered garbage and its memory can't be reclaimed. As freachable objects are marked, objects referred to by their reference type fields are also marked recursively; all these objects must survive the collection. At this point, the garbage collector has finished identifying garbage. Some of the objects identified as garbage have been reclassified as not garbage—in a sense, the object has become *resurrected*. The garbage collector compacts the reclaimable memory, and the special CLR thread empties the freachable queue, executing each object's **Finalize** method.

The next time the garbage collector is invoked, it will see that the finalized objects are truly garbage because the application's roots don't point to it and the freachable queue no longer points to it either. The memory for the object is simply reclaimed. The important point to get from all of this is that two garbage collections are required to reclaim memory used by objects that require finalization. In reality, more than two collections will be necessary because the objects get promoted to another generation (which I'll explain later). Figure 21-7 shows what the managed heap looks like after the second garbage collection.

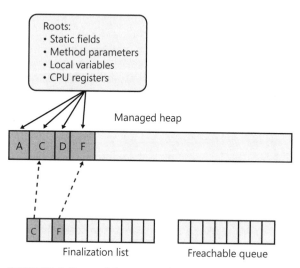

FIGURE 21-7 Status of the managed heap after second garbage collection

The Dispose Pattern: Forcing an Object to Clean Up

The **Finalize** method is incredibly useful because it ensures that native resources aren't leaked when managed objects have their memory reclaimed. However, the problem with the **Finalize** method is there is no guarantee of when it will be called, and because it isn't a public method, a user of the class can't call it explicitly.

The capability to deterministically dispose of or close an object is frequently useful when you're working with managed types that wrap native resources such as files, database connections, and bitmaps. For example, you might want to open a database connection, query some records, and close the database connection—you wouldn't want the database connection to stay open until the next garbage collection occurs, especially because the next garbage collection could occur hours or even days after you retrieve the database records.

Types that offer the capability to be deterministically disposed of or closed implement what is known as the *dispose pattern*. The dispose pattern defines conventions a developer should adhere to when defining a type that wants to offer explicit cleanup to a user of the type. In addition, if a type implements the dispose pattern, a developer using the type knows exactly how to explicitly dispose of the object when it's no longer needed.

> **Note** Any type that defines a **Finalize** method should also implement the dispose pattern as described in this section so that users of the type have a lot of control over the lifetime of the resource. However, a type can implement the dispose pattern and not define a **Finalize** method. For example, the **System.IO.BinaryWriter** class falls into this category. I'll explain the reason for this exception in the section "An Interesting Dependency Issue" later in this chapter.

Earlier I showed you the **SafeHandle** class. This class implements a **Finalize** method that ensures that a native resource wrapped by the object is closed (or released) when the object is collected. However, a developer using a **SafeHandle** object has a way to explicitly close the native resource because the **SafeHandle** class implements the **IDisposable** interface.

Let's take another look at the **SafeHandle** class. But for brevity, let's just focus on the parts that have to do with the dispose pattern:

```
// Implementing the IDisposable interface signals users of
// this class that it offers the dispose pattern.
public abstract class SafeHandle : CriticalFinalizerObject, IDisposable {

    // This public method can be called to deterministically close
    // the resource. This method implements IDisposable's Dispose.
    public void Dispose() {
        // Call the method that actually does the cleanup.
        Dispose(true);
    }

    // This public method can be called instead of Dispose.
    public void Close() {
        Dispose(true);
    }

    // When garbage collected, this Finalize method runs to close the resource
    ~SafeHandle() {
        // Call the method that actually does the cleanup.
        Dispose(false);
    }

    // This is the common method that does the actual cleanup.
    // Finalize, Dispose, and Close call this method.
    // Because this class isn't sealed, this method is protected & virtual.
    // If this class were sealed, this method should be private.
    protected virtual void Dispose(Boolean disposing) {
        if (disposing) {
            // The object is being explicitly disposed/closed, not
            // finalized. It is therefore safe for code in this if
            // statement to access fields that reference other
            // objects because the Finalize method of these other objects
            // hasn't yet been called.

            // For the SafeHandle class, there is nothing to do in here.
        }
```

```
        // The object is being disposed/closed or finalized, do the following:
        // If resource was already released, just return
        // If ownsHandle is false, return
        // Set flag indicating that this resource has been released
        // Call the virtual ReleaseHandle method
        // Call GC.SuppressFinalize(this) to prevent Finalize from being called
    }
}
```

Implementing the dispose pattern is hardly trivial. Now let me explain what all this code does. First, the **SafeHandle** class implements the **System.IDisposable** interface. This interface is defined in the FCL as follows:

```
public interface IDisposable {
    void Dispose();
}
```

Any type that implements this interface is stating that it adheres to the dispose pattern. Simply put, this means that the type offers a public, parameterless **Dispose** method that can be explicitly called to release the resource wrapped by the object. Note that the memory for the object itself is *not* freed from the managed heap's memory; the garbage collector is still responsible for freeing the object's memory, and there's no telling exactly when this will happen. The parameterless **Dispose** and **Close** methods should be both public and nonvirtual.

Note You might notice that this **SafeHandle** class also offers a public **Close** method. This method simply calls **Dispose**. Some classes that offer the dispose pattern also offer a **Close** method for convenience; but the dispose pattern doesn't require this method. For example, the **System.IO.FileStream** class offers the dispose pattern, and this class also offers a **Close** method. Programmers find it more natural to close a file rather than dispose of a file. However, the **System.Threading.Timer** class doesn't offer a **Close** method even though it adheres to the dispose pattern.

Important If a class defines a field in which the field's type implements the dispose pattern, the class itself should also implement the dispose pattern. The **Dispose** method should dispose of the object referred to by the field. This allows someone using the class to call **Dispose** on it, which in turn releases the resources used by the object itself. In fact, this is one of the main reasons why types might implement the dispose pattern but not implement the **Finalize** method.

For example, the **BinaryWriter** class implements the dispose pattern. When **Dispose** is called on a **BinaryWriter** object, **BinaryWriter**'s **Dispose** method calls **Dispose** on the stream object maintained as a field inside the **BinaryWriter** object. So when the **BinaryWriter** object is disposed, the underlying stream is disposed, which, in turn, releases the native stream resource.

So now you know three ways to clean up a **SafeHandle** object: a programmer can write code to call **Dispose**, a programmer can write code to call **Close**, or the garbage collector can call the object's **Finalize** method. The cleanup code is placed in a separate, protected, virtual method, which is also called **Dispose**, but this **Dispose** method takes a **Boolean** parameter named **disposing**.

This **Dispose** method is where you put all of the cleanup code. In the **SafeHandle** example, the method sets a flag indicating that the resource has been released and then calls the virtual **ReleaseHandle** method to actually perform the releasing of the resource. Note that the dispose pattern states that a single object can have **Dispose** or **Close** called on it multiple times; the first time, the resource should be released; for future calls, the method should just return (no exception should be thrown).

> **Note** It is possible to have multiple threads call **Dispose/Close** on a single object simultaneously. However, the dispose pattern states that thread synchronization is not required. The reason is because code should be calling **Dispose/Close** only if the code knows for a fact that no other thread is using the object. If you don't know if an object is still in use at a certain point in your code, you should not be calling **Dispose/Close**. Instead, wait for a garbage collection to kick in so that it can determine if the object is no longer being used, and then release the resource.

When an object's **Finalize** method is called by the CLR, the **Dispose** method's **disposing** parameter is set to **false**. This tells the **Dispose** method that it shouldn't execute any code that references other managed objects whose classes implement a **Finalize** method. Imagine that the CLR is shutting down, and inside a **Finalize** method, you attempt to write to a **FileStream**. This might not work because the **FileStream** might have already had its **Finalize** method called, closing the underlying disk file.

On the other hand, when you call **Dispose** or **Close** in your code, the **Dispose** method's **disposing** parameter must be set to **true**. This indicates that the object is being explicitly disposed of, not finalized. In this case, the **Dispose** method is allowed to execute code that references another object (such as a **FileStream**); because you have control over the program's logic, you know that the **FileStream** object is still open.

By the way, if the **SafeHandle** class were sealed, the **Dispose** method that takes a **Boolean** should be implemented as a private method instead of a protected virtual method. But since the **SafeHandle** class is not sealed, any class that derives from **SafeHandle** can override the **Dispose** method that takes a **Boolean** in order to override the cleanup code. The derived class wouldn't implement the parameterless **Dispose** or **Close** methods, and it wouldn't override the **Finalize** method. The derived class would simply inherit the implementation of all of these methods. Note that the derived class's override of the **Dispose** method that takes a **Boolean** should call the base class's version of the **Dispose** method that takes a **Boolean**, allowing the base class to perform whatever cleanup it needs to do. This is exactly the case of the **FileStream** type that I used as an example: it derives from **Stream** that implements the **Close** and the parameterless **IDisposable.Dispose** method. **FileStream** simply overrides the **Dispose** method, which takes a **Boolean** parameter to dispose of the **SafeHandle** field wrapping the unmanaged file resource.

> **Important** You need to be aware of some versioning issues here. If in version 1, a base type doesn't implement the **IDisposable** interface, it can never implement this interface in a later version. If the base type were to add the **IDisposable** interface in the future, all of the derived types wouldn't know to call the base type's methods, and the base type wouldn't get a chance to clean itself up properly. On the other hand, if in version 1 a base type implements the **IDisposable** interface, it can never remove this interface in a later version because the derived type would try to call methods that no longer exist in the base type.

Another noteworthy part of this code is the call to **GC**'s static **SuppressFinalize** method inside the **Dispose** method that takes a **Boolean**. You see, if code using a **SafeHandle** object explicitly calls **Dispose** or **Close**, there is no need for the object's **Finalize** method to execute, because if **Finalize** did execute, there would be an unnecessary attempt to release the resource a second time. The call to **GC**'s **SuppressFinalize** turns on a bit flag associated with the object referred to by its single **this** parameter. When this flag is on, the CLR knows not to move this object's pointer from the finalization list to the freachable queue, preventing the object's **Finalize** method from being called and ensuring that the object doesn't live until the next garbage collection. Note that the **SafeHandle** class calls **SuppressFinalize** even when the object is being finalized. This has no ill effect because the object is already in the process of being finalized.

Using a Type That Implements the Dispose Pattern

Now that you know how a type implements the dispose pattern, let's take a look at how a developer uses a type that offers the dispose pattern. Instead of talking about the **SafeHandle** class, let's talk about the more common **System.IO.FileStream** class. The **FileStream** class offers the ability to open a file, read bytes from the file, write bytes to the file, and close the file. When a **FileStream** object is constructed, the Win32 **CreateFile** function is called, the returned handle is saved in a **SafeFileHandle** object, and a reference to this object is maintained via a private field in the **FileStream** object. The **FileStream** class also offers several additional properties (such as **Length**, **Position**, **CanRead**) and methods (such as **Read**, **Write**, **Flush**).

Let's say that you want to write some code that creates a temporary file, writes some bytes to the file, and then deletes the file. You might start writing the code like this:

```
using System;
using System.IO;

public static class Program {
    public static void Main() {
        // Create the bytes to write to the temporary file.
        Byte[] bytesToWrite = new Byte[] { 1, 2, 3, 4, 5 };

        // Create the temporary file.
        FileStream fs = new FileStream("Temp.dat", FileMode.Create);
```

```
        // Write the bytes to the temporary file.
        fs.Write(bytesToWrite, 0, bytesToWrite.Length);

        // Delete the temporary file.
        File.Delete("Temp.dat");  // Throws an IOException
    }
}
```

Unfortunately, if you build and run this code, it might work, but most likely it won't. The problem is that the call to **File**'s static **Delete** method requests that Windows delete a file while it is still open. And so **Delete** throws a **System.IO.IOException** exception with the following string message: "**The process cannot access the file "Temp.dat" because it is being used by another process.**"

Be aware that in some cases, the file might actually be deleted! If another thread somehow caused a garbage collection to start after the call to **Write** and before the call to **Delete**, the **FileStream**'s **SafeFileHandle** field would have its **Finalize** method called, which would close the file and allow **Delete** to work. The likelihood of this situation is extremely rare, however, and therefore the previous code will fail more than 99 percent of the time.

Fortunately, the **FileStream** class implements the dispose pattern, allowing you to modify the source code to explicitly close the file. Here's the corrected source code:

```
using System;
using System.IO;

public static class Program {
    public static void Main() {
        // Create the bytes to write to the temporary file.
        Byte[] bytesToWrite = new Byte[] { 1, 2, 3, 4, 5 };

        // Create the temporary file.
        FileStream fs = new FileStream("Temp.dat", FileMode.Create);

        // Write the bytes to the temporary file.
        fs.Write(bytesToWrite, 0, bytesToWrite.Length);

        // Explicitly close the file when finished writing to it.
        fs.Dispose();

        // Delete the temporary file.
        File.Delete("Temp.dat");  // This always works now.
    }
}
```

The only difference here is that I've added a call to **FileStream**'s **Dispose** method. The **Dispose** method calls the **Dispose** method that takes a **Boolean** as parameter, which calls **Dispose** on the **SafeFileHandle** object, which ends up calling the Win32 **CloseHandle** function, which causes Windows to close the file. Now, when **File**'s **Delete** method is called, Windows sees that the file isn't open and successfully deletes it.

Because the **FileStream** class also offers a public **Close** method, the earlier code could be written as follows with identical results:

```
using System;
using System.IO;

public static class Program {
    public static void Main() {
        // Create the bytes to write to the temporary file.
        Byte[] bytesToWrite = new Byte[] { 1, 2, 3, 4, 5 };

        // Create the temporary file.
        FileStream fs = new FileStream("Temp.dat", FileMode.Create);

        // Write the bytes to the temporary file.
        fs.Write(bytesToWrite, 0, bytesToWrite.Length);

        // Explicitly close the file when finished writing to it.
        fs.Close();

        // Delete the temporary file.
        File.Delete("Temp.dat");   // This always works now.
    }
}
```

Note Again, remember that the **Close** method isn't officially part of the dispose pattern; some types will offer it and some won't.

Keep in mind that calling **Dispose** or **Close** simply gives the programmer a way to force the object to do its cleanup at a deterministic time; these methods have no control over the lifetime of the memory used by the object in the managed heap. This means you can still call methods on the object even though it has been cleaned up. The following code calls the **Write** method after the file is closed, attempting to write more bytes to the file. Obviously, the bytes can't be written, and when the code executes, the second call to the **Write** method throws a **System.ObjectDisposedException** exception with the following string message: **"Cannot access a closed file."**

```
using System;

using System.IO;

public static class Program {
    public static void Main() {
        // Create the bytes to write to the temporary file.
        Byte[] bytesToWrite = new Byte[] { 1, 2, 3, 4, 5 };

        // Create the temporary file.
        FileStream fs = new FileStream("Temp.dat", FileMode.Create);

        // Write the bytes to the temporary file.
```

```
        fs.Write(bytesToWrite, 0, bytesToWrite.Length);

        // Explicitly close the file when finished writing to it.
        fs.Close();

        // Try to write to the file after closing it.
        // The following line throws an ObjectDisposedException.
        fs.Write(bytesToWrite, 0, bytesToWrite.Length);

        // Delete the temporary file.
        File.Delete("Temp.dat");
    }
}
```

No memory corruption has occurred here because the memory for the **FileStream** object still exists; it's just that the object can't successfully execute its methods after it is explicitly disposed.

Important When defining your own type that implements the dispose pattern, be sure to write code in all of your methods and properties to throw a **System.ObjectDisposedException** if the object has been explicitly cleaned up. The **Dispose** and **Close** methods should never throw an **ObjectDisposedException** if called multiple times, though; these methods should just return.

Important In general, I strongly discourage calling a **Dispose** or **Close** method. The reason is that the CLR's garbage collector is well written, and you should let it do its job. The garbage collector knows when an object is no longer accessible from application code, and only then will it collect the object. When application code calls **Dispose** or **Close**, it is effectively saying that it knows when the application no longer has a need for the object. For many applications, it is impossible to know for sure when an object is no longer required.

For example, if you have code that constructs a new object, and you then pass a reference to this object to another method, the other method could save a reference to the object in some internal field variable (a root). There is no way for the calling method to know that this has happened. Sure, the calling method can call **Dispose** or **Close**, but later, some other code might try to access the object, causing an **ObjectDisposedException** to be thrown.

I recommend that you call **Dispose** or **Close** either at a place in your code where you know you must clean up the resource (as in the case of attempting to delete an open file) or at a place where you know it is safe to call one of the methods and you want to improve performance by removing the object from the finalization list, thus preventing object promotion.

C#'s using Statement

The previous code examples show how to explicitly call a type's **Dispose** or **Close** method. If you decide to call either of these methods explicitly, I highly recommend that you place the call in an exception-handling **finally** block. This way, the cleanup code is guaranteed to execute. So it would be better to write the previous code example as follows:

```
using System;
using System.IO;

public static class Program {
   public static void Main() {
      // Create the bytes to write to the temporary file.
      Byte[] bytesToWrite = new Byte[] { 1, 2, 3, 4, 5 };

      // Create the temporary file.
      FileStream fs = new FileStream("Temp.dat", FileMode.Create);
      try {
         // Write the bytes to the temporary file.
         fs.Write(bytesToWrite, 0, bytesToWrite.Length);
      }
      finally {
         // Explicitly close the file when finished writing to it.
         if (fs != null)   fs.Dispose();
      }

      // Delete the temporary file.
      File.Delete("Temp.dat");
   }
}
```

Adding the exception-handling code is the right thing to do, and you must have the diligence to do it. Fortunately, the C# language provides a **using** statement, which offers a simplified syntax that produces code identical to the code just shown. Here's how the preceding code would be rewritten using C#'s **using** statement:

```
using System;
using System.IO;

public static class Program {
   public static void Main() {
      // Create the bytes to write to the temporary file.
      Byte[] bytesToWrite = new Byte[] { 1, 2, 3, 4, 5 };

      // Create the temporary file.
      using (FileStream fs = new FileStream("Temp.dat", FileMode.Create)) {
         // Write the bytes to the temporary file.
         fs.Write(bytesToWrite, 0, bytesToWrite.Length);
      }

      // Delete the temporary file.
      File.Delete("Temp.dat");
   }
}
```

In the **using** statement, you initialize an object and save its reference in a variable. Then you access the variable via code contained inside **using**'s braces. When you compile this code, the compiler automatically emits the **try** and **finally** blocks. Inside the **finally** block, the compiler emits code to cast the object to an **IDisposable** and calls the **Dispose** method. Obviously, the compiler allows the **using** statement to be used only with types that implement the **IDisposable** interface.

> **Note** C#'s **using** statement supports the capability to initialize multiple variables as long as the variables are all of the same type. It also supports the capability to use just an already initialized variable. For more information about this topic, refer to the "Using Statements" topic in the C# Programmer's Reference.

The **using** statement also works with value types that implement the **IDisposable** interface. This allows you to create an extremely efficient and useful mechanism to encapsulate the code necessary to begin and end an operation. For example, let's say that you want to lock a block of code by using a **Mutex** object. The **Mutex** class does implement the **IDisposable** interface, but calling **Dispose** on it releases the native resource; it has nothing to do with the lock itself. To get simplified syntax to lock and unlock a **Mutex**, you can define a value type that encapsulates the locking and unlocking of a **Mutex** object. The **MutexLock** structure below is an example of this, and the **Main** method following it demonstrates how to use the **MutexLock** effectively:

```
using System;
using System.Threading;

// This value type encapsulates mutex locking and unlocking
internal struct MutexLock : IDisposable {
    private readonly Mutex m_mutex;

    // This constructor acquires a lock on the mutex
    public MutexLock(Mutex m) {
        m_mutex = m;
        m_mutex.WaitOne();
    }

    // This Dispose method releases the lock on the mutex
    public void Dispose() {
        m_mutex.ReleaseMutex();
    }
}

public static class Program {
    // This method demonstrates how to use the MutexLock effectively
    public static void Main() {
        // Construct a mutex object
        Mutex m = new Mutex();

        // Lock the mutex, do something, and unlock the mutex
        using (new MutexLock(m)) {
            // Perform some thread-safe operation in here...
        }
    }
}
```

An Interesting Dependency Issue

The **System.IO.FileStream** type allows the user to open a file for reading and writing. To improve performance, the type's implementation makes use of a memory buffer. Only when the buffer fills does the type flush the contents of the buffer to the file. A **FileStream** supports the writing of bytes only. If you want to write characters and strings, you can use a **System.IO.StreamWriter**, as is demonstrated in the following code:

```
FileStream fs = new FileStream("DataFile.dat", FileMode.Create);
StreamWriter sw = new StreamWriter(fs);
sw.Write("Hi there");

// The following call to Close is what you should do.
sw.Close();
// NOTE: StreamWriter.Close closes the FileStream;
// the FileStream doesn't have to be explicitly closed.
```

Notice that the **StreamWriter**'s constructor takes a reference to a **Stream** object as a parameter, allowing a reference to a **FileStream** object to be passed as an argument. Internally, the **StreamWriter** object saves the **Stream**'s reference. When you write to a **StreamWriter** object, it internally buffers the data in its own memory buffer. When the buffer is full, the **StreamWriter** object writes the data to the **Stream**.

When you're finished writing data via the **StreamWriter** object, you should call **Dispose** or **Close**. (Because the **StreamWriter** type implements the dispose pattern, you can also use it with C#'s **using** statement.) Both of these methods do exactly the same thing: cause the **StreamWriter** object to flush its data to the **Stream** object and close the **Stream** object. In my example, when the **FileStream** object is closed, it flushes its buffer to disk just prior to calling the Win32 **CloseHandle** function.

> **Note** You don't have to explicitly call **Dispose** or **Close** on the **FileStream** object because the **StreamWriter** calls it for you. However, if you do call **Dispose/Close** explicitly, the **FileStream** will see that the object has already been cleaned up—the methods do nothing and just return.

What do you think would happen if there were no code to explicitly call **Dispose** or **Close**? Well, at some point, the garbage collector would correctly detect that the objects were garbage and finalize them. But the garbage collector doesn't guarantee the order in which the **Finalize** methods are called. So if the **FileStream** object were finalized first, it would close the file. Then when the **StreamWriter** object was finalized, it would attempt to write data to the closed file, throwing an exception. If, on the other hand, the **StreamWriter** object were finalized first, the data would be safely written to the file.

How was Microsoft to solve this problem? Making the garbage collector finalize objects in a specific order would have been impossible because objects could contain references to each other, and there would be no way for the garbage collector to correctly guess the order in which to finalize these objects. Here is Microsoft's solution: the **StreamWriter** type does not implement a **Finalize** method, missing the opportunity to flush the data in its buffer to the underlying **FileStream** object. This means that if you forget to explicitly close the **StreamWriter** object, data is guaranteed to be lost. Microsoft expects developers to see this consistent loss of data and fix the code by inserting an explicit call to **Close/Dispose**.

> **Note** The .NET Framework offers a feature called Managed Debugging Assistants (MDAs). When an MDA is enabled, the .NET Framework looks for certain common programmer errors and fires a corresponding MDA. In the debugger, it looks like an exception has been thrown. There is an MDA available to detect when a **StreamWriter** object is garbage collected without having prior been explicitly closed. To enable this MDA in Microsoft Visual Studio, open your project and select the Debug.Exceptions menu item. In the Exceptions dialog box, expand the Managed Debugging Assistants node and scroll to the bottom. There you will see the StreamWriterBufferredDataLost MDA. Select the Thrown check box to have the Visual Studio debugger stop whenever a **StreamWriter** object's data is lost.

Monitoring and Controlling the Lifetime of Objects Manually

The CLR provides each AppDomain with a *GC handle table*. This table allows an application to monitor the lifetime of an object or manually control the lifetime of an object. When an AppDomain is created, the table is empty. Each entry on the table consists of a pointer to an object on the managed heap and a flag indicating how you want to monitor or control the object. An application adds and removes entries from the table via the **System.Runtime.InteropServices.GCHandle** type shown below. Since the GC handle table is used mostly in scenarios when you are interoperating with unmanaged code, most of GCHandle's members have the **[SecurityCritical]** attribute applied to them.

```
// This type is defined in the System.Runtime.InteropServices namespace
public struct GCHandle {
   // Static methods that create an entry in the table
   public static GCHandle Alloc(object value);
   public static GCHandle Alloc(object value, GCHandleType type);

   // Static methods that convert a GCHandle to an IntPtr
   public static explicit operator IntPtr(GCHandle value);
   public static IntPtr ToIntPtr(GCHandle value);

   // Static methods that convert an IntPtr to a GCHandle
   public static explicit operator GCHandle(IntPtr value);
   public static GCHandle FromIntPtr(IntPtr value);

   // Static methods that compare two GCHandles
   public static Boolean operator ==(GCHandle a, GCHandle b);
   public static Boolean operator !=(GCHandle a, GCHandle b);
```

```
    // Instance method to free the entry in the table (index is set to 0)
    public void Free();

    // Instance property to get/set the entry's object reference
    public object Target { get; set; }

    // Instance property that returns true if index is not 0
    public Boolean IsAllocated { get; }

    // For a pinned entry, this returns the address of the object
    public IntPtr AddrOfPinnedObject();

    public override Int32 GetHashCode();
    public override Boolean Equals(object o);
}
```

Basically, to control or monitor an object's lifetime, you call **GCHandle**'s static **Alloc** method, passing a reference to the object that you want to monitor/control, and a **GCHandleType**, which is a flag indicating how you want to monitor/control the object. The **GCHandleType** type is an enumerated type defined as follows:

```
public enum GCHandleType {
    Weak = 0,                      // Used for monitoring an object's existence
    WeakTrackResurrection = 1,     // Used for monitoring an object's existence
    Normal = 2,                    // Used for controlling an object's lifetime
    Pinned = 3                     // Used for controlling an object's lifetime
}
```

Now, here's what each flag means:

- **Weak**   This flag allows you to *monitor* the lifetime of an object. Specifically, you can detect when the garbage collector has determined this object to be unreachable from application code. Note that the object's **Finalize** method may or may not have executed yet and therefore, the object may still be in memory.

- **WeakTrackResurrection**   This flag allows you to *monitor* the lifetime of an object. Specifically, you can detect when the garbage collector has determined that this object is unreachable from application code. Note that the object's **Finalize** method (if it exists) has definitely executed, and the object's memory has been reclaimed.

- **Normal**   This flag allows you to *control* the lifetime of an object. Specifically, you are telling the garbage collector that this object must remain in memory even though there may be no variables (roots) in the application that refer to this object. When a garbage collection runs, the memory for this object can be compacted (moved). The **Alloc** method that doesn't take a **GCHandleType** flag assumes that **GCHandleType.Normal** is specified.

- **Pinned**   This flag allows you to *control* the lifetime of an object. Specifically, you are telling the garbage collector that this object must remain in memory even though there might be no variables (roots) in the application that refer to this object. When a garbage collection runs, the memory for this object cannot be compacted (moved). This is typically useful when you want to hand the address of the memory out to unmanaged code. The unmanaged code can write to this memory in the managed heap knowing that the location of the managed object will not be moved due to a garbage collection.

When you call **GCHandle**'s static **Alloc** method, it scans the AppDomain's GC handle table, looking for an available entry where the address of the object you passed to **Alloc** is stored, and a flag is set to whatever you passed for the **GCHandleType** argument. Then, **Alloc** returns a **GCHandle** instance back to you. A **GCHandle** is a lightweight value type that contains a single instance field, an **IntPtr**, which refers to the index of the entry in the table. When you want to free this entry in the GC handle table, you take the **GCHandle** instance and call the **Free** method (which also invalidates the instance by setting the **IntPtr** field to zero).

Here's how the garbage collector uses the GC handle table. When a garbage collection occurs:

1. The garbage collector marks all of the reachable objects (as described at the beginning of this chapter). Then, the garbage collector scans the GC handle table; all **Normal** or **Pinned** objects are considered roots, and these objects are marked as well (including any objects that these objects refer to via their fields).

2. The garbage collector scans the GC handle table looking for all of the **Weak** entries. If a **Weak** entry refers to an object that isn't marked, the pointer identifies an unreachable object (garbage), and the entry has its pointer value changed to **null**.

3. The garbage collector scans the finalization list. If a pointer in the list refers to an unmarked object, the pointer identifies an unreachable object, and the pointer is moved from the finalization list to the freachable queue. At this point, the object is marked because the object is now considered reachable.

4. The garbage collector scans the GC handle table looking for all of the **WeakTrackResurrection** entries. If a **WeakTrackResurrection** entry refers to an object that isn't marked (which now is an object pointed to by an entry in the freachable queue), the pointer identifies an unreachable object (garbage), and the entry has its pointer value changed to **null**.

5. The garbage collector compacts the memory, squeezing out the holes left by the unreachable objects. Note that the garbage collector sometimes decides not to compact memory if it determines that the amount of fragmentation isn't worth the time to compact. **Pinned** objects are not compacted (moved); the garbage collector will move other objects around them.

Now that you have an understanding of the mechanism, let's take a look at when you'd use them. The easiest flags to understand are the **Normal** and **Pinned** flags, so let's start with these two. Both of these flags are typically used when interoperating with unmanaged code.

The **Normal** flag is used when you need to hand a reference to a managed object to unmanaged code because, at some point in the future, the unmanaged code is going to call back into managed code, passing it the reference. You can't actually pass a pointer to a managed object out to unmanaged code because if a garbage collection occurs, the object could move in memory, invalidating the pointer. So to work around this, you would call **GCHandle**'s **Alloc** method, passing in a reference to the object and the **Normal** flag. Then you'd cast the returned **GCHandle** instance to an **IntPtr** and pass the **IntPtr** into the unmanaged code. When the unmanaged code calls back into managed code, the managed code would cast the passed **IntPtr** back to a **GCHandle** and then query the **Target** property to get the reference (or current address) of the managed object. When the unmanaged code no longer needs the reference, you'd call **GCHandle**'s **Free** method, which will allow a future garbage collection to free the object (assuming no other root exists to this object).

Notice that in this scenario, the unmanaged code is not actually using the managed object itself; the unmanaged code wants a way just to reference the object. In some scenarios, the unmanaged code needs to actually use the managed object. In these scenarios, the managed object must be pinned. Pinning prevents the garbage collector from moving/compacting the object. A common example is when you want to pass a managed **String** object to a Win32 function. In this case, the **String** object must be pinned because you can't pass the reference of a managed object to unmanaged code and then have the garbage collector move the object in memory. If the **String** object were moved, the unmanaged code would either be reading or writing to memory that no longer contained the **String** object's characters—this will surely cause the application to run unpredictably.

When you use the CLR's P/Invoke mechanism to call a method, the CLR pins the arguments for you automatically and unpins them when the unmanaged method returns. So, in most cases, you never have to use the **GCHandle** type to explicitly pin any managed objects yourself. You do have to use the **GCHandle** type explicitly when you need to pass the address of a managed object to unmanaged code and then, the unmanaged function returns, but unmanaged code might still need to use the object later. The most common example of this is when performing asynchronous I/O operations.

Let's say that you allocate a byte array that should be filled as data comes in from a socket. Then, you would call **GCHandle**'s **Alloc** method, passing in a reference to the array object and the **Pinned** flag. Then, using the returned **GCHandle** instance, you call the **AddrOfPinnedObject** method. This returns an **IntPtr** that is the actual address of the pinned object in the managed heap; you'd then pass this address into the unmanaged function, which will return back to managed code immediately. While the data is coming from the socket, this byte array buffer should not move in memory; preventing this buffer from moving is accomplished by using the **Pinned** flag. When the asynchronous I/O operation has completed, you'd call **GCHandle**'s **Free** method, which will allow a future garbage collection to move the buffer. Your managed code should still have a reference to the buffer so that you can access the data, and this reference will prevent a garbage collection from freeing the buffer from memory completely.

It is also worth mentioning that C# offers a **fixed** statement that effectively pins an object over a block of code. Here is some code that demonstrates its use:

```
unsafe public static void Go() {
   // Allocate a bunch of objects that immediately become garbage
   for (Int32 x = 0; x < 10000; x++) new Object();

   IntPtr  originalMemoryAddress;
   Byte[] bytes = new Byte[1000];    // Allocate this array after the garbage objects

   // Get the address in memory of the Byte[]
   fixed (Byte* pbytes = bytes) { originalMemoryAddress = (IntPtr) pbytes; }

   // Force a collection; the garbage objects will go away & the Byte[] might be compacted
   GC.Collect();

   // Get the address in memory of the Byte[] now & compare it to the first address
   fixed (Byte* pbytes = bytes) {
      Console.WriteLine("The Byte[] did{0} move during the GC",
         (originalMemoryAddress == (IntPtr) pbytes) ? " not" : null);
   }
}
```

Using C#'s **fixed** statement is more efficient that allocating a pinned GC handle. What happens is that the C# compiler emits a special "pinned" flag on the **pbytes** local variable. During a garbage collection, the garbage collector examines the contents of this root, and if the root is not **null**, it knows not to move the object referred to by the variable during the compaction phase. The C# compiler emits IL to initialize the **pbytes** local variable to the address of the object at the start of a **fixed** block, and the compiler emits an IL instruction to set the **pbytes** local variable back to **null** at the end of the **fixed** block so that the variable doesn't refer to any object, allowing the object to move when the next garbage collection occurs.

Now, let's talk about the next two flags, **Weak** and **WeakTrackResurrection**. These two flags can be used in scenarios when interoperating with unmanaged code, but they can also be used in scenarios that use only managed code. The **Weak** flag lets you know when an object has been determined to be garbage but the object's memory is not guaranteed to be reclaimed yet. The **WeakTrackResurrection** flag lets you know when an object's memory has been reclaimed. Of the two flags, the **Weak** flag is much more commonly used than the **WeakTrackResurrection** flag. In fact, I've never seen anyone use the **WeakTrackResurrection** flag in a real application.

Let's say that **Object-A** periodically calls a method on **Object-B**. However, the fact that **Object-A** has a reference to **Object-B** forbids **Object-B** from being garbage collected, and in some rare scenarios, this may not be desired; instead, we might want **Object-A** to call **Object-B**'s method if **Object-B** is still alive in the managed heap. To accomplish this scenario, **Object-A** would call **GCHandle**'s **Alloc** method, passing in the reference to **Object-B** and the **Weak** flag. **Object-A** would now just save the returned **GCHandle** instance instead of the reference to **Object-B**.

At this point, **Object-B** can be garbage collected if no other roots are keeping it alive. When **Object-A** wants to call **Object-B**'s method, it would query **GCHandle**'s read-only **Target** property. If this property returns a non-**null** value, then **Object-B** is still alive. **Object-A**'s code would then cast the returned reference to **Object-B**'s type and call the method. If the **Target** property returns **null**, then **Object-B** has been collected and **Object-A** would not attempt to call the method. At this point, **Object-A**'s code would probably also call **GCHandle**'s **Free** method to relinquish the **GCHandle** instance.

Since working with the **GCHandle** type can be a bit cumbersome and because it requires elevated security to keep or pin an object in memory, the **System** namespace includes a **WeakReference** class to help you. This class is really just an object-oriented wrapper around a **GCHandle** instance: logically, its constructor calls **GCHandle**'s **Alloc**, its **Target** property calls **GCHandle**'s **Target** property, and its **Finalize** method calls **GCHandle**'s **Free** method. In addition, no special permissions are required for code to use the **WeakReference** class because the class supports only weak references; it doesn't support the behavior provided by **GCHandle** instances allocated with a **GCHandleType** of **Normal** or **Pinned**.

The downside of the **WeakReference** class is that its object must be allocated on the heap. So the **WeakReference** class is a heavier-weight object than a **GCHandle** instance. Also, the **WeakReference** class doesn't implement the dispose pattern (which is a bug), so there is no way for you to free the **GCHandle** table entry explicitly; you have to wait for a garbage collection to kick in so that its **Finalize** method is called. The **WeakReference** class was introduced in version 1.0 of the .NET Framework; therefore, it is not generic (generics were introduced in version 2.0). So, I have created a little, lightweight structure that I sometimes use to put a compile-time type-safe wrapper around the **WeakReference** class:

```
internal struct WeakReference<T> : IDisposable where T : class {
   private WeakReference m_weakReference;

   public WeakReference(T target) { m_weakReference = new WeakReference(target); }
   public T Target { get { return (T)m_weakReference.Target; } }
   public void Dispose() { m_weakReference = null; }
}
```

Occasionally, developers ask me if there is a way to create a weak delegate where one object will register a callback delegate with some other object's event but the developer doesn't want the registering of the event to forcibly keep the object alive. For example, let's say that we have a class called **DoNotLiveJustForTheEvent**. We want to create an instance of this class and have it register a callback method with a **Button** object's **Click** event. However, we don't want the **Button** object's event to keep the **DoNotLiveJustForTheEvent** object alive. If the **DoNotLiveJustForTheEvent** object has no other reason to live, then we want it to get garbage collected, and it will just not receive a notification the next time the **Button** object raises its **Click** event. Let me show you how you might accomplish this:

First, here is the definition of the **DoNotLiveJustForTheEvent** class:

```
internal sealed class DoNotLiveJustForTheEvent {
    public void Clicked(Object sender, EventArgs e) {
        MessageBox.Show("Test got notified of button click.");
    }
}
```

Now, here is the code that creates a **Form** and two **Button** controls. The first **Button** control fills the left half of the **Form**'s client area and the second **Button** control fills the right half of the **Form**'s client area. Then, on the first **Button** control, I construct an instance of the **DoNotLiveJustForTheEvent** class and register this object's **Clicked** method as the event handler for this **Button** control's **Click** event. However, I do this by using my **WeakEventHandler** class, which turns an **EventHandler** delegate into a weak version of itself. I'll show how this class is implemented shortly. On the second **Button** control's **Click** event, I register a callback that will force a garbage collection to occur; I click this button to test that everything is working OK. Finally, I add the controls to the form's control collection, resize the form's client area, and then show the form:

```
public static void Go() {
    var form = new Form() {
        Text = "Weak Delegate Test",
        FormBorderStyle = FormBorderStyle.FixedSingle
    };

    var btnTest = new Button() {
        Text = "Click me",
        Width = form.Width / 2
    };

    var btnGC = new Button() {
        Text = "Force GC",
        Left = btnTest.Width,
        Width = btnTest.Width
    };

    // WeakEventHandler turns an EventHandler delegate into a weak version of itself
    btnTest.Click += new WeakEventHandler(new DoNotLiveJustForTheEvent().Clicked)
        { RemoveDelegateCode = eh => btnTest.Click -= eh };

    btnGC.Click += (sender, e) => { GC.Collect(); MessageBox.Show("GC complete."); };

    form.Controls.Add(btnTest);
    form.Controls.Add(btnGC);
    form.ClientSize = new Size(btnTest.Width * 2, btnTest.Height);
    form.ShowDialog();
}
```

Since I do not store the reference to the **DoNotLiveJustForEvent** object in a root variable, the object will be considered garbage when the next garbage collection runs. But, until then, I can click the left button multiple times and see that the **DoNotLiveJustForEvent** object's **Clicked** method is getting called. However, once I click the right button in the form, the **DoNotLiveJustForEvent** object is garbage collected. Now, when I click the left button, the

WeakEventHandler object determines that the **DoNotLiveJustForEvent** object is gone, and it unregisters itself with the **Button**'s **Click** event so that it never gets called again. Of course, the **WeakEventHandler** object will have its memory reclaimed during the next garbage collection.

To understand my **WeakEventHandler** class, you need to first understand its base class. **WeakEventHandler** is derived from my abstract generic **WeakDelegate** class:

```
public abstract class WeakDelegate<TDelegate> where TDelegate
   : class /* MulticastDelegate */ {
   private WeakReference<TDelegate> m_weakDelegate;
   private Action<TDelegate> m_removeDelegateCode;

   public WeakDelegate(TDelegate @delegate) {
      var md = (MulticastDelegate)(Object)@delegate;
      if (md.Target == null)
         throw new ArgumentException(
            "There is no reason to make a WeakDelegate to a static method.");

      // Save a WeakReference to the delegate
      m_weakDelegate = new WeakReference<TDelegate>(@delegate);
   }

   public Action<TDelegate> RemoveDelegateCode {
      set {
         // Save the delegate that refers to code that knows how to remove the
         // WeakDelegate object when the non-weak delegate object is GC'd
         m_removeDelegateCode = value;
      }
   }

   protected TDelegate GetRealDelegate() {
      // If the real delegate hasn't been GC'd yet, just return it
      TDelegate realDelegate = m_weakDelegate.Target;
      if (realDelegate != null) return realDelegate;

      // The real delegate was GC'd, we don't need our
      // WeakReference to it anymore (it can be GC'd)
      m_weakDelegate.Dispose();

      // Remove the delegate from the chain (if the user told us how)
      if (m_removeDelegateCode != null) {
         m_removeDelegateCode(GetDelegate());
         m_removeDelegateCode = null;  // Let the remove handler delegate be GC'd
      }
      return null;   // The real delegate was GC'd and can't be called
   }

   // All derived classes must return a delegate to
   // a private method matching the TDelegate type
   public abstract TDelegate GetDelegate();

   // Implicit conversion operator to convert a WeakDelegate object to an actual delegate
   public static implicit operator TDelegate(WeakDelegate<TDelegate> @delegate) {
```

```
        return @delegate.GetDelegate();
    }
}
```

Now, we can look at my **WeakEventHandler** class:

```
// This class provides support for the non-generic EventHandler delegate
public sealed class WeakEventHandler : WeakDelegate<EventHandler> {
    public WeakEventHandler(EventHandler @delegate) : base(@delegate) { }

    /// <summary>Returns a reference to the non-generic EventHandler delegate</summary>
    public override EventHandler GetDelegate() { return Callback; }

    // This private method must match the desired delegate's signature
    private void Callback(Object sender, EventArgs e) {
        // If the target hasn't been GC'd invoke it
        var eh = base.GetRealDelegate();
        if (eh != null) eh(sender, e);
    }
}
```

Solving this weak delegate problem turned out to be much more challenging than I first expected it to be. The CLR and C# have a lot of limitations that I had to work around; this makes the code bigger and more complex than I would have liked. Here are some of the problems:

- I want my **WeakDelegate** class to have its **TDelegate** generic argument constrained to accept only delegate objects that are derived from **System.MulticastDelegate**. However, C# doesn't allow you to constrain a generic argument to **MulticastDelegate** or even **System.Delegate** (the base class of **MulticastDelegate**). Therefore, the best I can do is constrain **TDelegate** to **class** (that is, any reference type).

- I wanted to have a **WeakDelegate** object automatically remove itself from the delegate chain that it is a member of when it sees that its target delegate has been garbage collected. However, a delegate has no way to know what chain it is a member of.

- I also thought about passing an event (like the **Button**'s **Click** event) to **WeakDelegate**'s constructor. Then I could have code inside my **WeakDelegate** class that automatically removes the **WeakDelegate** object from the event, but there is no way to create a variable that refers to an event. Therefore, the user of a **WeakDelegate** class can optionally set the **RemoveDelegateCode** property to some delegate referring to code that knows how to remove the delegate from a delegate chain or an event; at least I can pass the **WeakDelegate** object's delegate to remove into this code.

- The CLR treats each delegate type as different types and so you can't cast a reference to one delegate type to another delegate type even if the delegate types have the same signature. For example, I'd like to cast a reference to an **EventHandler** delegate to an **EventHandler<EventArgs>** delegate since these delegate signatures are actually identical. But the CLR treats these as different types, and the cast is not allowed.

Microsoft's CLR team knows about this delegate limitation and is considering ways to allow delegates with the same signature to be equivalent in a future version of the CLR. Due to this limitation, a different class has to be defined for each delegate's type.

I already showed you the **WeakEventHandler** type that corresponds to the **EventHandler** delegate. I also have a **WeakEventHandler<TEventArgs>** type that corresponds to the **EventHandler<TEventArgs>** delegate type:

```
// This WeakDelegate partial class provides support for the
// generic EventHandler<TEventArgs> delegate
public sealed class WeakEventHandler<TEventArgs> :
   WeakDelegate<EventHandler<TEventArgs>> where TEventArgs : EventArgs {

   public WeakEventHandler(EventHandler<TEventArgs> @delegate) : base(@delegate) { }

   /// <summary>
   /// Returns a reference to the generic
   /// EventHandler<typeparam name="TEventArgs"/> delegate
   /// </summary>
   public override EventHandler<TEventArgs> GetDelegate() { return Callback; }

   private void Callback(Object sender, TEventArgs e) {
      // If the target hasn't been GC'd invoke it
      var eh = base.GetRealDelegate();
      if (eh != null) eh(sender, e);
   }
}
```

If the CLR would treat delegate types that have the same signature as equivalent, I could use my **WeakEventHandler<TEventArgs>** type for non-generic **EventHandler** events, and I could delete my **WeakEventHandler** class entirely.

It would actually be pretty cool if the .NET Framework included a weak reference delegate mechanism, but no such thing exists today. However, it has been discussed by the CLR team at Microsoft, and it is likely that something like that will be part of a future version. If the CLR had first-class support for it, then they could easily work around all the limitations that I had to deal with, which would make the implementation easier to use and more efficient.

Important When developers start learning about weak references, they immediately start thinking that they are useful in caching scenarios. For example, they think it would be cool to construct a bunch of objects that contain a lot of data and then to create weak references to these objects. When the program needs the data, the program checks the weak reference to see if the object that contains the data is still around, and if it is, the program just uses it; the program experiences high performance. However, if a garbage collection occurred, the objects that contain the data will be destroyed, and when the program has to re-create the data, the program experiences lower performance.

The problem with this technique is the following: Garbage collections do not occur when memory is full or close to full. Instead, garbage collections occur whenever generation 0 is full, which occurs approximately after every 256 KB of memory is allocated. So objects are being tossed out of memory much more frequently than desired, and your application's performance suffers greatly.

Weak references can be used quite effectively in caching scenarios, but building a good cache algorithm that finds the right balance between memory consumption and speed is very complex. Basically, you want your cache to keep strong references to all of your objects and then, when you see that memory is getting tight, you start turning strong references into weak references. Currently, the CLR offers no mechanism to notify an application that memory is getting tight. But some people have had much success by periodically calling the Win32 **GlobalMemoryStatusEx** function and checking the returned **MEMORYSTATUSEX** structure's **dwMemoryLoad** member. If this member reports a value above 80, memory is getting tight, and you can start converting strong references to weak references based on whether you want a least-recently used algorithm, a most-frequently used algorithm, a time-base algorithm, or whatever.

Developers frequently want to associate a piece of data with another entity. For example, you can associate data with a thread or with an AppDomain. It is also possible to associate data with an individual object by using the **System.Runtime.CompilerServices. ConditionalWeakTable<TKey,TValue>** class, which looks like this:

```
public sealed class ConditionalWeakTable<TKey, TValue>
   where TKey : class where TValue : class {
   public ConditionalWeakTable();
   public void    Add(TKey key, TValue value);
   public TValue  GetValue(TKey key, CreateValueCallback<TKey, TValue> createValueCallback);
   public Boolean TryGetValue(TKey key, out TValue value);
   public TValue  GetOrCreateValue(TKey key);
   public Boolean Remove(TKey key);

   public delegate TValue CreateValueCallback(TKey key);  // Nested delegate definition
}
```

If you want to associate some arbitrary data with one or more objects, you would first create an instance of this class. Then, call the **Add** method passing in a reference to some object for the **key** parameter and the data you want to associate with the object in the **value** parameter. If you attempt to add a reference to the same object more than once, the **Add** method throws an **ArgumentException**; to change the value associated with an object, you must remove the key and then add it back in with the new value. Note that this class is thread-safe so multiple threads can use it concurrently, although this means that the performance of the class is not stellar; you should test the performance of this class to see how well it works for your scenario. Also, there is no good reason why **TValue** is constrained to class (only reference types). In the future, the CLR team might remove the constraint on **TValue** so that you can associate value type instances with an object without having to box the value types.

Of course, a table object internally stores a **WeakReference** to the object passed in as the key; this ensures that the table doesn't forcibly keep the object alive. But what makes the **ConditionalWeakTable** class so special is that it guarantees that the value remains in memory as long as the object identified by the key is in memory. So this is more than a normal **WeakReference** because if it were, the value could be garbage collected even though the key object continued to live. The **ConditionalWeakTable** class could be used to implement the dependency property mechanism of Silverlight and Windows Presentation Foundation

(WPF). It can also be used internally by dynamic languages to dynamically associate data with objects.

Here is some code that demonstrates the use of the **ConditionalWeakTable** class. It allows you to call the **GCWatch** extension method on any object passing in some **String** tag. Then it notifies you via the console window whenever that particular object gets garbage collected:

```
internal static class ConditionalWeakTableDemo {
   public static void Main() {
      Object o = new Object().GCWatch("My Object created at " + DateTime.Now);
      GC.Collect();      // We will not see the GC notification here
      GC.KeepAlive(o);   // Make sure the object o refers to lives up to here
      o = null;          // The object that o refers to can die now

      GC.Collect();      // We'll see the GC notification here
   }
}

internal static class GCWatcher {
   // NOTE: Be careful with Strings due to interning and MarshalByRefObject proxy objects
   private readonly static ConditionalWeakTable<Object, NotifyWhenGCd<String>> s_cwt =
      new ConditionalWeakTable<Object, NotifyWhenGCd<String>>();

   private sealed class NotifyWhenGCd<T> {
      private readonly T m_value;

      internal NotifyWhenGCd(T value) { m_value = value; }
      public override string ToString() { return m_value.ToString(); }
      ~NotifyWhenGCd() { Console.WriteLine("GC'd: " + m_value); }
   }

   public static T GCWatch<T>(this T @object, String tag) where T : class {
      s_cwt.Add(@object, new NotifyWhenGCd<String>(tag));
      return @object;
   }
}
```

Resurrection

When we talked about finalization, you'll recall that when an object requiring finalization is considered dead, the garbage collector forces the object back to life so that its **Finalize** method can be called. Then, after its **Finalize** method is called, the object is permanently dead. To summarize: An object requiring finalization dies, lives, and then dies again. Bringing a dead object back to life is called *resurrection*.

The act of preparing to call an object's **Finalize** method is a form of resurrection. When the garbage collector places a reference to the object on the freachable queue, the object is now reachable from a root and has come back to life. This is required so that the code in the **Finalize** method can access the object's fields. Eventually, the object's **Finalize** method returns, no roots point to the object because it is removed from the freachable queue, and the object is dead forever after.

But what if an object's **Finalize** method executed code that placed a pointer to the object in a static field, as demonstrated in the following code?

```
internal sealed class SomeType {
   ~SomeType() {
      Program.s_ObjHolder = this;
   }
}

public static class Program {
   public static Object s_ObjHolder;    // Defaults to null
   ...
}
```

In this case, when a **SomeType** object has its **Finalize** method called, a reference to the object is placed in a root, and the object is reachable from the application's code. This object is now resurrected, and the garbage collector won't consider the object to be garbage. The application is free to use the object—but you must remember that the object *has* been finalized, so using it can cause unpredictable results. Also keep in mind that if **SomeType** contained fields that referenced other objects (either directly or indirectly), all objects would be resurrected because they are all reachable from the application's roots. However, be aware that some of these other objects might also have had their **Finalize** method called.

In general, resurrection is not considered a good thing, and you should avoid writing code that takes advantage of this "feature" of the CLR. The few scenarios in which resurrection can be useful are when an application's architecture requires use of the same object over and over again. When the object is finished being used, a garbage collection will occur. In the object's **Finalize** method, it assigns its **this** pointer to another root, preventing the object from dying. But you'll want to tell the garbage collector to call the object's **Finalize** method again after the next usage. To make this possible, the **GC** type offers a static method named **ReRegisterForFinalize**. This method takes a single parameter: a reference to an object. The following code demonstrates how to fix **SomeType**'s **Finalize** method so that the **Finalize** method is called after each use of the object:

```
internal sealed class SomeType {
   ~SomeType() {
      Program.s_ObjHolder = this;
      GC.ReRegisterForFinalize(this);
   }
}
```

When the **Finalize** method is called, it resurrects the object by making a root refer to the object. The **Finalize** method then calls **ReRegisterForFinalize**, which appends the address of the specified object (**this**) to the end of the finalization list. When the garbage collector determines that this object is unreachable (some time in the future when the static field is set to **null**), it will move the object's pointer from the finalization list to the freachable queue, and the **Finalize** method will be called again. Again, remember that resurrecting an object resurrects all of the objects it refers to; you may need to call **ReRegisterForFinalize** for all of these objects, and in many situations, this is impossible because you won't have access to the private fields of the other objects!

This example shows how to create an object that constantly resurrects itself and never dies—but you don't usually want objects to do this. It's far more common to conditionally set a root to reference the object inside the **Finalize** method.

> **Note** Make sure that you call **ReRegisterForFinalize** no more than once per resurrection, or the object will have its **Finalize** method called multiple times. The reason is that each call to **ReRegisterForFinalize** appends a new entry to the end of the finalization list. When an object is determined to be garbage, all of these entries move from the finalization list to the freachable queue, making the object's **Finalize** method called multiple times.

At the end of this chapter's "Generations" section, I present a **GCNotification** class that uses resurrection in a useful and meaningful way.

Generations

As I mentioned near the beginning of the chapter, generations are a mechanism within the CLR garbage collector whose sole reason for being is to improve an application's performance. A *generational garbage collector* (also known as an *ephemeral garbage collector*, although I don't use the latter term in this book) makes the following assumptions:

- The newer an object is, the shorter its lifetime will be.

- The older an object is, the longer its lifetime will be.

- Collecting a portion of the heap is faster than collecting the whole heap.

Numerous studies have demonstrated the validity of these assumptions for a very large set of existing applications, and these assumptions have influenced how the garbage collector is implemented. In this section, I'll describe how generations work.

When initialized, the managed heap contains no objects. Objects added to the heap are said to be in generation 0. Stated simply, objects in generation 0 are newly constructed objects that the garbage collector has never examined. Figure 21-8 shows a newly started application with five objects allocated (A through E). After a while, objects C and E become unreachable.

FIGURE 21-8 A newly initialized heap containing some objects, all in generation 0. No collections have occurred yet.

When the CLR initializes, it selects a budget size for generation 0 of, say, 256 KB. (The exact size is subject to change.) So if allocating a new object causes generation 0 to surpass its budget, a garbage collection must start. Let's say that objects A through E occupy 256 KB. When object F is allocated, a garbage collection must start. The garbage collector will determine that objects C and E are garbage and will compact object D, causing it to be adjacent to object B. Incidentally, generation 0's budget of 256 KB was chosen because it is likely that all of these objects will fit entirely into a CPU's L2 cache so that compacting memory happens incredibly fast. The objects that survive the garbage collection (objects A, B, and D) are said to be in generation 1. Objects in generation 1 have been examined by the garbage collector once. The heap now looks like Figure 21-9.

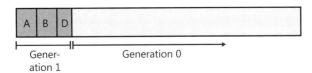

FIGURE 21-9 After one collection, generation 0 survivors are promoted to generation 1; generation 0 is empty

After a garbage collection, generation 0 contains no objects. As always, new objects will be allocated in generation 0. Figure 21-10 shows the application running and allocating objects F through K. In addition, while the application was running, objects B, H, and J became unreachable and should have their memory reclaimed at some point.

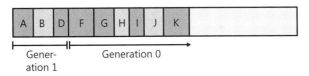

FIGURE 21-10 New objects are allocated in generation 0; generation 1 has some garbage

Now let's say that attempting to allocate object L would put generation 0 over its 256-KB budget. Because generation 0 has reached its budget, a garbage collection must start. When starting a garbage collection, the garbage collector must decide which generations to examine. Earlier, I said that when the CLR initializes, it selects a budget for generation 0. Well, it also selects a budget for generation 1. Let's say that the budget selected for generation 1 is 2 MB.

When starting a garbage collection, the garbage collector also sees how much memory is occupied by generation 1. In this case, generation 1 occupies much less than 2 MB, so the garbage collector examines only the objects in generation 0. Look again at the assumptions that the generational garbage collector makes. The first assumption is that newly created objects have a short lifetime. So generation 0 is likely to have a lot of garbage in it, and collecting generation 0 will therefore reclaim a lot of memory. The garbage collector will just ignore the objects in generation 1, which will speed up the garbage collection process.

Obviously, ignoring the objects in generation 1 improves the performance of the garbage collector. However, the garbage collector improves performance more because it doesn't traverse every object in the managed heap. If a root or an object refers to an object in an old generation, the garbage collector can ignore any of the older objects' inner references, decreasing the amount of time required to build the graph of reachable objects. Of course, it's possible that an old object's field refers to a new object. To ensure that the updated fields of these old objects are examined, the garbage collector uses a mechanism internal to the JIT compiler that sets a bit when an object's reference field changes. This support lets the garbage collector know which old objects (if any) have been written to since the last collection. Only old objects that have had fields change need to be examined to see whether they refer to any new object in generation 0.[2]

> **Note** Microsoft's performance tests show that it takes less than 1 millisecond to perform a garbage collection of generation 0. Microsoft's goal is to have garbage collections take no more time than an ordinary page fault.

A generational garbage collector also assumes that objects that have lived a long time will continue to live. So it's likely that the objects in generation 1 will continue to be reachable from the application. Therefore, if the garbage collector were to examine the objects in generation 1, it probably wouldn't find a lot of garbage. As a result, it wouldn't be able to reclaim much memory. So it is likely that collecting generation 1 is a waste of time. If any garbage happens to be in generation 1, it just stays there. The heap now looks like Figure 21-11.

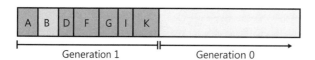

FIGURE 21-11 After two collections, generation 0 survivors are promoted to generation 1 (growing the size of generation 1); generation 0 is empty

As you can see, all of the generation 0 objects that survived the collection are now part of generation 1. Because the garbage collector didn't examine generation 1, object B didn't have its memory reclaimed even though it was unreachable at the time of the last garbage collection. Again, after a collection, generation 0 contains no objects and is where new objects will be placed. In fact, let's say that the application continues running and allocates

---

2 For the curious, here are some more details about this. When the JIT compiler produces native code that modifies a reference field inside an object, the native code includes a call to a write barrier method. This write barrier method checks if the object whose field is being modified is in generation 1 or 2 and if it is, the write barrier code sets a bit in what is called the card table. The card table has 1 bit for every 128-byte range of data in the heap. When the next GC starts, it scans the card table to know which objects in generations 1 and 2 have had their fields changed since the last GC. If any of these modified objects refer to an object in generation 0, then the generation 0 objects survive the collection. After the GC, the card table is reset to all zeroes. The write barrier code causes a slight performance hit when writing to a reference field in an object (as opposed to a local variable or static field) and that performance hit is slightly worse if that object is in generation 1 or 2.

objects L through O. And while running, the application stops using objects G, L, and M, making them all unreachable. The heap now looks like Figure 21-12.

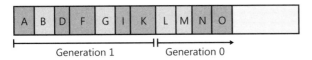

FIGURE 21-12 New objects are allocated in generation 0; generation 1 has more garbage

Let's say that allocating object P causes generation 0 to exceed its budget, causing a garbage collection to occur. Because the memory occupied by all of the objects in generation 1 is less than 2 MB, the garbage collector again decides to collect only generation 0, ignoring the unreachable objects in generation 1 (objects B and G). After the collection, the heap looks like Figure 21-13.

FIGURE 21-13 After three collections, generation 0 survivors are promoted to generation 1 (growing the size of generation 1 again); generation 0 is empty

In Figure 21-13, you see that generation 1 keeps growing slowly. In fact, let's say that generation 1 has now grown to the point in which all of the objects in it occupy 2 MB of memory. At this point, the application continues running (because a garbage collection just finished) and starts allocating objects P through S, which fill generation 0 up to its budget. The heap now looks like Figure 21-14.

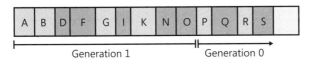

FIGURE 21-14 New objects are allocated in generation 0; generation 1 has more garbage

When the application attempts to allocate object T, generation 0 is full, and a garbage collection must start. This time, however, the garbage collector sees that the objects in generation 1 are occupying so much memory that generation 1's 2-MB budget has been reached. Over the several generation 0 collections, it's likely that a number of objects in generation 1 have become unreachable (as in our example). So this time, the garbage collector decides to examine all of the objects in generation 1 and generation 0. After both generations have been garbage collected, the heap now looks like Figure 21-15.

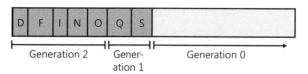

FIGURE 21-15 After four collections: generation 1 survivors are promoted to generation 2, generation 0 survivors are promoted to generation 1, and generation 0 is empty

As before, any objects that were in generation 0 that survived the garbage collection are now in generation 1; any objects that were in generation 1 that survived the collection are now in generation 2. As always, generation 0 is empty immediately after a garbage collection and is where new objects will be allocated. Objects in generation 2 are objects that the garbage collector has examined two or more times. There might have been several collections, but the objects in generation 1 are examined only when generation 1 reaches its budget, which usually requires several garbage collections of generation 0.

The managed heap supports only three generations: generation 0, generation 1, and generation 2; there is no generation 3.[3] When the CLR initializes, it selects budgets for all three generations. As I mentioned earlier, the budget for generation 0 is about 256 KB, and the budget for generation 1 is about 2 MB. The budget for generation 2 is around 10 MB. Again, the budget sizes are selected to improve performance. The larger the budget, the less frequently a garbage collection will occur. And again, the performance improvement comes because of the initial assumptions: new objects have short lifetimes, and older objects are likely to live longer.

The CLR's garbage collector is a self-tuning collector. This means that the garbage collector learns about your application's behavior whenever it performs a garbage collection. For example, if your application constructs a lot of objects and uses them for a very short period of time, it's possible that garbage collecting generation 0 will reclaim a lot of memory. In fact, it's possible that the memory for all objects in generation 0 can be reclaimed.

If the garbage collector sees that there are very few surviving objects after collecting generation 0, it might decide to reduce the budget of generation 0 from 256 KB to 128 KB. This reduction in the allotted space will mean that garbage collections occur more frequently but will require less work for the garbage collector, so your process's working set will be small. In fact, if all objects in generation 0 are garbage, a garbage collection doesn't have to compact any memory; it can simply set **NextObjPtr** back to the beginning of generation 0, and then the garbage collection is performed. Wow, this is a fast way to reclaim memory!

> **Note** The garbage collector works extremely well for applications with threads that sit idle at the top of their stack most of the time. Then, when the thread has something to do, it wakes up, creates a bunch of short-lived objects, returns, and then goes back to sleep. Many applications follow this architecture, including Windows Forms, WPF, ASP.NET Web Forms, and XML Web service applications.

---

[3] The **System.GC** class's static **MaxGeneration** method returns 2.

For ASP.NET applications, a client request comes in, a bunch of new objects are constructed, the objects perform work on the client's behalf, and the result is sent back to the client. At this point, all of the objects used to satisfy the client's request are garbage. In other words, each ASP.NET application request causes a lot of garbage to be created. Because these objects are unreachable almost immediately after they're created, each garbage collection reclaims a lot of memory. This keeps the process's working set very low, and the garbage collector's performance is phenomenal.

In fact, most of an application's roots live on the thread's stack in arguments or local variables. If a thread's stack is short, it takes very little time for the garbage collector to examine the roots and mark the reachable objects. In other words, garbage collections go much faster if you avoid deeps stacks. One way to avoid a deep stack is to avoid using recursive methods.

On the other hand, if the garbage collector collects generation 0 and sees that there are a lot of surviving objects, not a lot of memory was reclaimed in the garbage collection. In this case, the garbage collector will grow generation 0's budget to maybe 512 KB. Now, fewer collections will occur, but when they do, a lot more memory should be reclaimed. By the way, if insufficient memory has been reclaimed after a collection, the garbage collector will per- form a full collection before throwing an **OutOfMemoryException**.

Throughout this discussion, I've been talking about how the garbage collector dynamically modifies generation 0's budget after every collection. But the garbage collector also modi- fies the budgets of generation 1 and generation 2 by using similar heuristics. When these generations are garbage collected, the garbage collector again sees how much memory is reclaimed and how many objects survived. Based on the garbage collector's findings, it might grow or shrink the thresholds of these generations as well to improve the overall per- formance of the application. The end result is that the garbage collector fine-tunes itself automatically based on the memory load required by your application—this is very cool!

The **GCNotification** class shown below is similar to the **GCBeep** program discussed in the "Using Finalization with Managed Resources" section earlier in this chapter. However, the **GCNotification** class raises an event whenever a generation 0 or generation 2 collection occurs. With these events, you could have the computer beep whenever a collection or you calculate how much time passes between collections, how much memory is allocated be- tween collections, and more. With this class, you could easily instrument your application to get a better understanding of how your application uses memory.

```
public static class GCNotification {
   private static Action<Int32> s_gcDone = null;  // The event's field

   public static event Action<Int32> GCDone {
      add {
         // If there were no registered delegates before, start reporting notifications now
         if (s_gcDone == null) { new GenObject(0); new GenObject(2); }
         s_gcDone += value;
      }
      remove { s_gcDone -= value; }
   }
```

```
        private sealed class GenObject {
            private Int32 m_generation;
            public GenObject(Int32 generation) { m_generation = generation; }
            ~GenObject() { // This is the Finalize method
                // If this object is in the generation we want (or higher),
                // notify the delegates that a GC just completed
                if (GC.GetGeneration(this) >= m_generation) {
                    Action<Int32> temp = Interlocked.CompareExchange(ref s_gcDone, null, null);
                    if (temp != null) temp(m_generation);
                }

                // Keep reporting notifications if there is at least one delegated registered,
                // the AppDomain isn't unloading, and the process isn't shutting down
                if ((s_gcDone != null)
                    && !AppDomain.CurrentDomain.IsFinalizingForUnload()
                    && !Environment.HasShutdownStarted) {
                    // For Gen 0, create a new object; for Gen 2, resurrect the object & let
                    // the GC call Finalize again the next time Gen 2 is GC'd
                    if (m_generation == 0) new GenObject(0);
                    else GC.ReRegisterForFinalize(this);
                } else { /* Let the objects go away */ }
            }
        }
    }
}
```

Other Garbage Collection Features for Use with Native Resources

Sometimes, a native resource consumes a lot of memory, but the managed object wrapping that resource occupies very little memory. The quintessential example of this is the bitmap. A bitmap can occupy several megabytes of native memory, but the managed object is tiny because it contains only an **HBITMAP** (a 4- or 8-byte value). From the CLR's perspective, a process could allocate hundreds of bitmaps (using little managed memory) before performing a collection. But if the process is manipulating many bitmaps, the process's memory consumption will grow at a phenomenal rate. To fix this situation, the **GC** class offers the following two static methods:

```
public static void AddMemoryPressure(Int64 bytesAllocated);
public static void RemoveMemoryPressure(Int64 bytesAllocated);
```

A class that wraps a potentially large native resource should use these methods to give the garbage collector a hint as to how much memory is really being consumed. Internally, the garbage collector monitors this pressure, and when it gets high, a garbage collection is forced.

There are some native resources that are fixed in number. For example, Windows formerly had a restriction that it could create only five device contexts. There had also been a restriction on the number of files that an application could open. Again, from the CLR's perspective, a process could allocate hundreds of objects (that use little memory) before performing a collection. But if the number of these native resources is limited, attempting to use more than are available will typically result in exceptions being thrown. To fix this situation, the **System.Runtime.InteropServices** namespace offers the **HandleCollector** class:

```
public sealed class HandleCollector {
    public HandleCollector(String name, Int32 initialThreshold);
    public HandleCollector(String name, Int32 initialThreshold,  Int32 maximumThreshold);
    public void Add();
    public void Remove();

    public Int32 Count { get; }
    public Int32 InitialThreshold { get; }
    public Int32 MaximumThreshold { get; }
    public String Name { get; }
}
```

A class that wraps a native resource that has a limited quantity available should use an instance of this class to give the garbage collector a hint as to how many instances of the resource are really being consumed. Internally, this class object monitors the count, and when it gets high, a garbage collection is forced.

> **Note** Internally, the **GC.AddMemoryPressure** and **HandleCollector.Add** methods call **GC.Collect**, forcing a garbage collection to start prior to generation 0 reaching its budget. Normally, forcing a garbage collection to start is strongly discouraged because it usually has an adverse effect on your application's performance. However, classes that call these methods are doing so in an effort to keep limited native resources available for the application. If the native resources run out, the application will fail. For most applications, it is better to work with reduced performance than to not be working at all.

Here is some code that demonstrates the use and effect of the memory pressure methods and the **HandleCollector** class:

```
using System;
using System.Runtime.InteropServices;

public static class Program {
    public static void Main() {
        MemoryPressureDemo(0);                    // 0    causes infrequent GCs
        MemoryPressureDemo(10 * 1024 * 1024);  // 10MB causes frequent GCs

        HandleCollectorDemo();
    }

    private static void MemoryPressureDemo(Int32 size) {
        Console.WriteLine();
        Console.WriteLine("MemoryPressureDemo, size={0}", size);
        // Create a bunch of objects specifying their logical size
        for (Int32 count = 0; count < 15; count++) {
            new BigNativeResource(size);
        }

        // For demo purposes, force everything to be cleaned-up
        GC.Collect();
```

```
                GC.WaitForPendingFinalizers();
        }

        private sealed class BigNativeResource {
            private Int32 m_size;

            public BigNativeResource(Int32 size) {
                m_size = size;
                if (m_size > 0) {
                    // Make the GC think the object is physically bigger
                    GC.AddMemoryPressure(m_size);
                }
                Console.WriteLine("BigNativeResource create.");
            }

            ~BigNativeResource() {
                if (m_size > 0) {
                    // Make the GC think the object released more memory
                    GC.RemoveMemoryPressure(m_size);
                }
                Console.WriteLine("BigNativeResource destroy.");
            }
        }


        private static void HandleCollectorDemo() {
            Console.WriteLine();
            Console.WriteLine("HandleCollectorDemo");
            for (Int32 count = 0; count < 10; count++) {
                new LimitedResource();
            }

            // For demo purposes, force everything to be cleaned-up
            GC.Collect();
            GC.WaitForPendingFinalizers();
        }

        private sealed class LimitedResource {
            // Create a HandleCollector telling it that collections should
            // occur when two or more of these objects exist in the heap
            private static HandleCollector s_hc = new HandleCollector("LimitedResource", 2);

            public LimitedResource() {
                // Tell the HandleCollector that 1 more LimitedResource
                // object has been added to the heap
                s_hc.Add();
                Console.WriteLine("LimitedResource create.  Count={0}", s_hc.Count);
            }
            ~LimitedResource() {
                // Tell the HandleCollector that 1 less LimitedResource
                // object has been removed from the heap
                s_hc.Remove();
                Console.WriteLine("LimitedResource destroy. Count={0}", s_hc.Count);
            }
        }
    }
}
```

If you compile and run the code above, your output will be similar to the following output:

```
MemoryPressureDemo, size=0
BigNativeResource create.
BigNativeResource create.
BigNativeResource create.
BigNativeResource create.
BigNativeResource create.
BigNativeResource create.
BigNativeResource create.
BigNativeResource create.
BigNativeResource create.
BigNativeResource create.
BigNativeResource create.
BigNativeResource create.
BigNativeResource create.
BigNativeResource create.
BigNativeResource create.
BigNativeResource destroy.
BigNativeResource destroy.
BigNativeResource destroy.
BigNativeResource destroy.
BigNativeResource destroy.
BigNativeResource destroy.
BigNativeResource destroy.
BigNativeResource destroy.
BigNativeResource destroy.
BigNativeResource destroy.
BigNativeResource destroy.
BigNativeResource destroy.
BigNativeResource destroy.
BigNativeResource destroy.
BigNativeResource destroy.

MemoryPressureDemo, size=10485760
BigNativeResource create.
BigNativeResource create.
BigNativeResource create.
BigNativeResource create.
BigNativeResource create.
BigNativeResource create.
BigNativeResource create.
BigNativeResource create.
BigNativeResource destroy.
BigNativeResource destroy.
BigNativeResource destroy.
BigNativeResource destroy.
BigNativeResource destroy.
BigNativeResource create.
BigNativeResource create.
BigNativeResource destroy.
BigNativeResource destroy.
BigNativeResource destroy.
BigNativeResource destroy.
BigNativeResource create.
BigNativeResource create.
```

```
BigNativeResource create.
BigNativeResource destroy.
BigNativeResource destroy.
BigNativeResource create.
BigNativeResource create.
BigNativeResource destroy.
BigNativeResource destroy.
BigNativeResource destroy.
BigNativeResource destroy.

HandleCollectorDemo
LimitedResource create.   Count=1
LimitedResource create.   Count=2
LimitedResource create.   Count=3
LimitedResource destroy.  Count=3
LimitedResource destroy.  Count=2
LimitedResource destroy.  Count=1
LimitedResource create.   Count=1
LimitedResource create.   Count=2
LimitedResource destroy.  Count=2
LimitedResource create.   Count=2
LimitedResource create.   Count=3
LimitedResource destroy.  Count=3
LimitedResource destroy.  Count=2
LimitedResource destroy.  Count=1
LimitedResource create.   Count=1
LimitedResource create.   Count=2
LimitedResource destroy.  Count=2
LimitedResource create.   Count=2
LimitedResource destroy.  Count=1
LimitedResource destroy.  Count=0
```

Predicting the Success of an Operation that Requires a Lot of Memory

Occasionally you find yourself implementing an algorithm that you know will require a number of objects that together will occupy a good bit of memory. You could start executing the algorithm, and, if you run out of memory, the CLR will throw an **OutOfMemoryException**. In that case, you have done a lot of work that now must be thrown away. Plus, you need to catch this exception and allow your program to recover gracefully.

In the **System.Runtime** namespace, there is a **MemoryFailPoint** class that offers you the ability to check for sufficient memory prior to starting a memory-hungry algorithm. Here is what the class looks like:

```
public sealed class MemoryFailPoint : CriticalFinalizerObject, IDisposable {
    public MemoryFailPoint(Int32 sizeInMegabytes);
    ~MemoryFailPoint();
    public void Dispose();
}
```

The way you use this class is pretty simple. First, you construct an instance of it by passing in the number of megabytes that you think your algorithm is going to require (round up if you're not completely sure). Internally, the constructor performs the following checks that trigger actions in consequence:

1. Is there enough available space in the system's paging file, and is there enough contiguous virtual address space in the process to satisfy the request? Note that the constructor subtracts any amount of memory that has been logically reserved by another call to **MemoryFailPoint**'s constructor.

2. If there isn't enough space, a garbage collection is forced in an attempt to free up some space.

3. If there is still not enough paging file space, an attempt is made to expand the paging file. If the paging file cannot grow enough, an **InsufficientMemoryException** is thrown.

4. If there still isn't enough contiguous virtual address space, an **InsufficientMemoryException** is thrown.

5. If enough paging file space and virtual address space has been found, the requested number of megabytes are reserved by adding the number of megabytes to a private static field defined within the **MemoryFailPoint** class. The addition is done in a thread-safe way so that multiple threads can construct an instance of this class simultaneously and be guaranteed that they have logically reserved the memory they requested as long as no exception is thrown in the constructor.

If **MemoryFailPoint**'s constructor throws an **InsufficientMemoryException**, your application can release some resources it is currently using, or it can reduce its performance (perform less caching of data) in order to reduce the chance of the CLR throwing an **OutOfMemoryException** in the future. By the way, **InsufficientMemoryException** is derived from **OutOfMemoryException**.

> **Important** If **MemoryFailPoint**'s constructor doesn't throw an exception, you have logically reserved the memory you have requested and you can execute your memory-hungry algorithm. However, be aware that you have not physically allocated this memory. This means that it is just *more likely* for your algorithm to run successfully, getting the memory it needs. The **MemoryFailPoint** class cannot guarantee that your algorithm will get the memory it needs even if the constructor doesn't throw an exception. This class exists to *help* you make a more robust application.

When you have completed executing the algorithm, you should call **Dispose** on the **MemoryFailPoint** object you constructed. Internally, **Dispose** just subtracts (in a thread-safe way) the number of megabytes you reserved from the **MemoryFailPoint**'s static field. The code below demonstrates the use of the **MemoryFailPoint** class:

```
using System;
using System.Runtime;

public static class Program {
    public static void Main() {
        try {
            // Logically reserve 1.5 GB of memory
            using (MemoryFailPoint mfp = new MemoryFailPoint(1500)) {
                // Perform memory-hungry algorithm in here

            } // Dispose will logically free the 1.5 GB of memory
        }
        catch (InsufficientMemoryException e) {
            // The memory could not be reserved
            Console.WriteLine(e);
        }
    }
}
```

Programmatic Control of the Garbage Collector

The **System.GC** type allows your application some direct control over the garbage collector. For starters, you can query the maximum generation supported by the managed heap by reading the **GC.MaxGeneration** property; this property always returns 2.

You can also force the garbage collector to perform a collection by calling one of the following two static methods:

```
void GC.Collect(Int32 Generation)
void GC.Collect()
void Collect(Int32 generation, GCCollectionMode mode)
```

The first method allows you to specify which generation(s) to collect. You can pass any integer from 0 to **GC.MaxGeneration** inclusive. Passing 0 causes generation 0 to be collected, passing 1 causes generations 1 and 0 to be collected, and passing 2 causes generations 2, 1, and 0 to be collected. The version of the **Collect** method that takes no parameters forces a full collection of all generations and is equivalent to calling:

```
GC.Collect(GC.MaxGeneration);
```

The third overload of **Collect** allows you to pass a generation and a **GCCollectionMode**. Table 21-1 describes the various GC collection mode symbols.

TABLE 21-1 Symbols Defined by the GCCollectionMode Enumerated Type

Symbol Name	Description
Default	The same as calling **GC.Collect** with no flag. Today, this is the same as passing **Forced**, but this may change in a future version of the CLR.
Forced	Forces a collection to occur immediately for all generations up to and including the specified generation.
Optimized	The garbage collector will only perform a collection if the collection would be productive either by freeing a lot of memory or by reducing fragmentation. If the garbage collection would not be productive, then the call has no effect.

Under most circumstances, you should avoid calling any of the **Collect** methods; it's best just to let the garbage collector run on its own accord and fine-tune its generation budgets based on actual application behavior. However, if you're writing a console user interface (CUI) or graphical user interface (GUI) application, your application code owns the process and the CLR in that process. For these application types, you *might* want to suggest a garbage collection to occur at certain times using a **GCCollectionMode** of **Optimized**. Normally, modes of **Default** and **Forced** are used for debugging and testing.

For example, you might consider calling the **Collect** method if some non-recurring event has just occurred that has likely caused a lot of old objects to die. The reason that calling **Collect** in such a circumstance may not be so bad is that the garbage collector's predictions of the future based on the past are not likely to be accurate for non-recurring events.

For example, it might make sense for your application to force a full garbage collection of all generations after your application initializes or after the user saves a data file. When a Windows Form control is hosted on a Web page, a full collection is performed each time a page is unloaded. Don't explicitly call **Collect** to try to improve your application's response time; call it to reduce your process's working set.

The **GC** type also offers a **WaitForPendingFinalizers** method. This method simply suspends the calling thread until the thread processing the freachable queue has emptied the queue, calling each object's **Finalize** method. In most applications, it's unlikely that you'll ever have to call this method. Occasionally, though, I've seen code like this:

```
GC.Collect();
GC.WaitForPendingFinalizers();
GC.Collect();
```

This code forces a garbage collection. When the collection is complete, the memory for objects that don't require finalization is reclaimed. But the objects that do require finalization can't have their memory reclaimed yet. After the first call to **Collect** returns, the special, dedicated finalization thread is calling **Finalize** methods asynchronously. The call to **WaitForPendingFinalizers** puts the application's thread to sleep until all **Finalize** methods are called. When **WaitForPendingFinalizers** returns, all of the finalized objects are now truly garbage. At this point, the second call to **Collect** forces another garbage collection, which reclaims all of the memory occupied by the now-finalized objects.

For some applications (especially server applications that tend to keep a lot of objects in memory), the time required for the garbage collector to do a full collection that includes generation 2 can be excessive. In fact, if the collection takes a very long time to complete, then client requests might time out. To help these kinds of applications, the **GC** class offers a **RegisterForFullGCNotification** method. Using this method and some additional helper methods (**WaitForFullGCApproach**, **WaitForFullGCComplete**, and **CancelFullGCNotification**), an application can now be notified when the garbage collector is getting close to performing a full collection. The application can then call **GC.Collect** to force a collection at a more opportune time, or the application could communicate with another server to better load balance the client requests. For more information, examine these methods in the .NET Framework SDK documentation. Note that you should always call the **WaitForFullGCApproach** and **WaitForFullGCComplete** methods in pairs because the CLR handles them as pairs internally.

Finally, the **GC** class offers two static methods to allow you to determine which generation an object is currently in:

```
Int32 GetGeneration(Object obj)
Int32 GetGeneration(WeakReference wr)
```

The first version of **GetGeneration** takes an object reference as a parameter, and the second version takes a **WeakReference** reference as a parameter. The value returned will be between **0** and **GC.MaxGeneration** inclusively.

The following code will help you understand how generations work. The code also demonstrates the use of the **GC** methods just discussed.

```
using System;

internal sealed class GenObj {
    ~GenObj() {
        Console.WriteLine("In Finalize method");
    }
}

public static class Program {
    public static void Main() {
        Console.WriteLine("Maximum generations: " + GC.MaxGeneration);

        // Create a new GenObj in the heap.
        Object o = new GenObj();

        // Because this object is newly created, it is in generation 0.
        Console.WriteLine("Gen " + GC.GetGeneration(o)); // 0
```

```
            // Performing a garbage collection promotes the object's generation.
            GC.Collect();
            Console.WriteLine("Gen " + GC.GetGeneration(o)); // 1

            GC.Collect();
            Console.WriteLine("Gen " + GC.GetGeneration(o)); // 2

            GC.Collect();
            Console.WriteLine("Gen " + GC.GetGeneration(o)); // 2 (max)


            o = null; // Destroy the strong reference to this object.

            Console.WriteLine("Collecting Gen 0");
            GC.Collect(0);                      // Collect generation 0.
            GC.WaitForPendingFinalizers();      // Finalize is NOT called.

            Console.WriteLine("Collecting Gens 0, and 1");
            GC.Collect(1);                      // Collect generations 0 & 1.
            GC.WaitForPendingFinalizers();      // Finalize is NOT called.

            Console.WriteLine("Collecting Gens 0, 1, and 2");
            GC.Collect(2);                      // Same as Collect()
            GC.WaitForPendingFinalizers();      // Finalize IS called.
        }
    }
```

Building and running this code yields the following output:

```
Maximum generations: 2
Gen 0
Gen 1
Gen 2
Gen 2
Collecting Gen 0
Collecting Gens 0, and 1
Collecting Gens 0, 1, and 2
In Finalize method
```

Thread Hijacking

Earlier in this chapter, I explained the garbage collection algorithm. However, I made a big assumption during that discussion: that only one thread is running. In the real world, it's likely for multiple threads to be accessing the managed heap or at least manipulating objects allocated within the managed heap. When one thread sparks a garbage collection, other threads must not access any objects (including object references on its own stack) because the garbage collector is likely to move these objects, changing their memory locations.

So when the garbage collector wants to start a garbage collection, all threads executing managed code must be suspended. The CLR has a few different mechanisms that it uses to safely suspend threads so that a garbage collection can be performed. The reason that there are multiple mechanisms is to keep threads running as long as possible and to reduce overhead as much as possible. I don't want to get into all of the details here, but suffice it to say that Microsoft has done a lot of work to reduce the overhead involved with a garbage collection. Microsoft will continue to modify these mechanisms over time to ensure efficient garbage collections in the future.

When the CLR wants to start a garbage collection, it immediately suspends all threads that are executing managed code. The CLR then examines each thread's instruction pointer to determine where the thread is executing. The instruction pointer address is then compared with the JIT compiler–produced tables in an effort to determine what code the thread is executing.

If the thread's instruction pointer is at an offset identified by a table, the thread is said to have reached a *safe point*. A safe point is a place where it's OK to leave a thread suspended until a garbage collection completes. If the thread's instruction pointer isn't at an offset identified by an internal method table, the thread isn't at a safe point, and the CLR can't perform a garbage collection. In this case, the CLR *hijacks* the thread: the CLR modifies the thread's stack so that the return address points to a special function implemented inside the CLR. The thread is then resumed. When the currently executing method returns, the special function will execute, suspending the thread.

However, the thread might not return from its method for quite some time. So after the thread resumes execution, the CLR waits about 250 milliseconds for the thread to be hijacked. After this time, the CLR suspends the thread again and checks its instruction pointer. If the thread has reached a safe point, the garbage collection can start. If the thread still hasn't reached a safe point, the CLR checks to see whether another method has been called; if one has, the CLR modifies the stack again so that the thread is hijacked when it returns from the most recently executing method. Then the CLR resumes the thread and waits another few milliseconds before trying again.

When all of the threads have reached a safe point or have been hijacked, garbage collection can begin. When the garbage collection is completed, all threads are resumed, and the application continues running. The hijacked threads return to the method that originally called them.

This algorithm has one small twist. When the CLR wants to start a garbage collection, it suspends all threads that are executing managed code, but it does not suspend threads that are executing unmanaged code. Once all of the threads that are executing managed code are at a safe point or are hijacked, the garbage collection is allowed to start. The threads executing unmanaged code are allowed to continue running because any object that they are using should have been pinned. If a thread currently executing unmanaged code returns to managed code, the thread is immediately suspended until the garbage collection has completed.

As it turns out, the CLR uses hijacking most of the time rather than using the JIT compiler–produced tables to determine if the thread is at a safe point. The reason is the JIT compiler–

produced tables require a lot of memory and increase the working set, which in turn hurts performance significantly. So, the JIT compiler–produced tables contain information for sections of code having loops that do not call other methods. If the method has a loop that calls other methods or if there are no loops, the JIT compiler–produced tables do not have much information in them, and hijacking is used to suspend the threads.

Garbage Collection Modes

When the CLR starts, it selects a GC mode, and this mode cannot change during the lifetime of the process. There are two basic GC modes:

- **Workstation**   This mode fine-tunes the garbage collector for client-side applications. The garbage collector assumes that other applications are running on the machine and does not hog CPU resources. The Workstation mode can have two submodes: Workstation with the concurrent collector and Workstation without the concurrent collector. I'll describe the concurrent collector feature shortly.

- **Server**   This mode fine-tunes the garbage collector for server-side applications. The garbage collector assumes that no other applications (client or server) are running on the machine and it assumes that all the CPUs on the machine are available to do a garbage collection. This GC mode causes the managed heap to be split into several sections, one per CPU. When a garbage collection is initiated, the garbage collector has one thread per CPU; each thread collects its own section in parallel with the other threads. Parallel collections work well for server applications in which the worker threads tend to exhibit uniform behavior. This feature requires the application to be running on a computer with multiple CPUs so that the threads can truly be working simultaneously to attain a performance improvement.

By default, applications run with the Workstation GC mode, and the concurrent collector is turned on. However, a server application (such as ASP.NET or SQL Server) that hosts the CLR can request the CLR to load the Server GC. However, if the server application is running on a uniprocessor machine, then the CLR will load the Workstation GC mode without the concurrent collector.

An application that self-hosts the CLR can tell the CLR to use the server collector by creating a configuration file (as discussed in Chapter 2, "Building, Packaging, Deploying, and Administering Applications and Types," and Chapter 3, "Shared Assemblies and Strongly Named Assemblies") that contains a **gcServer** element for the application. Here's an example of a configuration file:

```
<configuration>
    <runtime>
        <gcServer enabled="true"/>
    </runtime>
</configuration>
```

When an application is running, it can ask the CLR if it is running in the Server GC mode by querying the **GCSettings** class's **IsServerGC** read-only **Boolean** property:

```
using System;
using System.Runtime; // GCSettings is in this namespace

public static class Program {
   public static void Main() {
      Console.WriteLine("Application is running with server GC=" + GCSettings.IsServerGC);
   }
}
```

The Workstation GC mode can run in concurrent or non-concurrent mode. In concurrent mode, the garbage collector has an additional background thread that collects objects concurrently while the application runs. When a thread allocates an object that pushes generation 0 over its budget, the garbage collector first suspends all threads and then determines which generations to collect. If the garbage collector needs to collect generation 0 or 1, it proceeds as normal. However, if generation 2 needs collecting, the size of generation 0 will be increased beyond its budget to allocate the new object, and then the application's threads are resumed.

While the application's threads are running, the garbage collector has a normal priority background thread that marks unreachable objects. This thread competes for CPU time with the application's threads, causing the application's tasks to execute more slowly. Once the objects are marked, the garbage collector suspends all threads again and decides whether to compact memory. If the garbage collector decides to compact memory, memory is compacted, root references are fixed up, and the application's threads are resumed. This garbage collection takes less time than usual because the set of unreachable objects has already been built. However, the garbage collector might decide not to compact memory; in fact, the garbage collector favors this approach. If you have a lot of free memory, the garbage collector won't compact the heap; this improves performance but grows your application's working set. When using the concurrent garbage collector, you'll typically find that your application is consuming more memory than it would with the non-concurrent garbage collector.

To summarize: Concurrent collection creates a better interactive experience for users and is therefore best for interactive CUI or GUI applications. For some applications, however, concurrent collection will actually hurt performance and will cause more memory to be used. When testing your application, you should experiment with and without concurrent collection and see which approach gives the best performance and memory usage for your application.

You can tell the CLR not to use the concurrent collector by creating a configuration file for the application (as discussed in Chapters 2 and 3) that contains a **gcConcurrent** element. Here's an example of a configuration file:

```
<configuration>
    <runtime>
        <gcConcurrent enabled="false"/>
    </runtime>
</configuration>
```

In addition to the modes just described, the garbage collector supports synchronization-free allocations. On a multiprocessor system, generation 0 of the managed heap is partitioned into multiple memory arenas, one arena per thread. This allows multiple threads to make allocations simultaneously so that exclusive access to the heap isn't required.

While the GC mode is configured for the process and it cannot change while the process runs, your application can have some control over the garbage collection by using the **GCSettings** class's **GCLatencyMode** property. This read/write property can be set to any of the values in the **GCLatencyMode** enumerated type, as shown in Table 21-2.

TABLE 21-2 **Symbols Defined by the GCLatencyMode Enumerated Type**

Symbol Name	Description
Batch (default for the Server GC mode)	In the Workstation GC mode, this latency mode turns off the concurrent GC. In the Server GC mode, this is the only valid latency mode.
Interactive (default for the Workstation GC mode)	In the Workstation GC mode, this latency mode turns on the concurrent GC. In the Server GC, this latency mode is not valid.
LowLatency	In the Workstation GC mode, you use this latency mode during short-term, time-sensitive operations (like drawing animations) where a generation 2 collection might be disruptive. In the Server GC, this latency mode is not valid.

The **LowLatency** mode requires some additional explanation. Typically, you would set this mode, perform a short-term, time-sensitive operation, and then set the mode back to either **Batch** or **Interactive**. While the mode is set to **LowLatency**, the garbage collector will really avoid doing any generation 2 collections because these could take a long time. Of course, if you call **GC.Collect()**, then generation 2 still gets collected. Also, the garbage collector will perform a generation 2 collection if Windows tells the CLR that system memory is low (see the "What Causes **Finalize** Methods to Be Called" section earlier in this chapter).

Under **LowLatency** mode, it is more likely that your application could get an **OutOfMemoryException** thrown. Therefore, stay in this mode for as short a time as possible, avoid allocating many objects, avoid allocating large objects, and set the mode back to **Batch** or **Interactive** using a *constrained execution region (CER)*, as discussed in Chapter 20, "Exceptions and State Management." Also, remember that the latency mode is a process-wide setting and threads may be running concurrently. These other threads could even change this setting while another thread is using it and so you may want to update some kind of counter (manipulated via **Interlocked** methods) when you have multiple threads manipulating this setting. Here is some code showing how to properly use the **LowLatency** mode:

```
private static void LowLatencyDemo() {
   GCLatencyMode oldMode = GCSettings.LatencyMode;
   System.Runtime.CompilerServices.RuntimeHelpers.PrepareConstrainedRegions();
   try {
      GCSettings.LatencyMode = GCLatencyMode.LowLatency;
      // Run your code here...
   }
   finally {
      GCSettings.LatencyMode = oldMode;
   }
}
```

Large Objects

There is one more performance improvement you might want to be aware of. Any objects that are 85,000 bytes or more in size are considered to be *large objects*. Large objects are allocated from a special large object heap. Objects in this heap are finalized and freed just as the small objects I've been talking about. However, large objects are never compacted because it would waste too much CPU time to shift 85,000-byte blocks of memory down in the heap. However, you should never write code that assumes that large objects do not move in memory because the size of large objects could change from 85,000 bytes to something else in the future. To guarantee that an object doesn't move in memory, pin it as discussed in the "Monitoring and Controlling the Lifetime of Objects Manually" section earlier in this chapter.

Large objects are always considered part of generation 2, so you should create large objects only for resources that you need to keep alive for a long time. Allocating short-lived large objects will cause generation 2 to be collected more frequently, which will hurt performance. The following program proves that large objects are always allocated in generation 2:

```
using System;

public static class Program {
   public static void Main() {
      Object o = new Byte[85000];
      Console.WriteLine(GC.GetGeneration(o));   // Displays 2; not 0
   }
}
```

All of these mechanisms are transparent to your application code. To you, the developer, it appears as if there is just one managed heap; these mechanisms exist simply to improve application performance.

Monitoring Garbage Collections

Within a process, there are a few methods that you can call to monitor the garbage collector. Specifically, the **GC** class offers the following static methods, which you can call to see how many collections have occurred of a specific generation or how much memory is currently being used by objects in the managed heap:

```
Int64 GetTotalMemory(Boolean forceFullCollection);
Int32 CollectionCount(Int32 generation);
```

To profile a particular code block, I have frequently written code to call these methods before and after the code block and then calculate the difference. This gives me a very good indication of how my code block has affected my process's working set and indicates how many garbage collections occurred while executing the code block. If the numbers are high, I know to spend more time tuning the algorithms in my code block.

You can also see how much memory is being used by individual AppDomains as opposed to the whole process. For more information about this, see the "AppDomain Monitoring" section in Chapter 22.

When you install the .NET Framework, it installs a set of performance counters that offer a lot of real-time statistics about the CLR's operations. These statistics are visible via the PerfMon.exe tool or the System Monitor ActiveX control that ships with Windows. The easiest way to access the System Monitor control is to run PerfMon.exe and click the + toolbar button, which causes the Add Counters dialog box shown in Figure 21-16 to appear.

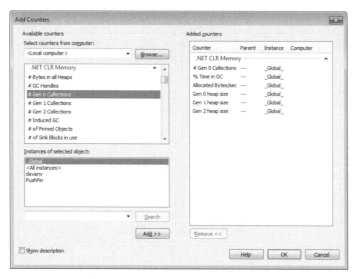

FIGURE 21-16 PerfMon.exe showing the .NET CLR Memory counters

To monitor the CLR's garbage collector, select the .NET CLR Memory performance object. Then select a specific application from the instance list box. Finally, select the set of counters that you're interested in monitoring, click Add, and then click OK. At this point, the System Monitor will graph the selected real-time statistics. For an explanation of a particular counter, select the desired counter and then select the Show Description check box.

Another great tool for monitoring your application's object allocations is the CLR Profiler. This tool offers call profiling, heap snapshots, and memory-use timelines. There is even an API that can be used from test code to start and stop profiling and inject comments into the logs. Also, the source code for this tool is available so that you can modify the tool for your own needs. The best way to acquire this tool is for you to search the Web for *CLR profiler*. This tool is invaluable, and I highly recommend it.

Finally, you should look into using the SOS Debugging Extension (SOS.dll), which can often offer great assistance when debugging memory problems and other CLR problems. For memory-related actions, the SOS Debugging Extension allows you to see how much memory is allocated within the process to the managed heap, displays all objects registered for finalization in the finalization queue, displays the entries in the GCHandle table per AppDomain or for the entire process, shows the roots that are keeping an object alive in the heap, and more.

Chapter 22
CLR Hosting and AppDomains

In this chapter, I'll discuss two main topics that really show off the incredible value provided by the Microsoft .NET Framework: *hosting* and *AppDomains*. Hosting allows any application to utilize the features of the common language runtime (CLR). In particular, this allows existing applications to be at least partially written using managed code. Furthermore, hosting allows applications the ability to offer customization and extensibility via programming.

Allowing extensibility means that third-party code will be running inside your process. In Microsoft Windows, loading a third party's DLLs into a process has been fraught with peril. The DLL could easily have code in it that could compromise the application's data structures and code. The DLL could also try to use the security context of the application to gain access to resources that it should not have access to. The CLR's AppDomain feature solves all of these problems. AppDomains allow third-party untrusted code to run in an existing process, and the CLR guarantees that the data structures, code, and security context will not be exploited or compromised.

Programmers typically use hosting and AppDomains along with assembly loading and reflection. Using these four technologies together makes the CLR an incredibly rich and powerful platform. In this chapter, I'll focus on hosting and AppDomains. In the next chapter, I'll focus on assembly loading and reflection. When you learn and understand all of these technologies, you'll see how your investment in the .NET Framework today will certainly pay off down the line.

CLR Hosting

The .NET Framework runs on top of Microsoft Windows. This means that the .NET Framework must be built using technologies that Windows can interface with. For starters, all managed module and assembly files must use the Windows portable executable (PE) file format and be either a Windows executable (EXE) file or a DLL.

When developing the CLR, Microsoft implemented it as a COM server contained inside a DLL; that is, Microsoft defined a standard COM interface for the CLR and assigned GUIDs to this interface and the COM server. When you install the .NET Framework, the COM server representing the CLR is registered in the Windows registry just as any other COM server would. If you want more information about this topic, refer to the MetaHost.h C++ header file that ships with the .NET Framework SDK. This header file defines the GUIDs and the unmanaged **ICLRMetaHost** interface definition.

Any Windows application can host the CLR. However, you shouldn't create an instance of the CLR COM server by calling **CoCreateInstance**; instead, your unmanaged host should call the **CLRCreateInstance** function declared in MetaHost.h. The **CLRCreateInstance** function is implemented in the MSCorEE.dll file, which is usually found in the C:\Windows\System32 directory. This DLL is affectionately referred to as the *shim*, and its job is to determine which version of the CLR to create; the shim DLL doesn't contain the CLR COM server itself.

A single machine may have multiple versions of the CLR installed, but there will be only one version of the MSCorEE.dll file (the shim).[1] The version of MSCorEE.dll installed on the machine is the version that shipped with the latest version of the CLR installed on the machine. Therefore, this version of MSCorEE.dll knows how to find any previous versions of the CLR that may be installed.

The actual CLR code is contained in a file whose name has changed with different versions of the CLR. For versions 1.0, 1.1, and 2.0, the CLR code is in a file called MSCorWks.dll, and for version 4.0, the CLR code is in a file called Clr.dll. Since you can have multiple versions of the CLR installed on a single machine, these files are installed into different directories as follows.[2]

- Version 1.0 is in C:\Windows\Microsoft.NET\Framework\v1.0.3705
- Version 1.1 is in C:\Windows\Microsoft.NET\Framework\v1.0.4322
- Version 2.0 is in C:\Windows\Microsoft.NET\Framework\v2.0.50727
- Version 4.0 is in C:\Windows\Microsoft.NET\Framework\v4.0.21006

---

[1] If you are using a 64-bit version of Windows, there are actually two versions of the MSCorEE.dll file installed. One version is the 32-bit x86 version, which will be in the C:\Windows\SysWOW64 directory. The other version is the 64-bit x64 or IA64 version (depending on your computer's CPU architecture), which will be in the C:\Windows\System32 directory.

[2] Note that versions 3.0 and 3.5 of the .NET Framework shipped with version 2.0 of the CLR; I do not show the directories for .NET Framework versions 3.0 and 3.5 because the CLR DLL loads from the v2.0.50727 directory.

The **CLRCreateInstance** function can return an **ICLRMetaHost** interface. A host application can call this interface's **GetRuntime** function, specifying the version of the CLR that the host would like to create. The shim then loads the desired version of the CLR into the host's process.

By default, when a managed executable starts, the shim examines the executable file and extracts the information indicating the version of the CLR that the application was built and tested with. However, an application can override this default behavior by placing **requiredRuntime** and **supportedRuntime** entries in its XML configuration file (described in Chapter 2, "Building, Packaging, Deploying, and Administering Applications and Types," and Chapter 3, "Shared Assemblies and Strongly Named Assemblies").

The **GetRuntime** function returns a pointer to the unmanaged **ICLRRuntimeInfo** interface from which the **ICLRRuntimeHost** interface is obtained via the **GetInterface** method. The hosting application can call methods defined by this interface to:

- Set Host managers. Tell the CLR that the host wants to be involved in making decisions related to memory allocations, thread scheduling/synchronization, assembly loading, and more. The host can also state that it wants notifications of garbage collection starts and stops and when certain operations time out.

- Get CLR managers. Tell the CLR to prevent the use of some classes/members. In addition, the host can tell which code can and can't be debugged and which methods in the host should be called when a special event—such as an AppDomain unload, CLR stop, or stack overflow exception—occurs.

- Initialize and start the CLR.

- Load an assembly and execute code in it.

- Stop the CLR, thus preventing any more managed code from running in the Windows process.

There are many reasons why hosting the CLR is useful. Hosting allows any application to offer CLR features and a programmability story and to be at least partially written in managed code. Any application that hosts the runtime offers many benefits to developers who are trying to extend the application. Here are some of the benefits:

- Programming can be done in any programming language.

- Code is just-in-time (JIT)–compiled for speed (versus being interpreted).

- Code uses garbage collection to avoid memory leaks and corruption.

- Code runs in a secure sandbox.

- The host doesn't need to worry about providing a rich development environment. The host makes use of existing technologies: languages, compilers, editors, debuggers, profilers, and more.

If you are interesting in using the CLR for hosting scenarios, I highly recommend that you get Steven Pratschner's excellent book, *Customizing the Microsoft .NET Framework Common Language Runtime* (Microsoft Press 2005), even though it focuses on pre-4.0 versions of the CLR.

> **Note** Of course, a Windows process does not need to load the CLR at all. It needs to be loaded only if you want to execute managed code in a process. Prior to .NET Framework 4.0, the CLR allowed only one instance of itself to reside within a Windows process. That is, a process could contain no CLR, v1.0 of the CLR, v1.1 of the CLR, or v2.0 of the CLR. Allowing only one CLR version per process is a huge limitation. For example, Microsoft Office Outlook couldn't load two add-ins that were built and tested against different versions of the .NET Framework.
>
> However, with .NET Framework 4.0, Microsoft now supports the ability to load v2.0 and v4.0 in a single Windows process, allowing components written for .NET Framework versions 2.0 and 4.0 to run side by side without experiencing any compatibility problems. This is a fantastic new feature, as it allows .NET Framework components to be used reliably in more scenarios than ever before. You can use the ClrVer.exe tool to see which CLR version(s) are loaded into any given process.
>
> Once a CLR is loaded into a Windows process, it can never be unloaded; calling the **AddRef** and **Release** methods on the **ICLRRuntimeHost** interface has no effect. The only way for the CLR to be unloaded from a process is for the process to terminate, causing Windows to clean up all resources used by the process.

AppDomains

When the CLR COM server initializes, it creates an *AppDomain*. An AppDomain is a logical container for a set of assemblies. The first AppDomain created when the CLR is initialized is called the *default AppDomain*; this AppDomain is destroyed only when the Windows process terminates.

In addition to the default AppDomain, a host using either unmanaged COM interface methods or managed type methods can instruct the CLR to create additional AppDomains. The whole purpose of an AppDomain is to provide isolation. Here are the specific features offered by an AppDomain:

- **Objects created by code in one AppDomain cannot be accessed directly by code in another AppDomain**   When code in an AppDomain creates an object, that object is "owned" by that AppDomain. In other words, the object is not allowed to live beyond the lifetime of the AppDomain whose code constructed it. Code in other AppDomains can access another AppDomain's object only by using marshal-by-reference or marshal-by-value semantics. This enforces a clean separation and boundary because code in one AppDomain can't have a direct reference to an object created by code in a different AppDomain. This isolation allows AppDomains to be easily unloaded from a process without affecting code running in other AppDomains.

- **AppDomains can be unloaded**   The CLR doesn't support the ability to unload a single assembly from an AppDomain. However, you can tell the CLR to unload an AppDomain, which will cause all of the assemblies currently contained in it to be unloaded as well.

- **AppDomains can be individually secured**   When created, an AppDomain can have a permission set applied to it that determines the maximum rights granted to assemblies running in the AppDomain. This allows a host to load some code and be ensured that the code cannot corrupt or read important data structures used by the host itself.

- **AppDomains can be individually configured**   When created, an AppDomain can have a bunch of configuration settings associated with it. These settings mostly affect how the CLR loads assemblies into the AppDomain. There are configuration settings related to search paths, version binding redirects, shadow copying, and loader optimizations.

> **Important**   A great feature of Windows is that it runs each application in its own process address space. This ensures that code in one application cannot access code or data in use by another application. Process isolation prevents security holes, data corruption, and other unpredictable behaviors from occurring, making Windows and the applications running on it robust. Unfortunately, creating processes in Windows is very expensive. The Win32 **CreateProcess** function is very slow, and Windows requires a lot of memory to virtualize a process's address space.
>
> However, if an application consists entirely of managed code that is verifiably safe and doesn't call out into unmanaged code, there are no problems related to running multiple managed applications in a single Windows process. And AppDomains provide the isolation required to secure, configure, and terminate each of these applications.

Figure 22-1 shows a single Windows process that has one CLR COM server running in it. This CLR is currently managing two AppDomains (although there is no hard-coded limit to the number of AppDomains that could be running in a single Windows process). Each AppDomain has its own loader heap, each of which maintains a record of which types have been accessed since the AppDomain was created. These type objects were discussed in Chapter 4, "Type Fundamentals"; each type object in the loader heap has a method table, and each entry in the method table points to JIT-compiled native code if the method has been executed at least once.

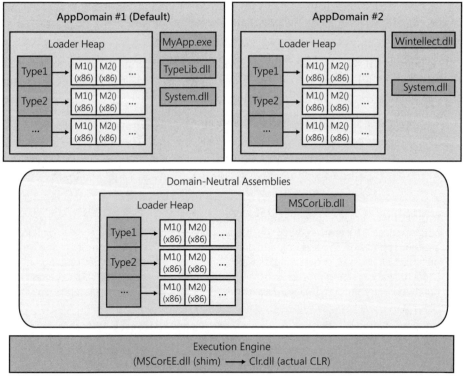

FIGURE 22-1 A single Windows process hosting the CLR and two AppDomains

In addition, each AppDomain has some assemblies loaded into it. AppDomain #1 (the default AppDomain) has three assemblies: MyApp.exe, TypeLib.dll, and System.dll. AppDomain #2 has two assemblies loaded into it: Wintellect.dll and System.dll.

You'll notice that the System.dll assembly has been loaded into both AppDomains. If both AppDomains are using a single type from System.dll, both AppDomains will have a type object for the same type allocated in each loader heap; the memory for the type object is not shared by all of the AppDomains. Furthermore, as code in an AppDomain calls methods defined by a type, the method's Intermediate Language (IL) code is JIT-compiled, and the resulting native code is associated with each AppDomain; the code for the method is not shared by all AppDomains that call it.

Not sharing the memory for the type objects or native code is wasteful. However, the whole purpose of AppDomains is to provide isolation; the CLR needs to be able to unload an AppDomain and free up all of its resources without adversely affecting any other AppDomain. Replicating the CLR data structures ensures that this is possible. It also ensures that a type used by multiple AppDomains has a set of static fields for each AppDomain.

Some assemblies are expected to be used by several AppDomains. The best example is MSCorLib.dll. This assembly contains **System.Object**, **System.Int32**, and all of the other types that are so integral to the .NET Framework. This assembly is automatically loaded when the CLR initializes, and all AppDomains share the types in this assembly. To reduce resource usage, MSCorLib.dll is loaded in an AppDomain-neutral fashion; that is, the CLR maintains a special loader heap for assemblies that are loaded in a domain-neutral fashion. All type objects in this loader heap and all native code for methods of these types are shared by all AppDomains in the process. Unfortunately, the benefit gained by sharing these resources does come with a price: assemblies that are loaded domain-neutral can never be unloaded. The only way to reclaim the resources used by them is to terminate the Windows process to cause Windows to reclaim the resources.

Accessing Objects Across AppDomain Boundaries

Code in one AppDomain can communicate with types and objects contained in another AppDomain. However, access to these types and objects is allowed only through well-defined mechanisms. The Ch22-1-AppDomains sample application below demonstrates how to create a new AppDomain, load an assembly into it, and construct an instance of a type defined in that assembly. The code shows the different behaviors when constructing a type that is marshaled by reference, a type that is marshaled by value, and a type that can't be marshaled at all. The code also shows how these differently marshaled objects behave when the AppDomain that created them is unloaded. The Ch22-1-AppDomains sample application has very little code in it, but I have added a lot of comments. After the code listing, I'll walk through the code, explaining what the CLR is doing.

```
private static void Marshalling() {
    // Get a reference to the AppDomain that that calling thread is executing in
    AppDomain adCallingThreadDomain = Thread.GetDomain();

    // Every AppDomain is assigned a friendly string name (helpful for debugging)
    // Get this AppDomain's friendly string name and display it
    String callingDomainName = adCallingThreadDomain.FriendlyName;
    Console.WriteLine("Default AppDomain's friendly name={0}", callingDomainName);

    // Get & display the assembly in our AppDomain that contains the 'Main' method
    String exeAssembly = Assembly.GetEntryAssembly().FullName;
    Console.WriteLine("Main assembly={0}", exeAssembly);

    // Define a local variable that can refer to an AppDomain
    AppDomain ad2 = null;

    // *** DEMO 1: Cross-AppDomain Communication using Marshal-by-Reference ***
    Console.WriteLine("{0}Demo #1", Environment.NewLine);

    // Create new AppDomain (security & configuration match current AppDomain)
    ad2 = AppDomain.CreateDomain("AD #2", null, null);
    MarshalByRefType mbrt = null;
```

```
// Load our assembly into the new AppDomain, construct an object, marshal
// it back to our AD (we really get a reference to a proxy)
mbrt = (MarshalByRefType)
   ad2.CreateInstanceAndUnwrap(exeAssembly, "MarshalByRefType");

Console.WriteLine("Type={0}", mbrt.GetType());   // The CLR lies about the type

// Prove that we got a reference to a proxy object
Console.WriteLine("Is proxy={0}", RemotingServices.IsTransparentProxy(mbrt));

// This looks like we're calling a method on MarshalByRefType but, we're not.
// We're calling a method on the proxy type. The proxy transitions the thread
// to the AppDomain owning the object and calls this method on the real object.
mbrt.SomeMethod();

// Unload the new AppDomain
AppDomain.Unload(ad2);
// mbrt refers to a valid proxy object; the proxy object refers to an invalid AppDomain

try {
   // We're calling a method on the proxy type. The AD is invalid, exception is thrown
   mbrt.SomeMethod();
   Console.WriteLine("Successful call.");
}
catch (AppDomainUnloadedException) {
   Console.WriteLine("Failed call.");
}


// *** DEMO 2: Cross-AppDomain Communication using Marshal-by-Value ***
Console.WriteLine("{0}Demo #2", Environment.NewLine);

// Create new AppDomain (security & configuration match current AppDomain)
ad2 = AppDomain.CreateDomain("AD #2", null, null);

// Load our assembly into the new AppDomain, construct an object, marshal
// it back to our AD (we really get a reference to a proxy)
mbrt = (MarshalByRefType)
   ad2.CreateInstanceAndUnwrap(exeAssembly, "MarshalByRefType");

// The object's method returns a COPY of the returned object;
// the object is marshaled by value (not be reference).
MarshalByValType mbvt = mbrt.MethodWithReturn();

// Prove that we did NOT get a reference to a proxy object
Console.WriteLine("Is proxy={0}", RemotingServices.IsTransparentProxy(mbvt));

// This looks like we're calling a method on MarshalByValType and we are.
Console.WriteLine("Returned object created " + mbvt.ToString());

// Unload the new AppDomain
AppDomain.Unload(ad2);
// mbvt refers to valid object; unloading the AppDomain has no impact.

try {
```

```
      // We're calling a method on an object; no exception is thrown
      Console.WriteLine("Returned object created " + mbvt.ToString());
      Console.WriteLine("Successful call.");
   }
   catch (AppDomainUnloadedException) {
      Console.WriteLine("Failed call.");
   }


   // DEMO 3: Cross-AppDomain Communication using non-marshalable type ***
   Console.WriteLine("{0}Demo #3", Environment.NewLine);

   // Create new AppDomain (security & configuration match current AppDomain)
   ad2 = AppDomain.CreateDomain("AD #2", null, null);

   // Load our assembly into the new AppDomain, construct an object, marshal
   // it back to our AD (we really get a reference to a proxy)
   mbrt = (MarshalByRefType)
      ad2.CreateInstanceAndUnwrap(exeAssembly, "MarshalByRefType");

   // The object's method returns an non-marshalable object; exception
   NonMarshalableType nmt = mbrt.MethodArgAndReturn(callingDomainName);
   // We won't get here...
}


// Instances can be marshaled-by-reference across AppDomain boundaries
public sealed class MarshalByRefType : MarshalByRefObject {
   public MarshalByRefType() {
      Console.WriteLine("{0} ctor running in {1}",
         this.GetType().ToString(), Thread.GetDomain().FriendlyName);
   }

   public void SomeMethod() {
      Console.WriteLine("Executing in " + Thread.GetDomain().FriendlyName);
   }

   public MarshalByValType MethodWithReturn() {
      Console.WriteLine("Executing in " + Thread.GetDomain().FriendlyName);
      MarshalByValType t = new MarshalByValType();
      return t;
   }

   public NonMarshalableType MethodArgAndReturn(String callingDomainName) {
      // NOTE: callingDomainName is [Serializable]
      Console.WriteLine("Calling from '{0}' to '{1}'.",
         callingDomainName, Thread.GetDomain().FriendlyName);
      NonMarshalableType t = new NonMarshalableType();
      return t;
   }
}


// Instances can be marshaled-by-value across AppDomain boundaries
[Serializable]
```

```
public sealed class MarshalByValType : Object {
    private DateTime m_creationTime = DateTime.Now; // NOTE: DateTime is [Serializable]

    public MarshalByValType() {
        Console.WriteLine("{0} ctor running in {1}, Created on {2:D}",
            this.GetType().ToString(),
            Thread.GetDomain().FriendlyName,
            m_creationTime);
    }

    public override String ToString() {
        return m_creationTime.ToLongDateString();
    }
}


// Instances cannot be marshaled across AppDomain boundaries
// [Serializable]
public sealed class NonMarshalableType : Object {
    public NonMarshalableType() {
        Console.WriteLine("Executing in " + Thread.GetDomain().FriendlyName);
    }
}
```

If you build and run the Ch22-1-AppDomains application, you get the following output:

```
Default AppDomain's friendly name= Ch22-1-AppDomains.exe
Main assembly=Ch22-1-AppDomains, Version=0.0.0.0, Culture=neutral, PublicKeyToken=null

Demo #1
MarshalByRefType ctor running in AD #2
Type=MarshalByRefType
Is proxy=True
Executing in AD #2
Failed call.

Demo #2
MarshalByRefType ctor running in AD #2
Executing in AD #2
MarshalByValType ctor running in AD #2, Created on Friday, August 07, 2009
Is proxy=False
Returned object created Friday, August 07, 2009
Returned object created Friday, August 07, 2009
Successful call.

Demo #3
MarshalByRefType ctor running in AD #2
Calling from 'Ch22-1-AppDomains.exe' to 'AD #2'.
Executing in AD #2

Unhandled Exception: System.Runtime.Serialization.SerializationException:
Type 'NonMarshalableType' in assembly 'Ch22-1-AppDomains, Version=0.0.0.0,
Culture=neutral, PublicKeyToken=null' is not marked as serializable.
at MarshalByRefType.MethodArgAndReturn(String callingDomainName)
at Program.Marshalling()
at Program.Main()
is not marked as serializable.
```

```
at MarshalByRefType.MethodArgAndReturn(String callingDomainName)
  at Program.Marshalling()
  at Program.Main()
```

Now, I will discuss what this code and the CLR are doing.

Inside the **Marshalling** method, I first get a reference to an **AppDomain** object that identifies the AppDomain the calling thread is currently executing in. In Windows, a thread is always created in the context of one process, and the thread lives its entire lifetime in that process. However, a one-to-one correspondence doesn't exist between threads and AppDomains. AppDomains are a CLR feature; Windows knows nothing about AppDomains. Since multiple AppDomains can be in a single Windows process, a thread can execute code in one AppDomain and then execute code in another AppDomain. From the CLR's perspective, a thread is executing code in one AppDomain at a time. A thread can ask the CLR what AppDomain it is currently executing in by calling **System.Threading.Thread**'s static **GetDomain** method. The thread could also query **System.AppDomain**'s static, read-only **CurrentDomain** property to get the same information.

When an AppDomain is created, it can be assigned a *friendly name*. A friendly name is just a **String** that you can use to identify an AppDomain. This is typically useful in debugging scenarios. Since the CLR creates the default AppDomain before any of our code can run, the CLR uses the executable file's file name as the default AppDomain's friendly name. My **Marshalling** method queries the default AppDomain's friendly name by using **System.AppDomain**'s read-only **FriendlyName** property.

Next, my **Marshalling** method queries the strong-name identity of the assembly (loaded into the default AppDomain) that defines the entry point method **Main** that calls **Marshalling**. This assembly defines several types: **Program**, **MarshalByRefType**, **MarshalByValType**, and **NonMarshalableType**. At this point, we're ready to look at the three demos that are all pretty similar to each other.

Demo #1: Cross-AppDomain Communication that Uses Marshal-by-Reference

In Demo #1, **System.AppDomain**'s static **CreateDomain** method is called, instructing the CLR to create a new AppDomain in the same Windows process. The **AppDomain** type actually offers several overloads of the **CreateDomain** method; I encourage you to study them and select the version that is most appropriate when you are writing code to create a new AppDomain. The version of **CreateDomain** that I call accepts three arguments:

- A **String** identifying the friendly name I want assigned to the new AppDomain   I'm passing in "AD #2" here.

- A **System.Security.Policy.Evidence** identifying the evidence that the CLR should use to calculate the AppDomain's permission set   I'm passing **null** here so that the new AppDomain will inherit the same permission set as the AppDomain creating it.

Usually, if you want to create a security boundary around code in an AppDomain, you'd construct a **System.Security.PermissionSet** object, add the desired permission objects to it (instances of types that implement the **IPermission** interface), and then pass the resulting **PermissionSet** object reference to the overloaded version of the **CreateDomain** method that accepts a **PermissionSet**.

- A **System.AppDomainSetup** identifying the configuration settings the CLR should use for the new AppDomain   Again, I'm passing **null** here so that the new AppDomain will inherit the same configuration settings as the AppDomain creating it. If you want the AppDomain to have a special configuration, construct an **AppDomainSetup** object, set its various properties to whatever you desire such as the name of the configuration file for example, and then pass the resulting **AppDomainSetup** object reference to the **CreateDomain** method.

Internally, the **CreateDomain** method creates a new AppDomain in the process. This AppDomain will be assigned the specified friendly name, security, and configuration settings. The new AppDomain will have its very own loader heap, which will be empty because there are currently no assemblies loading into the new AppDomain. When you create an AppDomain, the CLR does not create any threads in this AppDomain; no code runs in the AppDomain unless you explicitly have a thread call code in the AppDomain.

Now to create an instance of an object in the new AppDomain, we must first load an assembly into the new AppDomain and then construct an instance of a type defined in this assembly. This is precisely what the call to **AppDomain**'s public, instance **CreateInstanceAndUnwrap** method does. When calling **CreateInstanceAndUnwrap**, I pass two arguments: a **String** identifying the assembly I want loaded into the new AppDomain (referenced by the **ad2** variable) and another **String** identifying the name of the type that I want to construct an instance of. Internally, **CreateInstanceAndUnwrap** causes the calling thread to transition from the current AppDomain into the new AppDomain. Now, the thread (which is inside the call to **CreateInstanceAndUnwrap**) loads the specified assembly into the new AppDomain and then scans the assembly's type definition metadata table, looking for the specified type ("MarshalByRefType"). After the type is found, the thread calls the **MarshalByRefType**'s parameterless constructor. Now the thread transitions back to the default AppDomain so that **CreateInstanceAndUnwrap** can return a reference to the new**MarshalByRefType** object.

> **Note** There are overloaded versions of **CreateInstanceAndUnwrap** that allow you to call a type's constructor passing in arguments.

While this sounds all fine and good, there is a problem: the CLR cannot allow a variable (root) living in one AppDomain to reference an object created in another AppDomain. If **CreateInstanceAndUnwrap** simply returned the reference to the object, isolation would be broken, and isolation is the whole purpose of AppDomains! So just before **CreateInstanceAndUnwrap** returns the object reference, it performs some additional logic.

You'll notice that the **MarshalByRefType** type is derived from a very special base class: **System.MarshalByRefObject**. When **CreateInstanceAndUnwrap** sees that it is marshalling an object whose type is derived from **MarshalByRefObject**, the CLR will marshal the object by reference across the AppDomain boundaries. Here is what it means to marshal an object by reference from one AppDomain (the source AppDomain where the object is really created) to another AppDomain (the destination AppDomain from where **CreateInstanceAndUnwrap** is called).

When a source AppDomain wants to send or return the reference of an object to a destination AppDomain, the CLR defines a proxy type in the destination AppDomain's loader heap. This proxy type is defined using the original type's metadata, and therefore, it looks exactly like the original type; it has all of the same instance members (properties, events, and methods). The instance fields are not part of the type, but I'll talk more about this in a moment. This new type does have some instance fields defined inside of it, but these fields are not identical to that of the original data type. Instead, these fields indicate which AppDomain "owns" the real object and how to find the real object in the owning AppDomain. (Internally, the proxy object uses a **GCHandle** instance that refers to the real object. The **GCHandle** type is discussed in Chapter 21, "Automatic Memory Management (Garbage Collection)."

Once this type is defined in the destination AppDomain, **CreateInstanceAndUnwrap** creates an instance of this proxy type, initializes its fields to identify the source AppDomain and the real object, and returns a reference to this proxy object to the destination AppDomain. In my Ch22-1-AppDomains application, the **mbrt** variable will be set to refer to this proxy. Notice that the object returned from **CreateInstanceAndUnwrap** is actually not an instance of the **MarshalByRefType** type. The CLR will usually not allow you to cast an object of one type to an incompatible type. However, in this situation, the CLR does allow the cast because this new type has the same instance members as defined on the original type. In fact, if you use the proxy object to call **GetType**, it actually lies to you and says that it is a **MarshalByRefType** object.

However, it is possible to prove that the object returned from **CreateInstanceAndUnwrap** is actually a reference to a proxy object. To do this, my Ch22-1-AppDomains application calls **System.Runtime.Remoting.RemotingService**'s public, static **IsTransparentProxy** method passing in the reference returned from **CreateInstanceAndUnwrap**. As you can see from the output, **IsTransparentProxy** returns **true**, indicating that the object is a proxy.

Now, my Ch22-1-AppDomains application uses the proxy to call the **SomeMethod** method. Since the **mbrt** variable refers to a proxy object, the proxy's implementation of this method is called. The proxy's implementation uses the information fields inside the proxy object to transition the calling thread from the default AppDomain to the new AppDomain. Any actions now performed by this thread run under the new AppDomain's security and configuration settings. Then, the thread uses the proxy object's **GCHandle** field to find the real object in the new AppDomain, and then it uses the real object to call the real **SomeMethod** method.

There are two ways to prove that the calling thread has transitioned from the default AppDomain to the new AppDomain. First, inside the **SomeMethod** method, I call **Thread.GetDomain().FriendlyName**. This will return "AD #2" (as evidenced by the output) since the thread is now running in the new AppDomain created by using **AppDomain.CreateDomain** with "AD #2" as the friendly name parameter. Second, if you step through the code in a debugger and display the Call Stack window, the [AppDomain Transition] line marks where a thread has transitioned across an AppDomain boundary. See the Call Stack window near the bottom of Figure 22-2.

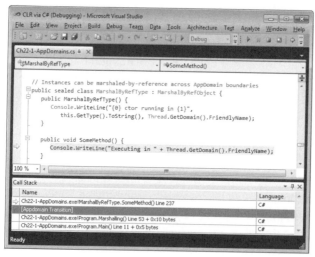

FIGURE 22-2 The Debugger's Call Stack window showing an AppDomain transition

When the real **SomeMethod** method returns, it returns to the proxy's **SomeMethod** method, which transitions the thread back to the default AppDomain, and then the thread continues executing code in the default AppDomain.

Note When a thread in one AppDomain calls a method in another AppDomain, the thread transitions between the two AppDomains. This means that method calls across AppDomain boundaries are executed synchronously. However, at any given time, a thread is considered to be in just one AppDomain, and it executes code using that AppDomain's security and configuration settings. If you want to execute code in multiple AppDomains concurrently, you should create additional threads and have them execute whatever code you desire in whatever AppDomains you desire.

The next thing that my Ch22-1-AppDomains application does is call **AppDomain**'s public, static **Unload** method to force the CLR to unload the specified AppDomain including all of the assemblies loaded into it, and a garbage collection is forced to free up any objects that were created by code in the unloading AppDomain. At this point, the default AppDomain's **mbrt** variable still refers to a valid proxy object; however, the proxy object no longer refers to a valid AppDomain (because it has been unloaded).

When the default AppDomain attempts to use the proxy object to call the **SomeMethod** method, the proxy's implementation of this method is called. The proxy's implementation determines that the AppDomain that contained the real object has been unloaded, and the proxy's **SomeMethod** method throws an **AppDomainUnloadedException** to let the caller know that the operation cannot complete.

Wow! The CLR team at Microsoft had to do a lot of work to ensure AppDomain isolation, but it is important work because these features are used heavily and are being used more and more by developers every day. Obviously, accessing objects across AppDomain boundaries by using marshal-by-reference semantics has some performance costs associated with it, so you typically want to keep the use of this feature to a minimum.

I promised you that I'd talk a little more about instance fields. A type derived from **MarshalByRefObject** can define instance fields. However, these instance fields are not defined as being part of the proxy type and are not contained inside a proxy object. When you write code that reads from or writes to an instance field of a type derived from **MarshalByRefObject**, the JIT compiler emits code that uses the proxy object (to find the real AppDomain/object) by calling **System.Object**'s **FieldGetter** or **FieldSetter** methods, respectively. These methods are private and undocumented; they are basically methods that use reflection to get and set the value in a field. So although you can access fields of a type derived from **MarshalByRefObject**, the performance is particularly bad because the CLR really ends up calling methods to perform the field access. In fact, the performance is bad even if the object that you are accessing is in your own AppDomain.[3]

The Performance of Accessing Instance Fields

To demonstrate the significance of this performance hit, I wrote the following code:

```
private sealed class NonMBRO : Object            { public Int32 x; }
private sealed class MBRO    : MarshalByRefObject { public Int32 x; }

private static void FieldAccessTiming(){
   const Int32 count = 10000000;
   NonMBRO nonMbro = new NonMBRO();
   MBRO mbro = new MBRO();

   Int64 time = Stopwatch.GetTimestamp();
   for (Int32 c = 0; c < count; c++) nonMbro.x++;
   Console.WriteLine("{0:N0}", Stopwatch.GetTimestamp() - time);  //  134,174

   time = Stopwatch.GetTimestamp();
   for (Int32 c = 0; c < count; c++) mbro.x++;
   Console.WriteLine("{0:N0}", Stopwatch.GetTimestamp() - time);  //  1,533,886
}
```

---

[3] If the CLR required that all fields be private (which is recommended for good data encapsulation), then the **FieldGetter** and **FieldSetter** methods wouldn't have to exist and accessing fields from methods could always have been direct, avoiding any performance penalty.

When I ran this code, it took 134,174 milliseconds to access the instance field of a **NonMBRO** class that is derived from **Object**, and it took 1,533,886 milliseconds to access the instance field of an **MBRO** class that is derived from **MarshalByRefObject**. So, accessing an instance field of a class derived from **MarshalByRefObject** takes more than 12 times longer!

From a usability standpoint, a type derived from **MarshalByRefObject** should really avoid defining any static members. The reason is that static members are always accessed in the context of the calling AppDomain. No AppDomain transition can occur because a proxy object contains the information identifying which AppDomain to transition to, but there is no proxy object when calling a static member. Having a type's static members execute in one AppDomain while instance members execute in another AppDomain would make a very awkward programming model.

Since there are no roots in the second AppDomain, the original object referred to by the proxy could be garbage collected. Of course, this is not ideal. On the other hand, if the original object is held in memory indefinitely, then the proxy could go away and the original object would still live; this is also not ideal. The CLR solves this problem by using a *lease manager*. When a proxy for an object is created, the CLR keeps the object alive for 5 minutes. If no calls have been made through the proxy after 5 minutes, then the object is *deactivated* and will have its memory freed at the next garbage collection. After each call into the object, the lease manager renews the object's lease so that it is guaranteed to remain in memory for another 2 minutes before being deactivated. If an application attempts to call into an object through a proxy after the object's lease has expired, the CLR throws a **System.Runtime. Remoting.RemotingException**.

It is possible to override the default lease times of 5 minutes and 2 minutes by overriding **MarshalByRefObject**'s virtual **InitializeLifetimeServices** method. For more information, see the section titled "Lifetime Leases" in the .NET Framework SDK documentation.

Demo #2: Cross-AppDomain Communication Using Marshal-by-Value

Demo #2 is very similar to Demo #1. Again, another AppDomain is created exactly as Demo #1 did it. Then, **CreateInstanceAndUnwrap** is called to load the same assembly into the new AppDomain and create an instance of a **MarshalByRefType** object in this new AppDomain. Next, the CLR creates a proxy to the object, and the **mbrt** variable (in the default AppDomain) is initialized referring to the proxy. Now, using the proxy, I call **MethodWithReturn**. This method, which takes no arguments, will execute in the new AppDomain to create an instance of the **MarshalByValType** type before returning a reference to the object to the default AppDomain.

MarshalByValType is not derived from **System.MarshalByRefObject**, and therefore, the CLR cannot define a proxy type to create an instance from; the object can't be marshaled by reference across the AppDomain boundary.

However, since **MarshalByValType** is marked with the **[Serializable]** custom attribute, **MethodWithReturn** is allowed to marshal the object by value. The next paragraph describes what it means to marshal an object by value from one AppDomain (the source AppDomain) to another AppDomain (the destination AppDomain). For more information about the CLR"s serialization and deserialization mechanisms, see Chapter 24, "Runtime Serialization."

When a source AppDomain wants to send or return a reference to an object to a destination AppDomain, the CLR serializes the object's instance fields into a byte array. This byte array is copied from the source AppDomain to the destination AppDomain. Then, the CLR deserializes the byte array in the destination AppDomain. This forces the CLR to load the assembly that defines the type being deserialized into the destination AppDomain if it is not already loaded. Then, the CLR creates an instance of the type and uses the values in the byte array to initialize the object's fields so that they have values identical to those they had in the original object. In other words, the CLR makes an exact duplicate of the source object in the destination's AppDomain. **MethodWithReturn** then returns a reference to this copy; the object has been marshaled by value across the AppDomain's boundary.

> **Important** When loading the assembly, the CLR uses the destination AppDomain's policies and configuration settings (for example, the AppDomain can have a different AppBase directory or different version binding redirections). These policy differences might prevent the CLR from locating the assembly. If the assembly cannot be loaded, an exception will be thrown, and the destination will not receive a reference to the object.

At this point, the object in the source AppDomain and the object in the destination AppDomain live separate lifetimes, and their states can change independently of each other. If there are no roots in the source AppDomain keeping the original object alive (as in my Ch22-1-AppDomains application), its memory will be reclaimed at the next garbage collection.

To prove that the object returned from **MethodWithReturn** is not a reference to a proxy object, my Ch22-1-AppDomains application calls **System.Runtime.Remoting.RemotingService**'s public, static **IsTransparentProxy** method passing in the reference returned from **MethodWithReturn**. As you can see from the output, **IsTransparentProxy** returns **false**, indicating that the object is a real object, not a proxy.

Now, my program uses the real object to call the **ToString** method. Since the **mbvt** variable refers to a real object, the real implementation of this method is called, and no AppDomain transition occurs. This can be evidenced by examining the debugger's Call Stack window, which will not show an [Appdomain Transition] line.

To further prove that no proxy is involved, my Ch22-1-AppDomains application unloads the new AppDomain and then attempts to call the **ToString** method again. Unlike in Demo #1, the call succeeds this time because unloading the new AppDomain had no impact on objects "owned" by the default AppDomain, and this includes the object that was marshaled by value.

Demo #3: Cross-AppDomain Communication Using Non-Marshalable Types

Demo #3 starts out very similar to Demos #1 and #2. Just as in Demos #1 and #2, an AppDomain is created. Then, **CreateInstanceAndUnwrap** is called to load the same assembly into the new AppDomain, create a **MarshalByValType** object in this new AppDomain, and have the **mbrt** variable refer to a proxy to this object.

Then, using this proxy, I call **MethodArgAndReturn**, which accepts an argument. Again, the CLR must maintain AppDomain isolation, so it cannot simply pass the reference to the argument into the new AppDomain. If the type of the object is derived from **MarshalByRefObject**, the CLR will make a proxy for it and marshal it by reference. If the object's type is marked as **[Serializable]**, the CLR will serialize the object (and its children) to a byte array, marshal the byte array into the new AppDomain, and then deserialize the byte array into an object graph, passing the root of the object graph into the **MethodArgAndReturn** method.

In this particular demo, I am passing a **System.String** object across AppDomain boundaries. The **System.String** type is not derived from **MarshalByRefObject**, so the CLR cannot create a proxy. Fortunately, **System.String** is marked as **[Serializable]**, and therefore the CLR can marshal it by value, which allows the code to work. Note that for **String** objects, the CLR performs a special optimization. When marshaling a **String** object across an AppDomain boundary, the CLR just passes the reference to the **String** object across the boundary; it does not make a copy of the **String** object. The CLR can offer this optimization because **String** objects are immutable; therefore, it is impossible for code in one AppDomain to corrupt a **String** object's characters. For more about **String** immutability, see Chapter 14, "Chars, Strings, and Working with Text."[4]

Inside **MethodArgAndReturn**, I display the string passed into it to show that the string came across the AppDomain boundary, and then I create an instance of the **NonMarshalableType** type and return a reference to this object to the default AppDomain. Since **NonMarshalableType** is not derived from **System.MarshalByRefObject** and is also not marked with the **[Serializable]** custom attribute, **MethodArgAndReturn** is not allowed to marshal the object by reference or by value—the object cannot be marshaled

---

[4] By the way, this is why the **System.String** class is sealed. If the class were not sealed, then you could define your own class derived from **String** and add your own fields. If you did this, there is no way that the CLR could ensure that your "string" class was immutable.

across an AppDomain boundary at all! To report this, **MethodArgAndReturn** throws a **SerializationException** in the default AppDomain. Since my program doesn't catch this exception, the program just dies.

AppDomain Unloading

One of the great features of AppDomains is that you can unload them. Unloading an AppDomain causes the CLR to unload all of the assemblies in the AppDomain, and the CLR frees the AppDomain's loader heap as well. To unload an AppDomain, you call **AppDomain**'s **Unload** static method (as the Ch22-1-AppDomains application does). This call causes the CLR to perform a lot of actions to gracefully unload the specified AppDomain:

1. The CLR suspends all threads in the process that have ever executed managed code.

2. The CLR examines all of the threads' stacks to see which threads are currently executing code in the AppDomain being unloaded or which threads might return at some point to code in the AppDomain that is being unloaded. The CLR forces any threads that have the unloading AppDomain on their stack to throw a **ThreadAbortException** (resuming the thread's execution). This causes the threads to unwind, executing any **finally** blocks on their way out so that cleanup code executes. If no code catches the **ThreadAbortException**, it will eventually become an unhandled exception that the CLR swallows; the thread dies, but the process is allowed to continue running. This is unusual because for all other unhandled exceptions, the CLR kills the process.

> **Important** The CLR will not immediately abort a thread that is currently executing code in a **finally** block, **catch** block, a class constructor, a critical execution region, or in unmanaged code. If the CLR allowed this, cleanup code, error recovery code, type initialization code, critical code, or arbitrary code that the CLR knows nothing about would not complete, resulting in the application behaving unpredictably and with potential security holes. An aborting thread is allowed to finish executing these code blocks and then, at the end of the code block, the CLR forces the thread to throw a **ThreadAbortException.**

3. After all threads discovered in step #2 have left the AppDomain, the CLR then walks the heap and sets a flag in each proxy object that referred to an object created by the unloaded AppDomain. These proxy objects now know that the real object they referred to is gone. If any code now calls a method on an invalid proxy object, the method will throw an **AppDomainUnloadedException**.

4. The CLR forces a garbage collection to occur, reclaiming the memory used by any objects that were created by the now unloaded AppDomain. The **Finalize** methods for these objects are called, giving the objects a chance to clean themselves up properly.

5. The CLR resumes all of the remaining threads. The thread that called **AppDomain.Unload** will now continue running; calls to **AppDomain.Unload** occur synchronously.

My Ch22-1-AppDomains application uses just one thread to do all of the work. Whenever my code calls **AppDomain.Unload**, there are no threads in the unloading AppDomain, and therefore, the CLR doesn't have to throw any **ThreadAbortException** exceptions. I'll talk more about **ThreadAbortException** later in this chapter.

By the way, when a thread calls **AppDomain.Unload**, the CLR waits 10 seconds for the threads in the unloading AppDomain to leave it. If after 10 seconds, the thread that called **AppDomain.Unload** doesn't return, it will throw a **CannotUnloadAppDomainException**, and the AppDomain may or may not be unloaded in the future.

> **Note** If a thread calling **AppDomain.Unload** is in the AppDomain being unloaded, the CLR creates another thread that attempts to unload the AppDomain. The first thread will forcibly throw the **ThreadAbortException** and unwind. The new thread will wait for the AppDomain to unload, and then the new thread terminates. If the AppDomain fails to unload, the new thread will process a **CannotUnloadAppDomainException**, but since you did not write the code that this new thread executes, you can't catch this exception.

AppDomain Monitoring

A host application can monitor the resources that an AppDomain consumes. Some hosts will use this information to decide when to forcibly unload an AppDomain should its memory or CPU consumption rise above what the host considers reasonable. Monitoring can also be used to compare the resource consumption of different algorithms to determine which uses fewer resources. Because AppDomain monitoring incurs additional overhead, hosts must explicitly turn the monitoring on by setting **AppDomain**'s static **MonitoringEnabled** property to **true**. This turns on monitoring for all AppDomains. Once monitoring is turned on, it cannot be turned off; attempting to set the **MonitoringEnabled** property to **false** causes an **ArgumentException** to be thrown.

Once monitoring is turned on, your code can query the following four read-only properties offered by the AppDomain class:

- **MonitoringSurvivedProcessMemorySize**   This static **Int64** property returns the number of bytes that are currently in use by all AppDomains controlled by the current CLR instance. The number is accurate as of the last garbage collection.

- **MonitoringTotalAllocatedMemorySize**   This instance **Int64** property returns the number of bytes that have been allocated by a specific AppDomain. The number is accurate as of the last garbage collection.

- **MonitoringSurvivedMemorySize**   This instance **Int64** property returns the number of bytes that are currently in use by a specific AppDomain. The number is accurate as of the last garbage collection.

- **MonitoringTotalProcessorTime**   This instance **TimeSpan** property returns the amount of CPU usage incurred by a specific AppDomain.

The following class shows how to use three of these properties to see what has changed within an AppDomain between two points in time:

```
private sealed class AppDomainMonitorDelta : IDisposable {
   private AppDomain m_appDomain;
   private TimeSpan m_thisADCpu;
   private Int64 m_thisADMemoryInUse;
   private Int64 m_thisADMemoryAllocated;

   static AppDomainMonitorDelta() {
      // Make sure that AppDomain monitoring is turned on
      AppDomain.MonitoringIsEnabled = true;
   }

   public AppDomainMonitorDelta(AppDomain ad) {
      m_appDomain = ad ?? AppDomain.CurrentDomain;
      m_thisADCpu = m_appDomain.MonitoringTotalProcessorTime;
      m_thisADMemoryInUse = m_appDomain.MonitoringSurvivedMemorySize;
      m_thisADMemoryAllocated = m_appDomain.MonitoringTotalAllocatedMemorySize;
   }

   public void Dispose() {
      GC.Collect();
      Console.WriteLine("FriendlyName={0}, CPU={1}ms", m_appDomain.FriendlyName,
         (m_appDomain.MonitoringTotalProcessorTime - m_thisADCpu).TotalMilliseconds);
      Console.WriteLine("   Allocated {0:N0} bytes of which {1:N0} survived GCs",
         m_appDomain.MonitoringTotalAllocatedMemorySize - m_thisADMemoryAllocated,
         m_appDomain.MonitoringSurvivedMemorySize - m_thisADMemoryInUse);
   }
}
```

The following code shows how to use the AppDomainMonitorDelta class:

```
private static void AppDomainResourceMonitoring() {
   using (new AppDomainMonitorDelta(null)) {
      // Allocate about 10 million bytes that will survive collections
      var list = new List<Object>();
      for (Int32 x = 0; x < 1000; x++) list.Add(new Byte[10000]);

      // Allocate about 20 million bytes that will NOT survive collections
      for (Int32 x = 0; x < 2000; x++) new Byte[10000].GetType();

      // Spin the CPU for about 5 seconds
      Int64 stop = Environment.TickCount + 5000;
      while (Environment.TickCount < stop) ;
   }
}
```

When I execute this code, I get the following output:

```
FriendlyName=03-Ch22-1-AppDomains.exe, CPU=5031.25ms
   Allocated 30,159,496 bytes of which 10,085,080 survived GCs
```

AppDomain First-Chance Exception Notifications

Each AppDomain can have associated with it a series of callback methods that get invoked when the CLR begins looking for **catch** blocks within an AppDomain. These methods can perform logging, or a host can use this mechanism to monitor exceptions being thrown within an AppDomain. The callbacks cannot handle the exception or swallow it in any way; they are just receiving a notification that the exception has occurred. To register a callback method, just add a delegate to AppDomain's instance **FirstChanceException** event.

Here is how the CLR processes an exception: When the exception is first thrown, the CLR invokes any **FirstChanceException** callback methods registered with the AppDomain that is throwing the exception. Then, the CLR looks for any **catch** blocks on the stack that are within the same AppDomain. If a **catch** block handles the exception, then processing of the exception is complete and execution continues as normal. If the AppDomain has no **catch** block to handle the exception, then the CLR walks up the stack to the calling AppDomain and throws the same exception object again (after serializing and deserializing it). At this point, it is as if a brand new exception is being thrown, and the CLR invokes any **FirstChanceException** callback methods registered with the now current AppDomain. This continues until the top of the thread's stack is reached. At that point, if the exception is not handled by any code, the CLR terminates the whole process.

How Hosts Use AppDomains

So far, I've talked about hosts and how they load the CLR. I've also talked about how the hosts tell the CLR to create and unload AppDomains. To make the discussion more concrete, I'll describe some common hosting and AppDomain scenarios. In particular, I'll explain how different application types host the CLR and how they manage AppDomains.

Executable Applications

Console UI applications, NT Service applications, Windows Forms applications, and Windows Presentation Foundation (WPF) applications are all examples of self-hosted applications that have managed EXE files. When Windows initializes a process using a managed EXE file, Windows loads the shim and the shim examines the CLR header information contained in the application's assembly (the EXE file). The header information indicates the version of the CLR that was used to build and test the application. The shim uses this information to determine which version of the CLR to load into the process. After the CLR loads and initializes, it again examines the assembly's CLR header to determine which method is the application's entry point (**Main**). The CLR invokes this method, and the application is now up and running.

As the code runs, it accesses other types. When referencing a type contained in another assembly, the CLR locates the necessary assembly and loads it into the same AppDomain. Any additionally referenced assemblies also load into the same AppDomain. When the application's **Main** method returns, the Windows process terminates (destroying the default AppDomain and all other AppDomains).

> **Note** By the way, you can call **System.Environment**'s static **Exit** method if you want to shut down the Windows process including all of its AppDomains. **Exit** is the most graceful way of terminating a process because it first calls the **Finalize** methods of all of the objects on the managed heap and then releases all of the unmanaged COM objects held by the CLR. Finally, **Exit** calls the Win32 **ExitProcess** function.

It's possible for the application to tell the CLR to create additional AppDomains in the process's address space. In fact, this is what my Ch22-1-AppDomains application did.

Microsoft Silverlight Rich Internet Applications

Microsoft's Silverlight runtime technology uses a special CLR that is different from the normal desktop version of the .NET Framework. Once the Silverlight runtime is installed, navigating to a Web site that uses Silverlight causes the Silverlight CLR (CoreClr.dll) to load in your browser (which may or may not be Windows Internet Explorer—you may not even be using a Windows machine). Each Silverlight control on the page runs in its own AppDomain. When the user closes a tab or navigates to another Web site, any Silverlight controls no longer in use have their AppDomains unloaded. The Silverlight code running in the AppDomain runs in a limited-security sandbox so that it cannot harm the user or the machine in any way.

Microsoft ASP.NET Web Forms and XML Web Services Applications

ASP.NET is implemented as an ISAPI DLL (implemented in ASPNet_ISAPI.dll). The first time a client requests a URL handled by the ASP.NET ISAPI DLL, ASP.NET loads the CLR. When a client makes a request of a Web application, ASP.NET determines if this is the first time a request has been made. If it is, ASP.NET tells the CLR to create a new AppDomain for this Web application; each Web application is identified by its virtual root directory. ASP.NET then tells the CLR to load the assembly that contains the type exposed by the Web application into this new AppDomain, creates an instance of this type, and starts calling methods in it to satisfy the client's Web request. If the code references more types, the CLR will load the required assemblies into the Web application's AppDomain.

When future clients make requests of an already running Web application, ASP.NET doesn't create a new AppDomain; instead, it uses the existing AppDomain, creates a new instance of the Web application's type, and starts calling methods. The methods will already be JIT-compiled into native code, so the performance of processing all subsequent client requests is excellent.

If a client makes a request of a different Web application, ASP.NET tells the CLR to create a new AppDomain. This new AppDomain is typically created inside the same worker process as the other AppDomains. This means that many Web applications run in a single Windows process, which improves the efficiency of the system overall. Again, the assemblies required by each Web application are loaded into an AppDomain created for the sole purpose of isolating that Web application's code and objects from other Web applications.

A fantastic feature of ASP.NET is that the code for a Web site can be changed on the fly without shutting down the Web server. When a Web site's file is changed on the hard disk, ASP.NET detects this, unloads the AppDomain that contains the old version of the files (when the last currently running request finishes), and then creates a new AppDomain, loading into it the new versions of the files. To make this happen, ASP.NET uses an AppDomain feature called *shadow copying*.

Microsoft SQL Server

Microsoft SQL Server is an unmanaged application because most of its code is still written in unmanaged C++. SQL Server allows developers to create stored procedures by using managed code. The first time a request comes in to the database to run a stored procedure written in managed code, SQL Server loads the CLR. Stored procedures run in their own secured AppDomain, prohibiting the stored procedures from adversely affecting the database server.

This functionality is absolutely incredible! It means that developers will be able to write stored procedures in the programming language of their choice. The stored procedure can use strongly typed data objects in its code. The code will also be JIT-compiled into native code when executed instead of being interpreted. And developers can take advantage of any types defined in the Framework Class Library (FCL) or in any other assembly. The result is that our job becomes much easier and our applications perform much better. What more could a developer ask for?!

Your Own Imagination

Productivity applications such as word processors and spreadsheets also allow users to write macros in any programming language they choose. These macros will have access to all of the assemblies and types that work with the CLR. They will be compiled, so they will execute fast, and, most important, these macros will run in a secure AppDomain so that users don't get hit with any unwanted surprises. Your own applications can use this ability, too, in any way you want.

Advanced Host Control

In this section, I'll mention some more advanced topics related to hosting the CLR. My intent is to give you a taste of what is possible, and this will help you to understand more of what the CLR is capable of. I encourage you to seek out other texts if you find this information particularly interesting.

Managing the CLR by Using Managed Code

The **System.AppDomainManager** class allows a host to override CLR default behavior by using managed code instead of using unmanaged code. Of course, using managed code makes implementing a host easier. All you need to do is define your class and derive it from the **System.AppDomainManager** class, overriding any virtual methods where you want to take over control. Your class should then be built into its very own assembly and installed into the global assembly cache (GAC) because the assembly needs to be granted full-trust, and all assemblies in the GAC are always granted full-trust.

Then, you need to tell the CLR to use your **AppDomainManager**-derived class. In code, the best way to do this is to create an **AppDomainSetup** object initializing its **AppDomainManagerAssembly** and **AppDomainManagerType** properties, both of which are of type **String**. Set the **AppDomainManagerAssembly** property to the string identifying the strong-name identity of the assembly that defines your **AppDomainManager**-derived class, and then set the **AppDomainManagerType** property to the full name of your **AppDomainManager**-derived class. Alternatively, **AppDomainManager** can be set in your application's XML configuration file by using the **appDomainManagerAssembly** and **appDomainManagerType** elements. In addition, a native host could query for the **ICLRControl** interface and call this interface's **SetAppDomainManagerType** function, passing in the identity of the GAC-installed assembly and the name of the **AppDomainManager**-derived class.[5]

Now, let's talk about what an **AppDomainManager**-derived class can do. The purpose of the **AppDomainManager**-derived class is to allow a host to maintain control even when an add-in tries to create AppDomains of its own. When code in the process tries to create a new AppDomain, the **AppDomainManager**-derived object in that AppDomain can modify security and configuration settings. It can also decide to fail an AppDomain creation, or it can decide to return a reference to an existing AppDomain instead. When a new AppDomain is created, the CLR creates a new **AppDomainManager**-derived object in the AppDomain. This object can also modify configuration settings, how execution context is flowed between threads, and permissions granted to an assembly.

---

[5]   It is also possible to configure an **AppDomainManager** by using environment variables and registry settings, but these mechanisms are more cumbersome than the methods mentioned in the text and should be avoided except for some testing scenarios.

Writing a Robust Host Application

A host can tell the CLR what actions to take when a failure occurs in managed code. Here are some examples (listed from least severe to most severe):

- The CLR can abort a thread if the thread is taking too long to execute and return a response. (I'll discuss this more in the next section.)

- The CLR can unload an AppDomain. This aborts all of the threads that are in the AppDomain and causes the problematic code to be unloaded.

- The CLR can be disabled. This stops any more managed code from executing in the process, but unmanaged code is still allowed to run.

- The CLR can exit the Windows process. This aborts all of the threads and unloads all of the AppDomains first so that cleanup operations occur, and then the process terminates.

The CLR can abort a thread or AppDomain gracefully or rudely. A graceful abort means that cleanup code executes. In other words, code in **finally** blocks runs, and objects have their **Finalize** methods executed. A rude abort means that cleanup code does not execute. In other words, code in **finally** blocks may not run, and objects may not have their **Finalize** methods executed. A graceful abort cannot abort a thread that is in a **catch** or **finally** block. However, a rude abort will abort a thread that is in a **catch** or **finally** block. Unfortunately, a thread that is in unmanaged code or in a constrained execution region (CER) cannot be aborted at all.

A host can set what is called an *escalation policy*, which tells the CLR how to deal with managed code failures. For example, SQL Server tells the CLR what to do should an unhandled exception be thrown while the CLR is executing managed code. When a thread experiences an unhandled exception, the CLR first attempts to upgrade the exception to a graceful thread abort. If the thread does not abort in a specified time period, the CLR attempts to upgrade the graceful thread abort to a rude thread abort.

What I just described is what usually happens. However, if the thread experiencing the unhandled exception is in a *critical region*, the policy is different. A thread that is in a critical region is a thread that has entered a thread synchronization lock that must be released by the same thread, for example, a thread that has called **Monitor.Enter**, **Mutex**'s **WaitOne**, or one of **ReaderWriterLock**'s **AcquireReaderLock** or **AcquireWriterLock** methods.[6] Successfully waiting for an **AutoResetEvent**, **ManualResetEvent**, or **Semaphore** doesn't cause the thread to be in a critical region because another thread can signal these synchronization objects. When a thread is in a critical region, the CLR believes that the thread is

---

[6] All of these locks internally call **Thread**'s **BeginCriticalRegion** and **EndCriticalRegion** methods to indicate when they enter and leave critical regions. Your code can call these methods too if you need to. Normally, this would be necessary only if you are interoperating with unmanaged code.

accessing data that is shared by multiple threads in the same AppDomain. After all, this is probably why the thread took the lock. If the thread is accessing shared data, just terminating the thread isn't good enough because other threads may then try to access the shared data that is now corrupt, causing the AppDomain to run unpredictably or with possible security vulnerabilities.

So when a thread in a critical region experiences an unhandled exception, the CLR first attempts to upgrade the exception to a graceful AppDomain unload in an effort to get rid of all of the threads and data objects that are currently in use. If the AppDomain doesn't unload in a specified amount of time, the CLR upgrades the graceful AppDomain unload to a rude AppDomain unload.

How a Host Gets Its Thread Back

Normally, a host application wants to stay in control of its threads. Let's take a database server as an example. When a request comes into the database server, a thread picks up the request and then dispatches the request to another thread that is to perform the actual work. This other thread may need to execute code that wasn't created and tested by the team that produced the database server. For example, imagine a request coming into the database server to execute a stored procedure written in managed code by the company running the server. It's great that the database server can run the stored procedure code in its own AppDomain, which is locked down with security. This prevents the stored procedure from accessing any objects outside of its own AppDomain, and it also prevents the code from accessing resources that it is not allowed to access, such as disk files or the clipboard.

But what if the code in the stored procedure enters an infinite loop? In this case, the database server has dispatched one of its threads into the stored procedure code, and this thread is never coming back. This puts the server in a precarious position; the future behavior of the server is unknown. For example, the performance might be terrible now because a thread is in an infinite loop. Should the server create more threads? Doing so uses more resources (such as stack space), and these threads could also enter an infinite loop themselves.

To solve these problems, the host can take advantage of thread aborting. Figure 22-3 shows the typical architecture of a host application trying to solve the runaway thread problem. Here's how it works (the numbers correspond to the circled numbers in the figure):

1. A client sends a request to the server.

2. A server thread picks up this request and dispatches it to a thread pool thread to perform the actual work.

3. A thread pool thread picks up the client request and executes trusted code written by the company that built and tested the host application.

4. This trusted code then enters a **try** block, and from within the **try** block, calls across an AppDomain boundary (via a type derived from **MarshalByRefObject**). This AppDomain contains the untrusted code (perhaps a stored procedure) that was not built and tested by the company that produced the host application. At this point, the server has given control of its thread to some untrusted code; the server is feeling nervous right now.

5. When the host originally received the client's request, it recorded the time. If the untrusted code doesn't respond to the client in some administrator-set amount of time, the host calls **Thread**'s **Abort** method asking the CLR to stop the thread pool thread, forcing it to throw a **ThreadAbortException**.

6. At this point, the thread pool thread starts unwinding, calling **finally** blocks so that cleanup code executes. Eventually, the thread pool thread crosses back over the AppDomain boundary. Since the host's stub code called the untrusted code from inside a **try** block, the host's stub code has a **catch** block that catches the **ThreadAbortException**.

7. In response to catching the **ThreadAbortException**, the host calls **Thread**'s **ResetAbort** method. I'll explain the purpose of this call shortly.

8. Now that the host's code has caught the **ThreadAbortException**, the host can return some sort of failure back to the client and allow the thread pool thread to return to the pool so that it can be used for a future client request.

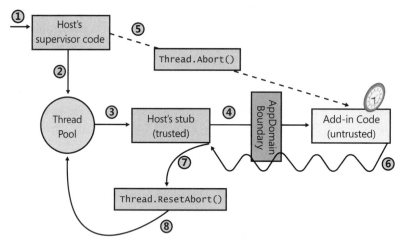

FIGURE 22-3 How a host application gets its thread back

Let me now clear up a few loose ends about this architecture. First, **Thread**'s **Abort** method is asynchronous. When **Abort** is called, it sets the target thread's **AbortRequested** flag and returns immediately. When the runtime detects that a thread is to be aborted, the runtime tries to get the thread to a *safe place*. A thread is in a safe place when the runtime feels that it can stop what the thread is doing without causing disastrous effects. A thread is in a safe place if it is performing a managed blocking operation such as sleeping or waiting. A thread can be corralled to a safe place by using hijacking (described in Chapter 21). A thread is not in a safe place if it is executing a type's class constructor, code in a **catch** or **finally** block, code in a CER, or unmanaged code.

Once the thread reaches a safe place, the runtime will detect that the **AbortRequested** flag is set for the thread. This causes the thread to throw a **ThreadAbortException**. If this exception is not caught, the exception will be unhandled, all pending **finally** blocks will execute, and the thread will kill itself gracefully. Unlike all other exceptions, an unhandled **ThreadAbortException** does not cause the application to terminate. The runtime silently eats this exception and the thread dies, but the application and all of its remaining threads continue to run just fine.

In my example, the host catches the **ThreadAbortException**, allowing the host to regain control of the thread and return it to the pool. But there is a problem: What is to stop the untrusted code from catching the **ThreadAbortException** itself to keep control of the thread? The answer is that the CLR treats the **ThreadAbortException** in a very special manner. Even when code catches the **ThreadAbortException**, the CLR doesn't allow the exception to be swallowed. In other words, at the end of the **catch** block, the CLR automatically rethrows the **ThreadAbortException** exception.

This CLR feature raises another question: If the CLR rethrows the **ThreadAbortException** at the end of a **catch** block, how can the host catch it to regain control of the thread? Inside the host's **catch** block, there is a call to **Thread**'s **ResetAbort** method. Calling this method tells the CLR to stop rethrowing the **ThreadAbortException** at the end of each **catch** block.

This raises yet another question: What's to stop the untrusted code from catching the **ThreadAbortException** and calling **Thread**'s **ResetAbort** method itself to keep control of the thread? The answer is that **Thread**'s **ResetAbort** method requires the caller to have the **SecurityPermission** with the **ControlThread** flag set to **true**. When the host creates the AppDomain for the untrusted code, the host will not grant this permission, and now, the untrusted code cannot keep control of the host's thread.

I should point out that there is still a potential hole in this story: While the thread is unwinding from its **ThreadAbortException**, the untrusted code can execute **catch** and **finally** blocks. Inside these blocks, the untrusted code could enter an infinite loop, preventing the host from regaining control of its thread. A host application fixes this problem by setting an escalation policy (discussed earlier). If an aborting thread doesn't finish in a reasonable amount of time, the CLR can upgrade the thread abort to a rude thread abort, a rude AppDomain unload, disabling of the CLR, or killing of the process. I should also note that the untrusted code could catch the **ThreadAbortException** and, inside the **catch** block, throw some other kind of exception. If this other exception is caught, at the end of the **catch** block, the CLR automatically rethrows the **ThreadAbortException**.

It should be noted, though, that most untrusted code is not actually intended to be malicious; it is just written in such a way so as to be taking too long by the host's standards. Usually, **catch** and **finally** blocks contain very little code, and this code usually executes quickly without any infinite loops or long-running tasks. And so it is very unlikely that the escalation policy will have to go into effect for the host to regain control of its thread.

By the way, the **Thread** class actually offers two **Abort** methods: One takes no parameters, and the other takes an **Object** parameter allowing you to pass anything. When code catches the **ThreadAbortException**, it can query its read-only **ExceptionState** property. This property returns the object that was passed to **Abort**. This allows the thread calling **Abort** to specify some additional information that can be examined by code catching the **ThreadAbortException**. The host can use this to let its own handling code know why it is aborting threads.

## Chapter 23

Assembly Loading and Reflection

This chapter is all about discovering information about types, creating instances of them, and accessing their members when you didn't know anything about them at compile time. The information in this chapter is typically used to create a dynamically extensible application. This is the kind of application for which one company builds a host application and other companies create add-ins to extend the host application. The host can't be built or tested against the add-ins because the add-ins are created by different companies and are likely to be created after the host application has already shipped. This is why the host needs to discover the add-ins at runtime.

A dynamically extensible application could take advantage of common language runtime (CLR) hosting and AppDomains as discussed in Chapter 22, "CLR Hosting and AppDomains." The host could run the add-in code in an AppDomain with its own security and configuration settings. The host could also unload the add-in code by unloading the AppDomain. At the end of this chapter, I'll talk a little about how to put all of this stuff together—CLR hosting, AppDomains, assembly loading, type discovery, type instance construction, and reflection—in order to build a robust, secure, dynamically extensible application.

Assembly Loading

As you know, when the just-in-time (JIT) compiler compiles the Intermediate Language (IL) for a method, it sees what types are referenced in the IL code. Then at runtime, the JIT compiler uses the assembly's TypeRef and AssemblyRef metadata tables to determine what assembly defines the type being referenced. The AssemblyRef metadata table entry contains all of the parts that make up the strong name of the assembly. The JIT compiler grabs all of these parts—name (without extension or path), version, culture, and public key token—concatenates them into a string, and then attempts to load an assembly matching this identity into the AppDomain (assuming that it's not already loaded). If the assembly being loaded is weakly named, the identity is just the name of the assembly (no version, culture, or public key token information).

Internally, the CLR attempts to load this assembly by using the **System.Reflection.Assembly** class's static **Load** method. This method is publicly documented, and you can call it to explicitly load an assembly into your AppDomain. This method is the CLR equivalent of Win32's **LoadLibrary** function. There are actually several overloaded versions of **Assembly**'s **Load** method. Here are the prototypes of the more commonly used overloads:

```
public class Assembly {
    public static Assembly Load(AssemblyName assemblyRef);
    public static Assembly Load(String assemblyString);
    // Less commonly used overloads of Load are not shown
}
```

Internally, **Load** causes the CLR to apply a version-binding redirection policy to the assembly and looks for the assembly in the global assembly cache (GAC), followed by the application's base directory, private path subdirectories, and codebase locations. If you call **Load** passing a weakly named assembly, **Load** doesn't apply a version-binding redirection policy to the assembly, and the CLR won't look in the GAC for the assembly. If **Load** finds the specified assembly, it returns a reference to an **Assembly** object that represents the loaded assembly. If **Load** fails to find the specified assembly, it throws a **System.IO.FileNotFoundException**.

Note In some extremely rare situations, you may want to load an assembly that was built for a specific CPU architecture. In this case, when specifying an assembly's identity, you can also include a process architecture part. For example, if my GAC happened to have an IL-neutral and an x86-specific version of an assembly, the CLR would favor the CPU-specific version of the assembly (as discussed in Chapter 3, "Shared Assemblies and Strongly Named Assemblies"). However, I can force the CLR to load the IL-neutral version by passing the following string to **Assembly**'s **Load** method:

```
"SomeAssembly, Version=2.0.0.0, Culture=neutral,
    PublicKeyToken=01234567890abcde, ProcessorArchitecture=MSIL"
```

Today, the CLR supports four possible values for ProcessorArchitecture: MSIL (Microsoft IL), x86, IA64, and AMD64.

Important Some developers notice that **System.AppDomain** offers a **Load** method. Unlike **Assembly**'s static **Load** method, AppDomain's **Load** method is an instance method that allows you to load an assembly into the specified AppDomain. This method was designed to be called by unmanaged code, and it allows a host to inject an assembly into a specific AppDomain. Managed code developers generally shouldn't call this method because when AppDomain's **Load** method is called, you pass it a string that identifies an assembly. The method then applies policy and searches the normal places looking for the assembly. Recall that an AppDomain has settings associated with it that tell the CLR how to look for assemblies. To load this assembly, the CLR will use the settings associated with the specified AppDomain, not the calling AppDomain.

> However, AppDomain's **Load** method returns a reference to an assembly. Because the
> **System.Assembly** class isn't derived from **System.MarshalByRefObject**, the assembly
> object must be marshaled by value back to the calling AppDomain. But the CLR will now use
> the calling AppDomain's settings to locate the assembly and load it. If the assembly can't be
> found using the calling AppDomain's policy and search locations, a **FileNotFoundException** is
> thrown. This behavior is usually undesirable and is the reason that you should avoid AppDomain's
> **Load** method.

In most dynamically extensible applications, **Assembly**'s **Load** method is the preferred way
of loading an assembly into an AppDomain. However, it does require that you have all of
the pieces that make up an assembly's identity. Frequently, developers write tools or utilities
(such as ILDasm.exe, PEVerify.exe, CorFlags.exe, GACUtil.exe, SGen.exe, SN.exe, XSD.exe) that
perform some kind of processing on an assembly. All of these tools take a command-line
argument that refers to the path name of an assembly file (including file extension). To load
an assembly specifying a path name, you call **Assembly**'s **LoadFrom** method:

```
public class Assembly {
   public static Assembly LoadFrom(String path);
   // Less commonly used overloads of LoadFrom are not shown
}
```

Internally, **LoadFrom** first calls **System.Reflection.AssemblyName**'s static **GetAssemblyName**
method, which opens the specified file, finds the AssemblyDef metadata table's entry,
and extracts the assembly identity information and returns it in a **System.Reflection.
AssemblyName** object (the file is also closed). Then, **LoadFrom** internally calls **Assembly**'s **Load**
method, passing it the **AssemblyName** object. At this point, the CLR applies version-binding
redirection policy and searches the various locations looking for a matching assembly. If **Load**
finds the assembly, it will load it, and an **Assembly** object that represents the loaded assembly will be returned; **LoadFrom** returns this value. If **Load** fails to find an assembly, **LoadFrom**
loads the assembly at the path name specified in **LoadFrom**'s argument. Of course, if an
assembly with the same identity is already loaded, **LoadFrom** simply returns an **Assembly**
object that represents the already loaded assembly.

By the way, the **LoadFrom** method allows you to pass a URL as the argument. Here is an
example:

```
Assembly a = Assembly.LoadFrom(@"http://Wintellect.com/SomeAssembly.dll");
```

When you pass an Internet location, the CLR downloads the file, installs it into the user's
download cache, and loads the file from there. Note that you must be online or an exception
will be thrown. However, if the file has been downloaded previously, and if Windows Internet
Explorer has been set to work offline (see Internet Explorer's Work Offline menu item in its
File menu), the previously downloaded file will be used, and no exception will be thrown. You
can also call **UnsafeLoadFrom**, which can load a Web-downloaded assembly, bypassing some
security checks.

> **Important** It is possible to have different assemblies on a single machine all with the same identity. Because **LoadFrom** calls **Load** internally, it is possible that the CLR will not load the specified file and instead will load a different file giving you unexpected behavior. It is highly recommended that each build of your assembly change the version number; this ensures that each version has its own identity, and because of this, **LoadFrom** will now work as expected.

Microsoft Visual Studio's UI designers and other tools typically use **Assembly**'s **LoadFile** method. This method can load an assembly from any path and can be used to load an assembly with the same identity multiple times into a single AppDomain. This can happen as changes to an application's UI are made in the designer/tool and the user rebuilds the assembly. When loading an assembly via **LoadFile**, the CLR will not resolve any dependencies automatically; your code must register with **AppDomain**'s **AssemblyResolve** event and have your event callback method explicitly load any dependent assemblies.

If you are building a tool that simply analyzes an assembly's metadata via reflection (as discussed later in this chapter), and you want to ensure that none of the code contained inside the assembly executes, the best way for you to load an assembly is to use **Assembly**'s **ReflectionOnlyLoadFrom** method, or in some rarer cases, **Assembly**'s **ReflectionOnlyLoad** method. Here are the prototypes of both methods:

```
public class Assembly {
    public static Assembly ReflectionOnlyLoadFrom(String assemblyFile);
    public static Assembly ReflectionOnlyLoad(String assemblyString);
    // Less commonly used overload of ReflectionOnlyLoad is not shown
}
```

The **ReflectionOnlyLoadFrom** method will load the file specified by the path; the strong-name identity of the file is not obtained, and the file is not searched for in the GAC or elsewhere. The **ReflectionOnlyLoad** method will search for the specified assembly looking in the GAC, application base directory, private paths, and codebases. However, unlike the **Load** method, the **ReflectionOnlyLoad** method does not apply versioning policies, so you will get the exact version that you specify. If you want to apply versioning policy yourself to an assembly identity, you can pass the string into **AppDomain**'s **ApplyPolicy** method.

When an assembly is loaded with **ReflectionOnlyLoadFrom** or **ReflectionOnlyLoad**, the CLR forbids any code in the assembly from executing; any attempt to execute code in an assembly loaded with either of these methods causes the CLR to throw an **InvalidOperationException**. These methods allow a tool to load an assembly that was delay-signed, would normally require security permissions that prevent it from loading, or was created for a different CPU architecture.

Frequently when using reflection to analyze an assembly loaded with one of these two methods, the code will have to register a callback method with **AppDomain**'s **ReflectionOnlyAssemblyResolve** event to manually load any referenced assemblies (calling **AppDomain**'s **ApplyPolicy** method, if desired); the CLR doesn't do it automatically for you. When the callback method is invoked, it must call **Assembly**'s **ReflectionOnlyLoadFrom** or **ReflectionOnlyLoad** method to explicitly load a referenced assembly and return a reference to this assembly.

> **Note** People often ask about assembly unloading. Unfortunately, the CLR doesn't support the ability to unload individual assemblies. If the CLR allowed it, your application would crash if a thread returned back from a method to code in the unloaded assembly. The CLR is all about robustness and security, and allowing an application to crash in this way would be counterproductive to its goals. If you want to unload an assembly, you must unload the entire AppDomain that contains it. This was discussed in great detail in Chapter 22.
>
> It would seem that assemblies loaded with either the **ReflectionOnlyLoadFrom** or the **ReflectionOnlyLoad** method could be unloaded. After all, code in these assemblies is not allowed to execute. However, the CLR also doesn't allow assemblies loaded via either of these two methods to be unloaded. The reason is that once an assembly is loaded this way, you can still use reflection to create objects that refer to the metadata defined inside these assemblies. Unloading the assembly would require the objects to be invalidated somehow. Keeping track of this would be too expensive in terms of implementation and execution speed.

Many applications consist of an EXE file that depends on many DLL files. When deploying this application, all the files must be deployed. However, there is a technique that you can use to deploy just a single EXE file. First, identify all the DLL files that your EXE file depends on that do not ship as part of the Microsoft .NET Framework itself. Then add these DLLs to your Visual Studio project. For each DLL file you add, display its properties and change its "Build Action" to "Embedded Resource". This causes the C# compiler to embed the DLL file(s) into your EXE file, and you can deploy this one EXE file.

At runtime, the CLR won't be able to find the dependent DLL assemblies, which is a problem. To fix this, when your application initializes, register a callback method with the **AppDomain**'s **ResolveAssembly** event. The code should look something like this:

```
AppDomain.CurrentDomain.AssemblyResolve += (sender, args) => {
   String resourceName = "AssemblyLoadingAndReflection." +
      new AssemblyName(args.Name).Name + ".dll";

   using (var stream =
      Assembly.GetExecutingAssembly().GetManifestResourceStream(resourceName)) {
      Byte[] assemblyData = new Byte[stream.Length];
      stream.Read(assemblyData, 0, assemblyData.Length);
      return Assembly.Load(assemblyData);
   }
};
```

Now, the first time a thread calls a method that references a type in a dependent DLL file, the **AssemblyResolve** event will be raised and the callback code shown above will find the embedded DLL resource desired and load it by calling an overload of **Assembly**'s **Load** method that takes a **Byte[]** as an argument.

Using Reflection to Build a Dynamically Extensible Application

As you know, metadata is stored in a bunch of tables. When you build an assembly or a module, the compiler that you're using creates a type definition table, a field definition table, a method definition table, and so on. The **System.Reflection** namespace contains several types that allow you to write code that reflects over (or parses) these metadata tables. In effect, the types in this namespace offer an object model over the metadata contained in an assembly or a module.

Using these object model types, you can easily enumerate all of the types in a type definition metadata table. Then for each type, you can obtain its base type, the interfaces it implements, and the flags that are associated with the type. Additional types in the **System.Reflection** namespace allow you to query the type's fields, methods, properties, and events by parsing the corresponding metadata tables. You can also discover any custom attributes (covered in Chapter 18, "Custom Attributes") that have been applied to any of the metadata entities. There are even classes that let you determine referenced assemblies and methods that return the IL byte stream for a method. With all of this information, you could easily build a tool very similar to Microsoft's ILDasm.exe.

Note You should be aware that some of the reflection types and some of the members defined by these types are designed specifically for use by developers who are producing compilers for the CLR. Application developers don't typically use these types and members. The Framework Class Library (FCL) documentation doesn't explicitly point out which of these types and members are for compiler developers rather than application developers, but if you realize that not all reflection types and their members are for everyone, the documentation can be less confusing.

In reality, very few applications will have the need to use the reflection types. Reflection is typically used by class libraries that need to understand a type's definition in order to provide some rich functionality. For example, the FCL's serialization mechanism (discussed in Chapter 24, "Runtime Serialization") uses reflection to determine what fields a type defines. The serialization formatter can then obtain the values of these fields and write them into a byte stream that is used for sending across the Internet, saving to a file, or copying to the clipboard. Similarly, Visual Studio's designers use reflection to determine which properties should be shown to developers when laying out controls on their Web Forms or Windows Forms at design time.

Reflection is also used when an application needs to load a specific type from a specific assembly at runtime to accomplish some task. For example, an application might ask the user to provide the name of an assembly and a type. The application could then explicitly load the assembly, construct an instance of the type, and call methods defined in the type. This usage is conceptually similar to calling Win32's **LoadLibrary** and **GetProcAddress** functions.

Binding to types and calling methods in this way is frequently referred to as *late binding*. (*Early binding* is when the types and methods used by an application are determined at compile time.)

Reflection Performance

Reflection is an extremely powerful mechanism because it allows you to discover and use types and members at runtime that you did not know about at compile time. This power does come with two main drawbacks:

- Reflection prevents type safety at compile time. Since reflection uses strings heavily, you lose type safety at compile time. For example, if you call **Type.GetType("Jef");** to ask reflection to find a type called "Jef" in an assembly that has a type called "Jeff," the code compiles but produces an error at runtime because you accidentally misspelled the type name passed as the argument.

- Reflection is slow. When using reflection, the names of types and their members are not known at compile time; you discover them at runtime by using a string name to identify each type and member. This means that reflection is constantly performing string searches as the types in the **System.Reflection** namespace scan through an assembly's metadata. Often, the string searches are case-insensitive comparisons, which can slow this down even more.

Invoking a member by using reflection will also hurt performance. When using reflection to invoke a method, you must first package the arguments into an array; internally, reflection must unpack these on to the thread's stack. Also, the CLR must check that the arguments are of the correct data type before invoking a method. Finally, the CLR ensures that the caller has the proper security permission to access the member being invoked.

For all of these reasons, it's best to avoid using reflection to access a field or invoke a method/property. If you're writing an application that will dynamically discover and construct type instances, you should take one of the following approaches:

- Have the types derive from a base type that is known at compile time. At runtime, construct an instance of the derived type, place the reference in a variable that is of the base type (by way of a cast), and call virtual methods defined by the base type.

- Have the type implement an interface that is known at compile time. At runtime, construct an instance of the type, place the reference in a variable that is of the interface type (by way of a cast), and call the methods defined by the interface.

I tend to prefer using the interface technique over the base type technique because the base type technique doesn't allow the developer to choose the base type that works best in a particular situation. Although the base type technique works better in versioning scenarios since you could always add a member to the base type and the derived types just inherit it;

you can't add a member to an interface without forcing all types that implement the interface to modify their code and recompile it.

When you use either of these two techniques, I strongly suggest that the interface or base type be defined in its own assembly. This will reduce versioning issues. For more information about how to do this, see the section titled "Designing an Application That Supports Add-Ins" in this chapter.

Discovering Types Defined in an Assembly

Reflection is frequently used to determine what types an assembly defines. The FCL offers many methods to get this information. By far, the most commonly used method is **Assembly**'s **GetExportedTypes**. Here is an example of code that loads an assembly and shows the names of all of the publicly exported types defined in it:

```
using System;
using System.Reflection;

public static class Program {
   public static void Main() {
      String dataAssembly = "System.Data, version=4.0.0.0, " +
         "culture=neutral, PublicKeyToken=b77a5c561934e089";
      LoadAssemAndShowPublicTypes(dataAssembly);
   }

   private static void LoadAssemAndShowPublicTypes(String assemId) {
      // Explicitly load an assembly in to this AppDomain
      Assembly a = Assembly.Load(assemId);

      // Execute this loop once for each Type
      // publicly-exported from the loaded assembly
      foreach (Type t in a.GetExportedTypes()) {
         // Display the full name of the type
         Console.WriteLine(t.FullName);
      }
   }
}
```

What Exactly Is a Type Object?

Notice that the previous code iterates over an array of **System.Type** objects. The **System.Type** type is your starting point for doing type and object manipulations. **System.Type** is an abstract base type derived from **System.Reflection.MemberInfo** (because a **Type** can be a member of another type). The FCL provides a few types that are derived from **System.Type:System.RuntimeType**, **System.ReflectionOnlyType**, **System.Reflection.TypeDelegator**, and some types defined in the **System.Reflection.Emit** namespace (**EnumBuilder**, **GenericTypeParameterBuilder**, and **TypeBuilder**).

> **Note** The **TypeDelegator** class allows code to dynamically subclass a **Type** by encapsulating the **Type**, allowing you to override some of the functionality while having the original **Type** handle most of the work. This powerful mechanism allows you to override the way reflection works.

Of all of these types, the **System.RuntimeType** is by far the most interesting. **RuntimeType** is a type that is internal to the FCL, which means that you won't find it documented in the FCL documentation. The first time a type is accessed in an AppDomain, the CLR constructs an instance of a **RuntimeType** and initializes the object's fields to reflect (pun intended) information about the type.

Recall that **System.Object** defines a public, nonvirtual instance method named **GetType**. When you call this method, the CLR determines the specified object's type and returns a reference to its **RuntimeType** object. Because there is only one **RuntimeType** object per type in an AppDomain, you can use equality and inequality operators to see whether two objects are of the same type:

```
private static Boolean AreObjectsTheSameType(Object o1, Object o2) {
    return o1.GetType() == o2.GetType();
}
```

In addition to calling **Object**'s **GetType** method, the FCL offers several more ways to obtain a **Type** object:

- The **System.Type** type offers several overloaded versions of the static **GetType** method. All versions of this method take a **String**. The string must specify the full name of the type (including its namespace). Note that the primitive type names supported by the compiler (such as C#'s **int**, **string**, **bool**, and so on) aren't allowed because these names mean nothing to the CLR. If the string is simply the name of a type, the method checks the calling assembly to see whether it defines a type of the specified name. If it does, a reference to the appropriate **RuntimeType** object is returned.

  If the calling assembly doesn't define the specified type, the types defined by MSCorLib.dll are checked. If a type with a matching name still can't be found, **null** is returned or a **System.TypeLoadException** is thrown, depending on which overload of the **GetType** method you called and what parameters you passed to it. The FCL documentation fully explains this method.

  You can pass an assembly-qualified type string, such as "System.Int32, mscorlib, Version=4.0.0.0, Culture=neutral, PublicKeyToken=b77a5c561934e089", to **GetType**. In this case, **GetType** will look for the type in the specified assembly (loading the assembly if necessary).

- The **System.Type** type offers a static **ReflectionOnlyGetType** method. This method behaves similarly to the **GetType** method mentioned in the previous bullet, except that the type is loaded so that it can be reflected over but cannot be executed.

- The **System.Type** type offers the following instance methods: **GetNestedType** and **GetNestedTypes**.

- The **System.Reflection.Assembly** type offers the following instance methods: **GetType**, **GetTypes**, and **GetExportedTypes**.

- The **System.Reflection.Module** type offers the following instance methods: **GetType**, **GetTypes**, and **FindTypes**.

> **Note** Microsoft has defined a Backus-Naur Form grammar for type names and assembly-qualified type names that is used for constructing strings that will be passed to reflection methods. Knowledge of the grammar can come in quite handy when you are using reflection, specifically if you are working with nested types, generic types, generic methods, reference parameters, or arrays. For the complete grammar, see the FCL documentation or do a Web search for "Backus-Naur Form Grammar for Type Names." You can also look at **Type**'s **MakeArrayType**, **MakeByRefType**, **MakeGenericType**, and **MakePointerType** methods.

Many programming languages also offer an operator that allows you to obtain a **Type** object from a type name that is known at compile time. When possible, you should use this operator to obtain a reference to a **Type** instead of using any of the methods in the preceding list, because the operator generally produces faster code. In C#, the operator is called **typeof**, and you use this operator typically to compare late-bound type information with early-bound (known at compile time) type information. The following code demonstrates an example of its use:

```
private static void SomeMethod(Object o) {
    // GetType returns the type of the object at runtime (late-bound)
    // typeof returns the type of the specified class (early-bound)
    if (o.GetType() == typeof(FileInfo))      { ... }
    if (o.GetType() == typeof(DirectoryInfo)) { ... }
}
```

> **Note** The first **if** statement in the code checks if the variable **o** refers to an object of the **FileInfo** type; it does not check if **o** refers to an object that is derived from the **FileInfo** type. In other words, the code above tests for an exact match, not a compatible match, which is what you would get if you use a cast or C#'s **is** or **as** operators.

Once you have a reference to a **Type** object, you can query many of the type's properties to learn more about it. Most of the properties, such as **IsPublic**, **IsSealed**, **IsAbstract**, **IsClass**, **IsValueType**, and so on, indicate flags associated with the type. Other properties, such as **Assembly**, **AssemblyQualifiedName**, **FullName**, **Module**, and so on, return the name of the type's defining assembly or module and the full name of the type. You can also query the **BaseType** property to obtain the type's base type, and a slew of methods will give you even more information about the type.

The FCL documentation describes all of the methods and properties that **Type** exposes. Be aware that there are a lot of them. In fact, **Type** offers about 60 public instance properties. This doesn't even include the methods and fields that **Type** also defines. I'll be covering some of these methods in the next section.

Building a Hierarchy of Exception-Derived Types

The code shown below uses many of the concepts discussed already in this chapter to load a bunch of assemblies into the AppDomain and display all of the classes that are ultimately derived from **System.Exception**. By the way, this is the program I wrote to build the exception hierarchy displayed in the "FCL-Defined Exception Classes" section in Chapter 20, "Exceptions and State Management."

```
public static void Go() {
    // Explicitly load the assemblies that we want to reflect over
    LoadAssemblies();

    // Recursively build the class hierarchy as a hyphen-separated string
    Func<Type, String> ClassNameAndBase = null;
    ClassNameAndBase = t => "-" + t.FullName +
        ((t.BaseType != typeof(Object)) ? ClassNameAndBase(t.BaseType) : String.Empty);

    // Define query to find all public Exception-derived types in this AppDomain's assemblies
    var exceptionTree =
        (from a in AppDomain.CurrentDomain.GetAssemblies()
         from t in a.GetExportedTypes()
         where t.IsClass && t.IsPublic && typeof(Exception).IsAssignableFrom(t)
         let typeHierarchyTemp = ClassNameAndBase(t).Split('-').Reverse().ToArray()
         let typeHierarchy =
             String.Join("-", typeHierarchyTemp, 0, typeHierarchyTemp.Length - 1)
         orderby typeHierarchy
         select typeHierarchy).ToArray();

    // Display the Exception tree
    Console.WriteLine("{0} Exception types found.", exceptionTree.Length);
    foreach (String s in exceptionTree) {
        // For this Exception type, split its base types apart
        String[] x = s.Split('-');

        // Indent based on # of base types and show the most-derived type
        Console.WriteLine(new String(' ', 3 * (x.Length - 1)) + x[x.Length - 1]);
    }
}


private static void LoadAssemblies() {
    String[] assemblies = {
        "System,                PublicKeyToken={0}",
        "System.Core,           PublicKeyToken={0}",
        "System.Data,           PublicKeyToken={0}",
        "System.Design,         PublicKeyToken={1}",
```

```
            "System.DirectoryServices,  PublicKeyToken={1}",
            "System.Drawing,            PublicKeyToken={1}",
            "System.Drawing.Design,     PublicKeyToken={1}",
            "System.Management,         PublicKeyToken={1}",
            "System.Messaging,          PublicKeyToken={1}",
            "System.Runtime.Remoting,   PublicKeyToken={0}",
            "System.Security,           PublicKeyToken={1}",
            "System.ServiceProcess,     PublicKeyToken={1}",
            "System.Web,                PublicKeyToken={1}",
            "System.Web.RegularExpressions, PublicKeyToken={1}",
            "System.Web.Services,       PublicKeyToken={1}",
            "System.Windows.Forms,      PublicKeyToken={0}",
            "System.Xml,                PublicKeyToken={0}",
        };

        String EcmaPublicKeyToken = "b77a5c561934e089";
        String MSPublicKeyToken = "b03f5f7f11d50a3a";

        // Get the version of the assembly containing System.Object
        // We'll assume the same version for all the other assemblies
        Version version = typeof(System.Object).Assembly.GetName().Version;

        // Explicitly load the assemblies that we want to reflect over
        foreach (String a in assemblies) {
            String AssemblyIdentity =
                String.Format(a, EcmaPublicKeyToken, MSPublicKeyToken) +
                    ", Culture=neutral, Version=" + version;
            Assembly.Load(AssemblyIdentity);
        }
    }
}
```

Constructing an Instance of a Type

Once you have a reference to a **Type**-derived object, you might want to construct an instance of this type. The FCL offers several mechanisms to accomplish this:

- **System.Activator's CreateInstance methods**   The **Activator** class offers several overloads of its static **CreateInstance** method. When you call this method, you can pass either a reference to a **Type** object or a **String** that identifies the type of object you want to create. The versions that take a type are simpler. You get to pass a set of arguments for the type's constructor, and the method returns a reference to the new object.

  The versions of this method in which you specify the desired type by using a string are a bit more complex. First, you must also specify a string identifying the assembly that defines the type. Second, these methods allow you to construct a remote object if you have remoting options configured properly. Third, these versions don't return a reference to the new object. Instead, they return a **System.Runtime.Remoting. ObjectHandle** (which is derived from **System.MarshalByRefObject**).

An **ObjectHandle** is a type that allows an object created in one AppDomain to be passed around to other AppDomains without forcing the object to materialize. When you're ready to materialize the object, you call **ObjectHandle**'s **Unwrap** method. This method loads the assembly that defines the type being materialized in the AppDomain where **Unwrap** is called. If the object is being marshaled by reference, the proxy type and object are created. If the object is being marshaled by value, the copy is deserialized.

- **System.Activator's CreateInstanceFrom methods**   The **Activator** class also offers a set of static **CreateInstanceFrom** methods. These methods behave just as the **CreateInstance** method, except that you must always specify the type and its assembly via string parameters. The assembly is loaded into the calling AppDomain by using **Assembly**'s **LoadFrom** method (instead of **Load**). Because none of these methods takes a **Type** parameter, all of the **CreateInstanceFrom** methods return a reference to an **ObjectHandle**, which must be unwrapped.

- **System.AppDomain's methods**   The **AppDomain** type offers four instance methods (each with several overloads) that construct an instance of a type: **CreateInstance**, **CreateInstanceAndUnwrap**, **CreateInstanceFrom**, and **CreateInstanceFromAndUnwrap**. These methods work just as **Activator**'s methods except that these methods are instance methods, allowing you to specify which AppDomain the object should be constructed in. The methods that end with **Unwrap** exist for convenience so that you don't have to make an additional method call.

- **System.Type's InvokeMember instance method**   Using a reference to a **Type** object, you can call the **InvokeMember** method. This method locates a constructor matching the parameters you pass and constructs the type. The type is always created in the calling AppDomain, and a reference to the new object is returned. I'll discuss this method in more detail later in this chapter.

- **System.Reflection.ConstructorInfo's Invoke instance method**   Using a reference to a **Type** object, you can bind to a particular constructor and obtain a reference to the constructor's **ConstructorInfo** object. Then you can use the reference to the **ConstructorInfo** object to call its **Invoke** method. The type is always created in the calling AppDomain, and a reference to the new object is returned. I'll also discuss this method in more detail later in this chapter.

Note   The CLR doesn't require that value types define any constructors. However, this is a problem because all of the mechanisms in the preceding list construct an object by calling its constructor. However, **Activator**'s **CreateInstance** methods will allow you to create an instance of a value type without calling a constructor. If you want to create an instance of a value type without calling a constructor, you must call the version of the **CreateInstance** method that takes a single **Type** parameter or the version that takes **Type** and **Boolean** parameters.

The mechanisms just listed allow you to create an object for all types except for arrays (**System.Array**-derived types) and delegates (**System.MulticastDelegate**-derived types). To create an array, you should call **Array**'s static **CreateInstance** method (several over-loaded versions exist). The first parameter to all versions of **CreateInstance** is a reference to the **Type** of elements you want in the array. **CreateInstance**'s other parameters allow you to specify various combinations of dimensions and bounds. To create a delegate, you should call **Delegate**'s static **CreateDelegate** method (several overloads exist). The first parameter to all versions of **CreateDelegate** is a reference to the **Type** of delegate you want to create. **CreateDelegate**'s other parameters allow you to specify which instance method of an object or which static method of a type the delegate should wrap.

To construct an instance for a generic type, first get a reference to the open type, and then call **Type**'s public, instance **MakeGenericType** method, passing in an array of types that you want to use as the type arguments. Then, take the returned **Type** object and pass it into one of the various methods listed above. Here is an example:

```
using System;
using System.Reflection;

internal sealed class Dictionary<TKey, TValue> { }

public static class Program {
    public static void Main() {
        // Get a reference to the generic type's type object
        Type openType = typeof(Dictionary<,>);

        // Close the generic type by using TKey=String, TValue=Int32
        Type closedType = openType.MakeGenericType(typeof(String), typeof(Int32));

        // Construct an instance of the closed type
        Object o = Activator.CreateInstance(closedType);

        // Prove it worked
        Console.WriteLine(o.GetType());
    }
}
```

If you compile the code shown above and run it, you get the following output:

```
Dictionary`2[System.String,System.Int32]
```

Designing an Application That Supports Add-Ins

When you're building extensible applications, interfaces should be the centerpiece. You could use a base class instead of an interface, but in general, an interface is preferred because it allows add-in developers to choose their own base class. Suppose, for example, that you're writing an application and you want others to be able to create types that your application can load and use seamlessly. Here's the way to design this application:

- Create a Host SDK assembly that defines an interface whose methods are used as the communication mechanism between the host application and the add-in components. When defining the parameters and return values for the interface methods, try to use other interfaces or types defined in MSCorLib.dll. If you want to pass and return your own data types, define them in this Host SDK assembly, too. Once you settle on your interface definitions, give this assembly a strong name (discussed in Chapter 3), and then package and deploy it to your partners and users. Once published, you should really avoid making any kind of breaking changes to the types in this assembly. For example, do not change the interface in any way. However, if you define any data types, it is OK to add new members. If you make any modifications to the assembly, you'll probably want to deploy it with a publisher policy file (also discussed in Chapter 3).

 Note You can use types defined in MSCorLib.dll because the CLR always loads the version of MSCorLib.dll that matches the version of the CLR itself. Also, only a single version of MSCorLib.dll is ever loaded into a CLR instance. In other words, different versions of MSCorLib.dll never load side by side (as described in Chapter 3). As a result, you won't have any type version mismatches, and your application will require less memory.

- The add-in developers will, of course, define their own types in their own Add-In assembly. Their Add-In assembly will reference the types in your Host SDK assembly. The add-in developers are able to put out a new version of their assembly as often as they'd like, and the host application will be able to consume the add-in types without any problem whatsoever.

- Create a separate Host Application assembly containing your application's types. This assembly will obviously reference the Host SDK assembly and use the types defined in it. Feel free to modify the code in the Host Application assembly to your heart's desire. Because the add-in developers don't reference the Host Application assembly, you can put out a new version of it every hour if you want to and not affect any of the add-in developers.

This section contains some very important information. When using types across assemblies, you need to be concerned with assembly-versioning issues. Take your time to architect this cleanly by isolating the types that you use for communication across assembly boundaries into their own assembly. Avoid mutating or changing these type definitions. However, if you really need to modify the type definitions, make sure that you change the assembly's version number and create a publisher policy file for the new version.

I'll now walk through a very simple scenario that puts all of this together. First, here is the code for the HostSDK.dll assembly:

```
using System;

namespace Wintellect.HostSDK {
   public interface IAddIn {
      String DoSomething(Int32 x);
   }
}
```

Second, here is the code for an AddInTypes.dll assembly defining two public types that implement the HostSDK's interface. To build this assembly, the HostSDK.dll assembly must be referenced:

```
using System;
using Wintellect.HostSDK;

public sealed class AddIn_A : IAddIn {
   public AddIn_A() {
   }
   public String DoSomething(Int32 x) {
      return "AddIn_A: " + x.ToString();
   }
}

public sealed class AddIn_B : IAddIn {
   public AddIn_B() {
   }
   public String DoSomething(Int32 x) {
      return "AddIn_B: " + (x * 2).ToString();
   }
}
```

Third, here is the code for a simple Host.exe assembly (a console application). To build this assembly, the HostSDK.dll assembly must be referenced. To discover usable add-in types, this host code assumes that the types are defined in assemblies ending with a .dll file extension and that these assemblies are deployed into the same directory as the host's EXE file. Microsoft's Managed Extensibility Framework (MEF) is built on top of the various mechanisms that I show here, and it also offers add-in registration and discovery mechanisms. I urge you to check MEF out if you are building a dynamically extensible application, as it can simplify some of the material in this chapter.

```
using System;
using System.IO;
using System.Reflection;
using System.Collections.Generic;
using Wintellect.HostSDK;

public static class Program {
   public static void Main() {
      // Find the directory that contains the Host exe
      String AddInDir = Path.GetDirectoryName(Assembly.GetEntryAssembly().Location);
```

```
        // Assume AddIn assemblies are in same directory as host's EXE file
        String[] AddInAssemblies = Directory.GetFiles(AddInDir, "*.dll");

        // Create a collection of usable add-in Types
        List<Type> AddInTypes = new List<Type>();

        // Load add-in assemblies; discover which types are usable by the host
        foreach (String file in AddInAssemblies) {
            Assembly AddInAssembly = Assembly.LoadFrom(file);

            // Examine each publicly exported type
            foreach (Type t in AddInAssembly.GetExportedTypes()) {
                // If the type is a class that implements the IAddIn
                // interface, then the type is usable by the host
                if (t.IsClass && typeof(IAddIn).IsAssignableFrom(t)) {
                    AddInTypes.Add(t);
                }
            }
        }

        // Initialization complete: the host has discovered the usable add-ins

        // Here's how the host can construct add-in objects and use them
        foreach (Type t in AddInTypes) {
            IAddIn ai = (IAddIn) Activator.CreateInstance(t);
            Console.WriteLine(ai.DoSomething(5));
        }
    }
}
```

The simple host/add-in scenario just shown doesn't use AppDomains. However, in a real-life scenario, you will likely create each add-in in its own AppDomain with its own security and configuration settings. And of course, each AppDomain could be unloaded if you wanted to remove an add-in from memory. To communicate across the AppDomain boundary, you'd either tell the add-in developers to derive their add-in types from **MarshalByRefObject** or, more likely, have the host application define its own internal type that is derived from **MarshalByRefObject**. As each AppDomain is created, the host would create an instance of its own **MarshalByRefObject**-derived type in the new AppDomain. The host's code (in the default AppDomain) would communicate with its own type (in the other AppDomains) to have it load add-in assemblies and create and use instances of the add-in types.

Using Reflection to Discover a Type's Members

So far, this chapter has focused on the parts of reflection—assembly loading, type discovery, and object construction—necessary to build a dynamically extensible application. In order to have good performance and compile-time type safety, you want to avoid using reflection as much as possible. In the dynamically extensible application scenario, once an object is constructed, the host code typically casts the object to an interface type or a base class that is known at compile time; this allows the object's members to be accessed in a high-performance and compile-time type-safe way.

In the remainder of this chapter, I'm going to focus on some other aspects of reflection that you can use to discover and then invoke a type's members. The ability to discover and invoke a type's members is typically used to create developer tools and utilities that analyze an assembly by looking for certain programming patterns or uses of certain members. Examples of tools/utilities that do this are ILDasm.exe, FxCopCmd.exe, and Visual Studio's Windows Forms and Web Forms designers. In addition, some class libraries use the ability to discover and invoke a type's members in order to offer rich functionality as a convenience to developers. Examples of class libraries that do so are serialization/deserialization and simple data binding.

Discovering a Type's Members

Fields, constructors, methods, properties, events, and nested types can all be defined as members within a type. The FCL contains a type called **System.Reflection.MemberInfo**. This class is an abstract base class that encapsulates a bunch of properties common to all type members. Derived from **MemberInfo** are a bunch of classes; each class encapsulates some more properties related to a specific type member. Figure 23-1 shows the hierarchy of these types.

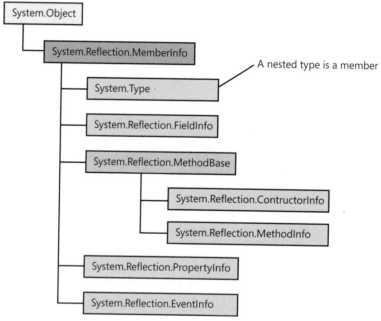

FIGURE 23-1 Hierarchy of the reflection types that encapsulate information about a type's member

The following program demonstrates how to query a type's members and display some information about them. This code processes all of the public types defined in all assemblies loaded in the calling AppDomain. For each type, the **GetMembers** method is called and

returns an array of **MemberInfo**-derived objects; each object refers to a single member
defined within the type. The **BindingFlags** variable, **bf**, passed to the **GetMembers** method
tells the method which kinds of members to return. I'll talk about **BindingFlags** later in this
chapter. Then, for each member, its kind (field, constructor, method, property, etc.) and its
string value (obtained by calling **ToString**) is shown.

```
using System;
using System.Reflection;

public static class Program {
    public static void Main() {
        // Loop through all assemblies loaded in this AppDomain
        Assembly[] assemblies = AppDomain.CurrentDomain.GetAssemblies();
        foreach (Assembly a in assemblies) {
            WriteLine(0, "Assembly: {0}", a);

            // Find Types in the assembly
            foreach (Type t in a.GetExportedTypes()) {
                WriteLine(1, "Type: {0}", t);

                // Discover the type's members
                const BindingFlags bf = BindingFlags.DeclaredOnly |
                    BindingFlags.NonPublic | BindingFlags.Public |
                    BindingFlags.Instance | BindingFlags.Static;

                foreach (MemberInfo mi in t.GetMembers(bf)) {
                    String typeName = String.Empty;
                    if (mi is Type)                  typeName = "(Nested) Type";
                    else if (mi is FieldInfo)        typeName = "FieldInfo";
                    else if (mi is MethodInfo)       typeName = "MethodInfo";
                    else if (mi is ConstructorInfo)  typeName = "ConstructoInfo";
                    else if (mi is PropertyInfo)     typeName = "PropertyInfo";
                    else if (mi is EventInfo)        typeName = "EventInfo";

                    WriteLine(2, "{0}: {1}", typeName, mi);
                }
            }
        }
    }
    private static void WriteLine(Int32 indent, String format, params Object[] args) {
        Console.WriteLine(new String(' ', 3 * indent) + format, args);
    }
}
```

When you compile and run this code, a ton of output is produced. Here is a small sampling
of what it looks like:

```
Assembly: mscorlib, Version=4.0.0.0, Culture=neutral, PublicKeyToken=b77a5c561934e089
    Type: System.Object
        MethodInfo: System.String ToString()
        MethodInfo: Boolean Equals(System.Object)
        MethodInfo: Boolean Equals(System.Object, System.Object)
        MethodInfo: Boolean ReferenceEquals(System.Object, System.Object)
```

```
    MethodInfo: Int32 GetHashCode()
    MethodInfo: System.Type GetType()
    MethodInfo: Void Finalize()
    MethodInfo: System.Object MemberwiseClone()
    MethodInfo: Void FieldSetter(System.String, System.String, System.Object)
    MethodInfo: Void FieldGetter(System.String, System.String, System.Object ByRef)
    MethodInfo: System.Reflection.FieldInfo GetFieldInfo(System.String, System.String)
    ConstructoInfo: Void .ctor()
Type: System.Collections.Generic.IComparer`1[T]
    MethodInfo: Int32 Compare(T, T)
Type: System.Collections.IEnumerator
    MethodInfo: Boolean MoveNext()
    MethodInfo: System.Object get_Current()
    MethodInfo: Void Reset()
    PropertyInfo: System.Object Current
Type: System.IDisposable
    MethodInfo: Void Dispose()
Type: System.Collections.Generic.IEnumerator`1[T]
    MethodInfo: T get_Current()
    PropertyInfo: T Current
Type: System.ArraySegment`1[T]
    MethodInfo: T[] get_Array()
    MethodInfo: Int32 get_Offset()
    MethodInfo: Int32 get_Count()
    MethodInfo: Int32 GetHashCode()
    MethodInfo: Boolean Equals(System.Object)
    MethodInfo: Boolean Equals(System.ArraySegment`1[T])
    MethodInfo: Boolean op_Equality(System.ArraySegment`1[T], System.ArraySegment`1[T])
    MethodInfo: Boolean op_Inequality(System.ArraySegment`1[T], System.ArraySegment`1[T])
    ConstructoInfo: Void .ctor(T[])
    ConstructoInfo: Void .ctor(T[], Int32, Int32)
    PropertyInfo: T[] Array
    PropertyInfo: Int32 Offset
    PropertyInfo: Int32 Count
    FieldInfo: T[] _array
    FieldInfo: Int32 _offset
```

Since **MemberInfo** is the root of the member hierarchy, it makes sense for us to discuss it a bit more. Table 23-1 shows several read-only properties and methods offered by the **MemberInfo** class. These properties and methods are common to all members of a type. Don't forget that **System.Type** is derived from **MemberInfo**, and therefore, **Type** also offers all of the properties shown in Table 23-1.

TABLE 23-1 Properties and Methods Common to All **MemberInfo**-Derived Types

Member Name	Member Type	Description
Name	**String** property	Returns the name of the member. In the case of a nested type, **Name** returns the concatenation of the name of the containing type, followed by '+', followed by the name of the nested type.

Member Name	Member Type	Description
MemberType	**MemberTypes** (enum) property	Returns the kind of member (field, constructor, method, property, event, type (non-nested type or nested type).
DeclaringType	**Type** property	Returns the **Type** that declares the member.
ReflectedType	**Type** property	Returns the **Type** used to obtain this member.
Module	**Module** property	Returns the **Module** that declares the member.
MetadataToken	**Int32** property	Returns the metadata token (within the module) that identifies the member.
GetCustomAttributes	Method returning **Object[]**	Returns an array in which each element identifies an instance of a custom attribute applied to this member. Custom attributes can be applied to any member. Use this method with assemblies that have not been loaded in the "reflection only" context.
GetCustomAttributesData	Method returning **IList<CustomAttributeData>**	Returns a collection in which each element identifies an instance of a custom attribute applied to this member. Custom attributes can be applied to any member. Even though **Assembly** does not derive from **MemberInfo**, it provides the same method that can be used with assemblies.
IsDefined	Method returning **Boolean**	Returns **true** if at least one instance of the specified custom attribute is applied to the member.

Most of the properties mentioned in Table 23-1 are self-explanatory. However, developers frequently confuse the **DeclaringType** and **ReflectedType** properties. To fully understand these properties, let's define the following type:

```
public sealed class MyType {
    public override String ToString() { return null; }
}
```

What would happen if the following line of code executed?

```
MemberInfo[] members = typeof(MyType).GetMembers();
```

The **members** variable is a reference to an array in which each element identifies a public member defined by **MyType** and any of its base types, such as **System.Object**. If you were to query the **DeclaringType** property for the **MemberInfo** element identifying the **ToString** method, you'd see **MyType** returned because **MyType** declares a **ToString** method. On the other hand, if you were to query the **DeclaringType** property for the **MemberInfo** element identifying the **Equals** method, you'd see **System.Object** returned because **Equals** is declared by **System.Object**, not by **MyType**. The **ReflectedType** property always returns **MyType** because this was the type specified when **GetMembers** was called to perform the reflection.

Each element of the array returned by calling **GetMembers** is a reference to one of the concrete types in the hierarchy (unless the **BindingFlags.DeclaredOnly** flag is specified). Although **Type**'s **GetMembers** method returns all of the type's members, **Type** also offers methods that return specific member types. For example, **Type** offers **GetNestedTypes**, **GetFields**, **GetConstructors**, **GetMethods**, **GetProperties**, and **GetEvents**. These methods all return arrays in which each element is a reference to a **Type** object, **FieldInfo** object, **ConstructorInfo** object, **MethodInfo** object, **PropertyInfo** object, or **EventInfo** object, respectively.

Figure 23-2 summarizes the types used by an application to walk reflection's object model. From an AppDomain, you can discover the assemblies loaded into it. From an assembly, you can discover the modules that make it up. From an assembly or a module, you can discover the types that it defines. From a type, you can discover its nested types, fields, constructors, methods, properties, and events. Namespaces are not part of this hierarchy because they are simply syntactical gatherings of types. If you want to list all of the namespaces defined in an assembly, you need to enumerate all of the types in this assembly and take a look at their **Namespace** property.

From a type, it is also possible to discover the interfaces it implements. (I'll show how to do this a little later.) And from a constructor, method, property accessor method, or event add/remove method, you can call the **GetParameters** method to obtain an array of **ParameterInfo** objects, which tells you the types of the member's parameters. You can also query the read-only **ReturnParameter** property to get a **ParameterInfo** object for detailed information about a member's return value. For a generic type or method, you can call the **GetGenericArguments** method to get the set of type parameters. Finally, for any of these items, you can call the **GetCustomAttributes** method to obtain the set of custom attributes applied to them.

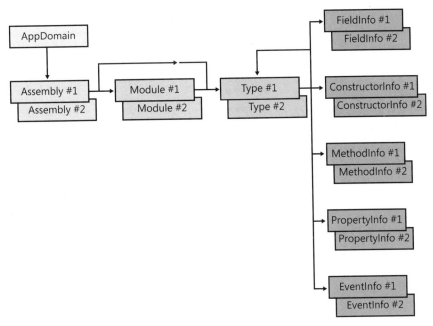

FIGURE 23-2 Types an application uses to walk reflection's object model

BindingFlags: Filtering the Kinds of Members That Are Returned

You query a type's members by calling **Type**'s **GetMembers**, **GetNestedTypes**, **GetFields**, **GetConstructors**, **GetMethods**, **GetProperties**, or **GetEvents** methods. When you call any of these methods, you can pass in an instance of a **System.Reflection.BindingFlags** enumerated type. The enumerated type identifies a set of bit flags OR'd together to help you filter the members that are returned from these methods. Table 23-2 shows the relevant symbols defined by the **BindingFlags** enumerated type.

All of the methods that return a set of members have an overload that takes no arguments at all. When you don't pass a **BindingFlags** argument, all of these methods return only the public members. In other words, the default is **BindingFlags.Public | BindingFlags. Instance | BindingFlags.Static**.

Note that **Type** also defines **GetMember**, **GetNestedType**, **GetField**, **GetConstructor**, **GetMethod**, **GetProperty**, and **GetEvent** methods. These methods allow you to pass in a **String** that identifies a member's name to look up. This is when **BindingFlags**'s **IgnoreCase** flag comes in handy.

TABLE 23-2 **Search Symbols Defined by the** `BindingFlags` **Enumerated Type**

Symbol	Value	Description
`Default`	0x00	A placeholder for no flags specified. Use this flag when you don't want to specify any of the flags listed in the remainder of this table.
`IgnoreCase`	0x01	Return members matching specified string regardless of case.
`DeclaredOnly`	0x02	Return only members of the reflected type, ignoring inherited members.
`Instance`	0x04	Return instance members.
`Static`	0x08	Return static members.
`Public`	0x10	Return public members.
`NonPublic`	0x20	Return non-public members.
`FlattenHierarchy`	0x40	Return static members defined by base types.

Discovering a Type's Interfaces

To obtain the set of interfaces that a type inherits, you can call **Type**'s **FindInterfaces**, **GetInterface**, or **GetInterfaces** method. All of these methods return **Type** objects that represent an interface. Note that these methods scan the type's inheritance hierarchy and return all of the interfaces defined on the specified type as well as all of its base types.

Determining which members of a type implement a particular interface is a little complicated because multiple interface definitions can all define the same method. For example, the **IBookRetailer** and **IMusicRetailer** interfaces might both define a method named **Purchase**. To get the **MethodInfo** objects for a specific interface, you call **Type**'s **GetInterfaceMap** instance method passing the interface type as an argument. This method returns an instance of a **System.Reflection.InterfaceMapping** (a value type). The **InterfaceMapping** type defines the four public fields listed in Table 23-3.

TABLE 23-3 **Public Fields Defined by the** `InterfaceMapping` **Type**

Field Name	Data Type	Description
`TargetType`	`Type`	This is the type that was used to call **GetInterfaceMapping**.
`InterfaceType`	`Type`	This is the type of the interface passed to **GetInterfaceMapping**.
`InterfaceMethods`	`MethodInfo[]`	This is an array in which each element exposes information about an interface's method.
`TargetMethods`	`MethodInfo[]`	This is an array in which each element exposes information about the method that the type defines to implement the corresponding interface's method.

The **InterfaceMethods** and **TargetMethods** arrays run parallel to each other; that is, **InterfaceMethods[0]** identifies the interface's **MethodInfo**, and **TargetMethods[0]** identifies the method defined by the type that implements this interface method. Here is some code that shows how to discover the interfaces and interface methods defined by a type:

```
using System;
using System.Reflection;

// Define two interfaces for testing
internal interface IBookRetailer : IDisposable {
   void Purchase();
   void ApplyDiscount();
}

internal interface IMusicRetailer {
   void Purchase();
}


// This class implements 2 interfaces defined by this assembly
// and 1 interface defined by another assembly
internal sealed class MyRetailer : IBookRetailer, IMusicRetailer, IDisposable {
   // IBookRetailer methods
   void IBookRetailer.Purchase() { }
   public void ApplyDiscount() { }

   // IMusicRetailer method
   void IMusicRetailer.Purchase() { }

   // IDisposable method
   public void Dispose() { }

   // MyRetailer method (not an interface method)
   public void Purchase() { }
}


public static class Program {
   public static void Main() {
      // Find interfaces implemented by MyRetailer where the interface is
      // defined in our own assembly. This is accomplished using a delegate
      // to a filter method that we pass to FindInterfaces.
      Type t = typeof(MyRetailer);
      Type[] interfaces = t.FindInterfaces(TypeFilter,  typeof(Program).Assembly);
      Console.WriteLine(
         "MyRetailer implements the following interfaces (defined in this assembly):");

      // Show information about each interface
      foreach (Type i in interfaces) {
         Console.WriteLine("\nInterface: " + i);

         // Get the type methods that map to the interface's methods
         InterfaceMapping map = t.GetInterfaceMap(i);
```

```
            for (Int32 m = 0; m < map.InterfaceMethods.Length; m++) {
                // Display the interface method name and which
                // type method implements the interface method.
                Console.WriteLine("   {0} is implemented by {1}",
                    map.InterfaceMethods[m], map.TargetMethods[m]);
            }
        }
    }


    // Returns true if type matches filter criteria
    private static Boolean TypeFilter(Type t, Object filterCriteria) {
        // Return true if the interface is defined in  assembly identified by filterCriteria
        return t.Assembly == filterCriteria;
    }
}
```

When you build and run the code above, you get the following output:

```
MyRetailer implements the following interfaces (defined in this assembly):

Interface: IBookRetailer
   Void Purchase() is implemented by Void IBookRetailer.Purchase()
   Void ApplyDiscount() is implemented by Void ApplyDiscount()

Interface: IMusicRetailer
   Void Purchase() is implemented by Void IMusicRetailer.Purchase()
```

Note that the **IDisposable** interface does not appear in the output because this interface is not declared in the EXE file's assembly.

Invoking a Type's Members

Now that you know how to discover the members defined by a type, you may want to invoke one of these members. What *invoke* means depends on the kind of member being invoked. Invoking a **FieldInfo** lets you get or set a field's value, invoking a **ConstructorInfo** lets you create an instance of the type passing arguments to a constructor, invoking a **MethodInfo** lets you call a method passing arguments and obtaining its return value, invoking a **PropertyInfo** lets you call the property's get or set accessor method, and invoking an **EventInfo** lets you add or remove an event handler.

Let's discuss how to invoke a method first because this is the most complex member you can invoke. Then we'll discuss how to invoke the other members. The **Type** class offers an **InvokeMember** method that lets you invoke a member. There are several overloaded versions of **InvokeMember**. I'll discuss one of the more common overloads; the other overloads work similarly.

```
public abstract class Type : MemberInfo, ... {
    public Object InvokeMember(
        String name,              // Name of member
        BindingFlags invokeAttr,  // How to look up members
        Binder binder,            // How to match members and arguments
        Object target,            // Object to invoke member on
        Object[] args,            // Arguments to pass to method
        CultureInfo culture);     // Culture used by some binders
    ...
}
```

When you call **InvokeMember**, it searches the type's members for a match. If no match is found, a **System.MissingMethodException**, **System.MissingFieldException**, or **System.MissingMemberException** exception is thrown. If a match is found, **InvokeMember** invokes the member. If the member returns something, **InvokeMember** returns it to you. If the member doesn't return anything, **InvokeMember** returns **null**. If the member you call throws an exception, **InvokeMember** catches the exception and throws a new **System.Reflection. TargetInvocationException**. The **TargetInvocationException** object's **InnerException** property will contain the actual exception that the invoked method threw. Personally, I don't like this behavior. I'd prefer it if **InvokeMember** didn't wrap the exception and just allowed it to come through.

Internally, **InvokeMember** performs two operations. First, it must select the appropriate member to be called—this is known as *binding*. Second, it must actually invoke the member —this is known as *invoking*. When you call **InvokeMember**, you pass a string as the **name** parameter, indicating the name of the member you want **InvokeMember** to bind to. However, the type might offer several members with the same name. After all, there might be several overloaded versions of a method, or a method and a field might have the same name. Of course, **InvokeMember** must bind to a single member before it can invoke it. All of the parameters passed to **InvokeMember** (except for the **target** parameter) are used to help **InvokeMember** decide which member to bind to. Let's take a closer look at these parameters.

The **binder** parameter identifies an object whose type is derived from the abstract **System.Reflection.Binder** type. A **Binder**-derived type is a type that encapsulates the rules for how **InvokeMember** should select a single member. The **Binder** base type defines abstract virtual methods such as **BindToField**, **BindToMethod**, **ChangeType**, **ReorderArgumentArray**, **SelectMethod**, and **SelectProperty**. Internally, **InvokeMember** calls these methods by using the **Binder** object passed via **InvokeMember**'s **binder** parameter.

Microsoft has defined an internal (undocumented) concrete type, called **System. DefaultBinder**, which is derived from **Binder**. This **DefaultBinder** type ships with the FCL, and Microsoft expects that almost everyone will use this binder. Some compiler vendors will define their own **Binder**-derived type and ship it in a runtime library used by code emitted by their compiler.[1] When you pass **null** to **InvokeMember**'s **binder** parameter, it will use a

---

[1] The code that accompanies this book includes the source code for a **SimpleBinder** class that demonstrates how to define your own **Binder**-derived type.

DefaultBinder object. **Type** offers a public, static, read-only property, **DefaultBinder**, that you can query to obtain a reference to a **DefaultBinder** object should you want one.

When a binder object has its methods called, the methods will be passed parameters to help the binder make a decision. Certainly, the binder is passed the name of the member that is being looked for. In addition, the binder's methods are passed the specified **BindingFlags** as well as the types of all of the parameters that need to be passed to the member being invoked.

Earlier in this chapter, Table 23-2 described the following **BindingFlags**: **Default**, **IgnoreCase**, **DeclaredOnly**, **Instance**, **Static**, **Public**, **NonPublic**, and **FlattenHierarchy**. The presence of these flags tells the binder which members to include in the search.

In addition to these flags, the binder examines the number of arguments passed via **InvokeMember**'s **args** parameter. The number of arguments limits the set of possible matches even further. The binder then examines the types of the arguments to limit the set even more. However, when it comes to the argument's types, the binder applies some automatic type conversions to make things a bit more flexible. For example, a type can define a method that takes a single **Int64** parameter. If you call **InvokeMember**, and in the **args** parameter, pass a reference to an array containing an **Int32** value, the **DefaultBinder** considers this a match. When invoking the method, the **Int32** value will be converted to an **Int64** value. The **DefaultBinder** supports the conversions listed in Table 23-4.

TABLE 23-4 **Conversions That DefaultBinder Supports**

Source Type	Target Type
Any type	Its base type
Any type	The interfaces it implements
Char	**UInt16, UInt32, Int32, UInt64, Int64, Single, Double**
Byte	**Char, UInt16, Int16, UInt32, Int32, UInt64, Int64, Single, Double**
SByte	**Int16, Int32, Int64, Single, Double**
UInt16	**UInt32, Int32, UInt64, Int64, Single, Double**
Int16	**Int32, Int64, Single, Double**
UInt32	**UInt64, Int64, Single, Double**
Int32	**Int64, Single, Double**
UInt64	**Single, Double**
Int64	**Single, Double**
Single	**Double**
A value type instance	A boxed version of the value type instance

There are two more **BindingFlags** that you can use to fine-tune the **DefaultBinder**'s behavior. These are described in Table 23-5.

TABLE 23-5 `BindingFlags` **Used with** `DefaultBinder`

Symbol	Value	Description
`ExactBinding`	0x010000	The binder will look for a member whose formal parameters exactly match the types of the supplied arguments.
`OptionalParamBinding`	0x040000	The binder will consider any member whose count of parameters matches the number of arguments passed. This flag is useful when there are members whose parameters have default values and for methods that take a variable number of arguments. Only **Type**'s **InvokeMember** method honors this flag.

InvokeMember's last parameter, **culture**, could also be used for binding. However, the **DefaultBinder** type completely ignores this parameter. If you define your own binder, you could use the culture parameter to help with argument type conversions. For example, the caller could pass a **String** argument with a value of "1,23." The binder could examine this string, parse it using the specified **culture**, and convert the argument's type to a **Single** (if the culture is "de-DE") or continue to consider the argument to be a **String** (if the culture is "en-US").

At this point, I've gone through all **InvokeMember**'s parameters related to binding. The one parameter I haven't discussed yet is **target**. This parameter is a reference to the object whose member you want to call. If you want to call a type's static member, you should pass **null** for this parameter.

The **InvokeMember** method is a very powerful method. It allows you to call a method (as I've been discussing), construct an instance of a type (basically by calling a constructor method), get or set a field, or get or set a property. You tell **InvokeMember** which of these actions you want to perform by specifying one of the **BindingFlags** listed in Table 23-6.

For the most part, the flags in Table 23-6 are mutually exclusive—you must pick one and only one when calling **InvokeMember**. However, you can specify both **GetField** and **GetProperty**, in which case **InvokeMember** searches for a matching field first and then for a matching property if it doesn't find a matching field. Likewise, **SetField** and **SetProperty** can both be specified and are matched the same way. The binder uses these flags to narrow the set of possible matches. If you specify the **BindingFlags.CreateInstance** flag, the binder knows that it can select only a constructor method.

TABLE 23-6 `BindingFlags` Used with `InvokeMember`

Symbol	Value	Description
`InvokeMethod`	0x0100	Tells **InvokeMember** to call a method
`CreateInstance`	0x0200	Tells **InvokeMember** to create a new object and call its constructor
`GetField`	0x0400	Tells **InvokeMember** to get a field's value
`SetField`	0x0800	Tells **InvokeMember** to set a field's value
`GetProperty`	0x1000	Tells **InvokeMember** to call a property's get accessor method
`SetProperty`	0x2000	Tells **InvokeMember** to call a property's set accessor method

Important With what I've told you so far, it would seem that reflection makes it easy to bind to a non-public member and invoke the member allowing application code a way to access private members that a compiler would normally prohibit the code from accessing. However, reflection uses code access security (CAS) to ensure that its power isn't abused or exploited.

When you call a method to bind to a member, the CLR first checks to see whether the member you're trying to bind to would be visible to you at compile time. If it would be, the bind is successful. If the member wouldn't normally be accessible to you, the method demands the **System.Security.Permissions.ReflectionPermission** permission, checking to see whether the **System.Security.Permissions.ReflectionPermissionFlags**'s **TypeInformation** bit is set. If this flag is set, the method will bind to the member. If the demand fails, a **System.Security.SecurityException** is thrown.

When you call a method to invoke a member, the method performs the same kind of check that it would when binding to a member. But this time, it checks whether the **ReflectionPermission** has **ReflectionPermissionFlag**'s **MemberAccess** bit set. If the bit is set, the member is invoked; otherwise, a **SecurityException** is thrown.

Of course, if your assembly has full-trust, security checks are assumed to be successful allowing binding and invoking to just work. However, you should never, ever use reflection to access any of a type's undocumented members because a future version of the assembly may easily break your code.

Bind Once, Invoke Multiple Times

Type's **InvokeMember** method gives you access to all of a type's members. However, you should be aware that every time you call **InvokeMember**, it must bind to a particular member and then invoke it. Having the binder select the right member each time you want to invoke a member is time-consuming, and if you do it a lot, your application's performance will suffer. So if you plan on accessing a member frequently, you're better off binding to the desired member once and then accessing that member as often as you want.

In this chapter, we've already discussed how to bind to a member by calling one of **Type**'s methods: **GetFields**, **GetConstructors**, **GetMethods**, **GetProperties**, **GetEvents**, or any similar method. All of these methods return references to objects whose type offers methods to access the specific member directly. Table 23-7 shows which method to call for each kind of member to invoke that member.

TABLE 23-7 How to Invoke a Member After Binding to It

Type of Member	Method to Invoke Member
`FieldInfo`	Call **GetValue** to get a field's value. Call **SetValue** to set a field's value.
`ConstructorInfo`	Call **Invoke** to construct an instance of the type and call a constructor.
`MethodInfo`	Call **Invoke** to call a method of the type.
`PropertyInfo`	Call **GetValue** to call a property's get accessor method. Call **SetValue** to call a property's set accessor method.
`EventInfo`	Call **AddEventHandler** to call an event's add accessor method. Call **RemoveEventHandler** to call an event's remove accessor method.

The **PropertyInfo** type represents metadata information about a property (as discussed in Chapter 10, "Properties"); that is, **PropertyInfo** offers **CanRead**, **CanWrite**, and **PropertyType** read-only properties. These properties indicate whether a property is readable or writeable and what data type the property is. **PropertyInfo** has a **GetAccessors** method that returns an array of **MethodInfo** elements: one for the get accessor method (if it exists), and one for the set accessor method (if it exists). Of more value are **PropertyInfo**'s **GetGetMethod** and **GetSetMethod** methods, each of which returns just one **MethodInfo** object. **PropertyInfo**'s **GetValue** and **SetValue** methods exist for convenience; internally, they get the appropriate **MethodInfo** and call it. To support parameterful properties (C# indexers), the **GetValue** and **SetValue** methods offer an **index** parameter of **Object[]** type.

The **EventInfo** type represents metadata information about an event (as discussed in Chapter 11, "Events"). The **EventInfo** type offers an **EventHandlerType** read-only property that returns the **Type** of the event's underlying delegate. The **EventInfo** type also has **GetAddMethod** and **GetRemoveMethod** methods, which return the **MethodInfo** corresponding to the method that adds or removes a delegate to/from the event. To add or remove a delegate, you can invoke these **MethodInfo** objects, or you can call **EventInfo**'s more convenient **AddEventHandler** and **RemoveEventHandler** methods.

When you call one of the methods listed in the right column of Table 23-7, you're not binding to a member; you're just invoking the member. You can call any of these methods multiple times, and because binding isn't necessary, the performance will be pretty good.

You might notice that **ConstructorInfo**'s **Invoke**, **MethodInfo**'s **Invoke**, and **PropertyInfo**'s **GetValue** and **SetValue** methods offer overloaded versions that take a reference to a **Binder**-derived object and some **BindingFlags**. This would lead you to believe that these methods bind to a member. However, they don't.

When calling any of these methods, the **Binder**-derived object is used to perform type conversions on the supplied method parameters, such as converting an **Int32** argument to an **Int64**, so that the already selected method can be called. As for the **BindingFlags** parameter, the only flag that can be passed here is **BindingFlags.SuppressChangeType**. However, binders are free to ignore this flag. Fortunately, the **DefaultBinder** class heeds this flag. When **DefaultBinder** sees this flag, it won't convert any arguments. If you use this flag and the arguments passed don't match the arguments expected by the method, an **ArgumentException** will be thrown.

Usually when you use the **BindingFlags.ExactBinding** flag to bind to a member, you'll specify the **BindingFlags.SuppressChangeType** flag to invoke the member. If you don't use these two flags in tandem, it's unlikely that invoking the member will be successful unless the arguments you pass happen to be exactly what the method expects. By the way, if you call **MemberInfo**'s **InvokeMethod** to bind and invoke a member, you'll probably want to specify both or neither of the two binding flags.

The following sample application demonstrates the various ways to use reflection to access a type's members. The **SomeType** class represents a type that has various members: a private field (**m_someField**), a public constructor (**SomeType**) that takes an **Int32** argument passed by reference, a public method (**ToString**), a public property (**SomeProp**), and a public event (**SomeEvent**). Having defined the **SomeType** type, I offer three different methods that use reflection to access **SomeType**'s members. Each method uses reflection in a different way to accomplish the same thing:

- The **UseInvokeMemberToBindAndInvokeTheMember** method demonstrates how to use **Type**'s **InvokeMember** to both bind and invoke a member.

- The **BindToMemberThenInvokeTheMember** method demonstrates how to bind to a member and invoke it later. This technique yields faster-performing code if you intend to invoke the same member on different objects multiple times.

- The **BindToMemberCreateDelegateToMemberThenInvokeTheMember** method demonstrates how to bind to an object or member, and then it creates a delegate that refers to that object or member. Calling through the delegate is very fast, and this technique yields even faster performance if you intend to invoke the same member on the same object multiple times.

- The **UseDynamicToBindAndInvokeTheMember** method demonstrates how to use C# **dynamic** primitive type (discussed at the end of Chapter 5, "Primitive, Reference, and Value Types") to simplify the syntax for accessing members. In addition, this technique can give reasonably good performance if you intend to invoke the same member on different objects that are all of the same type because the binding will happen once per type and be cached so that it can be invoked multiple times quickly. You can also use this technique to invoke a member on objects of different types.

```
using System;
using System.Reflection;
using Microsoft.CSharp.RuntimeBinder;


// This class is used to demonstrate reflection
// It has a field, constructor, method, property, and an event
internal sealed class SomeType {
   private Int32 m_someField;
   public SomeType(ref Int32 x) { x *= 2; }
   public override String ToString() { return m_someField.ToString(); }
   public Int32 SomeProp {
      get { return m_someField; }
set {
   if (value < 1)
      throw new ArgumentOutOfRangeException("value");
   m_someField = value;
}
   public event EventHandler SomeEvent;
   private void NoCompilerWarnings() { SomeEvent.ToString();}
}

public static class Program {
   private const BindingFlags c_bf = BindingFlags.DeclaredOnly | BindingFlags.Public |
      BindingFlags.NonPublic | BindingFlags.Instance;

   public static void Main() {
      Type t = typeof(SomeType);
      UseInvokeMemberToBindAndInvokeTheMember(t);
      Console.WriteLine();

      BindToMemberThenInvokeTheMember(t);
      Console.WriteLine();

      BindToMemberCreateDelegateToMemberThenInvokeTheMember(t);
      Console.WriteLine();

      UseDynamicToBindAndInvokeTheMember(t);
      Console.WriteLine();
   }


   private static void UseInvokeMemberToBindAndInvokeTheMember(Type t) {
      Console.WriteLine("UseInvokeMemberToBindAndInvokeTheMember");

      // Construct an instance of the Type
      Object[] args = new Object[] { 12 };   // Constructor arguments
      Console.WriteLine("x before constructor called: " + args[0]);
      Object obj = t.InvokeMember(null, c_bf | BindingFlags.CreateInstance,
         null, null, args);
      Console.WriteLine("Type: " + obj.GetType().ToString());
      Console.WriteLine("x after constructor returns: " + args[0]);
```

```
      // Read and write to a field
      t.InvokeMember("m_someField", c_bf | BindingFlags.SetField,
         null, obj, new Object[] { 5 });
      Int32 v = (Int32)t.InvokeMember("m_someField", c_bf | BindingFlags.GetField,
         null, obj, null);
      Console.WriteLine("someField: " + v);

      // Call a method
      String s = (String)
         t.InvokeMember("ToString", c_bf | BindingFlags.InvokeMethod, null, obj, null);
      Console.WriteLine("ToString: " + s);

      // Read and write a property
      try {
         t.InvokeMember("SomeProp", c_bf | BindingFlags.SetProperty,
            null, obj, new Object[] { 0 });
      }
      catch (TargetInvocationException e) {
         if (e.InnerException.GetType() != typeof(ArgumentOutOfRangeException)) throw;
         Console.WriteLine("Property set catch.");
      }
      t.InvokeMember("SomeProp", c_bf | BindingFlags.SetProperty,
         null, obj, new Object[] { 2 });
      v = (Int32)t.InvokeMember("SomeProp", c_bf | BindingFlags.GetProperty,
         null, obj, null);
      Console.WriteLine("SomeProp: " + v);

      // Add and remove a delegate from the event by invoking the event's add/remove methods
      EventHandler eh = new EventHandler(EventCallback);
      t.InvokeMember("add_SomeEvent", c_bf | BindingFlags.InvokeMethod,
         null, obj, new Object[] { eh });
      t.InvokeMember("remove_SomeEvent", c_bf | BindingFlags.InvokeMethod,
         null, obj, new Object[] { eh });
   }


   private static void BindToMemberThenInvokeTheMember(Type t) {
      Console.WriteLine("BindToMemberThenInvokeTheMember");

      // Construct an instance
      // ConstructorInfo ctor =
      //    t.GetConstructor(new Type[] { Type.GetType("System.Int32&") });
      ConstructorInfo ctor = t.GetConstructor(new Type[] { typeof(Int32).MakeByRefType() });
      Object[] args = new Object[] { 12 };  // Constructor arguments
      Console.WriteLine("x before constructor called: " + args[0]);
      Object obj = ctor.Invoke(args);
      Console.WriteLine("Type: " + obj.GetType().ToString());
      Console.WriteLine("x after constructor returns: " + args[0]);

      // Read and write to a field
      FieldInfo fi = obj.GetType().GetField("m_someField", c_bf);
      fi.SetValue(obj, 33);
      Console.WriteLine("someField: " + fi.GetValue(obj));
```

```
   // Call a method
   MethodInfo mi = obj.GetType().GetMethod("ToString", c_bf);
   String s = (String)mi.Invoke(obj, null);
   Console.WriteLine("ToString: " + s);

   // Read and write a property
   PropertyInfo pi = obj.GetType().GetProperty("SomeProp", typeof(Int32));
   try {
      pi.SetValue(obj, 0, null);
   }
   catch (TargetInvocationException e) {
      if (e.InnerException.GetType() != typeof(ArgumentOutOfRangeException)) throw;
      Console.WriteLine("Property set catch.");
   }
   pi.SetValue(obj, 2, null);
   Console.WriteLine("SomeProp: " + pi.GetValue(obj, null));

   // Add and remove a delegate from the event
   EventInfo ei = obj.GetType().GetEvent("SomeEvent", c_bf);
   EventHandler ts = new EventHandler(EventCallback); // See ei.EventHandlerType
   ei.AddEventHandler(obj, ts);
   ei.RemoveEventHandler(obj, ts);
}


// Callback method added to the event
private static void EventCallback(Object sender, EventArgs e) { }


private static void BindToMemberCreateDelegateToMemberThenInvokeTheMember(Type t) {
   Console.WriteLine("BindToMemberCreateDelegateToMemberThenInvokeTheMember");

   // Construct an instance (You can't create a delegate to a constructor)
   Object[] args = new Object[] { 12 };  // Constructor arguments
   Console.WriteLine("x before constructor called: " + args[0]);
   Object obj = Activator.CreateInstance(t, args);
   Console.WriteLine("Type: " + obj.GetType().ToString());
   Console.WriteLine("x after constructor returns: " + args[0]);

   // NOTE: You can't create a delegate to a field

   // Call a method
   MethodInfo mi = obj.GetType().GetMethod("ToString", c_bf);
   var toString = (Func<String>) Delegate.CreateDelegate(typeof(Func<String>), obj, mi);
   String s = toString();
   Console.WriteLine("ToString: " + s);

   // Read and write a property
   PropertyInfo pi = obj.GetType().GetProperty("SomeProp", typeof(Int32));
   var setSomeProp = (Action<Int32>)
      Delegate.CreateDelegate(typeof(Action<Int32>), obj, pi.GetSetMethod());
   try {
      setSomeProp(0);
   }
```

```
      catch (ArgumentOutOfRangeException) {
         Console.WriteLine("Property set catch.");
      }
      setSomeProp(2);
      var getSomeProp = (Func<Int32>)
         Delegate.CreateDelegate(typeof(Func<Int32>), obj, pi.GetGetMethod());
      Console.WriteLine("SomeProp: " + getSomeProp());

      // Add and remove a delegate from the event
      EventInfo ei = obj.GetType().GetEvent("SomeEvent", c_bf);
      var addSomeEvent = (Action<EventHandler>)
         Delegate.CreateDelegate(typeof(Action<EventHandler>), obj, ei.GetAddMethod());
      addSomeEvent(EventCallback);
      var removeSomeEvent = (Action<EventHandler>)
         Delegate.CreateDelegate(typeof(Action<EventHandler>), obj, ei.GetRemoveMethod());
      removeSomeEvent(EventCallback);
   }


   private static void UseDynamicToBindAndInvokeTheMember(Type t) {
      Console.WriteLine("UseDynamicToBindAndInvokeTheMember");

      // Construct an instance (You can't create a delegate to a constructor)
      Object[] args = new Object[] { 12 };  // Constructor arguments
      Console.WriteLine("x before constructor called: " + args[0]);
      dynamic obj = Activator.CreateInstance(t, args);
      Console.WriteLine("Type: " + obj.GetType().ToString());
      Console.WriteLine("x after constructor returns: " + args[0]);

      // Read and write to a field
      try {
         obj.m_someField = 5;
         Int32 v = (Int32)obj.m_someField;
         Console.WriteLine("someField: " + v);
      }
      catch (RuntimeBinderException e) {
         // We get here because the field is private
         Console.WriteLine("Failed to access field: " + e.Message);
      }

      // Call a method
      String s = (String)obj.ToString();
      Console.WriteLine("ToString: " + s);

      // Read and write a property
      try {
         obj.SomeProp = 0;
      }

      catch (ArgumentOutOfRangeException) {
         Console.WriteLine("Property set catch.");
      }
      obj.SomeProp = 2;
      Int32 val = (Int32)obj.SomeProp;
      Console.WriteLine("SomeProp: " + val);
```

```
        // Add and remove a delegate from the event
        obj.SomeEvent += new EventHandler(EventCallback);
        obj.SomeEvent -= new EventHandler(EventCallback);
    }
}
```

If you build and run this code, you'll see the following output:

```
UseInvokeMemberToBindAndInvokeTheMember
x before constructor called: 12
Type: SomeType
x after constructor returns: 24
someField: 5
ToString: 5
Property set catch.
SomeProp: 2

BindToMemberThenInvokeTheMember
x before constructor called: 12
Type: SomeType
x after constructor returns: 24
someField: 33
ToString: 33
Property set catch.
SomeProp: 2

BindToMemberCreateDelegateToMemberThenInvokeTheMember
x before constructor called: 12
Type: SomeType
x after constructor returns: 24
ToString: 0
Property set catch.
SomeProp: 2

UseDynamicToBindAndInvokeTheMember
x before constructor called: 12
Type: SomeType
x after constructor returns: 24
Failed to access field: 'SomeType.m_someField' is inaccessible due to its protection level
ToString: 0
Property set catch.
SomeProp: 2
```

Notice that **SomeType**'s constructor takes an **Int32** by reference as its only parameter. The previous code shows how to call this constructor and how to examine the modified **Int32** value after the constructor returns. Furthermore, near the top of the **BindToMemberThenInvokeTheMember** method is a call to **Type**'s **GetType** method passing in a string of **"System.Int32&"**. The ampersand (**&**) in the string allows me to identify a parameter passed by reference. This ampersand is part of the Backus-Naur Form grammar for type names, which you can look up in the FCL documentation. That line of code could also have been written like this:

```
ConstructorInfo ctor = t.GetConstructor(new Type[] { typeof(Int32).MakeByRefType() });
```

Using Binding Handles to Reduce Your Process's Memory Consumption

Many applications bind to a bunch of types (**Type** objects) or type members (**MemberInfo**-derived objects) and save these objects in a collection of some sort. Then later, the application searches the collection for a particular object and then invokes this object. This is a fine way of doing things except for one small issue: **Type** and **MemberInfo**-derived objects require a lot of memory. So if an application holds on to too many of these objects and invokes them occasionally, the application's memory consumption increases dramatically, having an adverse effect on the application's performance.

Internally, the CLR has a more compact way of representing this information. The CLR creates these objects for our applications only to make things easier for developers. The CLR doesn't need these big objects itself in order to run. Developers who are saving/caching a lot of **Type** and **MemberInfo**-derived objects can reduce their working set by using runtime handles instead of objects. The FCL defines three runtime handle types (all defined in the System namespace): **RuntimeTypeHandle**, **RuntimeFieldHandle**, and **RuntimeMethodHandle**. All of these types are value types that contain just one field, an **IntPtr**; this makes instances of these types extremely cheap (memory-wise). The **IntPtr** field is a handle that refers to a type, field, or method in an AppDomain's loader heap. So what you need now is an easy and efficient way to convert a heavyweight **Type/MemberInfo** object to a lightweight runtime handle instance and vice versa. Fortunately, this is easy using the following conversion methods and properties:

- To convert a **Type** object to a **RuntimeTypeHandle**, call **Type**'s static **GetTypeHandle** method passing in the reference to the **Type** object.

- To convert a **RuntimeTypeHandle** to a **Type** object, call **Type**'s static **GetTypeFromHandle** method passing in the **RuntimeTypeHandle**.

- To convert a **FieldInfo** object to a **RuntimeFieldHandle**, query **FieldInfo**'s instance read-only **FieldHandle** property.

- To convert a **RuntimeFieldHandle** to a **FieldInfo** object, call **FieldInfo**'s static **GetFieldFromHandle** method.

- To convert a **MethodInfo** object to a **RuntimeMethodHandle**, query **MethodInfo**'s instance read-only **MethodHandle** property.

- To convert a **RuntimeMethodHandle** to a **MethodInfo** object, call **MethodInfo**'s static **GetMethodFromHandle** method.

The program sample below acquires a lot of **MethodInfo** objects, converts them to **RuntimeMethodHandle** instances, and shows the working set difference:

```
using System;
using System.Reflection;
using System.Collections.Generic;
```

```
public sealed class Program {
   private const BindingFlags c_bf = BindingFlags.FlattenHierarchy | BindingFlags.Instance |
      BindingFlags.Static | BindingFlags.Public | BindingFlags.NonPublic;

   public static void Main() {
      // Show size of heap before doing any reflection stuff
      Show("Before doing anything");

      // Build cache of MethodInfo objects for all methods in MSCorlib.dll
      List<MethodBase> methodInfos = new List<MethodBase>();
      foreach (Type t in typeof(Object).Assembly.GetExportedTypes()) {
         // Skip over any generic types
         if (t.IsGenericTypeDefinition) continue;

         MethodBase[] mb = t.GetMethods(c_bf);
         methodInfos.AddRange(mb);
      }

      // Show number of methods and size of heap after binding to all methods
      Console.WriteLine("# of methods={0:N0}", methodInfos.Count);
      Show("After building cache of MethodInfo objects");

      // Build cache of RuntimeMethodHandles for all MethodInfo objects
      List<RuntimeMethodHandle> methodHandles =
         methodInfos.ConvertAll<RuntimeMethodHandle>(mb => mb.MethodHandle);

      Show("Holding MethodInfo and RuntimeMethodHandle cache");
      GC.KeepAlive(methodInfos); // Prevent cache from being GC'd early

      methodInfos = null;         // Allow cache to be GC'd now
      Show("After freeing MethodInfo objects");

      methodInfos = methodHandles.ConvertAll<MethodBase>(
         rmh=> MethodBase.GetMethodFromHandle(rmh));
      Show("Size of heap after re-creating MethodInfo objects");
      GC.KeepAlive(methodHandles);  // Prevent cache from being GC'd early
      GC.KeepAlive(methodInfos);    // Prevent cache from being GC'd early

      methodHandles = null;        // Allow cache to be GC'd now
      methodInfos = null;          // Allow cache to be GC'd now
      Show("After freeing MethodInfos and RuntimeMethodHandles");
   }
}
```

When I compiled and executed this program, I got the following output:

```
Heap size=    85,000 - Before doing anything
# of methods=48,467
Heap size= 7,065,632 - After building cache of MethodInfo objects
Heap size= 7,453,496 - Holding MethodInfo and RuntimeMethodHandle cache
Heap size= 6,732,704 - After freeing MethodInfo objects
Heap size= 7,372,704 - Size of heap after re-creating MethodInfo objects
Heap size=   192,232 - After freeing MethodInfos and RuntimeMethodHandles
```

Chapter 24
Runtime Serialization

Serialization is the process of converting an object or a graph of connected objects into a stream of bytes. *Deserialization* is the process of converting a stream of bytes back into its graph of connected objects. The ability to convert objects to and from a byte stream is an incredibly useful mechanism. Here are some examples:

- An application's state (object graph) can easily be saved in a disk file or database and then restored the next time the application is run. ASP.NET saves and restores session state by way of serialization and deserialization.

- A set of objects can easily be copied to the system's clipboard and then pasted into the same or another application. In fact, Windows Forms and Windows Presentation Foundation (WPF) use this.

- A set of objects can be cloned and set aside as a "backup" while a user manipulates the "main" set of objects.

- A set of objects can easily be sent over the network to a process running on another machine. The Microsoft .NET Framework's remoting architecture serializes and deserializes objects that are marshaled by value. It is also used to send objects across AppDomain boundaries, as discussed in Chapter 22, "CLR Hosting and AppDomains."

In addition to the above, once you have serialized objects in a byte stream in memory, it is quite easy to process the data in more useful ways, such as encrypting and compressing the data.

With serialization being so useful, it is no wonder that many programmers have spent count-less hours developing code to perform these types of actions. Historically, this code is difficult to write and is extremely tedious and error-prone. Some of the difficult issues that developers need to grapple with are communication protocols, client/server data type mismatches (such as little-endian/big-endian issues), error handling, objects that refer to other objects, in and out parameters, arrays of structures, and the list goes on.

Well, you'll be happy to know that the .NET Framework has fantastic support for serialization and deserialization built right into it. This means that all of the difficult issues mentioned above are now handled completely and transparently by the .NET Framework. As a developer, you can work with your objects before serialization and after deserialization and have the .NET Framework handle the stuff in the middle.

In this chapter, I explain how the .NET Framework exposes its serialization and deserialization services. For almost all data types, the default behavior of these services will be sufficient, meaning that it is almost no work for you to make your own types serializable. However, there is a small minority of types where the serialization service's default behavior will not be suf-ficient. Fortunately, the serialization services are very extensible, and I will also explain how to tap into these extensibility mechanisms, allowing you to do some pretty powerful things when serializing or deserializing objects. For example, I'll demonstrate how to serialize Version 1 of an object out to a disk file and then deserialize it a year later into an object of Version 2.

> **Note** This chapter focuses on the runtime serialization technology in the common language runtime (CLR), which has a deep understanding of CLR data types and can serialize all the public, protected, internal, and even private fields of an object to a compressed binary stream for high performance. See the **System.Runtime.Serialization.NetDataContractSerializer** class if you wish to serialize CLR data types to an XML stream. The .NET Framework also offers other serialization technologies that are designed more for interoperating between CLR data types and non-CLR data types. These other serialization technologies use the **System.Xml.Serialization.XmlSerializer** class and the **System.Runtime.Serialization.DataContractSerializer** class.

Serialization/Deserialization Quick Start

Let's start off by looking at some code:

```
using System;
using System.Collections.Generic;
using System.IO;
using System.Runtime.Serialization.Formatters.Binary;

internal static class QuickStart {
   public static void Main() {
      // Create a graph of objects to serialize them to the stream
      var objectGraph = new List<String> { "Jeff", "Kristin", "Aidan", "Grant" };
      Stream stream = SerializeToMemory(objectGraph);
```

```
        // Reset everything for this demo
        stream.Position = 0;
        objectGraph = null;

        // Deserialize the objects and prove it worked
        objectGraph = (List<String>) DeserializeFromMemory(stream);
        foreach (var s in objectGraph) Console.WriteLine(s);
    }

    private static MemoryStream SerializeToMemory(Object objectGraph) {
        // Construct a stream that is to hold the serialized objects
        MemoryStream stream = new MemoryStream();

        // Construct a serialization formatter that does all the hard work
        BinaryFormatter formatter = new BinaryFormatter();

        // Tell the formatter to serialize the objects into the stream
        formatter.Serialize(stream, objectGraph);

        // Return the stream of serialized objects back to the caller
        return stream;
    }

    private static Object DeserializeFromMemory(Stream stream) {
        // Construct a serialization formatter that does all the hard work
        BinaryFormatter formatter = new BinaryFormatter();

        // Tell the formatter to deserialize the objects from the stream
        return formatter.Deserialize(stream);
    }
}
```

Wow, look how simple this is! The **SerializeToMemory** method constructs a **System. IO.MemoryStream** object. This object identifies where the serialized block of bytes is to be placed. Then the method constructs a **BinaryFormatter** object (which can be found in the **System.Runtime.Serialization.Formatters.Binary** namespace). A formatter is a type (implementing the **System.Runtime.Serialization.IFormatter** interface) that knows how to serialize and deserialize an object graph. The Framework Class Library (FCL) ships with two formatters: the **BinaryFormatter** (used in this code example) and a **SoapFormatter** (which can be found in the **System.Runtime.Serialization.Formatters.Soap** namespace and is implemented in the System.Runtime.Serialization.Formatters.Soap.dll assembly).

> **Note** As of version 3.5 of the .NET Framework, the **SoapFormatter** class is obsolete and should not be used in production code. However, it can still be useful for debugging serialization code as it produces XML text which you can read. To use XML serialization and deserialization in production code, see the **XmlSerializer** and **DataContractSerializer** classes.

To serialize a graph of objects, just call the formatter's **Serialize** method and pass it two things: a reference to a stream object and a reference to the object graph that you wish to serialize. The stream object identifies where the serialized bytes should be placed and can be an object of any type derived from the **System.IO.Stream** abstract base class. This means that you can serialize an object graph to a **MemoryStream**, a **FileStream**, a **NetworkStream**, and so on.

The second parameter to **Serialize** is a reference to an object. This object could be anything: an **Int32**, a **String**, a **DateTime**, an **Exception**, a **List<String>**, a **Dictionary<Int32, DatTime>**, and so on. The object referred to by the **objectGraph** parameter may refer to other objects. For example, **objectGraph** may refer to a collection that refers to a set of objects. These objects may also refer to other objects. When the formatter's **Serialize** method is called, all objects in the graph are serialized to the stream.

Formatters know how to serialize the complete object graph by referring to the metadata that describes each object's type. The **Serialize** method uses reflection to see what instance fields are in each object's type as it is serialized. If any of these fields refer to other objects, then the formatter's **Serialize** method knows to serialize these objects, too.

Formatters have very intelligent algorithms. They know to serialize each object in the graph no more than once out to the stream. That is, if two objects in the graph refer to each other, then the formatter detects this, serializes each object just once, and avoids entering into an infinite loop.

In my **SerializeToMemory** method, when the formatter's **Serialize** method returns, the **MemoryStream** is simply returned to the caller. The application uses the contents of this flat byte array any way it desires. For example, it could save it in a file, copy it to the clipboard, send it over a wire, or whatever.

The **DeserializeFromStream** method deserializes a stream back into an object graph. This method is even simpler than serializing an object graph. In this code, a **BinaryFormatter** is constructed and then its **Deserialize** method is called. This method takes the stream as a parameter and returns a reference to the root object within the deserialized object graph.

Internally, the formatter's **Deserialize** method examines the contents of the stream, constructs instances of all the objects that are in the stream, and initializes the fields in all these objects so that they have the same values they had when the object graph was serialized. Typically, you will cast the object reference returned from the **Deserialize** method into the type that your application is expecting.

Note Here's a fun, useful method that uses serialization to make a deep copy, or clone, of an object:

```
private static Object DeepClone(Object original) {
   // Construct a temporary memory stream
   using (MemoryStream stream = new MemoryStream()) {
```

```
        // Construct a serialization formatter that does all the hard work
        BinaryFormatter formatter = new BinaryFormatter();

        // This line is explained in this chapter's "Streaming Contexts" section
        formatter.Context = new StreamingContext(StreamingContextStates.Clone);

        // Serialize the object graph into the memory stream
        formatter.Serialize(stream, original);

        // Seek back to the start of the memory stream before deserializing
        stream.Position = 0;

        // Deserialize the graph into a new set of objects and
        // return the root of the graph (deep copy) to the caller
        return formatter.Deserialize(stream);
    }
}
```

At this point, I'd like to add a few notes to our discussion. First, it is up to you to ensure that your code uses the same formatter for both serialization and deserialization. For example, don't write code that serializes an object graph using the **SoapFormatter** and then deserializes the graph using the **BinaryFormatter**. If **Deserialize** can't decipher the contents of the stream, then a **System.Runtime.Serialization.SerializationException** exception will be thrown.

The second thing I'd like to point out is that it is possible and also quite useful to serialize multiple object graphs out to a single stream. For example, let's say that we have the following two class definitions:

```
[Serializable] internal sealed class Customer { /* ... */ }
[Serializable] internal sealed class Order    { /* ... */ }
```

And then, in the main class of our application, we define the following static fields:

```
private static List<Customer> s_customers      = new List<Customer>();
private static List<Order>    s_pendingOrders  = new List<Order>();
private static List<Order>    s_processedOrders = new List<Order>();
```

We can now serialize our application's state to a single stream with a method that looks like this:

```
private static void SaveApplicationState(Stream stream) {
    // Construct a serialization formatter that does all the hard work
    BinaryFormatter formatter = new BinaryFormatter();

    // Serialize our application's entire state
    formatter.Serialize(stream, s_customers);
    formatter.Serialize(stream, s_pendingOrders);
    formatter.Serialize(stream, s_processedOrders);
}
```

To reconstruct our application's state, we would deserialize the state with a method that looks like this:

```
private static void RestoreApplicationState(Stream stream) {
    // Construct a serialization formatter that does all the hard work
    BinaryFormatter formatter = new BinaryFormatter();

    // Deserialize our application's entire state (same order as serialized)
    s_customers       = (List<Customer>) formatter.Deserialize(stream);
    s_pendingOrders   = (List<Order>)    formatter.Deserialize(stream);
    s_processedOrders = (List<Order>)    formatter.Deserialize(stream);
}
```

The third and last thing I'd like to point out has to do with assemblies. When serializing an object, the full name of the type and the name of the type's defining assembly are written to the stream. By default, **BinaryFormatter** outputs the assembly's full identity, which includes the assembly's file name (without extension), version number, culture, and public key information. When deserializing an object, the formatter first grabs the assembly identity and ensures that the assembly is loaded into the executing AppDomain by calling **System.Reflection.Assembly**'s **Load** method (discussed in Chapter 23, "Assembly Loading and Reflection").

After an assembly has been loaded, the formatter looks in the assembly for a type matching that of the object being deserialized. If the assembly doesn't contain a matching type, an exception is thrown and no more objects can be deserialized. If a matching type is found, an instance of the type is created and its fields are initialized from the values contained in the stream. If the type's fields don't exactly match the names of the fields as read from the stream, then a **SerializationException** exception is thrown and no more objects can be deserialized. Later in this chapter, I'll discuss some sophisticated mechanisms that allow you to override some of this behavior.

Important Some extensible applications use **Assembly.LoadFrom** to load an assembly and then construct objects from types defined in the loaded assembly. These objects can be serialized to a stream without any trouble. However, when deserializing this stream, the formatter attempts to load the assembly by calling **Assembly**'s **Load** method instead of calling the **LoadFrom** method. In most cases, the CLR will not be able to locate the assembly file, causing a **SerializationException** exception to be thrown. This catches many developers by surprise: Since the objects serialized correctly, they expect that they will deserialize correctly as well.

If your application serializes objects whose types are defined in an assembly that your application loads using **Assembly.LoadFrom**, then I recommend that you implement a method whose signature matches the **System.ResolveEventHandler** delegate and register this method with **System.AppDomain**'s **AssemblyResolve** event just before calling a formatter's **Deserialize** method. (Unregister this method with the event after **Deserialize** returns.) Now, whenever the formatter fails to load an assembly, the CLR calls your **ResolveEventHandler** method. This method is passed the identity of the assembly that failed to load. The method can extract the assembly file name from the assembly's identity and use this name to construct the path where the application knows the assembly file can be found. Then, the method can call **Assembly.LoadFrom** to load the assembly and return the resulting **Assembly** reference back from the **ResolveEventHandler** method.

This section covered the basics of how to serialize and deserialize object graphs. In the remaining sections, we'll look at what you must do in order to define your own serializable types, and we'll also look at various mechanisms that allow you to have greater control over serialization and deserialization.

Making a Type Serializable

When a type is designed, the developer must make the conscious decision as to whether or not to allow instances of the type to be serializable. By default, types are not serializable. For example, the following code does not perform as expected:

```
internal struct Point { public Int32 x, y; }

private static void OptInSerialization() {
    Point pt = new Point { x = 1, y = 2 };
    using (var stream = new MemoryStream()) {
        new BinaryFormatter().Serialize(stream, pt); // throws SerializationException
    }
}
```

If you were to build and run this code in your program, you'd see that the formatter's **Serialize** method throws a **System.Runtime.Serialization.SerializationException** exception. The problem is that the developer of the **Point** type has not explicitly indicated that **Point** objects may be serialized. To solve this problem, the developer must apply the **System.SerializableAttribute** custom attribute to this type as follows. (Note that this attribute is defined in the **System** namespace, not the **System.Runtime.Serialization** namespace.)

```
[Serializable]
internal struct Point { public Int32 x, y; }
```

Now, if we rebuild the application and run it, it does perform as expected and the **Point** objects will be serialized to the stream. When serializing an object graph, the formatter checks that every object's type is serializable. If any object in the graph is not serializable, the formatter's **Serialize** method throws the **SerializationException** exception.

> **Note** When serializing a graph of objects, some of the object's types may be serializable while some of the objects may not be serializable. For performance reasons, formatters do not verify that all of the objects in the graph are serializable before serializing the graph. So, when serializing an object graph, it is entirely possible that some objects may be serialized to the stream before the **SerializationException** is thrown. If this happens, the stream contains corrupt data. If you think you may be serializing an object graph where some objects may not be serializable, your application code should be able to recover gracefully from this situation. One option is to serialize the objects into a **MemoryStream** first. Then, if all objects are successfully serialized, you can copy the bytes in the **MemoryStream** to whatever stream (i.e. file, network) you really want the bytes written to.

The **SerializableAttribute** custom attribute may be applied to reference types (**class**), value types (**struct**), enumerated types (**enum**), and delegate types (**delegate**) only. (Note that enumerated and delegate types are always serializable so there is no need to explicitly apply the **SerializableAttribute** attribute to these types.) In addition, the **SerializableAttribute** attribute is not inherited by derived types. So, given the following two type definitions, a **Person** object can be serialized but an **Employee** object cannot:

```
[Serializable]
internal class Person { ... }

internal class Employee : Person { ... }
```

To fix this, you would just apply the **SerializableAttribute** attribute to the **Employee** type as well:

```
[Serializable]
internal class Person { ... }

[Serializable]
internal class Employee : Person { ... }
```

Note that this problem was easy to fix. However, the reverse—defining a type derived from a base type that doesn't have the **SerializableAttribute** attribute applied to it—is not easy to fix. But, this is by design; if the base type doesn't allow instances of its type to be serialized, its fields cannot be serialized since a base object is effectively part of the derived object. This is why **System.Object** has the **SerializableAttribute** attribute applied to it.

> **Note** In general, it is recommended that most types you define be serializable. After all, this grants a lot of flexibility to users of your types. However, you must be aware that serialization reads all of an object's fields regardless of whether the fields are declared as **public**, **protected**, **internal**, or **private**. You might not want to make a type serializable if it contains sensitive or secure data (like passwords) or if the data would have no meaning or value if transferred.
>
> If you find yourself using a type that was not designed for serialization and you do not have the source code of the type to add serialization support, all is not lost. In the "Overriding the Assembly and/or Type When Deserializing an Object" section later in this chapter, I will explain how you can make any non-serializable type serializable.

Controlling Serialization and Deserialization

When you apply the **SerializableAttribute** custom attribute to a type, all instance fields (**public**, **private**, **protected**, and so on) are serialized.[1] However, a type may define some instance fields that should not be serialized. In general, there are two reasons why you would not want some of a type's instance fields to be serialized:

---

[1]   Do not use C#'s automatically implemented property feature to define properties inside types marked with the **[Serializable]** attribute, because the compiler generates the names of the fields and the generated names can be different each time that you recompile your code, preventing instances of your type from being deserializable.

- The field contains information that would not be valid when deserialized. For example, an object that contains a handle to a Windows kernel object (such as a file, process, thread, mutex, event, semaphore, and so on) would have no meaning when deserialized into another process or machine since Windows kernel handles are process-relative values.

- The field contains information that is easily calculated. In this case, you select which fields do not need to be serialized, thus improving your application's performance by reducing the amount of data transferred.

The code below uses the **System.NonSerializedAttribute** custom attribute to indicate which fields of the type should not be serialized. (Note that this attribute is also defined in the **System** namespace, not the **System.Runtime.Serialization** namespace.)

```
[Serializable]
internal class Circle {
   private Double m_radius;

   [NonSerialized]
   private Double m_area;

   public Circle(Double radius) {
      m_radius = radius;
      m_area = Math.PI * m_radius * m_radius;
   }

   ...
}
```

In the code above, objects of **Circle** may be serialized. However, the formatter will serialize the values in the object's **m_radius** field only. The value in the **m_area** field will not be serialized because it has the **NonSerializedAttribute** attribute applied to it. This attribute can be applied only to a type's fields, and it continues to apply to this field when inherited by another type. Of course, you may apply the **NonSerializedAttribute** attribute to multiple fields within a type.

So, let's say that our code constructs a **Circle** object as follows:

```
Circle c = new Circle(10);
```

Internally, the **m_area** field is set to a value approximate to 314.159. When this object gets serialized, only the value of the **m_radius** field (10) gets written to the stream. This is exactly what we want, but now we have a problem when the stream is deserialized back into a **Circle** object. When deserialized, the **Circle** object will get its **m_radius** field set to 10, but its **m_area** field will be initialized to 0—not 314.159!

The code shown below demonstrates how to modify the **Circle** type to fix this problem:

```
[Serializable]
internal class Circle {
   private Double m_radius;

   [NonSerialized]
   private Double m_area;

   public Circle(Double radius) {
      m_radius = radius;
      m_area = Math.PI * m_radius * m_radius;
   }

   [OnDeserialized]
   private void OnDeserialized(StreamingContext context) {
      m_area = Math.PI * m_radius * m_radius;
   }
}
```

I've changed **Circle** so that it now contains a method marked with the **System.Runtime. Serialization.OnDeserializedAttribute** custom attribute.[2] Whenever an instance of a type is deserialized, the formatter checks if the type defines a method with this attribute on it and then the formatter invokes this method. When this method is called, all the serializable fields will be set correctly and they may be accessed to perform any additional work that would be necessary to fully deserialize the object.

In the modified version of **Circle** above, I made the **OnDeserialized** method simply calculate the area of the circle using the **m_radius** field and place the result in the **m_area** field. Now, **m_area** will have the desired value of 314.159.

In addition to the **OnDeserializedAttribute** custom attribute, the **System.Runtime.Serialization** namespace also defines **OnSerializingAttribute**, **OnSerializedAttribute**, and **OnDeserializingAttribute** custom attributes, which you can apply to your type's methods to have even more control over serialization and deserialization. Here is a sample class that applies each of these attributes to a method:

```
[Serializable]
public class MyType {
   Int32 x, y; [NonSerialized] Int32 sum;

   public MyType(Int32 x, Int32 y) {
      this.x = x; this.y = y; sum = x + y;
   }

   [OnDeserializing]
   private void OnDeserializing(StreamingContext context) {
```

---

[2] Use of the **System.Runtime.Serialization.OnDeserialized** custom attribute is the preferred way of invoking a method when an object is deserialized, as opposed to having a type implement the **System.Runtime.Serialization.IDeserializationCallback** interface's **OnDeserialization** method.

```
        // Example: Set default values for fields in a new version of this type
    }

    [OnDeserialized]
    private void OnDeserialized(StreamingContext context) {
        // Example: Initialize transient state from fields
        sum = x + y;
    }

    [OnSerializing]
    private void OnSerializing(StreamingContext context) {
        // Example: Modify any state before serializing
    }

    [OnSerialized]
    private void OnSerialized(StreamingContext context) {
        // Example: Restore any state after serializing
    }
}
```

Whenever you use any of these four attributes, the method you define must take a single **StreamingContext** parameter (discussed in the "Streaming Contexts" section later in this chapter) and return **void**. The name of the method can be anything you want it to be. Also, you should declare the method as **private** to prevent it from being called by normal code; the formatters run with enough security that they can call private methods.

Note When you are serializing a set of objects, the formatter first calls all of the objects' methods that are marked with the **OnSerializing** attribute. Next it serializes all of the objects' fields, and finally it calls all of the objects' methods marked with the **OnSerialized** attribute. Similarly, when you deserialize a set of objects, the formatter calls all of the objects' methods that are marked with the **OnDeserializing** attribute, then it deserializes all of the object's fields, and then it calls all of the objects' methods marked with the **OnDeserialized** attribute.

Note also that during deserialization, when a formatter sees a type offering a method marked with the **OnDeserialized** attribute, the formatter adds this object's reference to an internal list. After all the objects have been deserialized, the formatter traverses this list in reverse order and calls each object's **OnDeserialized** method. When this method is called, all the serializable fields will be set correctly, and they may be accessed to perform any additional work that would be necessary to fully deserialize the object. Invoking these methods in reverse order is important because it allows inner objects to finish their deserialization before the outer objects that contain them finish their deserialization.

For example, imagine a collection object (like **Hashtable** or **Dictionary**) that internally uses a hash table to maintain its sets of items. The collection object type would implement a method marked with the **OnDeserialized** attribute. Even though the collection object would start being deserialized first (before its items), its **OnDeserialized** method would be called last (after any of its items' **OnDeserialized** methods). This allows the items to complete deserialization so that all their fields are initialized properly, allowing a good hash code value to be calculated. Then, the collection object creates its internal buckets and uses the items' hash codes to place the items into the buckets. I show an example of how the **Dictionary** class uses this in the upcoming "Controlling the Serialized/Deserialized Data" section of this chapter.

If you serialize an instance of a type, add a new field to the type, and then try to deserialize the object that did not contain the new field, the formatter throws a **SerializationException** with a message indicating that the data in the stream being deserialized has the wrong number of members. This is very problematic in versioning scenarios where it is common to add new fields to a type in a newer version. Fortunately, you can use the **System.Runtime.Serialization.OptionalFieldAttribute** attribute to help you.

You apply the **OptionalFieldAttribute** attribute to each new field you add to a type. Now, when the formatters see this attribute applied to a field, the formatters will not throw the **SerializationException** if the data in the stream does not contain the field.

How Formatters Serialize Type Instances

In this section, I give a bit more insight into how a formatter serializes an object's fields. This knowledge can help you understand the more advanced serialization and deserialization techniques explained in the remainder of this chapter.

To make things easier for a formatter, the FCL offers a **FormatterServices** type in the **System.Runtime.Serialization** namespace. This type has only static methods in it, and no instances of the type may be instantiated. The following steps describe how a formatter automatically serializes an object whose type has the **SerializableAttribute** attribute applied to it:

1   The formatter calls **FormatterServices**'s **GetSerializableMembers** method:

```
public static MemberInfo[] GetSerializableMembers(Type type, StreamingContext context);
```

This method uses reflection to get the type's public and private instance fields (excluding any fields marked with the **NonSerializedAttribute** attribute). The method returns an array of **MemberInfo** objects, one for each serializable instance field.

2.   The object being serialized and the array of **System.Reflection.MemberInfo** objects are then passed to **FormatterServices**' static **GetObjectData** method:

```
public static Object[] GetObjectData(Object obj, MemberInfo[] members);
```

This method returns an array of **Object**s where each element identifies the value of a field in the object being serialized. This **Object** array and the **MemberInfo** array are parallel. That is, element 0 in the **Object** array is the value of the member identified by element 0 in the **MemberInfo** array.

3.   The formatter writes the assembly's identity and the type's full name to the stream.

4.   The formatter then enumerates over the elements in the two arrays, writing each member's name and value to the stream.

The following steps describe how a formatter automatically deserializes an object whose type has the **SerializableAttribute** attribute applied to it:

1. The formatter reads the assembly's identity and full type name from the stream. If the assembly is not currently loaded into the AppDomain, it is loaded (as described earlier). If the assembly can't be loaded, a **SerializationException** exception is thrown and the object cannot be deserialized. If the assembly is loaded, the formatter passes the assembly identity information and the type's full name to **FormatterServices**' static **GetTypeFromAssembly** method:

```
public static Type GetTypeFromAssembly(Assembly assem, String name);
```

This method returns a **System.Type** object indicating the type of object that is being deserialized.

2. The formatter calls **FormatterServices**'s static **GetUninitializedObject** method:

```
public static Object GetUninitializedObject(Type type);
```

This method allocates memory for a new object but does not call a constructor for the object. However, all the object's bytes are initialized to **null** or **0**.

3. The formatter now constructs and initializes a **MemberInfo** array as it did before by calling **FormatterServices**'s **GetSerializableMembers** method. This method returns the set of fields that were serialized and that need to be deserialized.

4. The formatter creates and initializes an **Object** array from the data contained in the stream.

5. The reference to the newly allocated object, the **MemberInfo** array, and the parallel **Object** array of field values is passed to **FormatterServices**' static **PopulateObjectMembers** method:

```
public static Object PopulateObjectMembers(
    Object obj, MemberInfo[] members, Object[] data);
```

This method enumerates over the arrays, initializing each field to its corresponding value. At this point, the object has been completely deserialized.

Controlling the Serialized/Deserialized Data

As discussed earlier in this chapter, the best way to get control over the serialization and deserialization process is to use the **OnSerializing**, **OnSerialized**, **OnDeserializing**, **OnDeserialized**, **NonSerialized**, and **OptionalField** attributes. However, there are some very rare scenarios where these attributes do not give you all the control you need. In addition, the formatters use reflection internally and reflection is slow, which increases the time it takes to serialize and deserialize objects. To get complete control over what data is serialized/deserialized or to eliminate the use of reflection, your type can implement the **System.Runtime.Serialization.ISerializable** interface, which is defined as follows:

```
public interface ISerializable {
    void GetObjectData(SerializationInfo info, StreamingContext context);
}
```

This interface has just one method in it, **GetObjectData**. But most types that implement this interface will also implement a special constructor that I'll describe shortly.

> **Important** The big problem with the **ISerializable** interface is that once a type implements it, all derived types must implement it too, and the derived types must make sure that they invoke the base class's **GetObjectData** method and the special constructor. In addition, once a type implements this interface, it can never remove it because it will lose compatibility with the derived types. It is always OK for **sealed** types to implement the **ISerializable** interface. Using the custom attributes described earlier in this chapter avoids all of the potential problems associated with the **ISerializable** interface.

> **Important** The **ISerializable** interface and the special constructor are intended to be used by the formatters. However, other code could call **GetObjectData**, which might then return potentially sensitive information, or other code could construct an object that passes in corrupt data. For this reason, it is recommended that you apply the following attribute to the **GetObjectData** method and the special constructor:
>
> ```
> [SecurityPermissionAttribute(SecurityAction.Demand, SerializationFormatter = true)]
> ```

When a formatter serializes an object graph, it looks at each object. If its type implements the **ISerializable** interface, then the formatter ignores all custom attributes and instead constructs a new **System.Runtime.Serialization.SerializationInfo** object. This object contains the actual set of values that should be serialized for the object.

When constructing a **SerializationInfo**, the formatter passes two parameters: **Type** and **System.Runtime.Serialization.IFormatterConverter**. The **Type** parameter identifies the object that is being serialized. Two pieces of information are required to uniquely identify a type: the string name of the type and its assembly's identity (which includes the assembly name, version, culture, and public key). When a **SerializationInfo** object is constructed, it obtains the type's full name (by internally querying **Type**'s **FullName** property) and stores this string in a private field. You can obtain the type's full name by querying **SerializationInfo**'s **FullTypeName** property. Likewise, the constructor obtains the type's defining assembly (by internally querying **Type**'s **Module** property followed by querying **Module**'s **Assembly** property followed by querying **Assembly**'s **FullName** property) and stores this string in a private field. You can obtain the assembly's identity by querying **SerializationInfo**'s **AssemblyName** property.

> **Note** While you can set a **SerializationInfo**'s **FullTypeName** and **AssemblyName** properties, this is discouraged. If you want to change the type that is being serialized, it is recommended that you call **SerializationInfo**'s **SetType** method, passing a reference to the desired **Type** object. Calling **SetType** ensures that the type's full name and defining assembly are set correctly. An example of calling **SetType** is shown in the "Serializing a Type as a Different Type and Deserializing an Object as a Different Object" section later in this chapter.

Once the **SerializationInfo** object is constructed and initialized, the formatter calls the type's **GetObjectData** method, passing it the reference to the **SerializationInfo** object. The **GetObjectData** method is responsible for determining what information is necessary to serialize the object and adding this information to the **SerializationInfo** object. **GetObjectData** indicates what information to serialize by calling one of the many overloaded **AddValue** methods provided by the **SerializationInfo** type. **AddValue** is called once for each piece of data that you wish to add.

The code below shows how the **Dictionary<TKey, TValue>** type implements the **ISerializable** and **IDeserializationCallback** interfaces to take control over the serialization and deserialization of its objects.

```
[Serializable]
public class Dictionary<TKey, TValue>: ISerializable, IDeserializationCallback {
   // Private fields go here (not shown)

   private SerializationInfo m_siInfo;  // Only used for deserialization

   // Special constructor (required by ISerializable) to control deserialization
   [SecurityPermissionAttribute(SecurityAction.Demand, SerializationFormatter = true)]
   protected Dictionary(SerializationInfo info, StreamingContext context) {
       // During deserialization, save the SerializationInfo for OnDeserialization
      m_siInfo = info;
   }

   // Method to control serialization
   [SecurityCritical]
   public virtual void GetObjectData(SerializationInfo info, StreamingContext context) {

      info.AddValue("Version", m_version);
      info.AddValue("Comparer", m_comparer, typeof(IEqualityComparer<TKey>));
      info.AddValue("HashSize", (m_ buckets == null) ? 0 : m_buckets.Length);
      if (m_buckets != null) {
         KeyValuePair<TKey, TValue>[] array = new KeyValuePair<TKey, TValue>[Count];
         CopyTo(array, 0);
         info.AddValue("KeyValuePairs", array, typeof(KeyValuePair<TKey, TValue>[]));
      }
   }

   // Method called after all key/value objects have been deserialized
   public virtual void IDeserializationCallback.OnDeserialization(Object sender) {
      if (m_siInfo == null) return; // Never set, return

      Int32 num = m_siInfo.GetInt32("Version");
      Int32 num2 = m_siInfo.GetInt32("HashSize");
      m_comparer = (IEqualityComparer<TKey>)
         m_siInfo.GetValue("Comparer", typeof(IEqualityComparer<TKey>));
      if (num2 != 0) {
         m_buckets = new Int32[num2];
         for (Int32 i = 0; i < m_buckets.Length; i++) m_buckets[i] = -1;
         m_entries = new Entry<TKey, TValue>[num2];
```

```
        m_freeList = -1;
        KeyValuePair<TKey, TValue>[] pairArray = (KeyValuePair<TKey, TValue>[])
            m_siInfo.GetValue("KeyValuePairs", typeof(KeyValuePair<TKey, TValue>[]));
        if (pairArray == null)
            ThrowHelper.ThrowSerializationException(
                ExceptionResource.Serialization_MissingKeys);

        for (Int32 j = 0; j < pairArray.Length; j++) {
            if (pairArray[j].Key == null)
                ThrowHelper.ThrowSerializationException(
                    ExceptionResource.Serialization_NullKey);

            Insert(pairArray[j].Key, pairArray[j].Value, true);
        }
    } else { m_buckets = null; }
    m_version = num;
    m_siInfo = null;
}
```

Each **AddValue** method takes a **String** name and some data. Usually, the data is of a simple value type like **Boolean**, **Char**, **Byte**, **SByte**, **Int16**, **UInt16**, **Int32**, **UInt32**, **Int64**, **UInt64**, **Single**, **Double**, **Decimal**, or **DateTime**. However, you can also call **AddValue**, passing it a reference to an **Object** such as a **String**. After **GetObjectData** has added all of the necessary serialization information, it returns to the formatter.

> **Note** You should *always* call one of the overloaded **AddValue** methods to add serialization information for your type. If a field's type implements the **ISerializable** interface, don't call the **GetObjectData** on the field. Instead, call **AddValue** to add the field; the formatter will see that the field's type implements **ISerializable** and the formatter will call **GetObjectData** for you. If you were to call **GetObjectData** on the field object, the formatter wouldn't know to create a new object when deserializing the stream.

The formatter now takes all of the values added to the **SerializationInfo** object and serializes each of them out to the stream. You'll notice that the **GetObjectData** method is passed another parameter: a reference to a **System.Runtime.Serialization.StreamingContext** object. Most types' **GetObjectData** methods will completely ignore this parameter, so I will not discuss it now. Instead, I'll discuss it in the "Streaming Contexts" section later in this chapter.

So now you know how to set all of the information used for serialization. At this point, let's turn our attention to deserialization. As the formatter extracts an object from the stream, it allocates memory for the new object (by calling the **System.Runtime.Serialize.FormatterServices** type's static **GetUninitializedObject** method). Initially, all of this object's fields are set to **0** or **null**. Then, the formatter checks if the type implements the **ISerializable** interface. If this interface exists, the formatter attempts to call a special constructor whose parameters are identical to that of the **GetObjectData** method.

If your class is **sealed**, then it is highly recommended that you declare this special constructor to be **private**. This will prevent any code from accidentally calling increasing security. If not, then you should declare this special constructor as **protected** so that only derived classes can call it. Note that the formatters are able to call this special constructor no matter how it is declared.

This constructor receives a reference to a **SerializationInfo** object containing all of the values added to it when the object was serialized. The special constructor can call any of the **GetBoolean**, **GetChar**, **GetByte**, **GetSByte**, **GetInt16**, **GetUInt16**, **GetInt32**, **GetUInt32**, **GetInt64**, **GetUInt64**, **GetSingle**, **GetDouble**, **GetDecimal**, **GetDateTime**, **GetString**, and **GetValue** methods, passing in a string corresponding to the name used to serialize a value. The value returned from each of these methods is then used to initialize the fields of the new object.

When deserializing an object's fields, you should call the **Get** method that matches the type of value that was passed to the **AddValue** method when the object was serialized. In other words, if the **GetObjectData** method called **AddValue**, passing it an **Int32** value, then the **GetInt32** method should be called for the same value when deserializing the object. If the value's type in the stream doesn't match the type you're trying to get, then the formatter will attempt to use an **IFormatterConvert** object to "cast" the stream's value to the desired type.

As I mentioned earlier, when a **SerializationInfo** object is constructed, it is passed an object whose type implements the **IFormatterConverter** interface. Since the formatter is responsible for constructing the **SerializationInfo** object, it chooses whatever **IFormatterConverter** type it wants. Microsoft's **BinaryFormatter** and **SoapFormatter** types always construct an instance of the **System.Runtime.Serialization.FormatterConverter** type. Microsoft's formatters don't offer any way for you to select a different **IFormatterConverter** type.

The **FormatterConverter** type calls the **System.Convert** class's static methods to convert values between the core types, such as converting an **Int32** to an **Int64**. However, to convert a value between other arbitrary types, the **FormatterConverter** calls **Convert**'s **ChangeType** method to cast the serialized (or original) type to an **IConvertible** interface and then calls the appropriate interface method. Therefore, to allow objects of a serializable type to be deserialized as a different type, you may want to consider having your type implement the **IConvertible** interface. Note that the **FormatterConverter** object is used only when deserializing objects and when you're calling a **Get** method whose type doesn't match the type of the value in the stream.

Instead of calling the various **Get** methods listed above, the special constructor could instead call **GetEnumerator**, which returns a **System.Runtime.Serialization.SerializationInfoEnumerator** object that can be used to iterate through all the values contained within the **SerializationInfo** object. Each value enumerated is a **System.Runtime.Serialization.SerializationEntry** object.

Of course, you are welcome to define a type of your own that derives from a type that implements **ISerializable**'s **GetObjectData** and special constructor. If your type also implements **ISerializable**, then your implementation of **GetObjectData** and your implementation of the special constructor *must* call the same functions in the base class in order for the object to be serialized and deserialized properly. Do not forget to do this or the objects will not serialize or deserialize correctly. The next section explains how to properly define an **ISerializable** type whose base type doesn't implement this interface.

If your derived type doesn't have any additional fields in it and therefore has no special serialization/deserialization needs, then you do not have to implement **ISerializable** at all. Like all interface members, **GetObjectData** is virtual and will be called to properly serialize the object. In addition, the formatter treats the special constructor as "virtualized." That is, during deserialization, the formatter will check the type that it is trying to instantiate. If that type doesn't offer the special constructor, then the formatter will scan base classes until it finds one that implements the special constructor.

Important The code in the special constructor typically extracts its fields from the **SerializationInfo** object that is passed to it. As the fields are extracted, you are not guaranteed that the objects are fully deserialized, so the code in the special constructor should not attempt to manipulate the objects that it extracts.

If your type must access members (such as call methods) on an extracted object, then it is recommended that your type also provide a method that has the **OnDeserialized** attribute applied to it or have your type implement the **IDeserializationCallback** interface's **OnDeserialization** method (as shown in the **Dictionary** example). When this method is called, all objects have had their fields set. However, there is no guarantee to the order in which multiple objects have their **OnDeserialized** or **OnDeserialization** method called. So, while the fields may be initialized, you still don't know if a referenced object is completely deserialized if that referenced object also provides an **OnDeserialized** method or implements the **IDeserializationCallback** interface.

How to Define a Type That Implements ISerializable when the Base Type Doesn't Implement This Interface

As mentioned earlier, the **ISerializable** interface is extremely powerful since it allows a type to take complete control over how instances of the type get serialized and deserialized. However, this power comes at a cost: The type is now responsible for serializing all of its base type's fields as well. Serializing the base type's fields is easy if the base type also implements the **ISerializable** interface; you just call the base type's **GetObjectData** method.

However, someday, you may find yourself defining a type that needs to take control of its serialization but whose base type does not implement the **ISerializable** interface. In this case, your derived class must manually serialize the base type's fields by grabbing their values and adding them to the **SerializationInfo** collection. Then, in your special constructor, you will also have to get the values out of the collection and somehow set the base class's fields. Doing all of this is easy (albeit tedious) if the base class's fields are **public** or **protected**, but it can be very difficult or impossible to do if the base class's fields are **private**.

This following code shows how to properly implement **ISerializable**'s **GetObjectData** method and its implied constructor so that the base type's fields are serialized:

```
[Serializable]
internal class Base {
   protected String m_name = "Jeff";
   public Base() { /* Make the type instantiable */ }
}

[Serializable]
internal class Derived : Base, ISerializable {
   private DateTime m_date = DateTime.Now;
   public Derived() { /* Make the type instantiable*/ }

   // If this constructor didn't exist, we'd get a SerializationException
   // This constructor should be protected if this class were not sealed
   [SecurityPermissionAttribute(SecurityAction.Demand, SerializationFormatter = true)]
   private Derived(SerializationInfo info, StreamingContext context) {
      // Get the set of serializable members for our class and base classes
      Type baseType = this.GetType().BaseType;
      MemberInfo[] mi = FormatterServices.GetSerializableMembers(baseType, context);

      // Deserialize the base class's fields from the info object
      for (Int32 i = 0; i < mi.Length; i++) {
         // Get the field and set it to the deserialized value
         FieldInfo fi = (FieldInfo)mi[i];
         fi.SetValue(this, info.GetValue(baseType.FullName + "+" + fi.Name, fi.FieldType));
      }

      // Deserialize the values that were serialized for this class
      m_date = info.GetDateTime("Date");
   }


   [SecurityPermissionAttribute(SecurityAction.Demand, SerializationFormatter = true)]
   public virtual void GetObjectData(SerializationInfo info, StreamingContext context) {
      // Serialize the desired values for this class
      info.AddValue("Date", m_date);

      // Get the set of serializable members for our class and base classes
      Type baseType = this.GetType().BaseType;
      MemberInfo[] mi = FormatterServices.GetSerializableMembers(baseType, context);

      // Serialize the base class's fields to the info object
      for (Int32 i = 0; i < mi.Length; i++) {
         // Prefix the field name with the fullname of the base type
         info.AddValue(baseType.FullName + "+" + mi[i].Name,
            ((FieldInfo)mi[i]).GetValue(this));
      }
   }
   public override String ToString() {
      return String.Format("Name={0}, Date={1}", m_name, m_date);
   }
}
```

In this code, there is a base class, **Base**, which is marked only with the **SerializableAttribute** custom attribute. Derived from **Base** is **Derived**, which also is marked with the **SerializableAttribute** attribute and also implements the **ISerializable** interface. To make the situation more interesting, you'll notice that both classes define a **String** field called **m_name**. When calling **SerializationInfo**'s **AddValue** method, you can't add multiple values with the same name. The code above handles this situation by identifying each field by its class name prepended to the field's name. For example, when the **GetObjectData** method calls **AddValue** to serialize **Base**'s **m_name** field, the name of the value is written as "Base+m_name."

Streaming Contexts

As mentioned earlier, there are many destinations for a serialized set of objects: same process, different process on the same machine, different process on a different machine, and so on. In some rare situations, an object might want to know where it is going to be deserialized so that it can emit its state differently. For example, an object that wraps a Windows semaphore object might decide to serialize its kernel handle if the object knows that it will be deserialized into the same process, because kernel handles are valid within a process. However, the object might decide to serialize the semaphore's string name if it knows that the object will be deserialized on the same machine but into a different process. Finally, the object might decide to throw an exception if it knows that it will be deserialized in a process running on a different machine because a semaphore is valid only within a single machine.

A number of the methods mentioned earlier in this chapter accept a **StreamingContext**. A **StreamingContext** structure is a very simple value type offering just two public read-only properties, as shown in Table 24-1.

TABLE 24-1 StreamingContext's Public Read-Only Properties

Member Name	Member Type	Description
State	StreamingContextStates	A set of bit flags indicating the source or destination of the objects being serialized/deserialized
Context	Object	A reference to an object that contains any user-desired context information

A method that receives a **StreamingContext** structure can examine the **State** property's bit flags to determine the source or destination of the objects being serialize/deserialized. Table 24-2 shows the possible bit flag values.

TABLE 24-2 `StreamingContextStates`'s **Flags**

Flag Name	Flag Value	Description
CrossProcess	0x0001	The source or destination is a different process on the same machine.
CrossMachines	0x0002	The source or destination is on a different machine.
File	0x0004	The source or destination is a file. Don't assume that the same process will deserialize the data.
Persistence	0x0008	The source or destination is a store such as a database or a file. Don't assume that the same process will deserialize the data.
Remoting	0x0010	The source or destination is remoting to an unknown location. The location may be on the same machine but may also be on another machine.
Other	0x0020	The source or destination is unknown.
Clone	0x0040	The object graph is being cloned. The serialization code may assume that the same process will deserialize the data, and it is therefore safe to access handles or other unmanaged resources.
CrossAppDomain	0x0080	The source or destination is a different AppDomain.
All	0x00FF	The source or destination may be any of the above contexts. This is the default context.

Now that you know how to get this information, let's discuss how you would set this information. The **IFormatter** interface (which is implemented by both the **BinaryFormatter** and the **SoapFormatter** types) defines a read/write **StreamingContext** property called **Context**. When you construct a formatter, the formatter initializes its **Context** property so that **StreamingContextStates** is set to **All** and the reference to the additional state object is set to **null**.

After the formatter is constructed, you can construct a **StreamingContext** structure using any of the **StreamingContextStates** bit flags, and you can optionally pass a reference to an object containing any additional context information you need. Now, all you need to do is set the formatter's **Context** property with this new **StreamingContext** object before calling the formatter's **Serialize** or **Deserialize** methods. Code demonstrating how to tell a formatter that you are serializing/deserialzing an object graph for the sole purpose of cloning all the objects in the graph is shown in the **DeepClone** method presented earlier in this chapter.

Serializing a Type as a Different Type and Deserializing an Object as a Different Object

The .NET Framework's serialization infrastructure is quite rich, and in this section, we discuss how a developer can design a type that can serialize or deserialize itself into a different type or object. Below are some examples where this is interesting:

■ Some types (such as **System.DBNull** and **System.Reflection.Missing**) are designed to have only one instance per AppDomain. These types are frequently called *singletons*. If you have a reference to a **DBNull** object, serializing and deserializing it should not cause a new **DBNull** object to be created in the AppDomain. After deserializing, the returned reference should refer to the AppDomain's already-existing **DBNull** object.

■ Some types (such as **System.Type**, **System.Reflection.Assembly**, and other reflection types like **MemberInfo**) have one instance per type, assembly, member, and so on. Imagine you have an array where each element references a **MemberInfo** object. It's possible that five array elements reference a single **MemberInfo** object. After serializing and deserializing this array, the five elements that referred to a single **MemberInfo** object should all refer to a single **MemberInfo** object. What's more, these elements should refer to the one **MemberInfo** object that exists for the specific member in the AppDomain. You could also imagine how this could be useful for polling database connection objects or any other type of object.

■ For remotely controlled objects, the CLR serializes information about the server object that, when deserialized on the client, causes the CLR to create a proxy object. This type of the proxy object is a different type than the server object, but this is transparent to the client code. When the client calls instance methods on the proxy object, the proxy code internally remotes the call to the server that actually performs the request.

Let's look at some code that shows how to properly serialize and deserialize a singleton type:

```
// There should be only one instance of this type per AppDomain
[Serializable]
public sealed class Singleton : ISerializable {
   // This is the one instance of this type
   private static readonly Singleton theOneObject = new Singleton();

   // Here are the instance fields
   public String Name = "Jeff";
   public DateTime Date = DateTime.Now;

   // Private constructor allowing this type to construct the singleton
   private Singleton() { }

   // Method returning a reference to the singleton
   public static Singleton GetSingleton() { return theOneObject; }

   // Method called when serializing a Singleton
   // I recommend using an Explicit Interface Method Impl. Here
   [SecurityPermissionAttribute(SecurityAction.Demand, SerializationFormatter = true)]
```

```
    void ISerializable.GetObjectData(SerializationInfo info, StreamingContext context) {
        info.SetType(typeof(SingletonSerializationHelper));
        // No other values need to be added
    }

    [Serializable]
    private sealed class SingletonSerializationHelper : IObjectReference {
        // Method called after this object (which has no fields) is deserialized
        public Object GetRealObject(StreamingContext context) {
            return Singleton.GetSingleton();
        }
    }
}

    // NOTE: The special constructor is NOT necessary because it's never called
}
```

The **Singleton** class represents a type that allows only one instance of itself to exist per AppDomain. The following code tests the **Singleton**'s serialization and deserialization code to ensure that only one instance of the **Singleton** type ever exists in the AppDomain:

```
private static void SingletonSerializationTest() {
    // Create an array with multiple elements referring to the one Singleton object
    Singleton[] a1 = { Singleton.GetSingleton(), Singleton.GetSingleton() };
    Console.WriteLine("Do both elements refer to the same object? "
        + (a1[0] == a1[1])); // "True"

    using (var stream = new MemoryStream()) {
        BinaryFormatter formatter = new BinaryFormatter();

        // Serialize and then deserialize the array elements
        formatter.Serialize(stream, a1);
        stream.Position = 0;
        Singleton[] a2 = (Singleton[])formatter.Deserialize(stream);

        // Prove that it worked as expected:
        Console.WriteLine("Do both elements refer to the same object? "
            + (a2[0] == a2[1])); // "True"
        Console.WriteLine("Do all  elements refer to the same object? "
            + (a1[0] == a2[0])); // "True"
    }
}
```

Now, let's walk through the code to understand what's happening. When the **Singleton** type is loaded into the AppDomain, the CLR calls its static constructor, which constructs a **Singleton** object and saves a reference to it in a static field, **s_theOneObject**. The **Singleton** class doesn't offer any public constructors, which prevents any other code from constructing any other instances of this class.

In **SingletonSerializationTest**, an array is created consisting of two elements; each element references the **Singleton** object. The two elements are initialized by calling **Singleton**'s static **GetSingleton** method. This method returns a reference to the one **Singleton** object. The first call to **Console**'s **WriteLine** method displays "True," verifying that both array elements refer to the same exact object.

Now, **SingletonSerializationTest** calls the formatter's **Serialize** method to serialize the array and its elements. When serializing the first **Singleton**, the formatter detects that the **Singleton** type implements the **ISerializable** interface and calls the **GetObjectData** method. This method calls **SetType**, passing in the **SingletonSerializationHelper** type, which tells the formatter to serialize the **Singleton** object as a **SingletonSerializationHelper** object instead. Since **AddValue** is not called, no additional field information is written to the stream. Since the formatter automatically detected that both array elements refer to a single object, the formatter serializes only one object.

After serializing the array, **SingletonSerializationTest** calls the formatter's **Deserialize** method. When deserializing the stream, the formatter tries to deserialize a **SingletonSerializationHelper** object since this is what the formatter was "tricked" into serializing. (In fact, this is why the **Singleton** class doesn't provide the special constructor that is usually required when implementing the **ISerializable** interface.) After constructing the **SingletonSerializationHelper** object, the formatter sees that this type implements the **System.Runtime.Serialization.IObjectReference** interface. This interface is defined in the FCL as follows:

```
public interface IObjectReference {
    Object GetRealObject(StreamingContext context);
}
```

When a type implements this interface, the formatter calls the **GetRealObject** method. This method returns a reference to the object that you really want a reference to now that deserialization of the object has completed. In my example, the **SingletonSerializationHelper** type has **GetRealObject** return a reference to the **Singleton** object that already exists in the AppDomain. So, when the formatter's **Deserialize** method returns, the **a2** array contains two elements, both of which refer to the AppDomain's **Singleton** object. The **SingletonSerializationHelper** object used to help with the deserialization is immediately unreachable and will be garbage collected in the future.

The second call to **WriteLine** displays "True," verifying that both of **a2**'s array elements refer to the exact same object. The third and last call to **WriteLine** also displays "True," proving that the elements in both arrays all refer to the exact same object.

Serialization Surrogates

Up to now, I've been discussing how to modify a type's implementation to control how a type serializes and deserializes instances of itself. However, the formatters also allow code that is not part of the type's implementation to override how a type serializes and deserializes its objects. There are two main reasons why application code might want to override a type's behavior:

- It allows a developer the ability to serialize a type that was not originally designed to be serialized.

- It allows a developer to provide a way to map one version of a type to a different version of a type.

Basically, to make this mechanism work, you first define a "surrogate type" that takes over the actions required to serialize and deserialize an existing type. Then, you register an instance of your surrogate type with the formatter telling the formatter which existing type your surrogate type is responsible for acting on. When the formatter detects that it is trying to serialize or deserialize an instance of the existing type, it will call methods defined by your surrogate object. Let's build a sample that demonstrates how all this works.

A serialization surrogate type must implement the **System.Runtime.Serialization. ISerializationSurrogate** interface, which is defined in the FCL as follows:

```
public interface ISerializationSurrogate {
   void GetObjectData(Object obj, SerializationInfo info, StreamingContext context);

   Object SetObjectData(Object obj, SerializationInfo info, StreamingContext context,
      ISurrogateSelector selector);
}
```

Now, let's walk through an example that uses this interface. Let's say your program contains some **DateTime** objects that contain values that are local to the user's computer. What if you want to serialize the **DateTime** objects to a stream but you want the values to be serialized in universal time? This would allow you to send the data over a network stream to another machine in another part of the world and have the **DateTime** value be correct. While you can't modify the **DateTime** type that ships with the FCL, you can define your own serialization surrogate class that can control how **DateTime** objects are serialized and deserialized. Here is how to define the surrogate class:

```
internal sealed class UniversalToLocalTimeSerializationSurrogate : ISerializationSurrogate {
   public void GetObjectData(Object obj, SerializationInfo info, StreamingContext context) {
      // Convert the DateTime from local to UTC
      info.AddValue("Date", ((DateTime)obj).ToUniversalTime().ToString("u"));
   }

   public Object SetObjectData(Object obj, SerializationInfo info, StreamingContext context,
      ISurrogateSelector selector) {
      // Convert the DateTime from UTC to local
      return DateTime.ParseExact(info.GetString("Date"), "u", null).ToLocalTime();
   }
}
```

The **GetObjectData** method here works just like the **ISerializable** interface's **GetObjectData** method. The only difference is that **ISerializationSurrogate**'s

GetObjectData method takes one additional parameter: a reference to the "real" object that is to be serialized. In the **GetObjectData** method above, this object is cast to **DateTime**, the value is converted from local time to universal time, and a string (formatted using universal full date/time pattern) is added to the **SerializationInfo** collection.

The **SetObjectData** method is called in order to deserialize a **DateTime** object. When this method is called, it is passed a reference to a **SerializationInfo** object. **SetObjectData** gets the string date out of this collection, parses it as a universal full date/time formatted string, and then converts the resulting **DateTime** object from universal time to the machine's local time.

The **Object** that is passed for **SetObjectData**'s first parameter is a bit strange. Just before calling **SetObjectData**, the formatter allocates (via **FormatterServices**'s static **GetUninitializedObject** method) an instance of the type that the surrogate is a surrogate for. The instance's fields are all **0/null** and no constructor has been called on the object. The code inside **SetObjectData** can simply initialize the fields of this instance using the values from the passed-in **SerializationInfo** object and then have **SetObjectData** return **null**. Alternatively, **SetObjectData** could create an entirely different object or even a different type of object and return a reference to this new object, in which case, the formatter will ignore any changes that may or may not have happened to the object it passed in to **SetObjectData**.

In my example, my **UniversalToLocalTimeSerializationSurrogate** class acts as a surrogate for the **DateTime** type which is a value type. And so, the **obj** parameter refers to a boxed instance of a **DateTime**. There is no way to change the fields in most value types (as they are supposed to be immutable) and so, my **SetObjectData** method ignores the **obj** parameter and returns a new **DateTime** object with the desired value in it.

At this point, I'm sure you're all wondering how the formatter knows to use this **ISerializationSurrogate** type when it tries to serialize/deserialize a **DateTime** object. The following code demonstrates how to test the **UniversalToLocalTimeSerializationSurrogate** class:

```
private static void SerializationSurrogateDemo() {
    using (var stream = new MemoryStream()) {
        // 1. Construct the desired formatter
        IFormatter formatter = new SoapFormatter();

        // 2. Construct a SurrogateSelector object
        SurrogateSelector ss = new SurrogateSelector();

        // 3. Tell the surrogate selector to use our surrogate for DateTime objects
        ss.AddSurrogate(typeof(DateTime), formatter.Context,
            new UniversalToLocalTimeSerializationSurrogate());
```

```
        // NOTE: AddSurrogate can be called multiple times to register multiple surrogates

        // 4. Tell the formatter to use our surrogate selector
        formatter.SurrogateSelector = ss;

        // Create a DateTime that represents the local time on the machine & serialize it
        DateTime localTimeBeforeSerialize = DateTime.Now;
        formatter.Serialize(stream, localTimeBeforeSerialize);

        // The stream displays the Universal time as a string to prove it worked
        stream.Position = 0;
        Console.WriteLine(new StreamReader(stream).ReadToEnd());

        // Deserialize the Universal time string & convert it to a local DateTime
        stream.Position = 0;
        DateTime localTimeAfterDeserialize = (DateTime)formatter.Deserialize(stream);

        // Prove it worked correctly:
        Console.WriteLine("LocalTimeBeforeSerialize ={0}", localTimeBeforeSerialize);
        Console.WriteLine("LocalTimeAfterDeserialize={0}", localTimeAfterDeserialize);
    }
}
```

After steps 1 through 4 have executed, the formatter is ready to use the registered surrogate types. When the formatter's **Serialize** method is called, each object's type is looked up in the set maintained by the **SurrogateSelector**. If a match is found, then the **ISerializationSurrogate** object's **GetObjectData** method is called to get the information that should be written out to the stream.

When the formatter's **Deserialize** method is called, the type of the object about to be deserialized is looked up in the formatter's **SurrogateSelector** and if a match is found, then the **ISerializationSurrogate** object's **SetObjectData** method is called to set the fields within the object being deserialized.

Internally, a **SurrogateSelector** object maintains a private hash table. When **AddSurrogate** is called, the **Type** and **StreamingContext** make up the key and the **ISerializationSurrogate** object is the key's value. If a key with the same **Type**/**StreamingContext** already exists, then **AddSurrogate** throws an **ArgumentException**. By including a **StreamingContext** in the key, you can register one surrogate type object that knows how to serialize/deserialize a **DateTime** object to a file and register a different surrogate object that knows how to serialize/deserialize a **DateTime** object to a different process.

> **Note** The **BinaryFormatter** class has a bug that prevents a surrogate from serializing objects with references to each other. To fix this problem, you need to pass a reference to your **ISerializationSurrogate** object to **FormatterServices**'s static **GetSurrogateForCyclicalReference** method. This method returns an **ISerializationSurrogate** object, which you can then pass to the **SurrogateSelector**'s **AddSurrogate** method. However, when you use the **GetSurrogateForCyclicalReference** method, your surrogate's **SetObjectData** method must modify the value inside the object referred to by **SetObjectData**'s **obj** parameter and ultimately return **null** or **obj** to the calling method. The downloadable code that accompanies this book shows how to modify the **UniversalToLocalTimeSerializationSurrogate** class and the **SerializationSurrogateDemo** method to support cyclical references.

Surrogate Selector Chains

Multiple **SurrogateSelector** objects can be chained together. For example, you could have a **SurrogateSelector** that maintains a set of serialization surrogates that are used for serializing types into proxies that get remoted across the wire or between AppDomains. You could also have a separate **SurrogateSelector** object that contains a set of serialization surrogates that are used to convert Version 1 types into Version 2 types.

If you have multiple **SurrogateSelector** objects that you'd like the formatter to use, you must chain them together into a linked list. The **SurrogateSelector** type implements the **ISurrogateSelector** interface, which defines three methods. All three of these methods are related to chaining. Here is how the **ISurrogateSelector** interface is defined:

```
public interface ISurrogateSelector {
   void ChainSelector(ISurrogateSelector selector);
   ISurrogateSelector GetNextSelector();
   ISerializationSurrogate GetSurrogate(Type type, StreamingContext context,
      out ISurrogateSelector selector);
}
```

The **ChainSelector** method inserts an **ISurrogateSelector** object immediately after the **ISurrogateSelector** object being operated on ('**this**' object). The **GetNextSelector** method returns a reference to the next **ISurrogateSelector** object in the chain or **null** if the object being operated on is the end of the chain.

The **GetSurrogate** method looks up a **Type/StreamingContext** pair in the **ISurrogateSelector** object identified by **this**. If the pair cannot be found, then the next **ISurrogateSelector** object in the chain is accessed, and so on. If a match is found, then **GetSurrogate** returns the **ISerializationSurrogate** object that handles the serialization/deserialization of the type looked up. In addition, **GetSurrogate** also returns the **ISurrogateSelector** object that contained the match; this is usually not needed and is ignored. If none of the **ISurrogateSelector** objects in the chain have a match for the **Type/StreamingContext** pair, **GetSurrogate** returns **null**.

> **Note** The FCL defines an **ISurrogateSelector** interface and also defines a
> **SurrogateSelector** type that implements this interface. However, it is extremely rare that
> anyone will ever have to define their own type that implements the **ISurrogateSelector**
> interface. The only reason to define your own type that implements this interface is if you need
> to have more flexibility over mapping one type to another. For example, you might want to
> serialize all types that inherit from a specific base class in a special way. The
> **System.Runtime.Remoting.Messaging.RemotingSurrogateSelector** class is a perfect
> example. When serializing objects for remoting purposes, the CLR formats the objects using the
> **RemotingSurrogateSelector**. This surrogate selector serializes all objects that derive from
> **System.MarshalByRefObject** in a special way so that deserialization causes proxy objects to
> be created on the client side.

Overriding the Assembly and/or Type When Deserializing an Object

When serializing an object, formatters output the type's full name and the full name of the type's defining assembly. When deserializing an object, formatters use this information to know exactly what type of object to construct and initialize. The earlier discussion about the **ISerializationSurrogate** interface showed a mechanism allowing you to take over the serialization and deserialization duties for a specific type. A type that implements the **ISerializationSurrogate** interface is tied to a specific type in a specific assembly.

However, there are times when the **ISerializationSurrogate** mechanism doesn't provide enough flexibility. Here are some scenarios when it might be useful to deserialize an object into a different type than it was serialized as:

■ A developer might decide to move a type's implementation from one assembly to a different assembly. For example, the assembly's version number changes making the new assembly different from the original assembly.

■ An object on a server that gets serialized into a stream that is sent to a client. When the client processes the stream, it could deserialize the object to a completely different type whose code knows how to remote method calls to the server's object.

■ A developer makes a new version of a type. We want to deserialize any already-serialized objects into the new version of the type.

The **System.Runtime.Serialization.SerializationBinder** class makes deserializing an object to a different type very easy. To do this, you first define your own type that derives from the abstract **SerializationBinder** type. In the code below, assume that version 1.0.0.0 of your assembly defined a class called **Ver1** and assume that the new version of your assembly defines the **Ver1ToVer2SerializationBinder** class and also defines a class called **Ver2**:

```
internal sealed class Ver1ToVer2SerializationBinder : SerializationBinder {
   public override Type BindToType(String assemblyName, String typeName) {
      // Deserialize any Ver1 object from version 1.0.0.0 into a Ver2 object

      // Calculate the assembly name that defined the Ver1 type
      AssemblyName assemVer1 = Assembly.GetExecutingAssembly().GetName();
      assemVer1.Version = new Version(1, 0, 0, 0);

      // If deserializing the Ver1 object from v1.0.0.0, turn it into a Ver2 object
      if (assemblyName == assemVer1.ToString() && typeName == "Ver1")
         return typeof(Ver2);

      // Else, just return the same type being requested
      return Type.GetType(String.Format("{0}, {1}", typeName, assemblyName));
   }
}
```

Now, after you construct a formatter, construct an instance of
Ver1ToVer2SerializationBinder and set the formatter's **Binder** read/write property to
refer to the binder object. After setting the **Binder** property, you can now call the formatter's
Deserialize method. During deserialization, the formatter sees that a binder has been set.
As each object is about to be deserialized, the formatter calls the binder's **BindToType** method,
passing it the assembly name and type that the formatter wants to deserialize. At this point,
BindToType decides what type should actually be constructed and returns this type.

> **Note** The **SerializationBinder** class also makes it possible to change the assembly/type
> information while serializing an object by overriding its **BindToName** method, which looks like
> this:
>
> ```
> public virtual void BindToName(Type serializedType,
>    out string assemblyName, out string typeName)
> ```
>
> During serialization, the formatter calls this method, passing you the type it wants to serialize.
> You can then return (via the two out parameters) the assembly and type that you want to serialize
> instead. If you return **null** and **null** (which is what the default implementation does), then no
> change is performed.

Chapter 25
Thread Basics

In this chapter, I introduce the basic concepts concerning threads, and I offer a way for developers to conceptualize about them and their use. I'll explain why Microsoft Windows introduced the concept of threads, CPU trends, the relationship between common language runtime (CLR) threads and Windows threads, the overhead associated with using threads, how Windows schedules threads, the Microsoft .NET Framework classes that expose thread properties, and much more.

The chapters in Part V of this book, "Threading," explain how Windows and the CLR work together to provide a threading architecture. It is my hope that after reading these chapters, you will take away a foundation of knowledge that will allow you to effectively use threads to design and build responsive, reliable, and scalable applications and components.

Why Does Windows Support Threads?

Back in the early days of computers, operating systems didn't offer the concept of a thread. In effect, there was just one thread of execution that ran throughout the entire system, which included both operating system code and application code. The problem with having only one thread of execution was that a long-running task would prevent other tasks from executing. For example, in the days of 16-bit Windows, it was very common for an application that was printing a document to stall the entire machine, causing the OS and all other applications to stop responding. And, sometimes applications would have a bug in them, resulting in an infinite loop that also stopped the entire machine from operating.

At this point, the end user would have no choice but to reboot the computer by pressing the reset button or power switch. Of course, end users hated doing this (they still do, in fact) because all running applications terminated; more importantly, any data that these applications were processing was thrown out of memory and lost. Microsoft knew that 16-bit Windows would not be a good enough operating system to keep Microsoft relevant as the computer industry progressed, so they set out to build a new OS to address the needs of corporations and individuals. This new OS had to be robust, reliable, scalable, and secure, and it had to improve the many deficiencies of 16-bit Windows. This OS kernel originally shipped in Microsoft Windows NT. Over the years, this kernel has had many tweaks and features added to it. The latest version of this kernel ships in the latest versions of the Microsoft client and server Windows operating systems.

When Microsoft was designing this OS kernel, they decided to run each instance of an application in what is called a *process*. A process is just a collection of resources that is used by a single instance of an application. Each process is given a virtual address space, ensuring that the code and data used by one process is not accessible to another process. This makes application instances robust because one process cannot corrupt code or data being used by another. In addition, the OS's kernel code and data are not accessible to processes; therefore, it's not possible for application code to corrupt operating system code or data. So now, application code cannot corrupt other applications or the OS itself, and the whole computing experience is much better for end users. In addition, the system is more secure because application code cannot access user names, passwords, credit card information, or other sensitive information that is in use by another application or the operating system itself.

This is all well and good, but what about the CPU itself? What if an application enters an infinite loop? Well, if there is only one CPU in the machine, then it executes the infinite loop and cannot execute anything else, so while the data cannot be corrupted and is more secure, the system could still stop responding to the end user. Microsoft needed to fix this problem, too, and threads were the answer. A *thread* is a Windows concept whose job is to virtualize the CPU. Windows gives each process its very own thread (which functions similar to a CPU), and if application code enters an infinite loop, the process associated with that code freezes up, but other processes (which have their own threads) are not frozen; they keep running!

Thread Overhead

Threads are awesome because they enable Windows to be responsive even when applications are executing long-running tasks. Also, threads allow the user to use one application (like Task Manager) to forcibly kill an application that appears frozen because it is executing a long-running task. But as with every virtualization mechanism, threads have space (memory consumption) and time (runtime execution performance) overhead associated with them. Let's explore this overhead in more detail now. Every thread has one of each of the following:

- **Thread kernel object**   The OS allocates and initializes one of these data structures for each thread created in the system. The data structure contains a bunch of properties (discussed later in this chapter) that describe the thread. This data structure also contains what is called the thread's context. The context is a block of memory that contains a set of the CPU's registers. When Windows is running on a machine with an x86 CPU, the thread's context uses about 700 bytes of memory. For x64 and IA64 CPUs, the context is about 1,240 and 2,500 bytes of memory, respectively.

- **Thread environment block (TEB)**   The TEB is a block of memory allocated and initialized in user mode (address space that application code can quickly access). The TEB consumes 1 page of memory (4 KB on x86 and x64 CPUs, 8 KB on an IA64 CPU). The TEB contains the head of the thread's exception-handling chain. Each **try** block that the thread enters inserts a node in the head of this chain; the node is removed from the chain when the thread exists in the **try** block. In addition, the TEB contains the thread's thread-local storage data as well as some data structures for use by Graphics Device Interface (GDI) and OpenGL graphics.

- **User-mode stack**   The user-mode stack is used for local variables and arguments passed to methods. It also contains the address indicating what the thread should execute next when the current method returns. By default, Windows allocates 1 MB of memory for each thread's user-mode stack.[1]

- **Kernel-mode stack**   The kernel-mode stack is also used when application code passes arguments to a kernel-mode function in the operating system. For security reasons, Windows copies any arguments passed from user-mode code to the kernel from the thread's user-mode stack to the thread's kernel-mode stack. Once copied, the kernel can verify the arguments' values, and since the application code can't access the kernel-mode stack, the application can't modify the arguments' values after they have been validated and the OS kernel code begins to operate on them. In addition, the kernel calls methods within itself and uses the kernel-mode stack to pass its own arguments, to store a function's local variables, and to store return addresses. The kernel-mode stack is 12 KB when running on a 32-bit Windows system and 24 KB when running on a 64-bit Windows system.

---

[1] For native applications, Windows reserves the 1 MB of address space and sparsely commits physical storage to it as the thread actually requires it when growing the stack. However, when managed applications create a thread, the CLR forces Windows to reserve and fully commit the stack immediately, so 1 MB of physical storage is fully allocated as each thread is created. The CLR team did this to make managed code behave more reliably in situations where the system was running low on memory. For example, the CLR and managed applications never have to worry about recovering from insufficient memory when attempting to grow a thread's stack. This was very important for Microsoft SQL Server when executing stored procedures implemented in managed code.

■ **DLL thread-attach and thread-detach notifications**   Windows has a policy that whenever a thread is created in a process, all DLLs loaded in that process have their **DllMain** method called, passing a **DLL_THREAD_ATTACH** flag. Similarly, whenever a thread dies, all DLLs in the process have their **DllMain** method called, passing it a **DLL_THREAD_DETACH** flag. Some DLLs need these notifications to perform some special initialization or cleanup for each thread created/destroyed in the process. For example, the C-Runtime library DLL allocates some thread-local storage state that is required should the thread use functions contained within the C-Runtime library.

In the early days of Windows, many processes had maybe 5 or 6 DLLs loaded into them, but today, some processes have several hundred DLLs loaded into them. Right now, on my machine, Microsoft Office Outlook has about 250 DLLs loaded into its process address space! This means that whenever a new thread is created in Office Outlook, 250 DLL functions must get called before the thread is allowed to do what it was created to do. And these 250 functions must be called again whenever a thread in Outlook dies. Wow—this can seriously affect the performance of creating and destroying threads within a process.[2]

So now, you see all the space and time overhead that is associated with creating a thread, letting it sit around in the system, and destroying it. But the situation gets even worse—now we're going to start talking about *context switching*. A computer with only one CPU in it can do only one thing at a time. Therefore, Windows has to share the actual CPU hardware among all the threads (logical CPUs) that are sitting around in the system.

At any given moment in time, Windows assigns one thread to a CPU. That thread is allowed to run for a time-slice (sometimes referred to as a *quantum*). When the time-slice expires, Windows context switches to another thread. Every context switch requires that Windows performs the following actions:

1. Save the values in the CPU's registers to the currently running thread's context structure inside the thread's kernel object.

2. Select one thread from the set of existing threads to schedule next. If this thread is owned by another process, then Windows must also switch the virtual address space seen by the CPU before it starts executing any code or touching any data.

3. Load the values in the selected thread's context structure into the CPU's registers.

After the context switch is complete, the CPU executes the selected thread until its time-slice expires, and then another context switch happens again. Windows performs context switches about every 30 ms. Context switches are pure overhead; that is, there is no memory or performance benefit that comes from context switches. Windows performs context switching to provide end users with a robust and responsive operating system.

---

[2] DLLs produced by C# and most other managed programming languages do not have a **DllMain** in them at all and so managed DLLs will not receive the **DLL_THREAD_ATTACH** and **DLL_THREAD_DETACH** notifications improving performance. In addition, unmanaged DLLs can opt out of these notifications by calling the Win32 **DisableThreadLibraryCalls** function. Unfortunately, many unmanaged developers are not aware of this function, so they don't call it.

Now, if an application's thread enters into an infinite loop, Windows will periodically preempt that thread, assign a different thread to an actual CPU, and let this other thread run for a while. This other thread could be Task Manager's thread and now, the end user can use Task Manager to kill the process containing the thread that is in an infinite loop. When doing this, the process dies and all the data it was working on is destroyed, too, but all other processes in the system continue to run just fine without losing their data. Of course, the user doesn't have to reset the machine and reboot, so context switches are required to provide end users with a much better overall experience at the cost of performance.

In fact, the performance hit is much worse than you might think. Yes, a performance hit occurs when Windows context switches to another thread. But the CPU was executing another thread, and the previously running thread's code and data reside in the CPU's caches so that the CPU doesn't have to access RAM memory as much, which has significant latency associated with it. When Windows context switches to a new thread, this new thread is most likely executing different code and accessing different data that is not in the CPU's cache. The CPU must access RAM memory to populate its cache so it can get back to a good execution speed. But then, about 30 ms later, another context switch occurs.

The time required to perform a context switch varies with different CPU architectures and speed. And the time required to build up a CPU's cache depends on what applications are running in the system, the size of the CPU's caches, and various other factors. So it is impossible for me to give you an absolute figure or even an estimate as to what time overhead is incurred for each context switch. Suffice it to say that you want to avoid using context switches as much as possible if you are interested in building high-performing applications and components.

Important At the end of a time-slice, if Windows decides to schedule the same thread again (rather than switching to another thread), then Windows does not perform a context switch. Instead, the thread is allowed to just continue running. This improves performance significantly, and avoiding context switches is something you want to achieve as often as possible when you design your code.

Important A thread can voluntarily end its time-slice early, which happens quite frequently because threads typically wait for I/O operations (keyboard, mouse, file, network, etc.) to complete. For example, Notepad's thread usually sits idle with nothing to do; this thread is waiting for input. If the user presses the J key on the keyboard, Windows wakes Notepad's thread to have it process the J keystroke. It may take Notepad's thread just 5 ms to process the key, and then it calls a Win32 function that tells Windows that it is ready to process the next input event. If there are no more input events, then Windows puts Notepad's thread into a wait state (relinquishing the remainder of its time-slice) so that the thread is not scheduled on any CPU until the next input stimulus occurs. This improves overall system performance since threads that are waiting for I/O operations to complete are not scheduled on a CPU and do not waste CPU time; other threads can be scheduled on the CPU instead.

In addition, when performing a garbage collection, the CLR must suspend all the threads, walk their stacks to find the roots to mark objects in the heap, walk their stacks again (updating roots to objects that moved during compaction), and then resume all the threads. So avoiding threads will greatly improve the performance of the garbage collector, too. And whenever you are using a debugger, Windows suspends all threads in the application being debugged every time a breakpoint is hit and resumes all the threads when you single-step or run the application. So the more threads you have, the slower your debugging experience will be.

From this discussion, you should conclude that you must avoid using threads as much as possible because they consume a lot of memory and they require time to create, destroy, and manage. Time is also wasted when Windows context switches between threads and when garbage collections occur. However, this discussion should also help you realize that threads must be used sometimes because they allow Windows to be robust and responsive.

I should also point out that a computer with multiple CPUs in it can actually run multiple threads simultaneously, increasing *scalability* (the ability to do more work in less time). Windows will assign one thread to each CPU core, and each core will perform its own context switching to other threads. Windows makes sure that a single thread is not scheduled on multiple cores at one time because this would wreak havoc. Today, computers that contain multiple CPUs, hyperthreaded CPUs, or multi-core CPUs are commonplace. But when Windows was originally designed, single-CPU computers were commonplace, and Windows added threads to improve system responsiveness and reliability. Today, threads are also being used to improve scalability, which can happen only on computers that have multiple cores in them.

The remaining chapters in this book discuss the various Windows and CLR mechanisms that exist so that you can effectively wrestle with the tension of creating as few threads as possible while still keeping your code responsive and allowing it to scale if your code is running on a machine with multiple cores.

Stop the Madness

If all we cared about was raw performance, then the optimum number of threads to have on any machine is identical to the number of CPUs on that machine. So a machine with one CPU would have only one thread, a machine with two CPUs would have two threads, and so on. The reason is obvious: If you have more threads than CPUs, then context switching is introduced and performance deteriorates. If each CPU has just one thread, then no context switching exists and the threads run at full speed.

However, Microsoft designed Windows to favor reliability and responsiveness as opposed to favoring raw speed and performance. And I commend this decision: I don't think any of us would be using Windows or the .NET Framework today if applications could still stop the OS and other applications. Therefore, Windows gives each process its own thread for improved system reliability and responsiveness. On my machine, for example, when I run Task Manager and select the Performance tab, I see the image shown in Figure 25-1.

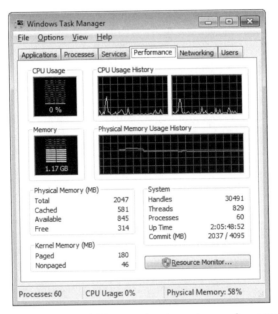

FIGURE 25-1 Task Manager showing system performance

It shows that my machine currently has 60 processes running on it, and so we'd expect that there were at least 60 threads on my machine since each process gets at least 1 thread. But Task Manager also shows that my machine currently has 829 threads in it! This means that there is about 829 MB of memory allocated for just the thread stacks, and my machine has only 2 GB of RAM in it. This also means that there is an average of approximately 13.8 threads per process.

Now, look at the CPU Usage reading: It shows that my CPU is busy 0 percent of the time. This means that 100 percent of the time, these 829 threads have literally nothing to do—they are just soaking up memory that is definitely not being used when the threads are not running. You have to ask yourself: Do these applications need all these threads to do nothing 100 percent of the time? The answer to this question has to be "No." Now, if you want to see which processes are the most wasteful, click the Processes tab, add the Threads column,[3] and sort this column in descending order, as shown in Figure 25-2.

---

[3] You add the column by selecting the View menu's Select Columns menu item.

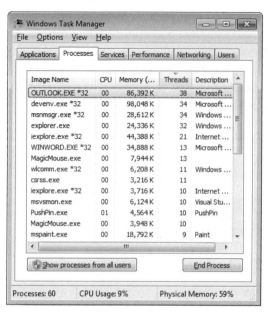

FIGURE 25-2 Task Manager showing processes

As you can see here, Outlook has created 38 threads and is using 0 percent of the CPU, Microsoft Visual Studio (Devenv.exe) has created 34 threads to use 0 percent of the CPU, Windows Live Messenger (Msnmsgr.exe) has created 34 threads to use 0 percent of the CPU, and so on. What is going on here?

When developers were learning about Windows, they learned that a process in Windows is very, very expensive. Creating a process usually takes several seconds, a lot of memory must be allocated, this memory must be initialized, the EXE and DLL files have to load from disk, and so on. By comparison, creating a thread in Windows is very cheap, so developers decided to stop creating processes and start creating threads instead. So now we have lots of threads. But even though threads are cheaper than processes, they are still very expensive compared to most other system resources, so they should be used sparingly and appropriately.

Well, without a doubt, we can say for sure that all of these applications we've just discussed are using threads inefficiently. There is just no way that all of these threads need to exist in the system. It is one thing to allocate resources inside an application; it's quite another to allocate them and then not use them. This is just wasteful, and allocating all the memory for thread stacks means that there is less memory for more important data, such as a user's document.[4]

---

[4] I just can't resist sharing with you another demonstration of how bad this situation is. Try this: Open Notepad.exe and use Task Manager to see how many threads are in it. Then select Notepad's File Open menu item to display the common File Open dialog box. Once the dialog box appears, look at Task Manager to see how many new threads just got created. On my machine, 22 additional threads are created just by displaying this dialog box! In fact, every application that uses the common File Open or File Save dialog box will get many additional threads created inside it that sit idle most of the time. A lot of these threads aren't even destroyed when the dialog box is closed.

To make matters worse, what if these were the processes running in a single user's Remote Desktop Services session—and what if there were actually 100 users on this machine? Then there would be 100 instances of Outlook, all creating 38 threads only to do nothing with them. That's 3,800 threads each with its own kernel object, TEB, user-mode stack, kernel-mode stack, etc. That is a lot of wasted resources. This madness has to stop, especially if Microsoft wants to give users a good experience when running Windows on netbook computers, many of which have only 1 GB of RAM. Again, the chapters in this part of the book will describe how to properly design an application to use very few threads in an efficient manner.

Now, I will admit that today, most threads in the system are created by native code. Therefore, the thread's user-mode stack is really just reserving address space and most likely, the stack is not fully committed to using storage. However, as more and more applications become managed or have managed components running inside them (which Outlook supports), then more and more stacks become fully committed, and they are allocating a full 1 MB of physical storage. Regardless, all threads still have a kernel object, kernel-mode stack, and other resources allocated to them. This trend of creating threads willy-nilly because they are cheap has to stop; threads are not cheap—rather, they are expensive, so use them wisely.

CPU Trends

In the past, CPU speeds used to increase with time, so an application that ran slowly on one machine would typically run faster on a newer machine. However, CPU manufacturers are unable to continue the trend of making CPUs faster. When you run CPUs at high speeds, they produce a lot of heat that has to be dissipated. A few years ago, I acquired a newly released notebook computer from a respected manufacturer. This computer had a bug in its firmware that made it not turn the fan on enough; as a result, after running the computer for a while, the CPU and the motherboard melted. The hardware manufacturer replaced the machine and then "improved" the firmware by making the fan run more frequently. Unfortunately, this had the effect of draining the battery faster, because fans consume a lot of power.

These are the kinds of problems that the hardware vendors face today. Since CPU manufacturers can't continuously produce higher-speed CPUs, they have instead turned their attention to making transistors smaller so that more of them can reside on a single chip. Today, we can have a single silicon chip that contains two or more CPU cores. The result is that our software only gets faster if we write our software to use the multiple cores. How do we do this? We use threads *in an intelligent fashion*.

Computers use three kinds of multi-CPU technologies today:

- **Multiple CPUs**   Some computers just have multiple CPUs in them. That is, the motherboard has multiple sockets on it, with each socket containing a CPU. Since the motherboard must be bigger, the computer case is bigger as well, and sometimes these machines have multiple power supplies in them due to the additional power drain. These kinds of computers have been around for a few decades, but they are not as popular today due to their increased size and cost.

- **Hyperthreaded chips**   This technology (owned by Intel) allows a single chip to look like two chips. The chip contains two sets of architectural states, such as CPU registers, but the chip has only one set of execution resources. To Windows, this looks like there are two CPUs in the machine, so Windows schedules two threads concurrently. However, the chip only executes one of the threads at a time. When one thread pauses due to a cache miss, branch misprediction, or data dependency, the chip switches to the other thread. This all happens in hardware, and Windows doesn't know that it is happening; Windows believes that both threads are running concurrently. Windows does know about hyperthreaded CPUs, and if you have multiple hyperthreaded CPUs in a single machine, Windows will first schedule one thread on each CPU so that the threads are truly running concurrently and then schedule other threads on the already-busy CPUs. Intel claims that a hyperthreaded CPU can improve performance by 10 percent to 30 percent.

- **Multi-core chips**   A few years ago, single chips containing multiple CPU cores have entered the scene. As I write this, chips with two, three, and four cores are readily available. Even my notebook computer has two cores in it; I'm sure it won't be long before our mobile phones have multiple cores in them too. Intel has even been working on a single chip with 80 cores on it! Wow, this is a lot of computing power! And Intel even has hyperthreaded multi-core chips.

NUMA Architecture Machines

While multi-core CPUs look great on the surface, they lead to a new problem. Now, multiple cores are accessing other system resources concurrently, so these other system resources become the bottleneck of the system's overall performance. For example, if two cores need to access RAM simultaneously, the memory bandwidth limits overall performance so that a dual-core system yields only a 30 percent to 70 percent performance improvement compared to a single-core system. To help mitigate this, computers are now employing what is called a *Cache-Coherent Non-Uniform Memory Access* architecture, or simply, NUMA.

Figure 25-3 shows the architecture of a NUMA-based computer system. This system has four nodes in it. Each node contains four CPUs, a north bridge, a south bridge, and local memory (RAM). Some nodes also have local devices connected. All of the memory is accessible to any node; however, the time it takes to access the memory is non-uniform. For example, any CPU on Node 1 can access local memory on Node 1 very quickly. A CPU on Node 1 can also access memory on Nodes 2 and 4, but only with a significant performance hit. A CPU in Node 1 can also access memory on Node 3, but the resulting performance hit is even worse since there is no direct line of communication between Nodes 1 and 3. Even though the 16 CPUs are spread across four different nodes, the hardware ensures that the caches of all CPUs remain coherent and in sync with each other.

The Win32 API offers many functions to unmanaged developers that allow their applications to specifically allocate memory on a particular NUMA node and to force threads to run on a specific NUMA node. Today, the CLR does nothing special to accommodate NUMA systems. In the future, I imagine the CLR will include things like having one garbage-collected heap per NUMA node and perhaps the ability for an application to indicate on which node an object should be allocated. Or perhaps the CLR will migrate objects from one node to another, depending on which CPU seems to be accessing the object the most.

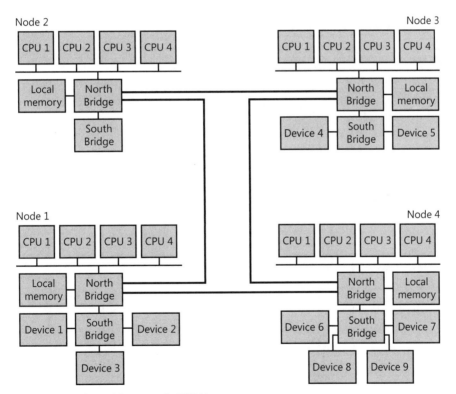

FIGURE 25-3 The architecture of a NUMA computer

Back in the early 1990s, it was hard to imagine that someday there would be computers that had 32 CPUs in them. Therefore, when 32-bit Windows was first created, it was designed to handle machines with up to 32 CPUs. Then, when Microsoft was making 64-bit Windows, it designed the system to handle up to 64 CPUs in a single machine. At the time, 64 CPUs seemed like a lot, but today it looks like machines are going to get even more CPUs in them in the not-so-far-off future.

Starting with Windows Server 2008 R2, Microsoft has designed Windows to support machines that have up to 256 logical processors in them. Figure 25-4 shows how Windows supports all these logical processors. Here's how to interpret the figure:

- A single machine has 1 or more processor groups where each group contains 1 to 64 logical processors.

- A processor group has one or more NUMA nodes. Each node contains some logical processors, cache memory, and local memory (all in proximity to each other).

- Each NUMA node has one or more sockets on it for silicon chips.

- Each socket's chip contains one or more CPU cores.

- Each core contains one or more logical processors. There can be more than one logical processor if the chip is hyperthreaded.

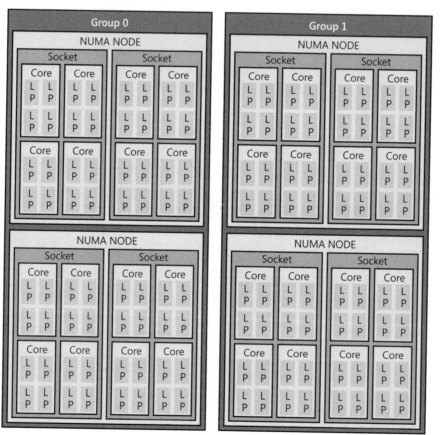

FIGURE 25-4 Windows uses processor groups to support machines with up to 256 logical processors in them

Today, the CLR doesn't take advantage of processor groups and so all of the threads it creates run in processor group 0 (the default) and can only use up to 64 cores when running on 64-bit Windows. Since 32-bit versions of Windows only support processor group 0 and since 32-bit versions of Windows only support 32 CPUs, managed applications can use up to 32 cores when running on a 32-bit version of Windows.

CLR Threads and Windows Threads

Today, the CLR uses the threading capabilities of Windows, so Part V of this book is really focusing on how the threading capabilities of Windows are exposed to developers who write code by using the CLR. I will explain about how threads in Windows work and how the CLR alters the behavior (if it does). However, if you'd like more information about threads, I recommend reading some of my earlier writings on the topic, such as my book *Windows via C/C++, 5th Edition* (Microsoft Press, 2007).

While a CLR thread maps directly to a Windows thread today, the Microsoft CLR team reserves the right to divorce itself from Windows threads in the future. Someday, the CLR may introduce its own logical thread concept so that a CLR logical thread doesn't necessarily map to a physical Windows thread. For example, there has been talk of creating logical threads that use much less resources than physical threads, and then you could have many logical threads running on top of a very small number of physical threads. For instance, the CLR could determine that one of your threads is in a wait state and reassign that thread to do a different task. The benefits of this include easier coding, less resources used, and potentially improved performance. Unfortunately, implementing this solution would be a huge amount of work for the CLR team, so I would not expect a feature like this to make it into the CLR anytime soon.

For you, all of this means that your code should make as few assumptions as possible when manipulating threads. For example, you should avoid P/Invoking to native Windows functions since these functions have no knowledge of a CLR thread.[5] By avoiding native Windows functions and sticking with Framework Class Library (FCL) types whenever possible, you're guaranteed that your code will easily take advantage of these performance enhancements as they become available in the future.

---

[5] If you need to P/Invoke out to native code and it is important that the code execute using the current physical operating system thread, then you should call **System.Threading.Thread**'s static **BeginThreadAffinity** method. When the thread no longer requires running by using the physical operating system thread, it can notify the CLR by calling **Thread**'s static **EndThreadAffinity** method.

Using a Dedicated Thread to Perform an Asynchronous Compute-Bound Operation

In this section, I will show you how to create a thread and have it perform an asynchronous compute-bound operation. While I am going to walk you through this, I highly recommend that you avoid the technique I show you here. Instead, you should use the CLR's thread pool to execute asynchronous compute-bound operations whenever possible, and I go into the details about doing this in Chapter 26, "Compute-Bound Asynchronous Operations."

However, there are some occasions when you might want to explicitly create a thread dedicated to executing a particular compute-bound operation. Typically, you'd want to create a dedicated thread if you're going to execute code that requires the thread to be in a particular state that is not normal for a thread pool thread. For example, explicitly create your own thread if any of the following is true:

- You need the thread to run with a non-normal thread priority. All thread pool threads run at normal priority. While you can change this, it is not recommended, and the priority change does not persist across thread pool operations.

- You need the thread to behave as a foreground thread, thereby preventing the application from dying until the thread has completed its task. For more information, see the "Foreground Threads versus Background Threads" section later in this chapter. Thread pool threads are always background threads, and they may not complete their task if the CLR wants to terminate the process.

- The compute-bound task is extremely long-running; this way, I would not be taxing the thread pool's logic as it tries to figure out whether to create an additional thread.

- I wanted to start a thread and possibly abort it prematurely by calling **Thread**'s **Abort** method (discussed in Chapter 22, "CLR Hosting and AppDomains").

To create a dedicated thread, you construct an instance of the **System.Threading.Thread** class, passing the name of a method into its constructor. Here is the prototype of **Thread**'s constructor:

```
public sealed class Thread : CriticalFinalizerObject, ... {
   public Thread(ParameterizedThreadStart start);
   // Less commonly used constructors are not shown here
}
```

The **start** parameter identifies the method that the dedicated thread will execute, and this method must match the signature of the **ParameterizedThreadStart** delegate.[6]

```
delegate void ParameterizedThreadStart(Object obj);
```

---

[6] For the record, **Thread** also offers a constructor that takes a **ThreadStart** delegate that accepts no arguments and returns **void**. Personally, I recommend that you avoid this constructor and delegate because they are more limiting. If your thread method takes an **Object** and returns **void**, then you can invoke your method using a dedicated thread or invoke it using the thread pool (as shown in Chapter 26).

Constructing a **Thread** object is a relatively lightweight operation because it does not actually create a physical operating system thread. To actually create the operating system thread and have it start executing the callback method, you must call **Thread**'s **Start** method, passing into it the object (state) that you want passed as the callback method's argument. The following code demonstrates how to create a dedicated thread and have it call a method asynchronously:

```
using System;
using System.Threading;

public static class Program {
    public static void Main() {
        Console.WriteLine("Main thread: starting a dedicated thread " +
            "to do an asynchronous operation");
        Thread dedicatedThread = new Thread(ComputeBoundOp);
        dedicatedThread.Start(5);

        Console.WriteLine("Main thread: Doing other work here...");
        Thread.Sleep(10000);       // Simulating other work (10 seconds)

        dedicatedThread.Join();  // Wait for thread to terminate
        Console.WriteLine("Hit <Enter> to end this program...");
        Console.ReadLine();
    }

    // This method's signature must match the ParameterizedThreadStart delegate
    private static void ComputeBoundOp(Object state) {
        // This method is executed by a dedicated thread

        Console.WriteLine("In ComputeBoundOp: state={0}", state);
        Thread.Sleep(1000);   // Simulates other work (1 second)

        // When this method returns, the dedicated thread dies
    }
}
```

When I compile and run this code, I get the following output:

```
Main thread: starting a dedicated thread to do an asynchronous operation
Main thread: Doing other work here...
In ComputeBoundOp: state=5
```

Sometimes when I run this code, I get the following output since I can't control how Windows schedules the two threads:

```
Main thread: starting a dedicated thread to do an asynchronous operation
In ComputeBoundOp: state=5
Main thread: Doing other work here...
```

Notice that the **Main** method calls **Join**. The **Join** method causes the calling thread to stop executing any code until the thread identified by **dedicatedThread** has destroyed itself or been terminated.

Reasons to Use Threads

There are really three reasons to use threads.

- **You can use threads to isolate code from other code.**   This can improve your application's reliability, and in fact, this is why Windows introduced the concept of threads into the operating system. Windows needs threads for reliability because your application is a third-party component to the operating system and Microsoft doesn't verify the quality of your code before you ship it. However, you should be testing all of your applications before you ship them, and since you are testing complete applications, you should know that they are robust and of high quality. Because of this, your application's need for robustness is not as high as the operating system's need for robustness, and therefore, your application should not use many threads for the purpose of maintaining robustness. If your application supports the loading of components produced by other parties, then your application's need for robustness increases and using threads can help satisfy this requirement.

- **You can use threads to make your coding easier.**   Sometimes coding is easier if you execute a task via its own thread. But of course, when you do this, you are using additional resources and not writing the code as efficiently as possible. Now, I'm all for having an easier coding process even at the expense of some resources. If I weren't OK with this, then I'd still be writing in machine language as opposed to being a C# developer. But sometimes I see people using threads thinking that they are choosing an easier programming methodology when, in fact, they are complicating their life (and their code) substantially. Usually, when you introduce threads, you introduce coordination code that may require thread synchronization constructs to know when the other thread has terminated. Once you start handling coordination, you are using even more resources and complicating your code. So make sure that threads are really going to help you before you start using them.

- **You can use threads to get concurrent execution.**   If and only if you know that your application is running on a machine with multiple CPUs in it, you can get improved performance by having multiple tasks executing simultaneously. Today, machines with multiple CPUs in them are quite common, so designing your application to use multiple cores makes sense and is the focus of Chapter 26 and Chapter 27, "I/O-Bound Asynchronous Operations."

Now, I'd like to share with you a theory of mine. Every computer has an incredibly powerful resource inside it: the CPU itself. If someone spends money on a computer, then that computer should be working all the time. In other words, I believe that all the CPUs in a computer should be running at 100 percent utilization all the time. I will qualify this statement with two caveats. First, you may not want the CPUs running at 100 percent utilization if the computer is on battery power because that may drain the battery too quickly. Second, some data centers would prefer to have 10 machines running at 50 percent CPU utilization rather than

5 machines running at 100 percent CPU utilization because running CPUs at full power tends to generate heat, which requires cooling systems, and powering a HVAC cooling system can be more expensive than powering more computers running at reduced capacity. Although data centers find it increasingly expensive to maintain multiple machines because each machine has to have periodic hardware and software upgrades and monitoring, this has to be weighed against the expense of running a cooling system.

Now, if you agree with my theory, then the next step is to figure out what the CPUs should be doing. Before I give you my ideas here, let me say something else first. In the past, developers and end users always felt that the computer was not powerful enough. Therefore, we developers would never just execute code unless the end users give us permission to do so and indicate that it is OK for the application to consume CPU resources via UI elements such as menu items, buttons, and check boxes.

But now, times have changed. Computers ship with phenomenal amounts of computing power, and even more computing power is being promised in the very near future. Earlier in this chapter, I showed you how Task Manager was reporting that my CPU was busy just 0 percent of the time. If my computer contained a quad-core CPU in it instead of the dual-core CPU that it now has, then Task Manager will report 0 percent more often. When an 80-core processor comes out, the machine will look like it's doing nothing almost all the time. To computer purchasers, it looks like they're spending more money for more powerful CPUs and the computer is doing less work!

This is the reason why the hardware manufacturers are having a hard time selling multi-core computers to users: the software isn't taking advantage of the hardware and users get no benefit from buying machines with additional CPUs. What I'm saying is that we now have an abundance of computing power available and more is on the way, so developers can aggressively consume it. That's right—in the past, we would never dream of having our applications perform some computation unless we knew the end user wanted the result of that computation. But now that we have extra computing power, we can dream like this.

Here's an example: When you stop typing in Visual Studio's editor, Visual Studio automatically spawns the compiler and compiles your code. This makes developers incredibly productive because they can see warnings and errors in their source code as they type and can fix things immediately. In fact, what developers think of today as the Edit-Build-Debug cycle will become just the Edit-Debug cycle because building (compiling) code will just happen all the time. You, as an end user, won't notice this because there is a lot of CPU power available and other things you're doing will barely be affected by the frequent running of the compiler. In fact, I would expect that in some future version of Visual Studio, the Build menu item will disappear completely because building will just become automatic. Not only does the application's UI get simpler, but the application also offers "answers" to the end user, making them more productive.

When we remove UI components like menu items, computers get simpler for end users. There are fewer options for them and fewer concepts for them to read and understand. It is the multi-core revolution that allows us to remove these UI elements, thereby making software so much simpler for end users that my grandmother might someday feel comfortable using a computer. For developers, removing UI elements usually results in less testing, and offering fewer options to the end user simplifies the code base. And if you currently localize the text in your UI elements and your documentation (like Microsoft does), then removing the UI elements means that you write less documentation and you don't have to localize this documentation anymore. All of this can save your organization a lot of time and money.

Here are some more examples of aggressive CPU consumption: spell checking and grammar checking of documents, recalculation of spreadsheets, indexing files on your disk for fast searching, and defragmenting your hard disk to improve I/O performance.

I want to live in a world where the UI is reduced and simplified, I have more screen real estate to visualize the data that I'm actually working on, and applications offer me information that helps me get my work done quickly and efficiently instead of me telling the application to go get information for me. I think the hardware has been there for software developers to use for the past few years. It's time for the software to start using the hardware creatively.

Thread Scheduling and Priorities

A preemptive operating system must use some kind of algorithm to determine which threads should be scheduled when and for how long. In this section, we'll look at the algorithm Windows uses. Earlier in this chapter, I mentioned how every thread's kernel object contains a context structure. The context structure reflects the state of the thread's CPU registers when the thread last executed. After a time-slice, Windows looks at all the thread kernel objects currently in existence. Of these objects, only the threads that are not waiting for something are considered schedulable. Windows selects one of the schedulable thread kernel objects and context switches to it. Windows actually keeps a record of how many times each thread gets context switched to. You can see this when using a tool such as Microsoft Spy++. Figure 25-5 shows the properties for a thread. Notice that this thread has been scheduled 31,768 times.[7]

---

[7] As a side note, you can also see that the thread has been in the system for more than 25 hours, but it actually used less than 1 second of CPU time, which wastes a lot of resources.

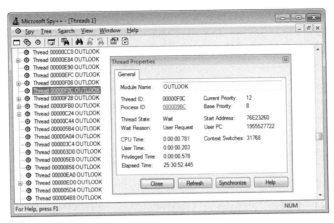

FIGURE 25-5 Spy++ showing a thread's properties

At this point, the thread is executing code and manipulating data in its process's address space. After another time-slice, Windows performs another context switch. Windows performs context switches from the moment the system is booted and continues until the system is shut down.

Windows is called a preemptive multithreaded operating system because a thread can be stopped at any time and another thread can be scheduled. As you'll see, you have some control over this, but not much. Just remember that you cannot guarantee that your thread will always be running and that no other thread will be allowed to run.

> **Note** Developers frequently ask me how they can guarantee that their thread will start running within some time period after some event—for example, how can you ensure that a particular thread will start running within 1 ms of data coming from the serial port? I have an easy answer: You can't.
>
> Real-time operating systems can make these promises, but Windows is not a real-time operating system. A real-time operating system requires intimate knowledge of the hardware it is running on so that it knows the latency associated with its hard disk controllers, keyboards, and other components. Microsoft's goal with Windows is to make it work on a wide variety of hardware: different CPUs, different drives, different networks, and so on. In short, Windows is not designed to be a real-time operating system. Let me also add that the CLR makes managed code behave even less in real time. There are many reasons for this, including just-in-time (JIT) loading of DLLs, JIT compiling of code, and the garbage collector kicking in at unpredictable times.

Every thread is assigned a priority level ranging from 0 (the lowest) to 31 (the highest). When the system decides which thread to assign to a CPU, it examines the priority 31 threads first and schedules them in a round-robin fashion. If a priority 31 thread is schedulable, it is assigned to a CPU. At the end of this thread's time-slice, the system checks to see whether there is another priority 31 thread that can run; if so, it allows that thread to be assigned to a CPU.

So long as priority 31 threads are schedulable, the system never assigns any thread with a priority of 0 through 30 to a CPU. This condition is called *starvation,* and it occurs when higher-priority threads use so much CPU time that they prevent lower-priority threads from executing. Starvation is much less likely to occur on a multiprocessor machine because a priority 31 thread and a priority 30 thread can run simultaneously on such a machine. The system always tries to keep the CPUs busy, and CPUs sit idle only if no threads are schedulable.

Higher-priority threads always preempt lower-priority threads, regardless of what the lower-priority threads are executing. For example, if a priority 5 thread is running and the system determines that a higher-priority thread is ready to run, the system immediately suspends the lower-priority thread (even if it's in the middle of its time-slice) and assigns the CPU to the higher-priority thread, which gets a full time-slice.

By the way, when the system boots, it creates a special thread called the *zero page thread.* This thread is assigned priority 0 and is the only thread in the entire system that runs at priority 0. The zero page thread is responsible for zeroing any free pages of RAM in the system when no other threads need to perform work.

Microsoft realized that assigning priority levels to threads was going to be too hard for developers to rationalize. Should this thread be priority level 10? Should this other thread be priority level 23? To resolve this issue, Windows exposes an abstract layer over the priority level system.

When designing your application, you should decide whether your application needs to be more or less responsive than other applications that may be running on the machine. Then you choose a process priority class to reflect your decision. Windows supports six process priority classes: Idle, Below Normal, Normal, Above Normal, High, and Realtime. Of course, Normal is the default and is therefore the most common priority class by far.

The Idle priority class is perfect for applications (like screen savers) that run when the system is all but doing nothing. A computer that is not being used interactively might still be busy (acting as a file server, for example) and should not have to compete for CPU time with a screen saver. Statistics-tracking applications that periodically update some state about the system usually should not interfere with more critical tasks.

You should use the High priority class only when absolutely necessary. You should avoid using the Realtime priority class if possible. Realtime priority is extremely high and can interfere with operating system tasks, such as preventing required disk I/O and network traffic from occurring. In addition, a Realtime process's threads could prevent keyboard and mouse input from being processed in a timely manner, causing the user to think that the system is completely frozen. Basically, you should have a good reason for using Realtime priority, such as the need to respond to hardware events with short latency or to perform some short-lived task.

Note To keep the overall system running smoothly, a process cannot run in the Realtime priority class unless the user has the Increase Scheduling Priority privilege. Any user designated as an administrator or a power user has this privilege by default.

Once you select a priority class, you should stop thinking about how your application relates to other applications and just concentrate on the threads within your application. Windows supports seven relative thread priorities: Idle, Lowest, Below Normal, Normal, Above Normal, Highest, and Time-Critical. These priorities are relative to the process's priority class. Again, Normal relative thread priority is the default, and it is therefore the most common.

So, to summarize, your process is a member of a priority class and within that process you assign thread priorities that are relative to each other. You'll notice that I haven't said anything about priority levels 0 through 31. Application developers never work with priority levels directly. Instead, the system maps the process's priority class and a thread's relative priority to a priority level. Table 25-1 shows how the process's priority class and the thread's relative priority maps to priority levels.

TABLE 25-1 **How Process Priority Class and Relative Thread Priorities Map to Priority Levels**

Relative Thread Priority	Process Priority Class					
	Idle	Below Normal	Normal	Above Normal	High	Realtime
Time-Critical	15	15	15	15	15	31
Highest	6	8	10	12	15	26
Above Normal	5	7	9	11	14	25
Normal	4	6	8	10	13	24
Below Normal	3	5	7	9	12	23
Lowest	2	4	6	8	11	22
Idle	1	1	1	1	1	16

For example, a Normal thread in a Normal process is assigned a priority level of 8. Because most processes are of the Normal priority class and most threads are of Normal thread priority, most threads in the system have a priority level of 8.

If you have a Normal thread in a high-priority process, the thread will have a priority level of 13. If you change the process's priority class to Idle, the thread's priority level becomes 4. Remember that thread priorities are relative to the process's priority class. If you change a process's priority class, the thread's relative priority will not change, but its priority number will.

Notice that the table does not show any way for a thread to have a priority level of 0. This is because the 0 priority is reserved for the zero page thread and the system does not allow any other thread to have a priority of 0. Also, the following priority levels are not obtainable: 17, 18, 19, 20, 21, 27, 28, 29, or 30. If you are writing a device driver that runs in kernel mode, you can obtain these levels; a user-mode application cannot. Also note that a thread in the Realtime priority class can't be below priority level 16. Likewise, a thread in a priority class other than Realtime cannot be above 15.

> **Note** The concept of a process priority class confuses some people. They think that this some-how means that Windows schedules processes. However, Windows never schedules processes; Windows only schedules threads. The process priority class is an abstract concept that Microsoft created to help you rationalize how your application compares with other running applications; it serves no other purpose.

> **Important** It is best to lower a thread's priority instead of raising another thread's priority. You would normally lower a thread's priority if that thread was going to execute a long-running compute-bound task like compiling code, spell checking, spreadsheet recalculations, etc. You would raise a thread's priority if the thread needs to respond to something very quickly and then run for a very short period of time and go back to its wait state. High-priority threads should be waiting for something most of their life so that they do not affect the responsiveness of the whole system. The Windows Explorer thread that responds to the user pressing the Windows key on the keyboard is an example of a high-priority thread. When the user presses this key, Windows Explorer preempts other lower-priority threads immediately and displays its menu. As the user navigates the menu, Windows Explorer's thread responds to each keystroke quickly, updates the menu, and then stops running until the user continues navigating the menu.

Normally, a process is assigned a priority class based on the process that starts it running. And most processes are started by Windows Explorer, which spawns all its child processes in the Normal priority class. Managed applications are not supposed to act as though they own their own processes; they are supposed to act as though they run in an AppDomain, so managed applications are not supposed to change their process's priority class because this would affect all code running in the process. For example, many ASP.NET applications run in a single process, with each application in its own AppDomain. The same is true for Silverlight applications, which run in an Internet browser process, and managed stored procedures, which run inside the Microsoft SQL Server process.

On the other hand, your application can change the relative thread priority of its threads by setting **Thread**'s **Priority** property, passing it one of the five values (**Lowest**, **BelowNormal**, **Normal**, **AboveNormal**, or **Highest**) defined in the **ThreadPriority** enumerated type. However, just as Windows has reserved the priority level 0 and the real-time range for itself, the CLR reserves the Idle and Time-Critical priority levels for itself. Today, the CLR has no threads that run at Idle priority level, but this could change in the future. However, the

CLR's finalizer thread, discussed in Chapter 21, "Automatic Memory Management (Garbage Collection)," runs at the Time-Critical priority level. Therefore, as a managed developer, you really only get to use the five highlighted relative thread priorities listed in Table 25-1.

> **Important** Today, most applications do not take advantage of thread priorities. However, in the world that I envision, where the CPUs are busy 100 percent of the time doing some kind of useful work, using thread priorities becomes critically important so that system responsiveness is unaffected. Unfortunately, end users have been trained to interpret a high-CPU usage number to mean that an application is out of control. In my new world, end users will need to be retrained to understand that high-CPU usage is a good thing—that it actually means that the computer is aggressively processing helpful pieces of information for users. The real problem would be if all the CPUs are busy running threads that are priority level 8 and above, as this would mean that applications are having trouble responding to end user input. Perhaps a future version of Task Manager will take thread priority levels into account when reporting CPU usage; this would be much more helpful in diagnosing a troubled system.

I should point out that the **System.Diagnostics** namespace contains a **Process** class and a **ProcessThread** class. These classes provide the Windows view of a process and thread, respectively. These classes are provided for developers wanting to write utility applications in managed code or for developers who are trying to instrument their code to help them debug it. In fact, this is why the classes are in the **System.Diagnostics** namespace. Applications need to be running with special security permissions to use these two classes. You would not be able to use these classes from a Silverlight application or an ASP.NET application, for example.

On the other hand, applications can use the **AppDomain** and **Thread** classes, which expose the CLR's view of an AppDomain and thread. For the most part, special security permissions are not required to use these classes, although some operations are still considered privileged.

Foreground Threads versus Background Threads

The CLR considers every thread to be either a foreground thread or a background thread. When all the foreground threads in a process stop running, the CLR forcibly ends any background threads that are still running. These background threads are ended immediately; no exception is thrown.

Therefore, you should use foreground threads to execute tasks that you really want to complete, like flushing data from a memory buffer out to disk. And you should use background threads for tasks that are not mission-critical, like recalculating spreadsheet cells or indexing records, because this work can continue again when the application restarts, and there is no need to force the application to stay active if the user wants to terminate it.

The CLR needed to provide this concept of foreground and background threads to better support AppDomains. You see, each AppDomain could be running a separate application and each of these applications would have its own foreground thread. If one application exits, causing its foreground thread to terminate, then the CLR still needs to stay up and running so that other applications continue to run. After all the applications exit and all their foreground threads terminate, the whole process can be destroyed.

The following code demonstrates the difference between foreground and background threads:

```
using System;
using System.Threading;

public static class Program {
    public static void Main() {
        // Create a new thread (defaults to foreground)
        Thread t = new Thread(Worker);

        // Make the thread a background thread
        t.IsBackground = true;

        t.Start(); // Start the thread
        // If t is a foreground thread, the application won't die for about 10 seconds
        // If t is a background thread, the application dies immediately
        Console.WriteLine("Returning from Main");
    }

    private static void Worker() {
        Thread.Sleep(10000);  // Simulate doing 10 seconds of work

        // The line below only gets displayed if this code is executed by a foreground thread
        Console.WriteLine("Returning from Worker");
    }
}
```

It is possible to change a thread from foreground to background and vice versa at any time during its lifetime. An application's primary thread and any threads explicitly created by constructing a **Thread** object default to being foreground threads. On the other hand, thread pool threads default to being background threads. Also, any threads created by native code that enter the managed execution environment are marked as background threads.

Important Try to avoid using foreground threads as much as possible. I was brought into a consulting job once where an application just wouldn't terminate. After I spent several hours researching the problem, it turned out that a UI component was explicitly creating a foreground thread (the default), and that was why the process wouldn't terminate. We changed the component to use the thread pool to fix the problem, and efficiency improved as well.

What Now?

In this chapter, I've explained the basics about threads, and I hope I've made it clear to you that threads are very expensive resources that should be used sparingly. The best way to accomplish this is by using the CLR's thread pool. The thread pool will manage thread creation and destruction for you automatically. The thread pool creates a set of threads that get reused for various tasks so your application requires just a few threads to accomplish all of its work.

In Chapter 26, I will focus on how to use the CLR's thread pool to perform compute-bound operations. Then, in Chapter 27, I will discuss how to use the thread pool in combination with the CLR's Asynchronous Programming Model to perform I/O-bound operations. In many scenarios, you can perform asynchronous compute-bound and I/O-bound operations in such a way that thread synchronization is not required at all. However, there are some scenarios where thread synchronization is required, and the way that the thread synchronization constructs work and the difference between these various constructs are discussed in Chapter 28, "Primitive Thread Synchronization Constructs," and Chapter 29, "Hybrid Thread Synchronization Constructs."

Before ending this discussion, I'd like to point out that I have been working extensively with threads since the first beta version of Windows NT 3.1 was available around 1992. And when .NET was in beta, I started producing a library of classes that can simplify asynchronous programming and thread synchronization. This library is called the *Wintellect Power Threading Library,* and it is freely downloadable and usable. Versions of the library exist for the desktop CLR, the Silverlight CLR, and the Compact Framework. The library, documentation, and sample code can be downloaded from *http://Wintellect.com/PowerThreading.aspx.* This Web site also contains links to a support forum, as well as to videos that show how to use various parts of the library.

Chapter 26
Compute-Bound Asynchronous Operations

In this chapter:

In this chapter, I'll talk about the various ways that you can perform operations asynchronously. When performing an asynchronous compute-bound operation, you execute it using other threads. Here are some examples of compute-bound operations: compiling code, spell checking, grammar checking, spreadsheet recalculations, transcoding audio or video data, and producing a thumbnail of an image. Certainly, compute-bound operations are common in financial and engineering applications.

I would say that most applications do not spend the bulk of their time processing in-memory data or performing calculations. You can verify that this is true by opening Task Manager and selecting the Performance tab. If your CPU usage is below 100% (which it tends to be most of the time), then the processes you have running are not using all the processing power made available by your machine's CPU cores. When the CPU usage is less than 100%, then some (if not all) of the threads within their processes are not running at all. Instead, these threads are waiting for some input or output operation to occur. For example, these threads are waiting for a timer to come due, waiting for data to be read from or written to a database, Web service, file, network, or other hardware device, or waiting for keystrokes, mouse movement, or mouse button clicks. When performing an I/O-bound operation, the Microsoft Windows device driver has the hardware device do the work for you and the CPU itself doesn't execute any threads that happen to exist in the system. Since threads are not running on a CPU, Task Manager indicates that CPU usage is low.

However, even in applications that are heavily I/O-bound, these applications perform some computation on data that has been received, and parallelizing this computation can greatly improve the application's throughput. This chapter introduces the common language runtime's (CLR's) thread pool and some basic concepts about how it works and how to use it. This information is critically useful, as the thread pool is the core technology that enables you to design and implement scalable, responsive, and reliable applications and components. Then this chapter shows the various mechanisms available that allow you to perform compute-bound operations via the thread pool. There are two reasons why you would want to execute compute-bound operations asynchronously: to keep the UI responsive in a GUI application or to scale a time-consuming calculation across multiple CPUs.

Introducing the CLR's Thread Pool

As stated in the previous chapter, creating and destroying a thread is an expensive operation in terms of time. In addition, having lots of threads wastes memory resources and also hurts performance due to the operating system having to schedule and context switch between the runnable threads. To improve this situation, the CLR contains code to manage its own thread pool. You can think of a thread pool as being a set of threads that are available for your application's own use. There is one thread pool per CLR; this thread pool is shared by all AppDomains controlled by that CLR. If multiple CLRs load within a single process, then each CLR has its own thread pool.

When the CLR initializes, the thread pool has no threads in it. Internally, the thread pool maintains a queue of operation requests. When your application wants to perform an asynchronous operation, you call some method that appends an entry into the thread pool's queue. The thread pool's code will extract entries from this queue and dispatch the entry to a thread pool thread. If there are no threads in the thread pool, a new thread will be created. Creating a thread has a performance hit associated with it (as already discussed). However, when a thread pool thread has completed its task, the thread is not destroyed; instead, the thread is returned to the thread pool, where it sits idle waiting to respond to another request. Since the thread doesn't destroy itself, there is no added performance hit.

If your application makes many requests of the thread pool, the thread pool will try to service all of the requests using just this one thread. However, if your application is queuing up several requests faster than the thread pool thread can handle them, additional threads will be created. Your application will eventually get to a point at which all of its requests can be handled by a small number of threads, so the thread pool should have no need to create a lot of threads.

If your application stops making requests of the thread pool, the pool may have a lot of threads in it that are doing nothing. This is wasteful of memory resources. So when a thread pool thread has been idle with nothing to do for some period of time (subject to change with different versions of the CLR), the thread wakes itself up and kills itself to free up resources.

As the thread is killing itself, there is a performance hit. However, this probably doesn't matter since the thread is killing itself because it has been idle, which means that your application isn't performing a lot of work.

The great thing about the thread pool is that it manages the tension between having a few threads, to keep from wasting resources, and having more threads, to take advantage of multiprocessors, hyperthreaded processors, and multi-core processors. And the thread pool is heuristic. If your application needs to perform many tasks and CPUs are available, the thread pool creates more threads. If your application's workload decreases, the thread pool threads kill themselves.

Internally, the thread pool categorizes its threads as either *worker threads* or *I/O threads*. Worker threads are used when your application asks the thread pool to perform an asynchronous compute-bound operation (which can include initiating an I/O-bound operation). I/O threads are used to notify your code when an asynchronous I/O-bound operation has completed. Specifically, this means that you are using the Asynchronous Programming Model (APM) to make I/O requests such as accessing a file, networked server, database, Web service, or other hardware device.

Performing a Simple Compute-Bound Operation

To queue an asynchronous compute-bound operation to the thread pool, you typically call one of the following methods defined by the **ThreadPool** class:

```
static Boolean QueueUserWorkItem(WaitCallback callBack);
static Boolean QueueUserWorkItem(WaitCallback callBack, Object state);
```

These methods queue a "work item" and optional state data to the thread pool's queue, and then all of these methods return immediately. A work item is simply a method identified by the **callback** parameter that will be called by a thread pool thread. The method can be passed a single parameter specified via the **state** (the state data) argument. The version of **QueueUserWorkItem** without the **state** parameter passes **null** to the callback method. Eventually, some thread in the pool will process the work item, causing your method to be called. The callback method you write must match the **System.Threading.WaitCallback** delegate type, which is defined as follows:

```
delegate void WaitCallback(Object state);
```

Note The signatures of the **WaitCallback** delegate, the **TimerCallback** delegate (discussed in this chapter's "Performing a Periodic Compute-Bound Operation" section), and the **ParameterizedThreadStart** delegate (discussed in Chapter 25, "Thread Basics") are all identical. If you define a method matching this signature, the method can be invoked by using **ThreadPool.QueueUserWorkItem**, by using a **System.Threading.Timer** object, or by using a **System.Threading.Thread** object.

The following code demonstrates how to have a thread pool thread call a method asynchronously:

```
using System;
using System.Threading;

public static class Program {
    public static void Main() {
        Console.WriteLine("Main thread: queuing an asynchronous operation");
        ThreadPool.QueueUserWorkItem(ComputeBoundOp, 5);
        Console.WriteLine("Main thread: Doing other work here...");
        Thread.Sleep(10000);  // Simulating other work (10 seconds)
        Console.WriteLine("Hit <Enter> to end this program...");
        Console.ReadLine();
    }

    // This method's signature must match the WaitCallback delegate
    private static void ComputeBoundOp(Object state) {
        // This method is executed by a thread pool thread

        Console.WriteLine("In ComputeBoundOp: state={0}", state);
        Thread.Sleep(1000);  // Simulates other work (1 second)

        // When this method returns, the thread goes back
        // to the pool and waits for another task
    }
}
```

When I compile and run this code, I get the following output:

```
Main thread: queuing an asynchronous operation
Main thread: Doing other work here...
In ComputeBoundOp: state=5
```

And, sometimes when I run this code, I get this output:

```
Main thread: queuing an asynchronous operation
In ComputeBoundOp: state=5
Main thread: Doing other work here...
```

The difference in the order of the lines in the output is attributed to the fact that the two methods are running asynchronously with respect to one another. The Windows scheduler determines which thread to schedule first, or it may schedule them both simultaneously if the application is running on a multi-CPU machine.

> **Note** If the callback method throws an exception that is unhandled, the CLR terminates the process (unless the host imposes its own policy). Unhandled exceptions are discussed in Chapter 20, "Exceptions and State Management."

Execution Contexts

Every thread has an execution context data structure associated with it. The execution context includes things such as security settings (compressed stack, **Thread**'s **Principal** property, and Windows identity), host settings (see **System.Threading. HostExecutionContextManager**), and logical call context data (see **System.Runtime. Remoting.Messaging.CallContext**'s **LogicalSetData** and **LogicalGetData** methods). When a thread executes code, some operations are affected by the values of the thread's execution context settings. This is certainly true for the security settings. Ideally, whenever a thread uses another (helper) thread to perform tasks, the issuing thread's execution context should flow (be copied) to the helper thread. This ensures that any operations performed by helper thread(s) are executing with the same security settings and host settings. It also ensures that any data stored in the initiating thread's logical call context is available to the helper thread.

By default, the CLR automatically causes the initiating thread's execution context to flow to any helper threads. This transfers context information to the helper thread, but it comes at a performance cost because there is a lot of information in an execution context, and accumulating all of this information and then copying it for the helper thread takes a fair amount of time. If the helper thread then employs additional helper threads, then more execution context data structures have to be created and initialized as well.

In the **System.Threading** namespace, there is an **ExecutionContext** class that allows you to control how a thread's execution context flows from one thread to another. Here is what the class looks like:

```
public sealed class ExecutionContext : IDisposable, ISerializable {
    [SecurityCritical] public static AsyncFlowControl SuppressFlow();
    public static void RestoreFlow();
    public static Boolean IsFlowSuppressed();

    // Less commonly used methods are not shown
}
```

You can use this class to suppress the flowing of an execution context, thereby improving your application's performance. The performance gains can be quite substantial for a server application. There is not much performance benefit for a client application, and the **SuppressFlow** method is marked with the **[SecurityCritical]** attribute, making it impossible to call in some client applications (like Silverlight). Of course, you should suppress the flowing of execution context only if the helper thread does not need or access the context information. If the initiating thread's execution context does not flow to a helper thread, the helper thread will use whatever execution context it last associated with it. Therefore, the helper thread really shouldn't execute any code that relies on the execution context state (such as a user's Windows identity).

Here is an example showing how suppressing the flow of execution context affects data in a thread's logical call context when queueing a work item to the CLR's thread pool[1]:

```
public static void Main() {
    // Put some data into the Main thread's logical call context
    CallContext.LogicalSetData("Name", "Jeffrey");

    // Initiate some work to be done by a thread pool thread
    // The thread pool thread can access the logical call context data
    ThreadPool.QueueUserWorkItem(
        state => Console.WriteLine("Name={0}", CallContext.LogicalGetData("Name")));


    // Now, suppress the flowing of the Main thread's execution context
    ExecutionContext.SuppressFlow();

    // Initiate some work to be done by a thread pool thread
    // The thread pool thread can NOT access the logical call context data
    ThreadPool.QueueUserWorkItem(
        state => Console.WriteLine("Name={0}", CallContext.LogicalGetData("Name")));

    // Restore the flowing of the Main thread's execution context in case
    // it employs more thread pool threads in the future
    ExecutionContext.RestoreFlow();
    ...
}
```

When I compile and run the code above, I get the following output:

```
Name=Jeffrey
Name=
```

While this discussion has focused on suppressing the flow of execution context when calling **ThreadPool.QueueUserWorkItem**, this technique is also useful when using **Task** objects (discussed in the "Tasks" section of this chapter) and is also useful when initiating asynchronous I/O operations (discussed in Chapter 27, "I/O-Bound Asynchronous Operations").

Cooperative Cancellation

The Microsoft .NET Framework offers a standard pattern for canceling operations. This pattern is *cooperative,* meaning that the operation that you wish to cancel has to explicitly support being canceled. In other words, the code performing the operation that you wish to cancel and the code that attempts to cancel the operation must both use the types mentioned in this section. It is nice when long-running compute-bound operations offer cancellation, so you should consider adding cancellation to your own compute-bound operations.

---

[1] The items that you add to the logical call context must be serializable, as discussed in Chapter 24, "Runtime Serialization." Flowing an execution context that contains logical call context data items can hurt performance dramatically because capturing the execution context requires serializing and deserializing all the data items.

In this section, I'll explain how to accomplish this. But, first, let me explain the two main types provided in the Framework Class Library (FCL) that are part of the standard cooperative cancellation pattern.

To cancel an operation, you must first create a **System.Threading. CancellationTokenSource** object. This class looks like this:

```
public sealed class CancellationTokenSource : IDisposable {  // A reference type
   public CancellationTokenSource();
   public void Dispose();  // Frees resources (like the WaitHandle)

   public Boolean IsCancellationRequested { get; }
   public CancellationToken Token { get; }

   public void Cancel();  // Internally, calls Cancel passing false
   public void Cancel(Boolean throwOnFirstException);
   ...
}
```

This object contains all the state having to do with managing cancellation. After constructing a **CancellationTokenSource** (a reference type), one or more **CancellationToken** (a value type) instances can be obtained from its **Token** property and passed around to your operations that allow themselves to be canceled. Here are the most useful members of the **CancellationToken** value type:

```
public struct CancellationToken {  // A value type
   // IsCancellationRequested is called by non-Task invoked operations
   public Boolean     IsCancellationRequested { get; }

   public void        ThrowIfCancellationRequested();  // Called by Task-invoked operations

   // WaitHandle is signaled when the CancellationTokenSource is canceled
   public WaitHandle WaitHandle { get; }
   // GetHashCode, Equals, operator== and operator!= members are not shown

   public static CancellationToken None { get; }
   public Boolean CanBeCanceled { get; }  // Rarely used

   public CancellationTokenRegistration Register(Action<Object> callback, Object state,
      Boolean useSynchronizationContext);  // Simpler overloads not shown
}
```

A **CancellationToken** instance is a lightweight value type as it contains a single private field: a reference to its **CancellationTokenSource** object. A compute-bound operation's loop can periodically call **CancellationToken**'s **IsCancellationRequested** property to know if the loop should terminate early, thereby ending the compute-bound operation. Of course, the benefit here is that CPU time is no longer being wasted on an operation whose result you know you're not interested in. Now, let me put all this together with some sample code:

```
internal static class CancellationDemo {
    public static void Go() {
        CancellationTokenSourcects = new CancellationTokenSource();

        // Pass the CancellationToken and the number-to-count-to into the operation
        ThreadPool.QueueUserWorkItem(o => Count(cts.Token, 1000));

        Console.WriteLine("Press <Enter> to cancel the operation.");
        Console.ReadLine();
        cts.Cancel();  // If Count returned already, Cancel has no effect on it
        // Cancel returns immediately, and the method continues running here...
    }

    private static void Count(CancellationToken token, Int32 countTo) {
        for (Int32 count = 0; count <countTo; count++) {
            if (token.IsCancellationRequested) {
                Console.WriteLine("Count is cancelled");
                break; // Exit the loop to stop the operation
            }

            Console.WriteLine(count);
            Thread.Sleep(200);   // For demo, waste some time
        }
        Console.WriteLine("Count is done");
    }
}
```

> **Note** If you want to execute an operation and prevent it from being canceled, you can pass
> the operation the **CancellationToken** returned from calling **CancellationToken**'s static
> **None** property. This property returns a special **CancellationToken** instance that is not
> associated with any **CancellationTokenSource** object (its private field is **null**). Since there is
> no **CancellationTokenSource**, no code can call **Cancel**, and the operation that is querying
> the special **CancellationToken**'s IsCancellationRequested property will always get back
> **false**. If you query **CancellationToken**'s CanBeCanceled property using one of these special
> **CancellationToken** instances, the property will return **false**. The property returns **true** for
> all other **CancellationToken** instances obtained by querying a **CancellationTokenSource**
> object's **Token** property.

If you'd like, you can register one or more methods to be invoked when a
CancellationTokenSource is canceled. However, you register each callback method using
CancellationToken's **Register** method. To this method, you pass an **Action<Object>**
delegate, a state value that will be passed to the callback via the delegate, and a
Boolean indicating whether or not to invoke the delegate using the calling thread's
SynchronizationContext. If you pass **false** for the **useSynchronizationContext**
parameter, then the thread that calls **Cancel** will invoke all the registered methods sequentially. If you pass **true** for the **useSynchronizationContext** parameter, then the callbacks
are sent (as opposed to posted) to the captured **SynchronizationContext** object which
governs which thread invokes the callback. The **SynchronizationContext** class is discussed
more in the "Applications and Their Threading Models" section in Chapter 27.

> **Note** If you register a callback method with a **CancellationTokenSource** after the **CancellationTokenSource** has already been canceled, then the thread calling **Register** invokes the callback (possible via the calling thread's **SynchronizationContext** if **true** is passed for the **useSynchronizationContext** parameter).

If **Register** is called multiple times, then multiple callback methods will be invoked. These callback methods could throw an unhandled exception. If you call **CancellationTokenSource**'s **Cancel**, passing it **true**, then the first callback method that throws an unhandled exception stops the other callback methods from executing, and the exception thrown will be thrown from **Cancel** as well. If you call **Cancel** passing it **false**, then all registered callback methods are invoked. Any unhandled exceptions that occur are added to a collection. After all callback methods have executed, if any of them threw an unhandled exception, then **Cancel** throws an **AggregateException** with its **InnerExceptions** property set to the collection of exception objects that were thrown. If no registered callback methods threw an unhandled exception, then **Cancel** simply returns without throwing any exception at all.

> **Important** There is no way to correlate an exception object from **AggregateException**'s **InnerExceptions** collection to a particular operation; you are basically just being told that *some* operation failed and the exception type tells you what the failure was. To track down the specific location of the failure will require examining the exception object's **StackTrace** property and manually scanning your source code.

CancellationToken's **Register** method returns a **CancellationTokenRegistration**, which looks like this:

```
public struct CancellationTokenRegistration :
   IEquatable<CancellationTokenRegistration>, IDisposable {
   public void Dispose();
   // GetHashCode, Equals, operator== and operator!= members are not shown
}
```

You can call **Dispose** to remove a registered callback from the **CancellationTokenSource** that it is associated with so that it does not get invoked when calling **Cancel**. Here is some code that demonstrates registering two callbacks with a single **CancellationTokenSource**:

```
varcts = new CancellationTokenSource();
cts.Token.Register(() => Console.WriteLine("Canceled 1"));
cts.Token.Register(() => Console.WriteLine("Canceled 2"));

// To test, let's just cancel it now and have the 2 callbacks execute
cts.Cancel();
```

When I run this code, I get the following output as soon as the **Cancel** method is called:

```
Canceled 2
Canceled 1
```

Finally, you can create a new **CancellationTokenSource** object by linking a bunch of other **CancellationTokenSource** objects. This new **CancellationTokenSource** object will be canceled when *any* of the linked **CancellationTokenSource** objects are canceled. The following code demonstrates:

```
// Create a CancellationTokenSource
var cts1 = new CancellationTokenSource();
cts1.Token.Register(() => Console.WriteLine("cts1 canceled"));

// Create another CancellationTokenSource
var cts2 = new CancellationTokenSource();
cts2.Token.Register(() => Console.WriteLine("cts2 canceled"));

// Create a new CancellationTokenSource that is canceled when cts1 or ct2 is canceled
var linkedCts = CancellationTokenSource.CreateLinkedTokenSource(cts1.Token, cts2.Token);
linkedCts.Token.Register(() => Console.WriteLine("linkedCts canceled"));

// Cancel one of the CancellationTokenSource objects (I chose cts2)
cts2.Cancel();

// Display which CancellationTokenSource objects are canceled
Console.WriteLine("cts1 canceled={0}, cts2 canceled={1}, linkedCts={2}",
    cts1.IsCancellationRequested, cts2.IsCancellationRequested,
linkedCts.IsCancellationRequested);
```

When I run the code above, I get the following output:

```
linkedCts canceled
cts2 canceled
cts1 canceled=False, cts2 canceled=True, linkedCts=True
```

Tasks

Calling **ThreadPool**'s **QueueUserWorkItem** method to initiate an asynchronous compute-bound operation is very simple. However, this technique has many limitations. The biggest problem is that there is no built-in way for you to know when the operation has completed, and there is no way to get a return value back when the operation completes. To address these limitations and more, Microsoft introduced the concept of *tasks,* and you use them via types in the **System.Threading.Tasks** namespace.

So, instead of calling **ThreadPool**'s **QueueUserWorkItem** method, you can do the same via tasks:

```
ThreadPool.QueueUserWorkItem(ComputeBoundOp, 5); // Calling QueueUserWorkItem
new Task(ComputeBoundOp, 5).Start();              // Equivalent of above using Task
```

In the code above, I am creating the **Task** object and then immediately call **Start** to schedule the task to run. Naturally, you can create the **Task** object and then call **Start** on it later. You could imagine code that creates a **Task** object and then passes it to some other method that decides when to call **Start** to schedule the task.

When creating a **Task**, you always call a constructor, passing it an **Action** or an **Action<Object>** delegate that indicates the operation that you want performed. If you pass a method that expects an **Object**, then you must also pass to **Task**'s constructor the argument that you ultimately want passed to the operation. You can also optionally pass to **Task**'s constructor a **CancellationToken**, which allows the **Task** to be canceled before it has been scheduled (see the "Cancelling a Task" section later in this chapter).

You can also optionally pass to the constructor some **TaskCreationOptions** flags that control how the **Task** executes. **TaskCreationOptions** is an enumerated type defining a set of flags that you can bitwise-OR together. It is defined as follows:

```
[Flags, Serializable]
public enumTaskCreationOptions {
    None              = 0x0000,// The default

    // Causes the default TaskScheduler to put the task in the thread pool's
    // global queue instead of a worker thread's local queue.
    PreferFairness    = 0x0001,

    // This flag is a hint to the TaskScheduler and it determines how to interpret this hint.
    // Today, the default TaskScheduler creates a thread for the task instead of queuing the
    // task to a thread pool thread. This behavior could change in the future.
    LongRunning       = 0x0002,

    // Always honored: Associates a Task with its parent Task (discussed shortly)
    AttachedToParent  = 0x0004,
}
```

Most of these flags are hints that may or may not be honored by the **TaskScheduler** that is being used to schedule a **Task**; the **AttachedToParent** flag is always honored, as it has nothing to do with the **TaskScheduler** itself. **TaskScheduler** objects are discussed later in the "Task Schedulers" section.

Waiting for a Task to Complete and Getting Its Result

With tasks, it is also possible to wait for them to complete and then get their result. Let's say that we have a **Sum** method that is computationally intensive if **n** is a large value:

```
private static Int32 Sum(Int32 n) {
    Int32 sum = 0;
    for (; n > 0; n--)
        checked { sum += n; }    // in n is large, this will throw System.OverflowException
    return sum;
}
```

We can now construct a **Task<TResult>**object (which is derived from **Task**), and we pass for the generic **TResult** argument the compute-bound operation's return type. Now, after starting the task, we can wait for it to complete and then get its result using the following code:

```
// Create a Task (it does not start running now)
Task<Int32> t = new Task<Int32>(n => Sum((Int32)n), 1000000000);

// You can start the task sometime later
t.Start();

// Optionally, you can explicitly wait for the task to complete
t.Wait(); // FYI: Overloads exist accepting timeout/CancellationToken

// You can get the result (the Result property internally calls Wait)
Console.WriteLine("The Sum is: " + t.Result); // An Int32 value
```

> **Important** When a thread calls the **Wait** method, the system checks if the **Task** that the thread is waiting for has started executing. If it has, then the thread calling **Wait** will block until the **Task** has completed running. But if the **Task** has not started executing yet, then the system *may* (depending on the **TaskScheduler**) execute the **Task** using the thread that called **Wait**. If this happens, then the thread calling **Wait** does not block; it executes the **Task** and returns immediately. This is good in that no thread has blocked, thereby reducing resource usage (by not creating a thread to replace the blocked thread) while improving performance (no time is spent to create a thread and there is no context switching). But it can also be bad if, for example, the thread has taken a thread synchronization lock before calling **Wait** and then the **Task** tries to take the same lock, resulting in a deadlocked thread!

If the compute-bound task throws an unhandled exception, the exception will be swallowed, stored in a collection, and the thread pool thread is allowed to return to the thread pool. When the **Wait** method or the **Result** property is invoked, these members will throw a **System.AggregateException** object.

The **AggregateException** type is used to encapsulate a collection of exception objects (which can happen if a parent task spawns multiple child tasks that throw exceptions). It contains an **InnerExceptions** property that returns a **ReadOnlyCollection<Exception>** object. Do not confuse the **InnerExceptions** property with the **InnerException** property, which the **AggregateException** class inherits from the **System.Exception** base class. For the example above, element **0** of **AggregateException**'s **InnerExceptions** property would refer to the actual **System.OverflowException** object thrown by the compute-bound method (**Sum**).

As a convenience, **AggregateException** overrides **Exception**'s **GetBaseException** method. **AggregateException**'s implementation returns the innermost **AggregateException** that is the root cause of the problem (assuming that there is just one innermost exception in the collection). **AggregateException** also offers a **Flatten** method that creates a new **AggregateException**, whose **InnerExceptions** property contains a list of exceptions produced by walking the original **AggregateException**'s inner exception hierarchy. Finally, **AggregateException** also provides a **Handle** method that invokes a callback method for each exception contained in the **AggregateException**. The callback can then decide, for each exception, how to handle the exception; the callback returns **true** to consider the exception handled and **false** if not. If, after calling **Handle**, at least one exception is not handled, then a new **AggregateException** object is created containing just the unhandled exceptions and the new **AggregateException** object is thrown. Later in this chapter, I show examples using the **Flatten** and **Handle** methods.

> **Important** If you never call **Wait** or **Result** or query a **Task**'s **Exception** property, then your code never observes that this exception has occurred. This is not ideal, as your program has experienced an unexpected problem that you are not aware of. So, when a **Task** object is garbage collected, its **Finalize** method checks to see if the **Task** experienced an unobserved exception; if it has, **Task**'s **Finalize** method throws the **AggregateException**. Since you cannot catch an exception thrown by the CLR's finalizer thread, your process is terminated immediately. You must fix your code by invoking one of the aforementioned members, ensuring that your code observes the exception and recovers from it.
>
> To help you detect unobserved exceptions, you can register a callback method with **TaskScheduler**'s static **UnobservedTaskException** event. This event is raised by the CLR's finalizer thread whenever a **Task** with an unobserved exception is garbage collected. When raised, your event handler method will be passed an **UnobservedTaskExceptionEventArgs** object containing the unobserved **AggregateException**. You can call **UnobservedTaskExceptionEventArgs**'s **SetObserved** method to indicate that you've processed the exception, thus preventing the CLR from terminating the process. However, you should not do this as a standard policy. As discussed in Chapter 20, it is better for a process to terminate instead of running with corrupted state.

In addition to waiting for a single task, the **Task** class also offers two static methods that allow a thread to wait on an array of **Task** objects. **Task**'s static **WaitAny** method blocks the calling thread until any of the **Task** objects in the array have completed. This method returns an **Int32** index into the array indicating which **Task** object completed, causing the thread to wake and continue running. The method returns **-1** if the timeout occurs and throws an **OperationCanceledException** if **WaitAny** is canceled via a **CancellationToken**.

Similarly, the **Task** class has a static **WaitAll** method that blocks the calling thread until all the **Task** objects in the array have completed. The **WaitAll** method returns **true** if all the **Task** objects complete and **false** if a timeout occurs; an **OperationCanceledException** is thrown if **WaitAll** is canceled via a **CancellationToken**.

Cancelling a Task

Of course, you can use a **CancellationTokenSource** to cancel a **Task**. First, we must revise our **Sum** method so that it accepts a **CancellationToken**:

```
private static Int32 Sum(CancellationTokenct, Int32 n) {
   Int32 sum = 0;
   for (; n > 0; n--) {
```

```
    // The following line throws OperationCanceledException when Cancel
    // is called on the CancellationTokenSource referred to by the token
    ct.ThrowIfCancellationRequested();

    checked { sum += n; }    // in n is large, this will throw System.OverflowException
  }
  return sum;
}
```

In this code, the compute-bound operation's loop periodically checks to see if the operation has been canceled by calling **CancellationToken**'s **ThrowIfCancellationRequested** method. This method is similar to **CancellationToken**'s **IsCancellationRequested** property shown earlier in the "Cooperative Cancellation" section. However, **ThrowIfCancellationRequested** throws an **OperationCanceledException** if the **CancellationTokenSource** has been canceled. The reason for throwing an exception is because, unlike work items initiated with **ThreadPool**'s **QueueUserWorkItem** method, tasks have the notion of having completed and a task can even return a value. So, there needs to be a way to distinguish a completed task from a faulting task, and having the task throw an exception lets you know that the task did not run all the way to completion.

Now, we will create the **CancellationTokenSource** and **Task** objects as follows:

```
CancellationTokenSourcects = new CancellationTokenSource();
Task<Int32> t = new Task<Int32>(() => Sum(cts.Token, 10000), cts.Token);

t.Start();

// Sometime later, cancel the CancellationTokenSource to cancel the Task
cts.Cancel(); // This is an asynchronous request, the Task may have completed already

try {
    // If the task got canceled, Result will throw an AggregateException
    Console.WriteLine("The sum is: " + t.Result);    // An Int32 value
}
catch (AggregateException x) {
    // Consider any OperationCanceledException objects as handled.
    // Any other exceptions cause a new AggregateException containing
    // only the unhandled exceptions to be thrown
    x.Handle(e => e is OperationCanceledException);

    // If all the exceptions were handled, the following executes
    Console.WriteLine("Sum was canceled");
}
```

When creating a **Task**, you can associate a **CancellationToken** with it by passing it to **Task**'s constructor (as shown above). If the **CancellationToken** gets canceled before the **Task** is scheduled, the **Task** gets canceled and never executes at all.[2] But if the **Task** has already been scheduled (by calling the **Start** method), then the **Task**'s code must explicitly support

---

[2] By the way, if you try to cancel a task before it is even started, an **InvalidOperationException** is thrown.

cancellation if it allows its operation to be canceled while executing. Unfortunately, while a **Task** object has a **CancellationToken** associated with it, there is no way to access it, so you must somehow get the *same* **CancellationToken** that was used to create the **Task** object into the **Task**'s code itself. The easiest way to write this code is to use a lambda expression and "pass" the **CancellationToken** as a closure variable (as I've done in the previous code example).

Starting a New Task Automatically When Another Task Completes

In order to write scalable software, you must not have your threads block. This means that calling **Wait** or querying a task's **Result** property when the task has not yet finished running will most likely cause the thread pool to create a new thread, which increases resource usage and hurts scalability. Fortunately, there is a better way to find out when a task has completed running. When a task completes, it can start another task. Here is a rewrite of the earlier code that doesn't block any threads:

```
// Create Task, defer starting it, continue with another task
Task<Int32> t = new Task<Int32>(n => Sum((Int32)n), 1000000000);

// You can start the task sometime later
t.Start();

// ContinueWith returns a Task but you usually don't care
Task cwt = t.ContinueWith(task => Console.WriteLine("The sum is: " + task.Result));
```

Now, when the task executing **Sum** completes, this task will start another task (also on some thread pool thread) that displays the result. The thread that executes the code above does not block waiting for either of these two tasks to complete; the thread is allowed to execute other code or, if it is a thread pool thread itself, it can return to the pool to perform other operations. Note that the task executing **Sum** could complete before **ContinueWith** is called. This will not be a problem because the **ContinueWith** method will see that the **Sum** task is complete and it will immediately start the task that displays the result.

Also, note that **ContinueWith** returns a reference to a new **Task** object (which my code placed in the **cwt** variable). Of course, you can invoke various members (like **Wait**, **Result**, or even **ContinueWith**) using this **Task** object, but usually you will ignore this **Task** object and will not save a reference to it in a variable.

I should also mention that **Task** objects internally contain a collection of **ContinueWith** tasks. So you can actually call **ContinueWith** several times using a single **Task** object. When the task completes, all the **ContinueWith** tasks will be queued to the thread pool. In addition, when calling **ContinueWith**, you can specify a bitwise OR'd set of **TaskContinuationOptions**. The first four flags—**None**, **PreferFairness**, **LongRunning**, and **AttachedToParent**—are identical to the flags offered by the **TaskCreationOptions** enumerated type shown earlier. Here is what the **TaskContinuationOptions** type looks like:

```
[Flags, Serializable]
public enumTaskContinuationOptions {
    None                    = 0x0000,// The default

    // Causes the default TaskScheduler to put the task in the thread pool's
    // global queue instead of a worker thread's local queue.
    PreferFairness          = 0x0001,

    // Causes the default TaskScheduler to create a thread for the task instead
    // of queuing the task to a thread pool thread
    LongRunning             = 0x0002,

    // Always honored: Associates a Task with its parent Task (discussed shortly)
    AttachedToParent        = 0x0004,

    // This flag indicates that you want the thread that executed the first task to also
    // execute the ContinueWith task. If the first task has already completed, then the
    // thread calling ContinueWith will execute the ContinueWith task.
    ExecuteSynchronously    = 0x80000,

    // These flags indicate under what circumstances to run the ContinueWith task
    NotOnRanToCompletion    = 0x10000,
    NotOnFaulted            = 0x20000,
    NotOnCanceled           = 0x40000,

    // These flags are convenient combinations of the above three flags
    OnlyOnCanceled          = NotOnRanToCompletion | NotOnFaulted,
    OnlyOnFaulted           = NotOnRanToCompletion | NotOnCanceld,
    OnlyOnRanToCompletion   = NotOnFaulted         | NotOnCanceled,
}
```

When you call **ContinueWith**, you can indicate that you want the new task to execute only if the first task is canceled by specifying the **TaskContinuationOptions.OnlyOnCanceled** flag. Similarly, you have the new task execute only if the first task throws an unhandled exception using the **TaskContinuationOptions.OnlyOnFaulted** flag. And, of course, you can use the **TaskContinuationOptions.OnlyOnRanToCompletion** flag to have the new task execute only if the first task runs all the way to completion without being canceled or throwing an unhandled exception. By default, if you do not specify any of these flags, then the new task will run regardless of how the first task completes. When a **Task** completes, any of its continue-with tasks that do not run are automatically canceled. Here is an example that puts all of this together:

```
Task<Int32> t = new Task<Int32>(n => Sum((Int32)n), 10000);

// You can start the task sometime later
t.Start();

// Each ContinueWith returns a Task but you usually don't care
```

```
t.ContinueWith(task => Console.WriteLine("The sum is: " + task.Result),
   TaskContinuationOptions.OnlyOnRanToCompletion);

t.ContinueWith(task => Console.WriteLine("Sum threw: " + task.Exception),
   TaskContinuationOptions.OnlyOnFaulted);

t.ContinueWith(task => Console.WriteLine("Sum was canceled"),
   TaskContinuationOptions.OnlyOnCanceled);
```

A Task May Start Child Tasks

Finally, tasks support parent/child relationships, as demonstrated by the following code:

```
Task<Int32[]> parent = new Task<Int32[]>(() => {
   var results = new Int32[3];    // Create an array for the results

   // This tasks creates and starts 3 child tasks
   new Task(() => results[0] = Sum(10000), TaskCreationOptions.AttachedToParent).Start();
   new Task(() => results[1] = Sum(20000), TaskCreationOptions.AttachedToParent).Start();
   new Task(() => results[2] = Sum(30000), TaskCreationOptions.AttachedToParent).Start();

   // Returns a reference to the array (even though the elements may not be initialized yet)
   return results;
});

// When the parent and its children have run to completion, display the results
varcwt = parent.ContinueWith(
   parentTask => Array.ForEach(parentTask.Result, Console.WriteLine));

// Start the parent Task so it can start its children
parent.Start();
```

Here, the parent task creates and starts three **Task** objects. By default, **Task** objects created by another task are top-level tasks that have no relationship to the task that creates them. However, the **TaskCreationOptions.AttachedToParent** flag associates a **Task** with the **Task** that creates it so that the creating task is not considered finished until all its children (and grandchildren) have finished running. When creating a **Task** by calling the **ContinueWith** method, you can make the continue-with task be a child by specifying the **TaskContinuationOptions.AttachedToParent** flag.

Inside a Task

Each **Task** object has a set of fields that make up the task's state. There is an **Int32** ID (see **Task**'s read-only **Id** property), an **Int32** representing the execution state of the **Task**, a reference to the parent task, a reference to the **TaskScheduler** specified when the **Task** was created, a reference to the callback method, a reference to the object that is to be passed to the callback method (queryable via **Task**'s read-only **AsyncState** property), a reference to an **ExecutionContext**, and a reference to a **ManualResetEventSlim** object. In addition, each **Task** object has a reference to some supplementary state that is created on demand.

The supplementary state includes a **CancellationToken**, a collection of **ContinueWithTask** objects, a collection of **Task** objects for child tasks that have thrown unhandled exceptions, and more. My point is that while tasks provide you a lot of features, there is some cost to tasks because memory must be allocated for all this state. If you don't need the additional features offered by tasks, then your program will use resources more efficiently if you use **ThreadPool.QueueUserWorkItem**.

The **Task** and **Task<TResult>** classes implement the **IDisposable** interface, allowing you to call **Dispose** when you are done with the **Task** object. Today, all the **Dispose** method does is close the **ManualResetEventSlim** object. However, it is possible to define classes derived from **Task** and **Task<TResult>**, and these classes could allocate their own resources, which would be freed in their override of the **Dispose** method. Of course, most developers will not explicitly call **Dispose** on a **Task** object in their code; instead, they will just let the garbage collector clean up any resources when it determines that they are no longer in use.

You'll notice that each **Task** object contains an **Int32** field representing a **Task**'s unique ID. When you create a **Task** object, the field is initialized to zero. Then the first time you query **Task**'s read-only **Id** property, the property assigns a unique **Int32** value to this field and returns it from the property. Task IDs start at 1 and increment by 1 as each ID is assigned. Just looking at a **Task** object in the Microsoft Visual Studio debugger will cause the debugger to display the **Task**'s ID, forcing the **Task** to be assigned an ID.

The idea behind the ID is that each **Task** can be identified by a unique value. In fact, Visual Studio shows you these task IDs in its Parallel Tasks and Parallel Stacks windows. But since you don't assign the IDs yourself in your code, it is practically impossible to correlate an ID number with what your code is doing. While running a task's code, you can query **Task**'s static **CurrentId** property, which returns a nullable **Int32** (**Int32?**). You can also call this from Visual Studio's Watch window or Immediate window while debugging to get the ID for the code that you are currently stepping through. Then you can find your task in the Parallel Tasks/Stacks windows. If you query the **CurrentId** property while a task is not executing, it returns **null**.

During a **Task** object's existence, you can learn where it is in its lifecycle by querying **Task**'s read-only **Status** property. This property returns a **TaskStatus** value that is defined as follows:

```
public enum TaskStatus {
   // These flags indicate the state of a Task during its lifetime:
   Created,            // Task created explicitly; you can manually Start() this task
   WaitingForActivation,// Task created implicitly; it starts automatically

   WaitingToRun,   // The task was scheduled but isn't running yet
   Running,        // The task is actually running

   // The task is waiting for children to complete before it considers itself complete
   WaitingForChildrenToComplete,
```

```
    // A task's final state is one of these:
    RanToCompletion,
    Canceled,
    Faulted
}
```

When you first construct a **Task** object, its status is **Created**. Later, when the task is started, its status changes to **WaitingToRun**. When the **Task** is actually running on a thread, its status changes to **Running**. When the task stops running and is waiting for any child tasks, the status changes to **WaitingForChildrenToComplete**. When a task is completely finished, it enters one of three final states: **RanToCompletion**, **Canceled**, or **Faulted**. When a **Task<TResult>** runs to completion, you can query the task's result via**Task<TResult>**'s **Result** property. When a **Task** or **Task<TResult>** faults, you can obtain the unhandled exception that the task threw by querying **Task**'s **Exception** property; which always returns an **AggregateException** object whose collection contains the set of unhandled exceptions.

For convenience, **Task** offers several read-only, **Boolean** properties: **IsCanceled**, **IsFaulted**, and **IsCompleted**. Note that **IsCompleted** returns **true** when the **Task** is in the **RanToCompleted**, **Canceled**, or **Faulted** state. The easiest way to determine if a **Task** completed successfully is to use code like this:

```
if (task.Status == TaskStatus.RanToCompletion) ...
```

A **Task** object is in the **WaitingForActivation** state if that **Task** is creating by calling one of these functions: **ContinueWith**, **ContinueWhenAll**, **ContinueWhenAny**, or **FromAsync**. A **Task** created by constructing a **TaskCompletionSource<TResult>** object is also created in the **WaitingForActivation** state. This state means that the **Task**'s scheduling is controlled by the task infrastructure. For example, you cannot explicitly start a **Task** object that was created by calling **ContinueWith**. This **Task** will start automatically when its antecedent task has finished executing.

Task Factories

Occasionally, you might want to create a bunch of **Task** objects that share the same state. To keep you from having to pass the same parameters to each **Task**'s constructor over and over again, you can create a task factory that encapsulates the common state. The **System.Threading.Tasks** namespace defines a **TaskFactory** type as well as a **TaskFactory<TResult>** type. Both of these types are derived from **System.Object**; that is, they are peers of each other.

If you want to create a bunch of tasks that have no return values, then you will construct a **TaskFactory**. If you want to create a bunch of tasks that have a specific return value, then you will construct a **TaskFactory<TResult>** where you pass the task's desired return type for the generic **TResult** argument. When you create one of these task factory classes, you pass to its constructor the defaults that you want the tasks that the factory creates to have. Specifically, you pass to the task factory the **CancellationToken**, **TaskScheduler**, **TaskCreationOptions**, and **TaskContinuationOptions** settings that you want factory-created tasks to have.

Here is some sample code demonstrating the use of a **TaskFactory**:

```
Task parent = new Task(() => {
   varcts = new CancellationTokenSource();
   vartf = new TaskFactory<Int32>(cts.Token,
   TaskCreationOptions.AttachedToParent,
   TaskContinuationOptions.ExecuteSynchronously,
   TaskScheduler.Default);

   // This tasks creates and starts 3 child tasks
   varchildTasks = new[] {
   tf.StartNew(() => Sum(cts.Token, 10000)),
   tf.StartNew(() => Sum(cts.Token, 20000)),
   tf.StartNew(() => Sum(cts.Token, Int32.MaxValue))  // Too big, throws OverflowException
   };

   // If any of the child tasks throw, cancel the rest of them
   for (Int32 task = 0; task <childTasks.Length; task++)
      childTasks[task].ContinueWith(
         t => cts.Cancel(), TaskContinuationOptions.OnlyOnFaulted);

   // When all children are done, get the maximum value returned from the
   // non-faulting/canceled tasks. Then pass the maximum value to another
   // task which displays the maximum result
   tf.ContinueWhenAll(
      childTasks,
      completedTasks => completedTasks.Where(
         t => !t.IsFaulted && !t.IsCanceled).Max(t => t.Result),
      CancellationToken.None)
      .ContinueWith(t =>Console.WriteLine("The maximum is: " + t.Result),
         TaskContinuationOptions.ExecuteSynchronously);
});


// When the children are done, show any unhandled exceptions too
parent.ContinueWith(p => {
   // I put all this text in a StringBuilder and call Console.WriteLine just once
   // because this task could execute concurrently with the task above & I don't
   // want the tasks' output interspersed
   StringBuildersb = new StringBuilder(
      "The following exception(s) occurred:" + Environment.NewLine);

   foreach (var e in p.Exception.Flatten().InnerExceptions)
      sb.AppendLine("   "+ e.GetType().ToString());
   Console.WriteLine(sb.ToString());
}, TaskContinuationOptions.OnlyOnFaulted);

// Start the parent Task so it can start its children
parent.Start();
```

With this code, I am creating a **TaskFactory<Int32>** object that I will use to create three **Task** objects. I want four things: for each **Task** object to share the same **CancellationTokenSource** token, for all three tasks to be considered children of their parent, for all continue-with tasks created by the **TaskFactory** object to execute synchronously, and for all the **Task** objects created by this **TaskFactory** to use the default **TaskScheduler**.

Then I create an array consisting of the three child **Task** objects, all created by calling **TaskFactory**'s **StartNew** method. This method conveniently creates and starts each child task. In a loop, I tell each child task that throws an unhandled exception to cancel all the other child tasks that are still running. Finally, using the **TaskFactory**, I call **ContinueWhenAll**, which creates a **Task** that runs when all the child tasks have completed running. Since this task is created with the **TaskFactory**, it will also be considered a child of the parent task and it will execute synchronously using the default **TaskScheduler**. However, I want this task to run even if the other child tasks were canceled, so I override the **TaskFactory**'s **CancellationToken** by passing in **CancellationToken.None**, which prevents this task from being cancelable at all. Finally, when the task that processes all the results is complete, I create another task that displays the highest value returned from all the child tasks.

Note When calling **TaskFactory**'s or **TaskFactory<TResult>**'s static **ContinueWhenAll** and **ContinueWhenAny** methods, the following **TaskContinuationOption** flags are illegal: **NotOnRanToCompletion**, **NotOnFaulted**, and **NotOnCanceled**. And of course, the convenience flags (**OnlyOnCanceled**, **OnlyOnFaulted**, and **OnlyOnRanToCompletion**) are also illegal. That is, **ContinueWhenAll** and **ContinueWhenAny** execute the continue-with task regardless of how the antecedent tasks complete.

Task Schedulers

The task infrastructure is very flexible, and **TaskScheduler** objects are a big part of this flexibility. A **TaskScheduler** object is responsible for executing scheduled tasks and also exposes task information to the Visual Studio debugger. The FCL ships with two **TaskScheduler**-derived types: the thread pool task scheduler and a synchronization context task scheduler. By default, all applications use the thread pool task scheduler. This task scheduler schedules tasks to the thread pool's worker threads and is discussed in more detail in this chapter's "How the Thread Pool Manages Its Threads" section. You can get a reference to the default task scheduler by querying **TaskScheduler**'s static **Default** property.

The synchronization context task scheduler is typically used for Windows Forms, Windows Presentation Foundation (WPF), and Silverlight applications. This task scheduler schedules all tasks onto the application's GUI thread so that all the task code can successfully update UI components like buttons, menu items, and so on. The synchronization context task scheduler does not use the thread pool at all. You can get a reference to a synchronization context task scheduler by querying **TaskScheduler**'s static **FromCurrentSynchronizationContext** method.

Here is a simple Windows Forms application that demonstrates the use of the synchronization context task scheduler:

```
internalsealed class MyForm : Form {
    public MyForm() {
        Text = "Synchronization Context Task Scheduler Demo";
        Visible = true; Width = 400; Height = 100;
    }

    // Get a reference to a synchronization context task scheduler
    private readonly TaskScheduler m_syncContextTaskScheduler =
        TaskScheduler.FromCurrentSynchronizationContext();

    private CancellationTokenSource m_cts;

    protected override void OnMouseClick(MouseEventArgs e) {
        if (m_cts != null) { // An operation is in flight, cancel it
            m_cts.Cancel();
            m_cts = null;
        } else { // An operation is not in flight, start it
            Text = "Operation running";
            m_cts = new CancellationTokenSource();

            // This task uses the default task scheduler and executes on a thread pool thread
            var t = new Task<Int32>(() => Sum(m_cts.Token, 20000), m_cts.Token);
            t.Start();

            // These tasks use the sync context task scheduler and execute on the GUI thread
            t.ContinueWith(task => Text = "Result: " + task.Result,
                CancellationToken.None, TaskContinuationOptions.OnlyOnRanToCompletion,
                m_syncContextTaskScheduler);

            t.ContinueWith(task => Text = "Operation canceled",
                CancellationToken.None, TaskContinuationOptions.OnlyOnCanceled,
                m_syncContextTaskScheduler);

            t.ContinueWith(task => Text = "Operation faulted",
                CancellationToken.None, TaskContinuationOptions.OnlyOnFaulted,
                m_syncContextTaskScheduler);
        }
        base.OnMouseClick(e);
    }
}
```

When you click in the client area of this form, a compute-bound task will start executing on a thread pool thread. This is good because the GUI thread is not blocked during this time and can therefore respond to other UI operations. However, the code executed by the thread pool thread should not attempt to update UI components or else an **InvalidOperationException** will be thrown.

When the compute-bound task is done, one of the three continue-with tasks will execute. These tasks are all issued against the synchronization context task scheduler corresponding to the GUI thread, and this task scheduler queues the tasks to the GUI thread, allowing the code executed by these tasks to update UI components successfully. All of these tasks update the form's caption via the inherited **Text** property.

Since the compute-bound work (**Sum**) is running on a thread pool thread, the user can interact with the UI to cancel the operation. In my simple code example, I allow the user to cancel the operation by clicking in the form's client area while an operation is running.

You can, of course, define your own class derived from **TaskScheduler** if you have special task scheduling needs. Microsoft has provided a bunch of sample code for tasks and includes the source code for a bunch of task schedulers in the Parallel Extensions Extras package, which can be downloaded from here: *http://code.msdn.microsoft.com/ParExtSamples*. Here are some of the task schedulers included in this package:

- **IOTaskScheduler**   This task scheduler queues tasks to the thread pool's I/O threads instead of its worker threads.

- **LimitedConcurrencyLevelTaskScheduler**   This task scheduler allows no more than *n* (a constructor parameter) tasks to execute simultaneously.

- **OrderedTaskScheduler**   This task scheduler allows only one task to execute at a time. This class is derived from **LimitedConcurrencyLevelTaskScheduler** and just passes 1 for *n*.

- **PrioritizingTaskScheduler**   This task scheduler queues tasks to the CLR's thread pool. After this has occurred, you can call **Prioritize** to indicate that a **Task** should be processed before all normal tasks (if it hasn't been processed already). You can call **Deprioritize** to make a **Task** be processed after all normal tasks.

- **ThreadPerTaskScheduler**   This task scheduler creates and starts a separate thread for each task; it does not use the thread pool at all.

Parallel's Static For, ForEach, and Invoke Methods

There are some common programming scenarios that can potentially benefit from the improved performance possible with tasks. To simplify programming, the static **System. Threading.Tasks.Parallel** class encapsulates these common scenarios while using **Task** objects internally. For example, instead of processing all the items in a collection like this:

```
// One thread performs all this work sequentially
for (Int32 i = 0; i < 1000; i++) DoWork(i);
```

you can instead get multiple thread pool threads to assist in performing this work by using the **Parallel** class's **For** method:

```
// The thread pool's threads process the work in parallel
Parallel.For(0, 1000, i => DoWork(i));
```

Similarly, if you have a collection, instead of doing this:

```
// One thread performs all this work sequentially
foreach (var item in collection) DoWork(item);
```

you can do this:

```
// The thread pool's threads process the work in parallel
Parallel.ForEach(collection, item => DoWork(item));
```

If you can use either **For** or **ForEach** in your code, then it is recommended that you use **For** because it executes faster.

And finally, if you have several methods that you need to execute, you could execute them all sequentially, like this:

```
// One thread executes all the methods sequentially
Method1();
Method2();
Method3();
```

or you could execute them in parallel, like this:

```
// The thread pool's threads execute the methods in parallel
Parallel.Invoke(
    () => Method1(),
    () => Method2(),
    () => Method3());
```

All of **Parallel**'s methods have the calling thread participate in the processing of the work, which is good in terms of resource usage because we wouldn't want the calling thread to just suspend itself while waiting for thread pool threads to do all the work. However, if the calling thread finishes its work before the thread pool threads complete their part of the work, then the call thread will suspend itself until all the work is done, which is also good because this gives you the same semantics as you'd have when using a **for** or **foreach** loop: The thread doesn't continue running until all the work is done. Also note that if any operation throws an unhandled exception, the **Parallel** method you called will ultimately throw an **AggregateException**.

Of course, you should not go through all your source code replacing **for** loops with calls to **Parallel.For** and **foreach** loops with calls to **Parallel.ForEach.** When calling the **Parallel** method, there is an assumption that it is OK for the work items to be performed concurrently. Therefore, do not use the **Parallel** methods if the work must be processed in sequential order. Also, avoid work items that modify any kind of shared data because the data could get corrupted if it is manipulated by multiple threads simultaneously. Normally, you would fix this by adding thread synchronization locks around the data access, but if you do this, then one thread at a time can access the data and you would lose the benefit of processing multiple items in parallel.

In addition, there is overhead associated with the **Parallel** methods; delegate objects have to be allocated, and these delegates are invoked once for each work item. If you have lots of work items that can be processed by multiple threads, then you might gain a performance increase. Also, if you have lots of work to do for each item, then the performance hit of calling through the delegate is negligible. You will actually hurt your performance if you use the **Parallel** methods for just a few work items or for work items that are processed very quickly.

I should mention that **Parallel**'s **For**, **ForEach**, and **Invoke** methods all have overloads that accept a **ParallelOptions** object, which looks like this:

```
public class ParallelOptions{
   public ParallelOptions();

   // Allows cancellation of the operation
   public CancellationTokenCancellationToken { get; set; } // Default=CancellationToken.None

   // Allows you to specify the maximum number of work items
   // that can be operated on concurrently
   public Int32MaxDegreeOfParallelism { get; set; }      // Default=-1 (# of available CPUs)

   // Allows you to specify which TaskScheduler to use
   public TaskSchedulerTaskScheduler { get; set; }      // Default=TaskScheduler.Default
}
```

In addition, there are overloads of the **For** and **ForEach** methods that let you pass three delegates:

- The task local initialization delegate (**localInit**) is invoked once for each task participating in the work. This delegate is invoked before the task is asked to process a work item.

- The body delegate (**body**) is invoked once for each item being processed by the various threads participating in the work.

- The task local finally delegate (**localFinally**) is invoked once for each task participating in the work. This delegate is invoked after the task has processed all the work items that will be dispatched to it. It is even invoked if the body delegate code experiences an unhandled exception.

Here is some sample code that demonstrates the use of the three delegates by adding up the bytes for all files contained within a directory:

```
private static Int64 DirectoryBytes(String path, String searchPattern,
   SearchOptionsearchOption) {
   var files = Directory.EnumerateFiles(path, searchPattern, searchOption);
   Int64 masterTotal = 0;

   ParallelLoopResult result = Parallel.ForEach<String, Int64>(
      files,

      () => { // localInit: Invoked once per task at start
         // Initialize that this task has seen 0 bytes
         return 0;    // Set taskLocalTotal initial value to 0
      },

      (file, loopState, index, taskLocalTotal) => { // body: Invoked once per work item
         // Get this file's size and add it to this task's running total
         Int64 fileLength = 0;
         FileStreamfs = null;
         try {
            fs = File.OpenRead(file);
            fileLength = fs.Length;
         }
         catch (IOException) { /* Ignore any files we can't access */ }
         finally { if (fs != null) fs.Dispose(); }
         return taskLocalTotal + fileLength;
      },

      taskLocalTotal => { // localFinally: Invoked once per task at end
         // Atomically add this task's total to the "master" total
         Interlocked.Add(ref masterTotal, taskLocalTotal);
      });

   return masterTotal;
}
```

Each task maintains its own running total (in the **taskLocalTotal** variable) for the files
that it is given. As each task completes its work, the master total is updated in a thread-safe
way by calling the **Interlocked.Add** method (discussed in Chapter 28, "Primitive Thread
Synchronization Constructs"). Since each task has its own running total, no thread synchronization is required during the processing of the item. Since thread synchronization would hurt
performance, not requiring thread synchronization is good. It's only after each task returns
that **masterTotal** has to be updated in a thread-safe way, so the performance hit of calling
Interlocked.Add occurs only once per task instead of once per work item.

You'll notice that the body delegate is passed a **ParallelLoopState** object, which looks like
this:

```
public class ParallelLoopState{
   public void Stop();
   public BooleanIsStopped { get; }

   public void Break();
   public Int64? LowestBreakIteration{ get; }
```

```
    public BooleanIsExceptional { get; }
    public BooleanShouldExitCurrentIteration { get; }
}
```

Each task participating in the work gets its own **ParallelLoopState** object, and it can use this object to interact with the other task participating in the work. The **Stop** method tells the loop to stop processing any more work, and future querying of the **IsStopped** property will return **true**. The **Break** method tells the loop to stop processing any items that are beyond the current item. For example, let's say that **ForEach** is told to process 100 items and **Break** is called while processing the fifth item, then the loop will make sure that the first five items are processed before **ForEach** returns. Note, however, that additional items may have been processed. The **LowestBreakIteration** property returns the lowest item number whose processing called the **Break** method. The **LowestBreakIteration** property returns **null** if **Break** was never called.

The **IsException** property returns **true** if the processing of any item resulted in an un-handled exception. If the processing of an item takes a long time, your code can query the **ShouldExitCurrentIteration** property to see if it should exit prematurely. This property returns **true** if **Stop** was called, **Break** was called, the **CancellationTokenSource** (referred to by the **ParallelOption**'s **CancellationToken** property) is canceled, or if the processing of an item resulted in an unhandled exception.

Parallel's **For** and **ForEach** methods both return a **ParallelLoopResult** instance, which looks like this:

```
publicstructParallelLoopResult{
    // Returns false if the operation was ended prematurely
    public Boolean IsCompleted { get; }
    public Int64? LowestBreakIteration{ get; }
}
```

You can examine the properties to determine the result of the loop. If **IsCompleted** returns **true**, then the loop ran to completion and all the items were processed. If **IsCompleted** is **false** and **LowestBreakIteration** is **null**, then some thread participating in the work called the **Stop** method. If **IsCompleted** is **false** and **LowestBreakIteration** is not **null**, then some thread participating in the work called the **Break** method and the **Int64** value returned from **LowestBreakIteration** indicates the index of the lowest item guaranteed to have been processed.

Parallel Language Integrated Query

Microsoft's Language Integrated Query (LINQ) feature offers a convenient syntax for per-forming queries over collections of data. Using LINQ, you can easily filter items, sort items, return a projected set of items, and much more. When you use LINQ to Objects, only one thread processes all the items in your data collection sequentially; we call this a *sequential query.* You can potentially improve the performance of this processing by using Parallel LINQ, which can turn your sequential query into a *parallel query,* which internally uses tasks (queued to the default **TaskScheduler**) to spread the processing of the collection's items across multiple CPUs so that multiple items are processed concurrently. Like **Parallel**'s methods, you will get the most benefit from Parallel LINQ if you have many items to process or if the processing of each item is a lengthy compute-bound operation.

The static **System.Linq.ParallelEnumerable** class (defined in System.Core.dll) implements all of the Parallel LINQ functionality, and so you must import the **System.Linq** namespace into your source code via C#'s **using** directive. In particular, this class exposes parallel versions of all the standard LINQ operators such as **Where**, **Select**, **SelectMany**, **GroupBy**, **Join**, **OrderBy**, **Skip**, **Take**, and so on. All of these methods are extension methods that extend the **System.Linq.ParallelQuery<T>** type. To have your LINQ to Objects query invoke the parallel versions of these methods, you must convert your sequential query (based on **IEnumerable** or **IEnumerable<T>**) to a parallel query (based on **ParallelQuery** or **ParallelQuery<T>**) using **ParallelEnumerable**'s **AsParallel** extension method, which looks like this[3]:

```
public static ParallelQuery<TSource>AsParallel<TSource>(this IEnumerable<TSource> source)
public static ParallelQueryAsParallel(this IEnumerablesource)
```

Here is an example of a sequential query that has been converted to a parallel query. This query returns all the obsolete methods defined within an assembly:

```
private static void ObsoleteMethods(Assembly assembly) {
var query =
    from type in assembly.GetExportedTypes().AsParallel()

    from method in type.GetMethods(BindingFlags.Public |
       BindingFlags.Instance | BindingFlags.Static)

    let obsoleteAttrType = typeof(ObsoleteAttribute)

    where Attribute.IsDefined(method, obsoleteAttrType)

    orderbytype.FullName

    let obsoleteAttrObj = (ObsoleteAttribute)
       Attribute.GetCustomAttribute(method, obsoleteAttrType)

       select String.Format("Type={0}\nMethod={1}\nMessage={2}\n",
          type.FullName, method.ToString(), obsoleteAttrObj.Message);

  // Display the results
  foreach (var result in query) Console.WriteLine(result);
}
```

---

[3] The **ParallelQuery<T>** class is derived from the **ParallelQuery** class.

While uncommon, within a query you can switch from performing parallel operations back to performing sequential operations by calling **ParallelEnumerable**'s **AsSequential** method:

```
public static IEnumerable<TSource> AsSequential<TSource>(this ParallelQuery<TSource> source)
```

This method basically turns a **ParallelQuery<T>** back to an **IEnumerable<T>** so that operations performed after calling **AsSequential** are performed by just one thread.

Normally, the resulting data produced by a LINQ query is evaluated by having some thread execute a **foreach** statement (as shown earlier). This means that just one thread iterates over all the query's results. If you want to have the query's results processed in parallel, then you should process the resulting query by using **ParallelEnumerable**'s **ForAll** method:

```
static void ForAll<TSource>(this ParallelQuery<TSource> source, Action<TSource> action)
```

This method allows multiple threads to process the results simultaneously. I could modify my code earlier to use this method as follows:

```
// Display the results
query.ForAll(Console.WriteLine);
```

However, having multiple threads call **Console.WriteLine** simultaneously actually hurts performance since the **Console** class internally synchronizes threads, ensuring that only one at a time can access the console window. This prevents text from multiple threads from being interspersed, making the output unintelligible. Use the **ForAll** method when you intend to perform calculations on each result.

Since Parallel LINQ processes items using multiple threads, the items are processed concurrently and the results are returned in an unordered fashion. If you need to have Parallel LINQ preserve the order of items as they are processed, then you can call **ParallelEnumerable**'s **AsOrdered** method. When you call this method, threads will process items in groups and then the groups are merged back together, preserving the order; this will hurt performance. The following operators produce unordered operations: **Distinct**, **Except**, **Intersect**, **Union**, **Join**, **GroupBy**, **GroupJoin**, and **ToLookup**. If you wish to enforce ordering again after one of these operators, just call the **AsOrdered** method.

The following operators produce ordered operations: **OrderBy**, **OrderByDescending**, **ThenBy**, and **ThenByDescending**. If you wish to go back to unordered processing again to improve performance after one of these operators, just call the **AsUnordered** method.

Parallel LINQ offers some additional **ParallelEnumerable** methods that you can call to control how the query is processed:

```
public static ParallelQuery<TSource> WithCancellation<TSource>(
   this ParallelQuery<TSource> source, CancellationTokencancellationToken)

public static ParallelQuery<TSource> WithDegreeOfParallelism<TSource>(
   this ParallelQuery<TSource> source, Int32degreeOfParallelism)

public static ParallelQuery<TSource> WithExecutionMode<TSource>(
   this ParallelQuery<TSource> source, ParallelExecutionModeexecutionMode)

public static ParallelQuery<TSource> WithMergeOptions<TSource>(
   this ParallelQuery<TSource> source, ParallelMergeOptionsmergeOptions)
```

Obviously, the **WithCancellation** method allows you to pass a **CancellationToken** so that the query processing can be stopped prematurely. The **WithDegreeOfParallelism** method specifies the maximum number of threads allowed to process the query; it does not force the threads to be created if not all of them are necessary. Usually you will not call this method, and, by default, the query will execute using one thread per core. However, you could call **WIthDegreeOfParallelism**, passing a number that is smaller than the number of available cores if you want to keep some cores available for doing other work. You could also pass a number that is greater than the number of cores if the query performs synchronous I/O operations because threads will be blocking during these operations. This wastes more threads but can produce the final result in less time. You might consider doing this in a client application, but I'd highly recommend against performing synchronous I/O operations in a server application.

Parallel LINQ analyzes a query and then decides how to best process it. Sometimes processing a query sequentially yields better performance. This is usually true when using any of these operations: **Concat**, **ElementAt(OrDefault)**, **First(OrDefault)**, **Last(OrDefault)**, **Skip(While)**, **Take(While)**, or **Zip**. It is also true when using overloads of **Select(Many)** or **Where** that pass a position index into your **selector** or **predicate** delegate. However, you can force a query to be processed in parallel by calling **WithExecutionMode**, passing it one of the **ParallelExecutionMode** flags:

```
public enum ParallelExecutionMode {
   Default = 0,           // Let Parallel LINQ decide to best process the query
   ForceParallelism = 1 // Force the query to be processed in parallel
}
```

As mentioned before, Parallel LINQ has multiple threads processing items, and then the results must be merged back together. You can control how the items are buffered and merged by calling **WithMergeOptions**, passing it one of the **ParallelMergeOptions** flags:

```
public enum ParallelMergeOptions {
   Default      = 0,    // Same as AutoBuffered today (could change in the future)
   NotBuffered  = 1,    // Results are processed as ready
   AutoBuffered = 2,    // Each thread buffers some results before processed
   FullyBuffered = 3    // Each thread buffers all results before processed
}
```

These options basically give you some control over speed versus memory consumption. **NotBuffered** saves memory but processes items slower. **FullyBuffered** consumes more memory while running fastest. **AutoBuffered** is the compromise in between **NotBuffered** and **FullyBuffered**. Really, the best way to know which of these to pick for any given query is to try them all and compare their performance results, or just accept the default, which tends to work pretty well for many queries. See the following blog posts for more information about how Parallel LINQ partitions work across CPU cores:

- *http://blogs.msdn.com/pfxteam/archive/2009/05/28/9648672.aspx*

- *http://blogs.msdn.com/pfxteam/archive/2009/06/13/9741072.aspx*

Performing a Periodic Compute-Bound Operation

The **System.Threading** namespace defines a **Timer** class, which you can use to have a thread pool thread call a method periodically. When you construct an instance of the **Timer** class, you are telling the thread pool that you want a method of yours called back at a future time that you specify. The **Timer** class offers several constructors, all quite similar to each other:

```
public sealed class Timer : MarshalByRefObject, IDisposable {
    public Timer(TimerCallback callback, Object state, Int32    dueTime, Int32    period);
    public Timer(TimerCallback callback, Object state, UInt32   dueTime, UInt32   period);
    public Timer(TimerCallback callback, Object state, Int64    dueTime, Int64    period);
    public Timer(TimerCallback callback, Object state, Timespan dueTime, TimeSpan period);
}
```

All four constructors construct a **Timer** object identically. The **callback** parameter identifies the method that you want called back by a thread pool thread. Of course, the callback method that you write must match the **System.Threading.TimerCallback** delegate type, which is defined as follows:

```
delegate void TimerCallback(Object state);
```

The constructor's **state** parameter allows you to pass state data to the callback method each time it is invoked; you can pass **null** if you have no state data to pass. You use the **dueTime** parameter to tell the CLR how many milliseconds to wait before calling your callback method for the very first time. You can specify the number of milliseconds by using a signed or unsigned 32-bit value, a signed 64-bit value, or a **TimeSpan** value. If you want the callback method called immediately, specify **0** for the **dueTime** parameter. The last parameter, **period**, allows you to specify how long, in milliseconds, to wait before each successive call to the callback method. If you pass **Timeout.Infinite** (**–1**) for this parameter, a thread pool thread will call the callback method just once.

Internally, the thread pool has just one thread that it uses for all **Timer** objects. This thread knows when the next **Timer** object's time is due. When the next **Timer** object is due, the thread wakes up, and internally calls **ThreadPool**'s **QueueUserWorkItem** to enter an entry into the thread pool's queue, causing your callback method to get called. If your callback method takes a long time to execute, the timer could go off again. This could cause multiple thread pool threads to be executing your callback method simultaneously. To work around this problem, I recommend the following: Construct the **Timer** specifying **Timeout.Infinite** for the **period** parameter. Now, the timer will fire only once. Then, in your callback method, call the **Change** method specifying a new due time and again specify **Timeout.Infinite** for the **period** parameter. Here is what the **Change** method overloads look like:

```
public sealed class Timer : MarshalByRefObject, IDisposable {
   public Boolean Change(Int32    dueTime, Int32    period);
   public Boolean Change(UInt32   dueTime, UInt32   period);
   public Boolean Change(Int64    dueTime, Int64    period);
   public Boolean Change(TimeSpan dueTime, TimeSpan period);
}
```

The **Timer** class also offers a **Dispose** method which allows you to cancel the timer altogether and optionally signal the kernel object identified by the **notifyObject** parameter when all pending callbacks for the time have completed. Here is what the **Dispose** method overloads look like:

```
public sealed class Timer : MarshalByRefObject, IDisposable {
   public Boolean Dispose();
   public Boolean Dispose(WaitHandle notifyObject);
}
```

> **Important** When a **Timer** object is garbage collected, its finalization code tells the thread pool to cancel the timer so that it no longer goes off. So when using a **Timer** object, make sure that a variable is keeping the **Timer** object alive or else your callback method will stop getting called. This is discussed and demonstrated in the "Garbage Collections and Debugging" section in Chapter 21, "Automatic Memory Management (Garbage Collection)."

The following code demonstrates how to have a thread pool thread call a method starting immediately and then every 2 seconds thereafter:

```
internal static class TimerDemo {
   private static Timer s_timer;

   public static void Go() {
      Console.WriteLine("Main thread: starting a timer");
      using (s_timer = new Timer(ComputeBoundOp, 5, 0, Timeout.Infinite)) {
         Console.WriteLine("Main thread: Doing other work here...");
         Thread.Sleep(10000);  // Simulating other work (10 seconds)
      } // Calls Dispose to cancel the timer now
   }
```

```
// This method's signature must match the TimerCallback delegate
private static void ComputeBoundOp(Object state) {
    // This method is executed by a thread pool thread
    Console.WriteLine("In ComputeBoundOp: state={0}", state);
    Thread.Sleep(1000);  // Simulates other work (1 second)

    // Have the Timer call this method again in 2 seconds
    s_timer.Change(2000, Timeout.Infinite);

    // When this method returns, the thread goes back
    // to the pool and waits for another work item
}
}
```

So Many Timers, So Little Time

Unfortunately, the FCL actually ships with several timers, and it is not clear to most programmers what makes each timer unique. Let me attempt to explain:

- **System.Threading's Timer class**   This is the timer discussed in the previous section, and it is the best timer to use when you want to perform periodic background tasks on a thread pool thread.

- **System.Windows.Forms's Timer class**   Constructing an instance of this class tells Windows to associate a timer with the calling thread (see the Win32 **SetTimer** function). When this timer goes off, Windows injects a timer message (**WM_TIMER**) into the thread's message queue. The thread must execute a message pump that extracts these messages and dispatches them to the desired callback method. Notice that all of the work is done by just one thread—the thread that sets the timer is guaranteed to be the thread that executes the callback method. This also means that your timer method will not be executed by multiple threads concurrently.

- **System.Windows.Threading's DispatcherTimer class**   This class is the equivalent of the **System.Windows.Forms**'s **Timer** class for Silverlight and WPF applications.

- **System.Timers's Timer class**   This timer is basically a wrapper around **System. Threading**'s **Timer** class that causes the CLR to queue events into the thread pool when the timer comes due. The **System.Timers.Timer** class is derived from **System. ComponentModel**'s **Component** class, which allows these timer objects to be placed on a design surface in Visual Studio. Also, it exposes properties and events, allowing it to be used more easily from Visual Studio's designer. This class was added to the FCL years ago while Microsoft was still sorting out the threading and timer stuff. This class probably should have been removed so that everyone would be using the **System. Threading.Timer** class instead. In fact, I never use the **System.Timers.Timer** class, and I'd discourage you from using it, too, unless you really want a timer on a design surface.

How the Thread Pool Manages Its Threads

Now I'd like to talk about how the thread pool code manages worker and I/O threads. However, I don't want to go into a lot of detail because the internal implementation has changed greatly over the years with each version of the CLR, and it will continue changing with future versions. It is best to think of the thread pool as a black box. The black box is not perfect for any one application, as it is a general-purpose thread scheduling technology designed to work with a large myriad of applications; it will work better for some applications than for others. It works very well today, and I highly recommend that you trust it because it would be very hard for you to produce a thread pool that works better than the one shipping in the CLR. And, over time, most applications should improve as the thread pool code internally changes how it manages threads.

Setting Thread Pool Limits

The CLR allows developers to set a maximum number of threads that the thread pool will create. However, it turns out that thread pools should never place an upper limit on the number of threads in the pool because starvation or deadlock might occur. Imagine queuing 1,000 work items that all block on an event that is signaled by the 1,001st item. If you've set a maximum of 1,000 threads, the 1,001st work item won't be executed, and all 1,000 threads will be blocked forever, forcing end users to terminate the application and lose all their work. Also, it is very unusual for developers to artificially limit the resources that they have available to their application. For example, would you ever start your application and tell the system you'd like to restrict the amount of memory that the application can use or limit the amount of network bandwidth that your application can use? Yet, for some reason, developers feel compelled to limit the number of threads that the thread pool can have.

Because customers have had starvation and deadlock issues, the CLR team has steadily increased the default maximum number of threads that the thread pool can have. The default maximum is now about 1,000 threads, which is effectively limitless since a 32-bit process has at most 2 GB of usable address space within it. After a bunch of Win32 DLLs load, the CLR DLLs load, the native heap and the managed heap is allocated, there is approximately 1.5 GB of address space left over. Since each thread requires more than 1 MB of memory for its user-mode stack and thread environment block (TEB), the most threads you can get in a 32-bit process is about 1,360. Attempting to create more threads than this will result in an **OutOfMemoryException** being thrown. Of course, a 64-bit process offers 8 terabytes of address space, so you could theoretically create hundreds of thousands of threads. But allocating anywhere near this number of threads is really just a waste of resources, especially when the ideal number of threads to have is equal to the number of CPUs in the machine. What the CLR team should do is remove the limits entirely, but they can't do this now because doing so might break some applications that expect thread pool limits to exist.

The **System.Threading.ThreadPool** class offers several static methods that you can call to manipulate the number of threads in the thread pool: **GetMaxThreads**, **SetMaxThreads**, **GetMinThreads**, **SetMinThreads**, and **GetAvailableThreads**. I highly recommend that you do not call any of these methods. Playing with thread pool limits usually results in making an application perform worse, not better. If you think that your application needs hundreds or thousands of threads, there is something seriously wrong with the architecture of your application and the way that it's using threads. This chapter and Chapter 27 demonstrate the proper way to use threads.

How Worker Threads Are Managed

Figure 26-1 shows the various data structures that make up the worker threads part of the thread pool. The **ThreadPool.QueueUserWorkItem** method and the **Timer** class always queue work items to the global queue. Worker threads pull items from this queue using a first-in-first-out (FIFO) algorithm and process them. Since multiple worker threads can be removing items from the global queue simultaneously, all worker threads contend on a thread synchronization lock to ensure that two or more threads don't take the same work item. This thread synchronization lock can become a bottleneck in some applications, thereby limiting scalability and performance to some degree.

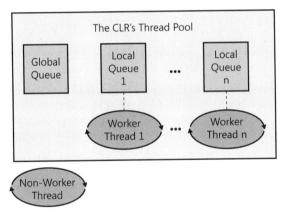

FIGURE 26-1 The CLR's thread pool

Now let's talk about **Task** objects scheduled using the default **TaskScheduler** (obtained by querying **TaskScheduler**'s static **Default** property).[4] When a non-worker thread schedules a **Task**, the **Task** is added to the global queue. But, each worker thread has its own local queue and when a worker thread schedules a **Task**, the **Task** is added to calling the thread's local queue.

---

4 Other **TaskScheduler**-derived objects may exhibit behavior different from what I describe here.

When a worker thread is ready to process an item, it always checks its local queue for a **Task** first. If a **Task** exists, the worker thread removes the **Task** from its local queue and processes the item. Note that a worker thread pulls tasks from its local queue using a last-in-first-out (LIFO) algorithm. Since a worker thread is the only thread allowed to access the head of its own local queue, no thread synchronization lock is required and adding and removing **Task**s from the queue is very fast. A side effect of this behavior is that **Task**s are executed in the reverse order that they were queued.

> **Important** Thread pools have never guaranteed the order in which queued items are processed, especially since multiple threads could be processing items simultaneously. However, this side effect exacerbates the problem. You must make sure that your application has no expectations about the order in which queued work items or **Task**s execute.

If a worker thread sees that its local queue is empty, then the worker thread will attempt to steal a **Task** from another worker thread's local queue. **Task**s are stolen from the tail of a local queue and require that a thread synchronization lock be taken, which hurts performance a little bit. Of course, the hope is that stealing rarely occurs, so this lock is taken rarely. If all the local queues are empty, then the worker thread will extract an item from the global queue (taking its lock) using the FIFO algorithm. If the global queue is empty, then the worker thread puts itself to sleep waiting for something to show up. If it sleeps for a long time, then it will wake itself up and destroy itself, allowing the system to reclaim the resources (kernel object, stacks, TEB) that were used by the thread.

The thread pool will quickly create worker threads so that the number of worker threads is equal to the value pass to **ThreadPool**'s **SetMinThreads** method. If you never call this method (and it's recommended that you never call this method), then the default value is equal to the number of CPUs that your process is allowed to use as determined by your process's affinity mask. Usually your process is allowed to use all the CPUs on the machine,[5] so the thread pool will quickly create worker threads up to the number of CPUs on the machine. After this many threads have been created, the thread pool monitors the completion rate of work items and if items are taking a long time to complete (the meaning of which is not documented), it creates more worker threads. If items start completing quickly, then worker threads will be destroyed.

Cache Lines and False Sharing

To improve the performance of repeatedly accessing memory, today's CPUs have on-chip cache memory. Accessing this memory is extremely fast, especially when compared to the speed of the CPU accessing motherboard memory. The first time that a thread reads some value in memory, the CPU fetches the desired value from the motherboard's memory and

---

[5] However, as of CLR version 4, 64 CPUs are used at most when running in a 64-bit process, and 32 CPUs are used at most when running in a 32-bit process.

stores it in the CPU's on-chip cache. In fact, to improve performance more, the CPU logically divides all memory into what is called a *cache line*. For the CPU in my computer, a cache line consists of 64 bytes, so the CPU fetches and stores 64-byte blocks from RAM.[6] Therefore, if your application needs to read an **Int32** value, the 64 bytes that contain the **Int32** will be fetched. Fetching more bytes than required usually results in a performance improvement because most applications tend to access data that is stored around other data the application is already accessing. This neighboring data will now be in the CPU's cache, avoiding RAM access.

However, if two or more cores access bytes in the same cache line, then the cores must communicate with each other and effectively pass the cache line from core to core so that multiple cores are not manipulating adjacent bytes at the same time. This can have an awful impact on the performance of your compute-bound operation. Let me demonstrate this with some code:

```
internal static class FalseSharing {
   private class Data {
      // These two fields are adjacent and (most likely) in the same cache line
      public Int32 field1;
      public Int32 field2;
   }

   private const Int32 iterations = 100000000; // 100 million
   private static Int32 s_operations = 2;
   private static Int64 s_startTime;

   public static void Main() {
      // Allocate an object and record the start time
      Data data = new Data();
      s_startTime = Stopwatch.GetTimestamp();

      // Have 2 threads access their own fields within the structure
      ThreadPool.QueueUserWorkItem(o => AccessData(data, 0));
      ThreadPool.QueueUserWorkItem(o => AccessData(data, 1));

      // For testing, block the Main thread
      Console.ReadLine();
   }

   private static void AccessData(Data data, Int32 field) {
      // The threads in here each access their own field within the Data object
      for (Int32 x = 0; x < iterations; x++)
         if (field == 0) data.field1++; else data.field2++;

      // Whichever thread finishes last, shows the time it took
      if (Interlocked.Decrement(ref s_operations) == 0)
         Console.WriteLine("Access time: {0:N0}", Stopwatch.GetTimestamp() - s_startTime);
   }
}
```

---

[6] You can determine the number of bytes in a CPU's cache line by calling Win32's **GetProcessorInformation** function. My Power Threading library contains a managed wrapper over this function, making it easy to call from managed code.

In this code, a **Data** object is constructed containing two fields. Most likely, these two fields will reside in the same cache line. Then, two thread pool threads go and execute the **AccessData** method. One thread will add **1** to **Data**'s **field1** field 100,000,000 times, and the other thread will do the same to the **field2** field. As each thread finishes, it decrements the value in the **s_Operations** field; whichever thread decrements the field to **0** is the last thread to finish, and this thread shows how long it took for both threads to complete their work. When I run this on my machine, I get a result of 15,856,074 milliseconds.

Now, let's change the **Data** class so it looks like this:

```
[StructLayout(LayoutKind.Explicit)]
private class Data {
    // These two fields are separated now and no longer in the same cache line
    [FieldOffset(0)]  public Int32 field1;
    [FieldOffset(64)] public Int32 field2;
}
```

What I have done here is separate the two fields by a cache line (64 bytes). Now, when I run the program, I get a result of 3,415,703 milliseconds. The first version is four times slower because the two fields were part of the same cache line and the CPUs had to keep handing the bytes back and forth to each other! From the program's point of view, the two threads were manipulating different data; but, from the CPU's cache line point of view, the CPUs were manipulating the same data. This is called *false sharing*. If the CPUs are on different Non-Uniform Memory Access (NUMA) nodes, then the performance impact can be substantially worse. In the second version, the fields were on different cache lines, so the CPUs could each work independently; nothing was shared.

I bring up this discussion to show you that cache lines and false sharing can have an enormous impact on the performance of an application when adjacent data is accessed by multiple threads simultaneously. This is something you should be aware of in performance-conscience scenarios and, if you detect it, you can usually devise a way to avoid it (like my use of the **FieldOffset** attribute).

Be aware that arrays maintain their length at the beginning of the array's memory, which is right next to the first few array elements. When you access any array element, the CLR verifies that the index you are using is within the array's length. This means that accessing an array's element always involves accessing the array's length, too. Therefore, to avoid additional false sharing, you should avoid having one thread write to the first few elements in the array while other threads are accessing other elements in the array.

## Chapter 27

I/O-Bound Asynchronous Operations

The previous chapter focused on ways to perform compute-bound operations asynchronously, allowing the thread pool to schedule the tasks onto multiple cores so that multiple threads can work concurrently, which increases throughput while using system resources efficiently. In this chapter, we'll focus on performing I/O-bound operations asynchronously, allowing hardware devices to handle the tasks so that threads and the CPU are not used at all. This, of course, uses system resources very efficiently because system resources are not required at all. However, the thread pool still plays an important role because, as you'll see, the thread pool threads will process the results of the various I/O operations.

How Windows Performs I/O Operations

Let's begin by discussing how Microsoft Windows performs synchronous I/O operations. Figure 27-1 represents a computer system with several hardware devices connected to it. Each of these hardware devices has its own circuit board, each of which contains a small, special-purpose computer that knows how to control its hardware device. For example, the hard disk drive has a circuit board that knows how to spin up the drive, seek the head to the right track, read or write data from or to the disk, and transfer the data to or from your computer's memory.

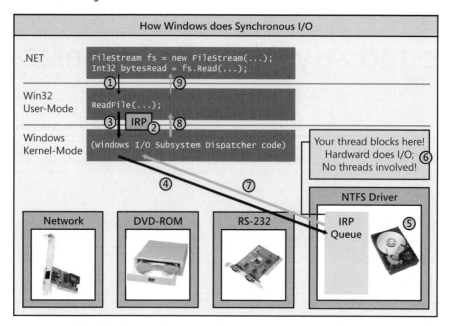

FIGURE 27-1 How Windows performs a synchronous I/O operation

In your program, you open a disk file by constructing a **FileStream** object. Then you call the **Read** method to read data from the file. When you call **FileStream**'s **Read** method, your thread transitions from managed code to native/user-mode code and **Read** internally calls the Win32 **ReadFile** function (#1). **ReadFile** then allocates a small data structure called an I/O Request Packet (IRP) (#2). The IRP structure is initialized to contain the handle to the file, an offset within the file where bytes will start to be read from, the address of a **Byte[]** that should be filled with the bytes being read, the number of bytes to transfer, and some other less interesting stuff.

ReadFile then calls into the Windows kernel by having your thread transition from native/user-mode code to native/kernel-mode code, passing the IRP data structure to the kernel (#3). From the device handle in the IRP, the Windows kernel knows which hardware device the I/O operation is destined for, and Windows delivers the IRP to the appropriate device driver's IRP queue (#4). Each device driver maintains its own IRP queue that contains I/O requests from all processes running on the machine. As IRP packets show up, the device driver passes the IRP information to the circuit board associated with the actual hardware device. The hardware device now performs the requested I/O operation (#5).

But here is the important part: While the hardware device is performing the I/O operation, your thread that issued the I/O request has nothing to do, so Windows puts your thread to sleep so that it is not wasting CPU time (#6). This is great, but while your thread is not wasting time, it is wasting space (memory), as its user-mode stack, kernel-mode stack, thread environment block (TEB), and other data structures are sitting in memory but are not being accessed at all. This is bad.

Ultimately, the hardware device will complete the I/O operation, and then Windows will wake up your thread, schedule it to a CPU, and let it return from kernel mode to user mode, and then back to managed code (#7, #8, and #9). **FileStream**'s **Read** method now returns an **Int32**, indicating the actual number of bytes read from the file so that you know how many bytes you can examine in the **Byte[]** that you passed to **Read**.

Let's imagine that you are implementing a Web application and as each client request comes in to your server, you need to make a database request. When a client request comes in, a thread pool thread will call into your code. If you now issue a database request synchronously, the thread will block for an indefinite amount of time waiting for the database to respond with the result. If during this time another client request comes in, the thread pool will have to create another thread and again this thread will block when it makes another database request. As more and more client requests come in, more and more threads are created, and all these threads block waiting for the database to respond. The result is that your Web server is allocating lots of system resources (threads and their memory) that are barely even used!

And to make matters worse, when the database does reply with the various results, threads become unblocked and they all start executing. But since you might have lots of threads running and relatively few CPU cores, Windows has to perform frequent context switches, which hurts performance even more. This is no way to implement a scalable application.

Now, let's discuss how Windows performs asynchronous I/O operations. In Figure 27-2, I have removed all the hardware devices except the hard disk from the picture, I introduce the common language runtime's (CLR's) thread pool, and I've modified the code slightly. I still open the disk file by constructing a **FileStream** object, but now I pass in the **FileOptions. Asynchronous** flag. This flag tells Windows that I want my read and write operations against the file to be performed asynchronously.

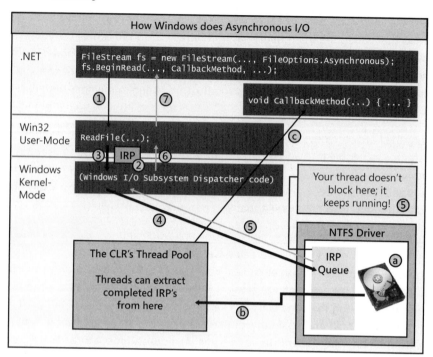

FIGURE 27-2 How Windows performs an asynchronous I/O operation

To read data from the file, I now call **BeginRead** instead of **Read**. Like **Read**, **BeginRead** calls Win32's **ReadFile** function (#1). **ReadFile** allocates its IRP, initializes it just like it did in the synchronous scenario (#2), and then passes it down to the Windows kernel (#3). Windows adds the IRP to the hard disk driver's IRP queue (#4), but now, instead of blocking your thread, your thread is allowed to return to your code; your thread immediately returns from its call to **BeginRead** (#5, #6, and #7). Now, of course, the IRP has not necessarily been processed yet, so you cannot have code after **BeginRead** that attempts to access the bytes in the passed-in **Byte[]**.

Now you might ask, when and how do you process the data that will ultimately be read? Well, when you call **BeginRead**, you pass it the name of a callback method as an argument (**CallbackMethod** in my example). The delegate referring to your callback method is effectively passed inside the IRP all the way down to the device driver. When the hardware device completes processing the IRP (a), it will queue the IRP's delegate into the CLR's thread pool (b). Sometime in the future, a thread pool thread will extract the completed IRP and invoke your callback method (c).[1] So now you know when the operation has completed, and inside this method, you can safely access the data inside the **Byte[]**.

---

[1] Completed IRPs are extracted from the thread pool using a first-in-first-out (FIFO) algorithm.

Now that you understand the basics, let's put it all into perspective. Let's say that a client request comes in, and our server makes an asynchronous database request. As a result, our thread won't block, and it will be allowed to return to the thread pool so that it can handle more incoming client requests. So now we have just *one* thread handling *all* incoming client requests. When the database server responds, its response is also queued into the thread pool, so our thread pool thread will just process it at some point and ultimately send the necessary data back to the client. At this point, we have just one thread processing all client requests and all database responses. Our server is using very few system resources and it is still running as fast as it can, especially since there are no context switches!

If items appear in the thread pool quicker than our one thread can process them all, then the thread pool might create additional threads. The thread pool will quickly create one thread per CPU on the machine. So on a quad-processor machine, four client requests/database responses (in any combination) are running on four threads without any context switching.[2]

However, if any of these threads voluntarily block (by invoking a synchronous I/O operation, calling **Thread.Sleep**, or waiting to acquire a thread synchronization lock), then Windows notifies the thread pool that one of its threads has stopped running. The thread pool now realizes that the CPUs are undersaturated and creates a new thread to replace the blocked thread. This, of course, is not ideal because creating a new thread is very expensive in terms of both time and memory.

What's worse is that the blocked thread might wake up and now the CPUs are oversaturated again and context switching must occur, decreasing performance. However, the thread pool is smart here. As threads complete their processing and return to the pool, the thread pool won't let them process new work items until the CPUs become exactly saturated again, thereby reducing context switches and improving performance. And if the thread pool later determines that it has more threads in it than it needs, it lets the extra threads kill themselves, thereby reclaiming the resources that these threads were using.

Internally, the CLR's thread pool uses a Windows resource called an *I/O Completion Port* to elicit the behavior that I've just described. The CLR creates an I/O Completion Port when it initializes and, as you open hardware devices, these devices can be bound to the I/O Completion Port so that device drivers know where to queue the completed IRPs. If you want to understand more about this mechanism, I recommend my book *Windows via C/C++, 5th Edition* (Microsoft Press, 2007).

---

2 This is assuming that other threads are not running on the computer, which is true most of the time since most computers are running at far less than 100% CPU usage. And CPU usage can be at 100% and this will still work as explained if the running threads have lower priorities. If other threads are running, then context switching does occur. This is bad for performance reasons, but it is good for reliability reasons. Remember that Windows gives each process at least one thread and performs context switches to ensure that an application whose thread is an infinite loop doesn't stop other applications' threads from running.

In addition to minimal resource usage and reduced context switches, we get many other benefits when performing I/O operations asynchronously. Whenever a garbage collection starts, the CLR must suspend all the threads in the process. Therefore, the fewer threads we have, the faster the garbage collector runs. In addition, when a garbage collection occurs, the CLR must walk all the threads' stacks looking for roots. Again, the fewer threads there are, the fewer stacks there are, and this also makes the garbage collection faster. But, in addition, if our threads don't block while processing work items, the threads tend to spend most of their time waiting in the thread pool. So when a garbage collection occurs, the threads are at the top of their stack, and walking each thread's stack for roots takes very little time.

Also, when you debug an application, Windows suspends all threads in the debuggee when you hit a breakpoint. Then, when you continue executing the debuggee, Windows has to resume all its threads, so if you have a lot of threads in an application, single-stepping through the code in a debugger can be excruciatingly slow. Using asynchronous I/O allows you to have just a few threads, improving your debugging performance.

And, here's yet another benefit: Let's say that your application wants to download 10 images from various Web sites, and that it takes 5 seconds to download each image. If you perform this work synchronously (downloading one image after another), then it takes you 50 seconds to get the 10 images. However, if you use just one thread to initiate 10 asynchronous download operations, then all 10 are being performed concurrently and all 10 images will come back in just 5 seconds! That is, when performing multiple synchronous I/O operations, the time it takes to get all the results is the sum of the times required for each individual result. However, when performing multiple asynchronous I/O operations, the time it takes to get all the results is the time required to get the single worst-performing operation.

For GUI applications, asynchronous operations offer yet another advantage: The application's user interface doesn't hang and remains responsive to the end user. In fact, if you are building a Silverlight application, you must perform all I/O operations asynchronously because the Silverlight version of the Framework Class Library (FCL) doesn't even offer methods that perform synchronous I/O operations. This was done purposely because Silverlight runs in a Web browser, like Windows Internet Explorer, and a thread issuing a synchronous I/O operation could block waiting for a Web server to reply. If this happens, the entire Web browser would be frozen. The user might not even be able to switch to another tab to work with a different Web site. In fact, this is a big reason why Windows Internet Explorer 8 creates a different process for each tab. Now one tab (not running Silverlight code) could stop responding, but other tabs still respond. But creating a separate process per tab is very resource-intensive, all in the name of keeping the UI responsive.[3]

---

[3] For the record, there is also a security advantage to having each tab run in its own process.

The CLR's Asynchronous Programming Model (APM)

Performing asynchronous operations is the key to building high-performance, scalable applications that allow you to use very few threads to execute a lot of operations. And when coupled with the thread pool, asynchronous operations allow you to take advantage of all of the CPUs that are in the machine. Realizing the enormous potential here, Microsoft's CLR team designed a pattern that would make it easy for developers to take advantage of this capability. This pattern is called the Asynchronous Programming Model (APM).

Personally, I love the APM because it is relatively easy to learn, simple to use, and is supported by many types in the FCL. Here are some examples:

- All **System.IO.Stream**-derived classes that communicate with hardware devices (including **FileStream** and **NetworkStream**) offer **BeginRead** and **BeginWrite** methods. Note that **Stream**-derived classes that do not communicate with hardware devices (including **BufferedStream**, **MemoryStream**, and **CryptoStream**) also offer **BeginRead** and **BeginWrite** methods to fit into the APM. However, the code in these methods performs compute-bound operations, not I/O-bound operations, and there-fore a thread is required to execute these operations.

- The **System.Net.Dns** class offers **BeginGetHostAddresses**, **BeginGetHostByName**, **BeginGetHostEntry**, and **BeginResolve** methods.

- The **System.Net.Sockets.Socket** class offers **BeginAccept**, **BeginConnect**, **BeginDisconnect**, **BeginReceive**, **BeginReceiveFrom**, **BeginReceiveMessageFrom**, **BeginSend**, **BeginSendFile**, and **BeginSendTo** methods.

- All **System.Net.WebRequest**-derived classes (including **FileWebRequest**, **FtpWebRequest**, and **HttpWebRequest**) offer **BeginGetRequestStream** and **BeginGetResponse** methods.

- The **System.IO.Ports.SerialPort** class has a read-only **BaseStream** property that returns a **Stream**, which, as you know, offers **BeginRead** and **BeginWrite** methods.

- The **System.Data.SqlClient.SqlCommand** class offers **BeginExecuteNonQuery**, **BeginExecuteReader**, and **BeginExecuteXmlReader** methods.

Furthermore, all delegate types define a **BeginInvoke** method for use with the APM. And finally, tools (such as WSDL.exe and SvcUtil.exe) that produce Web service proxy types also generate **BeginXxx** methods for use with the APM. By the way, there is a corresponding **EndXxx** method for each and every **BeginXxx** method. As you can see, support for the APM is pervasive throughout the FCL.

To synchronously read bytes from a **FileStream**, you'd call its **Read** method, which is proto-typed as follows:

```
public Int32 Read(Byte[] array, Int32 offset, Int32 count)
```

Calling a function that internally performs synchronous I/O puts your application in an unpredictable state as you have no idea when (or even if) the method will return. What if the file you opened was on a network server and just before calling **Read**, the server lost power? Now when will **Read** return?

And so, if you are interested in writing responsive, robust, and scalable software, you should not call methods that perform synchronous I/O; you should instead call methods that perform asynchronous I/O. To asynchronously perform an I/O operation, you would call a **BeginXxx** method like **FileStream**'s **BeginRead** method:

```
IAsyncResult BeginRead(Byte[] array, Int32 offset, Int32 numBytes,
    AsyncCallback userCallback, Object stateObject)
```

Notice that **BeginRead**'s first three parameters are identical to those of **Read**. And, in fact, every **BeginXxx** method has the same parameters as its synchronous counterpart method. But, every **BeginXxx** method has two additional parameters: **userCallback** and **stateObject**. The **userCallback** parameter is of the **AsyncCallback** delegate type:

```
public delegate void AsyncCallback(IAsyncResult ar);
```

For this parameter, you pass the name of a method (or lambda expression) representing code that you want to be executed by a thread pool thread when the asynchronous I/O operation completes. The last parameter to a **BeginXxx** method, **stateObject**, is a reference to any object you'd like forwarded on to your callback method. Inside your callback method, you access your **objectState** by querying the **IAsyncResult** interface's read-only **AsyncState** property.

All **BeginXxx** methods return an object that implements the **System.IAsyncResult** interface. When you call a **BeginXxx** method, it constructs an object that uniquely identifies your I/O request, queues up the request to the Windows device driver, and returns to you a reference to the **IAsyncResult** object. You can think of this object as your receipt. You can actually ignore the object reference returned from **BeginXxx** because the CLR internally holds a reference to the **IAsyncResult** object as well. When the operation completes, a thread pool thread will invoke your callback method, passing to it a reference to the internally held **IAsyncResult** object.

Inside your method, you'll call the corresponding **EndXxx** method, passing it the **IAsyncResult** object. The **EndXxx** method returns the same result that you would have gotten if you had called the synchronous method. For example, **FileStream**'s **Read** method returns an **Int32** that indicates the number of bytes actually read from the stream. **FileStream**'s **EndRead** method's return value has the same meaning:

```
Int32 EndRead(IAsyncResult result);  // Returns number of bytes read from the stream
```

Below is the code for a named-pipe server class, **PipeServer**, which is implemented using the APM:

```
internal sealed class PipeServer {
   // Each server object performs asynchronous operations on this pipe
   private readonly NamedPipeServerStream m_pipe = new NamedPipeServerStream(
      "Echo", PipeDirection.InOut, -1, PipeTransmissionMode.Message,
      PipeOptions.Asynchronous | PipeOptions.WriteThrough);

   public PipeServer() {
      // Asynchronously accept a client connection
      m_pipe.BeginWaitForConnection(ClientConnected, null);
   }

   private void ClientConnected(IAsyncResult result) {
      // A client connected, let's accept another client
      new PipeServer(); // Accept another client

      // Accept the client connection
      m_pipe.EndWaitForConnection(result);

      // Asynchronously read a request from the client
      Byte[] data = new Byte[1000];
      m_pipe.BeginRead(data, 0, data.Length, GotRequest, data);
   }

   private void GotRequest(IAsyncResult result) {
      // The client sent us a request, process it.
      Int32 bytesRead = m_pipe.EndRead(result);
      Byte[] data = (Byte[])result.AsyncState;

      // My sample server just changes all the characters to uppercase
      // But, you can replace this code with any compute-bound operation
      data = Encoding.UTF8.GetBytes(
         Encoding.UTF8.GetString(data, 0, bytesRead).ToUpper().ToCharArray());

      // Asynchronously send the response back to the client
      m_pipe.BeginWrite(data, 0, data.Length, WriteDone, null);
   }

   private void WriteDone(IAsyncResult result) {
      // The response was sent to the client, close our side of the connection
      m_pipe.EndWrite(result);
      m_pipe.Close();
   }
}
```

An instance of this class must be created *before* a client connects to the server because it is the constructor's call to **BeginWaitForConnection** that allows a client to connect. Once a client connects, the **ClientConnect** method will be called by a thread pool thread and a new instance of the **PipeServer** class is created so that additional clients can connect. Meanwhile, the **ClientConnected** method will call **BeginRead**, telling the network device driver to listen for incoming data from this client and put that data into the specified **Byte[]**.

When the client sends the data, some thread pool thread will call the **GotRequest** method. This method will gain access to the **Byte[]** (by querying the **AsyncState** property) and then process the data. In my example, I use a UTF-8 encoder to convert the **Byte[]** into a **String**, uppercase the characters in the **String**, and then convert the **String** back to a **Byte[]**. However, you can replace this code with your own compute-bound operation so that the server does whatever you need it to do. Then **GotRequest** sends the output data back to the client by calling **BeginWrite**. When the device driver has finished sending the data to the client, some thread pool thread will call **WriteDone**, which then closes the pipe and terminates the connection.

Notice that all the methods follow the same pattern: They end with a call to a **BeginXxx** method (except the last method, **WriteDone**) and they start with a call to an **EndXxx** method (except the constructor). Between the **EndXxx** and **BeginXxx** methods, I perform only compute-bound work; the I/O operations are at the "borders" of the methods, so now, threads never block. After each method, the threads return back to the thread pool where they can handle incoming client requests or incoming network responses. And if the thread pool gets busy with work, then it will automatically create multiple threads to handle the workload—my server scales automatically based on workload and based on the number of CPUs in the machine!

I created my server application as a console application and it initializes itself like this:

```
public static void Main() {
   // Start 1 server per CPU
   for (Int32 n = 0; n < Environment.ProcessorCount; n++)
      new PipeServer();

   Console.WriteLine("Press <Enter> to terminate this server application.");
   Console.ReadLine();
}
```

Now, let me show you the code for a named-pipe client class that is also implemented using the APM. Notice that the **PipeClient** class is structured identically to the **PipeServer** class.

```
internal sealed class PipeClient {
   // Each client object performs asynchronous operations on this pipe
   private readonly NamedPipeClientStream m_pipe;

   public PipeClient(String serverName, String message) {
      m_pipe = new NamedPipeClientStream(serverName, "Echo",
         PipeDirection.InOut, PipeOptions.Asynchronous | PipeOptions.WriteThrough);
      m_pipe.Connect(); // Must Connect before setting ReadMode
      m_pipe.ReadMode = PipeTransmissionMode.Message;

      // Asynchronously send data to the server
      Byte[] output = Encoding.UTF8.GetBytes(message);
      m_pipe.BeginWrite(output, 0, output.Length, WriteDone, null);
   }

   private void WriteDone(IAsyncResult result) {
      // The data was sent to the server
      m_pipe.EndWrite(result);
```

```
        // Asynchronously read the server's response
        Byte[] data = new Byte[1000];
        m_pipe.BeginRead(data, 0, data.Length, GotResponse, data);
    }

    private void GotResponse(IAsyncResult result) {
        // The server responded, display the response and close out connection
        Int32 bytesRead = m_pipe.EndRead(result);

        Byte[] data = (Byte[])result.AsyncState;
        Console.WriteLine("Server response: " + Encoding.UTF8.GetString(data, 0, bytesRead));
        m_pipe.Close();
    }
}
```

And, my client console application makes one hundred calls into the server using this code:

```
public static void Main() {
    // Now make 100 client requests against the server
    for (Int32 n = 0; n < 100; n++)
        new PipeClient("localhost", "Request #" + n);

    // Since all the requests are issued asynchronously, the constructors are likely
    // to return before all the requests are complete. The call below stops the
    // application from terminating until we see all the responses displayed.
    Console.ReadLine();
}
```

Frequently, developers implement servers to use one thread per client request. However, a 32-bit process can create no more than about 1,360 threads before running out of virtual address space. This means that a server using the one-thread-per-client model can't operate on more than 1,360 clients simultaneously. However, I modified my program to construct a bunch of **PipeServer** objects, and in a 32-bit process, I was able to create over 4 million of them before running out of memory. So the asynchronous model allows many more concurrent clients, uses fewer resources, processes clients faster (due to reduced context switches), improves garbage collection time, and improves debugging performance, too! What else could you ask for?

The AsyncEnumerator Class

Well, one thing you could ask for is an easier way to do asynchronous programming. The APM's programming model is cumbersome, which is the main reason why a lot of developers don't use it. Here are some of the problems with it:

- You must split your code up into many callback methods.

- You have to avoid using argument and local variables because these variables are allocated on a thread's stack and can't be accessed by another thread or by another method.

- Many C# language constructs, like **try/catch/finally**, **using**, **for**, **do**, **while**, and **foreach**, can't be used if you want to start the construct as one method and end it in another method. For example, in my **Server** class, I'd like to use C#'s **using** statement to open the pipe and then have it automatically be closed in a **finally** block. However, I can't use **using** because I open the pipe in **Server**'s constructor and I close it in a different method, **WriteDone**.

- It's hard to implement other features that many developers typically need such as coordinating multiple concurrent operations, supporting cancellation and timeout, and marshaling work to the GUI thread to update controls.

These are the main reasons why many developers avoid the APM. However, I have created a class, **AsyncEnumerator**, which simplifies all of this and fixes all the problems mentioned above. In a nutshell, my **AsyncEnumerator** class allows you to perform asynchronous operations using a synchronous programming model by leveraging C#'s iterator language feature. The class is part of my Power Threading library and is completely free to use. Versions of this library exist for the desktop CLR, Silverlight, and the Microsoft .NET Compact Framework. You can download the latest version of the library and sample code from *http://Wintellect.com/PowerThreading.aspx*. This Web page contains links to my *Concurrent Affairs* column in *MSDN Magazine*, where I explain how my **AsyncEnumerator** class works. There are also links to some videos I did showing how to use it, and a link to a newsgroup where I offer free technical support.

For now, let me just share some of the features that the **AsyncEnumerator** class offers:

- It implements the APM itself so it easily integrates with all the Microsoft .NET Framework technologies, such as ASP.NET and Windows Communication Foundation (WCF). This also allows composition of asynchronous subroutines, as one **AsyncEnumerator** can invoke another.

- It coordinates multiple concurrent asynchronous operations. That is, you can issue many asynchronous operations, and the **AsyncEnumerator** can notify you after all of them have completed or notify you as each one completes.

- It supports discard groups, which allow you to issue a set of asynchronous operations and have the **AsyncEnumerator** object automatically throw away the results as they complete. For example, you could request the temperature of London from three different Web servers within a single discard group. Whichever server responds the fastest gives your application the information it needs to continue processing. Then you can cancel the remaining operations that are part of that discard group.

- It allows you to cancel a set of asynchronous operations automatically by calling each operation's **EndXxx** methods (and swallowing exceptions) for you if you don't care about the results. This is particularly good for GUI applications because it allows users to cancel the operations if they get tired of waiting for the results. In addition, you can have the cancel occur automatically after a timeout interval that you specify. This is particularly good for server applications that want to respond to the client within a certain period of time with whatever information the server has.

- It frees you from having to worry about your application's threading model (as discussed in the "Applications and their Threading Models" section later in this chapter). For example, in a GUI application, the **AsyncEnumerator** invokes your code on the GUI thread by default so you can update UI controls. For an ASP.NET Web Form or XML Web Service application, the **AsyncEnumerator** automatically ensures that your code is running under the client's culture and identity.

- It has rich error-handling support. If your iterator returns and an asynchronous operation later completes, the **AsyncEnumerator** class throws an exception notifying you that there is no way for the **EndXxx** method to be called and therefore your application is leaking resources.

- It has rich debugging support. Typically, an application will have many **AsyncEnumerator** objects in memory. This is especially true of server applications. In a debugger, you can query the **AsyncEnumerator**'s static **GetInProgressList** method, which returns a list of all the **AsyncEnumerator** objects currently in existence. This list is sorted with the object that has been waiting the longest for an operation to complete at the top. If your application appears to be hung, looking at the item at the top of the list will usually take you right to the line in your code that is waiting for an operation to complete. In addition, when you look at an individual **AsyncEnumerator** object in the debugger, it displays a user-definable tag identifying the operation, the timestamp of the last asynchronous operation it performed, which operations have completed, and which operations have not completed yet. It also shows you the source code file and line within that file where the asynchronous operations were initiated.

Here is what the pipe server code looks like when implemented for use with my **AsyncEnumerator** class[4]:

```
private static IEnumerator<Int32> PipeServerAsyncEnumerator(AsyncEnumerator ae) {
   // Each server object performs asynchronous operations on this pipe
   using (var pipe = new NamedPipeServerStream(
      "Echo", PipeDirection.InOut, -1, PipeTransmissionMode.Message,
      PipeOptions.Asynchronous | PipeOptions.WriteThrough)) {

      // Asynchronously accept a client connection
      pipe.BeginWaitForConnection(ae.End(), null);
      yield return 1;

      // A client connected, let's accept another client
      var aeNewClient = new AsyncEnumerator();
      aeNewClient.BeginExecute(PipeServerAsyncEnumerator(aeNewClient),
         aeNewClient.EndExecute);

      // Accept the client connection
      pipe.EndWaitForConnection(ae.DequeueAsyncResult());

      // Asynchronously read a request from the client
      Byte[] data = new Byte[1000];
```

---

4 The sample code for this book contains the pipe client code re-implemented to use **AsyncEnumerator**. This version of the code follows the same structure shown here.

```
        pipe.BeginRead(data, 0, data.Length, ae.End(), null);
        yield return 1;

        // The client sent us a request, process it.
        Int32 bytesRead = pipe.EndRead(ae.DequeueAsyncResult());

        // My sample server just changes all the characters to uppercase
        // But, you can replace this code with any compute-bound operation
        data = Encoding.UTF8.GetBytes(
            Encoding.UTF8.GetString(data, 0, bytesRead).ToUpper().ToCharArray());

        // Asynchronously send the response back to the client
        pipe.BeginWrite(data, 0, data.Length, ae.End(), null);
        yield return 1;

        // The response was sent to the client, close our side of the connection
        pipe.EndWrite(ae.DequeueAsyncResult());
    } // Close happens in a finally block now!
}
```

There are several things to notice about this new version of the code:

- All the code is in one method as opposed to lots of methods spread out within a class. Since there is no class, there are no fields; all the variables are local variables.

- Where I would have had a method separation, I now have a **yield return 1** statement. This allows the thread to return to where it came from so that it can do more work.

- To every **BeginXxx** method, I pass **ae.End()**; this method returns a delegate referring to a method inside the **AsyncEnumerator** object. When the operation completes, the thread pool thread notifies the **AsyncEnumerator** object, which in turn continues executing your iterator method after the **yield return 1** statement.

- I always pass **null** as the last argument to every **BeginXxx** method. Therefore, I never need to call **IAsyncResult**'s **AsyncState** property and cast its return value to the right type; I just use the local variables directly.

- To every **EndXxx** method, I pass the result of calling **ae.DequeueAsyncResult()**. This method returns the **IAsyncResult** object that was passed to the **AsyncEnumerator** object by the thread pool thread when the asynchronous operation completed.

- And last, but not least, notice that now I can use C#'s **using** statement to control the lifetime of the **NamedPipeServerStream**. This also means that the **NamedPipeServerStream** object will be closed within a **finally** block should any other code throw an unhandled exception.

This gives you a good introduction as to what the **AsyncEnumerator** class can do for you and how it simplifies asynchronous programming. The code above doesn't even show some of the more exciting features. If you're interested in learning more about it, I encourage you to visit the Wintellect Web site mentioned earlier.

The APM and Exceptions

Whenever you call a **BeginXxx** method, it could throw an exception, of course. If this happens, you can assume that the asynchronous operation has not been queued, and therefore a thread pool thread will not invoke any callback method that you may have passed to the **BeginXxx** method.

When a Windows device driver is processing an asynchronous I/O request, it is possible for something to go wrong, and Windows will need to inform your application of this. For example, while sending bytes or waiting for bytes to come in over the network, a timeout could expire. If the data does not come in time, the device driver will want to tell you that the asynchronous operation completed with an error. To accomplish this, the device driver posts the completed IRP to the CLR's thread pool and effectively puts an error code in the **IAsyncResult** object that represents the asynchronous operation. A thread pool thread will then invoke your callback method, passing it the **IAsyncResult** object. Your callback method will then pass the **IAsyncResult** object to the appropriate **EndXxx** method, which will see the error code, convert it to an appropriate **Exception**-derived object, and then throw this exception object.

The result of all this is that exceptions work the same with asynchronous programming as they do with synchronous programming. However, you usually don't care about exceptions thrown from a **BeginXxx** call, and you usually do care about exceptions thrown from an **EndXxx** call. The following code demonstrates the use of exception handling and the APM:

```
internal static class ApmExceptionHandling {
   public static void Main() {
      // Try to access an invalid IP address
      WebRequest webRequest = WebRequest.Create("http://0.0.0.0/");
      webRequest.BeginGetResponse(ProcessWebResponse, webRequest);
      Console.ReadLine();
   }

   private static void ProcessWebResponse(IAsyncResult result) {
      WebRequest webRequest = (WebRequest)result.AsyncState;

      WebResponse webResponse = null;
      try {
         webResponse = webRequest.EndGetResponse(result);
         Console.WriteLine("Content length: " + webResponse.ContentLength);
      }
      catch (WebException we) {
         Console.WriteLine(we.GetType() + ": " + we.Message);
      }
      finally {
         if (webResponse != null) webResponse.Close();
      }
   }
}
```

When I run the above program, I get the following output:

```
System.Net.WebException: Unable to connect to the remote server
```

> **Note** A common problem exists when performing multiple asynchronous Hypertext Transfer Protocol (HTTP) requests that catches many developers by surprise. The HTTP (RFC 2616) states that a client application should not have more than two simultaneous connections to a single server. The classes in the FCL actually enforce this rule, and any thread trying to create additional connections to a particular server is blocked until one of the two existing connections is closed. You should either design your application to have no more than two outstanding connections to a single server at any one time or increase the maximum number of concurrent connections by setting **System.Net.ServicePointManager**'s static **DefaultConnectionLimit** property to whatever number your application needs.

Applications and Their Threading Models

The .NET Framework supports several different kinds of application models, and each application model might impose its own threading model. Console applications and Windows Services (which are really console applications; you just don't see the console) do not impose any kind of threading model; that is, any thread can do whatever it wants when it wants.

However, GUI applications, including Windows Forms, Windows Presentation Foundation (WPF), and Silverlight, impose a threading model where the thread that created the window is the only thread allowed to update that window. It is common for the GUI thread to spawn off an asynchronous operation so that the GUI thread doesn't block and stop responding to user input like mouse, keystroke, pen, and touch events. However, when the asynchronous operation completes, it completes using a thread pool thread which cannot update the UI showing the results. Somehow, the thread pool thread must have the GUI thread update the UI.

Like console applications, ASP.NET Web Form and XML Web Service applications allow any thread to do whatever it wants. When a thread pool thread starts to process a client's request, it can assume the client's culture (**System.Globalization.CultureInfo**), allowing the Web server to return culture-specific formatting for numbers, dates, and times.[5] In addition, the Web server can assume the client's identity (**System.Security.Principal. IPrincipal**) so that the server can access only the resources that the client is allowed to access. When a thread pool thread spawns an asynchronous operation, it will be completed by another thread pool thread, which will be processing the result of an asynchronous operation. While this work is being performed on behalf of the original client request, the culture and identity information doesn't flow to the new thread pool thread by default so any additional work done on behalf of the client is now not using the client's culture and identity information. Ideally, we want the culture and identity information to flow to the other thread pool threads that are still doing work on behalf of the same client.

---

[5] For more information, see http://msdn.microsoft.com/en-us/library/bz9tc508.aspx.

Fortunately, the FCL defines a base class, called **System.Threading.
SynchronizationContext**, which solves all these problems. Simply stated, a
SynchronizationContext-derived object connects an application model to its threading
model. The FCL defines several classes derived from **SynchronizationContext**, but usually
you will not deal directly with these classes; in fact, many of them are not publicly exposed
or documented. Here is what the **SynchronizationContext** class looks like (I show only the
members relevant to this discussion):

```
public class SynchronizationContext {
    public static SynchronizationContext Current { get; }
    public virtual void Post(SendOrPostCallback d, object state); // Call asynchronously
    public virtual void Send(SendOrPostCallback d, object state); // Call synchronously
}

// SendOrPostCallback is a delegate defined like this:
public delegate void SendOrPostCallback(Object state);
```

For Windows Forms applications, WPF applications, and Silverlight applications, the GUI
thread will have a **SynchronizationContext**-derived class associated with it. You can get a
reference to this object by having the GUI thread query **SynchronizationContext**'s static
Current property. You would then save a reference to this object in some shared variable
(like a **static** field of your own class). Then, whenever a thread pool thread needs to have
the GUI thread update the UI, you would have the thread pool thread reference the saved
SynchronizationContext-derived object and call its **Post** method, passing in the method
(matching the **SendOrPostCallback** delegate's signature) that should be invoked by the GUI
thread and an argument that should be passed to this method.

I recommend calling the **Post** method, as it queues up the callback to the GUI thread and
allows the thread pool thread to return immediately. **Send**, on the other hand, queues up the
callback to the GUI thread and then blocks the thread pool thread until the GUI thread has
completed calling the callback. Blocking the thread pool thread will most likely cause the
thread pool to create a new thread, increasing resource consumption while decreasing
performance. This is why I always avoid calling the **Send** method.

> **Note**   For the curious, here is how the various **SynchronizationContext**-derived classes get
> the GUI thread to invoke the **SendOrPostCallback** method. For Windows Forms, the **System.
> Windows.Forms.WindowsFormsSynchronizationContext** class's **Post** method internally
> calls **System.Windows.Forms.Control**'s **BeginInvoke** method, and its **Send** method internally
> calls **Control**'s **Invoke** method. For WPF and Silverlight, the **System.Windows.Threading.
> DispatcherSynchronizationContext** class's **Post** method internally calls **System.Windows.
> Threading.Dispatcher**'s **BeginInvoke** method, and its **Send** method internally calls
> **Dispatcher**'s **Invoke** method.

For ASP.NET Web Form and XML Web Service applications, the thread pool thread that starts running due to an incoming client request will have a **SynchronizationContext**-derived class associated with it. This object contains within it the client's culture and identity information. You can get a reference to this object by having the thread pool thread query **SynchronizationContext**'s static **Current** property. You would then save a reference to this object in some field that is a member of the object that is processing the client's request. When another thread pool thread calls back into a method of the class, you would have the thread pool thread reference the saved **SynchronizationContext**-derived object and call its **Post** method, passing in the method (matching the **SendOrPostCallback** delegate's signature) that should be invoked using the client's culture and identity information. This method will be executed by the same thread pool thread that called **Post**. For ASP.NET applications, the **SynchronizationContext**-derived type's **Post** and **Send** methods perform identically.

For a console or Windows Service application, there will not be a **SynchronizationContext**-derived object associated with the thread; querying **SynchronizationContext**'s static **Current** property will return **null**.

At first, all of this can be very confusing, so I wrote a little method that simplifies things greatly:

```
private static AsyncCallback SyncContextCallback(AsyncCallback callback) {
    // Capture the calling thread's SynchronizationContext-derived object
    SynchronizationContext sc = SynchronizationContext.Current;

    // If there is no SC, just return what was passed in
    if (sc == null) return callback;

    // Return a delegate that, when invoked, posts to the captured SC a method that
    // calls the original AsyncCallback passing it the IAsyncResult argument
    return asyncResult => sc.Post(result => callback((IAsyncResult)result), asyncResult);
}
```

This method turns a normal **AsyncCallback** method into an **AsyncCallback** method that is invoked via the calling thread's **SynchronizationContext**-derived object, ensuring that the right threading model is used no matter what application model I'm using.[6] Here is a Windows Forms example that uses the APM and my **SyncContextCallback** method to ensure that everything works correctly:

```
internal sealed class MyWindowsForm : Form {
    public MyWindowsForm() {
        Text = "Click in the window to start a Web request";
        Width = 400; Height = 100;
    }
```

---

[6] You might wonder why the .NET Framework doesn't just automatically provide what my **SyncContextCallback** method does. It wasn't until after .NET Framework version 1.0 shipped that everyone realized how big a problem this whole "application models have their own threading models" thing was. To address these problems, the **SynchronizationContext** class was added in .NET Framework version 2.0. To make this the default behavior now could have potentially broken existing applications, and this is why the "right" behavior isn't the default behavior.

```
protected override void OnMouseClick(MouseEventArgs e) {
    // The GUI thread initiates the asynchronous Web request
    Text = "Web request initiated";
    var webRequest = WebRequest.Create("http://Wintellect.com/");
    webRequest.BeginGetResponse(SyncContextCallback(ProcessWebResponse), webRequest);
    base.OnMouseClick(e);
}

private void ProcessWebResponse(IAsyncResult result) {
    // If we get here, this must be the GUI thread, it's OK to update the UI
    var webRequest = (WebRequest)result.AsyncState;
    using (var webResponse = webRequest.EndGetResponse(result)) {
        Text = "Content length: " + webResponse.ContentLength;
    }
}
}
```

Now, see how similar the WPF version is[7]:

```
private sealed class MyWpfWindow : System.Windows.Window {
    public MyWpfWindow() {
        Title = "Click in the window to start a Web request";
        Width = 400; Height = 100;
    }

    protected override void OnMouseDown(MouseButtonEventArgs e) {
        // The GUI thread initiates the asynchronous Web request
        Title = "Web request initiated";
        var webRequest = WebRequest.Create("http://Wintellect.com/");
        webRequest.BeginGetResponse(SyncContextCallback(ProcessWebResponse), webRequest);
        base.OnMouseDown(e);
    }

    private void ProcessWebResponse(IAsyncResult result) {
        // If we get here, this must be the GUI thread, it's OK to update the UI
        var webRequest = (WebRequest)result.AsyncState;
        using (var webResponse = webRequest.EndGetResponse(result)) {
            Title = "Content length: " + webResponse.ContentLength;
        }
    }
}
```

Implementing a Server Asynchronously

Earlier in this chapter, I showed my pipe server, which is implemented as a console application, and I implemented it taking advantage of the APM. Other servers using different application models can also be implemented using the APM. However, I have run into a lot of people who don't know that this is even possible. So, in this section, I just want to make you aware that you can implement all kinds of servers asynchronously. See the .NET Framework SDK documentation for more details.

---

[7] By the way, the Silverlight version is practically identical to this. The differences are all related to setting the title and detecting the mouse click; the code related to the APM is absolutely identical to the WPF version.

To implement an ASP.NET Web Form page asynchronously, open your .aspx file and add "Async=true" to your **Page** directive. Then, inside your code, call the **AddOnPreRenderCompleteAsync** method (your class inherits this method from **System.Web. UI.Page**), passing it the names of **BeginXxx** and **EndXxx** methods that you write yourself. In your **BeginXxx** method, start your asynchronous operation and let the thread pool thread return to the pool. Note that even though the thread is returning, the page is *not* sent back to the client. When the asynchronous operation completes, your **EndXxx** method will be called. Grab the data, update the page's controls, and now the page will be sent back to the client.

To implement an ASP.NET Web Service asynchronously, just implement your Web method as two methods, a **BeginXxx** method and an **EndXxx** method, following the pattern described in this chapter. Mark both methods with the **[WebMethod]** attribute.

To implement a Windows Communication Foundation Web Service asynchronously, define **BeginXxx** and **EndXxx** methods in your contracts following the pattern described in this chapter. Then, mark the **BeginXxx** method with the **[OperationContract(AsyncPattern= true)]** attribute.

Let me point out that my **AsyncEnumerator** class can really simplify your coding when you want to implement a server asynchronously.

The APM and Compute-Bound Operations

Chapter 26, "Compute-Bound Asynchronous Operations," showed how to perform compute-bound operations by calling **ThreadPool**'s **QueueUserWorkItem** method and also by using the **System.Threading.Tasks.Task** class. Well, in this section, I'll show you how to perform a compute-bound operation using the APM. It's unfortunate that the .NET Framework offers so many different programming models for accomplishing the same thing, as it is confusing to developers which one to use when. And since the multi-core revolution is still in its infancy, I suspect that even more programming models will show up in the future. This is just the way of the world. Eventually, many years from now, I'm sure things will get simpler; but for today and the near future, things will get more complicated. In this chapter's "Programming Model Soup" section, I attempt to compare and contrast the various APMs offered today by the .NET Framework.

You can call any method by using the APM, but first, you need to use a delegate that has the same signature as the method you want to call. For example, let's say you want to call a method that sums up the numbers from 1 to **n**. This computationally intensive task (which performs no I/O) could take a long time to execute if **n** is a large value.[8] Here is the **Sum** method:

---

[8] Yes, I know that a sum can be calculated quickly for any value of **n** using this formula: **n * (n + 1) / 2**. For this example, let's just forget that this formula exists and do it the old-fashioned way: manually adding up the numbers so that it takes a long time.

```
private static UInt64 Sum(UInt64 n) {
   UInt64 sum = 0;
   for (UInt64 i = 1; i <= n; i++) {
      checked {
         // I use checked code so that an OverflowException gets
         // thrown if the sum doesn't fit in a UInt64.
         sum += i;
      }
   }
   return sum;
}
```

If **n** is large, **Sum** could take a long time to execute. To keep the UI of my application responsive or to take advantage of other CPUs in the computer, I'd like to execute this method asynchronously. To do this, I use the generic **System.Func<T, TResult>** delegate that accepts
two type parameters; one for the argument and one for the return type:

```
public delegate TResult Func<T, TResult>(T arg);
```

You'll recall from the delegate discussion in Chapter 17, "Delegates," that the C# compiler
compiles this line of code into a class definition that logically looks like this:

```
public sealed class Func<T, TResult> : MulticastDelegate {
   public Func(Object object, IntPtr method);
   public TResult Invoke(T arg);
   public IAsyncResult BeginInvoke(T arg, AsyncCallback callback, Object object);
   public TResult EndInvoke(IAsyncResult result);
}
```

When you define a delegate in C# source code, the compiler always produces a class that has
BeginInvoke and **EndInvoke** methods. The **BeginInvoke** method has the same parameters
as the delegate definition, with two additional parameters at the end: **AsyncCallback** and
Object. All **BeginInvoke** methods return an **IAsyncResult**. The **EndInvoke** method has one
parameter, an **IAsyncResult**, and the **EndInvoke** method returns whatever data type the
delegate's signature returns.

Now that you understand all of this, using a delegate to execute a compute-bound operation
is trivial because it follows the APM pattern we've been talking about. Here is some code that
shows how to call **Sum** asynchronously:

```
public static void Main() {
   // Initialize a delegate variable to refer to the method we want to call asynchronously
   Func<UInt64, UInt64> sumDelegate = Sum;

   // Call the method using a thread pool thread
   sumDelegate.BeginInvoke(1000000000, SumIsDone, sumDelegate);

   // Executing some other code here would be useful...

   // For this demo, I'll just suspend the primary thread
   Console.ReadLine();
}
```

The **sumDelegate** variable is first initialized to refer to the method you want to call asynchronously. Then **BeginInvoke** is called to initiate the asynchronous calling of the method. Internally, the CLR constructs an **IAsyncResult** object to identify the asynchronous operation. As you know, I/O operations are queued to a Windows device driver; however, a delegate's **BeginInvoke** method queues compute-bound operations to the CLR's thread pool by internally calling **ThreadPool**'s **QueueUserWorkItem**. Finally, **BeginInvoke** returns the **IAsyncResult** object to its caller (which usually ignores it).

Since **BeginInvoke** queued the operation to the CLR's thread pool, a thread pool thread will wake, dequeue the work item, and call the compute-bound method (**Sum**, in this example). Normally, when a thread pool thread returns from executing a method, the thread returns back to the pool. However, in my example, **BeginInvoke** was called, passing in the name of a method (**SumIsDone**) for the second-to-last parameter. Because of this, when **Sum** returns, the thread pool thread does not return back to the pool; instead, it now calls **SumIsDone**. In other words, the callback is called when the compute-bound operation has completed, just as it would be called when an I/O-bound operation has completed. Here is what my **SumIsDone** method looks like:

```
private static void SumIsDone(IAsyncResult ar) {
   // Extract the sumDelegate (state) from the IAsyncResult object
   var sumDelegate = (Func<UInt64, UInt64>) ar.AsyncState;

   try {
      // Get the result and display it
      Console.WriteLine("Sum's result: " + sumDelegate.EndInvoke(result));
   }
   catch (OverflowException) {
      Console.WriteLine("Sum's result is too large to calculate");
   }
}
```

APM Considerations

All in all, I am a huge fan of the APM, but I must admit that it does have some shortcomings, and it would be nice if Microsoft solved some of these, or at least provided some guidance for developers. Let's discuss these issues.

Using the APM Without the Thread Pool

In this chapter, I have discussed how to use the APM and have thread pool threads invoke your callback methods with the asynchronous operations completed. What I have shown you is the preferred way to use the APM, as it uses little resources and offers excellent performance. However, the APM offers three other ways to know when the asynchronous operation has completed.

All **BeginXxx** methods return a reference to an object that implements the **IAsyncResult** interface:

```
public interface IAsyncResult {
    Object      AsyncState              { get; }
    WaitHandle AsyncWaitHandle          { get; } // Avoid using this
    Boolean     IsCompleted             { get; } // Avoid using this
    Boolean     CompletedSynchronously  { get; } // true if the op completed synchronously
}
```

First, if a thread calls **EndXxx**, passing in this **IAsyncResult** object before the operation is complete, the calling thread will block waiting for it to complete and the thread will wake with the result returned from **EndXxx**. Second, a thread can also block, waiting for the operation to complete, by calling **WaitOne** (discussed in Chapter 28, "Primitive Thread Synchronization Constructs") on the **WaitHandle** returned from querying **IAsyncResult**'s **AsyncWaitHandle** property. These first two techniques should be avoided, however, because they block a thread, potentially causing the thread pool to allocate another thread.

Third, a thread could continuously query **IAsyncResult**'s **IsCompleted** property in a loop to know when the operation is complete. This technique should also be avoided because it wastes CPU time while polling. If you poll waiting for a compute-bound operation to complete, then you steal CPU time away from the compute-bound operation, making it take longer to complete. Frequently, to reduce continuous polling, programmers call **Thread.Sleep** within each iteration of the polling loop. If you do this, now you are blocking threads and polling!

Always Call the EndXxx Method, and Call It Only Once

You must call **EndXxx** or else you will leak resources. Some developers have written code to call **BeginXxx** to write some data to a device, and there is no processing that needs to be done after the data has been written, so they don't care about calling **EndXxx**. However, calling **EndXxx** is required for two reasons. First, the CLR allocates some internal resources when you initiate an asynchronous operation. When the operation completes, the CLR will hold onto these resources until **EndXxx** is called. If **EndXxx** is never called, these resources remain allocated and will be reclaimed only when the process terminates. Second, when you initiate an asynchronous operation, you don't actually know if the operation eventually succeeded or failed. The only way you can discover this is by calling **EndXxx** and checking the return value or seeing if it throws an exception.

You should not call **EndXxx** more than once for any given asynchronous operation. When you call **EndXxx**, it could access some internal resources and then release them. If you call **EndXxx** again, the resources will have been released already, and the results will be unpredictable. In reality, calling **EndXxx** multiple times for a single operation may or may not work; it depends on how the class that implements the **IAsyncResult** interface has been written. Since Microsoft never told developers how this should behave, different developers implemented it in different ways. The only thing you can count on is that calling **EndXxx** just once will work.

Always Use the Same Object When Calling the **EndXxx** Method

Whatever object you use when calling **BeginXxx** should be the same object that you use to call **EndXxx**. For example, don't construct a delegate and call its **BeginInvoke** method and then construct another delegate (of the same type referring to the same object/method) and use it to call its **EndInvoke** method. While this seems as if it should work (since both delegate objects are identical in every way), it doesn't work because the **IAsyncResult** object internally keeps a reference to the original object used when calling **BeginInvoke**, and if they don't match, **EndInvoke** throws an **InvalidOperationException** with a string message of **"The IAsyncResult object provided does not match this delegate."** Again, using one object to call **BeginInvoke** and another object to call **EndInvoke** may work for some object types depending on how they were implemented.

Using **ref**, **out**, and **params** Arguments with **BeginXxx** and **EndXxx** Methods

The parameters of **BeginXxx** and **EndXxx** methods will deviate slightly from the patterns I've described in this chapter if the non-asynchronous version of the method uses any **out/ref** parameters or if it has a parameter marked with the **params** keyword. Since this is very rare, I won't show an example, but you should be aware of it. You'll easily figure out how to call the methods correctly when you need to.

You Can't Cancel an Asynchronous I/O-Bound Operation

There is currently no way to cancel an outstanding asynchronous I/O-bound operation. This is a feature that many developers would like, but it is actually quite hard to implement. After all, if you request 1,000 bytes from a server and then you decide you don't want those bytes anymore, there really is no way to tell the server to forget about your request. The way to deal with this is just to let the bytes come back to you and then throw them away. In addition, there is a race condition here: Your request to cancel the request could come just as the last byte is being read. Now what should your application do? You'd need to handle this potential race condition occurring in your own code and decide whether to throw the data away or act on it. Some **BeginXxx** methods might return an object that implements the **IAsyncResult** interface, as well as offering some kind of cancel method. In this case, you could cancel the operation. You'd have to check the documentation for the **BeginXxx** method or the class it returns to see whether cancellation is supported.

Memory Consumption

Whenever you call a **BeginXxx** method, it constructs an instance of a type that implements the **IAsyncResult** interface. This means that an object is created for every asynchronous operation that you want to perform. This adds more overhead and creates more objects on the heap, which causes more garbage collections to occur. The result: poorer application performance. So if you know for a fact that your I/O operations are going to execute extremely quickly, it may make more sense to perform them synchronously. Many developers (including myself) wish that the APM returned value types instead or had some other lightweight way of identifying a queued asynchronous operation; maybe Microsoft will improve the CLR someday by supporting this.

Some I/O Operations Must Be Done Synchronously

The Win32 API offers many functions that execute I/O operations. Unfortunately, some of these methods do not let you perform the I/O asynchronously. For example, the Win32 **CreateFile** method (called by **FileStream**'s constructor) always executes synchronously. If you're trying to create or open a file on a network server, it could take several seconds before **CreateFile** returns—the calling thread is idle all the while. An application designed for optimum performance and scalability would ideally call a Win32 function that lets you create or open a file asynchronously so that your thread is not sitting and waiting for the server to reply. Unfortunately, Win32 has no **CreateFile**-like function to let you do this, and therefore the FCL cannot offer an efficient way to open a file asynchronously.

Here is an example where this is a real problem. Imagine writing a simple UI control that allows the user to type a file path and provides automatic completion (similar to the common File Open dialog box). The control must use separate threads to enumerate directories looking for files because Windows doesn't offer any functions to enumerate files asynchronously. As the user continues to type in the UI control, you have to use more threads and ignore the results from any previously spawned threads. With Windows Vista, Microsoft introduced a new Win32 function called **CancelSynchronousIO**. This function allows one thread to cancel a synchronous I/O operation that is being performed by another thread. This function is not exposed by the FCL, but you can also P/Invoke to it if you want to take advantage of it from managed code. I show the P/Invoke signature for it in the next section of this chapter.

The point I want you to take away though is that many people think that synchronous APIs are easier to work with, and in many cases this is true. But in some cases, synchronous APIs can make things much harder. Microsoft's Windows team is looking at the synchronous-only APIs and deciding which function needs to be exposed with asynchronous APIs in future versions of Windows. Once they do this, the FCL will expose this functionality, too.

You can always call any method asynchronously via a delegate's **BeginInvoke** method, but when you do this, you are using a thread, so you are losing some efficiency. And actually, you can't use a delegate to call a constructor. So the only way to construct a **FileStream** object asynchronously is to call some other method asynchronously and have this other method construct the **FileStream** object. Windows doesn't offer functions to asynchronously access the registry, access the event log, get a directory's files/subdirectories, or change a file's/directory's attributes, to name just a few.

FileStream-Specific Issues

When you create a **FileStream** object, you get to specify whether you want to communicate using synchronous or asynchronous operations via the **FileOptions.Asynchronous** flag (which is equivalent to calling the Win32 **CreateFile** function and passing into it the **FILE_FLAG_OVERLAPPED** flag). If you do not specify this flag, Windows performs all operations against the file synchronously. Of course, you can still call **FileStream**'s **BeginRead** method, and to your application, it looks as if the operation is being performed asynchronously, but internally, the **FileStream** class uses another thread to emulate asynchronous behavior. This additional thread is wasteful and hurts performance.

On the other hand, you can create a **FileStream** object by specifying the **FileOptions. Asynchronous** flag. Then you can call **FileStream**'s **Read** method to perform a synchronous operation. Internally, the **FileStream** class emulates this behavior by starting an asynchronous operation and then immediately puts the calling thread to sleep until the operation is complete. This is also inefficient, but it is not as inefficient as calling **BeginRead** by using a **FileStream** constructed without the **FileOptions.Asynchronous** flag.

So, to summarize: When working with a **FileStream**, you must decide up front whether you intend to perform synchronous or asynchronous I/O against the file and indicate your choice by specifying the **FileOptions.Asynchronous** flag (or not). If you specify this flag, always call **BeginRead**. If you do not specify this flag, always call **Read**. This will give you the best performance. If you intend to make some synchronous and some asynchronous operations against the **FileStream**, it is more efficient to construct it using the **FileOptions.Asynchronous** flag. Alternatively, you can create two **FileStream** objects over the same file; open one **FileStream** for asynchronous I/O and open the other **FileStream** for synchronous I/O.

You should also be aware that the NTFS file system device driver performs some operations synchronously no matter how you open the file. For more information about this, see *http://support.microsoft.com/default.aspx?scid=kb%3Ben-us%3B156932*.

I/O Request Priorities

In Chapter 25, "Thread Basics," I showed how setting thread priorities affects how threads are scheduled. However, threads also perform I/O requests to read and write data from various hardware devices. If a low-priority thread gets CPU time, it could easily queue hundreds or thousands of I/O requests in a very short time. Because I/O requests typically require time to process, it is possible that a low-priority thread could significantly affect the responsiveness of the system by suspending high-priority threads, which prevents them from getting their work done. Because of this, you can see a machine become less responsive when executing long-running low-priority services such as disk defragmenters, virus scanners, content indexers, and so on.[9]

---

[9] The Windows SuperFetch feature takes advantage of low-priority I/O requests.

Starting with Windows Vista, it is now possible for a thread to specify a priority when making I/O requests. For more details about I/O priorities, refer to the white paper at *http://www.microsoft.com/whdc/driver/priorityio.mspx*. Unfortunately, the FCL does not include this functionality yet; hopefully, it will be added in a future version. However, you can still take advantage of this feature by P/Invoking out to native Win32 functions. Here is the P/Invoke code:

```
internal static class ThreadIO {
   public static BackgroundProcessingDisposer BeginBackgroundProcessing(
      Boolean process = false) {

      ChangeBackgroundProcessing(process, true);
      return new BackgroundProcessingDisposer(process);
   }

   public static void EndBackgroundProcessing(Boolean process = false) {
      ChangeBackgroundProcessing(process, false);
   }

   private static void ChangeBackgroundProcessing(Boolean process, Boolean start) {
      Boolean ok = process
         ? SetPriorityClass(GetCurrentWin32ProcessHandle(),
               start ? ProcessBackgroundMode.Start : ProcessBackgroundMode.End)
         : SetThreadPriority(GetCurrentWin32ThreadHandle(),
               start ? ThreadBackgroundgMode.Start : ThreadBackgroundgMode.End);
      if (!ok) throw new Win32Exception();
   }

   // This struct lets C#'s using statement end the background processing mode
   public struct BackgroundProcessingDisposer : IDisposable {
      private readonly Boolean m_process;
      public BackgroundProcessingDisposer(Boolean process) { m_process = process; }
      public void Dispose() { EndBackgroundProcessing(m_process); }
   }


   // See Win32's THREAD_MODE_BACKGROUND_BEGIN and THREAD_MODE_BACKGROUND_END
   private enum ThreadBackgroundgMode { Start = 0x10000, End = 0x20000 }

   // See Win32's PROCESS_MODE_BACKGROUND_BEGIN and PROCESS_MODE_BACKGROUND_END
   private enum ProcessBackgroundMode { Start = 0x100000, End = 0x200000 }

   [DllImport("Kernel32", EntryPoint = "GetCurrentProcess", ExactSpelling = true)]
   private static extern SafeWaitHandle GetCurrentWin32ProcessHandle();

   [DllImport("Kernel32", ExactSpelling = true, SetLastError = true)]
   [return: MarshalAs(UnmanagedType.Bool)]
   private static extern Boolean SetPriorityClass(
      SafeWaitHandle hprocess, ProcessBackgroundMode mode);

   [DllImport("Kernel32", EntryPoint = "GetCurrentThread", ExactSpelling = true)]
   private static extern SafeWaitHandle GetCurrentWin32ThreadHandle();
```

```
[DllImport("Kernel32", ExactSpelling = true, SetLastError = true)]
[return: MarshalAs(UnmanagedType.Bool)]
private static extern Boolean SetThreadPriority(
    SafeWaitHandle hthread, ThreadBackgroundgMode mode);

// http://msdn.microsoft.com/en-us/library/aa480216.aspx
[DllImport("Kernel32", SetLastError = true, EntryPoint = "CancelSynchronousIo")]
[return: MarshalAs(UnmanagedType.Bool)]
private static extern Boolean CancelSynchronousIO(SafeWaitHandle hThread);
}
```

And here is code showing how to use it:

```
public static void Main () {
    using (ThreadIO.BeginBackgroundProcessing()) {
        // Issue low-priority I/O requests in here (eg: calls to BeginRead/BeginWrite)
    }
}
```

You tell Windows that you want your thread to issue low-priority I/O requests by calling **ThreadIO**'s **BeginBackgroundProcessing** method. Note that this also lowers the CPU scheduling priority of the thread. You can return the thread to making normal-priority I/O requests (and normal CPU scheduling priority) by calling **EndBackgroundProcessing** or by calling **Dispose** on the value returned by **BeginBackgroundProcessing** (as shown above via C#'s **using** statement). A thread can only affect its own background processing mode; Windows doesn't allow a thread to change the background processing mode of another thread.

If you want all threads in a process to make low-priority I/O requests and have low CPU scheduling, you can call **BeginBackgroundProcessing**, passing in **true** for the **process** parameter. A process can only affect its own background processing mode; Windows doesn't allow a thread to change the background processing mode of another process.

> **Important** As a developer, it is your responsibility to use these new background priorities to allow the foreground applications to be more responsive, taking care to avoid *priority inversion*. In the presence of intense normal-priority I/Os, a thread running at background priority can be delayed for *seconds* before getting the result of its I/O requests. If a low-priority thread has grabbed a thread synchronization lock for which the normal-priority thread is waiting, the normal-priority threads might end up waiting for the background-priority thread until the low-priority I/O requests are completed. Your background-priority thread does not even have to submit I/Os for the problem to happen. So using shared synchronization objects between normal- and background-priority threads should be minimized (or eliminated if possible) to avoid these priority inversions where normal-priority threads are blocked on locks owned by background-priority threads.

Converting the `IAsyncResult` APM to a Task

In "The APM and Compute-Bound Operations" section earlier in this chapter, I showed how to use the APM to perform a compute-bound operation. In this section, I show how to do the opposite: use a **Task** to perform an I/O-bound operation.

In the **System.Threading.Tasks** namespace, there is a class called **TaskFactory**. This class was discussed in Chapter 26. However, this class offers a **FromAsync** method, which I did not discuss in Chapter 26. This method accepts four arguments and returns a reference to a **Task** object. The four arguments are a **BeginXxx** method, an **EndXxx** method, an **Object** state, and an optional **TaskCreationOptions**[10] value. So instead of initiating an asynchronous operation like this:

```
WebRequest webRequest = WebRequest.Create("http://Wintellect.com/");
webRequest.BeginGetResponse(result => {
   WebResponse webResponse = null;
   try {
      webResponse = webRequest.EndGetResponse(result);
      Console.WriteLine("Content length: " + webResponse.ContentLength);
   }
   catch (WebException we) {
      Console.WriteLine("Failed: " + we.GetBaseException().Message);
   }
   finally { if (webResponse != null) webResponse.Close(); }
}, null);
```

you can turn it into a **Task**, and then use it with the rest of the **Task** infrastructure like this:

```
WebRequest webRequest = WebRequest.Create("http://Wintellect.com/");
Task.Factory.FromAsync<WebResponse>(
   webRequest.BeginGetResponse, webRequest.EndGetResponse, null, TaskCreationOptions.None)
   .ContinueWith(task => {
   WebResponse webResponse = null;
   try {
      webResponse = task.Result;
      Console.WriteLine("Content length: " + webResponse.ContentLength);
   }
   catch (AggregateException ae) {
      if (ae.GetBaseException() is WebException)
         Console.WriteLine("Failed: " + ae.GetBaseException().Message);
      else throw;
   }
   finally { if (webResponse != null) webResponse.Close(); }
});
```

---

[10] The **FromAsync** method has additional overloads that allow you to pass up to three parameters to a **BeginXxx** method. If you need to call a **BeginXxx** method that takes more than three parameters, then there is a **FromAsync** overload that accepts an **IAsyncResult** parameter; you call the **BeginXxx** method yourself and its return value here. Avoid this overload if you can because it is less efficient than the overloads of **FromAsync** that do not take an **IAsyncResult**.

By the way, the **Task** class implements the **IAsyncResult** interface, so tasks support the APM to some extent. **Task**'s **AsyncState** property is the **IAsyncResult AsyncState** property, and this returns whatever state was passed in to **TaskFactory**'s **state** parameter. Since the **Task** is going to internally call the **EndXxx** method for you, the other **IAsyncResult** interface members that are potentially interesting are **AsyncWaitHandle**, **IsCompleted**, and maybe **CompletedSynchronously**. Well, as discussed earlier in this chapter in the "Using the APM Without the Thread Pool" section, the **AsyncWaitHandle** and **IsCompleted** properties should always be avoided, and the **CompletedSynchronously** property is more informative than actionable.

The Event-Based Asynchronous Pattern

When the .NET Framework was introduced, the only APM it offered is the one based on the **IAsyncResult** interface that I've been discussing this whole chapter. Microsoft's Windows Forms team felt that the **IAsyncResult** APM was too difficult for many Windows Form developers, so they created a new Event-based Asynchronous Pattern (EAP).[11] The main benefit of the EAP is that it integrates with the Microsoft Visual Studio UI designers. That is, you can drag most classes that implement the EAP to a Visual Studio design surface and then double-click event names and have Visual Studio automatically produce the event callback methods and wire the method up to the events themselves.

Many people, including me, believe that the EAP should never have been introduced into the .NET Framework. We believe that it adds more complication than it solves. For example, should classes that want to offer asynchronous behavior now implement both patterns? Or will two classes now be exposed that basically offer the same functionality, only differing by asynchronous pattern? How would users of a class choose which pattern to use and why? There are also some other technical problems that exist with this pattern, which I describe at the end of this section.

In fact, I'm often asked about the following MSDN Web page: *http://msdn2.microsoft.com /en-gb/library/ms228966.aspx*. This Web page actually instructs class developers to expose their asynchronous behavior using the EAP, not the APM. It also says, "It is rare for the **IAsyncResult** pattern to be implemented without the event-based pattern also being implemented." This Web page was produced by people on the Windows Forms team. There are very few people at Microsoft who actually agree with this Web page. And, in fact, Microsoft ships only three classes that actually implement both patterns and adhere to what this Web page says. Since I'm not a fan of this pattern and I discourage its use, I do not want to spend a lot of time on it. However, I know that some people do like and use the pattern, so I do want to spend some time on it.

---

[11] Many people from Microsoft's Windows Forms moved to Microsoft's WPF team, so WPF and Silverlight have also adopted this EAP.

Since the EAP was created for Windows Forms developers, let me show you some Windows Forms code that uses the pattern:

```
internal static class Eap {
    public static void Main() {
        // Create the form and show it
        Application.Run(new MyForm());
    }

    private sealed class MyForm : Form {
        protected override void OnClick(EventArgs e) {
            // The System.Net.WebClient class supports the Event-based Asynchronous Pattern
            WebClient wc = new WebClient();

            // When a string completes downloading, the WebClient object raises the
            // DownloadStringCompleted event which will invoke our ProcessString method
            wc.DownloadStringCompleted += ProcessString;

            // Start the asynchronous operation (this is like calling a BeginXxx method)
            wc.DownloadStringAsync(new Uri("http://Wintellect.com"));
            base.OnClick(e);
        }

        // This method is guaranteed to be called via the GUI thread
        private void ProcessString(Object sender, DownloadStringCompletedEventArgs e) {
            // If an error occurred, display it; else display the downloaded string
            MessageBox.Show((e.Error != null) ? e.Error.Message : e.Result);
        }
    }
}
```

In this sample, I manually wrote all the code, but I could have used Visual Studio to drag a **WebClient** control to my form. Then Visual Studio could have emitted the **ProcessString** method with no code in it and emitted the code to register this method with **WebClient**'s **DownloadStringCompleted** event. The EAP also guarantees that the event is raised on the application's GUI thread, allowing code in the event handler method to update UI controls. In addition to Visual Studio designer support, this is another big feature of the EAP. That is, classes that support the EAP automatically map the application model to its threading model; the EAP classes use the **SynchronizationContext** class internally. In addition, some of the EAP classes offer cancellation and progress reporting.

In the whole FCL, there are just 17 types that implement the EAP pattern. Some of these classes are derived from **System.ComponentModel.Component**, which allows them to be dragged and dropped onto a Visual Studio design surface, but most of the classes derive directly from **System.Object**. Here is the list of classes that support the EAP:

```
System.ComponentModel.Component-derived types
    System.ComponentModel.BackgroundWorker
    System.Media.SoundPlayer
    System.Net.WebClient
    System.Net.NetworkInformation.Ping
    System.Windows.Forms.PictureBox (derived from Control)
```

```
System.Object-derived types
    System.Net.Mail.SmtpClient
    System.Deployment.Application.ApplicationDeployment
    System.Deployment.Application.InPlaceHostingManager
    System.Activities.WorkflowInvoker
    System.ServiceModel.Activities.WorkflowControlClient
    System.Net.PeerToPeer.PeerNameResolver
    System.Net.PeerToPeer.Collaboration.ContactManager
    System.Net.PeerToPeer.Collaboration.Peer
    System.Net.PeerToPeer.Collaboration.PeerContact
    System.Net.PeerToPeer.Collaboration.PeerNearMe
    System.ServiceModel.Discovery.AnnouncementClient
    System.ServiceModel.Discovery.DiscoveryClient
```

The FCL ships 60 classes that implement the **IAsyncResult** pattern, including the following classes for which there is no equivalent class available that implements the EAP: the various **Stream**-derived classes (**FileStream**, **IsolatedStorageFileStream**, **DeflateStream**, **GZipStream**, and **PipeStream**), **SqlCommand**, and more.

I should also point out that tools that produce Web service proxy classes, like WSDL.exe and SvcUtil.exe, can produce proxy classes that support both the APM and the EAP.

If you look at the 17 classes listed above, they are all related to performing I/O-bound work except for one: **BackgroundWorker**. The **BackgroundWorker** class is designed for doing asynchronous compute-bound work, but unfortunately, a lot of developers use **BackgroundWorker** to perform synchronous I/O-bound work, which blocks a thread. I/O-bound work should be performed using one of the other 16 EAP classes or any of the classes that support the APM. The **BackgroundWorker** class offers the following three events:

- **DoWork**   The method that you register with this event should contain the compute-bound code. This event is raised by a thread pool thread.

- **ProgressChanged**   The method that you register with this event should contain the code that updates the UI with progress information. This event is always raised on the GUI thread. The **DoWork** event handler method must periodically call **BackgroundWorker**'s **ReportProgress** method to raise the **ProgressChanged** event.

- **RunWorkerCompleted**   The method that you register with this event should contain the code that updates the UI with the result of the compute-bound operation. This event is always raised on the GUI thread. The **DoWork** event handler method is passed a reference to a **DoWorkEventArgs** object. This object's **Result** property must be set to the value that the compute-bound operation wishes to return.

Converting the EAP to a Task

In the "Converting the **IAsyncResult** APM to a **Task**" section earlier in this chapter, I showed how to use the **IAsyncResult** APM to turn an asynchronous operation into a **Task** so that it could be used with the rest of the **Task** infrastructure. Well, it is also possible to turn an asynchronous operation using the EAP into a **Task**. The **System.Threading.Tasks** namespace defines a **TaskCompletionSource** class that looks like this:

```
public class TaskCompletionSource<TResult> {
    public TaskCompletionSource();
    public TaskCompletionSource(Object state, TaskCreationOptions creationOptions);

    public void SetCanceled();
    public void SetException(IEnumerable<Exception> exceptions);
    public void SetResult(TResult result);

    public Task<TResult> Task { get; }

    // Less important methods not shown
}
```

Constructing a **TaskCompletionSource** object also causes the creation of a **Task** that you can refer to by querying **TaskCompletionSource**'s **Task** property. Then, when an asynchronous operation completes, it uses the **TaskCompletionSource** object to set the reason for its completion: cancellation, unhandled exception, or its result. Calling one of the **SetXxx** methods sets the state of the underlying **Task** object. Here is code showing how to turn the EAP into a **Task**:

```
internal sealed class MyFormTask : Form {
    protected override void OnClick(EventArgs e) {
        // The System.Net.WebClient class supports the Event-based Asynchronous Pattern
        WebClient wc = new WebClient();

        // Create the TaskCompletionSource and its underlying Task object
        var tcs = new TaskCompletionSource<String>();

        // When a string completes downloading, the WebClient object raises the
        // DownloadStringCompleted event which will invoke our ProcessString method
        wc.DownloadStringCompleted += (sender, ea) => {
            // This code always executes on the GUI thread; set the Task's state
            if (ea.Cancelled) tcs.SetCanceled();
            else if (ea.Error != null) tcs.SetException(ea.Error);
            else tcs.SetResult(ea.Result);
        };

        // Have the Task continue with this Task that shows the result in a message box
        // NOTE: The ExecuteSynchronously flag is required to have this code run on the
        // GUI thread; without the flag, the code runs on a thread pool thread
        tcs.Task.ContinueWith(t => {
            try {
                MessageBox.Show(t.Result);
            }
            catch (AggregateException ae) {
                MessageBox.Show(ae.GetBaseException().Message);
            }}, TaskContinuationOptions.ExecuteSynchronously);

        // Start the asynchronous operation (this is like calling a BeginXxx method)
        wc.DownloadStringAsync(new Uri("http://Wintellect.com"));
        base.OnClick(e);
    }
}
```

Comparing the APM and the EAP

In this section, I compare the APM to the EPM. The biggest benefit of the EPM over the APM is that it can be used with the Visual Studio offering a design-time approach to invoke asynchronous operations. In addition, the EAP was introduced in the FCL at the same time as the **SynchronizationContext** class, and therefore it has built into it the ability to understand an application's threading model to ensure that, for GUI applications, the event handler method is invoked on the GUI thread.

However, the APM is closer to the metal and the EAP classes are typically implemented internally using the APM. This means that EAP classes tend to use more memory and perform slower than their APM equivalents. In fact, the EAP must allocate **EventArg**-derived objects for all progress reporting and completion events that are raised. Several EPM classes also contain a collection of **UserState** objects identifying separate operations and an **AsyncOperation** object, too. In a typical GUI application, these additional memory allocations (which cause additional garbage collections) are probably insignificant. However, the EPM would be an inappropriate choice for building a high-performance server application.

For simple scenarios, the EPM is easy to use and a fine choice. However, there are some scenarios where the EPM will actually be more complicated to use. If you call the **XxxAsync** method before registering the event handler method, it is possible that the asynchronous operation could complete before registering the event handler method and then the event handler method will not be invoked. Also, events are cumulative, and so you must unregister a method from the event and register a new method with the event if you want your next asynchronous operation to invoke a different method. Furthermore, static methods and singleton classes cannot offer the EPM for the same reason: different parts of an application may all register events at once, and all event handlers would be invoked when an operation completes regardless of which part of the application issued the asynchronous operation.

Error handling with the EAP is incongruous with the rest of the system. First, exceptions aren't thrown; in your event handler, you must query the **AsyncCompletedEventArgs**'s **Exception** property to see if it is **null** or not. If it is not **null**, then you have to use **if** statements to determine the type of the **Exception**-derived object instead of using **catch** blocks. And, if your code ignores the error, then no unhandled exception occurs, errors go undetected, and your application continues running with unpredictable results.

Programming Model Soup

Over the years, the .NET Framework has amassed a number of asynchronous programming models, each with its pros and cons, and I'm sure that new programming models will appear in the future. In an effort to help you, I have produced Table 27-1, which summarizes the various models that currently exist. For each model, I show what's its intended primary use is (compute-bound or I/O-bound operations), how it can emulate the other kind of operation, if the model supports parent/child relationships, if the model natively supports progress reporting, cancellation, blocking a thread until the operation completes (a feature you should avoid), notifying you when a timeout expires, and if you can get the result (or exception) of the operation when it completes. Here are some additional notes about Table 27-1:

- Tasks offer improved performance over **ThreadPool.QueueUserWorkItem** or a delegate's **BeginInvoke** if many tasks are being issued due to the work-stealing queues.

- You can use the **PreFairness** flag to get the same thread pool behavior as **ThreadPool.QueueUserWorkItem** or a delegate's **BeginInvoke**.

- You can use a customized **TaskScheduler**, allowing you to change scheduling algorithms without changing the code or programming model.

- **Task** objects consume more memory than just calling **ThreadPool.QueueUserWorkItem** or a delegate's **BeginInvoke**. Calling a delegate's **BeginInvoke** method has known performance issues, and while **Task** objects require more memory, tasks run faster and are probably a better choice than calling a delegate's **BeginInvoke** method.

- The **IAsyncResult** APM offers four rendezvous techniques, which complicates the model; however, if you mentally restrict yourself to the callback method technique (as I do), then the model is simplified.

- The **IAsyncResult** APM is generally faster and uses fewer resources than the EAP.

- Some of the classes that support the EAP support cancellation.

- The **IAsyncResult** APM doesn't support cancellation at all; however, you can always obtain cancellation behavior by setting a flag and throwing away the result when it does complete. Wrapping the **IAsyncResult** pattern in a **Task** and setting the proper **ContinueWith** callbacks can help you here.

- The EAP is event-based, so that you can easily use it from within Visual Studio's Windows Forms, WPF, and Silverlight forms designers, and the notifying methods are called in the right UI thread.

TABLE 27-1 Comparing the .NET Framework's Asynchronous Programming Models

Model	Primary Use	Emulate Secondary via What?	Parent /Child	Progress Reporting	Cancel	Wait	Timeout	Return/ Exception
QueueUser WorkItem	Compute	Sync I/O	No	No	No	No	No	No
Timer	Compute	Sync I/O	No	No	Via **Dispose**	No	Yes!	No
RegisterWaitFor SingleObject	Compute	Sync I/O	No	No	Via **Unregister**	No	Yes	No
Tasks	Compute	Sync I/O or **TaskCompletionSource** and **TaskScheduler**'s **FromAsync**	Yes	No	Compute: Before **Task** starts or if **Task** supports it I/O: Discard result	Yes	Yes	Yes
IAsyncResult APM	I/O	**Delegate**'s **BeginInvoke**	No	No	No	Yes	No	Yes
Event-based PM	I/O	**BackgroundWorker**	No	Some	Some types discard the result.	No	No	Yes
AsyncEnumerator	I/O	**Delegate**'s **BeginInvoke**	No	No	Yes	No	Yes	Yes

Chapter 28
Primitive Thread Synchronization Constructs

When a thread pool thread blocks, the thread pool creates additional threads, and the time and memory resources required to create, destroy, and schedule threads is very expensive. And when many developers see that they have threads in their program that are not doing anything useful, they tend to create more threads in hopes that the new threads will do something useful. The key to building scalable and responsive applications is to not block the threads you have so that they can be used and reused to execute other tasks. Chapter 26, "Compute-Bound Asynchronous Operations," focused on how to use existing threads to perform compute-bound operations, and Chapter 27, "I/O-Bound Asynchronous Operations," focused on how to use threads when performing I/O-bound operations.

In this chapter, I focus on thread synchronization. Thread synchronization is used to prevent corruption when multiple threads access shared data *at the same time*. I emphasize *at the same time* because thread synchronization is all about timing. If you have some data that is accessed by two threads and those threads cannot possibly touch the data simultaneously, then thread synchronization is not required at all. In Chapter 27, I showed some code that implements a named-pipe server. In the **ClientConnected** method, a thread allocates a **Byte[]** that will be filled with the data being sent from the client. When the client sends the data, a different thread pool thread will execute the **GotRequest** method, and this method will process the data in the **Byte[]**. Here we have two different threads accessing the same data. But the application is architected in such a way that it is impossible for two threads to access this same **Byte[]** at the same time. Therefore, no thread synchronization is used in the named-pipe application at all.

This is ideal because thread synchronization has many problems associated with it. First, it is tedious and extremely error-prone. In your code, you must identify all data that could potentially be touched by multiple threads at the same time. Then you must surround this code with additional code that acquires and releases a thread synchronization lock. The lock ensures that only one thread at a time can access the resource. If you forget to surround just one block of code with a lock, then the data will become corrupted. Also, there is no way to prove that you have added all your locking code correctly. You just have to run your application, stress-test it a lot, and hope that nothing goes wrong. In fact, you should test your application on a machine that has as many CPUs as possible because the more CPUs you have, the better chance that two or more threads will attempt to access the resource at the same time, making it more likely you'll detect a problem.

The second problem with locks is that they hurt performance. It takes time to acquire and release a lock because there are additional method calls and because the CPUs must coordinate with each other to determine which thread will acquire the lock first. Having the CPUs in the machine communicate with each other this way hurts performance. For example, let's say that you have code that adds a node to the head of a linked list:

```
// This class is used by the LinkedList class
public class Node {
   internal Node m_next;
   // Other members not shown
}

public sealed class LinkedList {
   private Node m_head;

   public void Add(Node newNode) {
      // The two lines below perform very fast reference assignments
      newNode.m_next = m_head;
      m_head = newNode;
   }
}
```

This **Add** method simply performs two reference assignments that can execute extremely fast. Now, if we want to make **Add** thread safe so that multiple threads can call it simultaneously without corrupting the linked list, then we need to have the **Add** method acquire and release a lock:

```
public sealed class LinkedList {
   private SomeKindOfLock m_lock = new SomeKindOfLock();
   private Node m_head;

   public void Add(Node newNode) {
      m_lock.Acquire();
      // The two lines below perform very fast reference assignments
      newNode.m_next = m_head;
      m_head = newNode;
      m_lock.Release();
   }
}
```

While **Add** is now thread safe, it has also become substantially slower. How much slower depends on the kind of lock chosen; I will compare the performance of various locks in this chapter and in Chapter 29, "Hybrid Thread Synchronization Constructs." But even the fastest lock could make the **Add** method several times slower than the version of it that didn't have any lock code in it at all. Of course, the performance becomes significantly worse if the code calls **Add** in a loop to insert several nodes into the linked list.

The third problem with thread synchronization locks is that they allow only one thread to access the resource at a time. This is the lock's whole reason for existing, but it is also a problem because blocking a thread causes more threads to be created. So, for example, if a thread pool thread attempts to acquire a lock that it cannot have, it is likely that the thread pool will create a new thread to keep the CPUs saturated with work. As discussed in Chapter 25, "Thread Basics," creating a thread is very expensive in terms of both memory and performance. And to make matters even worse, when the blocked threads gets to run again, it will run with this new thread pool thread; Windows is now scheduling more threads than there are CPUs, and this increases context switching, which also hurts performance.

The summary of all of this is that thread synchronization is bad, so you should try to design your applications to avoid as much of it as possible. To that end, you should avoid shared data such as **static** fields. When a thread uses the **new** operator to construct an object, the **new** operator returns a reference to the new object. At this point in time, only the thread that constructs the object has a reference to it; no other thread can access that object. If you avoid passing this reference to another thread that might use the object at the same time as the creating thread, then there is no need to synchronize access to the object.

Try to use value types because they are always copied, so each thread operates on its own copy. Finally, it is OK to have multiple threads accessing shared data simultaneously if that access is read-only. For example, many applications create some data structures during their initialization. Once initialized, the application can create as many threads as it wants; if all these threads just query the data, then all the threads can do this simultaneously without acquiring or releasing any locks. The **String** type is an example of this: Once a **String** object is created, it is immutable, so many threads can access a single **String** object at the same time without any chance of the **String** object becoming corrupted.

Class Libraries and Thread Safety

Now, I'd like to say a quick word about class libraries and thread synchronization. Microsoft's Framework Class Library (FCL) guarantees that all static methods are thread safe. This means that if two threads call a static method at the same time, no data will get corrupted. The FCL had to do this internally because there is no way that multiple companies producing different assemblies could coordinate on a single lock for arbitrating access to the resource. The **Console** class contains a **static** field, inside which many of its methods acquire and release to ensure that only one thread at a time is accessing the console.

For the record, making a method thread safe does not mean that it internally takes a thread synchronization lock. A thread-safe method means that data doesn't get corrupted if two threads attempt to access the data at the same time. The `System.Math` class has a `static` `Max` method implemented as follows:

```
public static Int32 Max(Int32 val1, Int32 val2) {
    return (val1 < val2) ? val2 : val1;
}
```

This method is thread safe even though it doesn't take any lock. Since `Int32` is a value type, the two `Int32` values passed to `Max` are copied into it and multiple threads could be calling `Max` simultaneously, but each thread is working on its own data, isolated from any other thread.

On the other hand, the FCL does not guarantee that instance methods are thread safe because adding all the locking code would hurt performance too much. And, in fact, if every instance method acquires and releases a lock, then you ultimately end up having just one thread running in your application at any given time, which hurts performance even more. As mentioned earlier, when a thread constructs an object, only this thread has a reference to the object, no other thread can access that object, and no thread synchronization is required when invoking instance methods. However, if the thread then exposes the reference to the object—by placing it in a static field, passing as the state argument to `ThreadPool.` `QueueUserWorkItem` or to a `Task`, and so on—then thread synchronization is required if the threads could attempt simultaneous non–read-only access.

It is recommended that your own class libraries follow this pattern; that is, make all your static methods thread safe and make all your instance methods not thread-safe. There is one caveat to this pattern: if the purpose of the instance method is to coordinate threads, then the instance method should be thread safe. For example, one thread can cancel an operation by calling `CancellationTokenSource`'s `Cancel` method, and another thread detects that it should stop what it's doing by querying the corresponding `CancellationToken`'s `IsCancellationRequested` property. These two instance members have some special thread synchronization code inside them to ensure that the coordination of the two threads goes as expected.[1]

Primitive User-Mode and Kernel-Mode Constructs

In this chapter, I explain the *primitive* thread synchronization constructs. By *primitive*, I mean the simplest constructs that are available to use in your code. There are two kinds of primitive constructs: user-mode and kernel-mode. Whenever possible, you should use the primitive user-mode constructs because they are significantly faster than the kernel-mode constructs as they use special CPU instructions to coordinate threads. This means that the coordination is occurring in hardware (which is what makes it fast). But this also means that the Microsoft

---

[1] Specifically, the field that both members access is marked as **volatile**, a concept that will be discussed later in this chapter.

Windows operating system never detects that a thread is blocked on a primitive user-mode construct. Since a thread pool thread blocked on a user-mode primitive construct is never considered blocked, the thread pool will not create a new thread to replace the temporarily blocked thread. In addition, these CPU instructions block the thread for an incredibly short period of time.

Wow! All of this sounds great, doesn't it? And it is great, which is why I recommend using these constructs as much as possible. However, there is a downside: Only the Windows operating system kernel can stop a thread from running so that it is not wasting CPU time. A thread running in user mode can be preempted by the system, but the thread will be scheduled again as soon as possible. So a thread that wants to acquire some resource but can't get it spins in user mode. This potentially wastes a lot of CPU time, which would be better spent performing other work or even just letting the CPU go idle to conserve power.

This brings us to the primitive kernel-mode constructs. The kernel-mode constructs are provided by the Windows operating system itself. As such, they require that your application's threads call functions implemented in the operating system kernel. Having threads transition from user mode to kernel mode and back incurs a big performance hit, which is why kernel-mode constructs should be avoided.[2] However, they do have a positive feature: When a thread uses a kernel-mode construct to acquire a resource that another thread has, Windows blocks the thread so that it is no longer wasting CPU time. Then, when the resource becomes available, Windows resumes the thread, allowing it to access the resource.

A thread waiting on a construct might block forever if the thread currently holding the construct never releases it. If the construct is a user-mode construct, the thread is running on a CPU forever, and we call this a *livelock*. If the construct is a kernel-mode construct, the thread is blocked forever, and we call this a *deadlock*. Both of these are bad, but of the two, a deadlock is always preferable to a livelock because a livelock wastes both CPU time and memory (the thread's stack, etc.), while a deadlock wastes only memory.[3]

In an ideal world, we'd like to have constructs that take the best of both worlds. That is, we'd like a construct that is fast and non-blocking (like the user-mode constructs) when there is no contention. But when there is contention for the construct, we'd like it to be blocked by the operating system kernel. Constructs that work like this do exist; I call them *hybrid constructs*, and I will discuss them in Chapter 29. It is very common for applications to use the hybrid constructs because in most applications, it is rare for two or more threads to attempt to access the same data at the same time. A hybrid construct keeps your application running fast most of the time, and occasionally it runs slowly to block the thread. The slowness usually doesn't matter at this point because your thread is going to be blocked anyway.

---

2 I'll show a program that measures the performance later in this chapter.

3 I say that the memory allocated for the thread is wasted because the memory is not being used in a productive manner if the thread is not making forward progress.

Many of the CLR's thread synchronization constructs are really just object-oriented class wrappers around Win32 thread synchronization constructs. After all, CLR threads are Windows threads, which means that Windows schedules and controls the synchronization of threads. Windows thread synchronization constructs have been around since 1992, and a ton of material has been written about them.[4] Therefore, I give them only cursory treatment in this chapter.

User-Mode Constructs

There are two kinds of primitive user-mode thread synchronization constructs:

- Volatile constructs, which perform an atomic read *or* write operation on a variable containing a simple data type

- Interlocked constructs, which perform an atomic read *and* write operation on a variable containing a simple data type

All the volatile and interlocked constructs require you to pass a reference (memory address) to a variable containing a simple data type. Some CPU architectures require that this memory address be properly aligned or else the constructs will throw a **DataMisalignedException**.

This means that a variable containing a 1-byte, 2-byte, and 4-byte value must be located at a memory address that is a multiple of 1, 2, or 4, respectively, and that a variable containing an 8-byte value is located at a memory address that allows the value to be manipulated atomically by the underlying hardware (a multiple of 4 or 8). Specifically, this means **(S)Byte** variables are on a 1-byte boundary, **(U)Int16** variables are on a 2-byte boundary, **(U)Int32** and **Single** variables are on a 4-byte boundary, and **(U)Int64** and **Double** variables are on a 4-byte or an 8-byte boundary. All reference variables and **(U)IntPtr** variables are 4 bytes wide in a 32-bit process and 8 bytes wide in a 64-bit process, so these variables are always aligned on 4-byte or 8-byte boundaries, depending on the type of process.

Fortunately, the CLR ensures that fields are properly aligned automatically unless the enclosing type has the **[StructLayout(LayoutKind.Explicit)]** attribute applied to it and **[FieldOffset(...)]** attributes applied to individual fields, forcing fields to be misaligned. If you avoid using these attributes, then you should have no trouble when using these user-mode constructs.

Accessing any properly aligned variable of the types mentioned above is always atomic. This means that all bytes within that variable are read from or written to all at once. So, for example, if you have the following class:

---

[4] In fact, my own book, *Windows via C/C++, 5th Edition* (Microsoft Press, 2007), has several chapters devoted to this subject.

```
internal static class SomeType {
   public static Int32 x = 0;
}
```

then, if some thread executes this line of code:

```
SomeType.x = 0x01234567;
```

the **x** variable will change from **0x00000000** to **0x01234567** all at once (atomically). Another thread cannot possibly see the value in an intermediate state. For example, it is impossible for some other read to query **SomeType.x** and get a value of **0x01230000**. However, while the reads and writes to a properly aligned variable are guaranteed to happen all at once, you are not guaranteed *when* they happen due to compiler and CPU optimizations. The volatile constructs ensure that the read or write operation is atomic and, more importantly, they also control the timing of these atomic operations. The interlocked constructs can perform operations that are slightly more complex than simple read and write operations, and they also control the timing of these operations.

Suppose that the **x** field in the **SomeType** class above is an **Int64** that is not properly aligned. If a thread executes this line of code:

```
SomeType.x = 0x0123456789abcdef;
```

it is possible that another thread could query **x** and get a value of **0x0123456700000000** or **0x0000000089abcdef** since the read and write operations are not atomic. This is called a *torn read*.

Volatile Constructs

Back in the early days of computing, software was written using assembly language. Assembly language is very tedious because programmers must explicitly state everything: Use this CPU register for this, branch to that, call indirect through this other thing, and so on. To simplify programming, higher-level languages were introduced. These higher-level languages introduced common useful constructs, like **if/else**, **switch/case**, various loops, local variables, arguments, virtual method calls, operator overloads, and much more. Ultimately, these language compilers must convert the high-level constructs down to the low-level constructs so that the computer can actually do what you want it to do.

In other words, the C# compiler translates your C# constructs into Intermediate Language (IL), which is then converted by the just-in-time (JIT) compiler into native CPU instructions, which must then be processed by the CPU itself. In addition, the C# compiler, the JIT compiler, and even the CPU itself can optimize your code. For example, the following ridiculous method can ultimately be compiled into nothing:

```
private static void OptimizedAway() {
    // Constant expression is computed at compile time resulting in zero
    Int32 value = (1 * 100) - (50 * 2);

    // If value is 0, the loop never executes
    for (Int32 x = 0; x < value; x++) {
        // There is no need to compile the code in the loop since it can never execute
        Console.WriteLine("Jeff");
    }
}
```

In this code, the compiler can see that **value** will always be **0**; therefore, the loop will never execute and consequently, there is no need to compile the code inside the loop. This method could be compiled down to nothing. In fact, when JITting a method that calls **OptimizedAway**, the JITter will try to inline the **OptimizedAway** method's code. Since there is no code, the JITter will even remove the code that tries to call **OptimizedAway**. We love this feature of compilers. As developers, we get to write the code in the way that makes the most sense to us. The code should be easy to write, read, and maintain. Then compilers translate our intentions into machine-understandable code. We want our compilers to do the best job possible for us.

When the C# compiler, JIT compiler, and CPU optimize our code, they guarantee us that the intention of the code is preserved. That is, from a single-threaded perspective, the method does what we want it to do, although it may not do it exactly the way we described in our source code. However, the intention might not be preserved from a multithreaded perspective. Here is an example where the optimizations make the program not work as expected:

```
internal static class StrangeBehavior {
    // As you'll see later, mark this field as volatile to fix the problem
    private static Boolean s_stopWorker = false;

    public static void Main() {
        Console.WriteLine("Main: letting worker run for 5 seconds");
        Thread t = new Thread(Worker);
        t.Start();
        Thread.Sleep(5000);
        s_stopWorker = true;
        Console.WriteLine("Main: waiting for worker to stop");
        t.Join();
    }

    private static void Worker(Object o) {
        Int32 x = 0;
        while (!s_stopWorker) x++;
        Console.WriteLine("Worker: stopped when x={0}", x);
    }
}
```

In this code, the **Main** method creates a new thread that executes the **Worker** method. This **Worker** method counts as high as it can before being told to stop. The **Main** method allows the **Worker** thread to run for 5 seconds before telling it to stop by setting the **static**

Boolean field to **true**. At this point, the **Worker** thread should display what it counted up to, and then the thread will terminate. The **Main** thread waits for the **Worker** thread to terminate by calling **Join**, and then the **Main** thread returns, causing the whole process to terminate.

Looks simple enough, right? Well, the program has a potential problem due to all the optimizations that could happen to it. You see, when the **Worker** method is compiled, the compiler sees that **s_stopWorker** is either **true** or **false**, and it also sees that this value never changes inside the **Worker** method itself. So the compiler could produce code that checks **s_stopWorker** first. If **s_stopWorker** is **true**, then **"Worker: stopped when x=0"** will be displayed. If **s_stopWorker** is **false**, then the compiler produces code that enters an infinite loop that increments **x** forever. You see, the optimizations cause the loop to run very fast because checking **s_stopWorker** only occurs once before the loop; it does not get checked with each iteration of the loop.

If you actually want to see this in action, put this code in a .cs file and compile the code using C#'s **/platform:x86** and **/optimize+** switches. Then run the resulting EXE file, and you'll see that the program runs forever. Note that you have to compile for x86 ensuring that the x86 JIT compiler is used at runtime. The x86 JIT compiler is more mature than the x64 or IA64 JIT compilers, so it performs more aggressive optimizations. The other JIT compilers do not perform this particular optimization, and therefore the program runs to completion with these other JIT compilers. This highlights another interesting point about all of this. Whether your program behaves as expected depends on a lot of factors, such as which compiler version and compiler switches are used, which JIT compiler is used, and which CPU your code is running on. In addition, to see the program above run forever, you must not run the program under a debugger because the debugger causes the JIT compiler to produce unoptimized code that is easier to step through.

Let's look at another example, which has two threads that are both accessing two fields:

```
internal sealed class ThreadsSharingData {
   private Int32 m_flag = 0;
   private Int32 m_value = 0;

   // This method is executed by one thread
   public void Thread1() {
      // Note: These could execute in reverse order
      m_value = 5;
      m_flag  = 1;
   }

   // This method is executed by another thread
   public void Thread2() {
      // Note: m_value could be read before m_flag
      if (m_flag == 1)
         Console.WriteLine(m_value);
   }
}
```

The problem with this code is that the compilers/CPU could translate the code in such a way as to reverse the two lines of code in the **Thread1** method. After all, reversing the two lines of code does not change the intention of the method. The method needs to get a **5** in **m_value** and a **1** in **m_flag**. From a single-threaded application's perspective, the order of executing this code is unimportant. If these two lines do execute in reverse order, then another thread executing the **Thread2** method *could* see that **m_flag** is **1** and then display **0**.

Let's look at this code another way. Let's say that the code in the **Thread1** method executes in *program order* (the way it was written). When compiling the code in the **Thread2** method, the compiler must generate code to read **m_flag** and **m_value** from RAM into CPU registers. It is possible that RAM will deliver the value of **m_value** first, which would contain a **0**. Then the **Thread1** method could execute, changing **m_value** to **5** and **m_flag** to **1**. But **Thread2**'s CPU register doesn't see that **m_value** has been changed to **5** by this other thread, and then the value in **m_flag** could be read from RAM into a CPU register and the value of **m_flag** becomes **1** now, causing **Thread2** to again display **0**.

This is all very exciting stuff and is more likely to cause problems in a release build of your program than in a debug build of your program, making it particularly tricky to detect these problems and correct your code. Now, let's talk about how to correct your code.

The **System.Threading.Thread** class offers three static methods that look like this[5]:

```
public sealed class Thread {
    public static void  VolatileWrite(ref Int32 address, Int32 value);
    public static Int32 VolatileRead(ref Int32 address);
    public static void  MemoryBarrier();
}
```

These methods are special. In effect, these methods disable some optimizations usually performed by the C# compiler, the JIT compiler, and the CPU itself. Here's how the methods work:

- The **VolatileWrite** method forces the value in **address** to be written to at the point of the call. In addition, any *earlier* program-order loads and stores must occur *before* the call to **VolatileWrite**.

- The **VolatileRead** method forces the value in **address** to be read from at the point of the call. In addition, any *later* program-order loads and stores must occur *after* the call to **VolatileRead**.

- The **MemoryBarrier** method doesn't access memory but it forces any *earlier* program-order loads and stores to be completed *before* the call to **MemoryBarrier**. And it also forces any *later* program-order loads and stores to be completed *after* the call to **MemoryBarrier**. **MemoryBarrier** is much less useful than the other two methods.

---

[5] There are also overloads of **VolatileRead** and **VolatileWrite** that operate on the following types: **(S)Byte**, **(U)Int16**, **UInt32**, **(U)Int64**, **(U)IntPtr**, **Single**, **Double**, and **Object**.

Important I know that this can be very confusing, so let me summarize it as a simple rule: When threads are communicating with each other via shared memory, write the last value by calling **VolatileWrite** and read the first value by calling **VolatileRead**.

So now we can fix the **ThreadsSharingData** class using these methods:

```
internal sealed class ThreadsSharingData {
    private Int32 m_flag = 0;
    private Int32 m_value = 0;

    // This method is executed by one thread
    public void Thread1() {
        // Note: 5 must be written to m_value before 1 is written to m_flag
        m_value = 5;
        Thread.VolatileWrite(ref m_flag, 1);
    }

    // This method is executed by another thread
    public void Thread2() {
        // Note: m_value must be read after m_flag is read
        if (Thread.VolatileRead(ref m_flag) == 1)
            Console.WriteLine(m_value);
    }
}
```

First, notice that we are following the rule. The **Thread1** method writes two values out to fields that are shared by multiple threads. The last value that we want written (setting **m_flag** to **1**) is performed by calling **VolatileWrite**. The **Thread2** method reads two values from fields shared by multiple threads, and the first value being read (**m_flag**) is performed by calling **VolatileRead**.

But what is really happening here? Well, for the **Thread1** method, the **VolatileWrite** call ensures that all the writes above it are completed before a **1** is written to **m_flag**. Since **m_value = 5** is before the call to **VolatileWrite**, it must complete first. In fact, if there were many variables being modified before the call to **VolatileWrite**, they would all have to complete before **1** is written to **m_flag**. Note that the writes before the call to **VolatileWrite** can be optimized to execute in any order; it's just that all the writes have to complete before the call to **VolatileWrite**.

For the **Thread2** method, the **VolatileRead** call ensures that all variable reads after it start after the value in **m_flag** has been read. Since reading **m_value** is after the call to **VolatileRead**, the value must be read after having read the value in **m_flag**. If there were many reads after the call to **VolatileRead**, they would all have to start after the value in **m_flag** has been read. Note that the reads after the call to **VolatileRead** can be optimized to execute in any order; it's just that the reads can't start happening until after the call to **VolatileRead**.

C#'s Support for Volatile Fields

Making sure that programmers call the **VolatileRead** and **VolatileWrite** methods correctly is a lot to ask. It's hard for programmers to keep all of this in their minds and to start imagining what other threads might be doing to shared data in the background. To simplify this, the C# compiler has the **volatile** keyword, which can be applied to static or instance fields of any of these types: **Byte, SByte, Int16, UInt16, Int32, UInt32, Char, Single,** or **Boolean**. You can also apply the **volatile** keyword to reference types and any enum field so long as the enumerated type has an underlying type of **Byte, SByte, Int16, UInt16, Int32, UInt32, Single,** or **Boolean**. The JIT compiler ensures that all accesses to a volatile field are performed as volatile reads and writes so that it is not necessary to explicitly call **Thread**'s static **VolatileRead** or **VolatileWrite** methods. Furthermore, the **volatile** keyword tells the C# and JIT compilers not to cache the field in a CPU register, ensuring that all reads to and from the field actually cause the value to be read from memory.

Using the **volatile** keyword, we can rewrite the **ThreadsSharingData** class as follows:

```
internal sealed class ThreadsSharingData {
    private volatile Int32 m_flag = 0;
    private          Int32 m_value = 0;

    // This method is executed by one thread
    public void Thread1() {
        // Note: 5 must be written to m_value before 1 is written to m_flag
        m_value = 5;
        m_flag = 1;
    }

    // This method is executed by another thread
    public void Thread2() {
        // Note: m_value must be read after m_flag is read
        if (m_flag == 1)
            Console.WriteLine(m_value);
    }
}
```

There are some developers (and I am one of them) who do not like C#'s **volatile** keyword, and they think that the language should not provide it. Our thinking is that most algorithms require few volatile read or write accesses to a field and that most other accesses to the field can occur normally, improving performance; seldom is it required that all accesses to a field be volatile. For example, it is difficult to interpret how to apply volatile read operations to algorithms like this one:

```
m_amount = m_amount + m_amount; // Assume m_amount is a volatile field defined in a class
```

Normally, an integer number can be doubled simply by shifting all bits left by 1 bit, and many compilers can examine the code above and perform this optimization. However, if **m_amount** is a **volatile** field, then this optimization is not allowed. The compiler must produce code to read **m_amount** into a register and then read it again into another register, add the two registers together, and then write the result back out to the **m_amount** field. The un-optimized code is certainly bigger and slower; it would be unfortunate if it were contained inside a loop.

Furthermore, C# does not support passing a **volatile** field by reference to a method. For example, if **m_amount** is defined as a **volatile Int32**, attempting to call **Int32**'s **TryParse** method causes the compiler to generate a warning as shown here:

```
Boolean success = Int32.TryParse("123", out m_amount);
// The above line causes the C# compiler to generate a warning:
// CS0420: a reference to a volatile field will not be treated as volatile
```

Interlocked Constructs

Thread's **VolatileRead** method performs an atomic read operation, and its **VolatileWrite** method performs an atomic write operation. That is, each method performs either an atomic read operation *or* an atomic write operation. In this section, we look at the static **System. Threading.Interlocked** class's methods. Each of the methods in the **Interlocked** class performs an atomic read *and* write operation. In addition, all the **Interlocked** methods are full memory fences. That is, any variable writes before the call to an **Interlocked** method execute before the **Interlocked** method, and any variable reads after the call execute after the call.

The static methods that operate on **Int32** variables are by far the most commonly used methods. I show them here:

```
public static class Interlocked {
    // return (++location)
    public static Int32 Increment(ref Int32 location);

    // return (--location)
    public static Int32 Decrement(ref Int32 location);

    // return (location1 += value)
    // Note: value can be a negative number allowing subtraction
    public static Int32 Add(ref Int32 location1, Int32 value);

    // Int32 old = location1; location1 = value; return old;
    public static Int32 Exchange(ref Int32 location1, Int32 value);

    // Int32 old = location1;
    // if (location1 == comparand) location1 = value;
    // return old;
    public static Int32 CompareExchange(ref Int32 location1,
        Int32 value, Int32 comparand);
    ...
}
```

There are also overloads of the above methods that operate on **Int64** values. Furthermore, the **Interlocked** class offers **Exchange** and **CompareExchange** methods that take **Object**, **IntPtr**, **Single**, and **Double**, and there is also a generic version in which the generic type is constrained to **class** (any reference type).

Personally, I love the **Interlocked** methods because they are relatively fast and you can do so much with them. Let me show you some code that uses the **Interlocked** methods to asynchronously query several Web servers for data. This code is pretty short, never blocks any threads, and uses thread pool threads to scale automatically, consuming up to the number of CPUs available if its workload could benefit from it. In addition, the code, as is, supports accessing up to 2,147,483,647 (**Int32.MaxValue**) Web servers. In other words, this code is a great model to follow for your own scenarios.

```
internal sealed class MultiWebRequests {
   // This helper class coordinates all the asynchronous operations
   private AsyncCoordinator m_ac = new AsyncCoordinator();

   // This is the set of Web servers we want to query
   private WebRequest[] m_requests = new WebRequest[] {
      WebRequest.Create("http://Wintellect.com/"),
      WebRequest.Create("http://Microsoft.com/")
   };

   // Create the response array: one response for each request
   private WebResponse[] m_results = new WebResponse[2];

   public MultiWebRequests(Int32 timeout = Timeout.Infinite) {
      // Asynchronously initiate all the requests all at once
      for (Int32 n = 0; n < m_requests.Length; n++) {
         m_ac.AboutToBegin(1);
         m_requests[n].BeginGetResponse(EndGetResponse, n);
      }

      // Tell the helper class that all operations have been initiated
      // and to call AllDone when all operations complete, Cancel is
      // called, or the timeout occurs
      m_ac.AllBegun(AllDone, timeout);
   }

   // Calling this method indicates that the results don't matter anymore
   public void Cancel() { m_ac.Cancel(); }

   // As each Web server responds, this method is called
   private void EndGetResponse(IAsyncResult result) {
      // Get the index corresponding to the request
      Int32 n = (Int32)result.AsyncState;

      // Store the response in the same index as the request
      m_results[n] = m_requests[n].EndGetResponse(result);

      // Tell the helper class that a Web server responded
      m_ac.JustEnded();
   }
```

```
    // This method is called after all Web servers respond,
    // Cancel is called, or the timeout occurs
    private void AllDone(CoordinationStatus status) {
        switch (status) {
            case CoordinationStatus.Cancel:
                Console.WriteLine("The operation was canceled"); break;

            case CoordinationStatus.Timeout:
                Console.WriteLine("The operation timed-out"); break;

            case CoordinationStatus.AllDone:
                Console.WriteLine("Here are the results from all the Web servers");
                for (Int32 n = 0; n < m_requests.Length; n++) {
                    Console.WriteLine("{0} returned {1} bytes.",
                        m_results[n].ResponseUri, m_results[n].ContentLength);
                }
                break;
        }
    }
}
```

OK, the code above doesn't actually use any **Interlocked** methods directly because I encapsulated all the coordination code in a reusable class called **AsyncCoordinator**, which I'll explain shortly. Let me first explain what this class is doing. When the **MultiWebRequest** class is constructed, it initializes an **AsyncCoordinator**, the array of **WebRequest** objects, and the array of **WebResponse** objects. It then issues all the Web requests asynchronously by calling **BeginGetResponse**. Just before issuing each request, it calls the **AsyncCoordinator**'s **AboutToBegin** method, passing it the number of requests about to be issued.[6]

After all the Web servers' requests have been made, **AsyncCoordinator**'s **AllBegun** method is called, passing it the name of the method that should execute when all the operations complete (**AllDone**) and a timeout value. As each Web server responds, various thread pool threads will call **MultiWebRequests**'s **EndGetResponse** method. This method determines which request it is processing (by examining the **IAsyncResult**'s **AsyncState** property) and then saves the **WebResponse** object in the **m_results** array. After storing each result, **AsyncCoordinator**'s **JustEnded** method is called to let the **AsyncCoordinator** object know that an operation completed.

If all the operations have completed, then the **AsyncCoordinator** will invoke the **AllDone** method to process the results from all the Web servers. The code executing the **AllDone** method will be the thread pool thread that just happened to get the last Web server response. If timeout or cancellation occurs, then **AllDone** will be invoked via whatever thread pool thread notifies the **AsyncCoordinator** of timeout or using whatever thread happened to call the **Cancel** method. There is also a chance that the thread issuing the Web server requests could invoke **AllDone** itself if the last request completes before **AllBegin** is called.

---

6   The code would still work correctly if it was rewritten calling **m_ac.AboutToBeging(m_requests.Length)** just
     once before the for loop instead of calling **AboutToBegin** inside the loop.

Note that there is a race because it is possible that all Web server requests complete, **AllBegun** is called, timeout occurs, and **Cancel** is called all at the exact same time. If this happens, then the **AsyncCoordinator** will select a winner and three losers, ensuring that the **AllDone** method is never called more than once. The winner is identified by the status argument passed into **AllDone**, which can be one of the symbols defined by the **CoordinationStatus** type:

```
internal enum CoordinationStatus { AllDone, Timeout, Cancel };
```

Now that you get a sense of what happens, let's take a look at how it works. The **AsyncCoordinator** class encapsulates all the thread coordination logic in it. It uses **Interlocked** methods for everything to ensure that the code runs extremely fast and that no threads ever block. Here is the code for this class:

```
internal sealed class AsyncCoordinator {
    private Int32 m_opCount = 1;        // Decremented by AllBegun
    private Int32 m_statusReported = 0; // 0=false, 1=true
    private Action<CoordinationStatus> m_callback;
    private Timer m_timer;

    // This method MUST be called BEFORE calling a BeginXxx method
    public void AboutToBegin(Int32 opsToAdd = 1) {
        Interlocked.Add(ref m_opCount, opsToAdd);
    }

    // This method MUST be called AFTER calling an EndXxx method
    public void JustEnded() {
        if (Interlocked.Decrement(ref m_opCount) == 0)
            ReportStatus(CoordinationStatus.AllDone);
    }

    // This method MUST be called AFTER calling ALL BeginXxx methods
    public void AllBegun(Action<CoordinationStatus> callback,
        Int32 timeout = Timeout.Infinite) {

        m_callback = callback;
        if (timeout != Timeout.Infinite)
            m_timer = new Timer(TimeExpired, null, timeout, Timeout.Infinite);
        JustEnded();
    }

    private void TimeExpired(Object o) { ReportStatus(CoordinationStatus.Timeout); }
    public void Cancel()               { ReportStatus(CoordinationStatus.Cancel); }

    private void ReportStatus(CoordinationStatus status) {
        // If status has never been reported, report it; else ignore it
        if (Interlocked.Exchange(ref m_statusReported, 1) == 0)
            m_callback(status);
    }
}
```

The most important field in this class is the **m_opCount** field. This field keeps track of the number of asynchronous operations that are still outstanding. Just before each asynchronous operation is started, **AboutToBegin** is called. This method calls **Interlocked.Add** to add the number passed to it to the **m_opCount** field in an atomic way. Adding to **m_opCount** must be performed atomically because Web servers could be responding on thread pool threads as more operations are being started. As Web servers respond, **JustEnded** is called. This method calls **Interlocked.Decrement** to atomically subtract **1** from **m_opCount**. Whichever thread happens to set **m_opCount** to **0** calls **ReportStatus**.

> **Note** The **m_opCount** field is initialized to **1** (not **0**); this is critically important as it ensures that **AllDone** is not invoked while the thread executing the constructor method is still issuing Web server requests. Before the constructor calls **AllBegun**, there is no way that **m_opCount** will ever reach **0**. When the constructor calls **AllBegun**, **AllBegun** internally calls **JustEnded**, which decrements **m_opCount** and effectively undoes the effect of having initialized it to **1**. Now, **m_opCount** can reach **0**, but only after we know that all the Web server requests have been initiated.

The **ReportStatus** method arbitrates the race that can occur among all the operations completing, the timeout occurring, and **Cancel** being called. **ReportStatus** must make sure that only one of these conditions is considered the winner so that the **m_callback** method is invoked only once. Arbitrating the winner is done via calling **Interlocked.Exchange**, passing it a reference to the **m_statusReported** field. This field is really treated as a Boolean variable; however, it can't actually be a **Boolean** variable because there are no **Interlocked** methods that accept a **Boolean** variable. So I use an **Int32** variable instead where **0** means **false** and **1** means **true**.

Inside **ReportStatus**, the **Interlocked.Exchange** call will change **m_statusReported** to **1**. But only the first thread to do this will see **Interlocked.Exchange** return a **0**, and only this thread will invoke the callback method. Any other threads that call **Interlocked.Exchange** will get a return value of **1**, effectively notifying these threads that the callback method has already been invoked and therefore it should not be invoked again.

Implementing a Simple Spin Lock

The **Interlocked** methods are great but they mostly operate on **Int32** values. What if you need to manipulate a bunch of fields in a class object atomically? In this case, we need a way to stop all threads but one from entering the region of code that manipulates the fields. Using **Interlocked** methods, we can build a thread synchronization lock:

```
internal struct SimpleSpinLock {
   private Int32 m_ResourceInUse; // 0=false (default), 1=true

   public void Enter() {
      // Set the resource to in-use and if this thread
      // changed it from Free, then return
      while (Interlocked.Exchange(ref m_ResourceInUse, 1) != 0) {
         /* Black Magic goes here... */
      }
   }

   public void Leave() {
      // Mark the resource as Free
      Thread.VolatileWrite(ref m_ResourceInUse, 0);
   }
}
```

And here is a class that shows how to use the **SimpleSpinLock**:

```
public sealed class SomeResource {
   private SimpleSpinLock m_sl = new SimpleSpinLock();

   public void AccessResource() {
      m_sl.Enter();
      // Only one thread at a time can get in here to access the resource...
      m_sl.Leave();
   }
}
```

The **SimpleSpinLock** implementation is very simple. If two threads call **Enter** at the same time, **Interlocked.Exchange** ensures that one thread changes **m_resourceInUse** from 0 to 1 and sees that **m_resourceInUse** was 0, and this thread then returns from **Enter** so that it can continue executing the code in the **AccessResource** method. The other thread will change **m_resourceInUse** from a 1 to a 1. This thread will see that it did not change **m_resourceInUse** from a **0**, and this thread will now start spinning continuously calling **Exchange** until the first thread calls **Leave**.

When the first thread is done manipulating the fields of the **SomeResource** object, it calls **Leave**, which internally calls **Thread.VolatileWrite** and changes **m_resourceInUse** back to a **0**. This causes the spinning thread to then change **m_resourceInUse** from a **0** to a **1** and this thread now gets to return from **Enter** so that it can access **SomeResource** object's fields.

There you have it. This is a simple implementation of a thread synchronization lock. The big potential problem with this lock is that it causes threads to spin when there is contention for the lock. This spinning wastes precious CPU time, preventing the CPU from doing other, more useful work. As a result, spin locks should only ever be used to guard regions of code that execute very quickly.

And spin locks should not typically be used on single-CPU machines, as the thread that holds the lock can't quickly release it if the thread that wants the lock is spinning. The situation becomes much worse if the thread holding the lock is at a lower priority than the thread wanting to get the lock because now the thread holding the lock may not get a chance to run at all, resulting in a livelock situation. Windows sometimes boosts a thread's priority dynamically for short periods of time. Therefore, boosting should be disabled for threads that are using spin locks; see the **PriorityBoostEnabled** properties of **System.Diagnostics.Process** and **System.Diagnostics.ProcessThread**. There are issues related to using spin locks on hyperthreaded machines, too. In an attempt to circumvent these kinds of problems, many spin locks have some addition logic in them; I refer to the additional logic as *Black Magic*. I'd rather not go into the details of Black Magic because it changes over time as more people study locks and their performance. However, I will say this: The FCL ships with a structure, **System.Threading.SpinWait**, which encapsulates the state-of-the-art thinking around this Black Magic.

Putting a Delay in the Thread's Processing

The Black Magic is all about having a thread that wants a resource to pause its execution temporarily so that the thread that currently has the resource can execute its code and relinquish the resource. To do this, the **SpinWait** struct internally calls **Thread**'s static **Sleep**, **Yield**, and **SpinWait** methods. I'll briefly describe these methods in this sidebar.

A thread can tell the system that it does not want to be schedulable for a certain amount of time. This is accomplished by calling **Thread**'s static **Sleep** method:

```
public static void Sleep(Int32 millisecondsTimeout);
public static void Sleep(TimeSpan timeout);
```

This method causes the thread to suspend itself until the specified amount of time has elapsed. Calling **Sleep** allows the thread to voluntarily give up the remainder of its time-slice. The system makes the thread not schedulable for *approximately* the amount of time specified. That's right—if you tell the system you want to sleep for 100 milliseconds, you will sleep approximately that long, but possibly several seconds or even minutes more. Remember that Windows is not a real-time operating system. Your thread will probably wake up at the right time, but whether it does depends on what else is going on in the system.

You can call **Sleep** and pass the value in **System.Threading.Timeout.Infinite** (defined as **-1**) for the **millisecondsTimeout** parameter. This tells the system to never schedule the thread, and it is not a useful thing to do. It is much better to have the thread exit and then recover its stack and kernel object. You can pass **0** to **Sleep**. This tells the system that the calling thread relinquishes the remainder of its current time-slice, and it forces the system to schedule another thread. However, the system can reschedule the thread that just called **Sleep**. This will happen if there are no more schedulable threads at the same priority or higher.

A thread can ask Windows to schedule another thread on the current CPU by calling **Thread**'s **Yield** method:

```
public static Boolean Yield();
```

If Windows has another thread ready to run on the current processor, then **Yield** returns **true** and the thread that called **Yield** ended its time-slice early, the selected thread gets to run for one time-slice, and then the thread that called **Yield** is scheduled again and starts running with a fresh new time-slice. If Windows does not have another thread to run on the current processor, then **Yield** returns **false** and the thread continues its time-slice.

The **Yield** method exists in order to give a thread of equal or lower priority that is starving for CPU time a chance to run. A thread calls this method if it wants a resource that is currently owned by another thread. The *hope* is that Windows will schedule the thread that currently owns the resource and that this thread will relinquish the resource. Then, when the thread that called **Yield** runs again, this thread can have the resource.

Yield is a cross between calling **Thread.Sleep(0)** and **Thread.Sleep(1)**. **Thread.Sleep(0)** will not let a lower-priority thread run whereas **Thread.Sleep(1)** will always force a context switch and Windows will force the thread to sleep longer than 1 millisecond due to the resolution of the internal system timer.

Hyperthreaded CPUs really let only one thread run at a time. So, when executing spin loops on these CPUs, you need to force the current thread to pause so that the CPU switches to the other thread, allowing it to run. A thread can force itself to pause, allowing a hyperthreaded CPU to switch to its other thread by calling **Thread**'s **SpinWait** method:

```
public static void SpinWait(Int32 iterations);
```

Calling this method actually executes a special CPU instruction; it does not tell Windows to do anything (since Windows already thinks that it has scheduled two threads on the CPU). On a non-hyperthreaded CPU, this special CPU instruction is simply ignored.

> **Note** For more information about these methods, see their Win32 equivalents: **Sleep**, **SwitchToThread**, and **YieldProcessor**. You can also learn more about adjusting the resolution of the system timer by looking up the Win32 **timeBeginPeriod** and **timeEndPeriod** functions.

The FCL also includes a **System.Threading.SpinLock** structure that is similar to my **SimpleSpinLock** class shown earlier except that it uses the **SpinWait** structure to improve performance. The **SpinLock** structure also offers timeout support. By the way, it is interesting to note that my **SimpleSpinLock** and the FCL's **SpinLock** are both value types. This means that they are lightweight, memory-friendly objects. A **SpinLock** is a good choice if you need to associate a lock with each item in a collection, for example. However, you must make sure that you do not pass **SpinLock** instances around because they are copied and you will lose any and all synchronization. And while you can define instance **SpinLock** fields, do not mark the field as **readonly** because its internal state must change as the lock is manipulated.

The Interlocked Anything Pattern

Many people look at the **Interlocked** methods and wonder why Microsoft doesn't create a richer set of interlocked methods that can be used in a wider range of scenarios. For example, it would be nice if the **Interlocked** class offered **Multiple**, **Divide**, **Minimum**, **Maximum**, **And**, **Or**, **Xor**, and a bunch of other methods. While the **Interlocked** class doesn't offer these methods, there is a well-known pattern that allows you to perform any operation on an **Int32** in an atomic way by using **Interlocked.CompareExchange**. In fact, since **Interlocked.CompareExchange** has additional overloads that operate on **Int64**, **Single**, **Double**, **Object**, and a generic reference type, this pattern will actually work for all these types, too.

Here is an example of the pattern that is being used to create an atomic **Maximum** method:

```
public static Int32 Maximum(ref Int32 target, Int32 value) {
    Int32 currentVal = target, startVal, desiredVal;

    // Don't access target in the loop except in an attempt
    // to change it because another thread may be touching it
    do {
        // Record this iteration's starting value
        startVal = currentVal;

        // Calculate the desired value in terms of startVal and value
        desiredVal = Math.Max(startVal, value);

        // NOTE: the thread could be preempted here!

        // if (target == startVal) target = desiredVal
        // Value prior to potential change is returned
        currentVal = Interlocked.CompareExchange(ref target, desiredVal, startVal);

        // If the starting value changed during this iteration, repeat
    } while (startVal != currentVal);

    // Return the maximum value when this thread tried to set it
    return desiredVal;
}
```

Now let me explain exactly what is going on here. Upon entering the method, **currentVal** is initialized to the value in **target** at the moment the method starts executing. Then, inside the loop, **startVal** is initialized to this same value. Using **startVal**, you can perform any operation you desire. This operation can be extremely complex, consisting of thousands of lines of code. But, ultimately, you must end up with a result that is placed into **desiredVal**. In my example, I simply determine whether **startVal** or **value** contains the larger value.

Now, while this operation is running, another thread could change the value in **target**. It is unlikely that this will happen, but it is possible. If this does happen, then the value in **derivedVal** is based off an old value in **startVal**, not the current value in **target**, and therefore, we should not change the value in **target**. To ensure that the value in **target** is changed to **desiredVal** if no thread has changed **target** behind our thread's back, we use **Interlocked.CompareExchange**. This method checks if the value in **target** matches the value in **startVal** (which identifies the value that we thought was in **target** before starting to perform the operation). If the value in **target** didn't change, then **CompareExchange** changes it to the new value in **desiredVal**. If the value in **target** did change, then **CompareExchange** does not alter the value in **target** at all.

CompareExchange returns the value that is in **target** at the time when **CompareExchange** is called, which I then place in **currentVal**. Then, a check is made comparing **startVal** with the new value in **currentVal**. If these values are the same, then a thread did not change **target** behind our thread's back, **target** now contains the value in **desiredVal**, the **while** loop does not loop around, and the method returns. If **startVal** is not equal to **currentVal**, then a thread did change the value in **target** behind our thread's back, **target** did not get changed to our value in **desiredVal**, and the **while** loop will loop around and try the operation again, this time using the new value in **currentVal** that reflects the other thread's change.

Personally, I have used this pattern in a lot of my own code and, in fact, I made a generic method, **Morph**, which encapsulates this pattern[7]:

```
delegate Int32 Morpher<TResult, TArgument>(Int32 startValue, TArgument argument,
   out TResult morphResult);

static TResult Morph<TResult, TArgument>(ref Int32 target, TArgument argument,
   Morpher<TResult, TArgument> morpher) {

   TResult morphResult;
   Int32 currentVal = target, startVal, desiredVal;
   do {
      startVal = currentVal;
      desiredVal = morpher(startVal, argument, out morphResult);
      currentVal = Interlocked.CompareExchange(ref target, desiredVal, startVal);
   } while (startVal != currentVal);
   return morphResult;
}
```

---

[7] Obviously, the **Morph** method incurs a performance penalty due to invoking the **morpher** callback method. For best performance, execute the operation inline, as in the **Maximum** example.

Kernel-Mode Constructs

Windows offers several kernel-mode constructs for synchronizing threads. The kernel-mode constructs are much slower than the user-mode constructs because they require coordination from the Windows operating system itself and because each method call on a kernel object causes the calling thread to transition from managed code to native user-mode code to native kernel-mode code and then return all the way back. These transitions require a lot of CPU time and, if performed frequently, can adversely affect the overall performance of your application.

However, the kernel-mode constructs offer some benefits over the primitive user-mode constructs, such as:

■ When a kernel-mode construct detects contention on a resource, Windows blocks the losing thread so that it is not spinning on a CPU, wasting processor resources.

■ Kernel-mode constructs can synchronize native and managed threads with each other.

■ Kernel-mode constructs can synchronize threads running in different processes on the same machine.

■ Kernel-mode constructs can have security applied to them to prevent unauthorized accounts from accessing them.

■ A thread can block until all kernel-mode constructs in a set are available or until any one kernel-mode construct in a set has become available.

■ A thread can block on a kernel-mode construct specifying a timeout value; if the thread can't have access to the resource it desires in the specified amount of time, then the thread is unblocked and can perform other tasks.

The two primitive kernel-mode thread synchronization constructs are events and semaphores. Other kernel-mode constructs, such as mutex, are built on top of the two primitive constructs. For more information about the Windows kernel-mode constructs, see my book *Windows via C/C++, 5th Edition* (Microsoft Press, 2007).

The **System.Threading** namespace offers an abstract base class called **WaitHandle**. The **WaitHandle** class is a simple class whose sole purpose is to wrap a Windows kernel object handle. The FCL provides several classes derived from **WaitHandle**. All classes are defined in the **System.Threading** namespace, and all classes are implemented in MSCorLib.dll except for **Semaphore**, which is implemented in System.dll. The class hierarchy looks like this:

```
WaitHandle
   EventWaitHandle
      AutoResetEvent
      ManualResetEvent
   Semaphore
   Mutex
```

Internally, the **WaitHandle** base class has a **SafeWaitHandle** field that holds a Win32 kernel object handle. This field is initialized when a concrete **WaitHandle**-derived class is constructed. In addition, the **WaitHandle** class publicly exposes methods that are inherited by all the derived classes. Every method called on a kernel-mode construct represents a full memory fence. **WaitHandle**'s interesting public methods are shown below (some overloads for some methods are not shown):

```
public abstract class WaitHandle : MarshalByRefObject, IDisposable {
    // Close & Dispose internally call the Win32 CloseHandle function.
    public virtual void Close();
    public void Dispose();

    // WaitOne internally calls the Win32 WaitForSingleObjectEx function.
    public virtual Boolean WaitOne();
    public virtual Boolean WaitOne(Int32 millisecondsTimeout);

    // WaitAny internally calls the Win32 WaitForMultipleObjectsEx function
    public static Int32 WaitAny(WaitHandle[] waitHandles);
    public static Int32 WaitAny(WaitHandle[] waitHandles, Int32 millisecondsTimeout);

    // WaitAll internally calls the Win32 WaitForMultipleObjectsEx function
    public static Boolean WaitAll(WaitHandle[] waitHandles);
    public static Boolean WaitAll(WaitHandle[] waitHandles, Int32 millisecondsTimeout);

    // SignalAndWait internally calls the Win32 SignalObjectAndWait function
    public static Boolean SignalAndWait(WaitHandle toSignal, WaitHandle toWaitOn);
    public static Boolean SignalAndWait(WaitHandle toSignal, WaitHandle toWaitOn,
        Int32 millisecondsTimeout, Boolean exitContext)

    // Use this to get access to the raw Win32 handle
    public SafeWaitHandle SafeWaitHandle { get; set; }

    // Returned from WaitAny if a timeout occurs
    public const Int32 WaitTimeout = 0x102;
}
```

There are a few things to note about these methods:

- You call **WaitHandle**'s **Close** (or **IDisposable**'s parameterless **Dispose** method) to close the underlying kernel object handle. Internally, these methods call the Win32 **CloseHandle** function.

- You call **WaitHandle**'s **WaitOne** method to have the calling thread wait for the underlying kernel object to become signaled. Internally, this method calls the Win32 **WaitForSingleObjectEx** function. The returned **Boolean** is **true** if the object became signaled or **false** if a timeout occurs.

- You call **WaitHandle**'s static **WaitAny** method to have the calling thread wait for any one of the kernel objects specified in the **WaitHandle[]** to become signaled. The returned **Int32** is the index of the array element corresponding to the kernel object that became signaled, or **WaitHandle.WaitTimeout** if no object became signaled while waiting. Internally, this method calls the Win32 **WaitForMultipleObjectsEx** function, passing **FALSE** for the **bWaitAll** parameter.

- You call **WaitHandle**'s static **WaitAll** method to have the calling thread wait for all the kernel objects specified in the **WaitHandle[]** to become signaled. The returned **Boolean** is **true** if all of the objects became signaled or **false** if a timeout occurs. Internally, this method calls the Win32 **WaitForMultipleObjectsEx** function, passing **TRUE** for the **bWaitAll** parameter.

- The array that you pass to the **WaitAny** and **WaitAll** methods must contain no more than 64 elements or else the methods throw a **System.NotSupportedException**.

- You call **WaitHandle**'s static **SignalAndWait** method to atomically signal one kernel object and wait for another kernel object to become signaled. The returned **Boolean** is **true** if the object became signaled or **false** if a timeout occurs. Internally, this method calls the Win32 **SignalObjectAndWait** function.

> **Note** In some cases, when a COM single-threaded apartment thread blocks, the thread can wake up internally to pump messages. For example, the blocked thread will wake to process a Windows message sent from another thread. This is done to support COM interoperability. For most applications, this is not a problem—in fact, it is a good thing. However, if your code takes another thread synchronization lock during the processing of the message, then deadlock could occur. As you'll see in Chapter 29, all the hybrid locks call these methods internally, so the same potential benefit or problem exists when using the hybrid locks as well.

The versions of the **WaitOne**, **WaitAll**, and **SignalAndWait** that do not accept a timeout parameter should be prototyped as having a **void** return type, not **Boolean**. The reason is because these methods will return only **true** since the implied timeout is infinite (**System.Threading.Timeout.Infinite**). When you call any of these methods, you do not need to check their return value.

As already mentioned, the **AutoResetEvent**, **ManualResetEvent**, **Semaphore**, and **Mutex** classes are all derived from **WaitHandle**, so they inherit **WaitHandle**'s methods and their behavior. However, these classes introduce additional methods of their own, and I'll address those now.

First, the constructors for all of these classes internally call the Win32 **CreateEvent** (passing **FALSE** for the **bManualReset** parameter) or **CreateEvent** (passing **TRUE** for the **bManualReset** parameter), **CreateSemaphore**, or **CreateMutex** functions. The handle value returned from all of these calls is saved in a private **SafeWaitHandle** field defined inside the **WaitHandle** base class.

Second, the **EventWaitHandle**, **Semaphore**, and **Mutex** classes all offer static **OpenExisting** methods, which internally call the Win32 **OpenEvent**, **OpenSemaphore**, or **OpenMutex** functions, passing a **String** argument that identifies an existing named kernel object. The handle value returned from all of these functions is saved in a newly constructed object that is returned from the **OpenExisting** method. If no kernel object exists with the specified name, a **WaitHandleCannotBeOpenedException** is thrown.

A common usage of the kernel-mode constructs is to create the kind of application that allows only one instance of itself to execute at any given time. Examples of single-instance applications are Microsoft Office Outlook, Windows Live Messenger, Windows Media Player, and Windows Media Center. Here is how to implement a single-instance application:

```
using System;
using System.Threading;

public static class Program {
    public static void Main() {
        Boolean createdNew;

        // Try to create a kernel object with the specified name
        using (new Semaphore(0, 1, "SomeUniqueStringIdentifyingMyApp", out createdNew)) {
            if (createdNew) {
                // This thread created the kernel object so no other instance of this
                // application must be running. Run the rest of the application here...
            } else {
                // This thread opened an existing kernel object with the same string name;
                // another instance of this application must be running now.
                // There is nothing to do in here, let's just return from Main to terminate
                // this second instance of the application.
            }
        }
    }
}
```

In this code, I am using a **Semaphore**, but it would work just as well if I had used an **EventWaitHandle** or a **Mutex** because I'm not actually using the thread synchronization behavior that the object offers. However, I am taking advantage of some thread synchronization behavior that the kernel offers when creating any kind of kernel object. Let me explain how the code above works. Let's say that two instances of this process are started at the same exact time. Each process will have its own thread, and both threads will attempt to create a **Semaphore** with the same string name ("SomeUniqueStringIdentifyingMyApp," in my example). The Windows kernel ensures that only one thread actually creates a kernel object with the specified name; the thread that created the object will have its **createdNew** variable set to **true**.

For the second thread, Windows will see that a kernel object with the specified name already exists; the second thread does not get to create another kernel object with the same name, although if this thread continues to run, it can access the same kernel object as the first process's thread. This is how threads in different processes can communicate with each other via a single kernel object. However, in this example, the second process's thread sees that its **createdNew** variable is set to **false**. This thread now knows that another instance of this process is running, and the second instance of the process exits immediately.

Event Constructs

Events are simply Boolean variables maintained by the kernel. A thread waiting on an event blocks when the event is **false** and unblocks when the event is **true**. There are two kinds of events. When an auto-reset event is **true**, it wakes up just one blocked thread because the kernel *automatically resets* the event back to **false** after unblocking the first thread. When a manual-reset event is **true**, it unblocks all threads waiting for it because the kernel does not automatically reset the event back to **false**; your code must *manually reset* the event back to **false**. The classes related to events look like this:

```
public class EventWaitHandle : WaitHandle {
    public Boolean Set();    // Sets Boolean to true; always returns true
    public Boolean Reset();  // Sets Boolean to false; always returns true
}

public sealed class AutoResetEvent : EventWaitHandle {
    public AutoResetEvent(Boolean initialState);
}

public sealed class ManualResetEvent : EventWaitHandle {
    public ManualResetEvent(Boolean initialState);
}
```

Using an auto-reset event, we can easily create a thread synchronization lock whose behavior is similar to the **SimpleSpinLock** class I showed earlier:

```
internal sealed class SimpleWaitLock : IDisposable {
    private AutoResetEvent m_ResourceFree = new AutoResetEvent(true); // Initially free

    public void Enter() {
        // Block efficiently in the kernel for the resource to be free, then return
        m_ResourceFree.WaitOne();
    }

    public void Leave() {
        m_ResourceFree.Set();// Mark the resource as Free
    }

    public void Dispose() { m_ResourceFree.Dispose(); }
}
```

You would use this **SimpleWaitLock** exactly the same way that you'd use the **SimpleSpinLock**. In fact, the external behavior is exactly the same; however, the performance of the two locks is radically different. When there is no contention on the lock, the **SimpleWaitLock** is much slower than the **SimpleSpinLock** because every call to **SimpleWaitLock**'s **Enter** and **Leave** methods forces the calling thread to transition from managed code to the kernel and back—which is bad. But when there is contention, the losing thread is blocked by the kernel and is not spinning and wasting CPU cycles—which is good. Note also that constructing the **AutoResetEvent** object and calling **Dispose** on it also cause managed to kernel transitions, affecting performance negatively. These calls usually happen rarely, so they are usually not something to be too concerned about.

To give you a better feel for the performance differences, I wrote the following code:

```
public static void Main() {
   Int32 x = 0;
   const Int32 iterations = 10000000;   // 10 million

   // How long does it take to increment x 10 million times?
   Stopwatch sw = Stopwatch.StartNew();
   for (Int32 i = 0; i < iterations; i++) {
      x++;
   }
   Console.WriteLine("Incrementing x: {0:N0}", sw.ElapsedMilliseconds);

   // How long does it take to increment x 10 million times
   // adding the overhead of calling a method that does nothing?
   sw.Restart();
   for (Int32 i = 0; i < iterations; i++) {
      M(); x++; M();
   }
   Console.WriteLine("Incrementing x in M: {0:N0}", sw.ElapsedMilliseconds);

   // How long does it take to increment x 10 million times
   // adding the overhead of calling an uncontended SimpleSpinLock?
   SimpleSpinLock ssl = new SimpleSpinLock();
   sw.Restart();
   for (Int32 i = 0; i < iterations; i++) {
      ssl.Enter(); x++; ssl.Leave();
   }
   Console.WriteLine("Incrementing x in SimpleSpinLock: {0:N0}", sw.ElapsedMilliseconds);

   // How long does it take to increment x 10 million times
   // adding the overhead of calling an uncontended SimpleWaitLock?
   using (SimpleWaitLock swl = new SimpleWaitLock()) {
      sw.Restart();
      for (Int32 i = 0; i < iterations; i++) {
         swl.Enter(); x++; swl.Leave();
      }
      Console.WriteLine("Incrementing x in SimpleWaitLock: {0:N0}", sw.ElapsedMilliseconds);
   }
}

[MethodImpl(MethodImplOptions.NoInlining)]
private static void M() { /* This method does nothing but return */ }
```

When I run the code above, I get the following output:

```
Incrementing x: 8
Incrementing x in M: 50
Incrementing x in SimpleSpinLock: 219
Incrementing x in SimpleWaitLock: 17,615
```

As you can clearly see, just incrementing **x** took only 8 milliseconds. To call a method around incrementing **x** added another 42 milliseconds. Then, executing code in a method that uses a user-mode construct caused the code to run 27 (219 / 8) times slower. But now see how much slower the program ran using a kernel-mode construct: 2,201 (17,615 / 8) times slower! So, if you can avoid thread synchronization, you should. If you need thread synchronization, then try to use the user-mode constructs. Always try to avoid the kernel-mode constructs, as this code ran 80 (17,615 / 219) times slower.

Semaphore Constructs

Semaphores are simply **Int32** variables maintained by the kernel. A thread waiting on a semaphore blocks when the semaphore is **0** and unblocks when the semaphore is greater than **0**. When a thread waiting on a semaphore unblocks, the kernel automatically subtracts **1** from the semaphore's count. Semaphores also have a maximum **Int32** value associated with them, and the current count is never allowed to go over the maximum count. Here is what the **Semaphore** class looks like:

```
public sealed class Semaphore : WaitHandle {
   public Semaphore(Int32 initialCount, Int32 maximumCount);
   public Int32 Release();   // Calls Release(1); returns previous count
   public Int32 Release(Int32 releaseCount);  // Returns previous count
}
```

So now let me summarize how these three kernel-mode primitives behave:

- When multiple threads are waiting on an auto-reset event, setting the event causes *only one* thread to become unblocked.

- When multiple threads are waiting on a manual-reset event, setting the event causes *all* threads to become unblocked.

- When multiple threads are waiting on a semaphore, releasing the semaphore causes **releaseCount** threads to become unblocked (where **releaseCount** is the argument passed to **Semaphore**'s **Release** method).

Therefore, an auto-reset event behaves very similarly to a semaphore whose maximum count is 1. The difference between the two is that **Set** can be called multiple times consecutively on an auto-reset event and still only one thread will be unblocked, whereas calling **Release** multiple times consecutively on a semaphore keeps incrementing its internal count, which could unblock many threads. By the way, if you call **Release** on a semaphore too many times, causing its count to exceed its maximum count, then **Release** will throw a **SemaphoreFullException**.

Using a semaphore, we can re-implement the **SimpleWaitLock** as follows, so that it gives multiple threads concurrent access to a resource (which is not necessarily a safe thing to do unless all threads access the resource in a read-only fashion):

```
public sealed class SimpleWaitLock : IDisposable {
   private Semaphore m_AvailableResources;

   public SimpleWaitLock(Int32 maximumConcurrentThreads) {
      m_AvailableResources =
         new Semaphore(maximumConcurrentThreads, maximumConcurrentThreads);
   }

   public void Enter() {
      // Wait efficiently in the kernel for resource access, then return
      m_AvailableResources.WaitOne();
   }

   public void Leave() {
      // This thread doesn't need access anymore; another thread can have it
      m_ AvailableResources.Release();
   }

   public void Dispose() { m_AvailableResources.Close(); }
}
```

Mutex Constructs

A mutex represents a mutual-exclusive lock. It works similar to an **AutoResetEvent** (or a **Semaphore** with a count of **1**) since all three constructs release only one waiting thread at a time. Here is what the **Mutex** class looks like:

```
public sealed class Mutex : WaitHandle {
   public Mutex();
   public void ReleaseMutex();
}
```

Mutexes have some additional logic in them which makes them more complex than the other constructs. First, **Mutex** objects record which thread obtained it by querying the calling thread's **Int32** ID. When a thread calls **ReleaseMutex**, the **Mutex** makes sure that the calling thread is the same thread that obtained the **Mutex**. If the calling thread is not the thread that obtained the **Mutex**, then the **Mutex** object's state is unaltered and **ReleaseMutex** throws a **System.ApplicationException**. Also, if a thread owning a **Mutex** terminates for any reason, then some thread waiting on the **Mutex** will be awakened by having a **System.Threading. AbandonedMutexException** thrown. Usually, this exception will go unhandled, terminating the whole process. This is good because a thread acquired the **Mutex** and it is likely that the thread terminated before it finished updating the data that the **Mutex** was protecting. If a thread catches **AbandonedMutexException**, then it could attempt to access the corrupt data, leading to unpredictable results and security problems.

Second, **Mutex** objects maintain a recursion count indicating how many times the owning thread owns the **Mutex**. If a thread currently owns a **Mutex** and then that thread waits on the **Mutex** again, the recursion count is incremented and the thread is allowed to continue running. When that thread calls **ReleaseMutex**, the recursion count is decremented. Only when the recursion count becomes 0 can another thread become the owner of the **Mutex**.

Most people do not like this additional logic. The problem is that these "features" have a cost associated with them. The **Mutex** object needs more memory to hold the additional thread ID and recursion count information. And, more importantly, the **Mutex** code has to maintain this information, which makes the lock slower. If an application needs or wants these additional features, then the application code could have done this itself; the code doesn't have to be built into the **Mutex** object. For this reason, a lot of people avoid using **Mutex** objects.

Usually a recursive lock is needed when a method takes a lock and then calls another method that also requires the lock, as the following code demonstrates:

```
internal class SomeClass : IDisposable {
   private readonly Mutex m_lock = new Mutex();

   public void Method1() {
      m_lock.WaitOne();
      // Do whatever...
      Method2();   // Method2 recursively acquires the lock
      m_lock.ReleaseMutex();
   }

   public void Method2() {
      m_lock.WaitOne();
      // Do whatever...
      m_lock.ReleaseMutex();
   }

   public void Dispose() { m_lock.Dispose(); }
}
```

In the code above, code that uses a **SomeClass** object could call **Method1**, which acquires the **Mutex**, performs some thread-safe operation, and then calls **Method2**, which also performs some thread-safe operation. Since **Mutex** objects support recursion, the thread will acquire the lock twice and then release it twice before another thread can own the **Mutex**. If **SomeClass** has used an **AutoResetEvent** instead of a **Mutex**, then the thread would block when it called **Method2**'s **WaitOne** method.

If you need a recursive lock, then you could create one easily by using an **AutoResetEvent**:

```
internal sealed class RecursiveAutoResetEvent : IDisposable {
   private AutoResetEvent m_lock = new AutoResetEvent(true);
   private Int32 m_owningThreadId = 0;
   private Int32 m_recursionCount = 0;

   public void Enter() {
      // Obtain the calling thread's unique Int32 ID
      Int32 currentThreadId = Thread.CurrentThread.ManagedThreadId;

      // If the calling thread owns the lock, increment the recursion count
      if (m_owningThreadId == currentThreadId) {
         m_recursionCount++;
         return;
      }
```

```
        // The calling thread doesn't own the lock, wait for it
        m_lock.WaitOne();

        // The calling now owns the lock, initialize the owning thread ID & recursion count
        m_owningThreadId = currentThreadId;
        m_recursionCount--;
    }

    public void Leave() {
        // If the calling thread doesn't own the lock, we have an error
        if (m_owningThreadId != Thread.CurrentThread.ManagedThreadId)
            throw new InvalidOperationException();

        // Subtract 1 from the recursion count
        if (--m_recursionCount == 0) {
            // If the recursion count is 0, then no thread owns the lock
            m_owningThreadId = 0;
            m_lock.Set();   // Wake up 1 waiting thread (if any)
        }
    }

    public void Dispose() { m_lock.Dispose(); }
}
```

While the behavior of the **RecursiveAutoResetEvent** class is identical to that of the **Mutex** class, a **RecursiveAutoResetEvent** object will have far superior performance when a thread tries to acquire the lock recursively because all the code that is required to track thread ownership and recursion is now in managed code. A thread has to transition into the Windows kernel only when first acquiring the **AutoResetEvent** or when finally relinquishing it to another thread.

Calling a Method When a Single Kernel Construct Becomes Available

Having a thread block indefinitely waiting for a kernel object to become available is wasteful of the thread's memory resources. Therefore, the thread pool offers a way to invoke a method of yours when a kernel object becomes available by using the **System.Threading. ThreadPool** class's static **RegisterWaitForSingleObject** method. There are several overloads of this method, but they are all very similar. Here is the prototype for one of the more commonly used overloads:

```
public static RegisteredWaitHandle RegisterWaitForSingleObject(
    WaitHandle waitObject, WaitOrTimerCallback callback, Object state,
    Int32 millisecondsTimeoutInterval, Boolean executeOnlyOnce);
```

When you call this method, the **waitObject** argument identifies the kernel object that you want the thread pool to wait for. Since this parameter is of the abstract base class **WaitHandle**, you can specify any class derived from this base class. Specifically, you can pass a reference to a **Semaphore**, **Mutex**, **AutoResetEvent**, or **ManualResetEvent** object. The second parameter, **callback**, identifies the method that you want the thread pool thread to call. The callback method that you write must match the **System.Threading. WaitOrTimerCallback** delegate, which is defined as follows:

```
public delegate void WaitOrTimerCallback(Object state, Boolean timedOut);
```

RegisterWaitForSingleObject's third parameter, **state**, allows you to specify some state data that should be passed to the callback method when the thread pool thread calls it; pass **null** if you have no special state data to pass. The fourth parameter, **millisecondsTimeoutInterval**, allows you to tell the thread pool how long it should wait for the kernel object to become signaled. It is common to pass **Timeout.Infinite (-1)** here to indicate an infinite timeout. If the last parameter, **executeOnlyOnce**, is **true**, a thread pool thread will execute the callback method just once. But if **executeOnlyOnce** is **false**, a thread pool thread will execute the callback method every time the kernel object becomes signaled. This is most useful when waiting for an **AutoResetEvent** object.

When the callback method is called, it is passed state data and a **Boolean** value, **timedOut**. If **timedOut** is **false**, the method knows that it is being called because the kernel object became signaled. If **timedOut** is **true**, the method knows that it is being called because the kernel object did not become signaled in the time specified. The callback method can perform whatever action it desires based on the value that it receives in the **timedOut** argument.

You'll notice that the **RegisterWaitForSingleObject** method returns a reference to a **RegisteredWaitHandle** object. This object identifies the kernel object that the thread pool is waiting on. If, for some reason, your application wants to tell the thread pool to stop watching the registered wait handle, your application can call **RegisteredWaitHandle**'s **Unregister** method:

```
public Boolean Unregister(WaitHandle waitObject);
```

The **waitObject** parameter indicates how you want to be notified when all queued work items for the registered wait have executed. You should pass **null** for this parameter if you don't want a notification. If you pass a valid reference to a **WaitHandle**-derived object, the thread pool will signal the object when all pending work items for the registered wait handle have executed.

The code below demonstrates how to have a thread pool thread call a method whenever an **AutoResetEvent** object becomes signaled:

```
internal static class RegisteredWaitHandleDemo {
   public static void Main() {
      // Construct an AutoResetEvent (initially false)
      AutoResetEvent are = new AutoResetEvent(false);

      // Tell the thread pool to wait on the AutoResetEvent
      RegisteredWaitHandle rwh = ThreadPool.RegisterWaitForSingleObject(
         are,               // Wait on this AutoResetEvent
         EventOperation,    // When available, call the EventOperation method
         null,              // Pass null to EventOperation
         5000,              // Wait 5 seconds for the event to become true
         false);            // Call EventOperation every time the event is true

      // Start our loop
      Char operation = (Char) 0;
      while (operation != 'Q') {
         Console.WriteLine("S=Signal, Q=Quit?");
         operation = Char.ToUpper(Console.ReadKey(true).KeyChar);
         if (operation == 'S') are.Set(); // User want to set the event
      }

      // Tell the thread pool to stop waiting on the event
      rwh.Unregister(null);
   }

   // This method is called whenever the event is true or
   // when 5 seconds have elapsed since the last callback/timeout
   private static void EventOperation(Object state, Boolean timedOut) {
      Console.WriteLine(timedOut ? "Timeout" : "Event became true");
   }
}
```

Chapter 29
Hybrid Thread Synchronization Constructs

In Chapter 28, "Primitive Thread Synchronization Constructs," I discussed the primitive user-mode and kernel-mode thread synchronization constructs. From these primitive constructs, all other thread synchronization constructs can be built. Typically, other thread synchronization constructs are built by combining the user-mode and kernel-mode constructs, and I call these *hybrid thread synchronization constructs*. Hybrid constructs provide the performance benefit of the primitive user-mode constructs when there is no thread contention. Hybrid constructs also use the primitive kernel-mode constructs to provide the benefit of not spinning (wasting CPU time) when multiple threads are contending for the construct at the same time. Since, in most applications, threads are rarely contending for a construct at the same time, the performance improvements can help your application greatly.

In this chapter, I will first show how hybrid constructs are built from the various primitive constructs. Then, I will introduce you to many of the hybrid constructs that ship with the Framework Class Library (FCL), describe their behavior, and give some insight as to how to use these constructs correctly. I will also mention some constructs that I have created and make available for free in Wintellect's Power Threading library, which can be downloaded from *http://Wintellect.com/*.

Toward the end of the chapter, I show how to minimize resource usage and improve performance by using the FCL's concurrent collection classes instead of using some of the hybrid constructs. And finally, I discuss the Power Threading library's **ReaderWriterGate** and **SyncGate** classes which offer reader-writer semantics without blocking any threads, thereby also reducing resource consumption and improving performance.

A Simple Hybrid Lock

So, without further ado, let me start off by showing you an example of a hybrid thread synchronization lock:

```
internal sealed class SimpleHybridLock : IDisposable {
   // The Int32 is used by the primitive user-mode constructs (Interlocked methods)
   private Int32 m_waiters = 0;

   // The AutoResetEvent is the primitive kernel-mode construct
   private AutoResetEvent m_waiterLock = new AutoResetEvent(false);

   public void Enter() {
      // Indicate that this thread wants the lock
      if (Interlocked.Increment(ref m_waiters) == 1)
         return; // Lock was free, no contention, just return

      // Another thread is waiting. There is contention, block this thread
      m_waiterLock.WaitOne();  // Bad performance hit here
      // When WaitOne returns, this thread now has the lock
   }

   public void Leave() {
      // This thread is releasing the lock
      if (Interlocked.Decrement(ref m_waiters) == 0)
         return; // No other threads are blocked, just return

      // Other threads are blocked, wake 1 of them
      m_waiterLock.Set();  // Bad performance hit here
   }

   public void Dispose() { m_waiterLock.Dispose(); }
}
```

The **SimpleHybridLock** contains two fields: an **Int32**, which will be manipulated via the primitive user-mode constructs, and an **AutoResetEvent**, which is a primitive kernel-mode construct. To get great performance, the lock tries to use the **Int32** and avoid using the **AutoResetEvent** as much as possible. Just constructing a **SimpleHybridLock** object causes the **AutoResetEvent** to be created, and this is a massive performance hit compared to the overhead associated with the **Int32** field. Later in this chapter, we'll see another hybrid construct (**AutoResetEventSlim**) that avoids the performance hit of creating the **AutoResetEvent** until the first time contention is detected from multiple threads accessing the lock at the same time. The **Dispose** method closes the **AutoResetEvent**, and this is also a big performance hit compared to the overhead of destroying the **Int32** field.

While it would be nice to improve the performance of constructing and disposing of a **SimpleHybridLock** object, it would be better to focus on the performance of its **Enter** and **Leave** methods because these methods tend to be called many, many times over the object's lifetime. Let's focus on these methods now.

The first thread to call **Enter** causes **Interlocked.Increment** to add one to the **m_waiters** field, making its value **1**. This thread sees that there were zero threads waiting before for this lock, so the thread gets to return from its call to **Enter**. The thing to appreciate here is that the thread acquired the lock very quickly. Now, if another thread comes along and calls **Enter**, this second thread increments **m_waiters** to **2** and sees that another thread has the lock, so this thread blocks by calling **WaitOne** using the **AutoResetEvent**. Calling **WaitOne** causes the thread to transition into the Windows' kernel, and this is a big performance hit. However, the thread must stop running anyway, so it is not too bad to have a thread waste some time to stop completely. The good news is that the thread is now blocked and so it is not wasting CPU time by spinning on the CPU, which is what the **SimpleSpinLock**'s **Enter** method, introduced in Chapter 28, does.

Now let's look at the **Leave** method. When a thread calls **Leave**, **Interlocked.Decrement** is called to subtract **1** from the **m_waiters** field. If **m_waiters** is now **0**, then no other threads are blocked inside a call to **Enter** and the thread calling **Leave** can simply return. Again, think about how fast this is: Leaving a lock means that a thread subtracts **1** from an **Int32**, performs a quick **if** test, and then returns! On the other head, if the thread calling **Leave** sees that **m_waiters** was not **1**, then the thread knows that there is contention and that there is at least one other thread blocked in the kernel. This thread must wake up one (and only one) of the blocked threads. It does this by calling **Set** on **AutoResetEvent**. This is a performance hit, as the thread must transition into the kernel and back, but this transition occurs only when there was contention. Of course, **AutoResetEvent** ensures that only one blocked thread wakes up; any other threads blocked on the **AutoResetEvent** will continue to block until the newly unblocked thread eventually calls **Leave**.

> **Note** In reality, any thread could call **Leave** at any time since the **Enter** method does not keep a record of which thread successfully acquired the lock. Adding the field and code to maintain this information is easy to do but it would increase the memory required for the lock object itself and hurt performance of the **Enter** and **Leave** methods because they would have to manipulate this field. I would rather have a fast-performing lock and make sure that my code uses it the right way. You'll notice that events and semaphores do not maintain this kind of information; only mutexes do.

Spinning, Thread Ownership, and Recursion

Since transitions into the kernel incur such a big performance hit and threads tend to hold on to a lock for very short periods of time, an application's overall performance can be improved by having a thread spin in user mode for a little while before having the thread transition to kernel mode. If the lock that the thread is waiting for becomes available while spinning, then the transition to kernel mode is avoided.

In addition, some locks impose a limitation where the thread that acquires the lock must be the thread that releases the lock. And some locks allow the currently owning thread to own the lock recursively. The **Mutex** lock is an example of a lock that has these characteristics.[1] Using some fancy logic, it is possible to build a hybrid lock that offers spinning, thread ownership, and recursion. Here is what the code looks like:

```
internal sealed class AnotherHybridLock : IDisposable {
    // The Int32 is used by the primitive user-mode constructs (Interlocked methods)
    private Int32 m_waiters = 0;

    // The AutoResetEvent is the primitive kernel-mode construct
    private AutoResetEvent m_waiterLock = new AutoResetEvent(false);

    // This field controls spinning in an effort to improve performance
    private Int32 m_spincount = 4000;    // Arbitrarily chosen count

    // These fields indicate which thread owns the lock and how many times it owns it
    private Int32 m_owningThreadId = 0, m_recursion = 0;

    public void Enter() {
        // If calling thread already owns the lock, increment recursion count and return
        Int32 threadId = Thread.CurrentThread.ManagedThreadId;
        if (threadId == m_owningThreadId) { m_recursion++; return; }

        // The calling thread doesn't own the lock, try to get it
        SpinWait spinwait = new SpinWait();
        for (Int32 spinCount = 0; spinCount < m_spincount; spinCount++) {
            // If the lock was free, this thread got it; set some state and return
            if (Interlocked.CompareExchange(ref m_waiters, 1, 0) == 0) goto GotLock;

            // Black magic: give other threads a chance to run
            // in hopes that the lock will be released
            spinwait.SpinOnce();
        }

        // Spinning is over and the lock was still not obtained, try one more time
        if (Interlocked.Increment(ref m_waiters) > 1) {
            // Other threads are blocked and this thread must block too
            m_waiterLock.WaitOne(); // Wait for the lock; performance hit
            // When this thread wakes, it owns the lock; set some state and return
        }

    GotLock:
        // When a thread gets the lock, we record its ID and
        // indicate that the thread owns the lock once
        m_owningThreadId = threadId; m_recursion = 1;
    }

    public void Leave() {
        // If the calling thread doesn't own the lock, there is a bug
```

[1] Threads do not spin when waiting on a **Mutex** object because the **Mutex**'s code is in the kernel. This means that the thread had to have already transitioned into the kernel to check the **Mutex**'s state.

```
    Int32 threadId = Thread.CurrentThread.ManagedThreadId;
    if (threadId != m_owningThreadId)
       throw new SynchronizationLockException("Lock not owned by calling thread");

    // Decrement the recursion count. If this thread still owns the lock, just return
    if (--m_recursion > 0) return;

    m_owningThreadId = 0;    // No thread owns the lock now

    // If no other threads are blocked, just return
    if (Interlocked.Decrement(ref m_waiters) == 0)
       return;

    // Other threads are blocked, wake 1 of them
    m_waiterLock.Set();      // Bad performance hit here
  }

  public void Dispose() { m_waiterLock.Dispose(); }
}
```

As you can see, adding extra behavior to the lock increases the number of fields it has, which increases its memory consumption. The code is also more complex, and this code must execute, which decreases the lock's performance. In Chapter 28's "Event Constructs" section, I compared the performance of incrementing an **Int32** without any locking, with a primitive user-mode construct, and with a kernel-mode construct. I repeat the results of those performance tests here and I include the results of using the **SimpleHybridlock** and the **AnotherHybridLock**. The results are in fastest to slowest order:

```
Incrementing x: 8                               Fastest
Incrementing x in M: 50                         6x slower
Incrementing x in SimpleSpinLock: 210           26x slower
Incrementing x in SimpleHybridLock: 211         26x slower (similar to SimpleSpinLock)
Incrementing x in AnotherHybridLock: 415        52x slower (due to ownership/recursion)
Incrementing x in SimpleWaitLock: 17,615        2,201x slower
```

It is worth noting that the **AnotherHybridLock** takes twice as much time as the **SimpleHybridLock**. This is due to the additional logic and error checking required managing the thread ownership and recursion behaviors. As you see, every behavior added to a lock impacts its performance.

A Potpourri of Hybrid Constructs

The FCL ships with many hybrid constructs that use fancy logic to keep your threads in user mode, improving your application's performance. Some of these hybrid constructs also avoid creating the kernel-mode construct until the first time threads contend on the construct. If threads never contend on the construct, then your application avoids the performance of creating the object and also avoids allocating memory for the object. A number of the constructs also support the use of a **CancellationToken** (discussed in Chapter 26, "Compute-

Bound Asynchronous Operations") so that a thread can forcibly unblock other threads that might be waiting on the construct. In this section, I introduce you to these hybrid constructs.

The `ManualResetEventSlim` and `SemaphoreSlim` Classes

The first two hybrid constructs are `System.Threading.ManualResetEventSlim` and `System.Threading.SemaphoreSlim`.[2] These constructs work exactly like their kernel-mode counterparts except that both employ spinning in user mode and they both defer creating the kernel-mode construct until the first time contention occurs. Their `Wait` methods allow you to pass a timeout and a `CancellationToken`. Here is what these classes look like (some method overloads are not shown):

```
public class ManualResetEventSlim : IDisposable {
    public ManualResetEventSlim(Boolean initialState, Int32 spinCount);
    public void Dispose();
    public void Reset();
    public void Set();
    public Boolean Wait(Int32 millisecondsTimeout, CancellationToken cancellationToken);

    public Boolean IsSet { get; }
    public Int32 SpinCount { get; }
    public WaitHandle WaitHandle { get; }
}
public class SemaphoreSlim : IDisposable {
    public SemaphoreSlim(Int32 initialCount, Int32 maxCount);
    public void Dispose();
    public Int32 Release(Int32 releaseCount);
    public Boolean Wait(Int32 millisecondsTimeout, CancellationToken cancellationToken);

    public Int32 CurrentCount { get; }
    public WaitHandle AvailableWaitHandle { get; }
}
```

The `Monitor` Class and Sync Blocks

Probably the most-used hybrid thread synchronization construct is the `Monitor` class, which provides a mutual-exclusive lock supporting spinning, thread ownership, and recursion. This is the most-used construct because it has been around the longest, C# has a built-in keyword to support it, the just-in-time (JIT) compiler has built-in knowledge of it, and the common language runtime (CLR) itself uses it on your application's behalf. However, as you'll see, there are many problems with this construct, making it easy to produce buggy code. I'll start by explaining the construct, and then I'll show the problems and some ways to work around these problems.

---

[2] While there is no **AutoResetEventSlim** class, in many situations you can construct a **SemaphoreSlim** object with a **maxCount** of **1**.

Every object on the heap can have a data structure, called a *sync block*, associated with it. A sync block contains fields similar to that of the **AnotherHybridLock** class that appeared earlier in this chapter. Specifically, it has fields for a kernel object, the owning thread's ID, a recursion count, and a waiting threads count. The **Monitor** class is a **static** class whose methods accept a reference to any heap object, and these methods manipulate the fields in the specified object's sync block. Here is what the most commonly used methods of the **Monitor** class look like:

```
public static class Monitor {
   public static void Enter(Object obj);
   public static void Exit(Object obj);

   // You can also specify a timeout when entered the lock (not commonly used):
   public static Boolean TryEnter(Object obj, Int32 millisecondsTimeout);

   // I'll discuss the lockTaken argument later
   public static void Enter(Object obj, ref Boolean lockTaken);
   public static void TryEnter(Object obj, Int32 millisecondsTimeout,
      ref Boolean lockTaken);
}
```

Now obviously, associating a sync block data structure with every object in the heap is quite wasteful, especially since most objects' sync blocks are never used. To reduce memory usage, the CLR team uses a more efficient way to offer the functionality just described. Here's how it works: When the CLR initializes, it allocates an array of sync blocks. As discussed elsewhere in this book, whenever an object is created in the heap, it gets two additional overhead fields associated with it. The first overhead field, the type object pointer, contains the memory address of the type's type object. The second overhead field, the *sync block index*, contains an integer index into the array of sync blocks.

When an object is constructed, the object's sync block index is initialized to -1, which indicates that it doesn't refer to any sync block. Then, when **Monitor.Enter** is called, the CLR finds a free sync block in the array and sets the object's sync block index to refer to the sync block that was found. In other words, sync blocks are associated with an object on the fly. When **Exit** is called, it checks to see if there are any more threads waiting to use the object's sync block. If there are no threads waiting for it, the sync block is free, **Exit** sets the object's sync block index back to -1, and the free sync block can be associated with another object in the future.

Figure 29-1 shows the relationship between objects in the heap, their sync block indexes, and elements in the CLR's sync block array. Object-A, Object-B, and Object-C all have their type object pointer member set to refer to Type-T (a type object). This means that all three objects are of the same type. As discussed in Chapter 4, "Type Fundamentals," a type object is also an object in the heap, and like all other objects, a type object has the two overhead members: a sync block index and a type object pointer. This means that a sync block can be associated with a type object and a reference to a type object can be passed to **Monitor**'s methods. By the way, the sync block array is able to create more sync blocks if necessary, so you shouldn't worry about the system running out of sync blocks if many objects are being synchronized simultaneously.

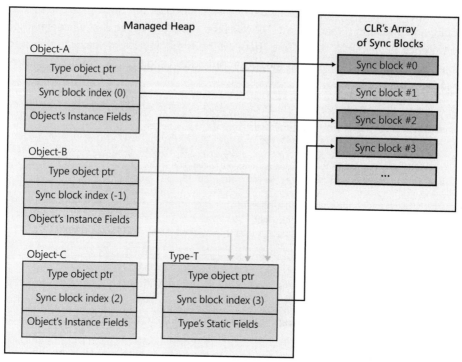

FIGURE 29-1 Objects in the heap (including type objects) can have their sync block indexes refer to an entry in the CLR's sync block array

Here is some code that demonstrates how the **Monitor** class was originally intended to be used:

```
internal sealed class Transaction {
    private DateTime m_timeOfLastTrans;

    public void PerformTransaction() {
        Monitor.Enter(this);
        // This code has exclusive access to the data...
        m_timeOfLastTrans = DateTime.Now;
        Monitor.Exit(this);
    }

    public DateTime LastTransaction {
        get {
            Monitor.Enter(this);
            // This code has shared access to the data...
            DateTime temp = m_timeOfLastTrans;
            Monitor.Exit(this);
            return temp;
        }
    }
}
```

On the surface, this seems simple enough, but there is something wrong with this code. The problem is that each object's sync block index is implicitly public. The code below demonstrates the impact of this.

```
public static void SomeMethod() {
    var t = new Transaction();
    Monitor.Enter(t); // This thread takes the object's public lock

    // Have a thread pool thread display the LastTransaction time
    // NOTE: The thread pool thread blocks until SomeMethod calls Monitor.Exit!
    ThreadPool.QueueUserWorkItem(o => Console.WriteLine(t.LastTransaction));

    // Execute some other code here...
    Monitor.Exit(t);
}
```

In this code, the thread executing **SomeMethod** calls **Monitor.Enter**, taking the **Transaction** object's publicly exposed lock. When the thread pool thread queries the **LastTransaction** property, this property also calls **Monitor.Enter** to acquire the same lock, causing the thread pool thread to block until the thread executing **SomeMethod** calls **Monitor.Exit**. Using a debugger, you can determine that the thread pool thread is blocked inside the **LastTransaction** property, but it is very hard to determine which other thread has the lock. If you do somehow figure out which thread has the lock, then you have to figure out what code caused it to take the lock. This is very difficult, and even worse, if you do figure it out, then the code might not be code that you have control over and you might not be able to modify this code to fix the problem. Therefore, my suggestion to you is to always use a private lock instead. Here's how I'd fix the **Transaction** class:

```
internal sealed class Transaction {
    private readonly Object m_lock = new Object(); // Each transaction has a PRIVATE lock now
    private DateTime m_timeOfLastTrans;

    public void PerformTransaction() {
        Monitor.Enter(m_lock);      // Enter the private lock
        // This code has exclusive access to the data...
        m_timeOfLastTrans = DateTime.Now;
        Monitor.Exit(m_lock);       // Exit the private lock
    }

    public DateTime LastTransaction {
        get {
            Monitor.Enter(m_lock);  // Enter the private lock
            // This code has shared access to the data...
            DateTime temp = m_timeOfLastTrans;
            Monitor.Exit(m_lock);   // Exit the private lock
            return temp;
        }
    }
}
```

If **Transaction**'s members were **static**, then simply make the **m_lock** field **static**, too, and now the **static** members are thread safe.

It should be clear from this discussion that **Monitor** should not have been implemented as a **static** class; it should have been implemented like all the other constructs: a class you instantiate and call instance methods on. In fact, **Monitor** has many other problems associated with it that are all because it is a **static** class. Here is a list of additional problems:

- A variable can refer to a proxy object if the type of object it refers to is derived from the **System.MarshalByRefObject** class (discussed in Chapter 22, "CLR Hosting and AppDomains"). When you call **Monitor**'s methods, passing a reference to a proxy object, you are locking the proxy object, not the actual object that the proxy refers to.

- If a thread calls **Monitor.Enter**, passing it a reference to a type object that has been loaded domain neutral (discussed in Chapter 22), the thread is taking a lock on that type across all AppDomains in the process. This is a known bug in the CLR that violates the isolation that AppDomains are supposed to provide. The bug is difficult to fix in a high-performance way, so it never gets fixed. The recommendation is to never pass a reference to a type object into **Monitor**'s methods.

- Because strings can be interned (as discussed in Chapter 14, "Chars, Strings, and Working with Text"), two completely separate pieces of code could unknowingly get references to a single **String** object in memory. If they pass the reference to the **String** object into **Monitor**'s methods, then the two separate pieces of code are now synchronizing their execution with each other unknowingly.

- When passing a string across an AppDomain boundary, the CLR does not make a copy of the string; instead, it simply passes a reference to the string into the other AppDomain. This improves performance, and in theory, it should be OK since **String** objects are immutable. However, like all objects, **String** objects have a sync block index associated with them, which is mutable, and this allows threads in different AppDomains to synchronize with each other unknowingly. This is another bug in CLR's AppDomain isolation story. The recommendation is never to pass **String** references to **Monitor**'s methods.

- Since **Monitor**'s methods take an **Object**, passing a value type causes the value type to get boxed, resulting in the thread taking a lock on the boxed object. Each time **Monitor.Enter** is called, a lock is taken on a completely different object and you get no thread synchronization at all.

- Applying the **[MethodImpl(MethodImplOptions.Synchronized)]** attribute to a method causes the JIT compiler to surround the method's native code with calls to **Monitor.Enter** and **Monitor.Exit**. If the method is an instance method, then **this** is passed to these methods, locking the implicitly public lock. If the method is static, then a reference to the type's type object is passed to these methods, potentially locking a domain-neutral type. The recommendation is to never use this attribute.

- When calling a type's type constructor (discussed in Chapter 8, "Methods"), the CLR takes a lock on the type's type object to ensure that only one thread initializes the type object and its static fields. Again, this type could be loaded domain neutral, causing a problem. For example, if the type constructor's code enters an infinite loop, then the type is unusable by all AppDomains in the process. The recommendation here is to avoid type constructors as much as possible or least keep them short and simple.

Unfortunately, the story gets worse. Since it is so common for developers to take a lock, do some work, and then release the lock within a single method, the C# language offers simplified syntax via its **lock** keyword. Suppose that you write a method like this:

```
private void SomeMethod() {
    lock (this) {
        // This code has exclusive access to the data...
    }
}
```

It is equivalent to having written the method like this:

```
private void SomeMethod() {
    Boolean lockTaken = false;
    try {
        //
        Monitor.Enter(this, ref lockTaken);
        // This code has exclusive access to the data...
    }
    finally {
        if (lockTaken) Monitor.Exit(this);
    }
}
```

The first problem here is that the C# team felt that they were doing you a favor by calling **Monitor.Exit** in a **finally** block. Their thinking was that this ensures that the lock is always released no matter what happens inside the **try** block. However, this is not a good thing. If an exception occurs inside the **try** block while changing state, then the state is now corrupted. When the lock is exited in the **finally** block, another thread will now start manipulating the corrupted state. It is better to have your application hang than it is to continue running with a corrupted state and potential security holes. The second problem is that entering and leaving a **try** block decreases the performance of the method. And some JIT compilers won't inline a method that contains a **try** block in it, decreasing performance even more. So now we have slower code that lets threads access corrupted state.[3] The recommendation is not to use C#'s **lock** statement.

Now we get to the **Boolean lockTaken** variable. Here is the problem that this variable is trying to solve. Let's say that a thread enters the **try** block and before calling **Monitor.Enter**,

---

[3]   By the way, while still a performance hit, it is safe to release a lock in a **finally** block if the code in the **try** block reads the state without attempting to modify it.

the thread is aborted (as discussed in Chapter 22). Now the **finally** block is called, but its code should not exit the lock. The **lockTaken** variable solves this problem. It is initialized to **false**, which assumes that the lock has not been entered into. Then, if **Monitor.Enter** is called and successfully takes the lock, it sets **lockTaken** to **true**. The **finally** block examines **lockTaken** to know whether to call **Monitor.Exit** or not.[4] By the way, the **SpinLock** structure also supports this **lockTaken** pattern.

The ReaderWriterLockSlim Class

It is common to have threads simply read the contents of some data. If this data is protected by a mutual exclusive lock (like the **SimpleSpinLock**, **SimpleWaitLock**, **SimpleHybridLock**, **AnotherHybridLock**, **Mutex**, or **Monitor**), then if multiple threads attempt this access concurrently, only one thread gets to run and all the other threads are blocked, which can reduce scalability and throughput in your application substantially. However, if all the threads want to access the data in a read-only fashion, then there is no need to block them at all; they should all be able to access the data concurrently. On the other hand, if a thread wants to modify the data, then this thread needs exclusive access to the data. The **ReaderWriterLockSlim** construct encapsulates the logic to solve this problem. Specifically, the construct controls threads like this:

- When one thread is writing to the data, all other threads requesting access are blocked.

- When one thread is reading from the data, other threads requesting read access are allowed to continue executing, but threads requesting write access are blocked.

- When a thread writing to the data has completed, either a single writer thread is unblocked so it can access the data or all the reader threads are unblocked so that all of them can access the data concurrently. If no threads are blocked, then the lock is free and available for the next reader or writer thread that wants it.

- When all threads reading from the data have completed, a single writer thread is unblocked so it can access the data. If no threads are blocked, then the lock is free and available for the next reader or writer thread that wants it.

Here is what this class looks like (some method overloads are not shown):

```
public class ReaderWriterLockSlim : IDisposable {
   public ReaderWriterLockSlim(LockRecursionPolicy recursionPolicy);
   public void Dispose();

   public void    EnterReadLock();
   public Boolean TryEnterReadLock(Int32 millisecondsTimeout);
   public void    ExitReadLock();
```

---

[4] The **try/finally** blocks and the **lockTaken** variable are potentially useful if what you're passing to **Monitor**'s methods is a reference to a domain-agile object, like a **String**, or a domain-neutral type object. Sure, state in one AppDomain might get corrupted, but threads in other AppDomains will be allowed to keep running.

```
    public void    EnterWriteLock();
    public Boolean TryEnterWriteLock(Int32 millisecondsTimeout);
    public void    ExitWriteLock();

    // Most applications will never query any of these properties
    public Boolean IsReadLockHeld              { get; }
    public Boolean IsWriteLockHeld             { get; }
    public Int32   CurrentReadCount            { get; }
    public Int32   RecursiveReadCount          { get; }
    public Int32   RecursiveWriteCount         { get; }
    public Int32   WaitingReadCount            { get; }
    public Int32   WaitingWriteCount           { get; }
    public LockRecursionPolicy RecursionPolicy { get; }
    // Members related to upgrading from a reader to a writer not shown
}
```

Here is some code that demonstrates the use of this construct:

```
internal sealed class Transaction : IDisposable {
    private readonly ReaderWriterLockSlim m_lock =
        new ReaderWriterLockSlim(LockRecursionPolicy.NoRecursion);
    private DateTime m_timeOfLastTrans;

    public void PerformTransaction() {
        m_lock.EnterWriteLock();
        // This code has exclusive access to the data...
        m_timeOfLastTrans = DateTime.Now;
        m_lock.ExitWriteLock();
    }

    public DateTime LastTransaction {
        get {
            m_lock.EnterReadLock();
            // This code has shared access to the data...
            DateTime temp = m_timeOfLastTrans;
            m_lock.ExitReadLock();
            return temp;
        }
    }

    public void Dispose() { m_lock.Dispose(); }
}
```

There are a few concepts related to this construct that deserve special mention. First, **ReaderWriterLockSlim**'s constructor allows you to pass in a **LockRecurionsPolicy** flag, which is defined as follows:

```
public enum LockRecursionPolicy { NoRecursion, SupportsRecursion }
```

If you pass the **SupportsRecursion** flag, then the lock will add thread ownership and recursion behaviors to the lock. As discussed earlier in this chapter, these behaviors negatively affect the lock's performance, so I recommend that you always pass **LockRecursionPolicy. NoRecursion** to the constructor (as I've done). For a reader-writer lock, supporting thread ownership and recursion is phenomenally expensive because the lock must keep track of all the reader threads that it has let into the lock and keep a separate recursion count for each reader thread. In fact, to maintain all this information in a thread-safe way, the **ReaderWriterLockSlim** internally uses a mutually exclusive spinlock! No, I'm not kidding.

The **ReaderWriterLockSlim** class offers additional methods (not shown earlier) that allow a reading thread to upgrade itself to a writer thread. Later, the thread can downgrade itself back to a reader thread. The thinking here is that a thread could start reading the data and based on the data's contents, the thread might want to modify the data. To do this, the thread would upgrade itself from a reader to a writer. Having the lock support this behavior deteriorates the lock's performance, and I don't think that this is a useful feature at all. Here's why: A thread can't just turn itself from a reader into a writer. Other threads may be reading, too, and these threads will have to exit the lock completely before the thread trying to up-grade is allowed to become a writer. This is the same as having the reader thread exit the lock and then immediately acquire it for writing.

> **Note** The FCL also ships a **ReaderWriterLock** construct, which was introduced in the Microsoft .NET Framework version 1.0. This construct had so many problems that Microsoft introduced the **ReaderWriterLockSlim** construct in .NET Framework version 2.0. The team didn't improve the **ReaderWriterLock** construct for fear of losing compatibility with applications that were using it. Here are the problems with the **ReaderWriterLock**. Even without thread contention, it is very slow. There is no way to opt out of the thread ownership and recursion behaviors, making the lock even slower. It favors reader threads over writer threads, and therefore writer threads can get queued up and are rarely serviced, resulting in denial of service problems.

The OneManyLock Class

I have created my own reader-writer construct that is faster than the FCL's **ReaderWriterLockSlim** class.[5] My class is called **OneManyLock** because it allows access to either one writer thread or many reader threads. The class basically looks like this:

```
public sealed class OneManyLock : IDisposable {
    public OneManyLock();
    public void Dispose();

    public void Enter(Boolean exclusive);
    public void Leave();
}
```

Now I'd like to give you a sense of how it works. Internally, the class has an **Int32** field for the state of the lock, a **Semaphore** object that reader threads block on, and an **AutoResetEvent**

---

[5] The code is inside the Ch29-1-HybridThreadSync.cs file that is part of the code that accompanies this book. You can download this code from *http://Wintellect.com/*.

object that writer threads block on. The **Int32** state field is divided into five subfields as follows:

- Three bits (a number from 0 to 7) represent the state of the lock itself. The possibilities are **0**=Free, **1**=OwnedByWriter, **2**=OwnedByReaders, **3**=OwnedByReadersAndWriterPending, and **4**=ReservedForWriter. The values 5, 6, and 7 are unused.

- Nine bits (a number from 0 to 511) represent the number of reader threads reading (RR) that the lock has currently allowed in.

- Nine bits (a number from 0 to 511) represent the number of reader threads waiting (RW) to get into the lock. These threads block on the auto-reset event object.

- Nine bits (a number from 0 to 511) represent the number of writer threads waiting (WW) to get into the lock. These threads block on the other semaphore object.

- The two remaining bits are unused and always have a value of **0**.

Now, since all the information about the lock fits in a single **Int32** field, I can manipulate this field using the methods of the **Interlocked** class so the lock is incredibly fast and causes a thread to block only when there is contention.

Here's what happens when a thread enters the lock for shared access:

- If the lock is Free: Set state to OwnedByReaders, RR=1, Return

- If the lock is OwnedByReaders: RR++, Return

- Else: RW++, Block reader thread. When the thread wakes, loop around and try again.

Here's what happens when a thread that has shared access leaves the lock:

- RR--

- If RR > 0: Return

- If WW > 0: Set state to ReservedForWriter, WW--, Release 1 blocked writer thread, Return

- If RW==0 && WW = 0: Set state to Free , Return

Here's what happens when a thread enters the lock for exclusive access:

- If the lock is Free: Set state to OwnedByWriter, Return

- If the lock is ReservedForWriter: Set state to OwnedByWriter, Return

- If the lock is OwnedByWriter: WW++, Block writer thread. When thread wakes, loop around and try again.

- Else: Set state to OwnedByReadersAndWriterPending, WW++, Block writer thread. When thread wakes, loop around and try again.

Here's what happens when a thread that has exclusive access leaves the lock:

- If WW==0 && RW==0: Set state to Free, Return

- If WW > 0: Set state to ReservedForWriter, WW--, Release 1 blocked writer thread, Return

- If WW==0 && RW>0: Set state to Free , RW=0, Wake all reader blocked read threads, Return

Let's say that there is currently one thread reading from the lock and another thread wants to enter the lock for writing. The writer thread will first check to see if the lock is Free, and since it is not, the thread will advance to perform the next check. However, at this point, the reader thread could leave the lock, and seeing that RR and WW are both 0, the thread could set the lock's state to Free. This is a problem because the writer thread has already performed this test and moved on. Basically what happened is that the reader thread changed the state that the writer thread was accessing behind its back. I needed to solve this problem so that the lock would function correctly.

To solve the problem, all of these bit manipulations are performed using the technique I showed in the "The Interlocked Anything Pattern" section from Chapter 28. If you recall, this pattern lets you turn any operation into a thread-safe atomic operation. This is what allows this lock to be so fast and have less state in it than other reader-writer locks. When I run performance tests comparing my **OneManyLock** against the FCL's **ReaderWriterLockSlim** and **ReaderWriterLock** classes I get the following results:

```
Incrementing x in OneManyLock: 406              Fastest
Incrementing x in ReaderWriterLockSlim: 999     ~2.5x slower
Incrementing x in ReaderWriterLock: 2,051       ~5.0x slower
```

Of course, since all reader-writer locks perform more logic than a mutually exclusive lock, their performance can be slightly worse. However, you have to weigh this against the fact that a reader-writer lock allows multiple readers into the lock simultaneously.

Before leaving this section, I'll also mention that my Power Threading library (download-able for free from *http://Wintellect.com/*) offers a slightly different version of this lock, called **OneManyResourceLock**. This lock and others in the library offer many additional features such as deadlock detection, the ability to turn on lock ownership and recursion (albeit at a performance cost), a unified programming model for all locks, and the ability to observe the runtime behavior of the locks. For observing behavior, you can see the maximum amount of time that a thread ever waited to acquire a lock and you can see the minimum and maximum amount of time that a lock was held.

The CountdownEvent Class

The next construct is **System.Threading.CountdownEvent**. Internally, this construct uses
a **ManualResetEventSlim** object. This construct blocks a thread until its internal counter
reaches **0**. In a way, this construct's behavior is the opposite of that of a **Semaphore** (which
blocks threads while its count is **0**). Here is what this class looks like (some method overloads
are not shown):

```
public class CountdownEvent : IDisposable {
   public CountdownEvent(Int32 initialCount);
   public void Dispose();
   public void Reset(Int32 count);              // Set CurrentCount to count
   public void AddCount(Int32 signalCount);     // Increments CurrentCount by signalCount
   public Boolean TryAddCount(Int32 signalCount); // Increments CurrentCount by signalCount
   public Boolean Signal(Int32 signalCount);    // Decrements CurrentCount by signameCount
   public Boolean Wait(Int32 millisecondsTimeout, CancellationToken cancellationToken);

   public Int32     CurrentCount { get; }
   public Boolean   IsSet        { get; }       // true if CurrentCount is 0
   public WaitHandle WaitHandle  { get; }
}
```

Once a **CountdownEvent**'s **CurrentCount** reaches **0**, it cannot be changed. The **AddCount**
method throws **InvalidOperationException** when **CurrentCount** is **0**, while the
TryAddCount method simply returns **false** if **CurrentCount** is **0**.

The Barrier Class

The **System.Threading.Barrier** construct is designed to solve a very rare problem, so it
is unlikely that you will have a use for it. **Barrier** is used to control a set of threads that are
working together in parallel so that they can step through phases of the algorithm together.
Perhaps an example is in order: When the CLR is using the server version of its garbage
collector, the GC algorithm creates one thread per core. These threads walk up different
application threads' stacks, concurrently marking objects in the heap. As each thread
completes its portion of the work, it must stop waiting for the other threads to complete
their portion of the work. After all threads have marked the objects, then the threads can
compact different portions of the heap concurrently. As each thread finishes compacting its
portion of the heap, the thread must block waiting for the other threads. After all the threads
have finished compacting their portion of the heap, then all the threads walk up the application's threads' stacks, fixing up roots to refer to the new location of the compacted object.
Only after all the threads have completed this work is the garbage collector considered
complete and the application's threads can be resumed.

This scenario is easily solved using the **Barrier** class, which looks like this (some method
overloads are not shown):

```
public class Barrier : IDisposable {
    public Barrier(Int32 participantCount, Action<Barrier> postPhaseAction);
    public void Dispose();
    public Int64 AddParticipants(Int32 participantCount);    // Adds participants
    public void RemoveParticipants(Int32 participantCount); // Subtracts participants
    public Boolean SignalAndWait(Int32 millisecondsTimeout, CancellationToken
      cancellationToken);

    public Int64 CurrentPhaseNumber     { get; }  // Indicates phase in process (starts at 0)
    public Int32 ParticipantCount       { get; }  // Number of participants
    public Int32 ParticipantsRemaining { get; }  // # of threads needing to call
      SignalAndWait
}
```

When you construct a **Barrier**, you tell it how many threads are participating in the work, and you can also pass an **Action<Barrier>** delegate referring to code that will be invoked whenever all participants complete a phase of the work. You can dynamically add and remove participating threads from the **Barrier** by calling the **AddParticipant** and **RemoveParticipant** methods but, in practice, this is rarely done. As each thread completes its phase of the work, it should call **SignalAndWait**, which tells the **Barrier** that the thread is done and the **Barrier** blocks the thread (using a **ManualResetEventSlim**). After all participants call **SignalAndWait**, the **Barrier** invokes the delegate (using the last thread that called **SignalAndWait**) and then unblocks all the waiting threads so they can begin the next phase.

Thread Synchronization Construct Summary

My recommendation always is to avoid writing code that blocks any threads. When performing asynchronous compute or I/O operations, hand the data off from thread to thread in such a way to avoid the chance that multiple threads could access the data simultaneously. I demonstrated this with the pipe server and client code shown in Chapter 27, "I/O-Bound Asynchronous Operations." If you are unable to fully accomplish this, then try to use the **VolatileRead**, **VolatileWrite**, and **Interlocked** methods because they are fast and they also never block a thread. Unfortunately, these methods manipulate only simple types, but you can perform rich operations on these types as described in the "The Interlocked Anything Pattern" section.

There are two main reasons why you would consider blocking threads:

- **The programming model is simplified.**   By blocking a thread, you are sacrificing some resources and performance so that you can write your application code sequentially without using callback methods.

- **A thread has a dedicated purpose.**   Some threads must be used for specific tasks. The best example is an application's primary thread. If an application's primary thread doesn't block, then it will eventually return and the whole process will terminate. Another example is an application's GUI thread or threads. Windows requires that a

window or control always be manipulated by the thread that created it, so we sometimes write code that blocks a GUI thread until some other operation is done and then
the GUI thread updates any windows and controls as needed. Of course, blocking the
GUI thread hangs the application and provides a bad end-user experience.

To avoid blocking threads, don't mentally assign a label to your threads. For example, don't
create a spell-checking thread, a grammar-checking thread, a thread that handles this particular client request, and so on. The moment you assign a label to a thread, you have also said
to yourself that that thread can't do anything else. But threads are too expensive a resource
to have them dedicated to a particular purpose. Instead, you should use the thread pool to
rent threads for short periods of time. So a thread pool thread starts out spell checking, then
it changes to grammar checking, and then it changes again to perform work on behalf of a
client request, and so on.

If, in spite of this discussion, you decide to block threads, then use the kernel object constructs
if you want to synchronize threads that are running in different AppDomains or processes.
To atomically manipulate state via a set of operations, use the **Monitor** class with a **private**
field.[6] Alternatively, you could use a reader-writer lock instead of **Monitor**. Reader-writer locks
are generally slower than **Monitor**, but they allow multiple reader threads to execute concurrently, which improves overall performance and minimizes the chance of blocking threads.

In addition, avoid using recursive locks (especially recursive reader-writer locks) because they
hurt performance. However, **Monitor** is recursive and its performance is very good.[7] Also,
avoid releasing a lock in a **finally** block because entering and leaving exception-handling
blocks incurs a performance hit, and if an exception is thrown while mutating state, then the
state is corrupted and other threads that manipulate it will experience unpredictable behavior
and security bugs.

Of course, if you do write code that holds a lock, your code should not hold the lock for a
long time because this increases the likelihood of threads blocking. In the "Using Collections
to Avoid Holding a Lock for a Long Time" section, I will show a technique that uses collection
classes as a way to avoid holding a lock for a long time.

Finally, for compute-bound work, you can use tasks (discussed in Chapter 26) to avoid a lot
of the thread synchronization constructs. In particular, I love that each task can have one or
more continue-with tasks associated with it that execute via some thread pool thread when
some operation completes. This is much better than having a thread block waiting for some
operation to complete. For I/O-bound work, the Asynchronous Programming Model (APM)
invokes your callback method when the I/O operation completes; this is similar to a task's
continue-with task.

---

[6] You could use a **SpinLock** instead of **Monitor** because **SpinLock**s are slightly faster. But a **SpinLock** is potentially
dangerous because it can waste CPU time and, in my opinion, it is not sufficiently faster than **Monitor** to justify its
use.

[7] This is partially because **Monitor** is actually implemented in native code, not managed code.

The Famous Double-Check Locking Technique

There is a famous technique called *double-check locking,* which is used by developers who want to defer constructing a singleton object until an application requests it (sometimes called *lazy initialization*). If the application never requests the object, it never gets constructed, saving time and memory. A potential problem occurs when multiple threads request the singleton object simultaneously. In this case, some form of thread synchronization must be used to ensure that the singleton object gets constructed just once.

This technique is not famous because it is particularly interesting or useful. It is famous because there has been much written about it. This technique was used heavily in Java, and later it was discovered that Java couldn't guarantee that it would work everywhere. The famous document that describes the problem can be found on this Web page: *www.cs.umd.edu/~pugh/java/memoryModel/DoubleCheckedLocking.html.*

Anyway, you'll be happy to know that the CLR supports the double-check locking technique just fine because of its memory model and volatile field access (described in Chapter 28). Here is code that demonstrates how to implement the double-check locking technique in C#:

```
internal sealed class Singleton {
   // s_lock is required for thread safety and having this object assumes that creating
   // the singleton object is more expensive than creating a System.Object object and that
   // creating the singleton object may not be necessary at all. Otherwise, it is more
   // efficient and easier to just create the singleton object in a class constructor
   private static readonly Object s_lock = new Object();

   // This field will refer to the one Singleton object
   private static Singleton s_value = null;

   // Private constructor prevents any code outside this class from creating an instance
   private Singleton() {
      // Code to initialize the one Singleton object goes here...
   }

   // Public, static method that returns the Singleton object (creating it if necessary)
   public static Singleton GetSingleton() {
      // If the Singleton was already created, just return it (this is fast)
      if (s_value != null) return s_value;

      Monitor.Enter(s_lock);  // Not created, let 1 thread create it
      if (s_value == null) {
         // Still not created, create it
         Singleton temp = new Singleton();

         // Save the reference in s_value (see discussion for details)
         Interlocked.Exchange(ref s_value, temp);
      }
      Monitor.Exit(s_lock);

      // Return a reference to the one Singleton object
      return s_value;
   }
}
```

The idea behind the double-check locking technique is that a call to the **GetSingleton** method quickly checks the **s_value** field to see if the object has already been created, and if it has, the method returns a reference to it. The beautiful thing here is that no thread synchronization is required once the object has been constructed; the application will run very fast. On the other hand, if the first thread that calls the **GetSingleton** method sees that the object hasn't been created, it takes a thread synchronization lock to ensure that only one thread constructs the single object. This means that a performance hit occurs only the first time a thread queries the singleton object.

Now, let me explain why this pattern didn't work in Java. The Java Virtual Machine read the value of **s_value** into a CPU register at the beginning of the **GetSingleton** method and then just queried the register when evaluating the second **if** statement, causing the second **if** statement to always evaluate to **true**, and multiple threads ended up creating **Singleton** objects. Of course, this happened only if multiple threads called **GetSingleton** at the exact same time, which in most applications is very unlikely. This is why it went undetected in Java for so long.

In the CLR, calling any lock method is a full memory fence, and any variable writes you have before the fence must complete before the fence and any variable reads after the fence must start after it. For the **GetSingleton** method, this means that the **s_value** field must be reread after the call to **Monitor.Enter**; it cannot be cached in a register across this method call.

Inside **GetSingleton**, you see the call to **Interlocked.Exchange**. Here's the problem that this is solving. Let's say that what you had inside the second **if** statement was the following line of code:

```
s_value = new Singleton();   // This is what you'd ideally like to write
```

You would expect the compiler to produce code that allocates the memory for a **Singleton**, calls the constructor to initialize the fields, and then assigns the reference into the **s_value** field. Making a value visible to other threads is called *publishing*. But the compiler could do this instead: allocate memory for the **Singleton**, publish (assign) the reference into **s_value**, and then call the constructor. From a single thread's perspective, changing the order like this has no impact. But what if, after publishing the reference into **s_value** and before calling the constructor, another thread calls the **GetSingleton** method? This thread will see that **s_value** is not **null** and start to use the **Singleton** object, but its constructor has not finished executing yet! This can be a very hard bug to track down, especially since it is all due to timing.

The call to **Interlocked.Exchange** fixes this problem. It ensures that the reference in **temp** can be published into **s_value** only after the constructor has finished executing. Another way to solve this problem would be to mark the **s_value** field with C#'s **volatile** keyword. This makes the write to **s_value** volatile, and again, the constructor has to finish running before the write can happen. Unfortunately, this makes all reads volatile, too, and since there is no need for this, you are hurting your performance with no benefit.

In the beginning of this section, I mentioned that the double-check locking technique is not that interesting. In my opinion, developers think it is cool, and they use it far more often than they should. In most scenarios, this technique actually hurts efficiency. Here is a much simpler version of the **Singleton** class that behaves the same as the previous version. This version does not use the double-check locking technique:

```
internal sealed class Singleton {
    private static Singleton s_value = new Singleton();

    // Private constructor prevents any code outside this class from creating an instance
    private Singleton() {
        // Code to initialize the one Singleton object goes here...
    }

    // Public, static method that returns the Singleton object (creating it if necessary)
    public static Singleton GetSingleton() { return s_value; }
}
```

Since the CLR automatically calls a type's class constructor the first time code attempts to access a member of the class, the first time a thread queries **Singleton**'s **GetSingleton** method, the CLR will automatically call the class constructor, which creates an instance of the object. Furthermore, the CLR already ensures that calls to a class constructor are thread safe. I explained all of this in Chapter 8. The one downside of this approach is that the type constructor is called when any member of a class is first accessed. If the **Singleton** type defined some other static members, then the **Singleton** object would be created when any one of them was accessed. Some people work around this problem by defining nested classes.

Let me show you a third way of producing a single **Singleton** object:

```
internal sealed class Singleton {
    private static Singleton s_value = null;

    // Private constructor prevents any code outside this class from creating an instance
    private Singleton() {
        // Code to initialize the one Singleton object goes here...
    }

    // Public, static method that returns the Singleton object (creating it if necessary)
    public static Singleton GetSingleton() {
        if (s_value != null) return s_value;

        // Create a new Singleton and root it if another thread didn't do it first
        Singleton temp = new Singleton();
        Interlocked.CompareExchange(ref s_value, temp, null);

        // If this thread lost, then the second Singleton object gets GC'd

        return s_value; // Return reference to the single object
    }
}
```

If multiple threads call **GetSingleton** simultaneously, then this version might create two (or more) **Singleton** objects. However, the call to **Interlocked.CompareExchange** ensures that only one of the references is ever published into the **s_value** field. Any object not rooted by this field will be garbage collected later on. Since, in most applications, it is unlikely that multiple threads will call **GetSingleton** at the same time, it is unlikely that more than one **Singleton** object will ever be created.

Now it might upset you that multiple **Singleton** objects could be created, but there are many benefits to this code. First, it is very fast. Second, it never blocks a thread; if a thread pool thread is blocked on a **Monitor** or any other kernel-mode thread synchronization construct, then the thread pool creates another thread to keep the CPUs saturated with work. So now, another megabyte or more of memory is allocated and initialized and all the DLLs get a thread attach notification. With **CompareExchange**, this can never happen. Of course, you can use this technique only when the constructor has no side effects.

The FCL offers two types that encapsulate the patterns described in this section. The generic **System.Lazy** class looks like this (some methods are not shown):

```
public class Lazy<T> {
    public Lazy(Func<T> valueFactory, LazyThreadSafetyMode mode);
    public Boolean IsValueCreated { get; }
    public T Value { get; }
}
```

This code demonstrates how it works:

```
public static void Main() {
    // Create a lazy-initialization wrapper around getting the DateTime
    Lazy<String> s = new Lazy<String>(
        () => DateTime.Now.ToLongTimeString(),
        LazyThreadSafetyMode.PublicationOnly);

    Console.WriteLine(s.IsValueCreated);   // Returns false since Value not queried yet
    Console.WriteLine(s.Value);            // The delegate is invoked now
    Console.WriteLine(s.IsValueCreated);   // Returns true since Value was queried
    Thread.Sleep(10000);                   // Wait 10 seconds and display the time again
    Console.WriteLine(s.Value);            // The delegate is NOT invoked now; same result
}
```

When I run this, I get the following output:

```
False
2:40:42 PM
True
2:40:42 PM     ← Notice that the time did not change 10 seconds later
```

The code above constructed an instance of the **Lazy** class and passed one of the **LazyThreadSafetyMode** flags into it. Here is what these flags look like and what they mean:

```
public enum LazyThreadSafetyMode {
    None,                          // No thread-safety support at all (good for GUI apps)
    ExecutionAndPublication        // Uses the double-check locking technique
    PublicationOnly,               // Uses the Interlocked.CompareExchange technique
}
```

In some memory-constrained scenarios, you might not even want to create an instance of the **Lazy** class. Instead, you can call static methods of the **System.Threading.LazyInitializer** class. The class looks like this:

```
public static class LazyInitializer {
    // These two methods use Interlocked.CompareExchange internally:
    public static T EnsureInitialized<T>(ref T target) where T: class;
    public static T EnsureInitialized<T>(ref T target, Func<T> valueFactory) where T: class;

    // These two methods pass the syncLock to Monitor's Enter and Exit methods internally
    public static T EnsureInitialized<T>(ref T target, ref Boolean initialized,
        ref Object syncLock);
    public static T EnsureInitialized<T>(ref T target, ref Boolean initialized,
        ref Object syncLock, Func<T> valueFactory);
}
```

Also, being able to explicitly specify a synchronization object to the **EnsureInitialized** method's **syncLock** parameter allows multiple initialization functions and fields to be protected by the same lock.

Here is an example using a method from this class:

```
public static void Main() {
    String name = null;
    // Since name is null, the delegate runs and initializes name
    LazyInitializer.EnsureInitialized(ref name, () => "Jeffrey");
    Console.WriteLine(name);    // Displays "Jeffrey"

    // Since name is not null, the delegate does not run; name doesn't change
    LazyInitializer.EnsureInitialized(ref name, () => "Richter");
    Console.WriteLine(name);    // Also displays "Jeffrey"
}
```

The Condition Variable Pattern

Let's say that a thread wants to execute some code when a complex condition is true. One option would be to let the thread spin continuously, repeatedly testing the condition. But this wastes CPU time, and it is also not possible to atomically test multiple variables that are making up the complex condition. Fortunately, there is a pattern that allows threads to efficiently synchronize their operations based on a complex condition. This pattern is called the *condition variable pattern,* and we use it via the following methods defined inside the **Monitor** class:

```
public static class Monitor {
   public static Boolean Wait(Object obj);
   public static Boolean Wait(Object obj, Int32 millisecondsTimeout);

   public static void Pulse(Object obj);
   public static void PulseAll(Object obj);
}
```

Here is what the pattern looks like:

```
internal sealed class ConditionVariablePattern {
   private readonly Object m_lock = new Object();
   private Boolean m_condition = false;

   public void Thread1() {
      Monitor.Enter(m_lock);          // Acquire a mutual-exclusive lock

      // While under the lock, test the complex condition "atomically"
      while (!m_condition) {
         // If condition is not met, wait for another thread to change the condition
         Monitor.Wait(m_lock);        // Temporarily release lock so other threads can get it
      }

      // The condition was met, process the data...

      Monitor.Exit(m_lock);           // Permanently release lock
   }

   public void Thread2() {
      Monitor.Enter(m_lock);          // Acquire a mutual-exclusive lock

      // Process data and modify the condition...
      m_condition = true;

      // Monitor.Pulse(m_lock);       // Wakes one waiter AFTER lock is released
      Monitor.PulseAll(m_lock);       // Wakes all waiters AFTER lock is released

      Monitor.Exit(m_lock);           // Release lock
   }
}
```

In this code, the thread executing the **Thread1** method enters a mutual-exclusive lock and
then tests a condition. Here, I am just checking a **Boolean** field, but this condition can be
arbitrarily complex. For example, you could check to see if it is a Tuesday in March and if a
certain collection object has 10 elements in it. If the condition is false, then you want the
thread to spin on the condition, but spinning wastes CPU time, so instead, the thread calls
Wait. **Wait** releases the lock so that another thread can get it and blocks the calling thread.

The **Thread2** method shows code that the second thread executes. It calls **Enter** to take
ownership of the lock, processes some data, which results in changing the state of the
condition, and then calls **Pulse(All)**, which will unblock a thread from its **Wait** call. **Pulse**
unblocks the longest waiting thread (if any), while **PulseAll** unblocks all waiting threads

(if any). However, any unblocked threads don't wake up yet. The thread executing **Thread2** must call **Monitor.Exit**, allowing the lock to be owned by another thread. Also, if **PulseAll** is called, the other threads do not unblock simultaneously. When a thread that called **Wait** is unblocked, it becomes the owner of the lock, and since it is a mutual-exclusive lock, only one thread at a time can own it. Other threads can get it after an owning thread calls **Wait** or **Exit**.

When the thread executing **Thread1** wakes, it loops around and tests the condition again. If the condition is still false, then it calls **Wait** again. If the condition is true, then it processes the data as it likes and ultimately calls **Exit**, leaving the lock so other threads can get it. The nice thing about this pattern is that it is possible to test several variables making up a complex condition using simple synchronization logic (just one lock), and multiple waiting threads can all unblock without causing any logic failure, although the unblocking threads might waste some CPU time.

Here is an example of a thread-safe queue that can have multiple threads enqueuing and dequeuing items to it. Note that threads attempting to dequeue an item block until an item is available for them to process.

```
internal sealed class SynchronizedQueue<T> {
   private readonly Object m_lock = new Object();
   private readonly Queue<T> m_queue = new Queue<T>();

   public void Enqueue(T item) {
      Monitor.Enter(m_lock);

      // After enqueuing an item, wake up any/all waiters
      m_queue.Enqueue(item);
      Monitor.PulseAll(m_lock);

      Monitor.Exit(m_lock);
   }

   public T Dequeue() {
      Monitor.Enter(m_lock);

      // Loop while the queue is empty (the condition)
      while (m_queue.Count == 0)
         Monitor.Wait(m_queue);

      // Dequeue an item from the queue and return it for processing
      T item = m_queue.Dequeue();
      Monitor.Exit(m_lock);
      return item;
   }
}
```

Using Collections to Avoid Holding a Lock for a Long Time

I'm not terribly fond of any of the thread synchronization constructs that use kernel-mode primitives because all of these primitives exist to block a thread from running, and threads are just too expensive to create and not have them run. Here is an example that hopefully clarifies the problem.

Imagine a Web site into which clients make requests. When a client request arrives, a thread pool thread starts processing the client's request. Let's say that this client wants to modify some data in the server in a thread-safe way, so it acquires a reader-writer lock for writing. Let's pretend that this lock is held for a long time. As the lock is held, another client request comes in, so that thread pool creates a new thread for the client request and then the thread blocks trying to acquire the reader-writer lock for reading. In fact, as more and more client requests come in, the thread pool creates more and more threads and all these threads are just blocking themselves on the lock. The server is spending all its time creating threads so that they can stop running! This server does not scale well at all.

Then, to make matters worse, when the writer thread releases the lock, all the reader threads unblock simultaneously and get to run, but now there may be lots of threads trying to run on relatively few CPUs, so Windows is context switching between the threads constantly. The result is that the workload is not being processed as quickly as it could because of all the overhead associated with the context switches.

If you look over all the constructs shown in this chapter, many of the problems that these constructs are trying to solve can be much better accomplished using the **Task** class discussed in Chapter 26. Take the **Barrier** class, for example: You could spawn several **Task** objects to work on a phase and then, when all these tasks complete, you could continue with one or more other **Task** objects. Compared to many of the constructs shown in this chapter, tasks have many advantages:

- Tasks use much less memory than threads and they take much less time to create and destroy.
- The thread pool automatically scales the tasks across available CPUs.
- As each task completes a phase, the thread running that task goes back to the thread pool where it can do other work if any is available for it.
- The thread pool has a process-global view of tasks and, as such, it can better schedule these tasks, reducing the number of threads in the process and also reducing context switching.

Reader-writer locks are very popular and useful.[8] Trying to build one of these out of **Task** objects would be quite challenging. However, my Power Threading library includes a non-blocking read-writer class, which I call **ReaderWriterGate**. It looks like this (some methods are not shown):

```
public sealed class ReaderWriterGate : IDisposable {
   public ReaderWriterGate();
   public void Dispose();

   public IAsyncResult BeginRead(ReaderWriterGateCallback callback, Object state,
       AsyncCallback asyncCallback, Object asyncState);
   public Object EndRead(IAsyncResult result);

   public IAsyncResult BeginWrite(ReaderWriterGateCallback callback, Object state,
       AsyncCallback asyncCallback, Object asyncState);
   public Object EndWrite(IAsyncResult result);
}
```

The **ReaderWriterGateCallback** is a delegate that looks like this:

```
public delegate object ReaderWriterGateCallback(ReaderWriterGateReleaser releaser);
```

The **ReaderWriterGateReleaser** class looks like this (some methods are not shown):

```
public sealed class ReaderWriterGateReleaser : IDisposable {
   public Object State { get; }  // Returns the 'state' passed to BeginRead/BeginWrite
   public void Dispose();
}
```

The **ReaderWriterGate** makes a lock look just like an asynchronous I/O operation. In fact, my class even offers **BeginRead** and **BeginWrite** methods that take an **AsyncCallback** delegate and return an **IAsyncResult**, as well as **EndRead** and **EndWrite** methods that accept an **IAsyncResult**. I designed the class to work exactly like the APM that was discussed in Chapter 27.

Here's how it works. Put the code that requires read access to a resource in its own method and then call **BeginRead**, passing this method for the **ReaderWriterGetCallback** delegate parameter. When it is safe to read from the resource, the **ReaderWriterGate** object will have a thread pool thread invoke your method. Note that several thread pool threads could be executing methods that read from the resource concurrently. Put the code that requires write access to a resource in its own method and then call **BeginWrite**, passing this method for the **ReaderWriterGetCallback** delegate parameter. When it is safe to write to the resource, the **ReaderWriterGate** object will have a thread pool thread invoke your method. Note that the **ReaderWriterGate** object ensures that there will be only one thread pool thread executing a method that writes to the resource at a particular time.

---

[8] Of course, if you only need mutual-exclusive access to a resource, you can always use a reader-writer lock and request only write access to the resource it protects.

When your method finishes processing the resource and returns, the **ReaderWriterGate** object will invoke whatever method you passed to **BeginRead**'s or **BeginWrite**'s **asyncCallback** parameter; this is how you know when the operation completed.

So now, let's return to our Web server discussion. A client makes a request to write to a resource, so a thread pool thread calls **ReaderWriterGate**'s **BeginWrite** method. While the thread is processing the callback method, another client makes a request. The thread pool creates a new thread, and this thread calls **BeginRead**. The **ReaderWriterGate** object sees that reading is not allowed at this time and it adds the **callback** delegate to an internal queue. The queue is a collection class, and it needs to be manipulated in a thread-safe way, so a lock is taken around the manipulation of the collection. However, the lock is held only while items are being added and removed from the queue, which requires a very short amount of time. This means that other threads also using the **ReaderWriterGate** will not block for long (if at all)!

After the **callback** delegate has been added to the queue, the thread pool thread returns to the pool. As more client requests come in, the *same* thread pool thread keeps waking up and calling **BeginRead**, adding more and more delegates to the internal queue. So now the server has only two threads in it doing all the work.

When the first thread finishes writing to the resource, it returns from the callback method to the **ReaderWriterGate** object. The **ReaderWriterGate** sees that there are a bunch of delegates in its internal queue, so it posts all these delegates to the CLR's thread pool. Again, a lock has to be taken around the manipulation of the queue, but the lock is held just long enough to queue its **callback** delegates into the thread pool. The thread pool then spans this work out over the cores using no more threads than there are cores, and so no context switching occurs.[9] Now, we have a scalable server that uses very little resources and runs with great performance.

A **ReaderWriterGate** object has another internal queue for delegates that wish to write to the resource. When a write request shows up, any incoming reader delegates get queued so that the current reader methods can finish and drain out of the gate. After the thread pool threads have finished processing the previously queued reader methods, a single writer delegate is queued to the thread pool. This is how I ensure that only other thread is calling a writer method at any given time.

More details about the **ReaderWriterGate** can be found here: *http://msdn.microsoft.com /en-us/magazine/cc163532.aspx*. After I came up with this idea, I sold the patent rights to

---

9 This is assuming that other threads are not running on the computer which, most of the time, is true since most computers are running at far less than 100 percent CPU usage. And CPU usage can be at 100 percent and this will still work as explained if the running threads have lower priorities. If other threads are running, then context switching occurs. This is bad for performance reasons, but it is good for reliability reasons. Remember that Windows gives each process at least one thread and performs context switches to ensure that a hung application doesn't stop other applications from running.

Microsoft, and in 2009, the Patent Office issued the patent (Patent #7,603,502). However, even though Microsoft owns the patent for this idea, the FCL does not provide any class that implements this idea. However, I provide an implementation in my Power Threading library. When I sold the rights to Microsoft, I acquired a license allowing Wintellect customers to use this "invention" with the caveat that it can be used only on a Microsoft platform.[10] By downloading the library from the Wintellect Web site, you are a Wintellect customer, and you can use the library subject to the license restriction.

In Chapter 27, I gave a brief introduction to my **AsyncEnumerator** class, which is also part of my Power Threading library. This class enabled you to use a synchronous programming model with classes that support the CLR's APM, and since my **ReaderWriterGate** supports the APM, you can use it with the **AsyncEnumerator**. However, when I first tried this, I discovered that I could simplify the programming model even more. So if you want to use my **AsyncEnumerator** and also have multiple iterators accessing shared data in a thread-safe way, use my **SyncGate** class instead of **ReaderWriterGate**. The **SyncGate** class is also in my Power Threading library, and it looks like this:

```
public sealed class SyncGate {
    public SyncGate();
    public void BeginRegion(SyncGateMode mode,
        AsyncCallback asyncCallback, Object asyncState);
    public void EndRegion(IAsyncResult result);
}
```

You should see the samples in my Power Threading library for examples of using these classes together, but I'll show a brief example here. I took the **PipeServerAsyncEnumerator** method shown in Chapter 27 and modified it to record the timestamp of the most recent client request in a static field accessible to all threads. Since multiple client requests can be running simultaneously using various threads, updating the static field must be done in a thread-safe way. To accomplish this, I create a static field that holds a reference to a **SyncGate** object, and I call its **BeginRegion** and **EndRegion** methods to acquire and release exclusive access, respectively. Here is the new version of the code with the added lines highlighted:

```
// This field records the timestamp of the most recent client's request
private static DateTime s_lastClientRequestTimestamp = DateTime.MinValue;

// The SyncGate enforces thread-safe access to the s_lastClientRequestTimestamp field
private static readonly SyncGate s_gate = new SyncGate();

private static IEnumerator<Int32> PipeServerAsyncEnumerator(AsyncEnumerator ae) {
    // Each server object performs asynchronous operations on this pipe
    using (var pipe = new NamedPipeServerStream(
```

---

[10] Silverlight is considered a Microsoft platform even if your Silverlight application is running in a non-Microsoft operating system. And, my Power Threading library does have a version of this class for Silverlight as well as the Microsoft .NET Compact Framework.

```
"Echo", PipeDirection.InOut, -1, PipeTransmissionMode.Message,
PipeOptions.Asynchronous | PipeOptions.WriteThrough)) {

    // Asynchronously accept a client connection
    pipe.BeginWaitForConnection(ae.End(), null);
    yield return 1;

    // A client connected, let's accept another client
    var aeNewClient = new AsyncEnumerator();
    aeNewClient.BeginExecute(
        PipeServerAsyncEnumerator(aeNewClient), aeNewClient.EndExecute);

    // Accept the client connection
    pipe.EndWaitForConnection(ae.DequeueAsyncResult());

    // Asynchronously read a request from the client
    Byte[] data = new Byte[1000];
    pipe.BeginRead(data, 0, data.Length, ae.End(), null);
    yield return 1;

    // The client sent us a request, process it.
    Int32 bytesRead = pipe.EndRead(ae.DequeueAsyncResult());

    // Get the timestamp of this client's request
    DateTime now = DateTime.Now;

    // We want to save the timestamp of the most recent client request. Since multiple
    // clients are running concurrently, this has to be done in a thread-safe way
    s_gate.BeginRegion(SyncGateMode.Exclusive, ae.End()); // Request exclusive access
    yield return 1;    // The iterator resumes when exclusive access is granted

    if (s_lastClientRequestTimestamp < now)
        s_lastClientRequestTimestamp = now;

    s_gate.EndRegion(ae.DequeueAsyncResult());    // Relinquish exclusive access

    // My sample server just changes all the characters to uppercase
    // But, you can replace this code with any compute-bound operation
    data = Encoding.UTF8.GetBytes(
        Encoding.UTF8.GetString(data, 0, bytesRead).ToUpper().ToCharArray());

    // Asynchronously send the response back to the client
    pipe.BeginWrite(data, 0, data.Length, ae.End(), null);
    yield return 1;
    // The response was sent to the client, close our side of the connection
    pipe.EndWrite(ae.DequeueAsyncResult());
  } // Close the pipe
}
```

The Concurrent Collection Classes

The FCL ships with four thread-safe collection classes, all of which are in the **System. Collections.Concurrent** namespace. **ConcurrentQueue**, **ConcurrentStack**, and **ConcurrentDictionary** are in MSCorLib.dll, while **ConcurrentBag** is in System.dll. Here is what some of their most commonly used members look like:

```
// Process items in a first-in, first-out order (FIFO)
public class ConcurrentQueue<T> : IProducerConsumerCollection<T>,
   IEnumerable<T>, ICollection, IEnumerable {

   public ConcurrentQueue();
   public void Enqueue(T item);
   public Boolean TryDequeue(out T result);
   public Int32 Count { get; }
   public IEnumerator<T> GetEnumerator();
}
// Process items in a last-in, first-out order (LIFO)
public class ConcurrentStack<T> : IProducerConsumerCollection<T>,
      IEnumerable<T>, ICollection, IEnumerable {

   public ConcurrentStack();
   public void Push(T item);
   public Boolean TryPop(out T result);
   public Int32 Count { get; }
   public IEnumerator<T> GetEnumerator();
}
// An unordered set of items where duplicates are allowed
public class ConcurrentBag<T> : IProducerConsumerCollection<T>,
   IEnumerable<T>, ICollection, IEnumerable {

   public ConcurrentBag();
   public void Add(T item);
   public Boolean TryTake(out T result);
   public Int32 Count { get; }
   public IEnumerator<T> GetEnumerator();
}
// An unordered set of key/value pairs
public class ConcurrentDictionary<TKey, TValue> : IDictionary<TKey, TValue>,
   ICollection<KeyValuePair<TKey, TValue>>, IEnumerable<KeyValuePair<TKey, TValue>>,
   IDictionary, ICollection, IEnumerable {

   public ConcurrentDictionary();
   public Boolean TryAdd(TKey key, TValue value);
   public Boolean TryGetValue(TKey key, out TValue value);
   public TValue this[TKey key] { get; set; }
   public Boolean TryUpdate(TKey key, TValue newValue, TValue comparisonValue);
   public Boolean TryRemove(TKey key, out TValue value);
   public TValue AddOrUpdate(TKey key, TValue addValue,
      Func<TKey, TValue> updateValueFactory);
   public TValue GetOrAdd(TKey key, TValue value);
   public Int32 Count { get; }
   public IEnumerator<KeyValuePair<TKey, TValue>> GetEnumerator();
}
```

All these collection classes are non-blocking. That is, if a thread tries to extract an element when no such element exists, the thread returns immediately; the thread does not block waiting for an element to appear. This is why methods like **TryDequeue**, **TryPop**, **TryTake**, and **TryGetValue** all return **true** if an item was obtained and **false** if not.

These non-blocking collections are not necessarily lock-free. The **ConcurrentDictionary** class uses **Monitor** internally, but the lock is held for a very short time while manipulating the item in the collection. **ConcurrentQueue** and **ConcurrentStack** are lock-free; these both internally use **Interlocked** methods to manipulate the collection. A single **ConcurrentBag** object internally consists of a mini-collection object per thread. When a thread adds an item to the bag, **Interlocked** methods are used to add the item to the calling thread's mini-collection. When a thread tries to extract an element from the bag, the bag checks the calling thread's mini-collection for the item. If the item is there, then an **Interlocked** method is used to extract the item. If the thread's mini-collection doesn't have the item, then a **Monitor** is taken internally to extract an item from another thread's mini-collection. We say that the thread is *stealing* the item from another thread.

You'll notice that all the concurrent classes offer a **GetEnumerator** method, which is typically used with C#'s **foreach** statement but can also be used with Language Integrated Query (LINQ). For the **ConcurrentStack**, **ConcurrentQueue**, and **ConcurrentBag**, the **GetEnumerator** method takes a snapshot of the collection's contents and returns elements from this snapshot; the contents of the actual collection may change while enumerating over the snapshot. **ConcurrentDictionary**'s **GetEnumerator** method does not take a snapshot of its contents, so the contents of the dictionary may change while enumerating over the dictionary; beware of this. Also note that the **Count** property returns the number of elements that are in the collection at the moment you query it. The count may immediately become incorrect if other threads are adding or removing elements from the collection at the same time.

Three of the concurrent collection classes, **ConcurrentStack**, **ConcurrentQueue**, and **ConcurrentBag**, implement the **IProducerConsumerCollection** interface, which is defined as follows:

```
public interface IProducerConsumerCollection<T> : IEnumerable<T>, ICollection, IEnumerable {
    Boolean TryAdd(T item);
    Boolean TryTake(out T item);
    T[] ToArray();
    void CopyTo(T[] array, Int32 index);
}
```

Any class that implements this interface can be turned into a blocking collection where threads producing (adding) items will block if the collection is full and threads consuming (removing) items will block if the collection is empty. Of course, I'd try to avoid using blocking collections as their purpose in life is to block threads. To turn a non-blocking collection into a blocking collection, you construct a **System.Collections.Concurrent.**

BlockingCollection class, passing in a reference to a non-blocking collection to its constructor. The **BlockingCollection** class (defined in the System.dll assembly) looks like this (some methods are not shown):

```
public class BlockingCollection<T> : IEnumerable<T>, ICollection, IEnumerable, IDisposable {
    public BlockingCollection(IProducerConsumerCollection<T> collection,
        Int32 boundedCapacity);

    public void Add(T item);
    public Boolean TryAdd(T item, Int32 msTimeout, CancellationToken cancellationToken);
    public void CompleteAdding();

    public T Take();
    public Boolean TryTake(out T item, Int32 msTimeout, CancellationToken cancellationToken);

    public Int32    BoundedCapacity   { get; }
    public Int32    Count             { get; }
    public Boolean IsAddingCompleted { get; }  // true if AddingComplete is called
    public Boolean IsCompleted       { get; }  // true if IsAddingComplete and Count==0

    public IEnumerable<T> GetConsumingEnumerable(CancellationToken cancellationToken);

    public void CopyTo(T[] array, int index);
    public T[] ToArray();
    public void Dispose();
}
```

When you construct a **BlockingCollection**, the **boundedCapacity** parameter indicates the maximum number of items that you want in the collection. If a thread calls **Add** when the underlying collection has reached its capacity, the producing thread will block. If preferred, the producing thread can call **TryAdd**, passing a timeout (in milliseconds) and/or a **CancellationToken** so that the thread blocks until the item is added, the timeout expires, or the **CancellationToken** is canceled (see Chapter 26 for more about the **CancellationToken** class).

The **BlockingCollection** class implements the **IDisposable** interface. When you call **Dispose**, it calls **Dispose** on the underlying collection and also disposes of two **SemaphoreSlim** objects that the class uses internally to block producers and consumers.

When producers will not be adding any more items into the collection, a producer should call the **CompleteAdding** method. This will signal the consumers that no more items will be produced. Specifically, this causes a **foreach** loop that is using **GetConsumingEnumerable** to terminate. The example code below demonstrates how to set up a producer/consumer scenario and signal completion:

```
public static void Main() {
   var bl = new BlockingCollection<Int32>(new ConcurrentQueue<Int32>());

   // A thread pool thread will do the consuming
   ThreadPool.QueueUserWorkItem(ConsumeItems, bl);

   // Add 5 items to the collection
   for (Int32 item = 0; item < 5; item++) {
      Console.WriteLine("Producing: " + item);
      bl.Add(item);
   }

   // Tell the consuming thread(s) that no more items will be added to the collection
   bl.CompleteAdding();

   Console.ReadLine();   // For testing purposes
}

private static void ConsumeItems(Object o) {
   var bl = (BlockingCollection<Int32>) o;

   // Block until an item shows up, then process it
   foreach (var item in bl.GetConsumingEnumerable()) {
      Console.WriteLine("Consuming: " + item);
   }

   // The collection is empty and no more items are going into it
   Console.WriteLine("All items have been consumed");
}
```

When I execute the above code, I get the following output:

```
Producing: 0
Producing: 1
Producing: 2
Producing: 3
Producing: 4
Consuming: 0
Consuming: 1
Consuming: 2
Consuming: 3
Consuming: 4
All items have been consumed
```

If you run this yourself, the **Producing** and **Consuming** lines could be interspersed, but the **All items have been consumed** line will always be last.

The **BlockingCollection** class also has static **AddToAny**, **TryAddToAny**, **TakeFromAny**, and **TryTakeFromAny** methods. All of these methods take a **BlockingCollection<T>[]**, as well as an item, a timeout, and a **CancellationToken**. The **(Try)AddToAny** methods cycle through all the collections in the array until they find a collection that can accept the item because it is below capacity. The **(Try)TakeFromAny** methods cycle through all the collections in the array until they find a collection to remove an item from.

Index

Symbols and Numbers

.NET Framework. See Microsoft .NET Framework

A

abstract keyword, 167, 187
accessor methods
  accessibility, 258
  AIP support, 241–242
  defined, 238
  generic, 258
  parameterless properties and, 239–241
  performance considerations, 257
Action delegate type, 422–423
Address Space Layout Randomization (ASLR), 2
administrative control
  advanced, 84–89
  simple, 61–64
AIPs (automatically implemented properties), 241–242
AL.exe. See Assembler Linker utility
anonymous types, 247–250
APM (Asynchronous Programming Model)
  AsyncEnumerator class and, 765–768
  BeginXxx methods, 761–762, 769, 774, 776, 778
  comparing to EAP, 788
  compute-bound operations, 774–776
  converting IAsyncResult to task, 783–784
  drawbacks, 765–766, 776–780
  EndXxx methods, 761–762, 769, 774, 777–778
  exceptions and, 769–770
  implementing servers asynchronously, 773–774
  overview, 761–765
AppDomain class, 622
AppDomainManager class, 615
AppDomains
  accessing objects across boundaries, 597–608
  advanced host control, 615–620
  first-chance exception notifications, 612
  GC handle tables, 555–557
  host support, 612–614
  monitoring, 610–611
  overview, 591, 594–597
  process performance, 16
  unhandled exceptions, 509
  unloading, 609–610
arguments. See type arguments
arithmetic operations, primitive types, 117–120

arity, defined, 284
Array class, 281, 385, 392
arrays
  access performance, 396–401
  casting, 390–391
  defined, 385
  derived from Array class, 392
  fixed-size, 401–403
  implementing interfaces, 393–394
  initializing elements, 388–389
  jagged, 387
  multidimensional, 387, 396
  non-zero-lower bounds, 395–396
  overview, 385–387
  passing/returning, 394–395
  SZ, 387, 396
  unsafe access, 401–403
as operator, casting with, 95–97
ASLR (Address Space Layout Randomization), 2
ASP.NET Web Form, 613–614, 770
Assembler Linker (AL.exe) utility
  adding resource files, 52–53
  building satellite assemblies, 59
  command-line switches, 88
  creating assemblies, 50–52
  delayed signaling, 78
  version resource information, 53–56
assemblies. See also strongly named assemblies
  adding modules, 46
  adding resource files, 52–53
  adding to projects, 49–50
  application development examples, 20–21
  binding, 77
  building, 43, 45
  characteristics, 43
  class support, 68
  combining managed code, 5–6
  combining modules, 43–53
  controlling member access, 23–24
  creating with Assembly Linker, 50–52
  culture tags, 58–59
  defined, 5, 43, 101
  delayed signaling, 77–79
  executing code, 9–17
  friend, 159–160
  kinds of, 66–67
  namespaces and, 97–101
  overriding, 689–690
  packaging, 59–60

861

W

X

About the Author

Jeffrey Richter is a cofounder of Wintellect (*http://www.Wintellect.com/*), a training, consulting, and debugging company dedicated to helping companies produce better software faster. Wintellect also offers its own twice-yearly Devscovery conference (*http://Devscovery.com/*). Jeffrey has written many books about Win32 and Microsoft .NET Framework programming, including *CLR via C#, 3rd Edition* (Microsoft Press, 2010), *Windows via C/C++, 5th Edition* (Microsoft Press, 2007), and *Programming Server-Side Applications for Microsoft Windows 2000* (Microsoft Press, 2000). Jeffrey is a contributing editor for *MSDN Magazine*, where he has written numerous feature articles and has been the *Win32 Q&A* columnist, *.NET Q&A* columnist, and *Concurrent Affairs* columnist. Jeffrey also speaks at various trade conferences worldwide, including Wintellect's Devscovery, VSLive!, and Microsoft's TechEd and Professional Developers Conference.

Jeffrey has consulted for many companies, including AT&T, DreamWorks, General Electric, Hewlett-Packard, IBM, and Intel. His code has shipped in many Microsoft products, among them Microsoft Visual Studio, Microsoft Golf, Windows Sound System, and various versions of Microsoft Windows. Jeff consulted with the .NET Framework team for eight years and maintains an ongoing close relationship with that team as well as the Windows team.

On the personal front, Jeffrey holds both airplane and helicopter pilot licenses, though he never gets to fly as often as he'd like. He is also a member of the International Brotherhood of Magicians and enjoys showing friends sleight-of-hand card tricks from time to time. Jeff's other hobbies include music (especially jazz and progressive rock from the 1970s), drumming, model railroading, and karate. He also enjoys traveling and theater. He lives in Kirkland, Washington, with his wife, Kristin, and his two sons, Aidan and Grant..

If you like the book you'll love the training

WINTELLECT TRAINING COURSES BY JEFFREY RICHTER

Effective Threading in C#: Mastering Responsive, Reliable and Scalable Applications

Duration and Format: 2 Day On-Site/ Virtual

Syllabus

Day 1
- Introduction, CPU industry trends
- Thread creation/destruction, overhead, scheduling and priorities
- Tools for monitoring and debugging threads
- Reasons to use threads and why
- Performing asynchronous compute-bound operations using the CLR's thread pool, Timers, and Tasks (new in .NET 4.0)
- Performing asynchronous I/O-bound operations using the CLR's Asynchronous Programming Model
- Using special language features (anonymous methods, lambda expressions, and iterators) to make asynchronous programming easier.

Day 2
- Performing asynchronous I/O-bound operations using the Event-based Asynchronous Programming Model
- Primitive (user-mode and kernel-mode) thread synchronization constructs including volatile fields, interlocked methods, SpinLocks
- Hybrid thread synchronization constructs including mutual exclusive locks, reader-writer locks, new .NET 4.0 locks
- Comparing the behavior and performance of locks
- How locks work internally and how to modify a lock's behavior
- The ReaderWriterGate: A lock that doesn't block any threads.

Mastering the .NET Framework

Duration and Format: 5 Day On-Site/ 3 Day On-Site/ Virtual

Syllabus

Day 1
- Introduction to the .NET Framework, Motivating its Use, and its Core Technologies
- The .NET Framework's Development Platform's Architecture
- Building, Deploying, Versioning, and Administering Applications and Components

Day 2
- Type Fundamentals (Type-safety, Value and Reference types, boxing)
- Type Members
- Essential Types

Day 3
- Working with Text (characters, strings, encodings, cultures, formatting, parsing)
- Generics (types, methods, interfaces, verifiability and constraints, collections)
- Exception Handling and State Management

Day 4
- Automatic Memory Management
- Language Enhancements (Iterators, LINQ , Dynamic)

Day 5
- Streams and Serialization (Stream composability, Binary, Soap, and XML serialization)
- Building Dynamically-Extensible Applications (AppDomains, Assemblies, Reflection)
- Interoperating with Unmanaged Code (COM and P/Invoke)

To learn more about Wintellect training offerings visit www.wintellect.com.

What do you think of this book?

We want to hear from you!

To participate in a brief online survey, please visit:

microsoft.com/learning/booksurvey

Tell us how well this book meets your needs—what works effectively, and what we can do better. Your feedback will help us continually improve our books and learning resources for you.

Thank you in advance for your input!

Stay in touch!

To subscribe to the *Microsoft Press® Book Connection Newsletter*—for news on upcoming books, events, and special offers—please visit:

microsoft.com/learning/books/newsletter